AutoCAD
and Its Applications
ADVANCED

by

Terence M. Shumaker
Faculty Emeritus
Former Chairperson
Drafting Technology
Autodesk Premier Training Center
Clackamas Community College, Oregon City, Oregon

David A. Madsen
President
Madsen Designs, Inc.

Faculty Emeritus
Former Chairperson
Drafting Technology
Autodesk Premier Training Center
Clackamas Community College, Oregon City, Oregon

Director Emeritus
American Design Drafting Association

Publisher
The Goodheart-Willcox Company, Inc.
Tinley Park, Illinois
www.g-w.com

Manufactured in the United States of America.

Library of Congress Catalog Card Number 2008016194
ISBN: 978-1-59070-991-7

1 2 3 4 5 6 7 8 9 – 09 – 13 12 11 10 09 08

The Goodheart-Willcox Company, Inc., Publisher Brand Disclaimer: Brand names, company names, and illustrations for products and services included in this text are provided for educational purposes only, and do not represent or imply endorsement or recommendation by the author or the publisher.

The Goodheart-Willcox Company, Inc., Safety Notice: The reader is expressly advised to carefully read, understand, and apply all safety precautions and warnings described in this book or that might also be indicated in undertaking the activities and exercises described herein to minimize risk of personal injury or injury to others. Common sense and good judgment should also be exercised and applied to help avoid all potential hazards. The reader should always refer to the appropriate manufacturer's technical information, directions, and recommendations; then proceed with care to follow specific equipment operating instructions. The reader should understand these notices and cautions are not exhaustive.

The publisher makes no warranty or representation whatsoever, either expressed or implied, including but not limited to equipment, procedures, and applications described or referred to herein, their quality, performance, merchantability, or fitness for a particular purpose. The publisher assumes no responsibility for any changes, errors, or omissions in this book. The publisher specifically disclaims any liability whatsoever, including any direct, indirect, incidental, consequential, special, or exemplary damages resulting, in whole or in part, from the reader's use or reliance upon the information, instructions, procedures, warnings, cautions, applications or other matter contained in this book. The publisher assumes no responsibility for the activities of the reader.

Library of Congress Cataloging-in-Publication Data
Shumaker, Terence M.
AutoCAD and its applications: advanced, 2009/ by Terence M. Shumaker, David A. Madsen—16th edition
p. cm.
Includes index
ISBN: 978-1-59070-991-7
1. Computer graphics. 2. AutoCAD. I. Madsen, David A. II. Title.
T385.S46124 2009
620'.00420285536—dc22
2008016194

Introduction

AutoCAD and Its Applications—Advanced provides complete instruction in mastering three-dimensional design and modeling using AutoCAD. This text also provides complete instruction in customizing AutoCAD and introduces programming AutoCAD. These topics are covered in an easy-to-understand sequence and progress in a way that allows you to become comfortable with the commands as your knowledge builds from one chapter to the next. In addition, *AutoCAD and Its Applications—Advanced* offers:

- Step-by-step use of AutoCAD commands.
- In-depth explanations of how and why commands function as they do.
- Examples and discussions of industrial practices and standards.
- Professional tips explaining how to effectively and efficiently use AutoCAD.
- Exercises to reinforce the chapter topics. These exercises should be completed where indicated in the text as they build on previously learned material.
- Chapter tests for review of commands and key AutoCAD concepts.
- A large selection of modeling and customizing problems supplement each chapter. Problems are presented as 3D illustrations, actual plotted drawings, and engineering sketches.
- Extensive use of font changes identify commands and keyboard entry. This is fully explained in the next section, Fonts Used in This Text.

With *AutoCAD and Its Applications—Advanced* you not only learn AutoCAD commands, but you also become acquainted with:

- 3D construction and layout techniques.
- Constructing models using different 3D coordinate systems.
- User coordinate systems.
- Model space viewports.
- 3D editing and display techniques.
- 3D text and dimensioning.
- Solid model construction, editing, and display.
- Modeling using sweeps and lofts.
- Model visualization and rendering.
- Customizing the AutoCAD environment.
- Customizing ribbon panels, menus, and toolbars.
- The basics of AutoLISP and dialog box (DCL) programming.
- Introduction to programming using Visual Basic for Applications (VBA).

Fonts Used in This Text

Different typefaces are used throughout each chapter to define terms and identify AutoCAD commands. Important terms appear in ***bold-italic face, serif*** type. AutoCAD menus, commands, variables, dialog box names, and toolbar button names are printed in **bold-face, sans serif** type. File names, folder names, paths, and keyboard-entry items appear in the body of the text in Roman, sans serif type. Keyboard keys are shown inside of square brackets [ ] and appear in Roman, sans serif type. For example, [Enter] means to press the enter (return) key.

Other Text References

This text focuses on advanced AutoCAD applications. Basic AutoCAD applications are covered in *AutoCAD and Its Applications—Basics,* which is also available from Goodheart-Willcox Publisher. *AutoCAD and Its Applications* texts are also available for previous releases of AutoCAD. For advanced AutoCAD programming applications, refer to the texts *Visual LISP Programming* and *VBA for AutoCAD,* which are both available from Goodheart-Willcox Publisher.

Introducing the AutoCAD Commands

HELIX

Ribbon
Home
> 3D Modeling
Helix
Menu Bar
Draw
> Helix
Type
HELIX

There are several ways to select AutoCAD drawing and editing commands. Selecting commands from the ribbon or menu is slightly different than entering them from the keyboard. When a command is introduced, the command-entry methods are illustrated in the margin next to the text reference. The example in the margin next to this paragraph illustrates the various methods of initiating the **HELIX** command to draw a helix.

Flexibility in Design

Flexibility is the keyword when using *AutoCAD and Its Applications—Advanced.* This text is an excellent training aid for both individual and classroom instruction. It is also an invaluable resource for any professional using AutoCAD. *AutoCAD and Its Applications—Advanced* teaches you how to apply AutoCAD to common modeling and customizing tasks.

When working through the text, you will see a variety of notices. These include Professional Tips, Notes, and Cautions that help you develop your AutoCAD skills.

PROFESSIONAL TIP

These ideas and suggestions are aimed at increasing your productivity and enhancing your use of AutoCAD commands and techniques.

NOTE

A note alerts you to important aspects of a command function, menu, or activity that is being discussed. These aspects should be kept in mind while you are working through the text.

CAUTION

A caution alerts you to potential problems if instructions or commands are incorrectly used or if an action can corrupt or alter files, folders, or storage media. If you are in doubt after reading a caution, always consult your instructor or supervisor.

AutoCAD and Its Applications—Advanced provides several ways for you to evaluate your performance. Included are:

- **Exercises.** The Student CD contains exercises for each chapter. These exercises allow you to perform tasks that reinforce the material just presented. You can work through the exercises at your own pace. However, the exercises are intended to be completed when called out in the text.
- **Chapter test.** Each chapter includes a written test at the end of the chapter. Questions require you to give the proper definition, command, option, or response to perform a certain task. You may also be asked to explain a topic or list appropriate procedures. An electronic version of the test is available on the Student CD.
- **Drawing problems.** There are a variety of drawing, design, and customizing problems at the end of each chapter. These are presented as real-world CAD drawings, 3D illustrations, and engineering sketches. The problems are designed to make you think, solve problems, use design techniques, research and use proper drawing standards, and correct errors in the drawings or engineering sketches. Graphics are used to represent the discipline to which a drawing problem applies.

These problems address mechanical drafting and design applications, such as manufactured part designs.

These problems address architectural and structural drafting and design applications, such as floor plans, furniture, and presentation drawings.

These problems address piping drafting and design applications, such as tank drawings and pipe layout.

These problems address a variety of general drafting, design, and customization applications. These problems should be attempted by everyone learning advanced AutoCAD techniques for the first time.

NOTE

Some problems presented in this text are given as engineering sketches. These sketches are intended to represent the kind of material from which a drafter is expected to work in a real-world situation. As such, engineering sketches often contain errors or slight inaccuracies and are most often not drawn according to proper drafting conventions and applicable standards. Errors in these problems are *intentional* to encourage you to apply appropriate techniques and standards in order to solve the problem. As in real-world applications, sketches should be considered preliminary layouts. Always question inaccuracies in sketches and designs and consult the applicable standards or other resources.

Student CD

At the back of this book is the Student CD. This CD contains the exercises and chapter test for each chapter and the appendix material. The appendix consists of:

- Appendix A Solid Modeling Tutorial
- Appendix B Common File Extensions
- Appendix C AutoCAD Command Aliases
- Appendix D Advanced Application Commands
- Appendix E Advanced Application System Variables
- Appendix F Basic AutoLISP Commands

As you work through each chapter, exercises on the Student CD are referenced. The exercises are intended to be completed as the references are encountered in the text. The solid modeling tutorial in Appendix A should be completed after Chapter 13. The remaining appendix material is intended as reference material.

Also included on the Student CD is the student software supplement. This contains a variety of student activities that are intended to supplement the exercises on the Student CD. These activities are referenced within the appropriate exercises and can be completed as additional practice.

About the Authors

Terence M. Shumaker is Faculty Emeritus, the former Chairperson of the Drafting Technology Department and former Director of the Autodesk Premier Training Center at Clackamas Community College. Terence taught at the community college level for over 28 years. He has professional experience in surveying, civil drafting, industrial piping, and technical illustration. He is the author of Goodheart-Willcox's *Process Pipe Drafting* and coauthor of the *AutoCAD and Its Applications* series (Releases 10 through 2008 editions) and *AutoCAD Essentials.*

David A. Madsen is the president of Madsen Designs, Inc. David is Faculty Emeritus, the former Chairperson of Drafting Technology and the Autodesk Premier Training Center at Clackamas Community College and former member of the American Design and Drafting Association (ADDA) Board of Directors. David was honored by the ADDA with Director Emeritus status at the annual conference in 2005. David was an instructor and a department chair at Clackamas Community College for nearly 30 years. In addition to community college experience, David was a Drafting Technology instructor at Centennial High School in Gresham, Oregon. David also has extensive experience in mechanical drafting, architectural design and drafting, and construction practices. He is the author of Goodheart-Willcox's *Geometric Dimensioning and Tolerancing* and coauthor of the *AutoCAD and Its Applications* series (Releases 10 through 2008 editions), *Architectural Drafting Using AutoCAD, AutoCAD Architecture and Its Applications, Architectural Desktop and Its Applications, Architectural AutoCAD,* and *AutoCAD Essentials.*

Acknowledgments

The authors and publisher would like to thank the following individuals and companies for their assistance and contributions.

Contributing Authors

The authors wish to acknowledge the following contributors for their professional expertise in providing in-depth research and testing, technical assistance, reviews, and development of new materials.

Jeffrey Laurich for Chapters 9 and 13 through 18 and consultation on other chapters. Jeff has been an instructor at Fox Valley Technical College in Appleton, WI, since 1991. He has worked in mechanical design and drafting since 1986. Jeff has taught classes in AutoCAD, Autodesk MAP, Autodesk VIZ, and other programs. He created a certificate program at FVTC entitled Computer Rendering and Animation that utilizes the 3D capabilities of AutoCAD and Autodesk VIZ. As a side occupation, Jeff uses Autodesk 3ds max to create renderings and animations for manufacturers and architects.

Adam Ferris for Chapters 20 through 24. Adam is the Director of Digital Technology at Wilson Architects in Boston, MA. Wilson Architects is a medium-size architecture firm specializing in the science and technology field. Adam is an award-winning Autodesk Certified Instructor with over 14 years of experience training Autodesk products in the Boston area. He has trained over 4000 students in New England. Prior to joining Wilson Architects, Adam owned an Autodesk products/CAD consulting firm aiding businesses in efficient AutoCAD configurations and management, network management, and 3D design with Autodesk 3ds max and Autodesk VIZ.

Mark Hagen for Chapters 25 through 29. Mark is currently an instructor in the Drafting Technology Department at Portland Community College. He teaches a wide variety of AutoCAD-related courses including beginning, intermediate, and advanced courses, as well as AutoLISP programming courses. Prior to working at Portland Community College, Mark worked as an Applications Consultant for KETIV Technologies, Inc., in Portland, Oregon. His responsibilities at KETIV included serving as an AutoCAD trainer\programmer\consultant for a large Pacific Northwest AutoCAD dealer and CAD\CAM\CAE company. Mark also has extensive experience in the drafting and design field. Before working for KETIV, Mark worked as a CAD Specialist for the Silver Eagle Manufacturing Company. His responsibilities primarily dealt with the design and drafting of steel fabrication weldments and assemblies. Mark is also certified in geometric dimensioning and tolerancing applications.

Contribution of Materials

Autodesk, Inc.
Bill Fane
CADENCE magazine
EPCM Services Ltd.
Fitzgerald, Hagan, & Hackathorn
Kunz Associates

Brief Contents

Three-Dimensional Design and Modeling

Model Visualization and Presentation

Customizing AutoCAD

Programming AutoCAD

Expanded Table of Contents

Three-Dimensional Design and Modeling

Model Visualization and Presentation

Customizing AutoCAD

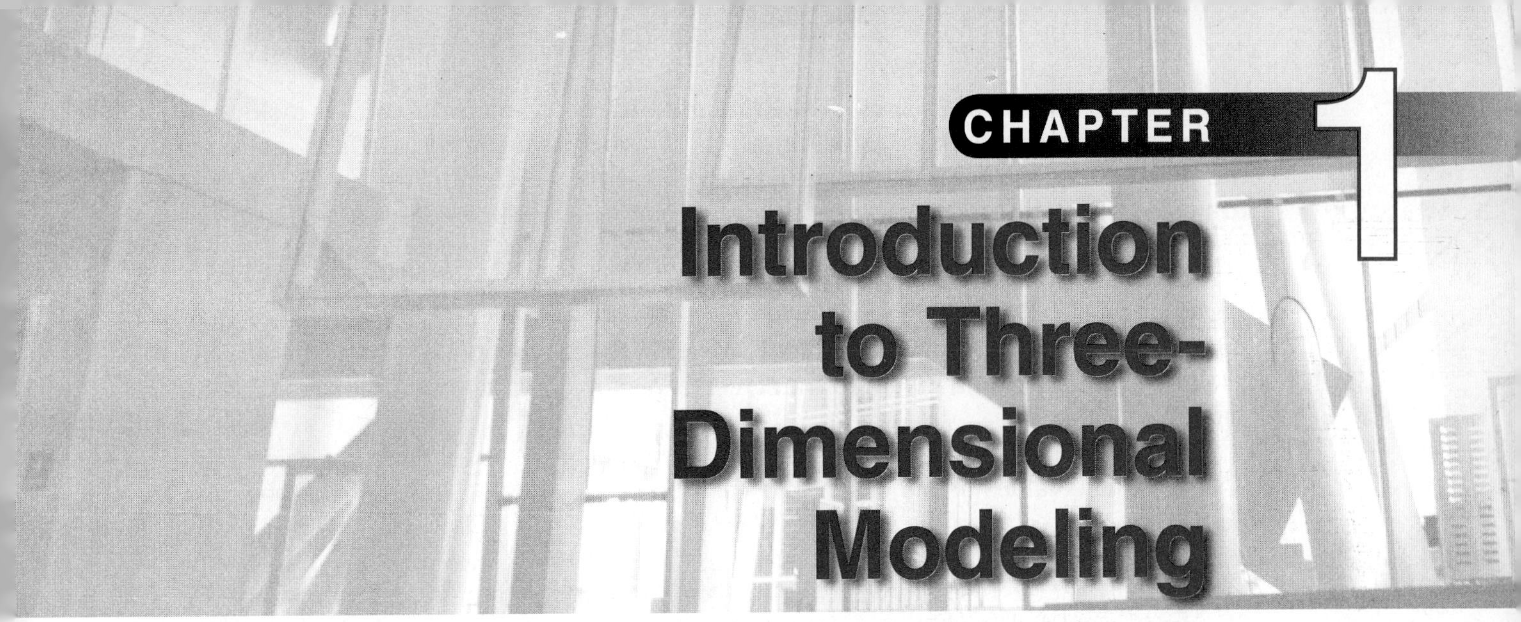

CHAPTER 1

Introduction to Three-Dimensional Modeling

Learning Objectives

After completing this chapter, you will be able to:
- ✓ Describe how to locate points in 3D space.
- ✓ Describe the right-hand rule of 3D visualization.
- ✓ Explain the function of the ribbon.
- ✓ Display 3D objects from preset isometric viewpoints.
- ✓ Display 3D objects from any desired viewpoint.
- ✓ Set a visual style current.

Three-dimensional (3D) design and modeling is a powerful tool for use in design, visualization, testing, analysis, manufacturing, assembly, and marketing. Three-dimensional models also form the basis of computer animations, architectural walk-throughs, and virtual worlds used with virtual reality systems and gaming platforms. Drafters who can design objects, buildings, and "worlds" in 3D are in demand for a wide variety of positions, both inside and outside of the traditional drafting and design disciplines.

The first eleven chapters of this book present a variety of techniques for drawing and designing in 3D. The skills you learn will provide you with the ability to construct any object in 3D and prepare you for entry into an exciting aspect of graphic communication.

To be effective in creating and using 3D objects, you must first have good 3D visualization skills. This includes the ability to see an object in three dimensions and to visualize it rotating in space. These skills can be obtained by using 3D techniques to construct objects and by trying to see two-dimensional sketches and drawings as 3D models. This chapter provides an introduction to several aspects of 3D drawing and visualization. Subsequent chapters expand on these aspects and provide a detailed examination of 3D drawing, editing, visualization, and display techniques.

Using Rectangular 3D Coordinates

In two-dimensional drawing, you see one plane defined by two dimensions. These dimensions are usually located on the X and Y axes, and what you see is the XY plane. However, in 3D drawing, another coordinate axis—the Z axis—is added. This results in two additional planes—the XZ plane and the YZ plane. If you are looking at a standard AutoCAD screen after AutoCAD is launched using the acad.dwt template, the positive Z axis comes directly out of the screen toward you. AutoCAD can only draw lines in 3D if it knows the X, Y, and Z coordinate values of each point on the object. For 2D drawing, only two of the three coordinates (X and Y) are needed.

Compare the 2D and 3D coordinate systems shown in **Figure 1-1.** Notice that the positive values of Z in the 3D coordinate system come up from the XY plane. In a new drawing based on the acad.dwt template, consider the surface of your computer screen as the XY plane. Anything behind the screen is negative Z and anything in front of the screen is positive Z.

The object in **Figure 1-2A** is a 2D drawing showing the top view of an object. The XY coordinate values of the origin and each point are shown. Think of the object as being drawn directly on the surface of your computer screen. However, this is actually a 3D object. When displayed in a pictorial view, the Z coordinates can be seen. Notice in **Figure 1-2B** that the first two values of each coordinate match the X and Y values of the 2D view. Three-dimensional coordinates are always expressed as (X,Y,Z). The 3D object was drawn using positive Z coordinates. Therefore, the object comes out of your computer screen when it is viewed from directly above. The object can also be drawn using negative Z coordinates. In this case, the object would extend behind, or into, the screen.

Study the nature of the rectangular 3D coordinate system. Be sure you understand Z values before you begin constructing 3D objects. It is especially important that you carefully visualize and plan your design when working with 3D constructions.

Figure 1-1.
A comparison of 2D and 3D coordinate systems.

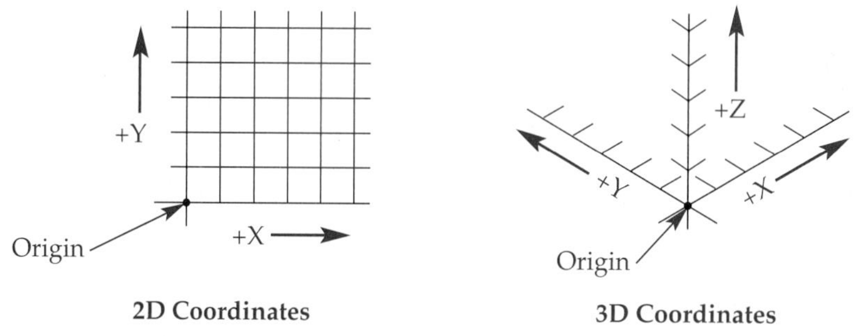

Figure 1-2.
A—The points making up a 2D object require only two coordinates. B—Each point of a 3D object must have an X, Y, and Z value. Notice that the first two coordinates (X and Y) are the same for each endpoint of a vertical line.

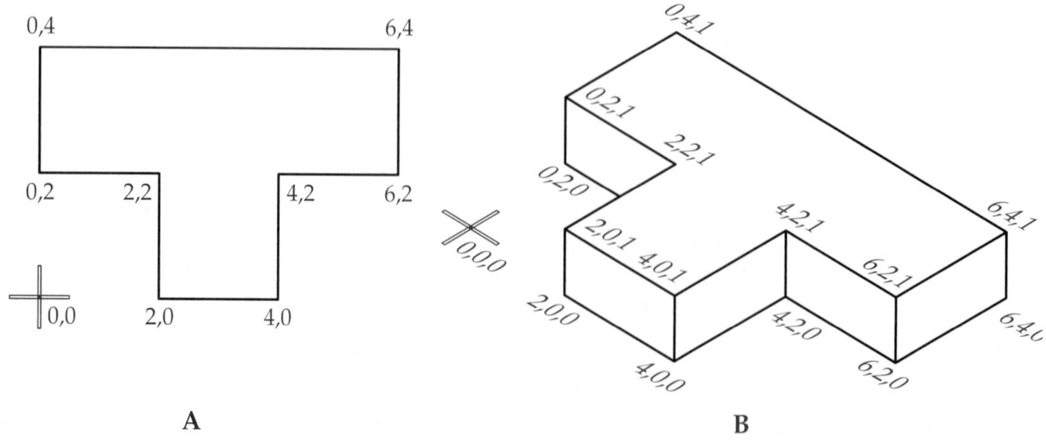

PROFESSIONAL TIP

All points in three-dimensional space can be drawn using one of three coordinate entry methods—rectangular, spherical, or cylindrical. This chapter uses the rectangular coordinate entry method. Complete discussions on the spherical and cylindrical coordinate entry methods are provided in Chapter 4.

Exercise 1-1

Complete the exercise on the Student CD.

Right-Hand Rule of 3D Drawing

In order to effectively draw in 3D, you must be able to visualize objects in 3D space. The ***right-hand rule*** is a simple method for visualizing the 3D coordinate system. It is a representation of the positive coordinate values in the three axis directions. AutoCAD's world coordinate system (WCS) and various user coordinate systems (UCS) are based on this concept of visualization.

To use the right-hand rule, position the thumb, index finger, and middle finger of your right hand as shown in **Figure 1-3.** Although this may seem a bit unusual, it can do wonders for your understanding of the three axes. Imagine that your thumb is the X axis, your index finger is the Y axis, and your middle finger is the Z axis. Hold your hand in front of you so that your middle finger is pointing directly at you, as shown in **Figure 1-3.** This is the plan view of the XY plane. The positive X axis is pointing to the right and the positive Y axis is pointing up. The positive Z axis comes toward you and the origin of this system is the palm of your hand.

The concept behind the right-hand rule can be visualized even better if you are sitting at a computer and the AutoCAD graphics window is displayed. Make sure the current drawing is based on the acad.dwt template. If the UCS icon is not displayed in the lower-left corner of the screen, turn it on by picking **View>Display>UCS Icon>On**

UCSICON

Type
UCSICON
Menu
View > Display > UCS Icon > On

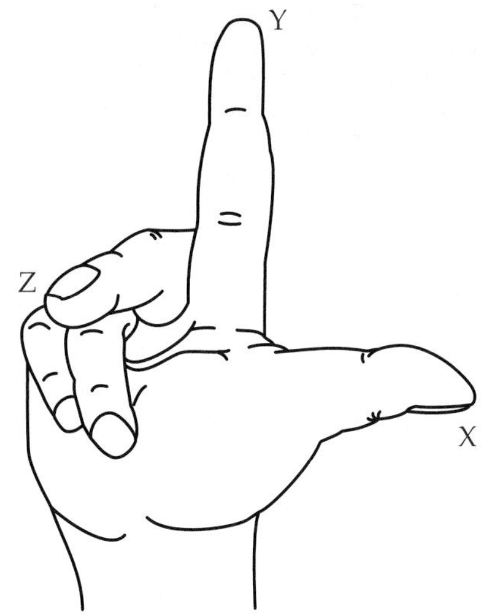

Figure 1-3. Positioning your hand to use the right-hand rule to understand the relationship of the X, Y, and Z axes.

Figure 1-4.
A comparison of the UCS icon and the right-hand rule.

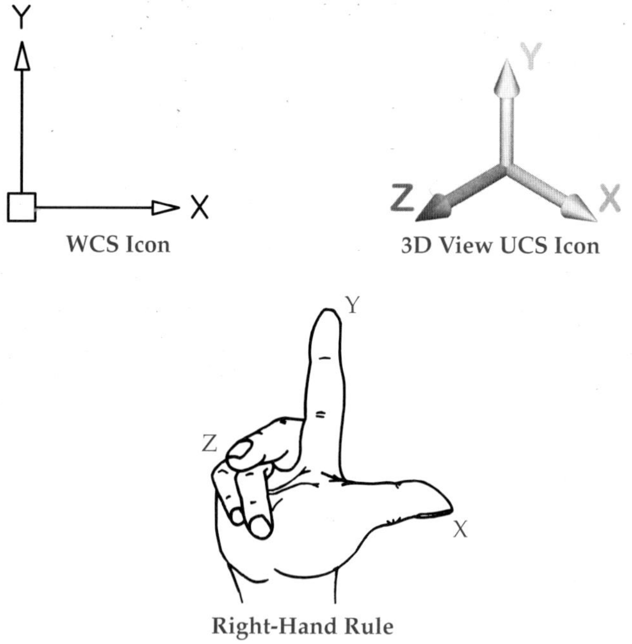

in the menu browser. Now, orient your right hand as shown in **Figure 1-3** and position it next to the UCS (or WCS) icon. Your index finger and thumb should point in the same directions as the Y and X axes, respectively, on the UCS icon. Your middle finger will be pointing out of the screen directly at you, which is the Z axis. See **Figure 1-4.** Notice the illustration on the right in the figure. This is the UCS icon shown when a 3D view is displayed using the view cube, which is discussed later in this chapter.

The right-hand rule can be used to eliminate confusion when rotating the UCS. The UCS can rotate on any of the three axes, just like a wheel rotates on an axle. Therefore, if you want to visualize how to rotate about the X axis, keep your thumb stationary and turn your hand either toward or away from you. If you wish to rotate about the Y axis, keep your index finger stationary and turn your hand to the left or right. When rotating about the Z axis, you must keep your middle finger stationary and rotate your entire arm.

If your 3D visualization skills are weak or you are having trouble visualizing different orientations of the UCS, use the right-hand rule. It is a useful technique for improving your 3D visualization skills. Rotating the UCS around one or more of the axes can become confusing if proper techniques are not used to visualize the rotation angles. A complete discussion of UCSs is provided in Chapter 4.

Basic Overview of the Interface

AutoCAD provides three working environments tailored to either 2D or 3D drawing or annotating a drawing. These environments are called *workspaces* and can be quickly restored. The workspace for 2D development based on the traditional AutoCAD screen layout is called AutoCAD Classic. The 2D Drafting & Annotation workspace is designed for drawing in 2D and annotating a drawing. It is similar to a streamlined version of the AutoCAD Classic layout with the ribbon displayed in place of toolbars and pull-down menus. The workspace for 3D development is called 3D Modeling.

Workspaces can be created, customized, and saved to allow a variety of graphical user interface configurations. The 3D Modeling workspace provides quick access to all of the tools required to construct, edit, view, and visualize 3D models. This section provides an overview of the 3D Modeling workspace and the layout of the ribbon and its panels.

NOTE

In order to use the default 3D "environment," you must start a new drawing file based on the acad3D.dwt template and set the **3D Modeling** workspace current. All discussions in the remainder of this book assume that AutoCAD is in this default 3D environment.

Workspaces

A ***workspace*** is a drawing environment in which, menus, toolbars, palettes, and ribbon panels are displayed for a specific task. A workspace stores not only which of these tools are visible, but also their on-screen locations. You can quickly change workspaces using the **Workspace Switching** tool on the status bar, **WSCURRENT** command, **Tools** menu, or **Workspaces** toolbar, as shown in **Figure 1-5.** By default, toolbars are not displayed. To display a toolbar, pick **Tools**>**Toolbars**>**AutoCAD** in the menu browser and then pick the specific toolbar. The default location for the **Workspaces** toolbar is docked below the **Quick Access** toolbar. When AutoCAD is closed, all displayed toolbars and their current locations are saved and restored the next time AutoCAD is launched. However, this status is not saved to the workspace. The default **3D Modeling** workspace is shown in **Figure 1-6.**

WSCURRENT

Type
WSCURRENT
Menu
Tools
> Workspaces
Toolbar
Status Bar
Workspace Switching

Figure 1-5.
Switching workspaces. A—Using the **Workspaces** toolbar. B—Using the **Workspaces Switching** tool.

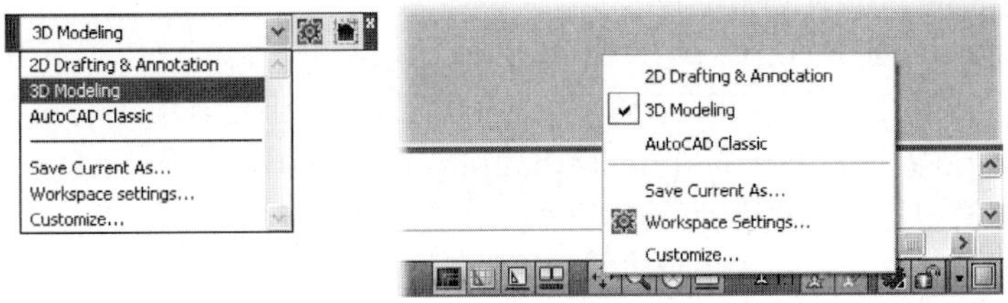

A B

Figure 1-6.
The **3D Modeling** workspace with a drawing file based on the acad3D.dwt template.

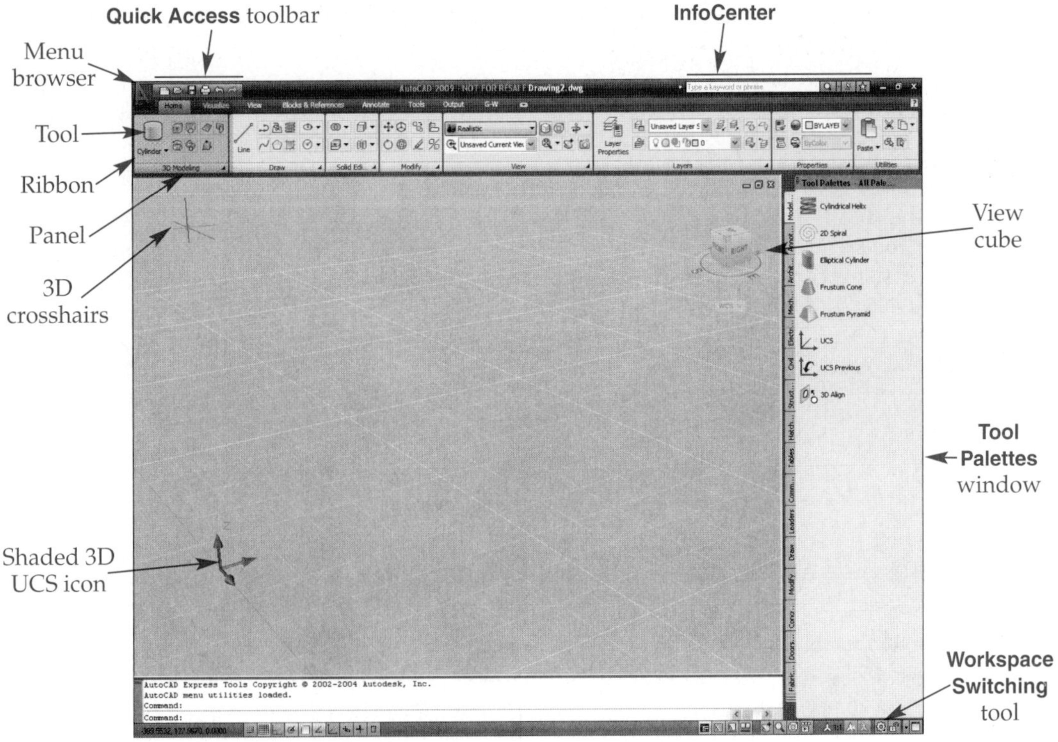

Ribbon Panels

RIBBON

Type
RIBBON DASHBOARD
Menu
Tools > Palettes > Ribbon

Within the 3D Modeling workspace, the **Home** tab on the ribbon displays eight panels. The tools in these panels provide all of the functions needed to design, view, and render your 3D model. See **Figure 1-7.** The title appears at the bottom of the panel. Panel titles can be hidden by right-clicking on any panel and unchecking **Show Panel Titles** in the shortcut menu.

Many panels contain more tools than displayed in the default view. These panels can be expanded by picking the flyout arrow in the lower-right corner of the panel. See **Figure 1-8A.** The flyout portion is displayed as long as the cursor remains over the panel. It retracts when the cursor moves off of the panel. To retain the flyout display, pick the pushpin icon in the lower-right corner of the expanded panel. See **Figure 1-8B.** The panel continues to be displayed until you pick the pushpin icon again to release it.

Multiple panel flyouts can be displayed using the pushpin, but may overlap in the process. This may obscure menu tools in adjacent panels. Simply pick on the panel you wish to use and its tools are displayed in full.

You can display only those control panels that you need. Right-click anywhere on the ribbon tab to display the shortcut menu. Select **Panels** to display a cascading menu that contains a list of the control panels available for that tab. See **Figure 1-9.** The panels that are currently displayed in the ribbon have a check mark next to their name. Select any of the checked control panels that you wish to remove from the current display. Unchecked panels can be turned on by selecting their name. Each tab has its own set of available control panels.

Figure 1-7.
The ribbon is composed of tabs and panels that provide access to 3D modeling, viewing, and presentation commands without using toolbars and menus.

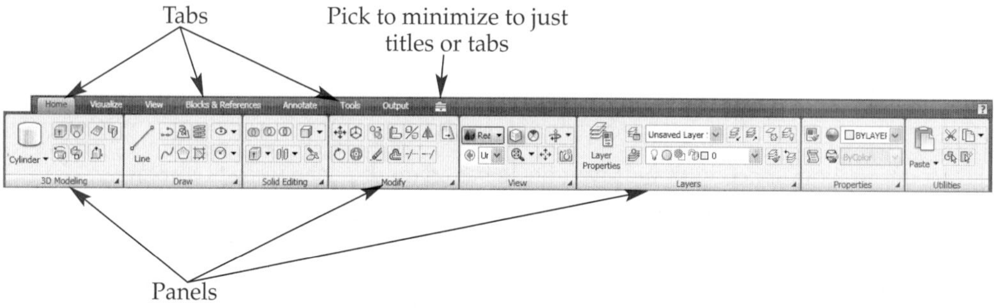

Figure 1-8.
A—Picking the flyout arrow expands the panel. The flyout is displayed as long as the cursor remains over the panel. It retracts when the cursor moves off the panel. B—Multiple panel flyouts can be displayed using the pushpin, but may overlap in the process. Pick the panel you wish to use to display its tools in full.

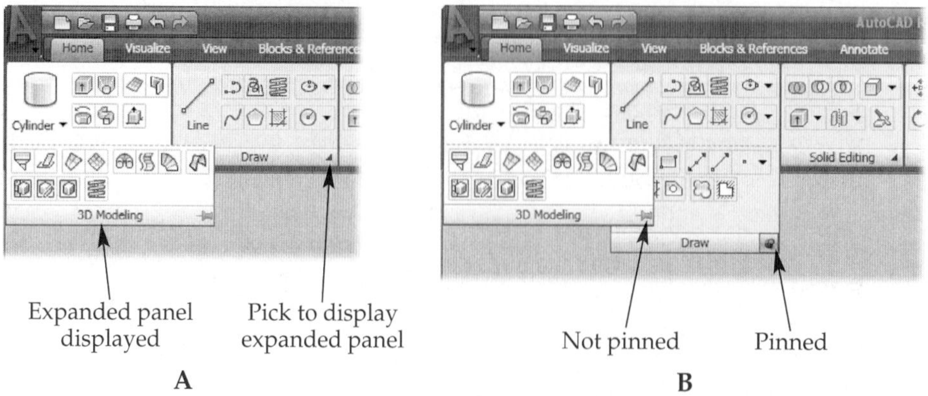

Figure 1-9.
Panels in a tab can be displayed or hidden using the shortcut menu.

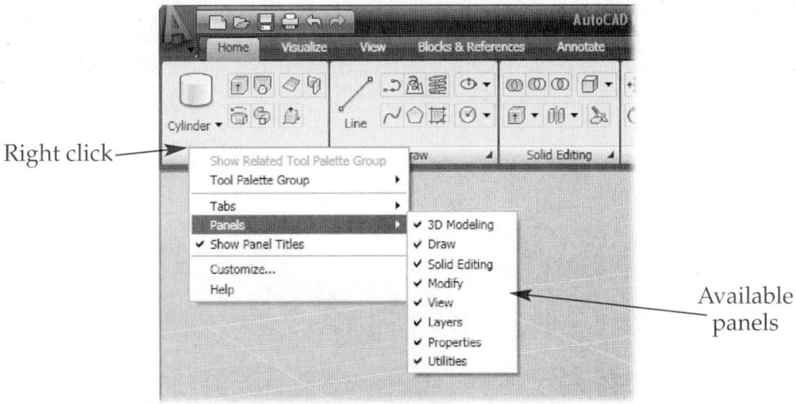

Each panel contains command tools. These are discussed in detail throughout the Modeling and Presentation sections of this book.

NOTE

The 2D Drafting & Annotation and 3D Modeling workspaces have the ribbon displayed by default. In each workspace, the ribbon displays a set of panels specifically related to that workspace. As soon as you select a different workspace, or re-select the current workspace, the panels associated with the workspace are displayed in the ribbon. The ribbon is not displayed by default in the AutoCAD Classic workspace. When the ribbon is displayed in this workspace, the available panels are the same as for the last-displayed workspace, either the 2D Drafting & Annotation or 3D Modeling. The panels associated with a workspace can be customized, as discussed in Chapter 19.

Displaying 3D Views

It does not do much good to understand how to draw in 3D space if you cannot see what you draw in three dimensions. The default view in the 2D environment based on the acad.dwt template is a plan, or top, view of the XY plane. The default view in the 3D environment based on the acad3D.dwt template is a pictorial, or 3D, view. AutoCAD provides several methods of changing your viewpoint to produce different pictorial views. The ***viewpoint*** is the location in space from which the object is viewed. The methods for changing your viewpoint include preset isometric and orthographic viewpoints, the view cube, and camera lens settings. Camera settings are discussed in detail in Chapter 15.

Isometric and Orthographic Viewpoint Presets

A 2D isometric drawing is based on angles of 120° between the three axes. AutoCAD provides preset viewpoints that allow you to view a 3D object from one of four isometric locations. See **Figure 1-10.** Each of these viewpoints produces an isometric view of the object. In addition, AutoCAD has presets for the six standard orthographic views of an object. The isometric and orthographic viewpoint presets are based on the WCS.

Figure 1-10.
There are four preset isometric viewpoints in AutoCAD. This illustration shows the direction from which the cube will be viewed for each of the presets. The grid represents the XY plane of the WCS.

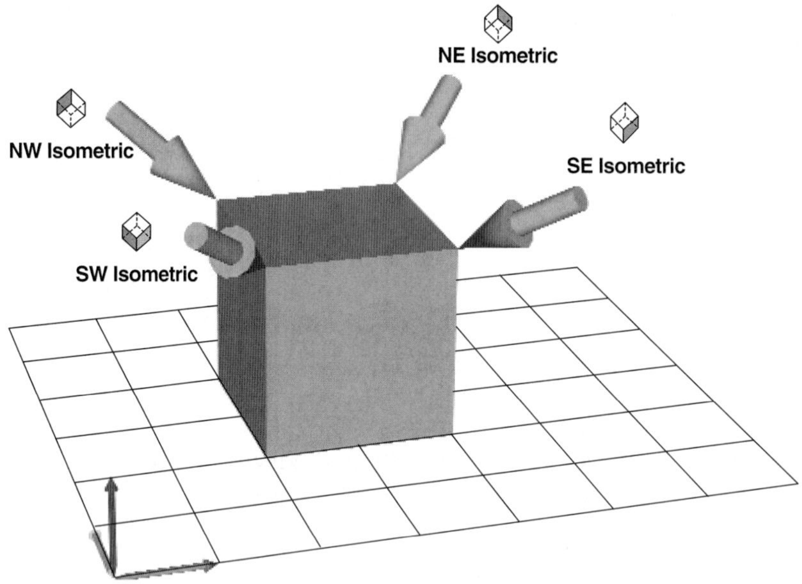

VIEW

Ribbon
Home
> View
> SW Isometric
> SE Isometric
> NE Isometric
> NW Isometric

Menu
View
> 3D Views
> SW Isometric
> SE Isometric
> NE Isometric
> NW Isometric

The four preset isometric views are southwest, southeast, northeast, and northwest. The six orthographic presets are top, bottom, left, right, front, and back. To switch your viewpoint to one of these presets, pick the drop-down list in the **View** panel in the **Home** tab of the ribbon and select the view name. See **Figure 1-11.** You can also pick **View**>**3D Views** in the menu browser or select the appropriate button on the **View** toolbar. This toolbar is not displayed by default.

Figure 1-11.
Selecting preset views. A—Using the **View** panel in the **Home** tab of the ribbon. B—Using the menu browser. C—Using the toolbar.

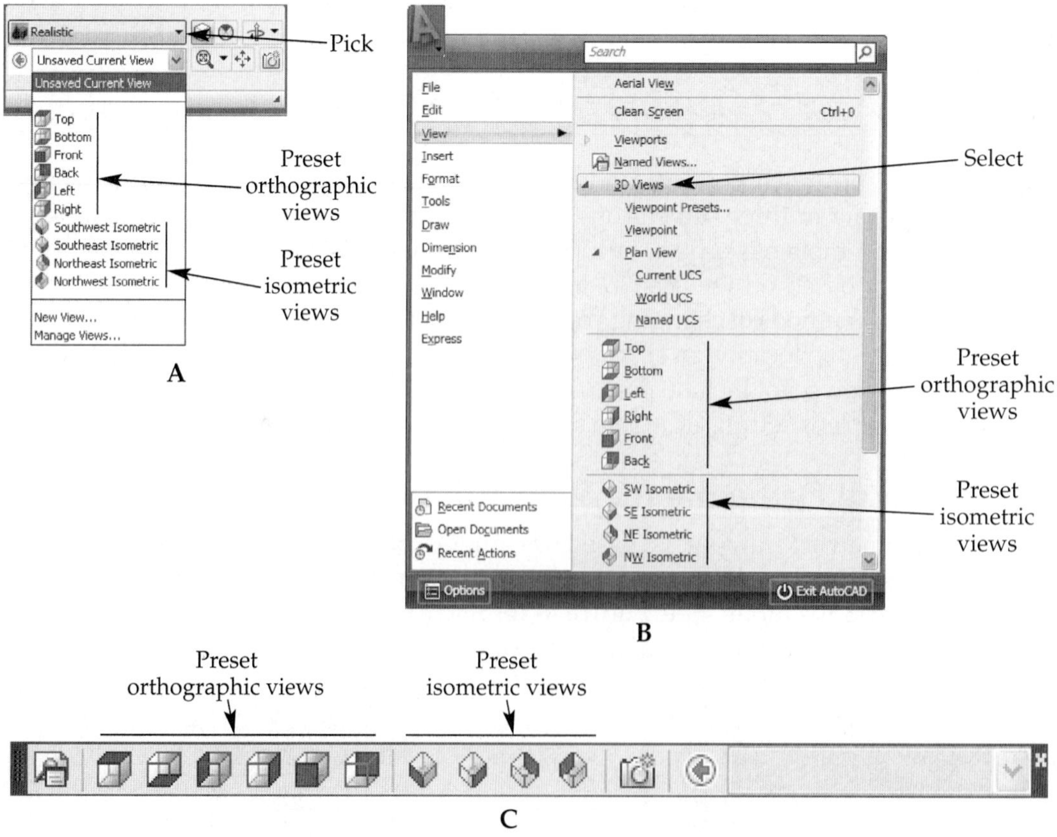

Once you select a view, the viewpoint in the current viewport is automatically changed to display an appropriate isometric or orthographic view. Since these presets are based on the WCS, selecting a preset produces the same view of the object regardless of the current UCS.

A view that looks straight down on the current drawing plane is called a ***plan view.*** An important aspect of the orthographic presets is that selecting one not only changes the viewpoint, but, by default, it also changes the UCS to be plan to the orthographic view. All new objects are created on that UCS instead of the WCS (or previous UCS). Working with UCSs is explained in detail in Chapter 4. However, to change the UCS to the WCS type UCS to access the **UCS** command and then type W for the **World** option.

When an isometric or other 3D view is displayed, you can easily switch to a plan view of the current UCS using the **PLAN** command. Using the menu browser, select **View**>**3D Views**>**Plan View**>**World UCS**. There are also **Current UCS** and **Named UCS** options in the cascading menu. The **PLAN** command is discussed in more detail in Chapter 3.

Ribbon
Home > **View** > **Top** > **Bottom** > **Left** > **Right** > **Front** > **Back**
Menu
View > **3D Views** > **Top** > **Bottom** > **Left** > **Right** > **Front** > **Back**

VIEW

View Manager Dialog Box

The **View Manager** dialog box **(View**>**Named Views...)** allows you to work with any named view, orthographic preset, or isometric preset. See **Figure 1-12.** To select a preset viewpoint, first expand the Preset Views branch in the tree on the left-hand side of the dialog box. The presets available here are the same as described above. To set a preset current, select its name in the tree and pick the **Set Current** button.

Using this dialog box, you can examine a view to determine if you like it before closing the dialog box. Select a view, such as SW Isometric, pick the **Set Current** button, and then pick the **Apply** button. You may have to move the dialog box to view the model. Use the same procedure to examine different views before you pick the **OK** button to close the dialog box.

NOTE

Selecting an orthographic view of a model using one of the methods described above produces a plan view, but it may not achieve the results you desire. Three-dimensional models can be displayed in AutoCAD using either parallel or perspective projection. Displaying a plan view in either projection is possible. However, a true plan view, as used in 2D orthographic projections, can only be created when the model is displayed as a parallel projection. You can quickly change the display from perspective to parallel, or vice versa, by right-clicking on the view cube, then picking either **Parallel** or **Perspective** in the shortcut menu. The current projection is checked in the shortcut menu.

Figure 1-12.
The **View Manager** dialog box allows you to work with any named view and orthographic and isometric preset views.

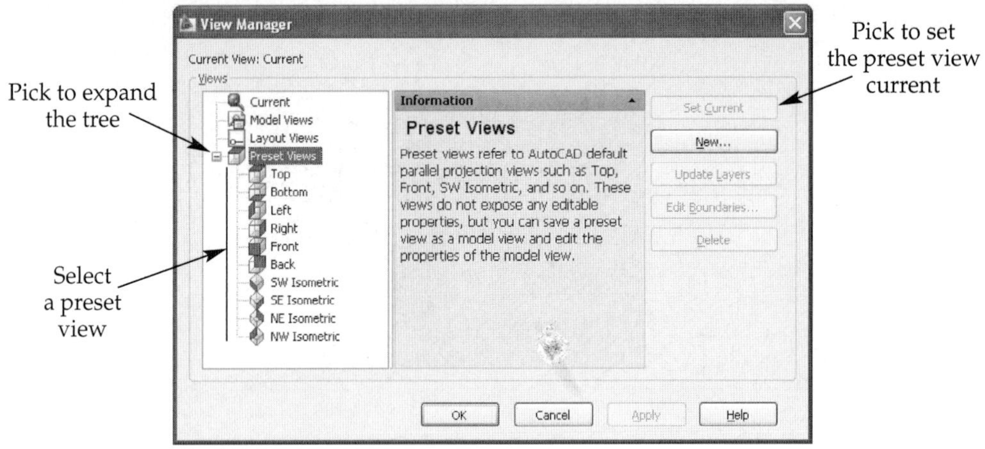

Exercise 1-2

Complete the exercise on the Student CD.

Introduction to the View Cube

You are not limited to the preset isometric viewpoints. In fact, you can view a 3D object from an unlimited number of viewpoints. The ***view cube*** allows you to display all of the preset isometric and orthographic views without making panel or menu selections. It also provides quick access to additional pictorial views and easy dynamic manipulation of all orthographic views. It allows you to dynamically rotate the view of the objects to create a new viewpoint.

The view cube is on by default in any 3D shaded or wireframe visual style. It is not displayed in the 2D Wireframe visual style, nor can it be displayed in this visual style. Visual styles are introduced later in this chapter and discussed in detail in Chapter 3.

NAVVCUBE

Ribbon
Home
> View
Toggle View Cube

Type
NAVVCUBE

Menu
View
> Display
> View Cube
> On

When displayed, the view cube appears in the upper-right corner of the screen. See Figure 1-13. The **NAVVCUBE** command controls the display of the view cube. It can also be quickly turned on and off using the **Toggle ViewCube** tool in the **View** panel of the **Home** tab on the ribbon.

As the cursor is moved over the view cube, individual faces, edges, and corners are highlighted. If you pick one of the named faces on the view cube, that orthographic plan view is displayed. However, the UCS is not changed. If you pick one of the corners, an isometric view is displayed that corresponds to one of the preset isometric views. If you pick an edge, an isometric view is displayed that looks at the edge you selected.

If you get lost while changing the viewpoint, just pick the **Home View** button on the view cube to display the view defined as the home view. By default, the southwest isometric view is the home view. You can test this by selecting the home view and looking at the compass at the base of the view cube. Note that the left face of the cube aligns with the west point on the compass. The front surface aligns with the south point on the compass. Therefore, the top-front corner points to the southwest.

Figure 1-13.
Using the view cube to change the viewpoint.

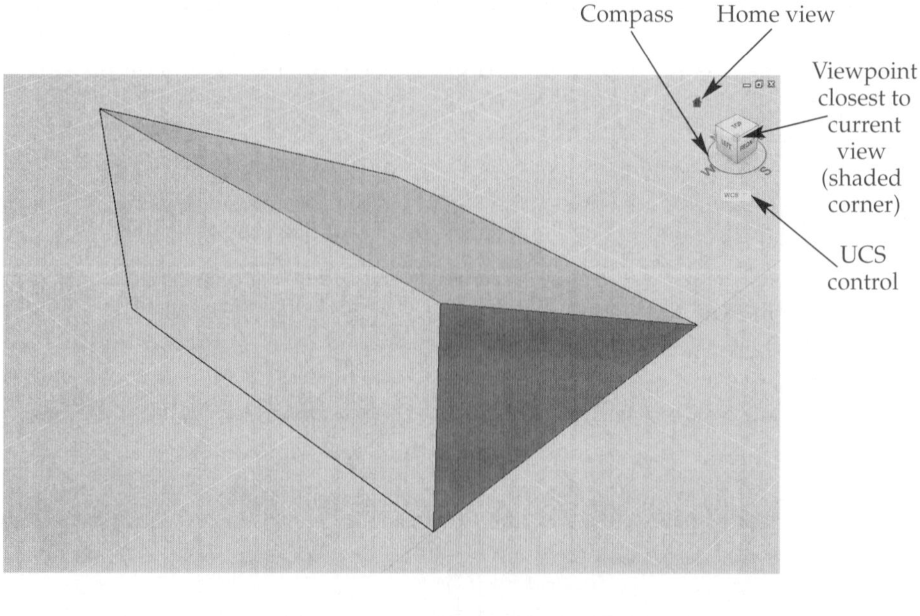

One edge, corner, or face of the view cube is always shaded or highlighted. Refer to **Figure 1-13.** This shading indicates the viewpoint on the cube that is closest to the current view.

The **NAVVCUBE** command has many options. This discussion is merely an introduction to the command. The command options and view cube features are covered in detail in Chapter 3.

PROFESSIONAL TIP

The **UNDO** command reverses the effects of the **NAVVCUBE** command.

Exercise 1-3

Complete the exercise on the Student CD.

Introduction to Visual Styles

VSCURRENT

Ribbon
Home
> View
> 2D Wireframe
> 3D Wireframe
> 3D Hidden
> Conceptual
> Realistic
Visualize
> Visual Styles
> 2D Wireframe
> 3D Wireframe
> 3D Hidden
> Conceptual
> Realistic

Type
VSCURRENT

Menu
View
> Visualize Styles
> 2D Wireframe
> 3D Wireframe
> 3D Hidden
> Conceptual
> Realistic

Toolbar
Visual Styles
2D Wireframe
3D Wireframe
3D Hidden
Conceptual
Realistic

A 3D model can be displayed in a variety of visual styles. A ***visual style*** controls the display of edges and shading in a viewport. There are five basic visual styles—2D wireframe, 3D wireframe, 3D hidden, conceptual, and realistic. A ***wireframe display*** shows all lines on the object, including those representing back or internal features. A ***hidden display*** suppresses the display of lines that would normally be hidden.

Examples of the visual styles are shown in **Figure 1-14.** To change styles, you can use the **VSCURRENT** command, **View** menu, **Visual Styles** toolbar, or the drop-down list in the **Visual Styles** panel on the **Visualize** tab in the ribbon. See **Figure 1-15.**

In the default 3D environment based on the acad3D.dwt template, the default display mode, or visual style, is Realistic. In this visual style, all objects appear as solids and are displayed in their assigned layer colors. Other display options are available. These options are discussed in detail in Chapter 3, but are given here as an introduction.

- **2D Wireframe.** Displays all lines of the model using assigned linetypes and lineweights. The 2D UCS icon and 2D grid are displayed, if turned on. If the **HIDE** command is used to display a hidden-line view, use the **REGEN** command to redisplay the wireframe view.
- **3D Wireframe.** Displays all lines of the model. The 3D grid and the 3D UCS icon are displayed, if turned on.
- **3D Hidden.** Displays all visible lines of the model from the current viewpoint and hides all lines not visible. Objects are not shaded or colored.
- **Conceptual.** The object is smoothed and shaded with transitional colors to help highlight details.
- **Realistic.** Displays the shaded and smoothed model using assigned layer colors and materials (see Chapter 14).

Figure 1-14.
The five AutoCAD default visual styles. A—**2D Wireframe**. B—**3D Wireframe**. C—**3D Hidden**. D—**Conceptual**. E—**Realistic**.

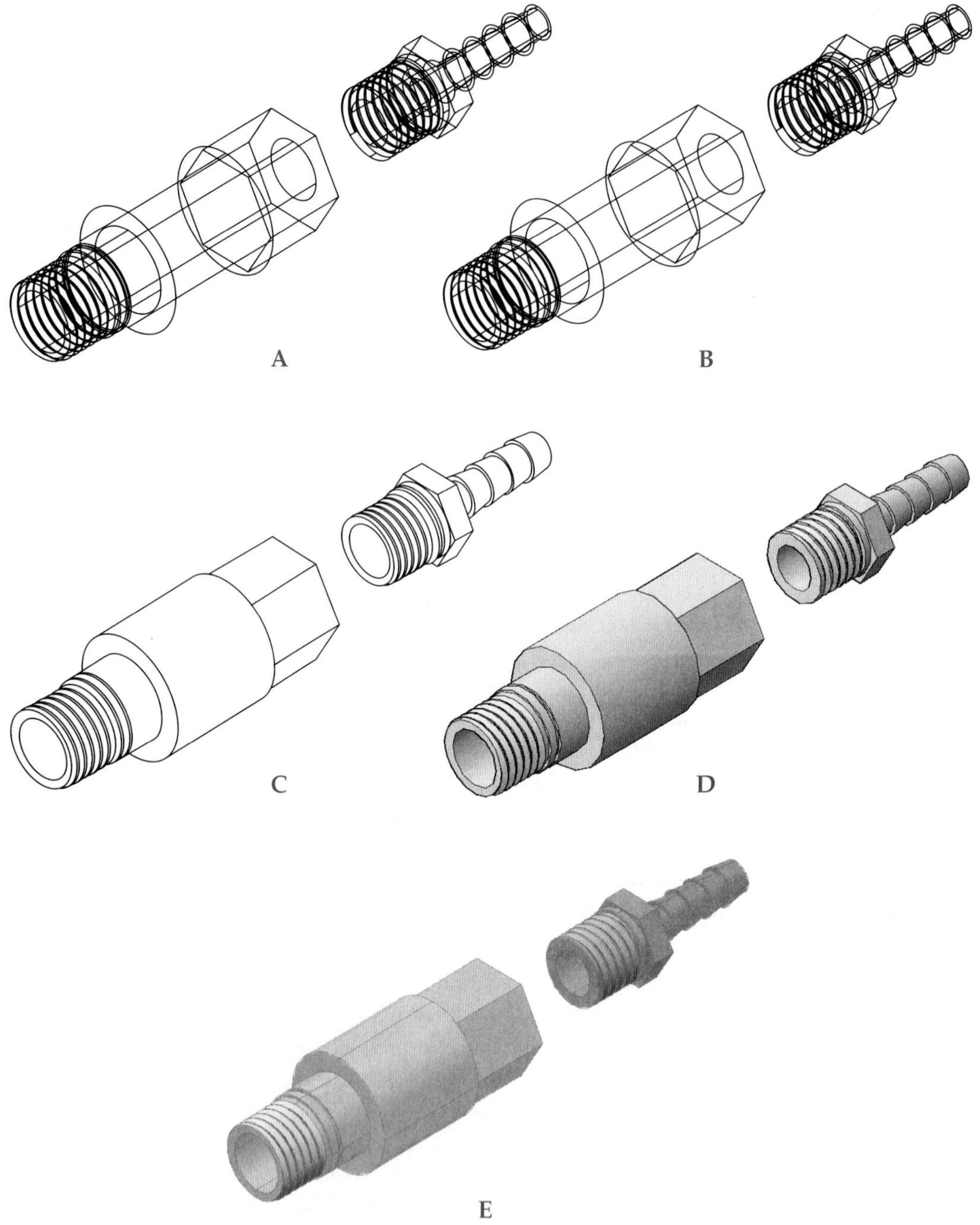

Figure 1-15.
A visual style can be set current using the drop-down list in the **View** panel in the **Home** tab or the **Visual Styles** panel in the **Visualize** tab of the ribbon.

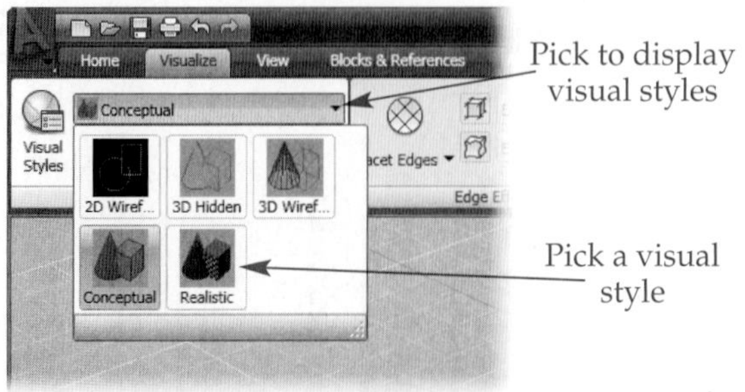

NOTE

When the visual style is 2D Wireframe, you can quickly view the model with hidden lines removed by selecting **Hide** from the **View** menu or typing HIDE. The **HIDE** command can be used at any time to remove hidden lines from a wireframe display. If **HIDE** is used when the current visual style is 3D Wireframe, Conceptual, or Realistic, the 3D Hidden visual style is set current.

Exercise 1-4

Complete the exercise on the Student CD.

Hidden Line Settings

By default, the **HIDE** command removes hidden lines from the display when the 2D Wireframe visual style is current. However, you can have hidden lines displayed in a different linetype and color instead of removed. To set this, open the **Visual Styles Manager** palette. See **Figure 1-16.** This can be accessed by typing the command or using the **Tools** menu, **Visual Style** panel in the **Visualize** tab of the ribbon, or **Visual Styles** toolbar. Using this palette, you can control all available settings for wireframe, hidden-line removed, and shaded displays in AutoCAD. See Chapter 13 for a detailed discussion of this palette.

To change the hidden line style in the 2D Wireframe visual style, select the corresponding image tile at the top of the **Visual Styles Manager**. In the **2D Hide - Obscured Lines** category of the palette are drop-down lists from which you can select a linetype and color.

VISUALSTYLES

Ribbon
Visualize
> Visual Styles
Visual Styles

Menu
Tools
> Palettes
> Visual Styles

Toolbar
Visual Styles
Manage Visual Styles

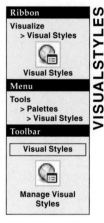

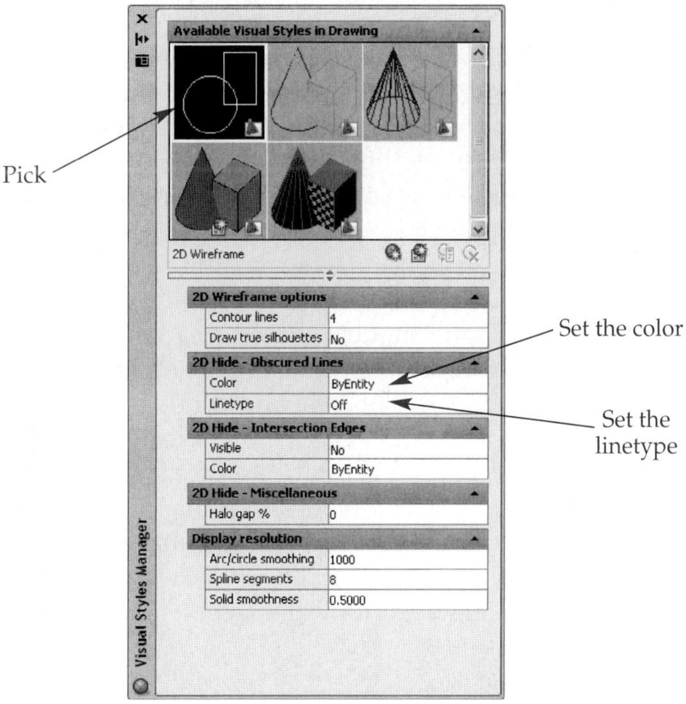

Figure 1-16.
The manner in which hidden lines appear in hidden displays when the **2D Wireframe** visual style is current is controlled in the **Visual Styles Manager** palette.

When the **Linetype** drop-down list is set to Off, the display of hidden lines is suppressed by the **HIDE** command. This is the default setting. When a linetype is selected from the drop-down list, hidden lines are displayed in that linetype after the **HIDE** command is used. The linetypes available in the drop-down list are not the same as the linetypes loaded into your drawing.

You can also change the display color of the hidden lines. Simply pick a color in the **Color** drop-down list. To have the hidden lines displayed in the same color as the object, select ByEntity, which is the default. The color setting has no effect when the **Linetype** drop-down list is set to Off.

NOTE

Making changes in the **Visual Styles Manager** redefines the visual style.

3D Construction Techniques

Before constructing a 3D model, you should determine the purpose of your design. What will the model be used for—presentation, analysis, or manufacturing? This helps you determine which tools you should use to construct and display the model. Three-dimensional objects can be drawn as solids or surfaces and displayed in wireframe, hidden-line removed, and shaded views.

A ***wireframe object,*** or model, is an object constructed of lines in 3D space. Wireframe models are hard to visualize because it is difficult to determine the angle of view and the nature of the surfaces represented by the lines. The **HIDE** command has no effect on a wireframe model because there is nothing to hide. All lines are always visible because there are no surfaces or faces between the lines. Wireframe models have very limited applications.

Surface modeling represents solid objects by creating a skin in the shape of the object. However, there is nothing inside of the object. Think of a surface model as a balloon filled with air. A surface model looks more like the real object than a wireframe and can be used for rendering. True surface models are constructed in specialized software used for applications such as civil engineering terrain modeling, automobile body design, sheet metal design and fabrication, and animation.

Like surface modeling, ***solid modeling*** represents the shape of objects, but also provides data related to the physical properties of the objects. Solid models can be analyzed to determine mass, volume, moments of inertia, and centroid. A solid model is not just a skin, it represents a solid object. Some third-party programs allow you to perform finite element analysis on the model. In addition, solid models can be rendered. Most 3D objects are created as solid models.

In AutoCAD, solid models can be created from primitives. ***Primitives*** are basic shapes used as the foundation to create complex shapes. Some of these basic shapes include boxes, cylinders, spheres, and cones. Primitives can be modified to create a finished product. See **Figure 1-17.**

Surface and solid models can be exported from AutoCAD for use in animation and rendering software, such as Autodesk 3ds max® or Autodesk VIZ®. Rendered models can be used in any number of presentation formats, including slide shows, black and white or color prints, and animation recorded to video files. Surface and solid models can also be used to create virtual worlds for virtual reality and gaming applications.

Figure 1-17.
A—These two cylinders and the box are solid primitives. B—With a couple of quick modifications, the large cylinder becomes a shaft with a machined keyway.

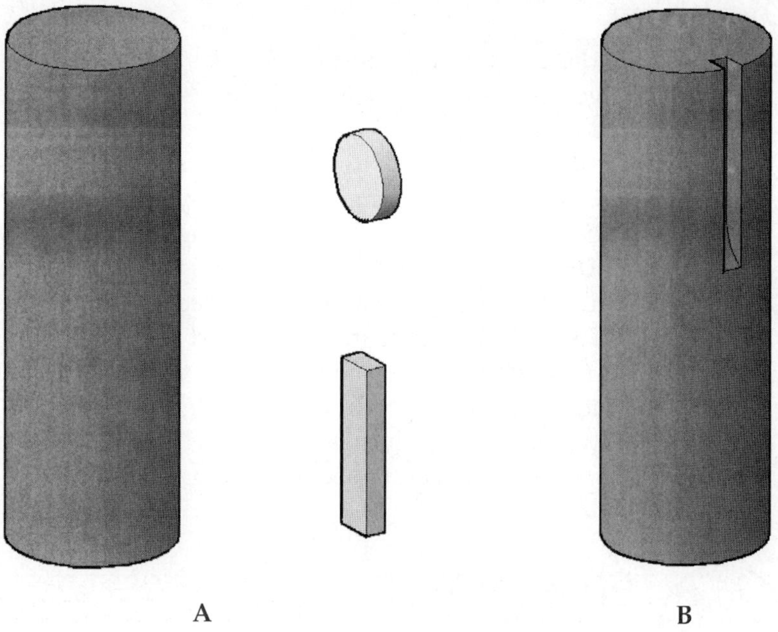

Guidelines for Working with 3D Drawings

Working in 3D, like working with 2D drawings, requires careful planning to efficiently produce the desired results. The following guidelines can be used when working in 3D.

Planning

- ✓ Determine the type of final drawing you need and the manner in which it will be displayed. Then, choose the method of 3D construction that best suits your needs—wireframe, surface, or solid.
- ✓ For an object requiring only one pictorial view, it may be actually quicker to draw an object in 3D rather than in AutoCAD's isometric mode. AutoCAD's 3D solid modeling tools enable you to quickly create an accurate model, then display it in the required isometric format using preset views. The **FLATSHOT** command can then be used to create a 2D drawing of the model.
- ✓ It is best to use AutoCAD's 3D commands to construct objects and layouts that need to be viewed from different angles for design purposes.
- ✓ Construct only the details needed for the function of the drawing. This saves space and time and makes visualization much easier.
- ✓ Use object snap modes in a pictorial view in conjunction with a dynamic UCS to save having to create new UCSs.
- ✓ Keep in mind that when the grid is displayed, the pattern appears at the current elevation and parallel to the XY plane of the current UCS.
- ✓ Create layers having different colors for different drawing objects. Turn them on and off as needed or freeze those not being used.

Editing

- ✓ Use the **Properties** palette to change the color, layer, or linetype of 3D objects.
- ✓ Use grips to edit a solid-modeled object (see Chapter 10).
- ✓ Do as much editing as possible from a 3D viewpoint. It is quicker and the results are immediately seen.

Displaying

- ✓ Use the **HIDE** command and visual styles to help visualize complex drawings.
- ✓ To change views quickly, use the preset isometric views, view cube, and **PLAN** command.
- ✓ Use the **VIEW** command to create and save 3D views for quicker pictorial displays. This avoids having to repeatedly use the **NAVVCUBE** command.
- ✓ Freeze unwanted layers before displaying objects in 3D, and especially before using **HIDE**. AutoCAD regenerates layers that are turned off, which may cause an inaccurate hidden display to be created. Frozen layers are not regenerated.
- ✓ Before using **HIDE**, zoom in on the part of a drawing to display. This saves time in regenerating the view because only the objects that are visible are regenerated.
- ✓ You may have to slightly move objects that touch or intersect if the display removes a line you need to see or plot.

Chapter Test

Answer the following questions. Write your answers on a separate sheet of paper or complete the electronic chapter test on the Student CD.

1. What are the three coordinates needed to locate any point in 3D space?
2. In a 2D drawing, what is the value for the Z coordinate?
3. What purpose does the right-hand rule serve?
4. Which three fingers are used in the right-hand rule?
5. What is the definition of a *viewpoint?*
6. What is the function of the *ribbon* and its panels?
7. How do you turn the display of individual panels on or off in the ribbon?
8. How can you quickly change the display from perspective projection to parallel projection, or vice versa?
9. How many preset isometric viewpoints does AutoCAD have? List them.
10. How does changing the UCS impact using one of the preset isometric viewpoints?
11. List the six preset orthographic viewpoints.
12. When selecting a preset orthographic viewpoint, what happens to the UCS?
13. Which command allows you to dynamically change your viewpoint using an on-screen cube icon?
14. Define *wireframe display.*
15. Define *hidden display.*
16. Define *wireframe object.*
17. Define *surface model.*
18. Define *solid model.*
19. Define *primitive.*
20. Briefly describe how to have hidden lines displayed in red when the **HIDE** command is used.

CHAPTER 2

Creating Primitives and Composites

Learning Objectives

After completing this chapter, you will be able to:

- ✓ Construct 3D solid primitives.
- ✓ Explain the dynamic feedback presented when constructing solid primitives.
- ✓ Create complex solids using the **UNION** command.
- ✓ Remove portions of a solid using the **SUBTRACT** command.
- ✓ Create a new solid from the interference volume between two solids.
- ✓ Create regions.

Overview of Solid Modeling

In Chapter 1 you were introduced to the three basic forms of 3D modeling—wireframe objects, solid models, and surface models. Solid models are probably the most useful and, hence, most common type of 3D modeling. A solid model accurately and realistically represents the shape and form of a final object. In addition, a solid model contains data related to the object's volume, mass, and centroid.

Solid modeling is very flexible. You can start with solid primitives, such as a box, cone, or cylinder, and perform a variety of editing functions. You can think of creating a solid model as working with modeling clay. Starting with a basic block of clay, you can add more clay, remove clay, cut holes, round edges, etc., until you have arrived at the final shape and form of the object.

PROFESSIONAL TIP

You can use snaps on solid objects. For example, you can snap to the center of a solid sphere using the **Center** object snap. The **Endpoint** object snap can be used to select the corners of a box, apex of a cone, corners of a wedge, etc.

Constructing Solid Primitives

As you learned in Chapter 1, a primitive is a basic building block. The eight ***solid primitives*** in AutoCAD are a box, cone, cylinder, polysolid, pyramid, sphere, torus, and wedge. These primitives can also be used as building blocks for complex solid models. This section provides detailed information on drawing all of the solid primitives. All of the 3D modeling primitive commands can be accessed using the **3D Modeling** panel in **Home** tab of the ribbon, the **Modeling** toolbar, the **Draw** menu, or by typing the name of the 3D modeling primitive. See **Figure 2-1.**

The information required to construct a solid primitive depends on the type of primitive being drawn. For example, to draw a solid cylinder you must provide a center point for the base, a radius or diameter of the base, and the height of the cylinder. A variety of command options are available when creating primitives, but each primitive is constructed using just a few basic dimensions. These are shown in **Figure 2-2.**

Figure 2-1.
A—The **Modeling** cascading menu in the **Draw** menu. B—The **Modeling** toolbar. C—The **3D Modeling** panel in the **Home** tab of the ribbon.

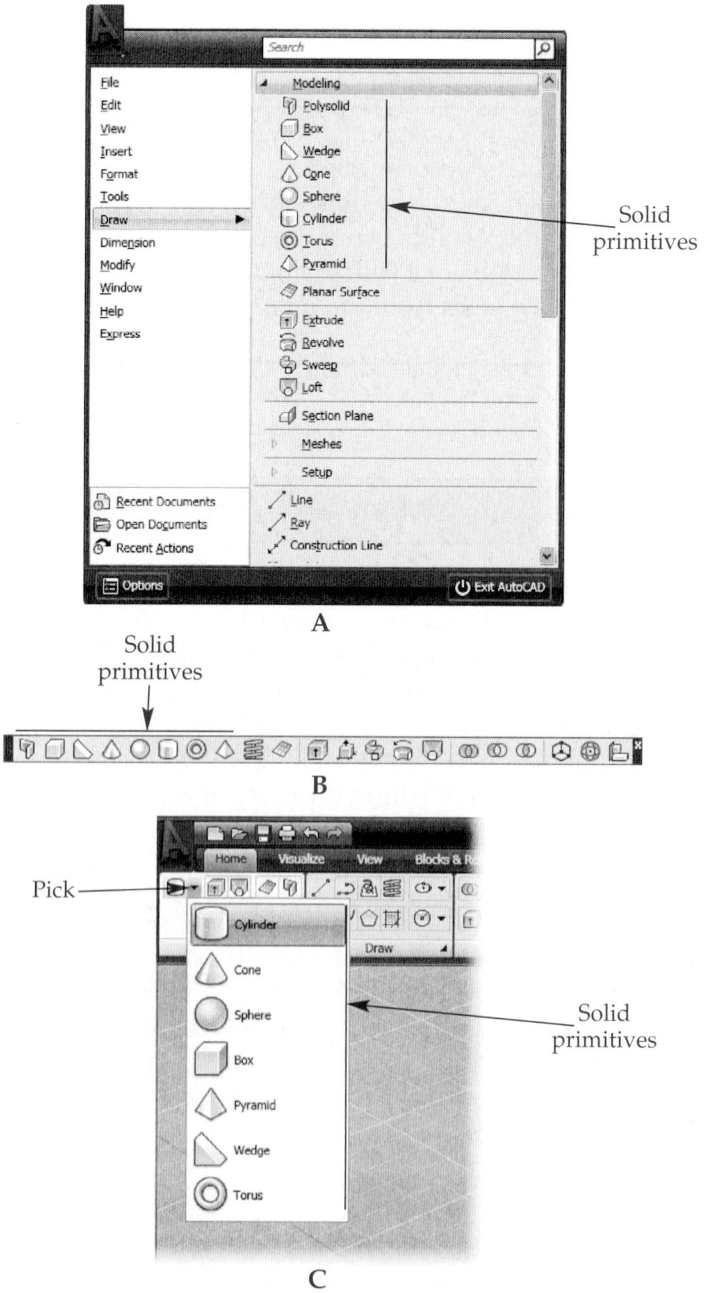

Certain familiar editing commands can be used on solid primitives. For example, you can fillet or chamfer the edges of a solid primitive. In addition, there are other editing commands that are specifically for use on solids. You can also perform Boolean operations on solids. These operations allow you to add one solid to another, subtract one solid from another, or create a new solid based on how two solids overlap.

Figure 2-2.
An overview of AutoCAD's solid primitives and the dimensions required to draw them.

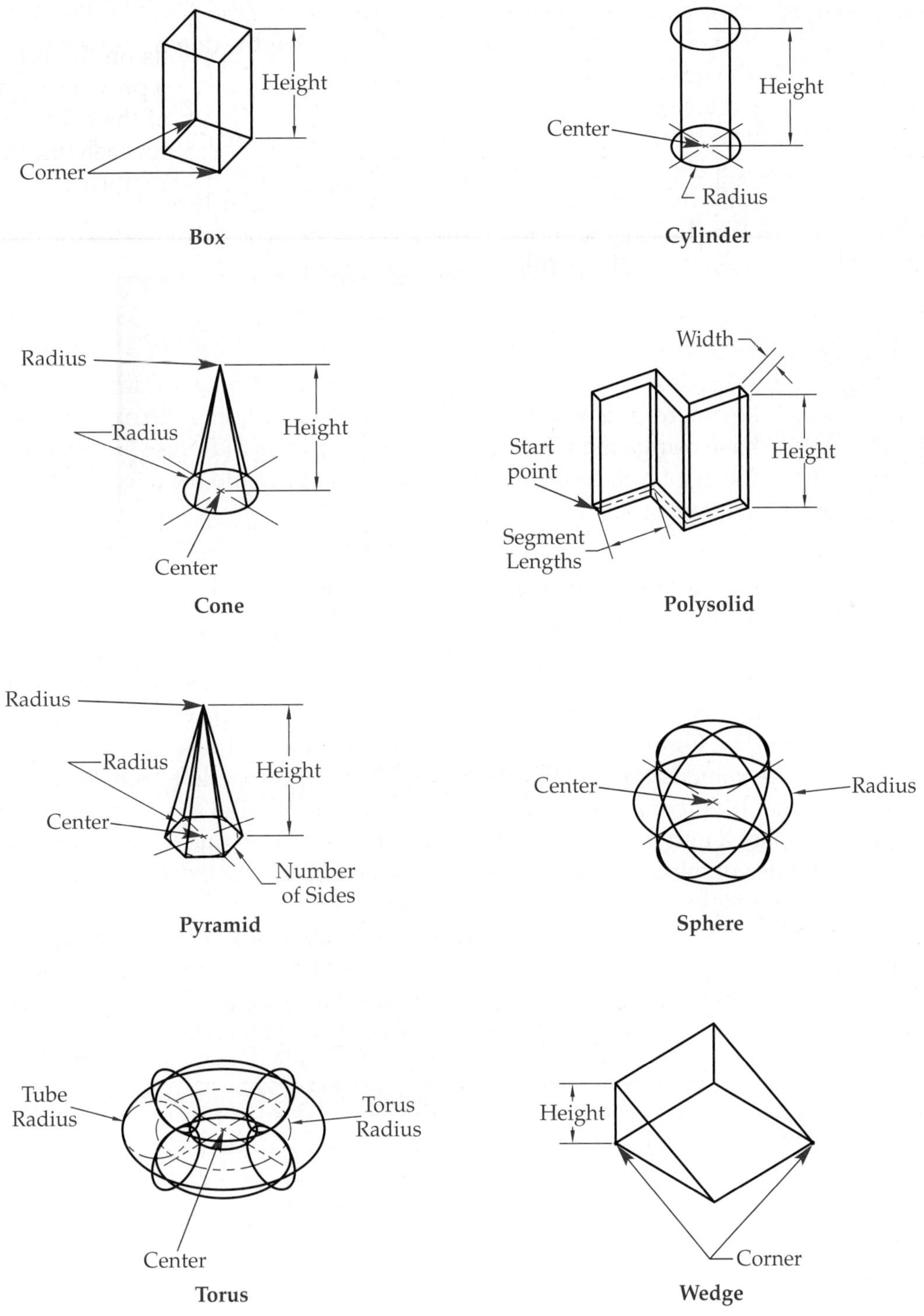

Using Dynamic Input and Dynamic Feedback

Dynamic input enables you to construct models in a "heads up" fashion with minimal eye movement around the screen. When a command is initiated, the command prompts are then displayed in the dynamic input area, which is at the lower-right corner of the crosshairs. As the pointer is moved, the dynamic input area follows it. The dynamic input area displays values of the cursor location, dimensions, command prompts, and command options (in a drop-down list). Coordinates and dimensions are displayed in boxes called *input fields.* When command options are available, a drop-down list arrow appears. Press the down arrow key on the keyboard to display the list. You can use your pointer to select the option or press the down arrow key until a dot appears by the desired option and press [Enter].

For example, after selecting a modeling command such as **BOX**, the first item that appears in the dynamic input area is the prompt to specify the first corner and a display of the X and Y coordinate values of the crosshairs. At this point you can use the pointer to specify the first corner or type coordinate values. Type the X value and then a comma or the [Tab] key to move to the Y value input box. This locks the typed value and any movement of the pointer will not change it.

CAUTION

When using dynamic input to enter coordinate values from the keyboard, it is important that you avoid pressing [Enter] until you have completed the coordinate entry. When you press [Enter], all of the displayed coordinate values are accepted and the next command prompt appears.

In addition to entering coordinate values for sizes of solid primitives, you can provide direct distance dimensions. For example, the second prompt of the **BOX** command is for the second corner of the base. When you move the pointer, two dimensional input fields appear. Also, notice that a preview of the base is shown in the drawing area. This is the ***dynamic feedback*** that AutoCAD provides as you create a solid primitive. See **Figure 2-3A.** If you enter a dimension at the keyboard and press the [Tab] key, the value is the length of the side. Then, press the left mouse button to set the base. But, if you enter a value followed by a comma, the dynamic input area changes to display X and Y coordinate boxes. In this case, the values entered are the X and Y coordinates of the opposite corner of the box base. If X, Y, *and* Z coordinates are entered, the point is the opposite corner of the box.

After establishing the location and size of the box base, the next prompt asks you to specify the height. Again, you can either enter a direct dimension value and press [Enter] or select the height with the pointer. See **Figure 2-3B.** AutoCAD provides dynamic feedback on the height of the box as the pointer is moved.

NOTE

The techniques described above can be used with any form of dynamic input. The current input field is always highlighted. You can always enter a value and use the [Tab] key to lock the input and move to the next field.

Figure 2-3.
A—Specifying the base of a box with dynamic input on. Notice the preview of the base.
B—Setting the height of a box with dynamic input on. Notice the preview of the height.

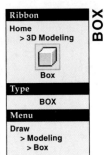

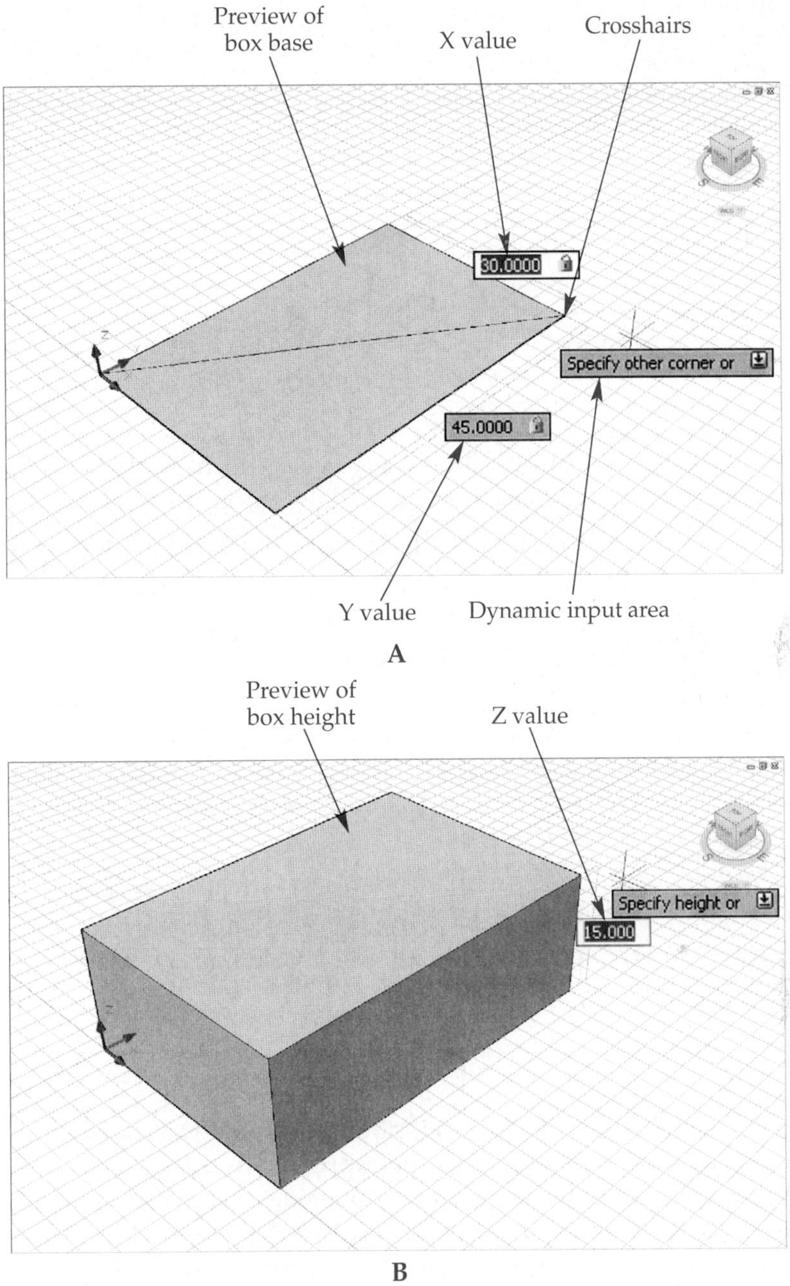

Box

A ***box*** has six flat sides forming square corners. It can be constructed starting from an initial corner or the center. See **Figure 2-4.** A cube can be constructed, as well as a box with unequal sides.

When the command is initiated, you are prompted to select the first corner or enter the **Center** option. The first corner is one corner on the base of the box. The center is the geometric center of the box, as shown in **Figure 2-4.** If you select the **Center** option, you are next prompted to select the center point.

After selecting the first corner or center, you are prompted to select the other corner or enter the **Cube** or **Length** option. The "other" corner is the opposite corner of the box base if you enter an XY coordinate, or the opposite corner of the box if you enter an XYZ coordinate. If the **Length** option is entered, you are first prompted for the length of one side. If dynamic input is on, you can also specify a rotation angle. After entering the length, you are prompted for the width of the box base. If the **Cube** option is selected, the length value is applied to all sides of the box.

BOX

Ribbon
Home
> 3D Modeling
Box
Type
BOX
Menu
Draw
> Modeling
> Box

Figure 2-4.
A—A box created using the **Cube** option. B—A box created by selecting the center point.

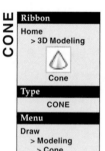

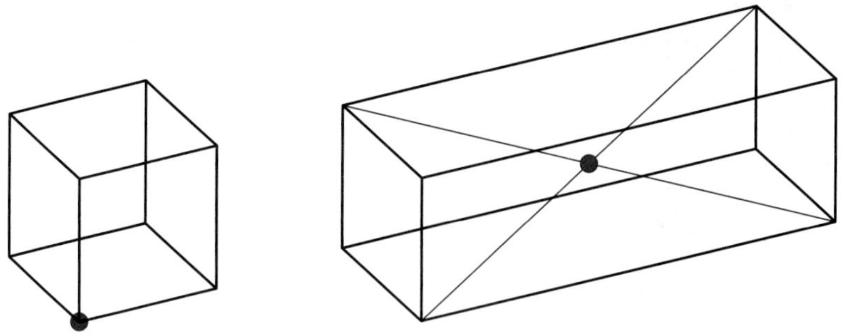

A B

Once the length and width of the base are established, you are prompted for the height, unless the **Cube** option was selected. Either enter the height or select the **2point** option. This option allows you to pick two points on screen to set the height. The box is created.

PROFESSIONAL TIP

If dynamic UCS is on, you can select a surface that is not parallel to the current UCS on which to locate the object. This feature is called a *dynamic UCS* and discussed in detail in Chapter 4.

Exercise 2-1

Complete the exercise on the Student CD.

Cone

CONE

Ribbon
Home > 3D Modeling Cone
Type
CONE
Menu
Draw > Modeling > Cone

A ***cone*** has a circular or elliptical base with edges that converge at a single point. The cone may be *truncated* so the top is flat and the cone does not have an apex. See **Figure 2-5.** When the command is initiated, you are prompted for the center point of the cone base or to enter an option. If you pick the center, you must then set the radius of the base. To specify a diameter, enter the **Diameter** option after specifying the center.

The **3P**, **2P**, and **Ttr** options are used to define a circular base using either three points on the circle, two points on the circle, or two points of tangency on the circle and a radius. The **Elliptical** option is used to create an elliptical base.

If the **Elliptical** option is entered, you are prompted to pick both endpoints of one axis and then one endpoint of the other axis of an ellipse that defines the base. If the **Center** option is entered after the **Ellipse** option, you are asked to select the center of the ellipse and then pick an endpoint on each of the axes.

After the base is defined, you are asked to specify a height. You can enter a height or enter the **2point**, **Axis endpoint**, or **Top radius** option. The **2point** option is used to set the height by picking two points on screen. The distance between the points is the height. The height is always applied perpendicular to the base.

The **Axis endpoint** option allows you to orient the cone at any angle, regardless of the current UCS. For example, to place a tapered cutout in the end of a block, first create a construction line. Refer to **Figure 2-6.** Then, locate the cone base and give a coordinate location of the apex, or axis endpoint. You can then use editing commands to subtract the cone from the box to create the tapered hole. See Chapters 10 and 11 for model editing details.

Figure 2-5.
A—A circular cone. B—A frustum cone. C—An elliptical cone.

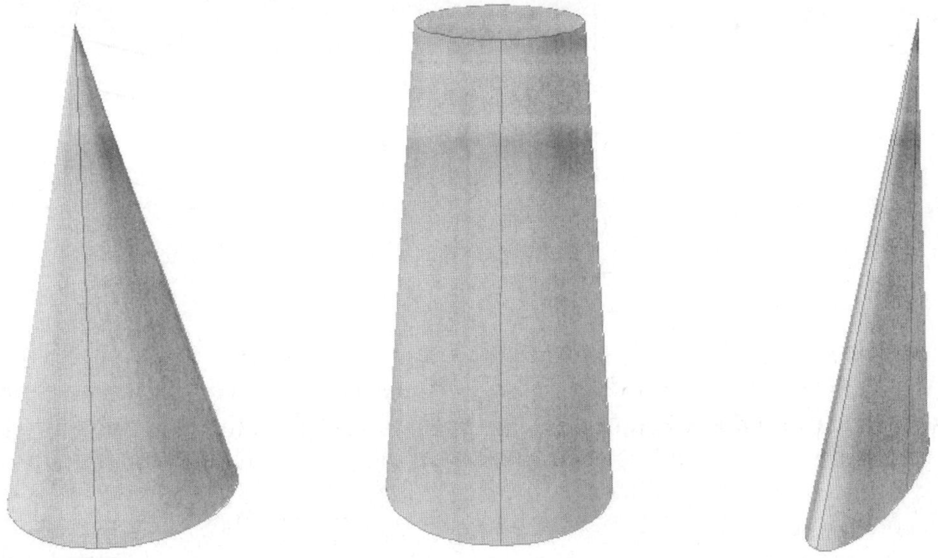

A B C

Figure 2-6.
A—Cones can be positioned relative to other objects using the **Axis endpoint** option. B—The cone is subtracted from the box.

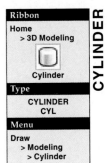

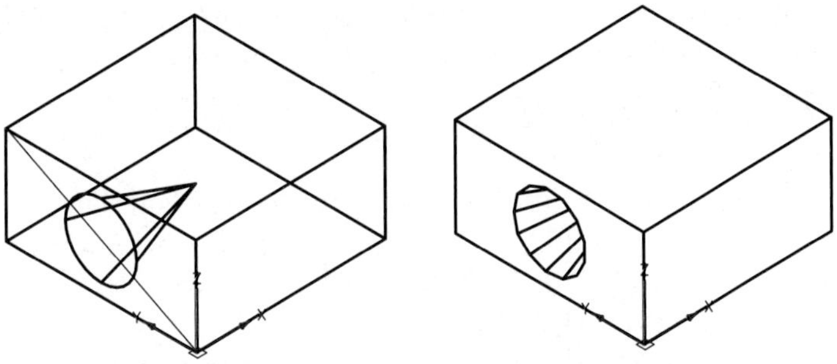

A B

The **Top radius** option allows you to specify the radius of the top of the cone. If this option is not used, the radius is zero, which creates a pointed cone. Setting the radius to a value other than zero produces a ***frustum cone,*** or a cone where the top is truncated and does not come to a point.

Cylinder

CYLINDER

Ribbon
Home > 3D Modeling Cylinder
Type
CYLINDER CYL
Menu
Draw > Modeling > Cylinder

A ***cylinder*** has a circular or elliptical base and edges that extend perpendicular to the base. See **Figure 2-7.** When the command is initiated, you are prompted for the center point of the cylinder base or to enter an option. If you pick the center, you must then set the radius of the base. To specify a diameter, enter the **Diameter** option after specifying the center.

The **3P**, **2P**, and **Ttr** options are used to define a circular base using either three points on the circle, two points on the circle, or two points of tangency on the circle and a radius. The **Elliptical** option is used to create an elliptical base.

If the **Elliptical** option is entered, you are prompted to pick both endpoints of one axis and then one endpoint of the other axis of an ellipse defining the base. If the **Center** option is entered, you are asked to select the center of the ellipse and then pick an endpoint on each of the axes.

Figure 2-7.
A—A circular cylinder. B—An elliptical cylinder.

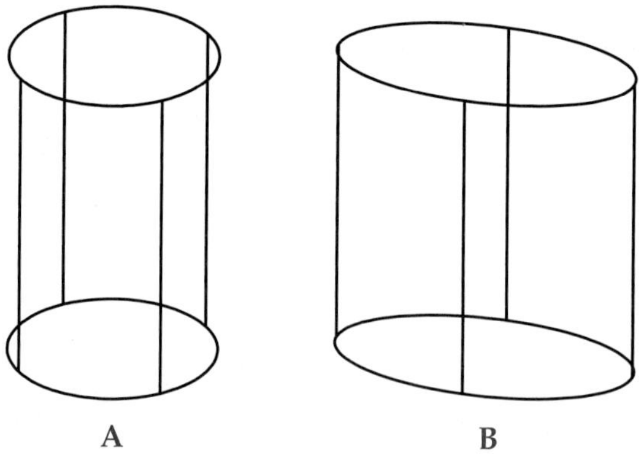

After the base is defined, you are asked to specify a height or to enter the **2point** or **Axis endpoint** option. The **2point** option is used to set the height by picking two points on screen. The distance between the points is the height. The **Axis endpoint** option allows you to orient the cylinder at any angle, regardless of the current UCS, just as with a cone.

The **Axis endpoint** option is useful for placing a cylinder inside of another object to create a hole. The cylinder can then be subtracted from the other object to create a hole. Refer to Figure 2-8. If the axis endpoint does not have the same X and Y coordinates as the center of the base, the cylinder is tilted from the XY plane.

If polar tracking is on when using the **Axis endpoint** option, you can rotate the cylinder axis 90° from the current UCS Z axis, and then turn the cylinder to any preset polar increment. See Figure 2-9A. If the polar tracking vector is parallel to the Z axis of the current UCS, the tooltip displays a positive or negative Z value. See Figure 2-9B.

Polysolid

POLYSOLID

Ribbon
Home
> 3D Modeling
Polysolid
Type
POLYSOLID
Menu
Draw
> Modeling
> Polysolid

The *polysolid* primitive is simply a polyline constructed as a solid object by applying a width and height to the polyline. Many of the options used to create polylines are used with the **POLYSOLID** command. The principal difference is that a solid object is constructed using **POLYSOLID**.

When the command is initiated, you are prompted to select the first point or enter an option. By default, the width of the polysolid is equally applied to each side of the line you draw. This is center justification. Using the **Justify** option, you can set the justification to center, left, or right. The justification applies to all segments created in this command session. See Figure 2-10. If you select the wrong justification option, you must exit the command and begin again.

Figure 2-8.
A—A cylinder is drawn inside of another cylinder using the **Axis endpoint** option. B—The large cylinder has a hole after **SUBTRACT** is used to remove the small cylinder.

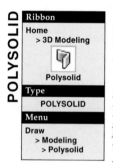

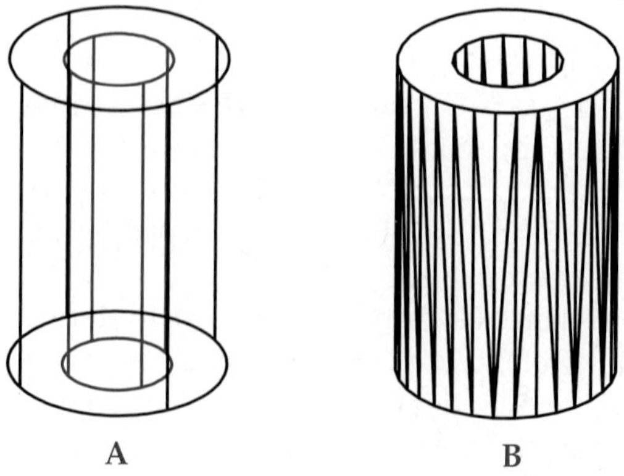

Figure 2-9.
A—If polar tracking is on, you can rotate the cylinder axis 90° from the current UCS Z axis and then move the cylinder to any angle in the XY plane. B—If the polar tracking vector is moved parallel to the current Z axis of the UCS, the tooltip displays a positive or negative Z dimension.

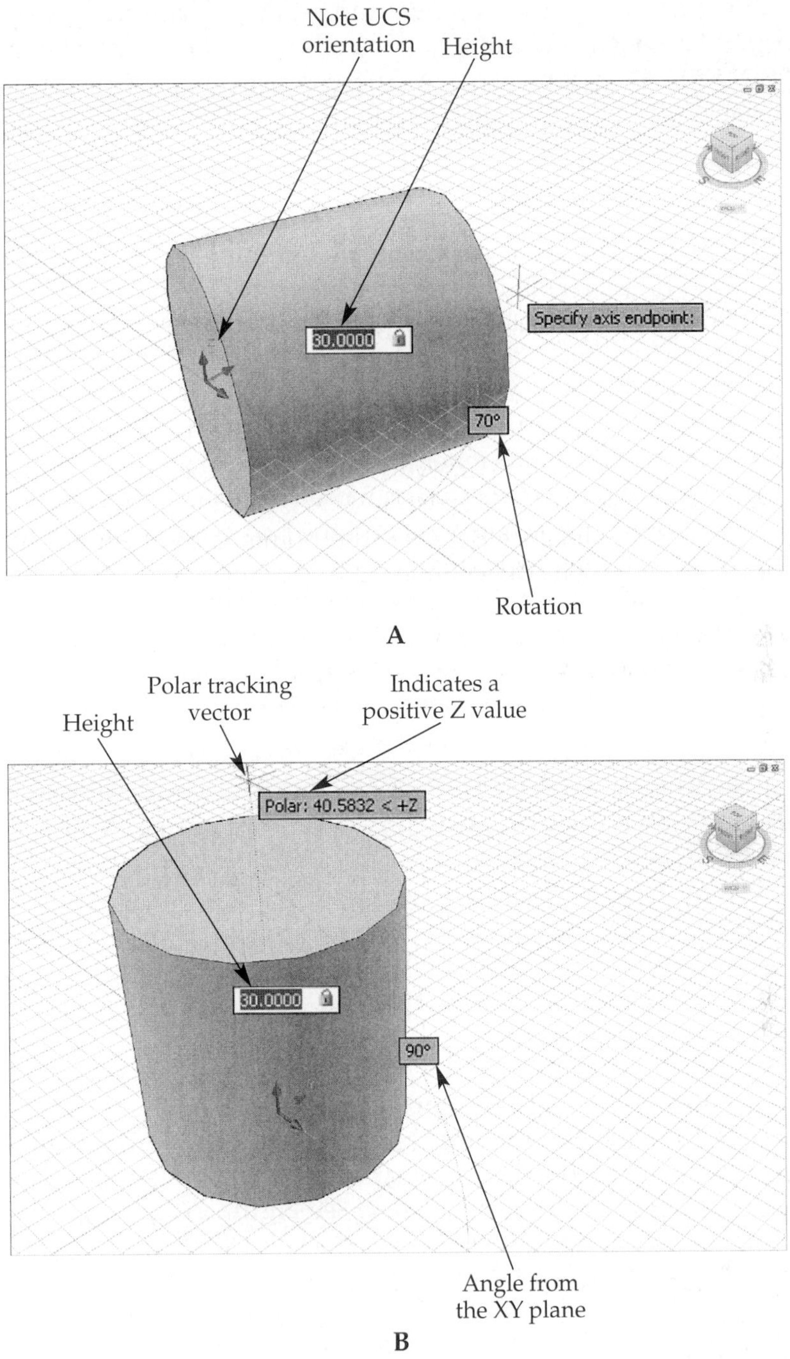

Figure 2-10.
When you begin the **POLYSOLID** command, use the **Justify** option to select the alignment.

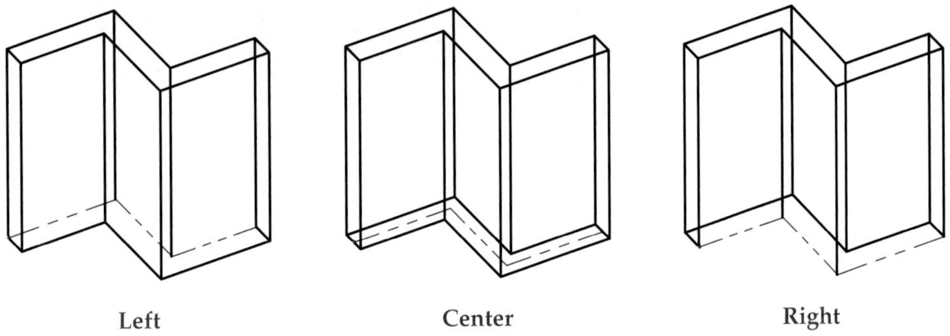

The default width is .25 units and height is four units. These values can be changed using the **Height** and **Width** options of the command. The height value is saved in the **PSOLHEIGHT** system variable. The width value is saved in the **PSOLWIDTH** system variable. Using these system variables, the default width and height can be set outside of the command.

The **Object** option allows you to convert an existing 2D object into a polysolid. AutoCAD entities such as lines, circles, arcs, polylines, polygons, and rectangles can be converted. The 2D object cannot be self intersecting. Some objects, such as 3D polylines and revision clouds, cannot be converted.

Once you have set the first point on the polysolid, pick the endpoint of the first segment. Continue adding segments as needed and press [Enter] to complete the command. After the first point is set, you can enter the **Arc** option. The current segment will then be created as an arc instead of a straight line. See **Figure 2-11.** Arc segments will be created until you enter the **Line** option. The suboptions for the **Arc** option are:

- **Close.** If there are two or more segments, this option creates an arc segment between the active point and the first point of the polysolid. You can also close straight-line segments.
- **Direction.** Specifies the tangent direction for the start of the arc.
- **Line.** Returns the command to creating straight-line segments.
- **Second point.** Locates the second point of a two-point arc. This is not the endpoint of the segment.

PROFESSIONAL TIP

The **Object** option of the **POLYSOLID** command is a powerful tool for converting 2D objects to 3D solids. For example, you can create a single-line wall plan using a polyline and then quickly convert it to a 3D model.

PYRAMID

Ribbon
Home > 3D Modeling
 Pyramid
Type
PYRAMID
Menu
Draw > Modeling > Pyramid

Pyramid

A ***pyramid*** has a base composed of straight-line segments and edges that converge at a single point. The pyramid base can be composed of three to 32 sides, much like a 2D polygon. A pyramid may be drawn with a pointed apex or as a ***frustum pyramid,*** which has a truncated, or flat, apex. See **Figure 2-12.**

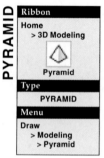

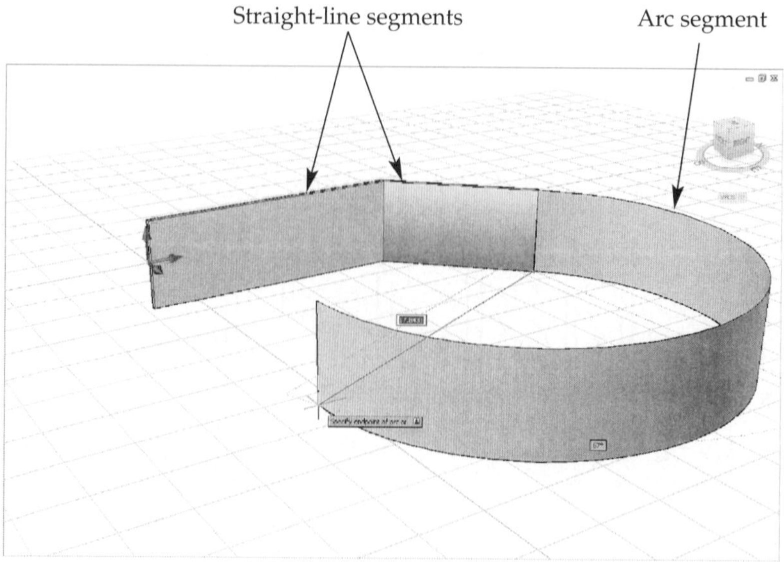

Figure 2-11.
The **Arc** option of the **POLYSOLID** command is used to create curved segments.

Figure 2-12.
A sampling of pyramids that can be constructed with the **PYRAMID** command.

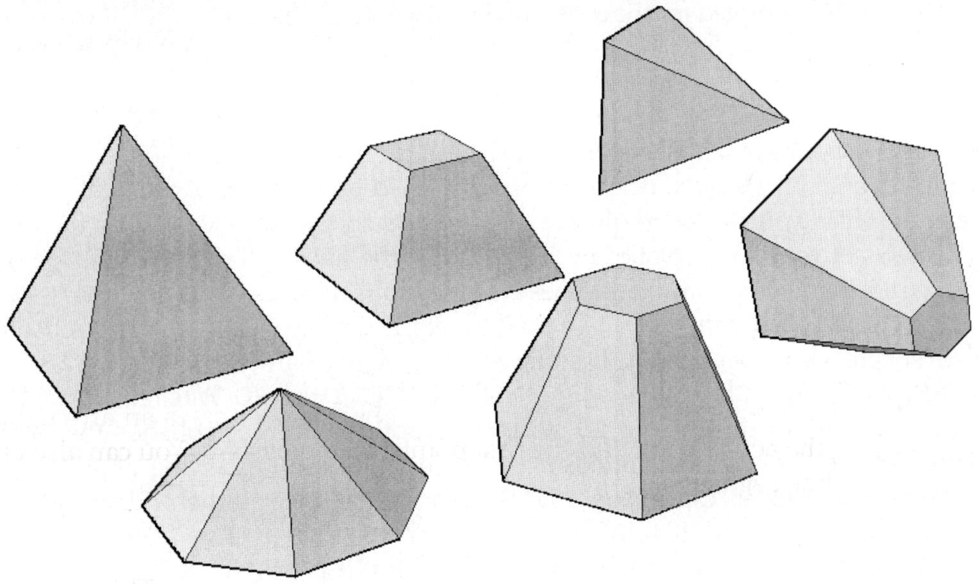

Once the command is initiated, you are prompted for the center of the base or to enter an option. To set the number of sides on the base, enter the **Sides** option. Then, enter the number of sides. You are returned to the first prompt.

The base of the pyramid can be drawn by either picking the center and the radius of a base circle or by picking the endpoints of one side. The default method is to pick the center. Simply specify the center and then set the radius. To pick the endpoints of one side, enter the **Edge** option. Then, pick the first endpoint of one side followed by the second endpoint. If dynamic input is on, you can also set a rotation angle for the pyramid.

If drawing the base from the center point, the polygon is circumscribed about the base circle by default. To inscribe the polygon on the base circle, enter the **Inscribed** option before setting the radius. To change back to a circumscribed polygon, enter the **Circumscribed** option before setting the radius.

After locating and sizing the base, you are prompted for the height. To create a frustum pyramid, enter the **Top radius** option. Then, set the radius of the top circle. The top will be either inscribed or circumscribed based on the base circle. You are then returned to the height prompt.

The height value can be set by entering a direct distance. You can also use the **2point** option to set the height. With this option, pick two points on screen. The distance between the two points is the height value. The **Axis endpoint** option can also be used to specify the center of the top in the same manner as for a cone or cylinder.

PROFESSIONAL TIP

Six-sided frustum pyramids can be used for bolt heads and as "blanks" for creating nuts.

SPHERE

Ribbon
Home > 3D Modeling  Sphere
Type
SPHERE
Menu
Draw > Modeling > Sphere

Sphere

A ***sphere*** is a round, smooth object like a baseball or globe. Once the command is initiated, you are prompted for the center of the sphere or to enter an option. If you pick the center, you must then set the radius of the sphere. To specify a diameter, enter the **Diameter** option after specifying the center. The **3P**, **2P**, and **Ttr** options are used to define the sphere using either three points on the surface of the sphere, two points on the surface of the sphere, or two points of tangency on the surface of the sphere and a radius.

Spheres and other curved objects can be displayed in a number of different ways. The manner in which you choose to display these objects should be governed by the display requirements of your work. Notice in Figure 2-13A the lines that define the shape of the spheres in a wireframe display. These lines are called ***contour lines,*** also known as *tessellation lines.* The **Visual Styles Manager** can be used to set the display of contour lines and silhouettes on spheres and other curved 3D surfaces for a given visual style. See Figure 2-14.

With the **Visual Styles Manager** displayed, select the 2D Wireframe image tile. The Contour lines setting in the **2D Wireframe options** area establishes the number of lines used to show the shape of curved objects. A similar setting appears in the 3D Wireframe, 3D Hidden, Conceptual, and Realistic visual styles if their Edge mode entry is set to Isolines. The default value is four, but can be set to a value from zero to 2047. Figure 2-13B displays spheres with 20 contour lines. It is best to use a lower number during construction and preliminary displays of the model and, if needed, higher settings for more realistic visualization. The contour lines setting is also available in the **Display** tab of the **Options** dialog box or by typing ISOLINES.

The Draw true silhouettes setting in the **2D Wireframe options** area controls the display of silhouettes on 3D solid curved surfaces. The setting is either Yes or No. Notice the sphere silhouette in Figures 2-13C and 2-13D. The Draw true silhouettes setting is stored in the **DISPSILH** system variable.

PROFESSIONAL TIP

The **Edge Effects** panel in the **Visualize** tab of the ribbon can also be used to change the contour lines and silhouettes without changing the visual style definition. This is discussed in Chapter 3.

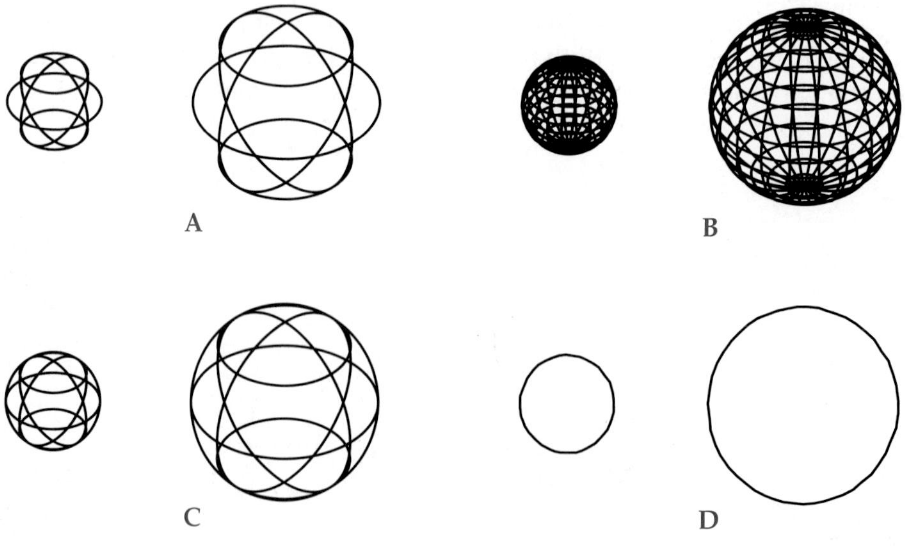

Figure 2-13.
A—The Draw true silhouettes setting is No and four contour lines are used. B—The Draw true silhouettes setting is No and 20 contour lines are used. C—The Draw true silhouettes setting is Yes and four contour lines are used. D—The Draw true silhouettes setting is Yes and the **HIDE** command is used with the 2D Wireframe visual style set current.

Figure 2-14.
The **2D Wireframe options** area of the **Visual Styles Manager** is used to control the display of contour lines and silhouettes on spheres and other curved 3D surfaces in a given visual style.

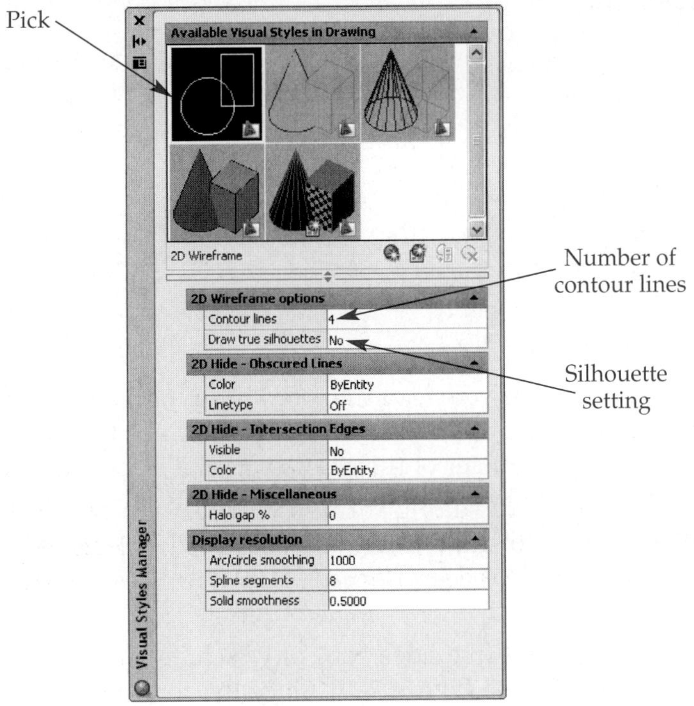

Torus

Ribbon
Home > 3D Modeling
Torus
Type
TORUS
Menu
Draw > Modeling > Torus

TORUS

A basic ***torus*** is a cylinder bent into a circle, similar to a doughnut or inner tube. There are three types of tori. See **Figure 2-15.** A torus with a tube diameter that touches itself has no center hole. This is the second type of torus and called ***self intersecting.*** To create a self-intersecting torus, the tube radius must be greater than the torus radius. The third type of torus looks like a football. It is drawn by entering a negative torus radius and a positive tube radius of greater absolute value, i.e. –1 and 1.1.

Once the command is initiated, you are prompted for the center of the torus or to enter an option. If you pick the center, you must then set the radius of the torus. To specify a diameter, enter the **Diameter** option after specifying the center. This defines a base circle that is the centerline of the tube. The **3P**, **2P**, and **Ttr** options are used to define the base circle of the torus using either three points, two points, or two points of tangency and a radius.

Figure 2-15.
The three types of tori are shown as wireframes and with hidden lines removed.

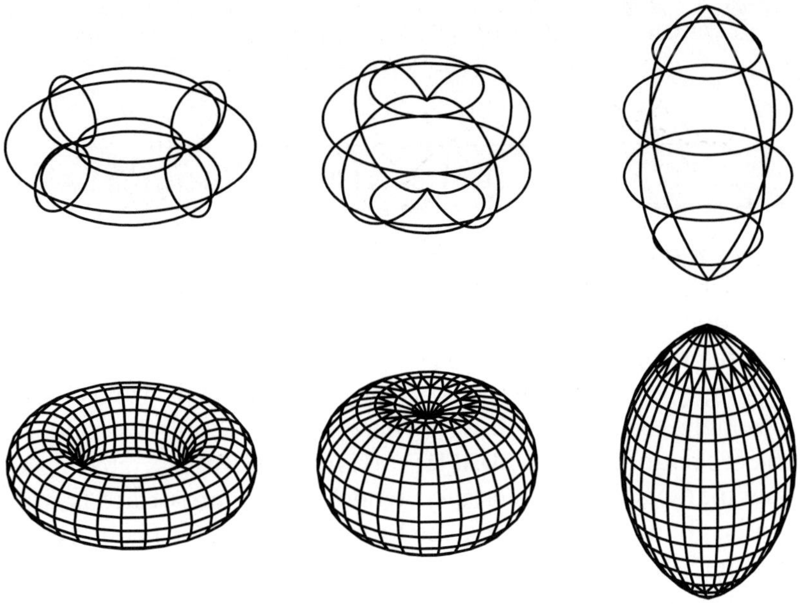

Figure 2-16.
A—A wedge drawn by picking corners and specifying a height. B—A wedge drawn using the **Center** option. Notice the location of the center.

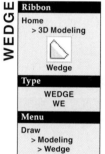

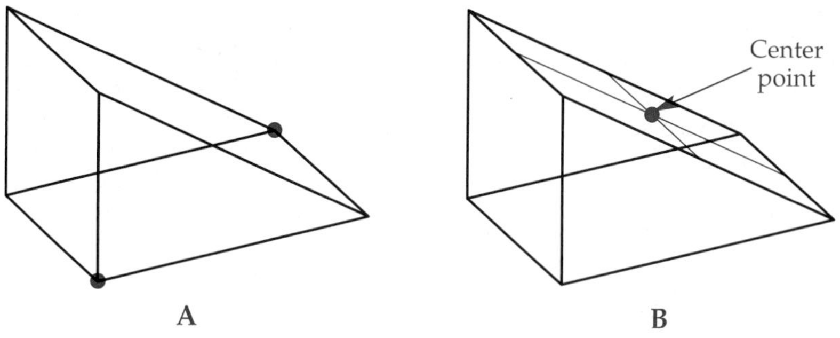

Once the base circle of the torus is defined, you are prompted for the tube radius or to enter an option. The tube radius defines the cross-sectional circle of the tube. To specify a diameter of the cross-sectional circle, enter the **Diameter** option. You can also use the **2point** option to pick two points on screen that define the diameter of the cross-sectional circle.

WEDGE

Ribbon
Home
> 3D Modeling
Wedge
Type
WEDGE
WE
Menu
Draw
> Modeling
> Wedge

Wedge

A ***wedge*** has five sides, four of which are at right angles and the fifth at an angle other than 90°. See **Figure 2-16.** Once the command is initiated, you are prompted to select the first corner of the base or to enter an option. By default, a wedge is constructed by picking diagonal corners of the base and setting a height. To pick the center point, enter the **Center** option. The center point of a wedge is the middle of the angled surface. You must then pick a point to set the width and length before entering a height.

After specifying the first corner or the center, you can enter the length, width, and height instead of picking a second corner. When prompted for the second corner, enter the **Length** option and specify the length. You are then prompted for the width. After the width is entered, you are prompted for the height.

To create a wedge with equal length, width, and height, enter the **Cube** option when prompted for the second corner. Then, enter a length. The same value is automatically used for the width and height.

Exercise 2-2
Complete the exercise on the Student CD.

Constructing a Planar Surface

PLANESURF

Ribbon
Home
> 3D Modeling
Planar Surface
Type
PLANESURF
Menu
Draw
> Modeling
> Planar Surface

A ***planar surface*** primitive is an object consisting of a single plane and is created parallel to the current XY plane. The surface that is created has zero thickness and is composed of a mesh of lines. It is created with the **PLANESURF** command. The command prompts you to specify the first corner and then the second corner of a rectangle. Once drawn, the surface is displayed as a mesh with lines in the X and Y directions. See **Figure 2-17A.** These lines are called *isolines* and do not include the object's boundary. The **SURFU** (Y axis) and **SURFV** (X axis) system variables determine how many isolines are created when the planar surface is drawn. The isoline values can be changed later using the **Properties** palette. The maximum number of isolines in either direction is 200.

Figure 2-17.
A—A rectangular planar surface with four isolines in the Y direction and eight isolines in the X direction. B—These two arcs and two lines form a closed area and lie on a single plane. C—The arcs and curves are converted into a planar surface. D—The planar surface is converted into a solid.

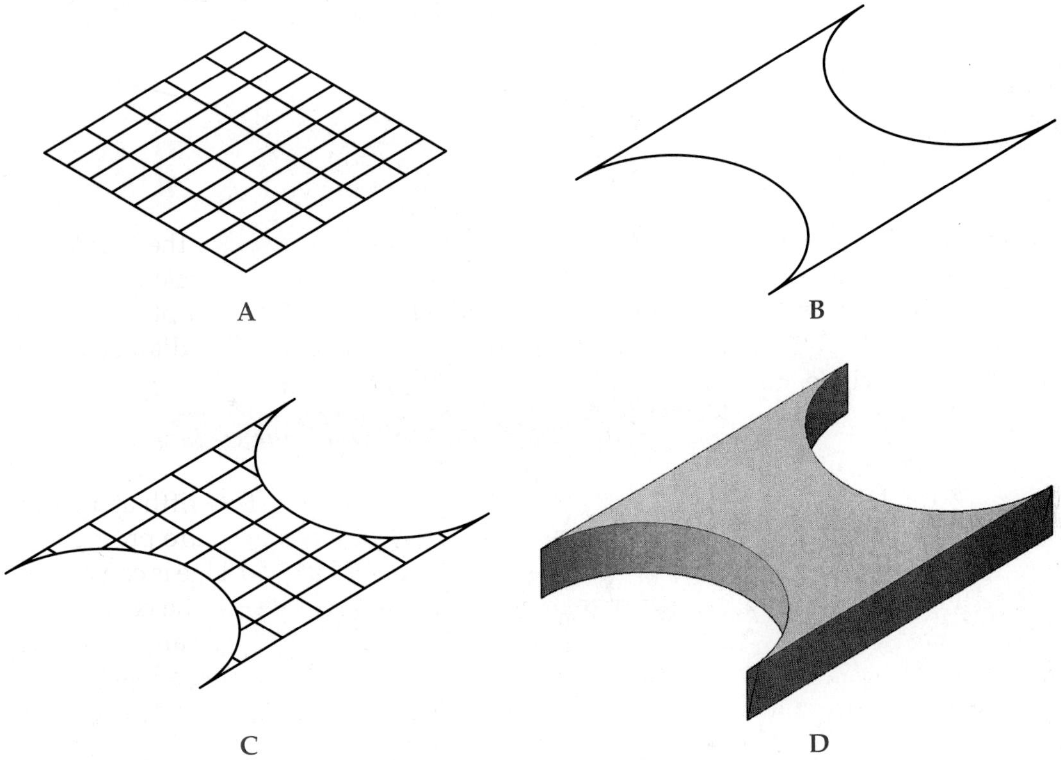

The **Object** option of the **PLANESURF** command allows you to convert a 2D object into a planar surface. Any existing object or objects lying in a single plane and forming a closed area can be converted to a planar surface. The objects in **Figure 2-17B** are two arcs and two lines connected at their endpoints. The resulting planar surface is shown in **Figure 2-17C.**

Although a planar surface is not a solid, it can be converted into a solid in a single step. For example, the object in **Figure 2-17C** is converted into a solid using the **THICKEN** command. See **Figure 2-17D.** The object that started as two arcs and two lines is now a solid model and can be manipulated and edited like any other solid. This capability allows you to create intricate planar shapes and quickly convert them to a solid for use in advanced modeling applications. Model editing procedures are discussed in detail in Chapters 7 through 11.

Creating Composite Solids

A ***composite solid*** is a solid model constructed of two or more solids, often primitives. Solids can be subtracted from each other, joined to form a new solid, or overlapped to create an intersection or interference. The commands used to create composite solids are found in the **3D Modeling** panel in the ribbon, in the **Solid Editing** cascading menu in the **Modify** menu, and on the **Solid Editing** toolbar. See **Figure 2-18.**

Figure 2-18.
Selecting a Boolean command. A—The **Solid Editing** cascading menu in the **Modify** menu. B—The **Solid Editing** toolbar. C—The **3D Modeling** panel in the **Home** tab of the ribbon.

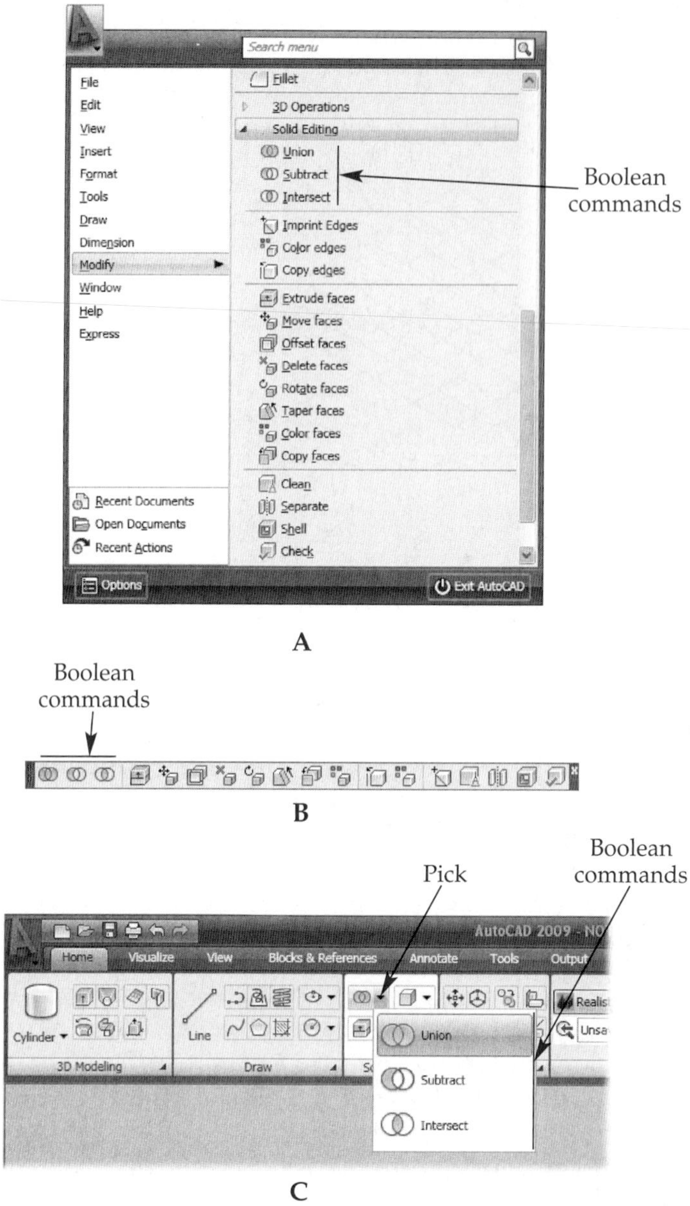

Introduction to Booleans

There are three operations that form the basis of constructing many complex solid models. Joining two or more solids is called a ***union*** operation. Subtracting one solid from another is called a ***subtraction*** operation. Forming a solid based on the volume of overlapping solids is called an ***intersection*** operation. Unions, subtractions, and intersections as a group are called ***Boolean operations.*** George Boole (1815–1864) was an English mathematician who developed a system of mathematical logic where all variables have the value of either one or zero. Boole's two-value logic, or *binary algebra,* is the basis for the mathematical calculations used by computers, and specifically for those required in the construction of composite solids.

UNION

Ribbon
Home
> Solid Editing
Union

Type
UNION
UNI

Menu
Modify
> Solid Editing
> Union

Joining Two or More Solid Objects

The **UNION** command is used to combine solid objects, **Figure 2-19.** The solids do not need to touch or intersect to form a union. Therefore, accurately locate the primitives when drawing them. After selecting the objects to join, just press [Enter] and the action is completed.

Figure 2-19.
A—The solid primitives shown here have areas of intersection and overlap. B—Composite solids after using the **UNION** command.

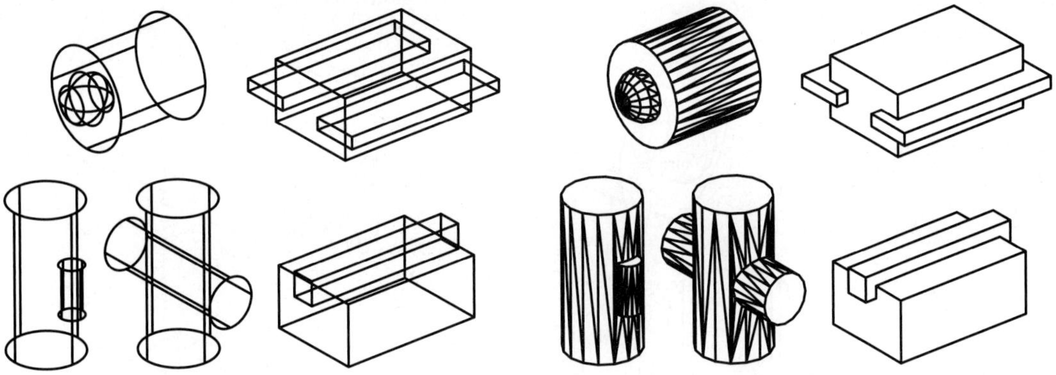

A B

In the examples shown in **Figure 2-19B,** notice that lines, or edges, are shown at the new intersection points of the joined objects. This is an indication that the features are one object, not separate objects.

Subtracting Solids

The **SUBTRACT** command allows you to remove the volume of one or more solids from another solid. Several examples are shown in **Figure 2-20.** The first object selected in the subtraction operation is the object *from* which volume is to be subtracted. The next object is the object to be subtracted from the first. The completed object will be a new solid. If the result is the opposite of what you intended, you may have selected the objects in the wrong order. Just undo the operation and try again.

SUBTRACT

Ribbon
Home
> Solid Editing
Subtract

Type
SUBTRACT
SU

Menu
Modify
> Solid Editing
> Subtract

Creating New Solids from the Intersection of Solids

When solid objects intersect, the overlap forms a common volume, a space that both objects share. This shared space is called an ***intersection.*** An intersection (common volume) can be made into a composite solid using the **INTERSECT** command. **Figure 2-21** shows several examples. A solid is formed from the common volume. The original objects are removed.

INTERSECT

Ribbon
Home
> Solid Editing
Intersect

Type
INTERSECT

Menu
Modify
> Solid Editing
> Intersect

Figure 2-20.
A—The solid primitives shown here have areas of intersection and overlap. B—Composite solids after using the **SUBTRACT** command.

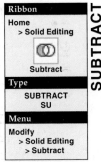

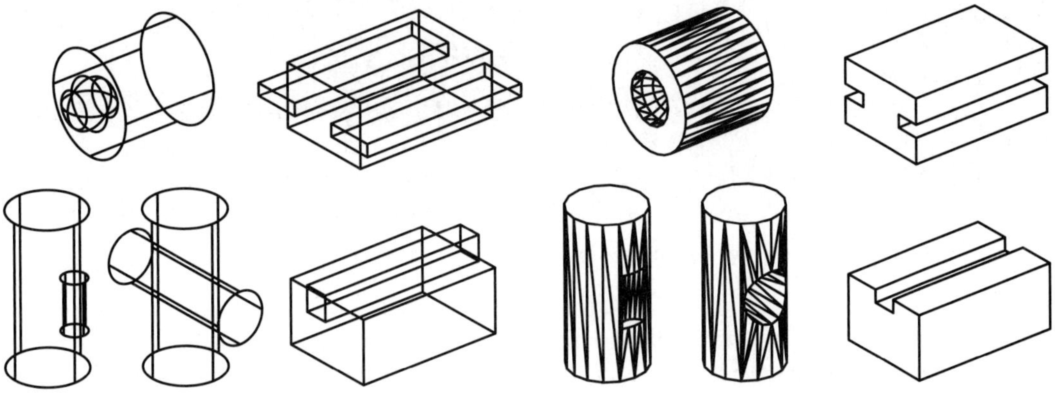

A B

Figure 2-21.
A—The solid primitives shown here have areas of intersection and overlap.
B—Composite solids after using the **INTERSECT** command.

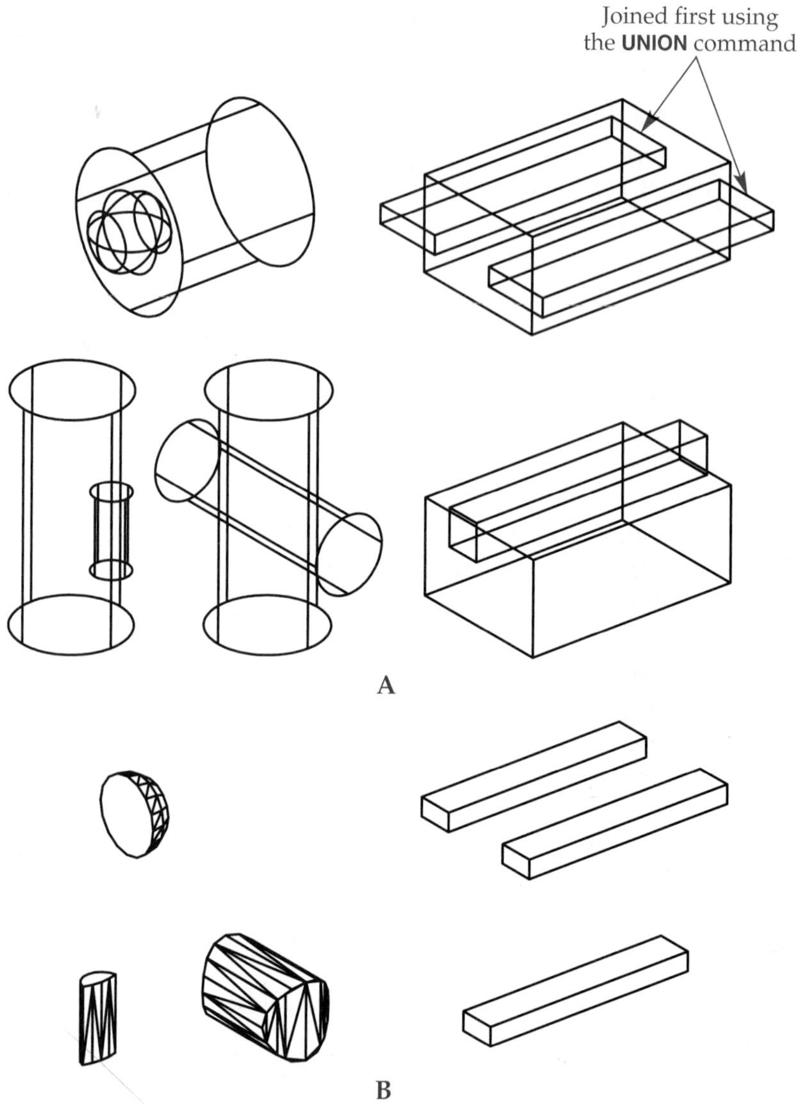

The **INTERSECT** command is also useful in 2D drawing. For example, if you need to create a complex shape that must later be used for inquiry calculations or hatching, draw the main object first. Then, draw all intersecting or overlapping objects. Next, create regions of the shapes. Finally, use **INTERSECT** to create the final shape. The resulting shape is a region and has solid properties. Regions are discussed later in this chapter.

Exercise 2-3
Complete the exercise on the Student CD.

INTERFERE

Ribbon
Home > Solid Editing
Interference Checking
Type
INTERFERE INF
Menu
Modify > 3D Operations > Interference Checking

Creating New Solids Using the Interfere Command

When you use the **SUBTRACT**, **UNION**, and **INTERSECT** commands, the original solids are deleted. They are replaced by the new composite solid. The **INTERFERE** command does not do this. A new solid is created from the interference (common volume) as if the **INTERSECT** command is used, but the original objects can be either deleted or retained.

Once the command is initiated, you are prompted to select the first set of solids or to enter an option. The **Settings** option opens the **Interference Settings** dialog box, which is used to change the visual style and color of the interference solid and the visual style of the viewport. The **Nested selection** option allows you to check the interference of separate solid objects within a nested block. A ***nested block*** is one that is composed of other blocks. When any needed options are set, select the first set of solids and press [Enter].

You are prompted to select the second set of solids or to enter an option. Entering the **Check first set** option tells AutoCAD to check the objects in the first set for interference. There is no second set when this option is used. Otherwise, select the second set of solids and press [Enter].

AutoCAD zooms in on the highlighted interference solid and displays the **Interference Checking** dialog box. See **Figure 2-22.** The visual style is set to a wireframe display by default and the interference solid is shaded in a color, which is red by default.

In the **Interfering objects** area of the **Interference Checking** dialog box, the number of objects selected in the first and second sets is displayed. The number of interfering pairs found in the selected objects is also displayed.

The buttons in the **Highlight** area of the dialog box are used to highlight the previous or next interference object. If the **Zoom to pair** check box is checked, AutoCAD zooms to the interference objects when the **Previous** or **Next** button is selected.

To the right of the **Highlight** area are three navigation buttons—**Zoom Realtime**, **Pan Realtime**, and **3D Orbit**. Selecting one of these display options temporarily hides the dialog box and activates the selected command. This allows you to navigate in the viewport. When the command is ended, the dialog box is redisplayed.

By default, the **Delete interference objects created on Close** check box is checked. This means that the object(s) created by interference is deleted. In order to retain the new solid(s), uncheck this box.

Figure 2-22.
The **Interference Checking** dialog box is used to check for interference between solids. To retain the interference solid, uncheck the **Delete interference objects created on Close** check box.

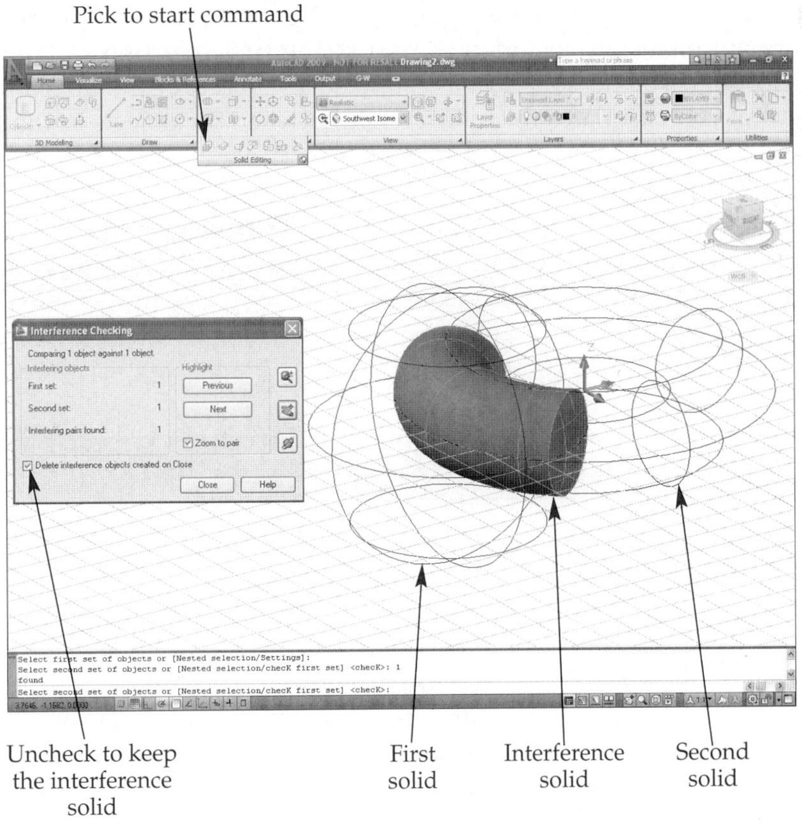

Figure 2-23.
A—Two solids form an area of intersection. B—After using **INTERFERE**, a new solid is defined (shown here in color) and the original solids remain. C—The new solid can be moved or copied.

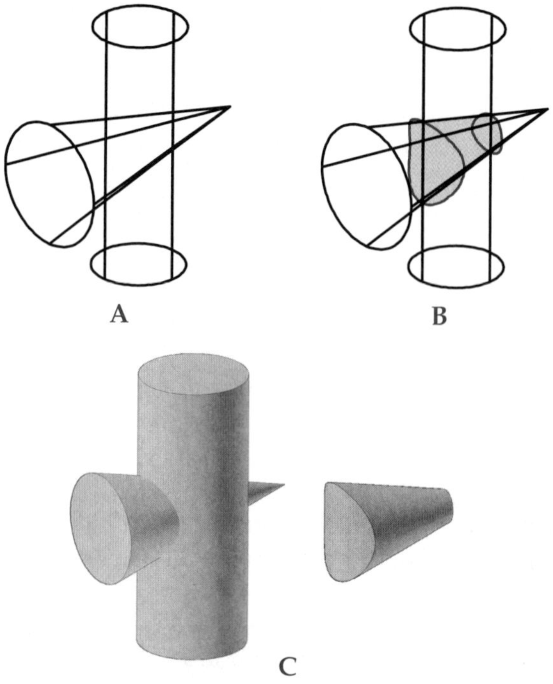

An example of interference checking and the result is shown in **Figure 2-23.** Notice that the original solids are intact, but new lines indicate the new solid. The new solid is retained as a separate object because the **Delete interference objects created on Close** check box was unchecked. The new solid can be moved, copied, and manipulated just like any other object. **Figure 2-23C** shows the new object after it has been moved and a conceptual display generated.

When the **INTERFERE** command is used, AutoCAD compares the first set of solids to the second set. Any solids that are selected for both the first and second sets are automatically included as part of the first selection set and eliminated from the second. If you do not select a second set of objects or the **Check first set** option is used, AutoCAD calculates the interference between the objects in the first selection set.

Exercise 2-4

Complete the exercise on the Student CD.

Creating a Helix

HELIX

Ribbon
Home
> 3D Modeling
Helix

Type
HELIX

Menu
Draw
> Helix

A ***helix*** is a spline in the form of a spiral and can be created as a 2D or 3D object. See **Figure 2-24.** It is not a solid object. However, it can be used as the path or framework for creating solid objects such as springs and spiral staircases.

When the command is initiated, you are prompted for the center of the helix base. After picking the center, you are prompted to enter the radius of the base. If you want to specify the diameter, enter the **Diameter** option. After the base is defined, you are prompted for the radius of the top. You can use the **Diameter** option to enter a diameter. The top and bottom can be different sizes. Entering different sizes creates a tapered helix, if the helix is 3D. A 2D helix should have different sizes for the top and bottom.

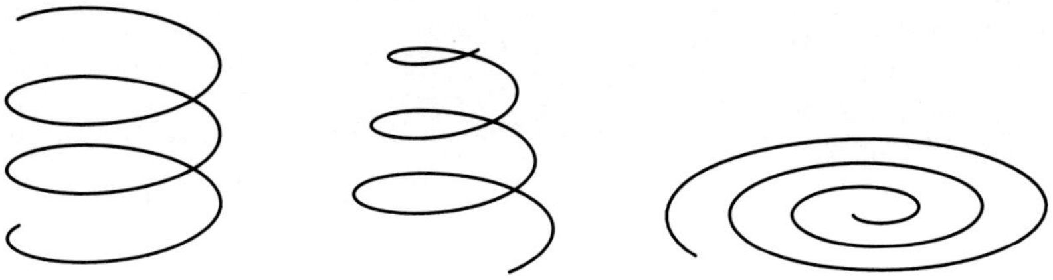

Figure 2-24.
Three types of helices. From left to right, equal top and bottom diameters, unequal top and bottom diameters, and unequal top and bottom diameters with the height set to zero.

After the top and bottom sizes are set, you are prompted to set the height or enter an option. To specify the number of turns in the helix, enter the **Turns** option. Then, enter the number of turns. The maximum is 500 and you can enter values less than one, but greater than zero.

By default, the helix turns in a counterclockwise manner. To change the direction in which the helix turns, enter the **Twist** option. Then, enter CW for clockwise or CCW for counterclockwise.

The height of the helix can be set in one of three ways. First, you can enter a direct distance. To do this, type the height value or pick with the mouse to set the height. To create a 2D helix, enter a height of zero.

You can also set the height for one turn of the helix using the **Turn height** option. In this case, the total height is the number of turns multiplied by the turn height. If you provide a value for the turn height and then specify the helix height, the number of turns is automatically calculated and the helix is drawn. Conversely, if you provide values for both the turn height and number of turns, the helix height is calculated by AutoCAD.

Finally, you can pick a location for the axis endpoint using the **Axis endpoint** option. This is the same option available with a cone, cylinder, or pyramid.

As an example, a solid model of a spring can be created by constructing a helix and a circle and then using the **SWEEP** command to sweep the circle along the helix path. See **Figure 2-25.** The **SWEEP** command is discussed in detail in Chapter 8.

First, determine the diameter of the spring wire and then draw a circle using that value. For this example, you will create two springs each with a wire diameter of .125 units, so draw two circles of that diameter, **Figure 2-26.** Their locations are not important. Next, determine the diameter of the spring and draw a corresponding helix. For this example, draw a helix anywhere on screen with a bottom diameter of one unit and a top diameter of one unit. Set the number of turns to eight and specify a height of two units. Draw another helix with the same settings, except make the top diameter .5 units.

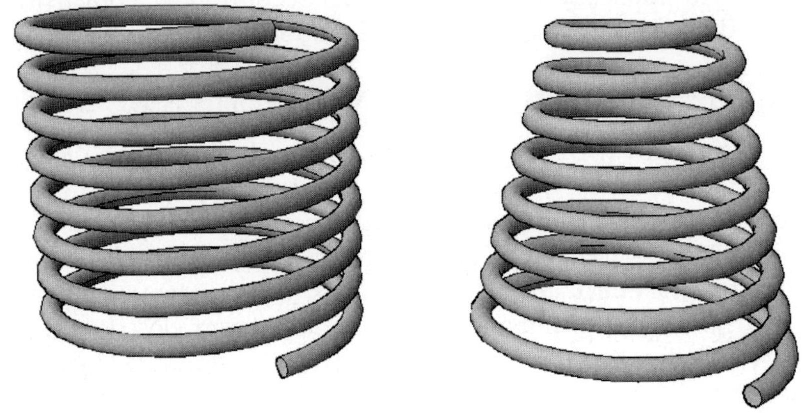

Figure 2-25.
A helix can be used as a path to create a spring.

Figure 2-26.
To create a spring, first draw a circle the same diameter as the spring wire. Then, draw the helix and sweep the circle along the helix. Shown here are the two helices used to create the springs in Figure 2-25.

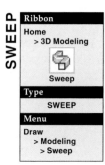

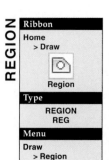

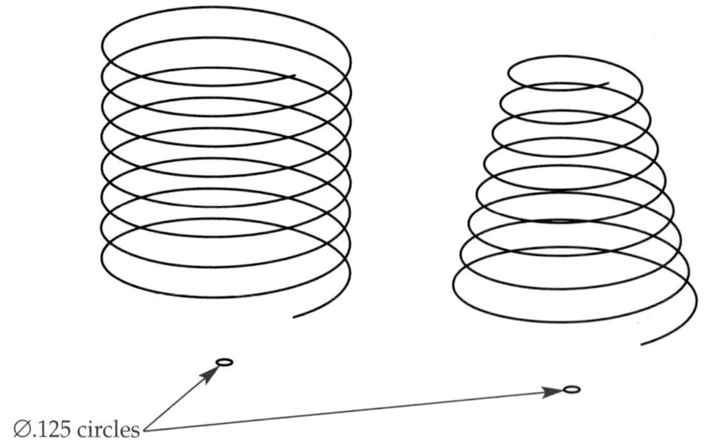

SWEEP

Ribbon
Home
> 3D Modeling
Sweep

Type
SWEEP

Menu
Draw
> Modeling
> Sweep

Initiate the **SWEEP** command. You are first prompted to select the objects to sweep; pick one circle and press [Enter]. Next, you are prompted to select the sweep path. Select one of the helices. The first sweep, or spring, is completed. Repeat the procedure for the other circle and helix. The drawing is now composed of the two original, single-line helices and the two new swept solids. The circles are consumed by the **SWEEP** command.

Exercise 2-5

Complete the exercise on the Student CD.

Working with Regions

A ***region*** is a closed, two-dimensional solid. It is a solid model without thickness (Z value). A region can be analyzed for its mass properties. Therefore, regions are useful for 2D applications where area and boundary calculations must be quickly obtained from a drawing.

Boolean operations can be performed on regions. When regions are unioned, subtracted, or intersected, a ***composite region*** is created. A composite region is also called a ***region model.***

A region can be quickly and easily given a thickness, or ***extruded*** into a 3D solid object. This means that you can convert a 2D shape into a 3D solid model in just a few steps. An application is drawing a 2D section view, converting it into a region, and extruding the region into a 3D solid model. Extruding is covered in Chapter 7.

Constructing a 2D Region Model

REGION

Ribbon
Home
> Draw
Region

Type
REGION
REG

Menu
Draw
> Region

The following example creates, as a region, the plan view of a base for a support bracket. In Chapter 7, you will learn how to extrude the region into a solid. First, start a new drawing. Next, create the profile geometry in **Figure 2-27** using the **RECTANGLE** and **CIRCLE** commands. These commands create 2D objects that can be converted into regions. The **PLINE** and **LINE** commands can also be used to create closed 2D objects.

The **REGION** command allows you to convert closed, two-dimensional objects into regions. When the command is initiated, you are prompted to select objects. Select the rectangle and four circles and then press [Enter]. The rectangle and each circle are now separate

Figure 2-27.
These 2D shapes can be made into a region. The region can then be made into a 3D solid.

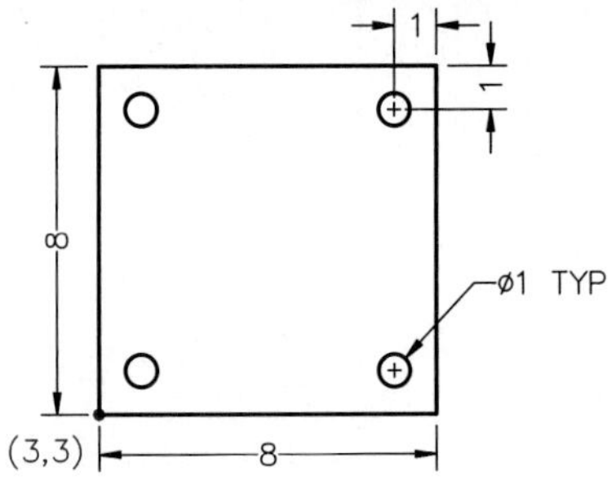

regions and the original objects are deleted. You may need to switch to a wireframe visual style in order to see the circles. You can individually pick the regions. If you pick a circle, notice that a grip is displayed in the center, but not at the four quadrants. This is because the object is not a circle anymore. However, you can still snap to the quadrants.

In order to create the proper solid, the circular regions must be subtracted from the rectangular region. Using the **SUBTRACT** command, select the rectangle as the object to be subtracted *from*, and then all of the circles as the objects to subtract. Now, if you select the rectangle or any of the circles, you can see that a single region has been created from the five separate regions. If you set the Conceptual or Realistic visual style current, you can see that the circles are now holes in the region. See **Figure 2-28.**

Using the Boundary Command to Create a Region

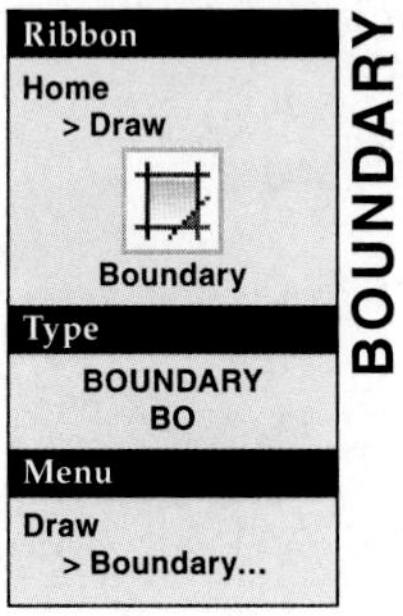

The **BOUNDARY** command is often used to create a polyline for hatching or an inquiry. In addition, this command can be used to create a region. When the command is initiated, the **Boundary Creation** dialog box is displayed. See **Figure 2-29.**

Next, select **Region** from the **Object type:** drop-down list in the **Boundary retention** area of the dialog box. Also, you can refine the boundary selection method by turning island detection on or off. When the **Island detection** check box above the **Boundary retention** area is checked, island detection is on.

- **On.** When an internal point is selected in the object, AutoCAD creates separate regions from any islands that reside within the object.
- **Off.** When an internal point is selected in the object, AutoCAD ignores islands that reside within the object when creating the region.

Finally, select the **Pick Points** button. The dialog box is closed and you are prompted to select an internal point. Pick a point inside of the object that you wish to convert to a region. Press [Enter] when you are finished and the region is created. You can always check to see if an object is a polyline or region by using the **LIST** command and selecting the object.

Figure 2-28.
Once the circular regions are subtracted from the rectangular region, they appear as holes. This is clear when the Conceptual or Realistic visual style is set current.

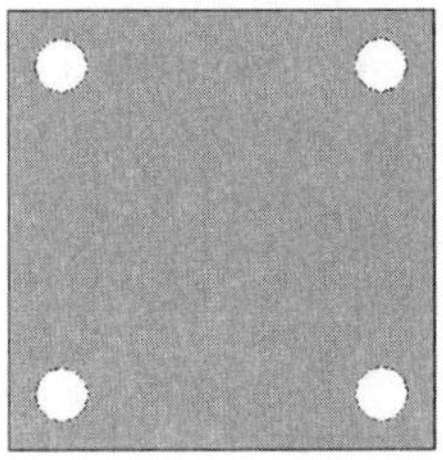

Figure 2-29.
Regions can be created using the **Boundary Creation** dialog box.

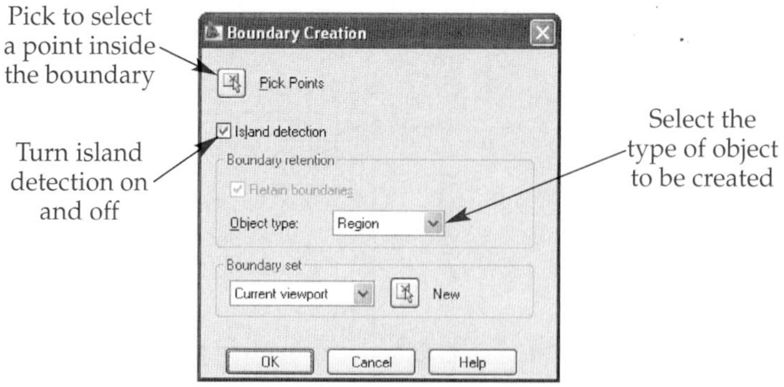

Calculating the Area of a Region

A region is not a polyline. It is an enclosed area called a ***loop.*** Certain properties of the region, such as area, are stored as a value of the region. The **AREA** command can be used to determine the length of all sides and the area of the loop. This can be a useful advantage of a region.

For example, suppose a parking lot is being repaved. You need to calculate the surface area of the parking lot to determine the amount of material needed. This total surface area excludes the space taken up by planting dividers, sidewalks, and lamp-posts because you will not be paving under these items. If the parking lot and all objects inside of it are drawn as a region, the **AREA** command can give you this figure in one step using the **Object** option. If a polyline is used to draw the parking lot, all internal features must be subtracted each time the **AREA** command is used.

PROFESSIONAL TIP

Regions can prove valuable when working with many items:

- Roof areas excluding chimneys, vents, and fans.
- Bodies of water, such as lakes, excluding islands.
- Lawns and areas of grass excluding flower beds, trees, and shrubs.
- Landscaping areas excluding lawns, sidewalks, and parking lots.
- Concrete surfaces, such as sidewalks, excluding openings for landscaping, drains, and utility covers.

You can find many other applications for regions that can help in your daily tasks.

Exercise 2-6

Complete the exercise on the Student CD.

Chapter Test

Answer the following questions. Write your answers on a separate sheet of paper or complete the electronic chapter test on the Student CD.

1. What is a *solid primitive?*
2. How is a solid cube created?
3. How is an elliptical cylinder created?
4. Where is the center of a wedge located?
5. What is a *frustum pyramid?*
6. What is a *polysolid?*
7. Name at least four AutoCAD 2D entities that can be converted to a polysolid.
8. What type of entity does the **HELIX** command create and how can it be converted into a solid model?
9. What is a *composite solid?*
10. Which type of mathematical calculations are used in the construction of solid models?
11. How are two or more solids combined to make a composite solid?
12. What is the function of the **INTERSECT** command?
13. How does the **INTERFERE** command differ from **INTERSECT** and **UNION**?
14. What is a *region?*
15. How can a 2D section view be converted to a 3D solid model?
16. What is created when regions are added to or subtracted from one another?
17. Which command allows you to remove the area of one region from another region?
18. When using the **BOUNDARY** command, what is the effect of unchecking the **Island detection** check box in the **Boundary Creation** dialog box?

Drawing Problems

Draw the objects in the following problems using the appropriate solid primitive commands and Boolean operations. Use your own measurements for objects shown without dimensions. Do not add dimensions to the models. Save the drawings as P2-(problem number). Display and plot the problems as indicated by your instructor.

1.

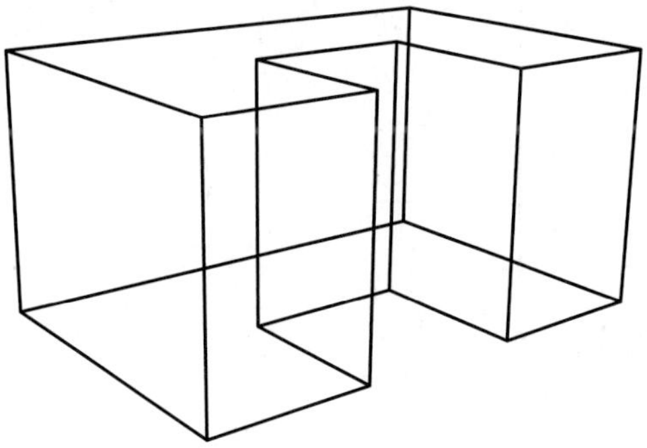

Drawing Problems - Chapter 2

2.

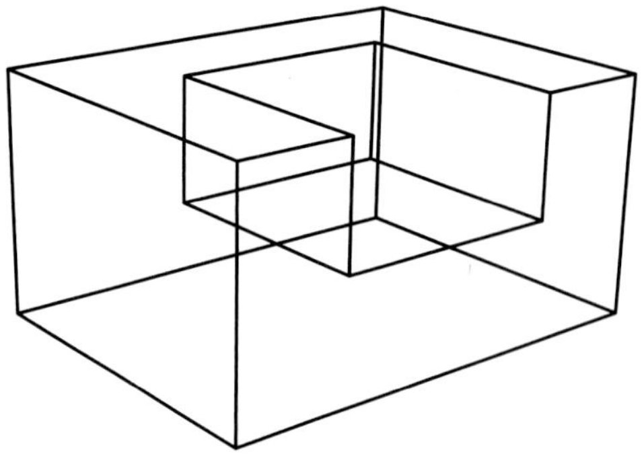

3.

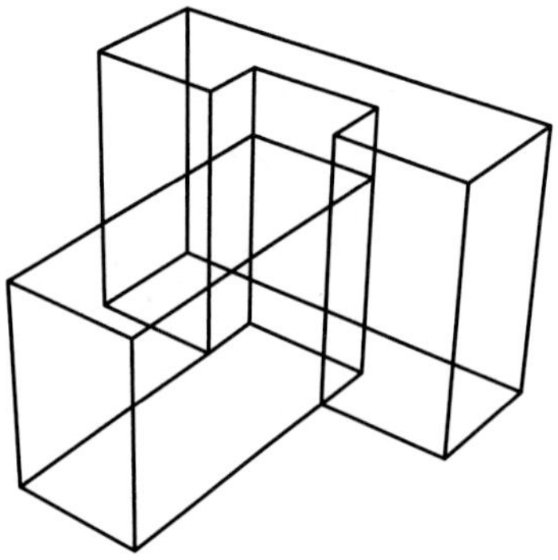

4.

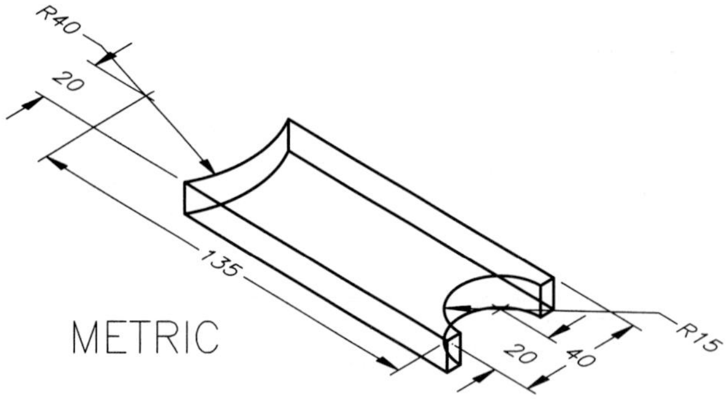

5.

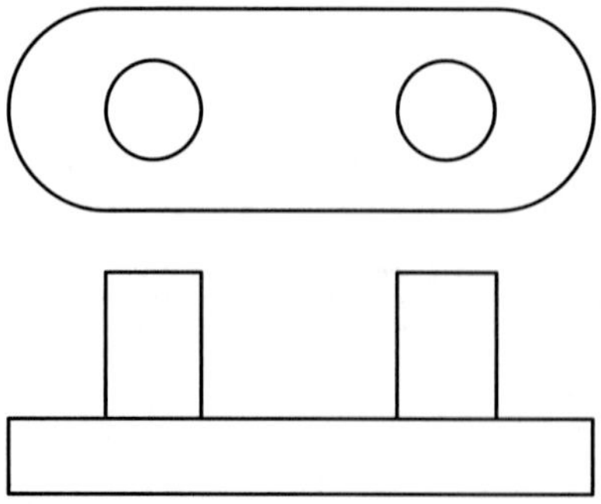

6.

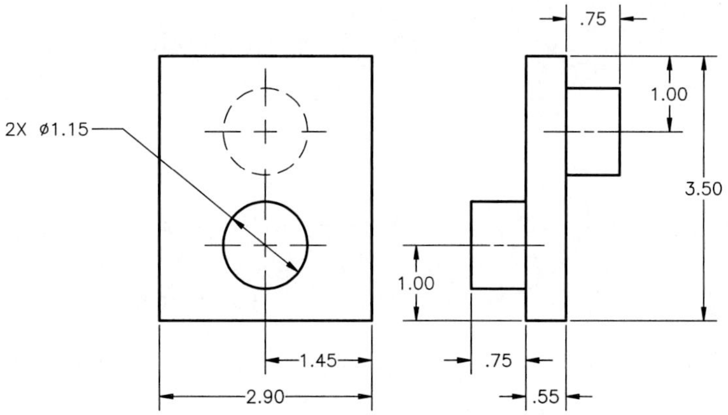

2X ⌀1.15
.75
1.00
3.50
1.00
1.45
2.90
.75
.55

7.

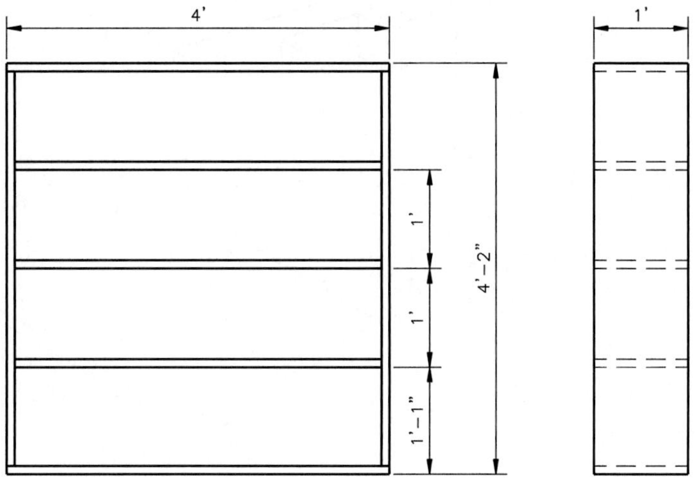

4'
1'
1'
1'
4'-2"
1'-1"

8.

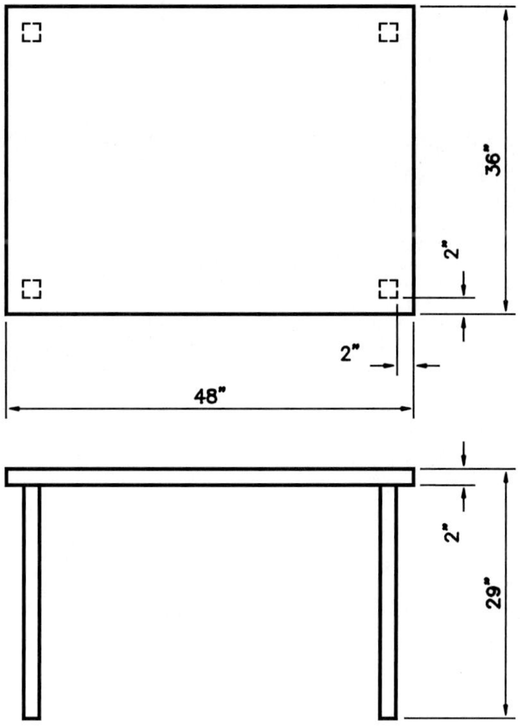

36"
2"
2"
48"
2"
29"

TABLE

9.

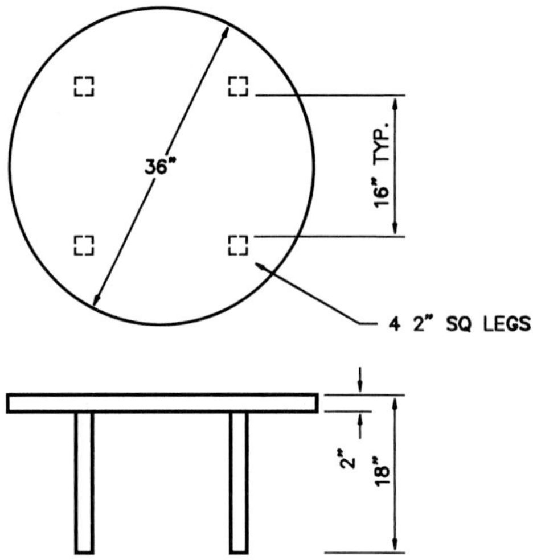

10.

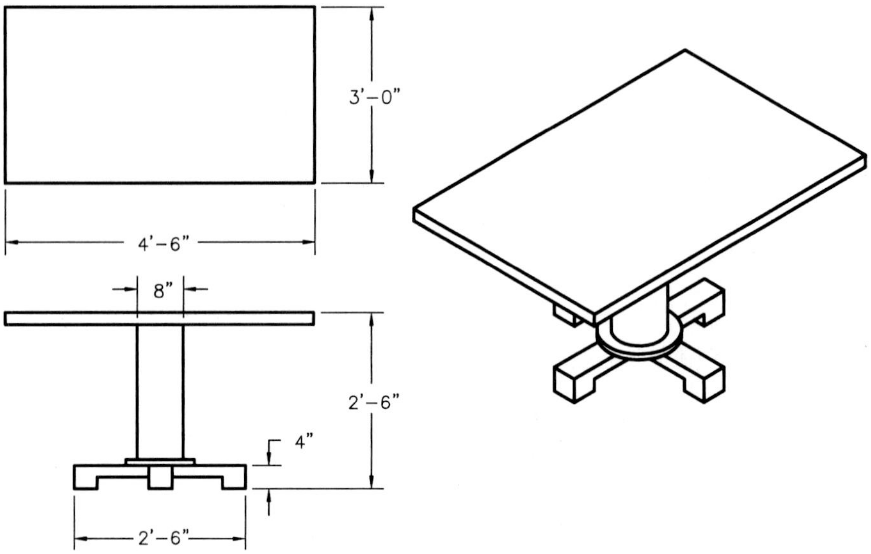

11. Draw the seat for a kitchen chair shown below. In later chapters, you will complete this chair. The seat is 1″ thick.

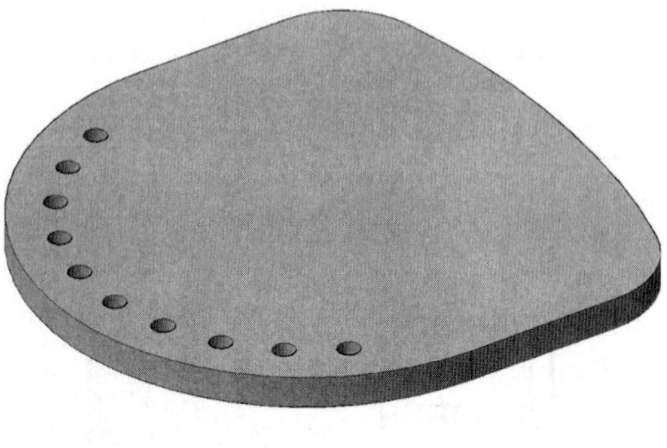

A

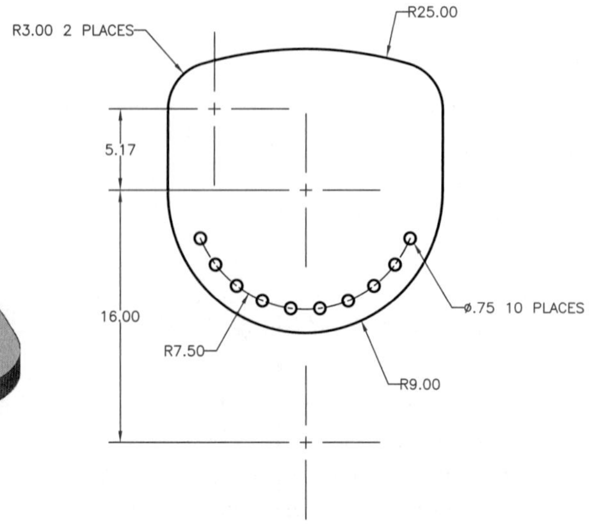

B

CHAPTER 3

Viewing and Displaying Three-Dimensional Models

Learning Objectives

After completing this chapter, you will be able to:

- ✓ Use the view cube to dynamically rotate the view of the model in 3D space.
- ✓ Use the view cube to display orthographic plan views of all sides on the model.
- ✓ Use steering wheels to display a 3D model from any angle.
- ✓ Use the visual style options to create face and edge style display variations.
- ✓ Render a 3D model.

AutoCAD provides several tools with which you can display and present 3D models in pictorial and orthographic views:

- Preset isometric viewpoints, discussed in Chapter 1.
- Dynamic model display using the view cube. This on-screen tool provides access to preset and dynamic display options.
- Complete 3D model display using steering wheels.
- The **3DORBIT** and **3DCORBIT** commands provide dynamic display and continuous orbiting tools for demonstrations and presentations.

Once a viewpoint has been selected, you can enhance the display by applying visual styles. The **View** panel in the **Home** tab of the ribbon provides a variety of ways to display a model, including wireframe, hidden line removal, and simple rendering. An introduction to visual styles is provided in Chapter 1 and additional details are discussed later in this chapter.

A more advanced rendering can be created with the **RENDER** command. It produces the most realistic image with highlights, shading, and materials, if applied. **Figure 3-1** shows a 3D model of a cast iron plumbing cleanout after using **HIDE**, setting the Conceptual visual style current, and using **RENDER**. Notice the difference in the three displays.

PROFESSIONAL TIP

AutoCAD has three powerful display tools: the view cube, steering wheels, and show motion. The power of these three tools has virtually eliminated the need for legacy display functions such as **DVIEW**, **VPOINT**, and **3DORBIT**. However, **3DORBIT** and **3DCORBIT** still possess some usefulness and are discussed later in this chapter.

Figure 3-1.
A—Hidden display (hidden lines removed). B—The **Conceptual** visual style set current. C—Rendered with lights and materials.

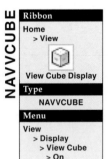

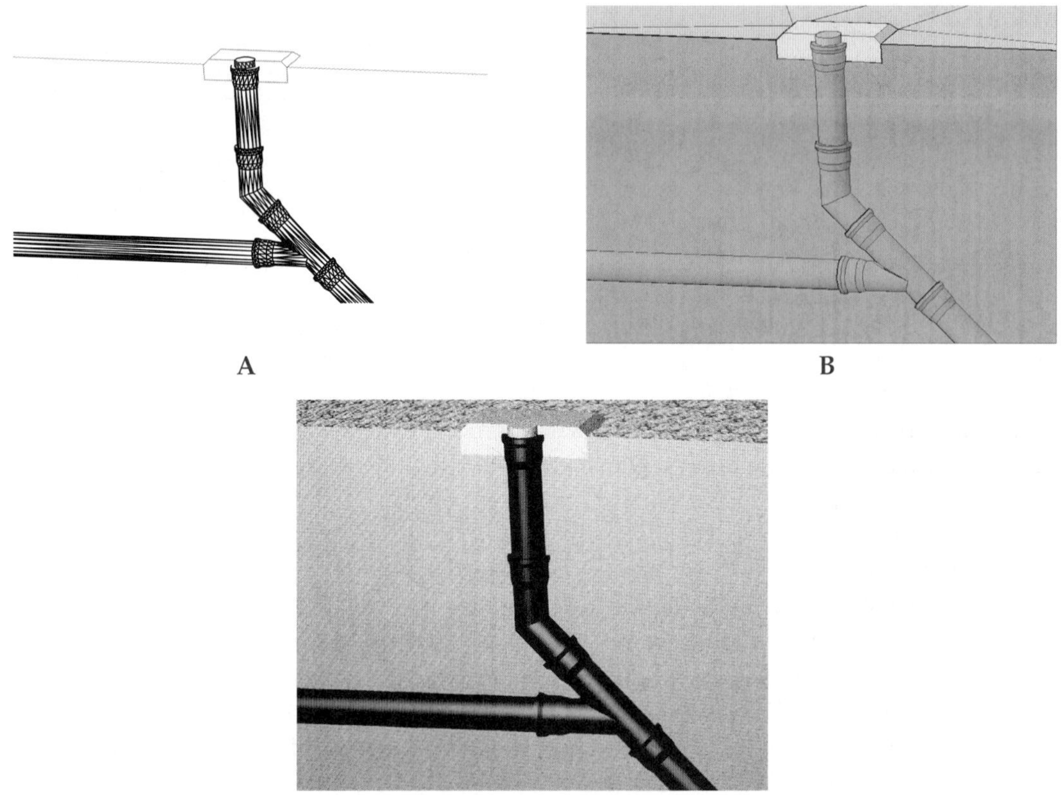

Dynamically Displaying Models with the View Cube

> **NAVVCUBE**
> **Ribbon**
> Home
> > View
> View Cube Display
> **Type**
> NAVVCUBE
> **Menu**
> View
> > Display
> > View Cube
> > On

The ***view cube*** navigation tool allows you to quickly change the current view of the model to a preset pictorial or orthographic view or any number of dynamically user-defined 3D views. The tool is displayed, by default, in the upper-right corner of the drawing area when a 3D visual style is set current. If the view cube is not displayed, pick the **View Cube Display** button from the **View** panel of the **Home** tab of the ribbon. The view cube cannot be displayed if the 2D Wireframe visual style is current.

The **View Cube Settings** dialog box offers many settings for expanding and enhancing the view cube. This dialog box is discussed in detail later in this chapter.

Understanding the View Cube

The view cube tool is composed of a cube labeled with the names of all six orthographic faces. See **Figure 3-2.** A compass rests at the base of the cube and is labeled with the four compass points (N, S, E, and W). The compass can be used to change the view. It also provides a visual cue to the orientation of the model in relation to the current user coordinate system (UCS). The ***user coordinate system*** describes the orientation of the X, Y, and Z axes. A complete discussion of user coordinate systems is given in Chapter 5.

Below the cube and compass is a button labeled WCS, which displays a shortcut menu. The label on this button displays the name of the current user coordinate system, which is, by default, the world coordinate system (WCS). This shortcut menu gives you the ability to switch from one user coordinate system to another. A user coordinate

Figure 3-2.
The cube in the view cube tool is labeled with the names of all six orthographic faces. The view cube also contains a **Home** icon, compass, and UCS shortcut menu.

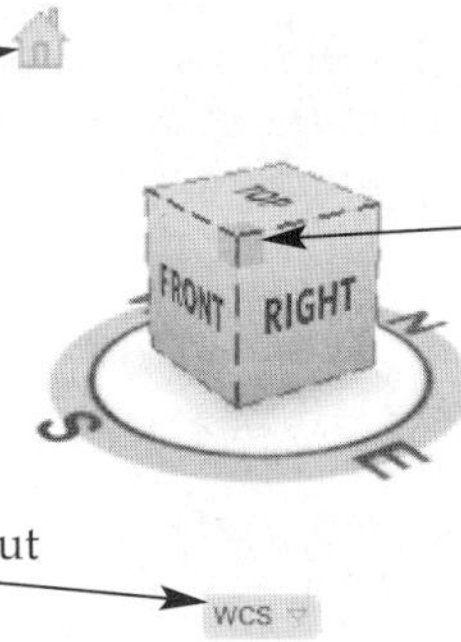

system is any coordinate system that is not the world coordinate system. The benefit of creating new user coordinate systems is the increase in efficiency and productivity when working on 3D models.

When the cursor is not over the view cube, the tool is displayed in its dimmed or ***inactive state.*** When the cursor is moved onto the view cube, the tool is displayed in its ***active state*** and a little house appears to the upper-left of the cube. This house is the **Home** icon. Picking this icon always restores the same view, called the ***home view.*** Later in this chapter, you will learn how to change the home view.

Notice that a corner, edge, or face on the cube is slightly shaded. In the default view of a drawing based on the acad3D.dwt template, the corner between the top, right, and front faces is shaded. The shaded part of the cube represents the standard view that is closest to the current view. Move the cursor over the cube and notice that edges, corners, and faces are highlighted as you move the pointer. If you pick a highlighted edge, corner, or face, a view is displayed that looks directly at the selected feature. By selecting standard views on the view cube, you can quickly move between pictorial and orthographic views.

PROFESSIONAL TIP

Picking the top face of the view cube displays a plan view of the current UCS XY plane. This is often quicker than using the **PLAN** command, which is discussed later in this chapter.

Dynamic displays

The easiest way to change the current view using the view cube is to pick and drag the cube. Simply move the cursor over the cube, press and hold the left mouse button, and drag the mouse to change the view. The view cube and model view dynamically change with the mouse movement. When you have found the view you want, release the mouse button. This is similar to the **Orbit** tool in steering wheels, which are discussed later in the chapter.

When dragging the view cube, you are not restricted to the current XY plane, as you are when using the compass. The compass is discussed later.

Pictorial displays

The view cube provides immediate access to 20 different preset pictorial views. When one of the corners of the cube is selected, a standard isometric pictorial view is displayed. See **Figure 3-3A.** There are eight corners that can be selected.

Picking on one of the four corners on the top face of the cube is the same as selecting **View>3D Views** from the menu and picking one of the preset isometric views, but requires only one pick. You can also select a preset isometric view from the drop-down list in the **View** panel on the **Home** tab of the ribbon, but you may need to first display the tab. Using the view cube may be a quicker method.

Figure 3-3.
A—When one of the corners of the cube is selected, a standard isometric view is displayed.
B—Selecting one of the edges of the cube produces the same rotation in the XY plane as an isometric view, but a zero elevation view in the Z plane.

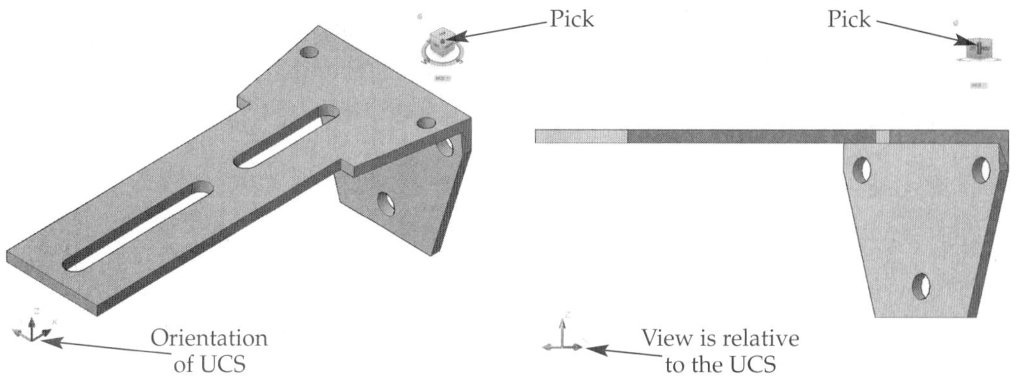

Selecting one of the edges of the cube sets the view perpendicular to that edge. See Figure 3-3B. There are 12 edges that can be selected. These standard views are not available in the menu or on the ribbon.

PROFESSIONAL TIP

The quickest method of dynamically rotating a 3D model is achieved by using the mouse wheel. Simply press and hold the [Shift] key while pressing down and holding the mouse wheel. Now move the mouse in any direction and the view rotates accordingly. This is a transparent function that executes the **3DORBIT** command and can be used at any time. Since it is transparent, it can even be used while you are in the middle of a command. It is an excellent technique to use because it does not require selecting another tool or executing a command.

Projection

The view displayed in the graphics window can be in one of two projections. The ***projection*** refers to how lines are applied to the viewing plane. In a pictorial view, lines in a ***perspective projection*** appear to converge as they recede into the background. The points at which the lines converge are called ***vanishing points.*** In 2D drafting, it is common to represent an object in pictorial as a one- or two-point perspective, especially in architectural drafting. In a ***parallel projection,*** lines remain parallel as they recede. This is how an orthographic or axonometric (isometric, dimetric, and trimetric) view is created.

To change the projection, right-click on the view cube to display the shortcut menu. Three display options are given:

- **Parallel.** Displays the model as a parallel projection. This creates an orthographic or axonometric view.
- **Perspective.** Displays the model in the more realistic, perspective projection. Lines recede into the background toward invisible vanishing points.
- **Perspective with Ortho Faces.** Displays the model in perspective projection when a pictorial view is displayed and parallel projection when an orthographic view is displayed. The parallel projection is only set current if a face on the view cube is selected to display the orthographic view. It is not set current if the **PLAN** command is used.

Figure 3-4 illustrates the difference between parallel and perspective projection.

Figure 3-4.
In a parallel projection, parallel lines remain parallel. In a perspective projection, parallel lines converge to a vanishing point. Notice the three receding lines on the boxes. If these lines are extended, they will intersect.

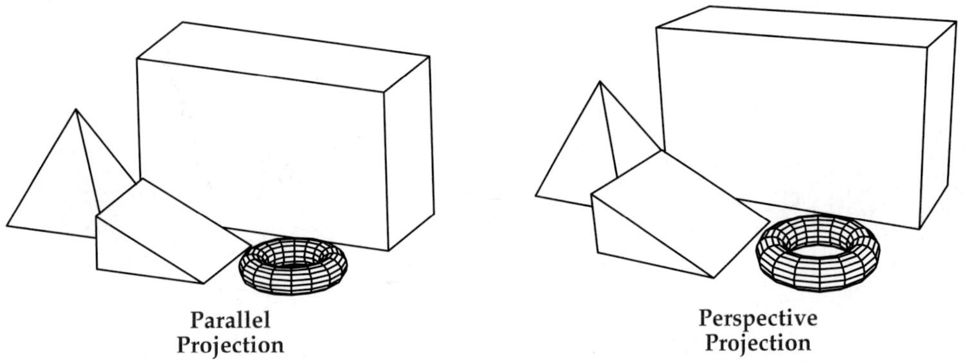

Exercise 3-1

Complete the exercise on the Student CD.

Orthographic displays

The view cube faces are labeled with orthographic view names, such as Top, Front, Left, and so on. Picking on a view cube face produces an orthographic display of that face. Keep in mind, if the current projection is perspective, the view will not be a true orthographic view. See **Figure 3-5.** If you plan to work in perspective projection, but also want to view proper orthographic faces, turn on **Perspective with Ortho Faces** in the view cube shortcut menu. Another way to achieve a proper orthographic view is to turn on parallel projection.

When a face is selected on the view cube, the cube rotates to orthographically display the named face. The view rotates accordingly. In addition, notice that a series of triangles point to the four sides of the cube (when the cursor is over the tool). See **Figure 3-6A.** Picking one of these triangles displays the orthographic view corresponding to the face to which the triangle is pointing, **Figure 3-6B.** This is a quick and efficient method to precisely rotate the display between orthographic views.

Figure 3-5.
A—To properly view orthographic faces using the view cube, turn on **Perspective with Ortho Faces** in the shortcut menu. B—When an orthographic view is set current with perspective projection on, the view is not a true orthographic view. Notice how you can see the receding surfaces.

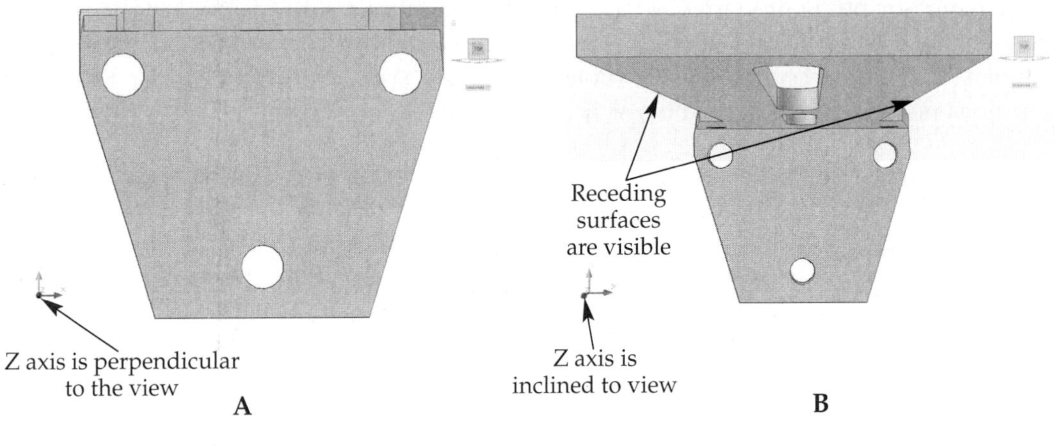

Figure 3-6.
A—The selected orthographic face is surrounded by triangles. Pick one of the triangles to display that orthographic face. B—The orthographic face corresponding to the picked triangle is displayed. Picking a roll arrow rotates the current view 90° in the selected direction. C—The rotated view.

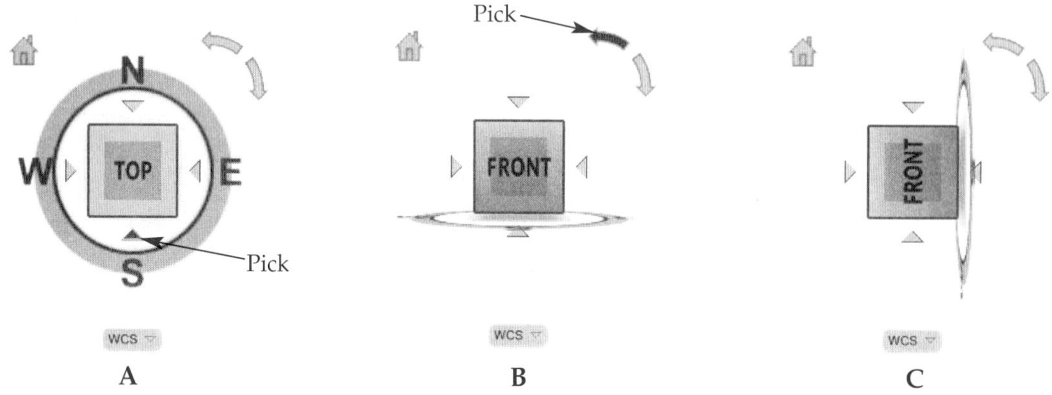

When an orthographic view is displayed, two ***roll arrows*** appear on the view cube. Picking either of these arrows rotates the current view 90° in the selected direction and about an axis perpendicular to the view. See **Figure 3-6C.** Using the triangles and roll arrows on the view cube provides the greatest flexibility in manipulating the model between orthographic views.

Setting views with the compass

The compass allows you to dynamically rotate the model in the XY plane. To do so, pick and hold on one of the four labels (N, S, E, or W). Then, drag the mouse to rotate the view. The view pivots about the Z axis of the current UCS. Try this a few times and notice that you can completely rotate the model by continuously moving cursor off of the screen. For example, pick the letter W and move the pointer either right or left (or up or down). Notice as you continue to move the mouse in one direction the model continues to rotate in that direction.

You can use the compass to display the model in a view plan to the right, left, front, or back face of the cube. When the pointer is moved to one of the four compass directions, the letter is highlighted, **Figure 3-7A.** Simply single pick on the compass label that is next to the face you wish to view. See **Figure 3-7B.**

Home view

The default home view is the southwest isometric view of the WCS. Picking the **Home** icon in the view cube always displays the view defined as the home view, regardless of the current UCS. You can easily set the home view to any display you wish. First, using any navigation method, display the model as required. Next, right-click on the view cube and pick **Set Current View as Home** from the shortcut menu. Now, when you pick the **Home** icon in the view cube, this view is set current. Remember, the **Home** icon does not appear until the cursor is over the view cube.

PROFESSIONAL TIP

Should you become disoriented after repeated use of the view cube, it is far more efficient to pick the **Home** icon than it is to use **UNDO** or try to select an appropriate location on the view cube.

Figure 3-7.
A—When the pointer is moved over one of the four compass directions, the letter is highlighted. B—If you pick the letter, the orthographic view from that compass direction is displayed.

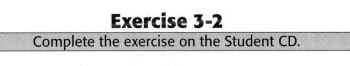

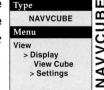

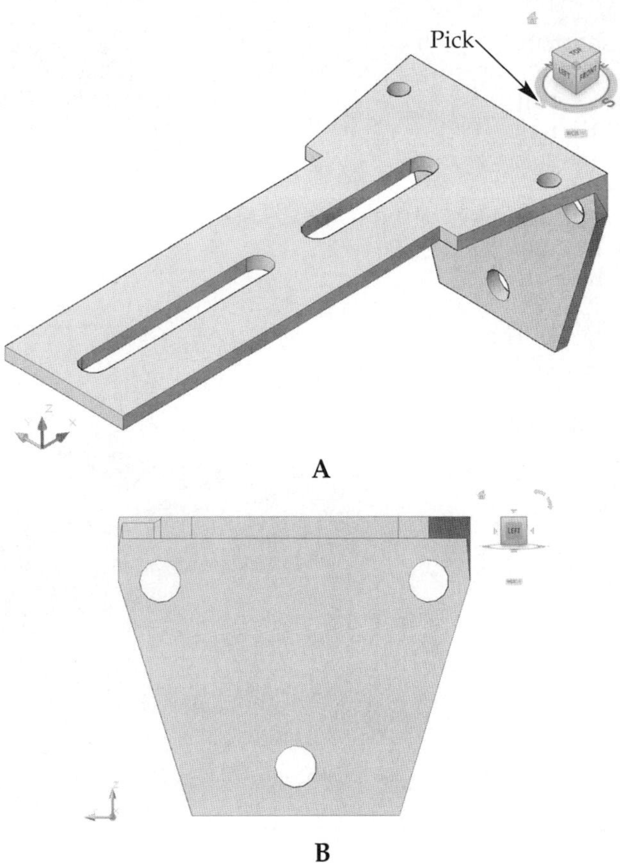

UCS settings

The UCS shortcut menu in the view cube shows the names of all named UCSs in the current drawing and the WCS. If there are no named UCSs, the listing is **WCS** and **New UCS**. See **Figure 3-8A.** To create a new UCS, pick **New UCS** from the shortcut menu. Next, use the appropriate UCS command options to create the new UCS. See Chapter 5 for complete coverage of the **UCS** command.

As new UCSs are created and saved, their names are added to the UCS shortcut menu. See **Figure 3-8B.** Now, if you wish to work on the model using a specific UCS, simply select it from the list. The UCS is then restored.

Exercise 3-2

Complete the exercise on the Student CD.

View Cube Settings Dialog Box

NAVVCUBE

Type
NAVVCUBE

Menu
View
> Display
View Cube
> Settings

The appearance and function of the view cube can be changed using the **View Cube Settings** dialog box, **Figure 3-9.** This dialog box is displayed by selecting **View Cube Settings...** from the view cube shortcut menu or by using the **Settings** option of the **NAVVCUBE** command. The next sections discuss the options found in the dialog box.

Display

Options in the **Display** area of the **View Cube Settings** dialog box control the appearance of the view cube tool. The thumbnail dynamically previews any changes made to the display options. There are four options in this area of the dialog box.

Figure 3-8.
The UCS shortcut menu below the view cube lists all named UCSs in the current drawing. A—The menu entries are **WCS** and **New UCS**. In this example, there are no saved UCSs in the drawing. B—The names of new UCSs are added to the UCS shortcut menu. The current UCS is indicated with a checkmark.

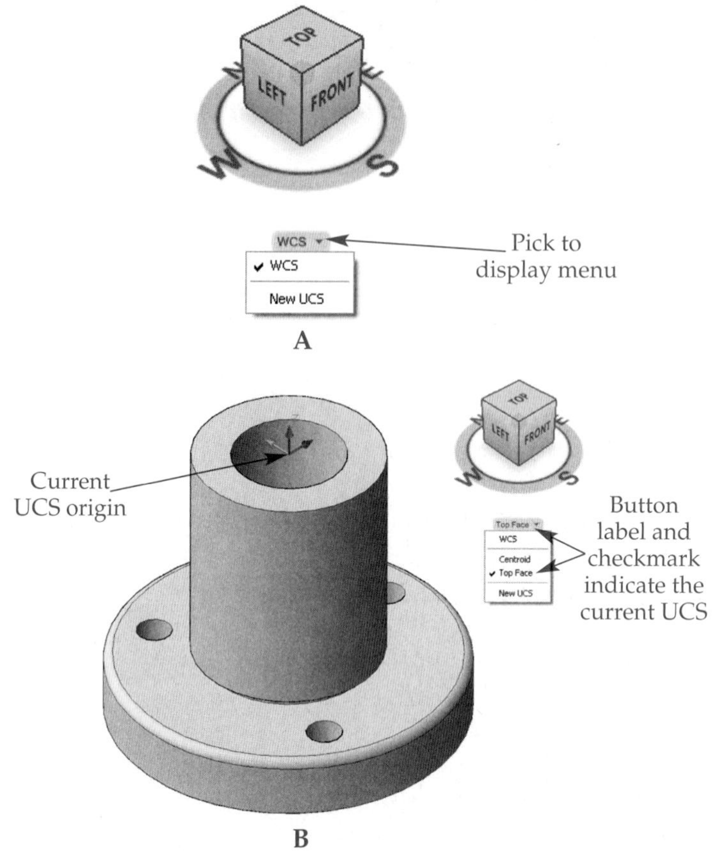

Figure 3-9.
The **View Cube Settings** dialog box.

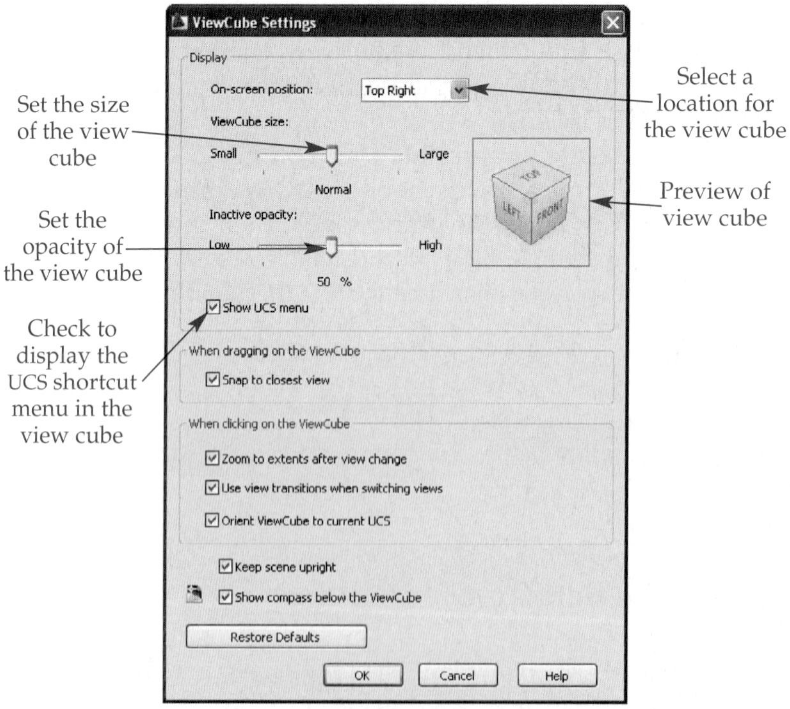

On-Screen Position. The view cube can be placed in one of four locations in the drawing area: top-right, bottom-right, top-left, or bottom-left corner. By default, it is located in the top-right corner of the screen. To change the location, select it in the **On-screen position:** drop-down list. The **NAVVCUBELOCATION** system variable controls this setting.

View Cube Size. The view cube can be displayed in one of three sizes. Use the **View Cube Size:** slider to set the size to either small, normal, or large. The **NAVVCUBESIZE** system variable controls this setting.

Inactive Opacity. When the view cube is inactive, it is displayed in a semitransparent state. Remember, the view cube is in the inactive state whenever the pointer is not over it. When the view cube is in the active state, it is displayed at 100% opacity. Use the **Inactive opacity:** slider to set the level of opacity (transparency). The value can be from 0% to 100% with a default value of 50%. The percentage is displayed below the slider. A value of zero results in the view cube being hidden until the cursor is moved over it. If opacity is set to 100%, there is no difference between the inactive and active states. The **NAVVCUBEOPACITY** system variable controls this setting.

Show UCS menu. By default, the UCS shortcut menu is displayed in the view cube. This menu is displayed by picking the UCS button below the cube. If you wish to remove the UCS menu from the view cube display, uncheck the **Show UCS menu** check box.

When dragging on the view cube

By default, when you drag the view cube, the view "snaps" to the closest standard view that can be displayed by the view cube. This is because the **Snap to closest view** check box is checked by default. Uncheck this check box if you want the view to freely rotate without snapping to a preset standard view as you drag the view cube.

When clicking on the view cube

Options in the **When clicking on the View Cube** area control how the final view is displayed and how the labels on the view cube can be related to the UCS. There are three options in this area.

Zoom to Extents After View Change. If the **Zoom to extents after change** check box is checked, the model is zoomed to the extents of the drawing whenever the view cube is used to change the view. Uncheck this if you want to use the view cube to change the display without fitting the model to the current viewport.

Use View Transitions When Switching Views. The default transition from one view to the next is a smooth rotation of the view. Although this transition may look nice, if you are working on a large model it may require more time and computer resources than you are willing to use. Therefore, if you are switching views a lot using view cube, it may be more efficient to uncheck the **Use view transitions when switching views** check box. When this is unchecked, a view change just cuts to the new view without a smooth transition. This option does not affect the view when dragging the view cube or its compass.

Orient View Cube to Current UCS. As you have seen, the view cube is aligned to the current UCS by default. In other words, the top face of the cube is always perpendicular to the Z axis of the UCS. However, this can be turned off by unchecking the **Orient View Cube to current UCS** check box. The **NAVVCUBEORIENT** system variable controls this setting. When unchecked, the faces of the view cube are not reoriented when the UCS is changed. It may be easier to visualize view changes if the view cube faces are oriented to the current UCS.

When the **Orient View Cube to current UCS** check box is unchecked, WCS is displayed above the UCS shortcut menu in the view cube (unless the WCS is current). See **Figure 3-10.** This is a reminder that the labels on the view cube relate to the WCS and not to the current UCS.

Figure 3-10.
When the **Orient View Cube to current UCS** option is off in the **View Cube Settings** dialog box, the UCS shortcut has WCS displayed above it.

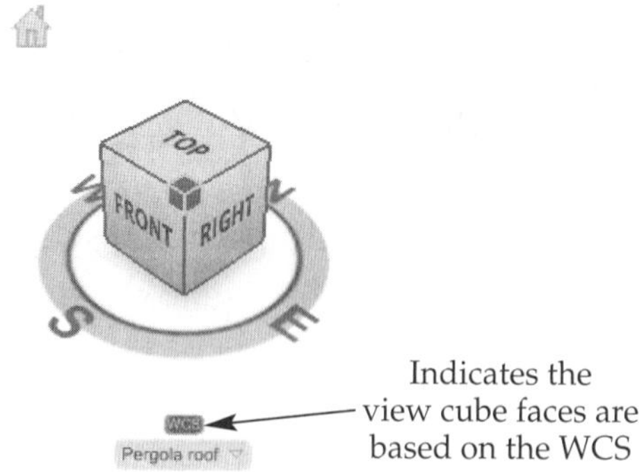

Keep Scene Upright. If the **Keep scene upright** check box is checked, the view of the model cannot be turned upside down. When unchecked, you may accidentally rotate the view so it is upside down. This can be confusing. It is best to leave this check box checked.

Show Compass below the View Cube. The compass is displayed by default in the view cube. However, if you do not find the compass useful, you can turn it off. To hide the compass, uncheck the **Show compass below the View Cube** check box.

Restore Defaults. After making several changes in the **View Cube Settings** dialog box you may get confused about the affect of different option settings on the model display. In this case, it is best to pick the **Restore Defaults** button to return all settings to their original values. Then change one setting at a time and test it to be sure the view cube functions as you intended.

Exercise 3-3

Complete the exercise on the Student CD.

Creating a Continuous 3D Orbit

3DCORBIT

Ribbon
Home
> View
Continuous Orbit

Type
3DCORBIT

Menu
View
> Orbit
> Continuous Orbit

The **3DCORBIT** command provides the ability to create a continuous orbit of a model. By moving your pointing device, you can set the model in motion in any direction and at any speed, depending on the power of your computer. An impressive display can be achieved using this command.

Once the command is initiated, the continuous orbit cursor is displayed. See **Figure 3-11.** Press and hold the pick button and move the pointer in the direction that you want the model to rotate and at the desired speed of rotation. Release the button when the pointer is moving at the appropriate speed. The model will continue to rotate until you pick the left mouse button, press [Enter] or [Esc], or right-click and pick **Exit** or another option. At any time while the model is orbiting, you can left-click and adjust the rotation angle and speed by repeating the process for starting a continuous orbit.

Figure 3-11.
This is the continuous orbit cursor in the **3DCORBIT** command (or **Continuous** option of the **3DORBIT** command). Pick and hold the left mouse button. Then, move the cursor in the direction in which you want the view to rotate and release the mouse button.

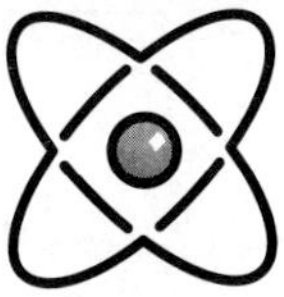

Plan Command Options

The **PLAN** command, introduced in Chapter 1, allows you to create a plan view of any user coordinate system (UCS) or the world coordinate system (WCS). The **PLAN** command automatically performs a **ZOOM Extents**. This fills the graphics window with the plan view. The command options are:

- **Current UCS.** This creates a view of the object that is plan to the current UCS.
- **World UCS.** This creates a view of the object that is plan to the WCS. If the WCS is the current UCS, this option and the **Current UCS** option produce the same results.
- **Named UCS.** This displays a view plan to a named UCS. The preset UCSs are not considered named UCSs. This option is **Ucs** when the **PLAN** command is typed.

This command may have limited usefulness when working with 3D models. The dynamic capabilities of the view cube are much more intuitive and may be quicker to use. However, you may find instances where the **PLAN** command is easier to use, such as when the view cube is not currently displayed.

PLAN

Type
PLAN
Menu
View
> 3D Views
> Plan View

Displaying Models with Steering Wheels

Steering wheels, or *wheels,* are dynamic menus that provide quick access to view-navigation tools. A steering wheel follows the cursor as it is moved around the drawing. Each wheel is divided into wedges and each wedge contains a tool. See **Figure 3-12.** The **NAVSWHEEL** command is used to display a steering wheel.

AutoCAD provides two basic types of wheels: View Object and Tour Building. The options contained in these two wheels are combined to form the Full Navigation wheel. Each of these three types can be used in a full wheel display or a minimized format. This section discusses the Full Navigation wheel and the two basic wheels in their full and mini formats. There is also a 2D Navigation wheel that is displayed in paper (layout) space or when the **NAVSWHEELMODE** system variable is set to 3. The functions of this wheel are covered in detail in *AutoCAD and Its Applications—Basics.*

NAVSWHEEL

Ribbon
Home
> View

Steering Wheels
Type
NAVSWHEEL
WHEEL
Menu
View
> Steering Wheels
Toolbar
Status Bar

Steering Wheel

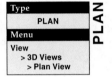

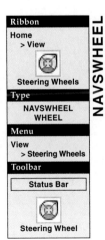

Using a Steering Wheel

When displayed the very first time, the steering wheel is pinned. This is discussed later in the Steering Wheel Settings section. Once a steering wheel is displayed, move the cursor around the screen. Notice as you move the cursor, the wheel follows it. When you stop the cursor, the wheel stops. If you move the cursor anywhere inside of the wheel, the wheel remains stationary. Note also that as you move the cursor inside of the wheel, a wedge (tool) is highlighted. If you pause the cursor over a tool, a tooltip is displayed that describes the tool.

Figure 3-12.
A—Full Navigation wheel. B—View Object wheel. C—Tour Building wheel.

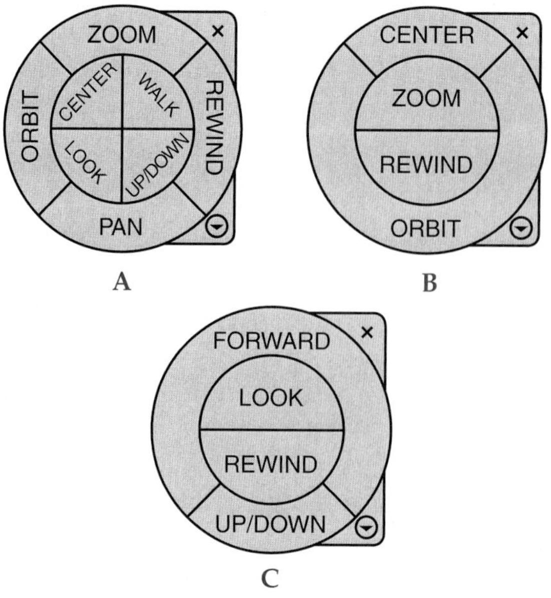

To use a specific tool, simply pick and hold on the highlighted wedge, then move the cursor as needed to change the view of the model. Once you release the pick button, the tool ends and the wheel is redisplayed. Some options display a *center point* about which the display will move. The **Center** tool is used to set the center point. These features are all discussed in the next sections.

To change between wheels, right-click to display the shortcut menu. Then, select **Full Navigation Wheel** from the menu to display that wheel. Or, select **Basic Wheels** to display a cascading menu. Select either **View Object Wheel** or **Tour Building Wheel** from the cascading menu to display that wheel. Refer to **Figure 3-13.**

PROFESSIONAL TIP

The view cube is a valuable visualization tool, especially when used in conjunction with a steering wheel. As you use the wheel options to manipulate the model, watch the view cube move. This provides you with a dynamic "map" of where your viewpoint is at all times in relation to the model, the UCS, and the view cube compass.

Exercise 3-4

Complete the exercise on the Student CD.

Figure 3-13.
The shortcut menu allows you to switch between steering wheels.

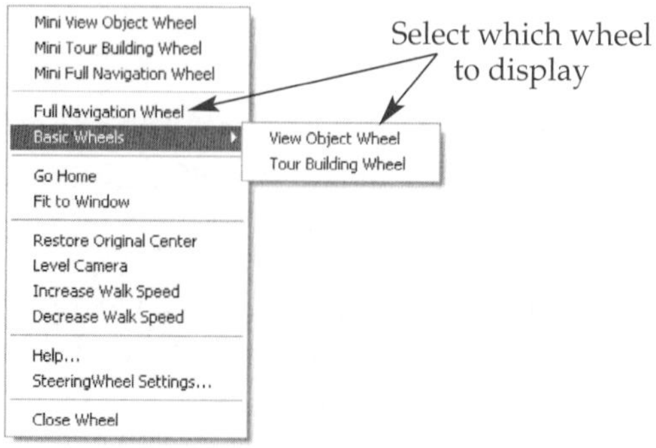

Full Navigation Wheel

The Full Navigation wheel contains all of the tools available in the View Object and Tour Building wheels. Refer to **Figure 3-12A.** These tools are discussed in the following sections. It also contains the **Pan** and **Walk** tools, which are not available in either of the other two wheels. These tools are discussed next. The tools shared with the View Object and Tour Building tools are discussed in the sections corresponding to those tools.

In addition, a number of settings are available to change the appearance of the steering wheel and the manner in which some of the tools function. Refer to the Steering Wheel Settings section later in this chapter for a complete discussion of these settings.

Pan

The **Pan** tool allows you to move the model in the direction that you drag the cursor. This tool functions exactly the same as the AutoCAD **RTPAN** command. When you pick and hold on the tool, the cursor changes to four arrows with the label Pan Tool below the cursor.

If you use the **Pan** tool with the perspective projection current, it may appear that the model is slowly rotating about a point. This is not the case. What you are seeing is merely the effect of the vanishing points. As you pan, the relationship between the viewpoint and the vanishing points changes. You can quickly test this by closing the wheel, right-clicking on the view cube, and picking **Parallel** from the shortcut menu. Now display the wheel again and use the **Pan** tool. Notice the difference. The model pans without appearing to rotate.

Walk

The **Walk** tool is used to simulate walking toward, through, or away from the model. When you pick and hold on the tool, the center circle icon is displayed at the bottom-center of the drawing area. See **Figure 3-14.** The cursor changes to an arrow pointing away from the center of the circle. This indicates the direction in which the view will move as you move the mouse. This gives the illusion of walking in that direction in relation to the model.

If you hold down the [Shift] key while clicking the **Walk** tool, the **Up/Down** slider is displayed. This allows you to change the Y axis orientation of the view. Releasing the [Shift] key returns you to the standard walk mode. The **Up/Down** slider is also used with the **Up/Down** tool on the Tour Building wheel. It is explained in that section.

View Object Wheel

If you think of your model as a building, the tools in the View Object wheel are used to view the outside of the building. This wheel contains four navigation tools: **Center, Zoom, Rewind,** and **Orbit**. Refer to **Figure 3-12B.**

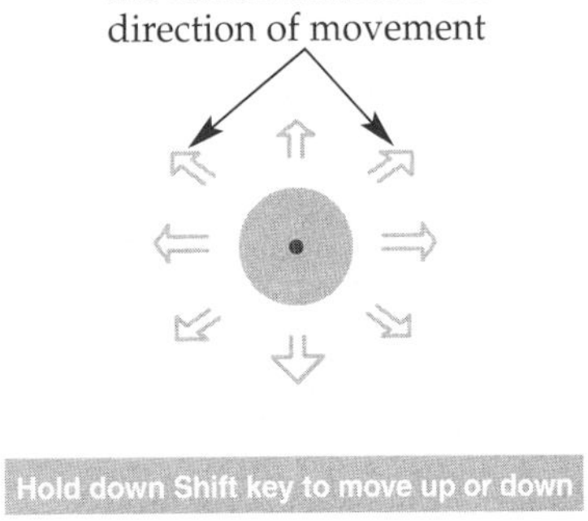

The arrow displayed as the cursor indicates the direction of movement
Hold down Shift key to move up or down

Figure 3-14.
The **Walk** tool displays the center circle icon. As you move the cursor around the icon, one of the arrows shown here is displayed to indicate the direction in which the view is being moved.

Center

The **Center** tool is used to set the center point for the current view. Many tools, such as **Zoom** and **Orbit**, are applied in relation to the center point. Pick and hold the **Center** tool, then move the cursor to a point on the model and release. The display immediately changes to center the model on that point. See **Figure 3-15.** The selected point must be on an object, but it does not need to be on a solid. Notice that the center point icon resembles a globe with three orbital axes. These axes relate to the three axes of the model shown on the UCS icon.

Zoom

The **Zoom** tool is used to dynamically zoom the view in and out, just as with the AutoCAD **RTZOOM** command. The tool uses the center point set with the **Center** tool. When you pick and hold the **Zoom** tool in the wheel, the center point is displayed at its current location. The cursor changes to a magnifying glass with the label Zoom Tool displayed below it. See **Figure 3-16.** There are three different ways to use the **Zoom** tool, as discussed in the next sections.

When the **Zoom** tool is accessed in the Full Navigation wheel, the center point is relocated to the position of the steering wheel. If you wish to zoom on the existing pivot point when using the Full Navigation wheel, first press the [Ctrl] key and then access the **Zoom** tool. This prevents the tool from relocating the center point. You can also move the center point using the **Center** tool, then switch to the View Object wheel and access the **Zoom** tool from that wheel. In either case, the zoom is relative to the location of the center point.

NOTE

Once you close the steering wheel, the center point is reset. The next time a steering wheel is displayed, the center point will be in the middle of the current view.

Pick and drag. To dynamically zoom, similar to realtime zoom, pick and drag the cursor. As the cursor is moved up or to the right, the viewpoint moves closer (zoom in). Move the pointer to the left or down and the viewpoint moves farther away (zoom out). The zooming is based on the current center point. When you have achieved the appropriate zoom location, release the pointer button.

Single click. If you select the **Zoom** tool with a single click, the view of the model zooms in by an incremental percentage. Each time you single click on the tool, the view is zoomed by 25%. The zoom is in relation to the center point.

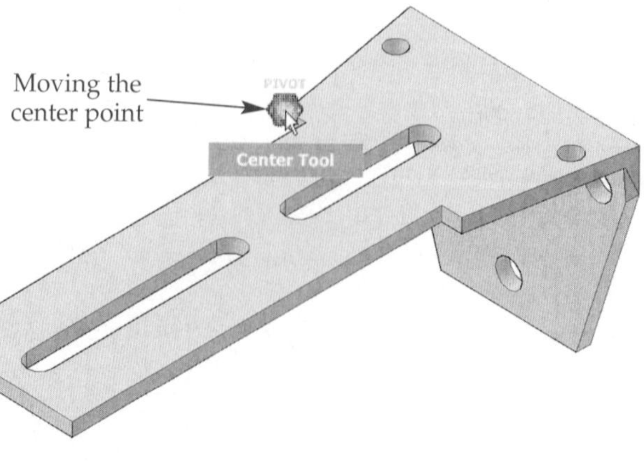

Figure 3-15.
The **Center** tool allows you to select a new center point for the current view. This becomes the point about which many steering wheel tools operate.

Figure 3-16.
The **Zoom** tool operates in relation to the center point. If the tool is selected from the Full Navigation wheel, the center point is automatically relocated to the cursor location.

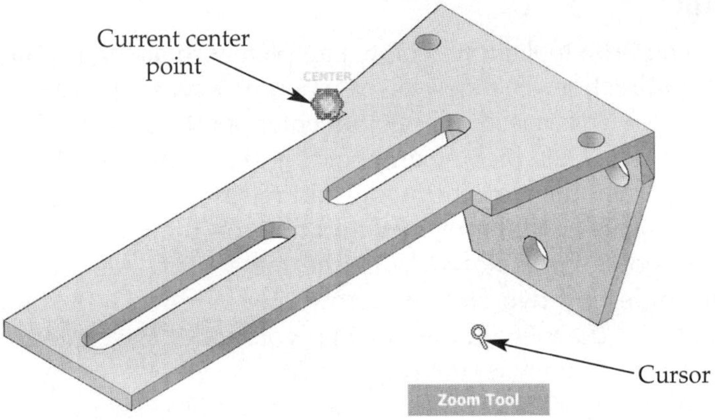

In order for this function to work when the **Zoom** tool is accessed from the Full Navigation wheel, you must check the **Enable single click incremental zoom** check box in the **Steering Wheel Settings** dialog box. This is discussed in detail later.

Shift and click. If you press and hold the [Shift] key and then pick the **Zoom** tool, the view is zoomed out by 25%. As with the single-click method, the **Enable single click incremental zoom** check box must be checked in order to use this with the Full Navigation wheel.

Rewind

The **Rewind** tool allows you to step back through previous views. A single pick on this tool displays the previous view. If you pick and hold the tool, a "slide show" of previous views is displayed as thumbnail images. See **Figure 3-17.** The most recent view is displayed on the right-hand side. The oldest view is displayed on the left-hand side. The slide representing the current view is highlighted with an orange frame and a set of brackets. While holding the pick button, move the cursor to the left. Notice that the set of brackets moves with the cursor. As a slide is highlighted, the corresponding view is restored in the viewport. Release the pick button when you find the view you want and it is set current.

The navigation history is maintained in the drawing file and is different for each open drawing. However, it is not saved when a drawing is closed. The **Steering Wheel Settings** dialog box allows you to control when thumbnail images are created and saved in the navigation history. This dialog box is discussed later in the chapter.

Figure 3-17.
A single pick on the **Rewind** tool displays the previous view. A "slide show" of previous views is displayed as thumbnail images if you press and hold the pick button.

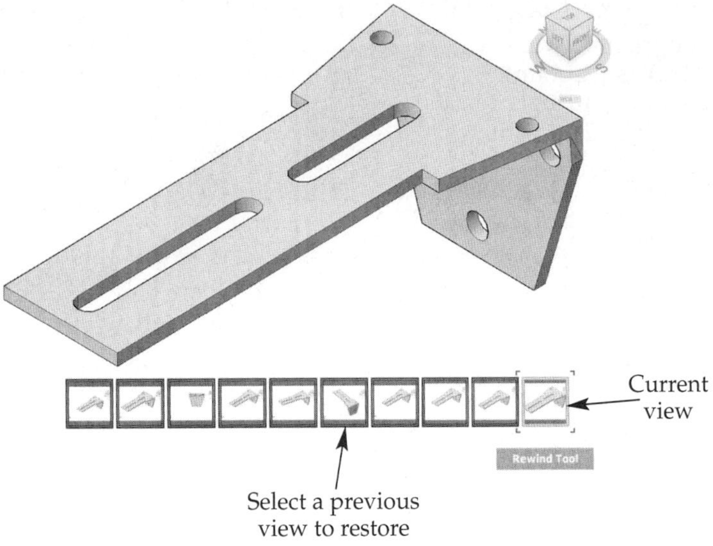

Orbit

The **Orbit** tool allows you to completely rotate your point of view around the model in any direction. The view pivots about the center point set with the **Center** tool. When using the Full Navigation wheel, the center point can be quickly set by pressing and holding the [Ctrl] key, then picking and holding the **Orbit** tool. Then, drag the center point to the desired pivot point on the model and release. Now you can use the **Orbit** tool.

To use the **Orbit** tool, pick and hold on the tool in the steering wheel. The current center point is displayed with the label Pivot. Also, the cursor changes to a point surrounded by two circular arrows. See **Figure 3-18A.** Move the cursor around the screen and the view of the model pivots about the center point. If this is not the result you wanted, just reset the pivot point.

When the **Orbit** tool is selected in the Full Navigation wheel, an option of the tool allows you to *roll* the view of the model, as opposed to orbiting (freely rotating). When rolling the view, the view axis parallel to your line of sight (perpendicular to the screen) is not altered.

To enable this option, first open the **Steering Wheels Settings** dialog box by right-clicking on the wheel and picking **Steering Wheel Settings...** from the shortcut menu. Uncheck the **Maintain Up direction for Orbit tool** check box in the lower-left corner of the dialog box and pick the **OK** button to exit the dialog. Now, pick and hold the **Orbit** tool in the Full Navigation wheel. You can orbit the view as described above. However, notice the message at the bottom of the view. Hold down the [Shift] key and the roll icon is displayed on the center point. See **Figure 3-18B.** As you move the cursor, the view only rotates in a circular or "rolling" manner about an axis perpendicular to the screen. Release the [Shift] key and you are returned to normal orbit mode. Remember, this option is *not* available when the **Orbit** tool is selected in the View Object wheel.

PROFESSIONAL TIP

Since the **Orbit** tool is most often used to quickly move your viewpoint to another side of the model, it is more intuitive to locate the pivot point somewhere on the model. First use the **Center** tool to establish the pivot point. Then, when you use the **Orbit** tool, the view pivots about that part of the model. If the center point is not set, it defaults to the center of the screen.

Figure 3-18.
A—The **Orbit** tool allows you to rotate your point of view completely around the model in any direction. This is the cursor displayed for the tool. B—Hold down the [Shift] key to roll the view when using the **Orbit** tool. The view will only rotate in a circular or "rolling" manner. This is the cursor displayed when rolling the view.

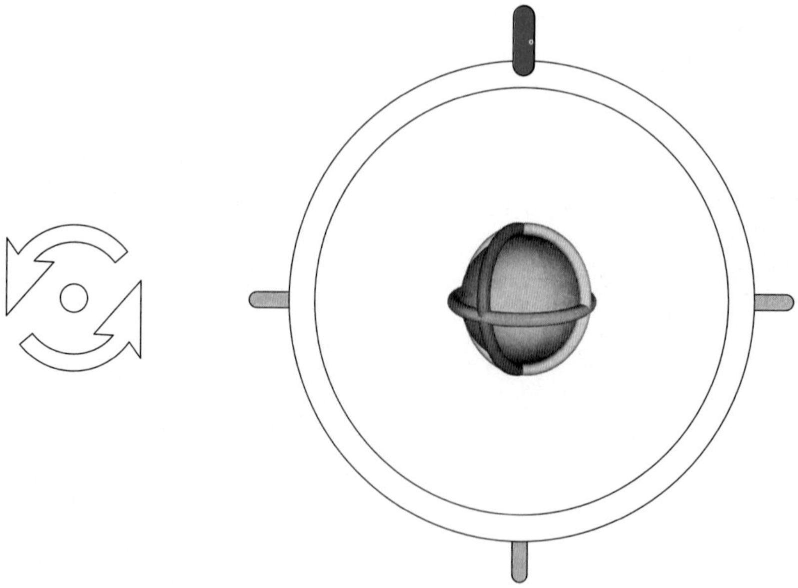

A B

CAUTION

When the **Zoom** tool is selected from the Full Navigation wheel, the center point is changed to the steering wheel location. Therefore, that center point is used as the pivot point for the **Orbit** tool. When the **Zoom** tool is selected from the View Object wheel, the center point is not changed. Therefore, it is best to switch to the View Object wheel to use the **Zoom** tool.

Tour Building Wheel

Where the tools in the View Object wheel are used to view the outside of the "building," the tools in the Tour Building wheel are used to move around inside of the "building." This wheel contains four navigation tools. The **Forward**, **Look**, and **Up/Down** tools are discussed here. The **Rewind** tool is discussed earlier.

Forward

The principal tool in the **Tour Building** wheel is the **Forward** tool. It is similar to the **Walk** tool in the Full Navigation wheel. However, it only allows forward movement from the current viewpoint. This tool requires a center point to be set on the model from within the tool. The existing center point cannot be used.

First, move the cursor and steering wheel to the point on the model that will be the target (center point). Next, pick and hold the **Forward** tool. The pick point becomes the center point and a drag distance indicator is displayed. See Figure 3-19. This indicator shows the starting viewpoint, the center point, and the surface of the model that you selected. Hold the mouse button down while moving the pointer up. The orange location slider moves to show the current viewpoint relative to the center point. As you move closer to the model, the green center point icon increases in size, which also provides a visual cue to the zoom level.

Look

The **Look** tool is used to rotate the view about the center of the view. When the tool is activated, the cursor appears as a half circle with arrows. See Figure 3-20. As you move the cursor down, the model moves up in the view as if you are actually tilting your head down to see the top of the model. Similarly, as you "look" away from the model to the right or left, the model appears to move away from your line of sight. The distance between you and the model remains the same and the orientation of the model does not change. Therefore, you would not want to use this tool if you wanted to see another side of the model.

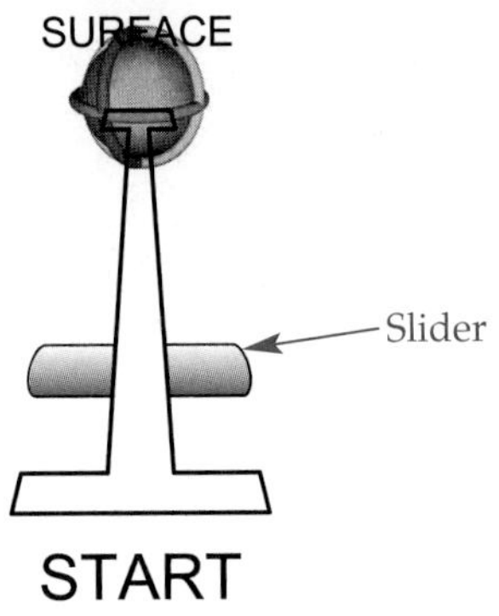

Figure 3-19.
The drag distance indicator is displayed when using the **Forward** tool. This indicator shows the start point of the view and the selected surface of the model. The slider indicates the current view position relative to the starting point.

Figure 3-20.
The **Look** tool cursor appears as a half circle with arrows.

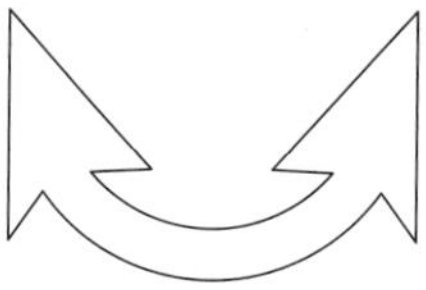

Up/Down

As the name indicates, the **Up/Down** tool moves the view up or down along the Y axis of the screen, regardless of the orientation of the current UCS. Pick and hold on the tool and the vertical distance indicator appears. See **Figure 3-21.** Two marks on this indicator show the upper and lower limits within which the view can be moved. The orange slider shows the position of the view as you move the cursor. When the tool is first activated, the view is at the top position. The **Up/Down** tool has limited value. The **Pan** tool is far more versatile.

PROFESSIONAL TIP

Using steering wheel tools such as **Forward**, **Look**, **Orbit**, and **Walk**, you can manipulate your view to fully explore the model. The **Rewind** tool can then be used to replay all of the previous views saved in the navigation history. This process allows you to find views of the model that you may want to save as named views for later use in model construction or for shots created with show motion (discussed in Chapter 4.) Remember, views created using steering wheels are not saved with the drawing file. Therefore, it may be a time-saver to create named views in this manner if there is a possibility they will be needed later.

Exercise 3-5

Complete the exercise on the Student CD.

Figure 3-21.
The indicator displayed when using the **Up/Down** tool shows the upper and lower limits within which the view can be moved. The top position is the location of the view when the tool is selected.

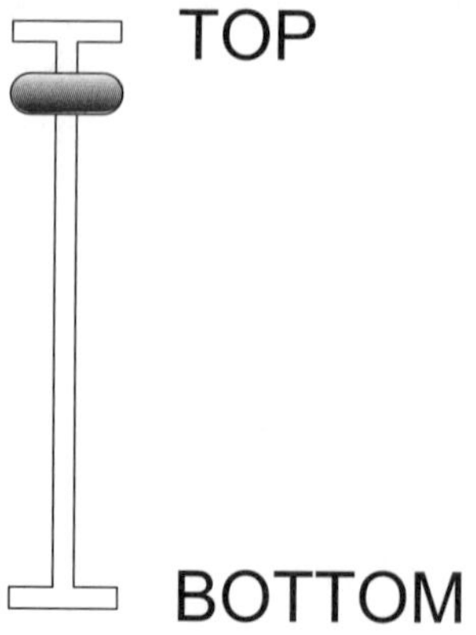

Figure 3-22.
In addition to full-size steering wheels, mini wheels can be used. A—Mini Full Navigation wheel. B—Mini View Object wheel. C—Mini Tour Building wheel.

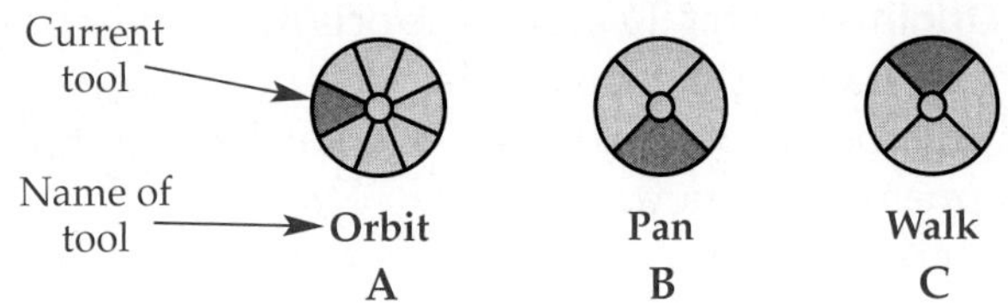

Mini Wheels

The three wheels discussed above were presented in their *full wheel* formats. As you gain familiarity with the use and function of each wheel and its tools, you may wish to begin using the abbreviated formats. The abbreviated formats are called ***mini wheels.*** See **Figure 3-22.** The mini wheels can be selected in the steering wheel shortcut menu. When you select a mini wheel, it replaces the cursor pointer.

As you move the mouse, the mini wheel follows. Slowly move the mouse in a small circle and notice that each wedge of the wheel is highlighted. The name of the currently highlighted tool appears below the mini wheel. When the tool you need is highlighted, simply click and hold to activate the tool. All tools in the mini wheels function the same as those in the full wheels. The only difference is the appearance of the wheels.

Steering Wheel Shortcut Menu

A quick method for switching between the different wheel formats is to use the steering wheel shortcut menu. Pick the menu arrow at the lower-right corner of a full wheel to display the menu. See **Figure 3-23.** Additionally, you can right-click when any full or mini wheel is displayed to access the menu. To select a wheel or change wheel formats, simply select the appropriate entry in the menu. Note that a check mark is *not* placed by the current wheel.

In addition to selecting a wheel, the shortcut menu provides options for viewing the model. Refer to **Figure 3-23.** These additional options are:

- **Go Home.** Returns the display to the home view. This is the same as picking the **Home** icon in the view cube.
- **Fit to Window.** Resizes the current view to fit all objects in the drawing inside of the window. This is essentially a zoom extents operation.

Figure 3-23.
Select the down arrow to display the steering wheel shortcut menu. Both full wheels and mini wheels can be displayed using this menu.

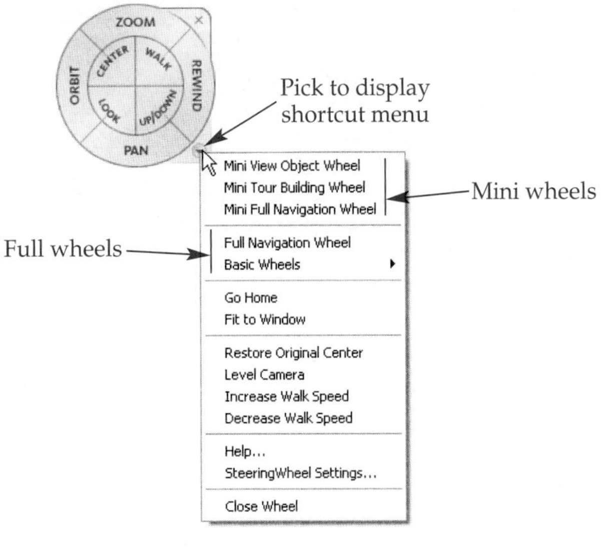

- **Restore Original Center.** Restores the original center point of the drawing using the current drawing extents. This does not change the current zoom factor. Therefore, if you are zoomed close into an object and pick this option, the object may disappear from view.
- **Level Camera.** The camera (your viewpoint) is rotated to be level with the XY ground plane.
- **Increase Walk Speed.** The speed used by the **Walk** tool is increased by 100%.
- **Decrease Walk Speed.** The speed used by the **Walk** tool is decreased by 50%.
- **Help.** Displays the online documentation (help file) for steering wheels.
- **Steering Wheel Settings.** Displays the **Steering Wheel Settings** dialog box, which is discussed in the next section.
- **Close Wheel.** Closes the steering wheel. This is the same as pressing [Esc] to close the wheel.

Exercise 3-6

Complete the exercise on the Student CD.

Steering Wheel Settings

The **Steering Wheels Settings** dialog box provides options for wheel appearance. See **Figure 3-24.** It also contains settings for the display and operation of several tools. It is displayed by picking **Steering Wheels Settings** in the shortcut menu.

Changing wheel appearance

The two areas at the top of the **Steering Wheels Settings** dialog box allow you to change the size and opacity of all wheels. The settings in the **Big Wheels** area are for the full wheels. The settings in the **Mini Wheels** area are for the mini wheels. The **Wheel size:** slider in each area is used to display the wheels in small, normal, or large size. The mini wheel has a fourth, extra large size. See **Figure 3-25.** These sliders set the **NAVSWHEELSIZEBIG** and **NAVSWHEELSIZEMINI** system variables.

Figure 3-24.
The **Steering Wheels Settings** dialog box provides options for wheel appearance and the display and operation of several tools.

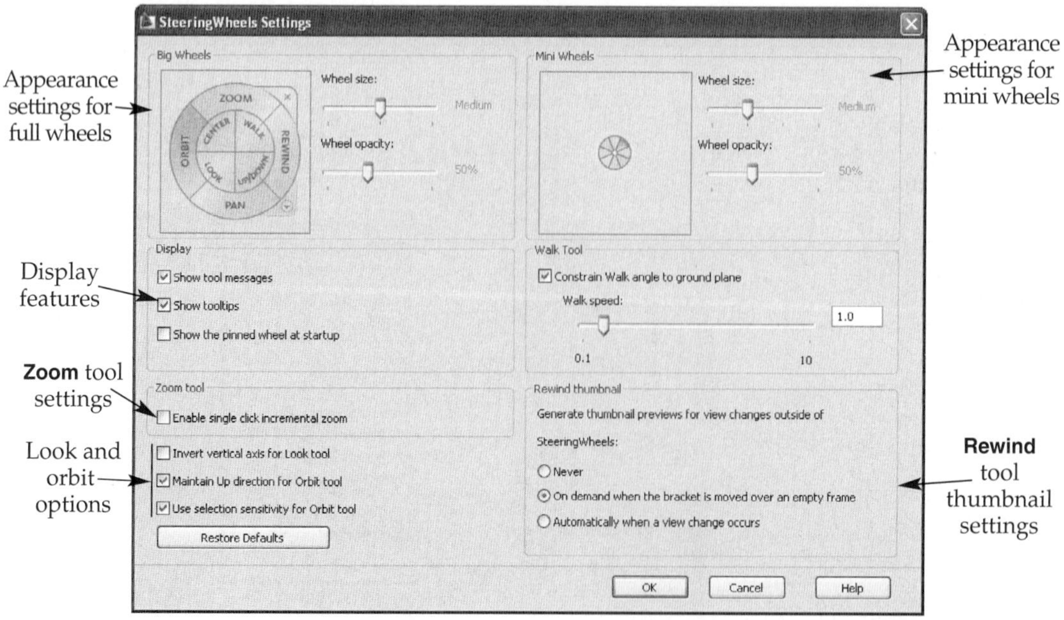

Figure 3-25.
The size of a steering wheel can be set in the **Steering Wheels Settings** dialog box or by using a system variable. A—The **NAVSWHEELSIZEBIG** system variable allows you to display full wheels in small, normal, or large size. B—The **NAVSWHEELSIZEMINI** system variable allows you to display mini wheels in small, normal, large, or extra large size.

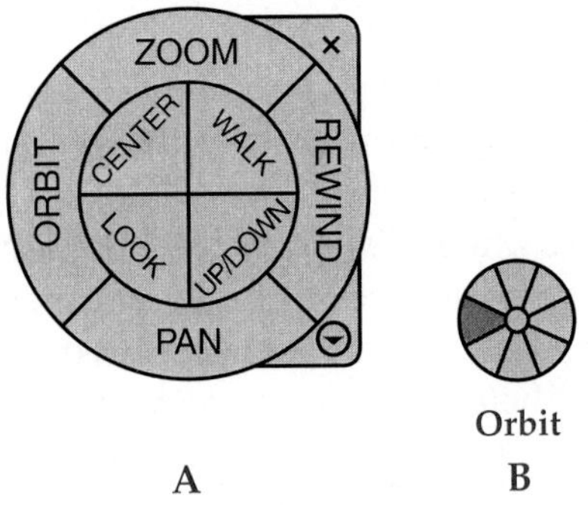

The **Wheel opacity:** slider in each area controls the transparency of the wheels. These sliders can be set to a value from 25% to 90% opacity. The sliders control the **NAVSWHEELOPACITYBIG** and the **NAVSWHEELOPACITYMINI** system variables. The appearance of the full wheel in three different opacity settings is shown in Figure 3-26.

Display features

The **Display** area of the **Steering Wheels Settings** dialog box controls three features of the wheel display. These settings determine whether messages and tooltips are displayed. There is also a setting for pinning the wheel at startup.

Figure 3-26.
The opacity of a steering wheel can be changed. A—Opacity of 25%. B—Opacity of 50%. C—Opacity of 90%.

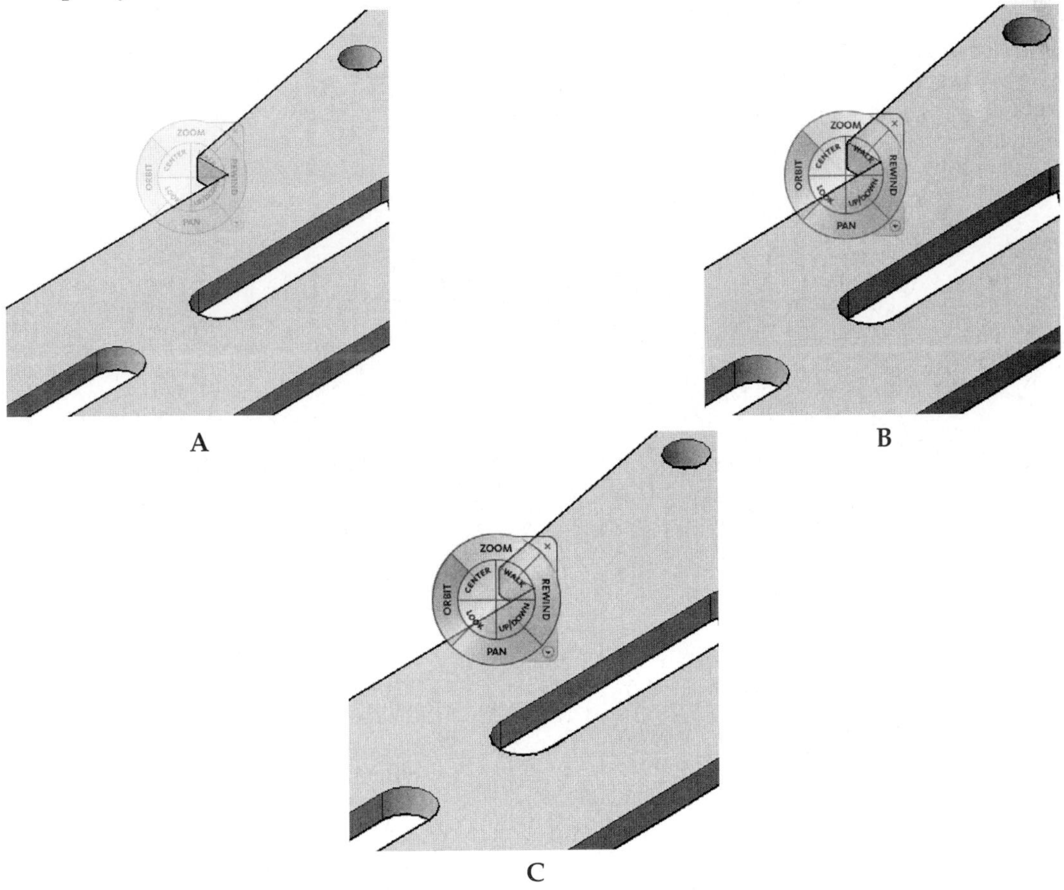

When a tool is selected, its name is displayed below the cursor. In addition, some tools have features or restrictions that can be indicated in a tool message. To see these messages, the **Show tool messages** check box must be checked. Otherwise, the messages are not displayed, but the restrictions remain in effect.

A tooltip is a short message that appears below the wheel when the cursor is hovered over the wheel. When the **Show tooltips** check box is checked, you can hold the cursor stationary over a tool for approximately three seconds and the tooltip will appear. Then, as you move the cursor over tools in the wheel, the appropriate tool tip is immediately displayed.

When the **Show the pinned wheel at startup** check box is checked, the steering wheel is displayed "pinned" in the lower-left corner of the graphics screen when the **NAVSWHEEL** command is used. This is how it appears the very first time a steering wheel is used when AutoCAD is installed. When the pointer is moved over the wheel, the "first contact" balloon is displayed. See **Figure 3-27.** You can select the **New to 3D** tab or **Familiar with 3D** tab. Each tab displays basic information on using steering wheels. This balloon is useful should you need reminders on the function and appearance of each type of wheel. To use the steering wheel, select an entry in the "first contact" balloon.

If you check the **Show the pinned wheel at startup** check box and exit the **Steering Wheels Settings** dialog box, the wheel is not pinned. This option will take affect the next time the **NAVSWHEEL** command is used. The steering wheel is pinned each time thereafter until the setting is changed.

PROFESSIONAL TIP

As soon as you become familiar with steering wheels, turn the **Show the pinned wheel at startup** option off. The "first contact" balloon is designed for a new user and quickly becomes a nuisance.

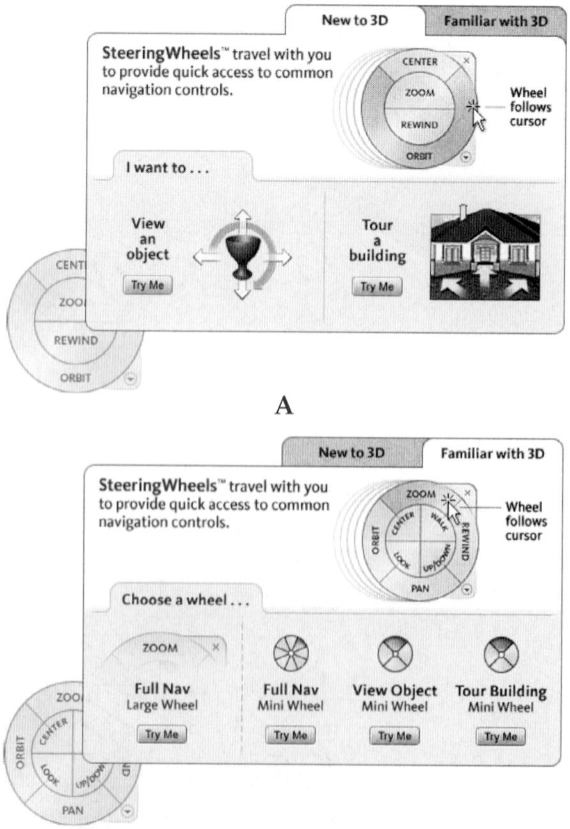

Figure 3-27.
The steering wheel "first contact" balloon. A—The **Familiar with 3D** tab. B—The **New to 3D** tab.

Walk tool

By default, when the **Walk** tool is used, you move parallel to the ground plane. This is because the **Constrain walk angle to ground plane** check box is checked. Test this by selecting the **Walk** tool and then move the cursor toward the top of the screen. You appear to be "walking" over the top of the model. Now, open the **Steering Wheels Settings** dialog box and uncheck the **Constrain walk angle to ground plane** box. This allows you to "fly" in the direction the cursor is moved when using the **Walk** tool. Exit the dialog box and again select the **Walk** tool. Move the cursor toward the top of the screen. This time it appears that you are flying directly toward or into the model.

The speed at which you walk through or around the model is controlled by the **Walk speed:** slider. The value can also be changed by typing in the text box at the right-hand end of the slider. The greater the value, the faster you will move as the cursor is moved away from the center circle icon.

Zoom tool

As discussed earlier, a single click on the **Zoom** tool zooms in on the current view by a factor of 25%. This is controlled by the **Enable single click incremental zoom** check box. When this check box is not checked, a single click on the tool has no effect. Some users find the single-click zoom confusing.

Look and orbit tool options

By default, when the **Look** tool is used and the cursor is moved downward, the view of the model moves up, just as if you were moving your eyes down. If you check the **Invert vertical axis for Look tool** option, this movement is reversed. In this case, the model moves in the same direction as the cursor.

If the **Maintain Up direction for Orbit tool** check box is not checked, it is possible to turn the model upside down while using the **Orbit** tool. This may not be desirable because it can be disorienting. To prevent this, be sure to leave the option checked. Uncheck this option only when you want to use **Orbit** in a "free-floating" mode.

By default, you can select objects in the model prior to using the wheel and the center of the selection is used as the pivot point for the **Orbit** tool. See **Figure 3-28.** First, select all objects about which you want the view to pivot. Next, display the wheel and

Figure 3-28.
A—When no objects are selected, the default center point is used as the pivot point. B—Select the objects about which you want the **Orbit** tool to pivot the view. Then, pick the **Orbit** tool at any point on the screen and notice that the pivot point is located in the middle of the selected objects.

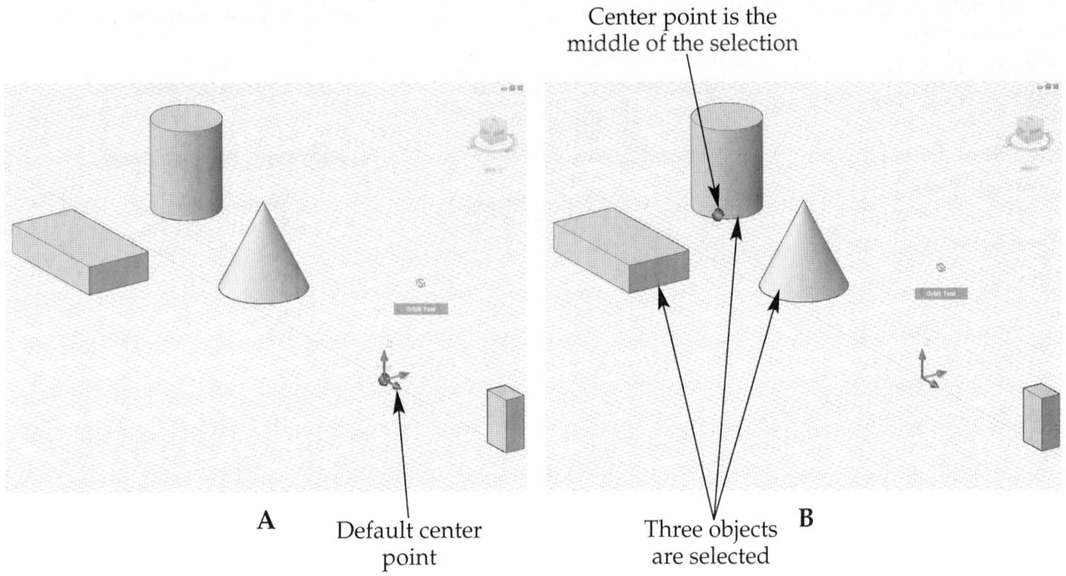

pick the **Orbit** tool. Notice that the pivot point is located in the middle of the selected objects. Now, rotate the view as needed. This behavior is controlled by the **Use selection sensitivity for Orbit tool** check box in the **Steering Wheels Settings** dialog box. When unchecked, the selection set has no effect on the center point.

NOTE

If you select objects, display the wheel, and use the **Center** tool to change the center point, that point is used for the **Orbit** tool, not the center of the selection.

Rewind thumbnail

Options in the **Rewind thumbnail** section of the **Steering Wheels Settings** dialog box control when and how thumbnail images are generated for use with the **Rewind** tool when view changes are made without using a wheel. There are three options in this area. Only one option can be on.

When the **Never** radio button is on, thumbnail images are never generated for view changes made outside of a wheel. Thumbnail images are created for view changes made with a wheel, which is true for all three options.

When the **On demand when the bracket is moved over an empty frame** radio button is on, thumbnail images are not automatically generated for view changes made outside of a wheel. The frames for these views display a double arrow icon when the **Rewind** tool in a wheel is used. However, as the brackets are moved over these frames, thumbnail images are generated. This is the default setting. See **Figure 3-29.**

When the **Automatically when a view change occurs** option is selected, a thumbnail image is generated any time a view change is made outside of a wheel. When the **Rewind** tool in a wheel is used, the frames for these views automatically display thumbnail images.

Restore defaults

Picking the **Restore Defaults** button in the **Steering Wheels Settings** dialog box returns all of the settings in the dialog box to their default values. Select this when at any time you are not sure how the settings are affecting the appearance and function of the steering wheel tools. Then, make changes one at a time as needed.

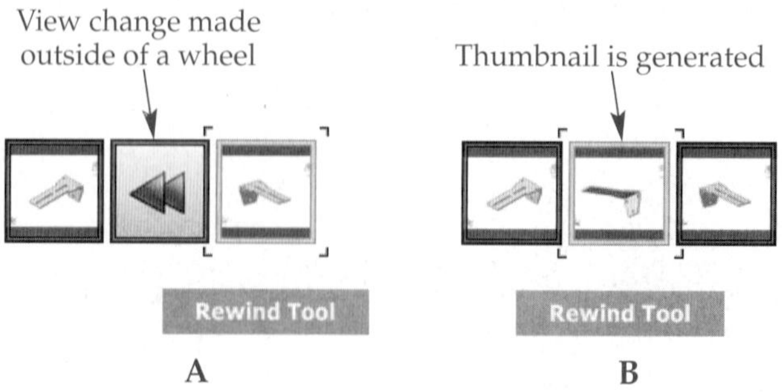

Figure 3-29.
A—By default, when the **Rewind** tool is selected, frames representing view changes made outside of a steering wheel display double-arrow icons. B—As the brackets are moved over the blank frames, thumbnail images are generated of the views created outside of a wheel.

PROFESSIONAL TIP

The view cube and steering wheels provide you with quick, dynamic methods of easily changing the viewpoint of the model. Prior versions of AutoCAD provided the **3DORBIT** command as the best dynamic method of changing your viewpoint. The functionality of this command has been replaced with the **Orbit** tool in the steering wheels. Although the **3DORBIT** command is still available for use, you may find that the view cube and wheels offer the most productive options for changing views.

Exercise 3-7

Complete the exercise on the Student CD.

Displaying a 3D Model in Different Visual Styles

The ***display*** of a 3D model is how the model is presented. This does not refer to the viewing angle, but rather colors, edge display, and shading or rendering. An object can be shaded from any viewpoint. A shaded model can be edited while still keeping the object shaded. This can make it easier to see how the model is developing without having to reshade the drawing. However, when editing a shaded object, it may also be more difficult to select features.

There are four basic ways in which a model can be displayed. The first is called a ***wireframe display.*** This is a display in which all lines are shown. The simplest "shaded" display technique is to remove hidden lines using the **HIDE** command or the 3D Hidden visual style to create a ***hidden display.*** However, this is not really a "shaded" display. A ***shaded display*** of the model can be created by setting either the Conceptual or Realistic visual style current. The Realistic visual style is considered the most realistic *shaded* display. A more detailed shaded model, a ***rendered display*** of the model, can be created with the **RENDER** command. A rendering is the most realistic presentation.

Visual styles are introduced in Chapter 1. The following sections discuss AutoCAD's visual styles and introduce rendering in AutoCAD. Detailed discussions on rendering, materials, lights, and animations appear in Chapter 14 through Chapter 18.

Exercise 3-8

Complete the exercise on the Student CD.

Using the Visual Styles and Edge Effects Panels

A ***visual style*** controls the manner in which the edges and shading of a model are displayed in a viewport. The **Visual Styles** and **Edge Effects** panels in the **Visualize** tab of the ribbon provide quick and dynamic access to a variety of settings that create instant changes to the model display. See **Figure 3-30.** This section presents all of the settings available for visual styles that do not rely on the use of lights and materials. The application of lights, cameras, and materials is presented in Chapters 14 through 16.

Figure 3-30.
The **Visual Styles** and **Edge Effects** panels in the **Visualize** tab of the ribbon provide access to options for setting a visual style current and modifying the properties set by a visual style.

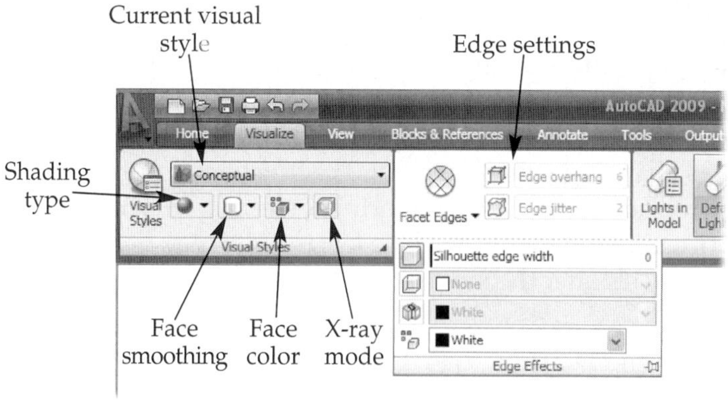

You learned in Chapter 1 that the **Visual Styles Manager** palette allows access to the full range of settings available to create a visual style. On the other hand, the **Visual Styles** and **Edge Effects** panels in the ribbon display a group of intuitive controls that enable you to quickly alter the display of the model on the screen without redefining the visual style. It may be easier and quicker to first use these panels to change settings when working with variations of model display. These changes provide instant visual feedback, not only while constructing a model, but also when displaying it for evaluation or presentation purposes. Then, should you wish to make detailed changes to the visual style using specific settings and values, use the **Visual Styles Manager** tool palette. A complete discussion of the **Visual Styles Manager** is provided in Chapter 14.

Visual style face settings

Four buttons below the visual styles drop-down list in the **Visual Styles** panel give you the ability to change the shading type, face smoothing, face colors, and transparency on the model when the 3D Hidden, Conceptual, or Realistic visual style is current.

Shading Type. The shading type flyout contains three buttons that determine the style in which the model faces are displayed. This flyout is located below the visual styles drop-down list in the **Visual Styles** panel. The use of these options is shown in **Figure 3-31.**

- **No Shading.** No colors or materials are displayed.
- **Realistic.** The default setting displays faces as realistically as possible without rendering.
- **Gooch.** Subdued colors eliminate darkness and highlights that might otherwise obscure or hide faces and details.

Face Smoothing. A ***facet*** is one flat portion, or plane, of a curved surface. Curved surfaces can be displayed faceted or smooth. See **Figure 3-32.** When displayed smooth, AutoCAD applies smoothing groups to the curved surfaces, which can increase regeneration time. The face smoothing flyout contains the **Facet Lighting**, **Smooth Lighting**, and **Smoothest Lighting** buttons. The **Smoothest Lighting** button uses per-pixel lighting. Per-pixel lighting must be enabled in the **Manual Performance Tuning** dialog box for this setting to have an effect. Otherwise, the **Smooth Lighting** setting is used when **Smoothest Lighting** is selected.

Face Colors. The face colors flyout contains four buttons that determine the manner in which the colors of the model faces are displayed. This flyout is located below the visual styles drop-down list in the **Visual Styles** panel. The color display is based on settings in the **Visual Styles Manager** palette, which is discussed in Chapter 14.

When the **Regular** button is selected in the flyout, face color options are not used. The faces are displayed in their assigned color. This may be ByLayer or an explicit color.

Faces are displayed in shades of a specified color when the **Monochrome** button is selected in the flyout. The default color is white, resulting in shades of gray. The color is controlled by the **VSMONOCOLOR** system variable.

When the **Tint** button is selected in the flyout, a tint is applied to the colors assigned to faces. The hue and saturation of the assigned colors is altered by applying a selected color. The color is controlled by the **VSMONOCOLOR** system variable.

Figure 3-31.
A—The Conceptual visual style is set current, then the **No Shading** button is selected in the **Visual Style** panel. No colors or materials are displayed. B—The **Gooch** button is selected. Subdued colors eliminate darkness and highlights that might otherwise obscure or hide faces and details. This is the default setting for the Conceptual visual style. C—The **Realistic** button is selected. The faces are displayed as realistically as possible without rendering.

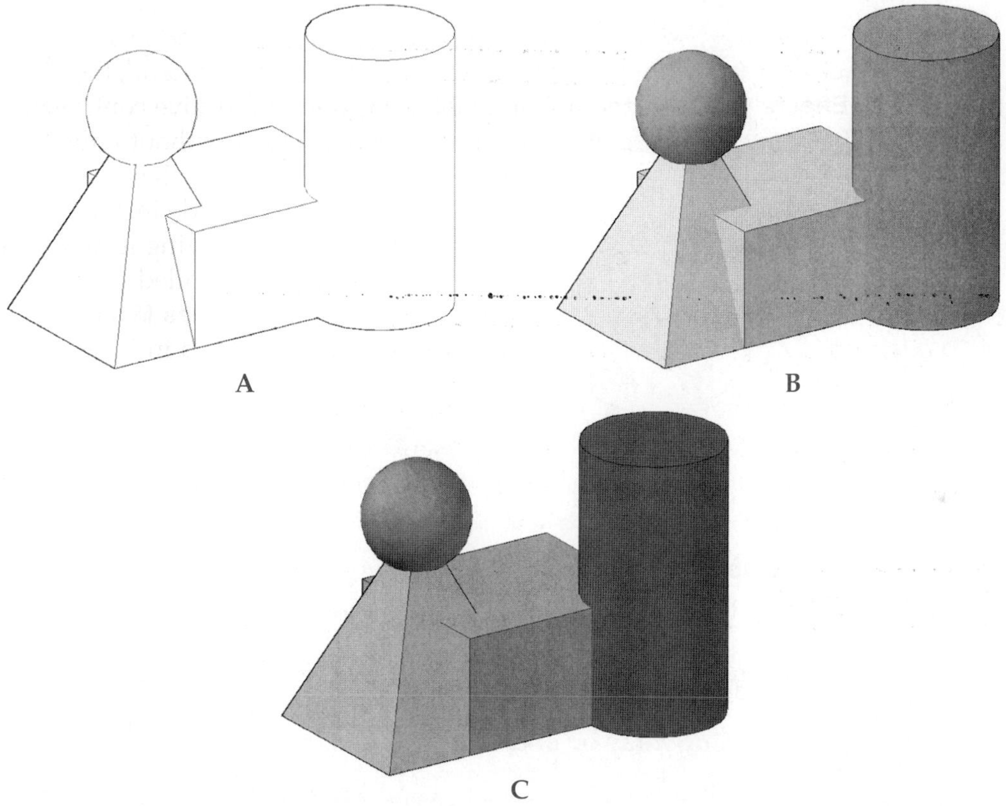

Figure 3-32.
A—The **Facet Lighting** button in the **Visual Styles** panel turns on the display of facets. B—The **Smooth Lighting** button in the **Visual Styles** panel turns the facet display off so that curved surfaces appear smooth.

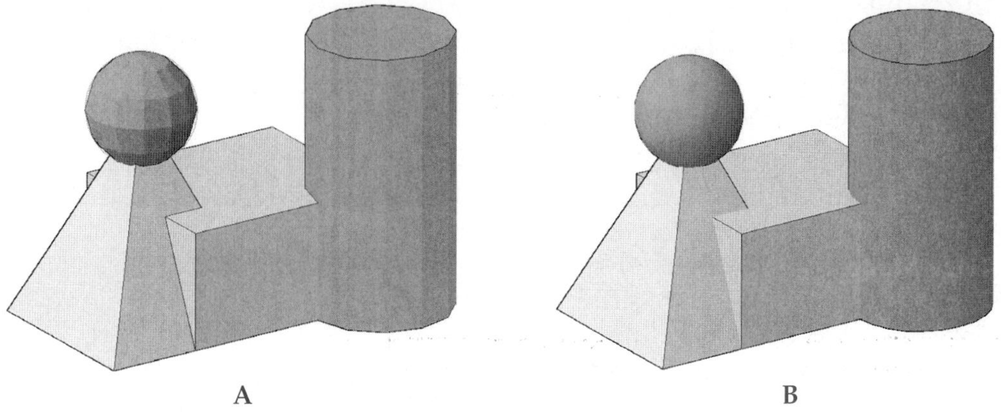

Figure 3-33.
A—The Conceptual visual style is set current. X-ray mode is off. B—X-ray mode is turned on. C—The 3D Hidden visual style is set current and X-ray mode is off. D—X-ray mode is turned on.

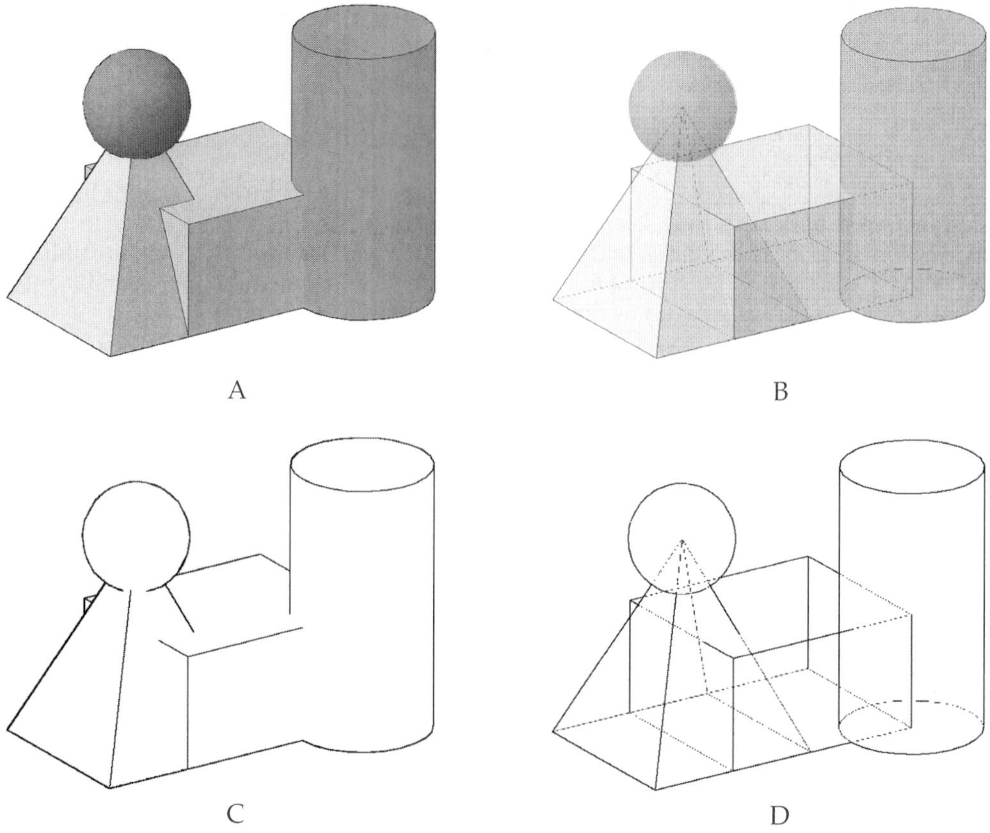

When the **Desaturate** button is selected in the flyout, the faces are displayed in their assigned colors. However, the colors are softened, or desaturated, and appear lighter.

Transparency. When the **X-Ray** button is on, all faces in the viewport are transparent. This is a toggle button that is off by default. When on, the button is highlighted in blue. The results of turning X-ray on and off are shown in **Figure 3-33.**

NOTE

Whenever you make a change to the face or edge settings, the name of the visual style in the visual styles drop-down list in the **Visual Styles** panel changes to *Current*. If you select a named visual style from the drop-down list, the settings of that visual style override the changes you made.

Visual style edge settings

There are six settings in the **Edge Effects** panel that control the appearance of both visible and obscured edges. Refer to **Figure 3-30.** Obscured edges are those that would normally be hidden by the object or other objects.

Edge Mode. The edge mode flyout at the left side of the **Edge Effects** panel in the **Visualize** tab of the ribbon controls the lines displayed to define solids. See **Figure 3-34.** The edge mode flyout contains three options:

- **No Edges.** Object edges are not shown. The edge option at the bottom of the panel are disabled. This is the same as setting the **VSEDGES** system variable to 0.

Figure 3-34.
The options in the expanded **Edge Effects** panel in the **Visualize** tab of the ribbon.

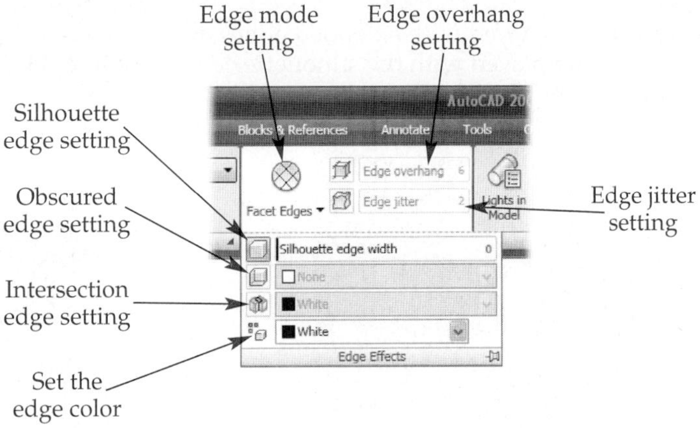

- **Isolines.** Displays isolines based on the current **ISOLINES** system variable setting. The isolines are shown in the color set in the color drop-down list at the bottom of the expanded **Edge Effects** panel. The **Obscured Edge** and **Intersection Edge** options at the bottom of the expanded panel are disabled. This is the same as setting the **VSEDGES** system variable to 1.
- **Facet Edges.** Edges of 3D faces are displayed in the color selected in the color drop-down list at the bottom of the expanded panel. The **Obscured Edge** and **Intersection Edge** options at the bottom of the panel are enabled. This is the same as setting the **VSEDGES** system variable to 2.

Edge Overhang. This setting determines if straight edges extend or "overhang" beyond corners. See **Figure 3-35A.** Extended edges are used to create the look of an architectural sketch. The **Edge Overhang** button is either on or off. When on, the button is highlighted in the **Edge Effects** panel. Use the **Edge overhang** slider bar next to the button to increase or decrease the amount of overhang. As you drag the slider, the overhang dynamically changes in the viewport. This setting is controlled by the **VSEDGEOVERHANG** system variable and can have a value from 1 to 100.

Edge Jitter. Edge jitter creates a sketch look along the entire length of edges by drawing multiple lines for the edges. See **Figure 3-35B.** The **Edge Jitter** button is either on or off. When on, the button is highlighted in the **Edge Effects** panel. The number of lines drawn for edges can be from zero to three. This can be set using the **Edge jitter** slider bar next to the button or by changing the **VSEDGEJITTER** system variable.

Silhouette Edges. The **Silhouette Edges** button in the expanded **Edge Effects** panel determines whether or not a highlighting line is applied to the silhouettes of objects. See **Figure 3-35C.** The button is either on or off. When on, the button is highlighted and the silhouette line width is applied. The intersecting edges of shapes are not silhouetted. Use the **Silhouette edge width** slider bar next to the button to set the thickness of the highlighting line. This is controlled by the **VSSILHEDGES** system variable and is independent of the **DISPSILH** system variable.

Obscured Edges. The **Obscured Edge** button in the expanded **Edge Effects** panel determines whether or not edges that are normally hidden in the current view are displayed. The button is either on or off. When on, the button is highlighted and hidden edges are displayed. See **Figure 3-35D.** This setting is controlled by the **VSOBSCUREDEDGES** system variable. Additionally, when the button is on, the edge color can be changed using the drop-down list next to the button.

Intersection Edges. The **Intersection Edge** button in the expanded **Edge Effects** panel determines whether or not lines are drawn where solids overlap. The button is either on or off. When on, the button is highlighted and a line is drawn at the intersection. This setting is controlled by the **VSINTERSECTIONEDGES** system variable. Additionally, when the button is on, the color of the intersecting edges can be changed using the drop-down list next to the button.

Figure 3-35.
A—The model is displayed with extended edges. B—The model is displayed with edge jitter. C—The model is displayed with the silhouette edges highlighted. D—The model is displayed with obscured edges visible.

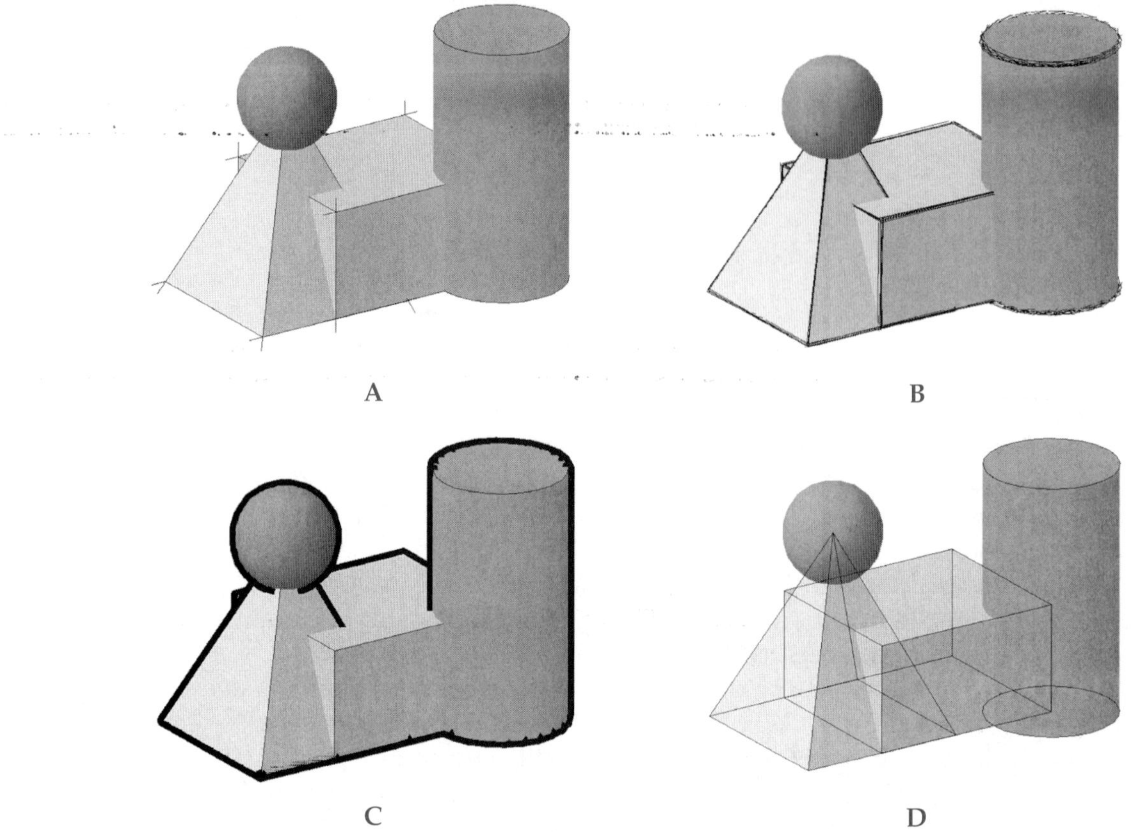

NOTE

The **ISOLINES**, **DISPSILH**, and **FACETRES** system variables are covered in detail in Chapter 14.

Exercise 3-9

Complete the exercise on the Student CD.

Rendering a Model

RENDER

Ribbon
Output > Render
Render
Type
RENDER RR
Menu
View > Render > Render

The **RENDER** command creates a realistic image of a model, **Figure 3-36.** However, rendering an image takes longer than shading an image. There are a variety of settings that you can change with the **RENDER** command that allow you to fine-tune renderings. These include lights, materials, backgrounds, fog, and preferences. Render settings are discussed in detail in Chapter 14 through Chapter 18.

When the command is initiated, the render window is displayed and the image is rendered. See **Figure 3-37.** The rendering that is produced is based on a variety of advanced render settings that are discussed in Chapter 14 through Chapter 18. The default render settings create an image using a single light source located behind the viewer. The light intensity is set to 1 and, if no materials are applied, the objects are rendered with a matte material that is the same color as the object display color.

Figure 3-36.
Rendering produces the most realistic display and can show shadows and materials.

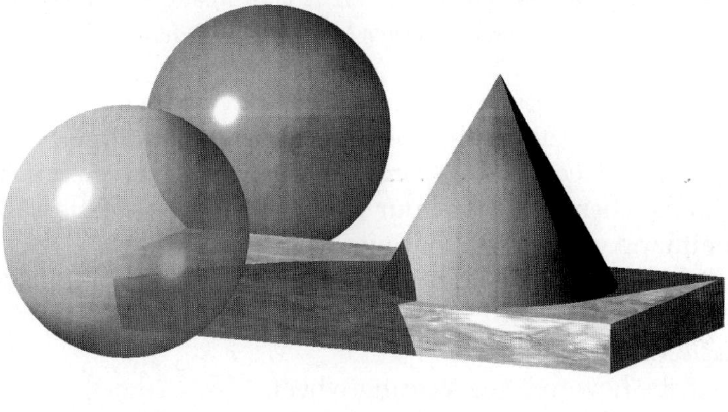

Figure 3-37.
The rendered model is displayed in the **Render** window.

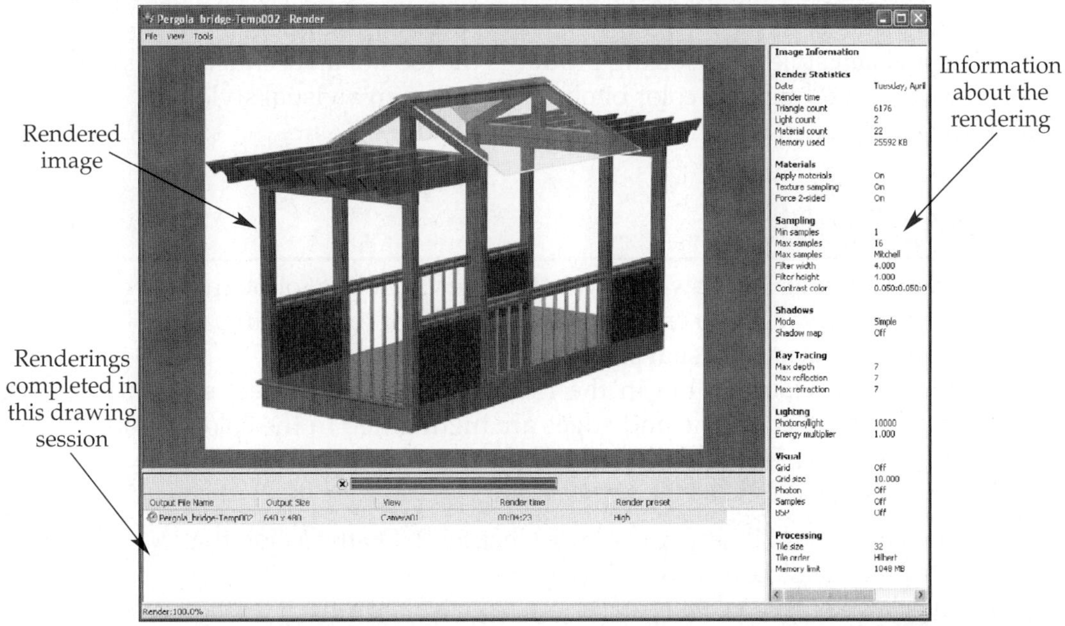

NOTE

If the image is rendered in the viewport, clean the screen using the **ZOOM**, **PAN**, **REGEN**, or **REDRAW** command. Setting the rendering destination as the viewport is discussed in Chapter 14.

Exercise 3-10

Complete the exercise on the Student CD.

Chapter Test

Answer the following questions. Write your answers on a separate sheet of paper or complete the electronic chapter test on the Student CD.

1. How do you select a standard isometric preset view using the view cube?
2. How is a standard orthographic view displayed using the view cube?
3. What is the difference between *parallel projection* and *perspective projection?*
4. What happens when one of the four view cube compass letters is picked?
5. Which command generates a continuous 3D orbit?
6. Which command can be used to produce a view that is parallel to the XY plane of the current UCS?
7. What is a *steering wheel?*
8. Briefly describe how to use a steering wheel.
9. The principal tool in the Tour Building wheel is the **Forward** tool. What is the purpose of this tool?
10. Which visual style is considered the highest level of shading?
11. What is the most realistic presentation?
12. Which visual style face setting produces a transparent image?
13. Which visual style edge setting produces the look of an architectural sketch?
14. How do you change the color of obscured edges in a visual style?
15. What is the function of the **RENDER** command?

Drawing Problems

1. Open one of your 3D drawings from Chapter 2. Do the following.
   A. Use the view cube to create a pictorial view of the drawing.
   B. Set the Conceptual visual style current.
   C. Using the **Visualize** tab in the ribbon, display the object so that faces are shown in object colors and edges are highlighted in the color of your choice. Change the edges to different colors.
   D. Save the drawing as P03_01.
2. Open one of your 3D drawings from Chapter 2. Do the following.
   A. Display the objects in Gooch face style.
   B. Toggle the projection from parallel to perspective and turn off the view cube compass.
   C. Pick an edge on the view cube. Set the parallel projection current. Create a named view based on this display.
   D. Create three additional views based on view cube edges. Alternate between parallel and perspective projection.
   E. Put the model into a continuous orbit.
   F. Save the drawing as P03_02.
3. Open one of your 3D drawings from Chapter 2 that was created with solid primitives. Do the following.
   A. Create three named views, each having a different viewpoint.
   B. Use a different visual style face color option in each view.
   C. Save the drawing as P03_03.
4. Open drawing P03_03 and do the following.
   A. Display one view and set obscured edges to blue.
   B. Change the edge display to isolines. What happened?
   C. Display a different view and turn facet edges on.
   D. Display intersection edges as black.
   E. Create a rendering of the object in one of the views.
   F. Save the drawing as P03_04.

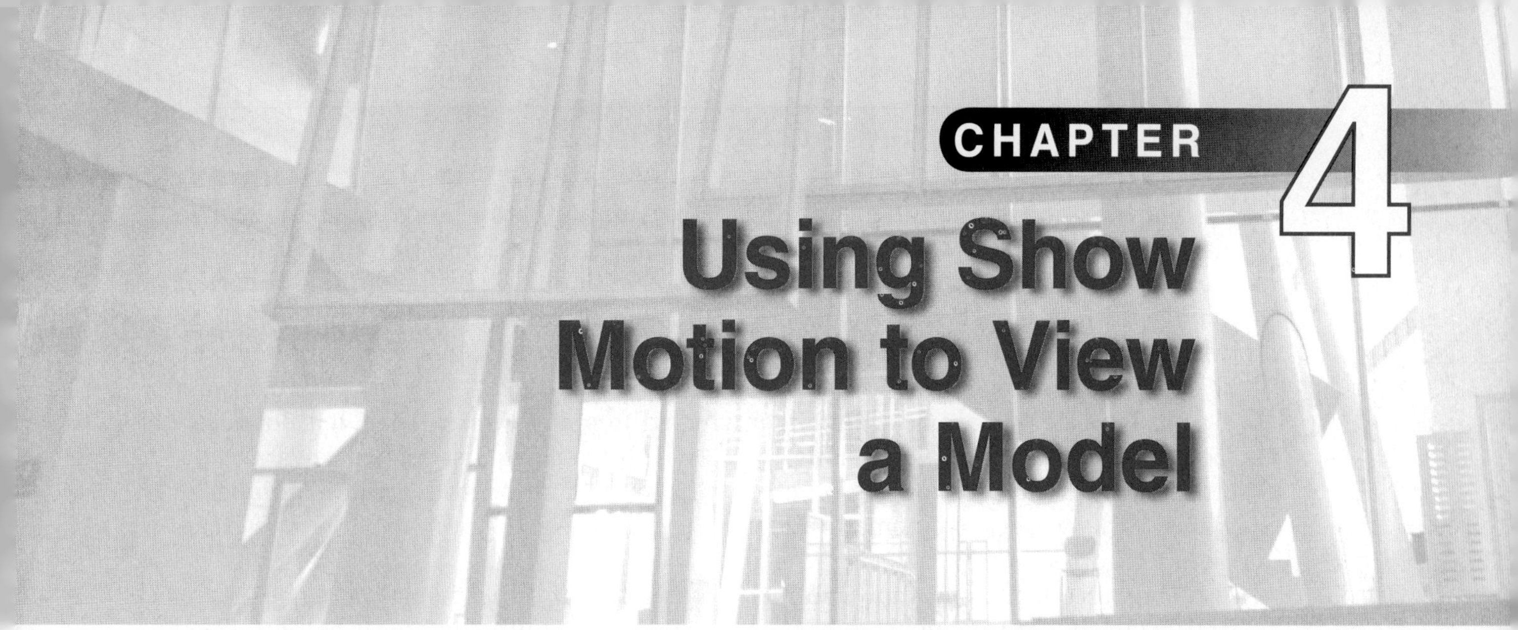

CHAPTER 4

Using Show Motion to View a Model

Learning Objectives

After completing this chapter, you will be able to:

✓ Explain the show motion tool.
✓ Create still shots of 3D models.
✓ Create walk shots of 3D models.
✓ Create cinematic shots of 3D models.
✓ Replay single shots and a sequence of shots.
✓ Change the properties of a shot.

AutoCAD's ***show motion*** tool is a powerful function that allows you to create named views, animated shots, and basic walkthroughs. It can quickly display a variety of named shots. It is also used to create basic animated presentations and displays. This capability is especially useful for animating 3D models that do not require the complexity and detail of fully textured, rendered animations and walkthroughs. Advanced rendering and walkthroughs are presented later in this book.

A ***view*** is a single-frame display of a model or drawing from any viewpoint. A ***shot*** is the manner in which the model is put in motion and the way the camera *moves* to that view. Therefore a single, named view can be modified to create several different shots using camera motion and movement techniques. Using show motion, you can create shots in one of three different formats:

- Still.
- Walk.
- Cinematic.

A ***still shot*** is exactly the same as a named view, but show motion allows you to add transition effects to display it. A ***walk shot*** requires that you use the **Walk** tool to define a camera motion path to create an animated shot. A ***cinematic shot*** is a single view to which you can add camera motion and movement effects to display the view. These shots are all created using the **New View/Shot Properties** dialog box. This is the same dialog box used to create named views.

Understanding Show Motion

Show motion is simply a means for creating, manipulating, and displaying named views. The **NAVSMOTION** command is used for show motion. The process involves the creation of shots using the **ShowMotion** toolbar and the **New View/Shot Properties** dialog box. Once a shot is created, you can give it properties that enable it to be displayed in many different ways. If a saved shot does not display in the manner you desire, it is easily modified.

A view category is a heading under which different views are filed. It is not necessary to create categories, especially if you will be making just a few views. On the other hand, if you are working on a complex model and need to create a number of views with a variety of cinematic and motion characteristics, it may be wise to create view categories.

The process of using show motion to create, modify, and display shots begins by first using the **ShowMotion** toolbar. All of your work with shots will be performed using the **New View/Shot Properties** dialog box. Options in this dialog box change based on the type of shot that is selected. These options are discussed in the sections that follow relating to each kind of shot.

PROFESSIONAL TIP

As you first start working with **ShowMotion**, you may want to create categories named Still, Cinematic, and Walk. As you create shots, file each under its appropriate category name. This will assist you in seeing how the different shot-creation techniques work. Later, you can apply the view categories to specific components of a complex model. In that case, for example, a subassembly of a 3D model may have a view category that contains all three types of shots for use in different types of modeling work or presentations. Creating and using view categories is discussed in detail at the end of this chapter.

Show Motion Toolbar

NAVSMOTION

Type
NAVSMOTION
Menu
View
> ShowMotion
Toolbar
Status Bar
ShowMotion

The **ShowMotion** toolbar is displayed at the bottom of the screen when the **NAVSMOTION** command is entered. See **Figure 4-1.** This toolbar provides controls for creating and manipulating views:

- **Unpin ShowMotion/Pin ShowMotion**
- **Play all**
- **Turn on Looping**
- **New Shot...**
- **Close ShowMotion**

When the toolbar is pinned, it remains displayed if you execute other commands, minimize the drawing, change ribbon panels, or switch to another software application. The **Unpin ShowMotion** button is used to unpin the toolbar. The **Pin ShowMotion** button is then displayed in its place. If you unpin the toolbar you must execute the **NAVSMOTION** command each time you wish to use show motion. If the drawing is saved with the **ShowMotion** toolbar pinned, the toolbar is pinned the next time the drawing is opened and **ShowMotion** is activated.

Figure 4-1.
The **ShowMotion** toolbar is displayed at the bottom of the screen and provides controls for creating and manipulating shots.

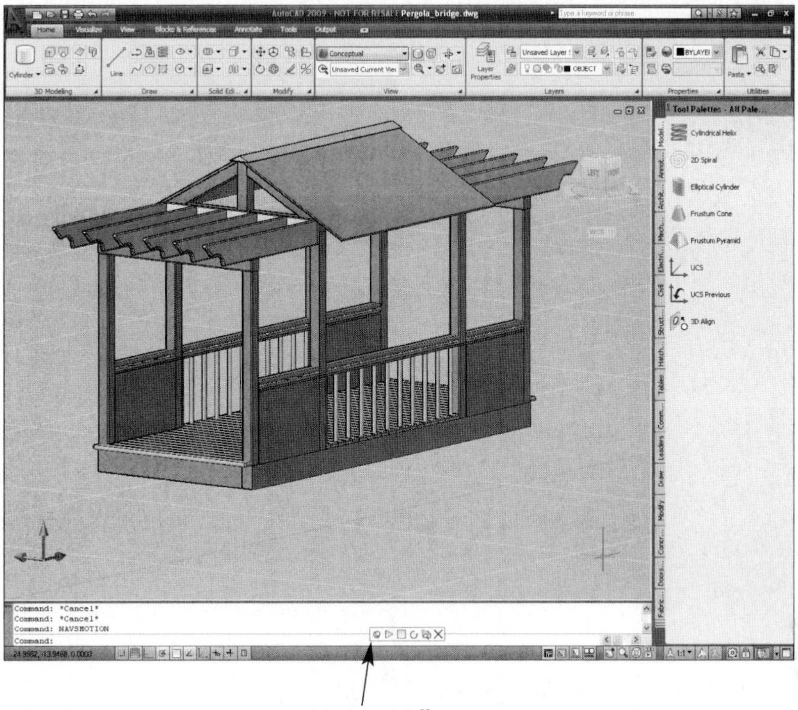

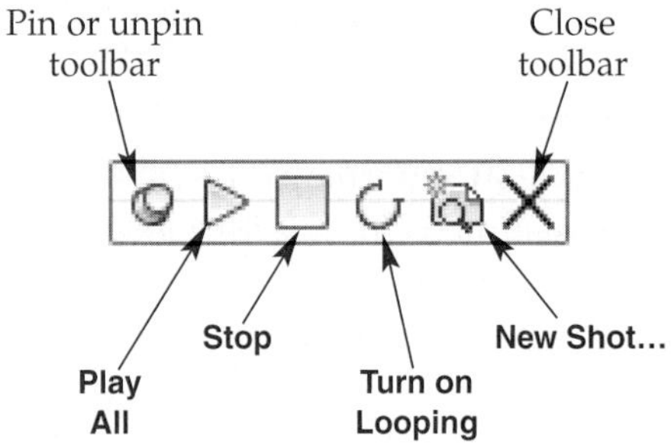

Press the **Play all** button to play all of the views and categories displayed as thumbnails above the toolbar. The playback of these views will loop (repeat) if the **Turn on Looping** button is selected. If looping is turned on, a view, category, or all categories are displayed in a loop whenever the **Play all** button is selected. The **Turn on Looping** button is a toggle. The image changes to indicate whether or not looping is turned on.

The **New Shot...** button opens the **New View/Shot Properties** dialog box. This dialog box is discussed in the next section. Picking the **Close ShowMotion** button closes the **ShowMotion** toolbar.

New View/Shot Properties Dialog Box

All shot creation takes place inside of the **New View/Shot Properties** dialog box. It is accessed by using the **ShowMotion** toolbar described above or using the **NEWSHOT** command. The dialog box can also be displayed from within the **View Manager** dialog box by picking the **New...** button. The **New View/Shot Properties** dialog box is shown in **Figure 4-2.**

Type
NEWSHOT
Toolbar
ShowMotion
New Shot...

NEWSHOT

Figure 4-2.
The **New View/Shot Properties** dialog box is used to create the three types of shots: still, walk, and cinematic.

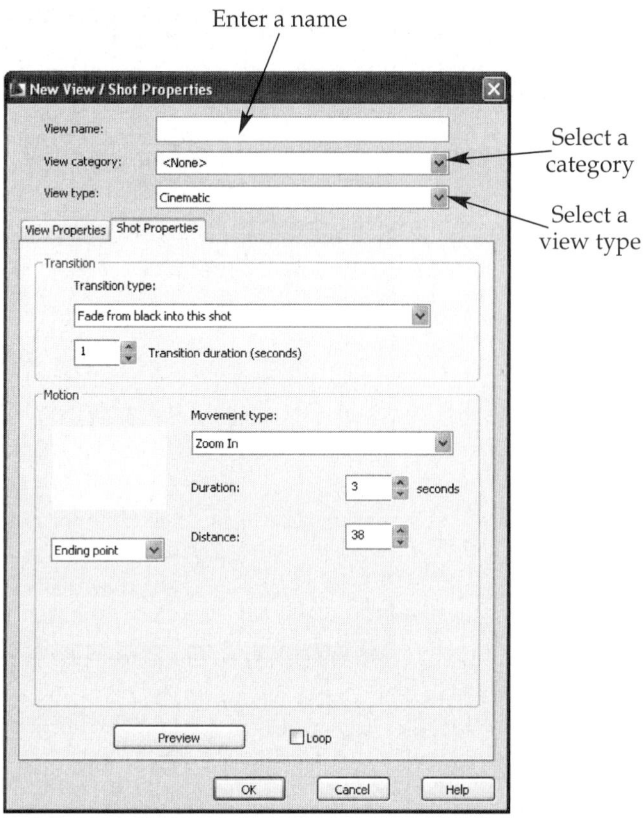

You must supply a shot name and a shot type. A view category is not required, but can help organize shots. This feature is discussed later in the chapter. The dialog box provides two tabs containing options that enable you to define the overall view and then specify the types of movement and motion desired in the shot. These tabs are discussed in the next sections.

View Properties Tab

The **View Properties** tab of the **New View/Shot Properties** dialog box is composed of three areas in which you can specify the overall presentation of the model view. See Figure 4-3. The overall presentation includes the view boundary, visual settings, and background.

Boundary settings

The setting in the **Boundary** area of the **View Properties** tab determines what is displayed in the shot. The **Current display** button is on by default. This means the shot will be composed of what is currently shown in the drawing area.

You can adjust the view by picking the **Define window** radio button. This temporarily closes the dialog box so you can draw a rectangular window to define the view. After picking the second corner, you can adjust the view by picking the first and second corners of the window again. Press [Enter] to accept the window and return to the dialog box.

Visual settings

The **Settings** area of the **View Properties** tab contains options that apply to the overall display of the model in the shot. When the **Save layer snapshot with view** check box is checked, all of the current layer visibility settings are saved with the new shot. This is checked by default.

Figure 4-3.
The **View Properties** tab of the **New View/ Shot Properties** dialog box.

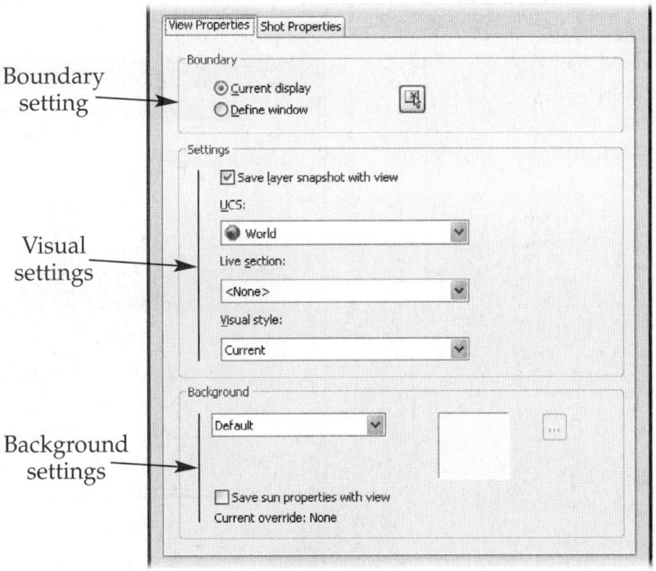

Any UCS currently defined in the drawing can be selected for use with the new shot. Use the **UCS:** drop-down list to select the UCS. When the shot is restored, that UCS is restored too. If you select <None> in the drop-down list, there is no UCS associated with the shot.

Live sectioning is a tool that enables you to view the internal features of 3D solids that are cut by a section plane object. This feature is covered in detail in Chapter 13. When a section plane object is created, it is given a name. Therefore, if a model contains one or more section plane objects, their names appear in the **Live section:** drop-down list. If a section plane object is selected in this list, the new shot shows the live sectioning for that plane.

A shot created with live sectioning on will be displayed in that manner even though live sectioning may be currently turned off in the drawing. However, live sectioning is reset to be on. Subsequent displays of the model that were created with live sectioning off are shown with it on. Keep this in mind as you develop shots for show motion.

The **Visual style:** drop-down list contains all visual styles in the drawing plus the options of Current and <None>. Selecting a visual style from the list results in that style being set current when the shot is played. Selecting Current or <None> will cause the shot to be displayed in the visual style currently displayed on the screen.

Background settings

The **Background** area of the **View Properties** tab provides options for changing the background of the new shot. The drop-down list in this area allows you to select a solid, gradient, image, or sun and sky background. You can also choose to retain the default background. If you pick Solid, Gradient, or Image, the **Background** dialog box appears. See **Figure 4-4.** If you select Sun & Sky, the **Adjust Sun & Sky Background** dialog box is displayed. See **Figure 4-5.** These dialog boxes are used to set the background. They are discussed in detail in Chapter 16.

The **Save sun properties with view** setting is used to have the sunlight data with the view. If you are displaying an architectural model using sunlight, you will likely want this check box checked for show motion. Sunlight and geographic location are discussed in detail in Chapter 16.

Figure 4-4.
The **Background** dialog box is used to add a background to the shot. Here, a gradient background is being created.

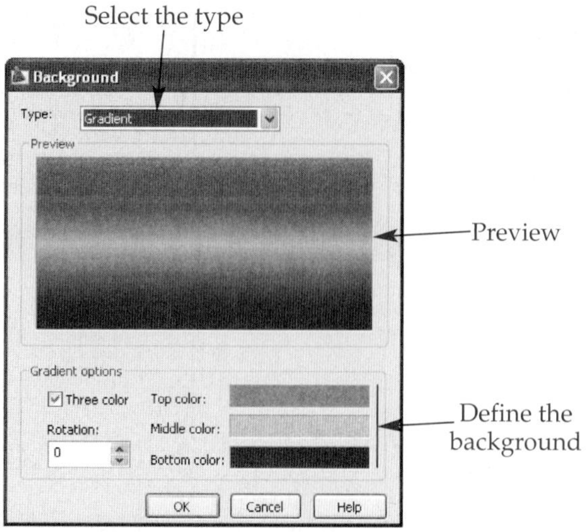

Figure 4-5.
When the background is set to Sun & Sky, the **Adjust Sun & Sky Background** dialog box is used to change settings for the background.

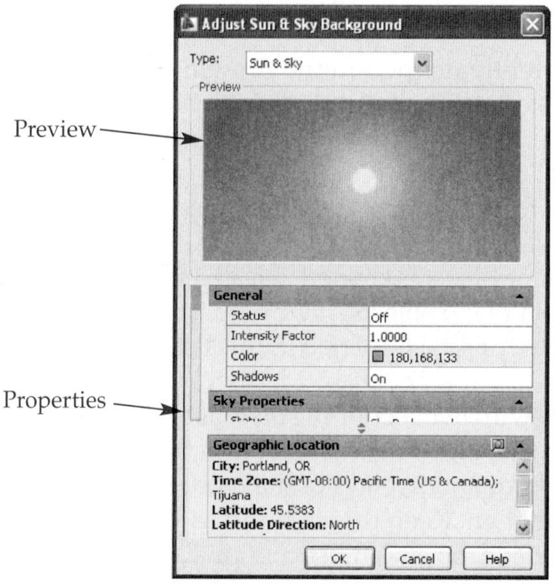

Shot Properties Tab

Settings in the **Shot Properties** tab of the **New View/Shot Properties** dialog box provide options for controlling the transition and motion of shots. There are numerous movement and motion options in this tab. The specific options available are based on the type of shot selected: still, walk, or cinematic. In addition, the cinematic shot contains a variety of motions that can be applied to the shot and each type of motion contains a number of variables. The options in the **Shot Properties** tab are discussed later in this chapter as they apply to different shots, movements, and motions.

Creating a Still Shot

A still shot is the same as a named view, but with a transition. Open the **New View/Shot Properties** dialog box and enter a name in the **View name:** text box. Next, pick in the text box for the **View category**: drop-down list and type a category name or select an existing category. Remember, it is not necessary to create or select a category at this time. Now, select Still from the **View type:** drop-down list.

In the **Shot Properties** tab, select a transition from the **Transition type:** drop-down list. You can select from one of three transitions:

- **Fade from black into this shot.** The screen begins totally black and fades into the current background color.
- **Fade from white into this shot.** The screen begins totally white and fades into the current background color.
- **Cut to shot.** The view is immediately displayed without a transition and the shot movements are applied.

The fade transitions will not function unless hardware acceleration is enabled. Turn on hardware acceleration in the following manner. Refer to **Figure 4-6.**

1. Enter the **3DCONFIG** command to display the **Adaptive Degradation and Performance Tuning** dialog box.
2. Pick the **Manual Tune** button to display the **Manual Performance Tuning** dialog box.
3. Check the **Enable hardware acceleration** check box.
4. Close both dialog boxes.

Next, in the **Transition duration (seconds)** text box, enter a length of time over which the transition will occur. If you want a fade transition to be complete, be sure to enter a value in the **Duration:** text box that is equal to or greater than the transition duration. Pick the **Preview** button to view the shot, then edit the transition and motion values as needed.

When finished, pick the **OK** button to close the **New View/Shot Properties** dialog box. The thumbnail image for the new shot is displayed above the **ShowMotion** toolbar. The large thumbnail image represents the category. Since there was no view category selected for the view, the name <None> is displayed. The small thumbnail image represents the shot just created. Its name may be truncated. See **Figure 4-7A.** Move the cursor into the shot thumbnail image and a large image is displayed. The name of the shot should appear in its entirety. The category thumbnail image is reduced to a small image. See **Figure 4-7B.**

Figure 4-6.
Hardware acceleration must be activated for the fade transitions to function.

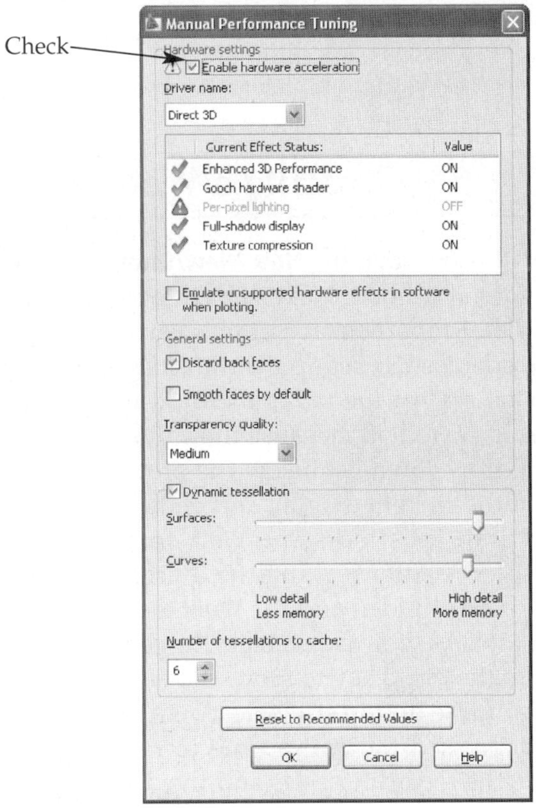

Figure 4-7.
A—The large thumbnail image on the bottom is for the category. The small thumbnail image is for the shot just created. Its name may be truncated. B—Move your cursor into the shot thumbnail image and it converts to a large image and the category thumbnail image is reduced to a small image.

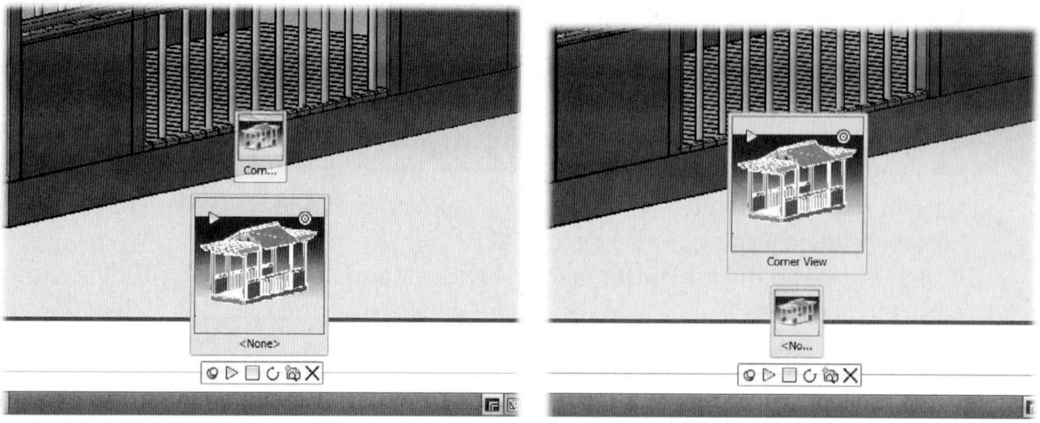

A B

NOTE

If the **Loop** check box at the bottom of the **Shot Properties** tab is checked, the shot will continuously loop through the transition during playback. This is similar to picking the **Turn on Looping** button in the **ShowMotion** toolbar. All three shot types have this option.

Exercise 4-1

Complete the exercise on the Student CD.

Creating a Walk Shot

To create a walk shot, open the **New View/Shot Properties** dialog box, enter a name, and select a category, if needed. Next, select Recorded Walk from the **View type:** drop-down list. In the **View Properties** tab, set up the view as described for a still shot.

In the **Shot Properties** tab, set up the transition as described for a still shot. The only option in the **Motion** area of the tab is the **Start recording** button. See Figure 4-8. The **Duration:** text box is grayed out because the value is based on how long you record the walk. The camera drop-down list below the preview image is also grayed out because the walk begins at the current display and ends at the point where you terminate it.

This type of shot uses the same **Walk** tool found in the steering wheels and discussed in Chapter 3. After picking the **Start recording** button, the **New View/Shot Properties** dialog box is hidden and the **Walk** tool message is displayed. Pick and drag to active the **Walk** tool. As soon as you pick, the center circle icon is displayed. If needed, you can hold down the [Shift] key to move the view up or down. When the [Shift] key is released (with the mouse button still held down), you can resume walking. The mouse button must be depressed the entire time to record all movements. As soon as you release the button, the recording ends and the dialog box is redisplayed.

Figure 4-8.
Creating a walk shot.

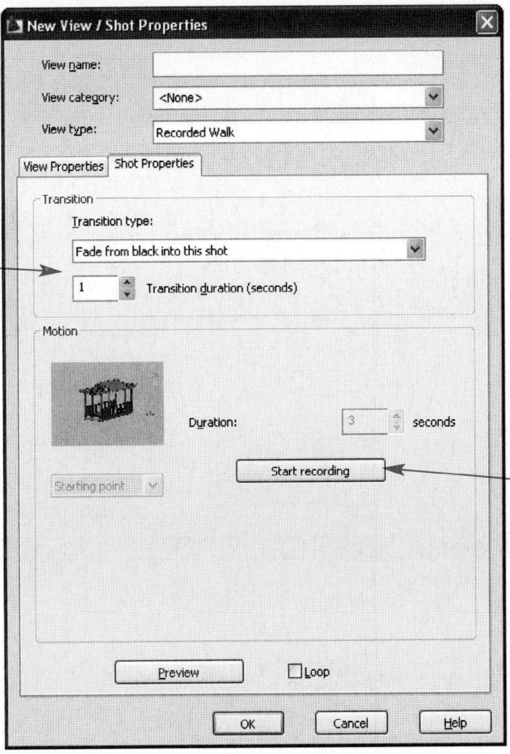

Finally, preview the shot. If you need to re-record it, pick the **Start recording** button and begin again. You cannot add to the shot; you must start over. Pick the **OK** button to save the shot and a new thumbnail is displayed in the **ShowMotion** toolbar.

NOTE

The walk shot capability of show motion is limited in its ability to produce a true "walkthrough." The path of your "walk" is inexact and it may take several times to create the effect you need. Should you wish to create a genuine walkthrough of an architectural or structural model, it is better to use tools such as **3DWALK** (walkthrough), **3DFLY** (flyby), or a **ANIPATH** (motion path animation). These powerful commands are used to create professional walkthroughs and animations and are covered in Chapter 18.

Exercise 4-2

Complete the exercise on the Student CD.

Creating a Cinematic Shot

To create a cinematic shot, open the **New View/Shot Properties** dialog box, enter a name, and select a category, if needed. Next, select Cinematic from the **View type:** drop-down list. In the **View Properties** tab, set up the view as described for a still shot. In the **Shot Properties** tab, pick a transition type and duration as described for a still shot.

Figure 4-9.
Creating a cinematic shot.

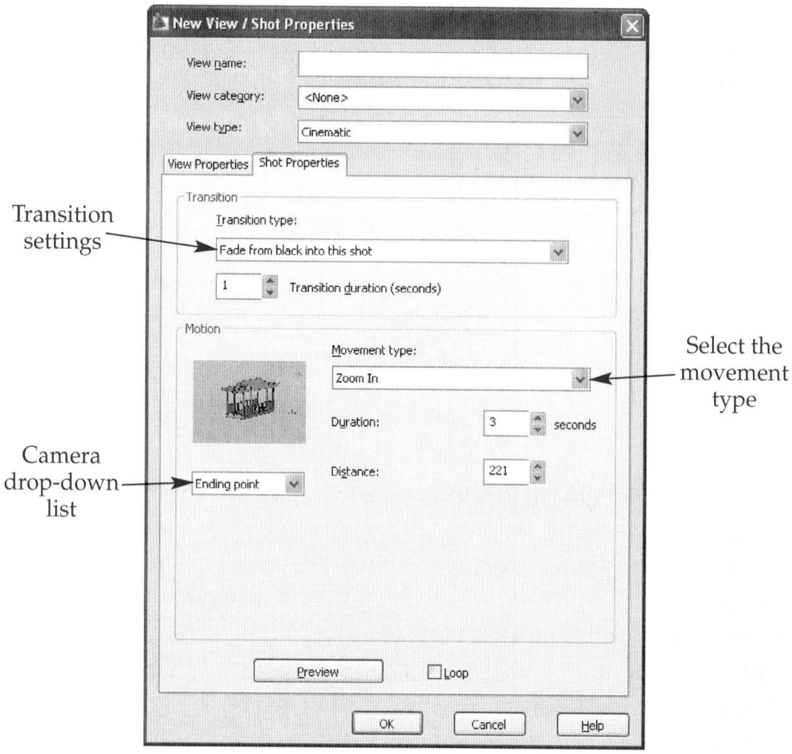

The specific options in the **Motion** area of the **Shot Properties** tab are discussed in the next sections, **Figure 4-9.** Pick a type of movement in the **Movement type:** drop-down list. The movement options available will change depending on the type of movement you select. Refer to the chart in **Figure 4-10** as a quick reference for movement options when creating a cinematic shot. Finally, pick the current position of the camera from the camera drop-down list below the preview image.

Pick the **Preview** button to view the shot. Make any changes required before picking the **OK** button to save the shot. Once the **OK** button is picked, the new view is displayed as a small thumbnail image above the large category thumbnail image. See **Figure 4-11.**

Figure 4-10.
This chart shows the different movement options based on the movement type selected in the **Movement type:** drop-down list in the **New View/Shot Properties** dialog box.

	Duration	Distance	Look at Camera Point	Distance Up	Distance Back	Distance Down
Zoom In	X	X				
Zoom out	X	X				
Track left	X	X	X			
Track right	X	X	X			
Crane up	X		X	X	X	
Crane down	X		X			X
Look	X					
Orbit	X					

Figure 4-11.
The thumbnail image for the new cinematic shot is displayed above the category thumbnail image.

Cinematic Basics

The motion and movement options available for a cinematic shot allow you to create a final display that appears to move into position as if the camera is traveling in a path toward the object. The **Motion** area of the **Shot Properties** tab contains a variety of options for creating an array of cinematic shots. Refer to **Figure 4-9.** The options can be confusing unless you understand some basics about essential components of a cinematic shot. Most important is the preview of the current view. All of the motion actions revolve around this view. This image tile is the current position of the camera and is also referred to as the ***key position*** of a shot. This is the position that is displayed when you pick the **Go** button on a thumbnail image above the **ShowMotion** toolbar.

The two elements of a cinematic shot are motion and movement. ***Motion*** relates to the behavior of the object and how it appears to be in motion during the cinematic shot. In addition, it refers to the position of the model at a specified point in the animation. ***Movement*** in a cinematic shot is the manner in which the camera moves in relation to the object.

PROFESSIONAL TIP

If your goal is to create a series of shots that blend together, it is a good idea to first develop a storyboard of the entire sequence. This could be as simple as a few notes indicating how you want the shots to move or even a few sketches noting the required movements and motion values. Planning your shots will save time when you begin creating them in AutoCAD.

Camera Drop-Down List

The camera drop-down list is located below the preview image in the **Motion** area of the **Shot Properties** tab. The preview image represents the position of the camera based on the option selected in the camera drop-down list. The following three options are available in the drop-down list, **Figure 4-12.**

- **Ending point.** The view in the preview image is the display that will be shown at the end of the cinematic shot. All movement options take the shot to this point.
- **Starting point.** The view in the preview image is the display that will be shown at the start of the cinematic shot. All movement options begin at this point.
- **Half-way point.** The view in the preview image is the display that will be shown at the half-way point of the cinematic shot.

Figure 4-12.
Selecting what the key position represents.

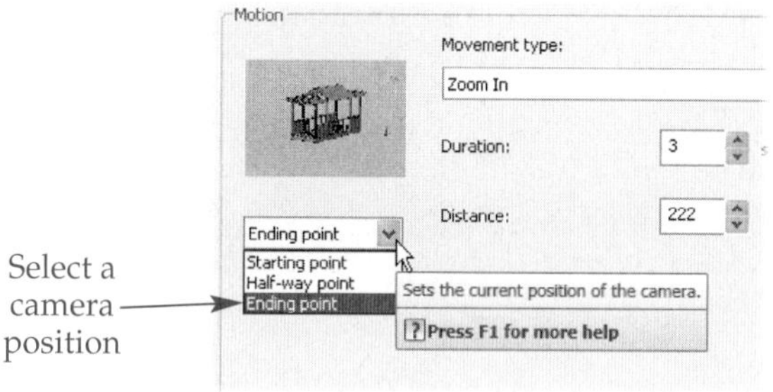

These options, in part, determine how the cinematic shot is created. If Starting point is selected, the cinematic shot begins with the current view. During the animation, the model may move off of the screen. If this happens, you may want to select Ending point so the model appears to move into position and stay there.

Exercise 4-3

Complete the exercise on the Student CD.

PROFESSIONAL TIP

The **Preview** button in the **New View/Shot Properties** dialog box is the best way to test any changes you make to the motion options. Each time you make a change, pick the button to see if the effect is what you want. Previewing each change is far more efficient than making several changes before you examine the results.

Movement Type

The **Movement type:** drop-down list in the **Shot Properties** tab of the **New View/ Shot Properties** dialog box is used to select the motion for the cinematic shot. There are eight types of camera movement that can be used with a cinematic shot:

- Zoom in.
- Zoom out.
- Track left.
- Track right.
- Crane up.
- Crane down.
- Look.
- Orbit.

The options available in the **Motion** area of the tab are based on which movement type is selected. The movement types and their options are discussed in the next sections.

Zoom In

When Zoom in is selected in the **Movement type:** drop-down list, the camera appears to zoom into the model in the shot. This movement type has two options, Figure 4-13. The value in the **Duration:** text box is the length of time over which the animation is recorded. The value in the **Distance:** text box is the distance the camera travels during the animation. The camera zooms in to cover the distance in the specified duration of time. When Zoom in is selected, the camera drop-down list is automatically set to Ending point. Keep in mind that the current position of the camera represents the final display after the cinematic shot is complete.

Figure 4-13.
The settings for the Zoom in movement type.

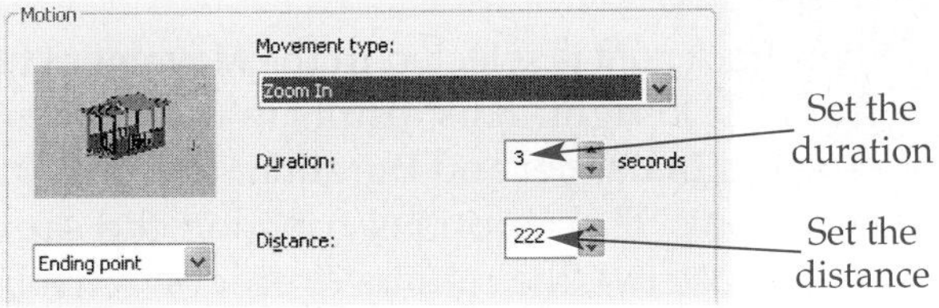

Zoom out

When Zoom out is selected in the **Movement type:** drop-down list, the camera appears to zoom away from the model in the shot. This movement type has **Duration:** and **Distance:** text options, as described for the Zoom in movement type.

When Zoom in is selected, the camera drop-down list is automatically set to Starting point. With this setting, the camera will zoom out the specified distance and the final image in the shot will be smaller than the preview image. If this is not the effect you want, it may be better to pick Ending point for the current position of the camera. Then, the model will appear to move from behind your view to stop at the current view.

Track left

When Track left is selected in the **Movement type:** drop-down list, the camera will move from right to left. This results in the view moving from left to right. This movement occurs over the specified distance and duration. This movement type has **Duration:** and **Distance:** text boxes, as described above, and the **Always look at camera pivot point** check box, Figure 4-14.

If the **Always look at camera pivot point** check box is checked, the center of the view remains stationary. As a result, the view in the shot appears to rotate about this point instead of sliding across the screen. The best way to visualize this motion is to use the **Preview** button with the option checked and then unchecked. This option is available for all "track" and "crane" movement types.

When Track left is selected, the camera drop-down list is automatically set to Half-way point. This means the preview image is the middle point of the animation. It will be displayed at the midpoint of the **Duration:** value.

PROFESSIONAL TIP

If the **Distance:** value is large, the screen may be blank for a few moments until the camera moves enough to bring the model into view. If this is not what you want, decrease the **Distance:** value or check the **Always look at camera pivot point** check box.

Figure 4-14.
The settings for the Track left movement type.

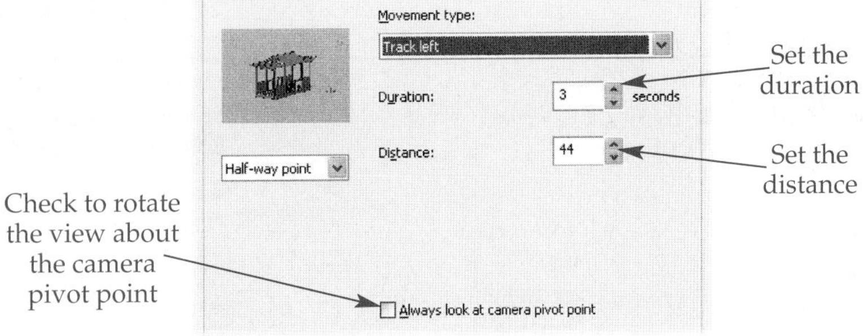

Track right

When Track right is selected in the **Movement type:** drop-down list, the camera will move from left to right. This results in the view moving from right to left. This movement type has **Distance:** and **Duration:** text boxes and the **Always look at camera pivot point** check box. These options function the same as described for Track left. When Track right is selected, the camera drop-down list is automatically set to Half-way point.

Crane up

Where the "track" movement types move the view left and right, the "crane" movement types move the view up and down. When Crane up is selected in the **Movement type:** drop-down list, the camera will move from bottom to top and then backward. This results in the view moving from top to bottom and zooming out. This movement type has **Distance:** and **Duration:** text boxes and the **Always look at camera pivot point** check box, as described above, which is checked by default.

This movement type has three additional options, **Figure 4-15.** The value in the **Distance Up:** text box is the distance the camera is moved upward. The value in the **Distance Back:** text box is the distance the camera is moved backward. The backward movement is typically short compared to the upward movement.

You can add more interest to the motion in the shot by shifting the view left or right. First, enable the option by checking the check box below the **Distance Back:** setting. Refer to **Figure 4-15.** Then, select either Shift left or Shift right from the drop-down list. Finally, enter a distance in the text box next to the drop-down list. The camera will be shifted left or right for the distance specified in this text box, resulting in the view shifting in the opposite direction. This shifting option is available for both "crane" motion types.

When Crane up is selected, the camera drop-down list is automatically set to Starting point. This means the preview image shows the beginning of the shot before the movement is applied. If the **Always look at camera pivot point** check box is not checked, and depending on the movement settings, the model may move off of the screen in the shot.

Crane down

When Crane down is selected in the **Movement type:** drop-down list, the camera will move from top to bottom and then forward. This results in the view moving from bottom to top and zooming in. This movement type has **Distance:** and **Duration:** text boxes and the **Always look at camera pivot point** check box, as described above, which is checked by default. It also has the left/right shifting option described in the previous section.

Instead of **Distance Up:** and **Distance Back:** settings, this movement type has **Distance Down:** and **Distance Forward:** settings. The value in the **Distance Down:** text box is the distance the camera cranes down in the shot. The value in the **Distance Forward:** text box is the distance the camera is moved forward in the shot.

Figure 4-15.
The settings for the Crane up movement type.

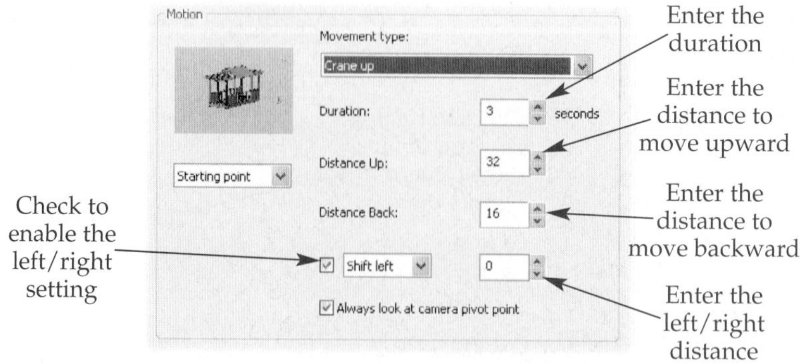

When Crane down is selected, the camera drop-down list is automatically set to Ending point. This means the preview image shows the end of the shot before the movement is applied. If the **Always look at camera pivot point** check box is not checked, and depending on the movement settings, the model may start off of the screen in the shot.

NOTE

All distance values related to the Crane up and Crane down movement types represent how far away from the view the camera must begin before the cinematic shot is started. For example, a large **Distance Back:** value means that the camera may have to begin at a point beyond or even around the view in order to travel the distance back to display the current view (when Ending point is selected in the camera drop-down list). It is always good practice to make a single change to the movements, then preview the shot. This is especially true for the Crane up and Crane down movement types.

Look

When Look is selected in the **Movement type:** drop-down list, the camera pans based on the values for left/right and up/down to display the view, **Figure 4-16.** For example, if the movement is set to look up 45° and Ending point is selected in the camera drop-down list, then the camera begins at a 45° angle below the view and looks up to display it.

The value in the **Duration:** text box is the length of time over which the animation is recorded. This option is the same as described for the other movement types.

The first drop-down list below the **Duration:** text box is used to specify either left or right movement. Select Degrees left in the drop-down list to have the camera move from right to left, resulting in the view moving from left to right. Select Degrees right to have the camera move from left to right and the view right to left. Next, specify the angular value for this movement in the degrees text box to the right of the drop-down list. For example, suppose you select Degrees left and enter an angle of 15°. In this case, the camera will start 15° to the *right* of the model and rotate to the left in the shot.

The second drop-down list below the **Duration:** text box is used to specify either up or down movement. Select Degrees up in the drop-down list to have the camera move from bottom to top, resulting in the view moving from top to bottom. Select Degrees down to have the camera and view move in the opposite direction. Specify the angular value for this movement in the degrees text box to the right of the drop-down list.

When Look is selected in the **Movement type:** drop-down list, the camera drop-down list is automatically set to Starting point. This means the shot will start with the current view and then apply the movement settings.

Figure 4-16.
The settings for the Look movement type.

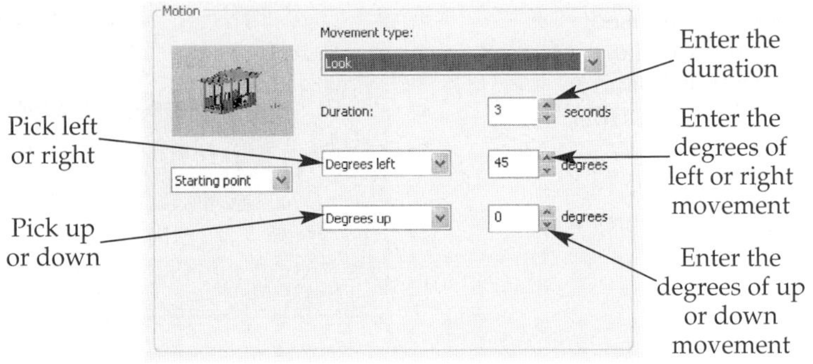

Orbit

When Orbit is selected in the **Movement type:** drop-down list, the camera rotates in place based on the values set for left/right and up/down movements. The Orbit movement type has the same options as the Look movement type, as described in the previous section.

When Orbit is selected in the **Movement type:** drop-down list, the camera drop-down list is automatically set to Starting point. This means the shot will start with the current view and then apply the movement settings. Unlike the Look movement type, the view center remains stationary in the shot. As a result, you do not need to worry about the model moving off of the screen.

Displaying or Replaying a Shot

As each shot is created, its thumbnail image is placed above the **ShowMotion** toolbar. The shot name is displayed below the thumbnail image. By default, the category thumbnail image is large and each shot thumbnail image is small. If the cursor is moved over one of the shot thumbnail images, all of the shot thumbnail images are enlarged and the category thumbnail image is reduced in size.

Each thumbnail image is composed of an image of the view in the shot, the shot name, and viewing controls. See Figure 4-17. The viewing controls are only displayed when the cursor is moved over the thumbnail image. The three viewing controls are:

VIEWPLAY
Type
VIEWPLAY

VIEWGO
Type
VIEWGO

- **Play.** Plays the shot. If looping is enabled, the shot repeats. Otherwise, the shot is played once. When this button is picked it changes to **Pause**. You can also play the shot by picking anywhere on its thumbnail image. The **VIEWPLAY** command can also be used to replay a shot.
- **Pause.** Pauses the shot. When this button is picked it changes to **Play**. Picking anywhere inside the image or on the **Play** button restarts playing of the shot.
- **Go.** Displays the key position of the view without playing the shot. The **VIEWGO** command also restores a named view.

You can play all of the shots in sequence by picking the **Play** button in the category thumbnail image or by picking anywhere inside of the category thumbnail image. Additionally, you can move to the key position of the first shot in a view category by picking the **Go** button on the view category thumbnail image.

Exercise 4-4
Complete the exercise on the Student CD.

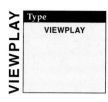

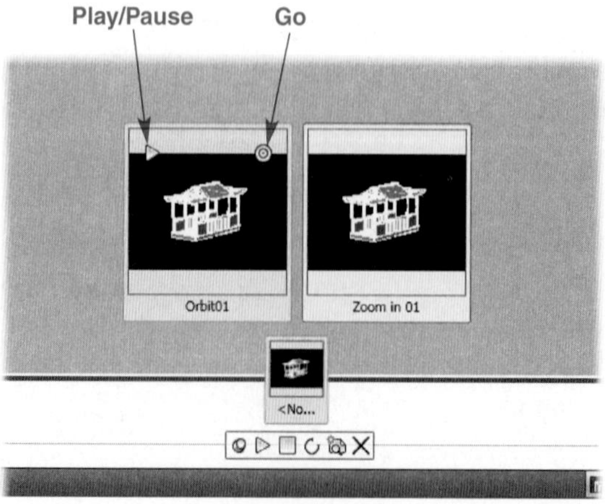

Figure 4-17.
Each thumbnail image is composed of the shot image, the shot name, and the viewing controls.

Thumbnail Shortcut Menu

Right-clicking on a shot or view category thumbnail image displays the shortcut menu shown in Figure 4-18. This menu provides quick access for modifying and manipulating shots and their thumbnail images.

Picking the **New View/Shot...** entry displays the **New View/Shot Properties** dialog box. Picking the **Properties...** entry displays the **View/Shot Properties** dialog box. This dialog box is the same as the **New View/Shot Properties** dialog box. However, all of the settings of the shot are displayed and can be changed. This option is only available to change the properties of a shot, not a category.

To rename a shot, pick the **Rename** entry in the shortcut menu. The name is highlighted below the thumbnail image. Type the new name and press [Enter]. To delete a shot, select **Delete** from the shortcut menu. There is no warning; the shot is simply deleted. The **UNDO** command can reverse this action.

If there is more than one shot in a category, you can rearrange the order. Right-click on a thumbnail image and pick either **Move left** or **Move right** in the shortcut menu. This moves the shot one step in the selected direction.

When a change is made to the model, it is not automatically reflected in the thumbnail images. If you do not update thumbnail images, they will remain in their original format, regardless of how many changes are made to the model. Selecting **Update the thumbnail for** in the shortcut menu displays a cascading menu with options for updating the thumbnail image:

- **This view.** Updates only the thumbnail image for the shot on which you right-clicked.
- **This category.** Updates all thumbnail images in the category. This option is only enabled when you right-click on a category thumbnail image.
- **All.** This option updates all thumbnail images in all categories and shots.

Creating and Using View Categories

A ***view category*** is a grouping that can be created in order to separate different types of shots. A view category can also contain shots arranged in a sequence that appear connected as they are played together. This is an optional feature, but an efficient method of separating different types of shots or grouping shots to use for a specific purpose. When a new category is created, it is represented by a category thumbnail image displayed above the **ShowMotion** toolbar.

To create a new view category, simply pick in the **View category:** drop-down list text box in the **New View/Shot Properties** dialog box. Then, enter a name. See Figure 4-19. The name is added to the drop-down list. If you wish to organize shots by categories, be sure to select the view category from the drop-down list before picking the **OK** button to exit the dialog box and create the shot.

You must create a shot to create a view category. If you delete the only shot in a view category, you also delete the category. The view category will no longer be available in the **New View/Shot Properties** dialog box.

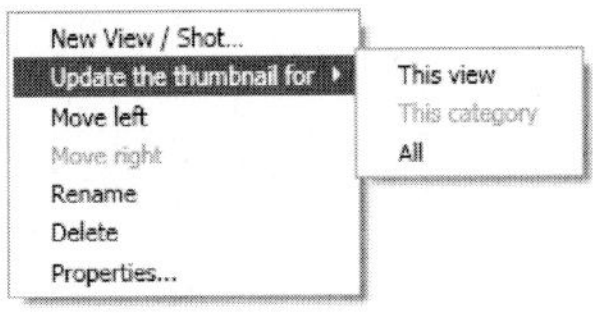

Figure 4-18.
Right-click on a shot or view category thumbnail image in the **ShowMotion** toolbar to display this shortcut menu.

Figure 4-19.
To create a new view category, type its name in the **View category:** drop-down list text box.

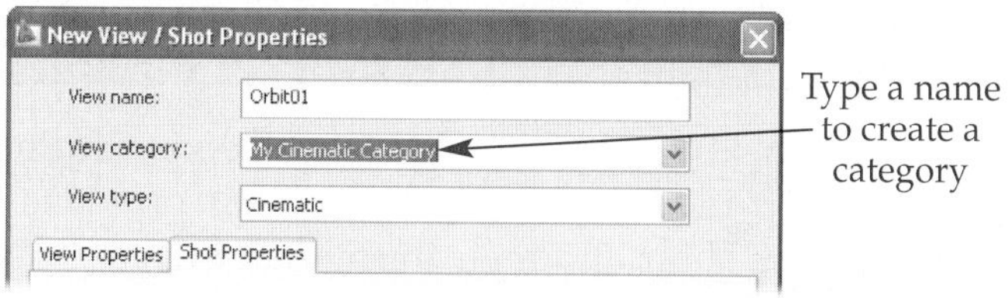

View Category Basics

After a new view category is created, it is represented by a thumbnail image above the **ShowMotion** toolbar. The category name is shown below the thumbnail image. As you create more shots within a category, the thumbnail images for the new shots are placed to the right of existing shots above the category thumbnail image. The thumbnail image for the first shot in a view category is displayed as the view category thumbnail image.

An entire view category and all of the views included in it can be quickly deleted. Simply right-click on the view category thumbnail image and pick **Delete** in the shortcut menu. An alert box appears asking you to confirm the deletion, **Figure 4-20.** The shots in a deleted view category cannot be recovered, so be sure there are no shots in the category you wish to save before deleting. However, you can use the **UNDO** command to reverse the deletion.

PROFESSIONAL TIP

Remember, you can change the order of the shots in a view category using the shortcut menu. Picking **Move left** or **Move right** moves the shot one step. Continue moving shots until the order is appropriate.

Playing and Looping Shots in a View Category

SEQUENCEPLAY

Type
SEQUENCEPLAY

A view category is a useful tool for grouping shots to be played together in a sequence. To play the shots in a view category, move the cursor over the view category thumbnail image above the **ShowMotion** toolbar. Then, pick the **Play** button in the thumbnail image. All shots in the category will be played. You can also use the **SEQUENCEPLAY** command to play the shots in a view category.

If you want the shots in a category to run on a continuous loop, pick the **Turn on Looping** button in the **ShowMotion** toolbar. Then, when the **Play** button is picked, the shots in the view category will display until the **Pause** button is picked either on the **ShowMotion** toolbar or in the view category thumbnail image. Pressing the [Esc] key also stops playback. To return to single-play mode, pick the **Turn off Looping** button on the **ShowMotion** toolbar. This button replaces the **Turn on Looping** button.

Changing a Shot's View Category and Properties

If you put a shot in the wrong view category, it is simple to move the shot to a different category. Right-click on the shot thumbnail image and select **Properties...** in the shortcut menu. This displays the **New View/Shot Properties** dialog box. Select the

Figure 4-20.
To remove a view category, right-click on its thumbnail image in the **ShowMotion** toolbar and pick **Delete** in the shortcut menu. This alert box appears to confirm the deletion.

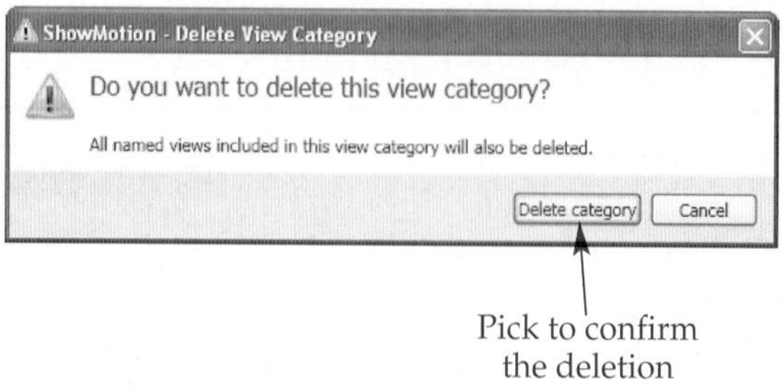

proper category name in the **View category:** drop-down list and pick the **OK** button. The shot thumbnail image will move into position above its new view category thumbnail image.

To change shot properties, first right-click on the shot thumbnail image and pick **Properties...** in the shortcut menu. The **New View/Shot Properties** dialog box is displayed. All properties of the shot can be changed. Change the settings as needed. Always preview the shot before you pick the **OK** button to save it.

Exercise 4-5

Complete the exercise on the Student CD.

PROFESSIONAL TIP

Try this procedure for creating a series of shots in a view category that are to be played in sequence.

1. Play each shot to determine where they should be located in the sequence.
2. Move shots left or right in the category as needed to create the proper sequence.
3. Play the category to determine if the shots properly transition from one to the next.
4. If a subsequent shot does not begin where the previous shot ended, right-click on that shot, pick **Properties...**, and make the necessary adjustments in the **View/Shot Properties** dialog box.
5. Play the category again.
6. Repeat the editing process with each shot until the category plays smoothly.

Chapter Test

Answer the following questions. Write your answers on a separate sheet of paper or complete the electronic chapter test on the Student CD.

1. For what is the *show motion tool* used?
2. Define *view* as it relates to the show motion tool.
3. Define *shot* as it relates to the show motion tool.
4. List the formats in which a shot can be created.
5. List the six buttons on the **ShowMotion** toolbar.
6. What is *live sectioning* and how can it be included in a shot?
7. Which type of shot is the same as a named view, but with a transition?
8. Which type of shot requires you to navigate through the view as you record the motion?
9. What is the *key position* of a cinematic shot?
10. Define *motion* and *movement* as they relate to a cinematic shot.
11. What is the purpose of the camera drop-down list in the **Shot Properties** tab of the **New View/Shot Properties** or **View/Shot Properties** dialog box?
12. List the eight types of camera movement for a cinematic shot.
13. Briefly describe two ways to play a single shot.
14. What is a *view category?*
15. How is an entire category of shots replayed?

Drawing Problems

1. Open one of your 3D drawings from Chapter 2. Do the following.
   A. Display a pictorial view of the drawing.
   B. Create a still shot. Use settings of your choice. Create a view category and place the shot in it.
   C. Display a different view of the drawing and create another still shot. Place the shot in the view category you created.
   D. Display a third view of the drawing and create a third still shot. Place the shot in the view category you created.
   E. Play each shot. If necessary, rearrange the shots. Then, play all shots in the category.
   F. Save the drawing as P04_01.

2. Open one of your 3D drawings from Chapter 2. Do the following.
   A. Display the objects in the Conceptual or Realistic visual style.
   B. Toggle the projection from parallel to perspective.
   C. Create two still shots and four cinematic shots of the model. Use a different motion type with each of the cinematic shots.
   D. Create two new categories and place one still and two cinematic shots in each category.
   E. Edit the shots in each category to create a smooth motion sequence.
   F. Save the drawing as P04_02.

3. Open one of your 3D drawings from Chapter 2 that was created with solid primitives. Do the following.
   A. Display a pictorial view.
   B. Create a walk shot. Place it in a view category named Walk Shots.
   C. Play the shot. How does this compare to a cinematic shot as far as ease of creation?
   D. Save the drawing as P04_03.

4. Open drawing P04_03 and do the following.
   A. Create a new cinematic shot using the Orbit motion type. Place it in a view category named Cinematic Shots.
   B. Create another cinematic shot using the Track left or Track right movement type. Check the **Always look at camera pivot** check box. Place the view in the Cinematic Shots category.
   C. Create a third cinematic shot using the Crane up or Crane down movement type. Make sure the **Always look at camera pivot** check box is checked. Place the view in the Cinematic Shots category.
   D. Play the Cinematic Shots category. Edit the shots as needed to create a smooth display.
   E. Create three still shots. Place them in a view category named Still Shots. Try creating three different gradient backgrounds to simulate dawn, noon, and dusk.
   F. Play the Still Shots category. Edit the shots as needed to create a smooth display.
   F. Save the drawing as P04_04.

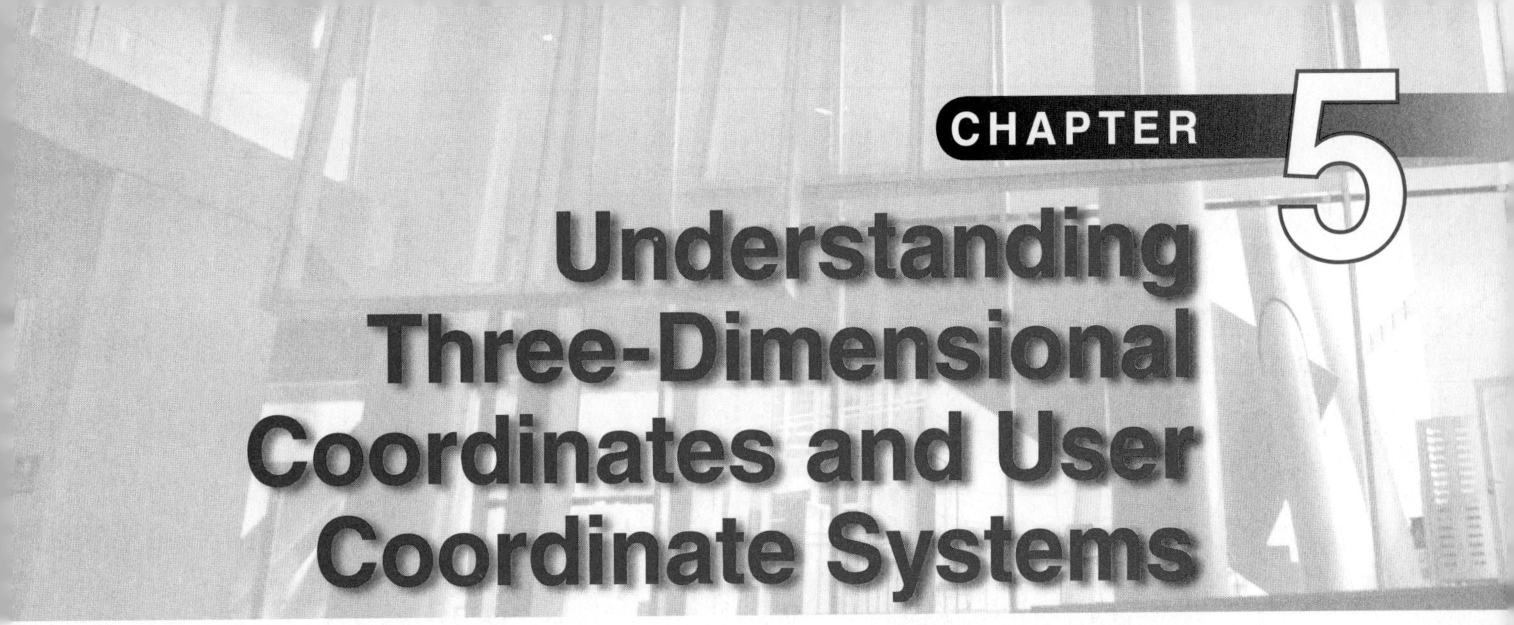

CHAPTER 5

Understanding Three-Dimensional Coordinates and User Coordinate Systems

Learning Objectives

After completing this chapter, you will be able to:

- ✓ Describe rectangular, spherical, and cylindrical methods of coordinate entry.
- ✓ Draw 3D polylines.
- ✓ Describe the function of the world and user coordinate systems.
- ✓ Move the user coordinate system to any surface.
- ✓ Rotate the user coordinate system to any angle.
- ✓ Change the user coordinate system to match the plane of a geometric object.
- ✓ Use a dynamic UCS.
- ✓ Save and manage user coordinate systems.
- ✓ Restore and use named user coordinate systems.
- ✓ Control user coordinate system icon visibility in viewports.

As you learned in Chapter 1, any point in space can be located using X, Y, and Z coordinates. This type of coordinate entry is called *rectangular coordinates.* Rectangular coordinates are most commonly used for coordinate entry. However, there are actually three ways in which to locate a point in space. The other two methods of coordinate entry are spherical coordinates and cylindrical coordinates. These two coordinate entry methods are discussed in the following sections. In addition, this chapter introduces working with user coordinate systems (UCSs).

Introduction to Spherical Coordinates

Locating a point in 3D space with ***spherical coordinates*** is similar to locating a point on Earth using longitudinal and latitudinal values, with the center of Earth representing the origin. Lines of longitude connect the North and South Poles and provide an east-west measurement on Earth's surface. Lines of latitude horizontally extend around Earth and provide a north-south measurement. The origin (Earth's center) can be that of the default world coordinate system (WCS) or the current user coordinate system (UCS). See **Figure 5-1A.**

Figure 5-1.
A—Lines of longitude, representing the highlighted latitudinal segments in the illustration, run from north to south. Lines of latitude, representing the highlighted longitudinal segments, run from east to west. B—Spherical coordinates require a distance, an angle in the XY plane, and an angle from the XY plane.

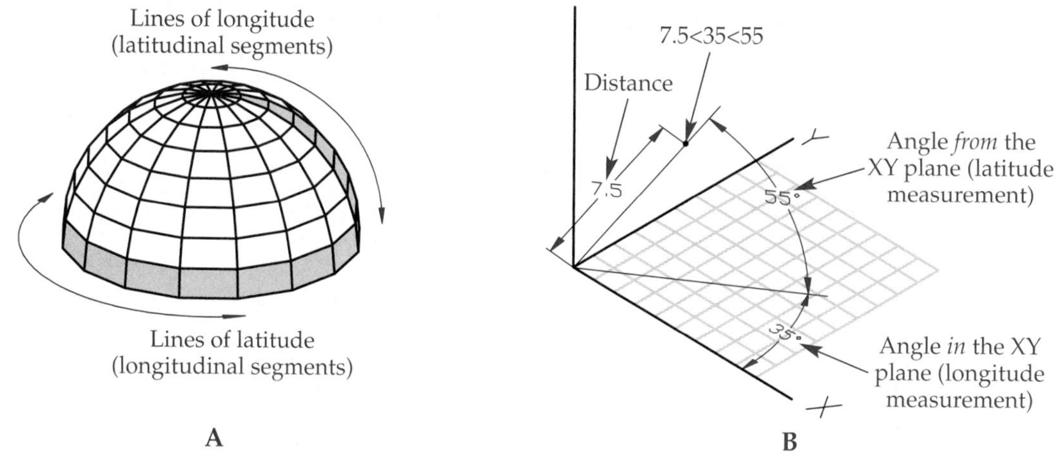

When entering spherical coordinates, the longitude measurement is expressed as the angle *in* the XY plane and the latitude measurement is expressed as the angle *from* the XY plane. See **Figure 5-1B.** A distance from the origin is also provided. The coordinates represent a measurement from the equator toward either the North or South Pole on Earth's surface. The following spherical coordinate entry is shown in **Figure 5-1B.**

7.5<35<55

This coordinate represents an absolute spherical coordinate, which is measured from the origin of the current UCS. Spherical coordinates can also be entered as relative coordinates. For example, a point drawn with the relative spherical coordinate @2<35<45 is located two units from the last point, at an angle of 35° *in* the XY plane, and at a 45° angle *from* the XY plane.

PROFESSIONAL TIP

Spherical coordinates are useful for locating features on a spherical surface. For example, they can be used to specify the location of a hole drilled into a sphere or a feature located from a specific point on a sphere. If you are working on such a spherical object, you might consider locating a UCS at the center of the sphere, then creating several different user coordinate systems rotated at different angles on the surface of the sphere. Any time a location is required, spherical coordinates can be used. Working with UCSs is introduced later in this chapter.

Using Spherical Coordinates

Spherical coordinates are well-suited for locating points on the surface of a sphere. In this section, you will draw a solid sphere and then locate a second solid sphere with its center on the surface of the first sphere.

To draw the first sphere, select the **SPHERE** command. Specify the center point as 7,5 and a radius of 1.5 units. Display a southeast isometric pictorial view of the sphere. Alternately, you can use the view cube to create a different pictorial view. Also, set the 3D Wireframe visual style current and switch to a parallel projection. Your drawing should look similar to **Figure 5-2A.**

Since you know the radius of the sphere, but the center of the sphere is not at the origin of the current UCS (the WCS), a relative spherical coordinate will be used to draw the second sphere. The sphere you drew is a solid and, as such, you can snap to its center using object snap. Set **Center** as a running object snap and then enter the **SPHERE** command again to draw the second sphere:

> Specify center point or [3P/2P/Ttr]: **FROM**↵
> Base point: *(use the **Center** object snap to select the center of the existing sphere)*
> <Offset>: **@1.5<30<60**↵ *(1.5 is the radius of the first sphere)*
> Specify radius or [Diameter]: **.4**↵

The objects should now appear as shown in **Figure 5-2B.** The center of the new sphere is located on the surface of the original sphere. This is clear after setting the Conceptual visual style current, **Figure 5-2C.** If you want the surfaces of the spheres to be tangent, add the radius value of each sphere (1.5 + .4) and enter this value when prompted for the offset from the center of the first sphere:

> <Offset>: **@1.9<30<60**↵

Notice in **Figure 5-2B** that the polar axes of the two spheres are parallel. This is because both objects were drawn using the same UCS, which can be misleading unless you understand how objects are constructed based on the current UCS. Test this by locating a cone on the surface of the large sphere, just below the small sphere. First, display a 3D wireframe view of the objects. Then, select the **CONE** command and continue as follows.

> Specify center point of base or [3P/2P/Ttr/Elliptical]: **FROM**↵
> Base point: **CEN**↵
> of *(pick the large sphere)*
> <Offset>: **@1.5<30<30**↵
> Specify base radius or [Diameter]: **.25**↵
> Specify height or [2Point/Axis endpoint/Top radius]: **1**↵

The result of this construction with the Conceptual visual style set current is shown in **Figure 5-3.** Notice how the axis of the cone is parallel to the polar axis of the sphere. To draw the cone so that its axis projects from the center of the sphere, you will need to change the UCS. This is discussed later in this chapter.

Figure 5-2.
A—A three-unit diameter sphere shown from the southeast isometric viewpoint.
B—A .8-unit diameter sphere is drawn with its center located on the surface of the original sphere. Also, lines have been drawn between the poles of the spheres. Notice how the polar axes are parallel. C—The objects after the Conceptual visual style is set current.

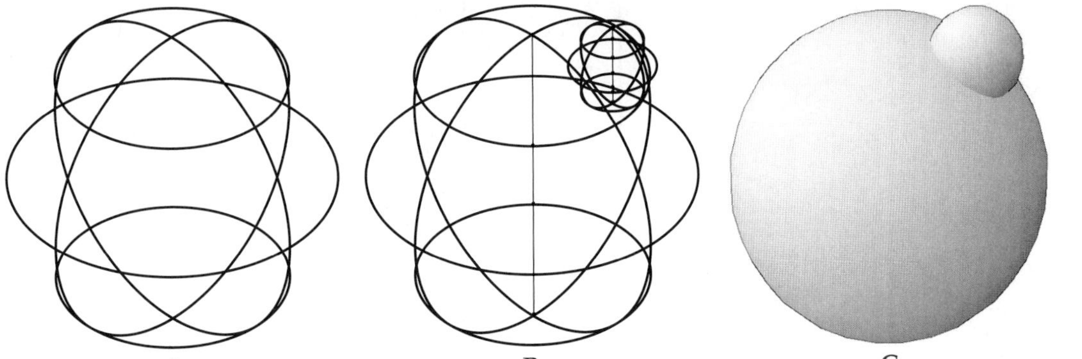

A B C

Figure 5-3.
The axis lines of objects drawn in the same user coordinate system are parallel. Notice that the cone does not project from the center of the large sphere.

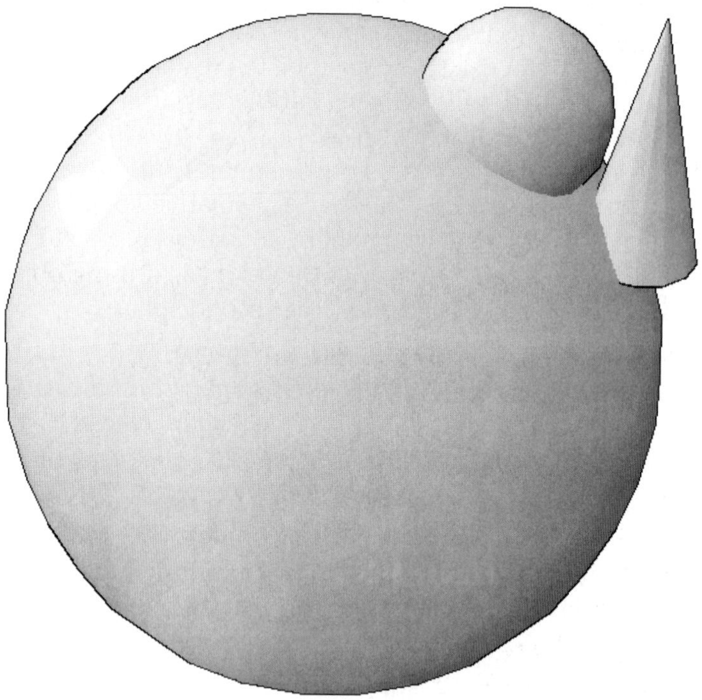

Introduction to Cylindrical Coordinates

Locating a point in space with ***cylindrical coordinates*** is similar to locating a point on an imaginary cylinder. Cylindrical coordinates have three values. The first value represents the horizontal distance from the origin, which can be thought of as the radius of a cylinder. The second value represents the angle in the XY plane, or the rotation of the cylinder. The third value represents a vertical dimension measured up from the polar coordinate in the XY plane, or the height of the cylinder. See **Figure 5-4**. The absolute cylindrical coordinate shown in the figure is:

7.5<35,6

Like spherical coordinates, cylindrical coordinates can also be entered as relative coordinates. For example, a point drawn with the relative cylindrical coordinate @1.5<30,4 is located 1.5 units from the last point, at an angle of 30° in the XY plane of the previous point, and at a distance of four units up from the XY plane of the previous point.

Figure 5-4.
Cylindrical coordinates require a horizontal distance from the origin, an angle in the XY plane, and a Z dimension.

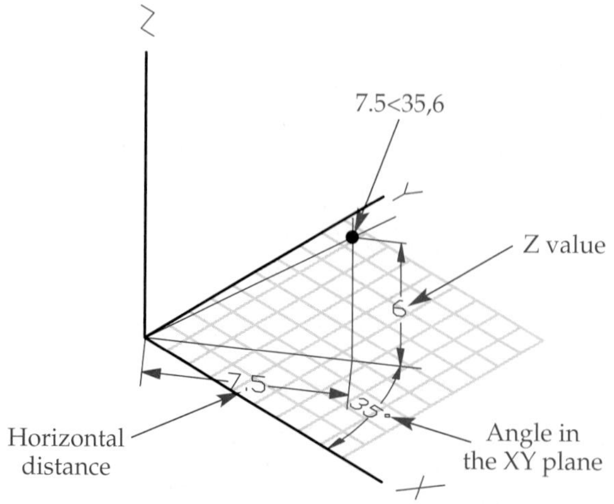

NOTE

Turn off dynamic input before entering cylindrical coordinates. Dynamic input does not correctly interpret the entry when cylindrical coordinates are typed.

Using Cylindrical Coordinates

Cylindrical coordinates work well for attaching new objects to a cylindrical shape. An example of this is specifying coordinates for a pipe that must be attached to another pipe, tank, or vessel. In **Figure 5-5,** a pipe must be attached to a 12′ diameter tank at a 30° angle from horizontal and 2′-6″ above the floor. In order to properly draw the pipe as a cylinder, you will have to change the UCS, which you will learn how to do later in this chapter. An attachment point for the pipe can be drawn using the **POINT** command and cylindrical coordinates. First, set the **PDMODE** system variable to 3. Then, enter the **POINT** command and continue:

Current point modes: PDMODE=3 PDSIZE=0.0000
Specify a point: **FROM**↵
Base point: **CEN**↵
of *(pick the base of the cylinder)*
<Offset>: **@6′<30,2′6″**↵ *(The radius of the tank is 6′.)*

The point can now be used as the center of the pipe (cylinder), **Figure 5-5B.** However, if you draw the pipe now, it will be parallel to the tank (large cylinder). By changing the UCS, as shown in **Figure 5-5C,** the pipe can be correctly drawn. Working with the UCS is introduced later in this chapter.

Exercise 5-1

Complete the exercise on the Student CD.

Figure 5-5.
A—A plan view of a tank shows the angle of the pipe attachment. B—A 3D view from the southeast quadrant shows the pipe attachment point located with cylindrical coordinates.
C—By creating a new UCS, the pipe can be drawn as a cylinder and correctly located without editing.

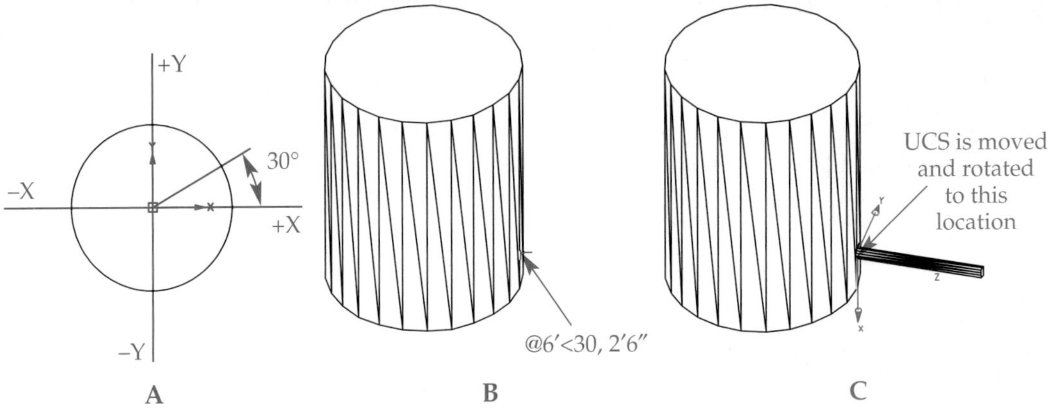

3D Polylines

A polyline drawn with the **PLINE** command is a 2D object. All segments of the polyline must be drawn parallel to the XY plane of the current UCS. A ***3D polyline,*** on the other hand, can be drawn in 3D space. The Z coordinate value can vary from point to point in the polyline.

3DPOLY

Ribbon
Home
> Draw

3D Polyline

Type
3DPOLY
3P

Menu
Draw
> 3D Polyline

The **3DPOLY** command is used to draw 3D polylines. Any form of coordinate entry is valid for drawing 3D polylines. If polar tracking is on when using the **3DPOLY** command, you can pick points in the Z direction if the polar tracking alignment path is parallel to the Z axis.

The **Close** option can be used to draw the final segment and create a closed shape. There must be at least two segments in the polyline to use the **Close** option. The **Undo** option removes the last segment without canceling the command.

The **PEDIT** command can be used to edit 3D polylines. The **PEDIT Spline** option is used to turn the 3D polyline into a B-spline curve based on the vertices of the polyline. A regular 3D polyline and the same polyline turned into a B-spline curve are shown in **Figure 5-6.** The **SPLFRAME** system variable controls the display of the original polyline frame and is either turned on (1) or off (0).

Exercise 5-2

Complete the exercise on the Student CD.

Introduction to Working with User Coordinate Systems

All points in a drawing or on an object are defined with XYZ coordinate values (rectangular coordinates) measured from the 0,0,0 origin. Since this system of coordinates is fixed and universal, AutoCAD refers to it as the ***world coordinate system (WCS).*** A ***user coordinate system (UCS),*** on the other hand, can be defined with its origin at any location and with its three axes in any orientation desired, while remaining at 90° to each other. The **UCS** command is used to change the origin, position, and rotation of the coordinate system to match the surfaces and features of an object under construction. When set up to do so, the UCS icon reflects the changes in the orientation of the UCS and placement of the origin.

Figure 5-6.
A regular 3D polyline and the B-spline curve version after using the **PEDIT** command.

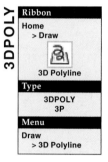

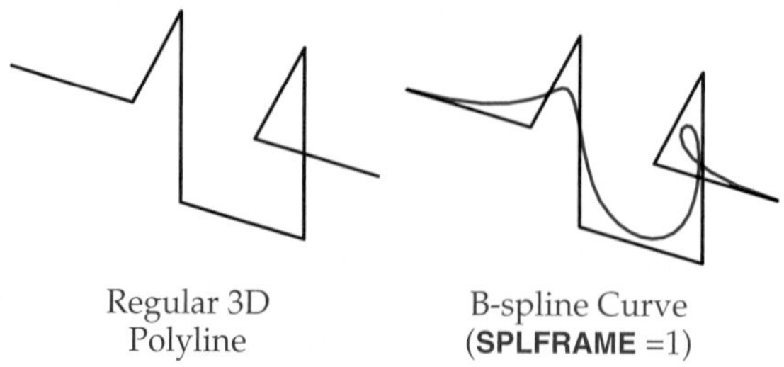

The **UCS** command is used to create and manage UCSs. This command and its options can be accessed on the ribbon, through the menu browser, by typing the command, or by using a toolbar (if displayed). Two selections in the **Tools** menu provide access to all UCS options. These selections are introduced here and discussed in detail later in this chapter.

- **New UCS.** This menu item displays a cascading menu containing most of the UCS command options found on the ribbon. The **New UCS** option can also be selected by picking on the UCS drop-down list below the view cube. All of these options are covered later in this chapter.
- **Named UCS.** This item displays the **UCS** dialog box. The **Named** button on the ribbon also displays this dialog box. The three tabs in the dialog box contain a variety of UCS and UCS icon options and settings. These options and settings are described as you progress through this chapter.

UCS

Ribbon
View > UCS
Type
UCS
Menu
Tools > New UCS
Tools > Named UCS

Earlier in this chapter, you used spherical coordinates to locate a small sphere on the surface of a larger sphere. You also drew a cone with the center of its base on the surface of the large sphere. However, the axis of the cone, which is a line from the center of the base to the tip of the cone, is not pointing to the center of the sphere. Refer to **Figure 5-3.** This is because the Z axes of the large sphere and cone are parallel to the world coordinate system (WCS) Z axis. The WCS is the default coordinate system of AutoCAD.

In order for the axis of the cone to project from the sphere's center point, the UCS must be changed using the **UCS** command. Working with different UCSs is discussed in the next section. However, the following is a quick overview and describes how to draw a cone with its axis projecting from the center of the sphere.

First, draw a three-unit diameter sphere with its center at 7,5. Display the drawing from the southeast isometric preset. To help see how the UCS is changing, make sure the UCS icon is displayed at the origin of the current UCS. Select **View**>**Display**>**UCS Icon** and make sure the icons next to the **On** and **Origin** entries have blue backgrounds. Also, set the 3D Wireframe visual style current.

Now, the sphere is drawn and the UCS icon is displayed at the origin of the current UCS (or at the lower-left corner of the screen, depending on the zoom level). However, the WCS is still the current user coordinate system. You are ready to start changing the UCS to meet your needs. Begin by moving the UCS origin to the center of the sphere using the **Origin** option of the **UCS** command. Notice that the UCS icon is now displayed at the center of the sphere, **Figure 5-7.** Also, if the grid is displayed, the red X and green Y axes intersect at the center of the sphere.

UCS

Ribbon
View > UCS

Origin
Type
UCS
Menu
Tools > New UCS > Origin

Study **Figure 5-8,** type the **UCS** command, and continue as follows. Keep in mind that the point you are locating—the center of the cone on the sphere's surface—is 30° from the X axis and 30° from the XY plane.

```
Current ucs name: *NO NAME*
Specify origin of UCS or [Face/NAmed/OBject/Previous/View/World/X/Y/Z/ZAxis]
  <World>: Z↵
```

UCS

Ribbon
View > UCS

Z
View > UCS

Y
Type
UCS
Menu
Tools > New UCS > Z
Tools > New UCS > Y

Figure 5-7.
The UCS origin is moved to the center of the sphere.

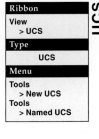

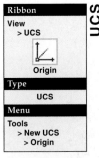

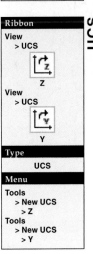

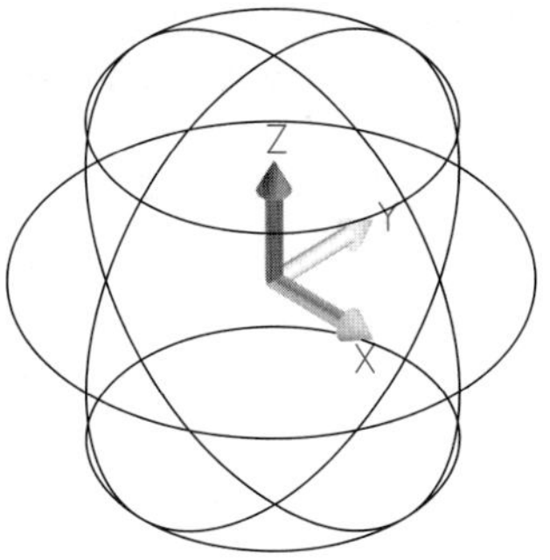

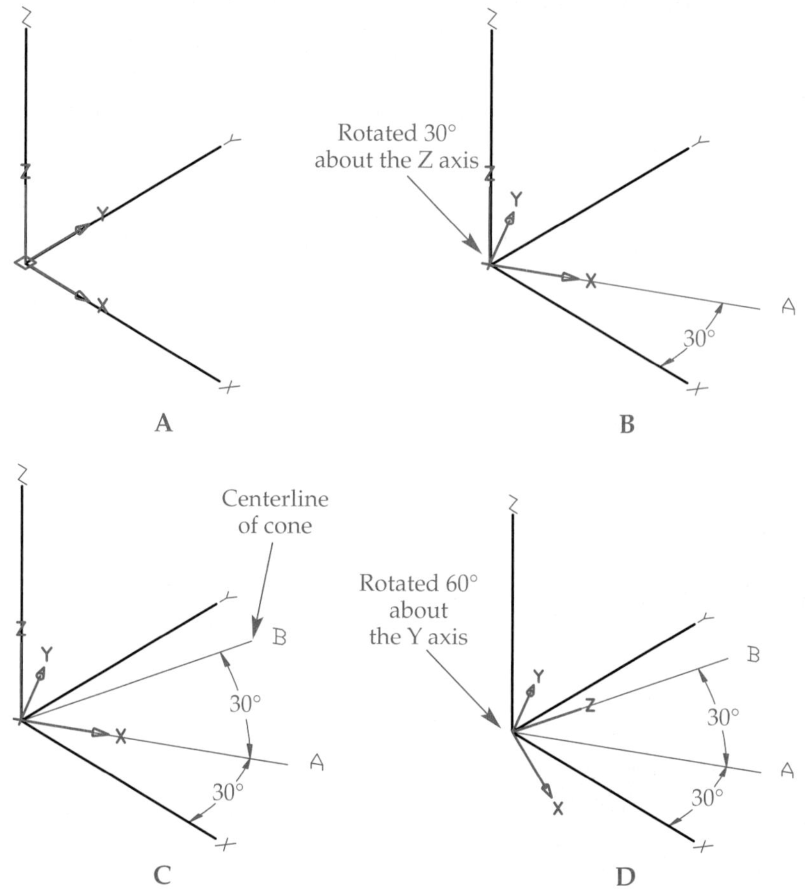

Figure 5-8.
A—The world coordinate system. B—The new UCS is rotated 30° in the XY plane about the Z axis. C—A line rotated up 30° from the XY plane represents the axis of the cone. D—The UCS is rotated 60° about the Y axis. The centerline of the cone coincides with the Z axis of this UCS.

Specify rotation angle about Z axis <90>: **30**↵ *(See Figure 5-8B.)*
Command: *(press [Enter] or the spacebar to reissue the* ***UCS*** *command)*
Current ucs name: *NO NAME*
Specify origin of UCS or [Face/NAmed/OBject/Previous/View/WorldX/Y/Z/ZAxis] <World>: **Y**↵
Specify rotation angle about Y axis <90>: **60**↵ *(See Figure 5-8D.)*

If the view cube is set to be oriented to the current UCS, then it rotates when the UCS is changed. Additionally, the grid rotates to match the new UCS. If the grid is not on, turn it on. Remember, the grid is displayed on the XY plane of the current UCS.

The new UCS can be used to construct a cone with its axis projecting from the center of the sphere. Figure 5-9A shows the new UCS located at the center of the sphere. With the UCS rotated, rectangular coordinates can be used to draw the cone. Enter the **CONE** command and specify the center as 0,0,1.5 (the radius of the sphere is 1.5 units). Enter a radius of .25 and a height of 1. The completed cone is shown in Figure 5-9B. You can see that the axis projects from the center of the sphere. Figure 5-9C shows the objects after setting the Conceptual visual style current.

This same basic procedure can be used in the tank and pipe example presented earlier in this chapter. To correctly locate the pipe (cylinder), first rotate the UCS 30° about the Z axis. Then, rotate the UCS 90° about the Y axis. The Z axis of this new UCS aligns with the long axis of the pipe. Finally, use rectangular coordinates to draw the cylinder with its center at the point drawn in Figure 5-5B.

Once you have changed to a new UCS, you can quickly return to the WCS by picking WCS in the view cube drop-down list or by using the **World** option of the **UCS** command. The WCS provides a common "starting place" for creating new UCSs.

Figure 5-9.
A—A new UCS is created with the Z axis projecting from the center of the sphere. B—A cone is drawn using the new UCS. The axis of the cone projects from the center of the sphere. C—The objects after the Conceptual visual style is set current.

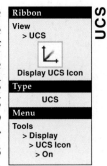

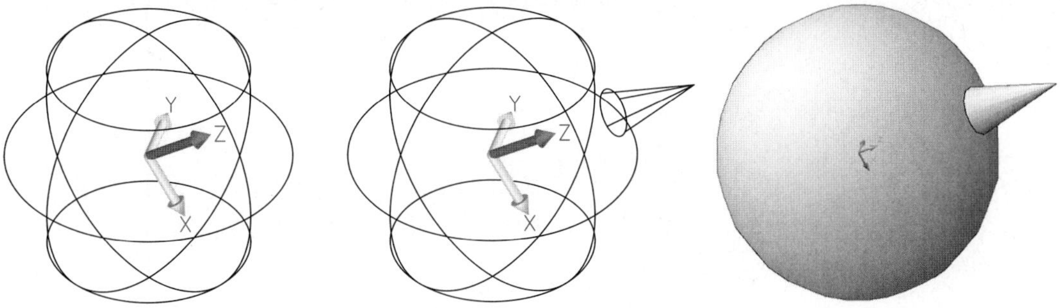

A B C

Exercise 5-3

Complete the exercise on the Student CD.

Working with User Coordinate Systems

Once you understand a few of the basic options of user coordinate systems, creating 3D models becomes an easy and quick process. The following sections show how to display the UCS icon, change the UCS in order to work on different surfaces of a model, and name and save a UCS. As you saw in the previous section, working with UCSs is easy.

Displaying the UCS Icon

The symbol that identifies the orientation of the coordinate system is called the ***UCS icon.*** When AutoCAD is first launched based on the acad3D.dwt template, the UCS icon is located at the WCS origin in the middle of the viewport. The display of this symbol is controlled by the **UCSICON** command. If your drawing does not require viewports and altered coordinate systems, you may want to turn the icon off using the **Off** option of the command. The icon disappears until you turn it on again using the **On** option of the command. You can also turn the icon on or off and set the icon to display at the origin using the options in the **Settings** tab of the **UCS** dialog box. Refer to Figure 5-10. This dialog box is displayed by picking the **Named** button on the **UCS** panel in the **View** tab of the ribbon, selecting **Tools>Named UCS...** from the menu, or typing the **UCSMAN** command.

UCS

Ribbon
View
> UCS
Display UCS Icon

Type
UCS

Menu
Tools
> Display
> UCS Icon
> On

PROFESSIONAL TIP

It is recommended that you have the UCS icon turned on at all times when working in 3D drawings. It provides a quick indication of the current UCS.

Figure 5-10.
Setting UCS and UCS icon options in the **UCS** dialog box.

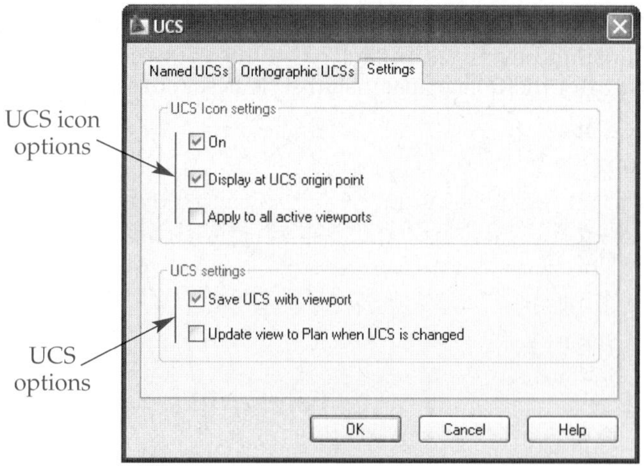

Modifying the UCS Icon

PROPERTIES

Type
PROPERTIES
Menu
View
> Display
> UCS Icon
> Properties...

The appearance of the wireframe UCS icon can be changed using the settings in the **UCS Icon** dialog box. See Figure 5-11. This dialog box is accessed using the **Properties** option of the **UCSICON** command. You can modify three characteristics of the UCS icon.

- **Style.** Select either a 2D or 3D icon in the **UCS icon style** area. The 2D style was used by earlier releases of AutoCAD. If the 3D style is selected, which is the default, the **Cone** and **Line width:** options are available. The line width can be one, two, or three pixels.
- **Size.** The **UCS icon size** area contains a text box and a slider. The value in the +text box is the size of the UCS icon expressed as a percentage of the viewport size. Enter a new value in the text box or adjust the slider.
- **Color.** Use the drop-down lists in the **UCS icon color** area to set the color of the UCS icon. Notice that different colors can be set for model space and paper (layout) space.

NOTE

The settings in the **UCS Icon** dialog box have no effect on the shaded 3D UCS icon. This icon is displayed when the 3D Wireframe, 3D Hidden, Conceptual, or Realistic visual style is set current. Also, if a perspective projection is set current when the dialog box is displayed, the preview is shown as dashed lines without arrowheads.

Figure 5-11.
The **UCS Icon** dialog box allows you to change the appearance of the wireframe UCS icon.

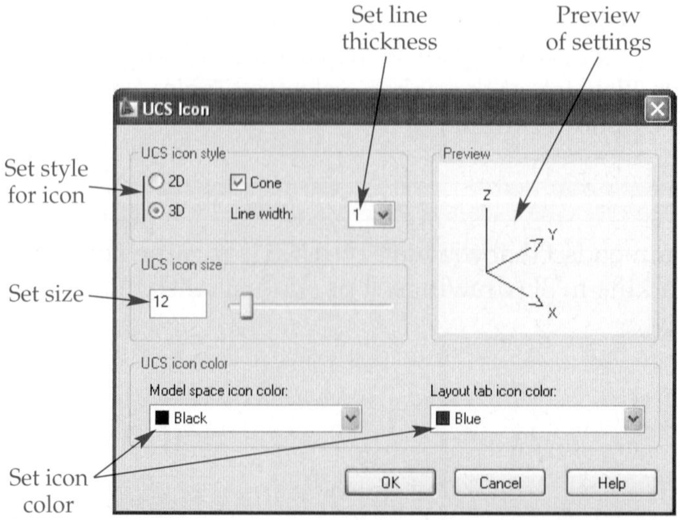

Changing the Coordinate System

To construct a three-dimensional object, you must draw shapes at many different angles. Different planes are needed to draw features on angled surfaces. To construct these features, it is easiest to rotate the UCS to match any surface on an object. The following example illustrates this process.

The object in **Figure 5-12** has a cylinder on the angled surface. A solid modeling command called **EXTRUDE**, which is discussed in Chapter 8, is used to create the base of the object. The cylinder is then drawn on the angled feature. In Chapter 7, you will learn how to dimension the object as shown in **Figure 5-12.**

The first step in creating this model is to draw the side view of the base as a wireframe. You could determine the X, Y, and Z coordinates of each point on the side view and enter the coordinates. However, a lot of typing can be saved if all points share a Z value of 0. By rotating the UCS, you can draw the side view entering only X and Y coordinates. Start a new drawing and display the southeast isometric view. If the UCS icon is off, turn it on and display it at the origin.

Now, rotate the UCS 90° about the X axis. The new UCS is parallel to the side of the object. The UCS icon is displayed at the origin of the UCS. If needed, you may want to pan the view so the UCS icon is near the center.

Next, use the **PLINE** command to draw the outline of the side view. Refer to the coordinates shown in **Figure 5-13.** The **PLINE** command is used instead of the **LINE** command because a closed polyline can be extruded into a solid. Be sure to use the **Close** option to draw the final segment. When entering coordinates, you may want to turn off dynamic input to disable direct-distance entry. A wireframe of one side of the object is created. Notice the orientation of the UCS icon.

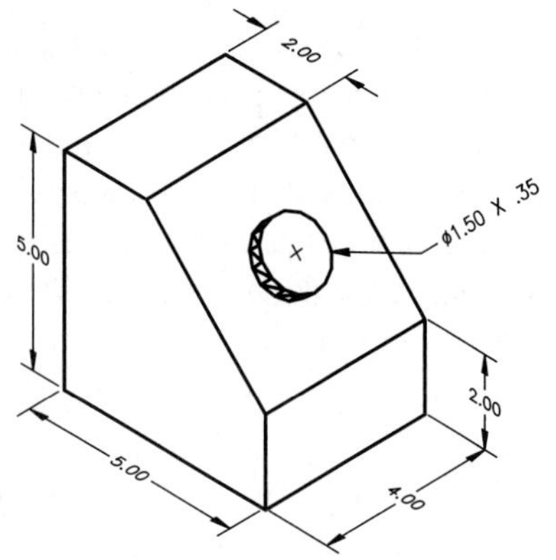

Figure 5-12.
This object can be constructed by changing the orientation of the coordinate system.

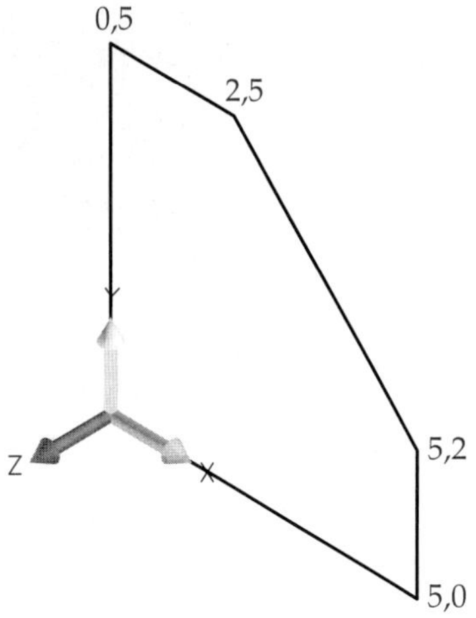

Figure 5-13.
A wireframe of one side of the base is created. Notice the orientation of the UCS.

Now, the **EXTRUDE** command is used to create the base as a solid. This command is covered in detail in Chapter 8. On the same UCS used to create the wireframe side, enter the command:

Command: **EXTRUDE**↵
Current wire frame density: ISOLINES = *current*
Select objects to extrude: *(pick the polyline)*
Select objects to extrude: ↵
Specify height of extrusion or [Direction/Path/Taper angle]: **–4**↵
Command:

By entering a negative value for the height of the extrusion, the resulting object extends behind (negative Z) the XY plane of the current UCS. You can also move the cursor so the preview extends below the UCS XY plane and enter positive 4. The base is created as a solid. See Figure 5-14. You may want to switch to a parallel projection, as shown in the figure.

Saving a Named UCS

UCS

Ribbon
View
> UCS
Named

Type
UCS

Menu
Tools
> Named UCS...

Once you have created a new UCS that may be used again, it is best to save it for future use. For example, you just created a UCS used to draw the wireframe of one side of the object. You can save this UCS using the **Save** option of the **UCS** command or the **UCS** dialog box.

If using the dialog box, right-click on the entry Unnamed and pick **Rename** in the shortcut menu. See Figure 5-15. You can also pick once or double-click on the highlighted name. Then, type the new name in place of Unnamed and press [Enter]. A name can have up to 255 characters. Numbers, letters, spaces, dollar signs ($), hyphens (–), and underscores (_) are valid. Use this method to save a new UCS or to rename an existing one. Now, the coordinate system is saved and can be easily recalled for future use.

PROFESSIONAL TIP

Most drawings can be created by rotating the UCS as needed without saving it. If the drawing is complex with several planes, each containing a large amount of detail, you may wish to save a UCS for each detailed face. Then, restore the proper UCS as needed. For example, when working with architectural drawings, you may wish to establish a different UCS for each floor plan and elevation view and for roofs and walls that require detail work.

Figure 5-14.
The wireframe is extruded to create the base as a solid.

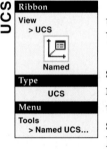

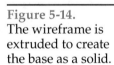

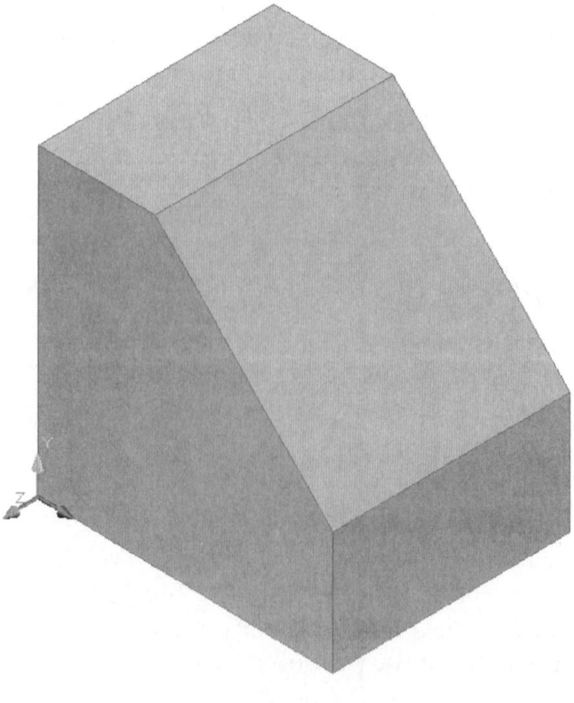

Figure 5-15.
Saving a new UCS. Select **Rename** to enter a name and save the Unnamed UCS.

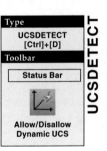

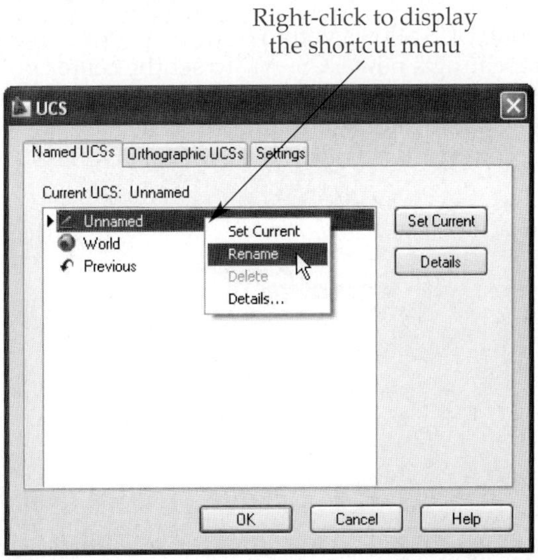

Dynamic UCS

A powerful tool for 3D modeling is the ***dynamic UCS function.*** A dynamic UCS is a UCS temporarily located on any existing face of a 3D model. The function is activated by picking the **Allow/Disallow Dynamic UCS** button in the status bar, pressing the [Ctrl]+[D] key combination, or setting the **UCSDETECT** system variable to 1. When the pointer is moved over a model surface, the XY plane of the UCS is aligned with that surface. This is especially useful when adding primitives or shapes to model surfaces. In addition, dynamic UCSs are useful when inserting blocks and xrefs, locating text, editing 3D geometry, editing with grips, and area calculations.

Type
UCSDETECT [Ctrl]+[D]
Toolbar
Status Bar
Allow/Disallow Dynamic UCS

UCSDETECT

An example of using dynamic UCS is to draw the cylinder on the angled face of the object shown in **Figure 5-12.** First, select the **CYLINDER** command. Make sure the dynamic UCS function is on. Then, move the pointer over one of the surfaces of the object. Notice that the 3D crosshairs change when they are moved over a new surface. The red (X) and green (Y) crosshairs are flat on the face. For ease of visualizing the 3D crosshairs as they are moved across different surfaces, right-click on the **Allow/Disallow Dynamic UCS** button in the status bar and select **Display crosshair labels** to turn on the XYZ labels on the crosshairs.

As you move the pointer over the object faces, note that hidden faces are not highlighted, therefore you cannot work on those faces. If you wish to work on a hidden face you must first change the viewpoint to make that face visible. The view cube can be used to dynamically change the viewpoint without interrupting the current command.

The **CYLINDER** command is currently prompting to select a center point of the base. If you pick a point, this sets the center of the cylinder base *and* temporarily relocates the UCS so its XY plane lies on the selected face. Once the point is selected and the dynamic UCS created, the UCS icon moves to the temporary UCS. When the command is ended, the UCS and UCS icon revert to their previous locations. To locate a 1.5″ diameter cylinder in the center of the angled face, use the following procedure.

1. At the "specify center point of base" prompt, [Shift] + right-click in the drawing area and pick **Mid Between 2 Points** from the shortcut menu. See **Figure 5-16A.**
2. Use the **Endpoint** snap to pick two opposite corners of the angled face. See **Figure 5-16B.** You can also use the **Midpoint** snap and pick the midpoint of the two sides or top and bottom edges. The UCS is temporarily moved to the angled face at the pick point, which is the center of the face.

Figure 5-16.
Using a dynamic UCS allows you to draw a cylinder on the angled face of the object shown here without creating a new UCS. A—To set the center point of the base and select the angled face for the dynamic UCS, use the **Mid Between 2 Points** snap and select corners or midpoints of the face. B—Set the radius or diameter of the base. C—Set the height of the cylinder. D—When the command is ended, the previous UCS is restored.

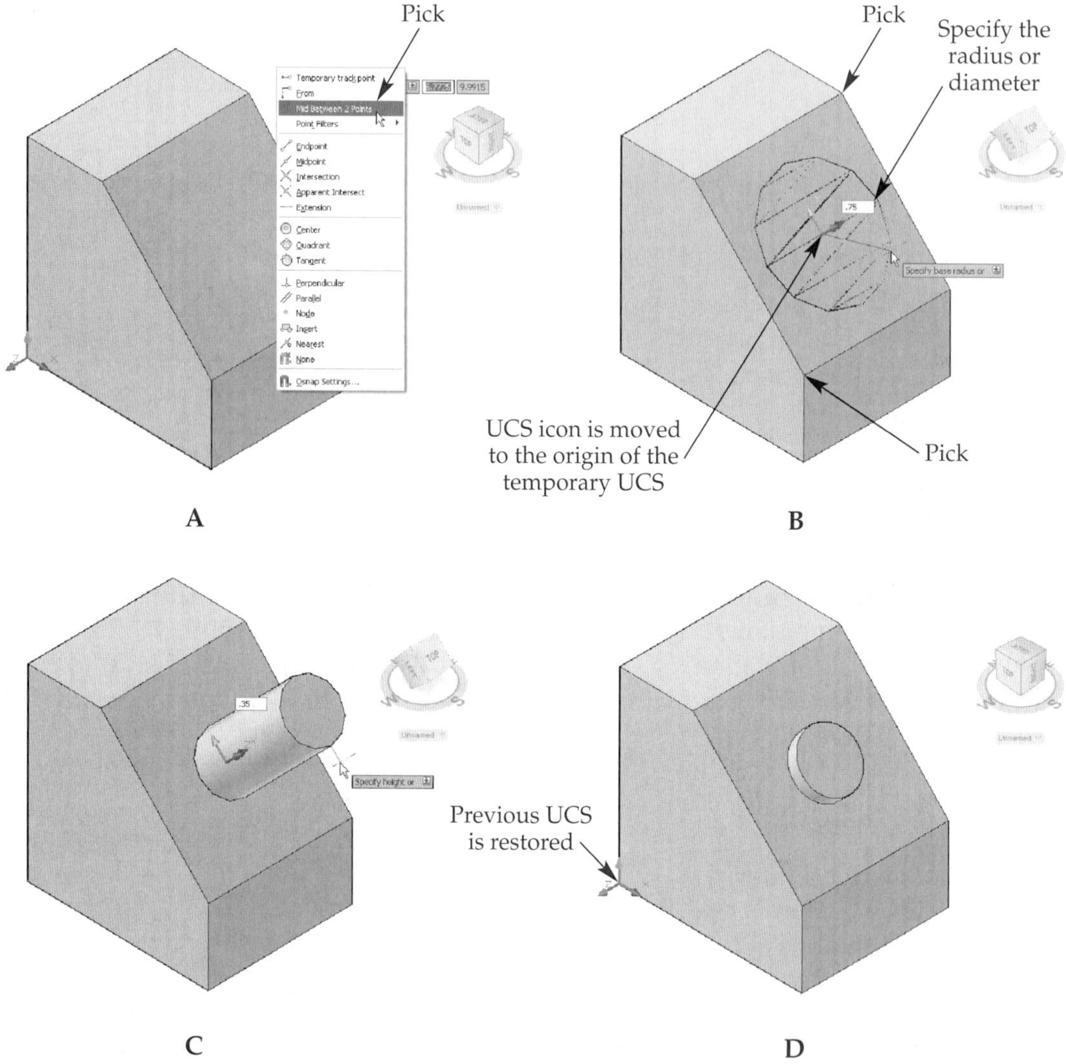

3. Specify the 1.5 unit diameter for the base.
4. Specify a cylinder height of .35 units. See **Figure 5-16C.**
5. The cylinder is properly located on the angled face and the UCS automatically returns to the previous location. See **Figure 5-16D.**

When setting a dynamic UCS, experiment with the behavior of the crosshairs as they are moved over different surfaces. The orientation of the crosshairs is related to the edge of the face that they are moved over. Can you determine the pattern by which the crosshairs are turned? The X axis of the crosshairs is always aligned with the edge that is crossed.

PROFESSIONAL TIP

If you want to temporarily turn off the dynamic UCS function while working in a command, press and hold the [Shift]+[Z] key combination while moving the pointer over a face. As soon as you release the keys, dynamic UCS function is reinstated.

Additional Ways to Change the UCS

There are other ways to change the UCS. These options include picking three points, selecting a new Z axis, and setting the UCS to an existing object. The next sections cover these options.

Selecting Three Points to Create a New UCS

The **3 Point** option of the **UCS** command can be used to change the UCS to any flat surface. This option requires that you first locate a new origin, then a point on the positive X axis, and finally a point on the XY plane that has a positive Y value. Refer to **Figure 5-17.** Use object snaps to select points that are not on the current XY plane. After you pick the third point—the point on the XY plane—the UCS icon changes its orientation to align with the angled surface of the base.

UCS

Ribbon
View
> UCS
3 Point

Type
UCS

Menu
Tools
> New UCS
> 3 Point

PROFESSIONAL TIP

When typing the **UCS** command, enter 3 at the Specify origin of UCS or [Face/NAmed/OBject/Previous/View/World/X/Y/Z/ZAxis] <World>: prompt. Notice that the option is not listed in the prompt.

Selecting a New Z Axis

The **ZAxis** option of the **UCS** command allows you to select the origin point and a point on the positive Z axis. Once the new Z axis is defined, AutoCAD sets the new X and Y axes.

UCS

Ribbon
View
> UCS
Z-Axis Vector

Type
UCS

Menu
Tools
> New UCS
> Z-Axis Vector

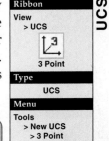

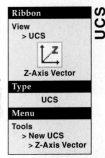

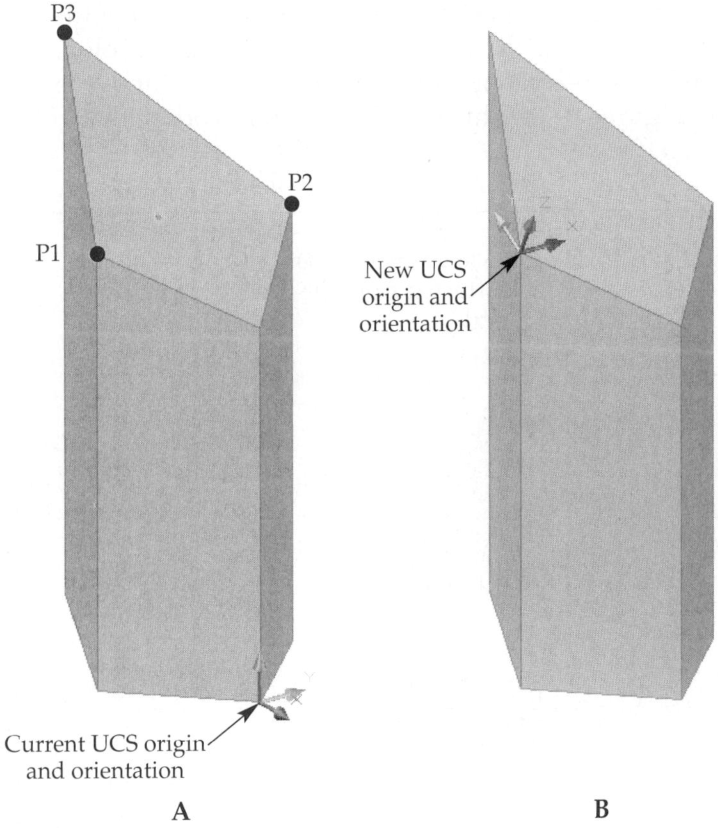

Figure 5-17. A—A new UCS can be established by picking three points. P1 is the origin, P2 is on the positive X axis, and P3 is on the XY plane and has a positive Y value. B—The new UCS is created.

You will now add a cylinder to the lower face of the base created earlier. The cylinder extends into the base. Refer to the location of the UCS in **Figure 5-16D.** This is the UCS after adding the cylinder to the angled face with a dynamic UCS. The Z axis does not project perpendicular to the lower face. Therefore, a new UCS must be created on the lower-right face. Change the UCS after entering the **ZAxis** option as follows.

1. Pick the origin of the new UCS. See **Figure 5-18A.** You may have to use an object snap to select the origin.
2. Pick a point on the positive portion of the new Z axis.
3. The new UCS is established and it can be saved if necessary.

Now, use auto-tracking or object snaps to draw a ∅.5″ cylinder centered on the lower face and extending 3″ into the base. Then, subtract the cylinder from the base part to create the hole, as shown in **Figure 5-18B.**

Setting the UCS to an Existing Object

UCS

Ribbon
View > UCS — Object
Type
UCS
Menu
Tools > New UCS > Object

The **Object** option of the **UCS** command can be used to define a new UCS on an object. However, there are some objects on which this option cannot be used: 3D polylines, 3D meshes, and xlines. There are also certain rules that control the orientation of the UCS. For example, if you select a circle, the center point becomes the origin of the new UCS. The pick point on the circle determines the direction of the X axis. The Y axis is relative to X and the UCS Z axis is the same as the Z axis of the selected object.

Look at **Figure 5-19A.** The circle shown is rotated an unknown number of degrees from the XY plane of the WCS. However, you need to create a UCS in which the circle is lying on the XY plane. Select the **Object** option of the **UCS** command and then pick the circle. The UCS icon may look like the one shown in **Figure 5-19B.** Notice how the X and Y axes are not aligned with the quadrants of the circle, as indicated by the grip locations. This may not be what you expected. The X axis orientation is determined by the pick point on the circle. Notice how the X axis is pointing at the pick point.

To rotate the UCS in the current plane so the X and Y axes of the UCS are aligned with the quadrants of the circle, use the **ZAxis** option of the **UCS** command. Select the center of the circle as the origin and then enter the absolute coordinate 0,0,1. This uses the current Z axis location, which also forces the X and Y axes to align with the object. Refer to **Figure 5-19C.** This method may not work with all objects.

Figure 5-18.
A—Using the **ZAxis** option to establish a new UCS. B—The new UCS is used to create a cylinder, which is then subtracted from the base to create a hole.

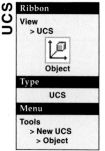

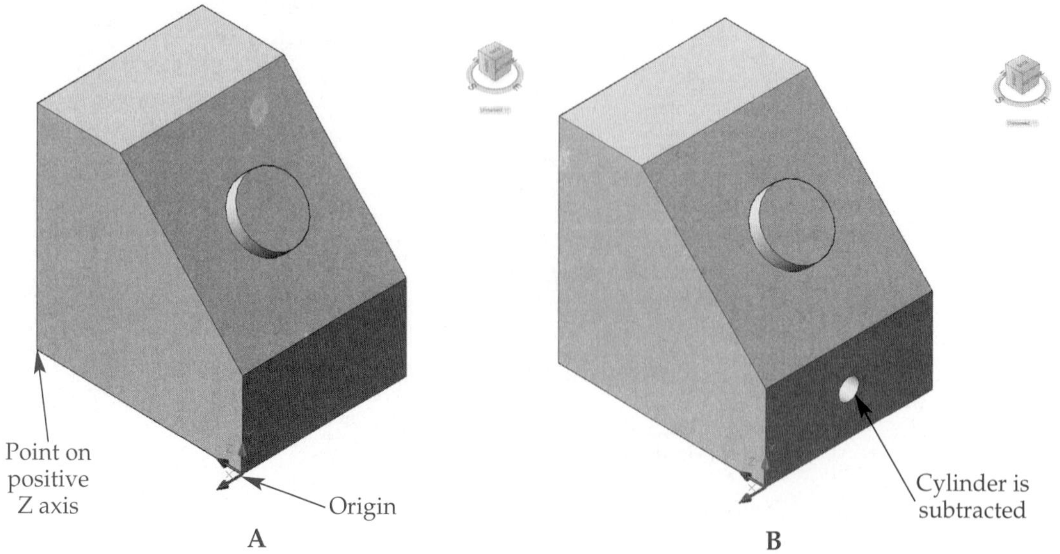

Figure 5-19.
A—This circle is rotated off of the WCS XY plane by an unknown number of degrees. It will be used to establish a new UCS. B—The circle is on the XY plane of the new UCS. However, the X and Y axes do not align with the circle's quadrants. C—The **ZAxis** option of the **UCS** command is used to align the UCS with the quadrants of the circle.

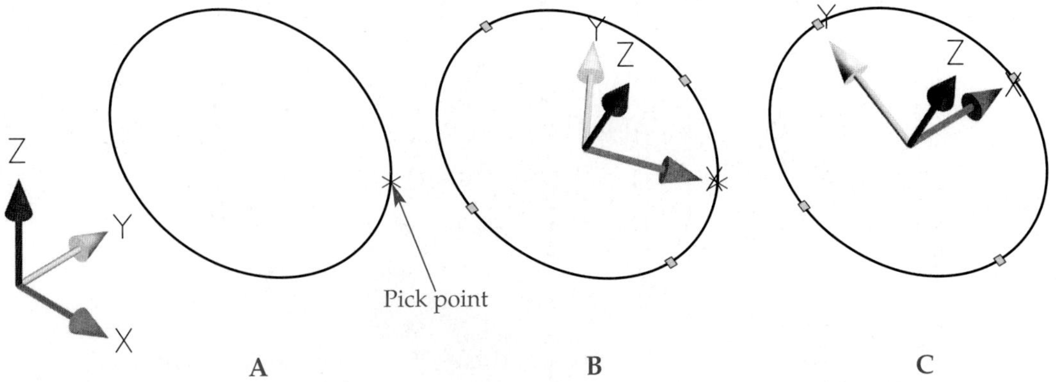

Setting the UCS to the Face of a 3D Solid

The **Face** option of the **UCS** command allows you to orient the UCS to any face on a 3D solid object. This option does not work on surface objects. Select the command and then pick a face on the solid. After you have selected a face on a 3D solid, you have the options of moving the UCS to the adjacent face or flipping the UCS 180° on the X, Y, or both axes. Use the **Next**, **Xflip**, or **Yflip** options to move or rotate the UCS as needed. Once you achieve the UCS orientation you want, press [Enter] to accept. Notice in **Figure 5-20** how many different UCS orientations can be selected for a single face.

UCS
Ribbon
View > UCS
Face
Type
UCS
Menu
Tools > New UCS > Face

Setting the UCS Perpendicular to the Current View

You may need to add notes or labels to a 3D drawing that are plan to the current view, such as that shown in **Figure 5-21.** The **View** option of the **UCS** command makes this easy to do. Immediately after selecting the **View** option, the UCS rotates to a position so the new XY plane is perpendicular to the current line of sight. Now, anything added to the drawing is plan to the current view. The command works on the current viewport only; other viewports are unaffected.

UCS
Ribbon
View > UCS
View
Type
UCS
Menu
Tools > New UCS > View

Applying the Current UCS to a Viewport

The **Apply** option of the **UCS** command allows you to apply the UCS in the current viewport to any or all model space or paper space viewports. Using the **Apply** option, you can have a different UCS displayed in every viewport or you can apply one UCS to all viewports. With the viewport that contains the UCS to apply active, enter the **Apply**

UCS
Type
UCS

Figure 5-20.
Several different UCSs can be selected from a single pick point using the **Face** option of the **UCS** command. Given the pick point, five of the eight possibilities are shown here.

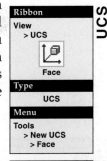

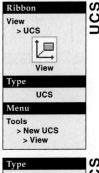

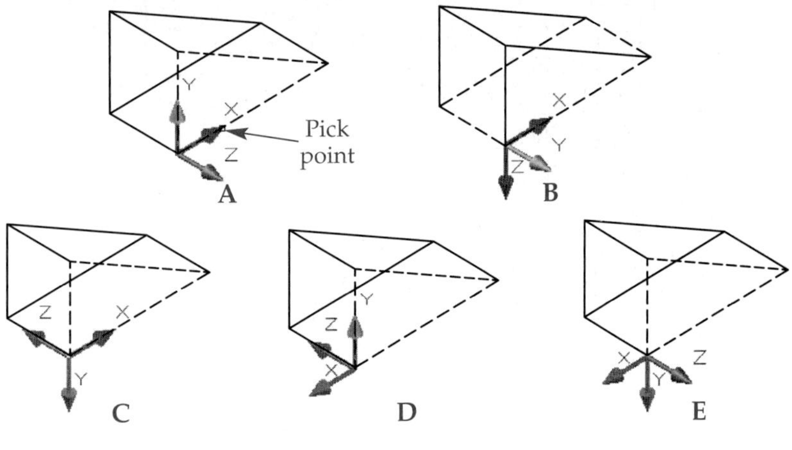

Figure 5-21.
The **View** option of the **UCS** command allows you to place text plan to the current view.

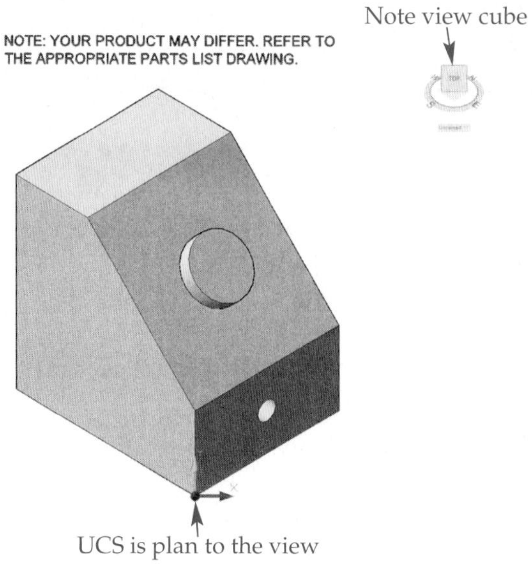

option. Then, pick a viewport to which the current UCS will be applied and press [Enter]. To apply the current UCS to all viewports, enter the **All** option. This option is only available on the command line. However, the option does not appear in the command prompt. Enter either A or APPLY to select the option.

Preset UCS Orientations

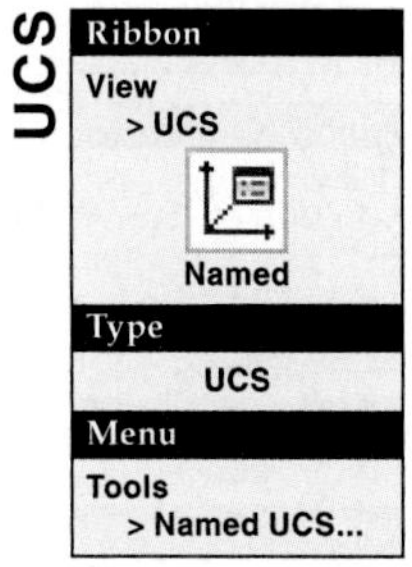

AutoCAD has six preset orthographic UCSs that match the six standard orthographic views. With the current UCS as the top view (plan), all other views are arranged as shown in Figure 5-22. These orientations can be selected by entering the command on the command

Figure 5-22.
The standard orthographic UCSs coincide with the six basic orthographic views.

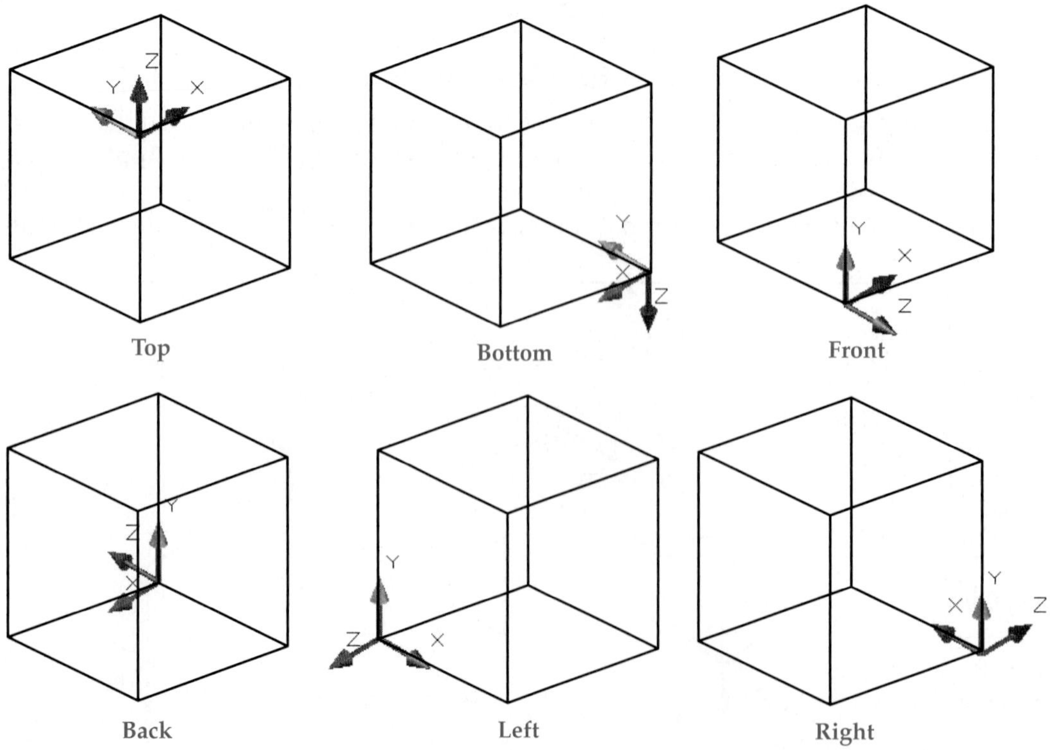

line or using the **Orthographic UCSs** tab of the **UCS** dialog box. When using the command line, type the name of the UCS (FRONT, BACK, RIGHT, etc.) at the first prompt:

Specify origin of UCS or [Face/NAmed/OBject/Previous/View/World/X/Y/Z/ZAxis] <World>: **FRONT** *or* **FR**↵

Note that there is no orthographic option listed for the command.

The **Relative to:** drop-down list at the bottom of the **Orthographic UCSs** tab of the **UCS** dialog box specifies whether the orthographic UCS is relative to a named UCS or absolute to the WCS. For example, suppose you have a saved UCS named Front Corner that is rotated 30° about the Y axis of the WCS. If you set current the top UCS relative to the WCS, the new UCS is perpendicular to the WCS, **Figure 5-23A.** However, if the top UCS is set current relative to the named UCS Front Corner, the new UCS is also rotated from the WCS, **Figure 5-23B.**

The Z value, or depth, of a preset UCS can be changed in the **Orthographic UCSs** tab of the **UCS** dialog box. First, right-click on the name of the UCS you wish to change. Then, pick **Depth** from the shortcut menu, **Figure 5-24A.** This displays the **Orthographic UCS depth** dialog box. See **Figure 5-25B.** You can either enter a new depth value or specify the new location on screen by picking the **Select new origin** button. Once the new depth has been selected, it is reflected in the preset UCS list.

PROFESSIONAL TIP

Changing the **Relative to:** setting affects *all* preset UCSs and *all* preset viewpoints! Therefore, leave this set to **World** unless absolutely necessary to change it.

Managing User Coordinate Systems and Displays

You can create, name, and use as many user coordinate systems as needed to construct your model or drawing. As you saw earlier, AutoCAD allows you to name (save) coordinate systems for future use. User coordinate systems can be created, renamed, set current, and deleted using the **Named UCSs** tab of the **UCS** dialog box, **Figure 5-25.**

The **Named UCSs** tab contains the **Current UCS:** list box. This list box contains the names of all saved coordinate systems plus World. If other coordinate systems have been used in the current drawing session, Previous appears in the list. Unnamed appears

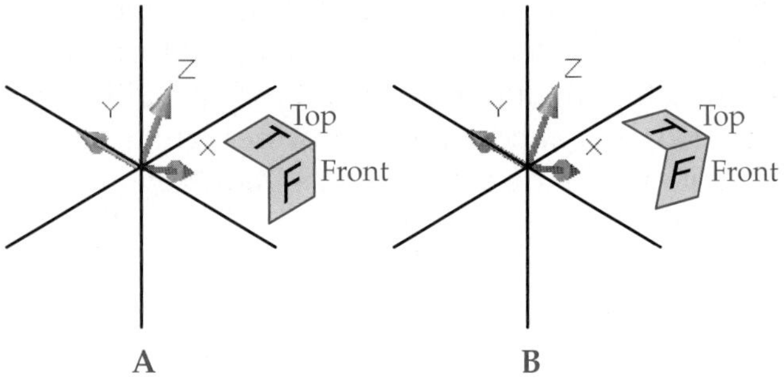

Figure 5-23. The **Relative to:** drop-down list entry in the **Orthographic UCSs** tab of the **UCS** dialog box determines whether the orthographic UCS is based on a named UCS or the WCS. The UCS icon here represents the named UCS. A—Relative to the WCS. B—Relative to the named UCS.

Figure 5-24.
A—The Z value, or depth, of a preset UCS can be changed by right-clicking on its name and selecting **Depth**. B—Enter a new depth value or pick the **Select new origin** button to pick a new location on screen.

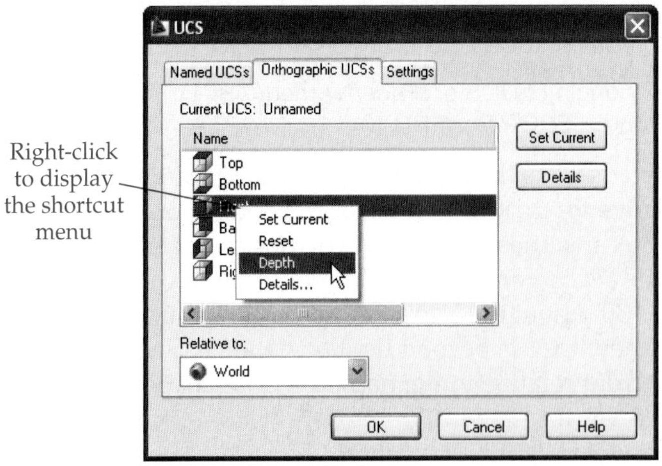

A

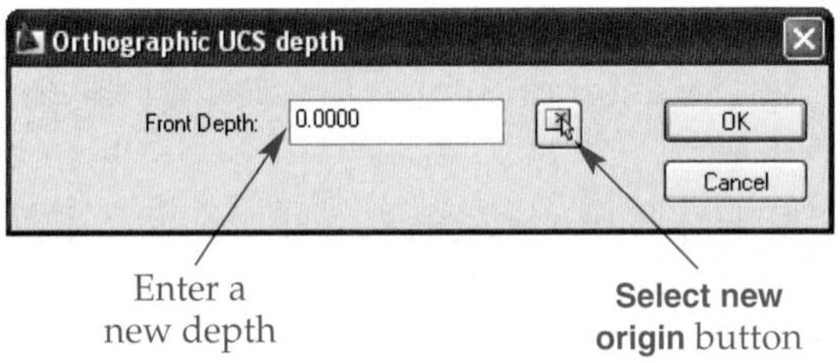

B

Figure 5-25.
The **UCS** dialog box allows you to rename, list, delete, and set current an existing UCS.

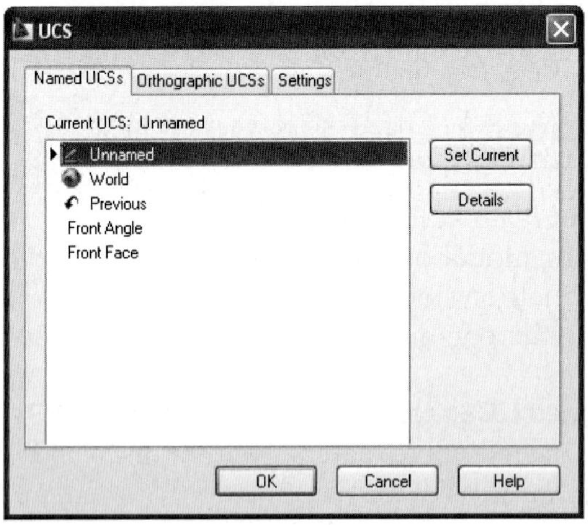

if the current coordinate system has not been named. The current UCS is indicated by a small triangle to the left of its name in the list. To make any of the listed coordinate systems active, highlight the name and pick the **Set Current** button.

A list of coordinate and axis values of the highlighted UCS can be displayed by picking the **Details** button. This displays the **UCS Details** dialog box shown in Figure 5-26.

If you right-click on the name of a UCS in the list in the **Named UCSs** tab, a shortcut menu is displayed. Using this menu, you can rename the UCS. Saving a UCS is discussed earlier in this chapter. You can also set the UCS current or delete it using the shortcut menu. The Unnamed UCS cannot be deleted, nor can World be deleted.

Figure 5-26.
The **UCS Details** dialog box displays the coordinate values of the selected UCS.

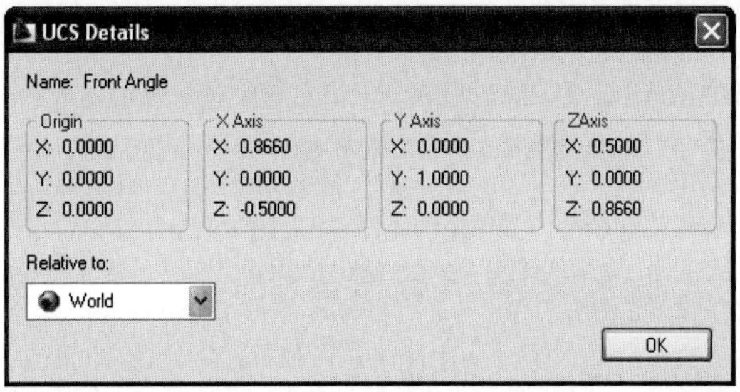

PROFESSIONAL TIP

You can also manage UCSs on the command line using the **UCS** command.

Exercise 5-4

Complete the exercise on the Student CD.

Setting an Automatic Plan Display

After changing the UCS, a plan view is often needed to give you a better feel for the XYZ directions. While you should try to draw in a pictorial view when possible as you construct a 3D object, some constructions may be much easier in a plan view. AutoCAD can be set to automatically make your view of the drawing plan to the current UCS. This is especially useful if you will be changing the UCS often, but want to work in a plan view.

The **UCSFOLLOW** system variable is used to automatically display a plan view of the current UCS. When it is set to 1, a plan view is automatically created in the current viewport when the UCS is changed. Viewports are discussed in Chapter 6. The default setting of **UCSFOLLOW** is 0 (off). After setting the variable to 1, a plan view will be automatically generated the next time the UCS is changed. The **UCSFOLLOW** variable generates the plan view only after the UCS is changed, not immediately after the variable is changed. However, if you select a different viewport, the previous viewport is set plan to the UCS if **UCSFOLLOW** has been set to 1 in that viewport. The **UCSFOLLOW** variable can be individually set for each viewport.

PROFESSIONAL TIP

To get the plan view displayed without changing the UCS, use the **PLAN** command, which is discussed in Chapter 3.

UCS Settings and Variables

As discussed in the previous section, the **UCSFOLLOW** system variable allows you to change how an object is displayed in relation to the UCS. There are also system variables that display a variety of information about the current UCS. These variables include:

- **UCSAXISANG.** (Stored value) The default rotation angle for the **X**, **Y**, or **Z** option of the **UCS** command.
- **UCSBASE.** The name of the UCS used to define the origin and orientation of the orthographic UCS settings. It can be any named UCS.
- **UCSDETECT.** (On or off) Turns the dynamic UCS function on and off. The **Allow/Disallow Dynamic UCS** button on the status bar controls this variable, as does the [Ctrl]+[D] key combination.
- **UCSORTHO.** (On or off) If set to 1 (on), the related orthographic UCS setting is automatically restored when an orthographic view is restored. If turned off, the current UCS is retained when an orthographic view is restored.
- **UCSNAME.** (Read only) Displays the name of the current UCS.
- **UCSORG.** (Read only) Displays the XYZ origin value of the current UCS.
- **UCSVIEW.** (On or off) If this variable is set to 1 (on), the current UCS is saved with the view when a view is saved. Otherwise, the UCS is not saved with the view.
- **UCSVP.** This controls which UCS is displayed in viewports. The default value is 1, which means that if you change a UCS in one viewport, the UCS changes in all of them. But, if you want the UCS of one or more viewports to remain unchanged, regardless of how you change the UCS in other viewports, set this variable to 0. Each viewport can be set to either 0 or 1.
- **UCSXDIR.** (Read only) Displays the XYZ value of the X axis direction of the current UCS.
- **UCSYDIR.** (Read only) Displays the XYZ value of the Y axis direction of the current UCS.

UCS options and variables can also be managed in the **Settings** tab of the **UCS** dialog box. See **Figure 5-10.** The settings in this tab are:

- **Save UCS with viewport.** If checked, the current UCS settings are saved with the viewport and the **UCSVP** system variable is set to 1. This variable can be set for each viewport in the drawing. Viewports in which this setting is turned off, or unchecked, will always display the UCS settings of the current active viewport.
- **Update view to Plan when UCS is changed.** This setting controls the **UCSFOLLOW** system variable. When checked, the variable is set to 1. When unchecked, the variable is set to 0.

Chapter Test

Answer the following questions. Write your answers on a separate sheet of paper or complete the electronic chapter test on the Student CD.

1. Explain *spherical coordinate entry.*
2. Explain *cylindrical coordinate entry.*
3. A new point is to be drawn 4.5″ from the last point. It is to be located at a 63° angle in the XY plane, and at a 35° angle from the XY plane. Write the proper spherical coordinate notation.
4. Write the proper cylindrical coordinate notation for locating a point 4.5″ in the horizontal direction from the origin, 3.6″ along the Z axis, and at a 63° angle in the XY plane.
5. Name the command that is used to draw 3D polylines.
6. Why is the command in question 5 needed?
7. Which command is used to change a 3D polyline into a B-spline curve?
8. How does the **SPLFRAME** system variable affect the B-spline curve created with the command in question 7?
9. What is the *WCS?*

10. What is a *user coordinate system (UCS)?*
11. What effect does the **Origin** option of the **UCSICON** command have on the UCS icon display?
12. Describe how to rotate the UCS so that the Z axis is tilted 30° toward the WCS X axis.
13. How do you return to the WCS from any UCS?
14. Which command controls the display of the user coordinate system icon?
15. What is a *dynamic UCS* and how is one activated?
16. What is the function of the **3 Point** option of the **UCS** command?
17. How do you automatically create a display that is plan to a new UCS?
18. What do you do so that the UCS icon is displayed at the origin of the current user coordinate system?
19. How do you move the UCS along the current Z axis?
20. What is the function of the **Object** option of the **UCS** command?
21. The **Face** option of the **UCS** command can be used on which types of objects?
22. What is the function of the **Apply** option of the **UCS** command?
23. In which dialog box is the **Orthographic UCSs** tab located?
24. Which command displays the **UCS** dialog box?
25. What appears in the **Named UCSs** tab of the **UCS** dialog box if the current UCS has not been saved?

Drawing Problems

For Problems 1–4, draw each object using solid primitives and Boolean commands to create composite solids. Measure the objects directly to obtain the necessary dimensions. Plot the drawings at a 3:1 scale using display methods specified by your instructor. Save the drawings as P05_(problem number).

1.

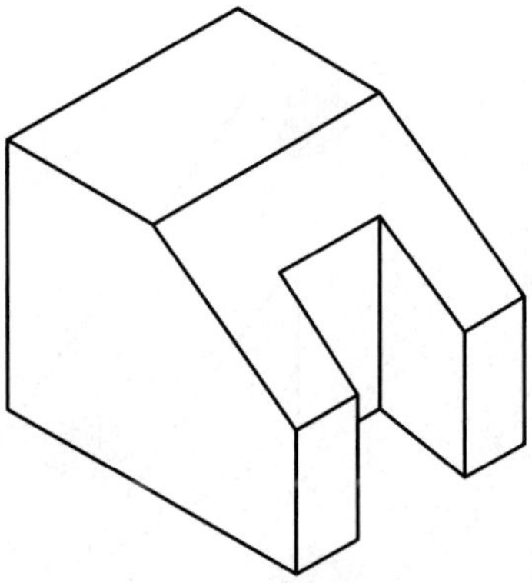

2.

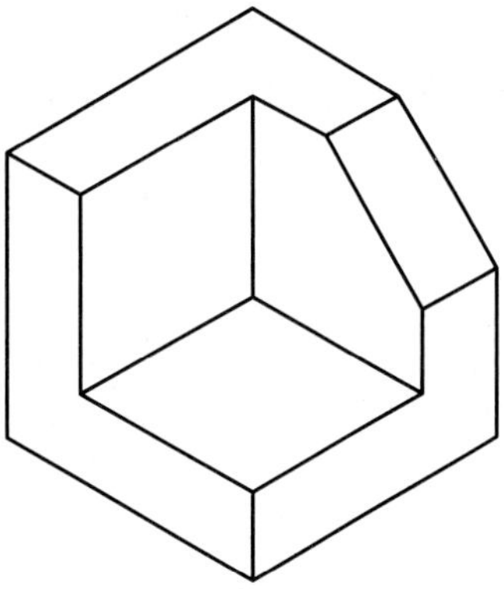

3.

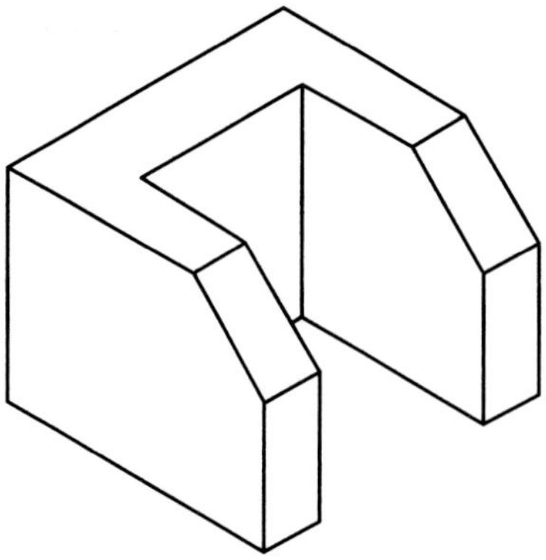

4.

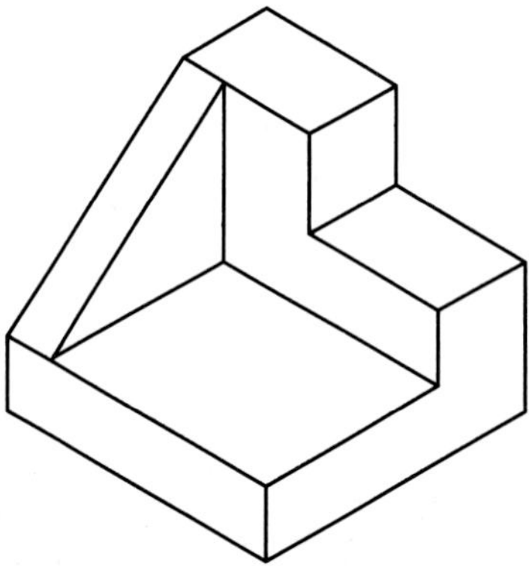

5. Create the mounting bracket shown below. Save the file as P05_05.

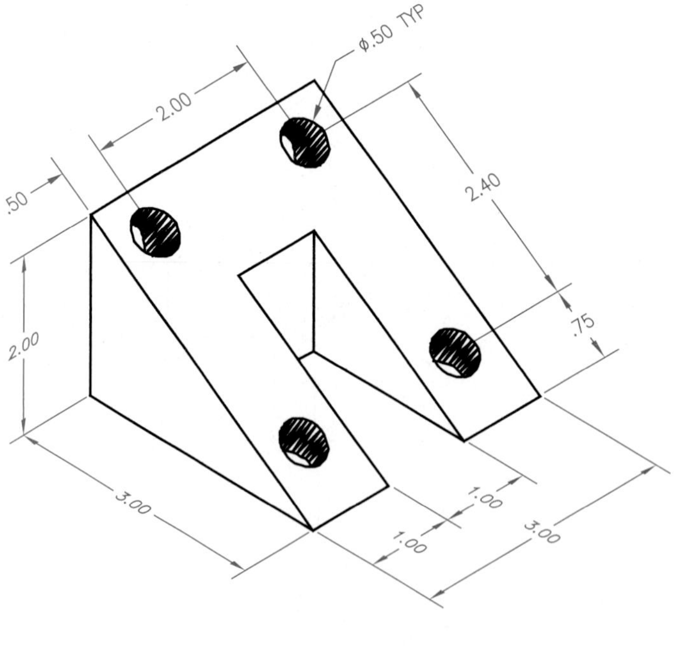

6. Create the computer speaker as shown below. The large-radius, arched surface is created by drawing a three-point arc. The second point of the arc passes through the point located by the .26 and 2.30 dimensions. Save the file as P05_06.

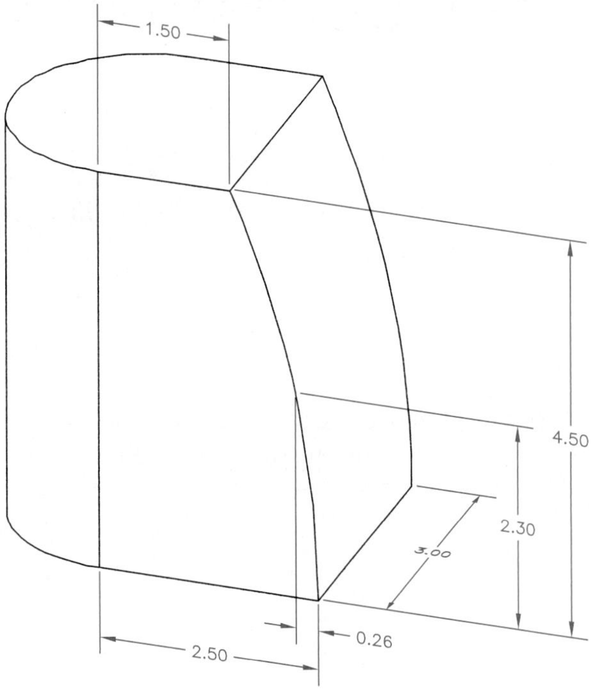

*For Problems 7–9, draw each object using solid primitives and Boolean commands to create composite solids. Use the dimensions provided. Save the drawings as **P05_**(problem number).*

7.

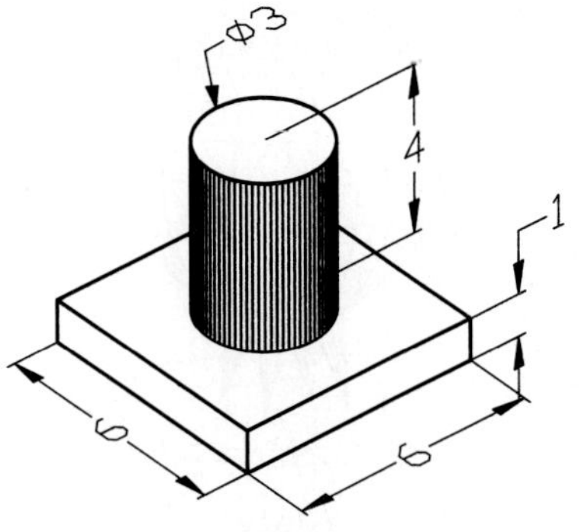

Pedestal #1

8.

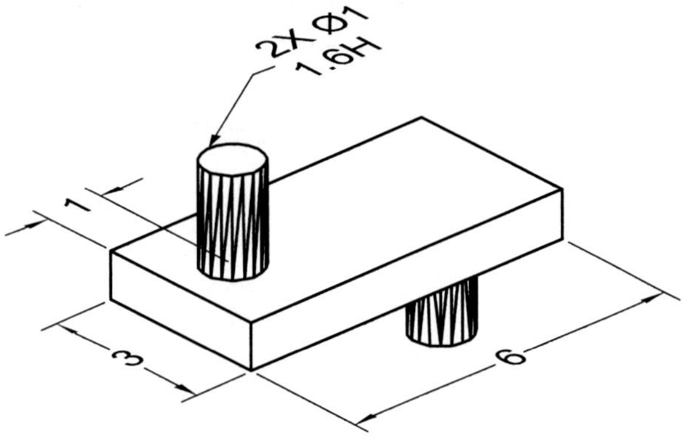

Locking Plate

9.

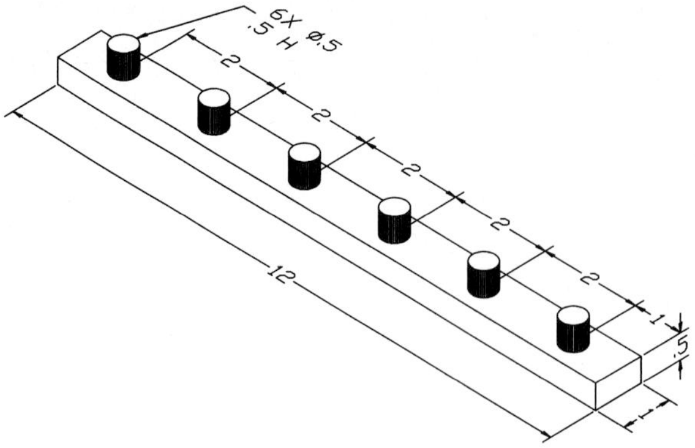

Pin Bar

10. Draw the ∅8″ pedestal shown. It is .5″ thick. The four feet are centered on a ∅7″ circle and are .5″ high. Save the drawing as P05_10.

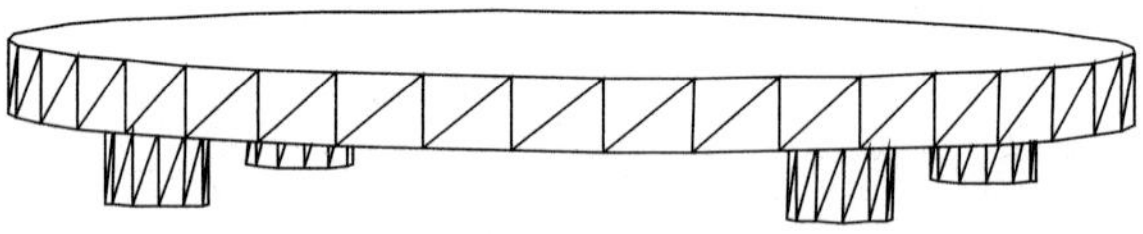

Pedestal #2

11. Four legs (cones), each 3″ high with a ∅1″ base, support this ∅10″ globe. Each leg tilts at an angle of 15° from vertical. The base is ∅12″ and .5″ thick. The bottom surface of the base is 8″ below the center of the globe. Save the drawing as P05_11.

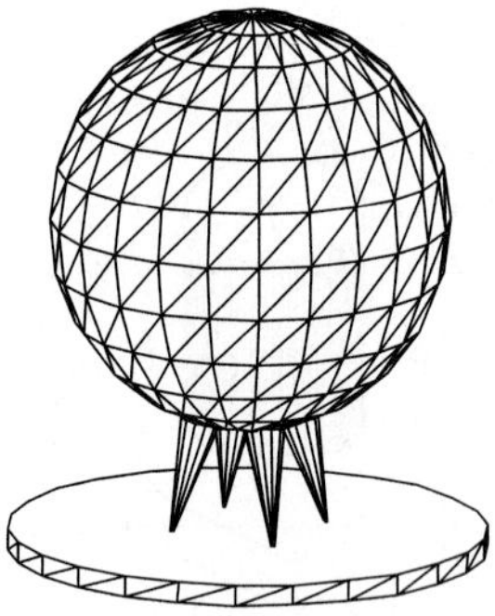

Globe

12. The table legs (A) are 2″ square and 17″ tall. They are 2″ in from each edge. The tabletop (B) is 24″ × 36″ × 1″. Save the drawing as P05_12.

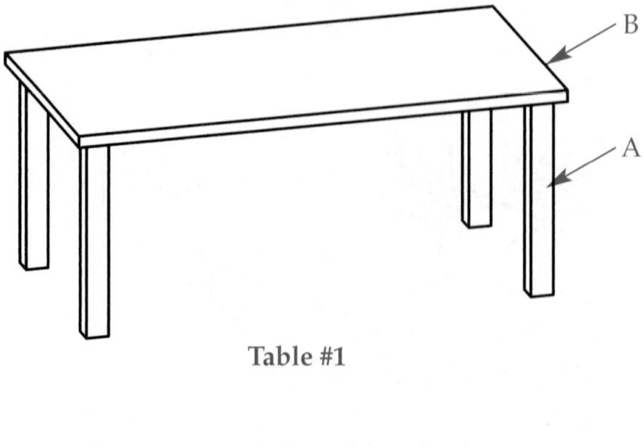

Table #1

13. The table legs (A) for the large table are ∅2″ and 17″ tall. The tabletop (B) is 24″ × 36″ × 1″. The table legs (C) for the small table are ∅2″ and 11″ tall. The tabletop (D) is 24″ × 14″ × 1″. All legs are 1″ in from the edges of the table. Save the drawing as P05_13.

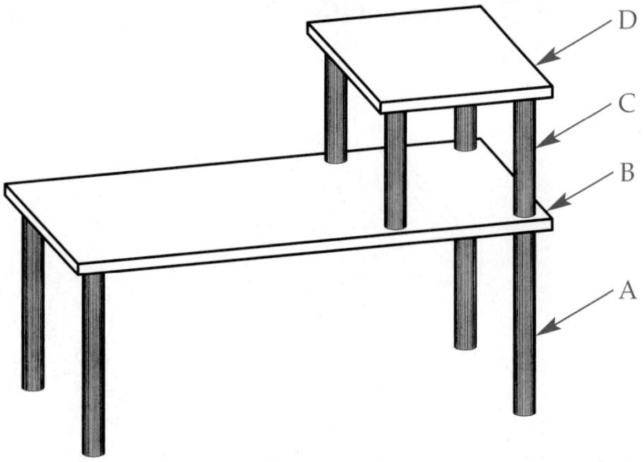

Table #2

14. The spherical objects (A) are ∅4″. Object B is 6″ long and ∅1.5″. Save the drawing as P05_14.

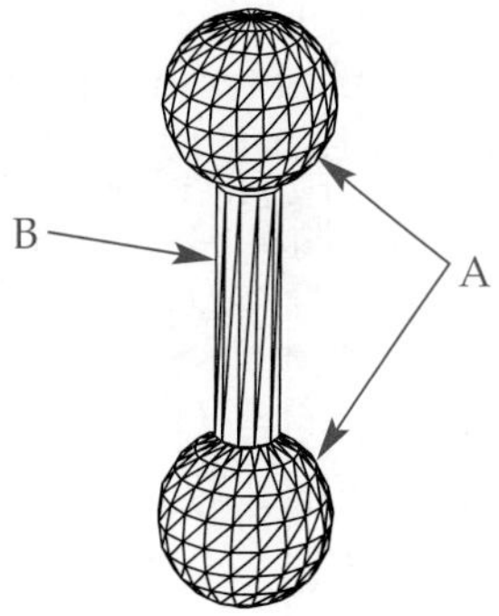

Dumbbell

15. Create the model of the globe using the dimensions shown. Save the file as P05_15.

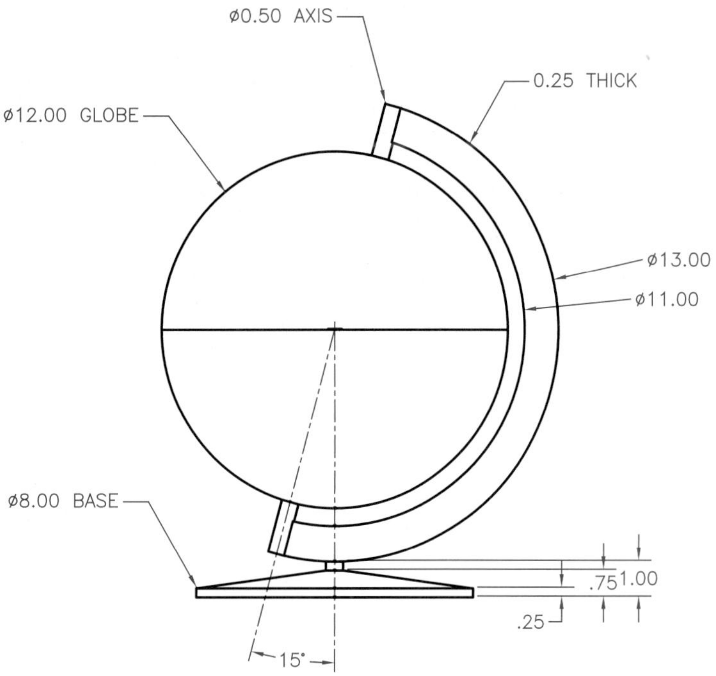

16. Object A is a ∅8″ cylinder that is 1″ tall. Object B is a ∅5″ cylinder that is 7″ tall. Object C is a ∅2″ cylinder that is 6″ tall. Object D is a .5″ × 8″ × .125″ box, and there are four pieces. The top surface of each piece is flush with the top surface of Object C. Object E is a ∅18″ cone that is 12″ tall. Create a smaller cone and hollow out Object E. Save the drawing as P05_16.

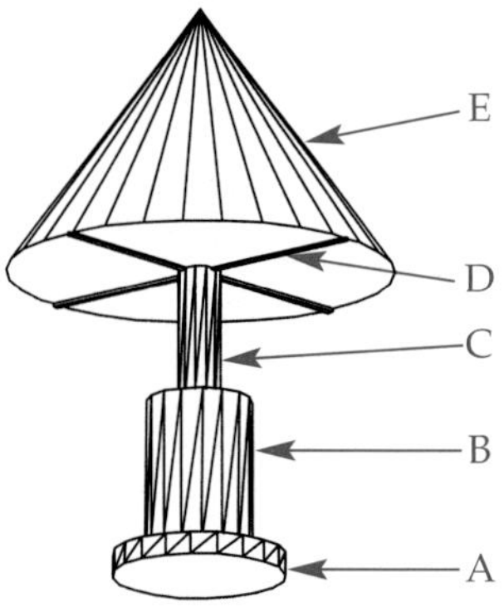

Table Lamp

17. Objects A and B are brick walls that are 5′ high. The walls are two bricks thick. Research the dimensions of standard brick and draw accordingly. Wall B is 7′ long and Wall A is 5′ long. Lamps are placed at each end of the walls. Object C is ∅2″ and 8″ tall. The center is offset from the end of the wall by a distance equal to the width of one brick. Object D is ∅10″. Save the drawing as P05_17.

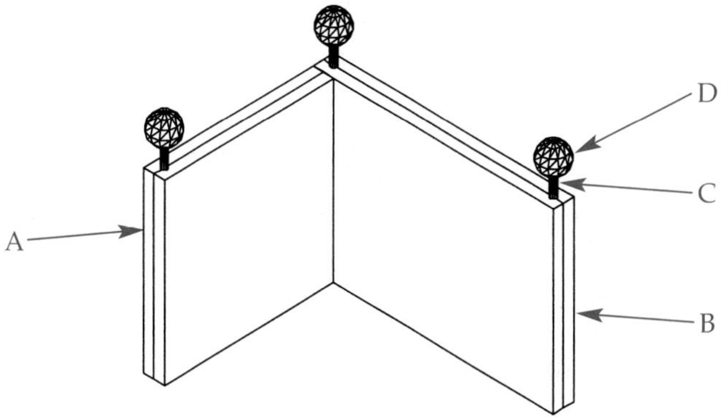

Garden Wall

18. Object A is Ø18″ and 1″ tall. Object B is Ø1.5″ and 6′ tall. Object C is Ø6″ and .5″ tall. Object D is a Ø10″ sphere. Object E is a U-shaped bracket to support the shade (Object F). There are two items; draw them an appropriate size. Object F has a Ø22″ base and is 12″ tall. Save the drawing as P05_18.

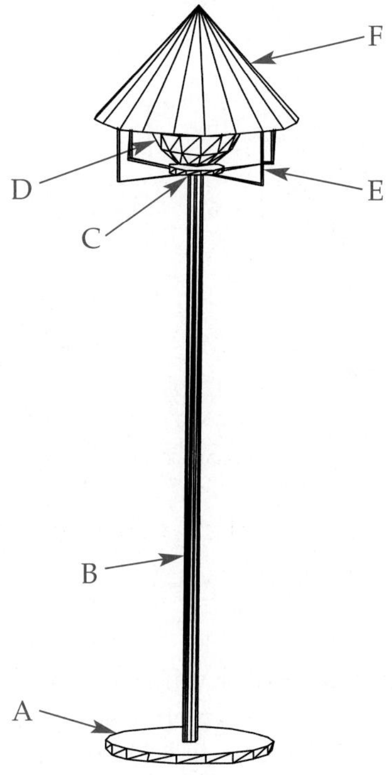

Floor Lamp

19. This is a concept sketch of a desk organizer. Create a solid model using the dimensions given. Use a dynamic UCS when appropriate or create and save new UCSs as needed. Inside dimensions of compartments can vary, but the thickness between compartments should be consistent. Do not add dimensions to the drawing. Plot your drawing on a B-size sheet of paper in a visual style specified by your instructor. Save the drawing as P05_19.

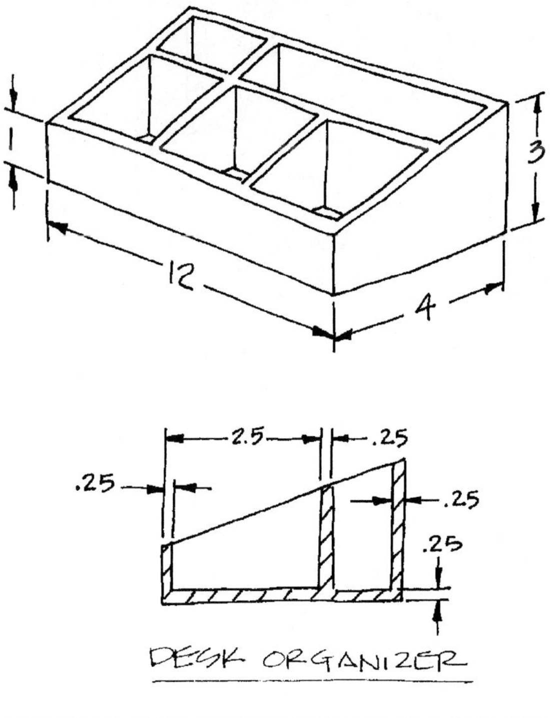

Drawing Problems - Chapter 5

20. This is a concept sketch of a pencil holder. Create a solid model using the dimensions given. Use a dynamic UCS when appropriate or create and save new UCSs as needed. Do not add dimensions to the drawing. Plot your drawing on a B-size sheet of paper in a visual style specified by your instructor. Save the drawing as P05_20.

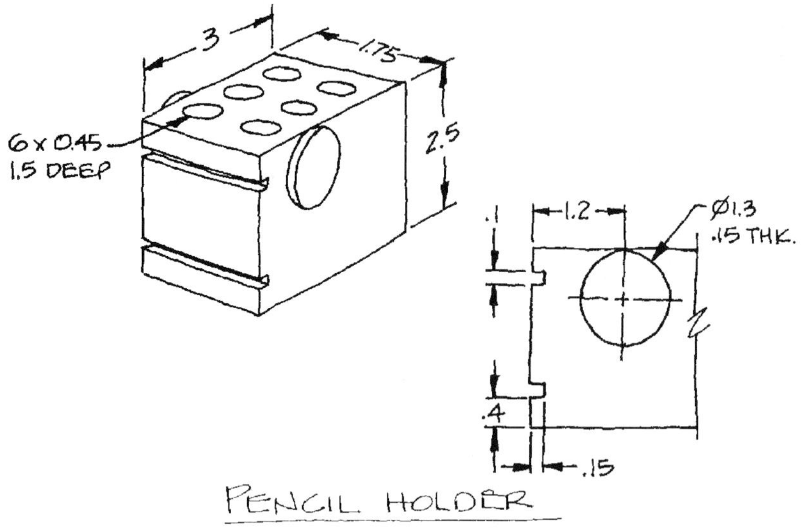

21. This is an engineering sketch of a window blind mounting bracket. Create a solid model using the dimensions given. Use a dynamic UCS when appropriate or create and save new UCSs as needed. Do not add dimensions to the drawing. Create two plots, each of a different view, on B-size paper in the visual styles specified by your instructor. Save the drawing as P05_21.

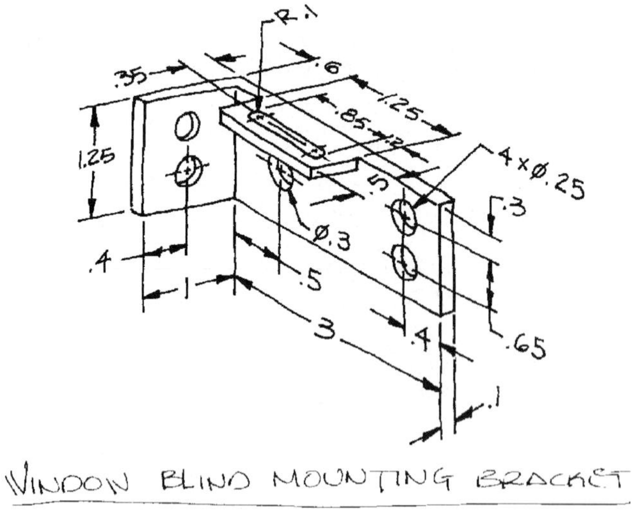

CHAPTER 6

Using Model Space Viewports

Learning Objectives

After completing this chapter, you will be able to:

- ✓ Describe the function of model space viewports.
- ✓ Create and save viewport configurations.
- ✓ Alter the current viewport configuration.
- ✓ Use multiple viewports to construct a drawing.

A variety of views can be displayed in a drawing at one time using model space viewports. This is especially useful when constructing 3D models. Using the **VPORTS** command, you can divide the drawing area into two or more smaller areas. These areas are called ***viewports.*** Each viewport can be configured to display a different 2D or 3D view of the model.

The ***active viewport*** is the viewport in which a command will be applied. Any viewport can be made active, but only one can be active at a time. As objects are added or edited, the results are shown in all viewports. A variety of viewport configurations can be saved and recalled as needed. This chapter discusses the use of viewports and shows how they can be used for 3D constructions.

Understanding Viewports

The AutoCAD drawing area can be divided into a maximum of 64 viewports. However, this is impractical due to the small size of each viewport. Four viewports are usually the maximum number practical to display at one time. The number of viewports you need depends on the model you are drawing. Each viewport can show a different view of an object. This makes it easier to construct 3D objects.

NOTE

The **MAXACTVP** (maximum active viewports) system variable sets the number of viewports that can be used at one time. The initial value is 64, which is the highest setting.

There are two types of viewports used in AutoCAD. The type of viewport created depends on whether it is defined in model space or paper space. ***Model space*** is the space, or mode, where the drawing is constructed. ***Paper space,*** or layout space, is the space where a drawing is laid out to be plotted. Viewports created in model space are called ***tiled viewports.*** Viewports created in paper space are called ***floating viewports.***

Model space is active by default when you start AutoCAD. Model space viewports are created with the **VPORTS** command. These viewport configurations cannot be plotted because they are for display purposes only. If you plot from model space, the contents of the active viewport are plotted. Tiled viewports are not AutoCAD objects. They are referred to as *tiled* because the edges of each viewport are placed side to side, as with floor tile, and they cannot overlap.

Floating (paper space) viewports are used to lay out the views of a drawing before plotting. They are described as *floating* because they can be moved around and overlapped. Paper space viewports are objects and they can be edited. These viewports can be thought of as "windows" cut into a sheet of paper to "see into" model space. You can then insert, or *reference,* different scaled drawings (views) into these windows. For example, architectural details or sections and details of complex mechanical parts may be referenced. Detailed discussions of paper space viewports are provided in *AutoCAD and Its Applications—Basics.*

The **VPORTS** command can be used to create viewports in a paper space layout. The process is very similar to that used to create model space viewports, which is discussed next. You can also use the **MVIEW** command to create paper space viewports.

Creating Viewports

Creating model space viewports is similar to working with a multiview layout in manual drafting. In a manual multiview layout, several views are drawn on the same sheet. You can switch from one view to another simply by moving your pencil. With model space viewports, you simply pick with your pointing device in the viewport in which you wish to work. The picked viewport becomes active. Using viewports is a good way to construct 3D models because all views are updated as you draw. However, viewports are also useful when creating 2D drawings.

The project on which you are working determines the number of viewports needed. Keep in mind that the more viewports you display on your screen, the smaller the view in each viewport. Small viewports may not be useful to you. Four different viewport configurations are shown in **Figure 6-1.** As you can see, when 16 viewports are displayed, the viewports are very small. Normally, two to four viewports are used.

VPORTS

Ribbon
View
> Viewports
New

Type
VPORTS

Menu
View
> Viewports

A layout of one to four viewports can be quickly created by using the **Viewports** dialog box, which is displayed with the **VPORTS** command, or by selecting from the options in the **Viewports** cascading menu of the **View** menu or the drop-down list in the **Viewports** tab on the **View** tab of the ribbon. See **Figure 6-2.** A list of preset viewport configurations is provided in the **New Viewports** tab of the **Viewports** dialog box, **Figure 6-3.**

There are 12 preset viewport configurations from which to choose in the **New Viewports** tab, including six different options for three-viewport configurations. See **Figure 6-4.** When you pick the name of a configuration in the **Standard viewports:** list, the viewport arrangement is displayed in the **Preview** area. After you have made a selection, you can save the configuration by entering a name in the **New name:** text box and then picking **OK** to close the dialog box. When the **Viewports** dialog box closes, the configuration is displayed on screen.

Figure 6-1.
A—Two vertical viewports. B—Two horizontal viewports. C—Three viewports, with the largest viewport positioned at the right. D—Sixteen viewports.

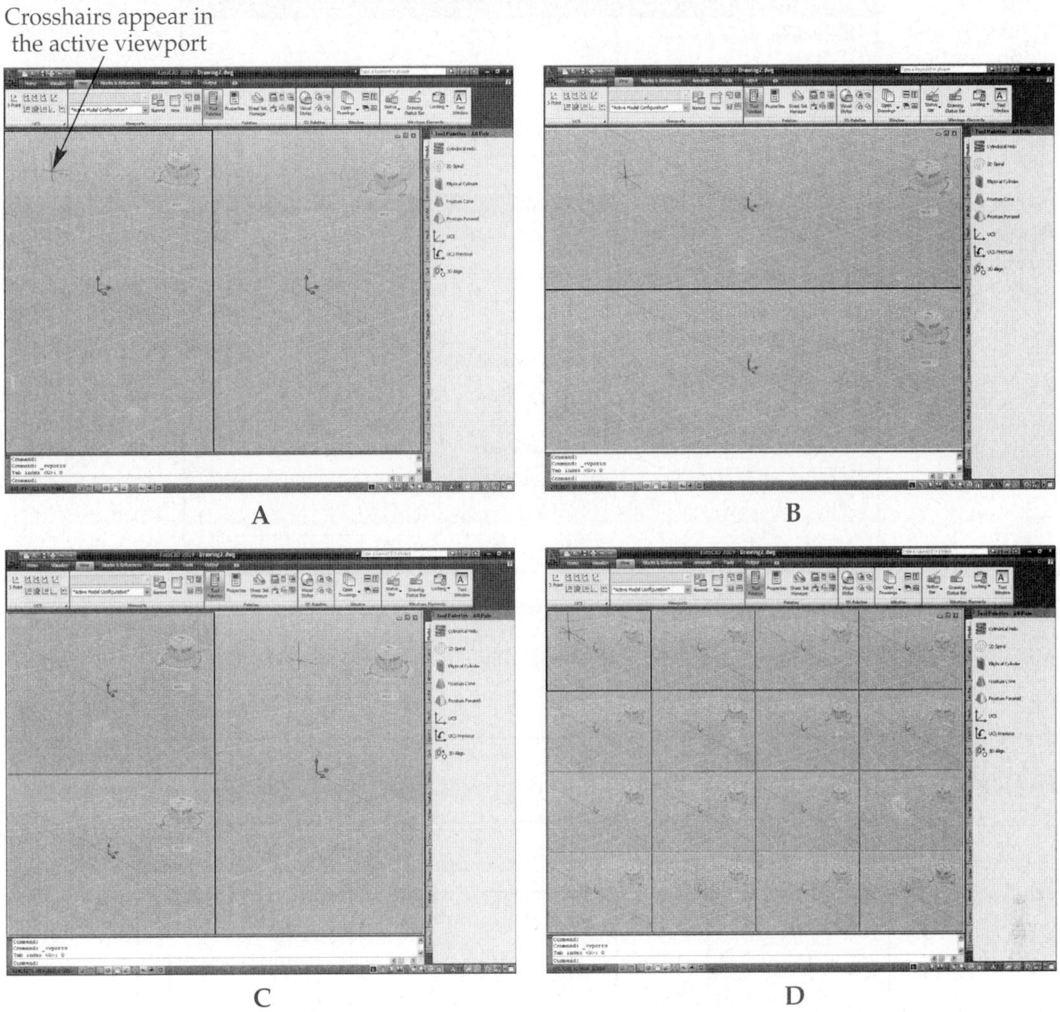

Figure 6-2.
Viewport configuration options can be selected from the **Viewports** cascading menu in the **View** menu.

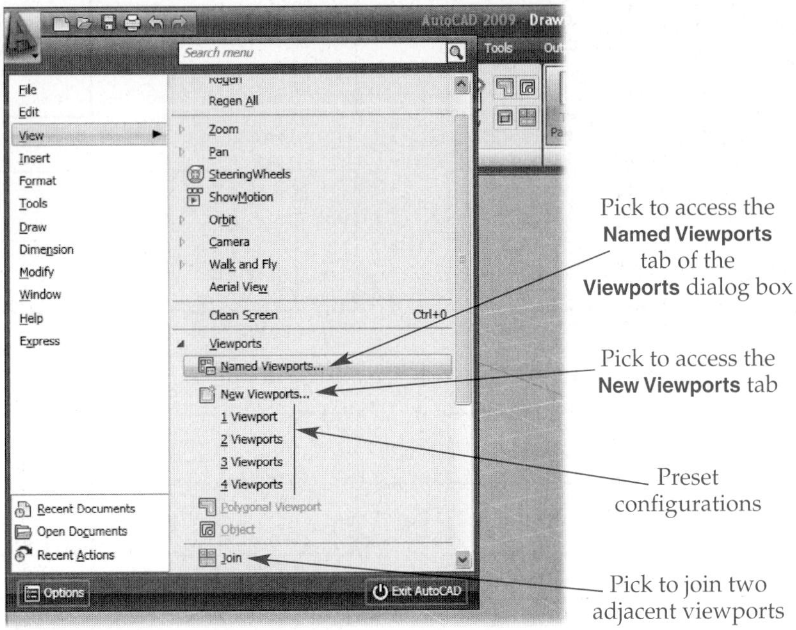

Figure 6-3.
Viewports are created using the **New Viewports** tab of the **Viewports** dialog box.

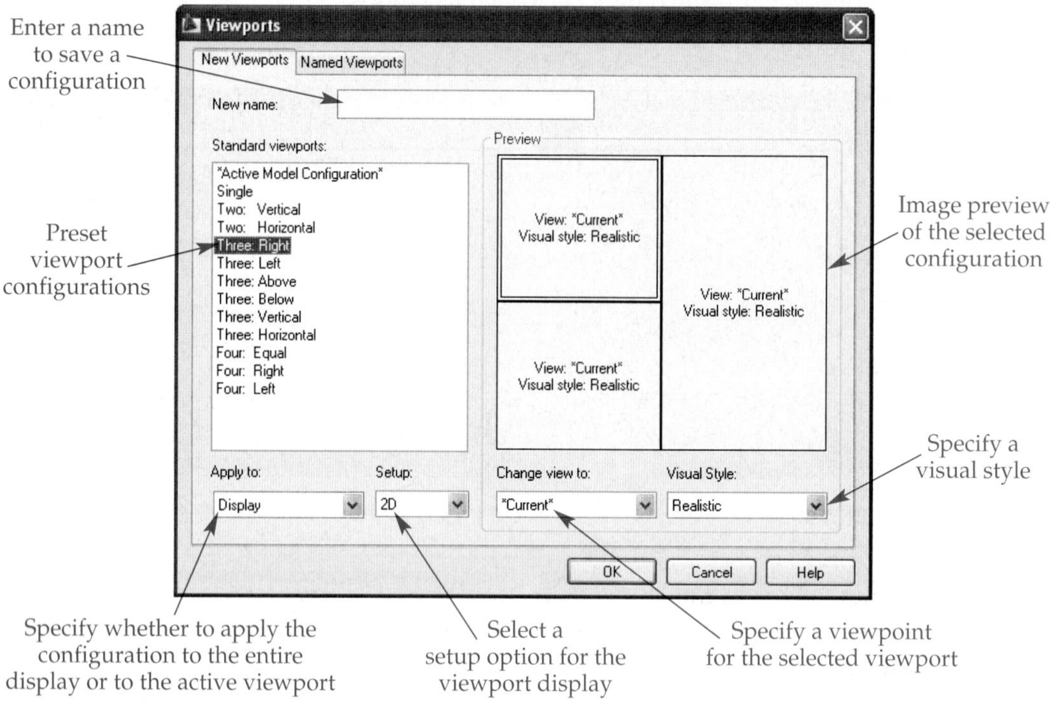

Figure 6-4.
Twelve preset tiled viewport configurations are provided in the **Viewports** dialog box.

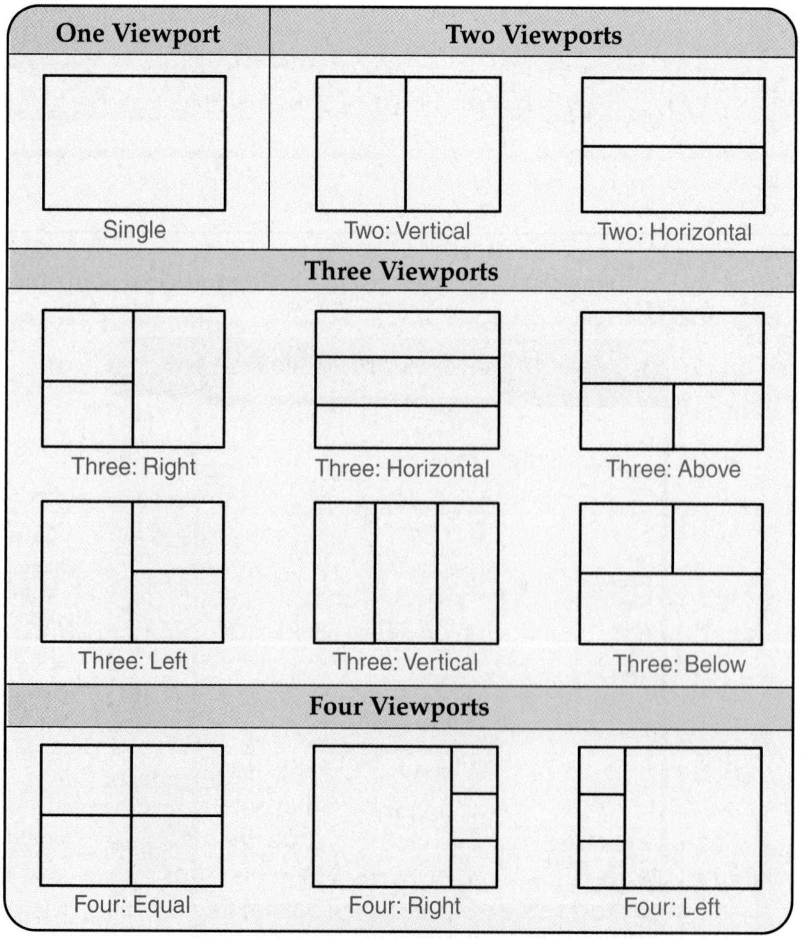

PROFESSIONAL TIP

Notice in **Figure 6-1** that the UCS icon is displayed in all viewports. This is an easy way to tell that several separate screens are displayed, rather than different views of the drawing.

Making a Viewport Active

After a viewport configuration has been created, a thick line surrounds the active viewport. When the screen cursor is moved inside of the active viewport, it appears as crosshairs. When moved into an inactive viewport, the screen cursor becomes an arrow.

Any viewport can be made active by moving the cursor into the desired viewport and pressing the pick button. You can also press the [Ctrl]+[R] key combination to switch viewports, or use the **CVPORT** (current viewport) system variable. Only one viewport can be active at a time.

Command: **CVPORT↵**
Enter new value for CVPORT <*current*>: **3↵**

The current value given is the ID number of the active viewport. The ID number is automatically assigned by AutoCAD, starting with 2. To change viewports with the **CVPORT** system variable, simply enter a different ID number. Using the **CVPORT** system variable is also a good way to determine the ID number of a viewport. The number 1 is not a valid viewport ID number.

PROFESSIONAL TIP

Each viewport can have its own view, viewpoint, UCS, zoom scale, limits, grid spacing, and snap setting. Specify the drawing aids in all viewports before saving the configuration. When a viewport is restored, all settings are restored as well.

Managing Defined Viewports

VPORTS

Ribbon
View
> Viewports
Named

Type
VPORTS

Menu
View
> Viewports
> Named Viewports...

If you are working with several different viewport configurations, it is easy to restore, rename, or delete existing viewports. You can do so using the **Viewports** dialog box. To access a list of named viewports, open the dialog box and select the **Named Viewports** tab. See **Figure 6-5.** To display a viewport configuration, highlight its name in the **Named viewports:** list and then pick the **OK** button.

Assume you have saved the current viewport configuration. Now, you want to work in a specific viewport, but do not need other viewports displayed on screen. First, pick the viewport you wish to work in to make it active. Open the **Viewports** dialog box, pick the **New Viewports** tab, and then pick **Single**. The **Preview** area displays the single viewport. Pick the **OK** button to exit. The active viewport you selected is displayed on screen. To restore the original viewport configuration, redisplay the **Viewports** dialog box, pick the **Named Viewports** tab, and then select the name of the saved viewport configuration. The **Preview** area displays the selected viewport configuration. Pick the **OK** button to exit.

Viewports can also be renamed and deleted using the **Named Viewports** tab of the **Viewports** dialog box. To rename a viewport, right-click on the viewport name and pick **Rename** from the shortcut menu. You can also single-click on a highlighted name. When the name becomes highlighted text, type the new name and press [Enter]. To delete a viewport configuration, right-click on the viewport name and pick **Delete** from the shortcut menu. You can also press the [Delete] key to delete the highlighted viewport. Press **OK** to exit the dialog box.

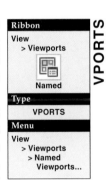

Apply to

When a preset viewport configuration is selected from the **Standard viewports:** list, it can be applied to either the entire display or the current viewport. The previous examples have shown how to create viewports that replace the entire display. Applying a configuration to the active viewport rather than the entire display can be useful when you need to display additional viewports.

For example, first create a configuration of three viewports using the Three:Right configuration option. Then, with the right (large) viewport active, open the **Viewports** dialog box again. Notice that the drop-down list under **Apply to:** is grayed out. Now, pick one of the standard configurations. This enables the **Apply to:** drop-down list. The default option is Display, which means the selected viewport configuration will replace the current display. Pick the drop-down list arrow to reveal the second option, Current Viewport. Pick this option and then pick the **OK** button. Notice that the selected viewport configuration has been applied to only the active (right) viewport. See **Figure 6-8.**

Setup

Viewports can be set up to display views in 2D or 3D. The 2D and 3D options are provided in the **Setup:** drop-down list. Displaying different views while working on a drawing allows you to see the results of your work on each view, since changes are reflected in each viewport as you draw. The selected viewport **Setup:** option controls the types of views available in the **Change view to:** drop-down list.

Change view to

The views that can be displayed in a selected viewport are listed in the **Change view to:** drop-down list. If the **Setup:** drop-down list is set to 2D, the views available to be displayed are limited to the current view and any named views. If 3D is active, the options include all of the standard orthographic and isometric views along with named views. When an orthographic or isometric view is selected for a viewport, the resulting orientation is shown in the **Preview** area. To assign a different viewpoint to a viewport, simply pick within a viewport in the **Preview** area to make it active and

Figure 6-8.
The selected viewport configuration has been applied to the active viewport within the original configuration.

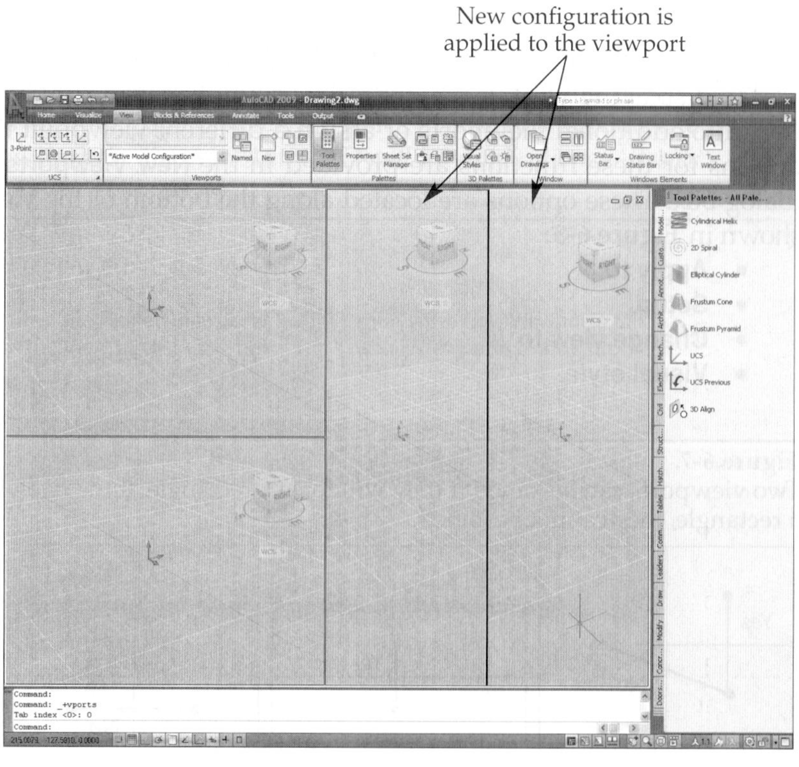

New configuration is applied to the viewport

then pick a viewpoint from the **Change view to:** drop-down list. Important: if you set a viewport to one of the orthographic preset views, the UCS is also (by default) changed in that viewport to the corresponding preset.

Visual style

A visual style can be specified for a viewport. Pick within a viewport in the **Preview** area to make it active and then select a visual style from the **Visual Style:** drop-down list. All preset and saved visual styles are available in the drop-down list.

PROFESSIONAL TIP

Displaying saved viewport configurations can be automated by using custom menus. Custom menus are easy to create. If a standard naming convention is used, these named configurations can be saved with template drawings. This creates a consistent platform that all students or employees can use.

Exercise 6-2

Complete the exercise on the Student CD.

Drawing in Multiple Viewports

When used with 2D drawings, viewports allow you to display a view of the entire drawing, plus views showing portions of the drawing. This is similar to using the **VIEW** command, except you can have several views on screen at once. You can also adjust the zoom magnification in each viewport to suit different areas of the drawing.

Viewports are also a powerful aid when constructing 3D models. You can specify different viewpoints in each viewport and see the model take shape as you draw. A model can be quickly constructed because you can switch from one viewport to another while drawing and editing. For example, you can draw a line from a point in one viewport to a point in another viewport simply by changing viewports while inside the **LINE** command. The result is shown in each viewport.

In Chapter 5, you constructed a solid object. It was a base that had an angled surface from which a cylinder projected. See Figure 6-9. Now, you will construct the object using two viewports. First, create a vertical configuration of two viewports. In the **Viewports** dialog box, set the right-hand viewport to display the southeast isometric. Also, select the Conceptual visual style. Set the left-hand viewport to display the front view. Remember, this will also set the UCS to the front preset orthographic UCS in that viewport. Also, select the 3D Wireframe visual style for the left-hand viewport. Close the dialog box and make the left-hand viewport active. You may also want to set the parallel projection current in both viewports.

VPORTS

Ribbon
View
> Viewports
New

Type
VPORTS

Menu
View
> Viewports

Next, draw a polyline using the coordinates shown in Figure 6-10. You may want to turn off dynamic input to disable direct-distance entry. Be sure to use the **Close** option for the last segment. As you construct the side view, you can clearly see its true size and shape in the left-hand viewport. At the same time, you can see the construction in 3D in the right-hand viewport. Notice that each viewport has a different UCS, as indicated by the UCS icon.

Figure 6-9.
You will construct the object from Chapter 5 using multiple viewports.

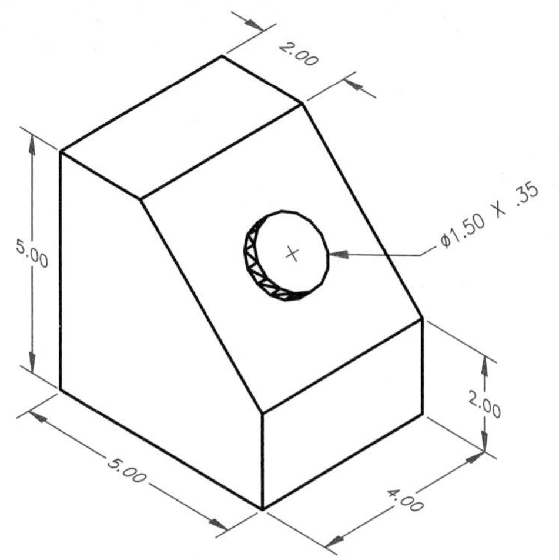

Figure 6-10.
The screen is divided into two viewports. A side view of the object appears in the left-hand viewport and a 3D view appears in the right-hand viewport. Notice the UCS icons.

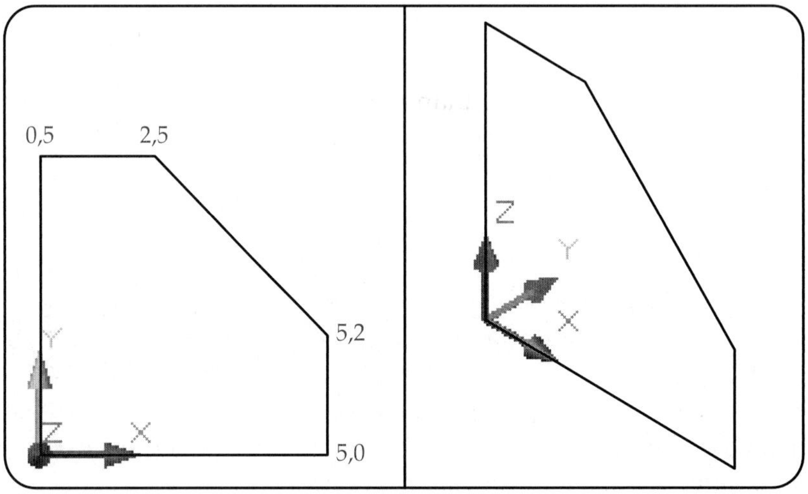

The next step is to extrude the shape to create the base. The **EXTRUDE** command is used to do so, as was the case in Chapter 5. In the left-hand viewport, select the **EXTRUDE** command, pick the polyline, and enter an extrusion height of –4 units. The front face of the object is now complete, Figure 6-11.

Now, the cylinder needs to be created on the angled face. First, split the left-hand viewport into two horizontal viewports (top and bottom) using the **New Viewports** tab of the **Viewports** dialog box. Set both of the new viewports to display the current view. Pick the **OK** button to close the dialog box. Then, make the upper-left viewport current and set it up to always display a plan view of the current UCS by setting the **UCSFOLLOW** system variable to 1.

Next, create a new UCS on the angled face. Use the **3 Point** option of the **UCS** command, which is described in Chapter 5. The pick points are shown in Figure 6-11; pick them in the right-hand viewport. Notice how the view in the upper-left viewport automatically changes to a plan view of the new current UCS.

Now, set the **Midpoint** object snap and turn on object snap tracking to draw the cylinder. Work in the right-hand viewport. When specifying the center of the base, acquire the midpoints of sides on the angled surface that are perpendicular to each other. Then, enter a diameter of 1.5 units and a height of .35 units. If you are having problems acquiring points, try switching to a parallel display instead of a perspective display.

Figure 6-11.
The base of the object is now complete. A new UCS will be created based on the pick points shown here. Alternately, a dynamic UCS can be used, as shown in Chapter 5.

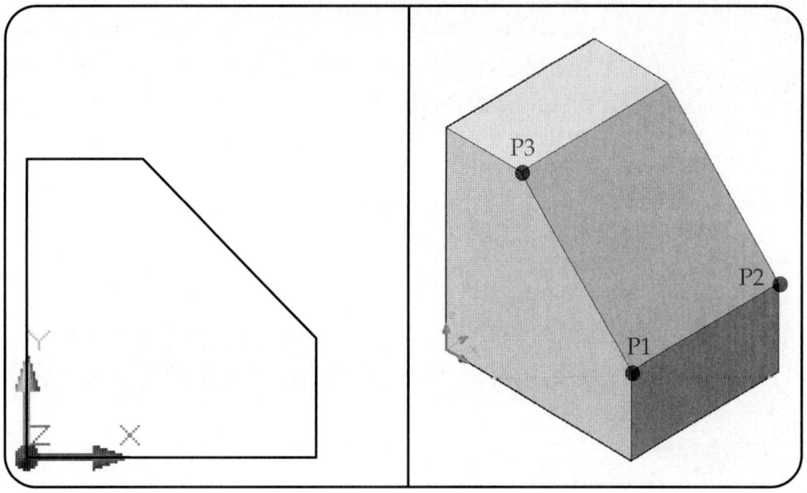

The object is now complete, **Figure 6-12.** Notice how the lower-left and right-hand viewports have different UCSs. Each viewport can have its own UCS. The view in the upper-left viewport is the plan view of the current UCS. If the lower-left viewport is made active, the plan view will be of the UCS in that viewport. By default, the UCS orientation in one viewport is not affected by a change to the UCS in another viewport unless the **UCSFOLLOW** system variable is set to 1 in a viewport. If a viewport arrangement is saved with several different UCS configurations, every named UCS remains intact and is displayed when the viewport configuration is restored.

The **REGEN** command affects only the current viewport. To regenerate all viewports at the same time, use the **REGENALL** command. This command can be entered by selecting **Regen All** from the **View** menu or typing REGENALL.

Type
REGENALL
Menu
View > Regen All

REGENALL

The Quick Text mode is controlled by the **REGEN** command. Therefore, if you are working with text displayed with the Quick Text mode in viewports, be sure to use the **REGENALL** command in order for the text to be regenerated in all viewports.

Figure 6-12.
The cylinder is drawn to complete the object. Notice the plan view in the upper-left viewport.

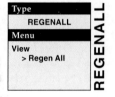

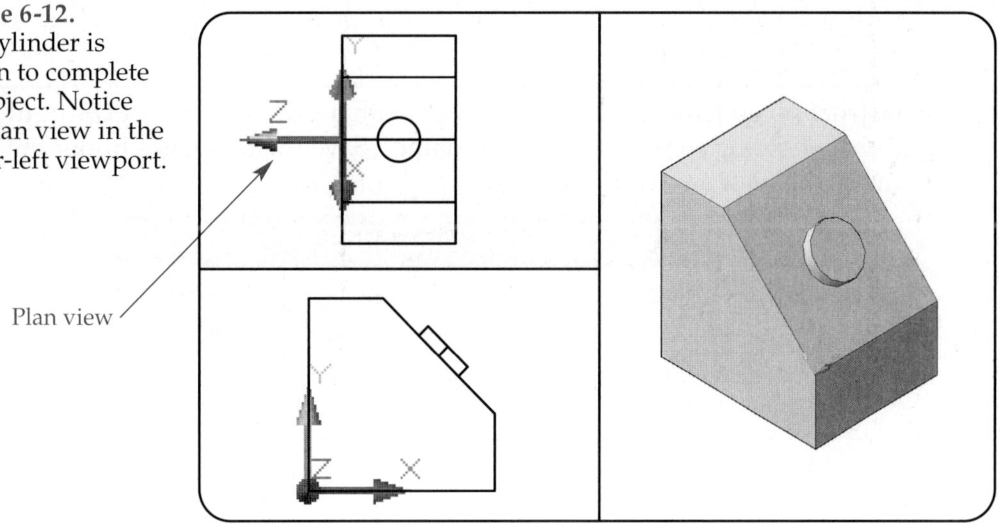

NOTE

The UCS configuration in each viewport is controlled by the **UCSVP** system variable. When **UCSVP** is set to 1 in a viewport, the UCS is independent from all other UCSs, which is the default. If **UCSVP** is set to 0 in a viewport, its UCS will change to reflect any changes to the UCS in the current viewport.

Exercise 6-3

Complete the exercise on the Student CD.

Chapter Test

Answer the following questions. Write your answers on a separate sheet of paper or complete the electronic chapter test on the Student CD.

1. What is the purpose of *viewports?*
2. How do you name a configuration of viewports?
3. What is the purpose of saving a configuration of viewports?
4. Explain the difference between *tiled* and *floating* viewports.
5. Name the system variable controlling the maximum number of viewports that can be displayed at one time.
6. How can a named viewport configuration be redisplayed on screen?
7. How can a list of named viewport configurations be displayed?
8. What relationship must two viewports have before they can be joined?
9. What is the significance of the dominant viewport when two viewports are joined?
10. When creating a new viewport configuration, how can you set a visual style in a viewport?

Drawing Problems

1. Construct seven template drawings, each with a preset viewport configuration. Use the following configurations and names. Save the templates under the same name as the viewport configuration.

Number of Viewports	Configuration	Name
2	Horizontal	TWO-H
2	Vertical	TWO-V
3	Right	THREE-R
3	Left	THREE-L
3	Above	THREE-A
3	Below	THREE-B
3	Vertical	THREE-V

2. Construct one of the problems from Chapter 3 using viewports. Use one of your template drawings from problem 6-1. Save the drawing as P06_02.

CHAPTER 7

Text and Dimensions in 3D

Learning Objectives

After completing this chapter, you will be able to:

✓ Create text with a thickness.
✓ Draw text that is plan to the current view.
✓ Dimension a 3D drawing.

Creating Text with Thickness

A thickness can be applied to text after it is created. This is done using the **Properties** palette. The thickness setting is located in the **General** section. Once a thickness is applied, the hidden lines can be removed using the **HIDE** command. **Figure 7-1** shows six different fonts as they appear with hidden lines removed after being given a thickness.

PROPERTIES

Ribbon
View > Palettes; Properties
Type
PROPERTIES; PR; [Ctrl]+[1]
Menu
Modify > Properties

Only text created using the **TEXT** and **DTEXT** commands (text object) can be assigned thickness. Text created with the **MTEXT** command (mtext object) cannot have thickness assigned to it. In addition, only AutoCAD SHX fonts can be given thickness. AutoCAD SHP shape fonts can be compiled into SHX fonts with the **COMPILE** command. The compiled fonts can then be used to create text with thickness. Windows TrueType fonts *cannot* be used to create text with thickness.

Figure 7-1.
Six different fonts with thickness after hidden lines are removed.

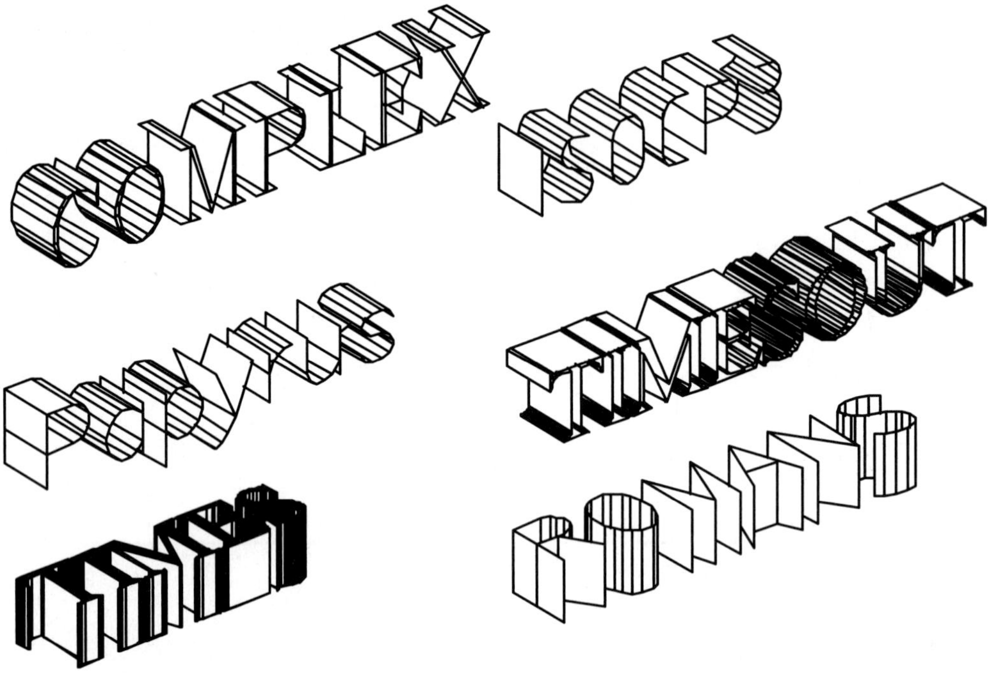

Text and the UCS

Text is created parallel to the XY plane of the UCS in which it is drawn. Therefore, if you wish to show text appearing on a specific plane, establish a new UCS on that plane before placing the text. Figure 7-2 shows several examples of text on different UCS XY planes.

Changing the Orientation of a Text Object

If text is improperly placed or created using the wrong UCS, it can be edited using grips or editing commands. Editing commands and grips are relative to the current UCS. For example, if text is drawn with the WCS current, you can use the **ROTATE** command to change the orientation of the text in the XY plane of the WCS. However, to

Figure 7-2.
Text located using three different UCSs.

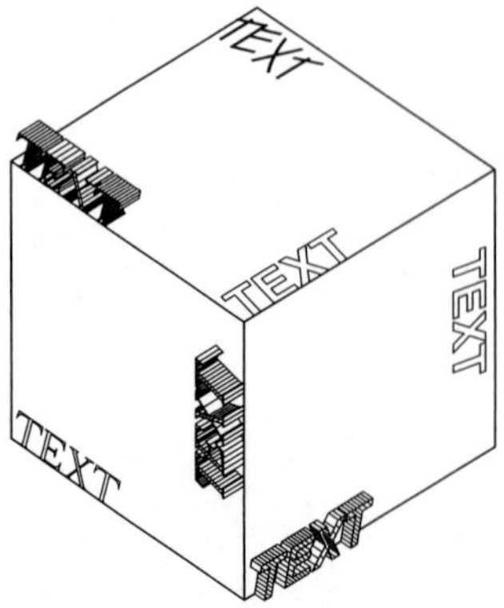

rotate the text so it tilts up from the XY plane of the WCS, you will need to change the UCS. Rotate the UCS as needed so the Z axis of the new UCS aligns with the axis about which you want to rotate. Then, the **ROTATE** command can be used to rotate the text. The **3DROTATE** command can also be used to avoid rotating the UCS. This command is discussed in Chapter 10.

Using the UCS View Option to Create a Title

It is often necessary to create a pictorial view of an object, but with a note or title that is plan to your point of view. For example, you may need to insert the title of a 3D view. See Figure 7-3. This is done with the **View** option of the **UCS** command, which is discussed in Chapter 5. With this option, a new UCS is created perpendicular to your viewpoint. However, the view remains unchanged. Inserted text will be horizontal (or vertical) in the current view. Name and save the UCS if you will use it again.

UCS

Ribbon
View
> UCS
View

Type
UCS

Menu
Tools
> New UCS
> View

Exercise 7-1

Complete the exercise on the Student CD.

Dimensioning in 3D

Three-dimensional objects are seldom dimensioned for manufacturing, but may be used for assembly. Dimensioned 3D drawings are most often used for some sort of presentation, such as displays, illustrations, parts manuals, or training manuals. All dimensions, including those shown in 3D, must be clear and easy to read. The most important aspect of applying dimensions to a 3D object is planning. That means following a few basic guidelines.

Creating a 3D Dimensioning Template Drawing

If you often create dimensioned 3D drawings, make a template drawing containing a few 3D settings. These are outlined on the following page.

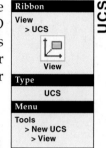

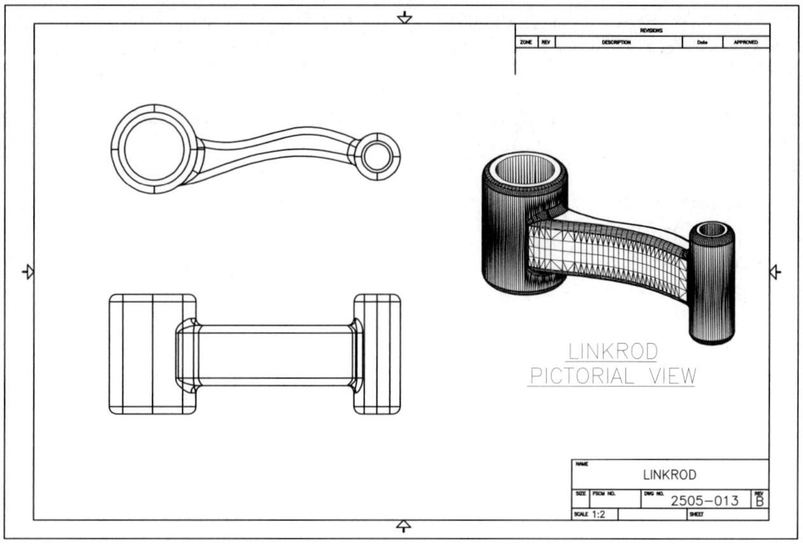

Figure 7-3.
This title (shown in color) has been correctly placed using the **View** option of the **UCS** command.

- Create named dimension styles with appropriate text heights. See *AutoCAD and Its Applications—Basics* for detailed information on dimensioning and dimension styles.
- Establish several named user coordinate systems that match the planes on which dimensions will be placed.
- If the preset isometric viewpoints will not serve your needs, establish and save several 3D viewpoints that can be used for different objects. These viewpoints will allow you to select the display that is best for reading dimensions.

Placing Dimensions in the Proper Plane

The location of dimensions and the plane on which they are placed are often a matter of choice. For example, **Figure 7-4** shows several options for placing a thickness dimension on an object. All of these are correct. However, several of the options can be eliminated when other dimensions are added. This illustrates the importance of planning.

The key to good dimensioning in 3D is to avoid overlapping dimension and extension lines in different planes. A freehand sketch can help you plan this. As you lay out the 3D sketch, try to group information items together. Dimensions, notes, and item tags should be grouped so that they are easy to read and understand. This technique is called ***information grouping.***

Figure 7-5A shows the object from **Figure 7-4** fully dimensioned using the aligned technique. Notice that the location dimension for the hole is placed on the top surface. This avoids dimensioning to hidden points. **Figure 7-5B** shows the same object dimensioned using the unilateral technique.

To create dimensions that properly display, it may be necessary to modify the dimension text rotation. The dimension shown in **Figure 7-6A** is inverted because the positive X and Y axes are incorrectly oriented. Using the **Properties** palette, change the text rotation value to 180. The dimension text is then properly displayed, **Figure 7-6B.** Alternately, you can rotate the UCS before drawing the dimension, but this may be more time-consuming.

PROFESSIONAL TIP

Prior to placing dimensions on a 3D drawing, you should determine the purpose of the drawing. For what will it be used? Just as dimensioning a drawing for manufacturing purposes is based on the function of the part, 3D dimensioning is based on the function of the drawing. This determines whether you use chain, datum, arrowless, architectural, or some other style of dimensioning. It also determines how completely the object is dimensioned.

Figure 7-4.
A thickness dimension can be located in many different places. All locations shown here are acceptable.

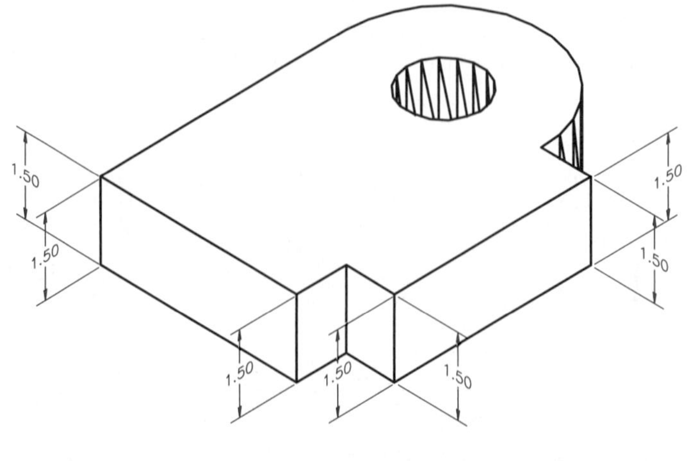

Figure 7-5.
A—An example of a 3D object dimensioned using the aligned technique. B—The object dimensioned with unilateral dimensions.

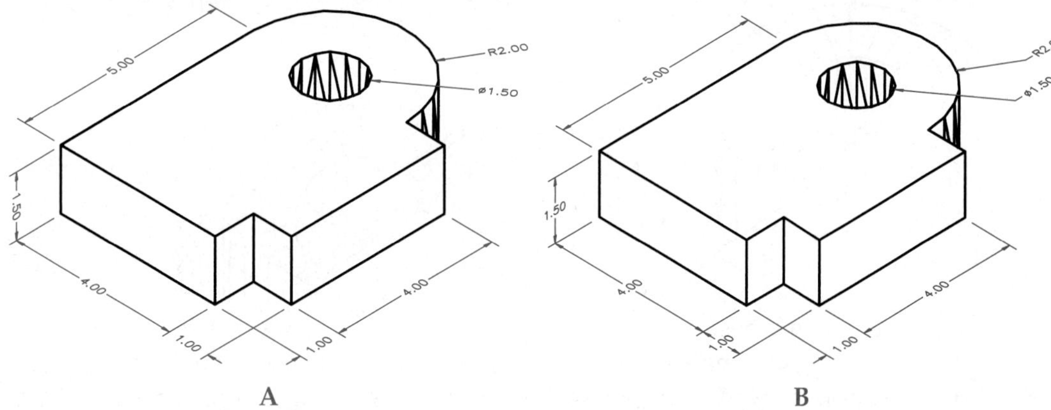

Figure 7-6.
A—This dimension text is inverted. B—The rotation value of the text is changed and the text reads correctly.

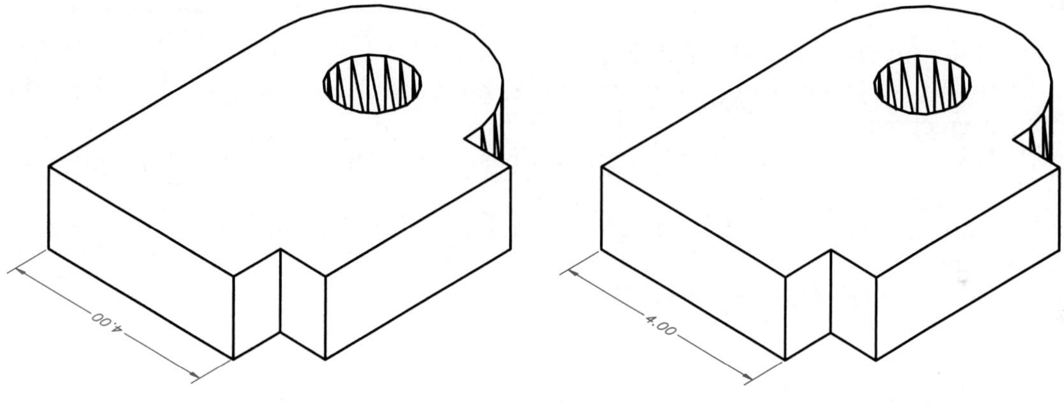

Placing Leaders and Radial Dimensions in 3D

Although standards such as ASME Y14.5M should be followed when possible, the nature of 3D drawing and the requirements of the project may determine how dimensions and leaders are placed. Remember, the most important aspect of dimensioning a 3D drawing is its presentation. Is it easy to read and interpret?

Leaders and radial dimensions can be placed on or perpendicular to the plane of the feature. Figure 7-7A shows the placement of leaders on the plane of the top surface. Figure 7-7B illustrates the placement of leaders and radial dimensions on two planes that are perpendicular to the top surface of the object. Remember that text, dimensions, and leaders are always created on the XY plane of the current UCS. Therefore, to create the layout in Figure 7-7B you must use more than one UCS.

Exercise 7-2

Complete the exercise on the Student CD.

Figure 7-7.
A—Leaders placed in the plane of the top surface. B—Leaders placed using two UCSs that are perpendicular to the top face.

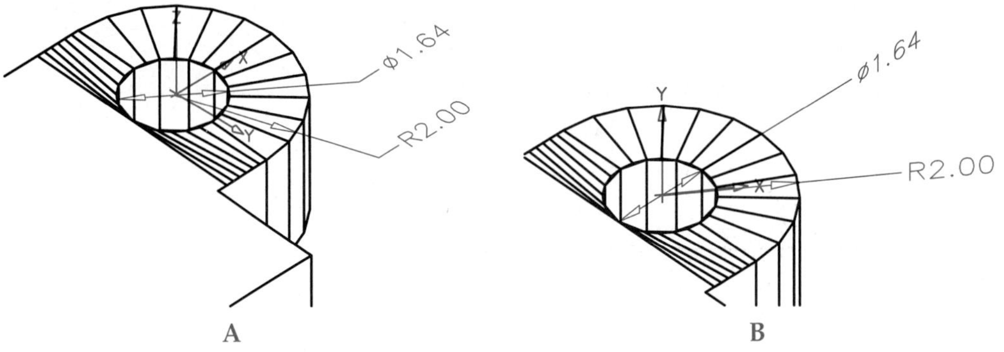

Chapter Test

Answer the following questions. Write your answers on a separate sheet of paper or complete the electronic chapter test on the Student CD.

1. How can you create 3D text with thickness?
2. If text is placed using the wrong UCS, how can it be edited to appear on the correct one?
3. How can text be horizontally placed based on your viewpoint if the object is displayed in 3D?
4. Name three items that should be a part of a 3D dimensioning template drawing.
5. What is *information grouping?*

Drawing Problems

1. This is a two-view orthographic drawing of a window valance mounting bracket. Create it as a solid model. Use solid primitives and Boolean commands as needed. Use the dimensions given. Similar holes have the same offset dimensions. Create new UCSs as needed. Display an appropriate pictorial view of the drawing. Then, add dimensions. Finally, add the material note so it is plan to the 3D view. Plot the drawing to scale on a C-size sheet of paper. Save the drawing as P07_01.

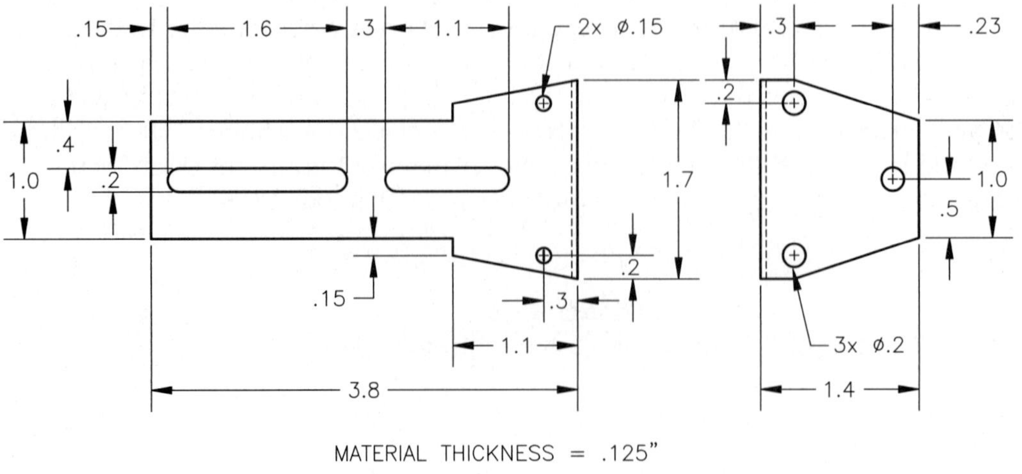

2. This is an orthographic drawing of a light fixture bracket. Create it as a solid model. Use solid primitives and Boolean commands as needed. Use the dimensions given. Similar holes have the same offset dimensions. Create new UCSs as needed. Display an appropriate pictorial view of the drawing. Then, add dimensions. Plot the drawing to scale on a C-size sheet of paper. Save the drawing as P07_02.

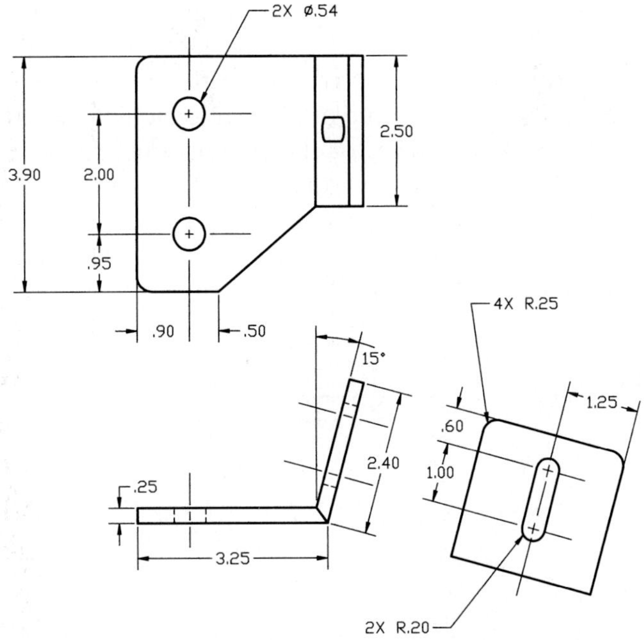

3. Create the end table as a solid model using solid primitives and Boolean commands as needed. The end result should be a single object. As a test of your object editing skills, try drawing the entire model by starting with only a single rectangle. You can copy, resize, extrude, and move objects as you create them from the single rectangle. Use the dimensions given and the following information to construct the model.
   A. Table height is 24″.
   B. Top of bottom shelf is 5″ off of the floor.
   C. Table legs must be located no less than 1/2″ from the tabletop edge.
   D. Shelf must be no closer than .75″ from the outside of table legs.
   E. Dimension the table as shown.
   F. Save the drawing as P07_03.

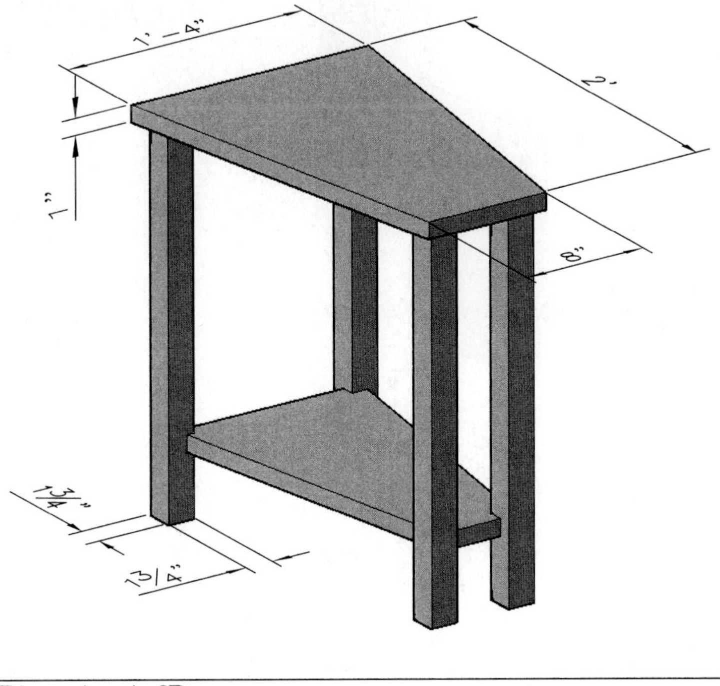

4. Shown below are the profiles of a roof gutter (for the collection of rainwater) and a gutter downspout. Draw the profiles in 3D using the dimensions shown. Use the following additional information to construct a 3D model like the one shown in the shaded view.
   A. Offset the gutter profile to create a material thickness of .025″. Be sure to close the ends to create a closed polyline so a 3D solid is created when it is extruded.
   B. Extrude the gutter profile 12″ to create a one-foot section.
   C. Relocate the downspout profile on the underside of the gutter.
   D. Construct an extrusion path for the downspout. Refer to the shaded view shown below, but use your own design.
   E. Extrude the downspout profile along the path.
   F. Dimension the end of the gutter profile in 3D.
   G. Save the drawing as P07_04.

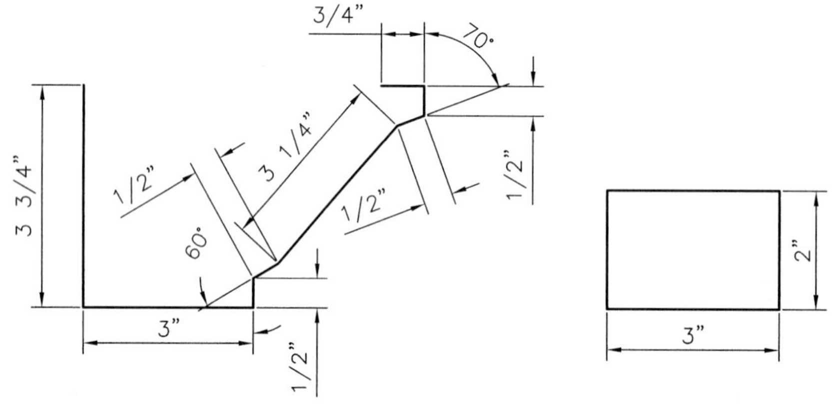

Gutter Profile

Downspout Profile

A

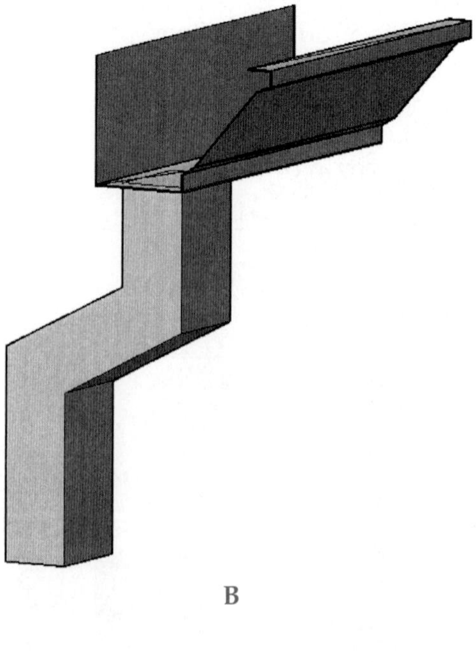
B

Problems 5–7. These problems are mechanical parts. Create a solid model of each part. Dimension each model. Place the title of each model so it is plan to the pictorial view. Plot the finished drawings on B-size paper. Save each drawing as P07_*(problem number).*

5.

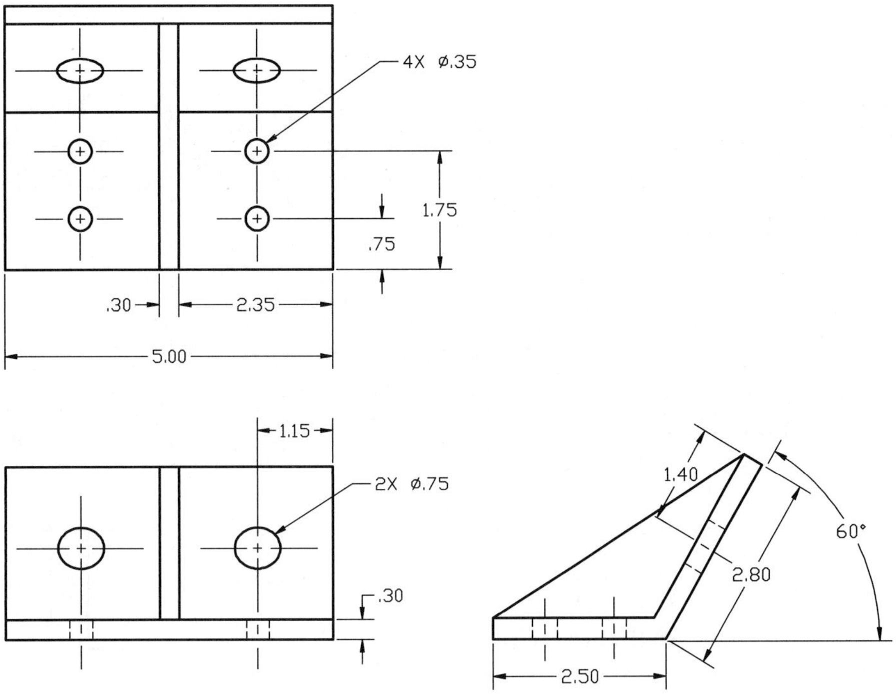

Angle Bracket

6.

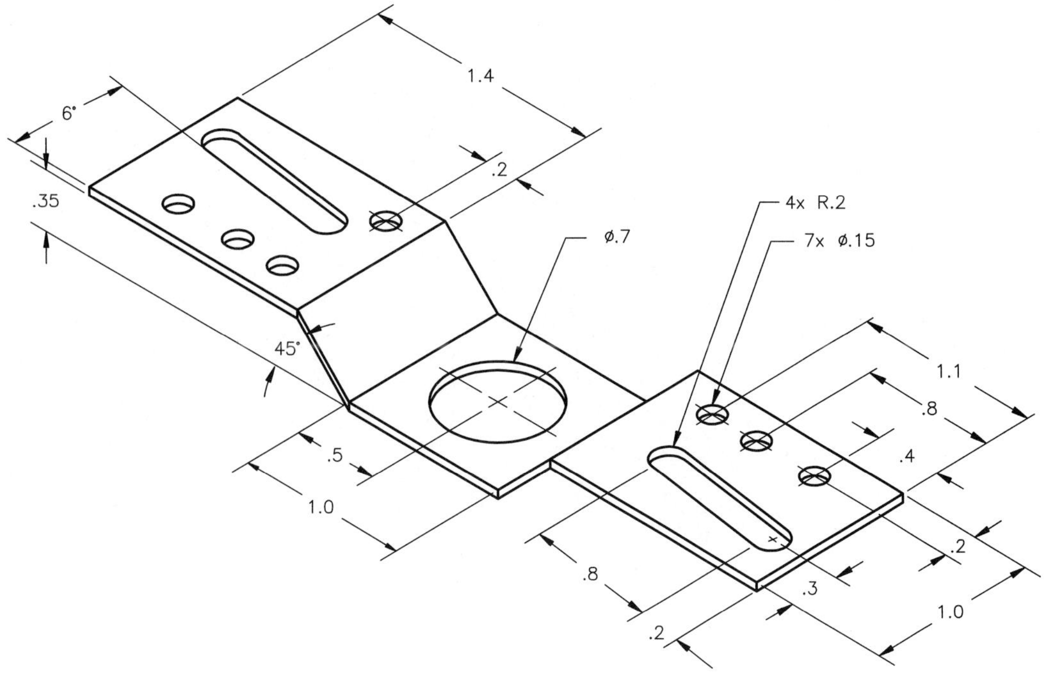

Guide Bracket

7.

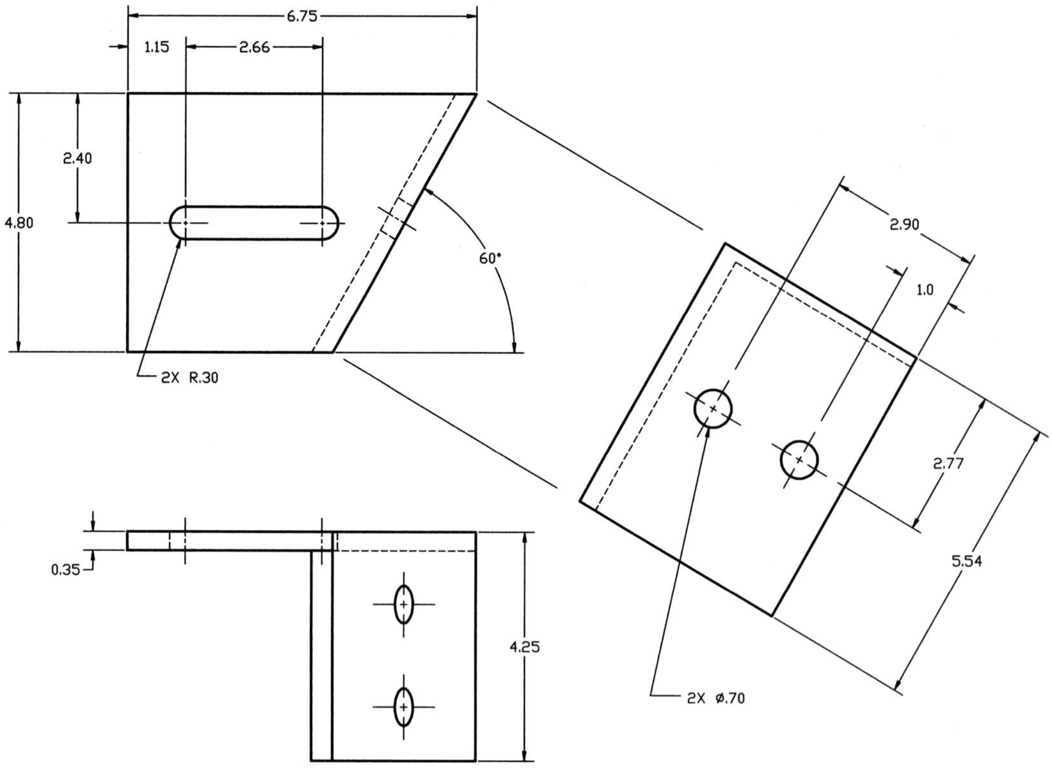

Angle Mount

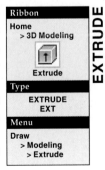

CHAPTER 8

Solid Model Extrusions and Revolutions

Learning Objectives

After completing this chapter, you will be able to:

- ✓ Create solids and surfaces by extruding 2D profiles.
- ✓ Extrude planar surfaces.
- ✓ Create symmetrical 3D solids and surfaces by revolving 2D profiles.
- ✓ Revolve planar surfaces.
- ✓ Use solid extrusions and revolutions as construction tools.

Complex shapes can be created by applying a thickness to a two-dimensional profile. This is called *extruding* the shape. You have been introduced to the operation in previous chapters. Two or more profiles can be extruded to intersect. The resulting union can form a new shape by performing a Boolean operation. Symmetrical objects can be created by revolving a 2D profile about an axis to create a new solid.

Creating Solid Model Extrusions

A ***solid extrusion*** is a closed, two-dimensional shape that has been given thickness. The **EXTRUDE** command allows you to create extrusions from lines, arcs, elliptical arcs, 2D polylines, 2D splines, circles, ellipses, 2D solids, regions, planar surfaces, and donuts. Objects in a block cannot be extruded. Closed objects, such as circles, polygons, closed polylines, and donuts, are converted to solids when they are extruded. Open-ended objects, such as lines, arcs, polylines, elliptical arcs, and splines, are converted to a ***surface extrusion*** when they are extruded. Surface extrusions have no mass properties.

EXTRUDE

Ribbon
Home
> 3D Modeling
Extrude

Type
EXTRUDE
EXT

Menu
Draw
> Modeling
> Extrude

Extrusions can be created along a straight line or along a path curve. A taper angle can also be applied as you extrude an object. **Figure 8-1** illustrates a polygon extruded into a solid.

When the **EXTRUDE** command is selected, you are prompted to select the objects to extrude. Select the objects and press [Enter]. You are then prompted for the extrusion height. The height is always applied along the Z axis of the object. A positive value extrudes above the XY plane of the object. A negative height value extrudes below the XY plane. If a pictorial view is displayed, you can drag the mouse to set the extrusion above or below the XY plane and then enter the height value.

Figure 8-1.
The **EXTRUDE** command creates a solid or surface by adding thickness to a 2D profile. A—The initial, closed 2D profile. B—The extruded solid object shown with hidden lines removed.

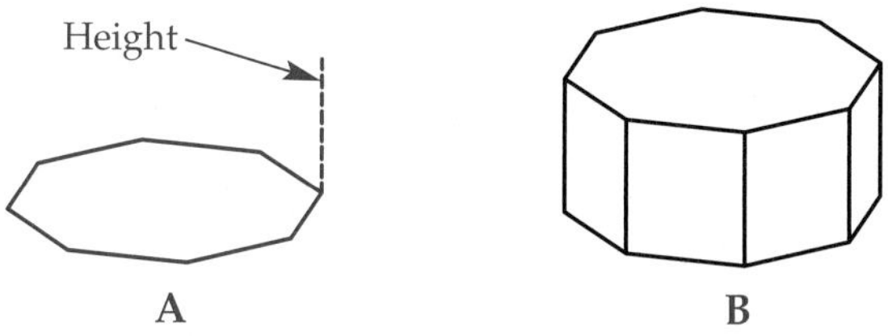

Before entering a height, you can specify a taper angle. The taper angle can be any value *between* +90° and –90°. A positive angle tapers to the inside of the object from the base. A negative angle tapers to the outside of the object from the base. See **Figure 8-2.** However, the taper angle cannot result in edges that "fold into" the extruded object.

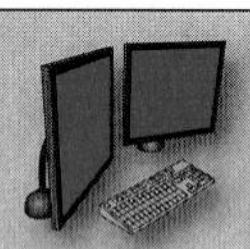

PROFESSIONAL TIP

Objects such as polylines, lines, and arcs that have a thickness can be converted to surfaces using the **CONVTOSURFACE** command. Circles and closed polylines with a thickness can be converted to solids using the **CONVTOSOLID** command.

Extrusions along a Path

A 2D shape can be extruded along a path to create a 3D solid or surface. The path can be a line, circle, arc, ellipse, polygon, polyline, or spline. Line segments and other objects can be first joined to form a polyline path. The corners of angled segments on the extruded object are mitered, while curved segments are smooth. See **Figure 8-3.**

When open objects, such as lines, arcs, polylines, elliptical arcs, and splines, are used as the profile, they are converted to a swept surface when extruded along a path. A *sweep* is a solid or surface that is created when an open or closed curve is pulled, or swept, along a 2D or 3D path. An extrusion is really a form of a sweep. Sweeps are discussed in detail in Chapter 9.

Figure 8-2.
A—A positive angle tapers to the inside of the object from the base.
B—A negative angle tapers to the outside of the object.

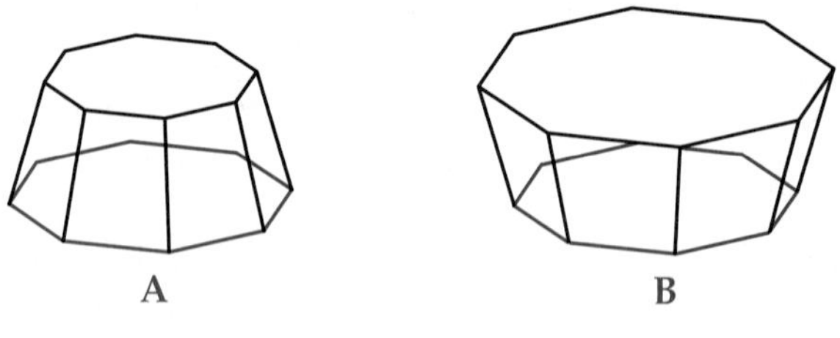

Figure 8-3.
A—Angled segments are mitered when extruded.
B—Curves are smoothed when extruded.

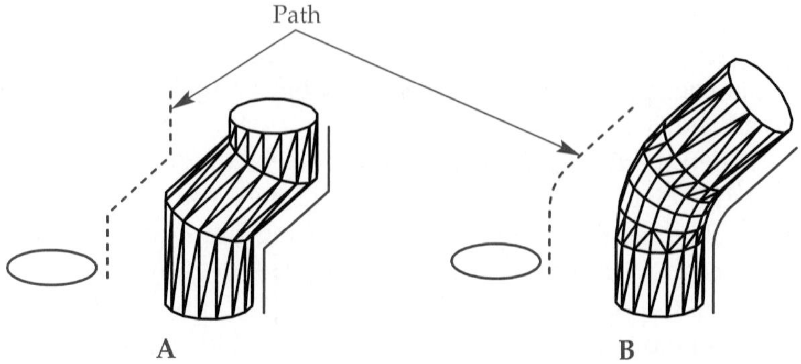

To extrude along a path, enter the **EXTRUDE** command and select the objects to extrude. When prompted for the height of the extrusion, enter the **Path** option. If needed, first enter a taper angle. Then, pick the object to be used as the extrusion path.

Objects can also be extruded along a line at an angle to the base object, **Figure 8-4.** Notice that the plane at the end of the extruded object is parallel to the original object. Also notice that the length of the extrusion is the same as that of the path. The path does not need to be perpendicular to the object.

If the path begins perpendicular to the profile, the cross section of the resulting extrusion is perpendicular to the path, regardless if the path is a straight line, curve, or spline. See **Figure 8-5.** If the path is a spline or curve that does not begin perpendicular to the profile, the profile may not remain perpendicular to the path as it is extruded.

If one of the endpoints of the path is not on the plane of the object to be extruded, the path is temporarily moved to the center of the profile. The extrusion is then created as if the path were connected to the original object, as shown in **Figure 8-4.**

NOTE

The **DELOBJ** system variable allows you to delete or retain the original extruded objects and path definitions. The settings are:

- 0 All original geometry and path definitions are retained.
- 1 Objects used for extrusion (profile curves) are deleted. This is the default.
- 2 All geometry used to define the extrusion, including path definitions, is deleted.
- –1 You are prompted to delete objects used for the extrusion (profile curves).
- –2 You are prompted to delete all geometry used to define the extrusion, including path definitions.

The **DELOBJ** system variable also affects the **REVOLVE, SWEEP,** and **LOFT** commands.

Extruding Regions

In Chapter 2, you learned how to create 2D regions. As an example, you created the top view of the base shown in **Figure 8-6A** as a region. Regions can be extruded to create 3D solids. The base you created in Chapter 2 can be extruded to create the final solid shown in **Figure 8-6B.** Any features of the region, such as holes, are extruded the same thickness as the rest of the object. If the profile was created as polylines, the holes

Figure 8-4.
A—An object extruded along a path. B—The end of an object extruded along an angled path is parallel to the original object.

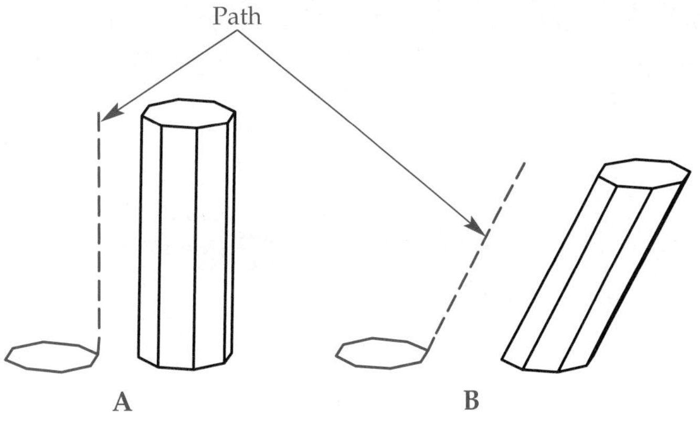

Figure 8-5.
A—Splines can be used as extrusion paths. Notice that the profile on the right is not perpendicular to the start of the path. B—The resulting extrusions.

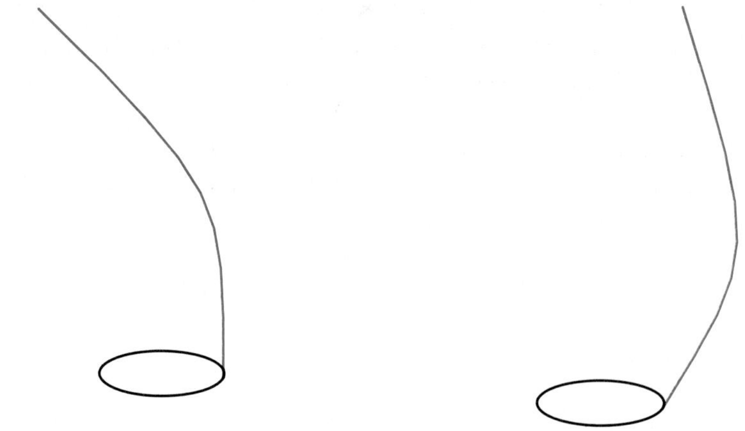

A

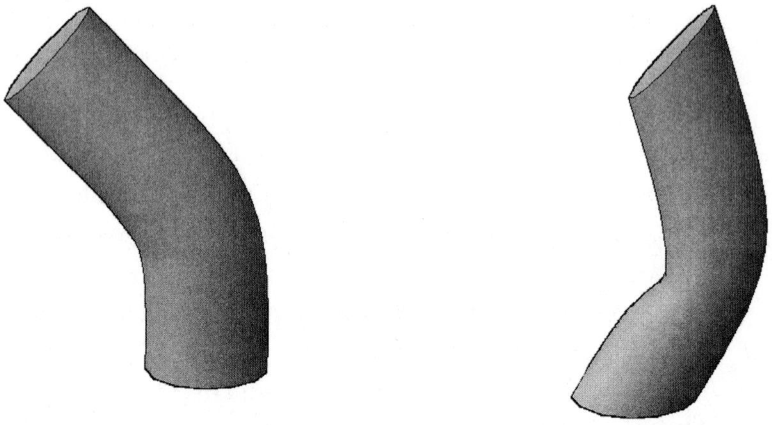

B

Figure 8-6.
A—The 2D region that will be extruded. B—The solid object created by extruding the region, shown in a 3D wireframe display.

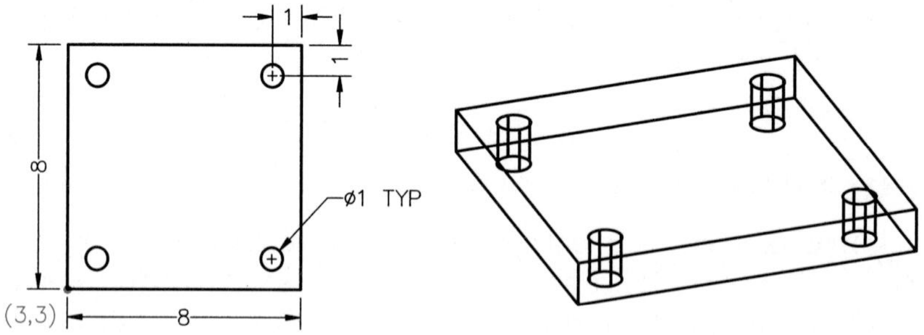

A B

must be separately extruded and then subtracted from the solid. Using this method, you can construct a fairly complex 2D region that includes curved profiles, holes, slots, etc. Then, a complex 3D solid can be quickly created. Additional details can be added using editing commands or Boolean operations.

Exercise 8-1

Complete the exercise on the Student CD.

Extruding a Planar Surface

A planar surface can be extruded into a solid object in the same manner as a region. Nonplanar (curved) surfaces cannot be extruded. Whereas both surfaces and regions have no thickness, the surface is an object composed of a mesh and the region is actually a solid that possesses mass properties. A surface can be quickly converted to a solid using the **EXTRUDE** command. Simply select the surface when prompted to select objects. The surface can be extruded in a specific direction, along a path, or at a taper angle.

Any closed object, such as a circle, rectangle, polygon, or polyline, can be converted into a surface with the **Object** option of the **PLANESURF** command. This surface can then be extruded into a 3D solid.

PROFESSIONAL TIP

You can also extrude a face on an existing solid into a new solid. When prompted to select objects, press the [Ctrl] key and pick the face to extrude. A face is a *subobject* of a solid. Subobject editing is covered in detail in Chapter 11.

Creating Solid Model Revolutions

Ribbon
Home > 3D Modeling > Revolve
Type
REVOLVE REV
Menu
Draw > Modeling > Revolve

REVOLVE

The **REVOLVE** command allows you to create solids and surfaces by revolving a shape about an axis. Shapes that can be revolved include lines, arcs, circles, ellipses, polygons, polylines, closed splines, regions, planar surfaces, and donuts. The selected object can be revolved at any angle up to 360°. A ***solid revolution*** is created when a closed shape is revolved about an axis. A ***surface revolution*** is created when an open shape is revolved about an axis. Surface revolutions have no mass properties.

When the command is selected, you are prompted to pick the objects to revolve. Then, you must define the axis of revolution. The default option is to pick the two endpoints of an axis of revolution. This is shown in Figure 8-7. You can also revolve about an object or the X, Y, or Z axis of the current UCS. Once the axis is defined, you are prompted to enter the angle through which the profile will be revolved. When the angle is specified, the revolution is created.

PROFESSIONAL TIP

When creating solid models, keep in mind that the final part will most likely need to be manufactured. Be aware of manufacturing processes and methods as you design parts. It is easy to create a part in AutoCAD with internal features that may be impossible to manufacture, especially when revolving a profile.

Figure 8-7.
Points P1 and P2 are selected as the axis of revolution for the profile.

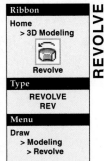

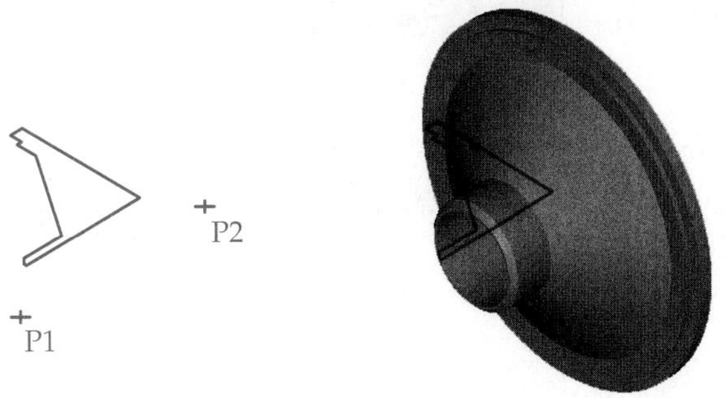

Figure 8-8.
An axis of revolution can be selected using the **Object** option of the **REVOLVE** command. Here, the line is selected as the axis.

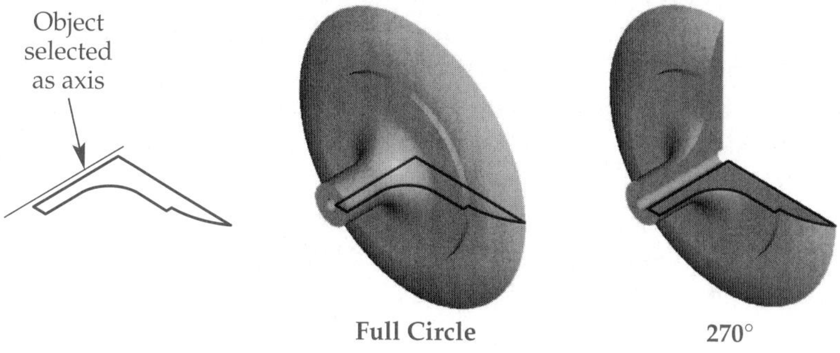

Revolving about an Axis-Line Object

You can select an object, such as a line, as the axis of revolution. Figure 8-8 shows a solid created using the **Object** option of the **REVOLVE** command. Both a full circle (360°) revolution and a 270° revolution are shown. Enter the **Object** option when prompted for the axis of revolution. Then, pick the axis object and enter the angle through which the profile will be rotated. You can use the **Start Angle** option before entering an angle of revolution. This allows you to specify the point at which the revolution starts and then the angle of revolution.

Revolving about the X, Y, or Z Axis

The X axis of the current UCS can be used as the axis of revolution by selecting the **X** option of the **REVOLVE** command. The origin of the current UCS is used as one end of the X axis line. Notice in Figure 8-9 that two different shapes can be created from the same 2D profile by changing the UCS origin. No hole appears in the object in Figure 8-9B because the profile was revolved about an edge that coincides with the X axis. The Y or Z axis can also be used as the axis of revolution. See Figure 8-10.

Exercise 8-2
Complete the exercise on the Student CD.

Figure 8-9.
A—A solid is created using the X axis as the axis of revolution. B—A different object is created with the same profile by changing the UCS origin.

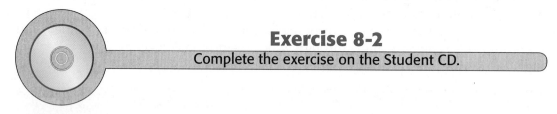

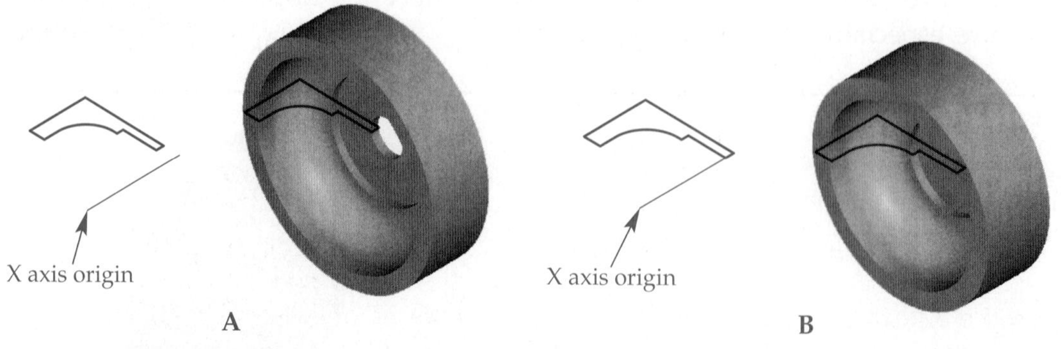

Figure 8-10.
A—A solid is created using the Y axis as the axis of revolution. B—A different object is created by changing the UCS origin.

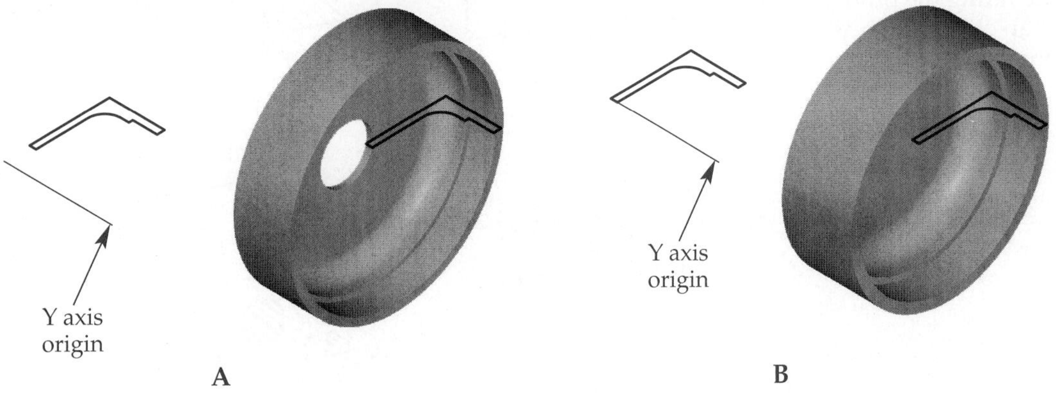

Revolving Regions

Earlier in this chapter, you learned that regions can be extruded. In this manner, holes, slots, keyways, etc., can be created. Regions can also be revolved. A complex 2D shape can be created using Boolean operations on regions. Then, the region can be revolved. One advantage of this method is it may be easier to create a region than trying to create a complex 2D profile as a single, closed polyline.

Revolving a Planar Surface

Just as a planar surface can be extruded into a solid object, it can also be revolved into a solid object. Nonplanar (curved) surfaces cannot be revolved. When the **REVOLVE** command is selected, simply pick the surface when prompted to select objects. The surface can be revolved about an axis defined by two pick points, an object, or the X, Y, or Z axis of the current UCS.

PROFESSIONAL TIP

You can also revolve a face on an existing solid into a new solid. When prompted to select objects, press the [Ctrl] key and pick the face to revolve.

Using Extrude and Revolve as Construction Tools

It is unlikely that an extrusion or revolution will result in a finished object. Rather, these operations will be used with other solid model construction methods, such as Boolean operations, to create the final object. The next sections discuss how to use **EXTRUDE** and **REVOLVE** with other construction methods to create a finished object.

Creating Features with Extrude

You can create a wide variety of features with the **EXTRUDE** command. Study the shapes shown in **Figure 8-11**. These detailed solid objects were created by drawing a profile and then using the **EXTRUDE** command. The objects in **Figure 8-11C** and **Figure 8-11D** must first be constructed as regions before they are extruded. For example, the five holes (circles) in **Figure 8-11D** must be removed from the base region using the **SUBTRACT** command.

Figure 8-11.
Detailed solids can be created by extruding the profile of an object. The profiles are shown here in color.

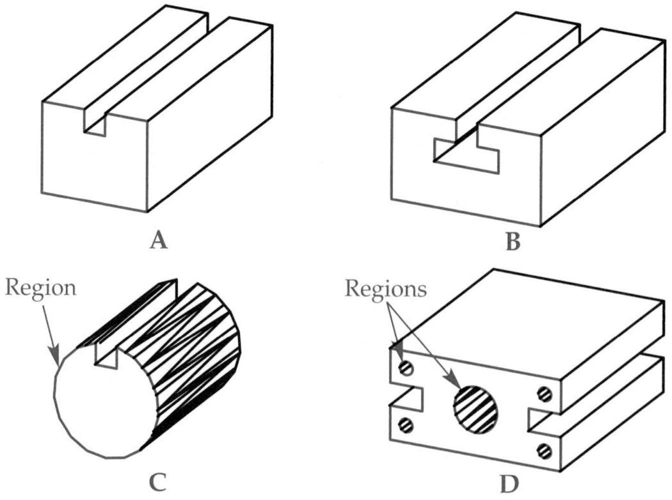

Look at Figure 8-12. This is part of a clamping device used to hold parts on a mill table. There is a T-slot milled through the block to receive a T-bolt and one side is stair-stepped, under which parts are clamped. If you look closely at the end of the object, most of the detail can be drawn as a 2D region and then extruded. However, there are also two holes in the top of the block to allow for bolting the clamp to the mill table. These features must be added to the extruded solid.

First, change the UCS to the front preset orthographic UCS. Display a plan view of the UCS. Then, draw the profile shown in Figure 8-13 using the **PLINE** command. You can draw it in stages, if you like, and then use the **PEDIT** command to join all segments into a single polyline.

Next, use the **EXTRUDE** command to create the 3D solid. Extrude the profile a distance of –6 units with a 0° taper. This will extrude the object away from you. Display the object from the southeast isometric preset viewpoint or use the view cube to display a pictorial view. The object should look similar to Figure 8-12 without the holes in the top. Set the Conceptual visual style current, if you like.

The two holes are ∅.5 units and evenly spaced on the surface through which they pass. Change to the WCS and draw a construction line from midpoint to midpoint, as shown in Figure 8-14. Then, set **PDMODE** to an appropriate value, such as 3, and use the **DIVIDE** command to divide the construction line into three parts. The two points created by the **DIVIDE** command are equally spaced on the surface and can be used to locate the two holes.

There are two ways to create a hole. You can draw a circle and extrude it or you can draw a solid cylinder. Either way, you need to subtract the cylinder to create the hole. Drawing a solid cylinder is probably easiest. When prompted for a center, use the

Figure 8-12.
Most of this object can be created by extruding a profile. However, the holes must be added after the extruded solid is created.

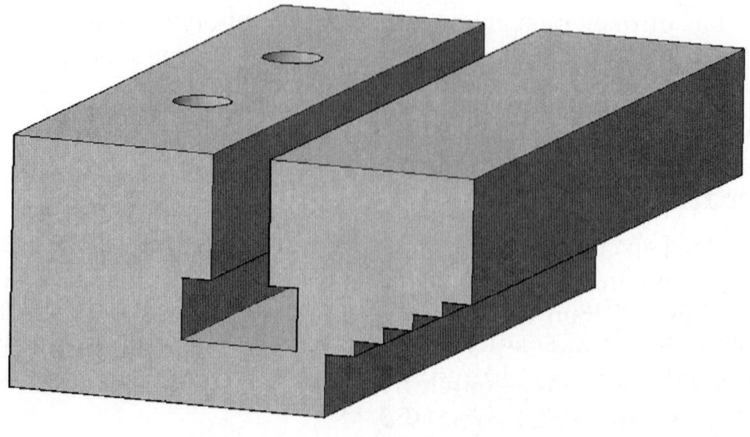

Figure 8-13.
This is the profile that will be extruded for the clamping block.

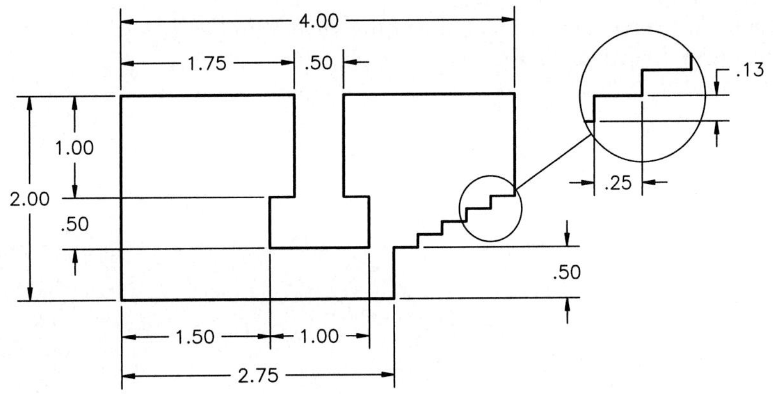

Figure 8-14.
Draw a construction line (shown here in color) and divide it into three parts.

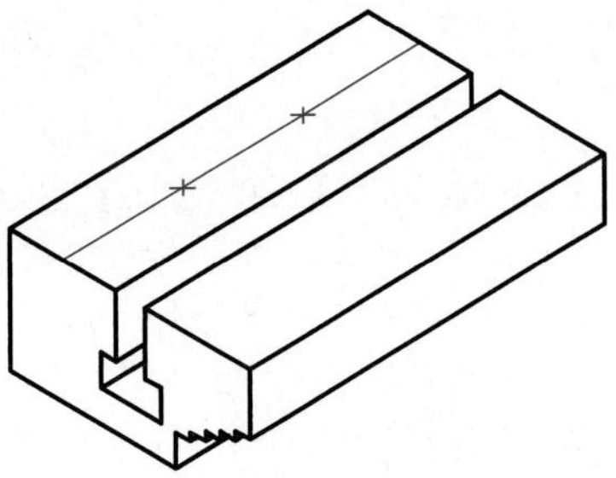

Node object snap to select the point. Then, enter the diameter. Finally, enter a negative height so that the cylinder extends into the solid or drag the cylinder down in the 3D view so it extends all of the way through the block. The actual height is not critical, as long as it extends through the block.

You can either copy the first cylinder to the second point or draw another cylinder. When both cylinders are located, use the **SUBTRACT** command to remove them from the solid. The object is now complete and should look like Figure 8-12.

Creating Features with Revolve

The **REVOLVE** command is very useful for creating symmetrical, round objects. However, many times the object you are creating is not completely symmetrical. For example, look at the camshaft in Figure 8-15. For the most part, this is a symmetrical, round object. However, the cam lobes are not symmetrical in relation to the shaft and bearings. The **REVOLVE** command can be used to create the shaft and bearings. Then, the cam lobes can be created and added.

Start a new drawing and make sure the WCS is the current UCS. Using the **PLINE** command, draw the profile shown in Figure 8-16A. This profile will be revolved through 360°, so you only need to draw half of the true plan view of the cam profile. The profile represents the shaft and three bearings.

Next, display the drawing from the southwest isometric preset viewpoint. Then, use the **REVOLVE** command to create the base camshaft. Pick the endpoints shown in Figure 8-16A as the axis of revolution. Revolve the profile through 360°. Zoom extents and set the Conceptual visual style current to clearly see the object.

Now, you need to create one cam lobe. Change the UCS to the left orthographic preset. Then, draw a construction point in the center of the left end of the camshaft. Use the **Center** object snap and an appropriate **PDMODE** setting. Next, draw the profile shown in Figure 8-16B. Use the construction point as the center of the large radius. You may want to create a new layer and turn off the display of the base camshaft.

Once the cam lobe profile is created, use the **REGION** command to create a region. Then, use the **EXTRUDE** command to extrude the region a height of –.5 units (into the camshaft). The extrusion should have a 0° taper. If you turned off the display of the base camshaft, turn it back on now.

Figure 8-15.
For the most part, this object is symmetrical about its center axis. However, the cam lobes are not symmetrical about the axis.

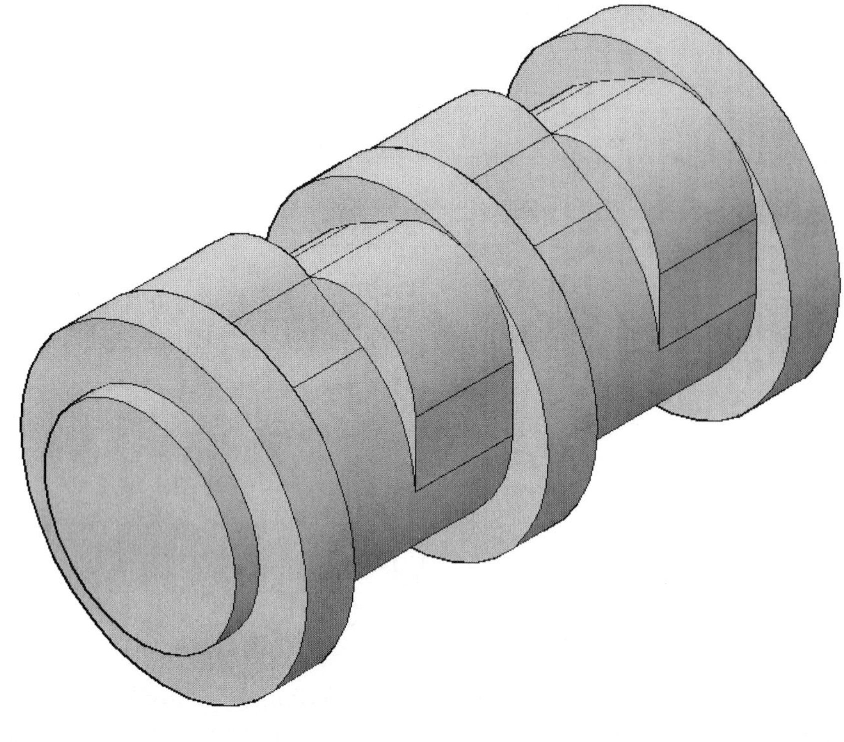

Figure 8-16.
A—This profile will be revolved to create the shaft and bearings. B—This is the profile of one cam lobe, which will be extruded.

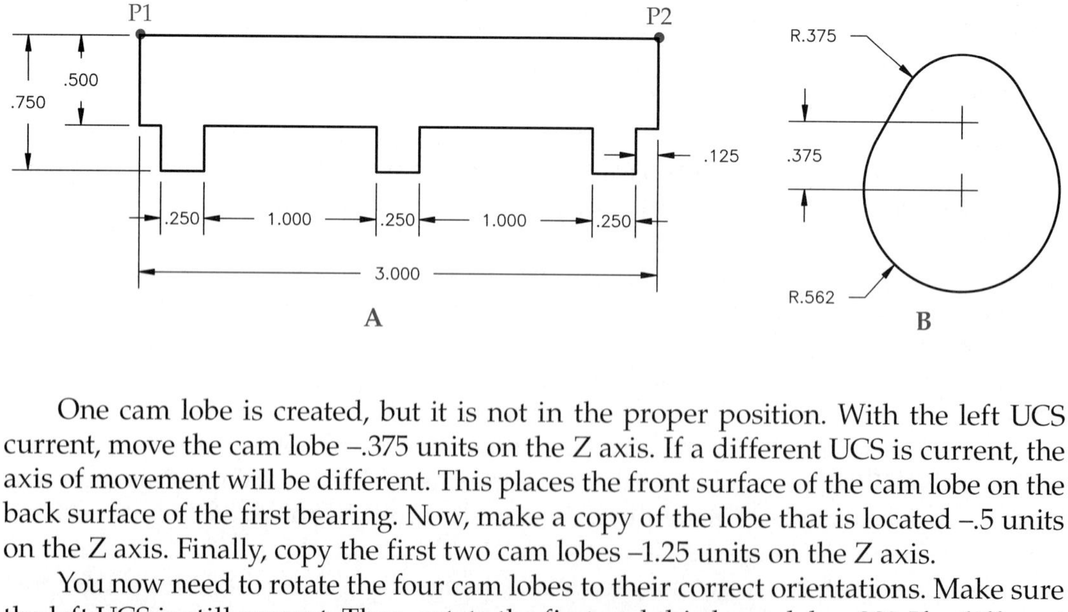

One cam lobe is created, but it is not in the proper position. With the left UCS current, move the cam lobe –.375 units on the Z axis. If a different UCS is current, the axis of movement will be different. This places the front surface of the cam lobe on the back surface of the first bearing. Now, make a copy of the lobe that is located –.5 units on the Z axis. Finally, copy the first two cam lobes –1.25 units on the Z axis.

You now need to rotate the four cam lobes to their correct orientations. Make sure the left UCS is still current. Then, rotate the first and third cam lobes 30°. If a different UCS is current , you can use the **3DROTATE** command. The center of rotation should be the center of the shaft. There are many points on the shaft to which the **Center** object snap can snap; they are all acceptable. You can also use the construction point as the center of rotation. Rotate the second and fourth cam lobes –30° about the same center.

Finally, use the **UNION** command to join all objects. The final object should appear as shown in Figure 8-15. Use the view cube to see all sides of the object. You can also create a rotating display using the **3DORBIT** command.

Multiple Intersecting Extrusions

Many solid objects have complex curves and profiles. These can often be constructed from the intersection of two or more extrusions. The resulting solid is a combination of only the intersecting volumes of the extrusions. The following example shows the construction of a coat hook.

1. Construct the first profile, Figure 8-17A.
2. Construct the second profile located on a common point with the first, Figure 8-17B.
3. Construct the third profile located on the common point, Figure 8-17C.
4. Extrude each profile the required dimension into the same area. Be careful to specify positive or negative heights for each extrusion, Figure 8-17D and Figure 8-17E.
5. Use the **INTERSECT** command to create a composite solid from the volume shared by the three extrusions, Figure 8-17F.

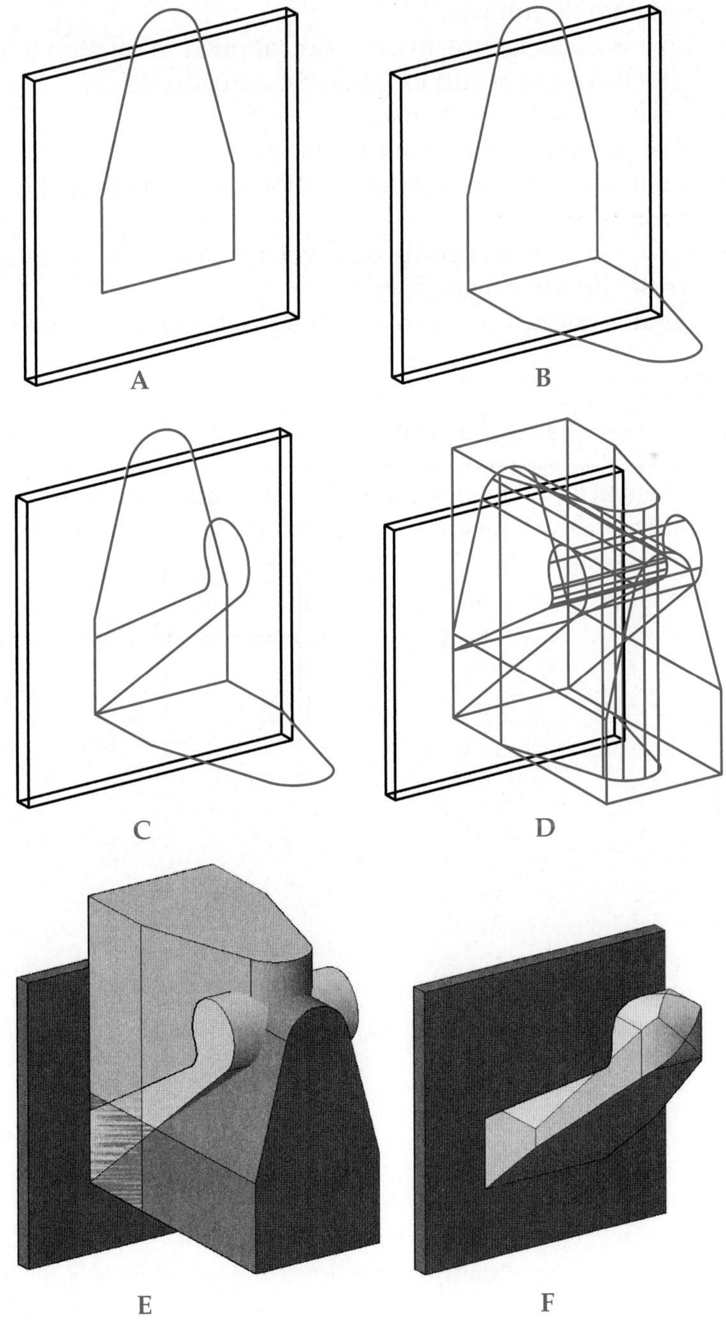

Figure 8-17. Constructing a coat hook. A—Draw the first profile. B—Draw the second profile. C—Draw the third profile. All three profiles should have a common origin. D—Extrude each profile so that the extruded objects intersect. E—The extruded objects after the Conceptual visual style is set current. F—Use the **INTERSECT** command to create the composite solid. The final solid is shown here with the Conceptual visual style set current.

Chapter Test

Answer the following questions. Write your answers on a separate sheet of paper or complete the electronic chapter test on the Student CD.

1. What is an *extrusion?*
2. How do you create a surface extrusion?
3. Briefly describe how to create a solid extrusion.
4. Which command can be used to convert circles and closed polylines with a thickness to solids?
5. How can an extrusion be constructed to extend below the XY plane of the current UCS?
6. What is the range in which a taper angle can vary?
7. How can a curved extrusion be constructed?
8. Which system variable allows you to delete or retain the original extruded objects and path definitions?
9. How is the height of an extrusion applied in relation to the original object?
10. Which type(s) of surface(s) can be extruded?
11. What is a *surface revolution?*
12. How do you create a solid revolution?
13. What are the five different options for selecting the axis of revolution for a revolved solid?
14. How can a given profile be revolved twice (or more) about the same axis and create different shaped solids?
15. What is one advantage of revolving a region over revolving a polyline?

Drawing Problems

1. Construct a 12′ long section of wide flange structural steel with the cross section shown below. Use the dimensions given. Save the drawing as P08_01.

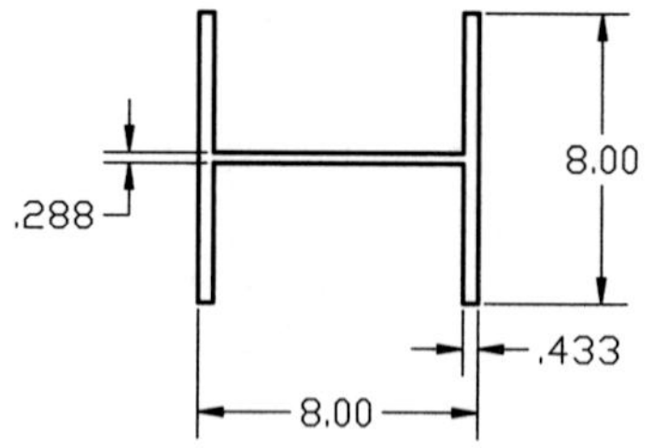

Problems 2–7. These problems require you to use a variety of solid modeling methods to construct the objects. Use **EXTRUDE**, **REVOLVE**, *solid primitives, new UCSs, and Boolean commands to assist in construction. Do not create section views. Save each as* **P08_***(problem number).*

2.

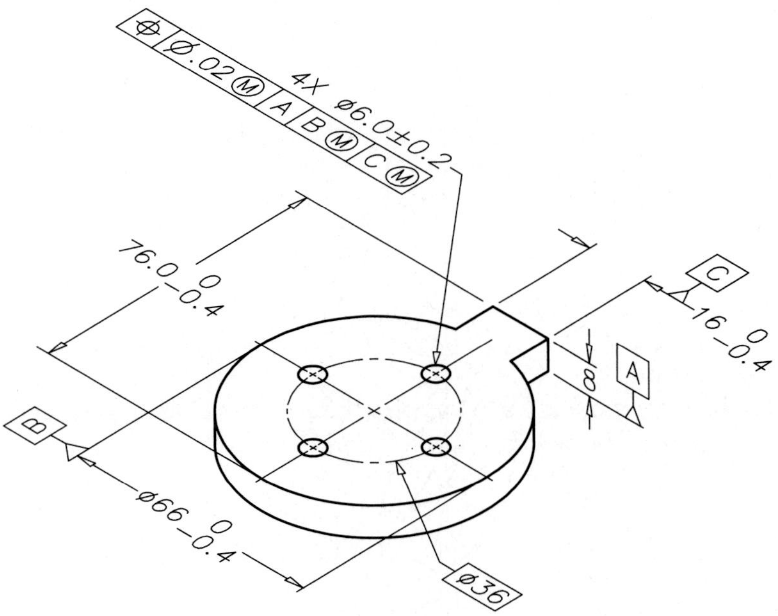

Spring Clip

3.

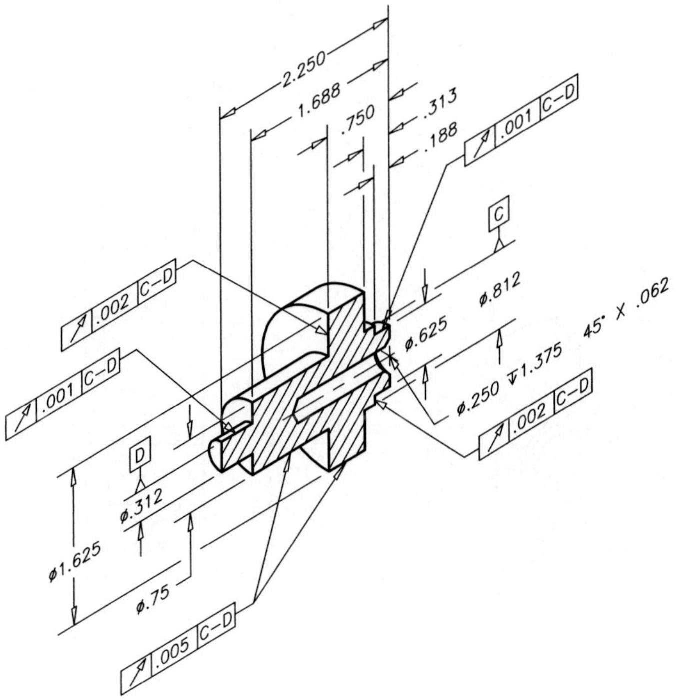

Valve Pin

4.

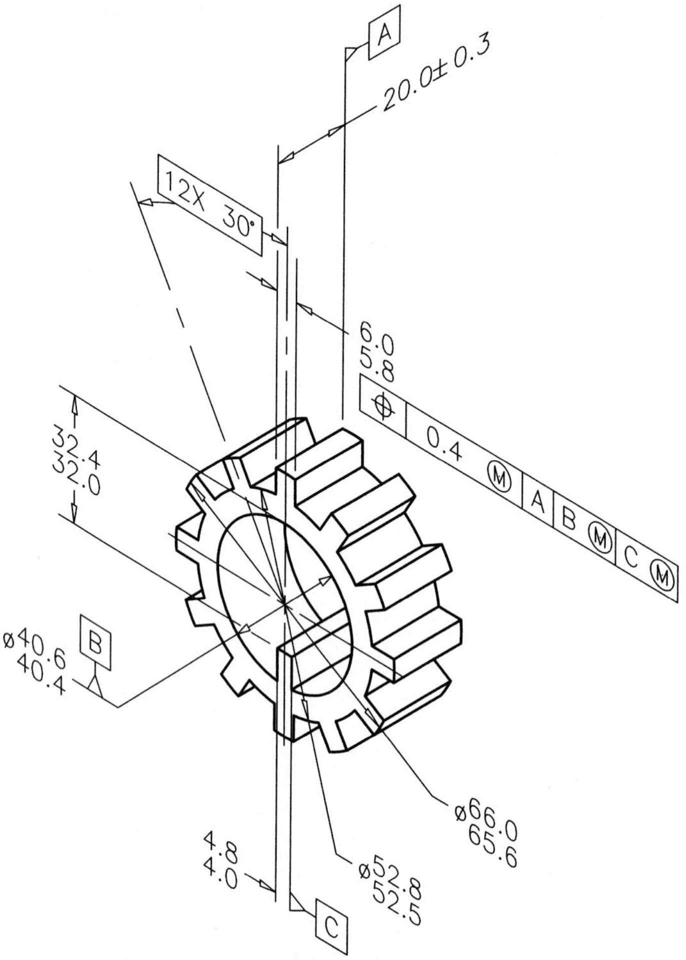

Spline

5.

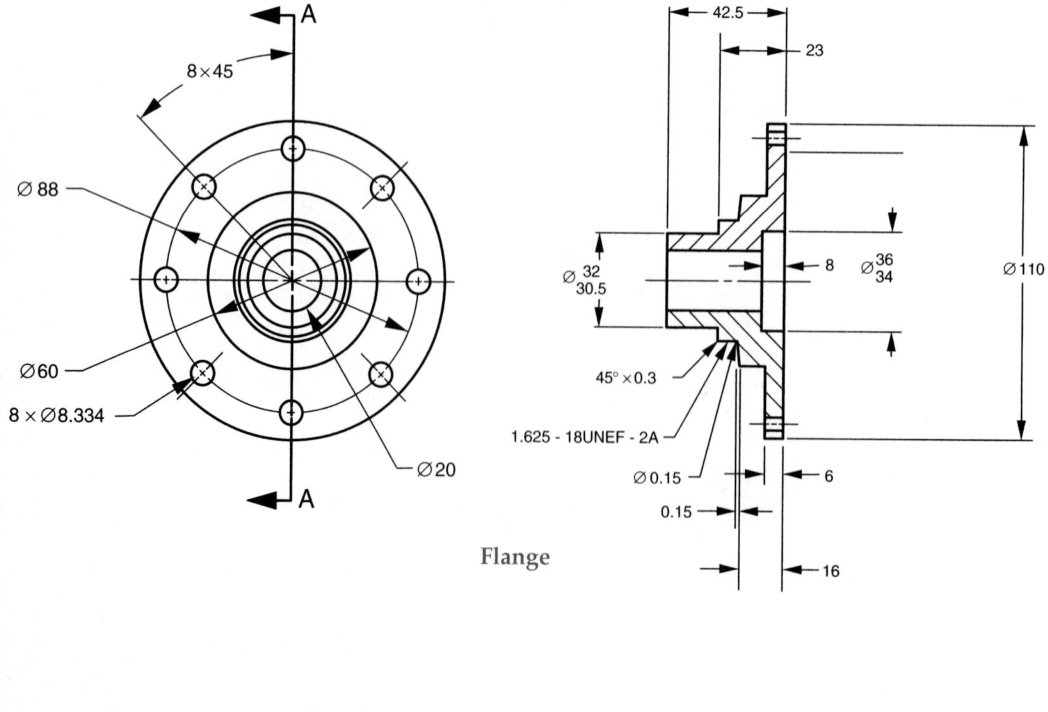

Flange

6.

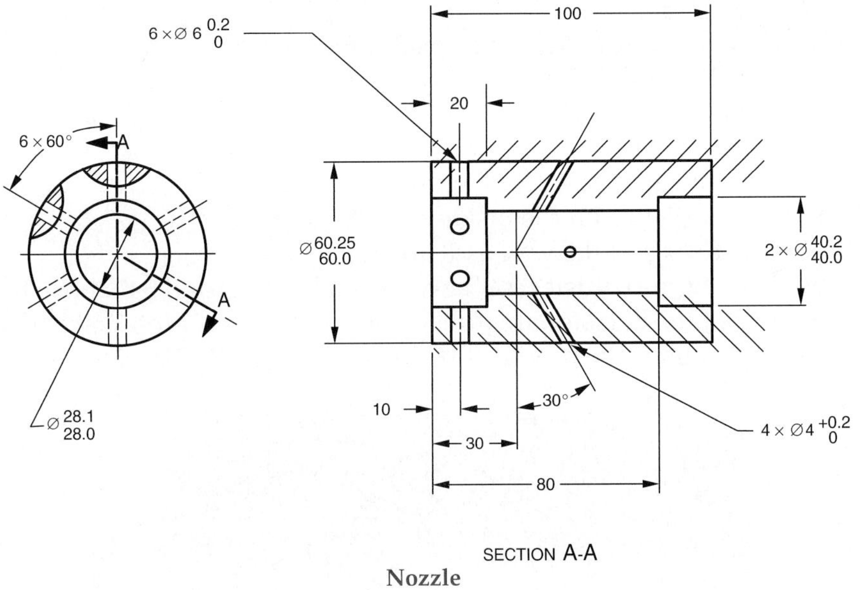

Nozzle

7.

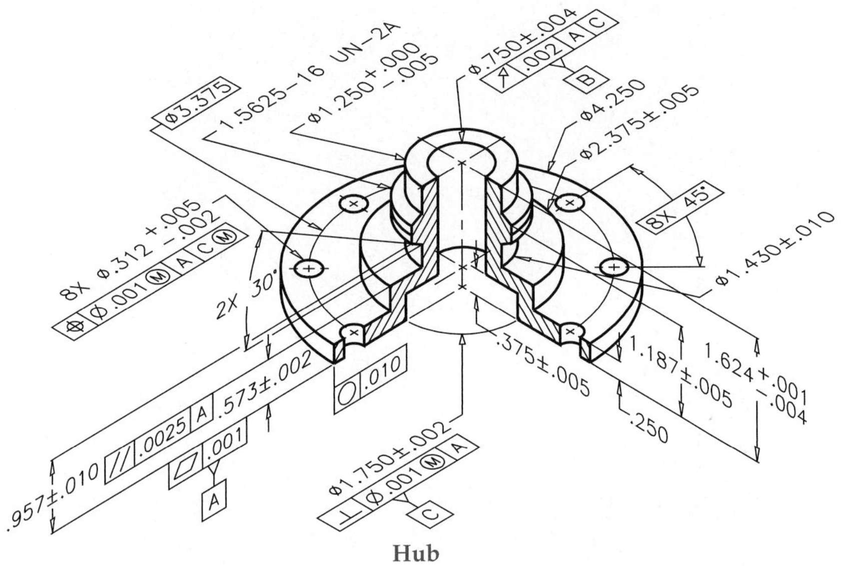

Hub

8. Create the stairway shown below using the following parameters. Save the file as P08_08.
   A. Use the detail for the riser and tread dimensions.
   B. There are 13 risers.
   C. The stairs are 42″ wide.
   D. The landing at the top of the stairs is 48″ long from the face of the last riser.
   E. The vertical wall is 15′-1″ high on the inside and 15′-7″ long.
   F. The floor is 8′ wide on the inside and 15′-7″ long.
   G. Draw the floor and the wall as 1″ thick.
   H. The center of the banister is 3″ away from the wall and 34″ above the steps.
   I. The ends of the banister are directly above the face of the first and last riser.
   J. Use the detail for the profile of the banister. Use **EXTRUDE** as needed.

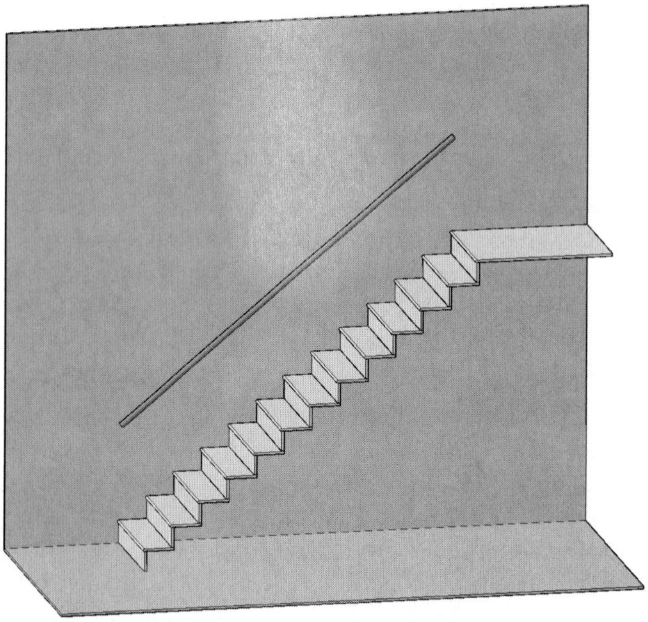

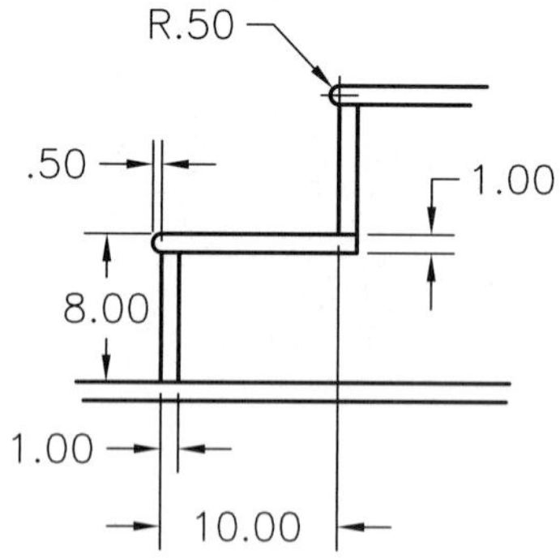

STAIR DETAIL

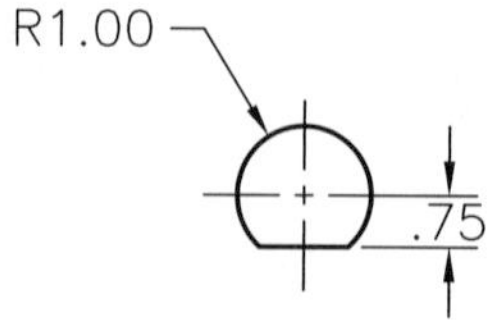

BANISTER DETAIL

9. Construct picture frame moldings using the profiles shown below.
   A. Draw each of the closed profiles shown. Use your own dimensions for the details of the moldings.
   B. The length and width of A and B should be no larger than 1.5″ × 1″.
   C. The length and width of C and D should be no larger than 3″ × 1.5″.
   D. Construct an 8″ × 12″ picture frame using moldings A and B.
   E. Construct a 12″ × 24″ picture frame using moldings C and D.
   F. Save the drawing as P08_09.

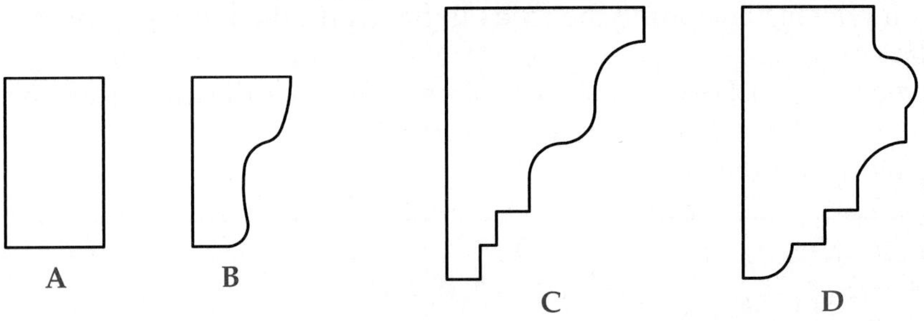

10. In this problem, you will refine the seat of the kitchen chair that you started in Chapter 2. You will use an extrusion following a path to create a curved, receding edge under the seat.
    A. Open P02_11 from Chapter 2. If you have not yet completed this model, do so now.
    B. Create a path for the extrusion by drawing a polyline that exactly matches either the upper or lower edge of the seat. Refer to the drawing shown below.
    C. Change the view and UCS as needed to display a plan view of the edge of the seat. Draw the profile shown below.
    D. Extrude the profile along the path and then subtract the extrusion from the seat.
    E. Save the drawing as P08_10.

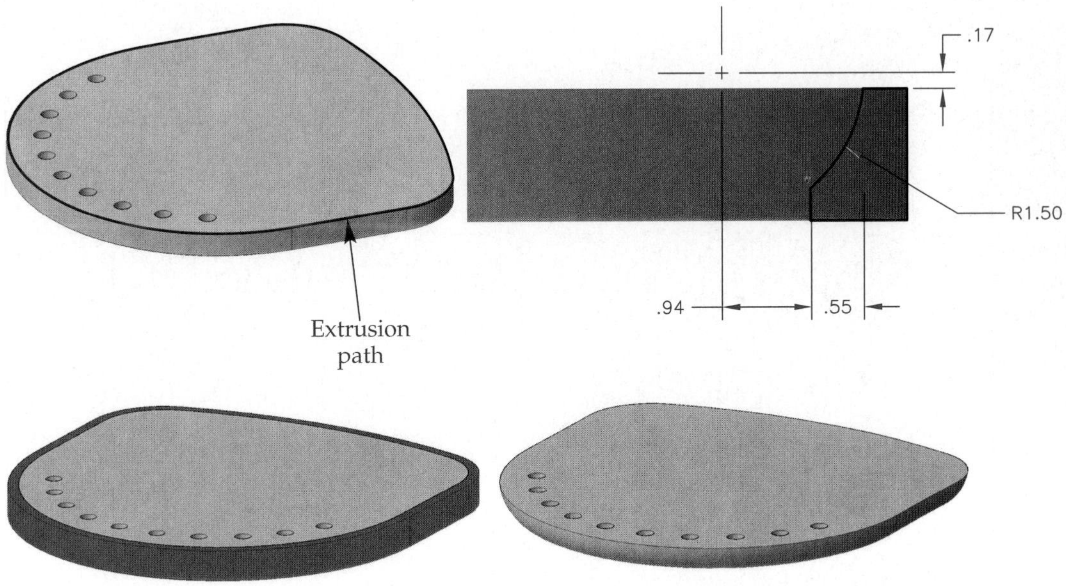

Seat with Extrusion in Place

Completed Seat

11. In this problem, you will be taking a manually drawn layout from an archive. You are to create a 3D model of the garage to update the archive.
    A. Review the manually drawn layout. Make note of the construction details shown.
    B. Research any additional details needed to construct the model. For example, the thickness of the doors is not listed as these are purchased items. However, you need to know these dimensions to draw the 3D model.
    C. Using what you have learned, create the garage as a solid model. Be sure to create all components, including the studs in the walls, the footings, and the anchor bolts.
    D. Create layers as needed. For example, you may wish to place the wall sheathing on a layer so it can be hidden to show the studs.
    E. Save the drawing as P08_11.

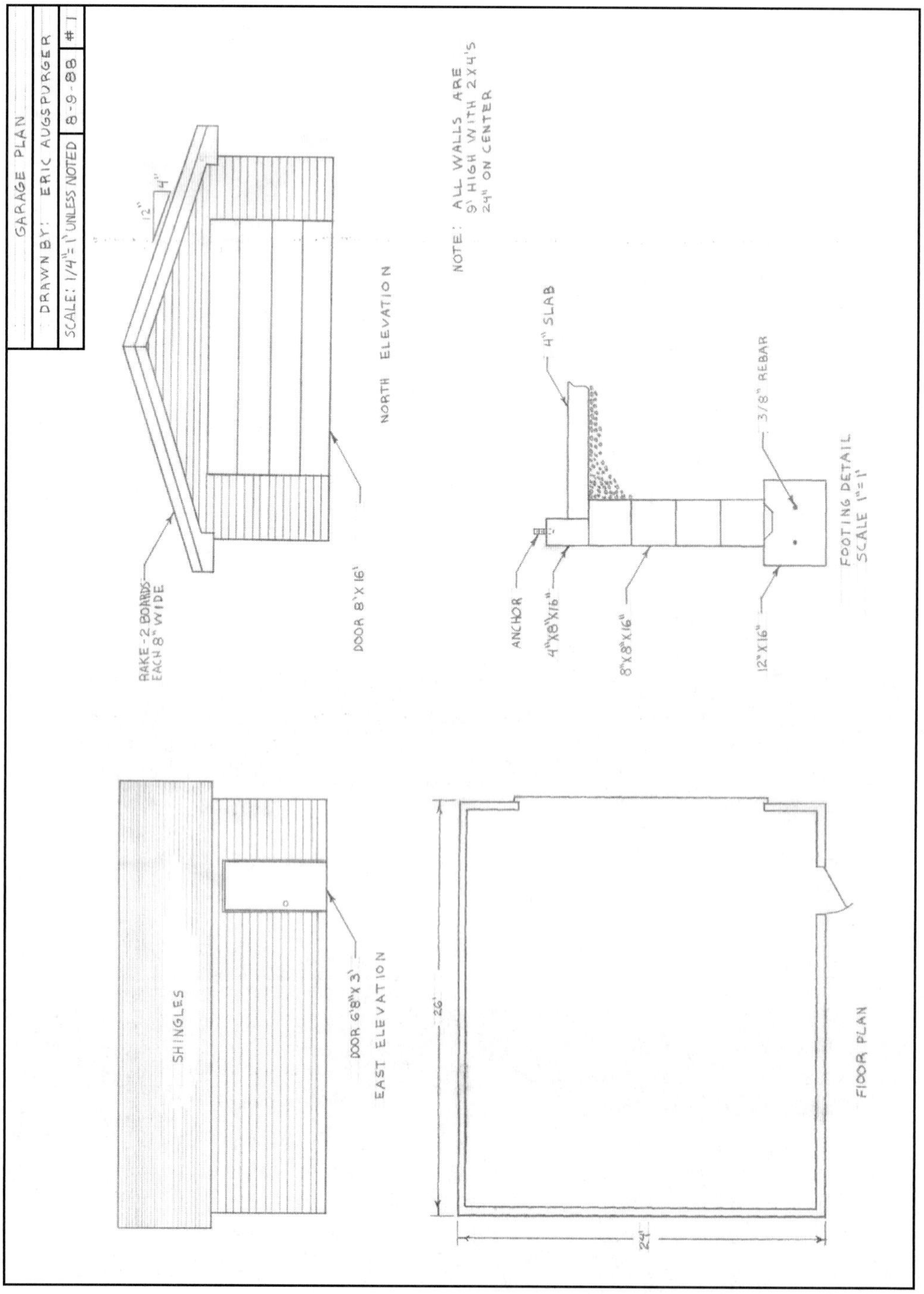

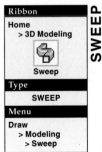

CHAPTER 9

Sweeps and Lofts

Learning Objectives

After completing this chapter, you will be able to:

- ✓ Sweep 2D shapes along a 2D or 3D path to create a solid or surface object.
- ✓ Create 3D solid or surface objects by lofting a series of cross sections.

In the previous chapter, you learned about extruded solids and surfaces. Sweeps and lofts are similar to extrusions. In fact, an extrusion is really just a type of sweep. A ***sweep*** is an object created by extruding a single 2D profile along a path object. Sweeping an open shape along the path results in a surface object. If a closed shape is swept, a solid object is created. A ***loft*** is an object created by extruding between two or more 2D profiles. The shape of the loft object blends from one cross-sectional profile to the next. The profiles can control the loft or it can be controlled by one path or multiple guide curves. As with a sweep, open shapes result in surfaces and closed shapes give you solids. Open and closed shapes cannot be used together in the same loft.

Creating Swept Surfaces and Solids

SWEEP

Ribbon
Home
> 3D Modeling
Sweep

Type
SWEEP

Menu
Draw
> Modeling
> Sweep

The **SWEEP** command is used to create swept surfaces and solids. The command requires at least two objects:

- 2D shape to be swept.
- 2D or 3D shape to be used as the sweep path.

The profile can be aligned with the path, you can specify the base point, a scale factor can be applied, and the profile can be twisted as it is swept. The command procedure and options are the same for both swept solids and surfaces.

Sweeping an open shape creates a surface. See Figure 9-1. The objects that can be swept to create surfaces include lines, arcs, elliptical arcs, 2D polylines, 2D splines, and traces. Sweeping a closed shape creates a solid. See Figure 9-2. The objects that can be swept to create a solid include circles, ellipses, closed 2D polylines, closed 2D splines, regions, planar surfaces, and planar faces of solids. The sweep path for either a surface or a solid can be a line, arc, circle, ellipse, elliptical arc, 2D polyline, 2D spline, 3D polyline, 3D spline, helix, or the edge of a surface or solid.

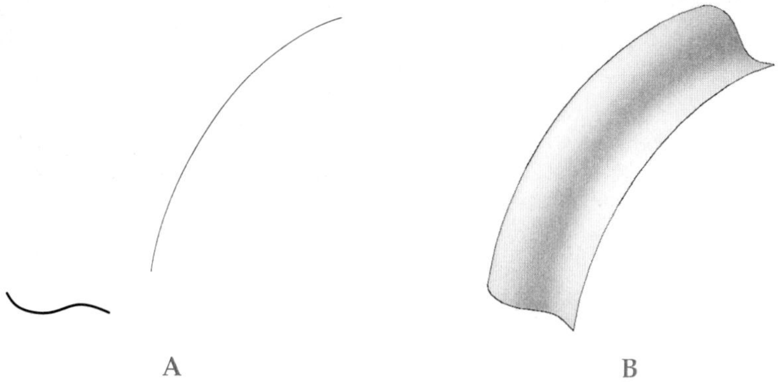

Figure 9-1.
A—This open shape will be swept along the path (shown in color). B—The resulting surface.

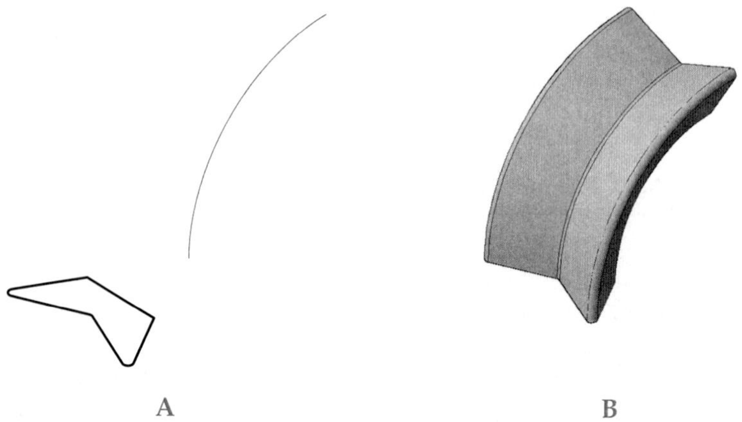

Figure 9-2.
A—This closed shape will be swept along the path (shown in color). B—The resulting solid.

When the command is initiated, you are prompted to select the objects to sweep. Select the profile(s) and press [Enter]. Planar faces of solids may be selected by holding the [Ctrl] key as you select. Multiple profiles can be selected. They are swept along the same path, but separate objects are created.

Next, you are prompted to select the path. The path and profile can lie on the same plane. Select the object to be used as the sweep path and press [Enter]. To select the edge of a surface or solid as the path, press the [Ctrl] key and then select the edge. The profile is then moved to be perpendicular to the path and extruded along the path. The sweep starts at the endpoint of the path nearest to where you selected it.

Exercise 9-1

Complete the exercise on the Student CD.

Changing the Alignment of the Profile

By default, the profile is aligned perpendicular to the sweep path. However, you can create a sweep where the profile is not perpendicular to the path. See Figure 9-3. After the **SWEEP** command is initiated, select the profile and press [Enter]. Before selecting the path, enter the **Alignment** option. The default setting of **Yes** means that profile will be moved so it is perpendicular to the path. If you select **No**, the profile is kept in the same position relative to the path as it is swept. The position of the 2D shape determines the alignment.

Figure 9-3.
A—The profile and path for the sweep. B—By default, the profile is aligned perpendicular to the path when swept. C—Using the **Alignment** option, the profile can be swept so it is not perpendicular to the path.

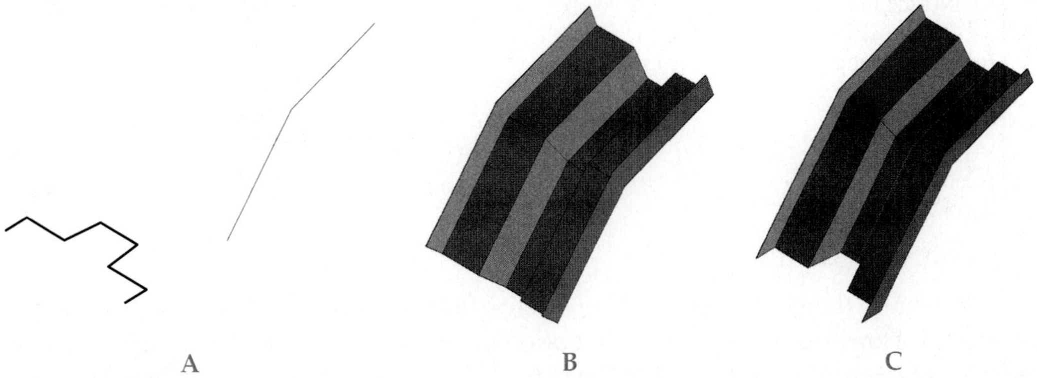

Changing the Base Point

The base point is the location on the shape that will be moved along the path to create the sweep. By default, if the 2D shape intersects the path, the profile is swept along the path at the point of intersection. If the 2D shape does not intersect the path, the default base point depends on the type of object being swept. When lines and arcs are swept, the default base point is their midpoint. Open polylines have a default base point at the midpoint of their total length.

The base point can be any point on the 2D shape or anywhere in the drawing. See Figure 9-4. To change the base point, use the **Base point** option of the **SWEEP** command. When the command is initiated, select the profile and press [Enter]. Before selecting the path, enter the **Base point** option. Next, pick the new base point. It does not have to be on an existing object. Once the new base point is selected, pick the path to create the sweep.

PROFESSIONAL TIP

If the location of the base point in relationship to the path is important, line up the shape with the path before starting the **SWEEP** command. Turn off the **Alignment** option in this situation.

Figure 9-4.
A—The profile and path for the sweep. B—The sweep is created with the default base point. C—The end of the path is selected as the base point. Notice the difference in this sweep and the one shown in B.

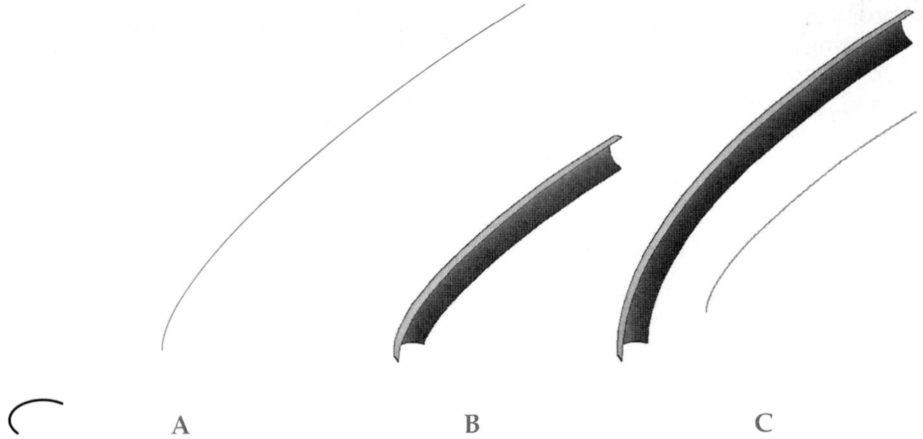

Figure 9-5.
A—The profile and path for the sweep. B—The resulting sweep. Notice how the .25 scale results in a tapered sweep.

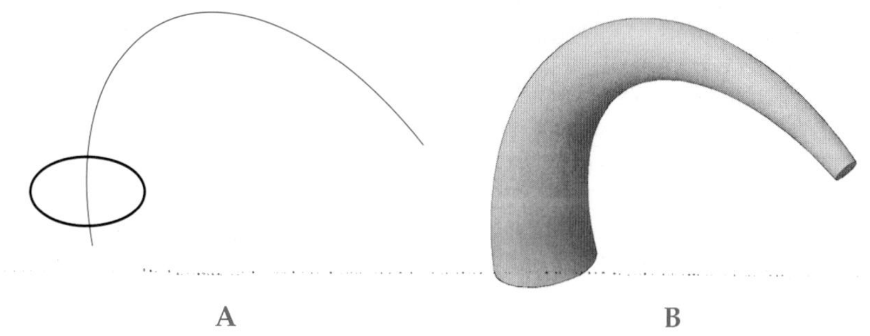

Scaling the Sweep Profile

By default, the size of the profile remains uniform from the beginning of the path to the end. However, using the **Scale** option of the **SWEEP** command, you can change the scale of the profile at the end of the path. This, in effect, tapers the sweep. Figure 9-5 shows a .25 scale applied to a sweep object. A 2D polyline path must be smooth; no sharp corners.

Once the **SWEEP** command is initiated, select the profile and press [Enter]. Before selecting the path, enter the **Scale** option. You are prompted for the scale. Enter the scale value and press [Enter]. The scale value must be greater than zero. You can also enter the **Reference** option. With this option, pick two points for the first reference line and then two points for the second reference line. The difference in scale between the two distances is the scale value. Once the scale is set, pick the path to create the sweep.

Twisting the Sweep

The profile can be rotated as it is swept along the length of the path by using the **Twist** option of the **SWEEP** command. The angle that you enter indicates the rotation of the shape along the path of the sweep. The higher the number, the more twists in the sweep. Figure 9-6 shows how a simple, closed profile and a straight line can be used to create a milling tool. The profile was swept with a 270° twist.

Once the **SWEEP** command is initiated, select the profile and press [Enter]. Then, before selecting the path, enter the **Twist** option. You are prompted for the twist angle or to enter the **Bank** option.

Banking is the natural rotation of the profile on a 3D sweep path, similar to a banked curve on a racetrack. See Figure 9-7. The path must be 3D to set banking. The banking option is disabled for a 2D path, although you can go through the motions of turning it on when creating the sweep. Once you use the **Bank** option to turn banking on, it is on by default the next time the **SWEEP** command is used. To turn it off, enter a twist angle of zero (or the twist angle you wish to use).

Figure 9-6.
A—The profile and path for creating the end mill. B—The resulting end mill model. Notice how the profile is twisted (rotated) as it is swept.

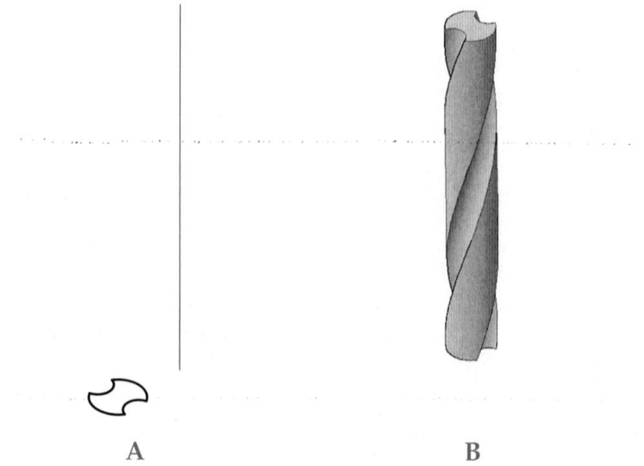

Figure 9-7.
A—The profile and path for the sweep are shown in red. B—Banking is off for this sweep. When viewed from the side, you can see that the profile does not bank through the curve. Look at the upper-right corner. C—Banking is on for this sweep. Notice how the profile banks, or leans, through the curve. Compare this to B.

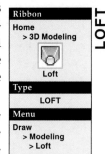

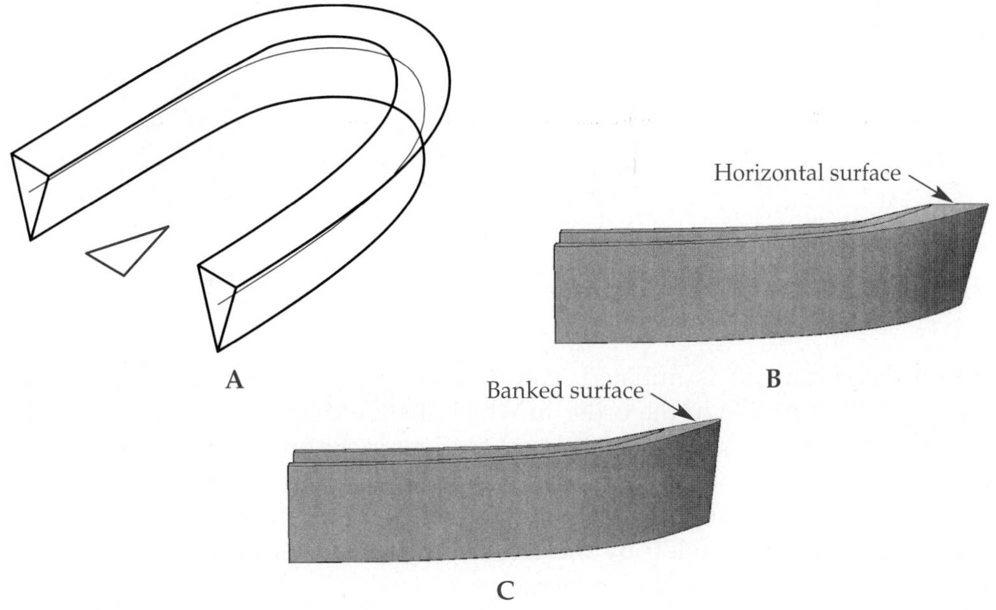

PROFESSIONAL TIP

The sweep options can be changed after the sweep is created using the **Properties** palette. In the **Geometry** section, you will find Profile rotation (alignment), Bank (banking), Twist along path (twist angle), and Scale along path (scale) settings.

Exercise 9-2
Complete the exercise on the Student CD.

Creating Lofted Objects

LOFT
Ribbon
Home > 3D Modeling > Loft
Type
LOFT
Menu
Draw > Modeling > Loft

The **LOFT** command is used to create lofted surfaces and solids based on a series of cross-sectional profiles. **Figure 9-8** shows an example of a loft formed from a rectangle, circle, and polygon. The loft may be guided by only the cross sections, as shown in the figure, by a path, or by guide curves. Lofting open shapes results in a surface object, while lofting closed shapes creates a solid. Open and closed shapes cannot be combined in the same loft.

Objects that can be used as cross sections include lines, circles, arcs, points, ellipses, elliptical arcs, 2D polylines, 2D splines, regions, planar faces of solids, planar surfaces, planar 3D faces, 2D solids, and traces. The loft path may be a line, circle, arc, ellipse, elliptical arc, spline, helix, or 2D or 3D polyline. Guide curves may be composed of lines, arcs, elliptical arcs, 2D or 3D splines, and 2D or 3D polylines. However, 2D polylines are limited to only one segment.

Figure 9-8.
A—The three profiles will be lofted to create a solid. B—The resulting loft with the default settings.

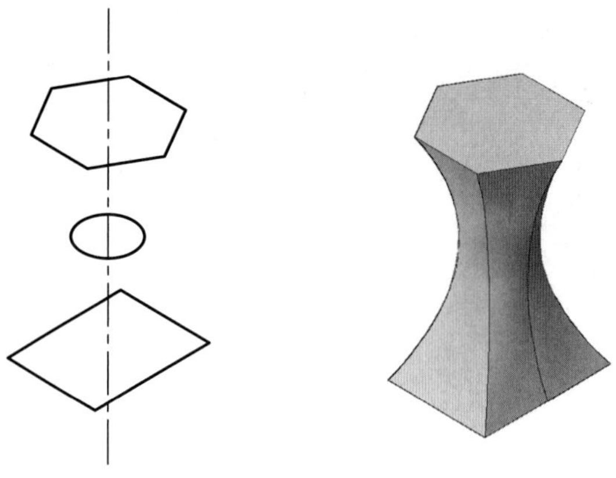

Once the command is initiated, you are prompted to select the cross-sectional profiles. Pick each profile in the order in which it should appear in the loft and press [Enter]. Be sure to individually select the cross sections in the order of the loft creation. You may not get the desired loft if you randomly select them or use a window selection.

Next, you are prompted to select how the loft is to be controlled. As mentioned earlier, you can control the loft by the cross sections, a path, or guide curves. These options are discussed in the next sections.

Controlling the Loft with Cross Sections

The **Cross-sections only** option of the **LOFT** command is useful when the 2D cross sections are drawn in their proper locations in space. The command determines the transition from one cross section to the next. The cross sections are not moved by the command.

When the **Cross-sections only** option is selected, the **Loft Settings** dialog box appears, Figure 9-9. The settings in this dialog box control the transition or contour between cross sections. If the **Preview changes** check box at the bottom of the dialog box is checked, the current settings are previewed in the drawing area. As settings are changed, the preview is updated. When all settings have been made, pick the **OK** button to close the dialog box and create the loft.

When the **Ruled** option is selected in the dialog box, the loft has straight transitions between the cross sections. Sharp edges are created at each cross section. Figure 9-10 shows the same cross sections in Figure 9-8A lofted with the **Ruled** option on. Compare this to Figure 9-8B.

Figure 9-9.
When the loft is controlled by cross sections only, the **Loft Settings** dialog box is used to control the transition between profiles.

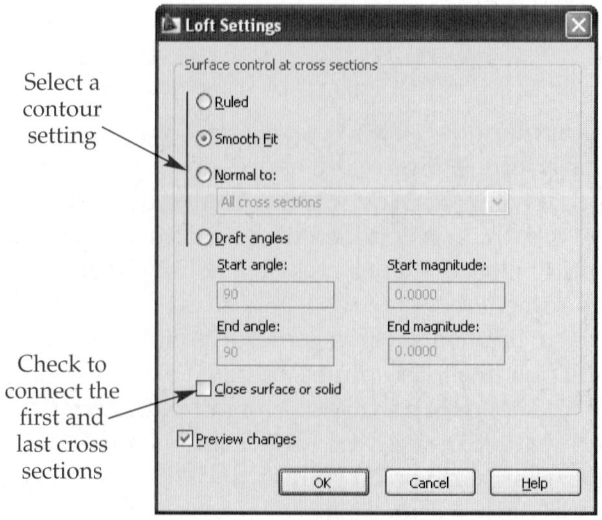

Figure 9-10.
The profiles in Figure 9-8A are lofted with the **Ruled** option on in the **Loft Settings** dialog box. Compare this to Figure 9-8B.

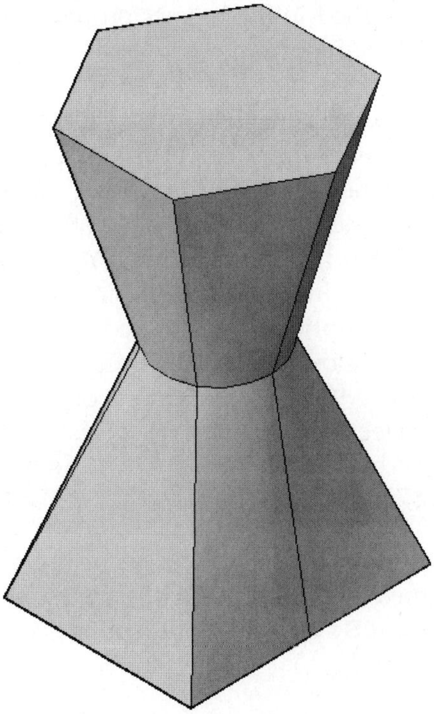

The **Smooth Fit** option creates a smooth transition between the cross sections. Sharp edges are only created at the first and last cross sections. This is the default setting and the one used to create the loft shown in **Figure 9-8B.**

When the **Normal to:** option is selected in the dialog box, you can choose how the normal of the transition is treated at the cross sections. A ***normal*** is a vector extending perpendicular to the cross section. When the transition is normal to a cross section, it is perpendicular to the cross section. You can set the transition normal to the first cross section, last cross section, both first and last cross sections, or all cross sections. See **Figure 9-11.** Select the normal setting in the drop-down list. You will have to experiment with these settings to get the desired loft shape.

Figure 9-11.
The profiles in Figure 9-8A are lofted with the **Normal to:** option on in the **Loft Settings** dialog box. Cross sections were selected from bottom to top. Compare these results with Figure 9-8B and Figure 9-10. A—**Start cross section.** B—**End cross section.** C—**Start and End cross sections.** D—**All cross sections.**

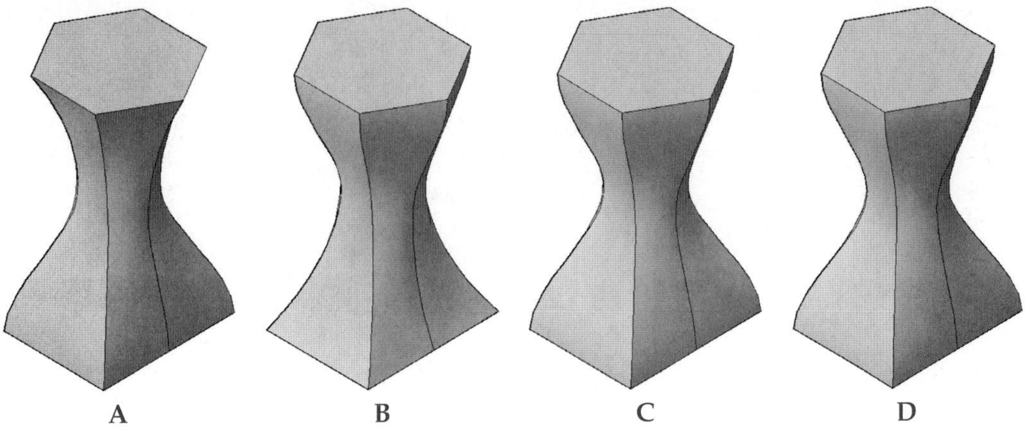

The **Draft angles** option allows you to add a taper to the beginning and end of the loft. A ***draft angle*** is a slight taper added to a part that allows the part to be removed from a mold. Plastic or metal parts are sometimes formed in a two-part mold. In order to remove the parts, a slight angle is designed into the parts on the inside and outside surfaces to make removing the part from the mold easier.

When setting the draft angle, you can set the angle and magnitude. See Figure 9-12. The default draft angle is 90°, which means the transition is perpendicular to the cross section. The magnitude represents the relative distance from the cross section, in the same direction as the draft angle, before the transition starts to curve toward the next cross section. Magnitude settings depend on the size of the cross sections, the draft angle values, and the distance between the cross sections. You may have to experiment with different magnitude and angle settings to get the desired loft shape.

The **Close surface or solid** option is used to connect the last cross section to the first cross section. This option "closes" the loft, similar to the **Close** option of the **LINE** or **PLINE** command. See Figure 9-13. This option is only available when the **Ruled** or **Smooth Fit** radio button is selected.

PROFESSIONAL TIP

The settings in the **Loft Settings** dialog box are retained as the default, so get in the habit of checking them each time you create a loft. The **LOFTNORMALS** system variable controls which surface control radio button is current.

Exercise 9-3

Complete the exercise on the Student CD.

Controlling the Loft with Guide Curves

Guide curves are lines that control the shape of the transition between cross sections. They do not have to be *curves.* They can be lines, arcs, elliptical arcs, splines (2D or 3D), or polylines (2D or 3D). There are four rules to follow when using guide curves:

Figure 9-12.
When setting the draft angle, you can set the angle and the magnitude. A—Draft angle of 90° and a magnitude of zero. B—Draft angle of 30° and a magnitude of 180. C—Draft angle of 60° and a magnitude of 180.

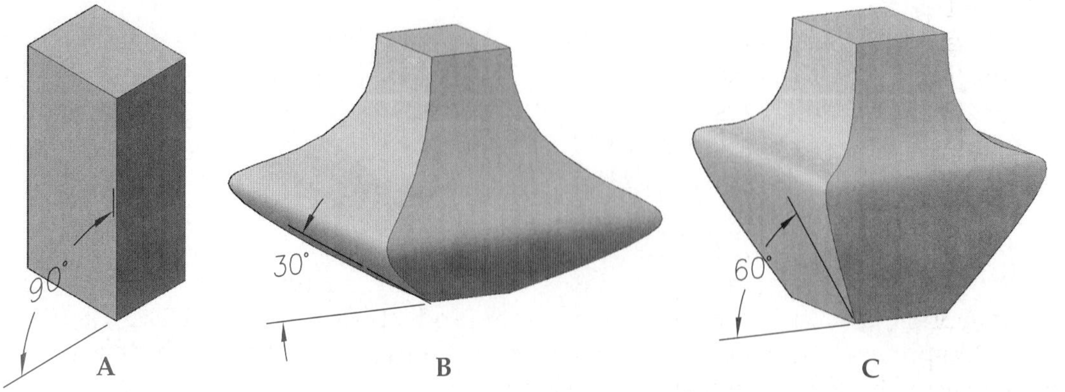

Figure 9-13.
A—These profiles will be used to create a sealing ring. They should be selected in a counterclockwise direction starting with the first cross section. B—The resulting loft with the default settings. Notice the gap between the first and last cross sections. C—By checking the **Close surface or solid** check box in the **Loft Settings** dialog box, the loft continues from the last cross section to the first cross section.

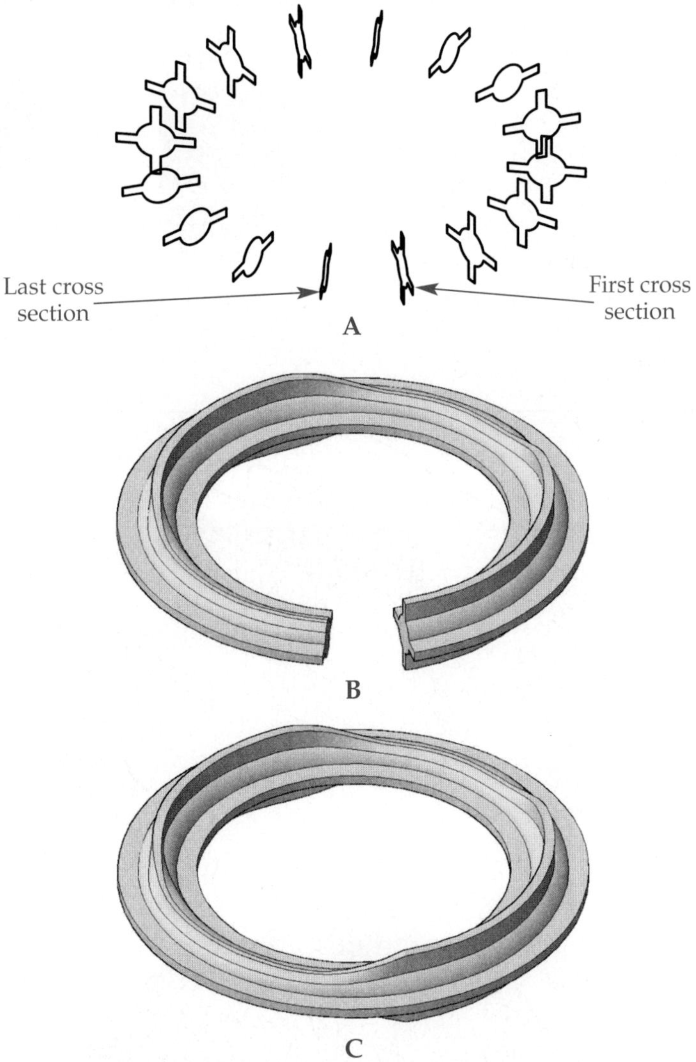

- The guide curve should start on the first cross section.
- The guide curve should end on the last cross section.
- The guide curve should intersect all other cross sections.
- The surface control in the **Loft Settings** dialog box must be set to **Smooth Fit** (**LOFTNORMALS** = 1).

When the **Guides** option is entered, you are prompted to select the guide curves. Select all of the guide curves and press [Enter]. The loft is created. The order in which guide curves are selected is not important.

For example, Figure 9-14A shows two circles that will be lofted. If the **Cross-sections only** option is used, a cylinder is created, Figure 9-14B. However, if the **Guides** option is used and the two guide curves shown in Figure 9-14A are selected, one side of the cylinder is deformed similar to a handle or grip. See Figure 9-14C.

Lofting is used to create open contour shapes such as fenders, automobile interior parts, fabrics, and other ergonomic consumer products. Figure 9-15 shows the use of open 2D splines in the construction of a fabric covering. Notice how each cross section is intersected by the guide curve. There is a cross section at the beginning of the guide curve and one at the end. These conditions fulfill the rules outlined earlier.

Figure 9-14.
A—These two circles will be lofted. The lines shown in color will be used as guide curves. B—When the circles are lofted using the **Cross-sections only** option, a cylinder is created. C—When the **Guides** option is used and the guide curves shown in A are selected, the resulting loft is shaped like a handle or grip.

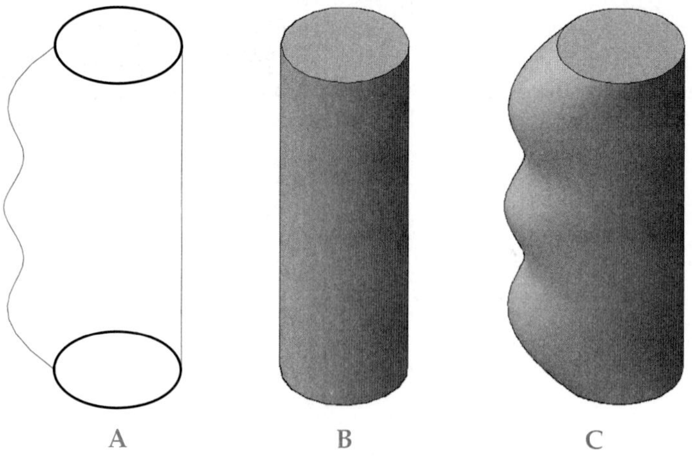

Figure 9-15.
A—The open profiles shown in black and the guide curve shown in color will be used to create a fabric covering for the three solid objects. B—The resulting fabric covering. This is a surface because the profiles were open.

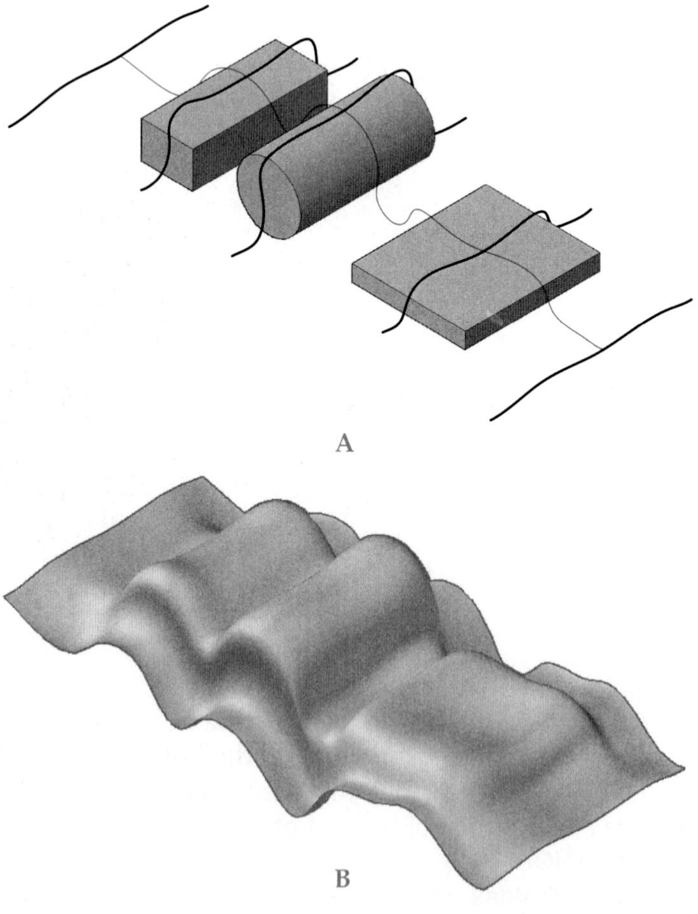

CAUTION

Guide curves only work well when the surface control is set to **Smooth Fit** (**LOFTNORMALS** = 1). Remember, the settings in the **Loft Settings** dialog box are retained after the previous **LOFT** command. If you get an error message when using guide curves or the curves are not reflected in the end result, make sure **LOFTNORMALS** is set to 1 and try it again.

Controlling the Loft with a Path

The **Path** option of the **LOFT** command places the cross sections along a single path. The path must intersect the planes on which each of the cross sections lie. However, the path does *not* have to physically touch the edge of each cross section, as is required of guide curves. When the **Path** option is entered, you are prompted to select the path. Once the path is picked, the loft is created. The cross sections remain in their original positions.

Figure 9-16 shows how 2D shapes can be positioned at various points on a path to create a loft. The rectangular shape does not cross the path. However, as long as the path intersects the plane of the rectangle, which it does, the shape will be included in the loft definition. The last shape at the top of the helix is a point object, causing the loft to taper.

PROFESSIONAL TIP

The **LOFT** command does not allow self-intersecting lofts to be created. Unfortunately, the error message you receive only states: The selected entities are not valid. If you see this message, look for areas where the path may be closing in on itself.

Exercise 9-4

Complete the exercise on the Student CD.

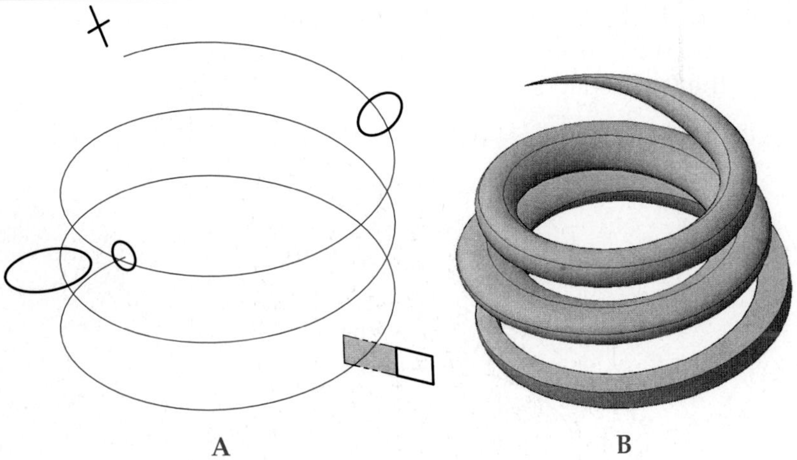

Figure 9-16.
A—The profiles shown in black will be lofted along the path shown in color. Notice how the rectangular profile is not intersected by the path, but the path does intersect the plane on which the rectangle lies. B—the resulting loft.

Chapter Test

Answer the following questions. Write your answers on a separate sheet of paper or complete the electronic chapter test on the Student CD.

1. What is a *loft?*
2. Which type of 2D shape results in a solid object when swept or lofted?
3. When using the **SWEEP** command, on which endpoint of the path does the sweep start?
4. What is the purpose of the **Base Point** option of the **SWEEP** command?
5. After the sweep or loft is created, how can the creation options be changed?
6. Which objects may be used as a sweep path?
7. How is the alignment of a sweep set to be perpendicular to the start of the path?
8. Which **SWEEP** command option is used to taper the sweep?
9. What is the difference between the **Ruled** and **Smooth Fit** options in the **LOFT** command?
10. What does the **Bank** option of the **LOFT** command do?
11. Where is the check box that will close the loft, similar to a polyline, and what is its name?
12. List five objects that may be used as guide curves in a loft.
13. What are the four rules that must be followed when using guide curves?
14. When using the **Path** option of the **LOFT** command, what must the path intersect?
15. How can a loft be created so it tapers to a point at its end?

Drawing Problems

1. Create the lamp shade shown below. Create two separate loft objects for the top and the bottom. Then, union the two pieces. Finally, scale a copy and hollow out the lamp shade. Save the drawing as P09_01.

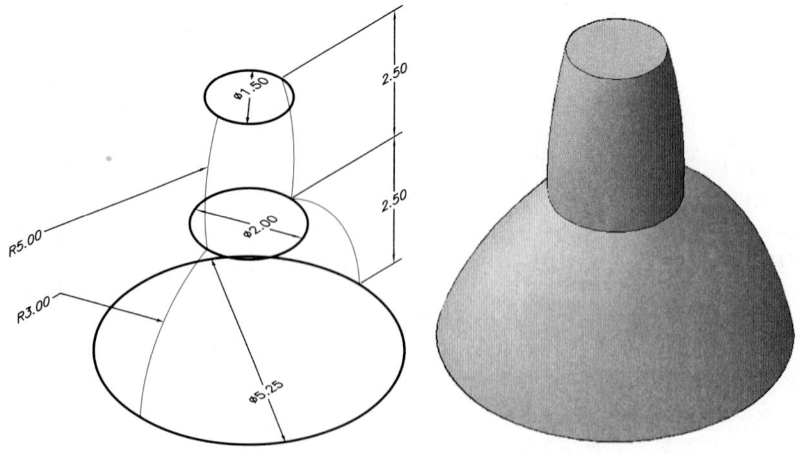

A B

2. Create the two shampoo bottles shown below. One design uses cross sections only and the other uses a guide curve. Each bottle is made up of two loft objects. Join the pieces so each bottle is one solid. Save the drawing as P09_02.

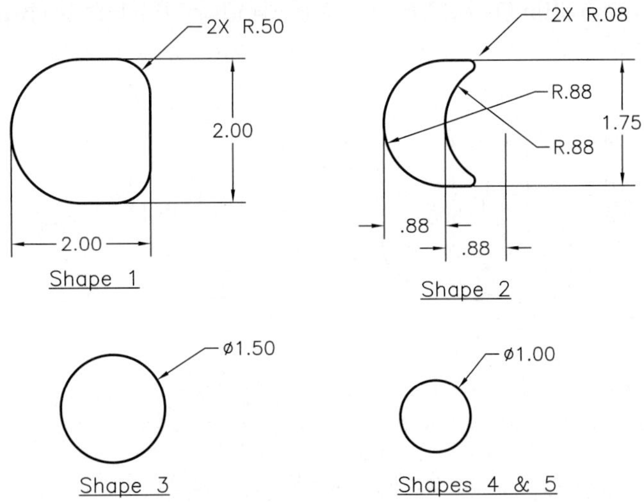

A

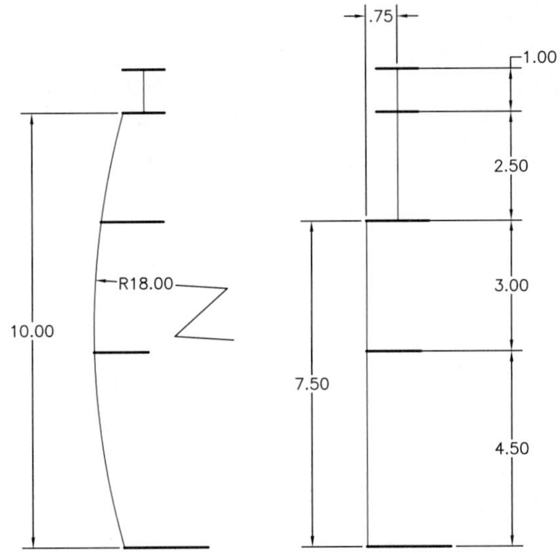

B

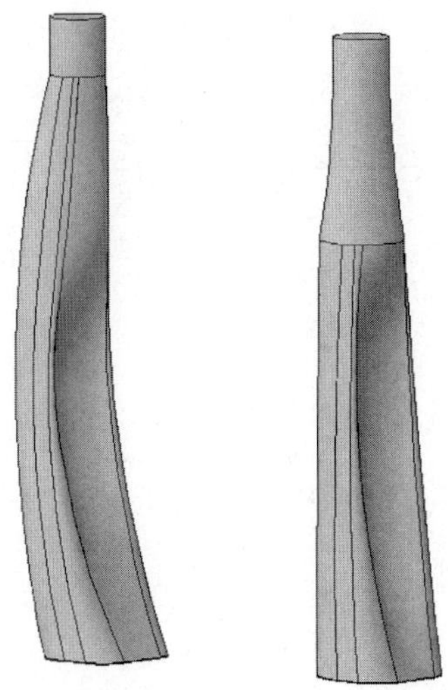

C

3. Create as a loft the automobile fender shown below. Use either the **Guide** or the **Path** option and the line shown in color. Save the drawing as P09_03.

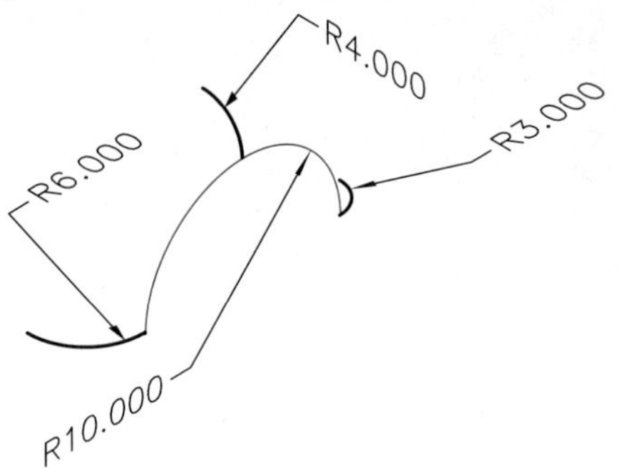

A

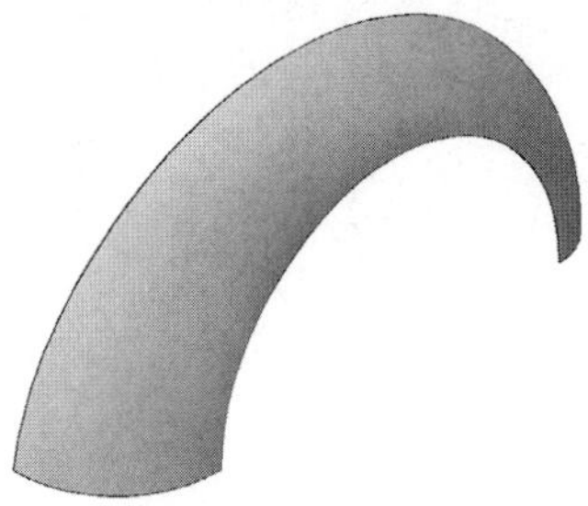

B

4. Draw as a loft the C-Clamp shown below. Use the shapes (A, B, C, and D) as the cross sections and the polyline (in color) as the guide curve. Add Ø1 unit cylinders to the ends. Make one cylinder .125H and the other 1.125H. The cylinders should be centered on profile D and located at the ends of the loft as shown. Make a Ø.625 hole through the larger cylinder. Save the drawing as P09_04.

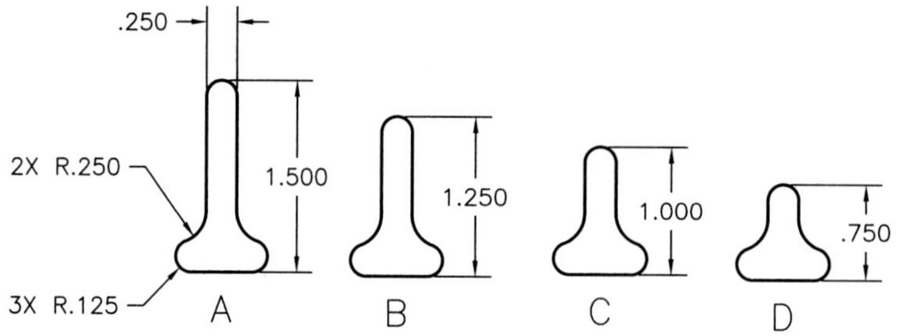

Cross Sections

A

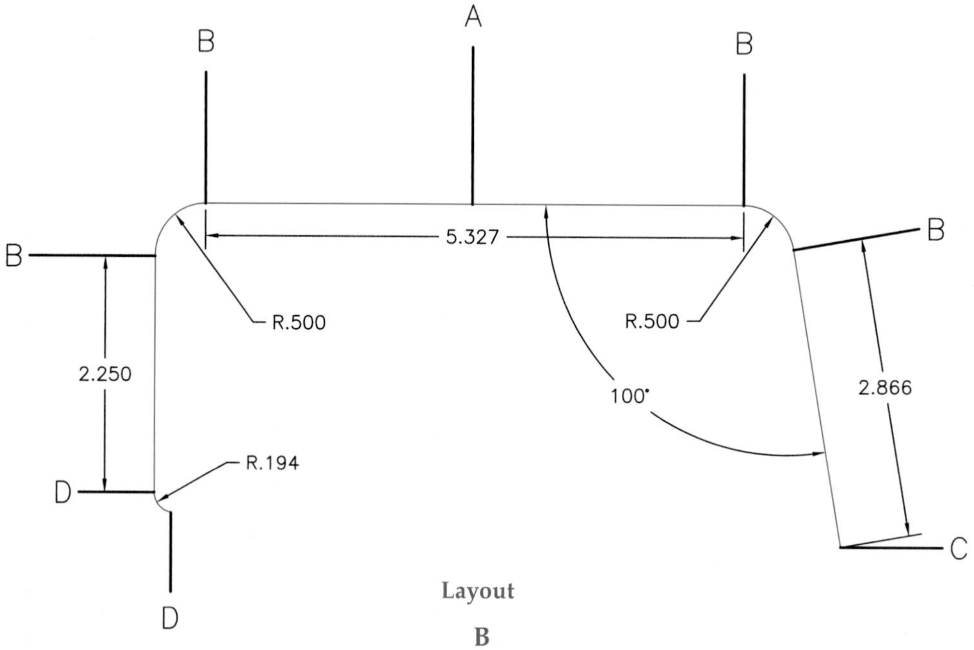

Layout

B

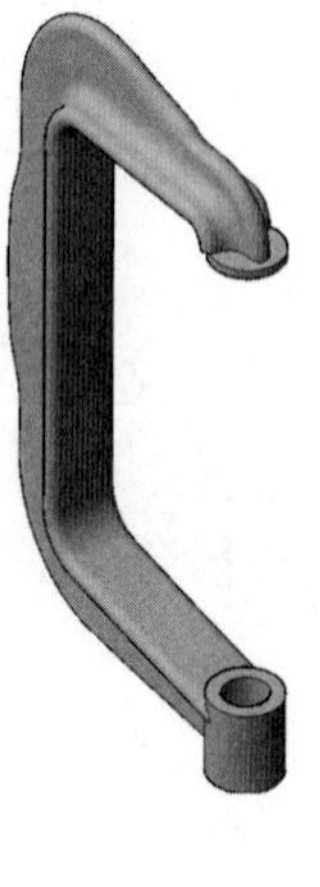

C

5. In this problem, you will draw a racetrack for toy cars by sweeping a 2D shape along a polyline path.
   A. Draw the polyline path shown with the coordinates given. Turn it into a spline.
   B. Draw the 2D profile shown using the dimensions given. Turn it into a region or a polyline.
   C. Use the **SWEEP** command to create the racetrack, as shown in the shaded view.
   D. You may have to use the **Properties** palette to adjust the sweep after it is drawn.
   E. Save the drawing as P09_05.

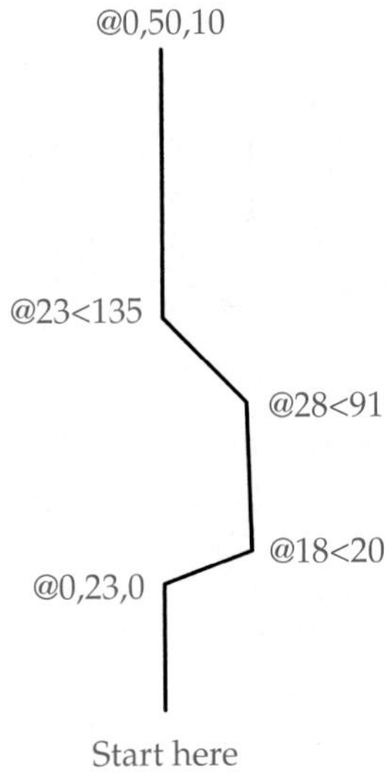

Polyline Path

A

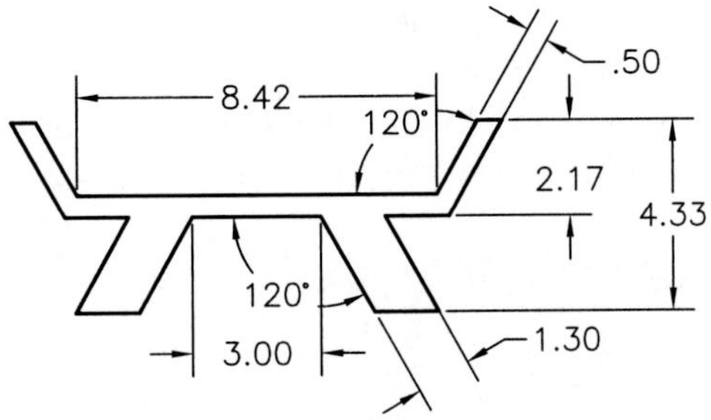

2D Profile

B

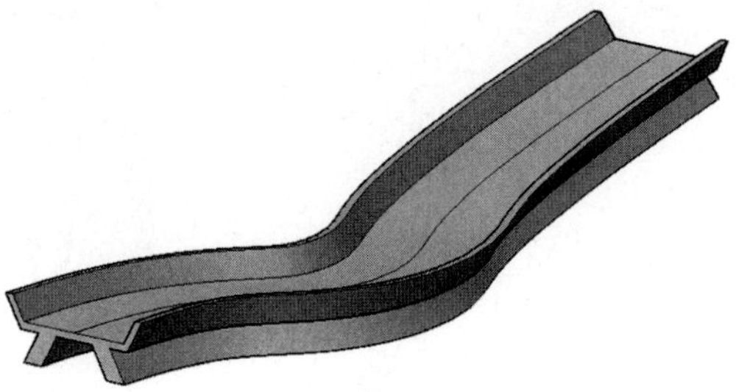

C

6. In this exercise, you will cut a UNC thread in a cylinder by sweeping a 2D shape around a helix and subtracting it.
   A. Draw a ∅.25 cylinder that is 1.00 in height.
   B. Draw the thread cutter profile shown below. The long edge of the cutter should be aligned with the vertical edge of the cylinder.
   C. Draw a helix centered on the cylinder with base and top radii of .125, turn height of .050, and a total height of 1.000.
   D. Sweep the 2D shape along the helix. Then, subtract the resulting solid from the cylinder. Refer to the shaded view shown below.
   E. If time allows, create another cutter profile to cut a .0313 × 45° chamfer on the end of the thread. Use a circle as a sweep path or revolve the profile about the center of the cylinder.
   F. Save the drawing as P09_06.

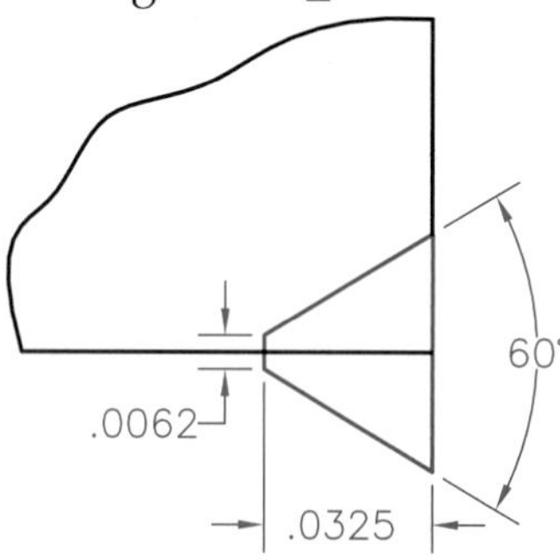

Thread Cutter
A

B

7. In this problem, you will add a seatback to the kitchen chair you started modeling in Chapter 2. In Chapter 8, you refined the seat.
   A. Open P08_10 from Chapter 8.
   B. Draw an arc for the top of the bow. Using a 14.25″ length of the arc, divide it into seven equal segments.
   C. Position eight ∅.50 circles at the division points.
   D. Draw circles at the top of each hole in the seat.
   E. Create a loft between each lower circle and each upper circle.
   F. Using the information in the drawings, create the outer bow for the seatback.
   G. Save the drawing as P09_07.

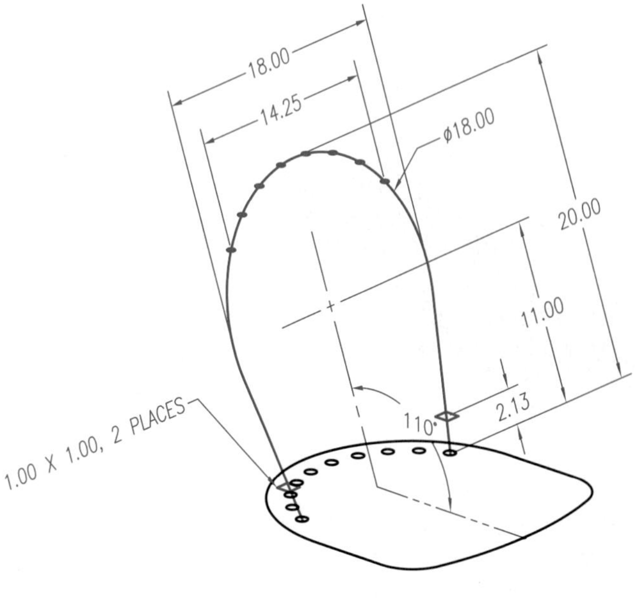

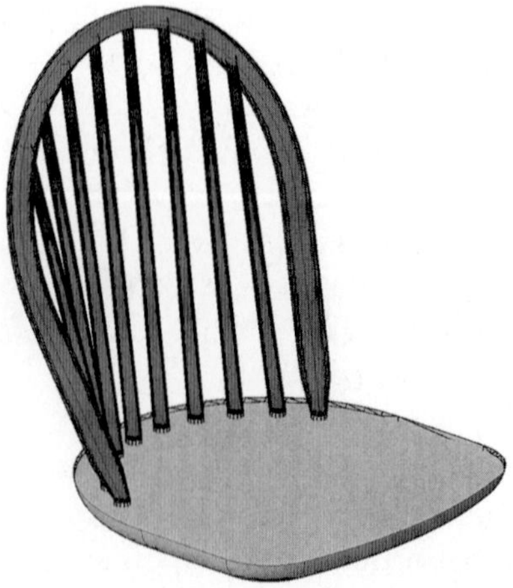
Completed Seatback

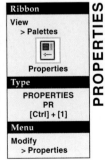

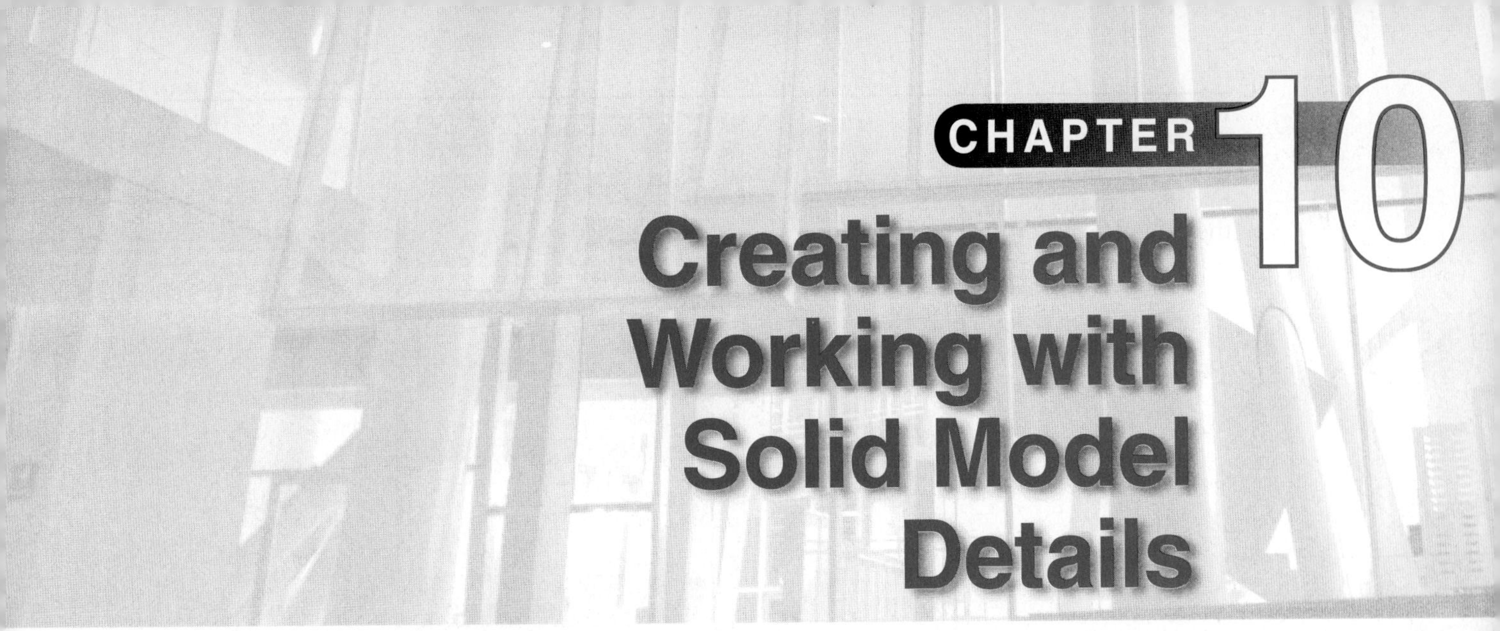

CHAPTER 10

Creating and Working with Solid Model Details

Learning Objectives

After completing this chapter, you will be able to:

- ✓ Change properties on solids.
- ✓ Align objects.
- ✓ Rotate objects in three dimensions.
- ✓ Mirror objects in three dimensions.
- ✓ Create 3D arrays.
- ✓ Fillet solid objects.
- ✓ Chamfer solid objects.
- ✓ Thicken a surface into a solid.
- ✓ Convert planar objects into surfaces.
- ✓ Slice a solid using various methods.
- ✓ Construct details on solid models.
- ✓ Remove features from solid models.

Changing Properties

Properties of 3D objects can be modified using the **Properties** palette, which is thoroughly discussed in *AutoCAD and Its Applications—Basics.* This palette is displayed using the **PROPERTIES** command. You can also double-click on a solid object or select the solid, right-click, and pick **Properties** from the shortcut menu.

PROPERTIES

Ribbon
View > Palettes
Properties
Type
PROPERTIES
PR
[Ctrl] + [1]
Menu
Modify > Properties

The **Properties** palette lists the properties of the currently selected object. For example, **Figure 10-1** lists the properties of a selected solid sphere. AutoCAD offers some parametric solid modeling options. A ***parametric solid modeling program*** allows you to change the parameters, such as a sphere's diameter, in the **Properties** palette. You can also change the sphere's position, linetype, linetype scale, color, layer, lineweight, and visual settings. The categories and properties available in the **Properties** palette depend on the selected object.

To modify an object property, select the property. Then, enter a new value in the right-hand column. The drawing is updated to reflect the changes. You can leave the **Properties** palette open as you continue with your work.

Figure 10-1.
The **Properties** palette can be used to change many of the properties of a solid.

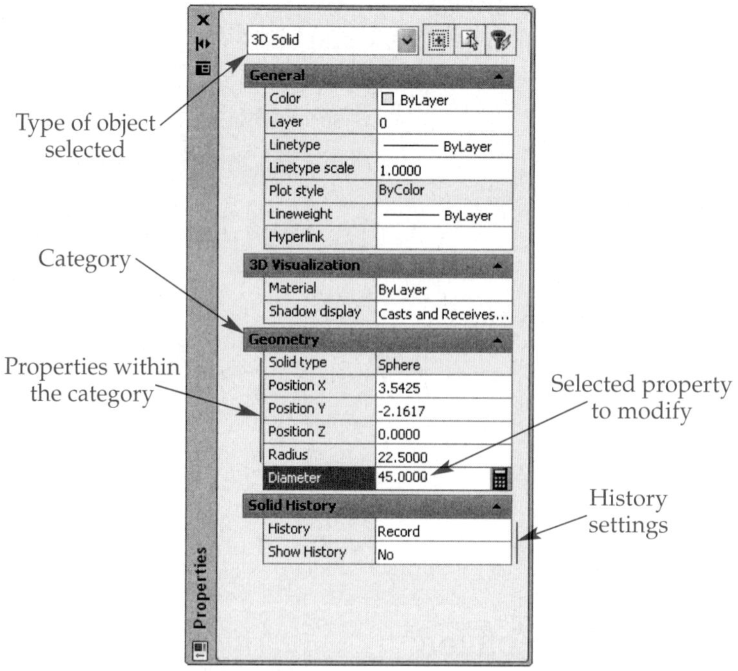

Solid Model History

AutoCAD can automatically record a history of a composite solid model's construction. The control of the history setting is found in the **Solid History** category of the **Properties** palette. By default, the History property in the **Properties** palette is set to Record, which means that the history will be saved. See Figure 10-1. It is generally a good idea to have the history recorded. Then, at any time, you can graphically display all of the geometry that was used to create the model.

If the **SOLIDHIST** system variable is set to a value of 1, all new solids have their History property set to Record. This is the default. If the system variable is set to 0, all new solids have their History property set to None (no recording). With either setting of the system variable, the **Properties** palette can be used to change the setting for individual solids.

To view the graphic history of the composite solid, set the Show History property in the **Properties** palette to Yes. All of the geometry used to construct the model is displayed. If the **SHOWHIST** system variable is set to 0, the Show History property is set to No for all solids and cannot be changed. If this system variable is set to 2, the Show History property is set to Yes for all solids and cannot be changed. A **SHOWHIST** setting of 1 allows the Show History property to be individually set for each solid.

An example of showing the history on a composite solid is provided in Figure 10-2. The object appears in its current edited format in Figure 10-2A. The Conceptual visual style is set current and the Show History property is set to No. In Figure 10-2B, the Show History property is set to Yes. Isolines have also been turned on. You can see the geometry that was used in the Boolean subtraction operations. Using subobject editing techniques, the individual geometry can be selected and edited. Subobject editing is discussed in detail in Chapter 11.

NOTE

If the Solid History property is set to Yes to display the components of the composite solid, as seen in Figure 10-2, the components will appear when the drawing is plotted. Be sure to set the Show History property to No before you print or plot.

Figure 10-2.
A—The object appears in its current edited format with **Show History** property turned off.
B—The **Show History** property is set to **Yes** and the display of isolines has been turned on.

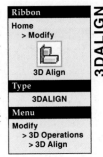

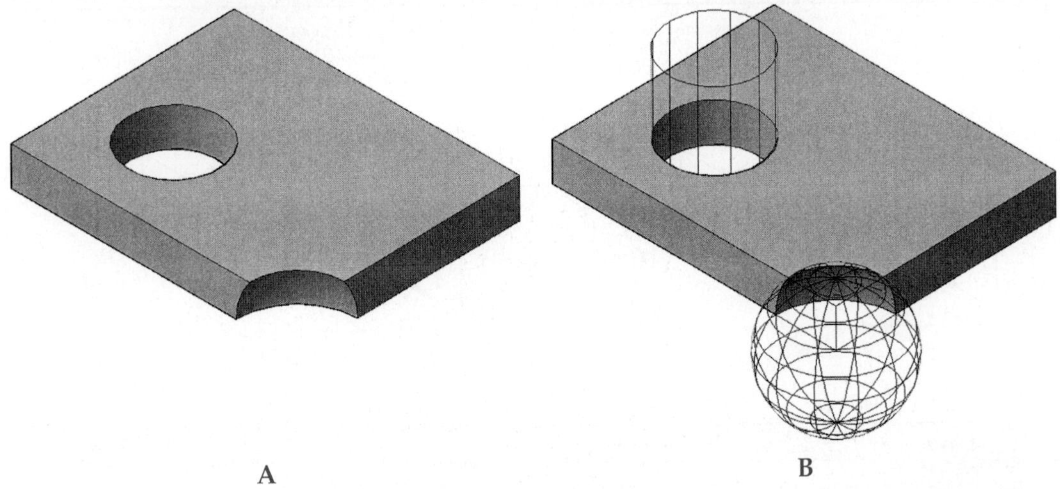

Aligning Objects in 3D

AutoCAD provides two different methods with which to move and rotate objects in a single command. This is called ***aligning*** objects. The simplest method is to align 3D objects by picking source points on the first object and then picking destination points on the object to which the first one is to be aligned. This is accomplished with the **3DALIGN** command, which allows you to both relocate and rotate the object. The second and much more versatile method allows you to not only move and rotate an object, but also to scale the object being aligned. This is possible with the **ALIGN** command.

Move and Rotate Objects in 3D Space

Ribbon
Home > Modify
3D Align
Type
3DALIGN
Menu
Modify > 3D Operations > 3D Align

3DALIGN

The basic function of moving and rotating an object relative to a second object or set of points is done with the **3DALIGN** command. It allows you to reorient an object in 3D space. Using this command, you can correct errors of 3D construction and quickly manipulate 3D objects. The **3DALIGN** command requires existing points (source) and the new location of those existing points (destination).

For example, refer to Figure 10-3. The wedge in Figure 10-3A is aligned in its new position in Figure 10-3B as follows. Set the **Intersection** or **Endpoint** running object snap to make point selection easier. Refer to the figure for the pick points.

Select objects: *(pick the wedge)*
1 found
Select objects: ↵
  Specify source plane and orientation...
Specify base point or [Copy]: *(pick P1)*
Specify second point or [Continue] <C>: *(pick P2)*
Specify third point or [Continue] <C>: *(pick P3)*
  Specify destination plane and orientation...
Specify first destination point: *(pick P4)*
Specify second destination point or [eXit] <X>: *(pick P5)*
Specify third destination point or [eXit] <X>: ↵

Figure 10-3.
The **3DALIGN** command can be used to properly orient 3D objects. A—Before aligning. Note the pick points. B—After aligning.

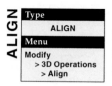

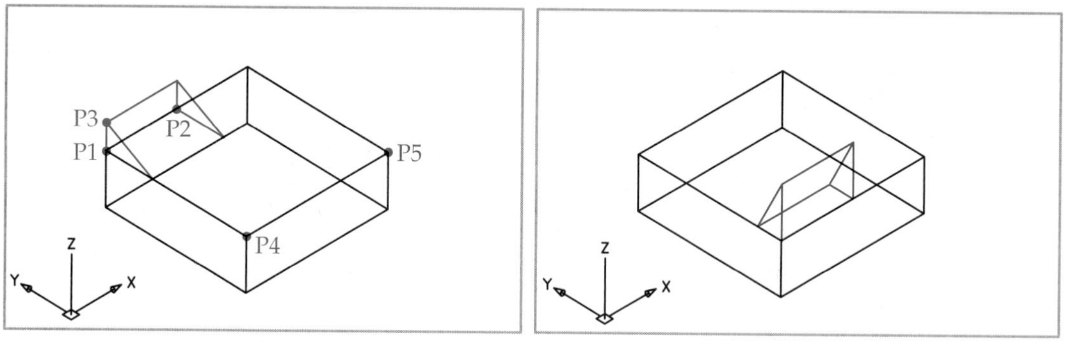

A　　　　B

PROFESSIONAL TIP

You can also use the **3DALIGN** command to copy, instead of move, an object and realign it at the same time. Just select the **Copy** option at the Specify base point or [Copy]: prompt. Then, continue selecting the points as shown above.

Exercise 10-1

Complete the exercise on the Student CD.

ALIGN

Type: ALIGN

Menu: Modify > 3D Operations > Align

Move, Rotate, and Scale Objects in 3D Space

The **ALIGN** command has the same functions of the **3DALIGN** command, but adds the ability to scale an object. Refer to **Figure 10-4**. The 90° bend must be rotated and scaled to fit onto the end of the HVAC assembly. Two source points and two destination points are required, **Figure 10-4A**. Then, you can choose to scale the object.

Select objects: *(pick the 90° bend)*
1 found
Select objects: ↵
Specify first source point: *(pick P1)*
Specify first destination point: *(pick P2; a line is drawn between the two points)*
Specify second source point: *(pick P3)*
Specify second destination point: *(pick P4; a line is drawn between the two points)*
Specify third source point or <continue>: ↵
Scale objects based on alignment points? [Yes/No] <N>: **Y**↵

The 90° bend is aligned and scaled to meet the existing ductwork object. See **Figure 10-4B.** You can also align using three source and three destination points. However, when doing so, you cannot scale the object.

PROFESSIONAL TIP

Before using 3D editing commands, set running object snaps to enhance your accuracy and speed.

Figure 10-4.
Using the **ALIGN** command. A—Two source points and two destination points are required. Notice how the bend is not at the proper scale. B—You can choose to scale the object during the operation. Notice how the aligned bend is also properly scaled.

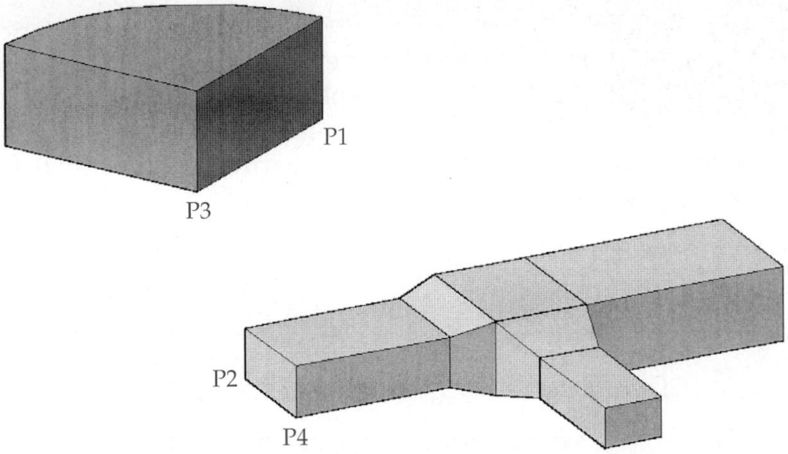

A

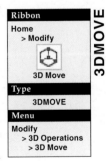

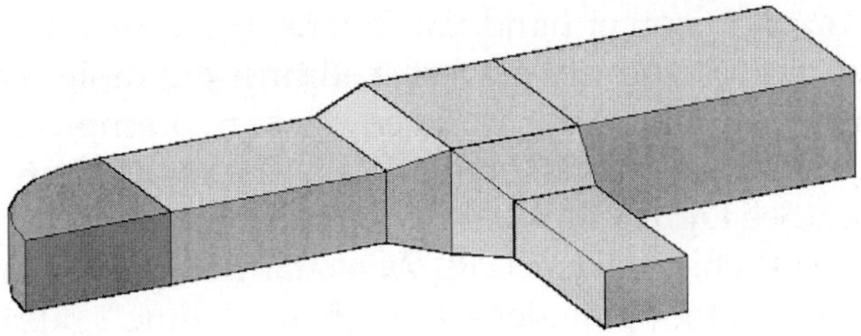

B

Exercise 10-2

Complete the exercise on the Student CD.

3D Moving

The **3DMOVE** command allows you to quickly move an object along any axis or plane of the current UCS. When the command is initiated, you are prompted to select the objects to move. After selecting the objects, press [Enter]. The ***move grip tool*** is displayed, attached to the cursor. The move grip tool is a tripod that appears similar to the shaded UCS icon. See **Figure 10-5A.** Pick a location to place the tool at the base of the move.

3DMOVE

Ribbon
Home
> Modify
3D Move
Type
3DMOVE
Menu
Modify
> 3D Operations
> 3D Move

If you move the pointer over the X, Y, or Z axis of the grip tool, the axis changes to yellow. To restrict movement along that axis, pick the axis. If you move the pointer over one of the right angles at the origin of the tool, the corresponding two axes turn yellow. Pick to restrict the movement to that plane. You can complete the movement by either picking a new point or by direct distance entry.

By default, when a solid is selected with no command active, the move grip tool is displayed. You can relocate the tool by selecting the grip at the tool's origin. Then, move the tool to a new location and pick. If the **Allow/Disallow Dynamic UCS** button is on, you can also realign the tool.

NOTE

If the **GTAUTO** system variable is set to 1, the move grip tool is displayed when a solid is selected with no command active. If the **GTLOCATION** system variable is set to 0, the grip tool is placed on the UCS icon (not necessarily the UCS *origin*). Both of these settings are the defaults.

3D Rotating

3DROTATE

Ribbon
Home
> Modify
3D Rotate
Type
3DROTATE
Menu
Modify
> 3D Operation
> 3D Rotate

As you have seen in earlier chapters, the **ROTATE** command can be used to rotate 3D objects. However, the command can only rotate objects in the XY plane of the current UCS. This is why you had to change UCSs to properly rotate objects. The **3DROTATE** command, on the other hand, can rotate objects on any axis regardless of the current UCS. This is an extremely powerful editing and design tool.

When the command is initiated, you are prompted to select the objects to rotate. After selecting the objects, press [Enter]. The ***rotate grip tool*** is displayed, attached to the cursor. See Figure 10-5B. If the 2D Wireframe visual style is current, the visual style is temporarily changed to the 3D Wireframe because the grip tool is not displayed in 2D mode. The grip tool provides you with a dynamic, graphic representation of the three axes of rotation. Pick a location that is to be the base point of the rotation.

Now, you can use the grip tool to rotate the objects about the tool's local X, Y, or Z axis. As you hover the cursor over one of the three circles in the grip tool, a vector is displayed that represents the axis of rotation. To rotate about the tool's X axis, pick the red circle on the grip tool. To rotate about the Y axis, pick the green circle. To rotate about the Z axis, pick the blue circle. Once you select a circle, it turns yellow and you are prompted for the start point of the rotation angle. You can enter a direct angle at this prompt or pick the first of two points defining the angle of rotation. When the rotation angle is defined, the object is rotated about the selected axis.

Figure 10-5.
A—The move grip tool is a tripod that appears similar to the shaded UCS icon. Pick a location to place the tool at the base of the move. B—This is the rotate grip tool. The three axes of rotation are represented by the circles. The origin of the rotation is where you place the center grip.

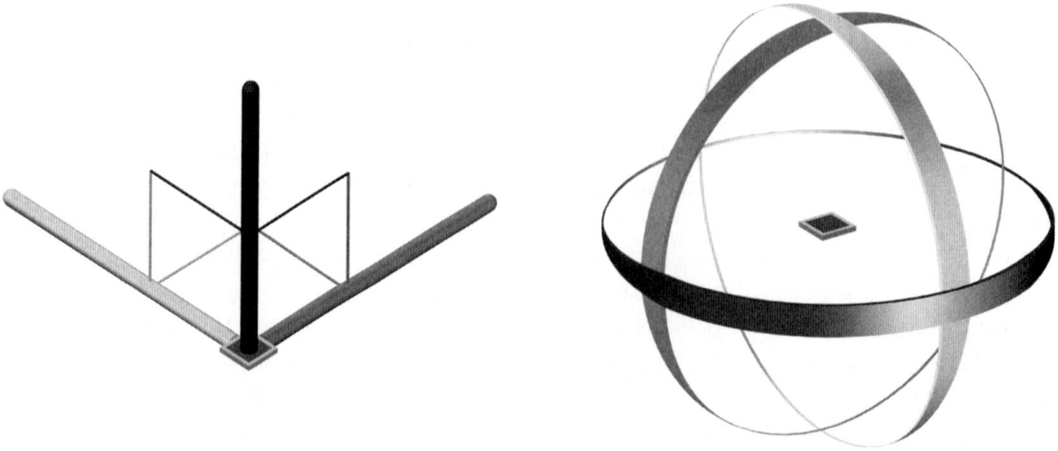

A B

Figure 10-6.
A—Use object tracking or object snaps to place the grip tool in the middle of the rectangular face. Then, select the axis of rotation. B—The completed rotation.

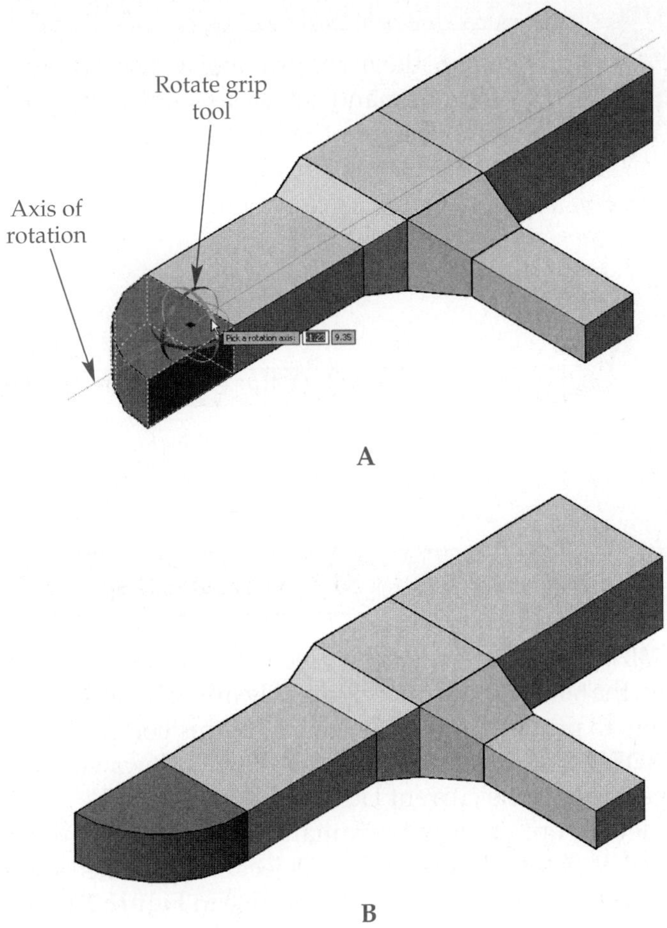

The following example rotates the bend in the HVAC assembly shown in Figure 10-6A. Set the **Midpoint** object snap and turn on object tracking. Then, select the command and continue:

Current positive angle in UCS: ANGDIR=*(current)* ANGBASE=*(current)*
Select objects: *(pick the bend)*
1 found
Select objects: ↵
Specify base point: *(acquire the midpoint of the vertical and horizontal edges, then pick to place the grip tool in the middle of the rectangular face)*
Pick a rotation axis: *(pick the green circle)*
Specify angle start point or type an angle: **180**↵

Note that the rotate grip tool remains visible through the base point and the angle of rotation selections. The rotated object is shown in Figure 10-6B.

If you need to rotate an object on an axis that is not parallel to the current X, Y, or Z axes, use a dynamic UCS with the **3DROTATE** command. Chapter 5 discussed the benefits of using a dynamic UCS when creating objects that need to be parallel to a surface other than the XY plane. With the object selected for rotation and the dynamic UCS option active (pick the **Allow/Disallow Dynamic UCS** button on the status bar), move the rotate grip tool over a face of the object. The grip tool aligns itself with the surface so that the Z axis is perpendicular to the face. Carefully place the grip tool over the point of rotation using object snaps. Make sure that the tool is correctly positioned before picking to locate it. Then, enter an angle or use polar tracking to rotate the object about the appropriate axis on the tool.

PROFESSIONAL TIP

By default, the move grip tool is displayed when an object is selected with no command active. To toggle between the move grip tool and the rotate grip tool, select the grip at the tool's origin and press the space bar. Then, pick a location for the tool's origin. You can toggle back to the move grip tool using the same procedure.

Exercise 10-3

Complete the exercise on the Student CD.

3D Mirroring

3DMIRROR

Ribbon
Home > Modify > 3D Mirror
Type
3DMIRROR
Menu
Modify > 3D Operation > 3D Mirror

The **MIRROR** command can be used to rotate 3D objects. However, like the **ROTATE** command, the **MIRROR** command can only mirror objects in the XY plane of the current UCS. Often, to properly mirror objects with this command, you have to change UCSs. The **MIRROR3D** command, on the other hand, allows you to mirror objects about any plane regardless of the current UCS.

The default option of the command is to define a mirror plane by picking three points on that plane, **Figure 10-7A.** Object snap modes should be used to accurately define the mirror plane. To mirror the wedge in **Figure 10-7A,** set the **Midpoint** running object snap, select the command, and use the following sequence. The resulting drawing is shown in **Figure 10-7B.**

Select objects: *(pick the wedge)*
1 found
Select objects: ↵
Specify first point of mirror plane (3 points) or
[Object/Last/Zaxis/View/XY/YZ/ZX/3points] <3points>: *(pick P1, which is the midpoint of the box's top edge)*
Specify second point on mirror plane: *(pick P2)*
Specify third point on mirror plane: *(pick P3)*
Delete source objects? [Yes/No] <N>: ↵

There are several different ways to define a mirror plane with the **MIRROR3D** command. These are:

- **Object.** The plane of the selected circle, arc, or 2D polyline segment is used as the mirror plane.
- **Last.** Uses the last mirror plane defined.
- **Zaxis.** Defines the plane with a pick point on the mirror plane and a point on the Z axis of the mirror plane.
- **View.** The viewing direction of the current viewpoint is aligned with a selected point to define the plane.
- **XY, YZ, ZX.** The mirror plane is placed parallel to one of the three basic planes of the current UCS and passes through a selected point.
- **3points.** Allows you to pick three points to define the mirror plane, as shown in the above example.

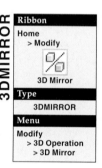

Figure 10-7.
The **MIRROR3D** command allows you to mirror objects about any plane regardless of the current UCS. A—The mirror plane defined by the three pick points is shown here in color. Point P1 is the midpoint of the top edge of the base. B—A copy of the original is mirrored.

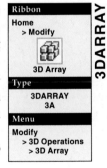

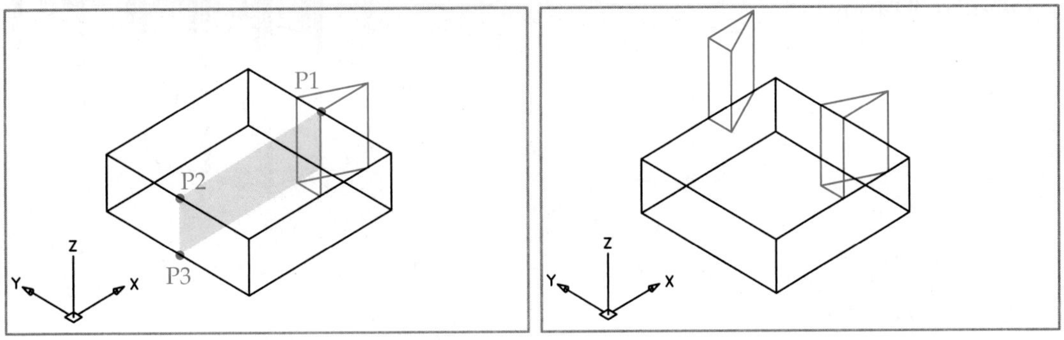

A B

Exercise 10-4

Complete the exercise on the Student CD.

Creating 3D Arrays

The **ARRAY** command can be used to create either a rectangular or polar array of a 3D object on the XY plane of the current UCS. You probably used this command to complete some of the problems in previous chapters. The **3DARRAY** command allows you to array an object in 3D space. There are two types of 3D arrays—rectangular and polar.

Rectangular 3D Arrays

In a ***rectangular 3D array,*** as with a rectangular 2D array, you must enter the number of rows and columns. However, you must also specify the number of ***levels,*** which represents the third (Z) dimension. The command sequence is similar to that used with the 2D array command, with two additional prompts.

3DARRAY

Ribbon
Home
> Modify
3D Array

Type
3DARRAY
3A

Menu
Modify
> 3D Operations
> 3D Array

An example of where a rectangular 3D array may be created is the layout of structural steel columns on multiple floors of a commercial building. In Figure 10-8A, you can see two concrete floor slabs of a building and a single steel column. It is now a simple matter of arraying the steel column in rows, columns, and levels.

To draw a rectangular 3D array, select the **3DARRAY** command. Pick the object to array and press [Enter]. Then, specify the **Rectangular** option:

Enter the type of array [Rectangular/Polar] <R>: **R**↵
Enter the number of rows (- - -) <1>: **3**↵
Enter the number of columns (¦¦¦) <1>: **5**↵
Enter the number of levels (...) <1>: **2**↵
Specify the distance between rows (- - -): **10'**↵
Specify the distance between columns (¦¦¦): **10'**↵
Specify the distance between levels (...): **12'8**↵

The result is shown in Figure 10-8B. Constructions like this can be quickly assembled for multiple levels using the **3DARRAY** command only once.

Figure 10-8.
A—Two floors and one steel column are drawn. B—A rectangular 3D array is used to place all of the required steel columns on both floors at the same time.

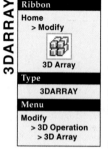

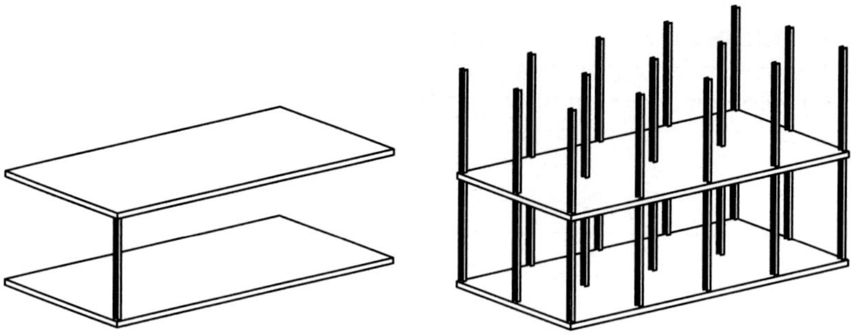

Polar 3D Arrays

3DARRAY

Ribbon
Home
> Modify
3D Array
Type
3DARRAY
Menu
Modify
> 3D Operation
> 3D Array

A ***polar 3D array*** is similar to a polar 2D array. However, the axis of rotation in a 2D polar array is parallel to the Z axis of the current UCS. In a 3D polar array, you can define a centerline axis of rotation that is not parallel to the Z axis of the current UCS. In other words, you can array an object in a UCS different from the current one. Unlike a rectangular 3D array, a polar 3D array does not allow you to create levels of the object. The object is arrayed in a plane defined by the object and the selected centerline (Z) axis.

To draw a polar 3D array, select the **3DARRAY** command. Pick the object to array and press [Enter]. Then, specify the **Polar** option:

Enter the type of array [Rectangular/Polar] <R>: **P**↵

For example, the four mounting flanges on the lower part of the duct in **Figure 10-9A** must be placed on the opposite end. However, notice the orientation of the UCS. First, copy one flange and rotate it to the proper orientation. Then, use the **3DARRAY** command as follows. Make sure ortho is on.

Select objects: *(select the copied flange)*
1 found
Select objects: ↵
Enter the type of array [Rectangular/Polar] <R>: **P**↵
Enter the number of items in the array: **4**↵
Specify the angle to fill (+=ccw, −=cw) <360>: ↵
Rotate arrayed objects? [Yes/No] <Y>: ↵
Specify center point of array: **CEN**↵
of: *(pick the center of the upper duct opening)*
Specify second point on axis of rotation: *(move the cursor so the ortho line projects out of the center of the duct opening and pick)*

The completed 3D polar array is shown in **Figure 10-9B**. If additional levels of a polar array are needed, they can be created by copying the array just created.

Exercise 10-5
Complete the exercise on the Student CD.

Figure 10-9.
A—A ductwork elbow with four flanges in place. Copies of these flanges need to be located on the opposite end. Start by creating one copy as shown. B—By creating a 3D polar array, the flanges are properly oriented without changing the UCS.

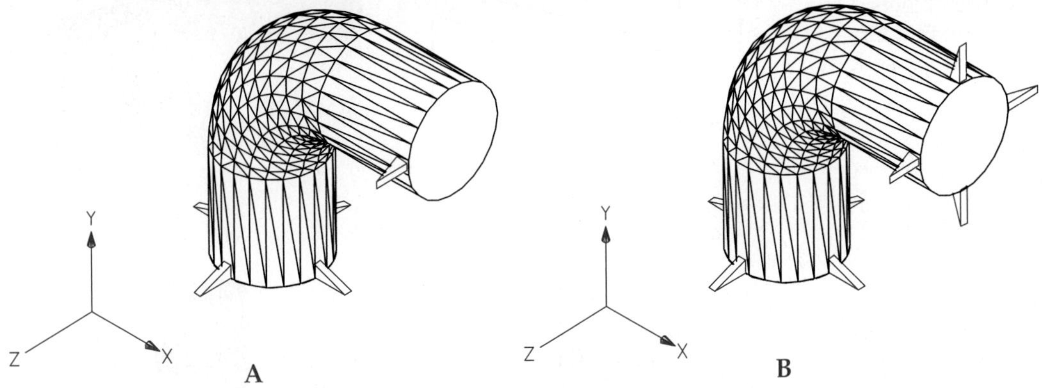

Filleting Solid Objects

Ribbon
Home
> Modify
Fillet
Type
FILLET
F
Menu
Modify
> Fillet

FILLET

A ***fillet*** is a rounded interior edge on an object, such as a box. A ***round*** is a rounded exterior edge. The **FILLET** command is used to create both fillets and rounds. Before a fillet or round is created at an intersection, the solid objects that intersect need to be joined using the **UNION** command. Then, use the **FILLET** command. See **Figure 10-10.** Since the object being filleted is actually a single solid and not two objects, only one edge is selected. In the following sequence, the fillet radius is set at .25, then the fillet is created. First, select the **FILLET** command and then continue as follows.

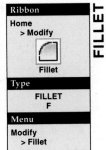

Current settings: Mode = *current*, Radius = *current*
Select first object or [Undo/Polyline/Radius/Trim/Multiple]: **R**↵
Specify fillet radius <*current*>: **.25**↵
Select first object or [Undo/Polyline/Radius/Trim/Multiple]: *(pick edge to be filleted or rounded)*
Enter fillet radius <0.2500>: ↵
Select an edge or [Chain/Radius]: ↵ *(this fillets the selected edge, but you can also select other edges at this point)*
1 edge(s) selected for fillet.

Examples of fillets and rounds are shown in **Figure 10-11.**

Figure 10-10.
A—Pick the edge where two unioned solids intersect to create a fillet. B—The fillet after rendering.

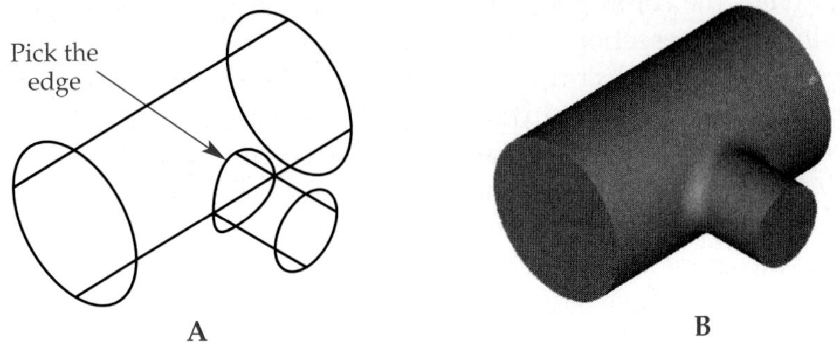

Figure 10-11.
Examples of fillets and rounds. The wireframe displays show the objects before the **FILLET** command is used.

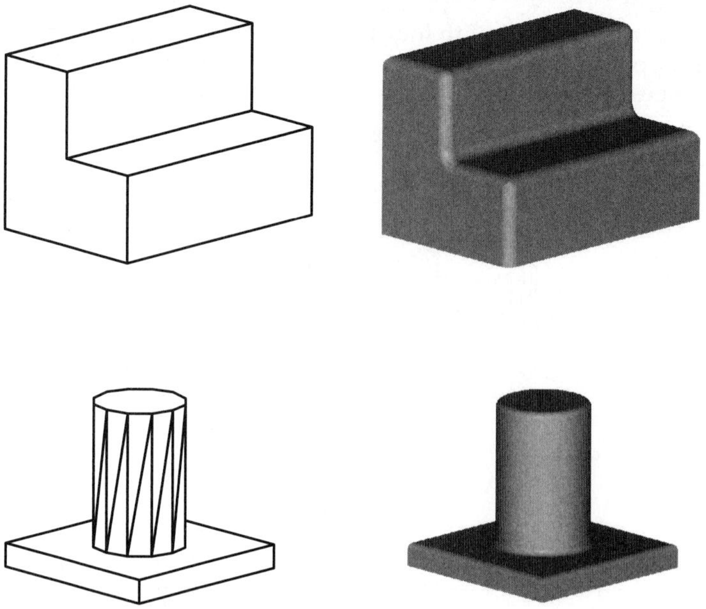

PROFESSIONAL TIP

You can construct and edit solid models while the object is displayed in a shaded view. If your computer has sufficient speed and power, it is often much easier to visualize the model in a 3D view with the Conceptual or Realistic visual style set current. This allows you to realistically view the model. If an edit or construction does not look right, just undo and try again.

Chamfering Solid Objects

CHAMFER

Ribbon
Home
> Modify
Chamfer

Type
CHAMFER
CHA

Menu
Modify
> Chamfer

A ***chamfer*** is a small square edge on the edges of an object. To create a chamfer on a 3D solid, use the **CHAMFER** command. Just as when chamfering a 2D line, there are two chamfer distances. Therefore, you must specify which surfaces correspond to the first and second distances. The detail to which the chamfer is applied must be constructed before chamfering. For example, if you are chamfering a hole, the object (cylinder) must first be subtracted to create the hole. If you are chamfering an intersection, the two objects must first be unioned.

After you enter the command, you must pick the edge you want to chamfer. The edge is actually the intersection of two surfaces of the solid. One of the two surfaces is highlighted when you select the edge. The highlighted surface is associated with the first chamfer distance. This surface is called the ***base surface.*** If the highlighted surface is not the one you want as the base surface, enter N at the [Next/OK] prompt and press [Enter]. This highlights the next surface. An edge is created by two surfaces. Therefore, when you enter N for the next surface, AutoCAD cycles through only two surfaces. When the proper base surface is highlighted, press [Enter].

Figure 10-12.
A—A hole is chamfered by picking the top surface, then the edge of the hole. B—The end of a cylinder is chamfered by first picking the side, then the end. Both ends can be chamfered at the same time, as shown here.

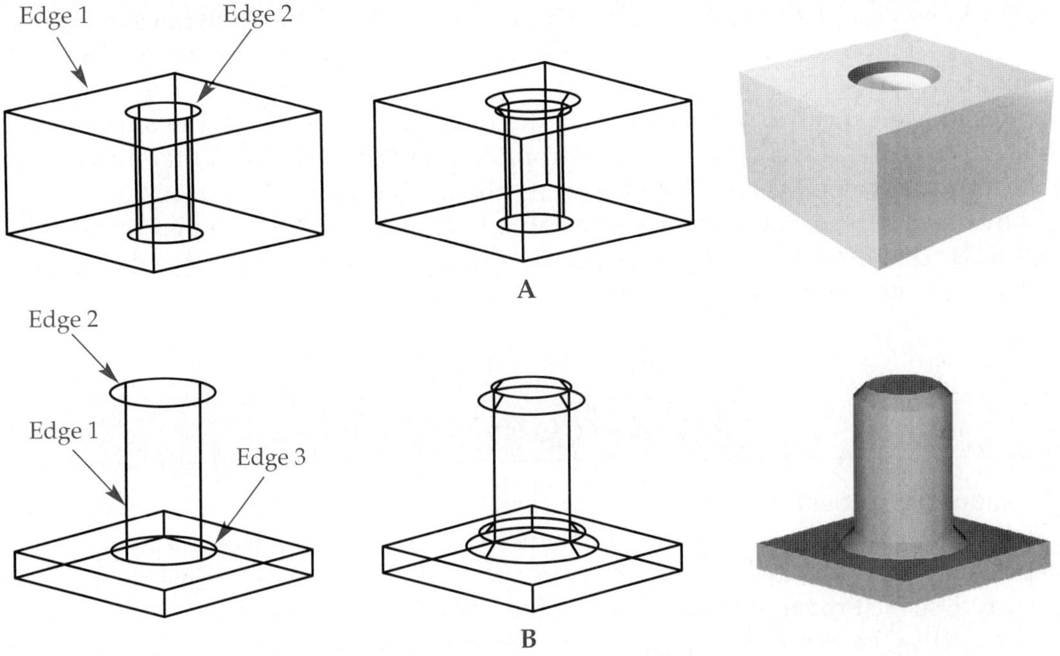

Chamfering a hole is shown in **Figure 10-12A.** The end of the cylinder in **Figure 10-12B** is chamfered by first picking one of the vertical isolines, then picking the top edge. The following command sequence is illustrated in **Figure 10-12A.**

(TRIM mode) Current chamfer Dist1 = *current*, Dist2 = *current*
Select first line or [Undo/Polyline/Distance/Angle/Trim/mEthod/Multiple]: *(pick edge 1)*
Base surface selection...
(if the side surface is highlighted, change to the top surface as follows)
Enter surface selection option [Next/OK (current)] <OK>: **N**↵
(the top surface should be highlighted)
Enter surface selection option [Next/OK (current)] <OK>: ↵
Specify base surface chamfer distance <*current*>: **.125**↵
Specify other surface chamfer distance <*current*>: **.125**↵
Select an edge or [Loop]: *(pick edge 2, the edge of the hole)*
Select an edge or [Loop]: ↵

PROFESSIONAL TIP

If you improperly create a fillet or chamfer, it is best to undo and try again as opposed to trying to fix it with editing methods. Faces and edges can be edited using the **SOLIDEDIT** command. Grips can also be used to edit solids. This procedure is discussed in Chapter 11; the **SOLIDEDIT** command is discussed in Chapter 12.

Exercise 10-6

Complete the exercise on the Student CD.

Thickening a Surface into a Solid

THICKEN

Ribbon
Home
> Solid Editing
Thicken
Type
THICKEN
Menu
Modify
> 3D Operation
> Thicken

A surface has no thickness. The value of the **THICKNESS** command does not affect the thickness of a planar surface, unlike for entities such as lines, polylines, polygons, and circles. But, a surface can be quickly converted to a 3D solid using the **THICKEN** command.

To add thickness to a surface, enter the command. Then, pick the surface(s) to thicken and press [Enter]. You are then prompted for the thickness. Enter a thickness value or pick two points on screen to specify the thickness. See Figure 10-13.

By default, the original surface object is deleted when the 3D solid is created with **THICKEN**. This is controlled by the **DELOBJ** system variable. To preserve the original surface, change the **DELOBJ** value to 0.

Converting to Surfaces

CONVTOSURFACE

Ribbon
Home
> Solid Editing
Convert to Surface
Type
CONVTOSURFACE
Menu
Modify
> 3D Operation
> Convert to Surface

AutoCAD provides a great deal of flexibility in converting and transforming objects. For example, a simple line can be quickly turned into a 3D solid in just a few steps. Refer to Figure 10-14.

1. Use the **Properties** palette to give the line a thickness. Notice that the object is still a line object, as indicated in the drop-down list at the top of the **Properties** palette.
2. Select the **CONVTOSURFACE** command.
3. Pick the thickened line. Its property type is now listed in the **Properties** palette as a surface extrusion.
4. Use the **THICKEN** command to give the surface a thickness. Its property type is now a 3D solid.

In this process, the **CONVTOSURFACE** and **THICKEN** commands were instrumental in creating a 3D solid from a line. Other objects that can be converted to surfaces using the **CONVTOSURFACE** command are 2D solids, arcs with thickness, open polylines with a thickness and no width, regions, and planar 3D faces.

Figure 10-13.
A—This surface will be thickened into a solid. B—The thickened surface is a 3D solid.

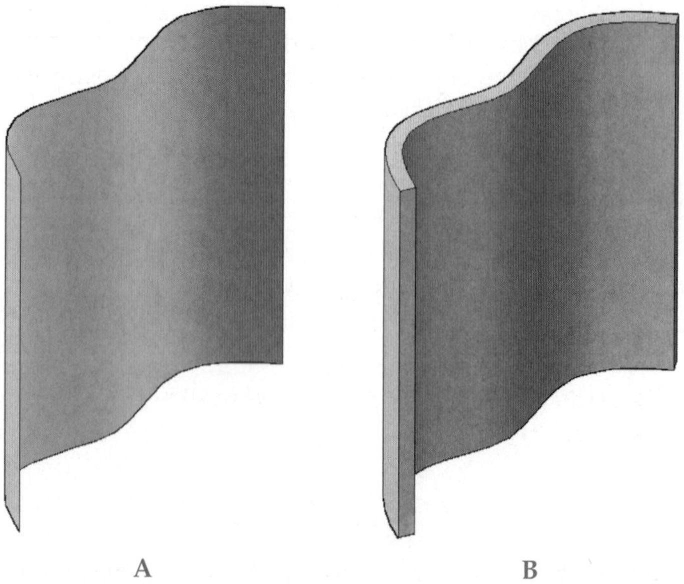

Figure 10-14.
The stages of converting a line into a solid. First, draw the line. Next, give the line a thickness using the **Properties** palette. Then, convert the line to a surface using the **CONVTOSURFACE** command. Finally, use the **THICKEN** command to give the surface a thickness.

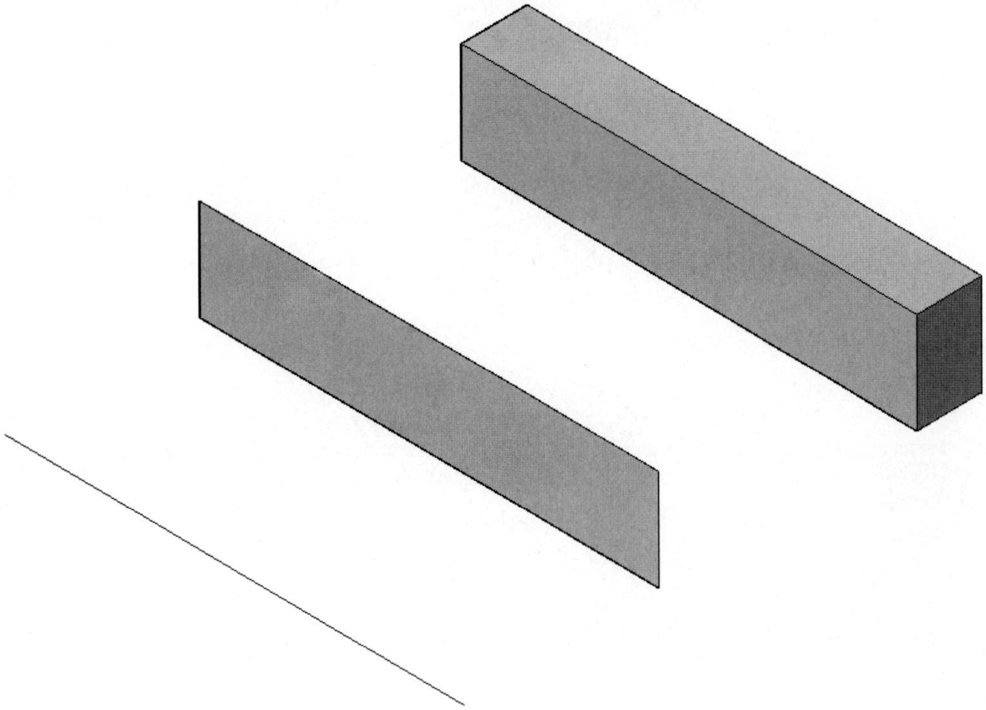

Exercise 10-7
Complete the exercise on the Student CD.

Converting to Solids

Ribbon
Home > Solid Editing
Convert to Solid
Type
CONVTOSOLID
Menu
Modify > 3D Operations > Convert to Solid

CONVTOSOLID

Additional flexibility in creating solids is provided by the **CONVTOSOLID** command. This command allows you to directly convert certain, closed objects into solids. You can convert:

- Circles with thickness.
- Wide, uniform-width polylines with thickness. This includes polygons and rectangles.
- Closed, zero-width polylines with thickness. This includes polygons, rectangles, and closed revision clouds.

First, select the command. Then, select the objects to convert and press [Enter]. The objects are instantly converted with no additional input required. Figure 10-15 shows the three different objects before and after conversion to a solid.

If an object that appears to be a closed polyline with a thickness does not convert to a solid and the command line displays the message Cannot convert an open curve, the polyline was not closed using the **Close** option of the **PLINE** command. Use the **PEDIT** or **PROPERTIES** command to close the polyline and use the **CONVTOSOLID** command again.

Figure 10-15.
A—From left to right, two polylines and a circle that will be converted into solids. B—The resulting solids.

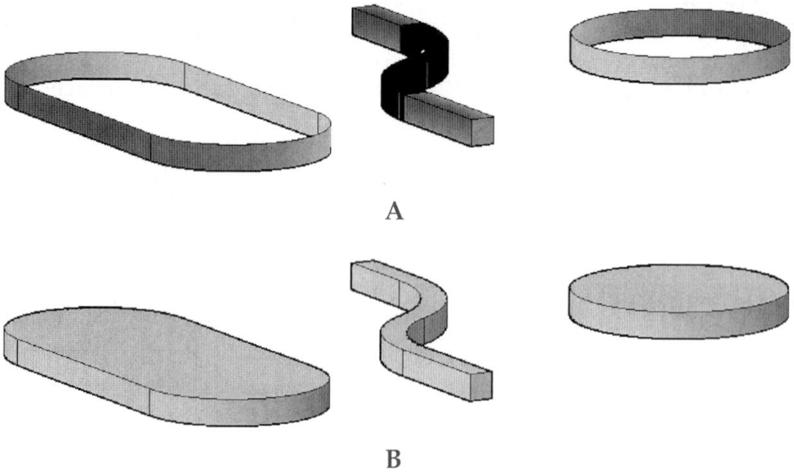

PROFESSIONAL TIP

To quickly create a straight section of pipe, draw a donut with the correct ID and OD of the pipe. Then, use the **Properties** palette to give the donut a thickness equal to the length of the section you are creating. Finally, use the **CONVTOSOLID** command to turn the donut into a solid.

Slicing a Solid

A 3D solid can be sliced at any location by using existing objects such as circles, arcs, ellipses, 2D polylines, 2D splines, or surfaces. Additionally, you can specify a slicing line by picking two points or specify a slicing plane by picking three points. After slicing the solid, you can choose to retain either or both sides of the model. The slices can then be used for model construction or display and presentation purposes.

SLICE

Ribbon
Home
> Solid Editing
Slice

Type
SLICE
SL

Menu
Modify
> 3D Operation
> Slice

The **SLICE** command is used to slice solids. When the command is initiated, you are asked to select the solids to be sliced. Select the objects and press [Enter]. Next, you must define the slicing path. The default method of defining a path requires you to specify two points on a slicing plane. The plane passes through the two points and is perpendicular to the XY plane of the current UCS. Refer to **Figure 10-16** as you follow this sequence:

1. Select the command and pick the object to be sliced.
2. Pick the start point of the slicing plane. See **Figure 10-16A.**
3. Pick the second point on the slicing plane.
4. You are prompted to specify a point on the desired side to keep. Select anywhere on the back half of the object. The point does not have to be *on* the object. It must simply be on the side of the cutting plane that you want to keep.
5. The object is sliced and the front half is deleted. See **Figure 10-16B.**

When prompted to select the side to keep, you can press [Enter] to keep both sides. If both sides are retained, two separate 3D solids are created. Each solid can then be manipulated for construction, design, presentation, or animation purposes.

Figure 10-16.
Slicing a solid by picking two points. A—Select two points on the cutting plane. The plane passes through these points and is perpendicular to the XY plane of the current UCS. B—The sliced solid.

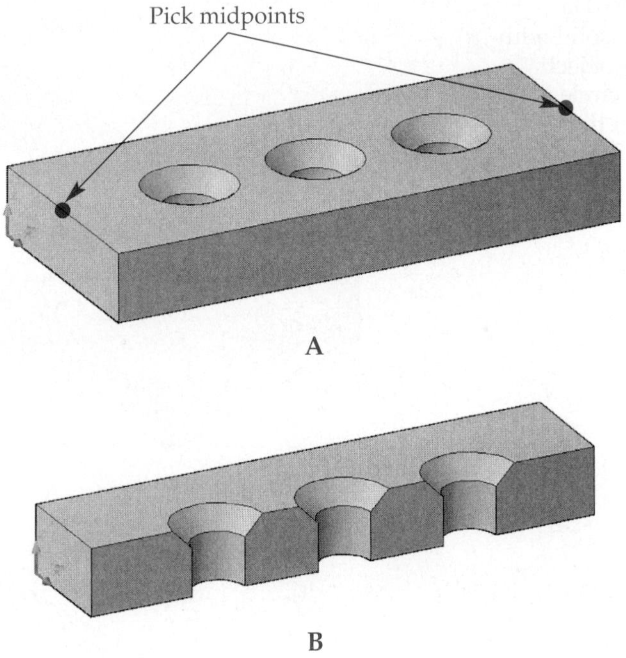

There are several additional options for specifying a slicing path. These options are listed here and described in the following sections.

- **Planar Object**
- **Surface**
- **Zaxis**
- **View**
- **XY**
- **YZ**
- **ZX**
- **3points**

NOTE

Once the **SLICE** command has been used, the history of the solid to that point is removed. If a history of the work is important, then save a copy of the file or place a copy of the object on a frozen layer prior to performing the slice.

Planar Object

A second method to create a slice through a 3D solid is to use an existing planar object. Planar objects include circles, arcs, ellipses, 2D polylines, and 2D splines. See **Figure 10-17A.** The plane on which the planar object lies must intersect the object to be sliced. The current UCS has no effect on this option.

Be sure that the object has been moved to the location of the slice. Then, select the **SLICE** command, pick the object to slice, and press [Enter]. Next, select the **Planar Object** option and select the slicing path object (the circle, in this case). Finally, specify which side is to be retained. See **Figure 10-17B.** Again, if both sides are kept, they are separate objects and can be individually manipulated.

Figure 10-17.
Slicing a solid with a planar object. A—The circle is drawn at the proper orientation and in the correct location. B—The completed slice.

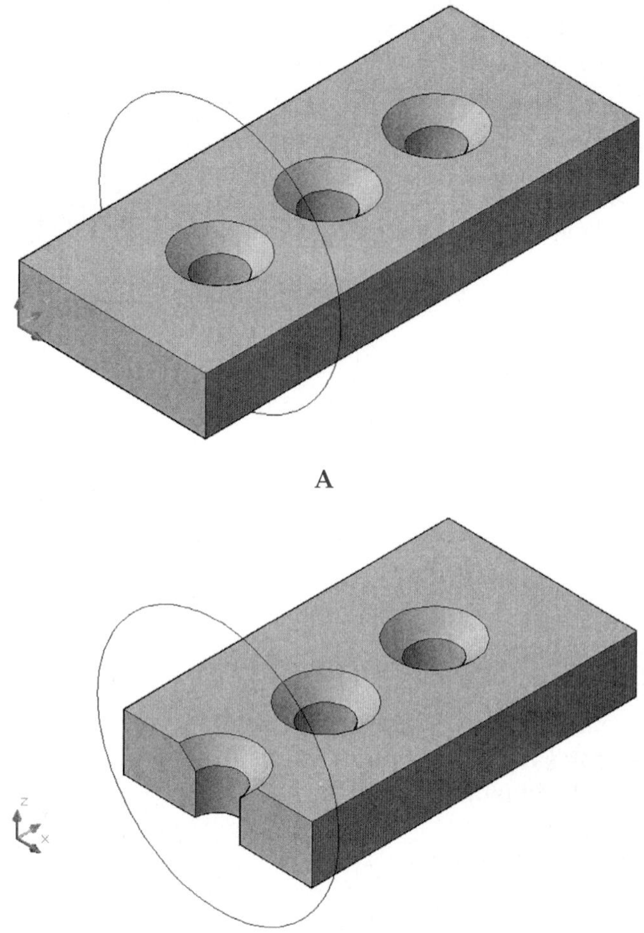
A
B

Surface

A surface object can be used as the slicing path. The surface can be planar or nonplanar (curved). This method can be used to quickly create a mating die. For example, refer to **Figure 10-18.** First, draw the required surface. The surface should exactly match the stamped part that will be manufactured, **Figure 10-18A.** Then, draw a box that encompasses the surface. Next, select the **SLICE** command, pick the box, and press [Enter]. Then, enter the **Surface** option and select the surface. You may need to do this in a wireframe display. Finally, when prompted to select the side to keep, press [Enter] to keep both sides. The two halves of the die can now be moved and rotated as needed, **Figure 10-18B.**

Z Axis

You can specify one point on the cutting plane and one point on the Z axis of the plane. See **Figure 10-19.** This allows you to have a cutting plane that is not parallel to the current UCS XY plane. First, select the **SLICE** command, pick the object to slice, and press [Enter]. Next, enter the **Zaxis** option. Then, pick a point on the XY plane of the cutting plane followed by a point on the Z axis of the cutting plane. Finally, pick the side of the object to keep.

Figure 10-18.
Slicing a solid with a surface. A—Draw the surface and locate it within the solid to be sliced. The solid is represented here by the wireframe. B—The completed slice with both sides retained. The top can now be moved and rotated as shown here.

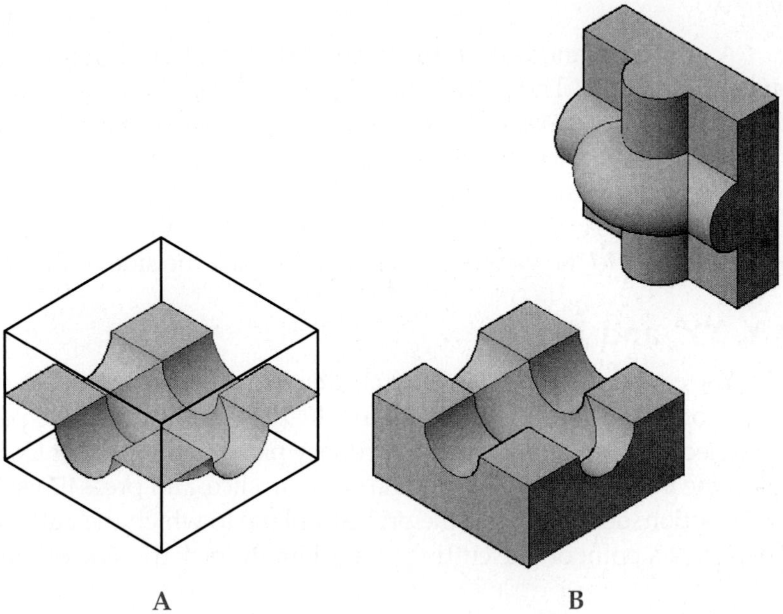

Figure 10-19.
Slicing a solid using the **Zaxis** option. A—Pick one point on the cutting plane and a second point on the Z axis of the cutting plane. B—The resulting slice.

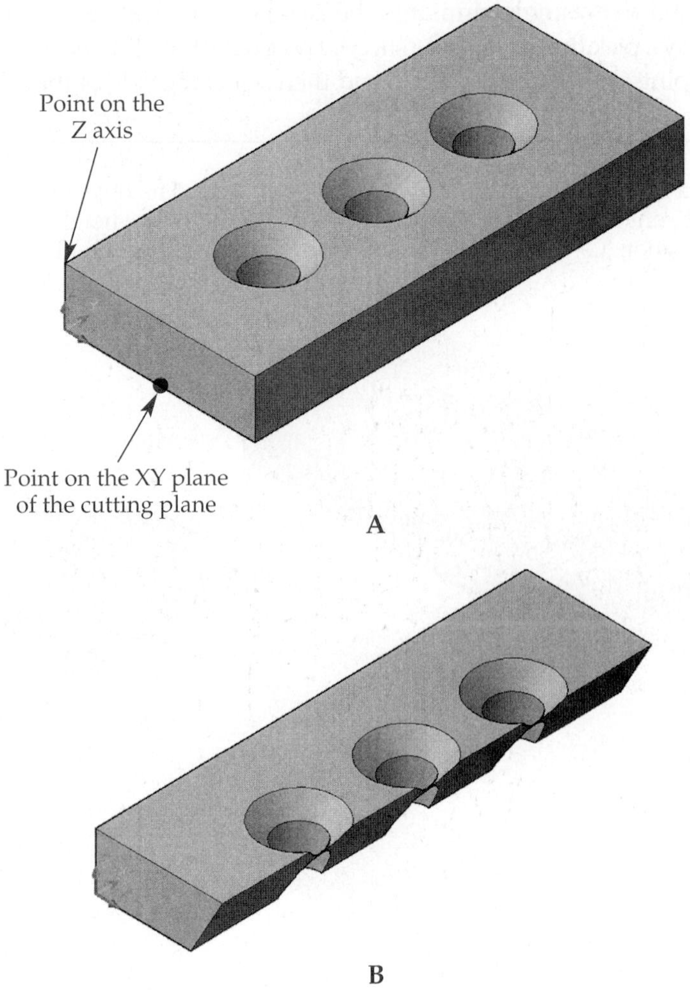

View

A cutting plane can be established that is aligned with the viewing plane of the current viewport. The cutting plane passes through a point you select, which sets the depth along the Z axis of the current viewing plane. First, select the **SLICE** command, pick the object to slice, and press [Enter]. Next, enter the **View** option. Then, pick a point in the viewport to define the location of the cutting plane on the Z axis of the viewing plane. Use object snaps to select a point on an object. The cutting plane passes through this point and is parallel to the viewing plane. Finally, pick the side of the object to keep.

XY, YZ, and ZX

You can slice an object using a cutting plane that is parallel to any of the three primary planes of the current UCS. See Figure 10-20. The cutting plane passes through the point you select and is aligned with the primary plane of the current UCS that you specify. First, select the **SLICE** command, pick the object to slice, and press [Enter]. Next, enter the **XY**, **YZ**, or **ZX** option, depending on the primary plane to which the cutting plane will be parallel. Then, pick a point on the cutting plane. Finally, pick the side of the object to keep.

Three Points

Three points can be used to define the cutting plane. This allows the cutting plane to be aligned at any angle, similar to the **Zaxis** option. See Figure 10-21. First, select the **SLICE** command, pick the object to be sliced, and press [Enter]. Then, enter the **3points** option. Pick three points on the cutting plane and then select the side of the object to keep.

Figure 10-20.
Slicing a solid using the **XY**, **YZ**, and **ZX** options. A—The object before slicing. The UCS origin is in the center of the first hole and at the midpoint of the height. B—The resulting slice using the **XY** option. C—The resulting slice using the **YZ** option. D—The resulting slice using the **ZX** option.

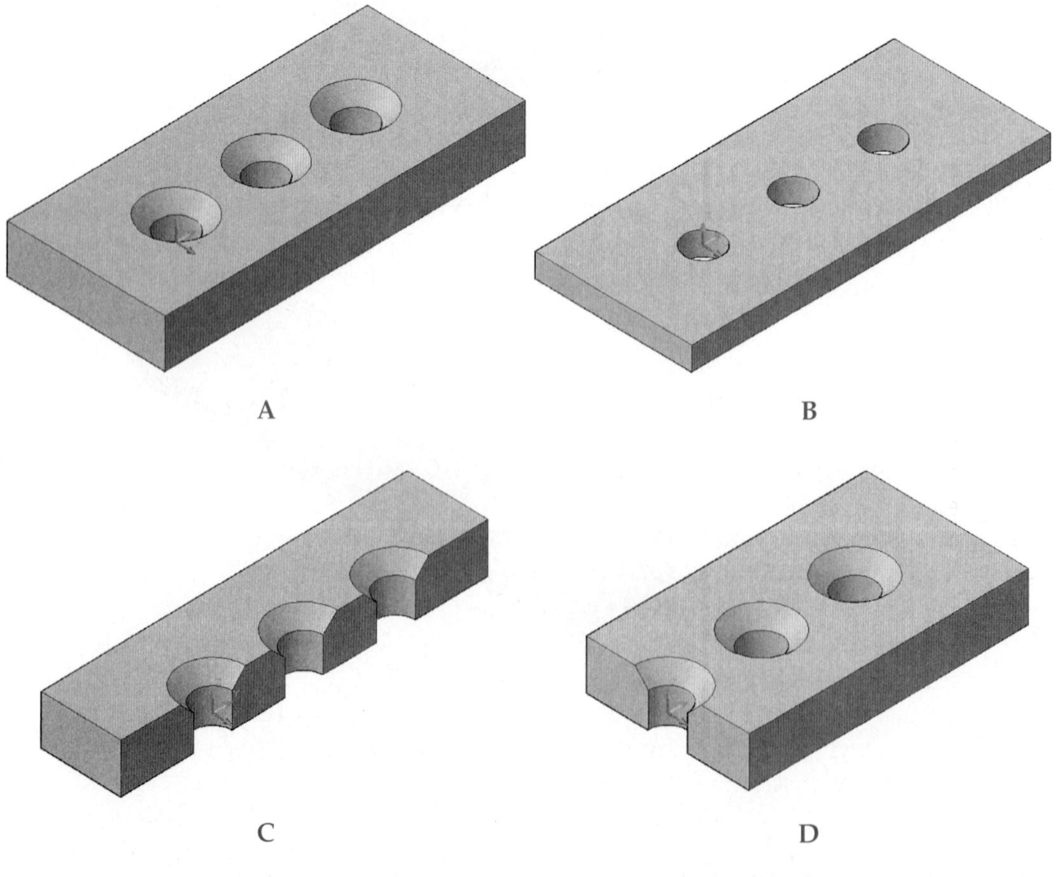

Figure 10-21.
Slicing a solid using the **3points** option. A—Specify three points to define the cutting plane. B—The resulting slice.

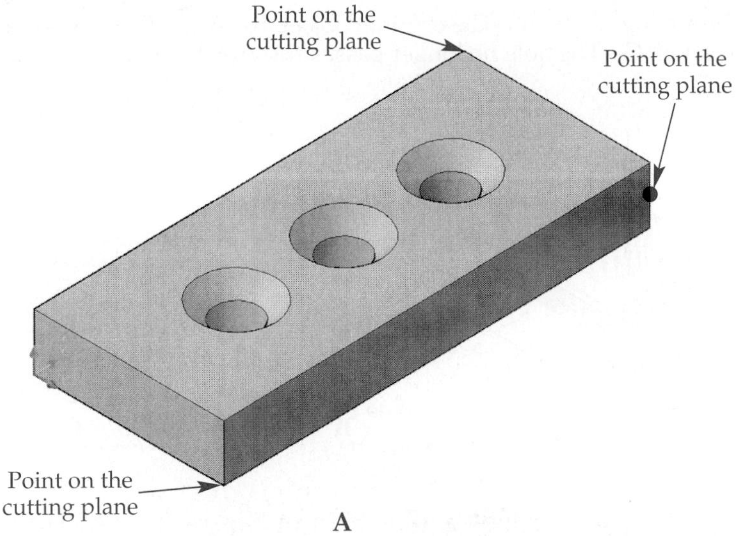

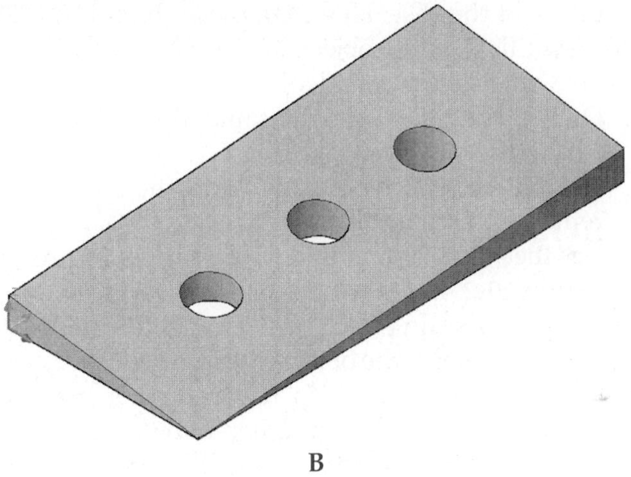

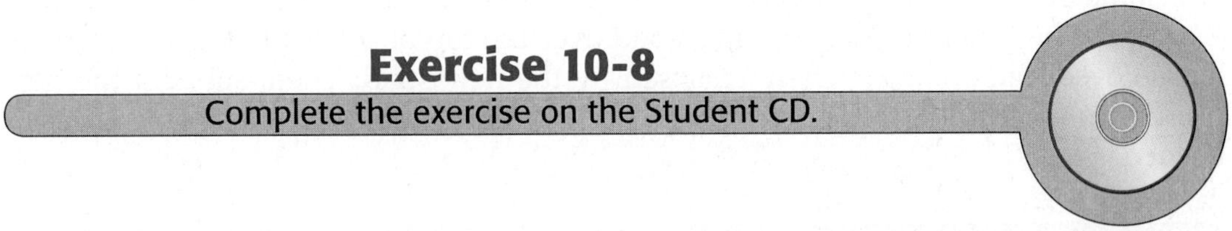

Exercise 10-8
Complete the exercise on the Student CD.

Removing Details and Features

Sometimes, it may be necessary to remove a detail that has been constructed. For example, suppose you placed a R.5 fillet on an object based on an engineering sketch. Then, the design is changed to a R.25 fillet. The **UNDO** command can only be used in the current drawing session. Also, even if the command can be used, you may have to step back through several other commands to undo the fillet. In another example, suppose an object has a bolt hole that is no longer needed. You will need to remove this feature.

In Chapter 2, solid modeling is described as working with modeling clay. If you think in these terms, you can remove features by adding "clay" to the object. Then, the new "clay" can be molded as needed.

Figure 10-22.
Removing fillets. A—The original object. B—A new base is added and the new fillets are created. C—The hole no longer passes through the object. D—The corrected object.

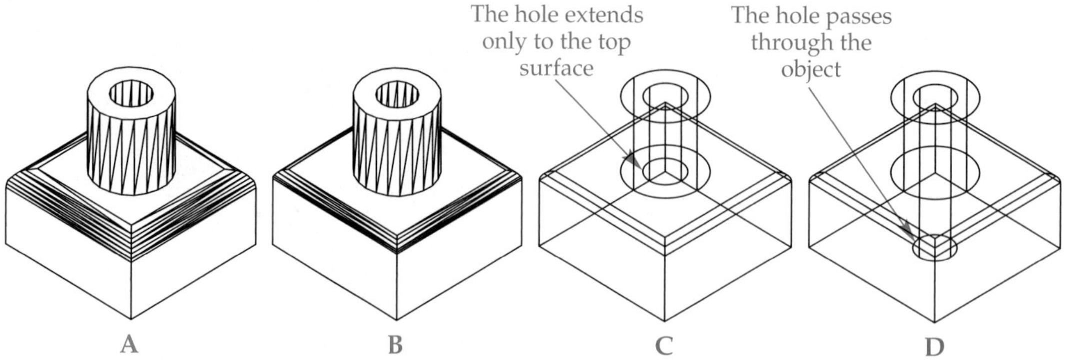

For example, look at the object in Figure 10-22A. There are R.5 rounds (fillets) on the top surface of the base. However, these should be R.25 rounds. You cannot simply place the new fillets on the object. You must first add material to create a square edge. Then, the new fillets can be added.

1. Draw a solid box with the same dimensions as the base without the rounds. Center the new box on the base.
2. Use the **UNION** command to add the new box to the object. This, in effect, removes the rounds.
3. Use the **FILLET** command to place the R.25 rounds on the top edge of the base, Figure 10-22B.

The rounds have now, in effect, been changed from R.5 to R.25. However, there is an unseen problem. Display the object in wireframe. Notice how the hole no longer passes through the object, Figure 10-22C. To correct this problem, draw a solid cylinder of the same dimensions as the hole and centered in the hole. Then, subtract the cylinder from the object. The hole now passes through the object, Figure 10-22D.

This technique of adding material can be used to remove any internal feature and some external features, such as fillets (rounds). Other external features, such as a boss, can be removed by drawing a solid over the top of the feature. The feature to be removed must be completely enclosed by the new solid. Then, subtract the new solid from the original object. Be sure to "redrill" holes and other internal features as needed.

PROFESSIONAL TIP

There are several other methods for editing solids. These are covered in detail in Chapters 11 and 12. The above procedure can be simplified with these editing methods.

Constructing Details and Features on Solid Models

A variety of machining, structural, and architectural details can be created using some basic solid modeling techniques. The features discussed in the next sections are just a few of the possibilities.

Figure 10-23.
Constructing a counterbore. A—Draw a cylinder to represent a hole. B—Draw a second cylinder to represent the counterbore. C—Subtract the two cylinders from the base object.

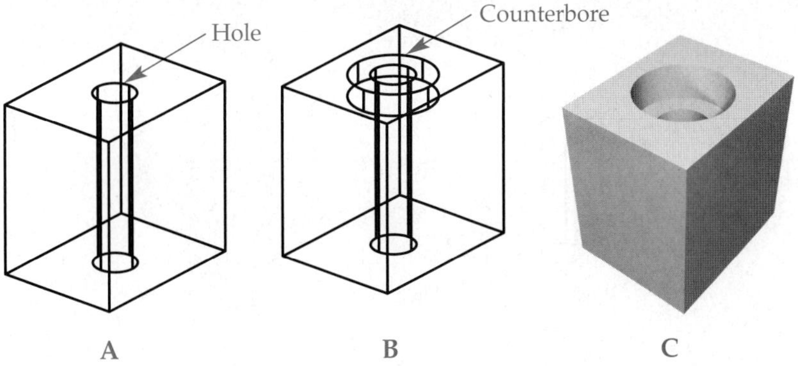

Counterbore and Spotface

A ***counterbore*** is a recess machined into a part, centered on a hole, that allows the head of a fastener to rest below the surface. Create a counterbore as follows.

1. Draw a cylinder representing the diameter of the hole, **Figure 10-23A.**
2. Draw a second cylinder that is the diameter of the counterbore and center it at the top of the first cylinder. Move the second cylinder so it extends below the surface of the object to the depth of the counterbore, **Figure 10-23B.**
3. Subtract the two cylinders from the base object, **Figure 10-23C.**

A ***spotface*** is similar to a counterbore, but is not as deep. See **Figure 10-24.** It provides a flat surface for full contact of a washer or underside of a bolt head. Construct it in the same way as a counterbore.

Countersink

A ***countersink*** is like a counterbore with angled sides. The sides allow a flat head machine screw or wood screw to sit flush with the surface of an object. A countersink can be drawn in one of two ways. You can draw an inverted cone centered on a hole and subtract it from the base, or you can chamfer the top edge of a hole. Chamfering is the quickest method.

1. Draw a cylinder representing the diameter of the hole, **Figure 10-25A.**
2. Subtract the cylinder from the base object.
3. Select the **CHAMFER** command.
4. Select the top edge of the base object.
5. Enter the chamfer distance(s).
6. Pick the top edge of the hole, **Figure 10-25B.**

Figure 10-24.
Constructing a spotface. A—The bottom of the second, larger-diameter cylinder should be located at the exact depth of the spotface. However, the height may extend above the surface of the base. Then, subtract the two cylinders from the base. B—The finished solid.

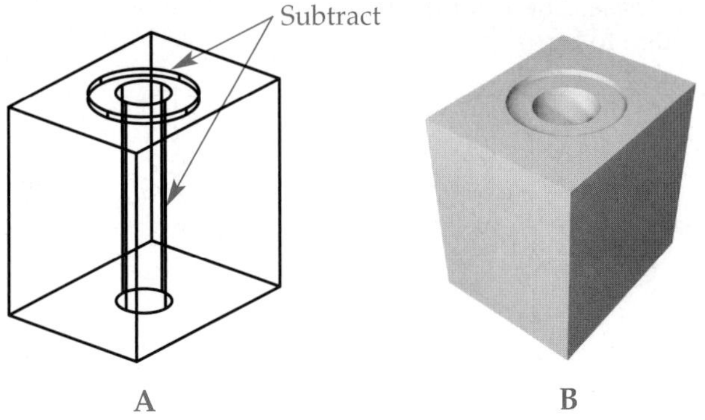

Figure 10-25.
Constructing a countersink. A—Subtract the cylinder from the base to create the hole. B—Chamfer the top of the hole to create a countersink.

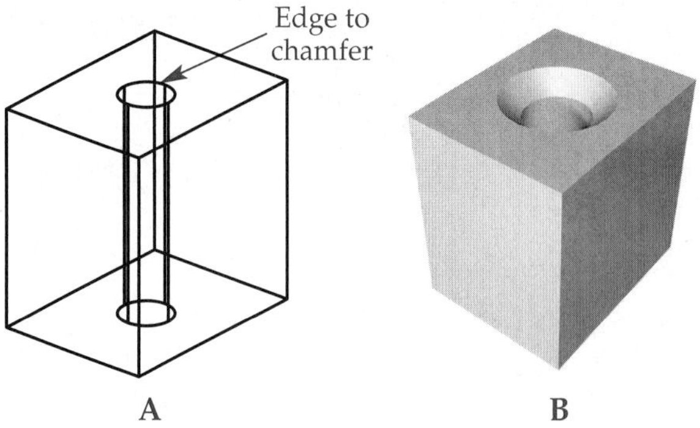

Boss

A ***boss*** serves the same function as a spotface. However, it is an area raised above the surface of an object. Draw a boss as follows.

1. Draw a cylinder representing the diameter of the hole. Extend it above the base object higher than the boss is to be, **Figure 10-26A.**
2. Draw a second cylinder the diameter of the boss. Place the base of this cylinder above the top surface of the base object a distance equal to the height of the boss. Give the cylinder a negative height value so that it extends inside of the base object, **Figure 10-26B.**
3. Union the base object and the second cylinder (boss). Subtract the hole from the unioned object, **Figure 10-26C.**
4. Fillet the intersection of the boss with the base object, **Figure 10-26D.**

O-Ring Groove

An ***O-ring*** is a circular seal that resembles a torus. It sits inside of a groove constructed so that part of the O-ring is above the surface. An ***O-ring groove*** can be constructed by placing the center of a circle on the outside surface of a cylinder. Then, revolve the circle around the cylinder. Finally, subtract the revolved solid from the cylinder.

1. Construct the cylinder to the required dimensions, **Figure 10-27A.**
2. Rotate the UCS on the X axis (or appropriate axis).
3. Draw a circle with a center point on the surface of the cylinder, **Figure 10-27B.**
4. Revolve the circle 360° about the center of the cylinder, **Figure 10-27C.**
5. Subtract the revolved object from the cylinder, **Figure 10-27D.**

Figure 10-26.
Constructing a boss. A—Draw a cylinder for the hole so it extends above the surface of the object. B—Draw a cylinder the height of the boss on the top surface of the object. C—Union the large cylinder to the base. Then, subtract the small cylinder (hole) from the unioned objects. D—Fillet the edge to form the boss.

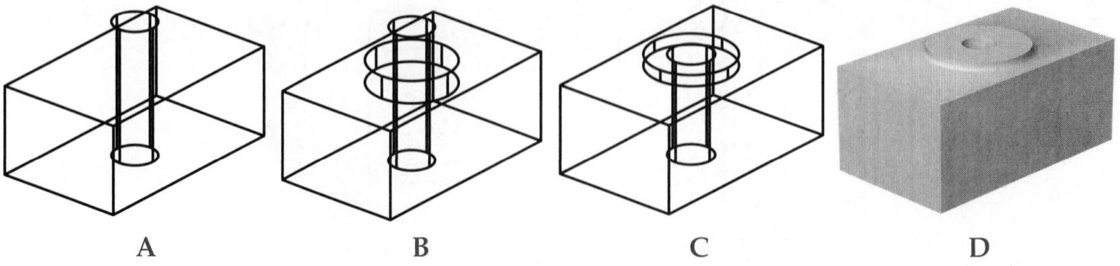

Figure 10-27.
Constructing an O-ring groove. A—Construct a cylinder; this one has a round placed on one end. B—Draw a circle centered on the surface of the cylinder. C—Revolve the circle 360° about the center of the cylinder. D—Subtract the revolved object from the cylinder. E—The completed O-ring groove.

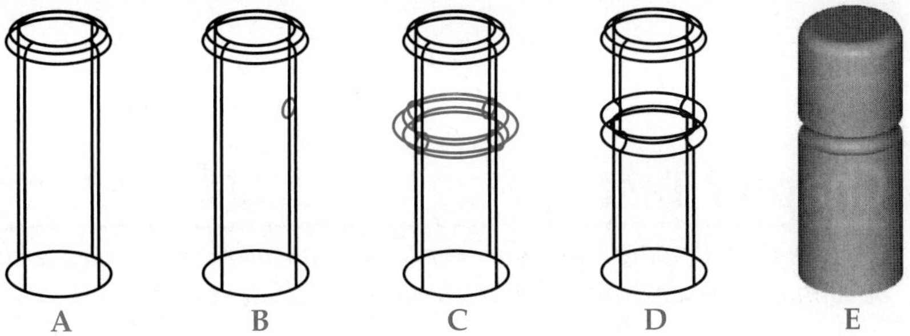

Figure 10-28.
A—The molding profile. B—The profile extruded to the desired length.

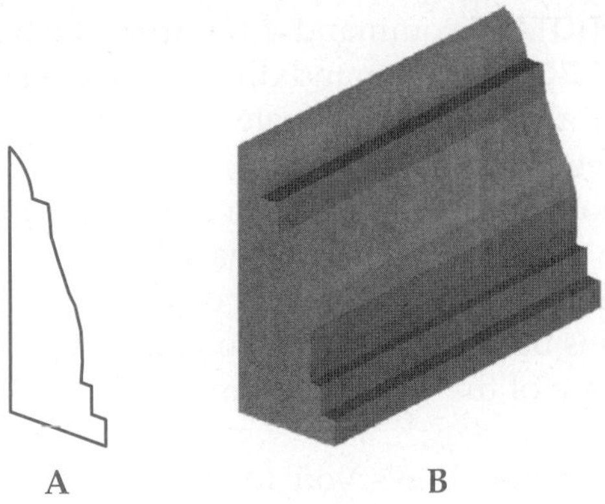

Architectural Molding

Architectural molding details can be quickly constructed using extrusions. First, construct the profile of the molding as a closed shape, Figure 10-28A. Then, extrude the profile the desired length, Figure 10-28B.

Corner intersections of molding can be quickly created by extruding the same shape in two different directions and then joining the two objects. First, draw the molding profile. Then, copy and rotate the profile to orient the Z axis in the desired direction, Figure 10-29A. Next, extrude the two profiles the desired lengths, Figure 10-29B. Finally, union the two extrusions to create the mitered corner molding, Figure 10-29C.

Figure 10-29.
Constructing corner molding. A—Copy and rotate the molding profile. B—Extrude the profiles to the desired lengths. C—Union the two extrusions to create the mitered corner. Note: The view has been rotated. D—The completed corner.

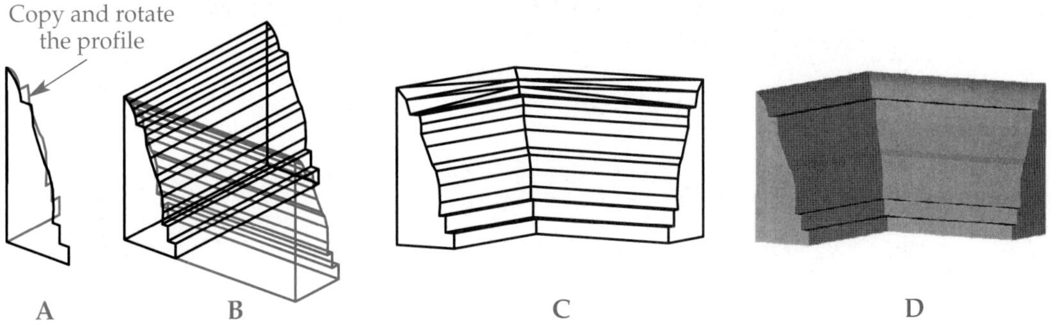

Exercise 10-9

Complete the exercise on the Student CD.

Chapter Test

Answer the following questions. Write your answers on a separate sheet of paper or complete the electronic chapter test on the Student CD.

1. Which properties of a solid can be changed in the **Properties** palette?
2. What does the History property control?
3. What is the purpose of the **ALIGN** command?
4. How does the **3DALIGN** command differ from the **ALIGN** command?
5. How does the **3DROTATE** command differ from the **ROTATE** command?
6. How does the **MIRROR3D** command differ from the **MIRROR** command?
7. Which command allows you to create a rectangular array by defining rows, columns, and levels?
8. How does a 3D polar array differ from a 2D polar array?
9. How many levels can a 3D polar array have?
10. Which command is used to fillet a solid object?
11. Which command is used to chamfer a solid object?
12. What is the purpose of the **THICKEN** command and which type of object does it create?
13. Which system variable allows you to preserve the original object when the **THICKEN** command is used?
14. List four objects that can be converted to surfaces using the **CONVTOSURFACE** command.
15. Briefly describe the function of the **SLICE** command.

Drawing Problems

1. Construct an 8″ diameter tee pipe fitting using the dimensions shown below. Hint: Extrude and union two solid cylinders before subtracting the cylinders for the inside diameters.
   A. Use **EXTRUDE** to create two sections of pipe at 90° to each other, then **UNION** the two pieces together.
   B. Use **FILLET** and **CHAMFER** to finish the object. The chamfer distance is .25″ × .25″.
   C. The outside diameter of all three openings is 8.63″ and the pipe wall thickness is .322″.
   D. Save the drawing as P10_01.

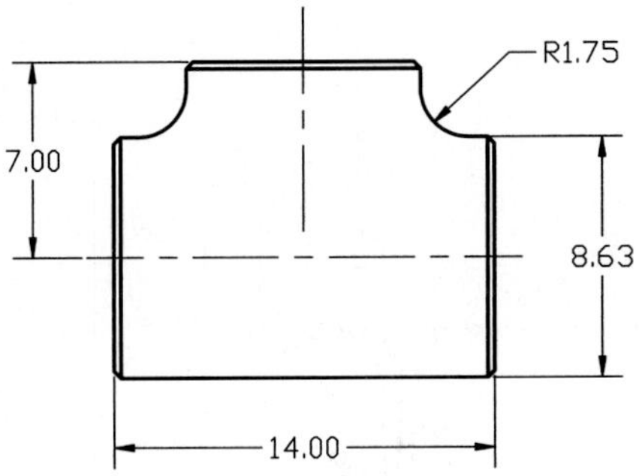

2. Construct an 8″ diameter, 90° elbow pipe fitting using the dimensions shown below.
   A. Use **EXTRUDE** or **SWEEP** to create the elbow.
   B. Chamfer the object. The chamfer distance is .25″ × .25″. Note: You cannot use the **CHAMFER** command.
   C. The outside diameter is 8.63″ and the pipe wall thickness is .322″.
   D. Save the drawing as P10_02.

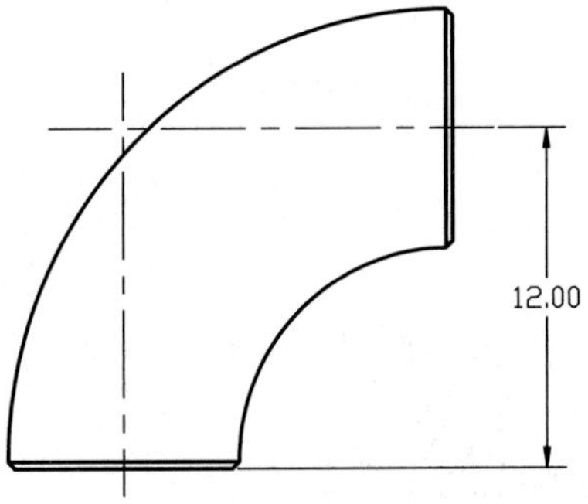

Problems 3–6. These problems require you to use a variety of solid modeling functions to construct the objects. Use all of the solid modeling and editing commands you have learned so far to assist in construction. Use a dynamic UCS when practical and create new UCSs as needed. Use **SOLIDHIST** *and* **SHOWHIST** *to record and view the steps used to create the solid models. Create copies of the completed models and split them as required to show the internal features visible in the section views. Save each drawing as* **P10_***(problem number).*

3.

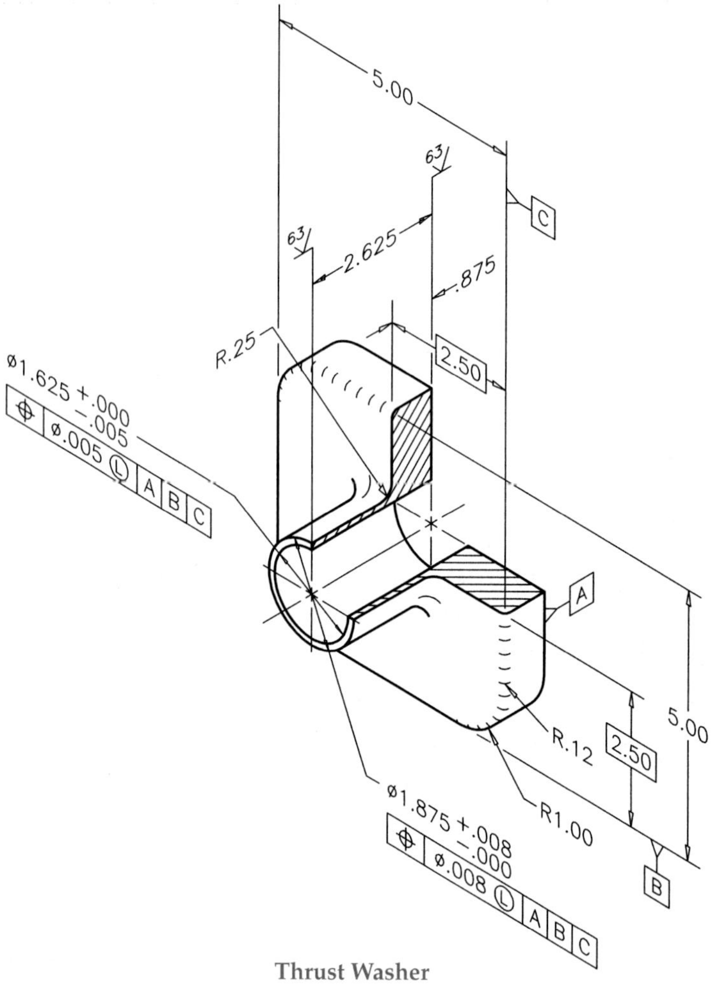

Thrust Washer

4.

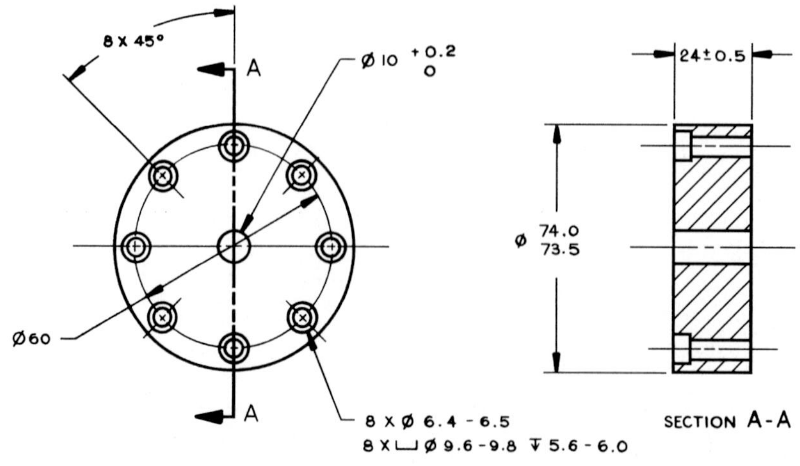

Collar

5.

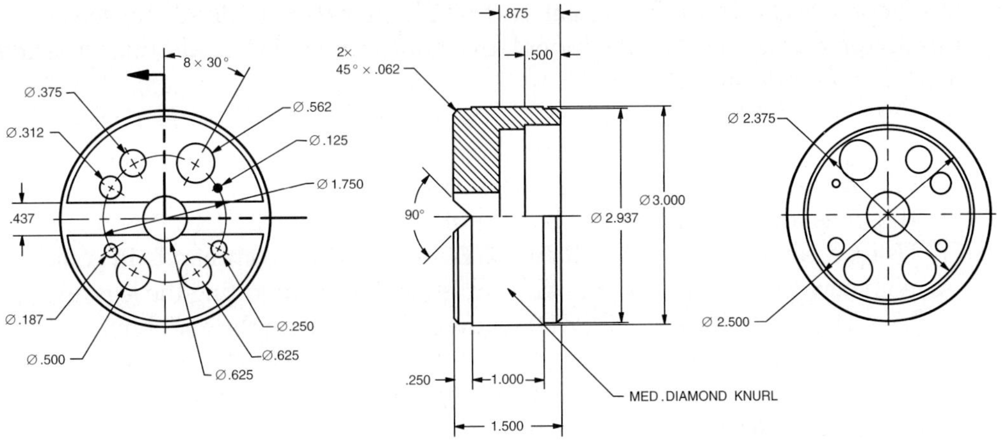

Diffuser

6.

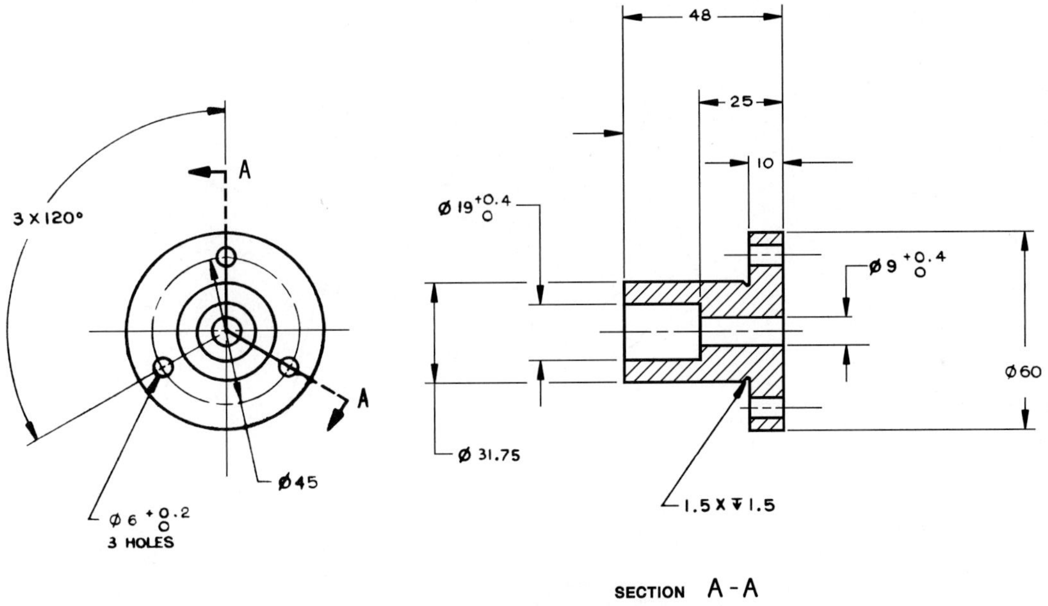

Bushing

7. In this problem, you will add legs to the kitchen chair you started in Chapter 2. In Chapter 8 you refined the seat and in Chapter 9 you added the seatback. In this chapter, you complete the model. In Chapter 16, you will add materials to the model and render it.
   A. Open P09_07 from Chapter 9.
   B. Using the **LINE** command, create the framework for lofting the legs and crossbars as shown below. The crossbars are at the midpoints of the legs. Position the lines for the double crossbar about 4.5″ apart.
   C. Using a combination of the **3DROTATE** and **3DMOVE** commands in conjunction with new UCSs, draw and position circles as shapes for lofting the legs and crossbars. The legs transition from ∅1.00 at the ends to ∅1.25 at the midpoints. The crossbars transition from ∅.75 at the ends to ∅1.00 at a position 2″ from each end.
   D. Create the legs and crossbars. The completed model is shown below.
   F. Save the drawing as P10_07.

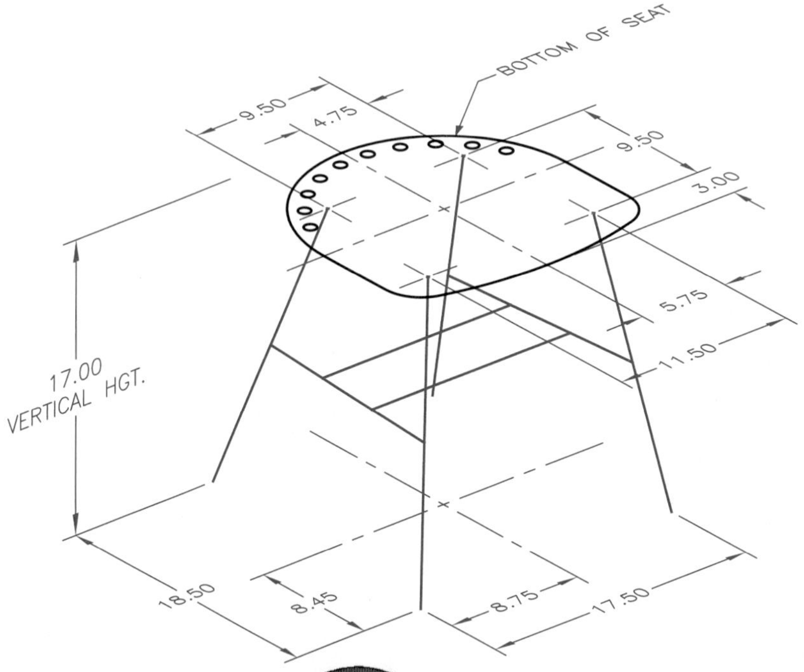

Completed Model

CHAPTER 11 Subobject Editing

Learning Objectives

After completing this chapter, you will be able to:

- ✓ Select subobjects (faces, edges, and vertices).
- ✓ Edit solids using grips.
- ✓ Edit face subobjects.
- ✓ Edit edge subobjects.
- ✓ Edit vertex subobjects.
- ✓ Extrude a closed boundary using the **PRESSPULL** command.
- ✓ Extract a wireframe from a 3D solid using the **XEDGES** command.

Grip Editing

There are three basic types of 3D solids in AutoCAD. The commands **BOX**, **WEDGE**, **CYLINDER**, **SPHERE**, etc., create 3D solid ***primitives***. ***Sweeps*** are 2D profiles given thickness by the **EXTRUDE**, **REVOLVE**, **SWEEP**, and **LOFT** commands to create a 3D solid. Finally, 3D solid ***composites*** are created by a Boolean operation or by using the **SOLIDEDIT** command. The **SOLIDEDIT** command is discussed in Chapter 12.

There are two types of grips—base and parameter—that may be associated with a solid object. These grips provide an intuitive means of modifying solids. Base grips are square and parameter grips are typically arrows. The editing that can be performed with these grips are discussed in the next sections.

Primitives

The 3D solid primitives (box, wedge, pyramid, cylinder, cone, sphere, and torus) all have basically the same grips. However, not all grips are available on all primitives. All primitives have a base grip at the centroid of the base. This grip functions like a standard grip in 2D work. It can be used to stretch, move, rotate, scale, or mirror the solid.

Boxes, wedges, and pyramids have square base grips at the corners that allow the size of the base to be changed. See **Figure 11-1.** Select one of these grips, move the cursor, and select a new point. The object dynamically changes in the viewport as you move the grip. You can also type the new coordinate location for the grip and press [Enter]. If ortho is off, the length and width can be changed at the same time by

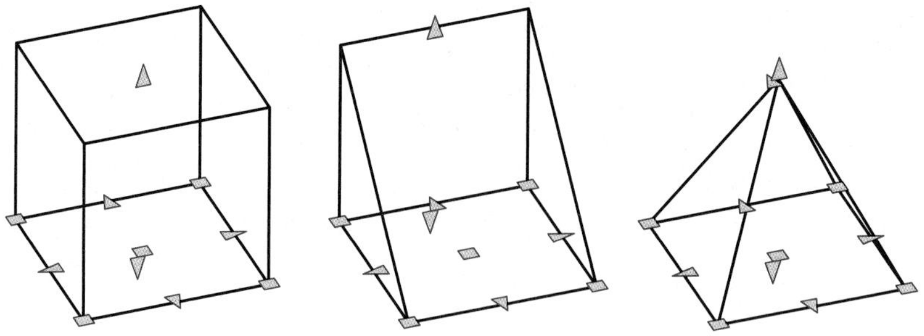

Figure 11-1.
Boxes, wedges, and pyramids have square base grips at the corners and parameter grips on the sides of the base and center of the top face, edge, or vertex.

dragging the grip, except in the case of a pyramid. The triangular parameter grips on the base allow the length or width to be changed. Additionally, the height of these objects can be changed using parameter grips. Each object has one parameter grip for changing the height of the apex and one for changing the height of the plane on which the base sits. A pyramid also has a parameter grip at the apex for changing the radius of the top.

Cylinders, cones, and spheres have four parameter grips for changing the radius of the base, or the cross section in the case of a sphere. See **Figure 11-2.** Cylinders and cones also have parameter grips for changing the height of the apex and the height of the plane on which the base sits. Additionally, a cone has a parameter grip at the apex for changing the radius of the top.

A torus has a parameter grip located at the center of the tube. See **Figure 11-3.** This grip is used to change the radius of the torus. There is also a parameter grip at each quadrant of the tube. These are used to change the radius of the tube.

A polysolid does not have parameter grips. Instead, a base grip appears at each corner of the starting face of the solid. See **Figure 11-4.** Use these grips to change the cross-sectional shape of the polysolid. The corners do not need to remain square. Base grips also appear at the endpoint of each segment centerline. Use these to change the location of each segment's endpoints.

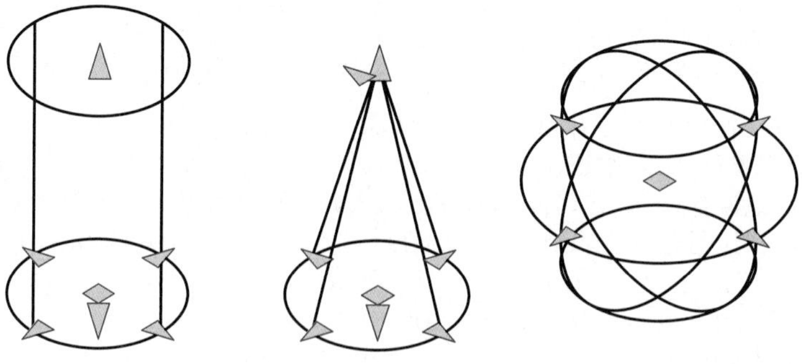

Figure 11-2.
Cylinders, cones, and spheres have four parameter grips for changing their radius. Cylinders and cones have parameter grips for changing their height. Cones also have a parameter grip for changing the radius of the top.

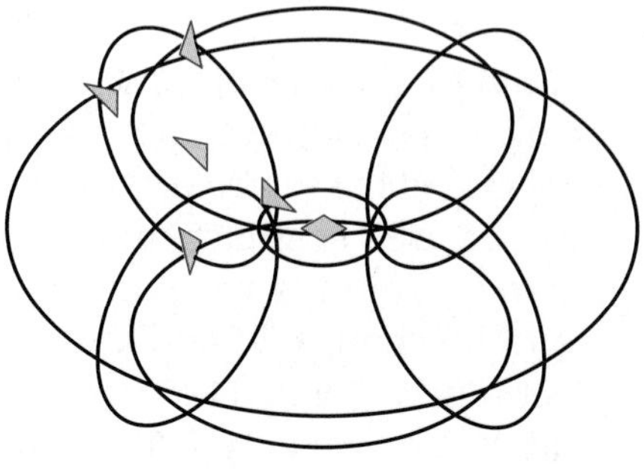

Figure 11-3.
A torus has a parameter grip located at the center of the tube for changing the radius of the torus. There are also parameter grips for changing the radius of the tube.

Figure 11-4.
A polysolid has a base grip at each corner of the starting face of the solid and one at the endpoint of each segment.

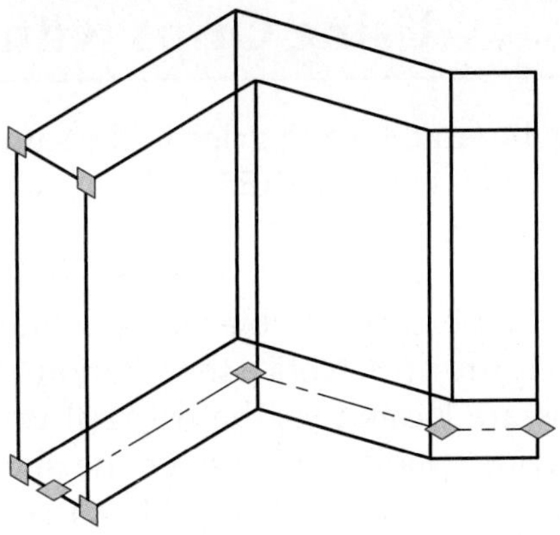

Swept Solids

Extrusions, revolutions, sweeps, and lofts are considered swept solids. Swept solids typically have base grips located at the vertices of the 2D profiles. These can be used to change the size of the profile and, thus, the solid. Other grips that appear include:

- A parameter grip appears on the upper face of extrusions for changing the height.
- A base grip appears on the axis of revolved solids for changing the location of the axis in relation to the profile.
- Base grips appear on the vertices of the path of sweeps for changing the shape of the path.

Composite Solids

The Boolean commands (**UNION**, **SUBTRACT**, and **INTERSECT**) create composite solids. Solids that have been modified using any of the options of the **SOLIDEDIT** command also become composite solids. The solid may still look like a primitive, sweep, loft, etc., but it is a composite. The grips available with the previous objects are no longer available, unless performing subobject editing on a composite created with a Boolean command (discussed later in this chapter). Composite solids have a base grip located at the centroid of the base surface. This grip can be used to stretch, move, rotate, scale, or mirror the solid.

NOTE

When performing grip editing on a solid, AutoCAD must be able to "solve" the end result. If it cannot, the edit is not applied.

Using Grips with Surfaces

Surfaces can be edited using grips in the same manner as discussed with solids. A planar surface created with **PLANESURF** can be moved, rotated, scaled, and mirrored, but not stretched. Base grips are located at each corner.

As you learned in Chapter 8, a variety of AutoCAD objects can be extruded to create a surface. Three of these objects—arc, line, and polyline—are shown extruded into surfaces in Figure 11-5. Notice the location and type of grips on the surface extrusions. Base grips are located on the original profile that was extruded to make the surface. These grips enable you to alter the shape of the surface. A parameter grip located on the top of the surface is used to change the height of the extrusion.

Surfaces that have been extruded, or swept, along a path can also be edited with grips. Also, the grips located on the path allow you to change the shape of the surface extrusion. See Figure 11-6.

Figure 11-5.
Surfaces extruded from an arc, line, and polyline. Notice the grips.

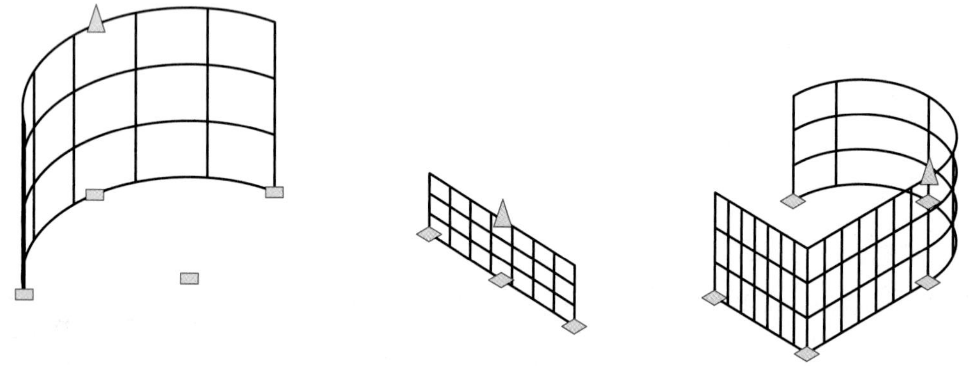

Figure 11-6.
A—Grips can be used to modify the path on this swept surface. B—The swept surface after grip editing.

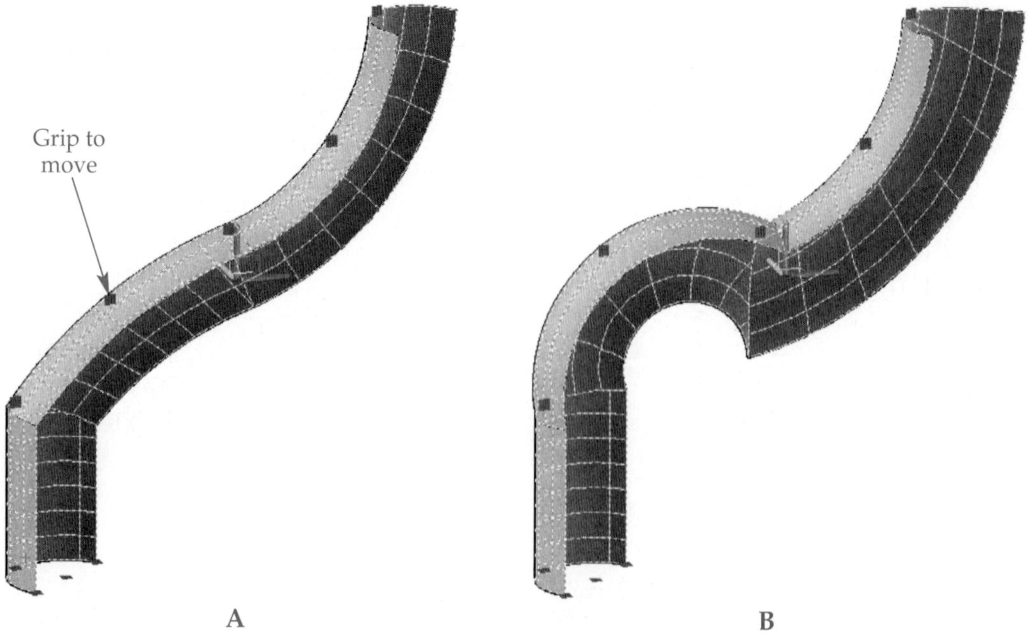

Exercise 11-1

Complete the exercise on the Student CD.

Overview of Subobject Editing

AutoCAD solid primitives, such as cylinders, wedges, and boxes, are composed of three types of subobjects: faces, edges, and vertices. In addition, the objects that are used with Boolean commands to create a composite solid are considered subobjects, if the history is recorded. The primitive subobjects can be edited. See **Figure 11-7**. Once selected, the primitive subobjects can even be deleted from the composite solid. **Figure 11-8** illustrates the difference between a composite solid model, the solid primitives used to construct it, and an individual subobject of one of the primitives.

Subobjects can be easily edited using grips, which provide an intuitive and flexible method of solid model design. For example, suppose you need to rotate a face subobject in the current XY plane. You can select the subobject, pick its base grip, and then cycle through the editing functions to **ROTATE**. You can also use the **ROTATE** command on the selected subobject.

Figure 11-7.
A—Selecting a subobject solid primitive within a composite solid displays its grips.
B—The grips on the primitive can be used to edit the primitive.

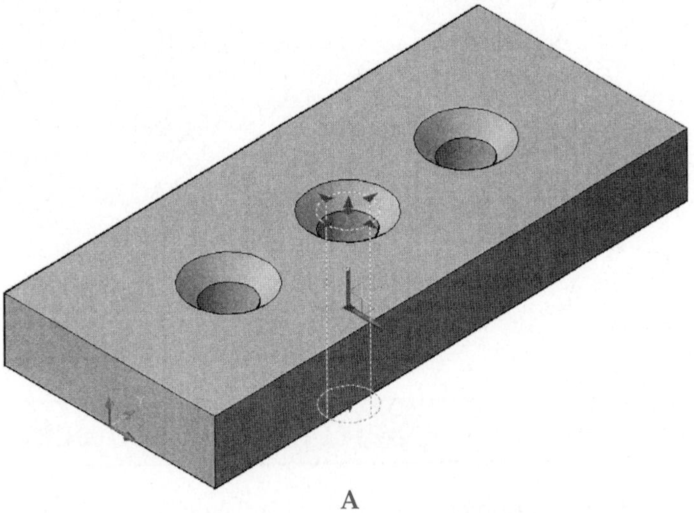

A

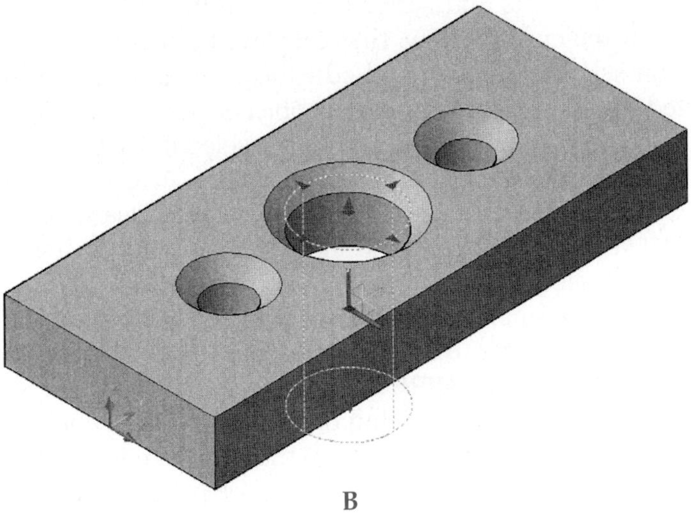

B

Figure 11-8.
A—The composite solid model is selected. Notice the single base grip. B—The wedge primitive subobject has been selected. Notice the grips associated with the primitive. C—An edge subobject within the primitive subobject is selected for editing.

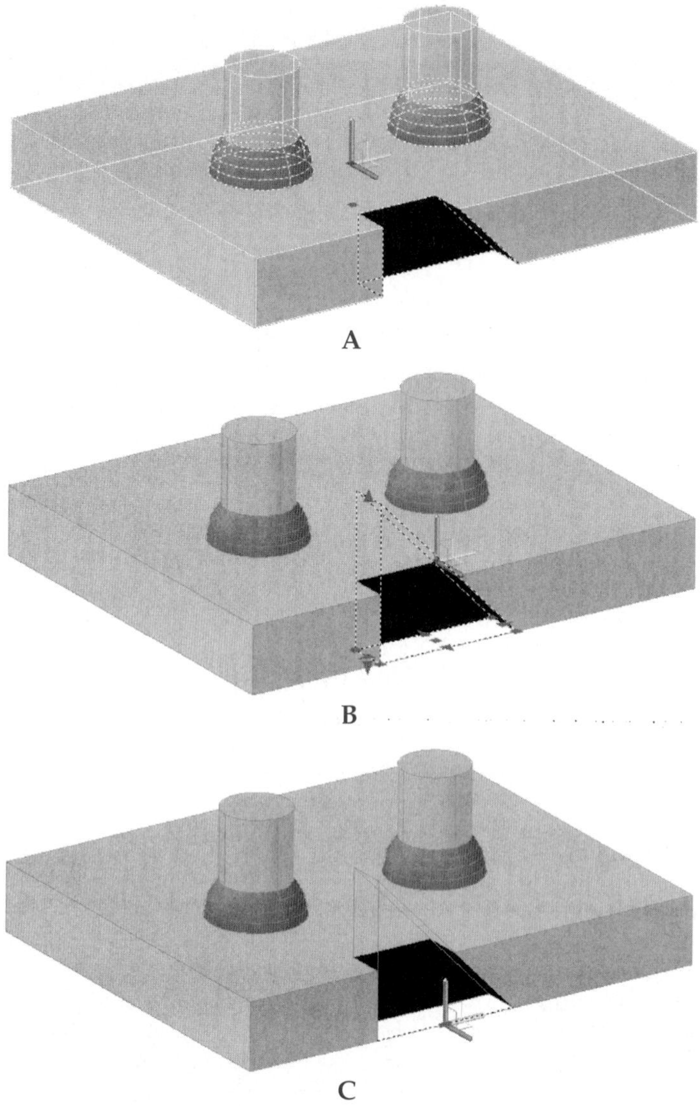

Selecting Subobjects

To select a subobject, press the [Ctrl] key and pick the subobject. You can select multiple subobjects and subobjects on multiple objects. To select a subobject that is hidden in the current view, first display the model as a wireframe. After creating a selection set, select a grip and edit the subobject as needed. Multiple objects can be selected in this manner. To deselect objects, press the [Shift]+[Ctrl] key combination and pick the objects to be removed from the selection set.

If objects or subobjects are overlapping, press the [Ctrl] key and the spacebar to turn on cycling and pick the subobject. Then, release the spacebar, continue holding the [Ctrl] key, and pick until the subobject you need is highlighted. Press [Enter] or the spacebar to select the highlighted subobject.

The [Ctrl] key method can be used to select subobjects for use with editing commands such as **MOVE**, **COPY**, **ROTATE**, **SCALE**, **ARRAY**, and **ERASE**. Some commands, like **ARRAY**, **STRETCH**, and **MIRROR**, are applied to the entire solid. Other operations may not be applied at all, depending on which type of subobject is selected. You can also use the **Properties** palette to change the color of edge and face subobjects or the material assigned to a face. The color of a subobject primitive can also be changed, but not the color of its subobjects.

CAUTION

Using the **SOLIDEDIT** command (discussed in Chapter 12) removes the history from a composite solid. Therefore, the original objects—the subobjects—are no longer available for subobject editing. However, you may still be able to perform some subobject edits, such as moving the original objects.

Face Subobject Editing

Faces of 3D solids can be modified using commands such as **MOVE**, **ROTATE**, and **SCALE**, or by using grips and grip tools. To select a face on a 3D solid, press the [Ctrl] key and pick within the boundary of the face. Do not pick the edge of the face. Face grips are circular and located in the center of the face, as shown in **Figure 11-9.** In the case of a sphere, the grip is located in the center of the sphere since there is only one face. The same is true of the curved face on a cylinder or cone.

By default, the history is recorded for all solid primitives and composites. If you select a primitive or a primitive subobject within a composite solid, all of the grips associated with that primitive are displayed. See **Figure 11-10A.** If you edit a 3D

Figure 11-9.
Face grips are located in the center of face subobjects.

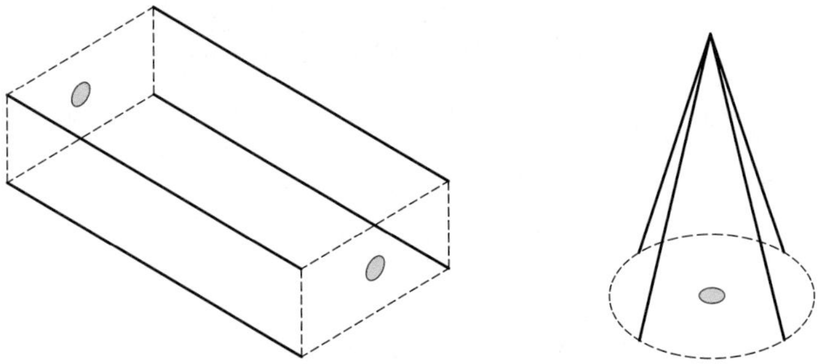

Figure 11-10.
A—This primitive is selected for editing. Notice the grips associated with the primitive. B—If the primitive is edited, the history of that primitive is deleted and a single base grip is displayed.

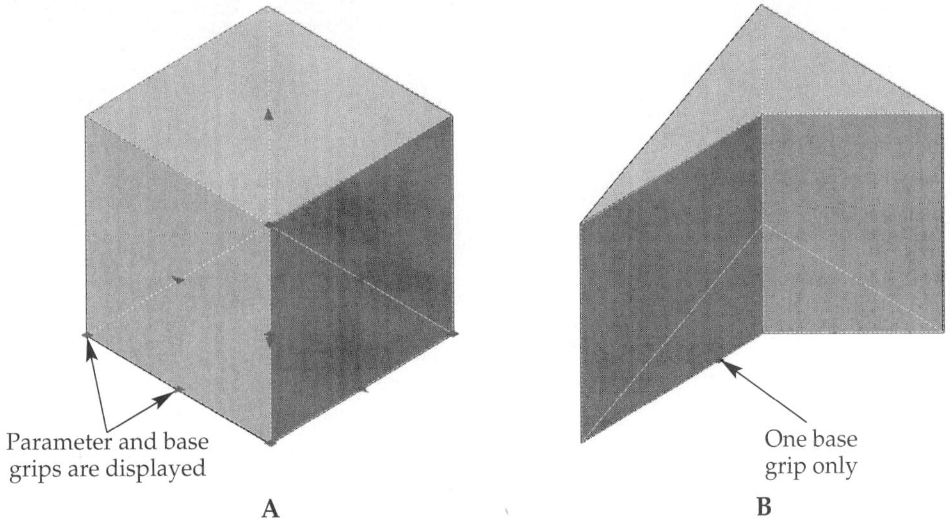

solid primitive face, the history of the primitive is deleted and the object becomes a composite solid. Then, when the object is selected, a single base grip is displayed. See **Figure 11-10B.**

While pressing the [Ctrl] key and selecting a face, you may pick faces that you do not want to edit. Depending on your viewpoint and current visual style, it may be difficult to select the face you want. Additionally, it may be almost impossible to deselect faces you do not need. Use the view cube to transparently change the viewpoint or use [Shift]+mouse wheel button to activate the transparent **3DORBIT** command and change your viewpoint.

NOTE

The recorded history of a solid composite can be displayed by selecting the solid, opening the **Properties** palette, and changing the Show History property in the **Solid History** category to Yes.

Moving Faces

When a face of a 3D solid is moved, all adjacent faces are dragged and stretched with it. The shape of the original 3D primitive or solid determines the manner in which the face can be moved and how adjacent faces react. A face can be moved using the **MOVE** command, **3DMOVE** command, move grip tool, or by dragging the face's base grip. When moving a face, use the grip tool, polar tracking, or direct distance entry. Otherwise, the results may appear correct in the view in which the edit is made, but, when the view is changed, the actual result may not be what you wanted. See **Figure 11-11.**

Figure 11-11.
A—The original solid primitives. B—The box and wedge are dynamically edited without using exact coordinates or distances. C—When the viewpoint is changed, you can see that dynamic editing has produced unexpected results.

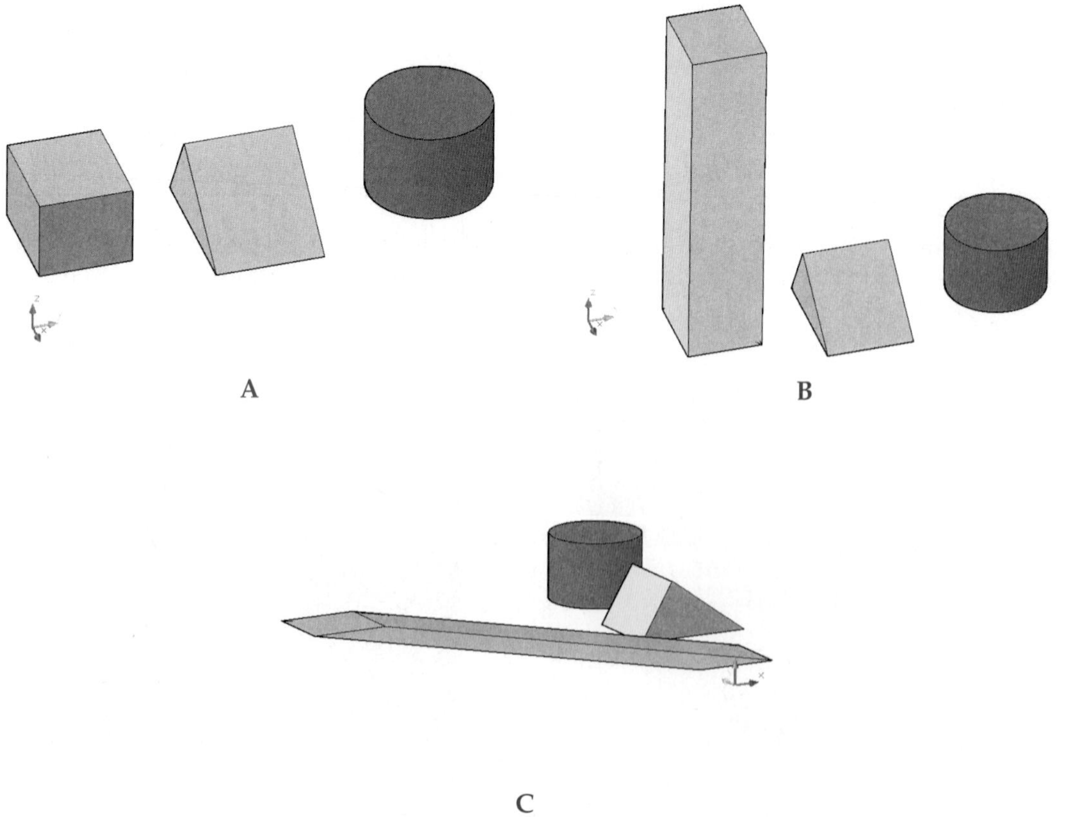

The move grip tool is displayed by default (**GTAUTO** = 1) when the face is selected. This tool is discussed in detail in Chapter 10. To use the move grip tool, move the pointer over the X, Y, or Z axis of the grip tool; the axis changes to yellow. To restrict movement along that axis, pick the axis. If you move the pointer over one of the right angles at the origin of the tool, the corresponding two axes turn yellow. Pick to restrict the movement to that plane. You can complete the movement by either picking a new point or by direct distance entry.

There are a few options to achieve different results when dynamically moving a face. The [Ctrl] key is used to access these options. First, select the face. See **Figure 11-12A.** Then, pick the face grip or grip tool and press and release the [Ctrl] key to cycle through the options.

If the [Ctrl] key is not pressed, the moved face maintains its size, shape, and orientation. The shape and plane of adjacent faces are changed. See **Figure 11-12B.** Pressing the [Ctrl] key three times resets the function, as if the [Ctrl] key had not been pressed.

If the [Ctrl] key is pressed once, the moved face maintains its shape and orientation. However, its size is modified because the planes of adjacent faces are maintained. See **Figure 11-12C.** Adjacent faces are not subdivided.

If the [Ctrl] key is pressed twice, the moved face maintains its size, shape, and orientation. However, adjacent faces are subdivided into triangular faces, if needed.

PROFESSIONAL TIP

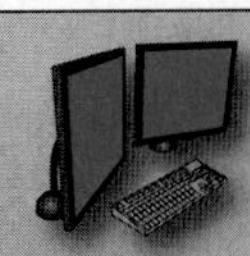

It is always important to keep the design intent of your solid model in mind. If you are creating a conceptual design, you may be able to use subobject grip editing and grip tools without entering precise coordinates. But, if you are working on a design for manufacturing or production, it is usually critical to use tools such as direct distance entry, grip tools with exact values, and polar tracking for greater accuracy.

Rotating Faces

Before rotating any primitive or subobject you must know in which plane the rotation is to occur. The **ROTATE** command permits a rotation in the current XY plane. But, you can get around this limitation by using the **3DROTATE** command. This command allows you to select a rotation plane by means of the rotate grip tool. This tool is discussed in detail in Chapter 10. When a subobject is selected, you cannot use the spacebar to switch to the rotate grip tool from the move grip tool. The rotate grip tool must be placed using the **3DROTATE** command.

Figure 11-12.
A—The original solid primitive. B—Without pressing the [Ctrl] key, the face maintains its shape and orientation. C—Pressing the [Ctrl] key once keeps the adjacent faces in their original planes, but alters the modified face.

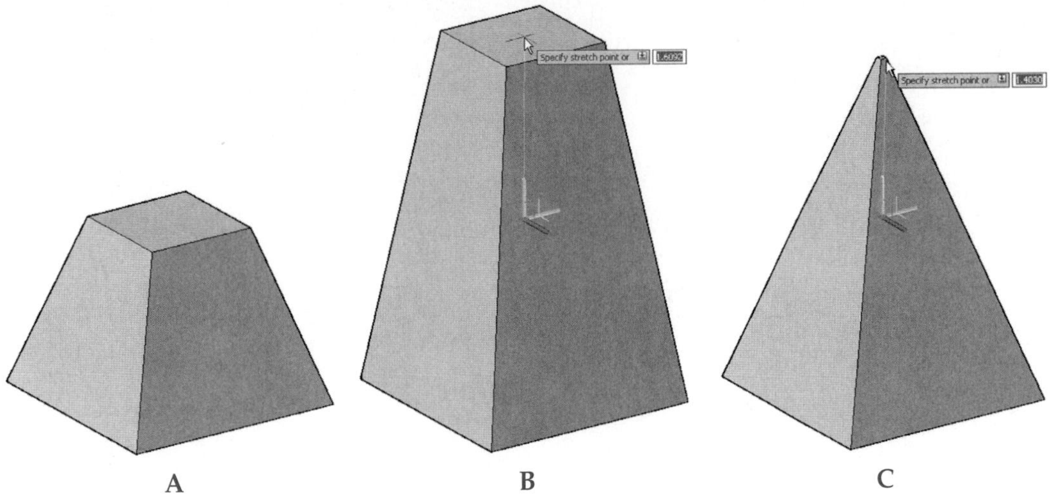

The rotate grip tool provides a dynamic, graphic representation of the three axes of rotation. To rotate about the tool's X axis, pick the red circle on the grip tool. To rotate about the Y axis, pick the green circle. To rotate about the Z axis, pick the blue circle. Once you select a circle, it turns yellow and you are prompted for the start point of the rotation angle. You can enter a direct angle at this prompt or pick the first of two points defining the angle of rotation. When the rotation angle is defined, the face is rotated about the selected axis.

For example, in **Figure 11-13A**, the top face is selected and the rotate grip tool is placed on a corner of the face. After picking the rotation axis on the grip tool, specify the angle start point and then the angle end point. Notice in **Figure 11-13B** that dynamic input is used to enter an exact angle value of –15. The result is shown in **Figure 11-13C**.

Figure 11-13.
Using the rotate grip tool to rotate a face. A—The top face is selected and the grip tool is placed on a base point of the face. B—The axis of rotation and a starting point for the angle are selected. C—The completed rotation.

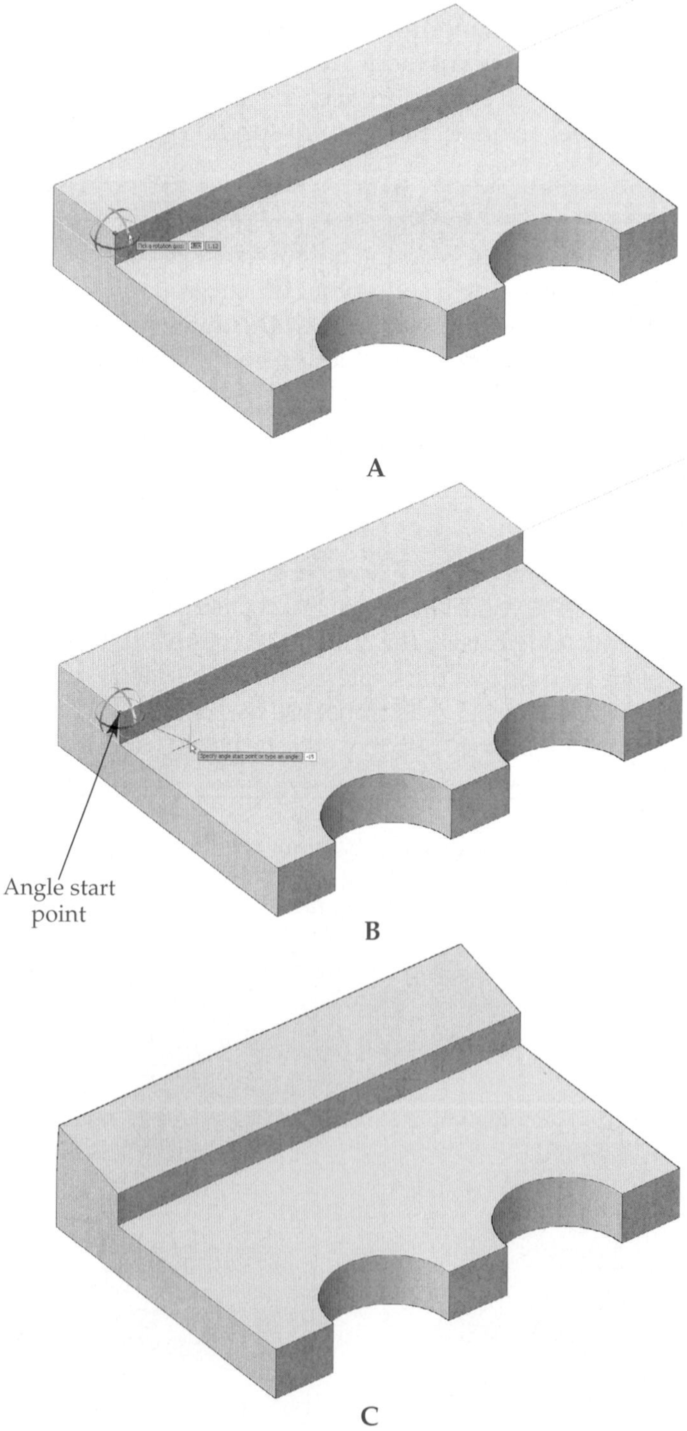

There are a few options to achieve different results when dynamically rotating a face. The [Ctrl] key is used to access these options. Pressing the [Ctrl] key while rotating a face affects adjacent faces in the same manner as discussed in moving faces. Figure 11-14A shows a rotation without pressing [Ctrl]. The shape and size of the face being rotated is maintained, while the adjacent faces change. Figure 11-14B shows a rotation after pressing [Ctrl] once. The shape and size of the face being rotated changes, while the plane and shape of adjacent faces are maintained. Pressing the [Ctrl] key a second time maintains the shape and orientation of the selected face, but triangular faces may be created on adjacent faces. Pressing the [Ctrl] key a third time resets the function.

PROFESSIONAL TIP

When you are working in a 3D view, you may want to use the **3DMOVE** and **3DROTATE** commands exclusively during editing sessions. If this is the case, set the **GTDEFAULT** variable to 1 (the default is 0). This automatically executes the **3DMOVE** and **3DROTATE** commands in a 3D view when you select the **MOVE** or **ROTATE** commands. If the 2D Wireframe visual style is current, the 3D Wireframe visual style is set current for the duration of the command.

Figure 11-14.
A—Rotating a face without pressing the [Ctrl] key. The large, top face on the object shown in Figure 10-13A has been selected for rotation.
B—Pressing the [Ctrl] key once keeps the adjacent faces in their original planes. The shape and size of the face being rotated changes.

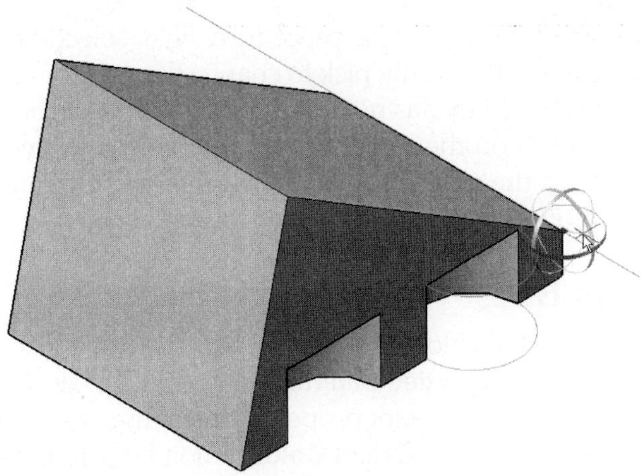

A

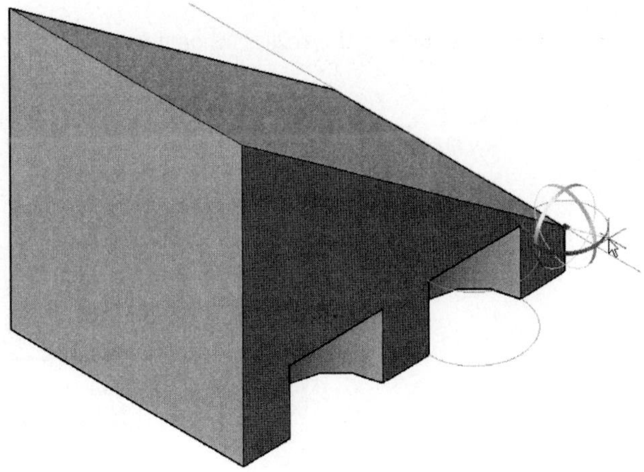

B

Figure 11-15.
Scaling a face. A—The original solid. B—The dark face is scaled down. C—The dark face is scaled up.

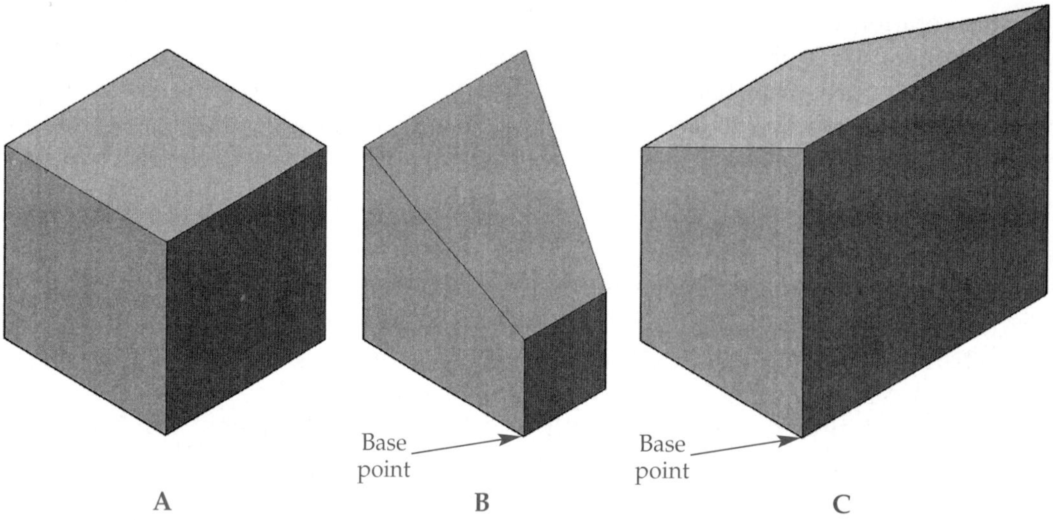

Scaling Faces

Scaling a face is a simple procedure. First, select the face to be scaled. Then, select a base point and dynamically pick to change the scale or use a scale factor. See Figure 11-15. Pressing the [Ctrl] key has no effect on the scaling process, except to turn it off or on, if the base point is on the same plane as the face. However, if the base point is not on the same plane as the selected face, then pressing the [Ctrl] key has the same effect as for the other face-editing operations.

Coloring Faces

To change the color of a face, use the [Ctrl] key selection method to select the face. Next, open the **Properties** palette. See Figure 11-16. In the **General** category, pick the drop-down list for the Color property. Select the desired color or pick Select Color... and choose a color from the **Select Color** dialog box. To change the material applied to the

Figure 11-16.
Changing the color of a face or the material assigned to it.

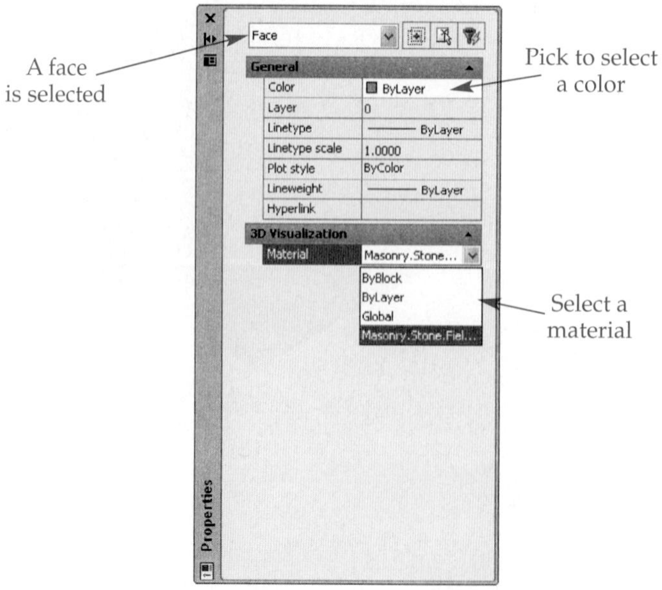

face, pick the drop-down list for the Material property in the **3D Visualization** category. Select a material from the list. A material must be loaded into the drawing to be available in this drop-down list. Materials are discussed in detail in Chapter 15.

Extruding a Solid Face

Planar faces on 3D solids can be extruded into new solids. Refer to the HVAC duct assembly shown in **Figure 11-17A.** A new, reduced trunk needs to be created on the left end of the assembly. This requires two pieces: a reducer and the trunk.

First, select the **EXTRUDE** command. At the "select objects" prompt, press the [Ctrl] key and pick the face subobject to be extruded. Next, since this is a reduced trunk, specify a taper angle. Enter the **Taper angle** option and specify the angle. In this case, a 15° angle is used. Finally, specify the extrusion height. The height of the reducer is 12". See **Figure 11-17B.**

Now, the new trunk needs to be created. Select the **EXTRUDE** command. Press the [Ctrl] key and pick the face to extrude. Since this piece is not tapered, enter the extrusion height, which in this case is 44". See **Figure 11-17C.** The two new pieces are separate solid objects. If the assembly is to be one solid, use the **UNION** command and join the two new solids to the assembly.

Figure 11-17.
A—A new, reduced trunk needs to be created on the left end of the HVAC assembly. The face shown in color will be extruded. B—The **Taper angle** option of the **EXTRUDE** command is used to create the reducer. The face shown in color will be extruded to create the extension. C—The **EXTRUDE** command is used to create an extension from the reducer.

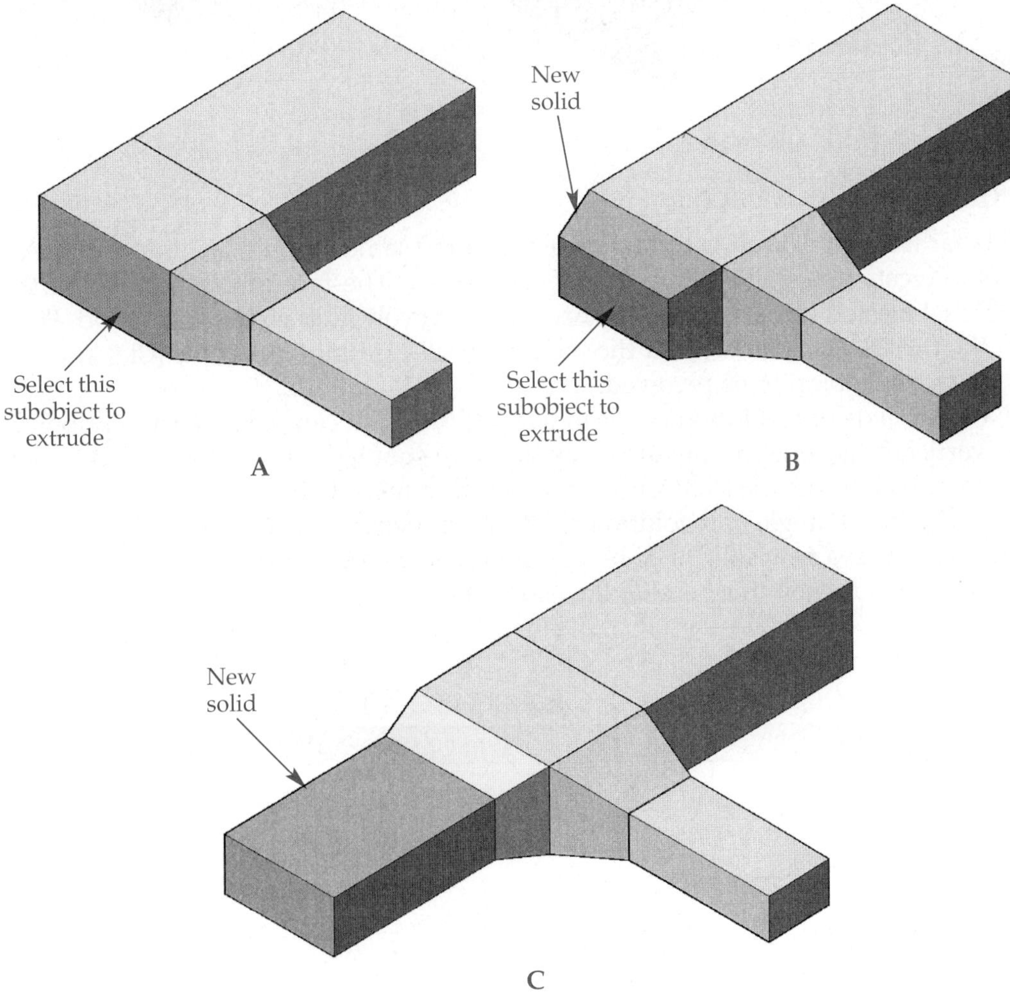

Figure 11-18.
A—The face on the left end of the HVAC duct (shown in color) needs to be revolved to create a 90° bend. B—Use the **REVOLVE** command and pick the face subobject to be revolved.

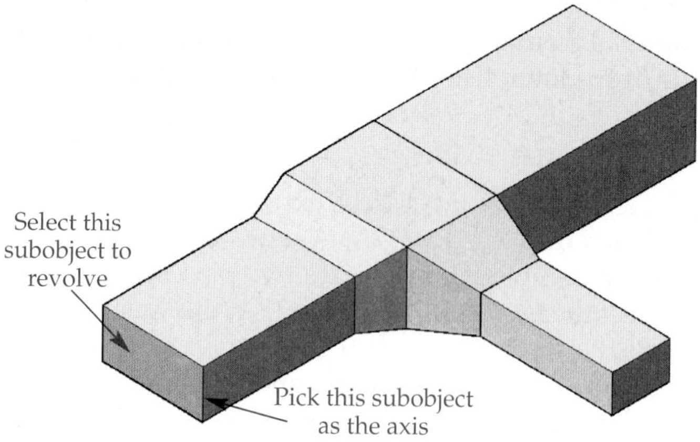

A

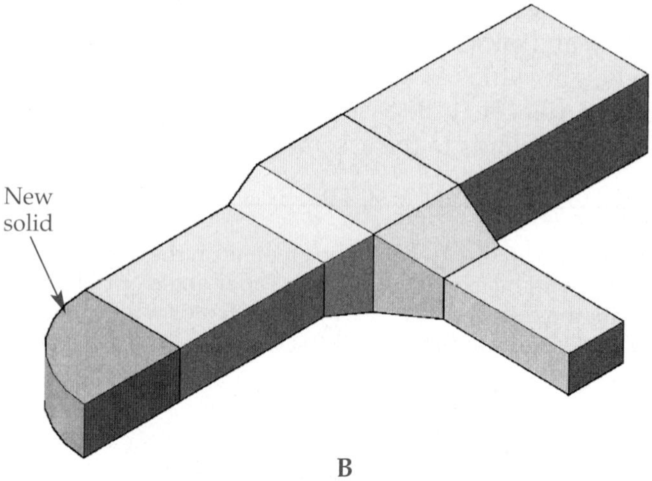

B

Revolving a Solid Face

Planar faces on 3D solids can be revolved in the same manner as other AutoCAD objects to create new solids. Refer to Figure 11-18A. The face on the left end of the HVAC duct created in the last section needs to be revolved to create a 90° bend. First, select the **REVOLVE** command. At the "select objects" prompt, press the [Ctrl] key and pick the face subobject to be revolved.

Next, the axis of revolution needs to be specified. You can pick the two endpoints of the vertical edge, but you can also pick the edge subobject. Enter the **Object** option of the command, press the [Ctrl] key, and select the edge subobject.

Finally, the 90° angle of revolution needs to be specified. Figure 11-18B shows the face revolved into a new solid. The bend is a new, separate solid. If necessary, use the **UNION** command to join the bend to the assembly.

Exercise 11-2

Complete the exercise on the Student CD.

Figure 11-19.
Edge grips are rectangular and displayed in the middle of the edge.

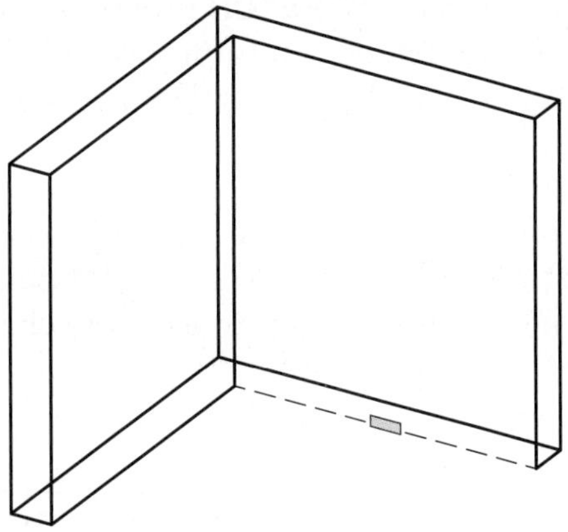

Edge Subobject Editing

Individual edges of a solid can be edited using grips and grip tools in the same manner as faces. To select an edge subobject, press the [Ctrl] key and pick the edge. Grips on linear edges are rectangular and appear in the middle of the edge, **Figure 11-19.** In addition to solid edges, the edges of regions can be altered using **MOVE**, **ROTATE**, and **SCALE**, but grips are not displayed on regions as they are on solid subobjects.

Remember, editing subobjects of a primitive removes the primitive's history. This should always be a consideration if it is important to preserve the solid primitives that were used to construct a 3D solid model. Instead of editing the primitive subobjects at their subobject level, it may be better to add or remove material with a Boolean operation, thus preserving the solid's history.

Moving Edges

To move an edge, select it using the [Ctrl] key, as previously discussed. By default (**GTAUTO** = 1), the move grip tool appears. See **Figure 11-20A.** Hover the cursor over the edge grip to set the tool on the grip. Then, select the appropriate axis handle and dynamically move the edge or use direct distance entry, **Figure 11-20B.** The move grip tool remains active until the [Esc] key is pressed.

Figure 11-20.
A—Select the edge subobject to be moved. B—The edge is moved. Notice how the size of the primitive used to subtract the cutout is not affected.

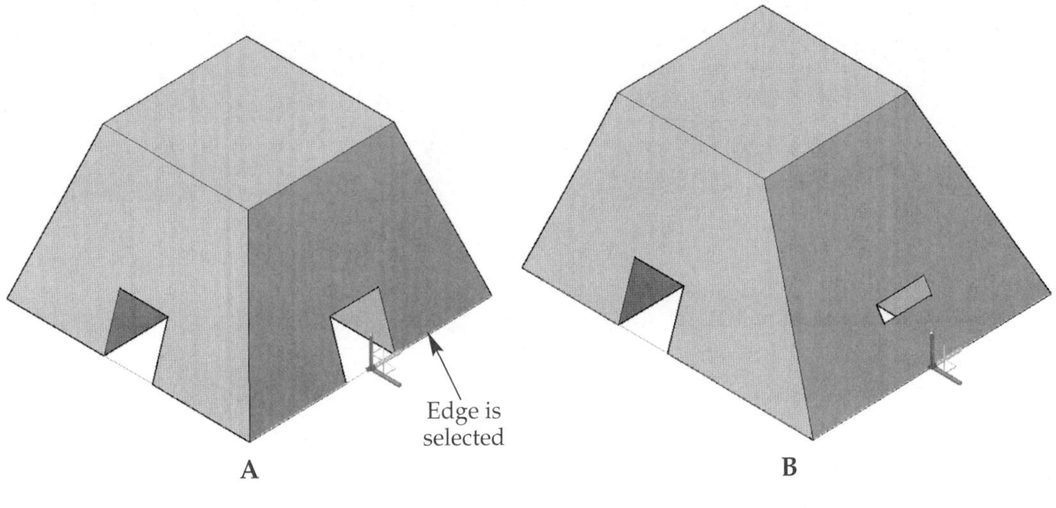

If you *pick* the edge grip to turn it hot, the move grip tool (if displayed) is bypassed. This places you in the standard grip editing mode. You can stretch, move, rotate, scale, and mirror the edge. In this case, the **STRETCH** function works the same as the move grip tool, but less reliably. You must be careful to use either ortho, polar tracking, or direct distance entry, but the possibility for error still exists.

There are a few options to achieve different results when dynamically moving an edge. The [Ctrl] key is used to access these options. First, select the edge. Then, pick the edge grip or grip tool and press and release the [Ctrl] key to cycle through the options.

If the [Ctrl] key is not pressed, the moved edge maintains its length and orientation. However, the shape and planes of adjacent faces are changed. See **Figure 11-21A.** If the [Ctrl] key is pressed three times, the function is reset, as if the [Ctrl] key had not been pressed.

Figure 11-21.
Moving an edge. A—If the [Ctrl] key is not pressed, the edge maintains its length and orientation, but the shape and planes of adjacent faces are changed. B—If the [Ctrl] key is pressed once, the moved edge maintains its orientation, but its length is modified because the planes of adjacent faces are maintained. C—If the [Ctrl] key is pressed twice, the adjacent faces may be triangulated.

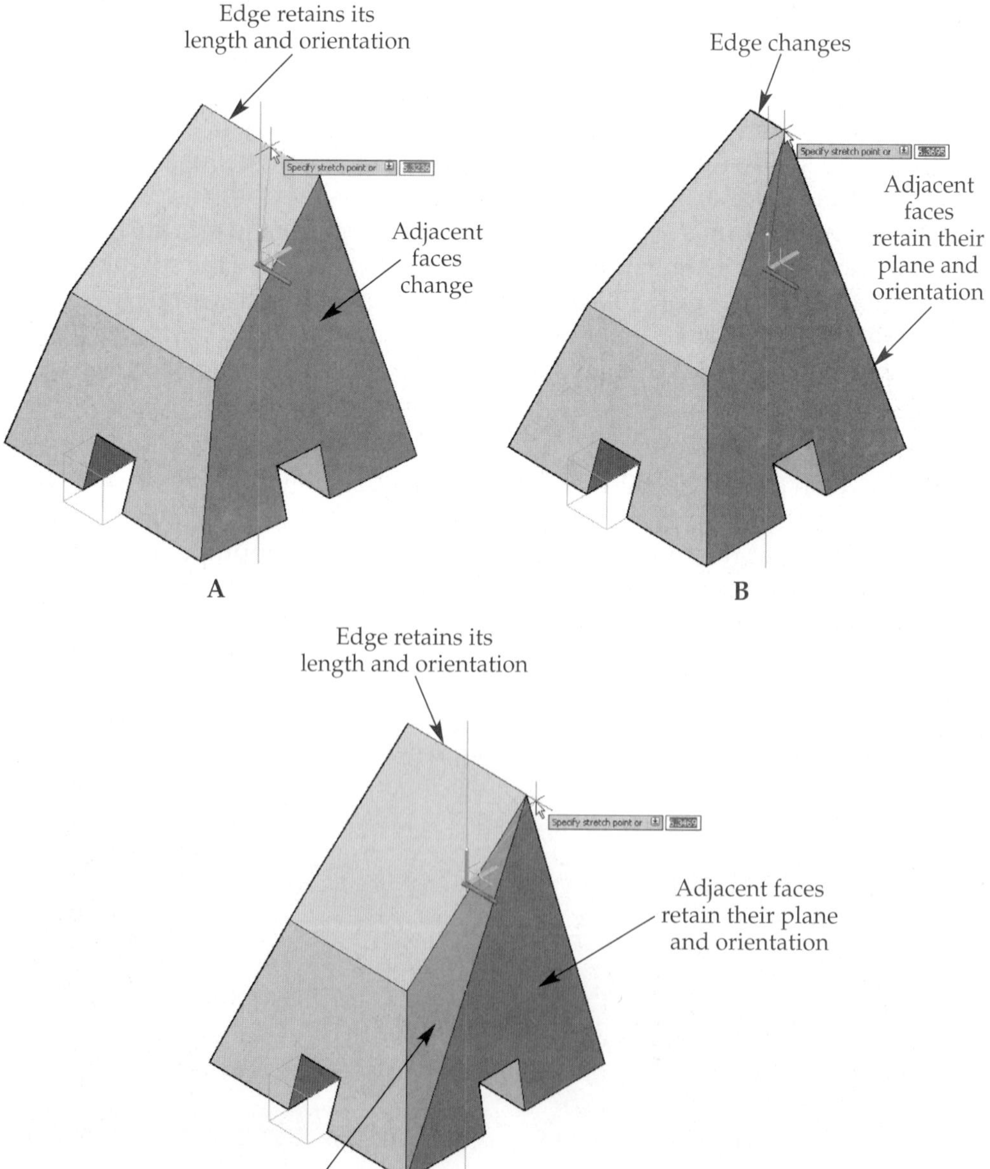

If the [Ctrl] key is pressed once, the moved edge maintains its orientation, but its length is modified. This is because the planes and orientation of adjacent faces are maintained. See **Figure 11-21B.**

If the [Ctrl] key is pressed twice, the moved edge maintains its length and orientation. But, if the move alters the planes of adjacent faces, those faces may become *nonplanar.* In other words, the face may now be located on two or more planes. If this happens, adjacent faces are divided into triangles, **Figure 11-21C.** This is visible when the object in **Figure 11-21C** is displayed in two orthographic views. See **Figure 11-22.**

PROFESSIONAL TIP

You can quickly enter the **MOVE**, **ROTATE**, or **SCALE** command for a subobject by selecting the subobject, right-clicking, and picking the command from the shortcut menu.

Rotating Edges

Before you select an edge to rotate, do a little planning. Since there are a wide variety of edge rotation options, it will save time if you first decide on the location of the base point about which the edge will rotate. Next, determine the direction and angle of rotation. Based on these criteria, choose the option that will accomplish the task the quickest.

To rotate an edge, enter the **ROTATE** or **3DROTATE** command. Then, pick the edge using the [Ctrl] key. Select a base point and then enter the rotation. You can also select the edge, pick the edge grip, and cycle to the **ROTATE** mode.

Edges are best rotated using the rotate grip tool. It provides a graphic visualization of the axis of rotation. If you select a dynamic UCS while using the **3DROTATE** command, you have a variety of rotation axes to use because the grip tool can be located on all planes adjacent to the selected edge.

There are a few options to achieve different results when dynamically rotating an edge. The [Ctrl] key is used to access these options. First, select the edge. Then, pick the edge grip or grip tool and press and release the [Ctrl] key to cycle through the options.

Figure 11-22.
Triangulated faces are clear in plan views. A—Front plan view. B—Side plan view.

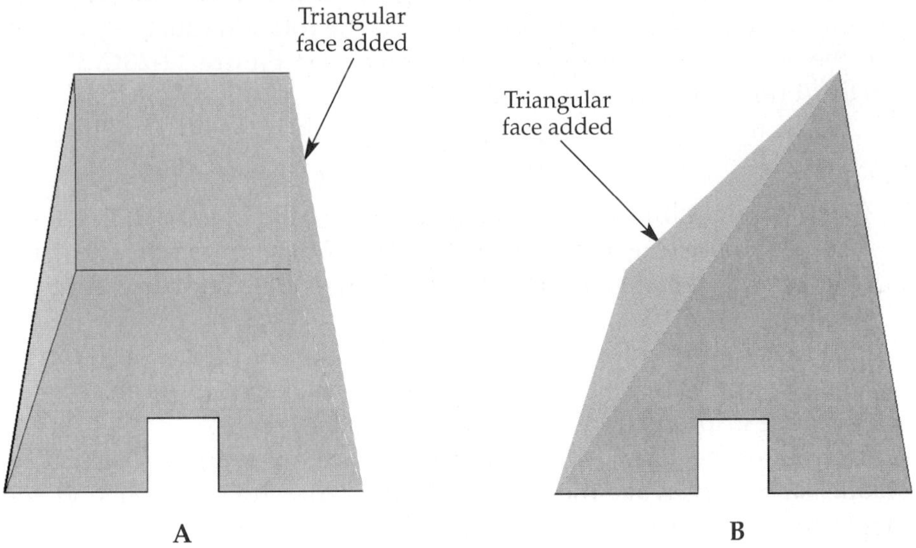

Figure 11-23.
Rotating an edge. A—The [Ctrl] key is not pressed. B—The [Ctrl] key is pressed once. Notice the top edge of the dark face. C—The [Ctrl] key is pressed twice.

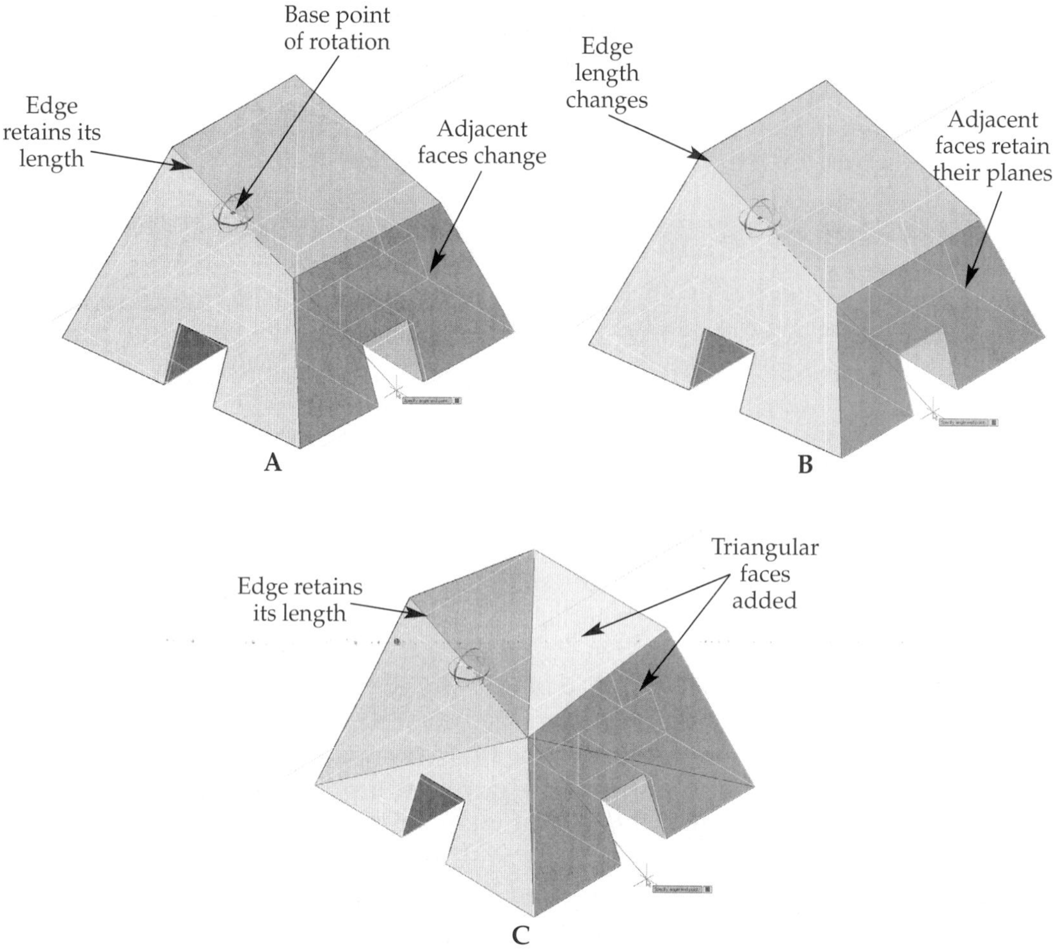

Pressing the [Ctrl] key while rotating a face affects adjacent faces in the same manner as discussed in moving faces. If the [Ctrl] key is not pressed, the rotated edge maintains its length, but the shape and planes of adjacent faces are changed. See **Figure 11-23A.** If the [Ctrl] key is pressed once, the length of the rotated edge is modified because the planes of adjacent faces are maintained. See **Figure 11-23B.** If the [Ctrl] key is pressed twice, the rotated edge maintains its length, but if the rotation causes faces to become nonplanar, the adjacent faces may be triangulated. See **Figure 11-23C.** Pressing the [Ctrl] key a third time resets the function.

Scaling Edges

Only linear (straight-line) edges can be scaled. Circular edges, such as the ends of cylinders, can be modified using grips or the **SOLIDEDIT** command. These tools can be used to change the diameter or establish taper angles. See Chapter 12 for a complete discussion of the **SOLIDEDIT** command.

To scale a linear edge, enter the **SCALE** command. Select the edge using the [Ctrl] key. Pick a base point for the operation and enter a scale factor. You can also select the edge, pick the edge grip, and cycle to the **SCALE** mode.

The direction of the scaled edge is related to the base point you select. The base point remains stationary, while the vertices in either direction are scaled. If you enter the **SCALE** command, you are prompted for the base point. If you select the edge grip, the grip becomes the base point. The differences in opposite end and midpoint scaling of an edge are shown in **Figure 11-24.**

Figure 11-24.
The differences in opposite end and midpoint scaling of an edge. A—The original object. B—The edge is scaled down with a base point on the left corner. C—The edge is scaled down to the same scale factor, but the base point is on the right corner. D—The edge is scaled down to the same scaled factor with the base point at the middle of the edge.

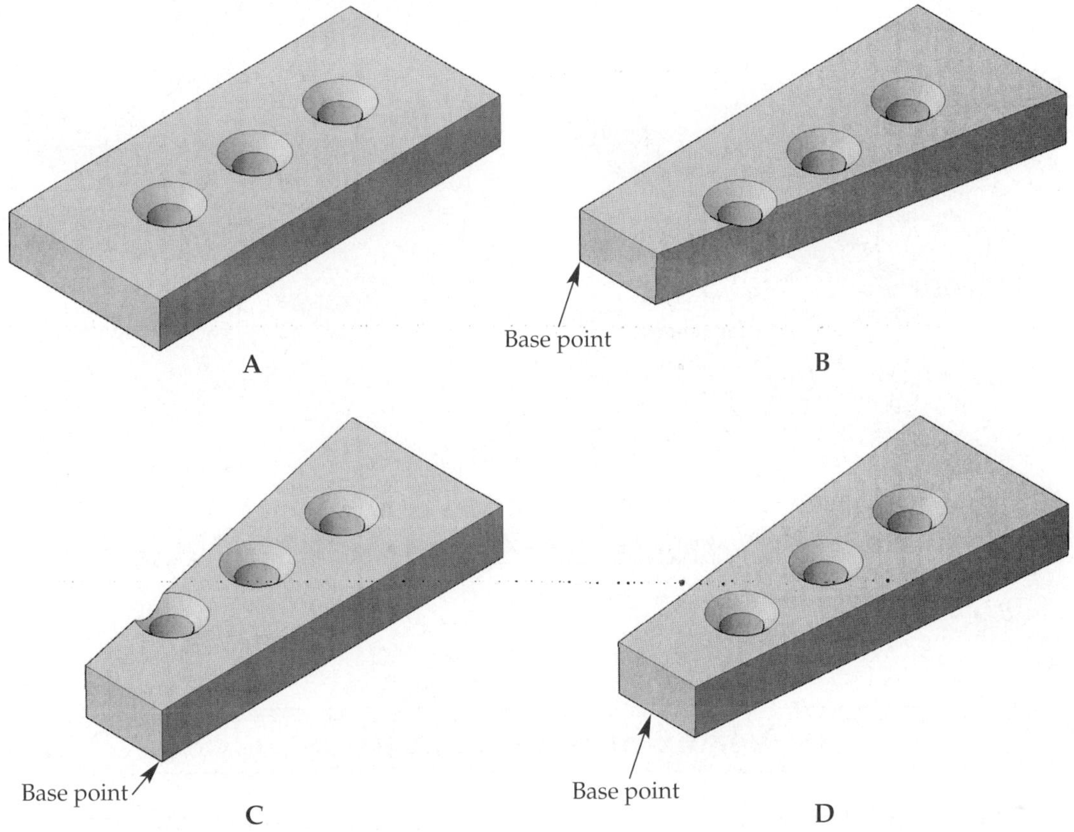

There are a few options to achieve different results when dynamically scaling an edge. The [Ctrl] key is used to access these options. First, select the edge. Then, pick the edge grip or enter the **SCALE** command and press and release the [Ctrl] key to cycle through the options.

If the [Ctrl] key is not pressed, the edge is scaled. The shape and planes of adjacent faces are changed to match the scaled edge. See **Figure 11-25A.**

If the [Ctrl] key is pressed once, the edge is, in effect, not scaled. This is because the planes of adjacent faces are maintained.

If the [Ctrl] key is pressed twice, the edge is scaled, as are edges attached to the modified edge. However, if the scaling causes faces to become nonplanar, they may be triangulated. See **Figure 11-25B.**

Coloring Edges

To change the color of an edge, use the [Ctrl] key selection method to select the edge. Next, open the **Properties** palette. In the **General** category, pick the drop-down list for the Color property. Select the desired color or pick Select Color… and choose a color from the **Select Color** dialog box. Edges cannot have materials assigned to them.

Deleting Edges

Edges can be deleted in certain situations. In order for an edge to be deleted, it must completely divide two faces that lie on the same plane. If this condition is met, the **ERASE** command or the [Delete] key can be used to remove the edge. The two faces become a single face.

Figure 11-25.
Scaling the front edge with the base point in the middle of the edge. The original object is shown in Figure 10-24A. A—If the [Ctrl] key is not pressed, the edge is scaled and the shape and planes of adjacent faces are changed. B—If the [Ctrl] key is pressed twice, the edge is scaled, as are edges attached to it. If the scaling causes faces to become nonplanar, the adjacent faces may be triangulated.

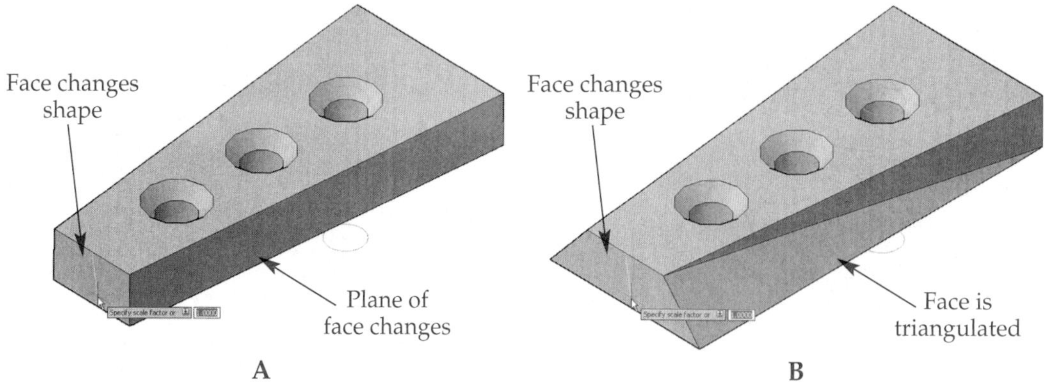

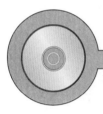

Exercise 11-3
Complete the exercise on the Student CD.

Vertex Subobject Editing

The modification of a single vertex involves moving the vertex and stretching all edges and planar faces attached to it. Vertex grips are circular and located on the vertex, as shown in **Figure 11-26**. A single vertex cannot be rotated or scaled, but you can select multiple vertices and perform rotating and scaling edits. When editing multiple vertices in this manner you are, in effect, editing edges.

As with other subobject editing functions performed on a 3D solid primitive, the solid's history is removed when a vertex is modified. The solid can no longer be edited using the primitive grips; only a single base grip is displayed. Further editing of the solid must be with the **SOLIDEDIT** command, discussed in Chapter 12, or through subobject editing.

Figure 11-26.
Vertex grips are circular and placed on the vertex.

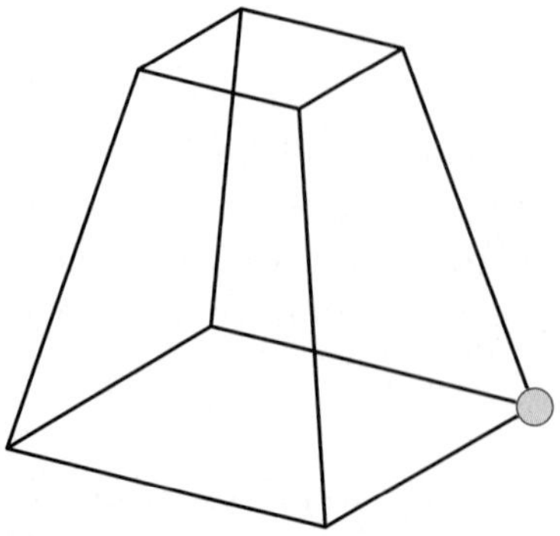

Moving Vertices

To move a vertex, select it using the [Ctrl] key method. By default (**GTAUTO** = 1), the move grip tool is displayed. You can use the move grip tool, the **MOVE** command, or standard grip editing modes to move the vertex. If the [Ctrl] key is not pressed while dynamically moving a vertex, adjacent faces are triangulated by the move. Pressing the [Ctrl] key once allows the vertex to be moved without triangulating adjacent faces, but the faces may change shape. In some cases, AutoCAD may deem it necessary to triangulate faces. See **Figure 11-27.**

PROFESSIONAL TIP

If you are dragging a vertex and faces become triangulated, you can transparently change your viewpoint to see the effect of the triangulation. Press and hold the [Shift] key. At the same time, press and hold the mouse wheel. Now, move the mouse to change the viewpoint. This is a transparent instance of the **3DORBIT** command.

Figure 11-27.
Moving a vertex. A—The original object. B—Without pressing the [Ctrl] key, adjacent faces are triangulated. C—Pressing the [Ctrl] key once moves the vertex and changes some of the adjacent faces.

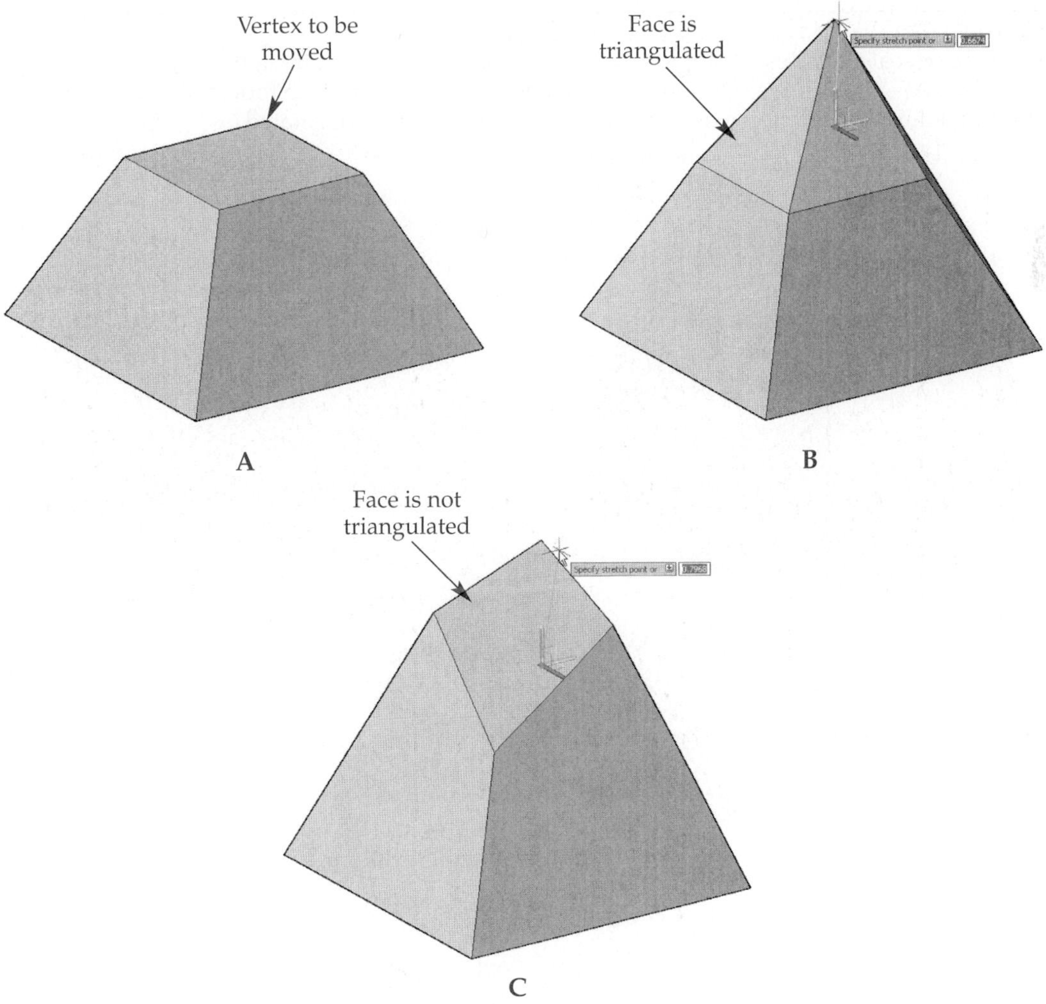

Rotating Vertices

As previously stated, a single vertex cannot be rotated or scaled, but two or more vertices can be. Since two vertices define a line, or edge, any edit is an edge modification. However, the process is slightly different than the edge modifications described earlier in this chapter.

To rotate an edge by selecting its endpoints, press the [Ctrl] key and select each vertex. See **Figure 11-28A.** You may need to use the [Ctrl]+space bar option to turn on cycling. Notice that grips appear at each selected vertex, but the edges between the vertices are not highlighted.

The **ROTATE** command can now be used to rotate the vertices (if **PICKFIRST** is set to 1). However, a more efficient method for rotating vertices is to use the **3DROTATE** command. The combination of the rotate grip tool and the UCS icon enable you to graphically view the rotation plane. Once the command is initiated, pick a location for the rotate grip tool, which is the base of rotation. See **Figure 11-28B.** Then, select the axis of revolution. Finally, pick the angle start point and enter the rotation. See **Figure 11-28C.**

If the [Ctrl] key is not pressed while dynamically rotating the vertices, the area of the selected vertices does not change and adjacent faces are triangulated. This is because the edges of the adjacent faces are attached to the selected vertices, so their edge length changes as the selected edge is rotated. If the [Ctrl] key is pressed once, the adjacent faces are not triangulated unless necessary, but the faces may change shape.

Figure 11-28.
To rotate or scale vertices, multiple vertices must be selected. In effect, the edges are modified. A—Vertices are selected to be rotated. B—The rotate grip tool is placed at the base of rotation and the rotation axis is selected. C—The vertices are rotated.

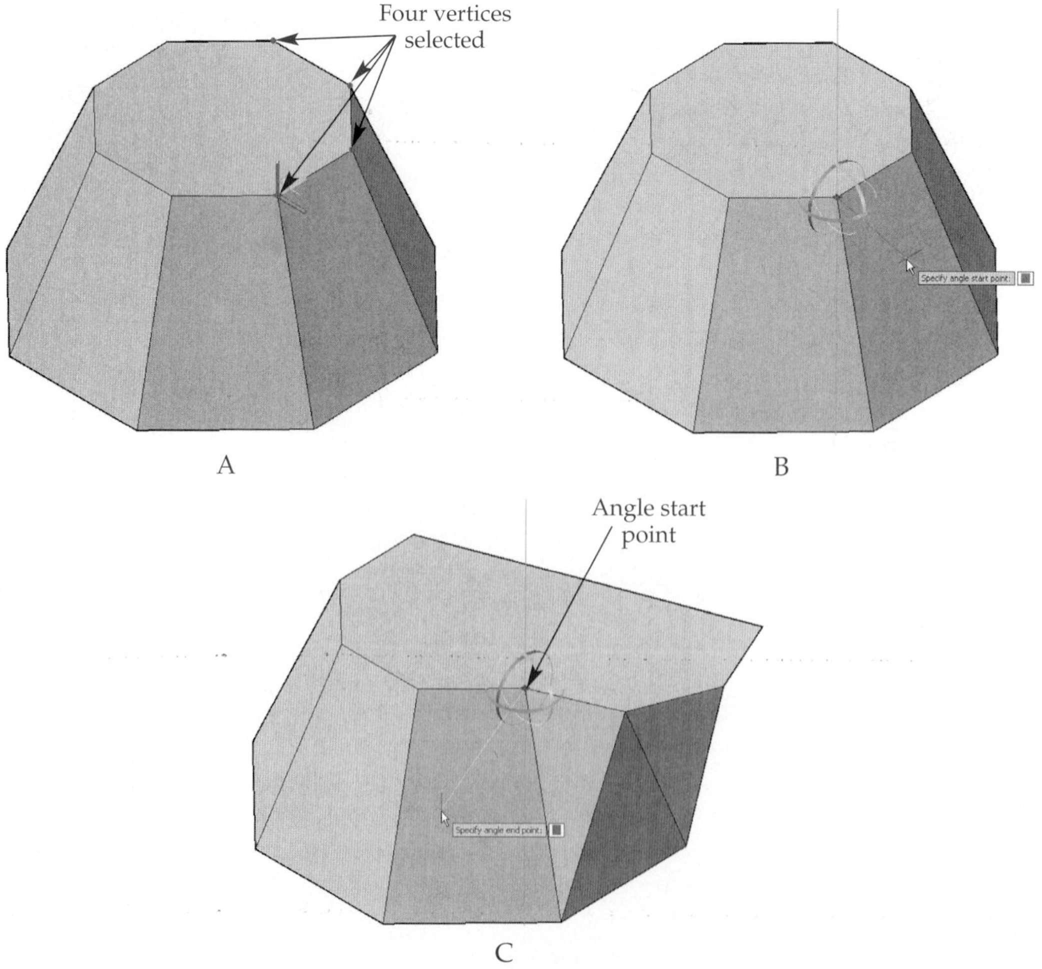

NOTE

If the selected edge does not dynamically rotate at the "angle end point" prompt, then the desired rotation is not possible.

Scaling Vertices

As mentioned earlier, it is not possible to scale a single vertex. However, two or more vertices can be selected for scaling. This, in effect, scales edges. The selection methods are the same as discussed for rotating vertices and the use of the [Ctrl] key while dragging produces the same effects. As the pointer is dragged, the dynamic display of scaled edges may be difficult to visualize. Therefore, it is best to use a scale factor or the **Reference** option to achieve properly scaled edges.

Exercise 11-4

Complete the exercise on the Student CD.

Using Subobject Editing as a Construction Tool

This section provides an example of how subobject editing can be used to not only make changes to existing solids and composites, but as a powerful construction tool. Some of the procedures of subobject editing, such as editing faces, edges, and vertices, are used to construct an HVAC assembly. The entire model is constructed from a single, solid cube. This is the only primitive you will draw.

Editing Faces

1. Begin by setting the units to Architectural and drawing a 24″ × 24″ cube. Display the model from the southeast isometric viewpoint.
2. Select the left-hand face and move it 60″ to the left. Also, select the front face and move it out 12″. This forms the first duct. See **Figure 11-29.**
3. Using the **EXTRUDE** command, select the left-hand face and extrude it 36″ to create a new solid. This is a tee junction from which two branches will extend.
4. Select the front face of the new solid and extrude it 28″ with a taper angle of 10° to create a new solid that is a reducer.
5. Select the left-hand face of the tee junction and extrude it 20″ with a taper angle of 10° to create a new solid that is a second reducer. See **Figure 11-30.**
6. Select the left-hand face of the 20″ reducer and move it 3 17/32″ along the positive Z axis. This places the top surface of the reducer level with the trunk of the duct. Next, extrude the left-hand face of this reducer 60″ into a new solid.
7. Use the **REVOLVE** command to turn the left-hand face of the 60″ extension into a new solid that is a 90° bend. Your drawing should now look like **Figure 11-31.**

Figure 11-29.
The left-hand face of the cube is moved 60″. The front face is then moved 12″.

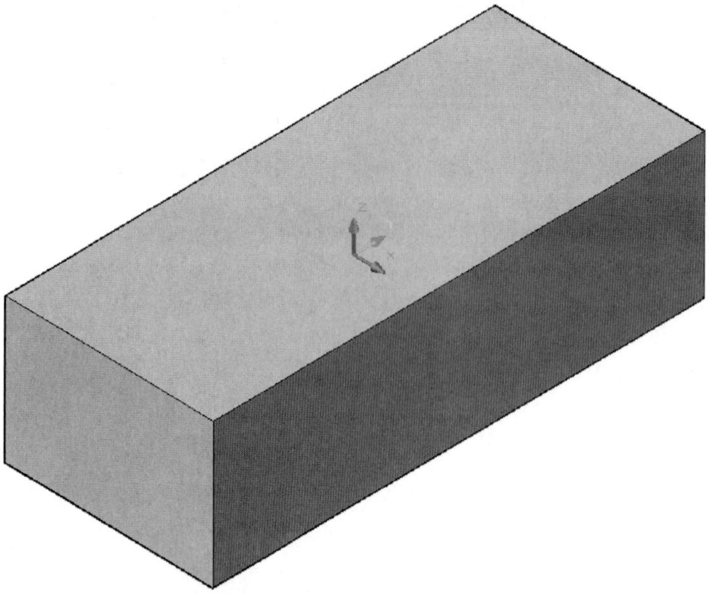

Figure 11-30.
Two reducers are created by extruding faces from the tee junction.

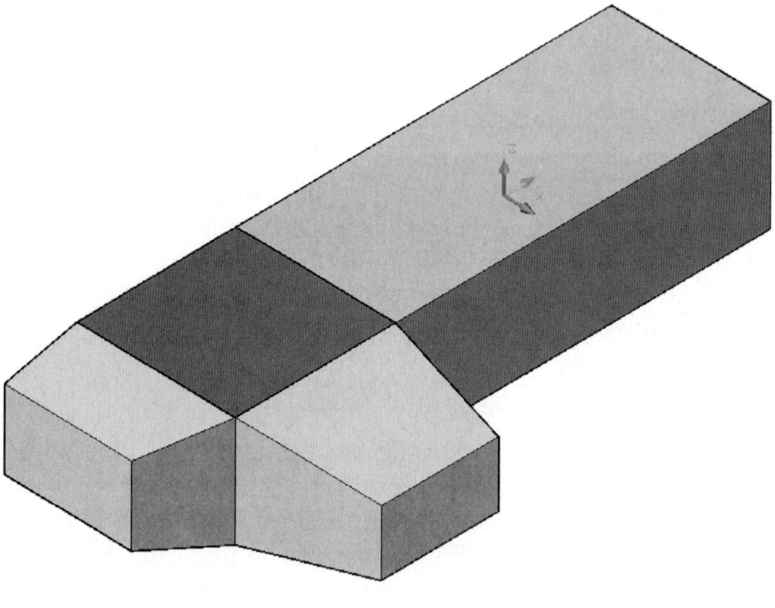

Editing Edges and Vertices

1. The bottom surface of the 28″ reducer must be level with the bottom of the tee junction and main trunk. Select the bottom edge of the reducer's front face and move it down 4 15/16″.
2. Select the two top vertices on the 28″ reducer's front face and move them down (negative Z) 6″.
3. Select the front, rectangular face of the 90° bend and extrude it 72″ into a new solid.
4. Select the front face of the 28″ reducer and extrude it 108″ into a new solid.
5. Select the front face of the new solid created in step 4 and extrude it 26″ to create a new solid that will be a tee junction.
6. Extrude the left-hand face of the tee junction 20″. See **Figure 11-32.**
7. Move the top edge of left-hand face on the 20″ extrusion created in step 6 down 4″.
8. Move each vertical edge of the 20″ extrusion 6″ toward the center of the duct.
9. Mirror a copy of the 20″ extrusion to the opposite side of the tee junction. The completed drawing should look like **Figure 11-33.**

Figure 11-31.
The left end of the 60″ extrusion is revolved 90° to create an elbow.

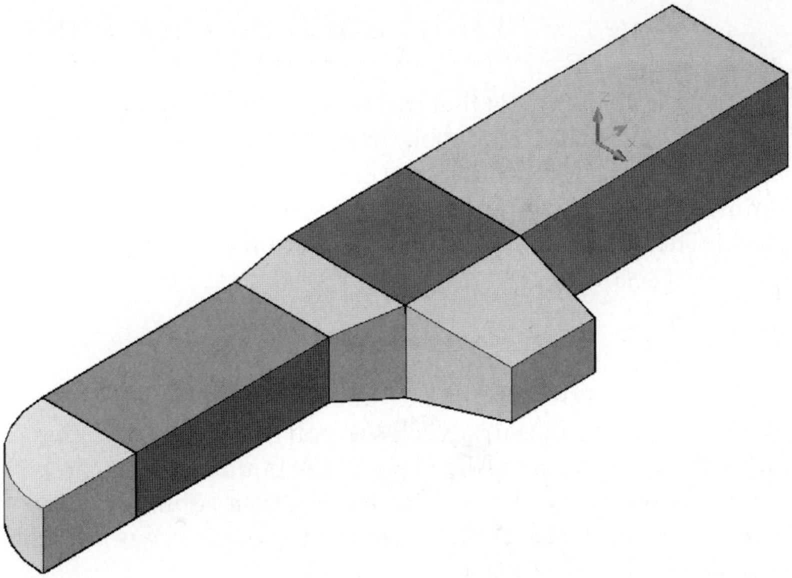

Figure 11-32.
The face of the revolved elbow is extruded 72″. The face of the right branch is extruded 108″. The right duct is then extruded 26″ and the left face of that extrusion is extruded by 20″.

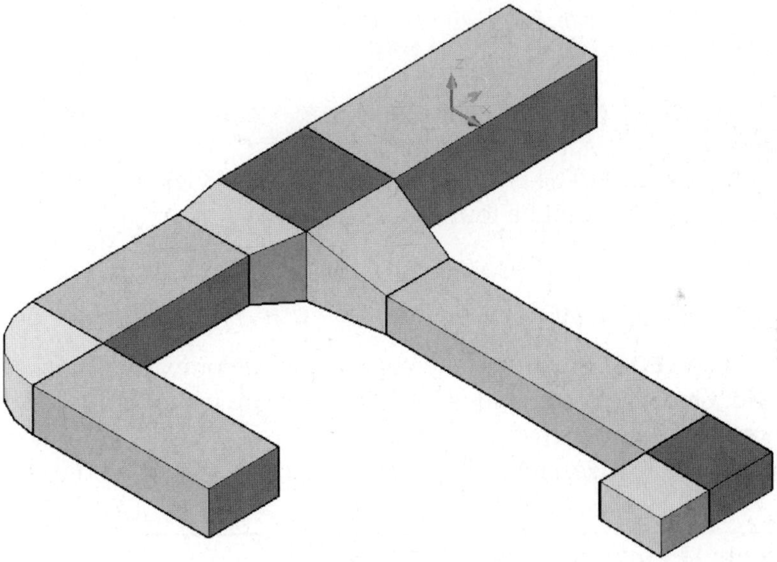

Figure 11-33.
The reducer is mirrored to create the final assembly.

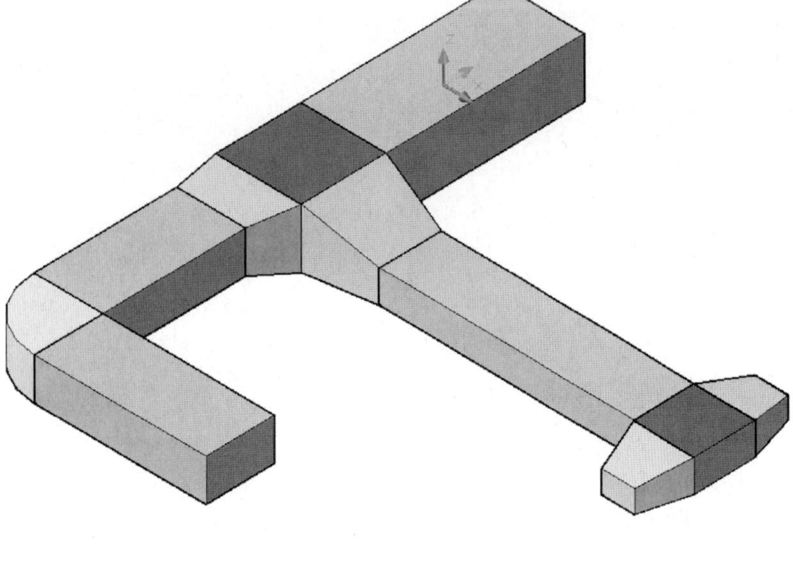

Other Solid Editing Tools

There are other tools that can be used in solid model editing. As you will learn in Chapter 12, the **SOLIDEDIT** tool can be used to edit faces, edges, and vertices much like subobject editing. In addition, you can extrude a closed boundary with the **PRESSPULL** command, extract a wireframe from a solid using the **XEDGES** command, and explode a solid. The **PRESSPULL** and **XEDGES** commands and exploding a solid are discussed in the next sections.

Presspull

PRESSPULL

Ribbon
Home
> 3D Modeling
Press/Pull
Type
PRESSPULL

The **PRESSPULL** command allows any closed boundary to be extruded. The boundary can be a flat surface, closed polyline, circle, or region. The extrusion is always applied perpendicular to the plane of the boundary, but can be in the positive or negative direction. When applied to the face of a solid, it is very similar to the **Extrude Face** option of the **SOLIDEDIT** command, though dynamic feedback is provided for the extrusion with **PRESSPULL**.

Once the command is initiated, you are prompted to pick inside of the bounded areas to extrude. Move the pointer inside of a boundary and pick. Then, drag the boundary to a new location and pick or, if dynamic input is on, enter the distance to extrude the face. See **Figure 11-34.**

NOTE

The entire boundary must be visible on the screen, or the loop will not be found.

Extracting a Wireframe

XEDGES

Ribbon
Home
> Solid Editing
Extract Edges
Type
XEDGES
Menu
Modify
> 3D Operations
> Extract Edges

The **XEDGES** command creates copies of, or extracts, all of the edges on a selected solid. Once the command is initiated, you are prompted to select objects. Select one or more solids and press [Enter]. The edges are extracted and placed on top of the existing edges. See **Figure 11-35.** The new objects are created on the current layer.

Figure 11-34.
Using the **PRESSPULL** command. A—Pick inside of a boundary (shown in color) and drag the boundary to a new location. B—The completed operation.

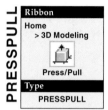

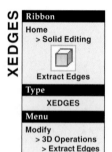

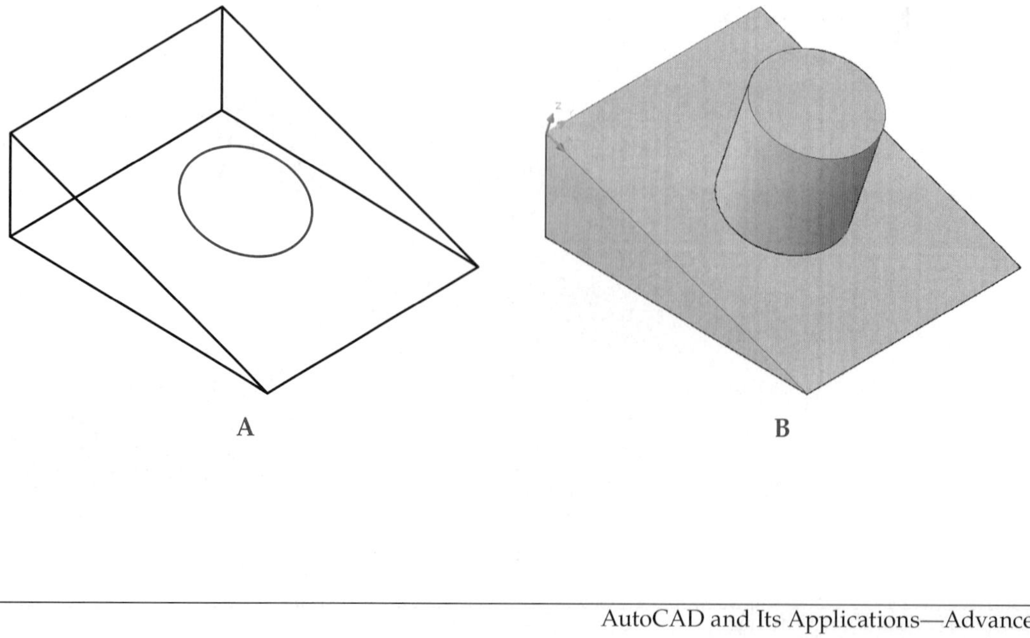

A B

Figure 11-35.
Extracting edges with the **XEDGES** command. A—The original object. B—The extracted wireframe (edges).

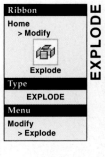

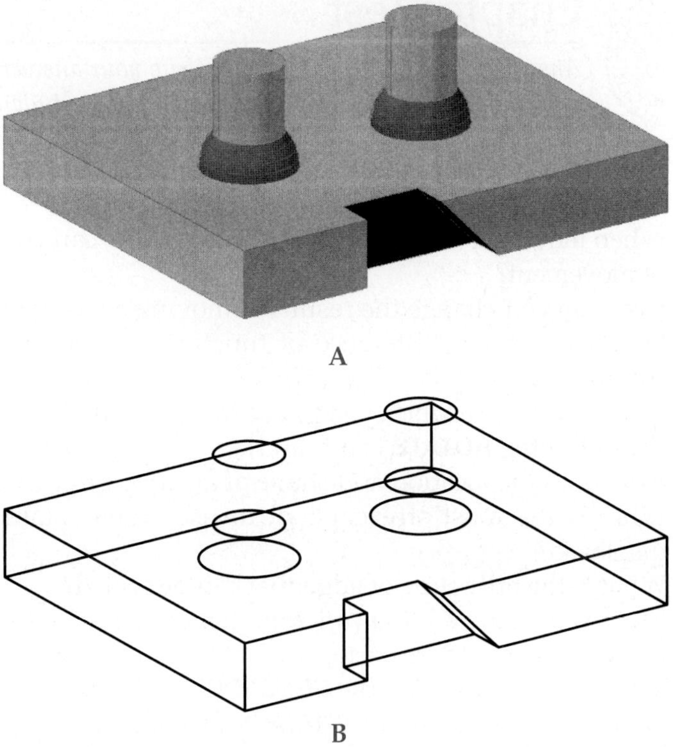

Straight edges and the curved edges where cylindrical surfaces intersect with flat or other cylindrical surfaces are the only edges extracted. Spheres and tori have no edges that can be extracted. The round bases of cylinders and cones are the only edges of those objects that will be extracted.

Exploding a Solid

A solid can be exploded. This turns the solid into surfaces and/or regions. Flat surfaces on the solid are turned into regions. Curved surfaces on the solid are turned into surfaces. To explode a solid, select the **EXPLODE** command. Then, pick the solid(s) to explode and press [Enter].

EXPLODE

Ribbon
Home
> Modify
Explode

Type
EXPLODE

Menu
Modify
> Explode

Exercise 11-5

Complete the exercise on the Student CD.

Chapter Test

Answer the following questions. Write your answers on a separate sheet of paper or complete the electronic chapter test on the Student CD.

1. How is a subobject selected?
2. How is a subobject deselected?
3. When moving a face on a solid primitive, how can you accurately control the axis of movement?
4. How can you change the results of moving a face while dragging it?
5. Describe a major difference of function between the **ROTATE** and **3DROTATE** commands.
6. Which variable enables you to use the **3DROTATE** command in a 3D view even if you select the **ROTATE** command?
7. How does the location and shape of an edge grip differ from a face grip?
8. What is the most efficient tool to use when rotating an edge and how is it displayed?
9. What is the only type of edge that can be scaled?
10. What is the only editing function that can be done to a single vertex?
11. How are two or more vertices selected for editing?
12. What is the function of the **PRESSPULL** command?
13. On which objects can the **PRESSPULL** command be used?
14. What is the purpose of the **XEDGES** command?
15. When a solid object is exploded, which type of object is created?

Drawing Problems - Chapter 11

Drawing Problems

1. Draw the bookcase shown below using the dimensions given. The final result should be a single solid object. Then, use grip and subobject editing procedures to edit the object as follows.
   A. Change the width of the bookcase to 3′.
   B. Change the height of the bookcase by eliminating the top section. The resulting height should be 3′-2″.
   C. Save the drawing as P11_01.

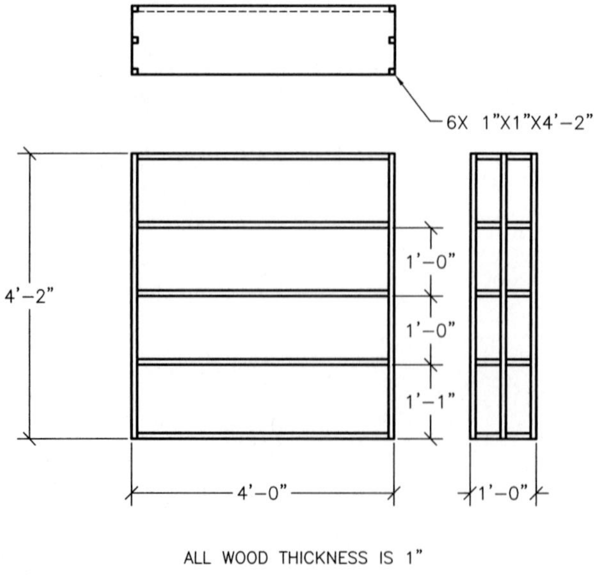

2. Open problem P11_01. Save it as P11_02. Use primitive and subobject editing procedures to create the following edits.
   A. Change the depth of the top of the bookcase to 6-1/2″.
   B. Change the depth of the bottom of the bookcase to 24″.
   C. Reduce the height of the front uprights so they are flush with the top surface of the next lower shelf.
   D. Extend the front of the second lowest shelf to match the front of the bottom. Add two uprights at the front corners between the bottom and this shelf.
   E. Save the drawing.

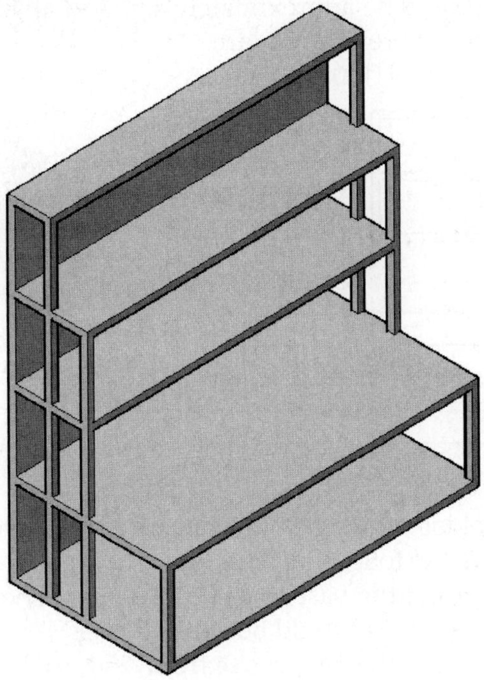

3. Draw the mounting bracket shown below. Then, use primitive and subobject editing procedures to create the following edits.
   A. Change the 3.00″ dimension to 3.50″.
   B. Change the 2.50″ dimension in the front view to 2.75″.
   C. Change the location of the slot in the auxiliary view from .60″ to .70″ and change the length of the slot to 1.15″.
   D. Change the width of each foot in the top view from 2.00″ to 1.50″. The overall dimension (5.00″) should not change.
   E. Change the angle of the bend from 15° to 45°.
   F. Save the drawing as P11_03.

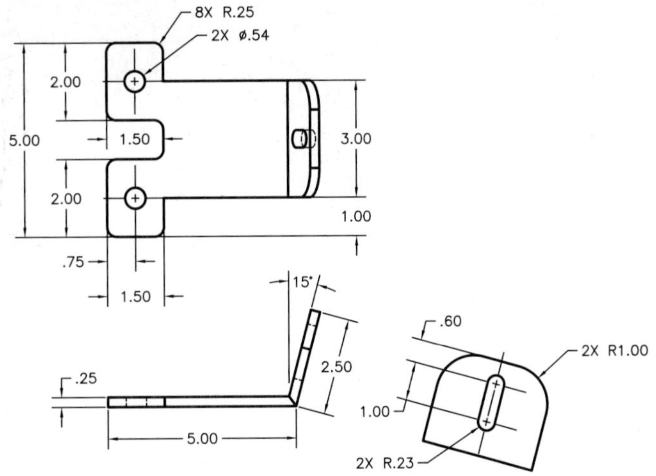

4. Draw as a single composite solid the desk organizer shown in the orthographic views below. Then, use primitive and subobject editing procedures to create the following edits. The final object should look like the shaded view below.
   A. Change the 3″ height to 3.25″.
   B. Change the 2″ height to 1.85″.
   C. Increase the thickness of the long compartment divider to .5″. The increase in thickness should be evenly applied along the centerline of the divider. Locate three evenly spaced, ∅5/16″ × 1.5″ holes in this divider.
   D. Angle the top face of the rear compartments by 30°. The height of the rear of the organizer should be approximately 4.5″ and all corners on the bottom of the organizer should remain square.
   E. Save the drawing as P11_04.

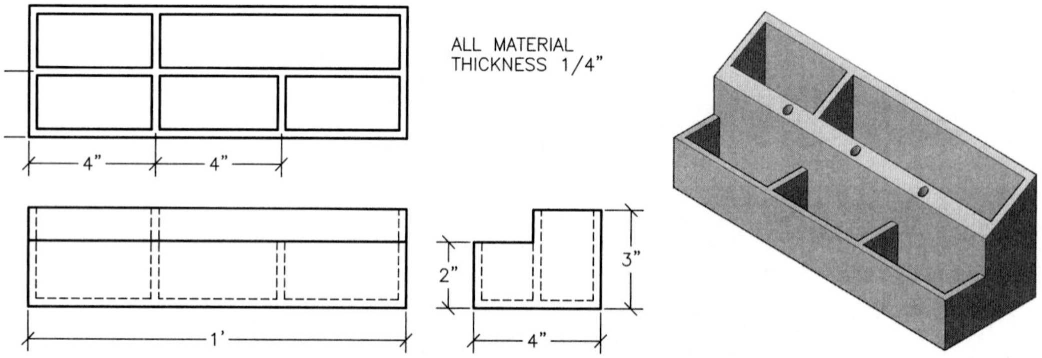

5. Draw the pencil holder shown below. Then, use primitive and subobject editing procedures to create the following edits.
   A. Change the depth of the base to 4.000″. The base should be rectangular, not square, and the grooves should become shorter.
   B. Change the height of the top groove from .250″ to .125″.
   C. Change the diameter of two holes from ∅.450″ to ∅.625″.
   D. Change the diameter of the other two holes from ∅.450″ to ∅1.000″.
   E. Rotate the top face 15° away from the side with the grooves. The planes of the adjoining faces should not change. Refer to the shaded view shown below.
   F. Save the drawing as P11_05.

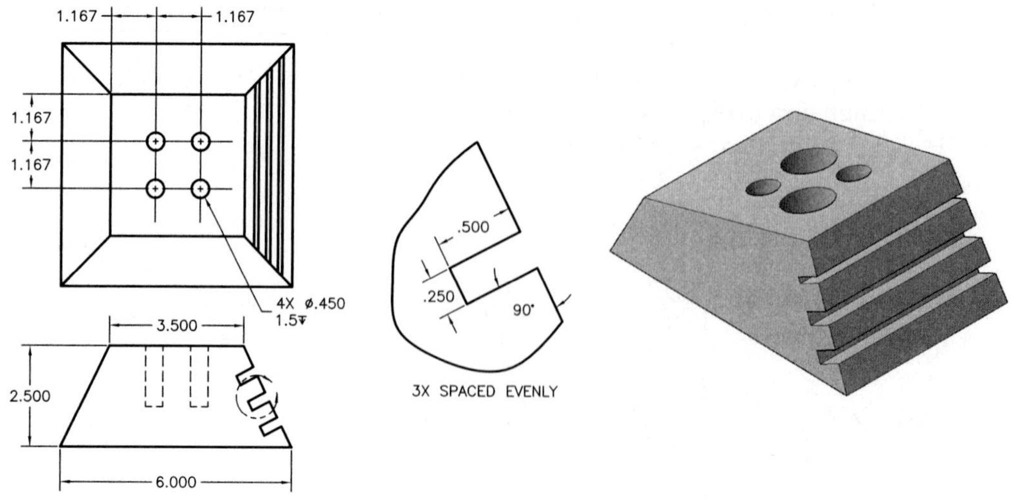

CHAPTER 12
Solid Model Editing

Learning Objectives

After completing this chapter, you will be able to:
- ✓ Change the shape and configuration of solid object faces.
- ✓ Copy and change the color of solid object edges and faces.
- ✓ Break apart a composite solid composed of physically separate entities.
- ✓ Use the **SOLIDEDIT** command to construct and edit a solid model.

AutoCAD provides expanded capabilities for editing solid models. As you saw in the previous chapter, grips can be used to edit a solid model. Also, the subobjects that make up a solid, such as faces, edges, and endpoints, can be edited. Additionally, a single command, **SOLIDEDIT**, enables you to edit faces, edges, or the entire body of the solid.

Overview of the SOLIDEDIT Command

The **SOLIDEDIT** command allows you to edit the faces, edges, and body of a solid. Many of the subobject editing functions can also be performed with the **SOLIDEDIT** command. The features of the **SOLIDEDIT** command can be accessed in the **Modify** menu, in the **Solid Editing** panel on the **Home** tab of the ribbon, or by typing SOLIDEDIT. See **Figure 12-1.**

When the **SOLIDEDIT** command is typed, you are first asked to select the component of the solid with which you wish to work. Specify either **Face**, **Edge**, or **Body**. The editing options for the selected component are then displayed. The editing function is directly entered when the option is selected from the menu or ribbon.

The following sections provide an overview of the solid model editing features of the **SOLIDEDIT** command. Each option is explained and the results of each are shown. A tutorial later in the chapter illustrates how these options can be used to construct a model.

Figure 12-1.
Accessing the **SOLIDEDIT** command options.

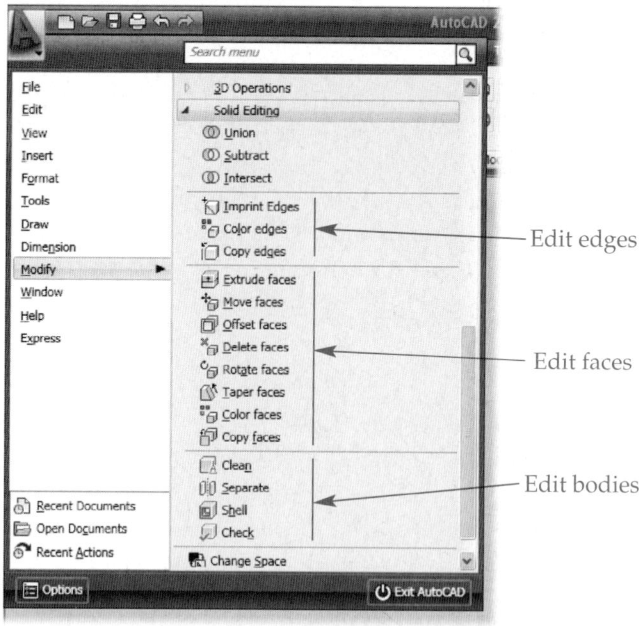

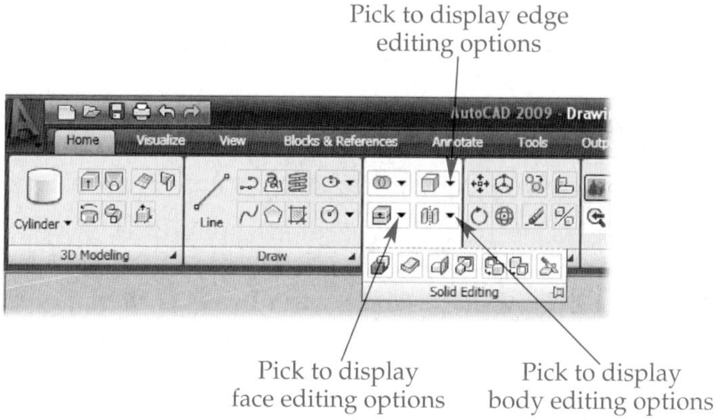

NOTE

AutoCAD displays a variety of error messages when illegal solid editing operations are attempted. Rather than trying to interpret the wording of these messages, just realize that what you tried to do will not work. Actions that may cause errors include trying to rotate a face into other faces or extruding and tapering an object at too great of an angle. When an error occurs, just try the operation again with different parameters.

Face Editing

The basic components of a solid are its faces and the greatest number of **SOLIDEDIT** options are for editing faces. All eight face editing options ask you to select faces. It is important to make sure you select the correct part of the model for editing. Remember the following three steps when using any of the face editing options.

1. First, select a face to edit. If you pick an edge, AutoCAD selects the two faces that share the edge. If this happens, use the **Remove** option to deselect the unwanted face. A more intuitive approach is to select the open space of the face as if you were touching the side of a part. AutoCAD highlights only that face.

2. Adjust the selection set at the Select faces or [Undo/Remove/ALL]: prompt. The following options are available.
   - **Undo.** Removes the previous selected face(s) from the selection set.
   - **Remove.** Allows you to select faces to remove from the selection set.
   - **ALL.** Adds all faces on the model to the selection set. This is only available after selecting at least one face. It can also be used to remove all faces if **Remove** is current.
   - **Add.** Allows you to add faces to the selection set. This is only available when **Remove** is current.
3. Press [Enter] to continue with face editing.

Extruding Faces

An extruded face is moved, or stretched, in a selected direction. The extrusion can be straight or have a taper. To extrude a face, select the command and pick the **Face>Extrude** option. You are then prompted to select the face(s) to extrude. Nonplanar (curved) faces cannot be extruded. As you pick faces, the prompt verifies the number of faces selected. For example, when an edge is selected, the prompt reads 2 faces found. When done selecting faces, press [Enter] to continue.

SOLIDEDIT

Ribbon
Home
> Solid Editing
Extrude Faces
Type
SOLIDEDIT
Menu
Modify
> Solid Editing
> Extrude Faces

Next, the height of the extrusion needs to be specified. A positive value adds material to the solid, while a negative value subtracts material from the solid. A taper can also be given.

Specify height of extrusion or [Path]: *(enter height)*
Specify angle of taper for extrusion <0>: *(enter an angle or accept the default)*
Solid validation started.
Solid validation completed.
Enter a face editing option
[Extrude/Move/Rotate/Offset/Taper/Delete/Copy/coLor/mAterial/Undo/eXit] <eXit>: **X**↵
Solids editing automatic checking: SOLIDCHECK=1
Enter a solids editing option [Face/Edge/Body/Undo/eXit] <eXit>: **X**↵

Figure 12-2 shows an original solid object and the result of extruding the top face with a 0° taper angle and a 30° taper angle. It also shows the original solid object with two adjacent faces extruded with 15° taper angles.

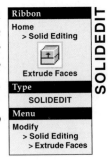

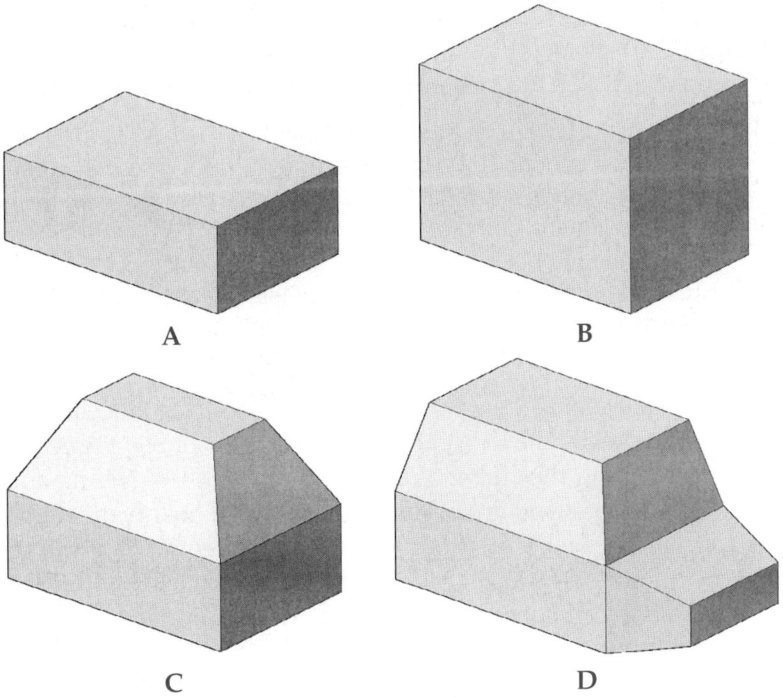

Figure 12-2. Extruding faces on an object. A—The original object. B—The top face is extruded with a 0° taper angle. C—The top face of the original is extruded with a 30° taper angle. D—The top and right-hand faces of the original are extruded with 15° taper angles.

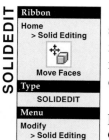

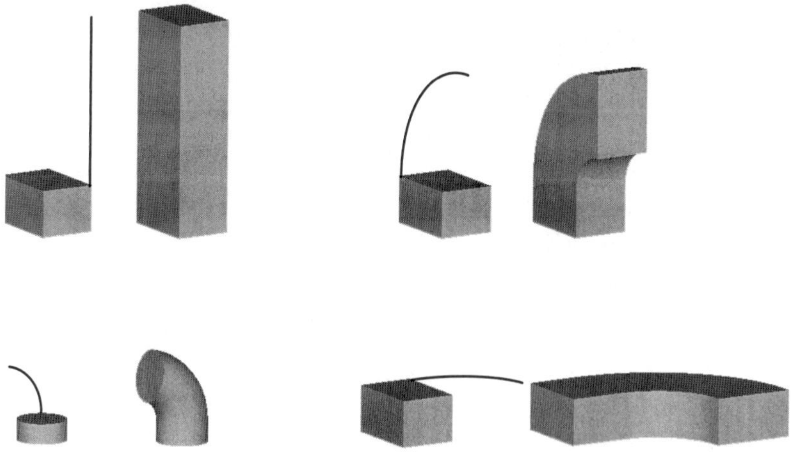

Figure 12-3.
The path of extrusion can be a line, circle, arc, ellipse, elliptical arc, polyline, or spline. Here, the paths are shown in color.

In addition to extruding a face perpendicular to itself, the extruded face can follow a path. Select the **Path** option at the Specify height of extrusion or [Path]: prompt. The path of extrusion can be a line, circle, arc, ellipse, elliptical arc, polyline, or spline. The extrusion height is the exact length of the path. See **Figure 12-3.**

Exercise 12-1
Complete the exercise on the Student CD.

Moving Faces

SOLIDEDIT

Ribbon
Home
> Solid Editing
Move Faces

Type
SOLIDEDIT

Menu
Modify
> Solid Editing
> Move Faces

The **Move Faces** option moves a face in the specified direction and lengthens or shortens the solid object. A solid model feature (such as a hole) that has been subtracted from an object to create a composite solid can be moved with this option. Object snaps may interfere with the operation of this option, so they may need to be toggled off during the operation.

To move a face, select the command and pick the **Face**>**Move** option. You are then prompted to select the face(s) to move. When done selecting faces, press [Enter] to continue. Next, you are prompted to select a base point of the operation:

Specify a base point or displacement: *(pick a base point)*
Specify a second point of displacement: *(pick a second point or enter coordinates)*
Solid validation started.
Solid validation completed.
Enter a face editing option
[Extrude/Move/Rotate/Offset/Taper/Delete/Copy/coLor/mAterial/Undo/eXit] <eXit>: **X**↵
Solids editing automatic checking: SOLIDCHECK=1
Enter a solids editing option [Face/Edge/Body/Undo/eXit] <eXit>: **X**↵

When adjacent faces are perpendicular, the edited face is moved in a direction so the new position keeps the face parallel to the original. See **Figures 12-4A** and **12-4B.** Faces that are normal to the current UCS can be moved by picking a new location or entering a direct distance. If you are moving a face that is not normal to the current UCS, you can enter coordinates for the second point of displacement, but it may be easier to first use the **Face** option of the **UCS** command to align the UCS with the face to be moved.

When adjacent faces join at angles other than perpendicular (90°), the moved face will be relocated as stated above, but only if the movement is less than the dimensional offset of the two faces. For example, in **Figure 12-4B** the top edge of the angled face

Figure 12-4.
A—The hole will be moved using the **Move** option of the **SOLIDEDIT** command. B—The hole is moved. C—When the angled face is moved, a portion of it is altered to be coplanar with the vertical face. D—If the angled face is moved more, it becomes completely coplanar to the vertical face. This is a new, single face.

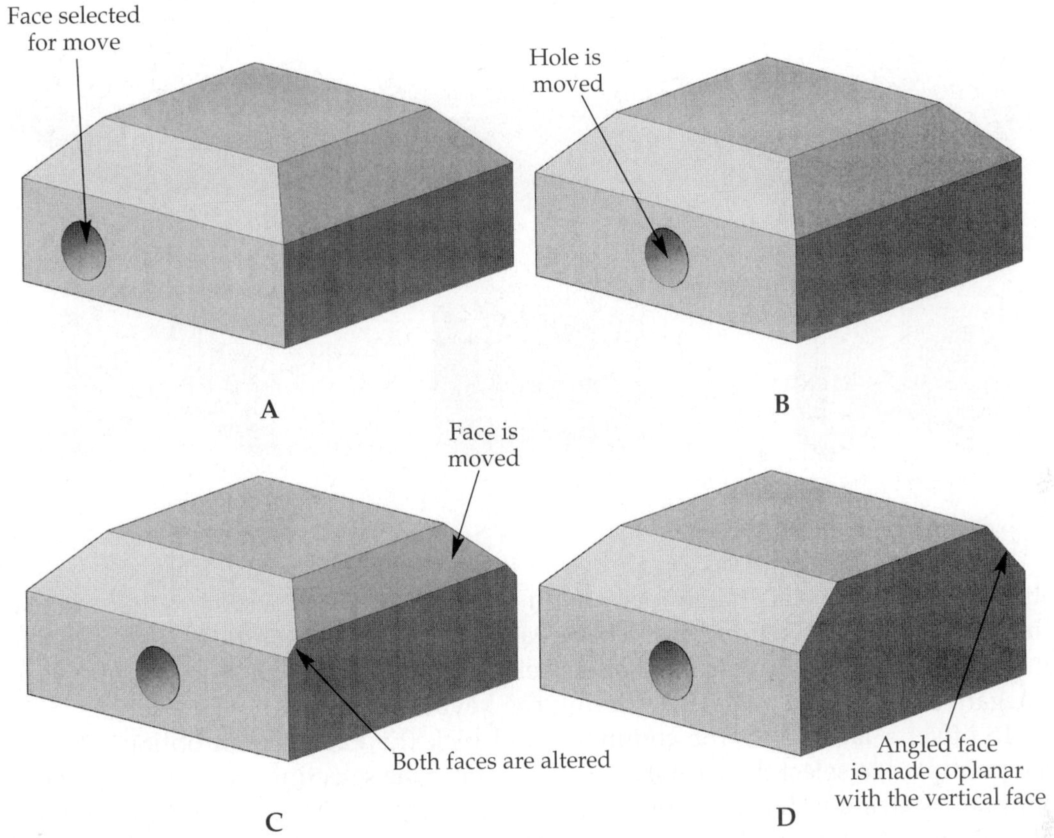

is in .5″ from the vertical face. If the angled face is moved outward a distance of less than .5″, it is altered as shown in **Figure 12-4C.** A portion of the angled face becomes coplanar with the vertical face. If the angled face is moved outward a distance greater than .5″, it is altered so that it forms a single plane with the adjacent face. What has actually happened is that the angled face is moved beyond the adjacent face, while remaining parallel to its original position. Thus, in effect, it has disappeared because the adjacent, vertical face cannot be altered. See **Figure 12-4D.** In this example, the angled face was moved .75″. The new vertical face that is created can now be moved.

Exercise 12-2

Complete the exercise on the Student CD.

Offsetting Faces

SOLIDEDIT

Ribbon
Home
> Solid Editing
Offset Faces

Type
SOLIDEDIT

Menu
Modify
> Solid Editing
> Offset Faces

The **Offset** option may seem the same as the **Extrude** option because it moves faces by a specified distance or through a specified point. Unlike the **OFFSET** command in AutoCAD, this option moves all selected faces a specified distance. It is most useful when you wish to change the size of features such as slots, holes, grooves, and notches in solid parts. A positive offset distance increases the size or volume of the solid (adds material), a negative distance decreases the size or volume of the

Figure 12-5.
Offsetting faces. A—The original objects. The hole is selected to offset. The interior of the L is also selected to offset. B—A positive offset distance increases the size or volume of the solid. C—A negative offset distance decreases the size or volume of the solid.

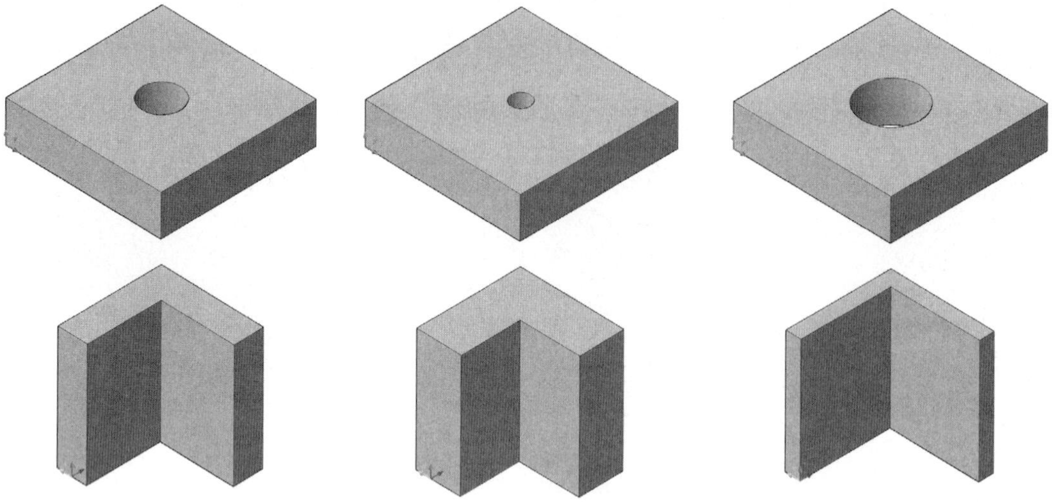

A B C

solid (removes material). Therefore, if you wish to make the width of a slot wider, provide a negative offset distance to decrease the size of the solid. Picking points to set the offset distance and direct distance entry are always taken as a positive value, so negative values must be entered using the keyboard.

To offset a face, select the command and pick the **Face**>**Offset** option. You are then prompted to select the face(s) to offset. When done selecting faces, press [Enter] to continue. Next, enter the offset distance and press [Enter] and then exit the command. See Figure 12-5 for examples of features edited with the **Offset** option.

PROFESSIONAL TIP

Nonplanar (curved) faces cannot be extruded, but can be offset. Using the **Offset** option, you can, in effect, "extrude" a nonplanar face.

Exercise 12-3

Complete the exercise on the Student CD.

Deleting Faces

SOLIDEDIT

Ribbon
Home
> Solid Editing
Delete Faces
Type
SOLIDEDIT
Menu
Modify
> Solid Editing
> Delete Faces

The **Delete** option deletes selected faces. This is a quick way to remove features such as chamfers, fillets, holes, and slots. To delete a solid face, select the command and pick the **Face**>**Delete** option. You are then prompted to select the face(s) to delete. When done selecting faces, press [Enter] to continue and then exit the command. When a face is deleted, existing faces extend to fill the gap. No additional faces are created. For instance, the inclined surface of a wedge cannot be deleted as there are no existing faces that can be extended to fill the gap. When deleting the face that is a chamfered or filleted edge, the adjacent edges are extended to fill the gap. See Figure 12-6.

Figure 12-6.
Deleting faces. A—The original objects with three rounds. B—The faces of two rounds have been deleted.

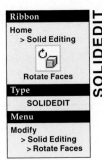

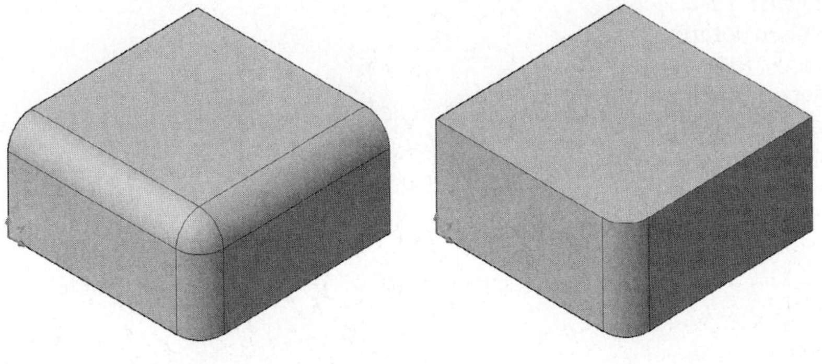

A B

Rotating Faces

The **Rotate** option rotates a face about a selected axis. To rotate a solid face, select the command and pick the **Face>Rotate** option. You are then prompted to select the face(s) to rotate. When done selecting faces, press [Enter] to continue. There are several methods by which a face can be rotated.

SOLIDEDIT
Ribbon
Home > Solid Editing
Rotate Faces
Type
SOLIDEDIT
Menu
Modify > Solid Editing > Rotate Faces

The **2points** option is the default. Pick two points to define the "hinge" about which the face will rotate. Then, provide the rotation angle and exit the command.

The **Axis by object** option allows you to use an existing object to define the axis of rotation. You can select the following objects. After selecting an object, enter the angle of rotation and exit the command.

- **Line.** The selected line becomes the axis of rotation.
- **Circle, arc, or ellipse.** The Z axis of the object becomes the axis of rotation. This Z axis is a line that passes through the center of the circle, arc, or ellipse and is perpendicular to the plane on which the 2D object lies.
- **Polyline or spline.** A line connecting the polyline or spline's start point and endpoint becomes the axis of rotation.

When you select the **View** option, the axis of rotation is perpendicular to the current view, with the positive direction coming out of the screen. This axis is identical to the Z axis when the **UCS** command **View** option is used. Next, enter the angle of rotation and exit the command.

The **Xaxis**, **Yaxis**, and **Zaxis** options prompt you to select a point. Either the X, Y, or Z axis that passes through that point is used as the axis of rotation. Then, enter the angle of rotation and exit the command.

Figure 12-7 provides several examples of rotated faces. Notice how the first and second pick points determine the direction of positive and negative rotation angles.

NOTE

A positive rotation angle moves the face in a clockwise direction looking from the first pick point to the second. Conversely, a negative angle rotates the face counterclockwise. If the rotated face will intersect or otherwise interfere with other faces, an error message indicates that the operation failed or that no solution was calculated. In this case, you may wish to try a negative angle if you previously entered a positive one. In addition, you can try selecting the opposite edge of the face as the axis of rotation.

Figure 12-7.
When rotating faces, the first and second pick points determine the direction of positive and negative rotation angles.

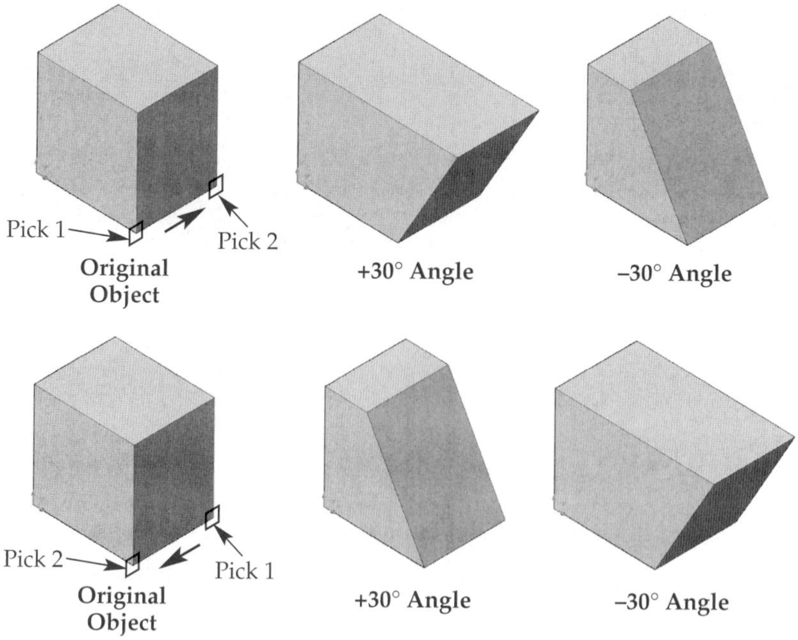

Exercise 12-4

Complete the exercise on the Student CD.

Tapering Faces

SOLIDEDIT

Ribbon
Home
> Solid Editing
Taper Faces
Type
SOLIDEDIT
Menu
Modify
> Solid Editing
> Taper Faces

The **Taper** option tapers a face at the specified angle, from the first pick point to the second. To taper a solid face, select the command and pick the **Face**>**Taper** option. You are then prompted to select the face(s) to taper. When done selecting faces, press [Enter] to continue:

Specify the base point: *(pick the base point)*
Specify another point along the axis of tapering: *(pick a point along the taper axis)*
Specify the taper angle: *(enter a taper value)*

Tapers work differently depending on whether the faces being tapered describe the outer boundaries of the solid, a cavity, or a removed portion of the solid. A positive taper angle always removes material. A negative taper angle always adds material. For example, if a positive taper angle is entered for a solid cylinder, the selected object is tapered in on itself from the base point along the axis of tapering, thus removing material. A negative angle tapers the object out away from itself to increase its size along the axis of tapering, thus adding material. See **Figure 12-8.**

On the other hand, if the faces of a feature such as a slot or hole are tapered, a positive taper angle increases the size of the feature along the axis of tapering. For example, if a round hole is tapered using a positive taper angle, its diameter increases from the base point along the axis of tapering, thus removing material from the solid. Conversely, if the same round hole is tapered using a negative taper angle, its diameter decreases from the base point along the axis of tapering, thus adding material to the solid. **Figure 12-9** shows some examples of this operation.

Figure 12-8. Tapering faces. A—The original objects. The dark face of the box and the circumference of the cylinder are selected. B—Positive taper angle. C—Negative taper angle.

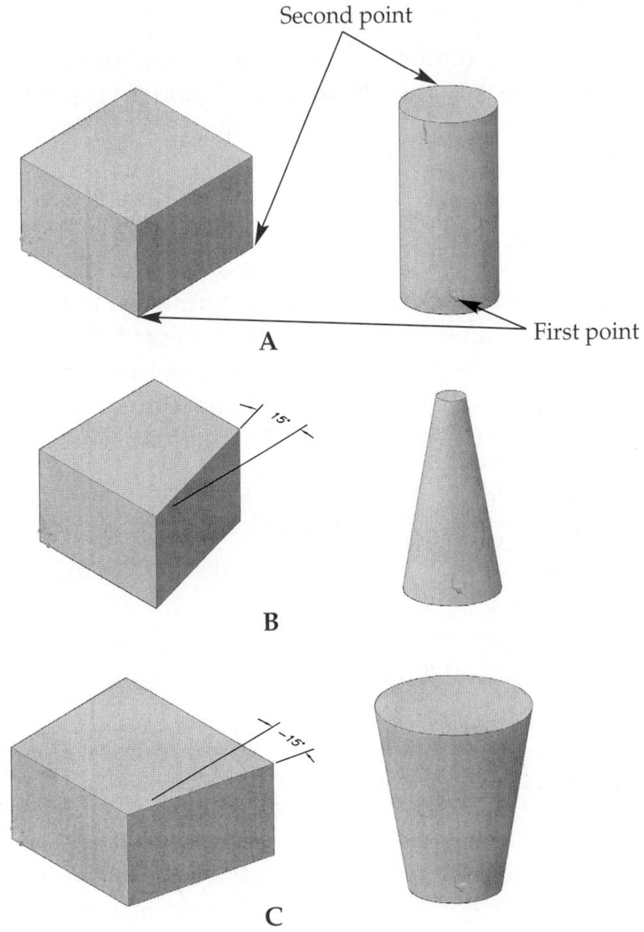

Figure 12-9. If a hole or slot is tapered using a positive taper angle, its diameter or width increases from the base point along the axis of tapering, thus removing material from the solid. A negative taper angle increases the volume of the solid.

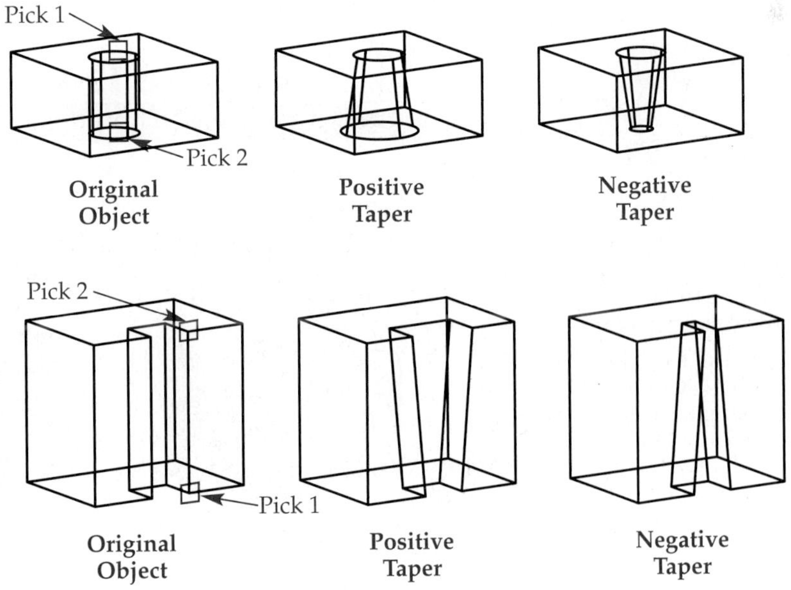

Exercise 12-5

Complete the exercise on the Student CD.

Copying Faces

SOLIDEDIT
Ribbon: Home > Solid Editing > Copy Faces
Type: SOLIDEDIT
Menu: Modify > Solid Editing > Copy Faces

The **Copy** option copies a face to the location or coordinates given. The copied face is *not* part of the original solid model. It is actually a region, which can later be extruded, revolved, swept, etc., into a solid. This may be useful when you wish to construct a mating part in an assembly that has the same features on the mating faces or the same outline. This option is quick to use because you can pick a base point on the face, then enter a single direct distance value for the displacement. Be sure an appropriate UCS is set if you wish to use direct distance entry.

To copy a solid face, select the command and pick the **Face**>**Copy** option. You are then prompted to select the face(s) to copy. When done selecting faces, press [Enter] to continue. You are prompted for a base point for the copy. Pick this point and then pick a second point of displacement or press [Enter] to use the first point as a displacement. See Figure 12-10 for examples of copied faces.

PROFESSIONAL TIP

Copied faces can also be useful for creating additional views. For example, you can copy a face to create a separate plan view with dimensions and notes. A copied face can also be enlarged to show details and to provide additional notation for design or assembly.

Coloring Faces

SOLIDEDIT
Ribbon: Home > Solid Editing > Color Faces
Type: SOLIDEDIT
Menu: Modify > Solid Editing > Color Faces

You can quickly change a selected face to a different color using the **Color** option. Select the command and pick the **Face**>**Color** option. You are then prompted to select the face(s) to color. When done selecting faces, press [Enter] to continue. Next, choose the desired color from the **Select Color** dialog box that is displayed. Remember, the color of the object (or face) determines the shaded color.

Exercise 12-6
Complete the exercise on the Student CD.

Figure 12-10.
A face can be quickly copied by picking a base point on the face and then entering a direct distance value for the displacement.

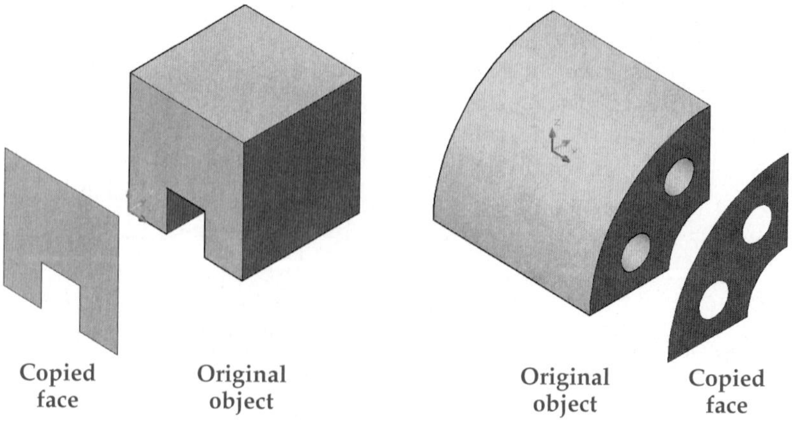

Edge Editing

Ribbon
Home
> Solid Editing
Copy Edges
Type
SOLIDEDIT
Menu
Modify
> Solid Editing
> Copy Edges

SOLIDEDIT

Edges can be edited in only two ways. They can be copied from the solid. Also, the color of an edge can be changed.

Copying an edge is similar to copying a face. To copy a solid edge, select the command and pick the **Edge>Copy** option. You are then prompted to select the edge(s) to copy. When done selecting edges, press [Enter] to continue. You are prompted for a base point for the copy. Pick this point and then pick a second point of displacement or press [Enter] to use the first point as a displacement. The edge is copied as a line, arc, circle, ellipse, or spline.

Ribbon
Home
> Solid Editing
Color Edges
Type
SOLIDEDIT
Menu
Modify
> Solid Editing
> Color Edges

SOLIDEDIT

To color a solid edge, select the command and pick the **Edge>Color** option. You are then prompted to select the edge(s) to color. When done selecting edges, press [Enter] to continue. Next, choose the desired color from the **Select Color** dialog box that is displayed and pick the **OK** button. The edges are now displayed with the new color. You may need to set a wireframe or hidden visual style current to see the change.

Body Editing

The body editing options of the **SOLIDEDIT** command perform editing operations on the entire body of the solid model. The body options are **Imprint**, **Separate**, **Shell**, **Clean**, and **Check**. The next sections cover these body editing options.

Imprint

Ribbon
Home
> Solid Editing
Imprint
Type
IMPRINT
SOLIDEDIT
Menu
Modify
> Solid Editing
> Imprint Edges

IMPRINT

Arcs, circles, lines, 2D and 3D polylines, ellipses, splines, regions, bodies, and 3D solids can be imprinted onto a solid, if the object intersects the solid. The imprint becomes a face on the surface based on the overlap between the two intersecting objects. Once the imprint has been made, the new face can be modified.

To imprint an object on a solid, select the command and pick the **Body>Imprint** option. If **IMPRINT** is typed, the option is directly entered. Also, in the menu and on the ribbon the **Imprint** option is grouped with the edge editing functions, not the body editing functions.

Once the option is activated, you are prompted to select the solid. This is the object on which the other objects will be imprinted. Then, select the objects to be imprinted. You have the option of deleting the source objects. The imprinted face can then be modified using face editing options. Figure 12-11 illustrates objects imprinted onto a solid model. Two of these are then extruded into the solid to create holes. The **PRESSPULL** command is used on the third object to create a cylindrical feature.

NOTE

Remember that objects are drawn on the XY plane of the current UCS unless you enter a specific Z value. Therefore, before you draw an object to be imprinted onto a solid model, be sure you have set an appropriate UCS for proper placement of the object by using a dynamic UCS or the **UCS** command. Alternately, you can draw the object on the XY plane and then move the object onto the solid object.

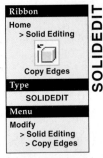

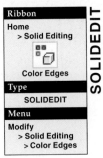

Figure 12-11.
Imprinted objects form new faces that can be extruded into the solid. A—A solid box with three objects on the plane of the top face. B—The objects are imprinted, then two of the new faces are extruded through the solid. The **PRESSPULL** command is used on the third new face to create the cylindrical feature.

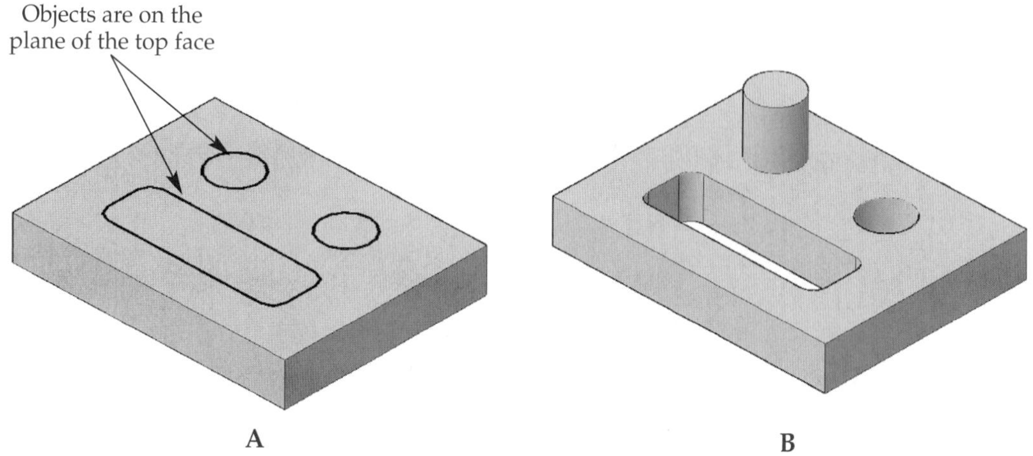

Separate

SOLIDEDIT

Ribbon
Home > Solid Editing
Separate
Type
SOLIDEDIT
Menu
Modify > Solid Editing > Separate

The **Separate** option separates two objects that are both a part of a single solid composite, but appear as separate physical entities. This can happen when modifying solids using the Boolean commands. The **Separate** option may be seldom used, but it has a specific purpose. If you select a solid model and an object physically separate from the model is highlighted, the two objects are parts of the same composite solid. If you wish to work with them as individual solids, they must first be separated.

To separate a solid body, select the command and pick the **Body**>**Separate** option. You are then prompted to select a 3D solid. After you pick the solid, it is automatically separated. No other actions are required and you can exit the command. However, if you select a solid in which the parts are physically joined, AutoCAD indicates this by prompting The selected solid does not have multiple lumps. A "lump" is a physically separate solid entity. In order to separate a solid, it must be composed of multiple lumps. See **Figure 12-12.**

Figure 12-12.
A—After the cylinder is subtracted from the box, the remaining solid is considered one solid. B—Use the **Separate** option to turn this single solid into two solids.

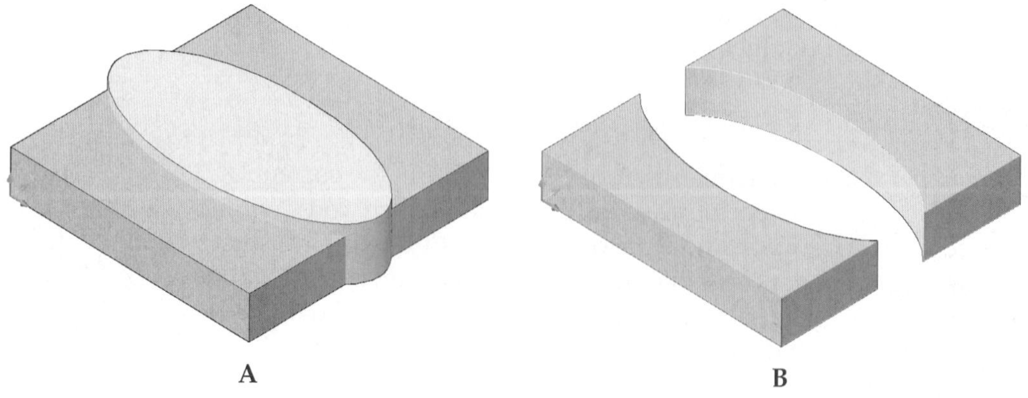

Shell

Ribbon
Home
> Solid Editing
Shell
Type
SOLIDEDIT
Menu
Modify
> Solid Editing
> Shell
SOLIDEDIT

A ***shell*** is a solid that has been "hollowed out." The **Shell** option creates a shell of the selected object using a specified offset distance, or thickness. To create a shell of a solid body, select the command and pick the **Body**>**Shell** option. You are prompted to select the solid. Only one solid can be selected.

After selecting the solid, you have the opportunity to remove faces. If you do not remove any faces, the new solid object will appear identical to the old solid object when shaded or rendered. The thickness of the shell will not be visible. If you wish to create a hollow object with an opening, select the face to be removed (the opening).

After selecting the object and specifying any faces to be removed, you are prompted to enter the shell offset distance. This is the thickness of the shell. A positive shell offset distance creates a shell on the inside of the solid body. A negative shell offset distance creates a shell on the outside of the solid body. See Figure 12-13. If you shell a solid that contains internal features, such as holes, grooves, and slots, a shell of the specified thickness is placed around those features. This is shown in Figure 12-14.

If the shell operation is not readily visible in the current view, you can rotate the view by using the [Shift] + the mouse wheel button to enter the transparent **3DORBIT** command or by using the view cube. You can also see the results by picking the **X-Ray** button in the **Visual Styles** panel on the **Visualize** tab of the ribbon.

PROFESSIONAL TIP

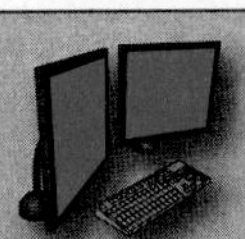

The **Shell** option of the **SOLIDEDIT** command is very useful in applications such as solid modeling of metal castings or injection-molded plastic parts.

Exercise 12-7

Complete the exercise on the Student CD.

Clean

Ribbon
Home
> Solid Editing
Clean
Type
SOLIDEDIT
Menu
Modify
> Solid Editing
> Clean
SOLIDEDIT

The **Clean** option removes all unused objects and shared surfaces. Imprinted objects are not removed. Select the command and pick the **Body**>**Clean** option. Then, pick the solid to be cleaned. No further input is required. You can exit the command.

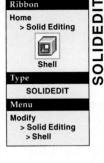

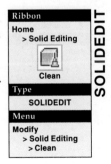

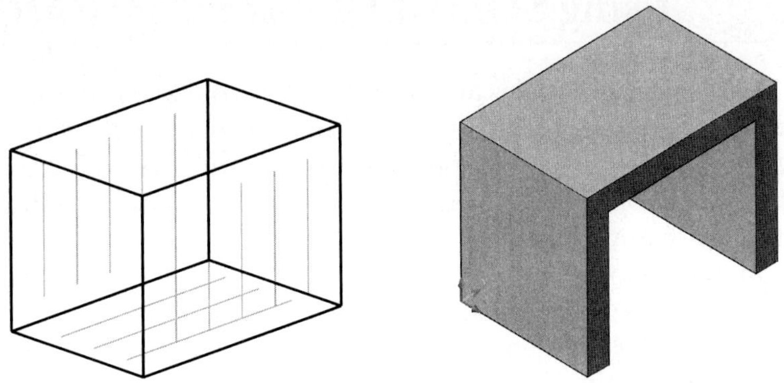

A B

Figure 12-13.
A—The right-front, bottom, and left-back faces (marked here by gray lines) are removed from the shell operation.
B—The resulting object after the shell operation.

Figure 12-14.
If you shell a solid that contains internal features, such as holes, grooves, and slots, a shell of the specified thickness is also placed around those features. A—Solid object with holes subtracted. B—Wireframe display after shelling with a negative offset. C—The Conceptual visual style is set current.

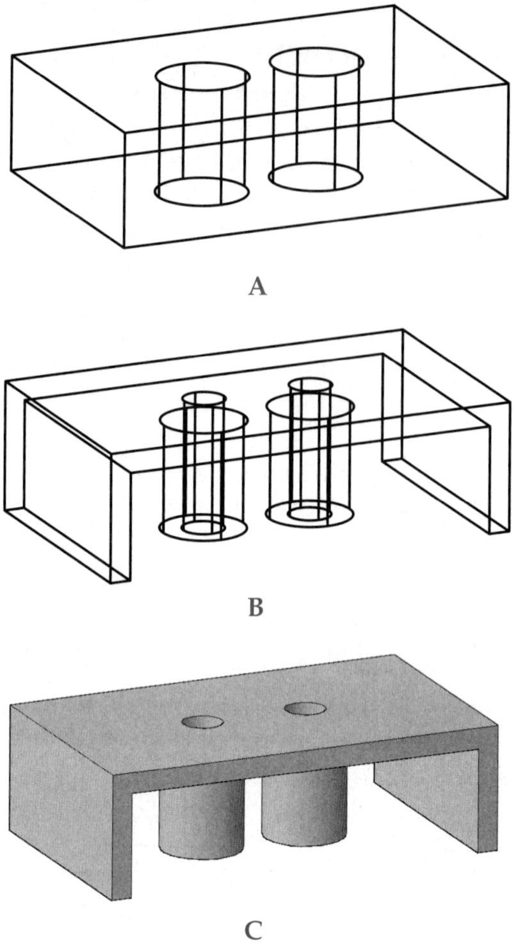

Check

SOLIDEDIT

Ribbon
Home
> Solid Editing
Check
Type
SOLIDEDIT
Menu
Modify
> Solid Editing
> Check

The **Check** option simply determines if the selected object is a valid 3D solid. If a true 3D solid is selected, AutoCAD displays the prompt This object is a valid ShapeManager solid. and you can exit the command. If the object selected is not a 3D solid, the prompt reads A 3D solid must be selected. and you are prompted to select a 3D solid. To access the **Check** option, select the command and pick the **Body**>**Check** option. Then, select the object to check.

Using SOLIDEDIT as a Construction Tool

This section provides an example of how the **SOLIDEDIT** command options can be used not only to edit, but also to construct a solid model. This makes it easy to design and construct a model without selecting a variety of commands. It also gives you the option of undoing a single editing operation or an entire editing session without ever exiting the command.

In the following example, **SOLIDEDIT** command options are used to imprint shapes onto the model body and then extrude those shapes into the body to create countersunk holes. Then, the model size is adjusted and an angle and taper are applied to one end. Finally, one end of the model is copied to construct a mating part.

Creating Shape Imprints on a Model

The basic shape of the solid model in this tutorial is drawn as a solid box, then shape imprints are added to it. Throughout this exercise, you may wish to change the UCS to assist in the construction of the part.

1. Draw a solid box using the dimensions shown in Figure 12-15.
2. Set the 3D Wireframe visual style current.
3. On the top surface of the box, locate a single ∅.4 circle using the dimensions given. Then, copy or array the circle to the other three corners as shown in the figure.
4. Use the **Imprint** option to imprint the circles onto the solid box. Delete the source objects.

Extruding Imprints to Create Features

The imprinted 2D shapes can now be extruded to create new 3D solid features on the model. Use the **Extrude Faces** option to extrude all four imprinted circles.

1. When you select the edge of the first circle, all features on that face are highlighted, but only the circle you picked and the top face have actually been selected. If you pick inside the circle, only the circle is selected and highlighted. In either case, be sure to also pick the remaining three circles.
2. Remove the top face of the box from the selection set, if needed.
3. The depth of the extrusion is .16 units. Remember to enter –.16 for the extrusion height since the holes remove material. The angle of taper for extrusion should be 35°. Your model should look like Figure 12-16A.
4. Extrude the small diameter of the four tapered holes so they intersect the bottom of the solid body. Select the holes by picking the small diameter circles. Instead of calculating the distance from the bottom of the chamfer to the bottom surface, you can simply enter a value that is greater than this distance, such as the original thickness of the object. Again, since the goal is to remove material, use a negative value for the height of the extrusion. There is no taper angle. Your model should now look like Figure 12-16B.

Figure 12-15.
The initial setup for the tutorial model.

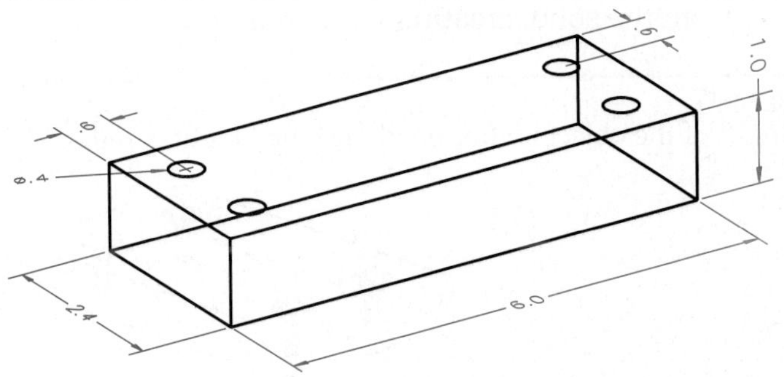

Figure 12-16.
A—The imprinted circles are extruded with a taper angle of 35°. B—Holes are created by further extrusion with a taper angle of 0°.

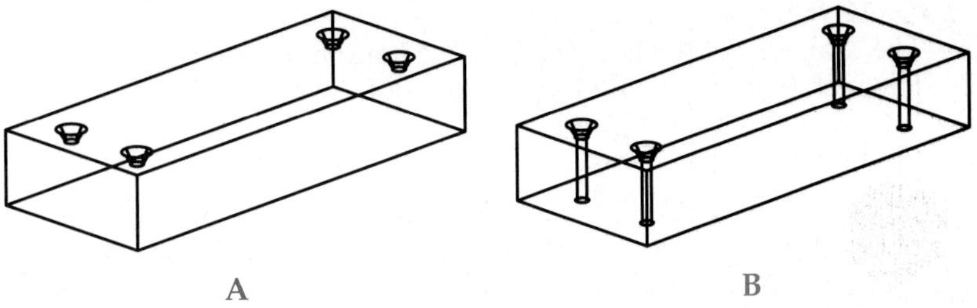

Moving Faces to Change Model Size

The next step is to use the **Move Faces** option to decrease the length and thickness of the solid body.

1. Select either end face and the two holes nearest to it. Be sure to select the holes *and* the countersinks. Move the two holes and end face two units toward the other end, thus changing the object length to four units.
2. Select the bottom face and move it .5 units up toward the top face, thus changing the thickness to .5 units. See Figure 12-17.

Offsetting a Feature to Change Its Size

Now, the **Offset Faces** option is used to increase the diameter of the four holes and to adjust a rectangular slot that will be added to the solid.

1. Using **Offset Faces**, select the four small hole diameters. Be sure to remove from the selection set any other faces that may be selected.
2. Enter an offset distance of –.05. This increases the hole diameter and decreases the solid volume. Exit the **SOLIDEDIT** command.
3. Select the **RECTANG** command. Set the fillet radius to .4 and draw a 2 × 1.6 rectangle centered on the top face of the solid. See Figure 12-18A.
4. Imprint the rectangle on the solid. Delete the source object.
5. Extrude the rectangle completely through the solid (.5 units). Remember to remove from the selection set any other faces that may be selected.
6. Offset the rectangular feature using an offset distance of .2 units. You will need to select all faces of the feature. This decreases the size of the rectangular opening and increases the solid volume. Your drawing should appear as shown in Figure 12-18B.

Tapering Faces

One side of the part is to be angled. The **Taper Faces** option is used to taper the left end of the solid.

1. Using **Taper Faces**, pick the face at the left end of the solid.
2. Pick point 1 in Figure 12-19 as the base point and point 2 as the second point along the axis of tapering.
3. Enter a value of –10 for the taper angle. This moves the upper-left end away from the solid, creating a tapered end.

Figure 12-17.
The length of the object is shortened and the height is reduced.

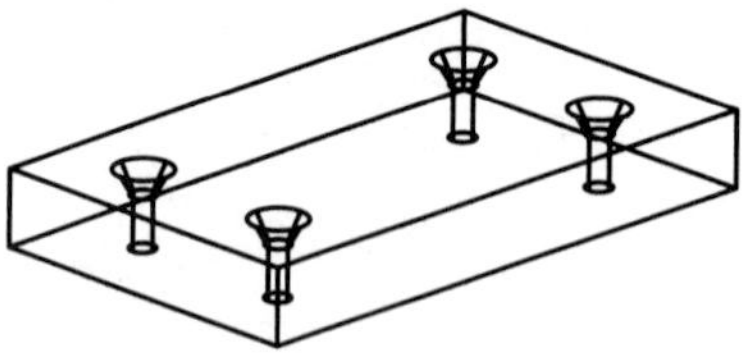

Figure 12-18.
A—The diameter of the holes is increased and a rectangle is imprinted on the top surface.
B—The rectangle is extruded to create a slot.

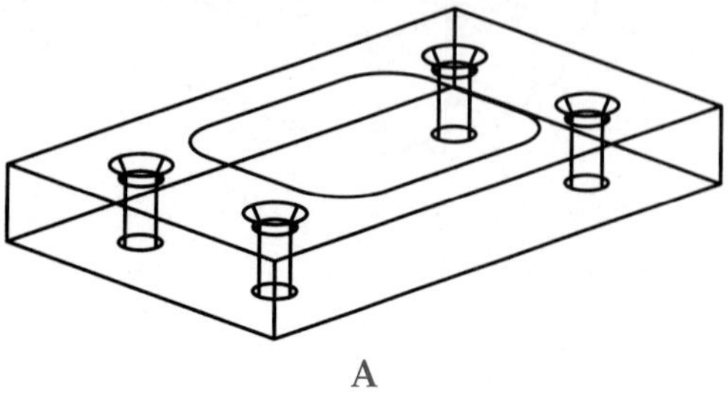

A

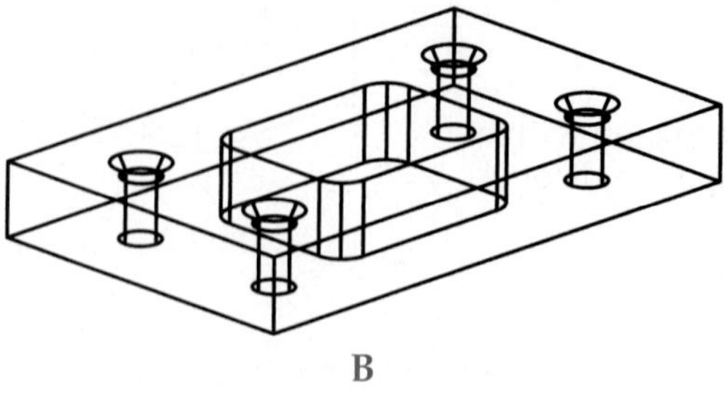

B

Rotating Faces

Next, use the **Rotate Faces** option to rotate the tapered end of the object. The top edge of the face will be rotated away from the holes, adding volume to the solid.

1. Using **Rotate Faces**, pick the face at the left end of the solid.
2. Pick point 1 in **Figure 12-19** as the first axis point and point 2 as the second point.
3. Enter a value of –30 for the rotation angle. This rotates the top edge of the tapered end away from the solid. See **Figure 12-20.**

Copying Faces

A mating part will now be created. This is done by first copying the face on the tapered end of the part.

1. Using the **Copy Faces** option, pick the angled face on the left end of the solid.
2. Pick one of the corners as a base point and copy the face one unit to the left. This face can now be used to create a new solid. See **Figure 12-21A.**
3. Draw a line four units in length on the negative X axis from the lower-right corner of the copied face. Use the **EXTRUDE** command on the copied face to create a new solid. Select the **Path** option and use the line as the extrusion path. See **Figure 12-21B.** If you do not use the **Path** option, the extrusion is projected perpendicular to the face.

NOTE

The **Extrude Faces** option of the **SOLIDEDIT** command cannot be used to turn a copied face into a solid body.

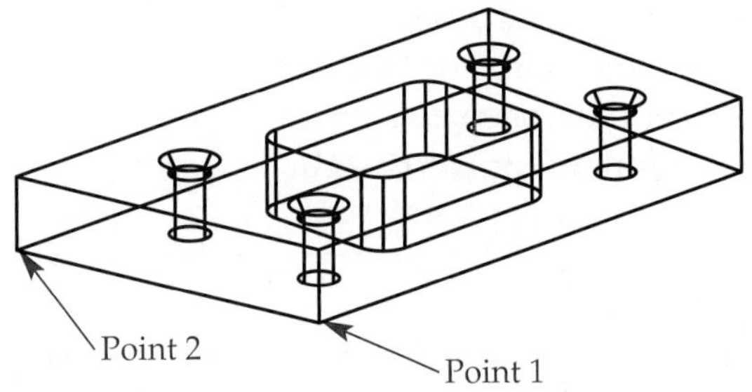

Figure 12-19.
The left end of the object is tapered. Notice the pick points. These points are also used when selecting an axis of rotation.

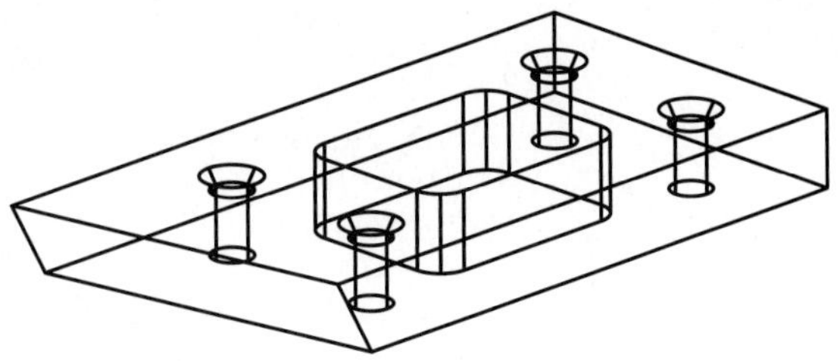

Figure 12-20.
The tapered end of the object is modified by rotating the face.

Figure 12-21.
Creating a mating part. A—The angled face is copied. B—The copied face is extruded into a solid.

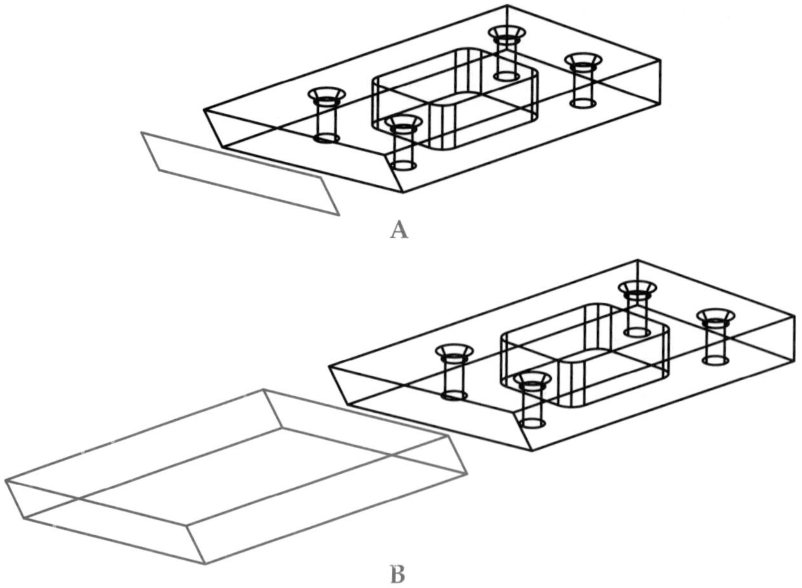

Creating a Shell

The bottom surface of the original solid will now be shelled out. Keep in mind that features such as the four holes and the rectangular slot will not be cut off by the shell. Instead, a shell will be placed around these features. This becomes clear when the operation is performed.

1. Select the **Shell** option and pick the original solid.
2. Remove the lower-left and lower-right edges of the solid. See Figure 12-22A. This removes the two side faces and the bottom face.
3. Enter a shell offset distance of .15 units. The shell is created and should appear similar to Figure 12-22A.
4. Use the view cube or **3DORBIT** command to view the solid from the bottom. Also, set the Conceptual visual style current. Your model should look like the one shown in Figure 12-22B.

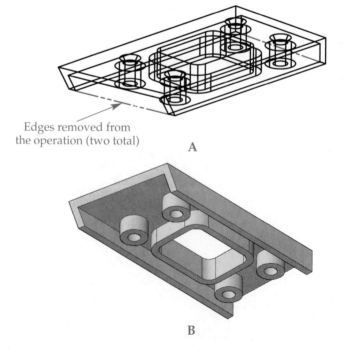

Figure 12-22.
A—The shelled object. B—The viewpoint is changed and the Conceptual visual style is set current.

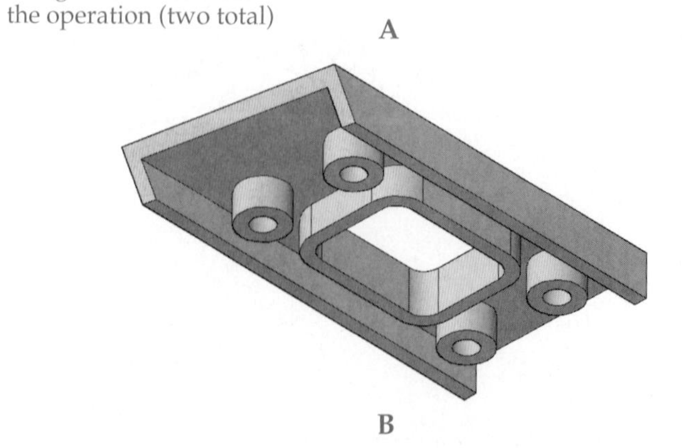

Chapter Test

Answer the following questions. Write your answers on a separate sheet of paper or complete the electronic chapter test on the Student CD.

1. What are the three components of a solid model?
2. When using the **SOLIDEDIT** command, how many faces are highlighted if you pick an edge?
3. How do you deselect a face that is part of the selection set?
4. How can you select a single face?
5. Which two operations can the **Extrude Faces** option perform?
6. How does the shape and length of an object selected as the path of an extrusion affect the final extrusion?
7. What is one of the most useful aspects of the **Offset Faces** option?
8. How do positive and negative offset distance values affect the volume of the solid?
9. How is a single object, such as a cylinder, affected by entering a positive taper angle when using the **Taper Faces** option?
10. When a shape is imprinted onto a solid body, which component of the solid does the imprinted object become and how can it be used?
11. In which situation would you use the **Separate** option?
12. How does the **Shell** option affect a solid that contains internal features such as holes, grooves, and slots?
13. How can you determine if an object is a valid 3D solid?
14. Describe two ways to change the view of your model while you are inside of a command.
15. How can you extrude a face in a straight line, but not perpendicular to the face?

Drawing Problems

1. Complete the tutorial presented in this chapter. Then, perform the following additional edits to the original solid.
   A. Lengthen the right end of the solid by .5 units.
   B. Taper the right end of the solid with the same taper angle used on the left end, but taper it in the opposite direction.
   C. Fillet the two long, top edges of the solid using a fillet radius of .2 units.
   D. Rotate the face at the right end of the solid with the same rotation angle used on the left end, but rotate it in the opposite direction.
   E. Save the drawing as P12_01.

2. Construct the solid part shown below using as many **SOLIDEDIT** options as possible. After completing the object, make the following modifications.
   A. Lengthen the 1.250″ diameter feature by .250″.
   B. Change the .750″ diameter hole to .625″ diameter.
   C. Change the thickness of the .250″ thick flange to .375″ (toward the bottom).
   D. Extrude the end of the 1.250″ diameter feature .250″ with a 15° taper inward.
   E. Save the drawing as P12_02.

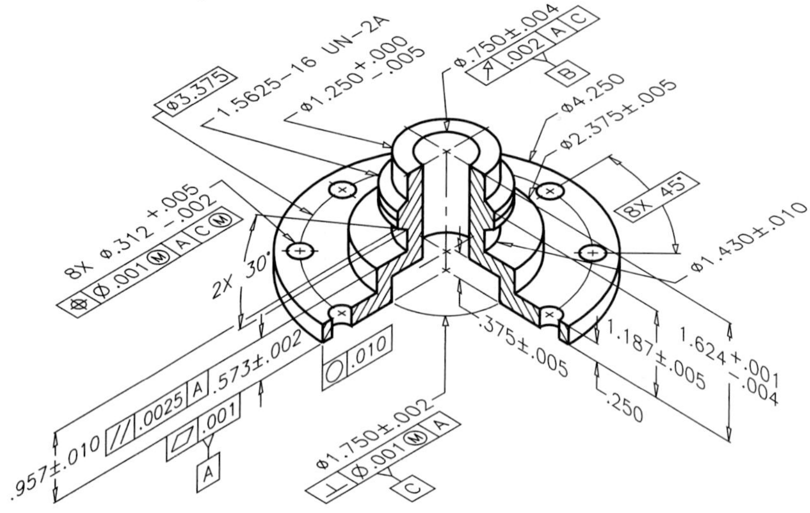

Hub

3. Construct the solid part shown below. Then, perform the following edits on the solid using the **SOLIDEDIT** command.
   A. Change the diameter of the hole to 35.6/35.4.
   B. Add a 5° taper to each inner side of each tooth (the bottom of each tooth should be wider while the top remains the same).
   C. Change the width of the 4.8/4.0 key to 5.8/5.0.
   D. Save the drawing as P12_03.

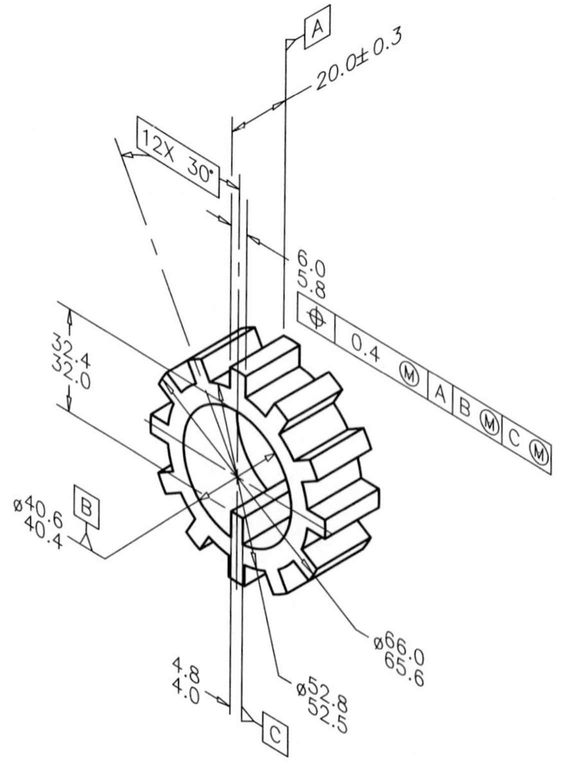

Spline

4. Construct the solid part shown below using as many **SOLIDEDIT** options as possible. Then, perform the following edits on the solid.
   A. Change the depth of the counterbore to 10 mm.
   B. Change the color of all internal surfaces to red.
   C. Save the drawing as P12_04.

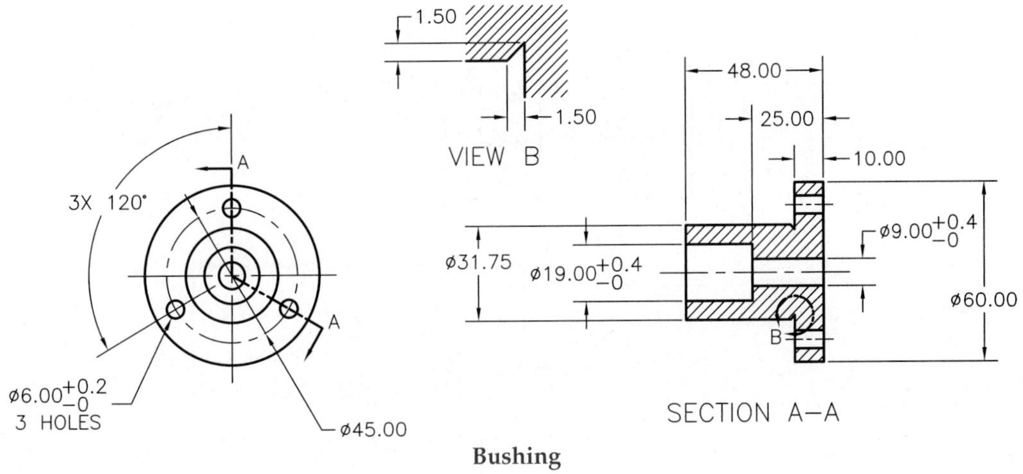

Bushing

5. Construct the solid part shown below using as many **SOLIDEDIT** options as possible. Then, perform the following edits on the solid.
   A. Change the 2.625″ height to 2.325″.
   B. Change the 1.625″ internal diameter to 1.425″.
   C. Taper the outside faces of the .875″ high base at a 5° angle away from the part. Hint: The base cannot be directly tapered.
   D. Save the drawing as P12_05.

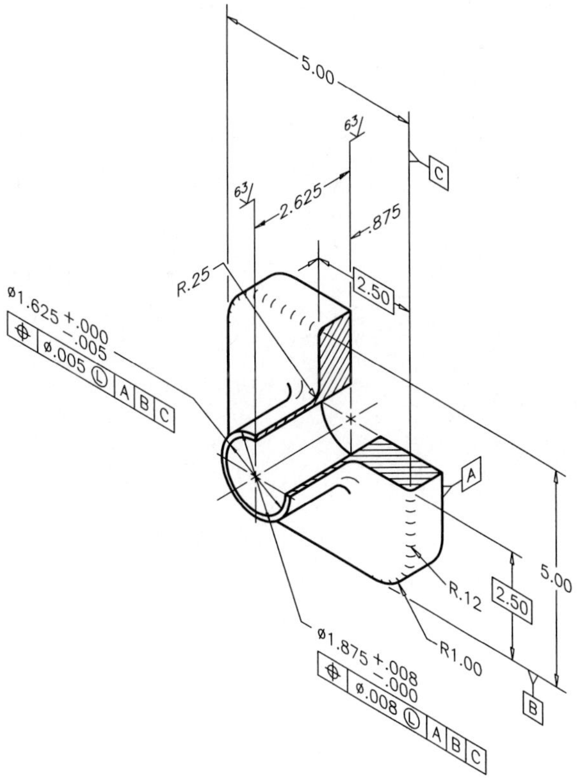

Thrust Washer

6. Construct the solid part shown below using as many **SOLIDEDIT** options as possible. Then, change the dimensions on the model as follows. Save the drawing as P12_06.

Existing	New
100	106
80	82
Ø60	Ø94
Ø40	Ø42
30°	35°

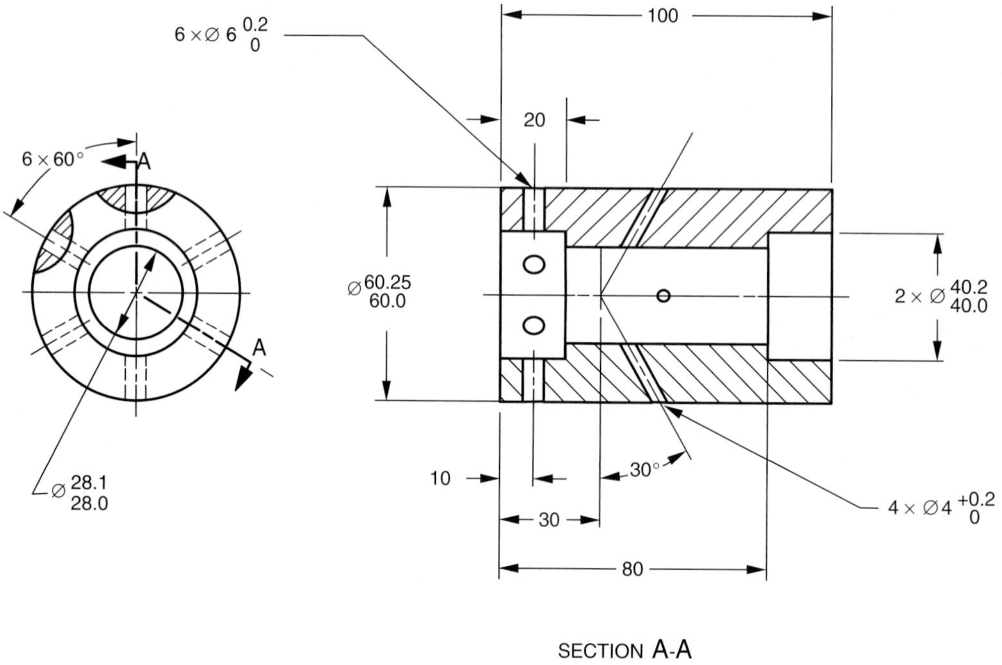

Nozzle

CHAPTER 13
Solid Model Display and Analysis

Learning Objectives

After completing this chapter, you will be able to:

✓ Construct a 3D section plane through a solid model.
✓ Adjust the size and location of section planes.
✓ Create a dynamic section of a 3D solid model.
✓ Construct 2D and 3D section blocks.
✓ Create a flat, 2D projection of a 3D solid model.
✓ Create a multiview layout of a solid model using **SOLVIEW** and **SOLDRAW**.
✓ Construct a profile of a solid using **SOLPROF**.
✓ Perform an analysis of a solid model.
✓ Export and import solid model data.

Certain aspects of a solid model's appearance are controlled by the **ISOLINES**, **DISPSILH**, and **FACETRES** system variables. The **ISOLINES** system variable, introduced in Chapter 3, controls the number of lines used to define solids in wireframe displays. The **FACETRES** system variable controls the number of lines used to define solids in hidden and shaded displays. The **DISPSILH** system variable is used to display a silhouette.

Internal features of the model can be shown using the **SECTIONPLANE** command. This command can create 2D and 3D section views on an object. The **FLATSHOT** command creates a 2D projection of the current view. This chapter also looks at how sections can be combined with 2D projections created with the **SOLVIEW** and **SOLDRAW** commands to create a drawing layout for plotting. This chapter also covers how a profile of a solid can be created using the **SOLPROF** command.

Controlling Solid Model Display

AutoCAD solid models can be displayed as wireframes, with hidden lines removed, shaded, or rendered. A wireframe is the default display when a drawing is started based on the acad.dwt template and is the quickest to display. The hidden, shaded, and rendered displays require a longer regeneration time. When a drawing is started based on the acad3D.dwt or acadiso3D.dwt template, the default display is the Realistic visual style, which is a shaded display.

Isolines

ISOLINES

Type
ISOLINES

The appearance of a solid model in a wireframe display is controlled by the **ISOLINES** system variable. *Isolines* represent the edges and curved surfaces of a solid model. This setting does *not* affect the final shaded or rendered object. However, if the Edge mode property for the visual style is set to Isolines, isolines are displayed when the visual style is set current. The default **ISOLINES** value is four. It can have a value from zero to 2047. All solid objects in the drawing are affected by changes to the **ISOLINES** value, as are all visual styles with their Edge mode property set to Isolines. **Figure 13-1** illustrates the difference between **ISOLINES** settings of four and 12.

The setting of the **ISOLINES** system variable can be changed in the **Visual Styles Manager** palette. For the 2D Wireframe visual style, change the Contour lines property in the **2D Wireframe Options** category. For all other visual styles, change the Number of lines property in the **Edge Settings** category. See **Figure 13-2A.** The Edge mode property must be set to Isolines to display the Number of lines property. The **ISOLINES** setting can also be changed in the **Contour lines per surface** text box found in the **Display resolution** area of the **Display** tab in the **Options** dialog box, or by typing ISOLINES and then entering a new value. See **Figure 13-2B.**

Creating a Display Silhouette

DISPSILH

Type
DISPSILH

When the Edge mode property of a 3D visual style is set to Facet Edges, objects are defined by ***tessellation lines.*** The **Facet Lighting** and **Smooth Lighting** buttons in the **Visual Styles** panel on the **Visualize** tab of the ribbon also control the Edge mode setting. When the **HIDE** command is used with the 2D Wireframe visual style current, tessellation lines are also displayed. The number of tessellation lines is controlled by the **FACETRES** system variable, which is discussed in the next section.

In the 2D Wireframe visual style, a model can also appear smooth with only a silhouette displayed, similar to the 3D Hidden visual style. This is controlled by the **DISPSILH** (display silhouette) system variable. The **DISPSILH** system variable has two values, 0 (off) and 1 (on). **Figure 13-3** shows solids with **DISPSILH** set to 0 and 1 after setting the 2D Wireframe visual style current and then using **HIDE**.

The setting can be changed by typing DISPSILH and entering a new value. You can also set the variable using the **Draw true silhouettes for solids and surfaces** check box in the **Display performance** area of the **Display** tab in the **Options** dialog box. Refer to **Figure 13-2B.** For the 2D Wireframe visual style, the **DISPSILH** variable can also be set in the **Visual Styles Manager** palette. The variable is controlled by the Draw true silhouettes property in the **2D Wireframe Options** category. Setting this property to Yes turns on silhouettes.

Figure 13-1.
Isolines define curved surfaces.
A—**ISOLINES** = 4.
B—**ISOLINES** = 12.

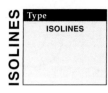

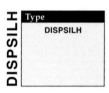

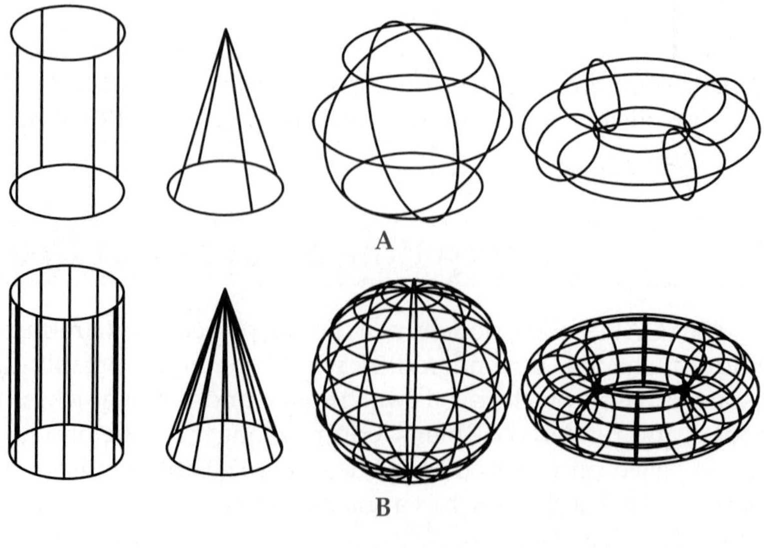

Figure 13-2.
A—The **ISOLINES** and **DISPSILH** values can be set in the **Visual Styles Manager**. B—The **ISOLINES**, **FACETRES**, and **DISPSILH** values can be set in the **Options** dialog box.

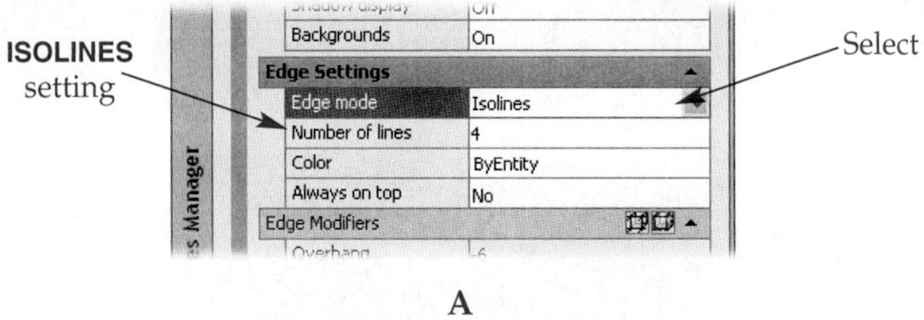

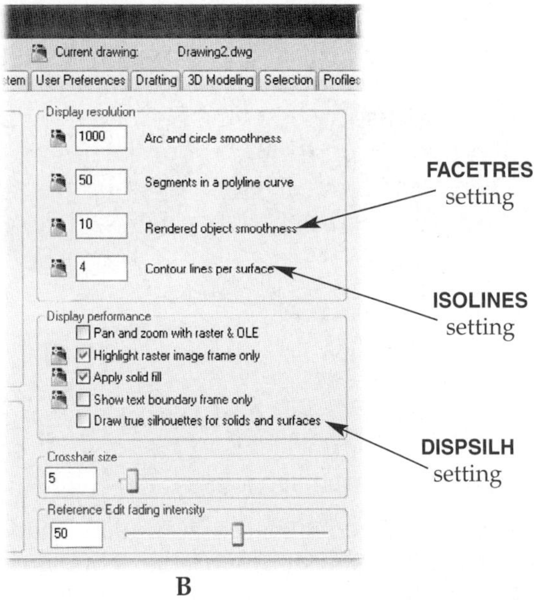

Figure 13-3.
A—The **HIDE** command used when **DISPSILH** is set to 0. Objects are displayed faceted. B—The **HIDE** command used when **DISPSILH** is set to 1. Facets are eliminated and only the silhouette is displayed.

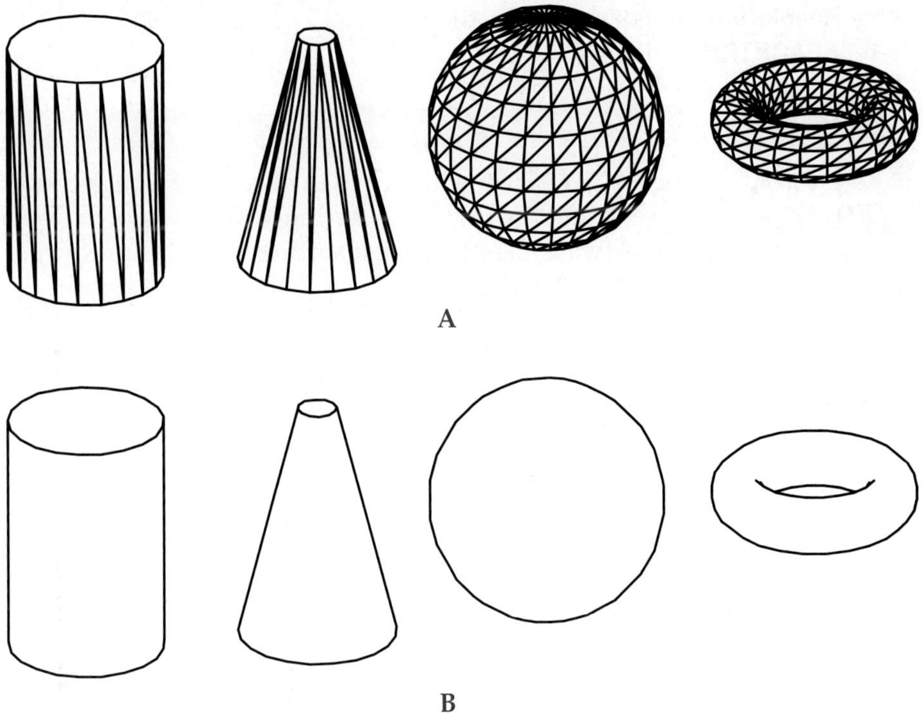

Figure 13-4.
A—The **FACETRES** setting is .5 and the Conceptual visual style set current.
B—The **FACETRES** setting is 5.0 and the Conceptual visual style is set current.

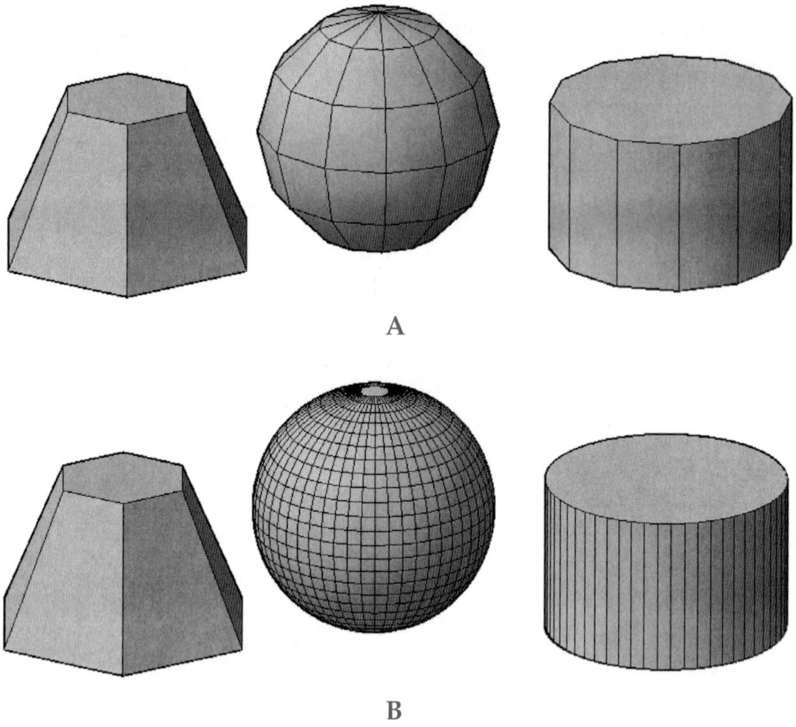

Controlling Surface Smoothness

FACETRES

Type
FACETRES

The smoothness of curved surfaces in hidden, shaded, and rendered displays is controlled by the **FACETRES** system variable. This variable determines the number of polygon faces applied to the solid model. The value can range from .01 to 10.0 and the default value is .5. This system variable can be changed by typing FACETRES or by changing the **Rendered object smoothness** setting in the **Display resolution** area in the **Options** dialog box. Refer to Figure 13-2B. For the 2D Wireframe visual style, the variable can be set in the **Visual Styles Manager** palette. The Solid Smoothness property in the **Display Resolution** category controls the variable. Figure 13-4 shows the effect of two different **FACETRES** settings.

CAUTION

Avoid setting **FACETRES** any higher than necessary. The additional edges and faces added by a higher setting will slow down system performance. Always use the lowest setting that will produce the results required by the project.

Exercise 13-1

Complete the exercise on the Student CD.

Creating Section Planes

The **SECTIONPLANE** command offers a powerful visualization and display tool. It enables you to construct a section plane, known as an AutoCAD ***section object,*** that can then be used as a plane to cut through a 3D model. Once the section object is drawn, it can be moved to any location, jogs can be added to it, and it can be rendered "live" so that internal features and sectioned material are dynamically visible as the cutting plane is moved. A variety of section settings allow you to customize the appearance of section features. Additionally, you can generate 2D sections/elevations or 3D sections that can be inserted into the drawing as a block. Once the command is initiated, you are prompted to select a face, the first point on the section object, or to enter an option.

Ribbon
Home > Solid Editing Section Plane
Type
SECTIONPLANE
Menu
Draw > Modeling > Section Plane

SECTIONPLANE

Pick a Face to Construct a Section Plane

The simplest way to create a section plane is to pick a flat face on the 3D object. Once the command is initiated, move the pointer until the face you wish to select is highlighted, then pick it. A transparent section object is placed on the face you selected and the model is cut at the plane. See Figure 13-5. The section plane can now be moved to create a section anywhere along the 3D model.

Pick Two Points to Construct a Section Plane

A second method for defining a section plane is to pick two points through which the section object passes. The section object is perpendicular to the XY plane of the current UCS. When the command is initiated, pick the first point, which cannot be on a face. See P1 in Figure 13-6. It may be best to turn off dynamic UCSs or you could end up picking a face as the first point instead of a point. After picking the first point, move the pointer and notice that the section plane rotates about the first point. Next, pick the second point (P2) to define a line that cuts through the model. After the second point is picked, the section object is created. The section plane extends just beyond the edges of the model.

Figure 13-5.
Creating a section object on a face. A—The object before the face is selected. B—The section object is created.

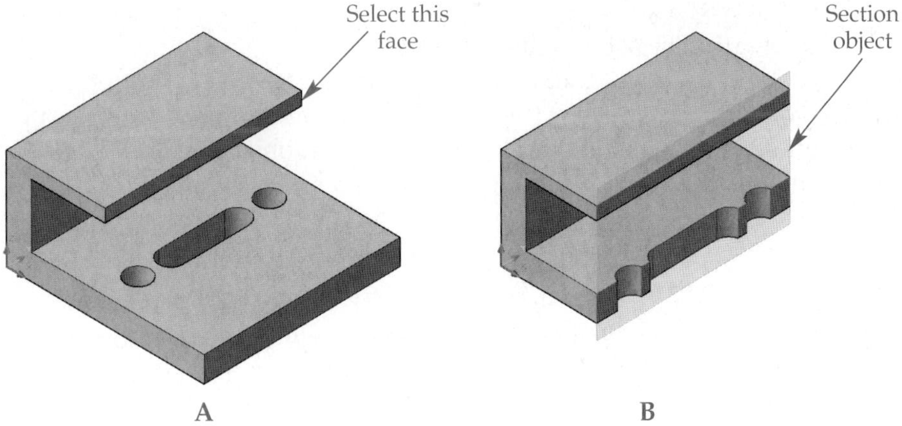

Figure 13-6.
Creating a section object by selecting two points.

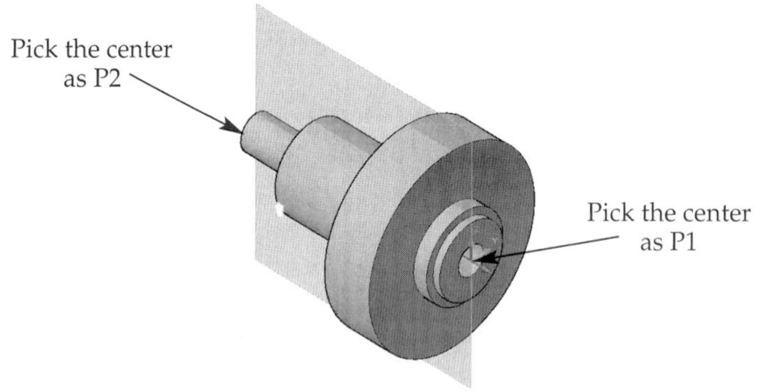

NOTE

When the section object is created by picking two points, notice that the model is not automatically cut as it is when a face is selected. This is because *live sectioning* is not turned on when picking two points, but is turned on when picking a face. To turn live sectioning on or off, select the section object, right-click, and select **Activate live sectioning** from the shortcut menu. Live sectioning is discussed later in this chapter.

Pick Multiple Points to Construct a Section Plane

The previous method accepts only two points to construct a single section plane. Using the **Draw section** option, you can specify multiple points in order to create section plane *jogs*. In engineering drawing terminology, a section object drawn in this manner can represent an ***offset*** or ***aligned*** section plane.

Once the command is initiated, select the **Draw section** option. Pick the start point, using object snaps if necessary. See **Figure 13-7.** Continue picking points as needed. After picking the last point to define the section plane, press [Enter]. You are then prompted to specify a point in the direction of the section view. This point is on the opposite side of the section object as the viewer. Pick a point on the model using object snaps if necessary. The section plane is created.

Notice in **Figure 13-7** that the pick points created a section object that does not extend beyond the boundary of the model. Also, the command "squares up" the section boundary to create a closed profile. Using section object grips, the section plane can be easily edited to include the entire solid. This is discussed in detail later in this chapter.

Create Orthographic Section Planes

The **Orthographic** option enables you to quickly place a section plane through the front, back, top, bottom, left, or right side of the object. See **Figure 13-8.** The origin is the center point of all objects in the model. Once the command is initiated, select the **Orthographic** option. Then, specify which orthographic plane you want to use as the section plane. The section object is created and all objects in the drawing are affected by it.

Figure 13-7.
Using the **Draw** option of the **SECTIONPLANE** command to create a section object with multiple segments.

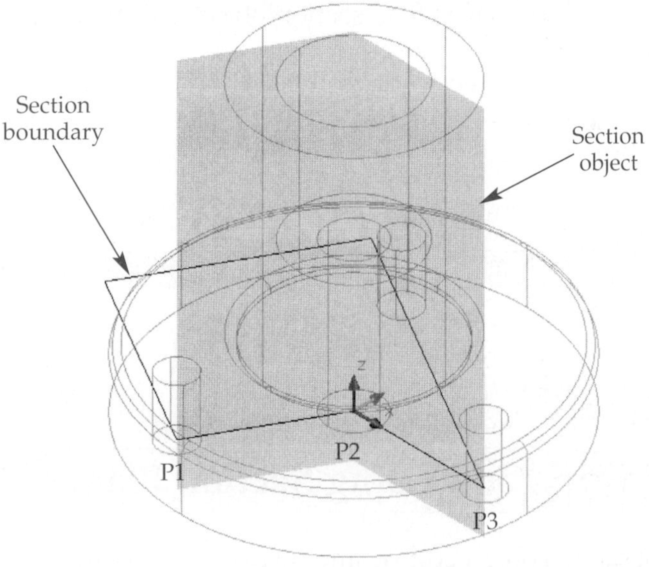

Figure 13-8.
Examples of orthographic **SECTIONPLANE** options. A—Top. B—Bottom. C—Left. D—Right.

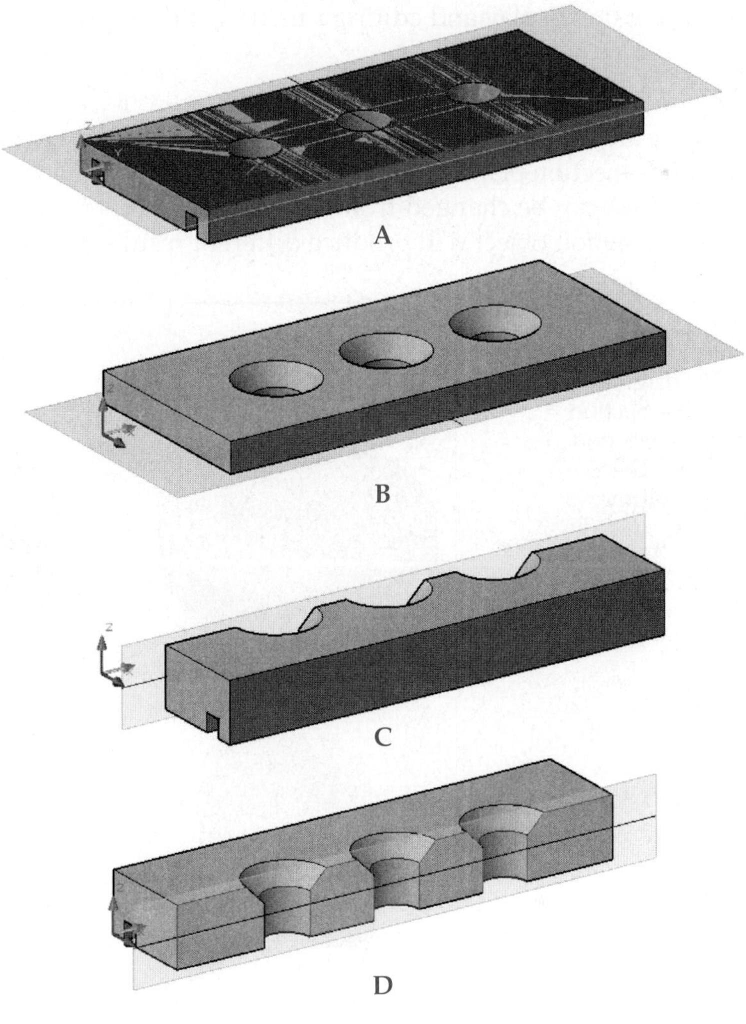

You may encounter a situation in which there is more than one solid on the screen and you want to use the **Orthographic** option to create a section object based on just one object. In this case, create a new layer, move objects you do not want to section to this layer, and then freeze the layer. The section object will be created based on the object that is visible. However, if the section plane passes through the objects on the frozen layers, those objects will be sectioned when the layers are thawed. A section plane affects all visible objects.

Exercise 13-2

Complete the exercise on the Student CD.

Editing and Using Section Planes

A wide range of section object editing and display options are available. However, there is no menu or ribbon access to these procedures. Instead, you must first select the section object, then right-click to display the shortcut menu. From this menu, you can access all of the display and editing functions that apply to the section object.

Section Object States

There are three possible states for the section object created by the **SECTIONPLANE** command—section plane, section boundary, and section volume. See Figure 13-9. The section object can be changed from one state to another. Depending on which state is active, the section object will produce different results on the solid(s).

Figure 13-9.
Section object states. A—The original object. B—Section plane. C—Section boundary. D—Section volume.

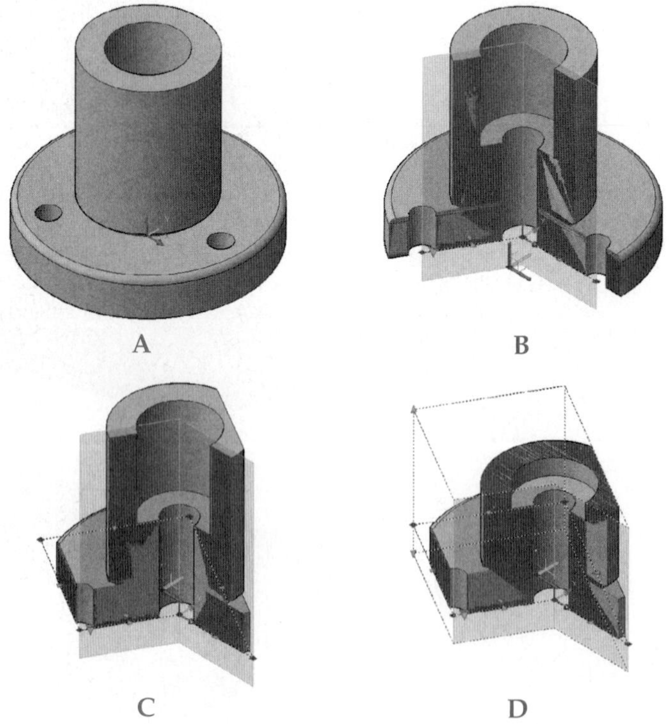

When the section object is created by picking a face, picking two points, or using the **Orthographic** option, the object is in the ***section plane state.*** A transparent plane is displayed on each segment of the section object and a line connects the pick points (or the edges of the section object). See **Figure 13-9B.** The section plane extends infinitely in the section object's Z direction and along the direction of the object segment (unless connected to other segments).

When the **Draw section** option is used, the ***section boundary state*** is applied. A transparent plane is displayed on each segment of the section object. A 2D box extends to the XY-plane boundaries of the section object. See **Figure 13-9C.** The sectioned object fits inside of this footprint. The section plane extends infinitely in the section object's Z direction.

The ***section volume state*** is not applied when the section object is created. The section object must be switched to this state once the object is created, as described in the next section. A transparent plane is displayed on each segment of the section object. In addition, a 3D box extends to the XYZ boundaries of the section object. The sectioned object fits inside of this box. See **Figure 13-9D.**

Section Object Properties

Once created, the properties of the section object can be changed. The **Section Object** category in the **Properties** palette contains properties specific to the section object. See **Figure 13-10.** These properties are described in the next sections.

Name

The default name of the first section object is Section Plane(1). Subsequent section planes are sequentially numbered, such as Section Plane(2), Section Plane(3), and so on. It may be beneficial to rename section objects so the name is representative of the section. For example, Front Half Section is much more descriptive than Section Plane(1). To rename a section object, select the Name property. Then, type a new name in the text box.

Figure 13-10.
The properties of a section object can be changed in the **Properties** palette.

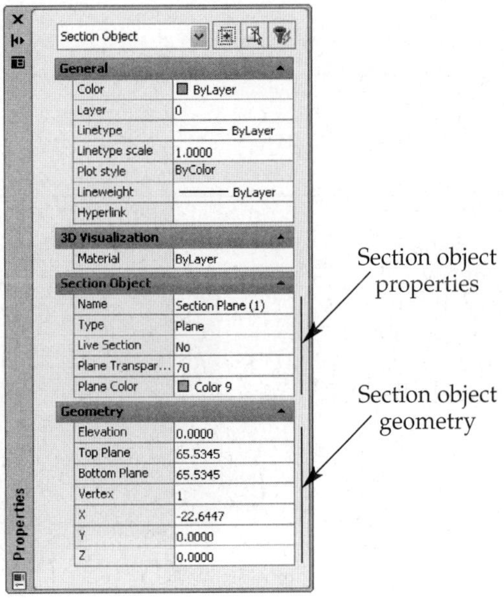

Type

As discussed earlier, the section object is in one of three states. The three states are section plane, section boundary, and section volume. To change the state of the section object, select the Type property. Then, pick the state in the drop-down list.

Live section

Live sectioning is a tool that enables you to dynamically view the internal features of a solid, surface, or region as the section object is moved. This tool is discussed later in the chapter. To turn live sectioning on or off, select the Live Section property. Then, pick either Yes (on) or No (off) in the drop-down list. This is the same as turning live sectioning on or off using the shortcut menu.

Plane transparency

The Plane Transparency property determines the opacity of the plane for the section object. The property value can range from 1 to 100. The lower the value, the more opaque the section plane object. See Figure 13-11.

Plane color

The plane of the section object can be set to any color available in the **Select Color** dialog box. To change the color, select the Plane Color property and then select a color from the drop-down list. To choose a color in the **Select Color** dialog box, pick the Select Color... entry in the drop-down list. This property only affects the plane of the section object, not the lines defining the boundary, volume, or section line. The color of these lines is controlled by the Color property in the **General** category.

Editing the Section Object

When the translucent planes of a section object or the lines representing the section object state are picked, grips are displayed. The specific grips displayed are related to the current section object state. Refer to Figure 13-9. The types of grips are:

- Base grip.
- Menu grip.
- Direction grip.
- Second grip.
- Arrow grips.
- Segment end grips.

Figure 13-11.
A—The Plane Transparency property of the section plane object is set to 1 (or 1% transparent). B—The Plane Transparency property of the section plane object is set to 85 (or 85% transparent).

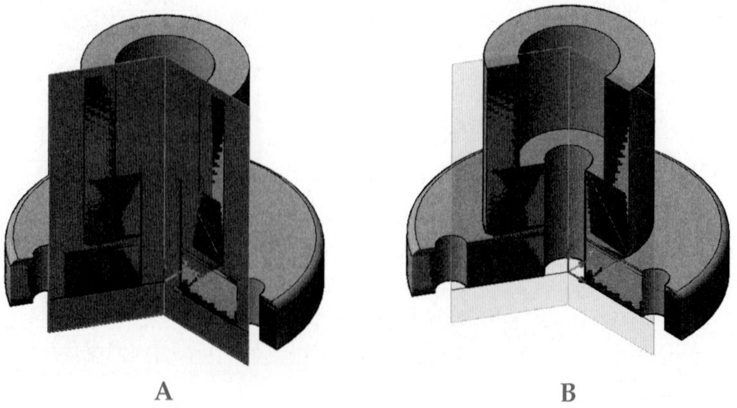

Figure 13-12.
The types of grips displayed on a section object.

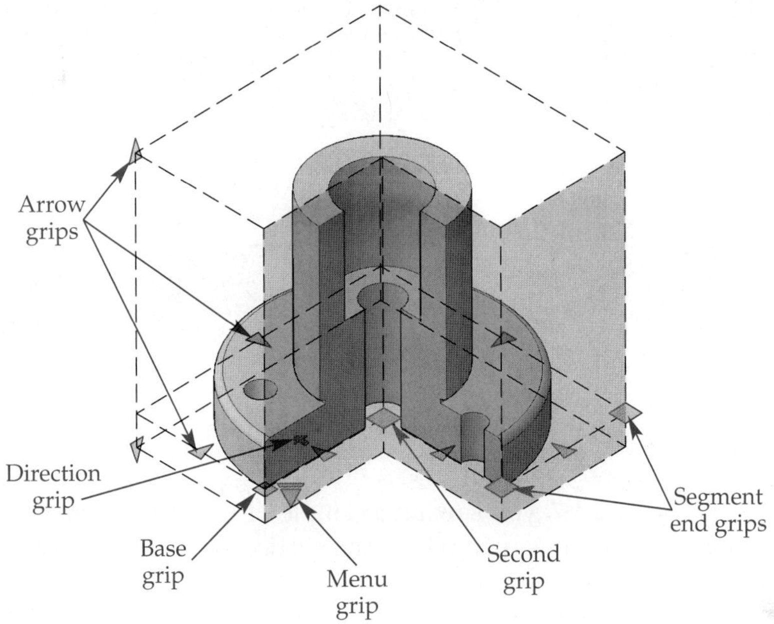

Base grip

The ***base grip*** appears at the first point picked when defining the section object. See **Figure 13-12.** It is the grip about which the section object can be rotated and scaled. The section object can also be moved using this grip.

Menu grip

The ***menu grip*** is always next to the base grip. Refer to **Figure 13-12.** Picking this grip displays the section state menu. See **Figure 13-13.** To switch the section object between states, pick the grip and then select the state from the menu.

Direction grip

The ***direction grip*** indicates the direction in which the section will be viewed. Refer to **Figure 13-12.** Pick the grip to rotate the view 180°. The direction grip also shows the direction of the live section. Live sectioning is discussed later in this chapter.

Second grip

The ***second grip*** appears at the second point picked when defining the section object. See **Figure 13-12.** The section object can be rotated and stretched about the base grip using the second grip.

Arrow grips

Arrow grips are located on all of the lines that represent the section plane, boundary, and volume. Refer to **Figure 13-12.** These grips are used to lengthen or shorten the section plane object segments or adjust the height of the section volume. The arrow grips at the top and bottom of the boundary box are used to change the height. Regardless of where the pointer is moved, the section object only extends in the segment's current plane. Changing the length of one segment of the section plane does not affect other segments.

Figure 13-13.
Changing section object states.

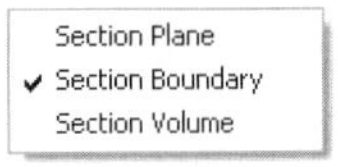

Figure 13-14.
A—The arrow grip is being used to extend the left side of the section plane past the boundary of the solid model. B—The edited section object. The right side can be corrected in the same manner.

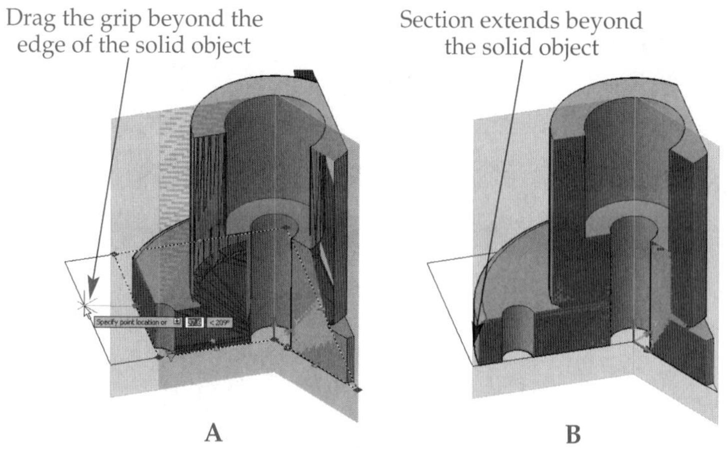

In Figure 13-7, you saw an example of using the **Draw section** option to create a section object. The way in which the section object was created resulted in the section plane not extending beyond the solid object. This can quickly be corrected using the arrow grips. Notice in Figure 13-14 that the arrow grip is being used to extend the left side of the section plane past the boundary of the solid model. This allows any subsequent section views to display the entire object rather than just a portion of it. The right side of the section plane can be extended in the same manner using the opposite arrow grip.

The arrow grips located on the line segments of the section plane move the position of the section plane. As a segment of the section plane is moved, it maintains its angular relationship and connection to any adjacent section plane segment.

Segment end grips

The ***segment end grips*** are located at the end of each line segment defining the section object state. Refer to Figure 13-12. The number of displayed segment end grips depends on whether the section object is in the section plane, section boundary, or section volume state. These grips provide access to the standard grip editing options of stretch, move, copy, rotate, scale, and mirror. If the rotate option is used, the section plane is rotated about the selected segment end grip. Moving a segment end grip can change the angle between section plane segments.

Adding Jogs to a Section

JOGSECTION

Type
JOGSECTION

You can quickly add a jog, or offset, to an existing section object. First, select the section object. Then, right-click to display the shortcut menu and select **Add jog to section**. You can also enter the **JOGSECTION** command. You are then prompted:

Specify a point on the section line to add jog:

Select a point directly on the section line. If any object snap is active, the **Nearest** object snap is temporarily turned on to ensure you pick the line. Once you pick, the jog is automatically added perpendicular to the line segment. See Figure 13-15A.

It is not critical that you pick the exact location on the line where you want the jog to occur. Remember, grips allow you to easily adjust the section plane location later. Notice in Figure 13-15B that the second jog barely cuts through the first hole. The intention is to run the section plane through the middle of the hole. To fix this, drag the arrow grip so the section plane segment is in the desired location, Figure 13-15C.

Figure 13-15.
Adding a jog to a section object. A—Pick a point on the section line to add a jog. B—The jog is added, but it is not in the proper location. C—Using the arrow grip, the jog is moved to the proper location.

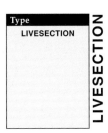

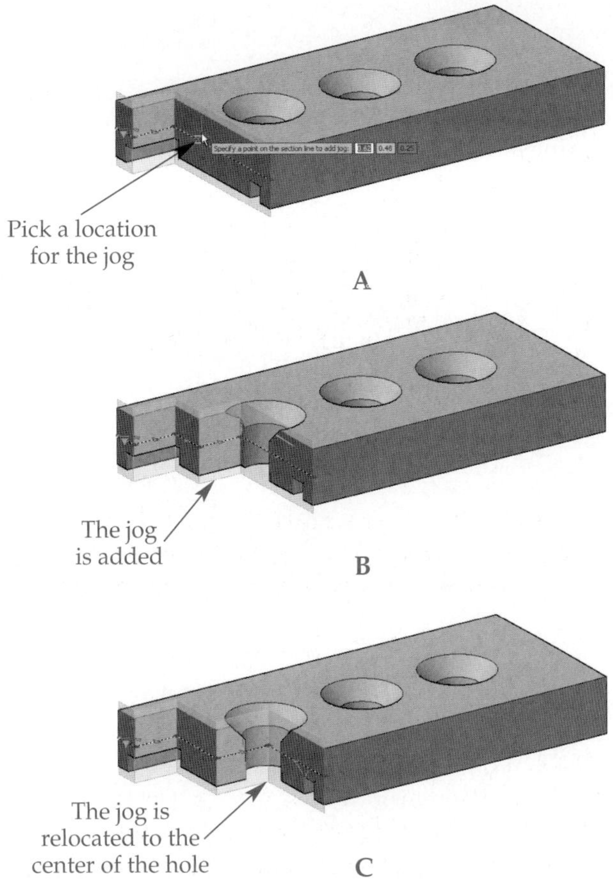

PROFESSIONAL TIP

If the section plane is not properly located, you can quickly change it. Simply pick the section object and right-click to display the shortcut menu. Then, select **Move**, **Scale**, or **Rotate** from the shortcut menu. Finally, adjust the section object location as needed.

Exercise 13-3

Complete the exercise on the Student CD.

Live Sectioning

Live sectioning is a tool that enables you to view the internal features of 3D solids, surfaces, and regions that are cut by the section plane of the section object. The view is dynamically updated as the section object is moved. This tool is used to visualize internal features and for establishing section locations from which 2D and 3D section views can be created. Live sectioning is either on or off.

Type
LIVESECTION

LIVESECTION

As you have seen, if the section plane is created by selecting a face, live sectioning is automatically turned on. However, when picking two points or using the **Draw** option of the **SECTIONPLANE** command, live sectioning is off. Live sectioning can be turned on and off for individual section objects, but only one section object can be "live" at any given time. To turn live sectioning on or off, select the section object. Then, right-click to display the shortcut menu and pick **Activate live sectioning**. See

Figure 13-16.
Live sectioning can be turned on for any section state by selecting the section object, right-clicking to display the shortcut menu, and picking **Activate live sectioning**.

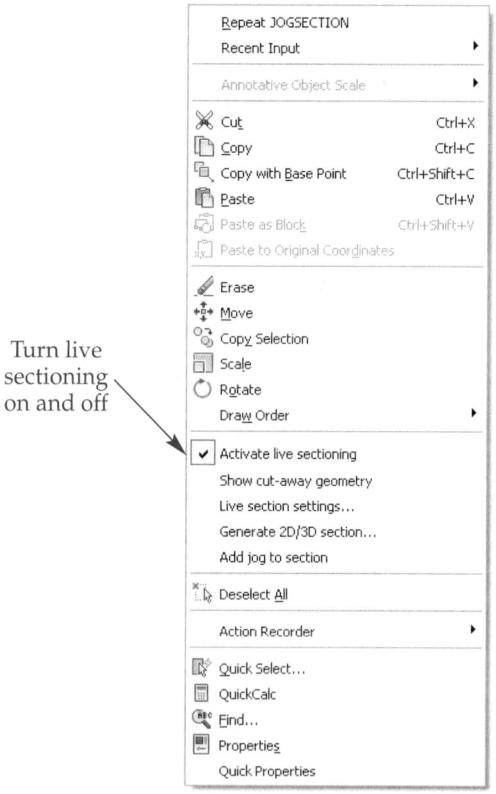

Figure 13-16. A check mark appears next to the menu item when live sectioning is on. You can also enter the **LIVESECTION** command and select the section object to toggle the on/off setting. When live sectioning is turned on, the material behind the viewing direction of the section plane is removed. The cross section of the 3D object is shown in gray and the internal shape of the 3D object is visible.

A wide variety of options allow you to change the appearance of not only the live sectioning display, but also of 2D and 3D section blocks that can be created from the sectioned display. These settings are found in the **Section Settings** dialog box. See **Figure 13-17.** To open this dialog box, select the section object, right-click, and pick **Live section settings...** in the shortcut menu.

To change the settings for live sectioning, pick the **Live section settings** radio button at the top of the **Section Settings** dialog box. The categories displayed in the dialog box contain properties related to live sectioning. Settings for 2D and 3D sections and elevations are discussed later in this chapter.

The three categories for live sectioning are **Intersection Boundary**, **Intersection Fill**, and **Cut-Away Geometry**. To display a brief description of any property, hover the cursor over the property in the **Section Settings** dialog box. The description is displayed in a tooltip. A check box at the bottom of the **Section Settings** dialog box allows you to apply the properties to all section objects or to just the selected section object.

PROFESSIONAL TIP

Live sectioning can be quickly turned on or off by double-clicking on the section plane object.

Figure 13-17.
Section settings. A—For a 2D block. B—For a 3D block. C—For live sectioning.

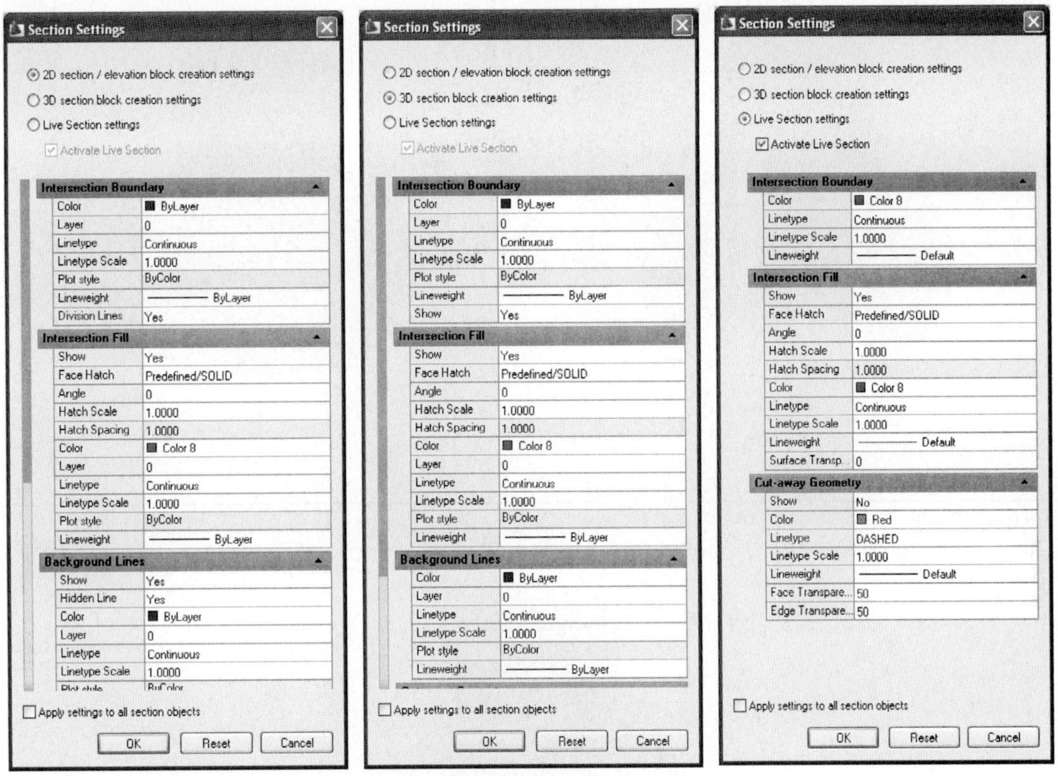

A B C

Intersection boundary

The intersection boundary is where the model is intersected by the section object. It is represented by line segments. You can set the color, linetype, linetype scale, and lineweight of the intersection boundary lines. Any linetype loaded into AutoCAD can be used.

Intersection fill

The intersection fill is the material visible on the model surface where the section object cuts. It is displayed as a solid fill, by default. Any hatch pattern available in AutoCAD can be used as the intersection fill. The angle, hatch scale, and hatch spacing, and color can be set. In addition, the linetype, linetype scale, and lineweight can be changed. The fill pattern can even be set to be transparent.

Cutaway geometry

The cutaway geometry is the part of the model removed by the live sectioning. By default, this geometry is not displayed. Changing the **Show** property to **Yes** displays the geometry. See **Figure 13-18.** You can set the color, linetype, linetype scale, and lineweight of the lines representing the cutaway geometry. In addition, the **Face Transparency** and **Edge Transparency** properties allow you to create a see-through effect, as seen in **Figure 13-19.** Each of these two properties is set to 50 by default.

PROFESSIONAL TIP

You can also display the cutaway geometry without using the **Section Settings** dialog box. Select the section object, right-click, and pick **Show cut-away geometry** in the shortcut menu.

Figure 13-18.
A—The intersection fill can be displayed as a hatch pattern in any specified color. B—The cutaway geometry is displayed.

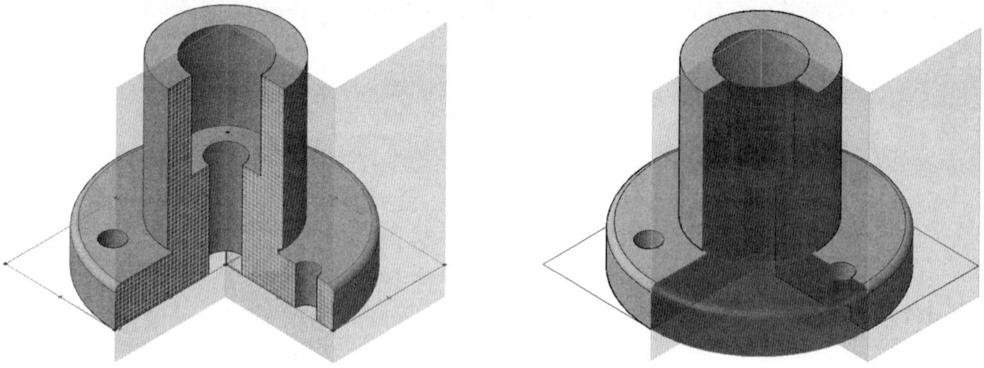

A B

Figure 13-19.
The cutaway geometry is displayed with 100% transparent faces and solid black lines.

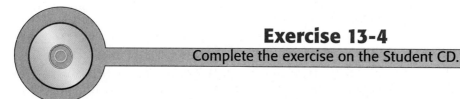

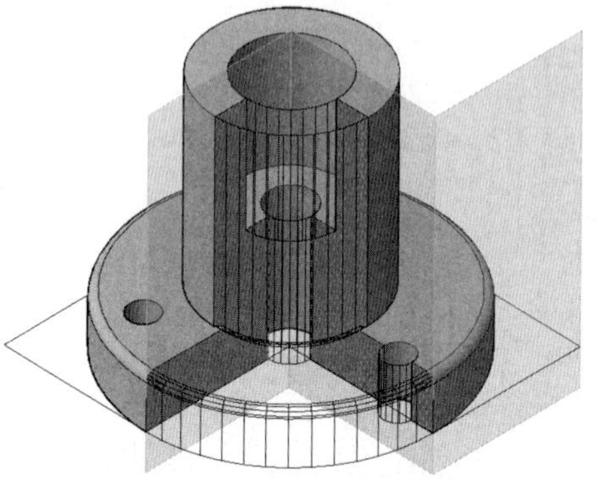

Exercise 13-4

Complete the exercise on the Student CD.

Generating 2D and 3D Sections and Elevations

The **SECTIONPLANE** command provides a fast and efficient method of creating sections. The sections can be either 2D or 3D. Not only can the sections be displayed on the current drawing, they can also be exported as a file that can then be used in any other drawing or document for display, technical drawing, or manufacturing purposes.

Creating sections

To create a section, select the section object, right-click, and pick **Generate 2D/3D section...** from the shortcut menu. The **Generate Section/Elevation** dialog box is displayed. See **Figure 13-20.** To expand the dialog box, pick the **Show details** button, which looks like a down arrow. In this dialog box, you can specify whether the section will be 2D or 3D, select what is included in the section, and specify a destination for the section.

To create a 2D section, pick the **2D Section/Elevation** radio button in the **2D/3D** area of the dialog box. A 2D section is projected onto the section plane, but is placed flat on the XY plane of the current UCS. To create a 3D section, pick the **3D Section** radio button. A 3D section is placed so its surfaces are parallel to the corresponding cut surfaces on the 3D object.

Figure 13-20.
The expanded **Generate Section/Elevation** dialog box.

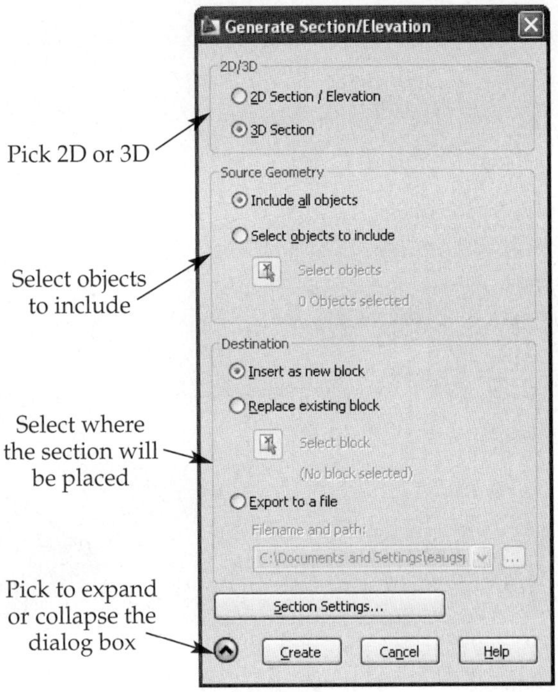

In the **Source Geometry** area of the dialog box, you can specify which geometry is included in the section. Picking the **Include all objects** radio button includes all 3D solids, surfaces, and regions in the section. To limit the section to certain objects, pick the **Select objects to include** radio button. Then, pick the **Select objects** button, select the objects on-screen, and press [Enter]. The number of selected objects is then displayed in the dialog box.

The **Destination** area of the dialog box is where you specify how the section will be placed. To place the section into the current drawing, pick the **Insert as new block** radio button. To update an existing section block, pick the **Replace existing block** radio button. Then, pick the **Select block** button, select the block on-screen, and press [Enter]. You will need to do this if the section object is changed. To save the section to a file for use in other drawings, pick the **Export to a file** radio button. Then, enter a path and file name in the text box.

Once all settings have been made, pick the **Create** button. The section is attached to the cursor and can be placed like a regular block. See **Figure 13-21.** Additionally, the options available are the same as if a regular block is being inserted. Once the block is inserted it can be moved, rotated, and scaled as needed.

Section settings

The **Section Settings...** button at the bottom of the **Generate Section/Elevation** dialog box opens the **Section Settings** dialog box discussed earlier. Using this dialog box, you can adjust all of the properties associated with the type of section being created. Depending on whether the **2D Section** or **3D Section** radio button is selected in the **Generate Section/Elevation** dialog box, the appropriate categories and properties are displayed in the **Section Settings** dialog box. Refer to **Figure 13-17.**

The categories discussed earlier related to the **Live Section Settings** radio button are available, although not all of the properties are displayed. Also, two additional categories are displayed for 2D and 3D sections:

- **Background Lines.** Available for 2D and 3D sections.
- **Curved Tangency Lines.** Only available for 2D sections.

Examples of 2D and 3D sections inserted as blocks in the drawing are shown in **Figure 13-22.** Notice how properties can be set to show cutaway geometry in a different color and to change the section pattern, color, and linetype scale.

Figure 13-21.
Inserting a 2D section block.

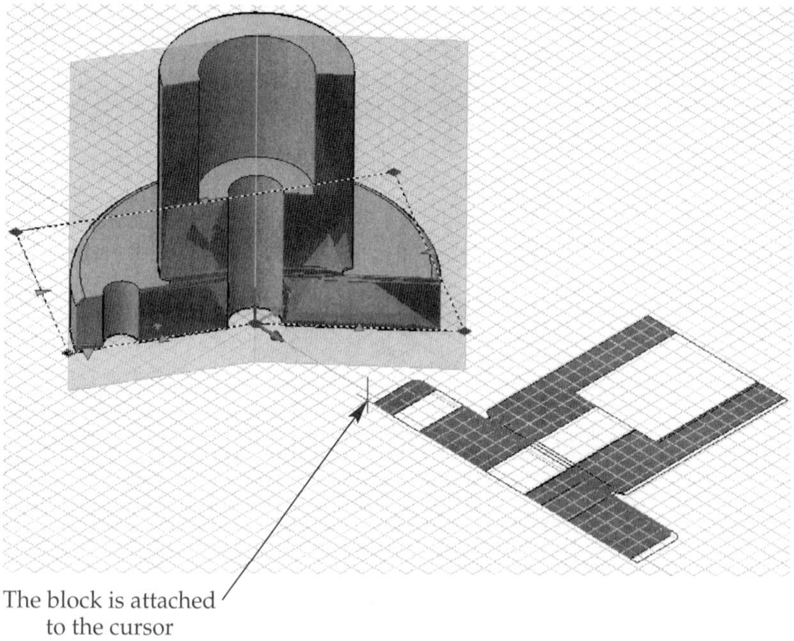

Figure 13-22.
A—The section object is created. B—A 2D section block is inserted into the drawing and the view is made plan to the block. C—A 3D section block is inserted into the drawing. Notice how the hatch pattern is displayed. D—The 3D section block is updated and now the cutaway geometry is displayed.

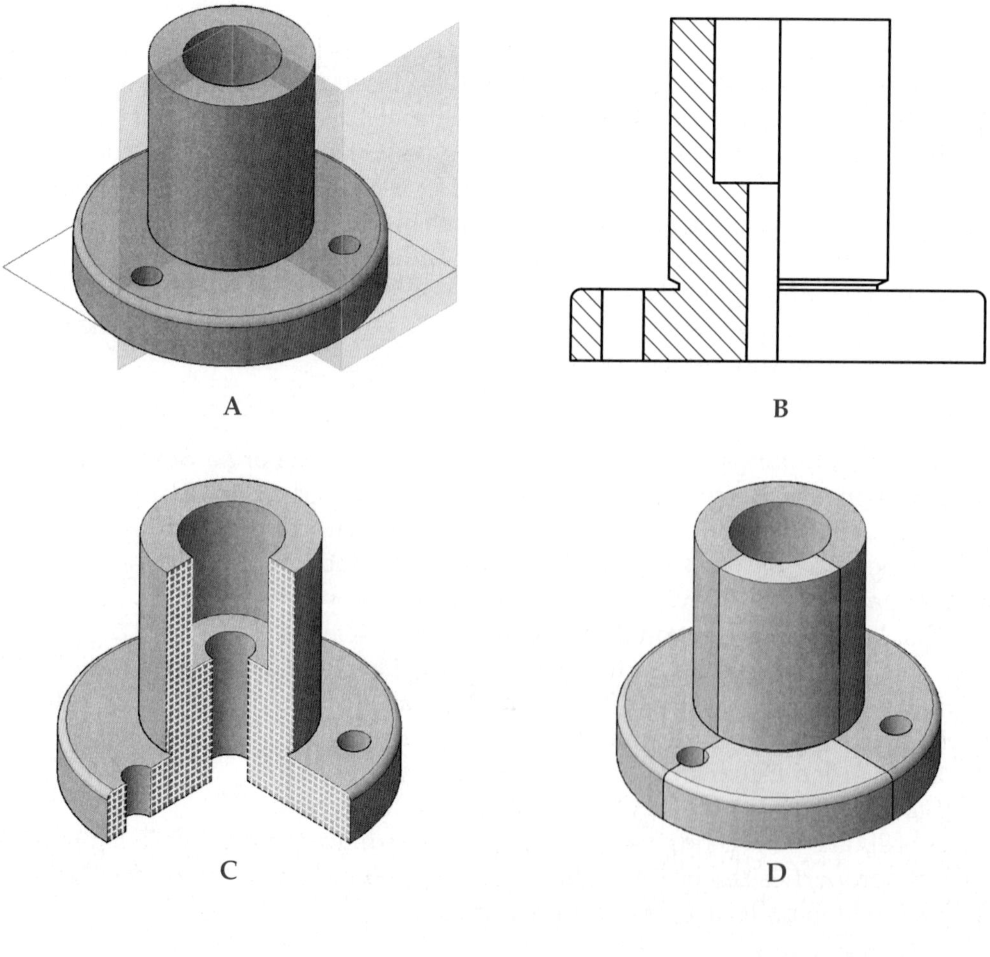

Background Lines. The properties in the **Background Lines** category provide control over the appearance of all lines that are not on the section plane. You can choose to have visible background lines, hidden background lines, or both displayed. They can be emphasized with color, linetype, or lineweight. The layer, linetype scale, and plot style can also be changed. These settings are applied to both visible and hidden background lines.

Curved Tangency Lines. The properties in the **Curved Tangency Lines** category apply to lines of tangency behind the section plane. For example, the object shown in **Figure 13-22** has a round on the top of the base. This results in a line of tangency behind the section plane where the round meets the vertical edge. You can have these lines displayed or suppressed. In general, lines of tangency are not shown in a section view. If you choose to display these lines, you can set the color, layer, linetype, linetype scale, plot style, and lineweight of the lines.

NOTE

When a 3D section is created, you must turn off live sectioning to see the complete sectioned object in the block. With live sectioning on, only the cut surfaces appear in the block.

Updating the section view

Once the section view is created, it is not automatically updated if the section object is changed. To update the section view, select the section object (not the block), right-click, and pick **Generate 2D/3D section...** from the shortcut menu. Then, in the **Destination** area of the **Generate Section/Elevation** dialog box, pick the **Replace existing block** radio button. If necessary, pick the **Select block** button and select the section block in the drawing. If you want to change the appearance of the section view, pick the **Section Settings...** button and adjust the properties as needed. Finally, pick the **Create** button in the **Generate Section/Elevation** dialog box to update the section block.

Exercise 13-5

Complete the exercise on the Student CD.

Creating a Flat Display of a 3D Model

The **FLATSHOT** command creates a flat projection of the 3D objects in the drawing from the current viewpoint. The view that is created is composed of 2D geometry and is projected onto the XY plane of the current UCS. This capability is useful for creating technical documents in which pictorial views of 3D objects are required.

Once the command is initiated, the **Flatshot** dialog box is displayed. See **Figure 13-23.** The options in this dialog box are similar to those found in the **Section Settings** dialog box. However, the display properties of foreground and obscured lines are limited to color and linetype. You can choose whether or not obscured lines are displayed in the flat view. You can also choose whether or not tangential edges are included.

Ribbon
Home > Solid Editing
Flatshot
Type
FLATSHOT

FLATSHOT

Select a destination for the flat view. Then, change the foreground and obscured lines settings as needed. Finally, pick the **Create** button. The flat view is inserted into the drawing as a block. Therefore, all of the ensuing prompts are those of a block insertion.

Figure 13-23.
The **Flatshot** dialog box.

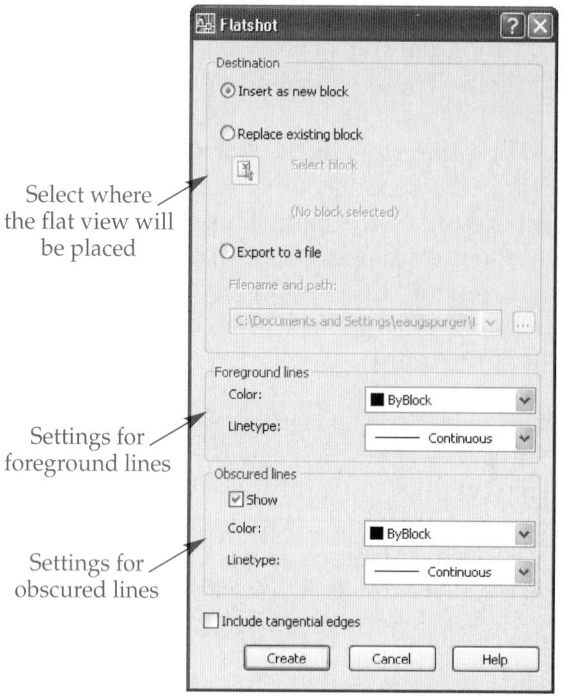

Use the **PLAN** command to obtain a plan view of the current UCS. Since the flat view is a block, it can be edited using the **BEDIT** command. Figure 13-24 shows a pictorial view of a 3D object and a plan view of the resulting flat view. To update the flat view to one from a different viewpoint, repeat the command and select the **Replace existing block** radio button in the **Destination** area of the dialog box.

PROFESSIONAL TIP

If the intention is to create a block to be used for a technical document, it may be best to export the flat view block to a file. It can then be inserted into a new AutoCAD drawing or copied into a document file.

Figure 13-24.
A—The 3D view from which a flat view will be generated. B—The inserted flat view. The viewpoint is plan to the block.

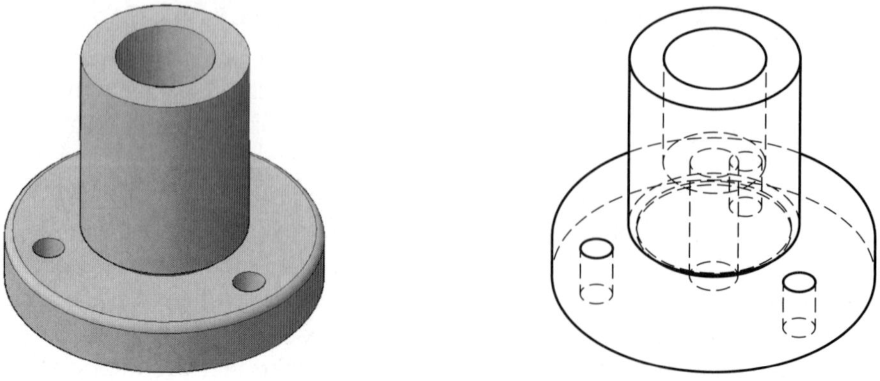

A B

Exercise 13-6

Complete the exercise on the Student CD.

Creating and Using Multiview Layouts

Once a solid model has been constructed, it is easy to create a multiview layout using the **SOLVIEW** command. This command allows you to create a layout containing orthographic, section, and auxiliary views. The **SOLDRAW** command can then be used to complete profile and section views. **SOLDRAW** must be used after **SOLVIEW**. The **SOLPROF** command can be used to create a profile of the solid in the current view.

Creating Views with SOLVIEW

SOLVIEW

Ribbon
Home
> 3D Modeling
Solid View

Type
SOLVIEW

Menu
Draw
> Modeling
> Setup
> View

The **SOLVIEW** command is used to create new floating viewports and to establish the display within those viewports. Therefore, you may want to delete the default viewport in the paper space tab before using the **SOLVIEW** command.

First restore the WCS. This will help avoid any confusion. Then, display a plan view. See **Figure 13-25.** It helps to have additional user coordinate systems created prior to using **SOLVIEW**. This allows you to construct orthographic views based on a specific named UCS.

Before using the **SOLVIEW** command, visualize which view is going to be the top view (or plan view) and how you would like the model rotated in relationship to the layout. With this in mind, look at the current UCS icon and make sure that the X axis is pointing to the "right" and the Y axis is pointing "up" in your imagined layout. If this is not the case, then you must restore the WCS, rotate the current UCS, or restore a saved UCS to correctly align the axes. Then, when you enter the **SOLVIEW** command in the layout, you can simply select the current UCS and you will be creating the top or plan view of your model.

When you enter the **SOLVIEW** command while in model space, AutoCAD automatically switches to paper space (layout space). Next, create an initial view from which other views can project. This is normally the top or front. In the following example, the top view is constructed first by using the plan view of a UCS named Leftside.

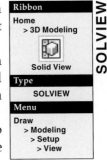

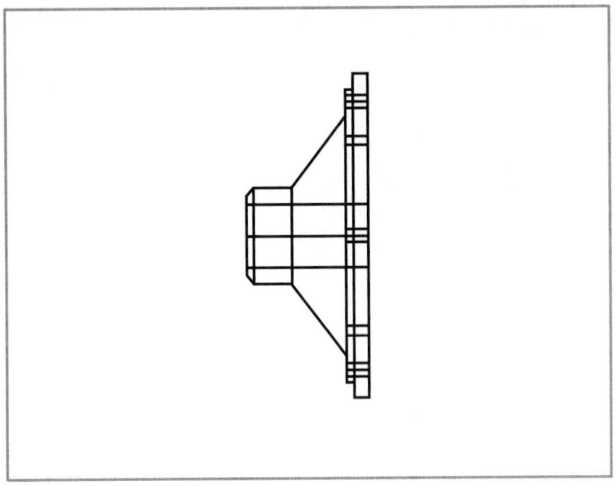

Figure 13-25. Before using **SOLVIEW**, display a plan view of the WCS.

Enter an option [Ucs/Ortho/Auxiliary/Section]: **U**↵
Enter an option [Named/World/?/Current] <Current>: **N**↵
Enter name of UCS to restore: **LEFTSIDE**↵
Enter view scale <1.0>: **.5**↵
Specify view center: *(pick a location in the layout for the center of the view)*
Specify view center <specify viewport>: ↵
Specify first corner of viewport: *(pick the first corner of a paper space viewport outside of the object)*
Specify opposite corner of viewport: *(pick the opposite corner of the viewport)*
Enter view name: **TOPVIEW**↵ *(the left of the object in AutoCAD is the top of the part)*
Enter an option [Ucs/Ortho/Auxiliary/Section]: *(leave the command active at this time)*

You must provide a name for the view. The result is shown in **Figure 13-26.**

The **SOLVIEW** command remains active until you press the [Enter] or [Esc] key. If you exit **SOLVIEW**, you can still return to the drawing and create additional orthographic viewports. With the command active, continue and create a section view to the right of the top view:

Enter an option [Ucs/Ortho/Auxiliary/Section]: **S**↵
Specify first point of cutting plane: *(pick the quadrant at point 1 in* **Figure 13-27***)*
Specify second point of cutting plane: *(pick the quadrant at point 2)*
Specify side to view from: *(pick point 3)*
Enter view scale <0.5>: ↵
Specify view center: *(pick the center of the new section view)*
Specify view center <specify viewport>: ↵ *(this prompt remains active until [Enter] is pressed to allow you to adjust the view location if necessary)*
Specify first corner of viewport: *(pick one corner of the viewport)*
Specify opposite corner of viewport: *(pick the opposite corner of the viewport)*
Enter view name: **SECTION**↵
Enter an option [Ucs/Ortho/Auxiliary/Section]: ↵

Notice in **Figure 13-27** that the new view is shown in the current visual style and not as a section. This is normal. **SOLVIEW** is used to create the views. The **SOLDRAW** command draws the section lines. **SOLDRAW** is discussed later in this chapter.

A standard orthographic view can be created using the **Ortho** option of **SOLVIEW**. This is illustrated in the following example. The new orthographic view is shown in **Figure 13-28.**

Enter an option [Ucs/Ortho/Auxiliary/Section]: **O**↵
Specify side of viewport to project: *(pick the bottom edge of the left viewport)*
Specify view center: *(pick the center of the new view)*
Specify view center <specify viewport>: ↵
Specify first corner of viewport: *(pick one corner of the viewport)*
Specify opposite corner of viewport: *(pick the opposite corner of the viewport)*
Enter view name: **FRONTVIEW**↵

Figure 13-26.
The initial view created with the **Ucs** option of **SOLVIEW**.

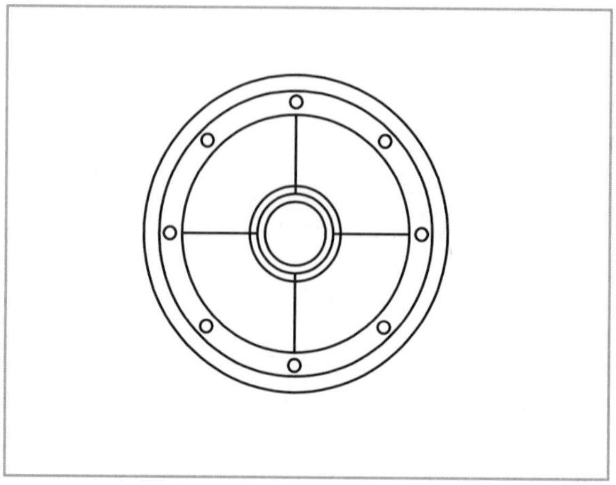

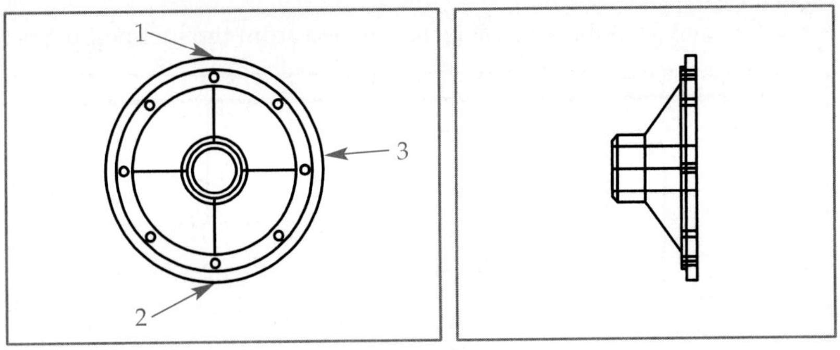

Figure 13-27.
The section view created with **SOLVIEW** (shown on the right) does not show projection lines. The pick points are shown on the left.

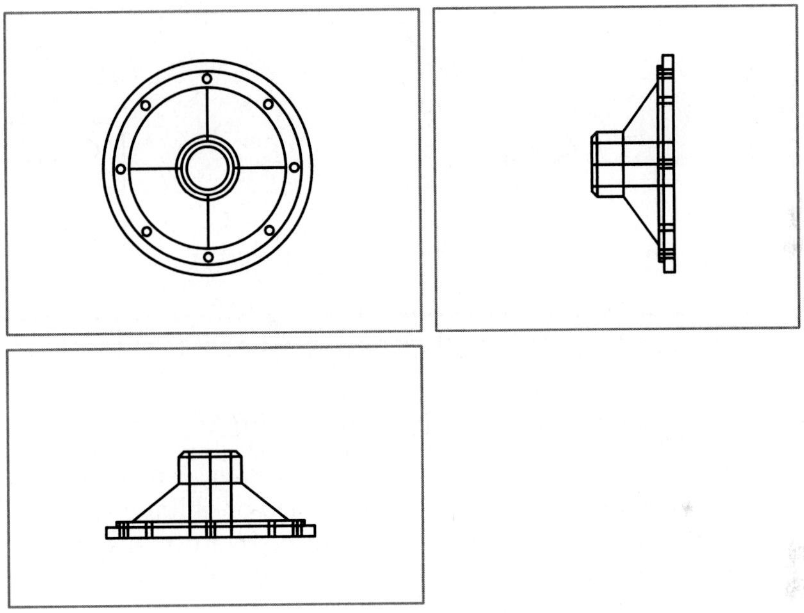

Figure 13-28.
An orthographic front view is created with the **Ortho** option of **SOLVIEW**. This is the view shown at the lower left.

The **SOLVIEW** command creates new layers that are used by **SOLDRAW** when profiles and sections are created. The layers are used for the placement of visible, hidden, dimension, and section lines. Each layer is named as the name of the view with a three letter tag, as shown in the following table. The use of these layers is discussed later in this chapter.

Layer Name	Object
View name-VIS	Visible lines
View name-HID	Hidden lines
View name-DIM	Dimension lines
View name-HAT	Hatch patterns (sections)

Exercise 13-7

Complete the exercise on the Student CD.

Figure 13-29.
An auxiliary view (shown in color) is created from the inclined plane in the front view.

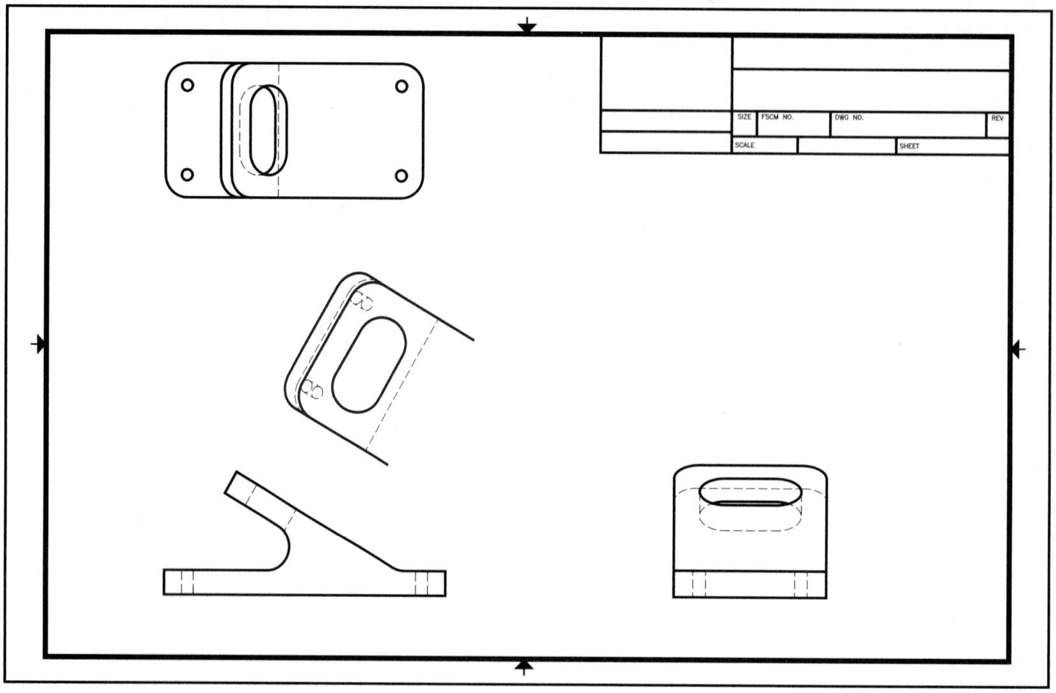

Creating Auxiliary Views with SOLVIEW

Auxiliary views are used to display a surface of an object that is not parallel to any of the standard views. It may be an inclined or oblique surface. Refer to **Figure 13-29.** Sometimes these views are necessary to show or dimension a feature that is not being displayed in true size in any other view. The slot in the inclined surface in **Figure 13-29** is not shown in true size in any of the standard views.

The auxiliary view is taken from one of the other views where the inclined surface is shown as an edge. The auxiliary view will be projected perpendicular to this surface. The auxiliary view is created by picking two points on the surface in the front view and another point to indicate the line of sight.

Enter an option [Ucs/Ortho/Auxiliary/Section]: **A**↵
Specify first point of inclined plane: *(using object snaps, pick a point on one end of the inclined surface)*
Specify second point of inclined plane: *(pick a point on the other end of the inclined surface)*
Specify side to view from: *(pick a point on the side of the surface from which you want to view it)*
Specify the view center: <specify viewport>↵
Specify first corner of viewport: *(pick one corner of the viewport)*
Specify opposite corner of viewport: *(pick the opposite corner of the viewport)*
Enter view name: **AUXILIARYVIEW**↵

Auxiliary views are often incomplete views, so it is acceptable to cut off portions of the view that are not necessary when you specify the corners of the viewport.

PROFESSIONAL TIP

When creating an auxiliary view, you may want to move other viewports that may be in the way to make room for the view.

Creating Finished Views with SOLDRAW

Ribbon
Home
> 3D Modeling
Solid Drawing
Type
SOLDRAW
Menu
Draw
> Modeling
> Setup
> Drawing

SOLDRAW

The **SOLVIEW** command saves information specific to each viewport when a new view is created. This information is used by the **SOLDRAW** command to construct a finished profile or section view. **SOLDRAW** first deletes any information currently on the *view name*-VIS, *view name*-HID, and *view name*-HAT layers for the selected view. Visible, hidden, and section lines are automatically placed on the appropriate layer. Therefore, you should avoid placing objects on any layer other than the *view name*-DIM layer.

The **SOLDRAW** command automatically creates a profile or section in the selected viewport. If you select a viewport that was created using the **Section** option of **SOLVIEW**, the **SOLDRAW** command uses the current values of the **HPNAME**, **HPSCALE**, and **HPANG** system variables to construct the section. These three variables control the angle, scale factor, and name of the hatch pattern.

If a view is selected that was not created as a section in **SOLVIEW**, the **SOLDRAW** command constructs a profile view. All new visible and hidden lines are placed on the *view name*-VIS or *view name*-HID layer. All existing objects on those layers are deleted.

Once the command is initiated, you are prompted to select objects. Pick the border of the viewport(s) for which you want the profile or section generated. When all viewports are selected, press [Enter] and the profiles and sections are created.

After the profile construction is completed, lines that should be a hidden linetype are still visible (solid). This is because the linetype set for the *view name*-HID layer is Continuous. Change the linetype for the layer to Hidden and the drawing should appear as shown in **Figure 13-30**, depending on the current visual style and hatch settings. You may also want to change other layer properties such as color, lineweight, and plot style.

Revising the 3D Model

If changes are needed after these views are created, the best practice is to modify the original 3D solid. However, the views created with **SOLVIEW** and **SOLDRAW** will not immediately reflect changes. To update the views, simply start the **SOLDRAW** command, select the viewports, and press [Enter]. The views are then updated with the changes.

When you go to model space to edit the solid, you may find it difficult to work on the original model. The 2D views created with **SOLDRAW** are projected on the top, bottom, left, and right, and sometimes within the model itself. It may be a good idea to set up a layer filter to temporarily freeze these layers while making changes. Remember to thaw the layers before updating the viewports with **SOLDRAW**.

Figure 13-30.
The new front profile view shows hidden lines after the linetype is set to Hidden for the FRONTVIEW-HID layer.

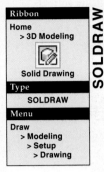

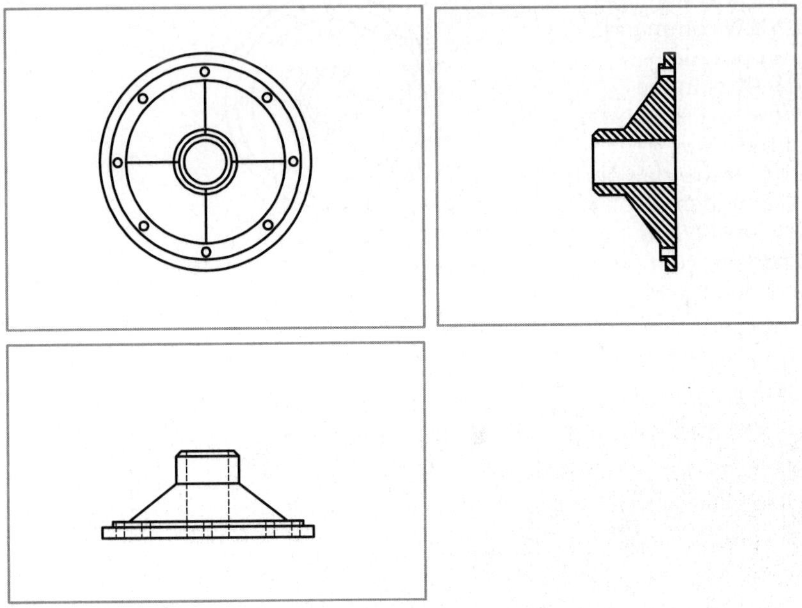

PROFESSIONAL TIP

If you wish to add dimensions in model space for the views created with **SOLVIEW** and **SOLDRAW**, use the view-specific DIM layers. These layers are created for that purpose and are only visible in one view. **SOLDRAW** does not delete information on the DIM layers when it constructs a view. If you prefer to dimension in paper space, use a layer other than the DIM layers created by **SOLVIEW**.

Adding a 3D View in Paper Space to the Drawing Layout

If you want to add a paper space viewport that contains a 3D (pictorial) view of the solid, use the **MVIEW** or **VPORTS** command. Create a single viewport by picking the corners. The object will appear in the viewport. Next, activate the viewport and use any of the "orbit" commands or a preset isometric viewpoint to achieve the desired 3D view. Pan and zoom as necessary. Change to the parallel or perspective projection if needed. You can also use the **Visual Style** control panel in the ribbon to adjust the display of the 3D viewport. The visual style set current for this viewport does not affect the displays in the other viewports. See Figure 13-31.

In order to have the hidden display correctly plotted, use the **MVIEW Shadeplot** option on the 3D viewport. Enter the command and select the **Shadeplot** option. Then, set the option to **Hidden**. If you have a hidden display shown in the viewport, you can also select **As displayed**. Then, pick the viewport when prompted to select objects.

Alternately, you can select the viewport and use the **Properties** palette to set the Shade plot property to As Displayed or Hidden. Any visual style display of the viewport can also be plotted in this manner by setting **MVIEW Shadeplot** to **As Displayed** (when the view is shaded) or **Rendered**.

Tips

Remember the following points when working with **SOLVIEW** and **SOLDRAW**.

- Use **SOLVIEW** first and then **SOLDRAW**.
- Do not draw on the *view name*-HID and *view name*-VIS layers.

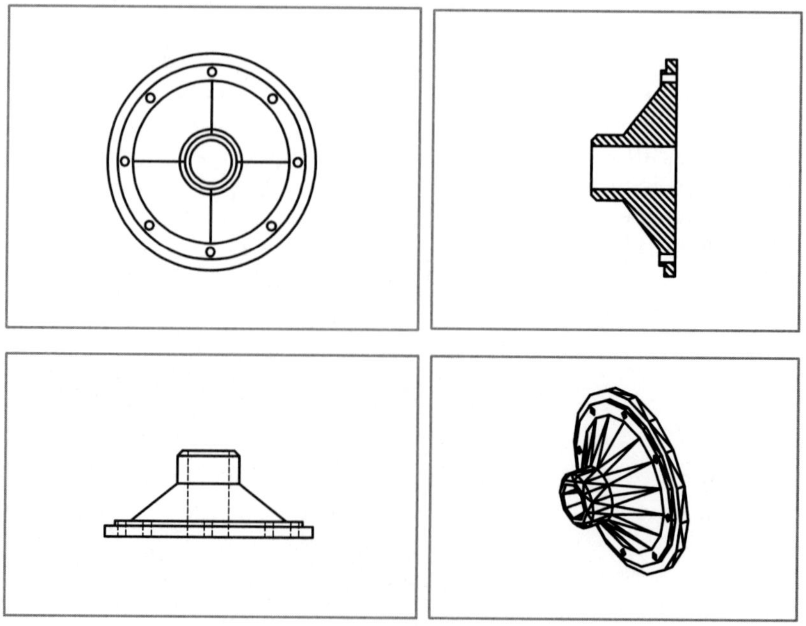

Figure 13-31.
Create a 3D viewport with the **MVIEW** command. You can hide the lines in the viewport, as shown at the lower right. To plot the viewport as a hidden display, use the **MVIEW Shadeplot** option and set it to Hidden.

- Place model space dimensions for each view on the *view name*-DIM layer for that specific view or simply dimension in paper space on a layer not created by **SOLVIEW**.
- After using **SOLVIEW**, use **SOLDRAW** on all viewports in order to create hidden lines or section views.
- Change the linetype on the *view name*-HID layer to Hidden and adjust other layer properties as needed.
- Create 3D viewports with the **MVIEW** or **VPORTS** command and an "orbit" command or a preset isometric view. Remove hidden lines when plotting with the **MVIEW Shadeplot** option set to **Hidden**.
- Plot the drawing in layout (paper) space at the scale of 1:1.

Exercise 13-8

Complete the exercise on the Student CD.

Creating a Profile with SOLPROF

Ribbon
Home > 3D Modeling Solid Profile
Type
SOLPROF
Menu
Draw > Modeling > Setup > Profile

SOLPROF

The **SOLPROF** command creates a profile view from a 3D solid model. This is similar to the **Profile** option of the **SOLVIEW** command. However, **SOLPROF** is limited to creating a profile view of the solid for the current view only.

SOLPROF creates a block of all lines forming the profile of the object. It also creates a block of the hidden lines of the object. The original 3D object is retained. Each of these blocks is placed on a new layer with the name of PH-*view handle* and PV-*view handle*. A ***view handle*** is a name composed of numbers and letters that is automatically given to a viewport by AutoCAD. For example, if the view handle for the current viewport is 2C9, the **SOLPROF** command creates the layers PH-2C9 and PV-2C9.

You must be in layout (paper) space and have a model space viewport active to use the command. Once the command is initiated, you are prompted to select objects:

Select objects: *(pick the solid)*
1 found
Select objects: ↵
Display hidden profile lines on separate layer? [Yes/No] <Y>: ↵
Project profile lines onto a plane? [Yes/No] <Y>: ↵

If you answer yes to this prompt, the 3D profile lines are projected to a 2D plane and converted to 2D objects. This produces a cleaner profile.

Delete tangential edges? [Yes/No] <Y>: ↵

Answering yes to this prompt produces a proper 2D view by eliminating lines that would normally appear at tangent points of arcs and lines. Once the profile is created, freeze the layer of the original object in the viewport. The original object and the profile created with **SOLPROF** are shown in **Figure 13-32.**

NOTE

When plotting views created with **SOLPROF**, hidden lines may not be displayed unless you freeze the layer that contains the original 3D object.

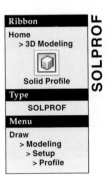

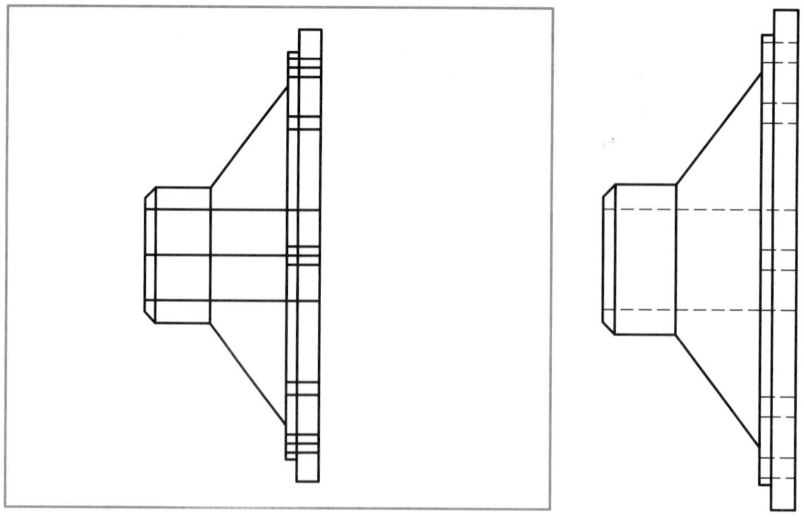

Figure 13-32.
A—The original solid. B—A profile created with **SOLPROF**.

Solid Model Analysis

MASSPROP

Ribbon
Tools > Inquiry
Region/Mass Properties
Type
MASSPROP
Menu
Tools > Inquiry > Region/Mass Properties

The **MASSPROP** command allows you to analyze a solid model for its physical properties. The data obtained from **MASSPROP** can be retained for reference by saving the data to a file. The default file name is the drawing name. The file is an ASCII text file with a .mpr (mass properties) extension. The analysis can be used for third party applications to produce finite element analysis, material lists, or other testing studies.

Once the command is initiated, you are prompted to select objects. Pick the objects for which you want the mass properties displayed and press [Enter]. AutoCAD analyzes the model and displays the results in the AutoCAD text window. See **Figure 13-33.** The following properties are listed.

- **Mass.** A measure of the inertia of a solid. In other words, the more mass an object has, the more inertia it has. Note: Mass is *not* a unit of measurement of inertia.
- **Volume.** The amount of 3D space the solid occupies.
- **Bounding box.** The dimensions of a 3D box that fully encloses the solid.
- **Centroid.** A point in 3D space that represents the geometric center of the mass.

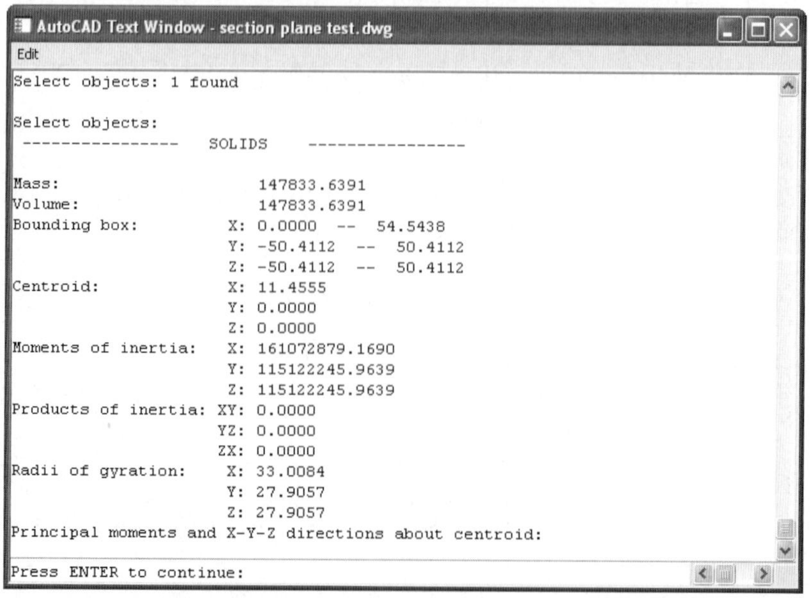
AutoCAD Text Window - section plane test.dwg
Edit

```
Select objects: 1 found

Select objects:
 ----------------   SOLIDS    ----------------

Mass:                       147833.6391
Volume:                     147833.6391
Bounding box:            X: 0.0000  --  54.5438
                         Y: -50.4112  --  50.4112
                         Z: -50.4112  --  50.4112
Centroid:                X: 11.4555
                         Y: 0.0000
                         Z: 0.0000
Moments of inertia:      X: 161072879.1690
                         Y: 115122245.9639
                         Z: 115122245.9639
Products of inertia:    XY: 0.0000
                        YZ: 0.0000
                        ZX: 0.0000
Radii of gyration:       X: 33.0084
                         Y: 27.9057
                         Z: 27.9057
Principal moments and X-Y-Z directions about centroid:

Press ENTER to continue:
```

Figure 13-33.
The **MASSPROP** command displays a list of solid properties in the AutoCAD text window.

- **Moments of inertia.** A solid's resistance when rotating about a given axis.
- **Products of inertia.** A solid's resistance when rotating about two axes at a time.
- **Radii of gyration.** Similar to moments of inertia. Specified as a radius about an axis.
- **Principal moments and X-Y-Z directions about a centroid.** The axes about which the moments of inertia are the highest and lowest.

PROFESSIONAL TIP

Advanced applications of solid model design and analysis are possible with Autodesk Inventor® software. This product allows you to create parametric designs and assign a wide variety of materials to the solid model.

Solid Model File Exchange

AutoCAD drawing files can be converted to files that can be used for testing and analysis. Use the **ACISOUT** command or **Export Data** dialog box to create a file with a .sat extension. These files can be imported into AutoCAD with the **ACISIN** or **IMPORT** command.

Solids can also be exported for use with stereolithography software. These files have a .stl extension. Use the **STLOUT** command or the **Export Data** dialog box to create STL files.

Importing and Exporting Solid Model Files

A solid model is frequently used with analysis and testing software or in the manufacture of a part. The **ACISOUT** and **EXPORT** commands allow you to create a type of file that can be used for these purposes. Once the **ACISOUT** command is initiated, you are prompted to select objects. After selecting objects and pressing [Enter], a standard save dialog box is displayed. See **Figure 13-34.** When using the **EXPORT** command, the standard save dialog box appears first. After entering a file name and selecting a file type (SAT), you are then prompted to select objects.

ACISOUT

Ribbon
Output
> Send
Export

Type
ACISOUT
EXPORT

Menu
File
> Export...

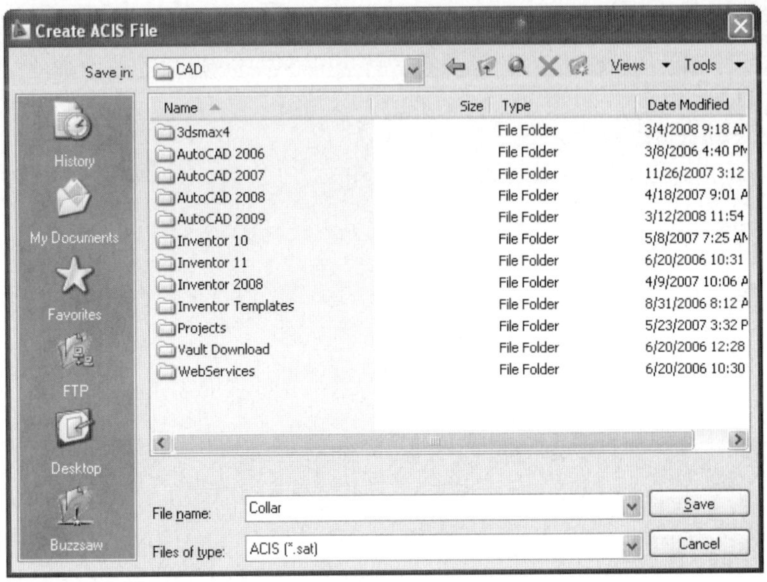

Figure 13-34.
Exporting an ACIS file.

ACISIN

Ribbon
Blocks & References
> Import
ACIS File

Type
ACISIN
IMPORT

Menu
Insert
> ACIS File

An SAT file can be imported into AutoCAD and automatically converted into a drawing file using the **ACISIN** and **IMPORT** commands. Once either command is initiated, a standard open dialog box appears. Change the file type to SAT, locate the file, and pick the **Open** button.

Stereolithography Files

Stereolithography is a technology that creates plastic, prototype 3D models using a computer-generated solid model, a laser, and a vat of liquid polymer. This technology is also called ***rapid prototyping*** or ***3D printing.*** A prototype 3D model can be designed and formed in a short amount of time without using standard manufacturing processes.

Most software used to create a stereolithograph can read STL files. AutoCAD can export a drawing file to the STL format, but *cannot* import STL files. Also, the solid model must be positioned in the current UCS in such a way so the entire object has positive XYZ coordinates.

STLOUT

Ribbon
Output
> Send
Export

Type
STLOUT
EXPORT

Menu
File
> Export...

The **STLOUT** and **EXPORT** commands can be used to create an STL file. Once the **STLOUT** command is initiated, you are prompted to select an object. You can only select a single object to be exported. You are then asked if you want to create a binary STL file. If you answer no to the prompt, an ASCII file is created. Keep in mind that a binary STL file may be as much as five times smaller than the same file in ASCII format. After you choose the type of file, a standard save dialog box is displayed. Type the file name in the **File name:** edit box and pick **Save** or press [Enter].

Once the **EXPORT** command is initiated, the standard save dialog box appears. Name the file and select the STL file type. Once the dialog box is closed, you are prompted to select an object. After you select the object and press [Enter], the file is created. You are not given the option of selecting a binary or ASCII format for the file. A binary file is automatically created.

PROFESSIONAL TIP

The **FACETRES** setting affects the "resolution" of the solid in an exported STL file and, thus, the final stereolithograph.

Exercise 13-9

Complete the exercise on the Student CD.

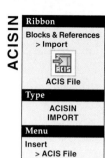

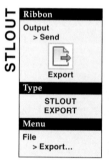

Chapter Test

Answer the following questions. Write your answers on a separate sheet of paper or complete the electronic chapter test on the Student CD.

1. What does the **SECTIONPLANE** command create?
2. How is the **Face** option of the **SECTIONPLANE** command used?
3. Which option of the **SECTIONPLANE** command is used to create sections with jogs?
4. When a section object is created by picking a face or two points or using the **Orthographic** option of the **SECTIONPLANE** command, which section object state is established?
5. Which section object grips are used to accomplish the following tasks?
   A. Change the section object state.
   B. Lengthen or shorten the section object segment.
   C. Rotate the section view 180°.
6. How is live sectioning turned on or off?
7. Which category in the **Section Settings** dialog box provides control over the material that is removed by the section object?
8. What are the two types of section view blocks that can be created from a section object?
9. Which command is used to create a flat view of the objects projected from the current viewpoint?
10. Which command should be used first, **SOLDRAW** or **SOLVIEW**?
11. Which option of the **SOLVIEW** command is used to create an orthographic view?
12. Name the layer(s) that the **SOLVIEW** command automatically create(s).
13. Which layer(s) in question 12 should you avoid drawing on?
14. Which command can automatically complete a section view using the current settings of **HPNAME**, **HPSCALE**, and **HPANG**?
15. Which command creates a profile view from a 3D model?
16. What is the function of the **MASSPROP** command?
17. What is the extension of the ASCII file that can be created by **MASSPROP**?
18. What is a *centroid?*
19. Which commands export and import solid models?
20. Which type of file has an .stl extension?

Drawing Problems

1. Open one of your solid model problems from a previous chapter and do the following.
   A. Use the **Face** option of the **SECTIONPLANE** command to create a section object.
   B. Alter the section so that the section plane object cuts through features of the model.
   C. Change the section settings to display an ANSI hatch pattern.
   D. Save the drawing as P13_01.

2. Open one of your solid model problems from a previous chapter and do the following.
   A. Construct a section through the model using the **Draw** option of the **SECTIONPLANE** command. Cut through as many features as possible.
   B. Display cutaway geometry with a 50% transparency.
   C. Display section lines using an appropriate hatch pattern.
   D. Generate a 3D section block that displays the cutaway geometry in a color of your choice.
   E. Create a layout with a viewport for the 3D block displayed at half the size of the original model.
   F. Save the drawing as P13_02.

3. Open one of your solid model problems from a previous chapter and do the following.
   A. Create a multiview layout of the model. One of the views should be a section view. Use a total of three 2D views.
   B. Use **SOLVIEW** and **SOLDRAW** to create the views. Be sure that section lines and hidden lines are properly displayed.
   C. Create a fourth viewport that contains a 3D view of the solid. Place the label PICTORIAL VIEW within the viewport.
   D. Plot the drawing so the 3D view is displayed with hidden lines removed.
   E. Save the drawing as P13_03.

4. Open one of your solid model problems from a previous chapter and do the following.
   A. Display the model in a plan view.
   B. Use **SOLPROF** to create a profile view. Save the profile view as a block in a file named P13_04PLN.
   C. Display the original model in a 3D view.
   D. Use **SECTIONPLANE** to construct a 2D front-view section of the model.
   E. Display the section as a plan view.
   F. Insert the block P13_04PLN above the section view. Adjust the views so they are properly aligned.
   G. Save the drawing as P13_04.

5. Choose five solid model problems from previous chapters and copy them to a new folder. Then, do the following.
   A. Open the first drawing. Export it as an SAT file.
   B. Do the same for the remaining four files.
   C. Compare the sizes of the SAT files with the DWG files. Compare the combined sizes of both types of files.
   D. Begin a new drawing and import one of the SAT files.

6. Draw the object shown below as a solid model. Do not dimension the object. Then, do the following.
   A. Construct a section object that creates a full section along the centerline of the hole.
   B. Generate a 2D section and display it on the drawing at half the size of the original. Specify section settings as desired.
   C. Generate a 3D section and display it on the drawing at half the size of the original. Do not display cutaway geometry. Specify section settings as desired.
   D. Activate live sectioning. Do not display the cutaway geometry.
   E. On the original solid model, display the intersection fill as an ANSI hatch pattern.
   F. Save the drawing as P13_06.

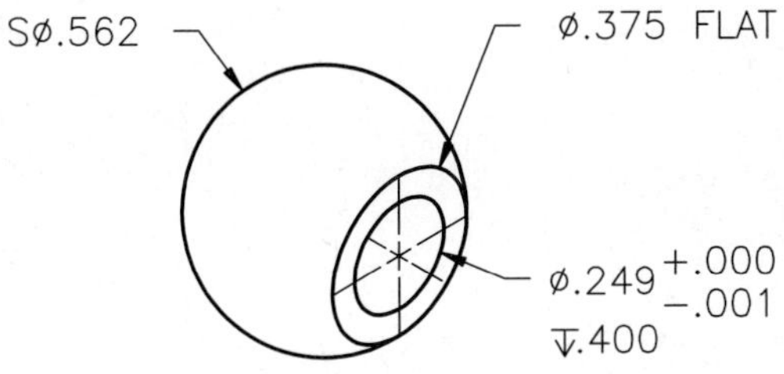

7. Draw the object shown below as a solid model. Only half of the object is shown; draw the complete object. Do not dimension the object. Then, do the following.
   A. Construct a section plane that creates a full section, as shown.
   B. Display the intersection fill as an ANSI hatch pattern.
   C. Activate live sectioning and view the cutaway geometry with a high level of transparency.
   D. Save the drawing as P13_07.

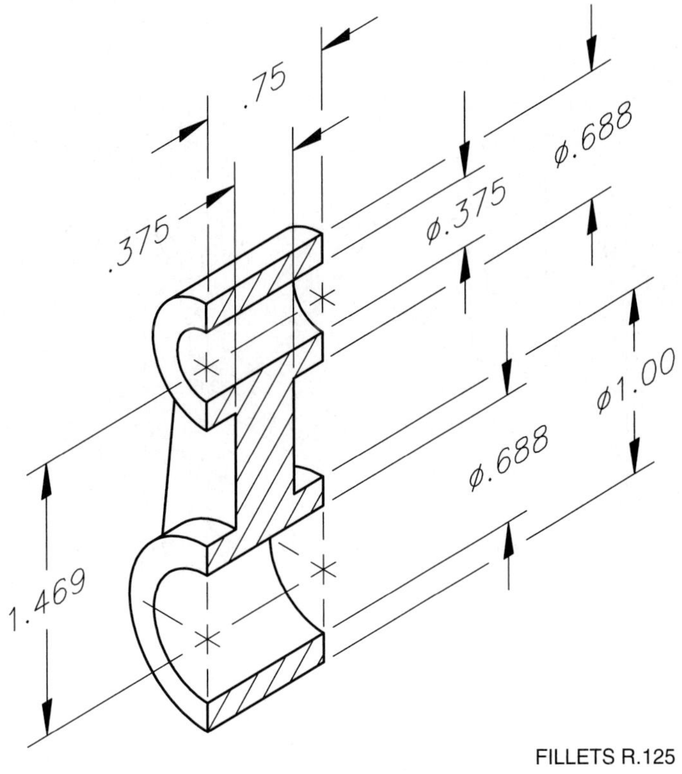

Drawing Problems - Chapter 13

8. Draw the object shown below as a solid model. Only half of the object is shown; draw the complete object. Do not dimension the object. Then, do the following.
   A. Construct a section plane that creates a half section.
   B. Display the intersection fill as an ANSI hatch pattern.
   C. Activate live sectioning and view the cutaway geometry with a low level of transparency.
   D. Generate a 3D section and save it as a block.
   E. Use **SOLVIEW** to create a two-view orthographic layout. Use an appropriate scale to plot on a B-size sheet.
   F. Create a third floating viewport and insert the 3D section block scaled to half the size of the drawing.
   G. Save the drawing as P13_08.

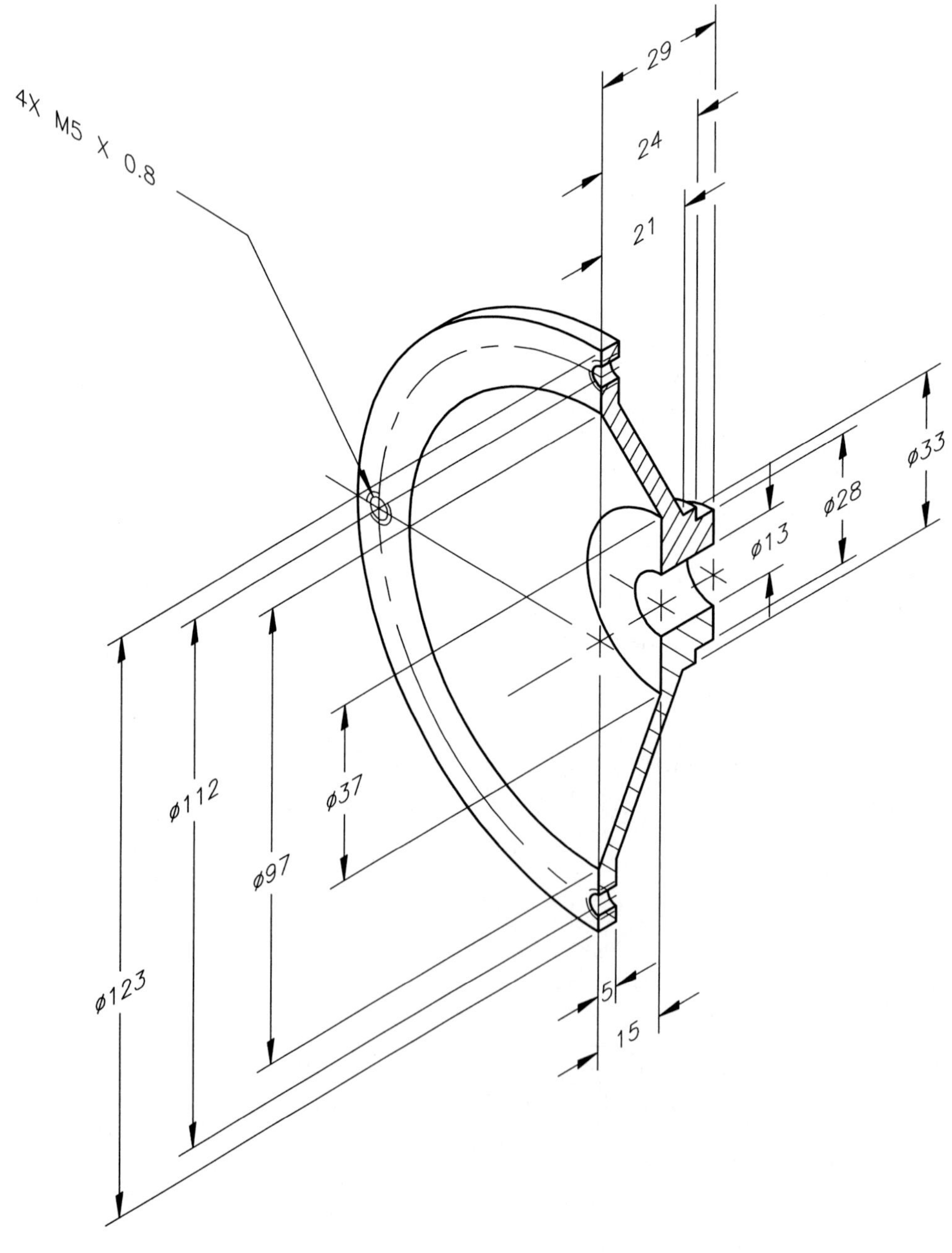

9. Draw the object shown below as a solid model. Use your own dimensions. Then, do the following.
   A. Construct a section plane that creates an offset section. The section should pass through the center of two holes in the base and through the large central hole.
   B. Display the intersection fill as an ANSI hatch pattern.
   C. Activate live sectioning and view the cutaway geometry with a low level of transparency in the color red.
   D. Generate a 3D section of the sectioned solid model and save it as a block.
   E. Use **SOLVIEW** to create a two-view orthographic layout. One view should be a half section. Use an appropriate scale to plot on a B-size sheet.
   F. Create a third floating viewport and insert the 3D section block scaled to half the size of the drawing.
   G. Save the drawing as P13_09.

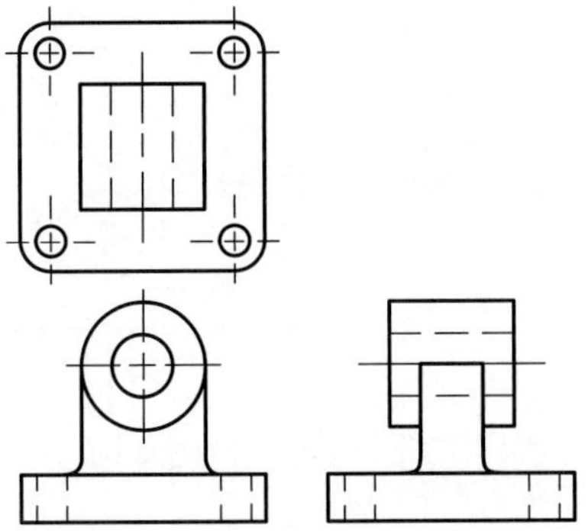

10. Draw the object shown below as a solid model. Do not dimension the object. Then, do the following.
   A. Display a 3D view of the model, generate a flat view, and save it as a block named P13_10_ FLATSHOT.
   B. Construct a section plane that creates a half section.
   C. Display the intersection fill as an ANSI hatch pattern.
   D. Activate live sectioning and view the cutaway geometry with a low level of transparency in the color red.
   E. Alter the section plane to create the section shown below.
   F. Generate a 3D section and save it as a block.
   G. Use **SOLVIEW** to create a two-view orthographic layout. One view should be a full section. Use an appropriate scale to plot on an A-size sheet.
   H. Create a third floating viewport and insert the 3D section block scaled to half the size of the drawing.
   I. Create a fourth viewport and insert the P13_10_FLATSHOT block scaled to half the size of the drawing.
   K. Save the drawing as P13_10.

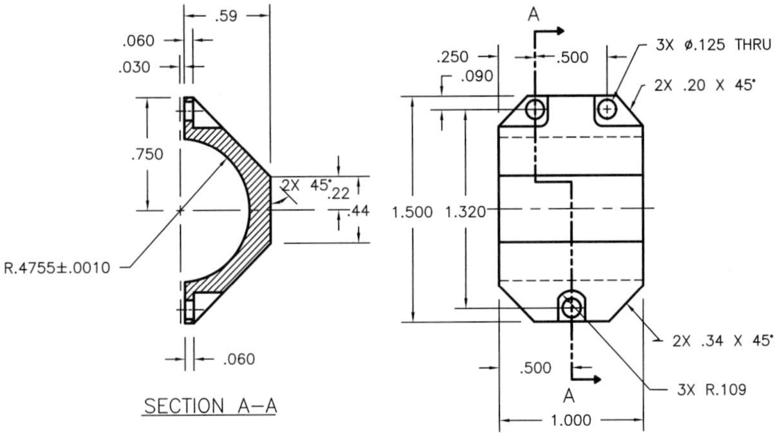

Using visual styles can help you better see your model as it develops. While a shadded visual style (top) is better than a wireframe display, a rending (bottom) can add realism to the model

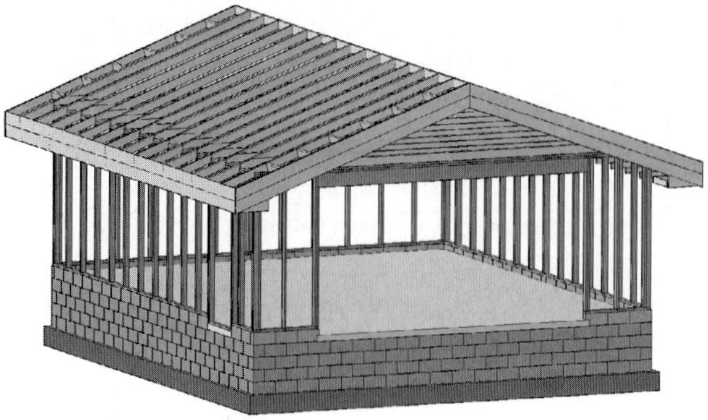

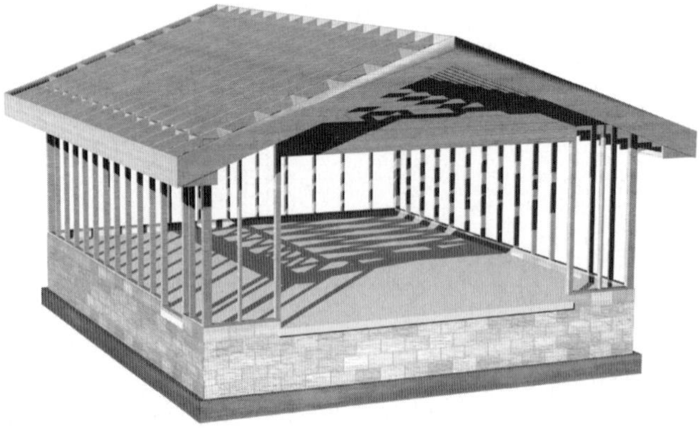

CHAPTER 14

Visual Style Settings and Basic Rendering

Learning Objectives

After completing this chapter, you will be able to:

- ✓ Describe the **Visual Style Manager** palette.
- ✓ Change the settings for visual styles.
- ✓ Create custom visual styles.
- ✓ Export visual styles to a tool palette.
- ✓ Render a scene using sunlight.
- ✓ Save a rendered image from the **Render** window.

In Chapter 1, you were introduced to the default visual styles. In Chapter 3, you learned how to use the **Visualize** tab on the ribbon to adjust several settings related to how the visual style represents objects. This is a way to quickly and easily change the appearance of the scene. In this chapter, you will learn about other visual style settings and how to redefine the visual style. You will also learn how to create your own visual style. Finally, this chapter provides an introduction to lights and rendering.

Overview of the Visual Styles Manager

The **Visual Styles Manager** palette provides access to all of the visual style settings. This palette is a floating window similar to the **Properties** palette. See Figure 14-1. Changes made in the **Visual Styles Manager** redefine the visual style.

Ribbon
View
> 3D Palettes
Visual Styles
Visualize
> Visual Styles
> Visual Styles

Type
VISUALSTYLES

Menu
View
> Visual Styles
> Visual Style Manager...

VISUALSTYLES

At the top of the **Visual Styles Manager** are image tiles for the defined visual styles. See Figure 14-2. The default visual styles are 2D Wireframe, 3D Hidden, 3D Wireframe, Conceptual, and Realistic. User-defined visual styles also appear as image tiles. The image on the image tile is a preview of the visual style settings. Selecting an image tile provides access to the properties of the visual style in the palette below. The name of the currently selected visual style appears below the image tiles and the corresponding image tile is surrounded by a yellow border.

To set a different visual style current using the **Visual Styles Manager**, double-click on the image tile. You can also select the image tile and pick the **Apply Selected Visual Style to Current Viewport** button immediately below the image tiles. An icon containing a white star is displayed in the image tile of the visual style that is current in the active viewport, as shown in Figure 14-2. A drawing icon appears in the image tile if the visual style is current in a viewport that is not active. The AutoCAD icon appears in the image tiles of the default visual styles.

Figure 14-1.
The **Visual Styles Manager** palette.

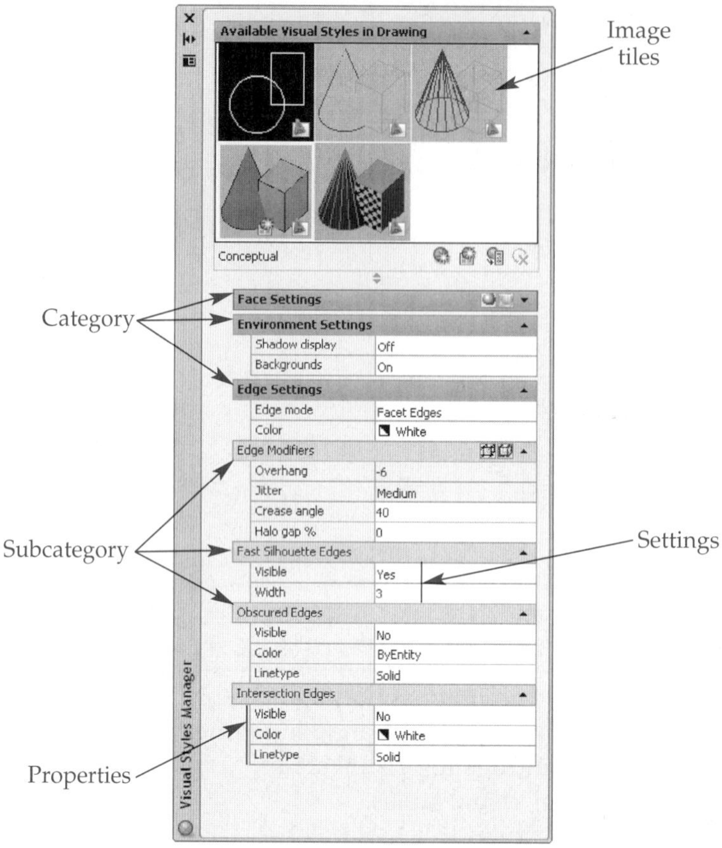

Figure 14-2.
The image tiles correspond to the visual styles. The image on the tile is a preview of the visual style's settings.

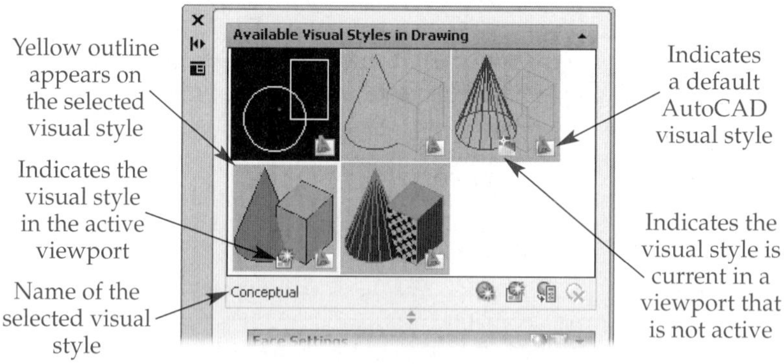

Exercise 14-1
Complete the exercise on the Student CD.

Visual Style Settings

As you saw in Chapter 3, the **Visual Styles** and **Edge Effects** panels on the **Visualize** tab of the ribbon provide several settings for altering the visual style. These settings are also available in the **Visual Styles Manager**. In addition, there are settings in the **Visual Styles Manager** that are not available on the ribbon. The next sections discuss settings available in the **Visual Styles Manager** for the default visual styles. Remember, changing any setting in the **Visual Styles Manager** redefines the visual style. Changes made using the ribbon are temporary.

2D Wireframe

When the 2D Wireframe visual style is set current, lines and curves are used to show the edges of 3D objects. Assigned linetypes and lineweights are displayed. All edges are visible as if the object is constructed of pieces of wire soldered together at the intersections (thus, the name *wireframe*). Either the 2D or 3D wireframe UCS icon is displayed and the 2D grid is displayed, if it is turned on. OLE objects will display normally. In addition, the drawing window display changes to the 2D Model Space context and parallel projection. For the 2D Wireframe visual style, the **Visual Styles Manager** displays the following categories. See Figure 14-3.

- **2D Wireframe Options**
- **2D Hide—Obscured Lines**
- **2D Hide—Intersection Edges**
- **2D Hide—Miscellaneous**
- **Display Resolution**

2D wireframe options

The Contour lines property controls the **ISOLINES** system variable. Isolines are the lines used to define curved surfaces on solid objects when displayed in a wireframe view. The setting is 4 by default and can range from 0 to 2047. Isolines are suppressed when the **HIDE** command is used with the 2D Wireframe visual style set current.

The Draw true silhouettes property controls the **DISPSILH** system variable. This determines whether or not silhouette edges are shown on curved surfaces. It is set to Off by default, which is equivalent to a **DISPSILH** setting of 0. This property is different from the **Silhouette Edges** setting in the **Edge Effects** panel in **Visualize** tab of the ribbon.

2D hide—obscured lines

The Color property in this category controls the **OBSCUREDCOLOR** system variable. This property determines the color of obscured lines when the **HIDE** command is used. The default setting is ByEntity. This means that, when displayed, obscured lines are shown in the same color as the object.

The Linetype property controls the **OBSCUREDLTYPE** system variable. This property determines whether or not obscured lines are displayed and in which linetype they are displayed. The default setting is Off, which means that obscured lines are not displayed when the **HIDE** command is used. The available linetypes are: Solid, Dashed, Dotted, Short Dash, Medium Dash, Long Dash, Double Short Dash, Double Medium Dash, Double Long Dash, Medium Long Dash, and Sparse Dot.

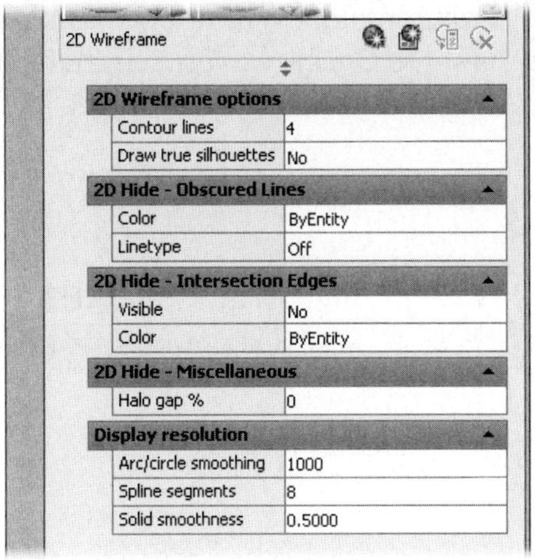

Figure 14-3.
The categories and properties available for the 2D Wireframe visual style.

NOTE

The above linetypes are not the same as the linetypes loaded into the **Linetype Manager** dialog box. They are independent of zoom levels, which means the dash size will stay the same when zooming in and out.

2D hide—intersection edges

This category is used to toggle the display of polylines at the intersection of 3D surfaces and set the color of the lines. The Visible property controls the **INTERSECTIONDISPLAY** system variable. This property determines whether or not polylines are displayed at the intersection of non-unioned 3D surfaces. The default setting is Off, which means that polylines are not displayed when the **HIDE** command is used.

The Color property in this category controls the **INTERSECTIONCOLOR** system variable. This property determines the color of the polylines displayed at intersection edges. By default, the setting is ByEntity. This means that, when displayed, the polylines at intersection edges are shown in the same color as the object.

2D hide—miscellaneous

The Halo Gap % property controls the **HALOGAP** system variable. This property determines the gap that is displayed where one object partially obscures another (between the foreground edge and where the background edge starts to show). The default setting is 0 and the value can range from 0 to 100. The value refers to a percentage of one unit. The gap is only displayed when the **HIDE** command is used. It is not affected by the zoom level.

Display resolution

The Arc/circle smoothing property controls the zoom percentage set by the **VIEWRES** command. This determines the resolution of circles and arcs. The value can range from 1 to 20,000. The higher the value, the higher the resolution of circles and arcs.

The Spline segments property controls the **SPLINESEGS** system variable. This property determines the number of line segments in a spline-fit polyline. The value can range from –32,768 to 32,767.

The Solid smoothness property controls the **FACETRES** system variable. This property determines the number of polygon faces applied to curved surfaces on solids. The default setting is .5 and the value can range from .01 to 10.0.

NOTE

Polygon faces will not be visible if the Draw true silhouettes property is set to On. However, a higher setting for the Solid smoothness property will make curved edges smoother.

Exercise 14-2

Complete the exercise on the Student CD.

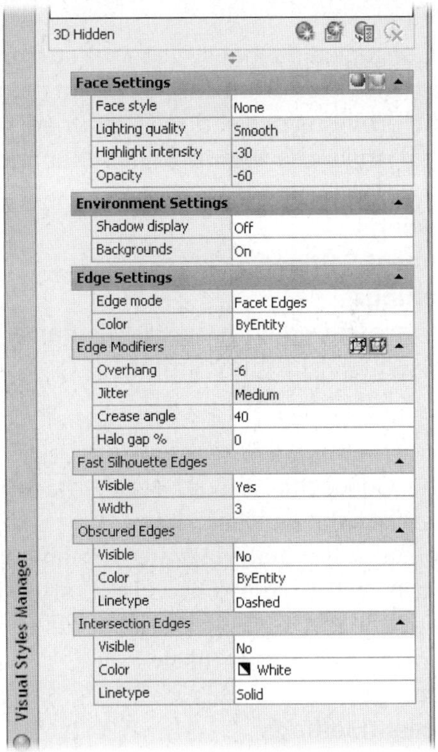

Figure 14-4.
The categories and properties available for the 3D Wireframe, 3D Hidden, Conceptual, and Realistic visual styles.

3D Hidden

The 3D Hidden visual style removes obscured lines from your view and makes 3D objects appear solid. The previous projection is retained and that context is set current. The benefit of using 3D Hidden is that you get sufficient 3D display, but it does not push the graphics system too hard. Objects are not shaded or colored. This is very useful when working on complex drawings and/or using a slow computer. For the 3D Hidden visual style, the **Visual Styles Manager** displays the following categories. See **Figure 14-4.**

- **Face Settings**
- **Environment Settings**
- **Edge Settings**

These categories are shared with the 3D Wireframe, Conceptual, and Realistic visual styles. They are discussed later in this chapter.

3D Wireframe

The 3D Wireframe visual style is similar to the 2D Wireframe visual style. All edges are visible and the shaded UCS icon is displayed. The previous projection is retained and that context is set current. When working in 3D, a wireframe view is sometimes necessary to select objects normally hidden from your view. While a 3D view can be displayed with the 2D Wireframe visual style, setting the 3D Wireframe current automatically displays grid lines and the shaded UCS icon (if they are turned on). For the 3D Wireframe visual style, the **Visual Styles Manager** displays the following categories. See **Figure 14-4.**

- **Face Settings**
- **Environment Settings**
- **Edge Settings**

These categories are shared with the 3D Hidden, Conceptual, and Realistic visual styles. They are discussed later in this chapter.

Conceptual

When the Conceptual visual style is set current, objects are smoothed and shaded. The shading is a transition from cool to warm colors. The transitional colors help highlight details. The previous projection is retained and that context is set current. For the Conceptual visual style, the **Visual Styles Manager** displays the following categories. See **Figure 14-4.**

- **Face Settings**
- **Environment Settings**
- **Edge Settings**

These categories are shared with the 3D Wireframe, 3D Hidden, and Realistic visual styles. They are discussed later in this chapter.

Realistic

As with the Conceptual visual style, the objects have smoothing and shading applied to them when the Realistic visual style is set current. In addition, if materials are applied to the objects, the materials are displayed. The previous projection is retained and that context is set current. This visual style is good for a final look at the scene before rendering. For the Realistic visual style, the **Visual Styles Manager** displays the following categories. See **Figure 14-4.**

- **Face Settings**
- **Environment Settings**
- **Edge Settings**

These settings are shared with the 3D Wireframe, 3D Hidden, and Conceptual visual styles. They are discussed in the next section.

VSFACESTYLE

Ribbon
Visualize
> Visual Style
No Shading
Visualize
> Visual Style
Realistic
Visualize
> Visual Style
Gooch
Type
VSFACESTYLE

VSLIGHTINGQUALITY

Ribbon
Visualize
> Visual Style
Facet Lighting
Visual
> Visual Style
Smooth Lighting
Visualize
> Visual Style
Smoothest Lighting
Type
VSLIGHTINGQUALITY

Settings for 3D Wireframe, 3D Hidden, Conceptual, and Realistic Visual Styles

The 3D Wireframe, 3D Hidden, Conceptual, and Realistic visual styles share similar categories and settings in the **Visual Styles Manager**. The visual styles have **Face Settings**, **Environmental Settings**, and **Edge Settings** categories. These categories and the properties available in them are discussed in the next sections.

Face settings

The Face style property controls the **VSFACESTYLE** system variable. This is also the same as selecting a button in the face style flyout in the **Visual Style** panel in the **Visualize** tab of the ribbon. These settings are discussed in Chapter 3. The default setting for the 3D Wireframe and 3D Hidden visual styles is None, for the Conceptual visual style is Gooch, and for the Realistic visual style is Real.

The Lighting quality property controls the **VSLIGHTINGQUALITY** system variable. This property determines whether curved surfaces are displayed smooth or as a series of flat faces. This is also the same as selecting the **Facet Lighting**, **Smooth Lighting**, or **Smoothest Lighting** button in the **Visual Styles** panel on the **Visualize** tab of the ribbon, as discussed in Chapter 3. No effect is produced if the Face style property is set to None. The default setting for the 3D Wireframe, 3D Hidden, Conceptual, and Realistic visual styles is Smooth. This property cannot be changed if the Face style property is set to None.

The Highlight intensity property controls the **VSFACEHIGHLIGHT** system variable. This property determines the size of the highlight on faces to which no material is assigned. A small highlight on an object makes it look smooth and hard. A large highlight on an object makes it look rough or soft. The initial value for the 3D Wireframe, 3D Hidden, Conceptual, and Realistic visual styles is –30, the value can range from –100 to 100. The higher the setting is above 0, the larger the highlight. Settings below 0 set

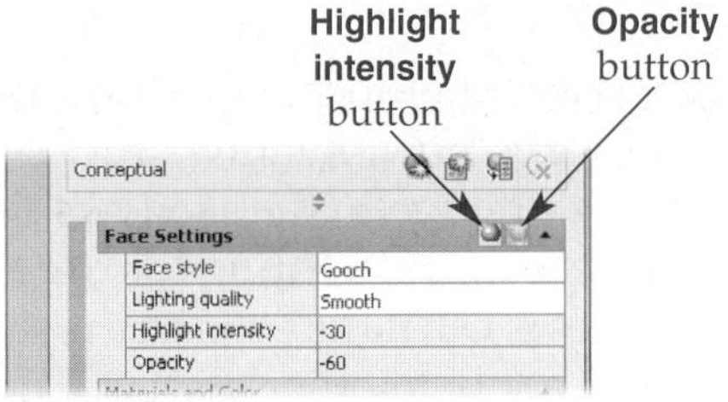

Figure 14-5.
The **Face Settings** category for the 3D Wireframe, 3D Hidden, Conceptual, and Realistic visual styles.

the value, but turn off the effect. To quickly turn the effect on or off, pick the **Highlight intensity** button on the **Face Settings** category title bar. See **Figure 14-5.** This changes the value from negative to positive, or vice versa. This property cannot be changed if the Face style property is set to None.

The Opacity property controls the **VSFACEOPACITY** system variable. This property determines how transparent or opaque faces are in the viewport. The default setting for the 3D Wireframe, 3D Hidden, Conceptual, and Realistic visual styles is –60. The value can range from –100 to 100. When the setting is 0, the faces are completely transparent. When the setting is 100, the faces are completely opaque. Settings below 0 set the value, but turn off the effect. To quickly turn the effect on or off, pick the **Opacity** button on the **Face Settings** category title bar. See **Figure 14-5.** This changes the value from negative to positive, or vice versa. This property cannot be changed if the Face style property is set to None.

The **Materials and Color** subcategory is only displayed when the **Face style** property is set to Real or Gooch. There are three properties in this subcategory—Material display, Face color mode, and Monochrome color or Tint color (depending on the Face color mode setting).

The Material display property controls the **VSMATERIALMODE** system variable. The default setting for the 3D Wireframe, 3D Hidden, Conceptual, and Realistic visual styles is Off. This means that objects display in their assigned color. When the setting is changed to Materials, the objects display the color of the material, but not the textures. When the setting is changed to Materials and textures, full materials are displayed.

The Face color mode property controls the **VSFACECOLORMODE** system variable. This property determines how color is applied to the faces of an object. It is the same as picking a button in the face colors flyout in the **Visual Styles** panel on the **Visualize** tab of the ribbon. The choices are:

- Normal. The object color is applied to faces.
- Monochrome. One color is applied to all faces. This also displays and enables the Monochrome color property.
- Tint. A combination of the object color and a specified color is applied to faces. This also displays and enables the Tint Color property. The Tint property only works when the Material display property is set to Materials.
- Desaturate. The object color is applied to faces, but the saturation of the color is reduced by 30%.

The Monochrome color and Tint Color properties control the **VSMONOCOLOR** system variable. This system variable determines the color that is applied when the Face color mode property is set to Monochrome or Tint.

VSFACECOLORMODE

Ribbon
Visualize > Visual Style — Regular
Visualize > Visual Style — Monochrome
Visualize > Visual Style — Tint
Visualize > Visual Style — Desaturate

Type
VSFACECOLORMODE

CAUTION

Displaying materials and textures on 3D objects in a complex drawing will slow system performance. Set the Face color mode property to Materials and textures only when it is absolutely necessary.

VSSHADOWS

Ribbon
Visualize
> Lights
Shadows Off
Visualize
> Lights
Ground Shadows
Visualize
> Lights
Full Shadows
Type
VSSHADOWS

Environment settings

The Shadow display property controls the **VSSHADOWS** system variable. This property controls if and how shadows are cast when the visual style is set current. It is the same as picking a button in the shadows flyout in the **Lights** panel on the **Visualize** tab of the ribbon. The default setting for the 3D Wireframe, 3D Hidden, Conceptual, and Realistic visual styles is Off. If the property is set to Ground shadow, objects cast shadows on the ground, but not onto other objects. The "ground" is the XY plane of the WCS. The Full shadows setting only works if lights have been placed in the scene and hardware acceleration is enabled.

The Backgrounds property controls the **VSBACKGROUNDS** system variable. This property determines whether or not the preselected background is displayed in the viewport. The default setting for the 3D Wireframe, 3D Hidden, Conceptual, and Realistic visual styles is On. Backgrounds can only be assigned to a view when a named view is created. After the view is created, restore the view to display the background.

VSEDGES

Ribbon
Visualize
> Edge Effects
No Edges
Visualize
> Edge Effects
Isolines
Visualize
> Edge Effects
Facet Edges
Type
VSEDGES

NOTE

Use the **3DCONFIG** command to enable hardware acceleration.

Edge settings

The Edge mode property controls the **VSEDGES** system variable. This property determines how edges on solid objects are represented when the visual style is set current. This is the same as picking a button in the edge flyout in the **Edge Effects** panel on the **Visualize** tab of the ribbon. The default for the 3D Wireframe and Realistic visual styles is Isolines. This means that isolines are displayed. The default for the 3D Hidden and Conceptual visual styles is Facet Edges. This means that faceted edges are displayed. Setting this property to None turns off isolines and facets and displays no edges. If the Face style property is set to None, this property cannot be set to None.

VSEDGEOVERHANG

Ribbon
Visualize
> Edge Effects
Edge Overhang
Type
VSEDGEOVERHANG

The Color property controls the **VSEDGECOLOR** system variable. This property determines the color of all edges on objects in the drawing. It is disabled when the Edge mode property is set to None.

The Number of lines and Always on top properties are displayed when the Edge mode property is set to Isolines. The Number of lines property controls the **ISOLINES** system variable. The Always on top property controls the **VSISOONTOP** system variable. This property determines if isolines are displayed when the model is shaded or hidden. The default for the 3D Wireframe, 3D Hidden, Conceptual, and Realistic visual styles is No. When set to Yes, edges are always displayed.

Edge Modifiers. This subcategory is not displayed if the Edge mode property is set to None. The Overhang property controls the **VSEDGEOVERHANG** system variable. This property can be used to create a hand-sketched appearance by extending the ends of edges. See **Figure 14-6A.** In order to make changes to this property, the **Overhanging edges** button must be on in the **Edge Modifiers** subcategory title bar. See **Figure 14-7.** The **Edge Overhang** button in the **Edge Effects** panel on the **Visualize** tab of the ribbon can also be turned on. The value for Overhang property can range from –100 to 100, which is the number of pixels. The higher the setting, the longer the overhang. A negative value sets the overhang length, but turns off the property. Picking either button makes the value positive and applies the effect (or makes the value negative and turns off the effect).

To adjust the overhang setting using the **Edge Effects** panel, first turn on the effect by picking the button. Then, move the cursor over the slider labeled **Edge overhang**. The cursor changes to left and right arrows and the tooltip reads Adjusts edge overhang.

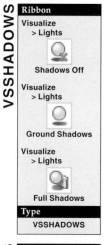

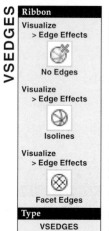

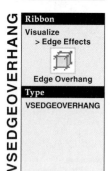

Figure 14-6.
A—Overhanging edges have been turned on for this visual style. B—Edge jitter has been turned on for this visual style.

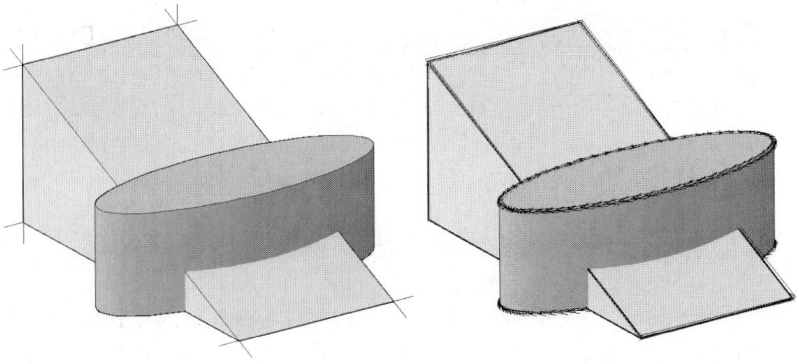

A B

Figure 14-7.
The **Edge Modifiers** subcategory for the 3D Wireframe, 3D Hidden, Conceptual, and Realistic visual styles.

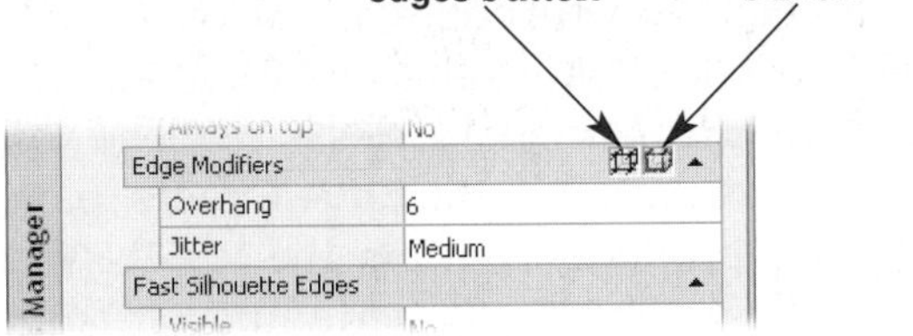

Pick and drag the slider to the left to decrease the overhang or to the right to increase the overhang. The value is displayed on the right-hand side of the slider.

The Jitter property controls the **VSEDGEJITTER** system variable. Jitter makes edges of objects look as if they were sketched with a pencil. See **Figure 14-6B.** In order to make changes to this property, the **Jitter edges** button must be on in the **Edge Modifiers** subcategory title bar. See **Figure 14-7.** The **Edge Jitter** button in the **Edge Effects** panel on the **Visualize** tab of the ribbon can also be turned on. There are four settings from which to choose: Off, Low, Medium, and High. The number of sketched lines increases at each higher setting.

VSEDGEJITTER

Ribbon
visualize
> Edge Effects

Edge Jitter

Type
VSEDGEJITTER

To adjust the jitter setting using the **Edge Effects** panel, first turn on the effect by picking the button. Then, move the cursor over the slider labeled **Edge jitter**. The cursor changes to left and right arrows and the tooltip reads Adjusts edge jitter. Pick and drag the slider to the left to decrease the jitter or to the right to increase the jitter. The value is displayed on the right-hand side of the slider. Remember, there are only four possible settings for jitter.

When the Edge mode property is set to Facet Edges, the Crease angle and Halo gap % properties are displayed in the **Edge Modifiers** subcategory. The Crease angle property controls the **VSEDGESMOOTH** system variable. This property determines how facet edges within a face are displayed based on the angle between adjacent faces. It does not affect edges between faces. See **Figure 14-8.** The value can range from 0 to 180. This is the number of degrees between edges below which a line is displayed. The Halo gap % property is the same as discussed earlier in the 2D Hide—Miscellaneous section.

PROFESSIONAL TIP

Remember, changing settings in the **Visual Styles Manager** redefines the style. Changing settings on the ribbon only changes the current display. It does not redefine the style.

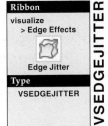

Figure 14-8.
A—The Crease angle property is set to 0. Notice the edges between facets within each face.
B—The Crease angle property is set to 10. The edges are no longer displayed.

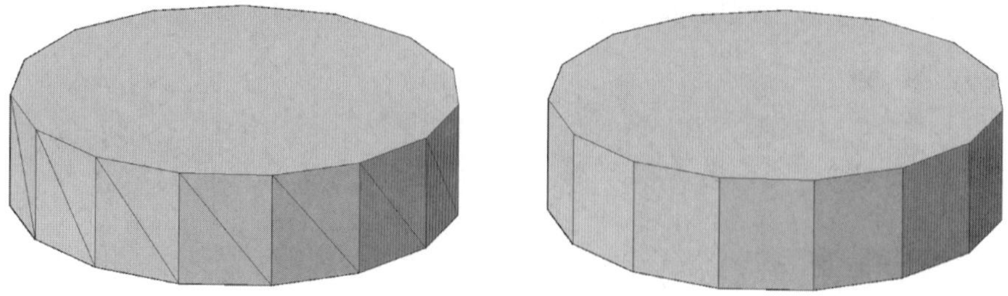

A B

VSSILHEDGES

Ribbon
Visualize
> Edge Effects
Silhouette Edges
Type
VSSILHEDGES

Fast Silhouette Edges. This subcategory is available for all of the Edge mode settings. The Visible property controls the **VSSILHEDGES** system variable. It determines whether or not silhouette edges are displayed around the outside edges of all objects. The default for the 3D Wireframe and Realistic visual styles is No. The default for the 3D Hidden and Conceptual visual styles is Yes. The Yes setting is the same as turning on the **Silhouette Edges** button in the **Edge Effects** panel on the **Visualize** tab of the ribbon.

The Width property controls the **VSSILHWIDTH** system variable. This property determines the width of silhouette lines. It is measured in pixels and the value can range from 1 to 25. Changing this property is the same as adjusting the **Silhouette edge width** slider on the **Edge Effects** panel. To adjust this slider, the **Silhouette Edges** button must be on (or the Visible property set to Yes).

VSOBSCUREEDGES

Ribbon
Visualize
> Edge Effects
Obscured Edge
Type
VSOBSCUREDEDGES

Obscured Edges. This subcategory is only available when the Edge mode property is set to Facet Edges. The Visible property controls the **VSOBSCUREDEDGES** system variable. This property determines whether or not obscured edges are displayed in a hidden or shaded view. See **Figure 14-9.** Setting this property is the same as picking the **Obscured Edge** button in the **Edge Effects** panel on the **Visualize** tab of the ribbon.

The Color property controls the **VSOBSCUREDCOLOR** system variable. Setting this color is the same as picking a color in the drop-down list next to the **Obscured Edge** button in the **Edge Effects** panel. The Linetype property controls the **VSOBSCUREDLTYPE** system variable. These properties function the same as those discussed earlier in this chapter in the 2D Hide—Obscured Lines section.

VSINTERSECTIONEDGES

Ribbon
Visualize
> Edge Effects
Intersection Edge
Type
VSINTERSECTIONEDGES

Intersection Edges. This subcategory is only available when the Edge mode property is set to Facet Edges. The Visible property controls the **VSINTERSECTIONEDGES** system variable. This property determines whether or not lines are displayed where one 3D object intersects another 3D object. See **Figure 14-10.** Setting this property to Yes is the same as turning on the **Intersection Edge** button in the **Edge Effects** panel on the Visualize tab of the ribbon.

Figure 14-9.
A—Obscured lines are not shown. B—The Visible property is set to Yes and obscured lines are shown.

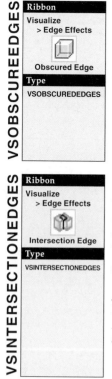

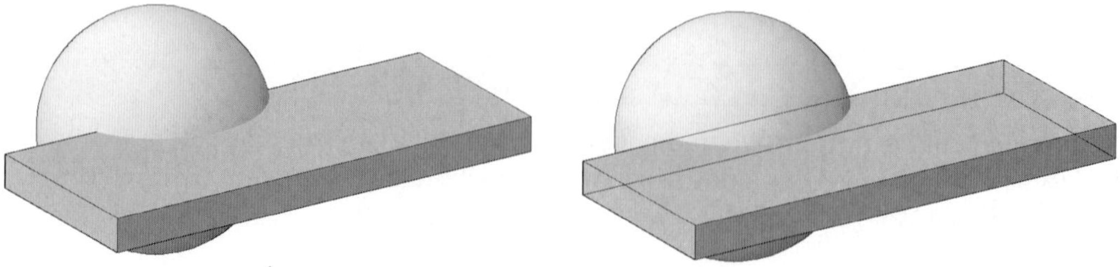

A B

Figure 14-10.
A—A line does not appear where these two objects intersect. B—The Visible property is set to Yes and a line appears at the intersection.

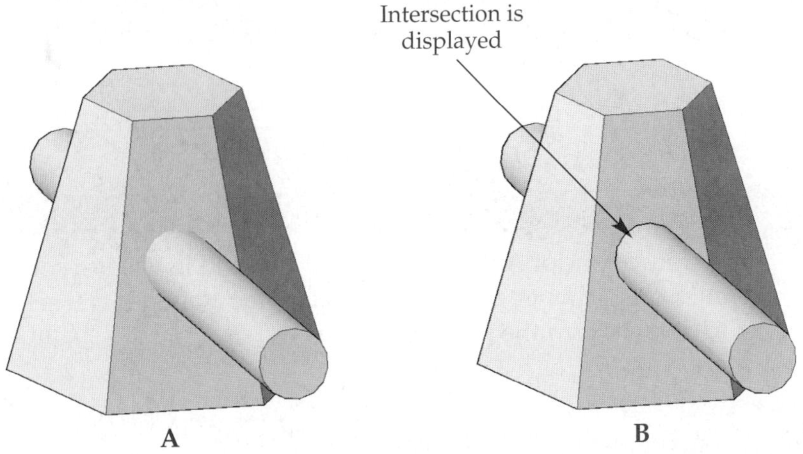

The Color property controls the **VSINTERSECTIONCOLOR** system variable. Setting this variable is the same as picking a color in the drop-down list next to the **Intersection Edge** button in the **Edge Effects** panel. The Linetype property controls the **VSINTERSECTIONLTYPE** system variable. These properties function the same as those discussed earlier in this chapter in the 2D Hide—Intersection Edges section.

PROFESSIONAL TIP

Setting the intersection edges Color property to a color that contrasts with the objects in your model is a good way to quickly check for interference between 3D objects.

Creating Your Own Visual Style

As you saw in the previous sections, you can customize the default AutoCAD visual styles. However, you may also want to create a number of different visual styles to quickly change the display of the scene. Custom visual styles are easy to create.

To create a custom visual style, open the **Visual Style Manager**. Then, pick the **Create New Visual Style** button below the image tiles. You can also right-click in the image tile area and select **Create New Visual Style...** from the shortcut menu. In the **Create New Visual Style** dialog box that appears, type a name for the new style and give it a description. See **Figure 14-11.** Then, pick the **OK** button to create the new visual style.

An image tile is created for the new visual style. The name and description of the visual style appear as help text when the cursor is over the image tile. Select the image tile to display the default properties for the new visual style. Then, change the settings as needed to meet your requirements.

Custom visual styles are only saved in the current drawing. They are not automatically available in other drawings. To use the new visual styles in any drawing, they must be exported to a tool palette. This is discussed in the next section.

Figure 14-11.
Creating a new visual style.

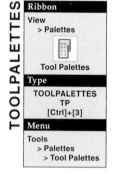

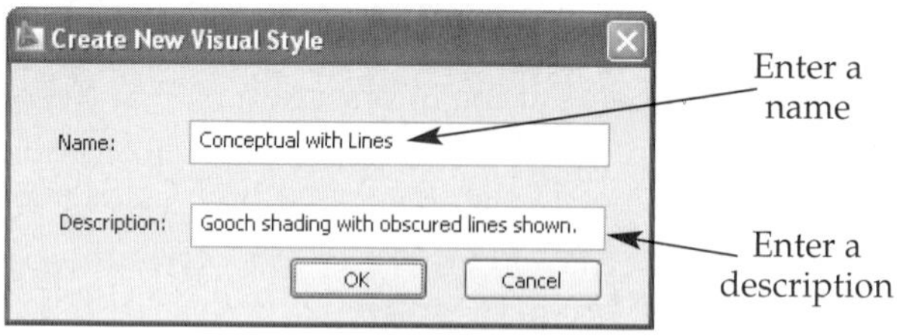

PROFESSIONAL TIP

To return one of AutoCAD's visual styles to its default settings, right-click on the image tile in the **Visual Styles Manager** and select **Restore to default** from the shortcut menu.

Exercise 14-3

Complete the exercise on the Student CD.

Steps for Exporting Visual Styles to a Tool Palette

TOOLPALETTES
Ribbon
View
> Palettes
Tool Palettes
Type
TOOLPALETTES
TP
[Ctrl]+[3]
Menu
Tools
> Palettes
> Tool Palettes

To have custom visual styles available in other drawings, export them to a tool palette. Use the following procedure.

1. Create and customize a visual style as described in the previous section.
2. Open the **Tool Palettes** window.
3. Right-click on the **Tool Palettes** title bar and pick **New Palette** from the shortcut menu.
4. Type the name of the new palette, such as My Visual Styles, in the text box that appears. See **Figure 14-12.**
5. The new palette is added and active. You are ready to export your custom visual styles into it.
6. Select the image tile of the visual style in the **Visual Styles Manager**. Remember, a yellow border appears around the selected image tile.
7. Pick the **Export the Selected Visual Style to the Tool Palette** button below the image tiles in the **Visual Styles Manager**. You can also right-click on the image tile and select **Export to Active Tool Palette** from the shortcut menu.

A new tool now appears in the palette with the same image, name, and description as the visual style in the **Visual Styles Manager**. See **Figure 14-13.** Selecting the tool applies the visual style to the current viewport. You can also right-click on the tool to display a shortcut menu. Using this menu, you can apply the visual style to the current viewport, all viewports, or add the visual style to the current drawing. The shortcut menu also allows you to rename the tool, access the properties of the visual style, and delete the visual style from the palette.

PROFESSIONAL TIP

A visual style can be added as a tool on a tool palette by dragging its image tile from the **Visual Styles Manager** and dropping it onto the tool palette.

Figure 14-12.
Creating a new tool palette on which to place visual style tools.

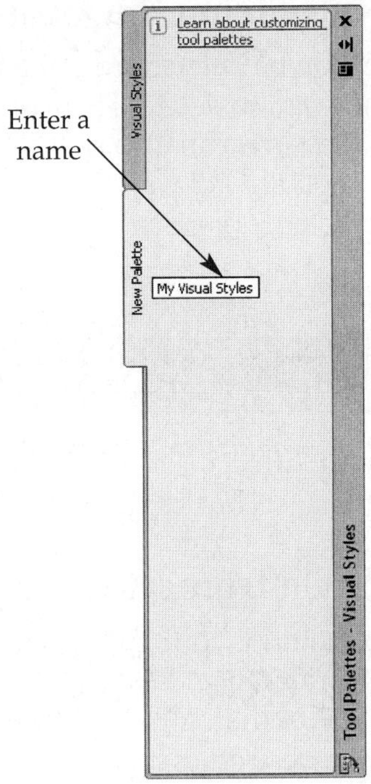

Figure 14-13.
A visual style has been copied to the tool palette as a tool.

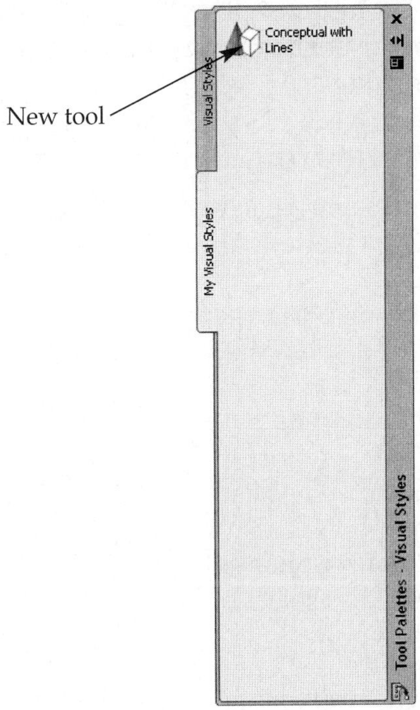

Exercise 14-4

Complete the exercise on the Student CD.

Deleting Visual Styles from the Visual Styles Manager

Custom visual styles can be deleted from the **Visual Styles Manager**. Pick the image tile of the visual style you want to delete. Then, pick the **Delete the Selected Visual Style** button below the image tiles. You can also right-click on the image tile and select **Delete** from the shortcut menu. You are *not* warned about the deletion. The default AutoCAD visual styles cannot be deleted, nor can a visual style that is currently in use.

Plotting Visual Styles

A visual style not only affects the on-screen display, it also affects plots. To plot objects with a specific visual style, use the following guidelines.

Plotting a Visual Style from Model Space

There are two basic methods for plotting from model space. The method you use strictly depends on your preference.

Method 1. Open the **Plot** dialog box and expand it by picking the **More Options** (>) button. Then, select the desired display from the **Shade plot** drop-down list in the **Shaded viewport options** area. Finally, plot the drawing. With this method, the current visual style is irrelevant.

Method 2. Set the desired visual style current. Then, open the **Plot** dialog box. Select **As displayed** from the **Shade plot** drop-down list in the **Shaded viewport options** area. Finally, plot the drawing.

Plotting a Visual Style from Paper Space

When plotting from paper space, the shade plot properties of the viewport(s) govern how the viewport is plotted. The viewport(s) can be set to plot visual styles in three different ways.

Method 1. Select the viewport in paper space and right-click to display the shortcut menu. Pick **Shade plot** to display the cascading menu. Then, select the appropriate visual style.

Method 2. Use the **Properties** palette to set the Shade plot property of the viewport. To do this, select the viewport in paper space and open the **Properties** palette. Pick the Shade plot property in the **Misc** category and change the setting to the desired option. The Shade plot property is also available in the **Quick Properties** palette.

Method 3. Use the **Visual Styles** suboption of the **Shadeplot** option of the **MVIEW** command. When prompted to select objects, pick the border of the viewport. Do not pick the objects in the viewport.

NOTE

The visual style of the viewport may also be selected when you create a viewport configuration in the **Viewports** dialog box (**VPORTS** command). Select the viewport in the **Preview** area of the dialog box. Then, pick the visual style desired from the **Visual Style:** drop-down list at the bottom of the dialog box. The **VPORTS** command can be used in model space or paper (layout) space.

Introduction to Rendering

Visual styles provide a way to plot your 3D scene to paper or a file, but control over the appearance is limited to the visual style settings. In Chapter 3, you were briefly introduced to the **RENDER** command. The **RENDER** command offers complete control over the scene and, with its features, you can create photorealistic images. In this chapter, you will be introduced to AutoCAD's rendering and lighting tools. Materials are discussed in later chapters along with more advanced rendering and lighting features.

Ribbon
Output
> Render

Render

Type
RENDER
RR

Menu
View
> Render
> Render

RENDER

When you render a scene, you are making a realistic image of your design that can be printed, displayed on a web page, or used in a presentation. To create an attractive rendering, you have to figure out what view you want to display, where the lights should be placed, what types of materials need to be applied to the 3D objects, and the kind of output that is needed. This section shows you how to create a quick rendering of your scene.

Introduction to Lights

Lights provide the illumination to a scene and are essential for rendering. There are three types of lighting in AutoCAD—default lighting, sunlight, and user-created lighting. AutoCAD automatically creates two default light sources in every scene. These lights ensure that all surfaces on the model are illuminated and visible. The types of lighting are discussed in more detail in Chapter 16.

A scene can be rendered with the default lights, but the results are usually not adequate to produce a photorealistic image. See **Figure 14-14.** The appearance is very artificial and no shadows are created. Shadows anchor objects to the scene and make them look real. See **Figure 14-15.** Without shadows, objects appear to float in space. Because the default lights do not cast shadows, other lights must be added to the scene and set to cast shadows. When a light is added to a scene, the default lights must be turned off. The first time you add a light, you receive a warning to this effect (unless the warning has been disabled).

In this section, you will learn how to add sunlight to the scene. Chapter 16 provides detailed information on lighting. Sunlight is produced by an automated distant light. Sunlight can be turned on by picking the **Sun Status** button in the **Sun** panel on the **Visualize** tab of the ribbon. The button background is blue when sunlight is on. See **Figure 14-16.**

Ribbon
Visualize
> Sun

Sun Status

Type
SUNSTATUS

SUNSTATUS

If the **Default Lighting** button is on in the **Lights** panel when the **Sun Status** button is turned on, a warning dialog box is displayed. This dialog box gives you choices to either turn off default lighting or keep it on. You cannot see the effects of sunlight with default lighting turned on, so it is recommended to turn it off.

If the current visual style is set to display full shadows, you should now see shadows in the scene, provided there are areas to receive shadows. Remember, hardware acceleration must be enabled to display full shadows.

The **Sun date** and **Sun time** sliders in the **Time & Location** panel on the **Visualize** tab of the ribbon are active when sunlight is turned on. You can drag the sliders to adjust the date and time. The current date and time are displayed on the right-hand end of the sliders. As you drag the sliders, the shadows in the scene change to reflect the settings.

Figure 14-14.
A scene rendered with the default AutoCAD lighting.

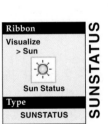

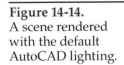

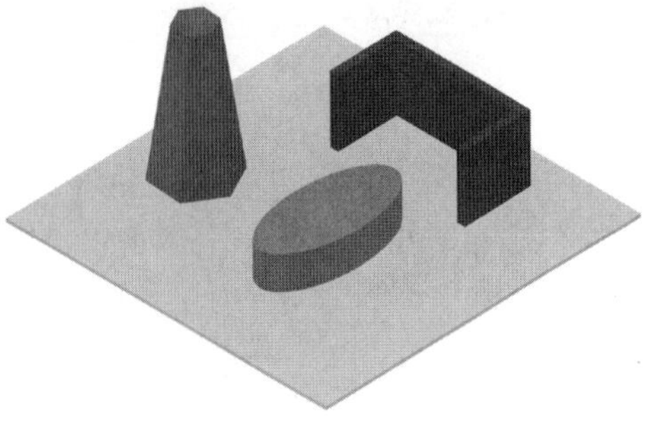

Figure 14-15.
A light has been added and set to cast shadows. Compare this rendering with Figure 14-14.

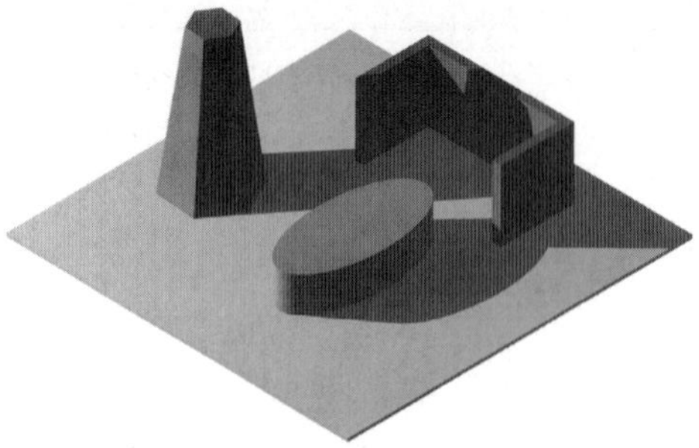

Figure 14-16.
The **Lights**, **Sun**, and **Time & Location** panels on the **Visualize** tab of the ribbon.

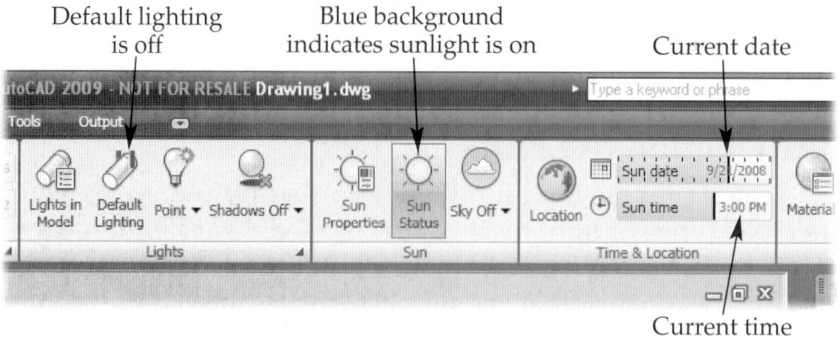

Rendering the Scene

The **Render** panel on the **Output** tab of the ribbon is shown in **Figure 14-17.** There are two buttons located in this control panel to initiate a rendering. If you pick the **Render** button, the **Render** window appears (by default) and AutoCAD immediately starts rendering the viewport. You will see the rendered tiles appear in the image pane as they are calculated. The **Render** window is explained more in the next section.

If you pick the **Region** button, you are prompted to pick two points in the viewport, similar to performing a window selection. The selected area is rendered in the viewport. Rendering a cropped area is often used to test areas of the scene for possible problems before performing the final rendering.

Also in the **Render** panel you will find the render preset drop-down list. This is located in the upper-right corner of the panel and its tooltip is Selects a render preset. This list gives you a selection of rendering presets based on image quality. The choices are:

- Draft
- Low
- Medium
- High
- Presentation

The Draft entry produces the lowest-quality rendering. The Presentation entry produces the highest-quality rendering. The better the quality, the longer it takes to complete the rendering process.

Figure 14-17.
The **Render** panel on the **Output** tab of the ribbon.

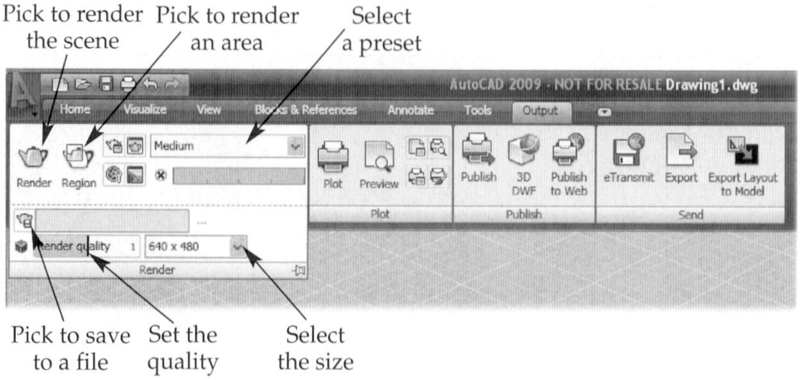

PROFESSIONAL TIP

Rendering a complex drawing may take a very long time and you do not want to repeat it because of some small error. It is important to make sure that everything in the scene is perfect before the final rendering. By rendering a cropped region and using lower-quality renderings, you can verify the appearance of any questionable areas without performing a full rendering.

Introduction to the Render Window

The **Render** window is composed of three main areas. See **Figure 14-18.** The image pane is where the rendering appears. The statistics pane shows the current rendering settings. The history pane shows a list of all of the images rendered from the drawing, with the most recent at the top.

You can zoom into the image in the image pane for detailed inspection. Use the mouse scroll wheel or the **Zoom +** and **Zoom –** entries in the **Tools** pull-down menu of the **Render** window. In the **File** pull-down menu of the **Render** window, select **Save...** to save the image selected in the history pane to an image file. The symbol in front of the image in the history pane changes to a folder with a red check mark on it. The **Save Copy...** option in the **File** pull-down menu of the **Render** window creates a copy of the image without modifying the original in the history pane.

NOTE

Advanced rendering is discussed in Chapter 17.

Exercise 13-5

Complete the exercise on the Student CD.

Figure 14-18.
The **Render** window.

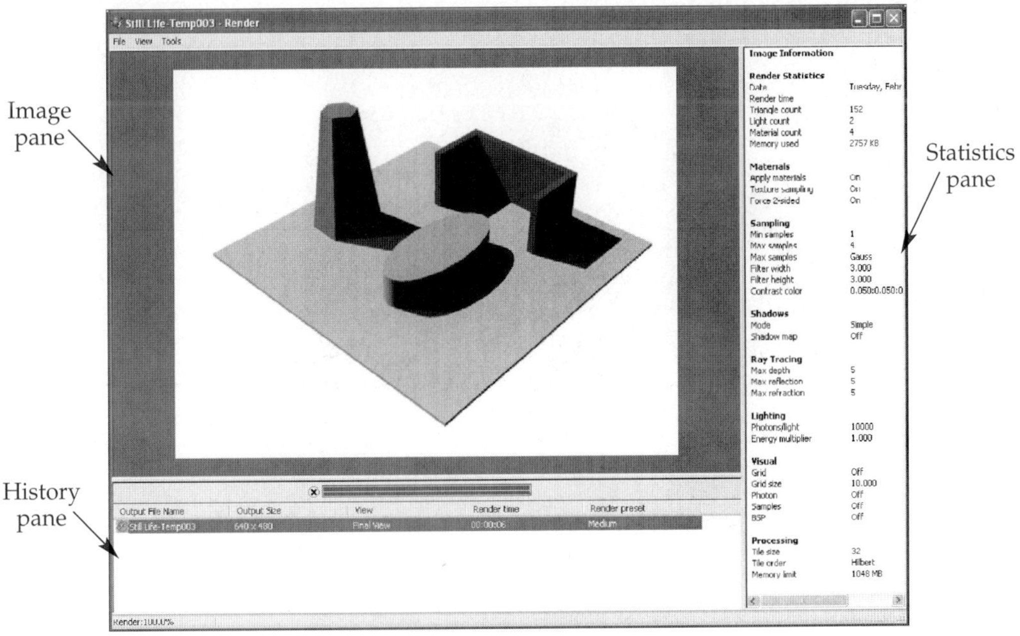

Chapter Test

Answer the following questions. Write your answers on a separate sheet of paper or complete the electronic chapter test on the Student CD.

1. What is the **Visual Styles Manager**?
2. Name the five default AutoCAD visual styles that can be edited in the **Visual Styles Manager**.
3. Describe the difference between setting the Lighting quality property to Smooth and Faceted.
4. What does the Desaturate setting of the Face color mode property do?
5. What has to be added to a scene before full shadows are displayed?
6. If you want to make your scene look hand sketched, but the Overhang and Jitter properties are not available, what other setting(s) do you have to change?
7. How do you set a visual style to display silhouette edges?
8. List the four settings for the Jitter property.
9. What is an *intersection edge?*
10. How do you make your own visual styles available in other drawings?
11. Which visual styles cannot be deleted?
12. How can you turn on sunlight?
13. Explain the function of the **Region** button in the **Render** panel on the ribbon.
14. Name the three main areas of the **Render** window.
15. How can you save a rendered image in the **Render** window?

Drawing Problems

1. In this problem, you will construct a living room scene using some simple shapes and blocks available through **DesignCenter**.
   A. Draw a 12′ × 12′ × 1″ box.
   B. Draw two boxes to represent walls, 12′ × 4″ × 8′. Position them as shown below.
   C. Open **DesignCenter** and select the **DC Online** tab. In the Standard Parts category listing area, expand the 3D Architectural tree.
   D. Find 3D blocks for the following objects, drag and drop them into the scene, and position them as shown: sofa, table, end table, lamp, plant, entertainment center, and chair.
   E. The blocks do not have to be exactly the same as shown below and may need to be scaled up or down.
   F. Apply each of the five default visual styles to the viewport and plot each. Use the As Displayed option in the **Plot** dialog box. Note the differences in each one.
   G. Save the drawing as P14_01.

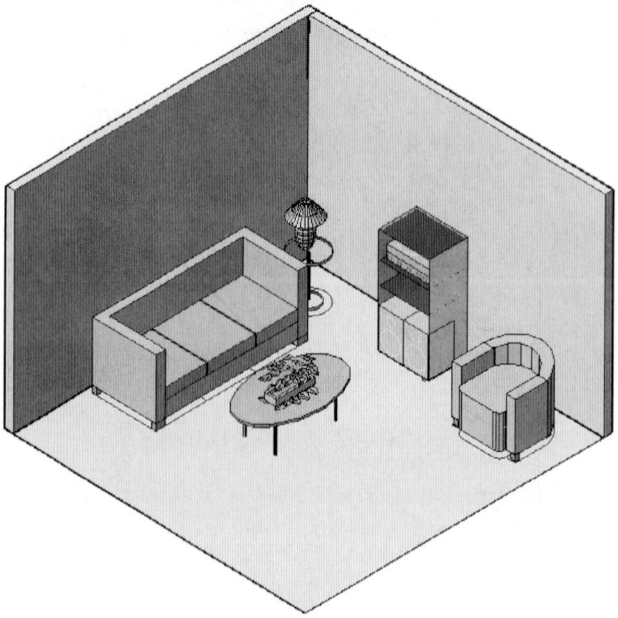

2. In this problem, you will create a new visual style to display the scene as if it is hand sketched.
   A. Open drawing P14_01.
   B. Create a new visual style named Hand Sketched with a description of Displays objects as sketched.
   C. Change the overhang and jitter settings to make the scene look as shown below.
   D. Change any other settings you like.
   E. Plot the scene. Select the new visual style in the **Shade plot** drop-down list.
   F. Export the new visual style to a tool palette so that it can be used in other drawings.
   G. Save the drawing as P14_02.

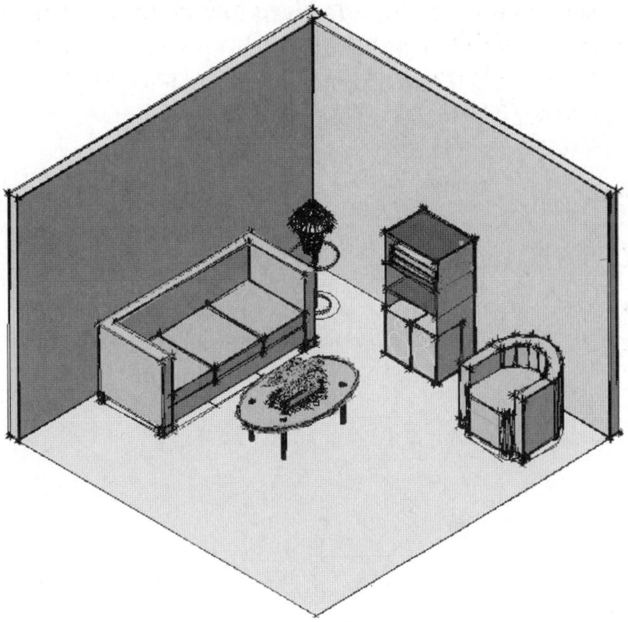

3. In this problem, you will create a realistic looking image of the car fender that you created in Chapter 9.
   A. Open drawing P09_03.
   B. Freeze any layers needed so that only the fender is displayed. Display the fender in the color you want it to be.
   C. Draw a planar surface to represent the ground.
   D. Set the Realistic visual style current. Then, turn on the highlight intensity and full shadows. Also, set the Edge Mode property to None.
   E. Turn on sunlight. Adjust the **Sun date** and **Sun time** sliders to make the shadows look as shown.
   F. Render the scene and save it as a JPEG image. Name the file P14_03.jpg.
   G. Save the drawing as P14_03.

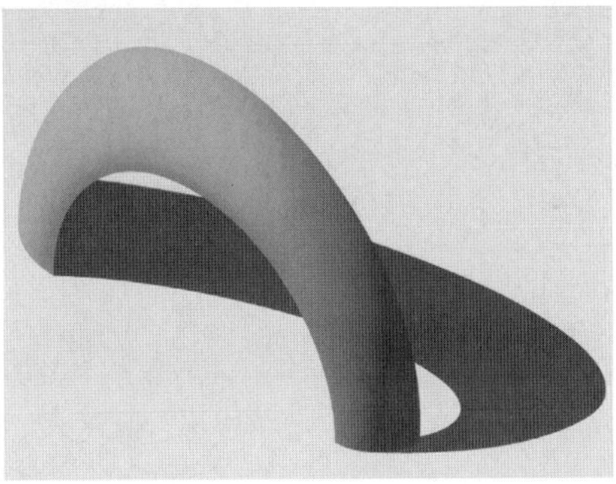

4. This problem demonstrates the differences in rendering time and image quality of the five different rendering presets.
   A. Open any 3D drawing from a previous chapter and display an appropriate isometric view. Change the projection to perspective, if it is not already current.
   B. Turn on sunlight and set the **Sun date** and **Sun time** sliders to place the shadows where you want them. Tip: Turning on full shadows allows you to locate the shadows without rendering.
   C. Render the scene once for each rendering preset: Draft, Low, Medium, High, and Presentation.
   D. In the history pane of the **Render** window, note the differences between the rendering time for each rendering.
   E. Save each image with a corresponding name: P14_04_Draft.jpg, P14_04_Low.jpg, P14_04_Medium.jpg, P14_04_High.jpg, and P14_04_Presentation.jpg.
   F. Save the drawing as P14_04.

CHAPTER 15

Materials in AutoCAD

Learning Objectives

After completing this chapter, you will be able to:

✓ Attach materials to the objects in a drawing.
✓ Change the properties of existing materials.
✓ Create new materials.

A ***material*** is simply an image stretched over an object to make it appear as though the object is made out of wood, marble, glass, brick, or various other materials. AutoCAD provides an assortment of materials that can be used in your drawings to create a realistic scene. The materials are grouped into categories to make them easier to find.

Materials are easy to attach. They can be dragged and dropped onto the objects, attached to all selected objects, and even attached based on the object's layer. Once the material is attached, you can adjust how the material is *mapped* to the object. If the current visual style is set to display materials in the viewport, you can immediately see the effects on the object. The properties of a material can also be changed to make it look shinier, softer, smoother, rougher, and so on. When you finally render the scene, you will see the full effect of the materials.

PROFESSIONAL TIP

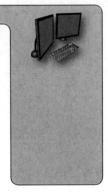

The "typical" installation of AutoCAD includes approximately 75 sample materials. However, approximately 425 materials are available if you choose to install the materials library. If you did not choose that option during installation of AutoCAD, you can use the installation CD to add the full materials library. For information describing how to do this, select **Help**>**Help** or press [F1] to display the online documentation. Then, in the **Contents** tab, select the **Installation and Licensing Guides** topic. Browse the topic for information on installing additional features such as the materials library.

Materials Library

TOOLPALETTES

Type
TOOLPALETTES
TP
[Ctrl]+[3]

Menu
Tools
> Palettes
> Tool Palettes

The ***materials library*** is the location where all materials are stored. AutoCAD uses tool palettes as the materials library. The **Materials** tool palette group contains eight sample palettes:

- **Concrete—Materials Sample**
- **Doors and Windows—Materials Sample**
- **Fabric—Materials Sample**
- **Finishes—Materials Sample**
- **Flooring—Materials Sample**
- **Masonry—Materials Sample**
- **Metals—Materials Sample**
- **Woods and Plastics—Materials Sample**

To display only the palettes in the **Materials** group, right-click on the title bar of the **Tool Palettes** window and select **Materials** from the shortcut menu, **Figure 15-1.** Each palette contains several material tools. See **Figure 15-2.** Each material is displayed in the palette as a sphere on a checkered background. The background is used to make the transparent materials, such as glass, more visible. The material name is, by default, shown to the right of the sphere. You may want to increase the width of the **Tool Palettes** window to see the complete name of each material. Tool palette options, such as display options, are covered in detail in Chapter 23.

Figure 15-1.
Displaying only the tool palettes in the **Materials** group. Notice that the materials library has also been installed.

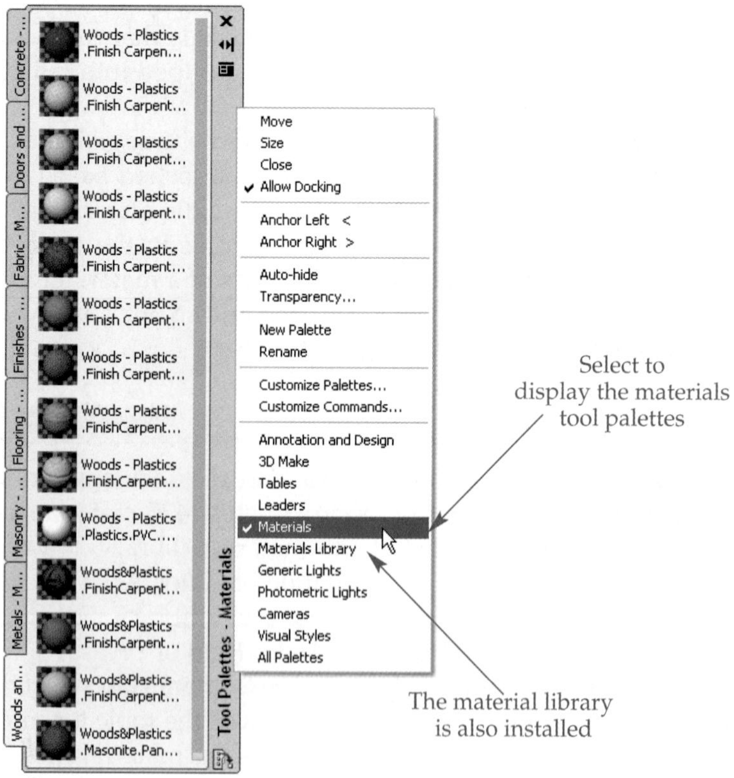

Figure 15-2.
Selected tool palettes in the **Materials** group. A—**Doors and Windows**. B—**Flooring**. C—**Masonry**. D—**Woods and Plastics**.

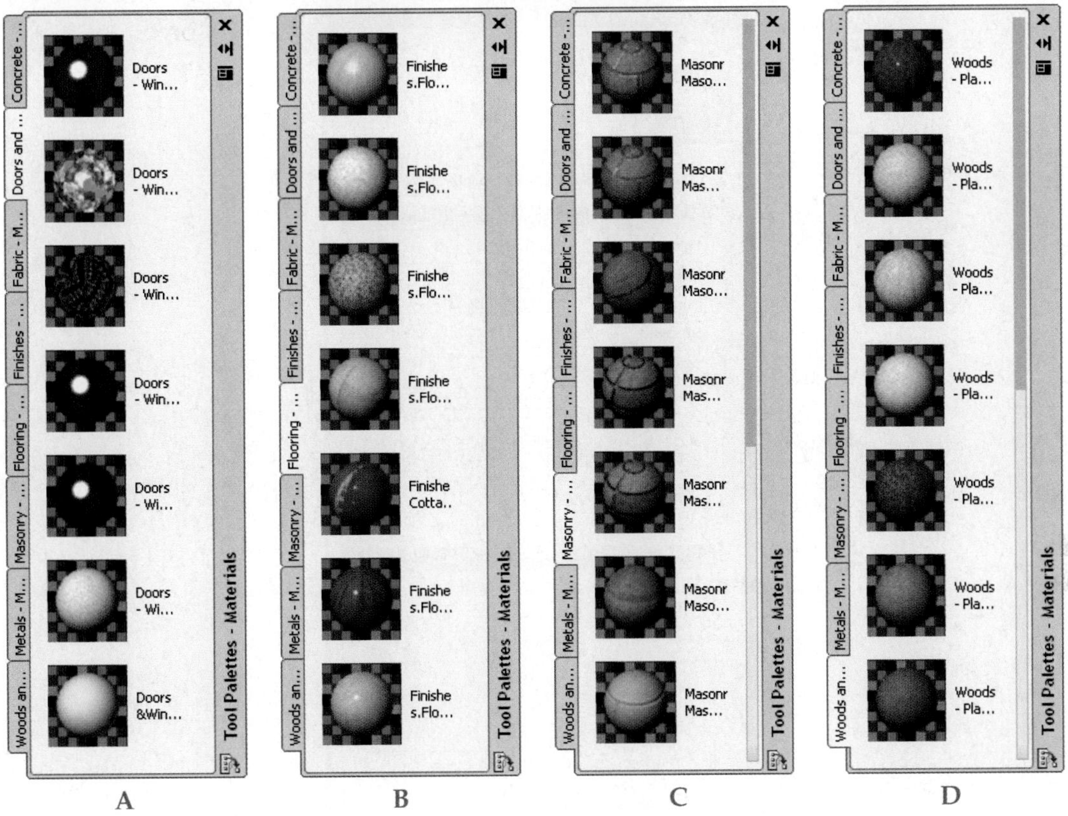

The properties of the individual materials can be accessed by right-clicking on the tool in the palette and picking **Properties...** from the shortcut menu. In the **Tool Properties** dialog box that is displayed, you can change the name, description of the material, and material properties. See **Figure 15-3.** The **Tool Properties** dialog box is discussed in more detail in Chapter 23. Changes made to the material in this dialog box only affect the material tool. To apply these changes to objects in the current scene, the material must be reattached to the objects. The features in the material editor in the **Tool Properties** dialog box are identical to those found in the **Materials** palette, which is discussed later in this chapter.

Exercise 15-1

Complete the exercise on the Student CD.

Applying and Removing Materials

To attach a material to an object in the drawing, pick once on the material image or name in the tool palette. As the cursor is moved into the drawing area, a paint brush icon appears next to the cursor. Pick the object to which you want the material applied. You can also drag the material from the tool palette and drop it onto an object. To apply a material only to a face on an object, hold the [Ctrl] key and pick the face. To apply a different material to an object, simply select the new material in the tool palette and pick the object again.

Figure 15-3.
The properties of a material tool.

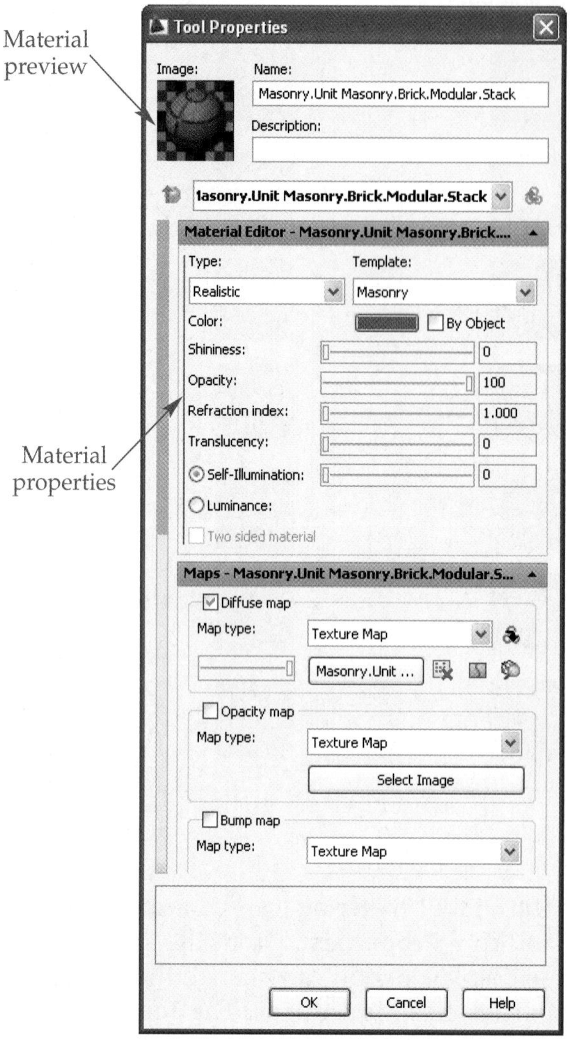

If you use the tool palette to assign a material that has already been loaded into the drawing, an AutoCAD alert appears warning of a material name conflict. AutoCAD needs to know how to handle the duplicate material. If you pick **Save this Material as a Copy**, the material is added to the drawing as Copy of *material name* (or Copy 1 of *material name*, Copy 2 of *material name*, and so on). Picking **Overwrite the Material** replaces the material in the drawing with the one you are attempting to attach. This is probably the best option in most cases, but any changes made to the existing material in the drawing are lost. The **Cancel** button in the alert dialog box allows you to cancel the operation. To avoid this naming-conflict situation, use the **Materials** palette to apply any materials already existing in the drawing to other objects. The **Materials** palette is discussed later.

MATERIALATTACH

Ribbon
Visualize
> Materials
Attach By Layer
Attach By Layer

You can use the **MATERIALATTACH** command to assign materials to the layers in your drawing. Once a material is assigned to a layer, any object on that layer is displayed in the material, as long as the object's material property is set to ByLayer. When objects are created in AutoCAD, the default "material" assigned to them is ByLayer. If your objects are organized on layers, this is the easiest way to attach materials. You can override the layer material by applying a material to individual objects.

Figure 15-4 shows the **Material Attachment Options** dialog box displayed by the **MATERIALATTACH** command. The list on the left side of the dialog box shows the materials loaded into the drawing. The right side of the dialog box shows the layers in

Figure 15-4.
Attaching materials to layers.

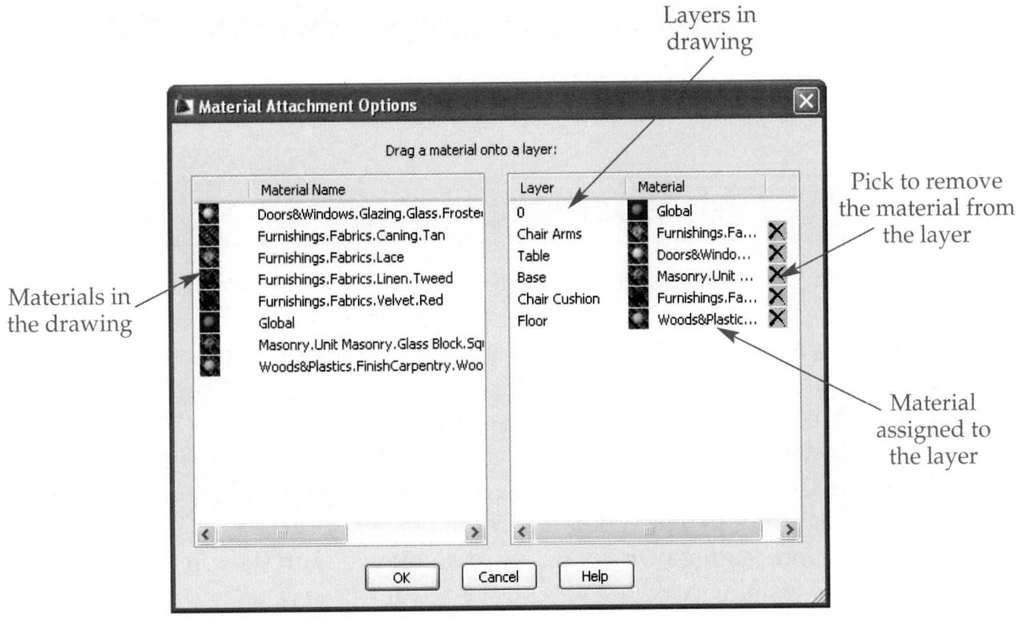

the drawing and the material attached to each layer. When no material is attached to a layer, the material is listed as Global. The Global material is a "blank" material in every drawing. To attach a material to a layer, drag the material from the list on the left and drop it onto the layer name on the right. To remove a material from a layer, pick the **X** button next to the material name on the right side of the dialog box. When all settings have been made, pick the **OK** button to close the dialog box.

The easiest way to remove a material is with the **Properties** palette. To remove a material from an object or subobject, simply change its Material property in the **3D Visualization** category to Global. If a material has not been assigned to the object's layer, the property can also be set to ByLayer. See **Figure 15-5.**

PROFESSIONAL TIP

A material can be applied to an object by dragging the material from the tool palette and dropping it onto the object. Also, a material can be loaded into the drawing without attaching it to an object by picking the material tool once in the tool palette and pressing [Enter] or by dragging and dropping it into a blank area of the drawing. This makes the material available in the drawing.

Figure 15-5.
Removing a material from an object. A—The material is assigned. B—The material is removed.

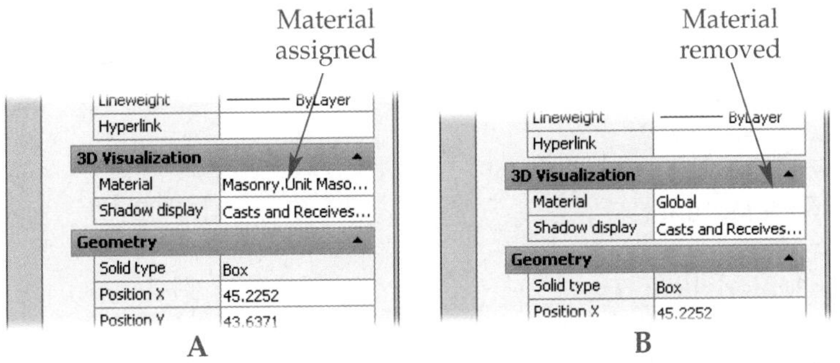

Exercise 15-2

Complete the exercise on the Student CD.

VSMATERIALMODE

Ribbon
Visualize > Materials — Materials and Textures Off
Visualize > Materials — Materials On/Textures Off
Visualize > Materials — Materials and Textures On
Type
VSMATERIALMODE

Material Display Options

As you learned in the previous chapter, visual styles control how materials are displayed in the viewport. The Material display property of a visual style can be set to display materials and textures, materials only, or neither materials nor textures. The **Materials** panel on the **Visualize** tab of the ribbon has three buttons in a flyout that correspond to, but override, this property setting:

- **Materials and Textures Off.** Objects are displayed in their assigned colors.
- **Materials On/Textures Off.** Objects are displayed in the basic color of the material, but no other material details are displayed.
- **Materials and Textures On.** Objects are displayed with the effects of all material properties visible.

Materials Palette

MATERIALS

Ribbon
Visualize > Materials — Materials
Type
MATERIALS
MAT
Menu
Tools > Palettes > Materials
View > Render > Materials...

When materials are attached to objects, subobjects, or layers, they are automatically added to the **Materials** palette. The **Materials** palette contains all of the materials loaded into the current drawing. It also provides a material editor for modifying the materials. See Figure 15-6.

At the top of the window is the **Available Materials in Drawing** pane. Samples (swatches) are displayed in this pane representing the materials that have been loaded into the drawing. A drawing icon in the lower-right corner of a swatch indicates that the material is currently in use in the drawing. In addition to the loaded materials, the default AutoCAD material Global appears in the list of swatches. The swatch outlined in yellow is the currently selected material. Its properties are displayed in the material editor. The material editor consists of several panes, including the **Material Editor**, **Maps**, **Advanced Lighting Override**, **Material Scaling & Tiling**, and **Material Offset & Preview** panes.

Swatch Options

Above the material swatches, at the right-hand end of the **Available Materials in Drawing** title bar, there is a square button. This is the **Toggle Display Mode** button, which toggles the swatch area between the display of multiple materials to a single material. See Figure 15-7. The single-swatch display mode provides a much better view of the details of the selected material. Arrow buttons on either side of the single material swatch allow you to select the next or previous material swatch. Immediately below the swatches are several buttons:

- **Swatch Geometry**
- **Checkered Underlay**
- **Preview Swatch Lighting Model**
- **Create New Material**
- **Purge from Drawing**
- **Indicate Materials in Use**
- **Apply Material to Objects**
- **Remove Materials from Selected Objects**

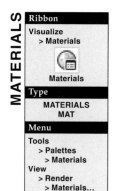

Figure 15-6.
The **Materials** palette provides swatches of the materials in the drawing and a material editor for modifying material properties.

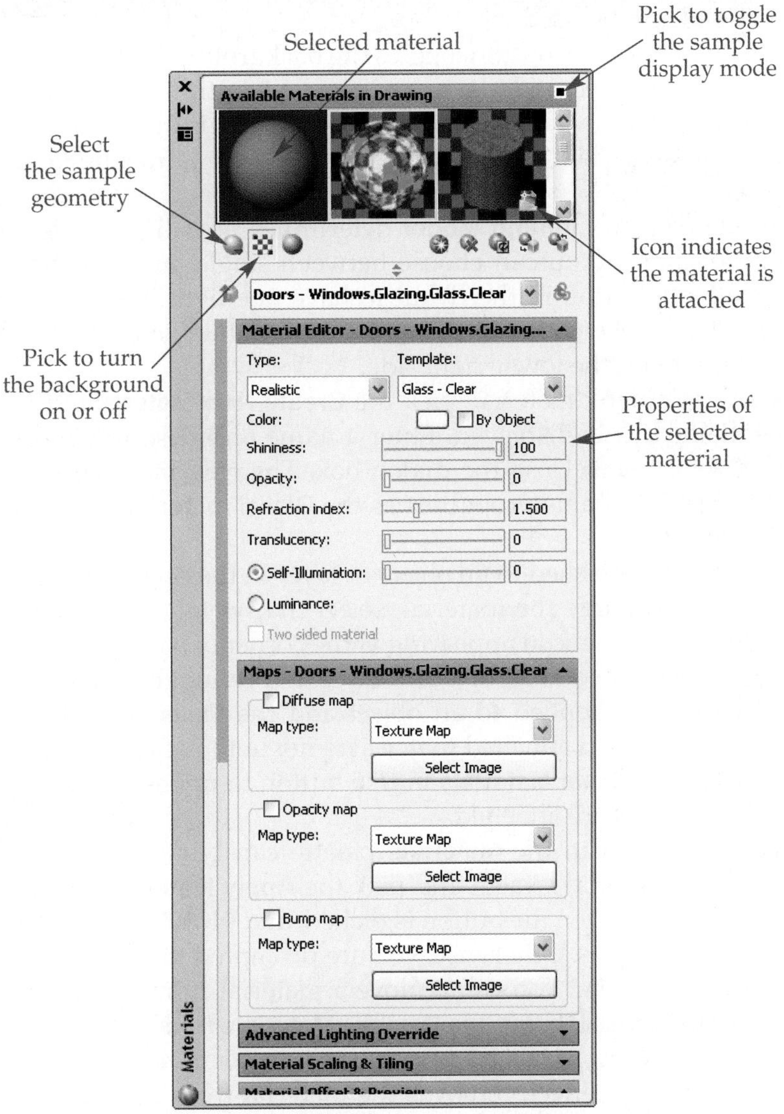

Figure 15-7.
The material swatches in the **Materials** palette can be displayed in different sizes. A—The medium setting. B—The full setting.

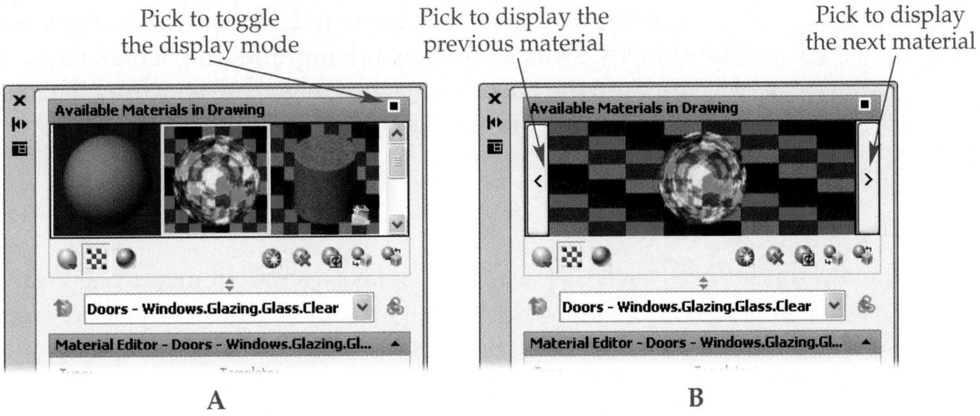

The sample geometry in the swatch can be displayed as a sphere, box, or cylinder. Pick the **Swatch Geometry** flyout and select the geometry to display in the swatch. This allows you to preview the material on an object of a similar shape to the object on which the material will be used.

The **Checkered Underlay** button toggles the background in the swatch from checkered to black. The checkered underlayment is needed for transparent, semitransparent, and dark-colored materials. These materials may not be visible on a black background. The checkered underlayment also allows you to view the refraction quality of a transparent material.

The **Preview Swatch Lighting Model** determines how lighting is applied to the geometry in the sample. You can choose between single and dual lighting sources. Pick the **Single Light** button in the flyout to have one light illuminate the geometry from the upper-left side. Pick the **Back Light** button in the flyout to add a second light behind the geometry on the lower-right side.

To create a new, blank material, pick the **Create New Material** button. The **Create New Material** dialog box is displayed. Enter a name and description for the material and pick the **OK** button to close the dialog box. The new material is displayed as a new swatch and has the same properties as the Global material. Changing properties is discussed later.

If a material is not attached to an object or layer in the drawing, it can be removed from the drawing. To purge the material, select the swatch and pick the **Purge from Drawing** button. A drawing icon appearing at the corner of a material swatch indicates that the material is attached to an object or layer and cannot be purged.

When a material is applied to an object and the **Materials** palette is open, the drawing icon indicating an attached material is not automatically added to the material swatch. Pick the **Indicate Materials in Use** button to update the material swatches to show which materials are attached.

Any material shown in the **Materials** palette can be attached to objects in the drawing. Select the material swatch and pick the **Apply Material to Objects** button. If any objects are selected when the button is picked, and **PICKFIRST** is set to 1, the material is applied to the objects. Otherwise, you are prompted to select objects.

You learned earlier that you can remove a material from an object by setting its Material property to Global. Picking the **Remove Materials from Selected Objects** button allows you to set an object's Material property to ByLayer. If no material is assigned to the object's layer, this, in effect, removes the material from the object. However, if a material is assigned to the object's layer, the object is displayed in that material.

PROFESSIONAL TIP

A material can be assigned to an object by dragging and dropping from the **Materials** palette. Select the material swatch in the **Materials** palette, drag the swatch into the drawing, and drop it onto the object to which you want the material attached. If you are attaching the material to a subobject, press the [Ctrl] key before dropping the material.

Swatch Shortcut Menu

Right-clicking in the swatch display area displays a shortcut menu. See Figure 15-8. This shortcut menu provides some options that are not available anywhere else:

- **Select Objects with Material.** This selects all objects in the drawing that have the current material attached to them. This option only selects objects that have the material attached *explicitly*. In other words, if the material is attached to an object's layer and the object's Material property is set to ByLayer, this option will *not* select the object.

Figure 15-8.
The shortcut menu displayed by right-clicking in the swatch display area of the **Materials** palette.

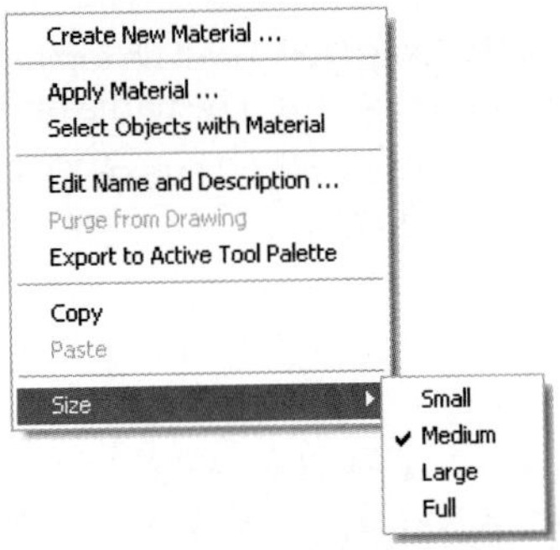

- **Edit Name and Description.** Displays a dialog box in which the name and description of the material can be changed.
- **Export to Active Tool Palette.** Exports the selected material to the current tool palette, as long as the palette is not read only. Tool palettes are discussed in detail in Chapter 23.
- **Copy and Paste options.** These two options allow you to copy the selected material and paste it back into the swatch area as a new material with the same properties. These options are very useful when creating a group of similar materials.
- **Size.** Displays a cascading menu with options for the display size of the material swatches—**Small**, **Medium**, **Large**, and **Full**.

Exercise 15-3

Complete the exercise on the Student CD.

Creating and Modifying Materials

Before creating and modifying materials, it is important to know your way around the **Materials** palette. There are six panes in the **Materials** palette:

- **Available Materials in Drawing**
- **Material Editor**
- **Maps**
- **Advanced Lighting Override**
- **Material Scaling & Tiling**
- **Material Offset & Preview**

The **Available Materials in Drawing** pane, discussed in the previous section, contains the material-preview swatches and related buttons. Depending on the material, some or all of the other five panes will be displayed.

Below the **Available Materials in Drawing** pane and above the **Material Editor** pane are three controls for working with nested maps. See **Figure 15-9A.** Maps are discussed later in this chapter. The drop-down list contains the ***mapping tree.*** The name in bold at the top of the list is the name of the current level of navigation. See **Figure 15-9B.** Picking one of the other levels in the tree navigates to that level. The name of that level is moved to the top of the drop-down and displayed in bold. The panes displayed in the **Materials** palette are only those containing property settings for the currently selected level.

Figure 15-9.
Navigating the material mapping tree. A—The top level. Note the navigation tools. B—The mapping tree is displayed in the drop-down list. The name of the current level is displayed in bold.

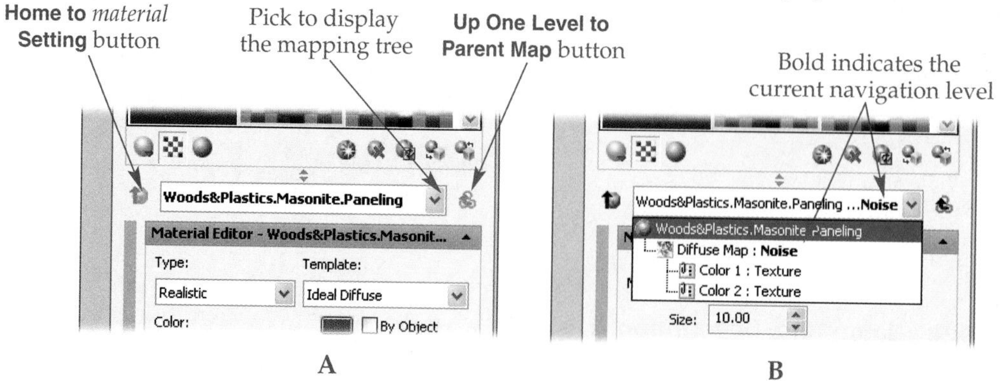

The button to the right of the drop-down list is **Up One Level to Parent Map**. Picking this button navigates up one step in the mapping tree. On the left side of the drop-down list is the **Home to** *material* **Setting** button. Picking this button navigates to the top level of the mapping tree, or the top of the material definition, no matter where you are in the mapping tree.

Creating New Materials

The basic properties of the material selected in the **Materials** palette are displayed in the **Material Editor** pane. Additional properties are displayed in the other panes in the **Materials** palette. Every material created in AutoCAD is based on a template. The specific properties available in the various panes are determined by the template on which the material is based. Templates are discussed in the next section.

To create a new material, open the **Materials** palette. Then, pick the **Create New Material** button below the material swatches or right-click on a swatch and select **Create New Material...** from the shortcut menu. In the **Create New Material** dialog box that appears, name the material and provide a description, Figure 15-10. When you pick the **OK** button, the material is automatically selected in the **Materials** palette and ready to be modified. To modify an existing material, simply select the material swatch and it is ready to be modified.

Types and Templates

A material can be one of four material types—realistic, realistic metal, advanced, or advanced metal. The ***material type*** determines the basic properties available for the material. It is set in the **Type:** drop-down list at the upper-left corner of the **Material Editor** pane. See Figure 15-11A.

In addition to a material type, you can select a material template. A ***material template*** provides you with a starting point for creating your own materials. It has settings already established that can be easily modified to give you the appearance

Figure 15-10.
Creating a new material.

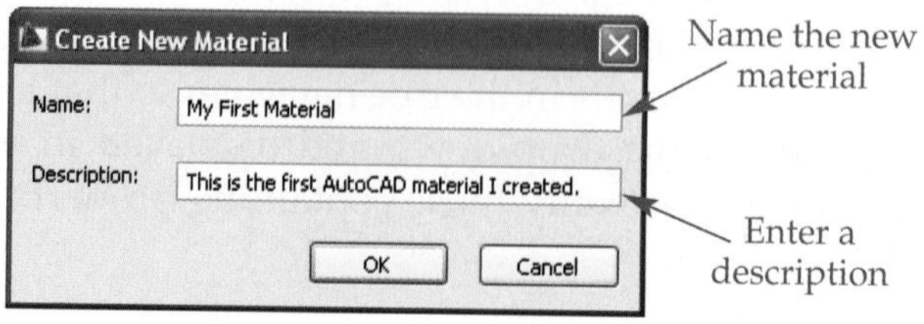

Figure 15-11.
Selecting a material type and a template on which to base the new material. A—Selecting the material type. B—Selecting a template.

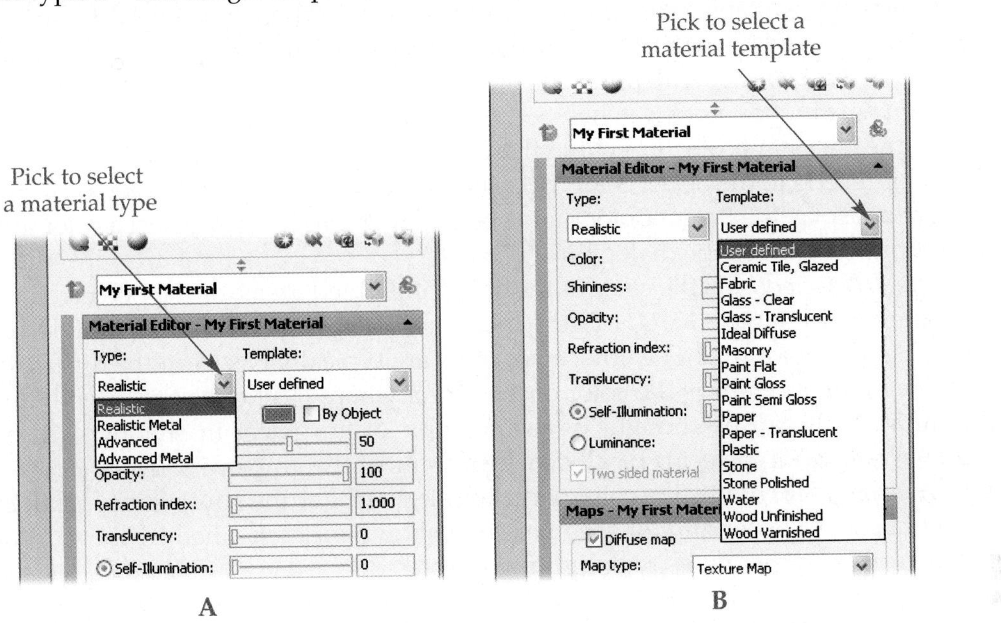

that you are looking for. To select a template, pick it in the **Template:** drop-down list at the upper-right corner of the **Material Editor** pane, **Figure 15-11B.** Material templates are only available for the realistic and realistic metal material types. Each has its own set of templates. The advanced and advanced metal material types do not display the **Template:** drop-down list.

The realistic or realistic metal material type is a good starting point if you are new to material creation. Each provides basic material properties. Realistic materials are based on the physical qualities of the material: color, shininess, opacity, refraction index, translucency, self illumination, and luminance. If a template other than User defined is selected, some of these properties have preset values applied to them. This gives you a starting point to create your own fabric, glass, metal, and various other materials.

When you get comfortable with creating basic materials, the two advanced material types—advanced and advanced metal—offer more material properties to provide additional control over the material appearance. The main difference between a realistic material type and an advanced material type is the addition of ambient, diffuse, and specular color settings and a reflection property.

PROFESSIONAL TIP

AutoCAD provides fantastic-looking materials to dress up the scene and make it look real. However, after you get comfortable with these materials and creating your own materials, start a library of your own materials. If your project is presented to a customer along with projects from competitors, and your competitors are using standard AutoCAD materials, your project will stand out from the crowd.

Color

There are three possible color settings: ambient, diffuse, and specular. All three properties are available with the advanced material types, but only diffuse is available with the realistic material types. For the advanced material types, the three color properties can be independently controlled or locked together. To lock colors, pick the lock icon next to the color swatches. See **Figure 15-12.** When locked, the diffuse color is always the dominant color. Checking the **By Object** check box turns off the color swatch. The color reverts to the object color (ByLayer, for example). To set the color, pick the color swatch to display the **Select Color** dialog box, **Figure 15-13.** Then, select a color and pick the **OK** button to close the dialog box.

The ***diffuse color*** is the color of the object in lighted areas, or the perceived color of the material. See **Figure 15-14.** It is the predominant color you see when you look at the object. Set this color first. The other two colors are typically based on the diffuse color.

The ***ambient color*** is the color of the object where light does not directly provide illumination. It can be thought of as the color of an object in shadows. In nature, shadows cast by an object typically contain some of the ambient color.

The ***specular color*** is the color of the highlight (the shiny spot). It is typically white or a light color. The amount of specular color shown is determined by the shininess of the material and the intensity of lighting in the scene.

Figure 15-12.
The ambient and diffuse colors are locked. The diffuse and specular colors are not locked.

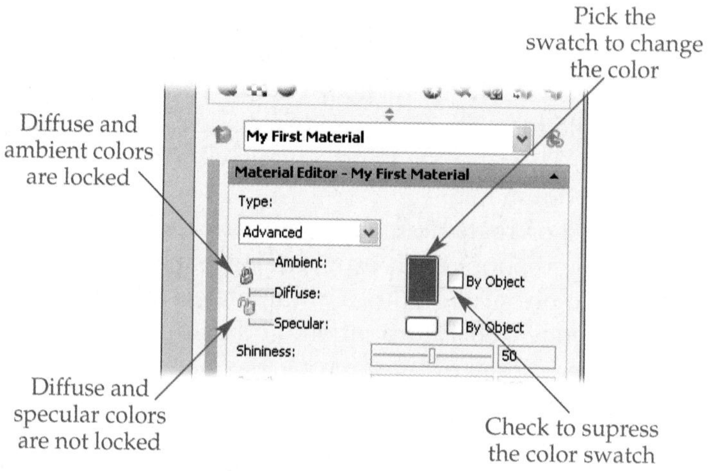

Figure 15-13.
Setting a color for a material property.

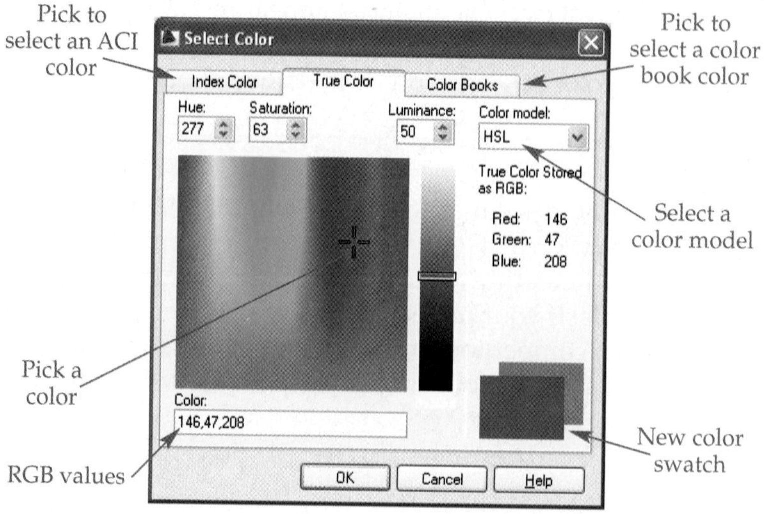

Figure 15-14.
The three colors of a material are illustrated here.

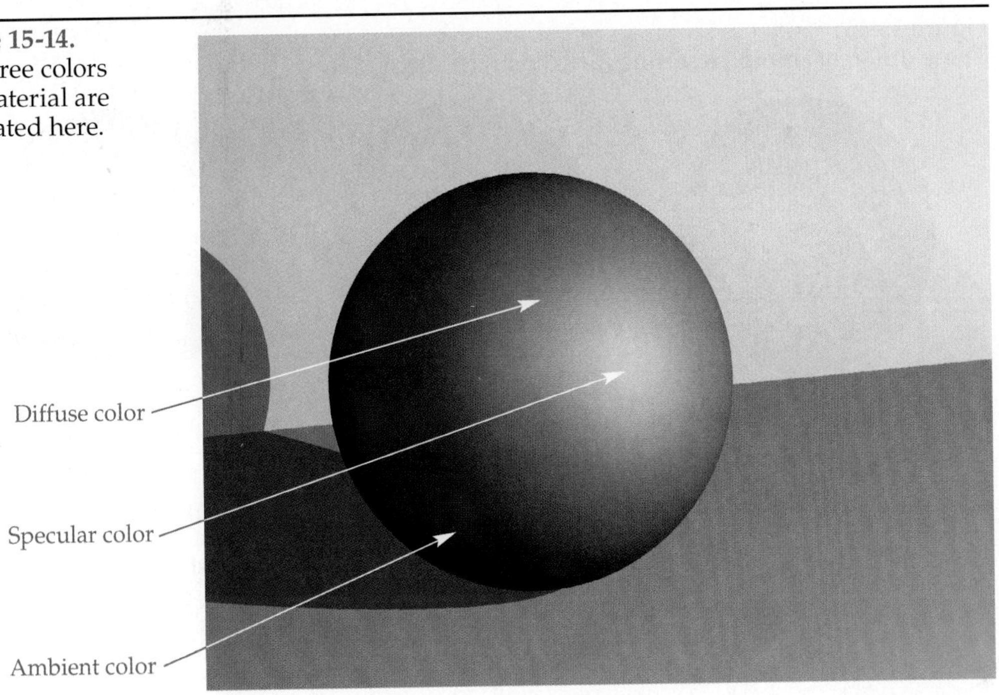

PROFESSIONAL TIP

Specular highlights can be seen everywhere. Look around you right now at edges and inclined surfaces. The diffuse color of the surface typically has little to do with the color of the highlight. The color of the light source usually determines the predominant highlight color. The majority of highlights are white or near white because most light sources are white or nearly white. However, highlights in the interior of a home may have a yellow cast to them because incandescent lightbulbs generally cast yellow light. Outside with a clear sky and bright sun, highlights may have a slight blue cast. These small details are what make a scene realistic.

Shininess

Shininess is a measure of the surface roughness. Smooth surfaces are very shiny and have a small, sharp highlight. These surfaces reflect in one direction most of the light that hits the surface. Rough surfaces tend to diffuse, or break up, light as it is reflected. Therefore, these surfaces do not appear very shiny and have a large, soft highlight. See **Figure 15-15.** To set the shininess, drag the **Shininess:** slider left to decrease the value or right to increase the value. You can also enter a value in the text box at the right-hand end of the slider.

Opacity

Opacity is a measure of a material's transparency, or how "see through" the material is. **Figure 15-16** shows an example of using transparent materials to show the internal workings of a mechanical assembly. To change the opacity value, drag the **Opacity:** slider to the left to make the material more transparent or right to make it more opaque. You can also enter a value in the text box at the right-hand end of the slider. A value of 100 creates an opaque material. Lower values create semitransparent materials. Realistic and advanced material types have an opacity property.

Figure 15-15.
Three different shininess settings are illustrated here.

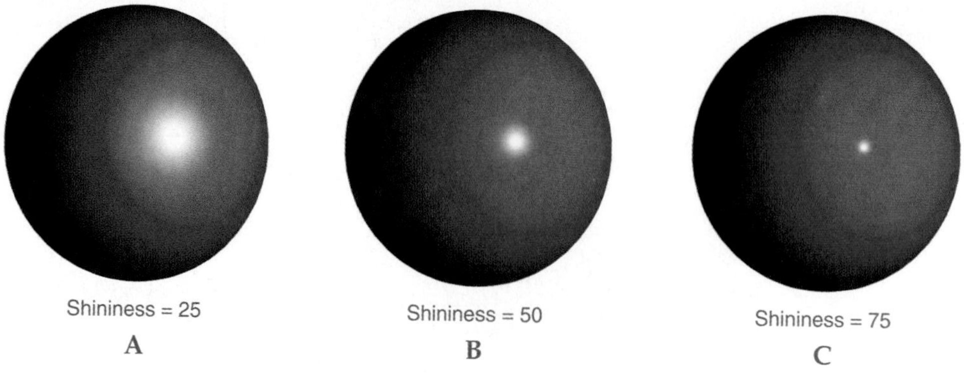

Figure 15-16.
The material used for the housing on this mechanism has an opacity setting of five.

Reflection

The ***reflection*** is a mirror image of the other objects in the scene. See **Figure 15-17.** Only the advanced and advanced metal material types have a reflection property. To make a material reflective, drag the **Reflection:** slider. Dragging the slider to the right increases the reflectivity of the material and to the left decreases reflectivity. You can also enter a value in the text box at the right-hand end of the slider.

Refraction Index

The ***refraction index,*** also know as the index of refraction (IOR), is a measure of how much light is bent (refracted) as it passes through transparent or semitransparent materials. The refraction index is what causes objects to appear distorted when viewed through a bottle or glass of water. See **Figure 15-18.** The higher the refraction index value, the more light is bent as it passes through the material. To set the value, drag the **Refraction index:** slider to the right to increase the value or left to decrease the value. You can also enter a value in the text box at the right-hand end of the slider. A value of 1.000 is the refraction index of a vacuum. The value of water is 1.3333 and glass is around 1.500. Generally, the refraction index is not set much above 1.700 and is usually somewhere between 1.000 and 1.500. Realistic and advanced material types have a refraction index property.

Figure 15-17.
The effect of increasing reflectivity. A—The reflection value of the material on the box is zero. B—The reflection value is increased to 100.

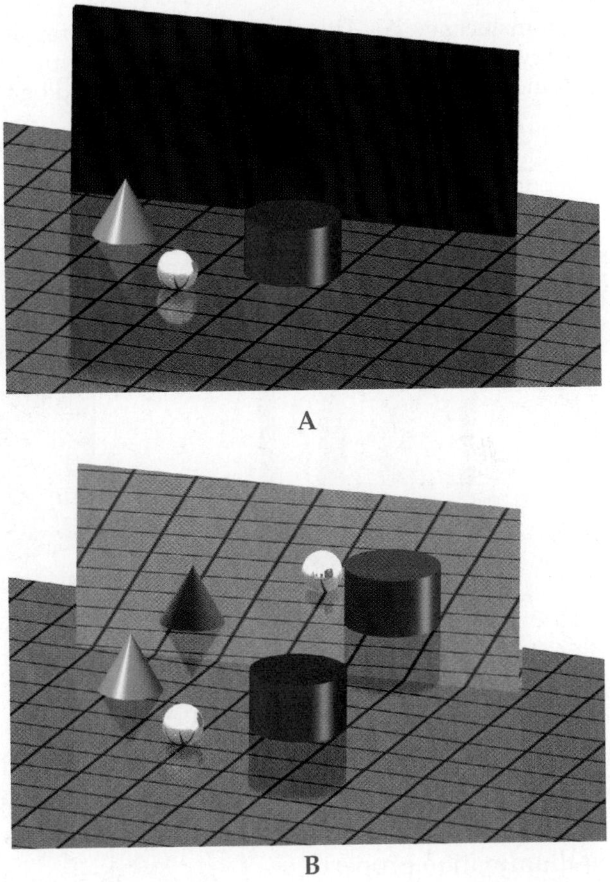

Figure 15-18.
The effect of refraction. A—The transparent material on the sphere has a refraction index of zero. B—When the refraction index is increased, the cylinder behind the sphere is distorted as light is refracted by the material.

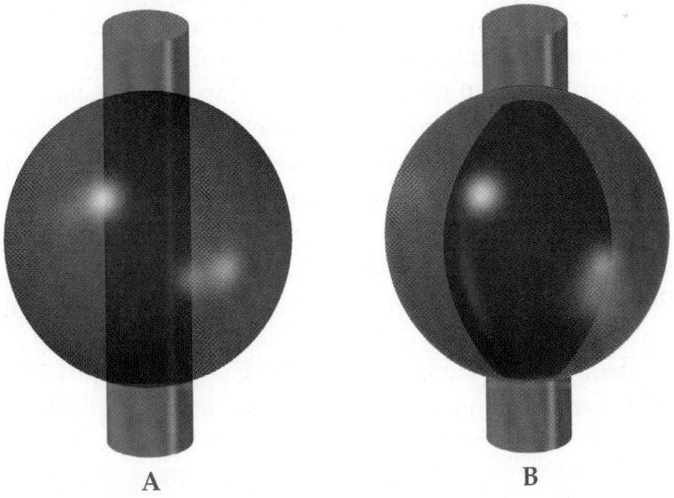

Translucency

Translucency is a quality of transparent and semitransparent materials that causes light to be diffused (scattered) as it passes through the material. See **Figure 15-19.** This makes any object with the material applied to it appear as if it is being illuminated from within, or glowing. The thicker the material, the more pronounced the effect. In AutoCAD, the translucency setting affects transparent, semitransparent, and opaque materials. With a higher setting, light appears to travel through an object lighting the opposite side. To change the translucency value, drag the **Translucency:** slider to the right to increase the value or left to decrease the value. You can also enter a value in the text box at the right-hand end of the slider. Realistic and advanced material types have a translucency property.

Figure 15-19.
The effect of translucency. A—The glass material has a translucency setting of zero. B—When the translucency setting is increased, light is diffused within the material. In this case, since the glass is thin, the effect is not as "glowing" as it would be for a thicker material.

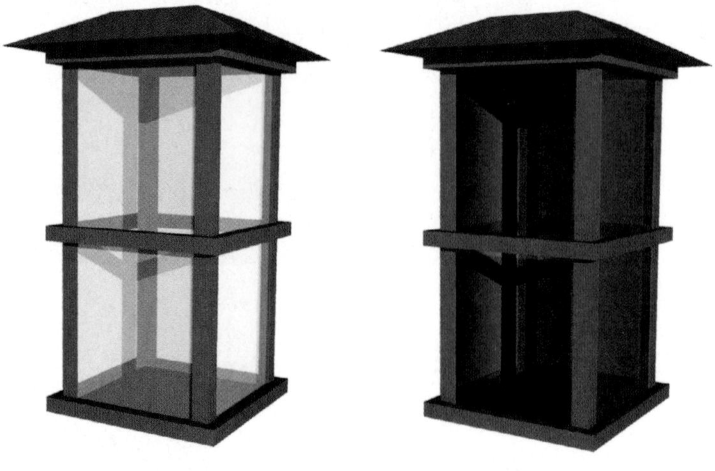

A B

Self Illumination and Luminance

Self illumination is an effect of a material producing illumination. See Figure 15-20. For example, the surface of a neon tube glows. However, in AutoCAD, a material with self illumination will not actually add illumination to a scene. All four material types have a self illumination property.

Luminance is defined as the value of light reflected off a surface. For realistic and realistic metal material types, you have the choice of using either self illumination or luminance. They both have a similar affect on the material. To use self illumination, pick the **Self-Illumination:** radio button. To use luminance, pick the **Luminance:** radio button.

To set the self illumination value, drag the **Self-Illumination:** slider to the right to increase the value or left to decrease the value. You can also enter a value in the text box at the right-hand end of the slider. Valid values for self illumination are from 1 to 100.

Luminance is expressed in candelas per square meter (cd/m^2). For example, 1 cd/m^2 is the equivalent of 1 candela of light radiating from a surface that is 1 square meter. To set luminance, enter a value in the text box that is displayed when the **Luminance:** radio button is picked. You may want to use luminance if the maximum self

Figure 15-20.
The effect of self illumination/luminance. A—The globe of this lightbulb does not have any self illumination. B—Self illumination is applied to the globe material.

A B

illumination setting of 100 is not making the material bright enough for you. A luminance setting of 1500 cd/m^2 is about the same as a self illumination setting of 100. Luminance can be set as high as 100 million cd/m^2.

Material Maps

Below the **Material Editor** pane in the **Materials** palette is the **Maps** pane. A ***texture map*** is simply an image applied to a material property. This type of map is known as a *2D map* because it is applied to the surface of an object and does not extend into it. On the other hand, a ***procedural map*** is mathematically generated based on the colors and values you select. This type of map is known as a *3D map* because it extends through the object. A material that has a map applied to at least one of its properties is called a ***mapped material.***

Maps

There are nine types of maps that can be applied to material properties: texture, checker, gradient ramp, marble, noise, speckle, tiles, waves, and wood. Each map has unique settings. A material can have separate diffuse, reflection, opacity, and bump maps, as discussed later in this chapter.

Texture Map. A texture map is an image file, such as a digital photograph, that is applied to one of the material's properties. **Figure 15-21** shows a box object with an image of a forest applied to the diffuse color of the material attached to it. To specify a texture map, first select Texture Map in the drop-down list in the appropriate area of the **Maps** pane. Then, pick the **Select Image** button in the same area. The **Select Image File** dialog box is displayed, which is a standard open dialog box. Browse to the folder where the image file is saved, select the file, and pick the **Open** button.

The "select image" button is now labeled with the file name of the image file. Also, a slider is displayed to the left of the button. See **Figure 15-22.** The slider is used to set the percentage of the image file that is applied to the property. At 100% (fully right), the entire image is applied to the property. At 50% (in the middle), the image appears to be 50% transparent, which is applied to the property. All of the map types have this slider for adjusting the amount of the map that is applied to the property.

The image settings are controlled by picking the **Click for Texture Map settings** button to the right of the **Map type:** drop-down list. This navigates to the map level of the material tree. Three additional buttons are also displayed to the right of the "select image" button. These are used to adjust and delete the map from the property. These buttons are available for all map types and are discussed later in the section Adjusting Material Maps.

Figure 15-21.
A material with a texture map. A—The background object's material does not have any maps applied. B—A texture map has been applied to the diffuse color component of the background object's material.

A B

Figure 15-22.
Use the slider to adjust the percentage of the texture map that is contributed to the property. All properties that can be mapped have this slider once a map is applied.

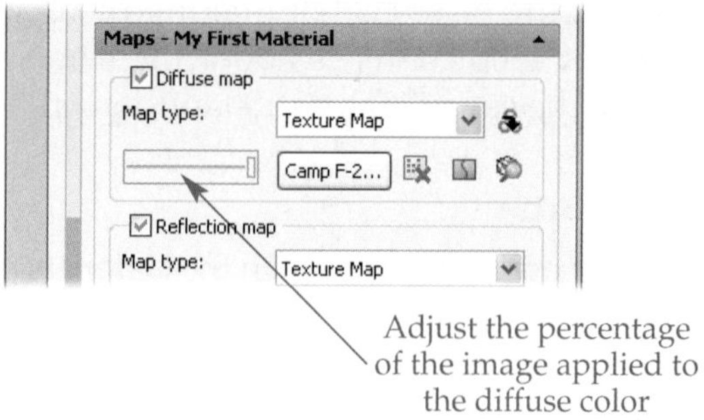

Checker. A ***checker map*** creates a two-color checkerboard pattern. By default, the colors are black and white, but different colors or images can be used as well. This map type can be used for checkerboard pattern floor materials. However, by changing various properties, you can simulate many different effects and use the map for other materials.

To specify a checker map, first select Checker in the drop-down list in the appropriate area of the **Maps** pane. Then, pick the **Click for Checker settings** button next to the **Map type:** drop-down list to navigate to the checker map level of the mapping tree. The **Checker** pane is now displayed in the **Materials** palette. See Figure 15-23. In this pane, the two colors that make up the checker pattern are defined. By default, they are both solid colors. Pick on the color swatch to change the color. To swap the color definitions, pick the **Swaps the Map Types** button in the middle of the pane. You are not limited to solid colors. All of the map types are listed in the **Map type:** drop-down list, along with Solid Color. For example, you can add a texture map to the color 1 definition and a noise map to the color 2 definition. The possibilities are endless.

The **Soften:** setting is used to blur the edges between the checkers. To change the setting, enter a value in the text box or use the up and down arrows. A value of 0.00 creates sharp edges between the checkers. The maximum setting is 5.00 and produces edges that are very blurred.

PROFESSIONAL TIP

Remember to use the **Up One Level to Parent Map**, **Home to Material Settings** button, and the drop-down list below the material samples to navigate through the mapping tree.

Figure 15-23.
The map-level properties of a checker map.

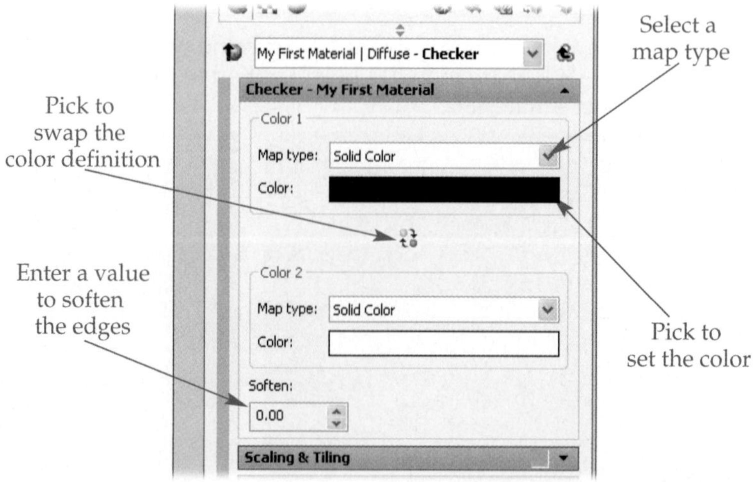

Gradient Ramp. The gradient ramp map is a texture map that allows you to create a material blending colors and textures in different patterns. It is similar to the **HATCH** command's **Gradient color** option. Select Gradient Ramp in the **Map type:** drop-down list. Then, pick the **Click for Gradient Ramp settings** button to navigate to the map level of the material tree.

The **Gradient Ramp** panel is now displayed in the **Materials** palette. See **Figure 15-24.** The gradient ramp is represented with three nodes at the bottom edge of the ramp. Each node represents a different color in the ramp. By default, the left node (node 1) is black, the middle node (node 3) is gray, and the right node (node 2) is white. The middle node can be moved left or right to change where the color transitions from black to gray to white.

There must be at least three nodes, but you are not limited to three nodes. Picking anywhere in the ramp creates a new node. It can then be moved and its properties changed. Right-clicking on a node opens a shortcut menu. This menu contains options to copy, paste, or delete the node.

Selecting a node by picking on it changes the panel directly below the ramp to the properties for that node. The **Map type:** drop-down list contains all of the map types. This means you are not limited to creating gradients of colors. You can blend patterns and images to create many different variations of gradients. See **Figure 15-25.**

Above the ramp are the **Gradient Type:** and **Interpolation:** drop-down lists. The setting in the **Gradient Type:** drop-down list controls the pattern of the gradient ramp. See **Figure 15-26.** The default pattern is linear. This results in a typical pattern similar to the ramp display. The other options are:

- **4 Corner.** Creates a linear transition that is asymmetrical.
- **Box.** The transition of colors or maps is in the shape of a square.
- **Diagonal.** This transition is linear, but rotated on the surface.
- **Lighting.** The intensity of the light source determines where the transition takes place. The right side of the ramp corresponds to the highest intensity of light and the left side of the ramp is equal to no light.

Figure 15-24.
The map-level properties of a gradient map.

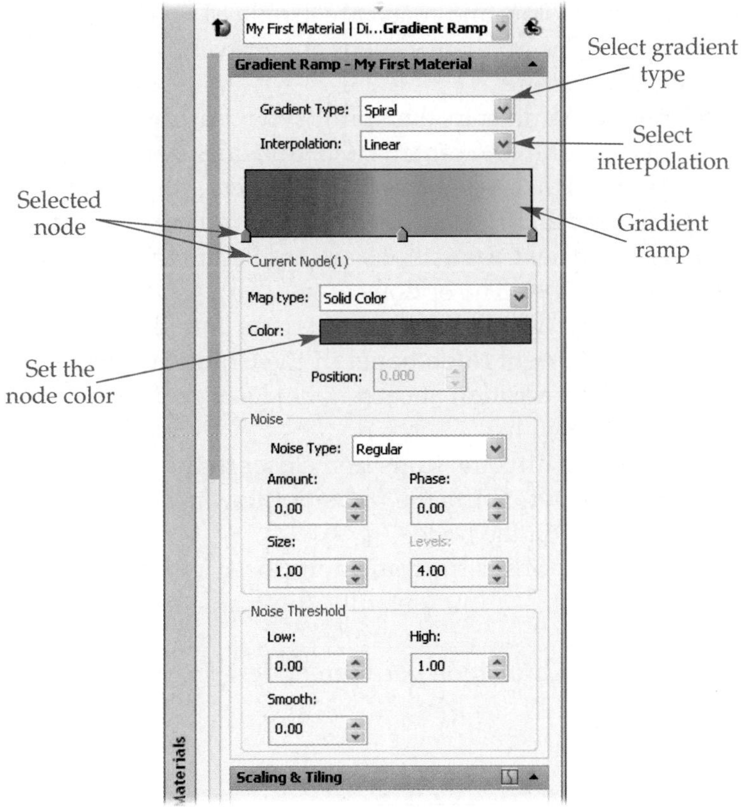

Figure 15-25.
This floor tile material is created using a gradient map. A texture map is alternated with solid white stripes. The box type and solid interpolation are used.

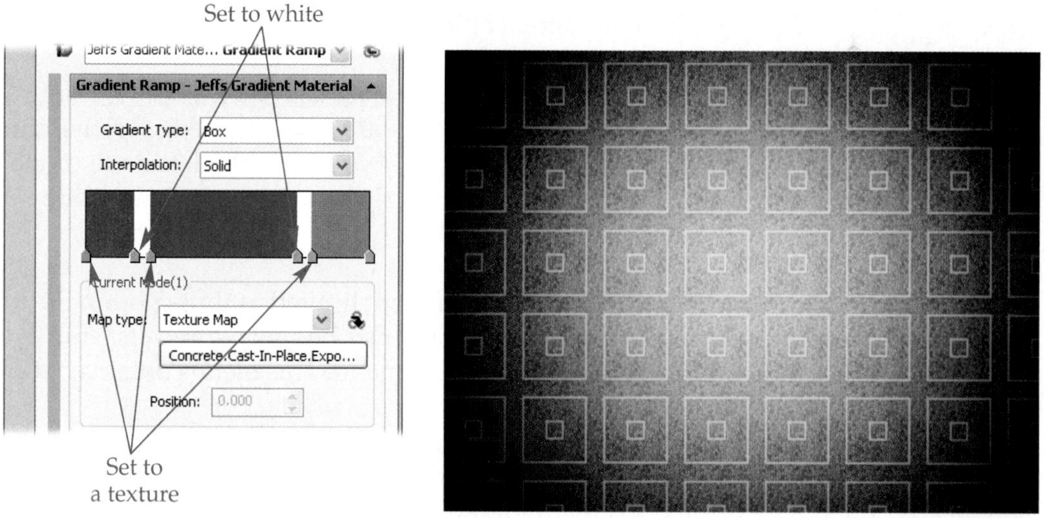

- **Linear.** This is the default. It is a smooth transition from one node to the next.
- **Mapped.** With this type you can assign one of the maps to determine the gradient. When selected, the **Gradient Map** area appears just below the **Gradient Type:** drop-down list. Use this area to select the map and change its properties.
- **Normal.** The angle between the camera direction and the surface normal controls how the pattern is displayed. The left side of the ramp is 0° between the normal and the camera viewpoint. The right side is 90° between the normal and the camera viewpoint.
- **Pong.** This gradient is a rotated linear transition, similar to the diagonal type, but it pivots about the corner of a box and reverses in the middle of the pattern.
- **Radial.** Colors and maps are arranged in a circular pattern similar to a target.
- **Spiral.** The gradient sweeps about a central point similar to the movement on a radar screen.
- **Sweep.** Similar to the spiral type, but the center of the sweep is at a corner instead of in the center. Also, this does not repeat like the pong type.
- **Tartan.** This resembles a plaid pattern. It is very similar to the box type.

The **Interpolation:** drop-down list controls the transition of colors and maps from one node to the next. Transitions are applied to the nodes from left to right, regardless of the node number. The options are:

- **Custom.** When this is selected, an **Interpolation** drop-down list is displayed in the **Current Node** panel in the **Gradient Ramp** pane. This is used to select a specific transition at each node. Each node can have a different setting in this drop-down list.
- **Ease In.** Shifts the transition closer to the node on the right.
- **Ease In Out.** Shifts the transition toward the node, but it remains more or less centered on the node.
- **Ease Out.** Shifts the transition closer to the node on the left.
- **Linear.** This is the default. The transition is constant from one node to the next.
- **Solid.** No transition between nodes. There is an abrupt change at each node.

Figure 15-26.
There are 12 different gradient types available for use in a gradient ramp map. The eight shown here are applied to the same object with the same lighting and mapping coordinates. A—4 Corner. B—Box. C—Diagonal. D—Lighting. E—Linear. F—Pong. G—Radial. H—Spiral.

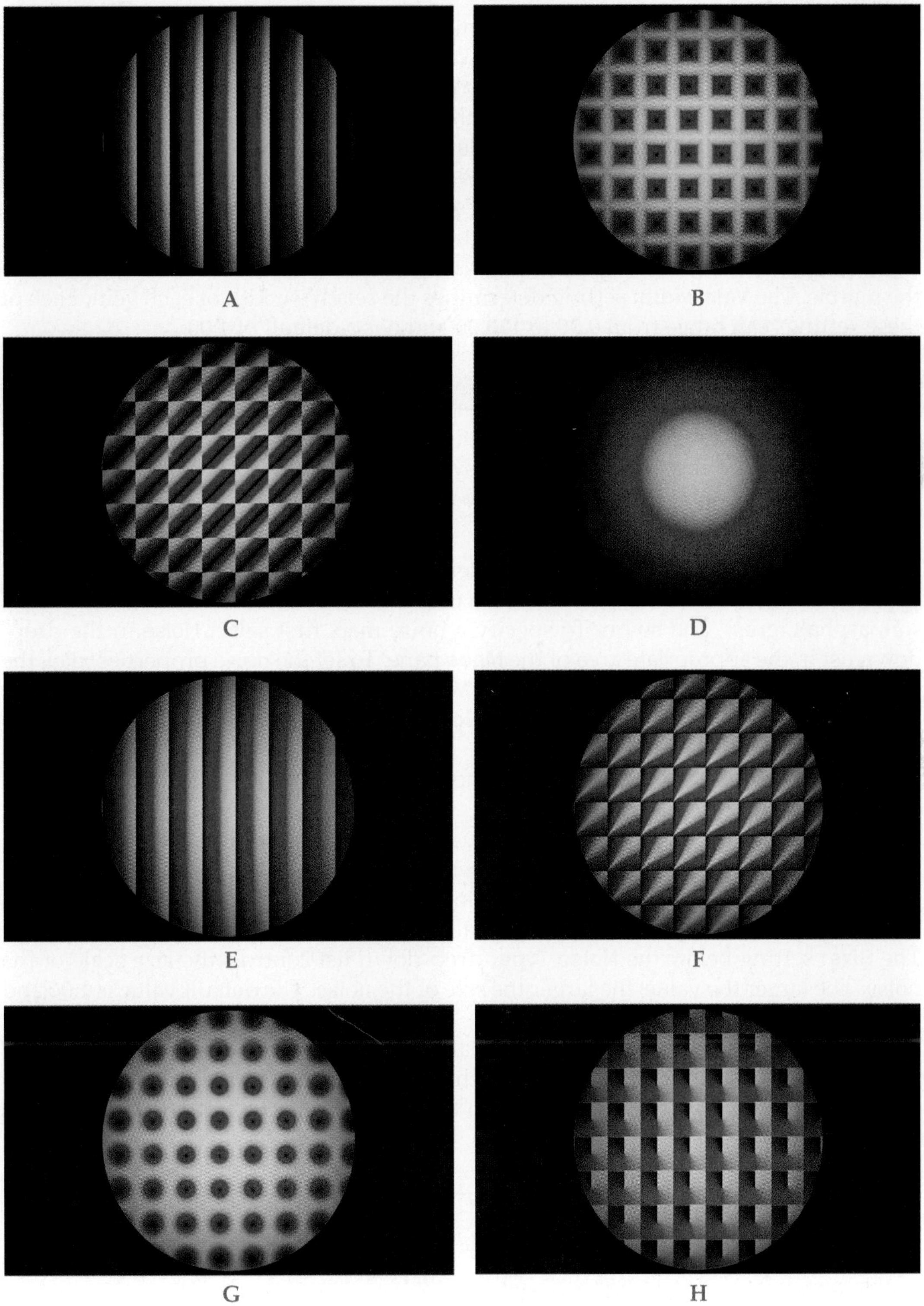

Below the **Current Node** area in the **Gradient Ramp** panel are the **Noise** and **Noise Threshold** areas. Noise may be added to the gradient map to create an uneven appearance. The settings are similar to those for the noise map. The noise map is described later in this section.

Marble. A ***marble map*** is a procedural map based on the colors and values you select. To specify a marble map, first select Marble in the drop-down list in the appropriate area of the **Maps** pane. To set the marble properties, pick the **Click for Marble settings** button next to the **Map type:** drop-down list to navigate to the marble map level of the mapping tree. The **Marble** pane is now displayed in the **Materials** palette. See Figure 15-27.

A marble map is based on two colors—stone and vein. The two color swatches in the **Marble** pane are used to specify these colors. You can swap the vein and stone colors by picking the **Swaps the Colors** button to the right of the swatches.

The **Vein spacing:** setting determines the relative distance between each vein in the marble. The **Vein width:** setting determines the relative width of each vein. Each of these settings can range from 0.00 to 100.00 and has a default of 1.00.

NOTE

The mathematical calculations that create the marble map are based on the world coordinate system. If you move or rotate the object, a different vein result is produced.

Noise. A ***noise map*** is a random pattern of two colors used to create an uneven appearance on the material. It is most often used to simulate materials such as concrete, soil, asphalt, grass, and so on. To specify a noise map, first select Noise in the drop-down list in the appropriate area of the **Maps** pane. To set the noise properties, pick the **Click for Noise settings** button next to the **Map type:** drop-down list to navigate to the noise map level of the mapping tree. The **Noise** pane is now displayed in the **Materials** palette. See Figure 15-28.

First, you need to select the type of noise. The options in the **Noise Type:** drop-down list are:

- **Regular.** This is "plain" noise and useful for most applications.
- **Fractal.** This creates the noise pattern using a fractal algorithm. When this is selected, the **Level:** control in the **Noise Threshold** area of the pane is enabled.
- **Turbulence.** This is similar to fractal, except that it creates fault lines.

The **Size:** setting below the **Noise Type:** drop-down list controls the size scale of the noise. The larger the value, the larger the size of the noise. The default value is 1.00 and the value can range from 0.00 to 1 billion.

The **Color 1** and **Color 2** areas of the pane control the color of the pattern of noise. To change the color, pick the color swatch. You can also select a map for the color definition using the **Map type:** drop-down list. To swap the color definitions, pick the **Swaps the Map Types** button.

Figure 15-27.
The map-level properties of a marble map.

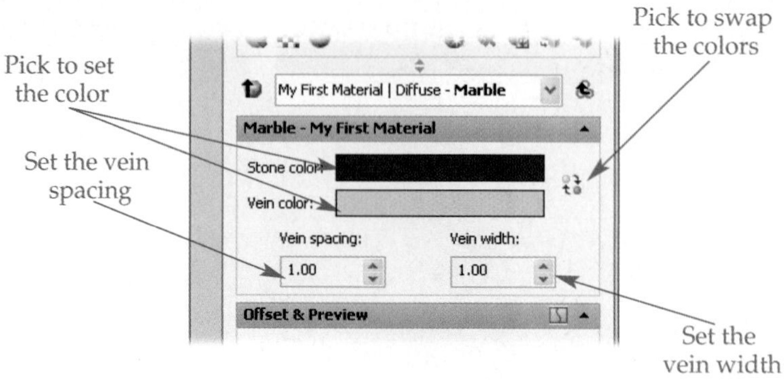

Figure 15-28.
The map-level properties of a noise map.

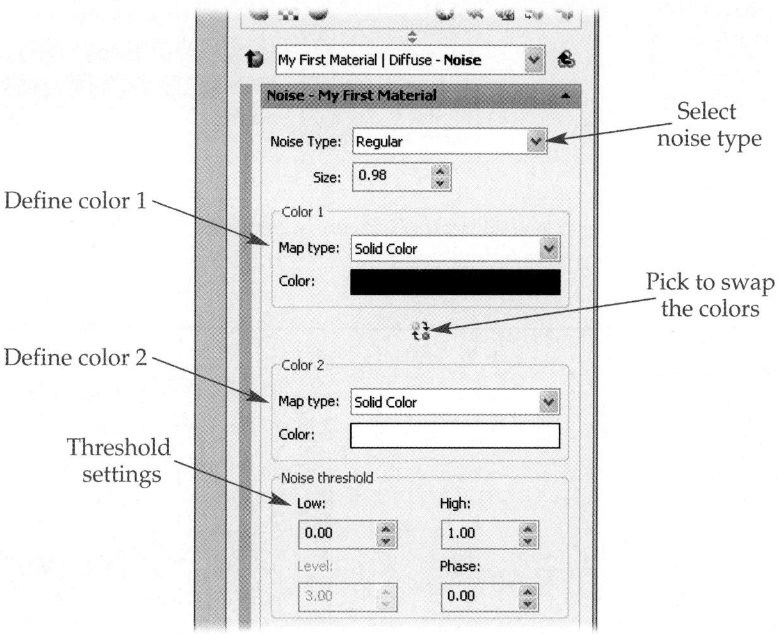

The settings in the **Noise Threshold** area of the **Noise** pane are used to fine-tune the noise effect. The settings in this area are:

- **Low.** The closer this setting is to 1.00, the more dominate color 1 is. The default setting is 0.00 and it can range from 0.00 to 1.00.
- **High.** The closer this setting is to 0.00, the more dominate color 2 is. The default setting is 1.00 and it can range from 0.00 to 1.00.
- **Level.** Sets the energy amount for fractal and turbulence. Lower values make the fractal noise appear blurry and the turbulence lines more defined. The default setting is 3.00 and it can range from 0.00 upward.
- **Phase.** Randomly changes the noise pattern with each value. This allows you to have materials with the same noise map settings look slightly different. You should have different patterns on different materials. This adds a level of realism to your scene.

Speckle. A ***speckle map*** is a random pattern of dots based on two colors. This map is great for textured walls, sand, granite, and so on. To specify a speckle map, first select Speckle in the drop-down list in the appropriate area of the **Maps** pane. To set the speckle map properties, pick the **Click for Speckle settings** button next to the **Map type:** drop-down list to navigate to the speckle map level of the mapping tree. The **Speckle** pane is now displayed in the **Materials** palette. See **Figure 15-29.** The settings for a speckle map are very simple. Pick colors for the color 1 and color 2 definitions. You cannot use maps, only colors. The **Size:** setting controls the size of the speckles.

Tiles. A ***tile map*** is a pattern of rectangular, colored blocks surrounded by colored grout lines. This may be the most versatile map in the whole collection. Tiles are used to simulate tile floors, ceiling grids, hardwood floors, and many different types of brick walls. To specify a tile map, first select Tiles in the drop-down list in the appropriate area of the **Maps** pane. To set the tile map properties, pick the **Click for Tile settings** button next to the **Map type:** drop-down list to navigate to the tile map level of the mapping tree. The **Tiles** pane is now displayed in the **Materials** palette. See **Figure 15-30.**

In the **Tiles** pane, first you need to select the pattern for the map. In the **Pattern type:** drop-down list, select one of the seven predefined tile patterns or Custom Pattern to create your own. The names of the predefined patterns bring to mind brick walls. For example, a mason may use a stack bond to build a brick wall. However, remember these are only *patterns.* You can also use a brick pattern to create tile floors and acoustic ceiling panels. The tile patterns are shown in **Figure 15-31.**

Figure 15-29. The map-level properties of a speckle map.

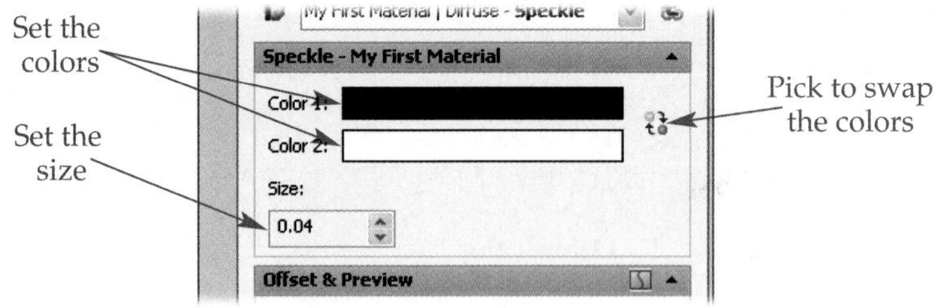

Figure 15-30. The map-level properties of a tile map.

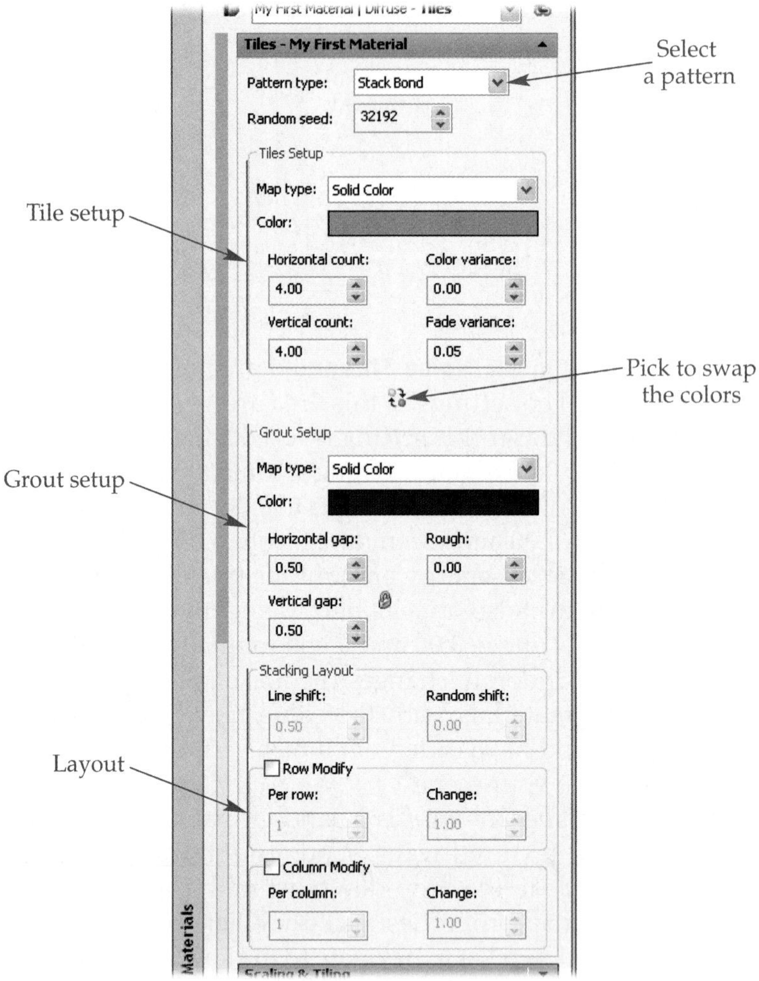

The **Random seed:** setting below the **Pattern type:** drop-down list is used to create a random color variation in the tiles. Ceramic tile floors, for example, look more realistic if each tile is slightly different in color. This variation is automatically applied, but entering a different random seed changes the pattern. Each material that uses a tile pattern should have a different random seed.

A tile pattern is really made up of tiles and grout. The **Tiles** pane contains **Tiles Setup** and **Grout Setup** areas in which these elements are defined. Each area has a drop-down list for selecting a map type and, if the map type is Solid Color, a color swatch for setting the color. The number and size of the tiles is controlled by the **Horizontal count:** and **Vertical count:** settings in the **Tiles Setup** area. The **Color variance:** setting in the **Tiles Setup** area can be used to slightly alter the color of each tile to create a more realistic appearance. The **Fade variance:** setting in the **Tiles Setup** area is used to slightly fade the color of each tile. You will have to experiment with the color variance

Figure 15-31.
A tile map can have a custom pattern or one of the predefined patterns shown here. A—Running bond. B—Common Flemish. C—English bond. D—Half running bond. E—Stack bond. F—Fine running bond. G—Fine stack bond.

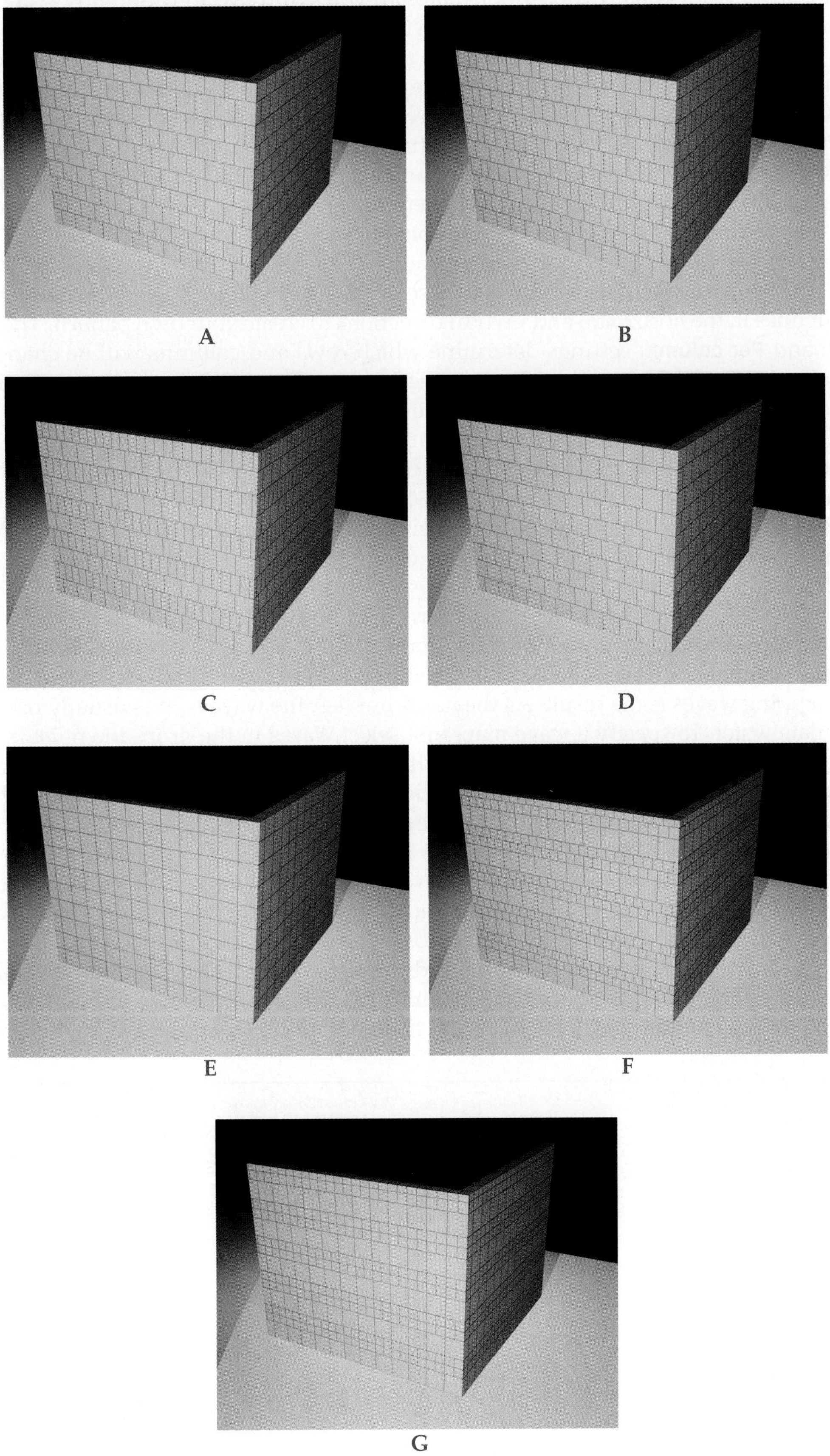

and fading to create the look you need. The grout setup is mainly just controlling size of the grout with the **Horizontal gap:** and **Vertical gap:** settings. Most of the time, these values will be the same and they can be locked together with the lock button. In some cases, such as for a hardwood floor material, you will have to differently scale the pattern on the horizontal and vertical axes to make the gap thicker in one direction.

In the **Stacking Layout** area, the value in the **Line shift:** text box changes the location of the vertical grout lines in every other row to create an alternate pattern of tiles. The default value is 0.50 and the range is from 0.00 to 100.00. The value in the **Random shift:** text box randomly moves the same lines. This works nicely for hardwood floor materials. Default value is 0.00 and the range is 0.00 to 100.00. The **Stacking Layout** area is only available with the Custom Pattern type.

The settings in the **Row Modify** and **Column Modify** areas are available with all tile pattern types, but may be disabled by default. To enable the settings, check the check box by the area name. The settings in these areas allow you to change the number of grout lines in the horizontal and vertical directions to create your own pattern. The **Per row:** and **Per column:** settings determine which rows and columns will be changed. When set to 0, no changes take place in the row or column. When set to 1, every row or column will be changed. When set to 2, every other row or column will be changed, and so on. The value must be a whole number. The setting in the **Change:** text box controls the size of the tiles in the row or column. A setting of 1 means that the tiles remain their original size. A setting of 0.50 makes the tiles one-half of their original size, a setting of 2 makes the tiles twice their original size, and so on. A setting of 0.00, in effect, completely turns off the row or column and the underlying color (usually black) shows through.

Waves. A ***wave map*** creates a pattern of concentric circles. Imagine dropping two or three stones into a pool of water and watching the ripples intersect with each other. A number of wave centers are randomly generated and a pattern created by the overlapping waves is the result. As the name implies, the wave map is usually used to simulate water. To specify a wave map, first select Waves in the drop-down list in the appropriate area of the **Maps** pane. To set the wave map properties, pick the **Click for Waves settings** button next to the **Map type:** drop-down list to navigate to the wave map level of the mapping tree. The **Waves** pane is now displayed in the **Materials** palette. See **Figure 15-32.**

In the **Waves** pane, first specify the two colors that will be used in the pattern. Maps cannot be used for the color definitions. To set a color, pick on the swatch and choose a color in the **Select Color** dialog box.

Below the color swatches are two radio buttons next to the **Distribution:** label. The radio button that is selected determines how the wave centers are distributed on the object. Picking the **3D** radio button means that the wave centers are randomly

Figure 15-32.
The map-level properties for a wave map.

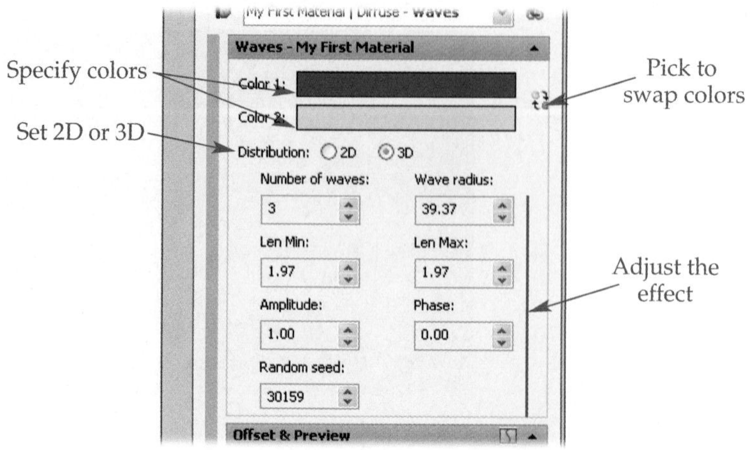

distributed over the surface of an imaginary sphere. This distribution affects all sides of an object. On the other hand, picking the **2D** radio button means that the wave centers are distributed on the XY plane. This is much better for nearly flat surfaces, such as the surface of a pond or lake.

The remaining settings in the **Waves** pane define the pattern of waves. The value in the **Number of waves:** text box is the number of wave centers that are generating the waves. The **Wave radius:** value is the radius of the circle or sphere from which the waves originate. The **Len Min:** and **Len Max:** settings define the minimum and maximum interval for each wave. The value in the **Amplitude:** text box can be thought of as the "power" of the wave. The default is 1.00, but the value can range from 0.00 to 10000.00. A value less than 1.00 makes color 1 more dominant. For a value greater than 1.00, color 2 is more dominant. The **Phase:** text box is used to shift the pattern and the **Random seed:** text box is used to redistribute the wave centers.

PROFESSIONAL TIP

To see how your changes affect the map, check the **Auto-regen** check box in the **Offset & Preview** pane. This will automatically update the preview in that pane when you change a setting. You can also change the swatch geometry to a cube, sphere, or cylinder. Some maps, like a wave map, are easier to understand when displayed on a cube.

Wood. A ***wood map*** is a procedural map that generates a wood grain based on the colors and values you select. See **Figure 15-33.** To specify a wood map, first select Wood in the drop-down list in the appropriate area of the **Maps** pane. To set the wood map properties, pick the **Click for Wood settings** button next to the **Map type:** drop-down list to navigate to the wave map level of the mapping tree. The **Wood** pane is now displayed in the **Materials** palette. See **Figure 15-34.**

A wood map is based on two colors. The two color swatches in the **Wood** pane are used to specify these colors, usually one dark and one light color. You can swap the two colors by picking the **Swaps the Colors** button to the right of the swatches. The **Radial noise:** setting determines the waviness of the wood's rings. The rings are found by cutting a tree crosswise. The **Axial noise:** setting determines the waviness of the length of the tree trunk. The **Grain thickness:** setting determines the relative width of the grain.

Figure 15-33.
A wood map is a procedural, or 3D, map. This type of map passes through the entire object to which it is applied.

Figure 15-34.
The map-level properties of a wood map.

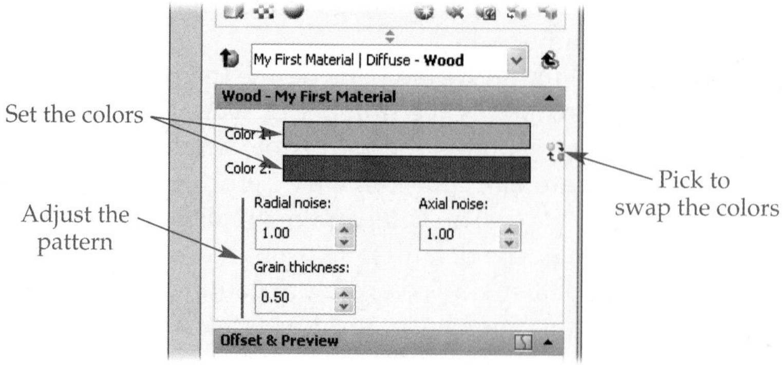

NOTE

The mathematical calculations that create the wood map are based on the world coordinate system. If you move or rotate the object, a different grain pattern is produced.

Diffuse map

A ***diffuse map*** is applied to the diffuse color property of a material. See Figure 15-35. This is assigned in the **Maps** pane, which is displayed at the top of the material mapping tree. The **Diffuse map** check box in the pane toggles the specified diffuse map off and on. When unchecked, the object color defined in the **Material Editor** pane controls the color of the object. If no map is specified, the toggle has no affect.

To assign a diffuse map, select the type of map to apply using the **Map type:** drop-down list in the **Diffuse map** area of the **Maps** pane. Then, define the map as described earlier. Once the map is defined, return to the top of the material mapping tree. In the **Diffuse map** area of the **Maps** pane, use the slider to adjust how much of the map is applied to the diffuse color.

Exercise 15-4

Complete the exercise on the Student CD.

Figure 15-35.
A—The diffuse color property of the material applied to this box has no map. B—A texture map is applied to the diffuse color property of the material.

A B

Reflection map

The advanced and advanced metal material types have a reflection property. A ***reflection map*** is applied to this property. This is often done for shiny materials in outdoor scenes. An image of clouds or blue sky is applied as a reflection map because the sky is not modeled. A reflection map is assigned in the **Maps** pane, which is displayed at the top of the material mapping tree. The **Reflection map** check box in the pane toggles the specified reflection map off and on.

To assign a reflection map, select the type of map to apply using the **Map type:** drop-down list in the **Reflection map** area of the **Maps** pane. Then, define the map as described earlier. Once the map is defined, return to the top of the material mapping tree. In the **Reflection map** area of the **Maps** pane, use the slider to adjust how much of the map is applied to the reflection property. Often, only a small percentage of the reflection map is applied to the material.

Opacity map

An ***opacity map*** is applied to the opacity property of a material to make an object appear transparent in different areas. Without an opacity map, the opacity property is equally applied to the object. Black areas of the map are transparent, white areas are opaque, and gray areas are semitransparent. See **Figure 15-36.** If a color appears in the map, the grayscale value of the color is used to calculate transparency. An opacity map is assigned in the **Maps** pane, which is displayed at the top of the material mapping tree. The **Opacity map** check box in the pane toggles the specified opacity map off and on.

To assign an opacity map, select the type of map to apply using the **Map type:** drop-down list in the **Opacity map** area of the **Maps** pane. Then, define the map as described earlier. Once the map is defined, return to the top of the material mapping tree. In the **Opacity map** area of the **Maps** pane, use the slider to adjust how much of the map is applied to the opacity property.

Bump map

A ***bump map*** is a map applied to the material to make some areas of the material appear raised and other areas depressed. The black, white, and grayscale values of the map are used to determine raised and depressed areas. Dark areas of the map make the material surface appear depressed and light areas make the material surface appear unchanged. For example, to show the texture of a brick wall, you could physically model the grooves into the wall. This would take a lot of time to model and would immensely increase the rendering time because of the increased complexity of the geometry. Using a bump map is an easier and more efficient way to accomplish the same task. **Figure 15-37** shows a bump map used to represent an embossed stamp on a

Figure 15-36.
The effect of an opacity map. A—This black and white image will be used as the opacity map. B—The material on the plane is completely opaque. C—When the opacity map is applied to the material, the dark areas of the map produce transparent areas on the object.

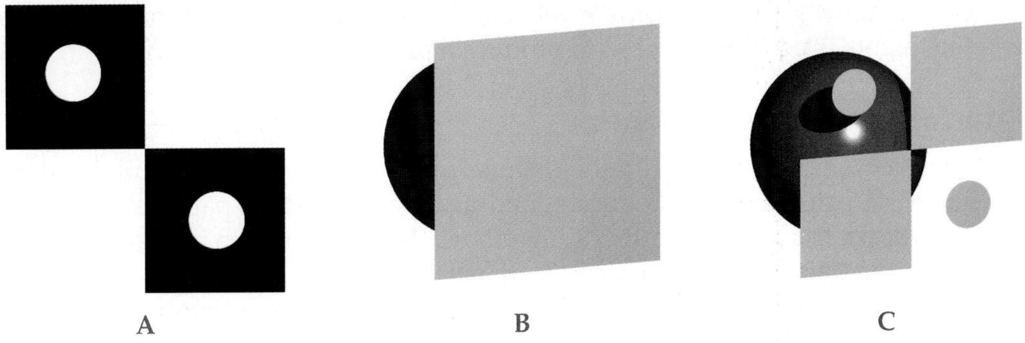

Figure 15-37.
The effect of a bump map. A—This image will be used as the bump map. B—When applied to the material, the bump map simulates louvers stamped into the metal case.

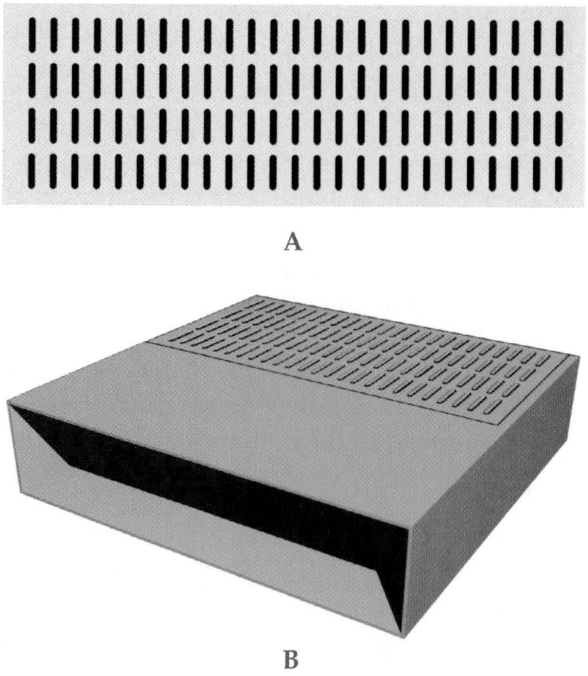

metal case. A bump map is assigned in the **Maps** pane, which is displayed at the top of the material mapping tree. The **Bump map** check box in the pane toggles the specified bump map off and on.

To assign a bump map, select the type of map to apply using the **Map type:** drop-down list in the **Bump map** area of the **Maps** pane. Then, define the map as described earlier. Once the map is defined, return to the top of the material mapping tree. In the **Bump map** area of the **Maps** pane, use the slider to adjust how much of the map is applied to the bump property. Typically, the bump map is set to a low percentage.

Exercise 15-5

Complete the exercise on the Student CD.

Adjusting Material Maps

Simply applying a map to a material rarely results in a realistic scene when the scene is rendered. The maps often need to be adjusted to produce the desired results. Maps can be adjusted at the material level or at the object level. A combination of these two adjustments is usually required to produce a photorealistic rendering.

Material-Level Adjustments

Whenever a map is applied to the diffuse, reflection, opacity, or bump property, three buttons are displayed in the corresponding area in the **Maps** pane below the **Map type:** drop-down list. See Figure 15-38. To remove the map from the material property, simply pick the **Delete map information from material** button. A warning may appear indicating that subtextures will also be deleted. Once the map is removed, the three buttons and the slider are removed from the area. If a texture map was removed, the

Figure 15-38.
The controls for a map. Once applied to a property, all maps display these controls.

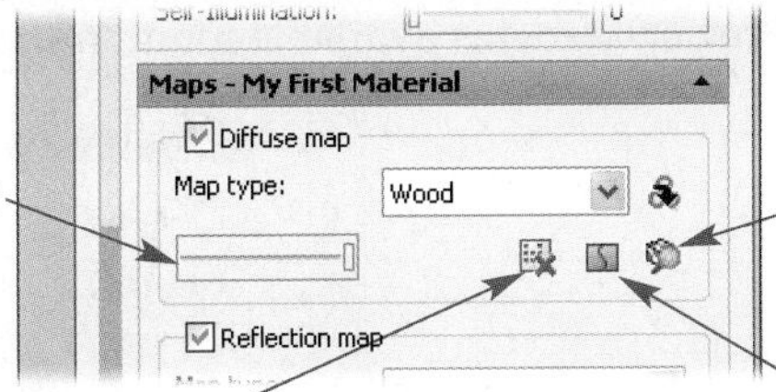

"select image" button is again labeled **Select Image**, which indicates that there is no map attached to the property.

The middle button below the **Map type:** drop-down list is used to synchronize or unsynchronize the map channels within the same material definition. For example, to make a realistic tile floor, a tile map is applied as a diffuse map. Another tile map is also used as a bump map to make the grout look recessed. If the scaling is changed for the bump map, but not synchronized, the grout colors and indentations will not match. See Figure 15-39. The synchronize button ensures that all of these settings are the same. Maps are synchronized by default. When synchronized, the button appears closed. When unsynchronized, the button appears open. When the button is picked to turn off synchronization, a warning message is displayed indicating that the other properties will be unaffected. It is recommended that you leave the synchronize feature on.

The right-hand button below the **Map type:** drop-down list opens the **Map Preview** dialog box. This dialog box displays the map channel in a larger, 2D view. This dialog box remains open until you close it. Checking the **Auto-update** check box forces the image to automatically update when a change is made to the map. If it is unchecked, the image is not updated until you manually update it by picking the **Update** button in the same dialog box.

The **Material Scaling & Tiling** and **Material Offset & Preview** panes in the **Materials** palette allow adjustments to be made that affect how the map image fits on the material. See Figure 15-40. Settings made in these panes impact all objects in the drawing that have this material applied to them. Each property map has similar panes at the map level in the mapping tree. These are named **Scaling & Tiling** and **Offset & Preview**

Figure 15-39.
A—This material has diffuse color and bump maps. B—If the bump map is not synchronized with the material, it will not align with the grout lines if scaled.

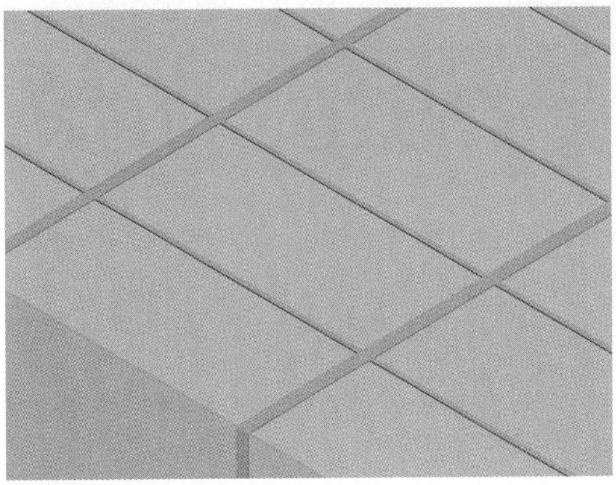

A

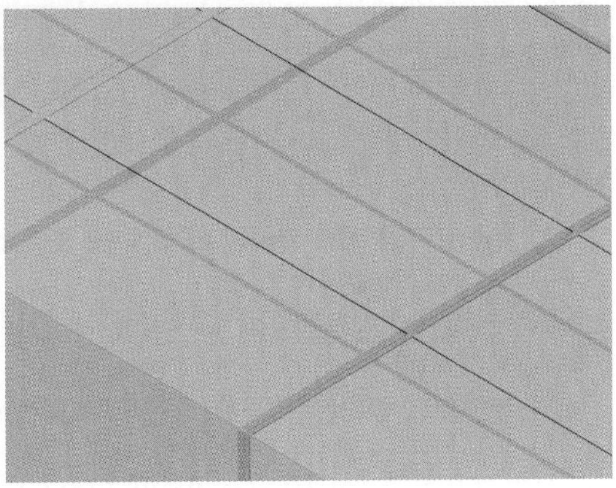

B

Figure 15-40.
Making map adjustments to the material. A—The **Material Scaling & Tiling** pane (or map-level **Scaling & Tiling** pane) is available for texture (2D) maps. B—The **Material Offset & Preview** pane (or map-level **Offset & Preview** pane) is available for all maps.

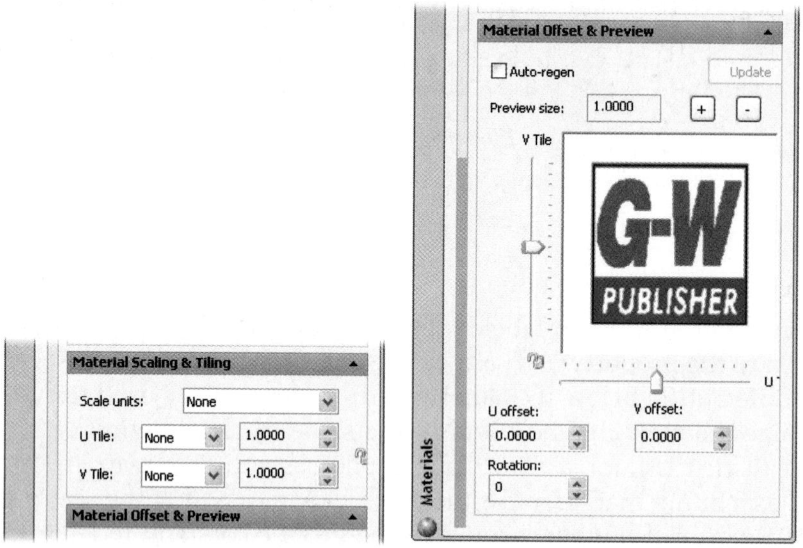

A B

and contain the same controls. Notice the title bars of the panes at the map level have synchronize buttons, which are the same buttons found in the **Maps** pane at the top of the material mapping tree. If unsynchronized, the settings in the **Scaling & Tiling** and **Offset & Preview** panes at the map level affect only the map. The settings in the **Material Scaling & Tiling** and **Material Offset & Preview** panes at the top of the material mapping tree are applied to all maps in the material definition.

Scaling and tiling

The map-level **Scaling & Tiling** pane is only available for texture maps (2D maps): texture map, checker, gradient ramp, and tiles. By the same token, the **Material Scaling & Tiling** pane is only displayed if one of the material properties has a texture map.

At the top of the **Material Scaling & Tiling** pane (or map-level **Scaling & Tiling** pane), select the units that will be used to apply the scaling. In the **Scale units:** drop-down list, you can select None, Fit to Gizmo, or a standard unit of measure. The gizmo is used for object-level material adjustments, as described in the next section.

After selecting the units for the scale, select the type of tiling for the U and V axes using the left-hand drop-down lists. The U and V axes are similar to the X and Y axes in a 2D drawing, but are relative to the map image. You can select None, Tile, or Mirror. None means the map will not be repeated. Mirror means the map is repeated, but each tile is a mirror image of its neighbor. Finally, enter the scale on the U and V axes using the right-hand text boxes. The value is the number of times the map fits within a one-unit square (defined by the selected units). The aspect ratio can be locked using the lock button to the right of the text boxes.

Offset and preview

At the top of the **Material Offset & Preview** pane (or map-level **Offset & Preview** pane) there is the **Auto-regen** check box. With this checked, the image automatically updates when changes are made. If it is not checked, you must pick the **Update** button to see the changes.

The value in the **Preview size:** text box is a zoom factor for the preview image. If the image is not properly displaying in the preview window, use this to zoom in or out. You can also use the **Zoom the preview in** (the + button) and the **Zoom the preview out** (the – button) to zoom in and out.

The **V Tile** and **U Tile** sliders change the scale of the map. As the slider is moved, the corresponding text box value in the **Material Scaling & Tiling** pane changes. These sliders are not displayed if a real-world unit is selected in the **Scale units:** drop-down list in the **Material Scaling & Tiling** pane.

The **U Offset:** and **V Offset:** text boxes at the bottom of the **Material Offset & Preview** pane set the location of the map image within the material. The offsets can also be changed by picking and dragging the image in the preview pane.

The value in the **Rotation:** text box determines the rotation of the map about the W axis. The W axis is similar to the Z axis, but is local to the image. When spherical or cylindrical mapping is applied to an object, this setting has no effect. Object-level mapping is discussed in the next section.

Object-Level Adjustments

Material mapping refers to specifying how a mapped material is applied to an object. When a mapped material is attached to an object, a default set of mapping coordinates, or simply *default mapping*, is used to apply the map to the object. Many times, the **Material Scaling & Tiling** and **Material Offset & Preview** panes (or the corresponding map-level panes) can be used to alter how the map is applied to the default mapping. But, since these changes affect all objects to which the material is applied, this may not be acceptable.

Fortunately, AutoCAD allows you to adjust mapping at the object level for texture-mapped (2D-mapped) materials. The **MATERIALMAP** command applies a grip tool, or ***gizmo***, based on one of four mapping types: planar, box, spherical, or cylindrical. See Figure 15-41. The colored edge represents the start and end of the map. For best results, select the mapping type based on the general shape of the object to which mapping is applied. Do not be afraid to experiment with other mapping types, however. Any mapping type can be used on any object, regardless of the object's shape. However, only one mapping type can be applied to an object at any given time.

MATERIALMAP

Ribbon
Visualize > Materials — Planar Mapping
Visualize > Materials — Box Mapping
Visualize > Materials — Cylindrical Mapping
Visualize > Materials — Spherical Mapping

Type
MATERIALMAP

Menu
View > Render > Mapping > Planar Mapping
View > Render > Mapping > Box Mapping
View > Render > Mapping > Cylindrical Mapping
View > Render > Mapping > Spherical Mapping

After one of the mapping types is selected, you are prompted to select the faces or objects. You can select multiple objects or faces. After making a selection, the gizmo is placed on the section set. The command remains active for you to adjust the mapping or enter an option.

Drag the grips on the gizmo to stretch or scale the material. The effects of editing a diffuse color map are dynamically displayed if the current visual style is set to display materials and textures. Otherwise, exit the command and render the scene to see the effect of the edit. To readjust the mapping, select the same mapping type and pick the object again. The gizmo is displayed in the same location as before.

The **Move** and **Rotate** options of the command toggle between the move and rotate grip tools. Using the grip tools, you can move and rotate the map on the object. The **Reset** option of the command restores the default mapping to the object. The **Switch mapping mode** option allows you to change between the four types of mapping.

If the command is typed, there is an additional option. The **Copy mapping to** option is a quick and easy way to apply the changes made to the current object to other objects in the scene. Enter this option and then select the objects to which the current mapping will be copied. This option is also available if the **Switch mapping mode** option is entered.

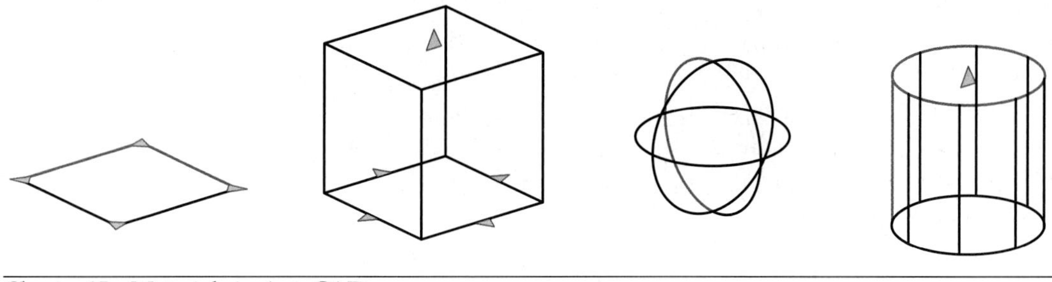

Figure 15-41.
These are the four material map gizmos. From left to right: planar, box, spherical, and cylindrical. The colored edge represents the start and end of the map.

For example, look at **Figure 15-42A.** The grain on the stair risers is running vertically when it should run horizontally. First, apply a planar map to the bottom riser. Next, rotate the mapping 90°, **Figure 15-42B.** Finally, use the **Copy mapping to** option to copy the mapping to the other risers, **Figure 15-42C.**

PROFESSIONAL TIP

If you are using a bump, reflection, or opacity map and need to adjust it at the object level, apply the same map as a diffuse color map. Also, set the visual style to display materials and textures. Then, adjust the object mapping as needed. The edits are dynamically displayed in the viewport. When the image is in the correct location, remove the diffuse color map from the material.

Exercise 15-6

Complete the exercise on the Student CD.

Figure 15-42.
Correcting material mapping. A—The grain on the risers runs vertically instead of horizontally. B—Rotating the map with the rotate gizmo. C—The corrected rendering. (Model courtesy of Arcways, Inc., Neenah, WI)

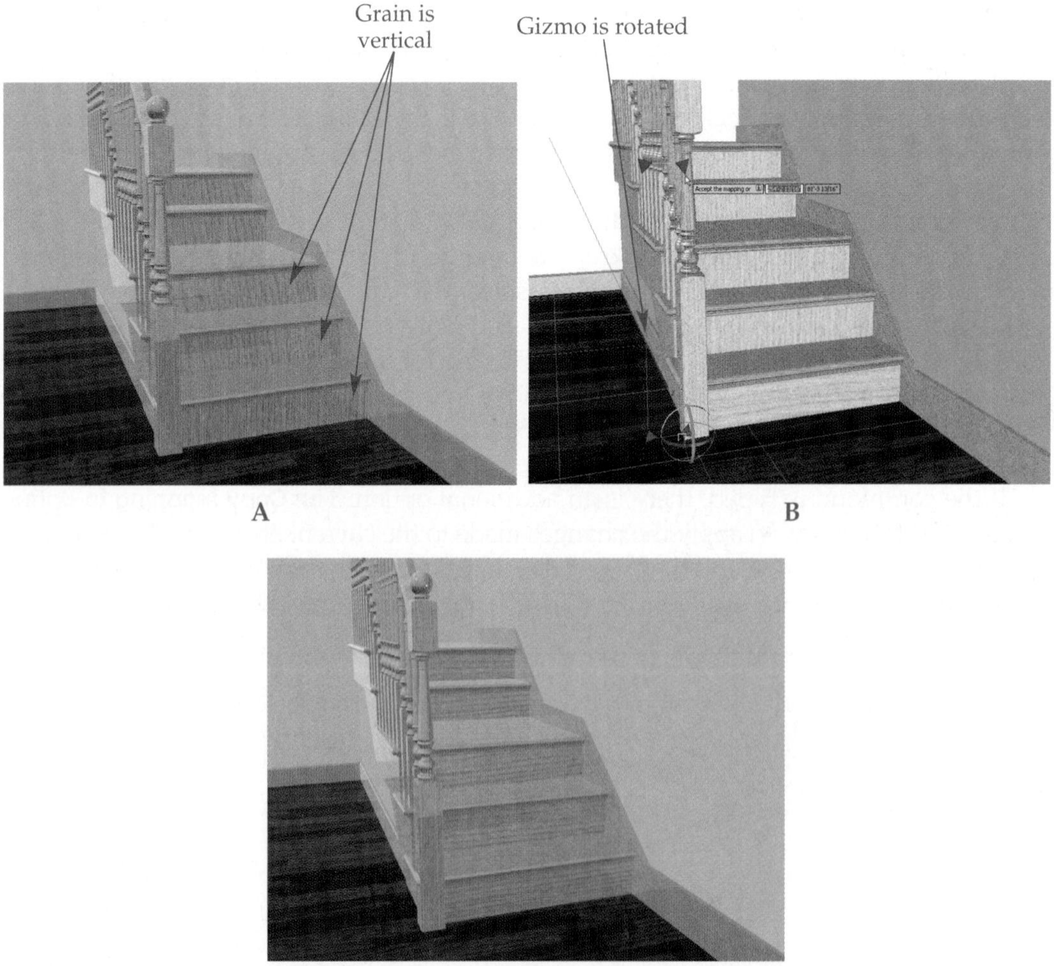

Chapter Test

Answer the following questions. Write your answers on a separate sheet of paper or complete the electronic chapter test on the Student CD.

1. Define *material.*
2. Define *materials library.*
3. Why do the materials in the tool palettes and **Materials** palette have a checkered background?
4. Describe how to attach a material using a tool palette.
5. How can materials be attached to layers?
6. By default, which material is attached to newly created objects?
7. Which material is used as the base material for creating new materials?
8. Name the three material display options for a visual style that can also be set using the **Materials** panel on the ribbon.
9. How do you know if a material in the **Materials** palette is being used in the drawing?
10. How can the name and description of an existing material be changed?
11. Name the four basic material types.
12. What are the templates available for the realistic metal material type?
13. To create a reflective material, which material type(s) can be used?
14. What are the three material color settings? Explain each.
15. Describe the difference between a transparent material and a translucent material.
16. How much illumination does a self-illuminated material add to a scene?
17. How is a marble material created?
18. Explain how black and white areas of an opacity map affect the transparency of a material.
19. Which objects do changes made in the **Material Offset & Preview** pane affect?
20. Name the four types of mapping available for adjusting texture maps at the object level.

Drawing Problems

1. In this problem, you will create a scene with basic 3D objects, attach materials to the objects, and adjust the settings of the materials.
   A. Start a new drawing and set the units to architectural.
   B. Draw a 15′ × 15′ planar surface to represent the floor.
   C. Draw two boxes to represent two walls. Make the boxes 15′ × 4″ × 9′. Position them to form a 90° corner. Alternately, you can draw a polysolid of the same dimensions.
   D. Draw a R2′ × 5′H cone in the center of the room.
   E. Open the **Tool Palettes** window, display the **Materials** palette group, and display the **Flooring** tool palette. Attach the material Finishes.Flooring.Tile.Square.Terra Cotta to the floor.
   F. Using the **Finishes** material tool palette, attach the material Finishes.Plaster.Stucco.Troweled.White to the wall.
   G. Using the same material tool palette, attach the material Finishes.Wall Covering.Stripes.Vertical.Blue-Grey to the cone.
   H. Turn on the sun and adjust the time to create good shadows. Refer to Chapter 14 for an introduction to sun settings.
   I. Render the scene. Save the rendering as P15_01.jpg.
   J. Save the drawing as P15_01.

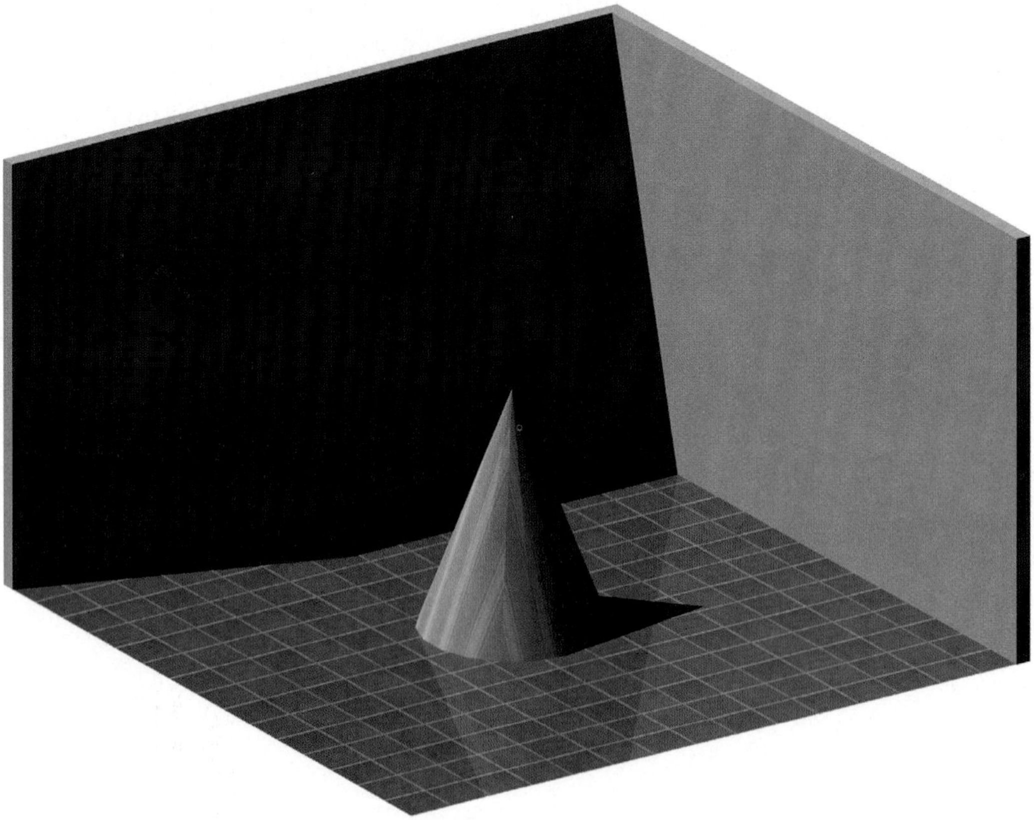

2. In this problem, you will attach materials to the objects in an existing drawing and render the scene.
   A. Open the drawing P14_01 from Chapter 14. If you did not complete this problem, do so now. Save the drawing as P15_02.
   B. Open the **Tool Palettes** window and display the **Materials** palette group.
   C. Attach the materials of your choice to the objects in the scene. Do not be restricted by the names of the materials. For example, a concrete material may be suitable for foliage or even carpet with a simple color change. Be creative.
   D. If the items in the scene were inserted using the **DC Online** tab in **DesignCenter**, they may be blocks with nested layers. Instead of exploding the blocks, use the **MATERIALATTACH** command and attach materials to the layers on which the nested objects reside.
   E. Turn on the sun and adjust the time to create good shadows. Refer to Chapter 14 for an introduction to sun settings.
   F. Render the scene. Save the rendering as P15_02.jpg.
   G. Save the drawing.

3. In this problem, you will create custom wood and marble materials.
   A. Start a new drawing and save it as P15_03.
   B. Draw two 5 × 5 × 5 boxes and position them near each other. Using other primitives, cut notches and holes in the boxes. The boxes will be used to test the custom materials.
   C. In the **Materials** palette, create two new materials. Name one Wood-*your initials* and the other Marble-*your initials*.
   D. Attach the wood material to one of the boxes and the marble material to the other box.
   E. Render the scene and make note of the wood grain and marble veins.
   F. Use the **Wood** and **Marble** panes in the material editor to change the properties of the materials.
   G. Render the scene again and make note of the changes. Using the **Render Region** button on the **Render** panel in the **Output** tab of the ribbon can save time when testing material changes.
   H. When you are satisfied with the materials, save the rendering as P15_03.
   I. Save the drawing.

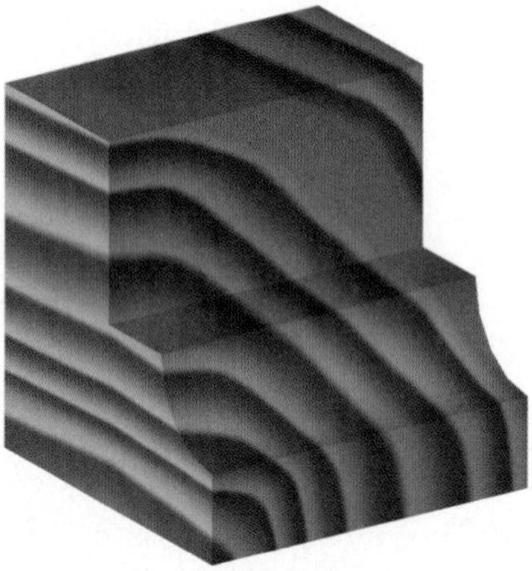

4. In this problem, you will create a bitmap and use it as opacity and bump maps.
   A. Draw a rectangle with an array of smaller rectangles inside of it, as shown below. Sizes are not important and the pattern can be varied if you like.
   B. Display a plan view of the rectangles. Then, copy all of the objects to the Windows clipboard by pressing [Ctrl]+[C] and selecting the objects.
   C. Launch Windows Paint. Then, paste the objects into the blank file. Notice how the AutoCAD background outside of the large rectangle is also included.
   D. Use the select tool (rectangle) in Paint to draw a window around the large rectangle created in AutoCAD and the smaller rectangles within it. Copy this to the Windows clipboard by pressing [Ctrl]+[C].
   E. Close Paint without saving. Start a new Paint file and paste the image from the clipboard into the blank file. Now, the unwanted AutoCAD background is no longer displayed. If needed, change the small rectangles to black and the lattice to white using the tools in Paint. The colors should be the reverse of what is shown below. Then, save the image file as P15_04.bmp and close Paint.
   F. In AutoCAD, draw a solid box of any size.
   G. Using the **Materials** palette, create a new material.
   H. Assign the P15_04.bmp image file you just created as an opacity map. Adjust the map so that it is scaled to fit to the object.
   I. Render the scene and note the effect.
   J. Turn off the opacity map.
   K. Assign the P15_04.bmp image file as a bump map. Adjust the map so that it is scaled to fit to the object.
   L. Render the scene and note the effect.
   M. Save the drawing as P15_04.

Lighting can have a dramatic effect on the scene. Notice how lighting is used in this model. One light is placed inside of the lamp and casts shadows. Another light is used to create sunlight. This is also set to cast shadows.

CHAPTER 16 Lighting

Learning Objectives

After completing this chapter, you will be able to:

- ✓ Describe the types of lighting in AutoCAD.
- ✓ List the user-created lights available in AutoCAD.
- ✓ Change the properties of lights.
- ✓ Generate and modify shadows.
- ✓ Add a background to your scene and control its appearance.

In Chapter 14, you were introduced to lighting. You learned how to adjust lighting by turning off the default lights and adding sunlight. In this chapter, you will learn all about the lights available in AutoCAD. You will learn lighting tips and tricks to help make the scene look its best.

Types of Lights

Ambient light is like natural light just before sunrise. It is the same intensity everywhere. All faces of the object receive the same amount of ambient light. Ambient light cannot create highlights, nor can it be concentrated in one area. AutoCAD does not have an ambient light setting. Instead, it relies on indirect illumination, which is discussed in Chapter 17.

A ***point light*** is like a lightbulb. Light rays from a point light shine out in all directions. A point light can create highlights. The intensity of a point light falls off, or weakens, over distance. Other programs, such as Autodesk 3ds max®, may call these lights *omni lights.* A ***target point light*** is the same as a standard point light except that a target is specified. The illumination of the target point light is directed toward the target.

A ***distant light*** is a directed light source with parallel light rays. This acts much like the Sun. Rays from a distant light strike all objects in your model on the same side and with the same intensity. The direction and intensity of a distant light can be changed.

A ***spotlight*** is like a distant light, but it projects in a cone shape. Its light rays are not parallel. A spotlight is placed closer to the object than a distant light. Spotlights have a hotspot and a falloff. The light from a standard spotlight is directed toward a target. A ***free spotlight*** is the same as a standard spotlight, but without a target.

A ***weblight*** is a directed light that represents real-world distribution of light. The illumination is based on photometric data that can be entered for each light. The light from a standard weblight is directed toward a target. A ***free weblight*** is the same as a standard weblight, but without a target point.

Properties of Lights

There are several factors that affect how a light illuminates an object. These include the angle of incidence, reflectivity of the object's surface, and the distance that the light is from the object. In addition, the ability to cast shadows is a property of light. Shadows are discussed in detail later in this chapter.

Angle of Incidence

AutoCAD renders the faces of a model based on the angle at which light rays strike the faces. This angle is called the ***angle of incidence.*** See **Figure 16-1.** A face that is perpendicular to light rays receives the most light. As the angle of incidence decreases, the amount of light striking the face also decreases.

Reflectivity

The angle at which light rays are reflected off of a surface is called the ***angle of reflection.*** The angle of reflection is always equal to the angle of incidence. Refer to **Figure 16-1.**

The "brightness" of light reflected from an object is actually the number of light rays that reach your eyes. A surface that reflects a bright light, such as a mirror, is reflecting most of the light rays that strike it. The amount of reflection you see is called the ***highlight.*** The highlight is determined by the angle from the viewpoint relative to the angle of incidence. Refer to **Figure 16-1.**

The surface quality of the object affects how light is reflected. A smooth surface has a high specular factor. The ***specular factor*** indicates the number of light rays that have the same angle of reflection. Surfaces that are not smooth have a low specular factor. These surfaces are called ***matte.*** Matte surfaces ***diffuse,*** or "spread out," the light as it strikes the surface. This means that few of the light rays have the same angle of reflection. **Figure 16-2** illustrates the difference between matte and high specular

Figure 16-1.
The amount of reflection, or highlight, you see depends on the angle from which you view the object.

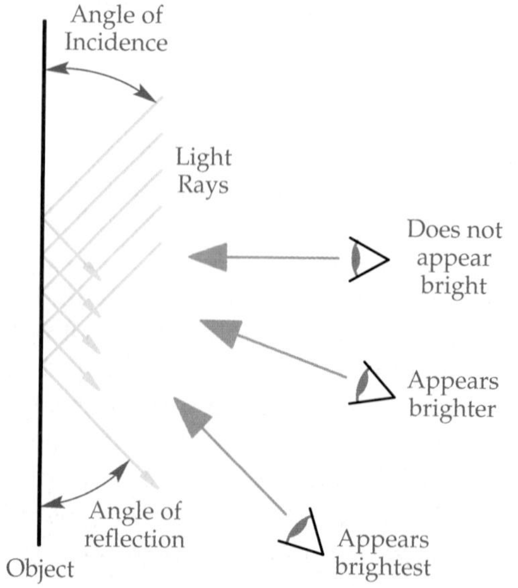

Figure 16-2.
Matte surfaces produce diffuse light. This is also referred to as having a low specular factor. Shiny surfaces evenly reflect light and have a high specular factor.

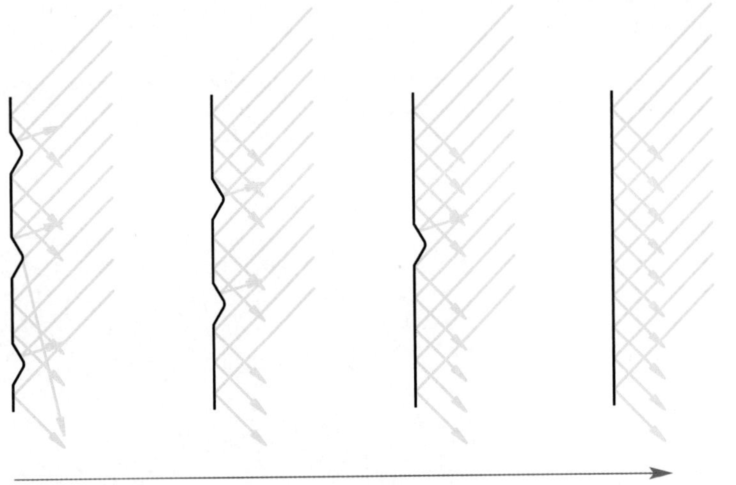

finishes. Surfaces can also vary in ***roughness.*** Roughness is a measure of the polish on a surface. This also affects how diffused the reflected light is.

Hotspot and Falloff

A spotlight produces a cone of light. The ***hotspot*** is the central portion of the cone, where the light is brightest. See **Figure 16-3.** The ***falloff*** is the outer portion of the cone, where the light begins to blend to shadow. The hotspot and falloff of a spotlight are not affected by the distance the light is from an object. Spotlights are the only lights with hotspot and falloff properties.

Attenuation

The farther an object is from a point light or spotlight, the less light will reach the object. See **Figure 16-4.** The intensity of light decreases over distance. This decrease is called ***attenuation.*** All lights in AutoCAD, except distant lights, have some kind of attenuation. Often, attenuation is called *falloff* or *decay.* However, do not confuse this

Figure 16-3.
The hotspot of a spotlight is the area that receives the most light. The smaller cone is the hotspot. The falloff receives light, but less than the hotspot. The larger cone is the falloff.

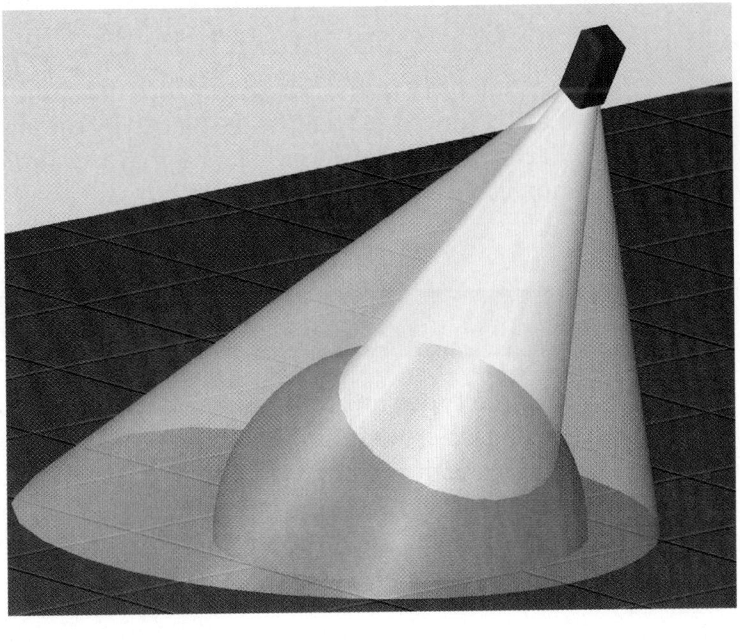

Figure 16-4. Attenuation is the intensity of light decreasing over distance. Attenuation has been turned on in this scene.

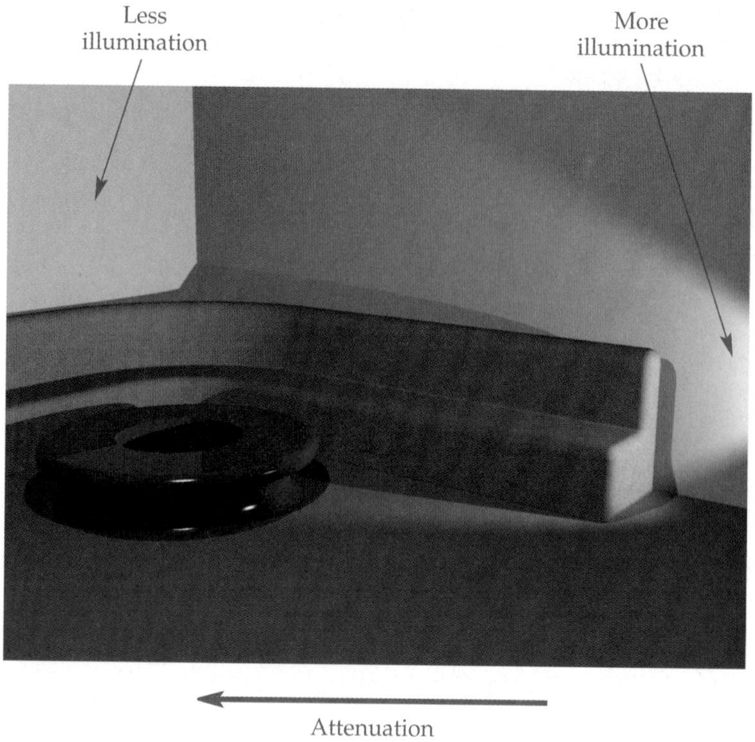

with the falloff of a spotlight, which is the outer edge of the cone of illumination. The following attenuation settings are available in AutoCAD.

- **None.** Applies the same light intensity regardless of distance. In other words, no attenuation is calculated.
- **Inverse Linear.** The illumination of an object decreases in inverse proportion to the distance. For example, if an object is two units from the light, it receives 1/2 of the full light. If the object is four units away, it receives 1/4 of the full light.
- **Inverse Squared.** The illumination of an object decreases in inverse proportion to the square of the distance. For example, if an object is two units from the light, it receives $(1/2)^2$, or 1/4, of the full light. If the object is four units away, it receives $(1/4)^2$, or 1/16, of the full light. As you can see, attenuation is greater for each unit of distance with the **Inverse Squared** option than with the **Inverse Linear** option.

PROFESSIONAL TIP

The intensity of the Sun's rays does not diminish from one point on Earth to another. They are weakened by the angle at which they strike Earth. Therefore, since distant lights are similar to the Sun, attenuation is not a factor with distant lights.

AutoCAD Lights

AutoCAD has three types of lighting: default lighting, sunlight with or without sky illumination, and user-created lighting. ***Default lighting*** is the lighting automatically available in the scene. It is composed of two light sources that evenly illuminate all surfaces. As the viewpoint is changed, the light sources follow to maintain an even illumination of the scene. There is no control over default lighting and it must be shut off whenever one of the other types of lighting is used.

As you saw in Chapter 14, ***sunlight*** may be added to any scene. AutoCAD uses a distant light to simulate the parallel rays of the Sun. The date and time of day can be adjusted to create different sunlight illumination. ***Sky illumination*** may also be added with sunlight to simulate light bouncing off of objects in the scene and particles in the atmosphere. This helps create a more-natural feel.

User-created lighting results when you add AutoCAD light objects to the drawing. There are four types of user-created lights: distant light, weblight, point light, and spotlight. See Figure 16-5. A distant light is a directed light source with parallel light rays. A weblight is a directional point light containing light intensity (photometric) data. A point light is like a lightbulb with light rays shining out in all directions. A spotlight is like a distant light, but it projects light in a cone shape instead of having parallel light rays.

LIGHTGLYPHDISPLAY
Ribbon
Visualize > Lights
Light Glyph Display
Type
LIGHTGLYPHDISPLAY
Menu
View > Render > Light > Light Glyphs

When created, point lights, weblights, and spotlights are represented by ***light glyphs,*** or icons, in the drawing. To suppress the display of light glyphs, pick the **Light Glyph Display** button in the expanded area of the **Lights** panel on the **Visualize** tab of the ribbon. The button is blue when light glyphs are displayed. The default lights, sun, and distant lights are not represented by glyphs.

In this section, you will learn how to add lights. You will also learn how to adjust the various properties of sunlight and AutoCAD light objects. The tools for working with lights can be accessed using the command line, menu browser, **Lights** toolbar, **Generic Lights** tool palette, the tool palettes in the **Photometric Lights** tool palette group, and **Lights** panel on the **Visualize** tab of the ribbon. See Figure 16-6.

So that you will never work with a completely dark scene, default lighting is applied in the viewport and to the rendering if no other lights are added. In order for your lights to be applied, you must switch between default lighting and user lighting. To do this, pick the **Default Lighting** button in the **Lights** panel on the **Visualize** tab of the ribbon. This button toggles the lighting between default lighting and whatever lights are available in the scene. When default lighting is on, the button is blue. When off, the button is grey. If you elected to do so, AutoCAD will automatically shut off default lighting when sunlight is turned on or a user-created light is added to the scene.

DEFAULTLIGHTING
Ribbon
Visualize > Light
Default Lighting
Type
DEFAULTLIGHTING

Lighting Units

There are three types of lighting units available in AutoCAD: standard (generic), international (SI), and US customary (American). Generic lighting is the type of lighting that was used in AutoCAD prior to AutoCAD 2008. This lighting provides very nice results, but the settings are not based on any real measurements. International or US customary lighting is called photometric lighting. ***Photometric lighting*** is physically correct and attenuates at the square of the distance from the source. For more accuracy, photometric data files can be imported from lighting manufacturers.

The **LIGHTINGUNITS** system variable sets which type of lighting is used. A setting of 0 means that standard (generic) lighting is used. This is the default setting for the

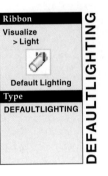

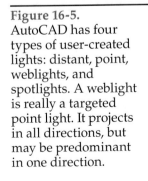

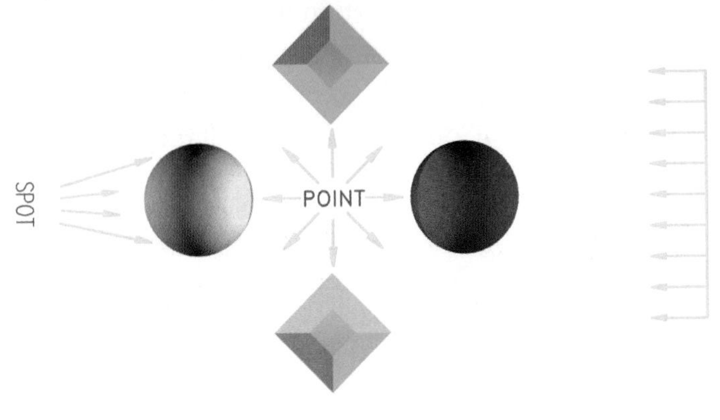

Figure 16-5.
AutoCAD has four types of user-created lights: distant, point, weblights, and spotlights. A weblight is really a targeted point light. It projects in all directions, but may be predominant in one direction.

Figure 16-6.
The tools for adding and controlling lights. A—**Generic Lights** tool palette. B—The four tool palettes in the **Photometric Lights** tool palette group. C—**Lights**, **Sun**, and **Time & Location** panels in the ribbon.

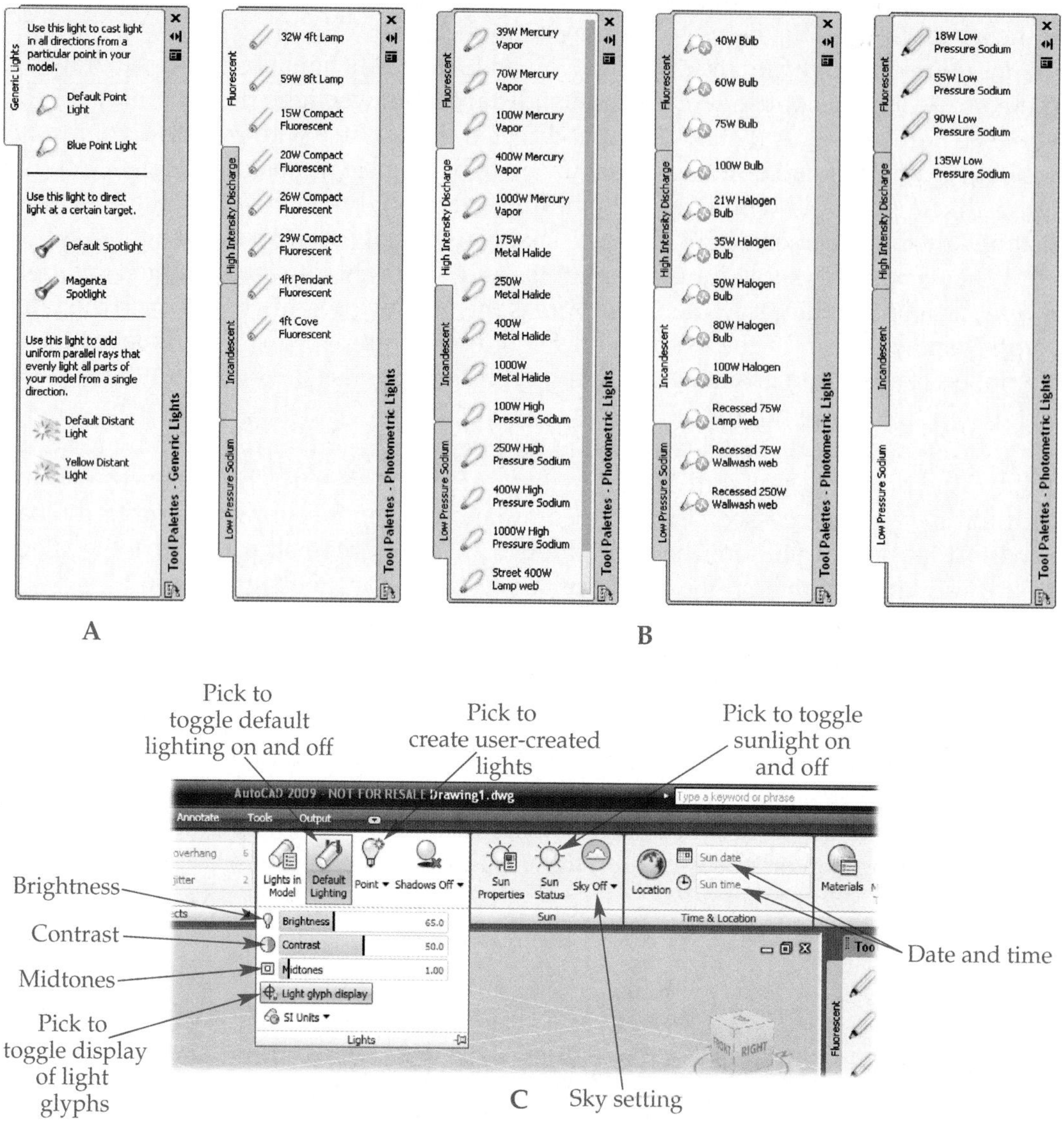

system variable. However, for more realistic lighting, it is recommended that photometric lighting be used. Enter a value of 1 and American lighting units are used. A setting of 2 turns on international lighting units. Both of these settings result in photometric lighting. The only difference between a setting of 1 and 2 is that American units are displayed as *candelas* and international units are displayed as *lumens*.

Sunlight

SUNSTATUS

Ribbon
Visualize > Sun
Sun Status
Type
SUNSTATUS

To turn sunlight on or off, pick the **Sun Status** button in the **Sun** panel on the **Visualize** tab of the ribbon. This button is blue when sunlight is on. Sunlight can also be turned on or off in the **Sun Properties** palette, which is discussed later. Sunlight is not represented by a light glyph. The date, time, and geographic location can be set in the **Time & Location** panel on the **Visualize** tab of the ribbon. These properties determine how the scene is illuminated by the sun.

To change the current date, pick the **Sun date** slider and drag it left or right. Sunlight must be on for the slider to be enabled. As you drag the slider, the date is displayed on the right-hand end of the slider. The time is changed in the same manner as the date. Drag the **Sun time** slider left or right. As you drag the slider, the time is displayed on the right-hand end of the slider.

The location of the scene can be set to an actual geographic location. This is important if you want to replicate the lighting and shadows of an actual site. Picking the **Location** button on the **Time & Location** panel in the **Visualize** tab of the ribbon opens a dialog box titled **Geographic Location – Define Geographic Location**. See **Figure 16-7.** The first option in this dialog box allows you to specify the location by importing a KML or a KMZ file. *KML* stands for Keyhole Markup Language. This file contains latitude, longitude, and, sometimes, other data to pinpoint a location on Earth. A KMZ file is a zipped KML file. The second option is to import the current location from Google Earth. In order for this to work, Google Earth must be installed and open with the location selected. The third option opens the **Geographic Location** dialog box. See **Figure 16-8.**

Ribbon
Visualize
> Time & Location
Location

Type
GEOGRAPHICLOCATION

GEOGRAPHICLOCATION

Figure 16-7.
This dialog box provides the options for defining the geographic location of the model.

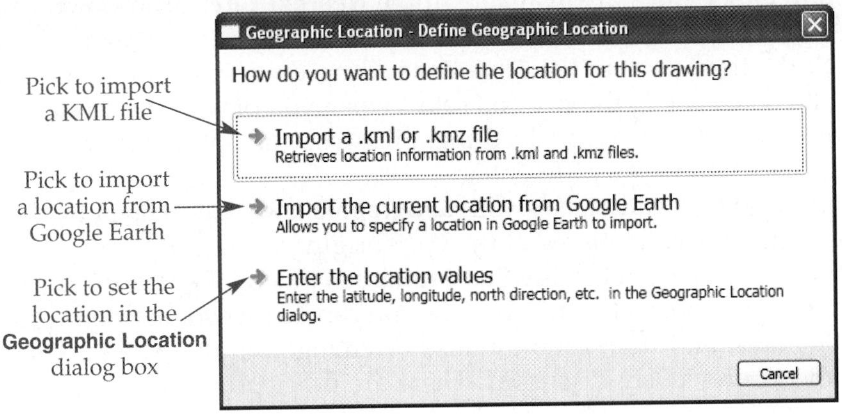

Figure 16-8.
The **Geographic Location** dialog box is used to input geographic location data.

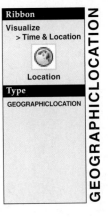

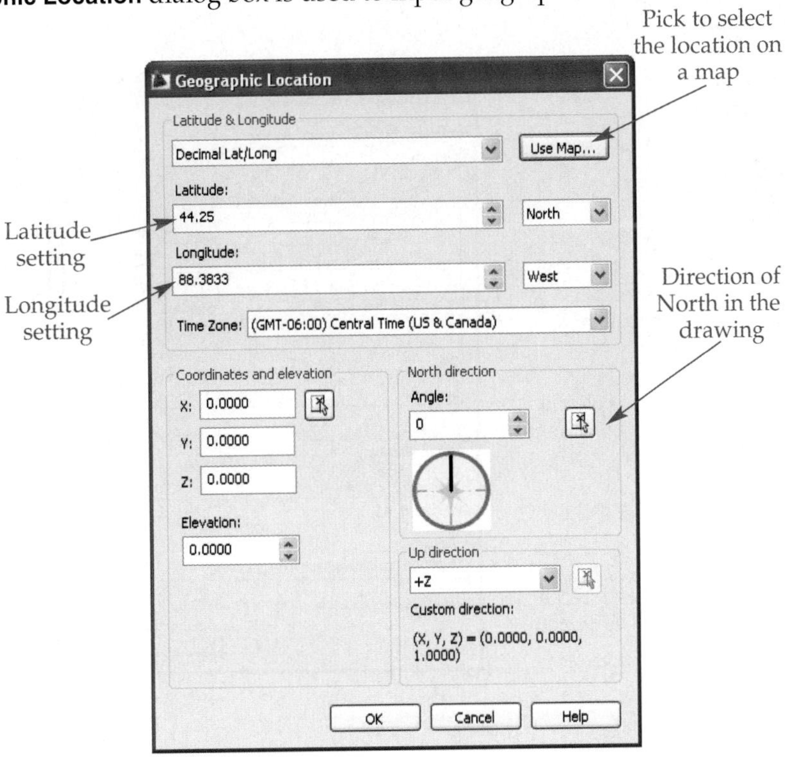

When a location is imported from Google Earth, you are asked to select a location in the drawing for the location. After picking a point in the drawing, you are asked for the North vector. Pick a point that should be in the direction of North. Once this is set, a ***geographic marker*** is added at the point selected for the location. This marker looks like a red and white thumbtack. Its visibility is controlled with the **GEOMARKERVISIBILITY** system variable.

To set the location, enter the latitude and longitude. You can select to use either decimal or degrees/minutes/seconds values for these settings. Also, pick a time zone in the **Time Zone:** drop-down list and set XYZ coordinates and elevation for AutoCAD's world coordinate system. You can specify the angle for North in the text box or by picking points in the drawing window. The "up direction" is normally +Z, but you can change it to –Z. You can also set it to anything you want if you select Custom in the drop-down list in the **Up direction** area.

The quickest way to set the location is to select it on a map. Pick the **Use Map...** button to open the **Location Picker** dialog box. See Figure 16-9. The crosshairs on the map indicates the current location. By default, picking a point on the map selects the nearest big city. Many other cities are available in the **Nearest City:** drop-down list. The **Region:** drop-down list is used to change the map to one of different areas of the world. You can pick the time zone in the **Time Zone:** drop-down list, but AutoCAD attempts to match the time zone to the city you select when you pick the **OK** button to close the dialog box. An alert box is displayed that gives you the option to accept the new time zone or go back and pick a different one.

Once you have selected a location, close the **Geographic Location** dialog box. The geographic marker is automatically placed at the WCS origin.

SUNPROPERTIES

Ribbon
Visualize
> Sun
Sun Properties

Type
SUNPROPERTIES

Menu
View
> Render
> Light
> Sun Properties

The properties of the sun are set in the **Sun Properties** palette, Figure 16-10. The **SUNPROPERTIES** command opens this palette. The sun can be turned on or off using the palette. The date, time, and time zone can also be changed in the palette. These settings are the same as previously discussed. There are other properties of the sun

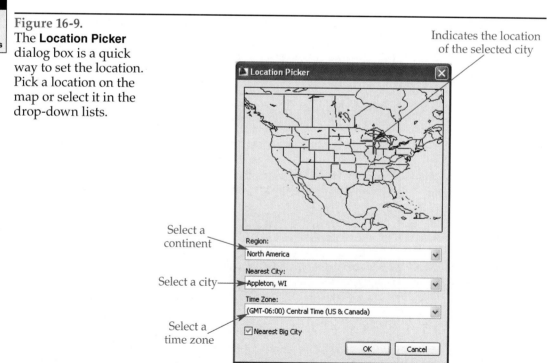

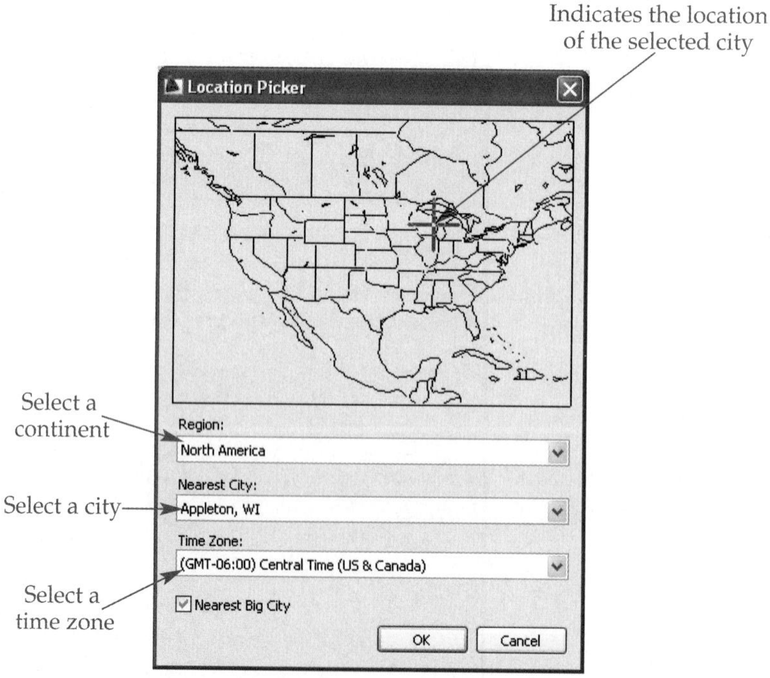

Figure 16-9.
The **Location Picker** dialog box is a quick way to set the location. Pick a location on the map or select it in the drop-down lists.

Figure 16-10.
The **Sun Properties** palette.

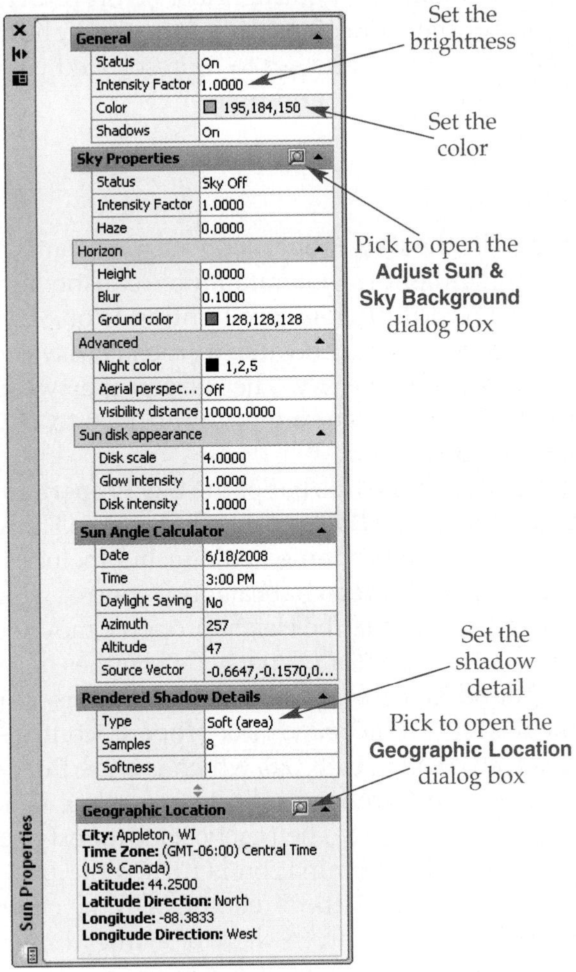

that are only available in the **Sun Properties** palette. This palette contains several categories, which are discussed in the next sections.

General

The Intensity Factor property in the **General** category determines the brightness of the sun. Setting this property to zero, in effect, turns off sunlight. Increasing the property makes the sunlight brighter. The maximum value for the property is determined by the capabilities of your computer.

The Color property in the **General** category is used to set the color of the sun, if photometric lighting is off. By default, sunlight is white (true color 255, 255, 255). To change the color, pick the drop-down list and choose a new color. If you pick the Select Color... entry, the **Select Color** dialog box is displayed for selecting a color. Sunlight can be changed to any color, but be aware that changing the color of the light may drastically alter the appearance of a scene. This is especially true if materials are attached to objects in the drawing. The color of sunlight is often set to a very light blue for an outdoor scene to help convey a bright blue sky.

The Shadows property in the **General** category determines whether or not the sun casts shadows. The property is either on or off. Shadows are discussed in detail later in this chapter.

NOTE

Photometric lighting must be off (**LIGHTINGUNITS** = 0) in order to set the sun color. If photometric lighting is on, the Color property is disabled and set to a preselected color based on the geographic location, date, and time.

Sky properties

The settings in the **Sky Properties** category control the sky. The sky is used in conjunction with sunlight to generate more-realistic lighting in the scene. This category is only displayed if photometric lighting is on. The Status property determines if the sky effect is on or off. The value in the Intensity property is a multiplier for the illumination provided by the sky. The Haze property controls how the sky illumination is diffused. The value can range from 0.0000 to 15.0000. The preset sun color is affected by this value.

Notice the button in the title bar of the **Sky Properties** category. Picking this button opens the **Adjust Sun & Sky Background** dialog box. This dialog box contains the same settings found in the **Sun Properties** palette, but includes a preview of the sun disk.

The settings in the **Horizon** subcategory control what the horizon looks like and where it is located. Changing the Height property moves the horizon up or down. The default value is 0.0000. The Blur property determines how much the horizon is blurred between the ground and the sky. The range for this value is from 0.0000 to 10.0000 with a default of 0.1000. The Ground color property controls the color of the ground. The default color is true color 128,128,128, which is a medium gray.

The settings in the **Advanced** subcategory allow you to control some of the more artistic settings of your scene. The Night color property sets the color of the night sky. This is only visible if sky illumination is turned on. In a city, the night sky may have an orange tint to it because of the streetlamps in the city. However, in the country, the night sky is nearly black due to the lack of artificial illumination. The Aerial perspective property determines whether or not aerial perspective is applied. This is a way of simulating distance between the camera and the sky/background. The setting is either on or off. The Visibility distance property sets the distance from the camera at which haze obscures 10% of the objects in the background. This is a very useful tool for creating the illusion of depth in a scene. The default value is 10000.0000, but it can range from 0.0000 to whatever is needed.

Normally, lights do not appear in the rendered scene at all, only the illumination provided by the lights. The settings in the **Sun disk appearance** subcategory control what the sun looks like in the sky, or on the background. The **Disk scale** property sets the size of the sun, or solar disk, as it appears on the background. The default value is 4.0000 with the range of values being from 0.0000 to 25.0000. The Glow intensity value determines the size of the glowing halo around the sun in the sky. Default value is 1.0000 and can range from 0.0000 to 25.0000. The Disk intensity property controls the brightness of the sun on the background. The default value is 1.0000 and the range of values is from 0.0000 to 25.0000.

Sun angle calculator

The settings in the **Sun Angle Calculator** category determine the angle of the sun in relationship to the XY plane. The Date and Time properties are discussed earlier and can be controlled from the **Time & Location** panel in the **Visualize** tab of the ribbon. This category in the **Sun Properties** palette also includes the Daylight Saving property. This property is used to turn daylight saving on or off. The Azimuth, Altitude, and Source Vector properties display the current settings, but are read only in the **Sun Properties** palette. These values are automatically calculated by the settings in the **Geographic Location** dialog box.

Rendered shadow details

The Type property in the **Rendered Shadow Details** category determines the type of shadow cast by the sun, if shadows are cast. When the property is set to Sharp, raytraced shadows are cast. These shadows have sharp edges. Raytracing produces accurate shadows, but rendering may take longer. When the property is set to either Soft (mapped) or Soft (area), shadow-mapped shadows are cast. This type of shadow has soft edges. Shadow-mapped shadows may be calculated quicker than raytraced shadows, but the resulting shadows are less precise. In addition, soft shadows do not work with transparent surfaces like windows. When the Type property is set to Soft (mapped), two additional settings are available in the category:

- Map Size. This property determines the number of subdivisions, or samples, used to create the shadow. By default, shadow maps are 256 × 256 pixels in size. If shadows look grainy, increasing this setting will make them look better.
- Softness. This property determines the sharpness of the shadow's edge. The value ranges from 1 to 10. The higher the value, the softer (less sharp) the edge of the shadow.

When the Type property is set to Soft (area), the two additional settings are:

- Samples. This property sets the number of samples used on the solar disk. The value can be from 0.0000 to 1000.0000.
- Softness. This property determines the sharpness of the shadow's edge, as described above.

When the Type property is set to Sharp, the other settings are read only and not applied.

NOTE

With photometric lighting on (**LIGHTINGUNITS** = 1 or 2), only the Soft (area) selection is available in the Type property drop-down list.

Geographic location

The **Geographic Location** category at the bottom of the **Sun Properties** palette displays the current geographic location settings. Changes cannot be made here, but picking the **Launch Geographic Location** button in the category's title bar opens the **Geographic Location** dialog box, which is described earlier.

Exercise 16-1

Complete the exercise on the Student CD.

Distant Lights

Distant lights are user-created lights that have parallel light rays. See **Figure 16-11.** When a distant light is created, the location from where the light is originating must be specified along with the direction of the light rays. Distant lights are not represented in the drawing by light glyphs. Distant lights are often used to create even, uniform, overhead illumination, such as you would encounter in an office situation. The distance of the objects in the scene to the distant light has no effect on the intensity of the illumination. Distant lights do not attenuate. A distant light can also be used to simulate sunlight without having to set up a time and location. However, the light must be manually moved to change the illuminating effect.

Figure 16-11.
This example shows the use of a distant light to simulate sunlight shining through a window. Notice how the edges of the shadows of the grill are parallel.

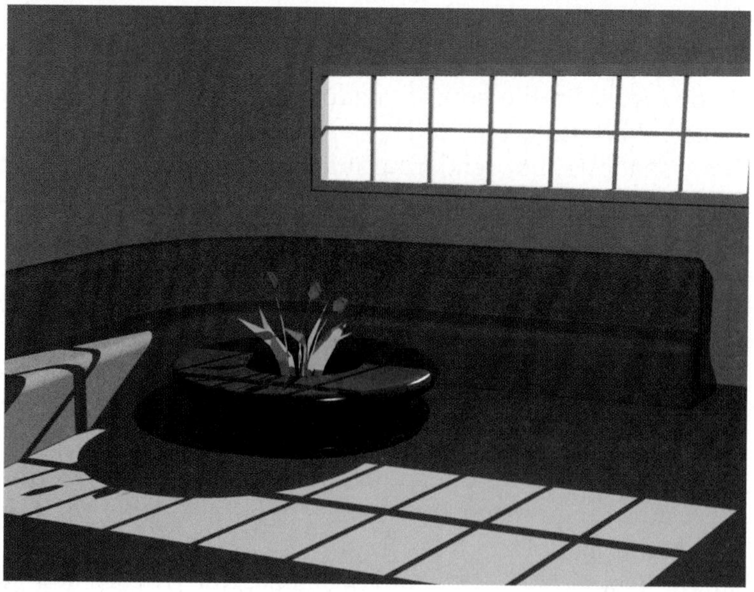

DISTANTLIGHT

Ribbon
Visualize
> Lights
Distant

Type
DISTANTLIGHT
LIGHT

Menu
View
> Render
> Light
> New Distant Light

The **DISTANTLIGHT** or **LIGHT** command is used to create a distant light. You are first prompted to specify the direction from which the light is originating or to enter the **Vector** option. If you pick a point, it is the location of the light. Next, you are prompted to specify the direction to which the light is pointing. This is simply the location where the light is aimed.

If you enter the **Vector** option instead of picking a "from" point, you must type the endpoint coordinates (in WCS units) of the direction vector. The light will point from the WCS origin to the entered endpoint.

After the light location and direction are determined, several other options are available. You can name the light, set the intensity, turn the light on or off, determine if and how shadows are cast, and set the light color.

AutoCAD provides a default name for new lights based on the type of light and a sequential number, such as Distantlight1, Distantlight2, and so on. It is a good idea to provide a meaningful name for a light. This is especially true if there are other lights in the scene. To rename a light, enter the **Name** option. Then, type the name of the light and press [Enter].

To set the brightness of the light, enter the **Intensity** option. Then, type a value and press [Enter]. The default value is 1.00. Setting the value to 0.00, in effect, turns off the light. The maximum value depends on the capabilities of your computer. This option is called **Intensity Factor** if photometric lighting is enabled.

When a light is created, it is on. To turn the light off, enter the **Status** option. Then, change the setting to **Off**.

The **Photometry** option is available when photometric lighting is active. It controls the luminous qualities of visible light sources. Once you enter the **Photometry** options, you can select one of three settings:

- **Intensity**. This is the power of the light source and can be entered as candelas (cd), luminous flux (lx), or foot-candles (fc), depending on the current lighting units.
- **Color**. This is the color of the light source and can be changed by typing in a name (to get a list of color names, enter ?) or by the Kelvin temperature value (k).
- **Exit**. Exits the command option.

The **Shadow** option is used to determine if and how shadows are cast by the distant light. To turn off shadow casting, enter the option and select the **Off** setting. The **Sharp** setting creates raytraced shadows. The **Softmapped** setting casts shadow-mapped shadows. Shadows are discussed later in this chapter.

By default, new distant lights cast white light (true color 255, 255, 255). To change the color of the light, enter the **Color** option. This option is called **Filter Color** if photometric lighting is enabled. To specify a new true color, simply specify the values and press [Enter]. To specify a color based on hue, saturation, and luminance (HSL), enter the **Hsl** option and specify the values. To enter an AutoCAD color index (ACI) number, enter the **Index color** option and specify the ACI number. To specify a color book color, enter the **Color Book** option and then specify the name of the color book followed by the name of the color.

Once all settings for the distant light have been made, use the **Exit** option to end the command and create the light. Do not press [Esc] to end the command. Doing so actually cancels the command and the light is not created.

PROFESSIONAL TIP

To provide a visual cue to a distant light's location and direction, draw a line with one endpoint at the "from" coordinate and the other endpoint at the "to" coordinate. Then, when creating the distant light, select the endpoints of the line. Since a distant light is not represented by a light glyph, the line serves the purpose of the glyph.

NOTE

If you attempt to create a distant light with photometric lighting on (**LIGHTINGUNITS** = 1 or 2), you will receive a warning to the effect that photometric distant lights may overexpose the scene. Also, the **Distant** button is not displayed in the flyout on the ribbon. When photometric lighting is on, enter the command by typing or selecting it in the menu browser.

Exercise 16-2

Complete the exercise on the Student CD.

Point Lights

Point lights are user-created lights that have light rays projecting in all directions. See Figure 16-12. When a point light is created, its location must be specified. Since point lights illuminate in all directions, there is no "to" location for a point light. A light glyph represents point lights in the drawing. See Figure 16-13. Point lights can be set to attenuate. In this case, the distance of the objects in the scene to the point light affects the intensity of the illumination.

The **POINTLIGHT** or **LIGHT** command is used to create a point light. You are first prompted to specify the location of the point light. Once the location is established, several options for the light are available. You can name the light, set the intensity, turn the light on or off, adjust the photometry settings, determine if and how shadows are cast, set the attenuation, and set the light color. The **Name**, **Intensity** (or **Intensity Factor**), **Status**, **Photometry**, **Shadow**, and **Color** (or **Filter Color**) options work the same as the corresponding options for a distant light.

POINTLIGHT

Ribbon
Visualize
> Lights
Point

Type
POINTLIGHT
LIGHT

Menu
View
> Render
> Light
> New Point Light

The **Attenuation** option is used to set attenuation for the point light. When this option is selected, five more options are available:

- **Attenuation Type**
- **Use Limits**
- **Attenuation Start Limit**
- **Attenuation End Limit**
- **Exit**

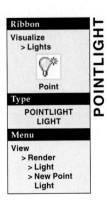

Figure 16-12.
A—A point light is placed inside of the lamp fixture. Notice how the light projects in all directions. B—When shadow casting is turned on for the light, the lampshade blocks the light from illuminating objects below the shade.

A

B

Figure 16-13.
This is the light glyph for a point light.

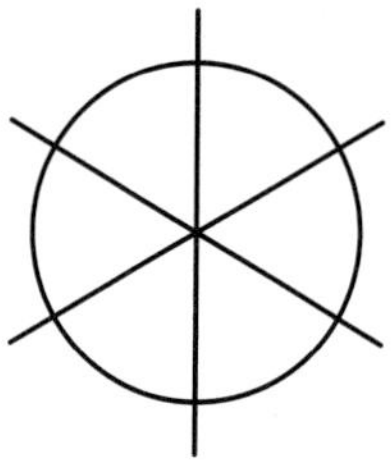

The **Exit** option returns you to the previous prompt.

The **Attenuation Type** option is used to turn attenuation on and off and to set the type of attenuation. To turn attenuation off, select the option and then enter **None**. To turn attenuation on, select the option and then enter either **Inverse Linear** or **Inverse Squared**. Attenuation is discussed in detail earlier in this chapter.

The **Use Limits** option determines if the attenuation of the light has a beginning and an end. When this option is set to **Off**, attenuation starts at the light and ends when the illumination reaches zero. When set to **On**, attenuation begins at the starting limit and ends at the ending limit.

To set the starting point for attenuation, enter the **Attenuation Start Limit** option. Then, specify the distance from the point light where attenuation will begin. The full intensity of the light provides illumination up to this point. From this point to the attenuation end limit, the light falls off.

To set the point where the illumination attenuates to zero, enter the **Attenuation End Limit** option. Then, specify the distance from the point light where the illumination is zero. Beyond this point, AutoCAD does not calculate the effect of the light.

TARGETPOINT

Type
TARGETPOINT LIGHT

Target Point Lights

The target point light is like a regular point light except that the command starts by asking for a *source* location and a *target* location. The rest of the options are the same. You can type TARGETPOINT to access this command or pick the **Targetpoint** option in the **LIGHT** command.

CAUTION

It is important to set attenuation limits. If there is no end limit for the light, AutoCAD may calculate the illumination beyond the boundary of the scene, even if there is nothing there to see. To speed processing time, tell AutoCAD where illumination stops for point and spotlights.

PROFESSIONAL TIP

A point light may be used as an incandescent lightbulb, such as in a table lamp. Most of these lightbulbs cast a yellow light. In these cases, you may want to change the color of the light to a light yellow. Compact fluorescent lightbulbs may cast white, light blue, or light yellow light. LED-based lights cast a color based on the color of the LED. Other colors can be used to give the impression of heat or colored lights.

Exercise 16-3

Complete the exercise on the Student CD.

Spotlights

Spotlights are user-created lights that have light rays projecting in a cone shape in one direction. See **Figure 16-14.** When a spotlight is created, the location from where the light is originating must be specified along with the direction in which the light rays travel. A light glyph represents spotlights in the drawing. See **Figure 16-15.** Spotlights can be set to attenuate. In this case, the distance of the objects in the scene to the spotlight affects the intensity of the illumination.

The **SPOTLIGHT** or **LIGHT** command is used to create a spotlight. You are first prompted to specify the location of the light. This is from where the light rays will originate. Next, you are prompted for the target location. This is simply the location where the light is aimed.

SPOTLIGHT

Ribbon
Visualize
> Lights
Spot

Type
SPOTLIGHT
LIGHT

Menu
View
> Render
> Light
> New
Spotlight

Figure 16-14.
Three spotlights are used to simulate recessed ceiling lights. Notice how the light from each spotlight projects in a cone.

Figure 16-15.
This is the light glyph for a spotlight.

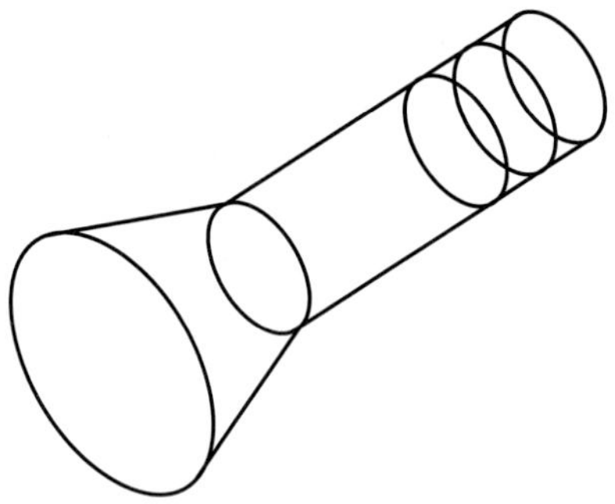

Once the location and target are established, several options for the light are available. Spotlights and point lights have similar settings. You can change the name, intensity, status, photometry settings, shadow, attenuation, and color. The **Name**, **Intensity** (or **Intensity Factor**), **Status**, **Photometry**, **Shadow**, and **Color** (or **Filter Color**) options work the same as the corresponding options for a point light. However, a spotlight also has hotspot and falloff settings.

The ***hotspot*** is the inner cone of illumination for a spotlight. Refer to Figure 16-16. This is measured in degrees. To set the hotspot, enter the **Hotspot** option and then specify the number of degrees for the hotspot.

The ***falloff,*** not to be confused with attenuation, is the outer cone of illumination for a spotlight. Like the hotspot, it is measured in degrees. The falloff value must be greater than or equal to the hotspot value. It cannot be less than the hotspot value. In practice, the falloff value is often much greater than the hotspot value. To set the falloff, enter the **Falloff** option and then specify the number of degrees for the falloff.

Once the light is created and you select it in the viewport, grips are displayed. If you hover the cursor over a grip, a tooltip is displayed indicating what the grip will modify. You can use grips to change the location of the spotlight and its target, the hotspot, and the falloff. If you hover over a falloff or hotspot grip, the current angle is displayed in the wireframe cone.

Free Spotlight

FREESPOT

Type
FREESPOT LIGHT

A free spotlight is like a standard spotlight except that you do not specify a target, only the light location. The rest of the options are the same. You can type FREESPOT to access this command or pick the **Freespot** option in the **LIGHT** command. When created, a free spotlight points down the Z axis (from positive to negative) of the current UCS. A free spotlight may be easier to control than a standard spotlight because you do not have to worry about the target point. If you want to change the angle or position of the light, use the **3DMOVE** and **ROTATE3D** commands.

Figure 16-16.
Hotspot and falloff for a spotlight are angular measurements.

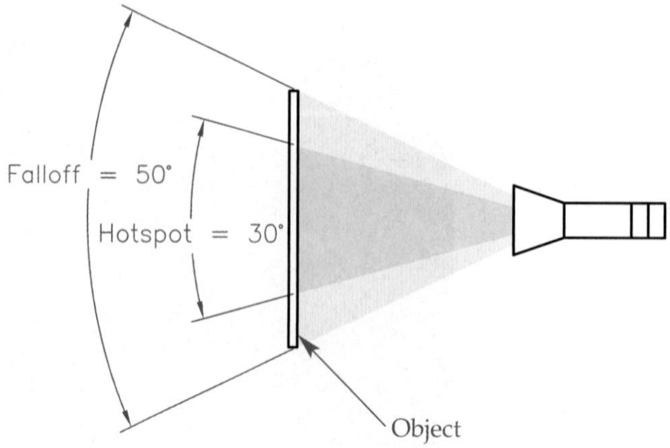

PROFESSIONAL TIP

The best way to see how colored lights affect your model is to experiment. Remember, you can render selected areas of the scene. This allows you to see how light intensity and color change objects without performing a full render.

Exercise 16-4

Complete the exercise on the Student CD.

Weblight

A photometric weblight is really just a targeted point light. The difference is that a weblight provides a more precise representation of the light. Real-world lights appear to evenly illuminate from their source, but, in reality, the shape of the light, the material used in its manufacture, and other factors make all lights distribute their energy in different ways. These data are provided by light manufacturers in the form of light distribution data. Light distribution data can be loaded into the **Photometric Web** subcategory of the **General** category in the **Properties** palette when the light is selected. Select the Web file property, then pick the browse button (**...**) and select an IES file. IES stands for Illuminating Engineering Society. AutoCAD's online documentation has additional information on IES files.

Think of the web of a weblight as a spherical cage surrounding the light source. If the light is evenly distributed from its source, the cage is a true sphere. In actuality, a light may emit more light energy in the X direction than in the Z direction. In this case, the cage bulges out further in the X direction. The position of this bulge may be important to the illumination of the scene and you may need to rotate the web to apply more or less light in one direction or another.

WEBLIGHT

Type
WEBLIGHT
LIGHT

To add a weblight to the scene, you can type WEBLIGHT or pick the **Web** option in the **LIGHT** command. You are prompted for source and target locations. The **Name**, **Intensity Factor**, **Status**, **Photometry**, **Shadow**, and **Filter Color** options work the same as the corresponding options for the previously discussed lights. However, weblights have an additional **Web** option. When this option is activated, these options are presented:

- **File.** Allows you to select an IES file.
- **X.** Rotates the web around the X axis.
- **Y.** Rotates the web around the Y axis.
- **Z.** Rotates the web around the Z axis.
- **Exit.** Exits the **Web** option.

Point and spotlights can be converted to weblights, and vice versa, using the **Properties** palette. Simply select an existing light and open the **Properties** palette. In the **General** category, the Type property determines whether the light is a point light, spotlight, or weblight. Select the type in the drop-down list. Using the **Properties** palette with lights is discussed in detail later in this chapter.

Free Weblight

FREEWEB

Type
FREEWEB
LIGHT

A free weblight is the same as a standard weblight except that there is no target. Only the source location is specified when placing the light. To change the location and direction of the light, use the **ROTATE3D** and **3DMOVE** commands.

NOTE

To create either standard or free weblights, photometric lighting must be enabled (**LIGHTINGUNITS** = 1 or 2).

Photometric Lights Tool Palette Group

Photometric lights may be easily added to the drawing using the tool palettes in the **Photometric Lights** tool palette group. Refer to Figure 16-6B. This palette group contains four palettes: **Fluorescent**, **High Intensity Discharge**, **Incandescent**, and **Low Pressure Sodium**. Lights created with these tools have preset properties for **Intensity Factor**, **Shadow**, and **Filter Color**. The glyph for the long fluorescent lights has a yellow line passing through its center indicating the direction of the light. The high intensity discharge and low-pressure sodium lights are point lights. The incandescent lights are free spotlights.

Lights in Model and Properties Palettes

The **Lights in Model** palette is extremely useful for controlling the lights in your scene, Figure 16-17. Used in conjunction with the **Properties** palette, you can manage and edit all of the lights in a scene.

Light list

LIGHTLIST

Ribbon
Visualize > Lights
Lights in Model
Type
LIGHTLIST
Menu
View > Render > Light > Light List

The **LIGHTLIST** command displays the **Lights in Model** palette. All user-created lights in the scene are displayed in the list. To modify the properties of a light, either double-click on the light name or right-click on it and select **Properties** from the shortcut menu. This opens the **Properties** palette. See Figure 16-18. If the **Properties** palette is already open, you can simply select a light in the **Lights in Model** palette. You can select more than one light by pressing the [Ctrl] key and selecting the names in the **Lights in Model** palette. This allows you to change all of their settings at the same time. This is an excellent way to make the lighting in your scene uniform or to control a series of lights with a single edit.

A light can be deleted from the scene using the **Lights in Model** palette. To do so, simply right-click on the name of the light and select **Delete Light** from the shortcut menu. The light is removed from the drawing. Using the **UNDO** command restores the light.

Figure 16-17.
All user-created lights are listed in the **Lights in Model** palette.

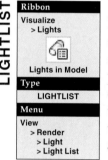

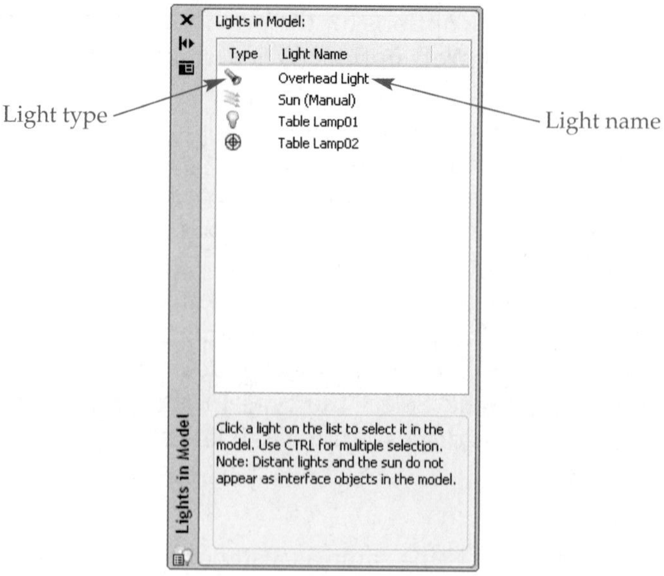

Figure 16-18.
The **Properties** palette with a weblight selected.

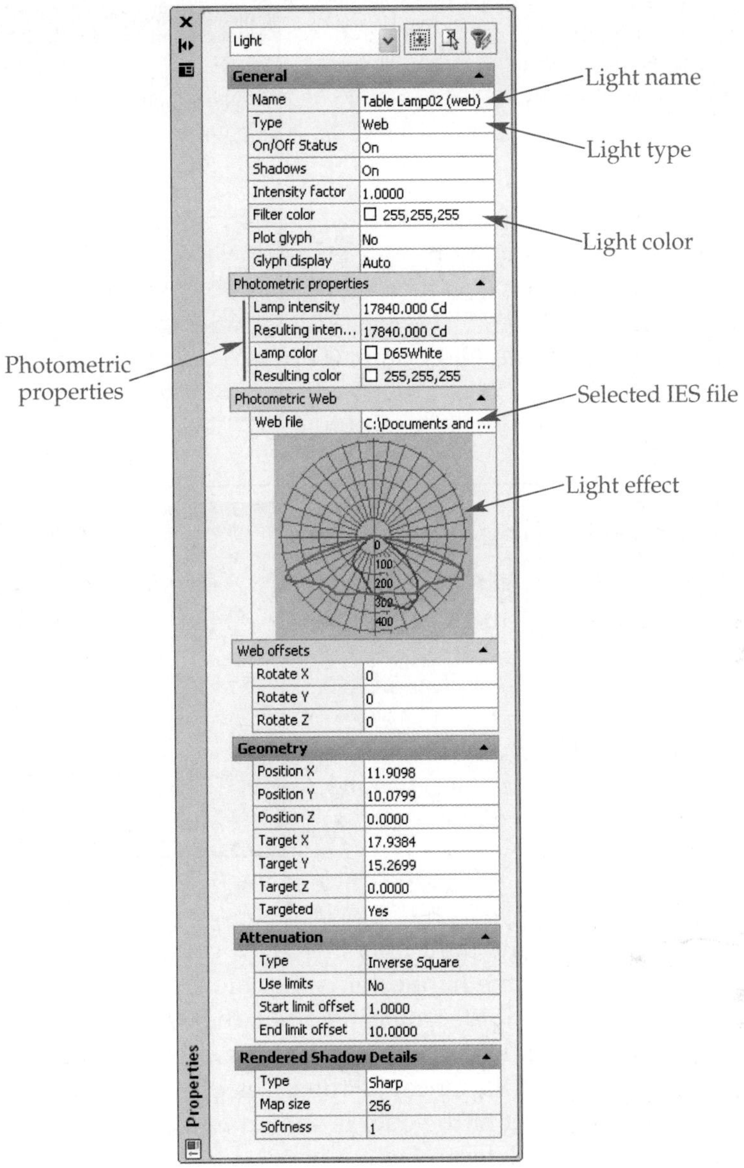

Properties palette

The **Photometric Properties** subcategory of the **General** category in the **Properties** palette has special settings for photometric lights. The Lamp intensity property determines the brightness of the light. The value may be expressed in candelas (cd), lumens (lm), or illuminance (lux) values. When you select the Lamp intensity property, a button is displayed to the right of the value. Picking this button opens the **Lamp Intensity** dialog box, Figure 16-19. In this dialog box, you can change the illumination units and set the intensity (Lamp intensity property). You can also set an intensity scale factor. This is multiplied by the Lamp intensity property to obtain the actual illumination supplied by the light. The read-only Resulting intensity property in the **Properties** palette displays the result.

The Lamp color property in the **Photometric Properties** subcategory in the **General** category controls the color of the light. If you select the property, a button is displayed to the right of the value. Picking this button opens the **Lamp Color** dialog box. See Figure 16-20. This dialog box gives you the option to control the color of the light by either standard spectra colors or Kelvin colors. The color selected in the **Filter color:** drop-down list is applied to the color of the light. The **Resulting color:** swatch displays

Figure 16-19.
The **Lamp Intensity** dialog box is used to set the intensity for a light.

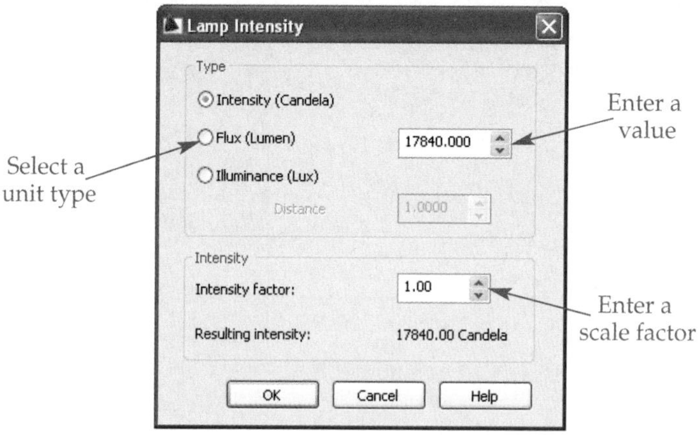

Figure 16-20.
The **Lamp Color** dialog box is used to set the color for the light and a filter color, if needed.

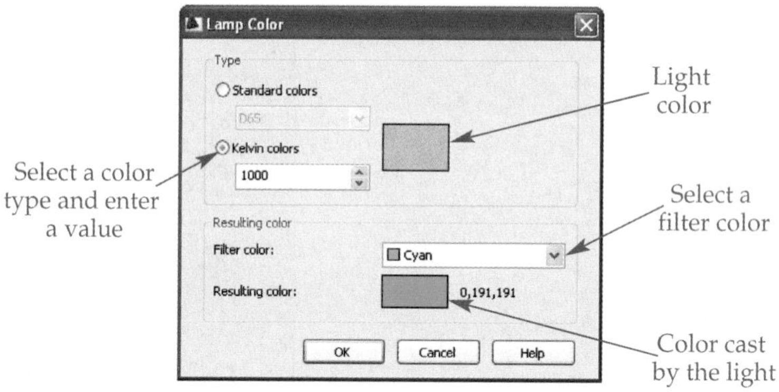

the color cast by the light once the filter color is applied. If the filter color is white (255,255,255), then the light color is the color cast by the light.

The **Photometric Web** subcategory in the **General** category is where you can specify an IES file for the light. Select the Web file property, then pick the browse button (**...**) and select the IES file. Once the file is selected, its location is displayed in the Web file property. The effect of the data is shown in a graph at the bottom of the **Photometric Web** subcategory. Refer to Figure 16-18.

The **Web offsets** subcategory in the **General** category allows you to rotate the web around the X, Y, and Z axes. This is discussed earlier in the Weblight section.

In the **Geometry** category, you can change the X, Y, and Z coordinates of the light. You can also change the X, Y, and Z coordinates of the light's target. If the light is not targeted, the Target X, Target Y, and Target Z properties are not displayed. To change the light from targeted to free, and vice versa, select Yes or No in the Targeted property drop-down list.

The properties in the **Attenuation** category are the same as those discussed earlier in this chapter in the Point Lights section. In order to change these properties in the **Properties** palette, photometric lighting must be off (**LIGHTINGUNITS** = 0).

The last category in the **Properties** palette is **Rendered Shadow Details**. The properties in this category are used to control shadows. Shadows are discussed later in this chapter.

PROFESSIONAL TIP

It is important to give your lights names that make them easy to identify in a list. If you accept the default names for lights, they will be called Pointlight1, Spotlight5, Distantlight7, Weblight2, etc., making them difficult to identify. Use the **Name** option when creating the light or, after the light is created, the **Properties** palette to change the name of the light.

Determining Proper Light Intensity

As a general rule, the object nearest to a point light or spotlight should receive the full illumination, or full intensity, of the light. Full intensity of any light that has an attenuation property is a value of one. Remember, attenuation is calculated using either the inverse linear or inverse square method. Therefore, you must calculate the appropriate intensity.

For example, suppose you have drawn an object and placed a point light and a spotlight. The point light is 55 units from the object. The spotlight is 43 units from the object. Use the following calculations to determine the correct intensity settings for the lights.

- **Inverse linear.** If the point light is 55 units from the object, the object receives 1/55 of the light. Therefore, set the intensity of the point light to 55 so the light intensity striking the object has a value of 1 (55/55 = 1). Since the spotlight is 43 units from the object, set its light intensity to 43 (43/43 = 1).
- **Inverse square.** If the point light is 55 units from the object, the object receives $(1/55)^2$, or 1/3025 ($55^2 = 3025$), of the light. Therefore, set the intensity of the point light to 3025 (3025/3025 = 1). The object receives $(1/43)^2$, or 1/1849 ($43^2 = 1849$), of the spotlight's illumination. Therefore, set the intensity of the spotlight to 1849 (1849/1849 = 1).

However, it should be noted that these settings are merely a starting point. You will likely spend some time adjusting lighting to produce the desired results. In some cases, it may take longer to light the scene than it did to model it.

PROFESSIONAL TIP

If you render a scene and the image appears black, all of the lights may have been turned off or have their intensity set to zero. A scene with no lights placed in it will be rendered with default lighting.

Shadows

Shadows are critical to the realism of a rendered 3D model. A model without shadows appears obviously fake. On the other hand, a model with realistic materials and shadows may be hard to recognize as computer generated. In AutoCAD, the sun, distant lights, point lights, spotlights, and weblights all can cast shadows. AutoCAD's default lighting does not cast shadows. There are two types of shadows that AutoCAD can create: shadow mapped and raytrace. The **Advanced Rendering Settings** palette provides settings for controlling the creation of shadows when rendering. This window and its options are discussed in the next chapter.

The options for creating shadows are the same for all lights. The options can be set when the light is created or adjusted later using the **Properties** palette. In the case of sunlight, the **Sun Properties** palette is used to set the options.

Shadow-Mapped Shadow Settings

A ***shadow-mapped shadow*** is a bitmap generated by AutoCAD. A shadow map has soft edges that can be adjusted. Creating shadow-mapped shadows is the only way to produce a soft-edge shadow. However, shadow maps do not transmit object color from transparent objects onto the surfaces behind the object. Figure 16-21 shows the difference between shadow-mapped shadows and raytraced shadows.

To specify shadow-mapped shadows and set the quality, or resolution, of the shadow, select the light and open the **Properties** palette (or **Sun Properties** palette). Use the **Lights in Model** palette to select a distant light and open the **Properties** palette for it. At the bottom of the **Properties** palette is the **Rendered Shadow Details** category, Figure 16-22. To specify shadow-mapped shadows, set the Type property to Soft (shadow map).

The Map size property determines the quality of the shadow. The value is the number of samples used to create the shadow. The higher the setting, the better quality of the generated shadow. However, the higher the setting, the longer it will take to render.

The value of the Softness property determines how soft the edge of the shadow is. The higher the value, the softer or blurrier the edge of the shadow. A low value can produce a very hard edge. The value can range from 1 to 5.

A variation of shadow-mapped shadows is created when the Type property is set to Soft (sampled). This type of shadow map must be used with photometric lighting (**LIGHTINGUNITS** = 1 or 2). In this case, different properties are displayed. The Samples property determines the number of "rays" used to generate the shadows. However, this is not considered raytracing. The Visible in rendering property determines whether the shape of the light is rendered. The Shape property sets the shape of the light. For spotlights, the shape can be either rectangular or circular (disk). For point and weblights, the shape can be linear, rectangular, circular (disk) cylindrical, or spherical. The remaining properties are based on the selected shape and are used to define the size of the shape.

NOTE

For standard shadow-mapped shadows to be created, the Shadow Map property in the **Advanced Render Settings** palette must be set to On. However, for the photometric shadow maps—the Soft (sampled) setting—the Shadow Map property does not affect the shadow generation. Advanced render settings are covered in the next chapter.

Figure 16-21.
The shadow from the object in the foreground is a shadow-mapped shadow. The shadow from the object in the background is a raytraced shadow.

Figure 16-22.
The **Rendered Shadow Details** category in the **Properties** palette.

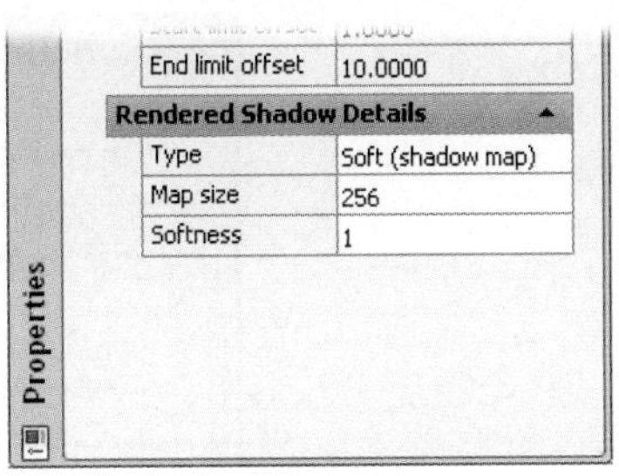

Raytrace Shadow Settings

A ***raytrace shadow*** is created by beams, or rays, from the light source. These rays trace the path of light as they strike objects to create a shadow. In addition, rays can pass through transparent objects, such as green glass, and project color onto surfaces behind the object. Raytrace shadows have a well-defined edge. They cannot be adjusted to produce a soft edge. Raytrace shadows can be used with standard and photometric lighting.

All lights set to cast shadows, except those set for shadow-mapped shadows, cast raytraced shadows. To switch from shadow-mapped shadows to raytrace shadows, select the light object and open the **Properties** palette. In the **Rendered Shadow Details** category, set the Type property to Sharp. The other properties are disabled because they only apply to shadow-mapped shadows.

PROFESSIONAL TIP

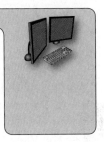

Turning on shadow casting will increase rendering time because of the calculations that AutoCAD has to perform. It is difficult to determine if raytraced or shadow-mapped shadows will be quicker to render because every scene is different and there are many variables that come into play. You will have to experiment with your scene to determine the acceptable level of shadow detail versus rendering time.

Adding a Background

A ***background*** is the backdrop for your 3D model. The background can be a solid color, a gradient of colors, a bitmap file, the sun and sky, or the current AutoCAD drawing background color. By default, the background is the drawing background color.

Type	VIEW
Menu	View > Named Views...

VIEW

To change the background for your drawing, you must first create a named view with the **VIEW** command. In the **View Manager** dialog box, pick the **New...** button to display the **New View/Shot Properties** dialog box. See **Figure 16-23.** The view name, category, and type are specified at the top of the dialog box. Near the bottom of the **View Properties** tab is the **Background** area. The drop-down list in this area is used to specify the type of background. The choices are: Default, Solid, Gradient, Image, and Sun & Sky. The Default setting uses the current AutoCAD viewport color. Photometric lighting must be on (**LIGHTINGUNITS** = 1 or 2) for Sun & Sky to appear in the drop-down list.

PROFESSIONAL TIP

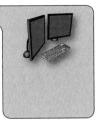

Before you create the named view, establish the viewpoint from which you want to see the final rendering. Set the perspective projection current, if desired. These settings are saved with the view. The drop-down list in the **Viewports** panel on the **View** tab of the ribbon makes it very easy to recall the view.

Figure 16-23.
The **View Properties** tab of the **New View/Shot Properties** dialog box. A named view must be created before you can use a background in your scene.

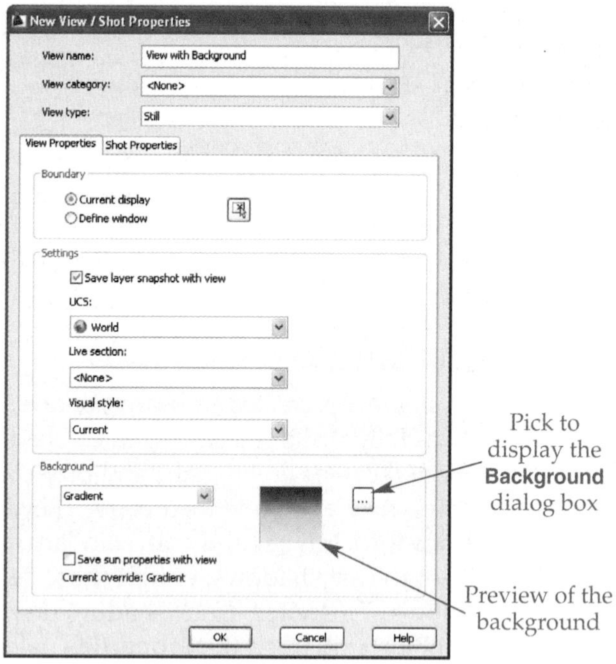

Solid Backgrounds

If you select Solid in the drop-down list, the **Background** dialog box is displayed. The Type: drop-down list in this dialog box is automatically set to Solid and the default color is displayed in the **Preview** area. See Figure 16-24. In the **Solid options** area of the dialog box, pick the horizontal **Color:** bar to open the **Select Color** dialog box. Then, select the background color that you desire. When the **Select Color** dialog box is closed, the color you picked is displayed in the **Preview** area of the **Background** dialog box. Close the **Background** dialog box, save the view, set the new view current, and close the **View Manager** dialog box.

NOTE

Make sure to do a test rendering with the background color you selected. The final result may look quite different than your expectations.

Gradient Backgrounds

A gradient background can be composed of two or three colors. If you select Gradient in the drop-down list in the **New View/Shot Properties** dialog box, the **Background** dialog box is displayed with Gradient selected and the default gradient colors displayed in the **Preview** area. See Figure 16-25. The **Top color:**, **Middle color:**, and **Bottom color:** swatches are displayed on the right side of the **Gradient options** area. Selecting a swatch opens the **Select Color** dialog box for changing the color. To create a two-color gradient composed of the top and bottom colors, uncheck the **Three Color** check box. The **Rotation:** text box provides the option of rotating the gradient. Close the **Background** dialog box, save the view, set the view current, and close the **View Manager** dialog box.

Convincing, clear blue skies can be simulated using the **Gradient** option. Initially, set the **Top**, **Middle**, and **Bottom** color values the same. Then, change the lightness (luminance) in the **True Color** tab in the **Select Colors** dialog box. Preview the background and make adjustments as needed.

Figure 16-24.
Creating a solid background.

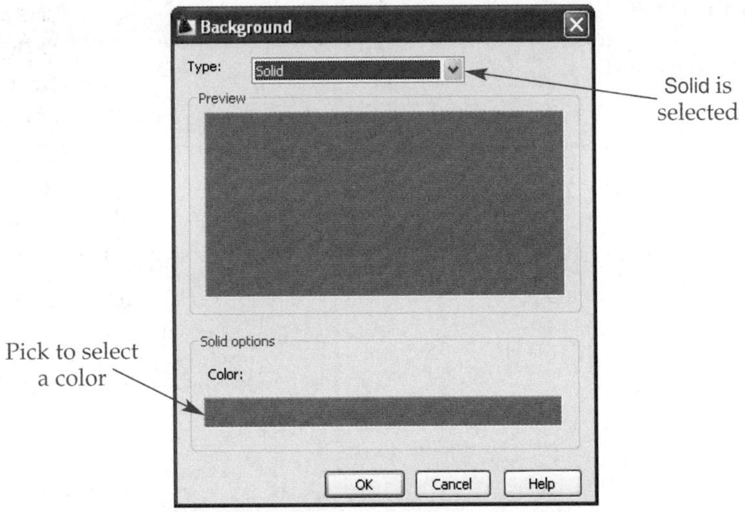

Figure 16-25.
Creating a gradient background.

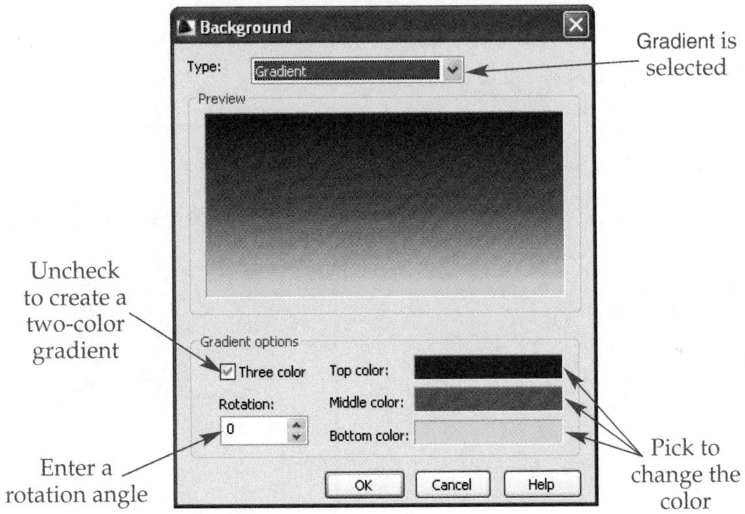

Using an Image as a Background

An image can be used as a background. This technique can be used to produce realistic or imaginative settings for your models. If you select Image in the drop-down list in the **New View/Shot Properties** dialog box, the **Background** dialog box is displayed with Image selected and a blank image displayed in the **Preview** area. See **Figure 16-26.** If you know the name and path of the image file, this can be typed in the text box. To locate the image file, pick the **Browse...** button to display a standard open dialog box. These image file types may be used for the background: TGA, BMP, PNG, JFIF (JPEG), TIFF, GIF, and PCX.

Once the image file is selected, it must be adjusted. The **Preview** area of the **Background** dialog box shows the image with a preview of a drawing sheet. This drawing sheet indicates how the image is going to be positioned in the view. Pick the **Adjust Image...** button to open the **Adjust Background Image** dialog box. See **Figure 16-27.**

In the **Image position:** drop-down list, pick how the image is applied to the viewport. The Center option centers the image in the view without changing its aspect ratio or scale. The Stretch option centers the image and stretches or shrinks it to fill the entire view. This is one way to plot an image file from AutoCAD. The Tile option keeps the image at its original size and shape, but moves it to the upper-left corner and duplicates it, if needed, to fill the view.

Figure 16-26.
Setting an image as the background.

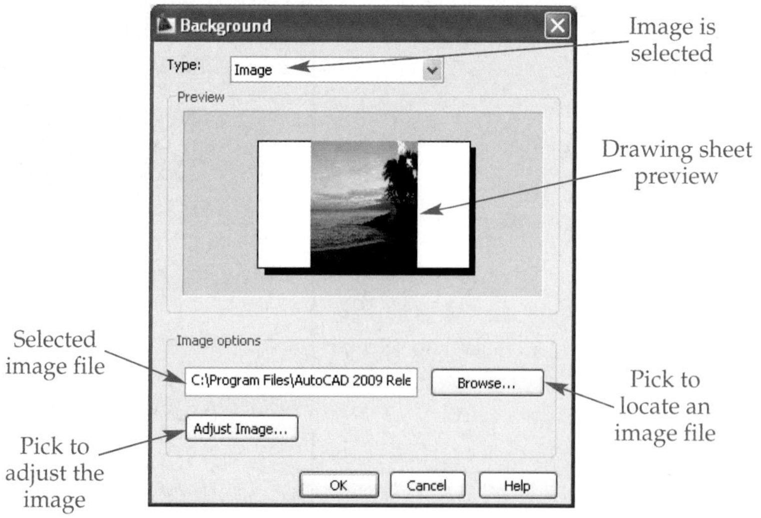

Figure 16-27.
Adjusting the background image.

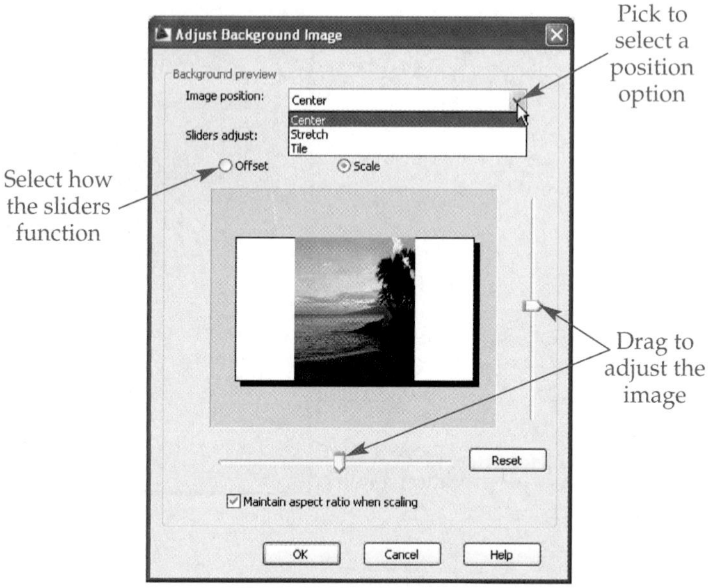

After the image is positioned, use the sliders to adjust it further. The sliders are disabled if Stretch is selected in the **Image position:** drop-down list. The slider function is based on which radio button is picked above the image:

- **Offset.** The sliders move the image in the X or Y direction.
- **Scale.** The sliders scale the image in the X or Y direction. This may distort the image if it is scaled too much in one direction. To prevent distortion, check the **Maintain aspect ratio when scaling** check box at the bottom.

The **Reset** button is located at the bottom-right corner of the preview pane. Picking this button returns the scale and offset settings to their original values.

Once the image is adjusted, pick the **OK** button to close the **Adjust Background Image** dialog box. Then, close the **Background** dialog box, save the view, set the view current, and close the **View Manager** dialog box.

Sun and Sky

If you select Sun & Sky in the drop-down list in the **New View** dialog box, the **Adjust Sun & Sky Background** dialog box is displayed. See **Figure 16-28.** AutoCAD uses the settings in this dialog box to simulate the sun in the sky. This dialog box

Figure 16-28.
The **Adjust Sun & Sky Background** dialog box contains settings for the sun and sky illumination.

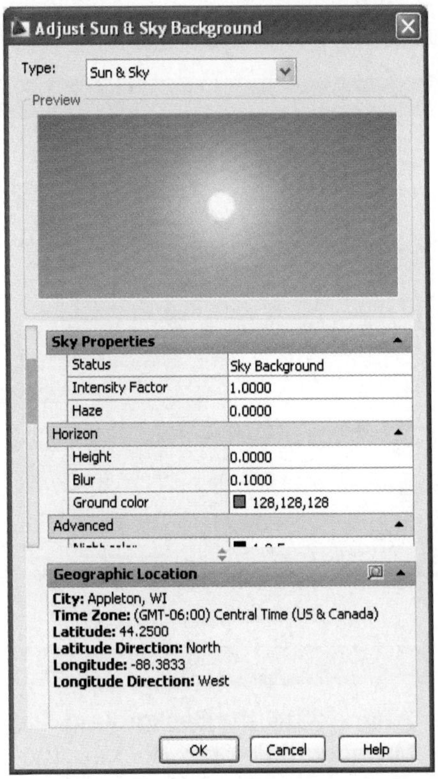

has a preview tile at the top and the **General**, **Sky Properties**, **Sun Angle Calculator**, **Rendered Shadow Details**, and **Geographic Location** categories. The settings in these categories are discussed earlier in this chapter in the Sky Properties section.

Once the sky is set, pick the **OK** button to close the **Adjust Sun & Sky Background** dialog box. Then, save the view, set the view current, and close the **View Manager** dialog box.

Changing the Background on an Existing View

To change the background of existing named views, open the **View Manager** dialog box. Select the view name in the **Views** tree on the left-hand side of the dialog box. Then, in the **General** category in the middle of the dialog box, select the Background override property. See Figure 16-29. Next, pick the drop-down list for the property and select the type of background you want applied: None, Solid, Gradient, Image, Sun & Sky, and Edit. Picking None sets the background to the AutoCAD default background. Setting the property to Solid, Gradient, or Image opens the **Background** dialog where you can make settings for that type. Selecting Sun & Sky opens the **Adjust Sun & Sky Background** dialog box. Picking Edit opens the **Background** or the **Adjust Sun & Sky Background** dialog box with the settings of the current background. Once the background type has been changed or the existing background edited, pick the **OK** button to save the view and close the **View Manager** dialog box.

Figure 16-29.
Changing the background of an existing, named view.

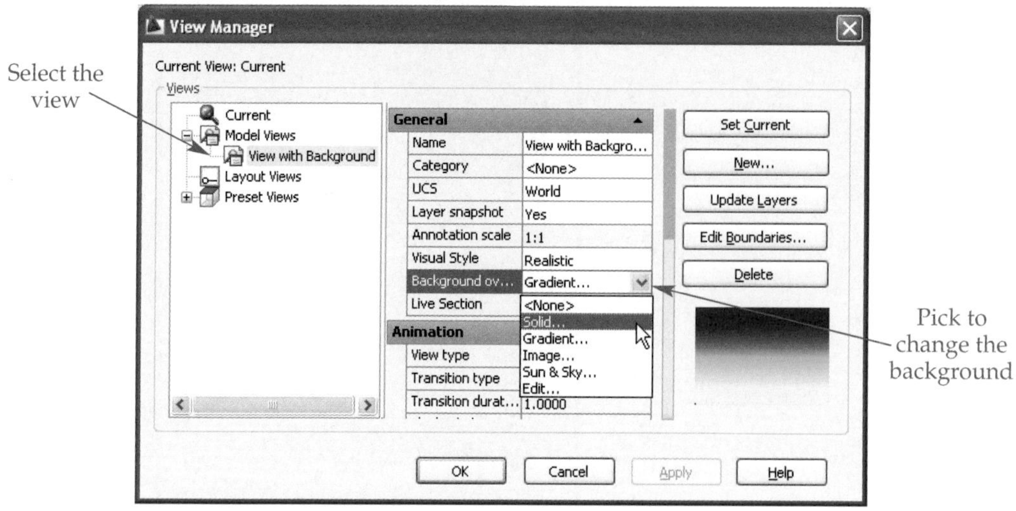

NOTE

After exiting the **Background** dialog box, you are returned to the **View Manager** dialog box. Picking the **OK** button to exit the **View Manager** dialog box does not necessarily activate the view that you just created or modified. The view must be set current to see the effects of the changes to the background. A view can be set current using the drop-down list on the **Viewports** panel in the **View** tab of the ribbon or it can be set current in the **View Manager** dialog box.

Exercise 16-5

Complete the exercise on the Student CD.

Chapter Test

Answer the following questions. Write your answers on a separate sheet of paper or complete the electronic chapter test on the Student CD.

1. Compare and contrast *ambient light, distant lights, point lights, spotlights,* and *weblights.*
2. Define *angle of incidence.*
3. Define *angle of reflection.*
4. A smooth surface has a(n) _____ specular factor.
5. Describe *hotspot* and *falloff.* Which lights have these properties?
6. What is *attenuation?*
7. What are the three types of lighting in AutoCAD?
8. What are the four types of light objects in AutoCAD?
9. What are light glyphs and which lights have them?
10. List the types of shadows that can be created in AutoCAD. Which type(s) can have soft edges?
11. Which type of shadow must be created for light to pass through transparent objects?
12. What must be created before a background can be added to a scene?
13. What are the four types of backgrounds in AutoCAD, other than the default background?
14. Why would you draw a line between the "from" point and "to" point of a distant light?
15. Describe how a gradient background can be used to represent a clear blue sky.

Drawing Problems

1. In this problem, you will draw some basic 3D shapes to create a building similar to an ancient structure, place lights in the drawing, and render the scene with shadows.
   A. Begin a new drawing and set the units to architectural. Save the drawing as P16_01.
   B. Draw a 32′ × 22′ planar surface to represent the floor. Using the tool palettes in the **Materials Library** palette group (or **Materials** group if the materials library is not installed), attach a material of your choice to the floor.
   C. Draw cylinders to represent pillars. Make each ∅2′ × 15′ tall. There are ten pillars per side. Attach a suitable material to the pillars.
   D. The roof is 32′ × 22′ and 5′ tall at the ridge. Attach an appropriate material.
   E. Create a perspective viewpoint looking into the building.
   F. Turn on sunlight and turn off the default lighting. Set the geographic location to Athens, Greece. Change the date and time to whatever you wish. Make sure the sun is set to cast shadows.
   G. Render the scene.
   H. Save the drawing.

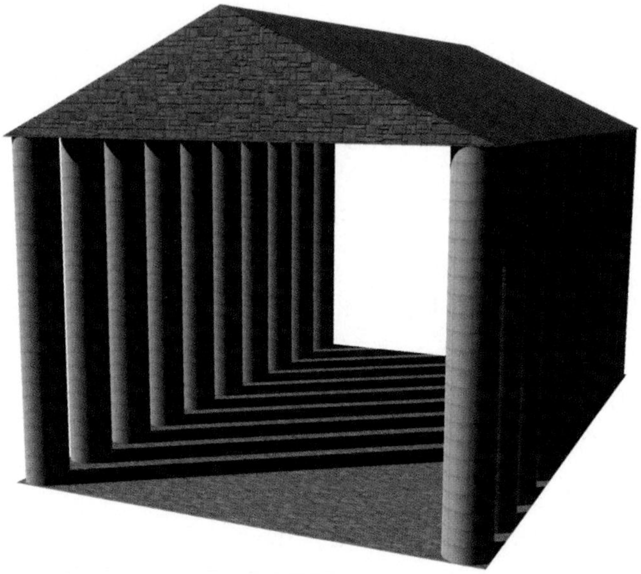

Drawing Problems - Chapter 16

2. Using the drawing from problem 1, you will experiment with different lighting types.
   A. Open drawing P16_01 and save it as P16_02.
   B. Turn off the sun.
   C. Place three point lights inside of the building. Evenly space the lights along the centerline of the ceiling. Adjust the light intensity so that the interior is not washed out. Set the color of the middle light to white. Set the color of the outside lights to red or blue. Render the scene.
   D. Turn off the point lights.
   E. Place two spotlights, one pointing from the front corner to the rear corner and the other pointing between the pillars on the left side of the building. Target them at the floor. Render the scene. Adjust the intensity, hotspot, and falloff as needed.
   F. Turn the point lights back on and render the scene with all six lights active. Adjust the light intensities again if the rendering is too washed out with light.
   G. Save the drawing.

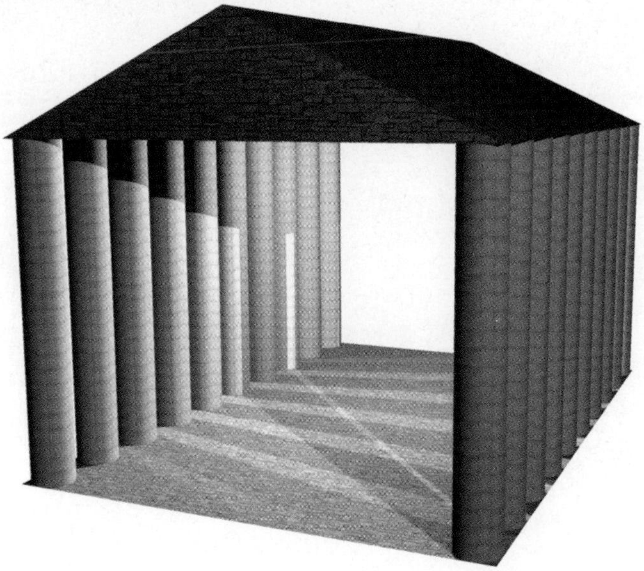

3. Using a previously created mechanical model, you will apply materials and lights to make it ready for presentation.
   A. Open drawing P08_05 created in Chapter 8. Save it as P16_03.
   B. Draw a planar surface below the flange to represent a tabletop.
   C. Using the tool palettes, attach an appropriate material, such as a wood or tile material, to the plane.
   D. Create a new material based on the Advanced material type. Attach a diffuse color map from the "all users" AutoCAD folder. There are several metal texture maps located in the \Textures folder. Apply a low reflection value to the material.
   E. Place two spotlights in the drawing and target them at the flange from different angles. Adjust their hotspot, falloff, and intensity to get the proper lighting.
   F. Create a perspective view of the scene. Then, render the scene.
   G. Save the drawing.

4. The building shown below will be used to study passive solar heating at different times of the year. Model the building using the overall dimensions given. Use your own dimensions for everything else. The side with the windows should be facing South (–Y in AutoCAD).
   A. Set the geographical location to a city in the northern hemisphere.
   B. Set the date to midsummer and the time to noon.
   C. Turn on sunlight and the default lighting off.
   D. Render the scene and note the location of the shadows inside the building.
   E. Change the date to late winter, render the scene again, and note the new location of the shadows. You can easily switch between the rendered images in the **Render** window by selecting each rendering in the **History** pane (this is discussed more in the next chapter).
   F. Observing the changes in the shadow locations, what design changes can be made to maximize sun exposure in the cold winter months? What design changes can be made to minimize sun exposure in the heat of summer?
   G. Change the geographical location to somewhere closer to the equator. Then, render the scene in summer and follow. How do the shadows compare to those in your location?
   H. Save the drawing as P16_04.

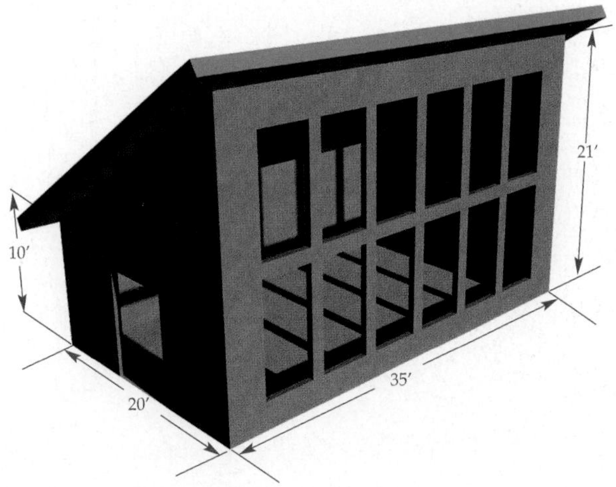

5. In this problem, you will be adding lights to a model and controlling their properties to create a pleasing scene. Model the courtyard shown below. The overall dimensions are 15′ × 16′ × 4′ (wall height). Use your own dimensions for everything else. Add lights as follows.
   A. Turn on the sun and turn off the default lighting. Set the time to late in the day so that the sun is close to the horizon.
   B. In the **Sky Properties** category of the **Sun Properties** palette, select Sky Background and Illumination for the Status property.
   C. Add a point light at the center of each sphere.
   D. Attach the Doors & Windows.Glazing.Glass.Frosted material to the spheres.
   E. Create a fill light above to illuminate the scene. This can be a point or spotlight.
   F. Render the scene using the low preset to see the lighting effects.
   G. Adjust the sun properties to create the look that you want.
   H. Adjust the properties of the point lights and any other lights in the scene. You may have to increase the intensity of the lights quite a bit to properly illuminate the scene.
   I. When the scene is illuminated the way you want it, render the scene using medium or high preset.
   J. Save the drawing as P16_05.

6. In Chapter 9, you completed the kitchen chair model that you started in Chapter 2. In this problem, you will be adding lights to the model and attaching materials to the various components in the chair.
   A. Open P10_07 from Chapter 10.
   B. Create a layer for each of the chair components: seat, legs/crossbars, seatback bow, and seatback spindles.
   C. Draw a planar surface to represent the floor. Place this on its own layer.
   D. Assign materials to each of the layers. You can use materials from the materials library or create your own materials.
   E. Set the Realistic visual style current.
   F. Adjust material mapping as needed.
   G. Add lighting to the scene.
   H. Render the scene. If you experience problems with the materials, try attaching by object instead of by layer.
   I. Save the drawing as P16_06.

Advanced lighting and rendering techniques can have a dramatic effect on the scene. The upper rendering shows an office building represented at the first light of day. The lower rendering shows the same office building represented near midday. Notice the dramatic difference achieved with just lighting and depth cueing.

CHAPTER 17 Advanced Rendering

Learning Objectives

After completing this chapter, you will be able to:

✓ Make advanced rendering settings.
✓ Set the resolution for a rendering.
✓ Save a rendering to an image file.
✓ Add fog/depth cueing to a scene.

In Chapter 14, you learned how to create a view of your scene that is more realistic than a visual style. In that chapter, you used AutoCAD's sunlight feature to create a simple rendering with mostly default settings. However, in this chapter you will learn about the advanced rendering features that allow you to create photorealistic renderings. You will learn all of the features related to rendering in AutoCAD. You will learn how to make your renderings look their best while conserving rendering time.

Render Window

By default, a drawing is rendered in the **Render** window, unless you are rendering a cropped area. This window allows you to inspect the rendering, save it to a file, compare it with previous renderings, and take note of the statistics. See **Figure 17-1.** There are three main areas of the **Render** window—the image, history, and statistics panes.

Image Pane

As AutoCAD processes the scene, the image begins to appear in the image pane in its final form. There may be as many as four phases that the rendering goes through as it is being processed:

- **Translation.** Processes the drawing information and determines light intensity, shadow placement, colors, and so on. This phase is always completed.
- **Photon emission.** ***Photon emission*** is a technique for calculating indirect illumination that traces photons emitted by the light source until they come to rest on a diffuse surface. It determines which areas will be illuminated by indirect, or bounced, light. The photon emission phase may or may not be processed, depending on settings in the **Advanced Render Settings** palette.

Figure 17-1.
The **Render** window.

- **Final gather.** ***Final gather*** increases the number of rays used to calculate global illumination (GI). This phase will be processed if it is turned on in the **Advanced Render Settings** palette.
- **Render.** Converts the data into an image. This phase is always completed.

Immediately below the image pane is the progress meter/status bar. The top bar displays the progress of the current phase and the bottom bar indicates the progress of the entire rendering. Also, at the very bottom of the **Render** window, below the history pane, the status of the phase is shown with its percentage complete. You can also hover the cursor over the progress meter/status bar during the rendering and a tooltip displays the percentage of completion for the current process and the overall render. The rendering can be cancelled at any time by pressing the [Esc] key or picking the **X** button to the left of the progress meter.

As discussed in Chapter 14, you can zoom the rendering in and out to inspect it. You can also save it to an image file using the **File** pull-down menu in the **Render** window.

History Pane

The history pane contains a list of all of the renderings that were created in this drawing since it was created, not just in this drawing session. The items in this list are called ***history entries.*** There are two types of history entries, which are indicated by icons. See Figure 17-2.

- **Normal.** The entry is saved to file. A link is maintained to that file. If the drawing is saved, closed, and reopened, you can pick the entry to view the rendering in the image pane.
- **Temporary.** The entry is available in the current drawing session, but is not saved to a file. If the drawing is closed, the image is lost. The name of the entry in the Output File Name column ends with -Temp*x*.

Right-clicking on an entry in the history pane displays a shortcut menu. The options in this menu can be used to save the image, render the image again, and manage the entry. The options in the shortcut menu are:

Figure 17-2.
The icon in front of the name indicates if the entry is normal or temporary.

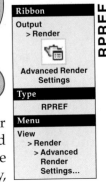

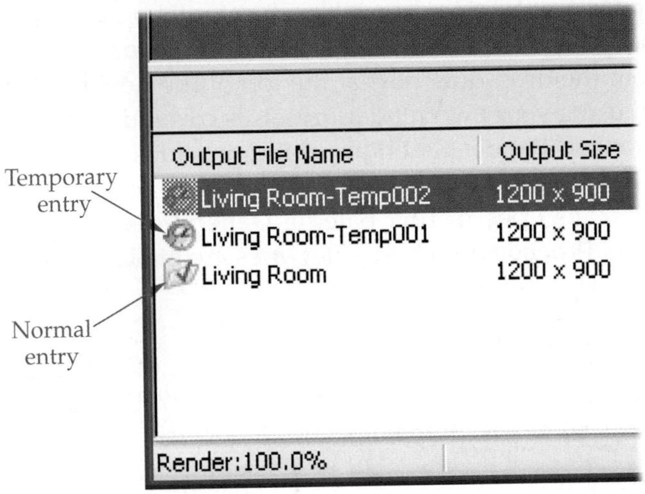

- **Render Again.** Renders the scene again using the same settings. A new entry is not added to the history pane.
- **Save.** Saves the rendered image to a file using a standard save dialog box. This turns the entry from a temporary entry into a normal entry.
- **Save Copy.** Saves the rendered image to a new file without changing the current entry.
- **Make Render Settings Current.** Sets all of the rendering settings of the entry as the current rendering settings in the drawing. This allows you to render the current scene using the settings of the entry.
- **Remove From the List.** Deletes the entry from the history pane, but any image files saved from the entry remain.
- **Delete Output File.** Deletes the image file created by saving the entry. The entry remains in the history pane and any image files that were created as copies are retained.

Statistics Pane

The statistics pane shows the details of the rendering that is selected in the history pane. By selecting renderings in the history pane, you can see in the image pane which version provides the best result. Then, you can use the statistics pane to view the settings. The information under the Render Statistics heading (date, render time, etc.) is added when the rendering is completed. The rest of the information reflects the settings in the **Advanced Render Settings** palette and the **Render Presets Manager** dialog box at the time the rendering was created.

Exercise 17-1

Complete the exercise on the Student CD.

Advanced Render Settings

RPREF

Ribbon
Output
> Render
Advanced Render Settings
Type
RPREF
Menu
View
> Render
> Advanced Render Settings...

The quickest and easiest way to control the quality of a rendering is with render presets. AutoCAD provides five standard render presets: Draft, Low, Medium, High, and Presentation. The Draft preset provides the lowest-quality rendering. Each preset above Draft changes the advanced render settings to gradually improve the rendering quality, peaking with the Presentation preset. However, as the quality is improved, the rendering time increases. The presets can be selected in the **Render** panel on the **Output** tab of the ribbon or from the drop-down list at the top of the **Advanced Render Settings** palette. Creating and using your own render presets is covered later in this chapter.

The **Advanced Render Settings** palette provides settings that give you complete control over how a rendering is created. The **RPREF** command opens the palette. There are five main categories in this palette: **General, Ray Tracing, Indirect Illumination, Diagnostic**, and **Processing**. These categories are explained in the next sections.

General

The **General** category provides properties for controlling the rendering destination, materials, sampling, and shadows, Figure 17-3. It contains four subcategories: **Render Context**, **Materials**, **Sampling**, and **Shadows**.

Render context

The **Render Context** subcategory contains general properties that control the rendering. The Procedure property determines what will be rendered. The settings are View, Crop, and Selected. View is the default and renders whatever you see in the drawing window. Crop allows you to specify an area of the scene to render. This is very useful when you want to do a test rendering, but do not want to wait for the whole scene. The Selected setting allows you to pick which objects to render.

The Destination property determines where the rendered scene will be displayed. You can choose to have the rendering placed in the viewport or **Render** window.

If the save button in the subcategory title bar is picked, the Output File Name property is enabled. This property sets the name and location of the file to which the rendering will automatically be saved.

The Output Size property sets the resolution, measured in pixels × pixels, for the rendered image. You can select standard resolutions or pick Specify Output Size... for a custom resolution. In the **Output Size** dialog box that is displayed when Specify Output Size... is selected, you can enter any resolution that you want. See Figure 17-4. If you want to prevent the image from stretching, make sure the **Lock image aspect** button is selected in the dialog box so that the height and width remain proportional. When you change the resolution, it is stored with the drawing.

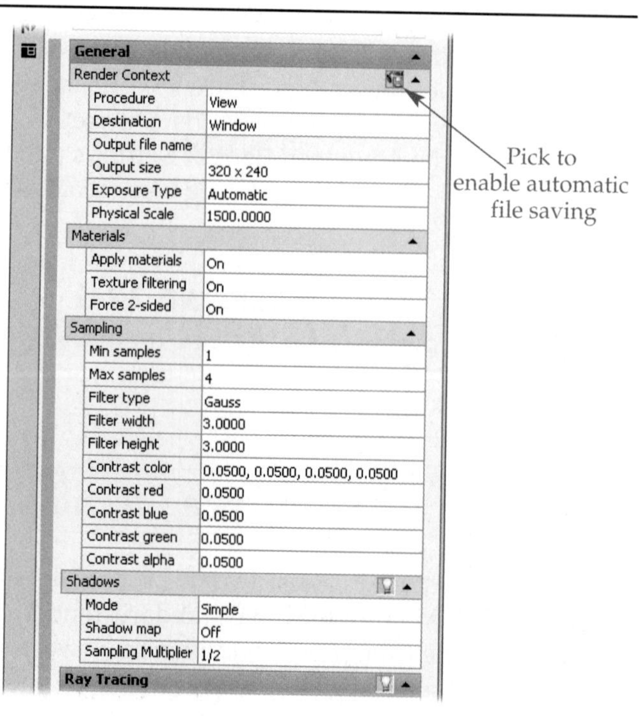

Figure 17-3.
The **General** category of the **Advanced Render Settings** palette.

Figure 17-4.
Setting a custom resolution.

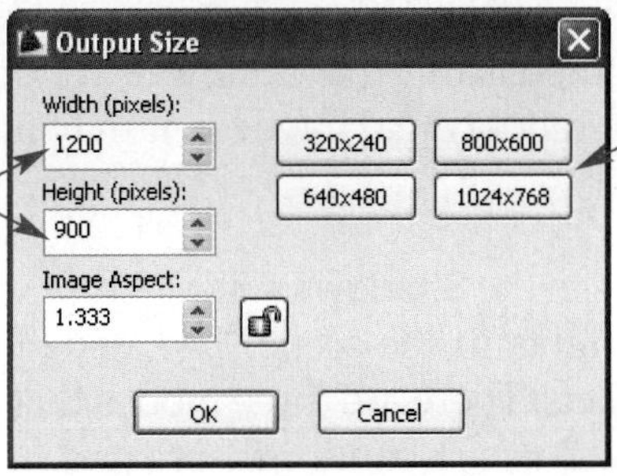

The Exposure Type property can be set to Automatic or Logarithmic. When set to Automatic, the entire image is sampled and some of the dim lighting effects are enhanced to make them more visible. When set to Logarithmic, the brightness and contrast are used to map physical values to RGB values. This is better for scenes with high dynamic ranges.

Exposure control needs a scale to work with and, if you are using non-physical lights (**LIGHTINGUNITS** set to 0), the Physical Scale property provides a scale. Standard lights have an Intensity Factor property that is multiplied by the Physical Scale value to determine the actual brightness of the light. The default value is 1500. In other words, a point light with an Intensity Factor value of 2 has an actual lamp intensity of 3000 candelas when the Physical Scale property is set to 1500.

Materials

The properties in the **Materials** subcategory determine how materials are handled in the rendering. The Apply Materials property controls whether or not materials attached to objects are rendered. The property can be set to On or Off. If set to Off, objects are rendered in their own colors. The Texture Filtering property determines whether or not antialiasing is applied to texture maps when rendered. Antialiasing is a way of reducing "jaggies" in the rendered image. The Force 2-sided property determines if AutoCAD renders both sides of all faces. This can fix problems where objects disappear in a rendering, but will increase rendering time.

Sampling

Sampling is a technique that tests the scene color at each pixel and then determines what the final color should be. This is most important in transition areas, such as edges of objects or shadows. Increasing the sampling will smooth out the jagged edges and incorrect coloring, but increase rendering time. You may also notice thicker lines.

The Min samples and Max samples properties set the minimum and maximum number of samples computed per pixel. A value of 1 means one sample per pixel. A value of 1/4 means one sample for every four pixels. The Filter type property determines how the samples are brought together to determine the pixel value:

- Box. Quickest method; evenly combines samples and gives them equal weight.
- Triangle. Weights the samples based on a pyramid with samples in the center of the filter area receiving the most weight.
- Gauss. Weights the samples based on a bell curve with samples in the center of the filter area receiving the most weight.
- Mitchell. Most accurate. Weights samples based on a curve centered on the filter area, like Gauss; however, this curve is steeper.
- Lanczos. Weights samples based on a curve centered on the filter area, like Mitchell, but it diminishes the weight of samples at the edge of the filter area.

The Filter width and Filter height properties determine the size of the filter area. A larger filter area softens the image, but increases rendering time.

The Contrast color, Contrast red, Contrast blue, Contrast green, and Contrast alpha properties specify the threshold value of the colors involved in sampling. If a sample differs from the sample next to it by more than this color, AutoCAD takes more than one sample per pixel up to the Max samples property. Values can be from 0.0 (black) to 1.0 (fully saturated). Increasing the value can reduce the amount of sampling and, therefore, speed up the rendering. However, it may also reduce the quality of the image.

Shadows

The properties in the **Shadows** subcategory control how the renderer handles shadows generated by the lights in the scene. The Mode property controls a shader function that calculates light effects. There are three modes that determine how shading is calculated:

- Simple. Shaders are randomly created.
- Sorted. Shaders are called in order from the object to the light.
- Segment. Shaders are called in order from the volume shaders to the segments of the light rays between the object and the light.

The Shadow Map property determines whether shadow-mapped or raytraced shadows are created. When this property is set to On, shadow-mapped shadows are generated. When it is set to Off, raytraced shadows are created.

The Sampling Multiplier property limits shadow sampling for area lights. The values are preset for the rendering presets: Draft = 0, Low = 1/4, Medium = 1/2, High = 1, and Presentation = 1. However, these values can be changed. This is the same principle that is described in the Sampling section, but instead of sampling pixels for object color, it is sampling for shadows.

Ray Tracing

The **Ray Tracing** category provides properties for controlling how the rendered image is shaded, Figure 17-5. ***Raytracing*** is a method of calculating reflections, refractions, and shadows by tracing the path of the light rays from the light sources. This is more accurate at producing shadows than shadow mapping, but it takes more time and the shadow edge is always sharp. To enable raytracing, pick the button in the category's title bar. If this is off, there will be no raytracing and the properties are disabled.

The Max reflections property is the maximum number of times that a ray can be reflected. The Max refractions property is the maximum number of times that a ray can be refracted. The Max depth property is the maximum number of reflections and refractions. For example, if this property is set to 5 and the Max reflections property is set to 3, then no more than two refractions will occur. A good way to figure out the required maximum depth is to imagine a light ray traveling through transparent objects or bouncing off of reflective objects in your scene. Count how many surfaces the object must contact and that is the maximum depth.

Indirect Illumination

Indirect illumination is a method in AutoCAD that simulates natural, bounced light. If indirect illumination is turned off and light does not directly strike an object, the object is dark. Without indirect illumination enabled, other lights must be added to the scene to simulate indirect illumination. The properties in the **Indirect Illumination** category allow you to create a natural-looking scene. There are three subcategories in the **Indirect Illumination** category: **Global Illumination**, **Final Gather**, and **Light Properties**. See Figure 17-6.

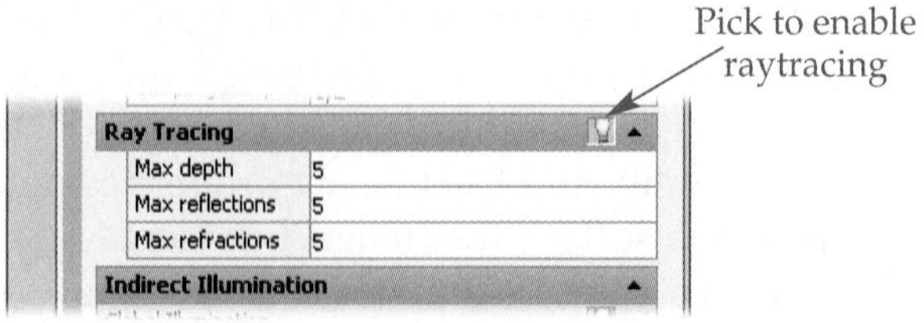

Figure 17-5.
The **Ray Tracing** category of the **Advanced Render Settings** palette.

Figure 17-6.
The **Indirect Illumination** category of the **Advanced Render Settings** palette.

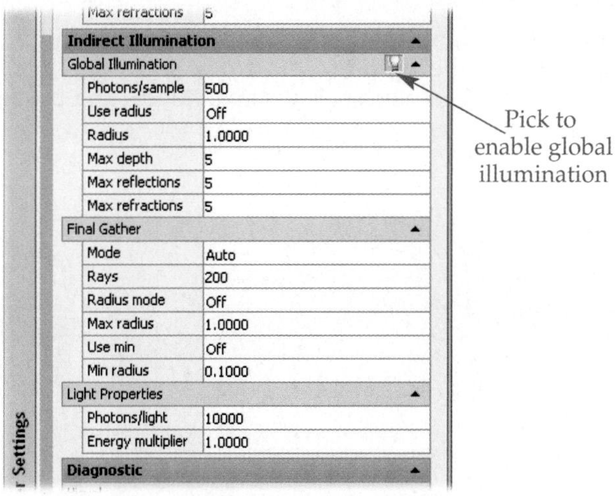

Global illumination

Global illumination (GI) is indirect illumination. Bounced light is simulated by generating photon maps on surfaces in the scene. These maps are created by tracing photons from the light source. Photons bounce around the scene from one object to the next until they finally strike a diffuse surface. When a photon strikes a surface, it is stored in the photon map. To enable global illumination, pick the button in the subcategory's title bar. If this button is off, there will be no indirect illumination.

The Photons/sample property sets the number of photons used to generate the photon map. The higher the value, the less noise global illumination produces. However, rendering time is longer and the image is blurrier.

The Use radius property determines whether the photons are a default radius or a user-specified radius. When the property is set to On, the Radius property sets the size of the photon. When set to Off, the radius of each photon is 1/10th of the scene's radius.

The Max reflections property is the maximum number of times that a photon can be reflected. The Max refractions property is the maximum number of times that a photon can be refracted. The Max depth property is the maximum number of reflections and refractions. For example, if this property is set to 5 and the Max reflections property is set to 3, then no more than two refractions will occur.

Final gather

The settings in the **Global Illumination** subcategory may result in dark and light areas in the scene. ***Final gathering*** increases the number of rays in the rendering and cleans up these artifacts. It will also greatly increase rendering time. Final gathering works the best with scenes that contain overall diffuse lighting. See Figure 17-7. The Mode property for final gathering can be set to:

- On. Turns on global illumination for final gathering.
- Off. Turns off global illumination for final gathering.
- Auto. Global illumination is turned on or off based on the sky light status. This is the default setting.

The Rays property sets the number of rays used to calculate indirect illumination. The higher the value, the better the result, but the longer the scene takes to render.

The Radius mode property determines how the Max radius property is applied during final gathering. There are three possible settings:

- On. The Max radius value is used for final gathering and it is measured in world units.
- Off. The radius of each area processed by final gathering is 10% of the maximum model radius.
- View. The Max radius value is used for final gathering, but it is measured in pixels instead of world units.

Figure 17-7.
A—This scene has a single point light. B—Global illumination is turned on. Notice the unevenness of the lighting. This can be seen especially on the sofa and in the corner of the walls. C—Final gathering cleans up artifacts and provides a more even illumination.

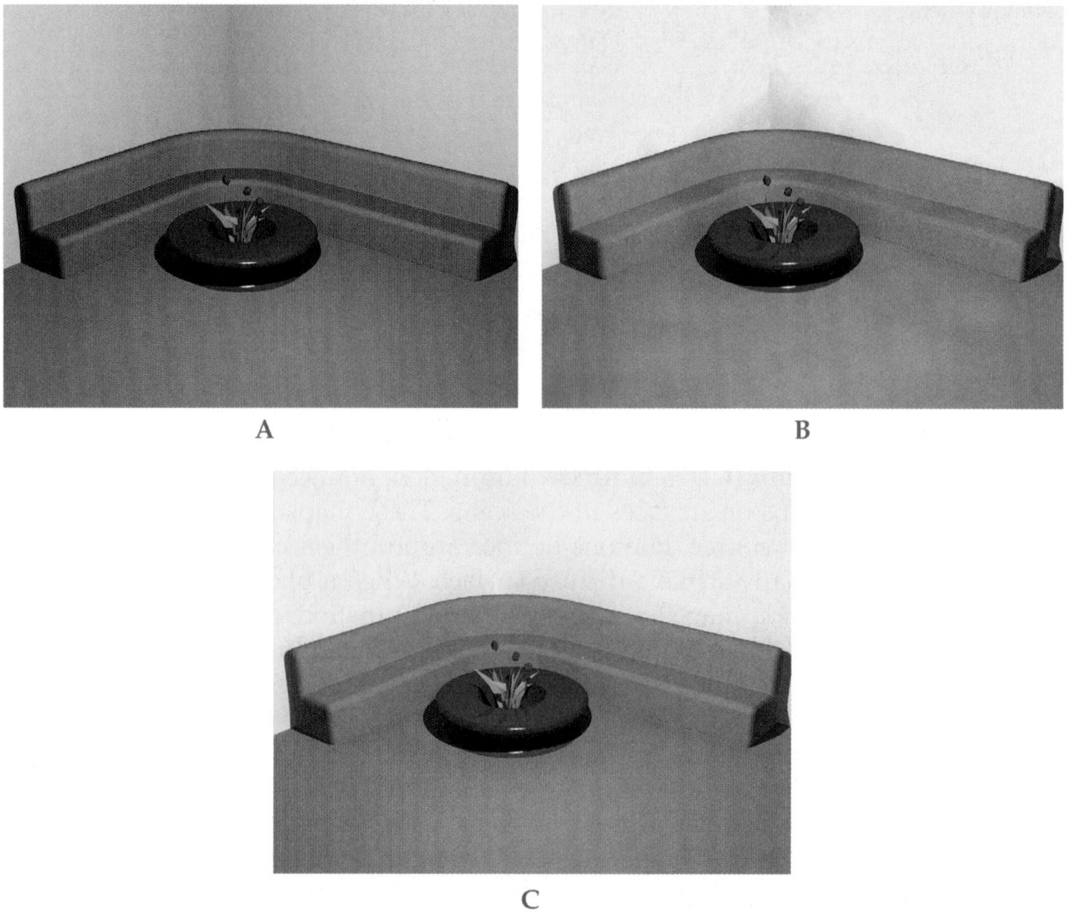

The Max radius property determines the maximum radius of each area processed during final gathering. The lower this value, the higher the quality of the rendering because a larger number of smaller areas is processed. However, rendering time is higher.

The Use min property determines whether or not the Min radius property is applied for final gathering. The Min radius property sets the minimum radius of the processed areas. Increasing this improves quality, but increases rendering time.

Light properties

The properties in the **Light Properties** subcategory control how the lights in the scene are applied when calculating indirect illumination. The Photons/light property sets the number of photons emitted by each light. Increasing this number makes each light cast more photons and improves the rendering quality. The Energy multiplier property determines how much light energy is used in global illumination. The default value of 1.0000 does not increase or decrease the light energy. Values less than the default decrease the light energy. Values greater than the default increase the light energy.

PROFESSIONAL TIP

If your scene looks washed out (flooded with light) with indirect illumination enabled, experiment with reducing the energy multiplier. This can have a dramatic effect on the scene.

Diagnostic

The properties in the **Diagnostic** category control tools to help you understand why the rendering produced the results it did, **Figure 17-8.** The scene can be rendered with photon maps, grids, and irradiance shown. These tools can help you diagnose and correct problems.

The Grid property determines if a coordinate grid is shown in the rendered image. The Grid size property sets the size of the grid. When the Grid property is set to Off, which is the default, the grid is not shown. There are three other settings:

- Object. A colored grid displays local coordinates (UVW). Each object has its own set of local coordinates.
- World. World coordinates (XYZ) are displayed in a colored grid, **Figure 17-9A.**
- Camera. Coordinates of a UCS corresponding to the camera or current view are displayed in a colored grid, **Figure 17-9B.**

The Photon property controls whether or not the effect of a photon map is shown in the rendering. When the property is set to Density or Irradiance and global illumination is on, the scene is rendered and overlaid with an image representing the photon map. See **Figure 17-10.**

- Density. Shows the photon map projected onto the scene. Higher-density areas are red and lower-density areas are the cooler colors.
- Irradiance. Similar to density, but the photons are shaded based on their irradiance value. Maximum irradiance is red and lower irradiance values are shown in the cooler colors.

The Samples property can be set to On or Off. When set to On, a grid is rendered plan to the view and varying shades of gray and white are displayed in the scene. This tool is another way to evaluate the lighting in the scene.

The BSP property determines whether or not the effects of *binary space partitioning (BSP)* are shown. BSP is a raytrace acceleration method. When rendering, if you receive

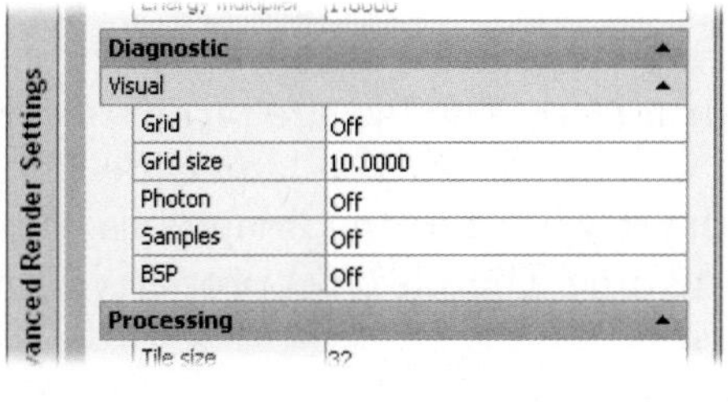

Figure 17-8.
The **Diagnostic** category of the **Advanced Render Settings** palette.

Figure 17-9.
Applying a grid to the rendering. A—The Grid property is set to World. B—The Grid property is set to Camera.

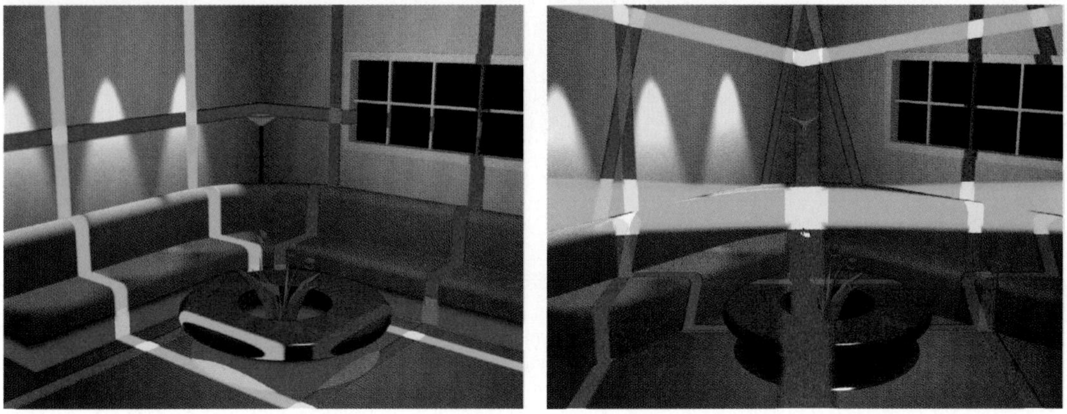

A B

Figure 17-10.
A photon map is applied to the rendering (Photon property set to Density).

a message about large depth or size values or the rendering is very slow, this tool may help you locate the problem.

- Depth. The depth of the raytrace tree is displayed. Top faces are displayed in bright red. The deeper the faces are in the tree, the cooler the colors in which they are displayed, Figure 17-11A.
- Size. The size of the leaves in the raytrace tree are displayed. Different colors are used to identify different leaf sizes, Figure 17-11B.

Processing

The properties in the **Processing** category control how the final render processing takes place, Figure 17-12. The Tile size property controls the size of the tiles into which the total image is subdivided. The larger the tile size, the fewer tiles that have to be rendered and the fewer times the image has to update. Larger tiles usually mean a shorter rendering time. The Tile order property controls the order in which the tiles are rendered:

Figure 17-11.
Showing the effects of binary space partitioning. A—The BSP property is set to Depth. B—The BSP property is set to Size.

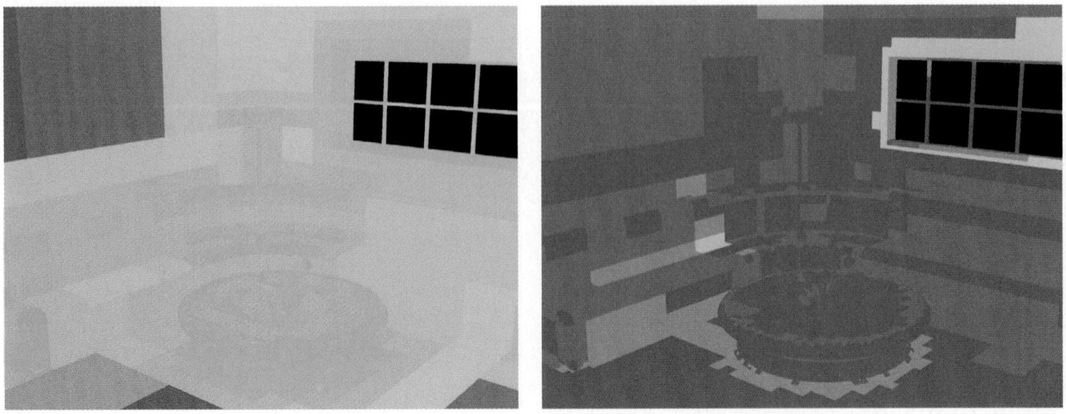

A B

Figure 17-12.
The **Processing** category of the **Advanced Render Settings** palette.

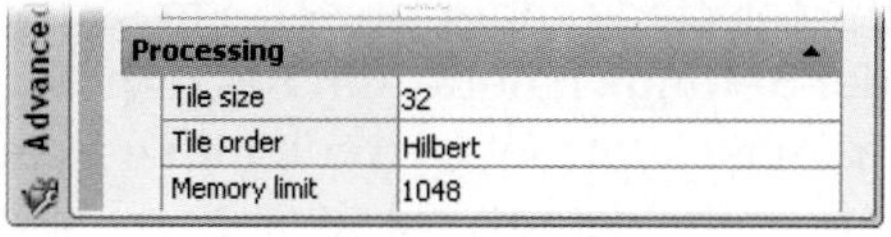

- Hilbert. The "cost" of switching to the next tile determines which tile is rendered next.
- Spiral. The rendering begins with the tiles in the center of the image and then spirals outward.
- Left to Right. The tiles are rendered from bottom to top and left to right in columns.
- Right to Left. The tiles are rendered from bottom to top and right to left in columns.
- Top to Bottom. The tiles are rendered from right to left and top to bottom in rows.
- Bottom to Top. The tiles are rendered from right to left and bottom to top in rows.

The Memory limit property specifies the maximum memory allocated for the rendering process. When this limit is reached, some objects may be removed from rendering.

Exercise 17-2

Complete the exercise on the Student CD.

Render Presets

Once settings have been established that create a rendering with the desired results, the settings can be saved to a custom render preset. The **Render Presets** dialog box is used to create custom render presets, Figure 17-13. The **RENDERPRESETS** command opens this dialog box.

The left side of the dialog box displays a tree that contains the standard render presets and any custom render presets. In the middle of the dialog box are all of the

Ribbon
Output > Render > Manage Render Presets...
Type
RENDERPRESETS RP

RENDERPRESETS

Figure 17-13.
The **Render Presets Manager** dialog box.

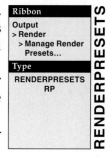

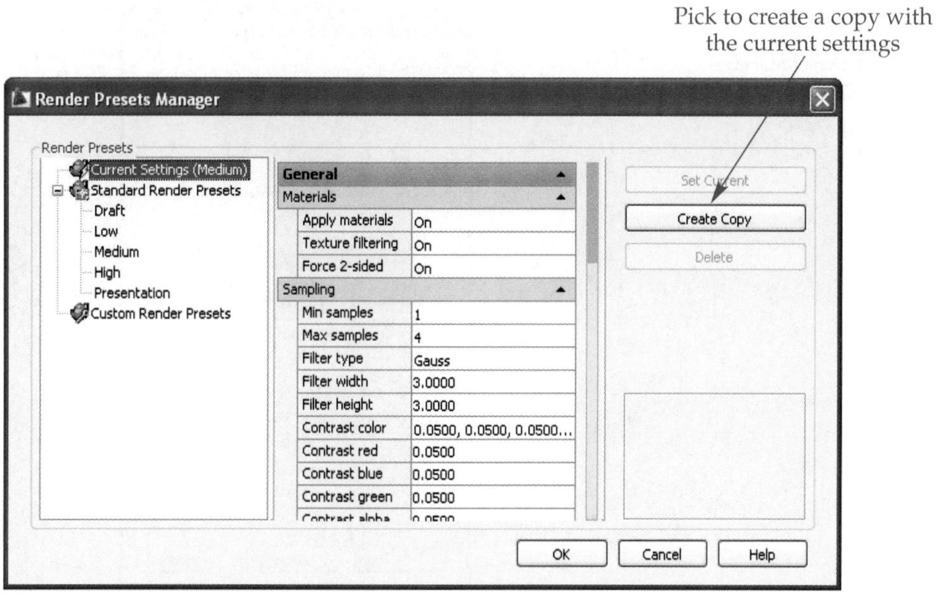

properties for the selected render preset. These are the same properties available in the **Advanced Render Settings** palette. On the right side of the dialog box are three buttons that allow you to make a preset current, make a copy of a preset, or delete a preset. You cannot delete one of the default presets.

The easiest way to create a custom preset is to start with a standard render preset and modify the properties until the desired result is produced. This preset will be indicated as the current preset in the **Render Presets** dialog box, but there will be an asterisk (*) in front of its name. The asterisk indicates that the preset has been changed from its original settings. Next, pick the **Create Copy** button in the **Render Presets** dialog box to make a copy. In the **Copy Render Preset** dialog box that appears, name the new render preset, provide a description, and pick the **OK** button. The new preset is saved in the Custom Render Presets branch of the tree.

Render Exposure

RENDEREXPOSURE

Type
RENDEREXPOSURE

The **RENDEREXPOSURE** command displays the **Adjust Rendered Exposure** dialog box. See Figure 17-14. In this dialog box, you can globally adjust the brightness, contrast, midtones, and exterior daylight of the scene. In order to use this command, photometric lighting must be on (**LIGHTINGUNITS** = 1 or 2) or the Exposure Type property in the **General** category of the **Advanced Render Settings** palette must be set to Logarithmic.

The **Preview** area in the **Adjust Rendered Exposure** dialog box displays the rendered scene with the changes you make in the dialog box so you can see how the scene will be altered. This saves the step of re-rendering the scene. Simply change the settings until the preview looks correct and then close the dialog box. The properties in this dialog box are:

- Brightness. Controls the brightness of the colors. The default value is 65.0000 and it can range from 0.0000 to 200.0000. Increasing the value increases how light the colors in the scene appear.
- Contrast. Controls the contrast of the colors in the scene. The default value is 50.0000 and it can range from 0.0000 to 100.0000. Increasing the value increases the difference between similar colors, in effect increasing the brightness of the scene.

Figure 17-14.
Using the **RENDEREXPOSURE** command to adjust the rendering.

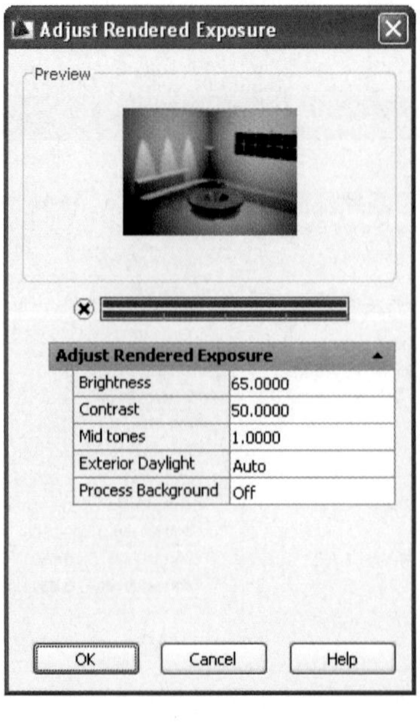

- Mid tones. Controls the midtone values of the colors. The midtone colors are neither light nor dark. The default value is 1.0000 and it can range from 0.0000 to 20.0000.
- Exterior Daylight. Sets the exposure for scenes illuminated with sunlight. It is either on, off, or automatic. The default setting is Auto.
- Process Background. Specifies whether or not the background is processed by exposure control when the scene is rendered. It is either on or off. The default setting is On.

To force the preview to update, pick the small X to the left of the rendering progress bars below the preview. The preview is updated with the current settings.

Render Environment

Ribbon
Output > Render Environment
Type
RENDER ENVIRONMENT
Menu
View > Render > Render Environment...

RENDERENVIRONMENT

The render environment allows for the addition of fog or depth cueing to the scene. ***Fog*** and ***depth cueing*** in AutoCAD are actually ways of using color to visually represent the distance between the camera (viewer) and objects in the model. See **Figure 17-15.** This is similar to looking at an object from a distance and seeing that the object is a little obscured from haze in the air. The only difference between fog and depth cueing is the color. Fog uses white or another light color and depth cueing generally uses black. The **Render Environment** dialog box is used to add fog/depth cueing, **Figure 17-16.**

Figure 17-15.
A—This scene has no fog/depth cueing applied. B—The scene has white fog applied (including the background). C—The scene has black depth cueing applied (including the background).

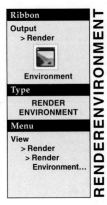

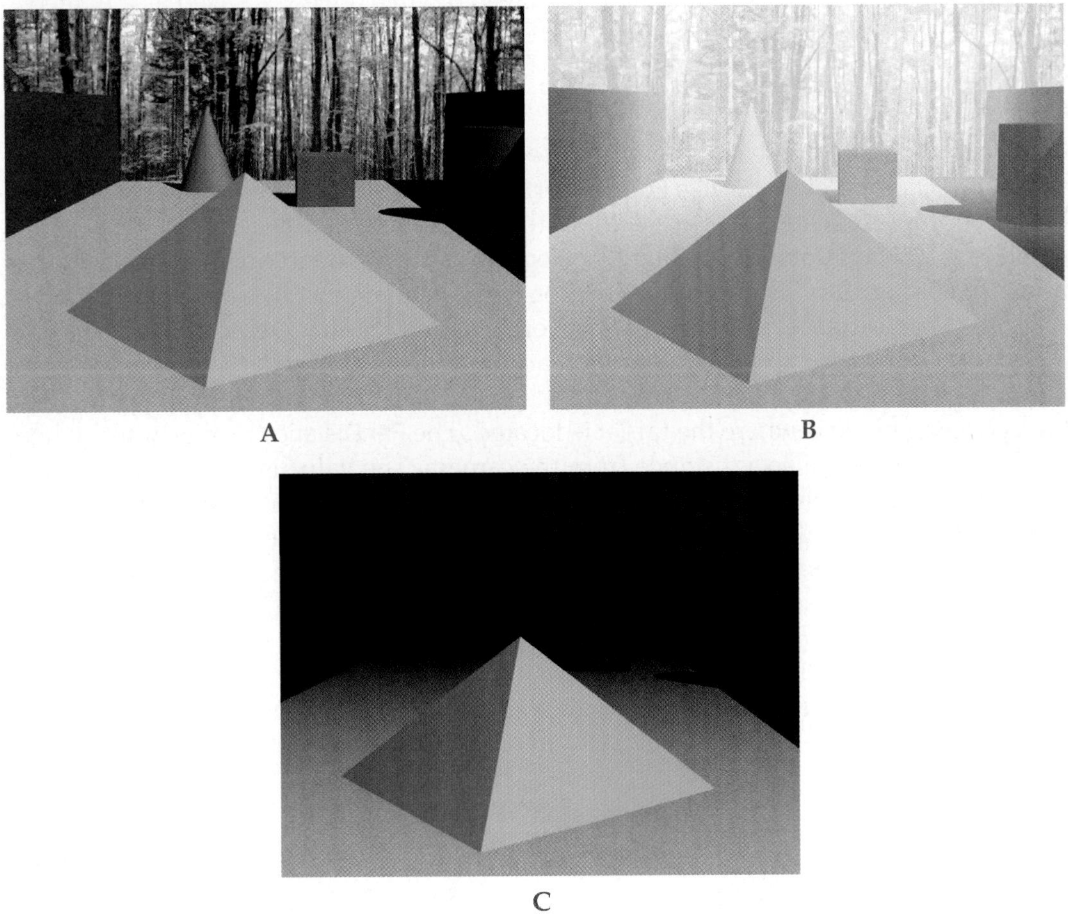

Figure 17-16.
The **Render Environment** dialog box is used to add fog/depth cueing to the scene.

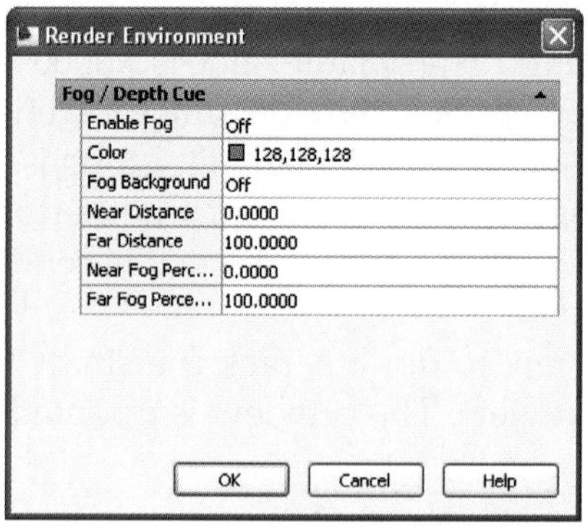

Creating a Camera

CAMERA

Ribbon
Home
> View
Create Camera
Type
CAMERA
CAM
Menu
View
> Create Camera

Before adding fog/depth cueing, a camera must be created that shows the view you want. Then, start the **3DCLIP** command and adjust the back clipping plane to where you want the effect to end. Only the back clipping plane needs to be active. The fog/depth cueing references this plane and the camera location.

Creating a camera and adjusting clipping planes is discussed in detail in Chapter 18. However, to create a camera and turn on the clipping plane(s), first select the command. Then, pick a location for the camera followed by the location for its target. Next, enter the **Clipping** option. Turn on the front clipping plane, if desired, and enter the offset distance. Then, turn on the back clipping plane and enter the offset distance. Finally, end the command (do not press [Esc]).

PROFESSIONAL TIP

A camera is automatically created when a view is saved as a named view. This is another good reason to save your views.

Adding Fog

Once a camera is created, open the **Render Environment** dialog box. To turn on fog/depth cueing, set the Enable Fog property to On. To set the color of the effect, select the Color property. Then, choose a color in the drop-down list. The Select Color... entry displays the **Select Color** dialog box. The Fog Background property determines whether or not the background is affected by the fog/depth cueing just like everything else.

The Near Distance property sets where the fog/depth cueing begins. This is a distance from the camera. The value can be from 0.0000 to 100.0000, which is a percentage of the total distance between the camera and the back clipping plane. The back clipping plane is where the target is located. The Far Distance property sets where the fog ends. This is also a distance from the camera. The value is also a percentage of the total distance from the camera to the back clipping plane and can be from 0.0000 to 100.0000. In other words, 100% ends at the back clipping plane.

The Near Fog Percentage property determines the opacity of the fog at its starting location. A value of 100 means the fog is 100% opaque. The near percentage is usually set to 0, or 0% opaque. The Far Fog Percentage property determines the opacity of the fog at its ending location. The fog/depth cueing will increase in opacity from the near distance to the far distance starting with the near fog percentage and ending with the far fog percentage.

Exercise 17-3

Complete the exercise on the Student CD.

Chapter Test

Answer the following questions. Write your answers on a separate sheet of paper or complete the electronic chapter test on the Student CD.

1. Describe the three panes of the **Render** window.
2. What are the three possible destinations for render output?
3. What is *sampling* and what do the properties in the **Sampling** subcategory in the **Advanced Render Settings** palette control?
4. Raytracing calculates shadows, _____, and _____.
5. How does global illumination simulate bounced light?
6. What is the benefit of final gathering?
7. For what is the Energy multiplier property in the **List Properties** subcategory in the **Advanced Render Settings** palette used?
8. For what are the properties in the **Diagnostic** category of the **Advanced Render Settings** palette used?
9. Describe how to create a custom render preset.
10. What is *fog/depth cueing?*

Drawing Problems

1. Using the drawing from problem 2 in Chapter 16, you will experiment with advanced render settings.
   A. Open drawing P16_02 and save it as P17_01.
   B. Make sure all of the lights are active and render the scene to the **Render** window using the Medium or High render preset.
   C. In the **Advanced Render Settings** palette, enable global illumination. Then, render the scene again.
   D. Enable final gathering and render the scene again. This time it will probably take much longer to render.
   E. Which rendering has the best quality?
   F. Which setting impacted render time the most?
   G. Save the last image as P17_01.jpg.
   H. Save the drawing.

2. In this problem, you will set up fog/depth cueing.
   A. Start a new drawing and save it as P17_02.
   B. Draw a planar surface that is 50 units × 20 units.
   C. Randomly place various objects (cones, boxes, spheres, etc.) on the plane. Assign a different color or material to each object.
   D. Create a viewpoint that is almost at ground level looking down the length of the plane. Try to get as many objects in the view as possible. Save this as a named view and add a background of some type.
   E. Add a distant light source. Position it and adjust its intensity so that interesting shadows are created in the scene, but the objects are sufficiently illuminated.
   F. With the **3DCLIP** command, set up clipping planes with the back clipping plane at the far end of the plane. Make sure the back clipping plane is on.
   G. In the **Render Environment** dialog box, turn on fog and set the color to black. The far distance should be 100 and the percentage should be around 75.
   H. Render the scene.
   I. Change the fog color to white and render the scene again.
   J. Set the fog to affect the background and render the scene again.
   K. Save the image as P17_02.jpg.
   L. Save the drawing.

3. In this problem, you will experiment with the **RENDEREXPOSURE** command and final gathering. Open P16_05 created in Chapter 16 and save it as P17_03. If you did not complete this problem, do so now.
   A. Open the **Advanced Render Settings** palette. In the **General** category, set the Exposure Type property to Logarithmic.
   B. In the **Indirect Illumination** category, change the Mode property in the **Final Gather** subcategory to Off.
   C. Render the scene and note the appearance.
   D. Use the **RENDEREXPOSURE** command to display the **Adjust Rendered Exposure** dialog box. Note the appearance of the preview image.
   E. Change the brightness setting to 80 and note how the preview changes.
   F. Pick the **OK** button to close the **Adjust Rendered Exposure** dialog box and render the scene again. Does the rendered scene match the preview in the **Adjust Rendered Exposure** dialog box?
   G. Turn on final gathering (Mode property = On) and open the **Adjust Rendered Exposure** dialog box. How does the preview look different? Why?
   H. Adjust the brightness setting to get the exposure that you want in the preview. Then, close the dialog box and render the scene again.
   I. Experiment with the other settings in the **Adjust Rendered Exposure** dialog box until you get the scene the way you want it.
   J. Render the scene one last time and save the image as a file called P17_03.jpg.
   K. Save the drawing.

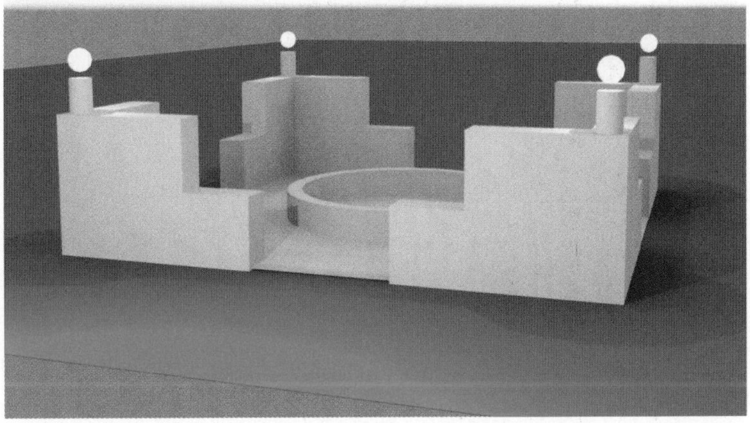

4. Using the same drawing from problem 17-3, you will perform diagnostics to determine the effects of the lights on the final rendering.
   A. Open drawing P17_03 and save it as P17_04.
   B. In the **Advanced Render Settings** palette, select the Medium rendering preset. In the **Indirect Illumination** category, turn off final gathering (Mode property = Off).
   C. In the **Diagnostic** category of the **Advanced Render Settings** palette, set the Grid property to Object. Render the scene.
   D. In the **Diagnostic** category of the **Advanced Render Settings** palette, set the Grid property to World. Render the scene.
   E. In the **Diagnostic** category of the **Advanced Render Settings** palette, set the Grid property to Camera. Render the scene.
   F. Describe the differences and explain why this is helpful in analyzing a scene.
   G. In the **Indirect Illumination** category of the **Advanced Render Settings** palette, turn on global illumination. In the **Diagnostic** category, turn off the grid and set the Photon property to Density.
   H. Render the scene. Describe the effect and what can be learned from it.
   I. Set the Photon property to Irradiance and render the scene. What does this effect tell about the lighting in the scene?
   J. Which diagnostic worked the best and why?
   K. Save the drawing.

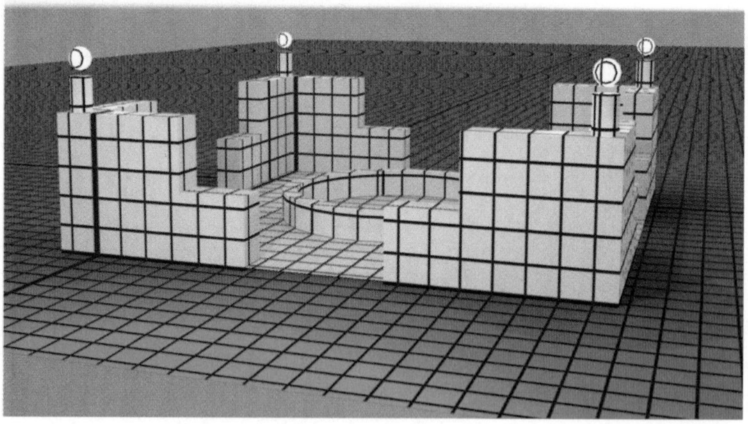

CHAPTER 18

Cameras, Walkthroughs, and Flybys

Learning Objectives

After completing this chapter, you will be able to:

- ✓ Create a camera to define a static 3D view.
- ✓ Activate and adjust front and back clipping planes.
- ✓ Record a walkthrough of a 3D model to a movie file.
- ✓ Record a flyby of a 3D model to a movie file.
- ✓ Create walkthroughs and flybys by following a path.
- ✓ Control the viewpoint, speed, and quality of the animation.

Once you have a 3D design complete, or even while still in the conceptual phase of design, you may want to take a stroll through the model and have a look around. You may also want to strap on some wings and fly over and around the model to see it from above. A ***walkthrough animation*** shows a scene as a person would view it walking through the scene. Walkthroughs often show the interior of a building. However, walkthroughs can be created for exterior scenes as well. A ***flyby animation*** is similar to a walkthrough, except that the person is not bound by gravity. In other words, the scene is viewed as a bird would see it flying through the scene. Flybys often show the exterior of a building.

The **3DWALK** command is used to create a walkthrough by recording views as a camera "walks" through the scene. The **3DFLY** command is very similar, but the movement of the camera is not limited to a single Z value. A path can also be drawn and the camera linked to the path. This chapter discusses these commands and other methods needed to create the animation you need. In addition, creating and using cameras are discussed.

Creating Cameras

Cameras are used in AutoCAD to store a viewpoint and easily recall it later when needed for viewing or rendering the scene. After the camera is established, you can zoom, pan, and orbit as needed and then come back to the camera view. It is not necessary to create a camera before using the **3DWALK**, **3DFLY**, and **ANIPATH** commands (discussed later) because these commands create their own cameras.

CAMERA

Ribbon
Home
> View

Create Camera
Type
CAMERA
CAM
Menu
View
> Create Camera

The **CAMERA** command allows you to add a camera to the scene. Cameras are normally placed in the plan view of the scene to make it easy for you to pick where you want to "stand" and where you want to "look." Once the command is selected, you are first prompted to specify the camera location. A camera glyph is placed in the scene at the camera location, **Figure 18-1.** Next, you must specify the target location. As you move the cursor before picking the target location, a pyramid-shaped field of view indicates what will be seen in the view. Once you select the target location, the command remains active for you to select an option:

Enter an option [?/Name/LOcation/Height/Target/LEns/Clipping/View/eXit]<eXit>:

The list, or **?**, option allows you to list the cameras in the drawing. Type an asterisk (*) to show all of the cameras in the drawing. You can also enter a name or part of a name and an asterisk. For example, entering HOUSE* will list all of the cameras whose name begins with HOUSE, such as HOUSE_SW, HOUSE_SE, and HOUSE_PLAN.

The **Name** option allows you to change the name of the camera as you create it. If you do not rename the camera, it is given a default, sequential name, such as Camera1, Camera2, Camera3, and so on. It is always a good idea to provide meaningful names for cameras. Names such as Living Room_SW, Corner, or Hallway_Looking East leave no doubt as to what the camera shows. If you choose not to rename the camera at this point, it can be renamed later using the **Properties** palette.

The **Location** option allows you to change the placement of the camera. Enter the option and then specify the new location. You can enter coordinates or pick a location in the drawing.

The **Height** option allows you to change the vertical location of the camera. Enter the option and then enter the height of the camera. The value you enter is the number of units from the current XY plane. If you are placing the camera in a plan view, this option is used to tilt the view up or down from the current XY plane.

The **Target** option allows you to change the placement of the camera target. Enter the option and then specify the new location. You can enter coordinates or pick a location in the drawing.

The **Lens** option allows you to change the focal length of the camera lens. If you change the lens focal length, you are really changing the field of view, or the area of the drawing that the camera covers. The lower the lens focal length, the wider the field of view angle. The focal length is measured in millimeters.

The **Clipping** option is used to turn the front and back clipping planes on or off. These planes are used to limit what is shown in the camera view. Clipping planes are discussed later in this chapter.

The **View** option is used to change the current view to that shown by the camera. This option has two choices—**Yes** or **No**. If you select Yes, the active viewport switches to the camera view and the **CAMERA** command ends. If you select **No**, the previous prompt returns.

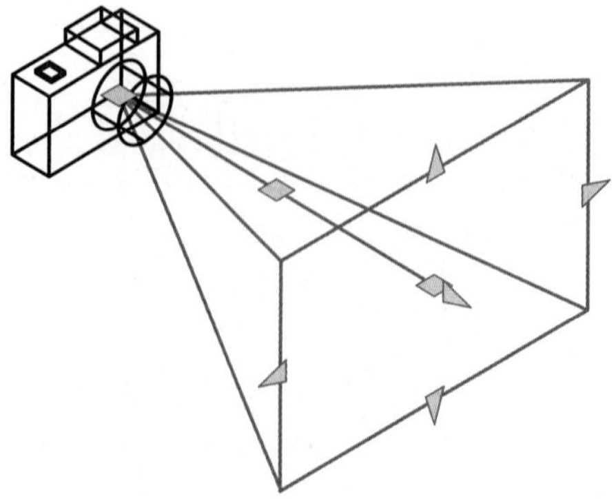

Figure 18-1.
A camera is represented by a glyph. When the camera is selected, the field of view (shown in color) and grips are displayed.

Once you have made all settings, press [Enter] or select the **Exit** option to end the command. The view (camera) is listed with the other saved views in the drop-down list in the **View** panel on the **Home** tab of the ribbon. It is also listed under the Model Views branch in the **View Manager** dialog box. Selecting the view makes it the current view in the active viewport.

PROFESSIONAL TIP

In addition to the camera name, many other camera properties can be changed in the **Properties** palette. The camera and target locations can be changed, the lens focal length and field of view can be adjusted, and the clipping planes can be modified. Also, you can change the roll angle, which is the rotation about a line from the camera to the target, and set the camera glyph to plot.

Camera System Variables

The **CAMERADISPLAY** system variable controls the visibility of camera glyphs. When set to 1, which is the default, camera glyphs are displayed. When set to 0, camera glyphs are not displayed. Creating a camera automatically sets the variable to 1.

When creating a camera, if you pick the camera and target locations without using object snaps, you may assume that the camera and target are located on the XY plane (Z coordinate of 0) of the current UCS. This may or may not be true. The **CAMERAHEIGHT** system variable determines the default height of the camera if a Z coordinate is not provided. It is a good idea to set this variable to a typical eye height before placing cameras. There is no corresponding system variable for the target because the target is usually placed by snapping to an object of interest. If X and Y coordinates are entered for the target location, but a Z coordinate is not provided, the Z value is automatically 0. If a camera was previously created in the drawing session and the **Height** option was used, that height value becomes the default camera height.

Camera Tool Palette

The **Camera** tool palette provides a quick way to add a camera, but the default tools do not allow for the options described earlier. The **Normal Camera** tool creates a camera with a 50 mm focal length. This camera simulates normal human vision. The **Wide-angle Camera** tool creates a camera with a 35 mm focal length. This type of view is commonly used for scenery or interior views where it is important to show as much as possible with minimal distortion. The **Extreme Wide-angle Camera** tool creates a camera with a 6 mm focal length. This camera produces a fish-eye view, which is very distorted and mainly useful for special effects.

Changing the Camera View

Once the camera is placed, it is easy to manipulate. If you select a camera, the **Camera Preview** window is displayed by default. This window shows the view through the camera, **Figure 18-2.** The view in the window can be displayed in the 3D Hidden, 3D Wireframe, Conceptual, Realistic, or any other named visual style. Select the visual style in the drop-down list in the window. If the **Display this window when editing a camera** check box at the bottom of the window is unchecked, the window is not displayed the next time a camera is selected. The next time the drawing is opened, this setting is restored (checked).

When a camera is selected, grips are displayed. Refer to **Figure 18-1.** If you hover the cursor over a grip, a tooltip appears indicating what the grip will alter. Picking the base grip on the camera allows you to reposition the camera in the scene. If the

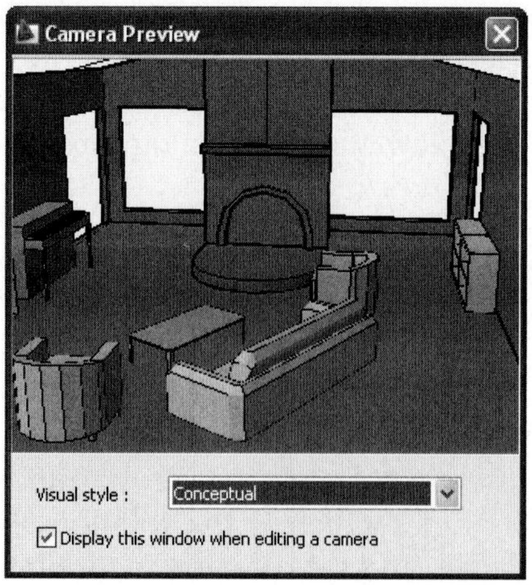

Figure 18-2.
The **Camera Preview** window is displayed, by default, when a camera is selected.

Camera Preview window is open, watch the preview as you move the camera to help guide you. Selecting the grip on the target allows the target to be repositioned. Again, use the preview in the **Camera Preview** window as a guide. The grip at the midpoint between the camera and target can be used to reposition the camera and target at the same time. If you pick and move one of the arrow grips on the end of the field of view, the lens focal length and field of view are changed.

Camera Clipping Planes

Clipping planes allow you to suppress objects in the foreground or background of your scene. Picture these clipping planes as flat, 2D objects perpendicular to the line of sight that can be moved closer to or farther from the viewer. Only the objects between the front and back clipping planes and within the field of view are seen in the camera view. This is helpful for eliminating walls, roofs, or any other clutter that may take away from the focus of the scene. Also, as mentioned in Chapter 17, the back clipping plane should be enabled when applying fog/depth cueing using the **Render Environment** dialog box. Clipping planes can be set while creating the camera or later using the **Properties** palette.

To set the clipping planes while creating the camera, enter the **Clipping** option. You are prompted:

Enable the front clipping plane? [Yes/No] <No>:

To enable the front clipping plane, enter YES. You are then asked to specify the offset from the target plane. This is described next. Once you enter the offset, or if you answer **No**, you are prompted:

Enable the back clipping plane? [Yes/No] <No>:

To enable the back clipping plane, enter YES and then specify the offset from the target plane.

The ***target plane*** is the 2D plane that is perpendicular to the line of sight and passing through the target point. Offsets for both front and back clipping planes are from this plane. Positive values place the clipping planes between the camera and the target plane. Negative values place the planes on the opposite side of the target plane from the camera. You can place the clipping planes anywhere in the scene from the camera location to infinity. You cannot, however, place the back clipping plane in front of the front clipping plane.

The best way to adjust clipping planes is using the **Properties** palette. Create the camera and then display a plan view of the camera and target (an approximate plan view is okay). Select the camera and open the **Properties** palette. In the **Clipping**

Figure 18-3.
Adjusting the clipping planes for a camera.

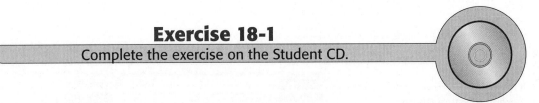

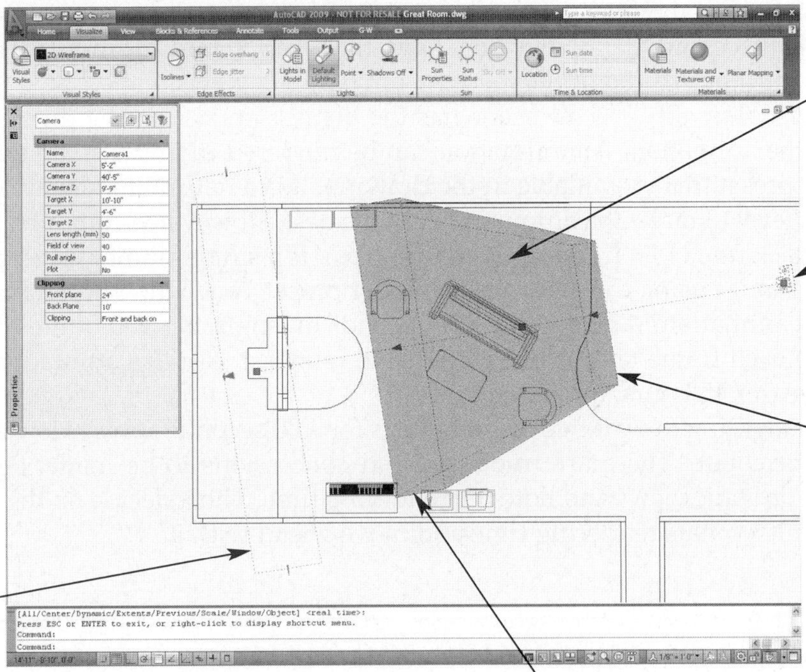

category, select the Clipping property. In the property drop-down list, select Front on, Back on, or Front and back on to turn on the appropriate clipping plane(s). Notice that the clipping planes are visible in the viewport, **Figure 18-3.** Next, enter offset values for the Front plane and Back plane properties, as appropriate. By displaying a plan view of the camera and target, you can see where the clipping planes are located and visualize their effect on the scene. If the **Camera Preview** window is open, the clipping is reflected in the preview.

Exercise 18-1

Complete the exercise on the Student CD.

Animation Preparation

The tools presented in this chapter make it easy to lay out a path, plan camera angles, and record the movement of the camera. The resulting animation can be directly output to a number of movie file types that can be shared with others. However, there are some decisions to make first.

It is important to exactly plan out what you want to see in the animation. Think like a movie director and plan the "shots." Ask these questions:

- What will be visible from each camera angle?
- Is there a background in place?
- Is the lighting appropriate?
- Will a simple walkthrough suffice or will a flyby be necessary?
- How close is the viewer (camera) going to be to the objects in the scene?

The answers to these questions will help determine the modeling detail required. Do not model anything that will not be seen. Also, do not place detailed materials on objects that are not the focus of the animation. Processing the animation may take a long time. Unnecessary detail may bog down the computer. In addition, walkthroughs and flybys must be created in perspective, not parallel, views.

The "visual quality" of the scene has the biggest impact on the time involved in rendering the animation. An animation can be rendered in any visual style or using any render preset that is available in the drawing. It is a natural tendency to render at the highest level to make the animation look the best. However, a computer animation has a playback rate of 30 frames per second (fps). If a single frame (view) takes three minutes to render using the **Presentation** render preset, how long will it take to render a 30 second animation? An animation 30 seconds in length has 900 frames (30 fps × 30 seconds). If each frame takes three minutes to render, the entire animation will take 2700 minutes, or 45 hours, to render.

Are you willing to wait two or three days for a 30 second movie? How about your boss or your client? There are trade-offs and concessions to be made. Perform test renderings on static views and note the rendering time. Then, decide on the acceptable level of quality versus rendering time and move ahead with it.

Walking and Flying

3DWALK

Ribbon
Tools
> Animations

Walk

Type
3DWALK

Menu
View
> Walk and Fly
> Walk

3DFLY

Ribbon
Tools
> Animations

Fly

Type
3DFLY

Menu
View
> Walk and Fly
> Fly

The process for creating a walkthrough or a flyby is the same. First, the command is initiated. Then, the movement is defined and recorded. Finally, the recorded movement is saved to an animation file.

When using the **3DWALK** and **3DFLY** commands, you can move through the scene using the arrow keys or the [W], [A], [S], and [D] keys on the keyboard to control your movements. Once either command is initiated, a message appears from the **Communication Center**, if the notification is turned on. If you expand this message, the key movements are explained. See **Figure 18-4.** To redisplay this message while the command is active, press the [Tab] key.

- **Move forward.** Up arrow or [W].
- **Move left.** Left arrow or [A].
- **Move right.** Right arrow or [D].
- **Back up.** Down arrow or [S].

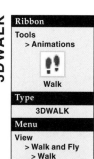

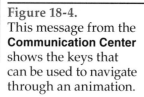

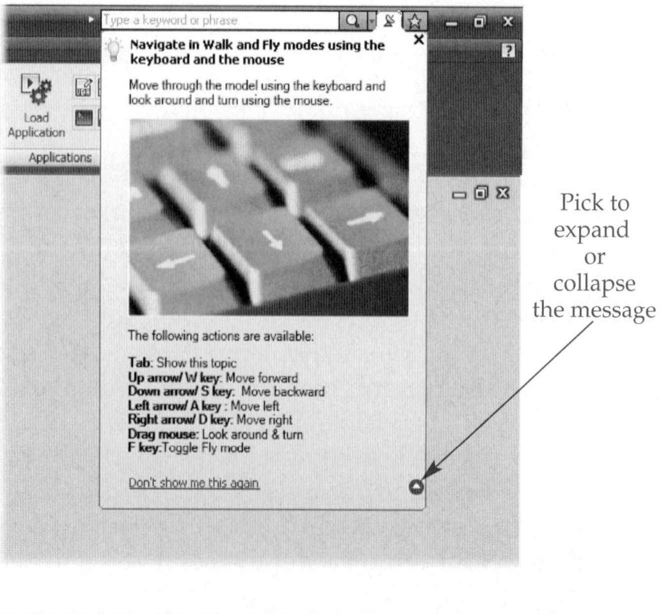

Figure 18-4.
This message from the **Communication Center** shows the keys that can be used to navigate through an animation.

You can also navigate through the scene using the mouse. Press and hold the left mouse button and then drag the mouse in the active viewport to "steer" through the scene. With the **3DWALK** command, the camera remains at the same Z value. With the **3DFLY** command, the Z position of the camera can change. The steps for creating a walkthrough or flyby are provided at the end of this section.

Position Locator

When the **3DWALK** or **3DFLY** command is initiated, the **Position Locator** palette appears. See **Figure 18-5.** This window shows a plan view of the scene. The purpose of this window is to provide an overview of the scene, in plan, while you develop the animation. It does not need to be displayed to create an animation and can be closed if it takes up too much space or slows down the rendering.

Position and target indicators appear in the plan view to show the location of the camera and its target. The green triangular shape displays the field of view. The ***field of view*** is the area within the camera's "vision." The field of view indicator is only displayed when the target indicator is displayed. By default, the position indicator is red. The target indicator is green by default. These properties can be changed in the **General** category at the bottom of the **Position Locator** palette.

You can reposition the camera and the target in the plan view simply by picking and dragging either indicator. The effect of the change is visible in the active viewport. Moving the position and target indicators closer together reduces the field of view. Picking the field of view lines and dragging moves the position and target indicators at the same time.

In addition to changing the color of the position and target indicators, the properties in the **General** category can be used to modify the display in the **Position Locator** palette. The Position indicator size property determines if the indicators are displayed small, medium, or large. If the Position indicator blink property is set to On, the indicators flash on and off in the preview. The Preview visual style property sets the visual style for the preview. This setting does not affect the current viewport or the animation. The Preview transparency property is set to 50% by default, but can be changed to whatever you want. If the view in the **Position Locator** palette is obscured by something (a roof, perhaps), you may want to set the Preview visual style property to 3D Hidden and the Preview transparency property to 80% or 90%. This will make the objects under the roof visible.

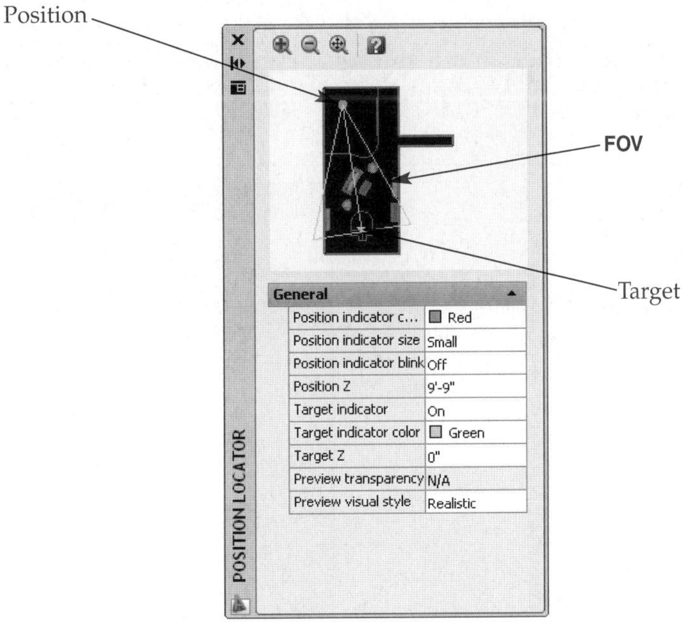

Figure 18-5.
The **Position Locator** palette.

Exercise 18-2

Complete the exercise on the Student CD.

Walk and Fly Settings

WALKFLYSETTINGS

Ribbon
Tools > Animations
Walk and Fly Settings
Type
WALKFLY SETTINGS
Menu
View > Walk and Fly > Walk and Fly Settings...

General settings for walkthroughs and flybys are made in the **Walk and Fly Settings** dialog box. See **Figure 18-6.** Open this dialog box by picking the **Walk and Fly Settings** button in the **Animations** panel on the ribbon (in the **Walk** flyout). It can also be displayed by picking the **Walk and Fly...** button in the **3D Modeling** tab of the **Options** dialog box.

The three radio buttons at the top of the dialog box are used to determine when the message shown in **Figure 18-4** is displayed. The check box determines if the **Position Locator** palette is automatically displayed when the **3DWALK** or **3DFLY** command is entered.

The text boxes in **Current drawing settings** area determine the size of each step and the number of steps per second. The **Walk/fly step size:** setting controls the **STEPSIZE** system variable. This is the number of units that the camera moves in one step. The **Steps per second:** setting controls the **STEPSPERSEC** system variable. This is the number of steps the camera takes each second. Together, these two settings determine how fast the camera moves in the animation.

PROFESSIONAL TIP

You will have to experiment with step size and steps per second values to make an animation that is easy to watch. Start with low numbers and work your way up. Fast movements are disorienting and make the viewer feel like they are missing something. The viewer should be able to take their time and get a good look at your design.

To get a feel for the proper speed for a walkthrough, pay attention to the next movie or TV show that you watch. When the director wants you to get a good look at the setting for the scene, the camera very slowly pans around the room. To emphasize distance, the camera slowly zooms in to a target object or person.

Camera tools

The expanded **View** panel on the **Home** tab of the ribbon contains some tools for quickly adjusting the camera before starting the animation. See **Figure 18-7.** The **Lens length** slider controls how much of the scene is seen by the camera. The ***lens length***

Figure 18-6.
General settings for the walkthrough or flyby are made in the **Walk and Fly Settings** dialog box.

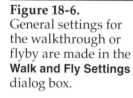

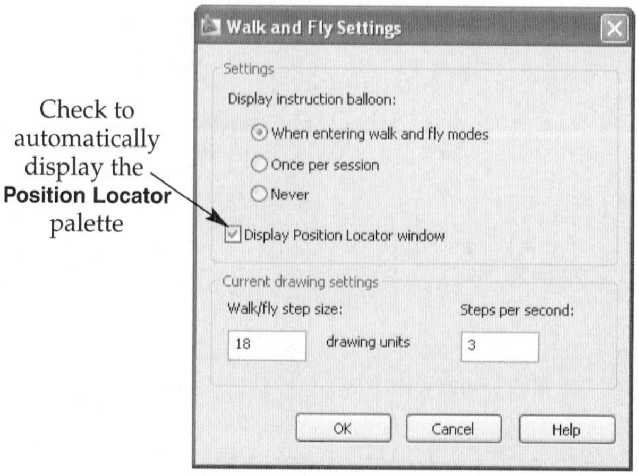

Figure 18-7.
Camera tools are located in the expanded **View** panel on the **Home** tab of the ribbon.

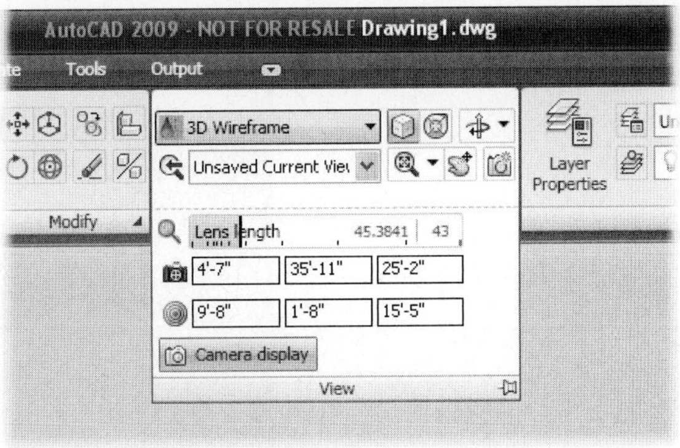

refers to the focal length of the camera lens. The higher the number, the closer you are to the subject. The range is from about 1 to 100000; 50 is a good starting point. There are stops on the slider for standard lens lengths. You can enter a specific value for the lens length or field of view by selecting the text in the slider, typing the value, and pressing [Enter].

Below the **Lens length** slider are text boxes for the camera and target positions. These can be used to change the X, Y, and Z coordinates of the camera or target. It is usually easier to change the X and Y locations in the **Position Locator** palette, but the Z coordinate cannot be set there. The Z coordinate determines eye level.

In Chapter 16, you learned that some lights are represented in viewports by light glyphs. Cameras are also represented by glyphs. The **Camera display** button toggles the display of camera glyphs on and off. The button is blue when camera glyphs are displayed. This is the default.

Animation tools

The **Animations** panel on the **Tools** tab of the ribbon contains the tools for controlling the recording and playback of the animation. See **Figure 18-8.** The **Start Recording Animation** button is used to initiate recording of camera movement. After the **3DWALK** or **3DFLY** command is activated, pick the button to start recording. Make sure that you are ready to start moving when you pick the button because recording starts as soon as it is picked.

Picking the **Pause Animation** button temporarily stops recording. This allows you to make adjustments to the view without recording the adjustment. When you are ready to begin recording again, pick the record button to resume.

Picking the **Play** button stops the recording and opens the **Animation Preview** dialog box in which the animation is played, **Figure 18-9.** The controls in this dialog

Figure 18-8.
The **Animations** panel on the **Tools** tab of the ribbon is where you can record and play back the walkthrough or flyby animation.

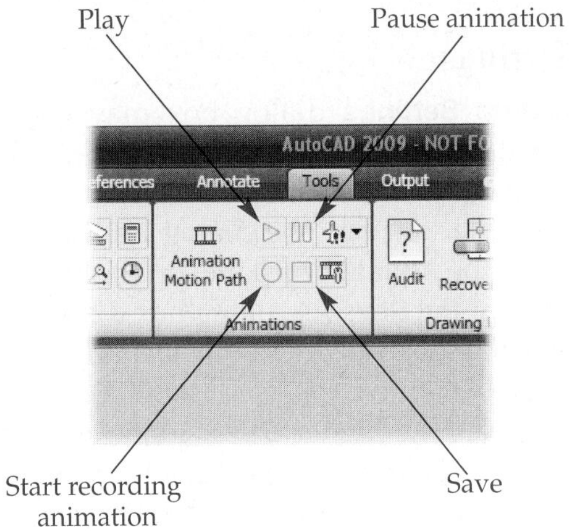

Figure 18-9.
The animation is played in the **Animation Preview** dialog box.

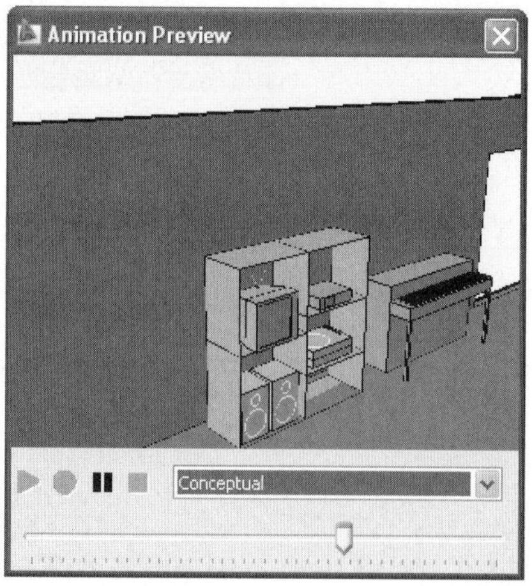

box can be used to rewind, pause, and play the animation. The slider can be dragged to preview part of the animation or move to a specific frame. The visual style can also be set using the drop-down list. If the animation is created using a render preset, the file must be played in Windows Media Player or another media player to view the rendered detail.

Picking the **Save** button stops recording and opens the **Save As** dialog box. Name the animation file, navigate to a location, and pick the **Save** button.

Picking the **Animation Settings** button opens the **Animation Settings** dialog box. The next section describes this dialog box in detail.

CAUTION

While the **3DWALK** or **3DFLY** command is active and the record button is on, you are creating an animation. If you move the camera in the **Position Locator** palette and start re-recording the animation to correct a problem, but do not first exit the current **3DWALK** or **3DFLY** command session, you are adding another segment to the animation you just previewed. To start over, first exit the current command session.

Exercise 18-3

Complete the exercise on the Student CD.

Animation settings

Ribbon
Tools
> Animations
Animation Settings

The **Animation Settings** dialog box may contain the most important settings pertaining to walkthroughs and flybys. See Figure 18-10. These animation settings determine how good the animation looks, how long it is going to take to complete, and how big the file will be. The dialog box is displayed by picking the **Animation Settings** button in the **Animations** panel on the **Tools** tab of the ribbon or the **Animation settings...** button in the **Save As** dialog box displayed when saving an animation.

The **Visual style:** drop-down list is used to set the shading level in the animation. The name of this drop-down list is a little misleading because visual styles and render presets are available. The higher the shading or rendering level selected in this drop-down list, the longer the rendering will take to process and the bigger the file will be. If you have numerous lights casting shadows, detailed materials, and global illumination

Figure 18-10.
The **Animation Settings** dialog box contains important settings pertaining to walkthroughs and flybys.

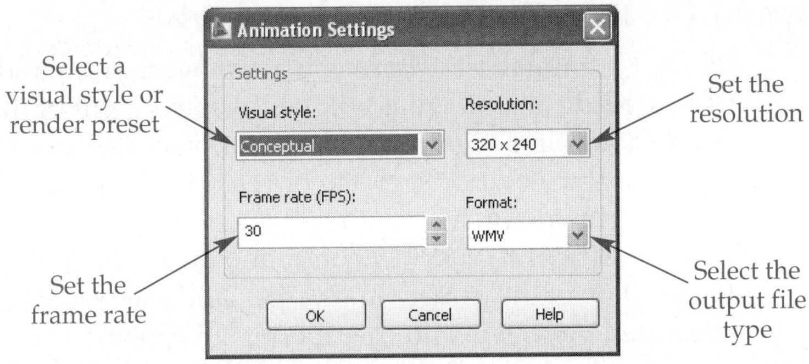

and final gathering enabled, settle in for a long wait. A simple, straight-ahead walkthrough of 10 or 15 feet can easily result in 300 frames of animation. If each frame takes about five seconds to render, that equals 1500 seconds, or 25 minutes, to create an animation file that is only 10 seconds long.

The **Frame rate (FPS):** text box sets the number of frames per second for the playback. In other words, this sets the speed of the animation playback. The default is 30 fps, which is a common playback rate.

The **Resolution:** drop-down list offers standard choices of resolution, from 160 × 120 to 1024 × 768. These are measured in pixels × pixels. Remember, higher resolutions mean longer processing times and larger file sizes.

The **Format:** drop-down list is used to select the output file type. The file type must be set in this dialog box. It cannot be changed in the **Save As** dialog box. The choices of output file type are:

- **WMV.** The standard movie file format for Windows Media Player.
- **AVI.** Audio-Video Interleaved is the Windows standard for movie files.
- **MOV.** QuickTime® Movie is the standard file format for Apple® movie files.
- **MPG.** Moving Picture Experts Group (MPEG) is another very common movie file format.

Depending on the configuration of your computer, you may not have all of these options or you may have additional options not listed here.

PROFESSIONAL TIP

Other AutoCAD navigation modes may be used to create a walkthrough or flyby. Anytime that you enter constrained, free, or continuous orbit, you can pick the **Start Recording Animation** button to record the movements. After you activate the **3DWALK** or **3DFLY** command, right-click and experiment with some of the other options as you record your animation. You can even combine some of these navigation modes with walking or flying. For example, use **3DFLY** to zoom into a scene, pause the animation, switch to constrained orbit, restart the recording, and slowly circle around your model. Animation settings are also available in this shortcut menu.

Exercise 18-4

Complete the exercise on the Student CD.

Steps to Create a Walkthrough or Flyby

1. Plan your animation: where you are moving from and to, what you are going to be looking at, and what will be the focal point of the scene.
2. Set up a multiple viewport configuration of three or four viewports.
3. In one of the viewports, create or restore a named view with the appropriate starting viewpoint. Make sure a background is set up, if desired.
4. Start the **3DWALK** or **3DFLY** command and note in the **Position Locator** palette the location of the camera and target, and the field of view. Adjust these in the expanded **View** panel on the ribbon, if necessary.
5. Open the **Animation Settings** dialog box and set up the desired shading, frame rate, resolution, and output file format.
6. Position your fingers over the navigation keys on the keyboard.
7. Pick the **Start Recording Animation** button.
8. Practice navigating through the view and then pick the **Play** button to preview your animation. When you are done practicing, make sure to cancel the command.
9. Pick the **Start Recording Animation** button to start over.
10. Start navigating through the view. Try to keep the movements as smooth as possible. Any jerks and shakes will be visible in the animation.
11. When you are done, stop moving forward and then pick the stop (**Save**) button. In the **Save As** dialog box, name and save the file.
12. The **Creating Video** dialog box is displayed as AutoCAD processes the frames, **Figure 18-11.**
13. When the **Creating Video** dialog box is automatically closed, the animation file is saved and you can take a look at it. Pick the **Play** button and watch the animation in the **Animation Preview** window. You can also locate the file using Windows Explorer. Then, double-click on the file to play the animation in Media Player (or whichever program is associated with the file type).
12. Exit the command. If you are not satisfied with the results and want to try it again, make sure to exit the command before you make another attempt at the walkthrough or flyby.

Motion Path Animation

You may have found it hard to create smooth motion using the keyboard and mouse. Fortunately, AutoCAD provides an easy way to create a nice, smooth animated walkthrough or flyby. This is done through the use of a motion path. A ***motion path*** is simply a line along which the camera, target, or both travel during the animation.

One method of using a motion path is to link the camera and target to a single path. The camera and its line of sight then follow the path much like a train follows tracks. See **Figure 18-12.**

Another option when using a motion path is to link the camera to a single point in the scene and the target to a path. For example, the target can be set to follow a circle or arc. The camera swivels on the point and "looks at" the path as if it is being rotated on a tripod. See **Figure 18-13.**

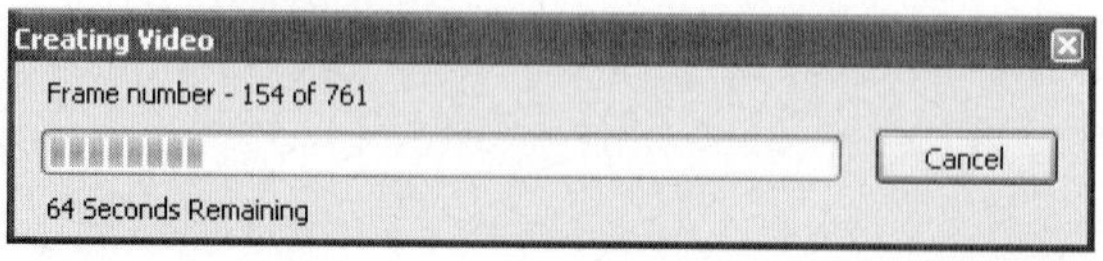

Figure 18-11.
The **Creating Video** dialog box is displayed as AutoCAD generates the animation.

Figure 18-12.
A—The camera and target are linked to the same path (shown in color). B—The camera looks straight ahead as it moves along the path.

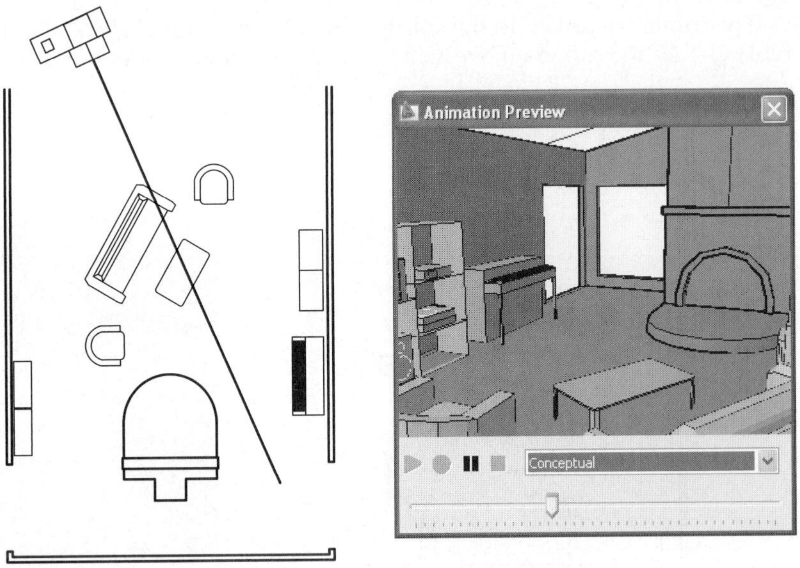

A B

Figure 18-13.
A—The camera is linked to a point so it remains stationary. The target is linked to the circle.
B—The camera view rotates around the room as if the camera is on a swivel tripod.

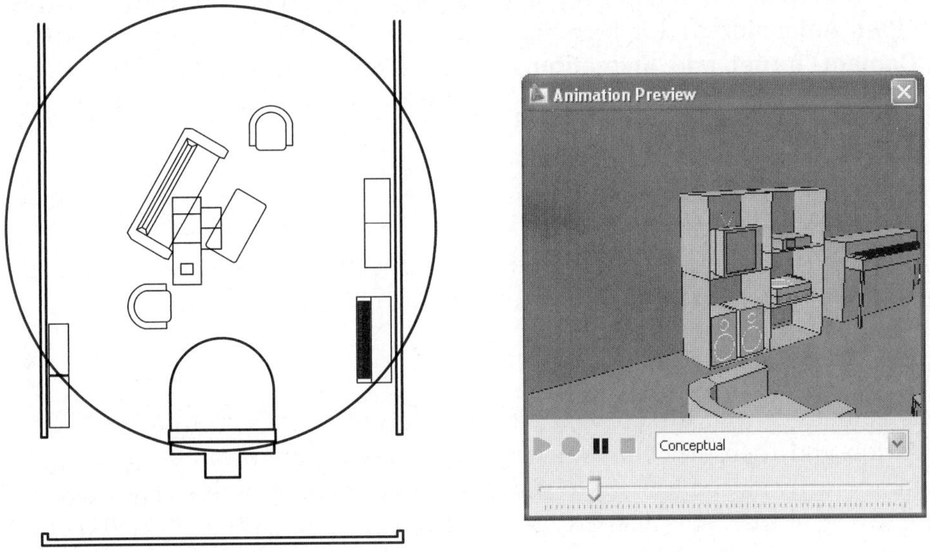

A B

A third way to use a motion path is to have the camera follow a path, but have the target locked onto a stationary point. This is similar to riding in a vehicle and watching an object of interest on the side of the road. As the vehicle moves, your gaze remains fixed on the object. See **Figure 18-14.**

The fourth method of using a motion path is to have both the camera and target follow separate paths. Picture yourself walking into an unfamiliar room. As you walk into the center of the room, your gaze sweeps left and right across the room. In this case, the camera (you) follows a straight line path and the target (your gaze) follows an arc from one side of the room to the other.

Figure 18-14.
A—The camera is linked to the spline path and the target is linked to the point (shown in color). B—As the camera moves along the path, it always looks at the point.

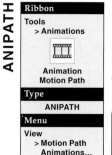

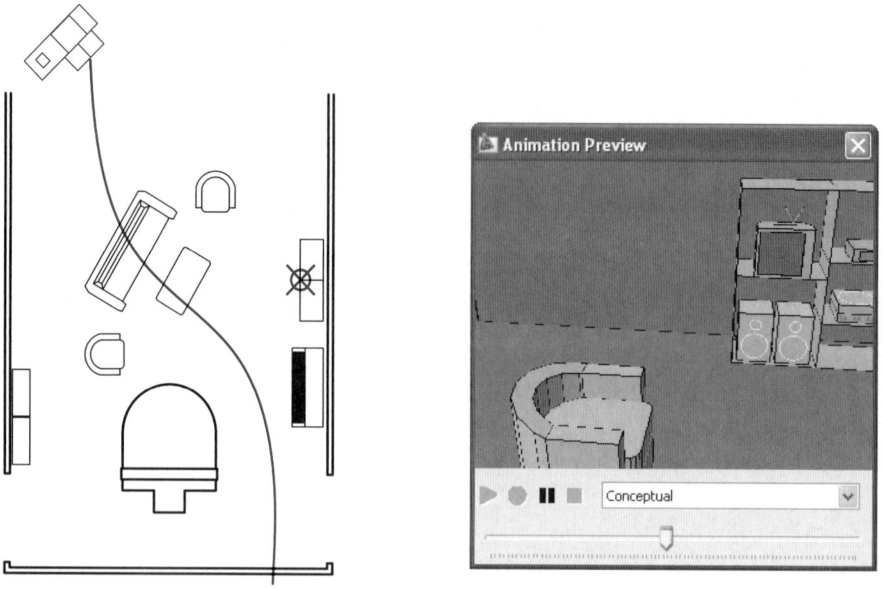

A B

ANIPATH

Ribbon
Tools
> Animations
Animation Motion Path
Type
ANIPATH
Menu
View
> Motion Path Animations...

The **ANIPATH** command is used to assign motion paths. The command opens the **Motion Path Animation** dialog box. See **Figure 18-15.** This dialog box has three main areas: **Camera**, **Target**, and **Animation settings**. These areas are described in detail in the next sections. The steps for creating a motion path animation are provided at the end of this section.

NOTE

Selecting a motion path automatically creates a camera. You cannot add a motion path to an existing camera.

Camera Area

The camera can be linked to a path or a point. To select a path, pick the **Path** radio button and then pick the "select" button next to the radio buttons. The dialog box is temporarily closed for you to select the path in the drawing. The path may be a line, arc, circle, ellipse, elliptical arc, polyline, 3D polyline, spline, or helix, but it must be drawn before the **ANIPATH** command is used. Splines are nice for motion paths because they are smooth and have gradual curves. The camera moves from the first point on the path to the last point on the path, so create paths with this in mind.

To select a stationary point, pick the **Point** radio button. Then, pick the "select" button next to the radio buttons. When the dialog box is hidden, specify the location in the drawing. You can use object snaps or enter coordinates. It may be a good idea to have a point drawn and use object snaps to select the point.

The camera must be linked to either a path or a point. If neither is selected, the command cannot be completed. If you want the camera to remain stationary as the target moves, select the **Point** radio button and then pick the stationary point in the drawing.

Once a point or path has been selected, it is added to the drop-down list. All named motion paths and selected motion points in the drawing appear in this list. Instead of using the "select" button, you can select the path or point in this drop-down list.

Figure 18-15.
The **Motion Path Animation** dialog box is used to create an animation that follows a path.

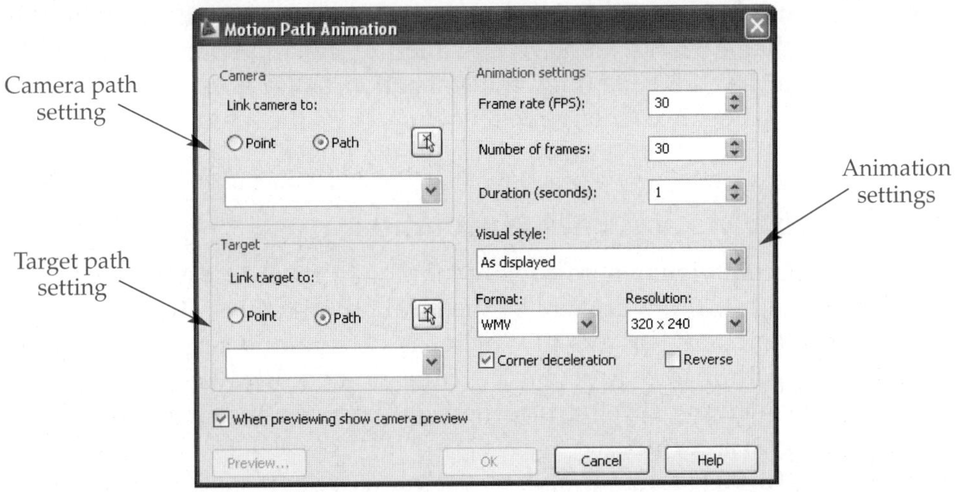

Target Area

The target is the location where the camera points. Like the camera, the target can be linked to a point or a path. To link the target to a path, select the **Path** radio button. Then, pick the "select" button and select the path in the drawing. If the camera is linked to a point, the target must be linked to a path. If the camera is set to follow a path, then you actually have three choices for the target. It can be linked to a path, point, or nothing. To link the target to a point, pick the **Point** radio button. Then, pick the "select" button to select the point in the drawing. The None option, which is selected in the drop-down list, means that the camera will look straight ahead down the path as it moves.

Animation Settings Area

Most of the settings in this area have the same effect as the corresponding settings in the **Animation Settings** dialog box. However, there are four settings unique to the **Motion Path Animation** dialog box.

The **Number of frames:** text box is used to set the total number of frames in the animation. Remember, a computer has a playback rate of 30 fps. Therefore, if the frame rate is set to 30, set the number of frames to 450 to create an animation that is 15 seconds long ($30 \times 15 = 450$).

The value in the **Duration (seconds):** text box is the total time of the animation. This value is automatically calculated based on the frame rate and number of frames. However, you can enter a duration value. Doing so will automatically change the number of frames based on the frame rate.

By default, the **Corner deceleration** check box is checked. This slows down the movement of the camera and target as they reach corners and curves on the path. If this is unchecked, the camera and target move at the same speed along the entire path, creating very jerky motion on curves and at corners. It is natural to decelerate on curves.

The **Reverse** check box simply switches the starting and ending points of the animation. If the camera (or target) travels from the first endpoint to the second endpoint, checking this check box makes the camera (or target) travel from the second endpoint to the first.

Previewing and Completing the Animation

To preview the animation, pick the **Preview...** button at the bottom of the **Motion Path Animation** dialog box. The camera glyph moves along the path in all viewports.

If the **When previewing show camera preview** check box is checked, the **Animation Preview** window is also displayed and shows the animation.

To finish the animation, pick the **OK** button in the **Motion Path Animation** dialog box. The **Save As** dialog box is displayed. Name the file and specify the location. If you need to change the file type, pick the **Animation settings...** button to open the **Animation Settings** dialog box. Change the file type, close the dialog box, and continue with the save.

Steps to Create a Motion Path Animation

1. Plan your animation: where you are moving from and to, what you are going to be looking at, and what will be the focal point of the scene.
2. Draw the paths and points to which the camera and target will be linked. Draw the path in the direction the camera should travel (first point to last point). Do not draw any sharp corners on the paths and make sure that the Z value (height) is correct.
3. Start the **ANIPATH** command.
4. Pick the camera path or point.
5. Pick the target path or point (or None).
6. Adjust fps, number of frames, and duration to set the length and speed of the animation.
7. Select a visual style, the file format, and the resolution.
8. Preview the animation. Adjust settings, if needed.
9. Save the animation to a file.

Exercise 18-5

Complete the exercise on the Student CD.

Chapter Test

Answer the following questions. Write your answers on a separate sheet of paper or complete the electronic chapter test on the Student CD.

1. Which system variable controls the display of camera glyphs?
2. Name the three camera tools available on the **Camera** tool palette and explain the differences between them.
3. When is the **Camera Preview** window displayed, by default?
4. From where is the offset distance for the camera clipping planes measured?
5. What is the difference between the **3DWALK** and **3DFLY** commands?
6. How do you "steer" your movement when creating a walkthrough or flyby animation?
7. What is the *field of view?*
8. What is the purpose of the **Position Indicator** palette?
9. In the **Walk and Fly Settings** dialog box, which settings combine to control the speed of the animation?
10. How do you start recording a walkthrough or flyby?
11. What must be done before correcting a motion error in a walkthrough or flyby?
12. Motion path animation involves linking a camera or target to _____ or _____.
13. Which types of objects may be used as a motion path?
14. If None is selected as the target "path," what does the camera do in the animation?
15. Explain *corner deceleration.*

Drawing Problems

1. In this problem, you will create and manipulate a camera in a drawing from a previous chapter.
   A. Open drawing P17_02 from Chapter 17 and save it as P18_01.
   B. Create at least two viewports and display a plan view in one of them.
   C. Use the **CAMERA** command to create a camera looking at the objects from the southwest quadrant. Change the camera settings as needed to display a pleasing view of the scene.
   D. Name the camera SW View.
   E. Turn on both the front and back clipping planes. Adjust them to eliminate one object in the front and one object in the back.
   F. Open the **Camera** tool palette and, using the tools in the palette, create three more cameras looking at the scene from various locations. Change their names to Normal, Wide-angle, and Fish-eye to match the type of camera.
   G. Save the drawing.

2. In this problem, you will draw some basic 3D shapes to represent equipment in a small workshop. Then, you will create an animated walkthrough.
   A. Start a new drawing and set the units to architectural. Save it as P18_02.
   B. Draw a planar surface that is 15′ × 30′.
   C. Draw three 9′ tall walls enclosing the two long sides and one short side.
   D. Use boxes and a cylinder to represent equipment. Refer to the illustration shown below. Use your own dimensions.
   E. Use the **3DWALK** command to create an animation of walking into the workshop. Turn and look at the shelves at the end of the animation.
   F. Set the visual style to Conceptual and the resolution to 640 × 480.
   G. Save the animation to a file named P18_02.avi (or the format of your choice).
   H. Save the drawing.

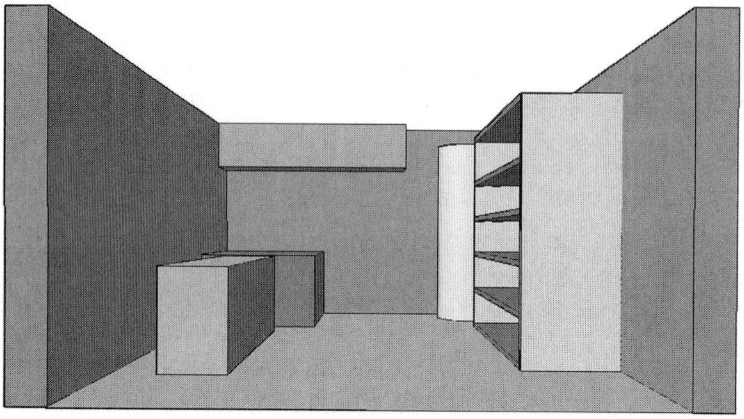

3. In this problem, you will create a motion path animation for the workshop drawn in problem 18-2.
   A. Open drawing P18_02 and save it as P18_03.
   B. Draw a line and an arc similar to those shown in color below. The dimensions are not important.
   C. Move both objects so they are 4′ off of the floor.
   D. Using the **ANIPATH** command, link the camera to the line and the target to the arc. Set the resolution to 640 × 480.
   E. Preview the animation. Adjust the animation settings as necessary. You may need to slow down the animation quite a bit. How do you do this?
   F. Save the animation as a file named P18_03.wmv (or the file format of your choice).
   G. Save the drawing.

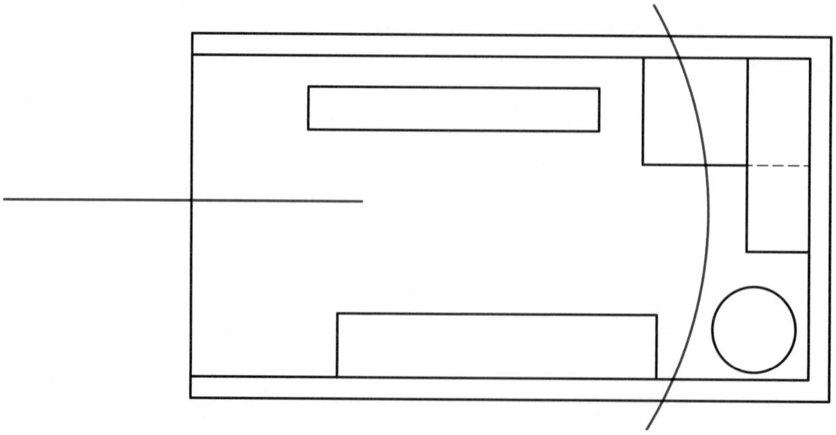

4. In this problem, you will create a motion path animation for presentation of a mechanical drawing from a previous chapter.
   A. Open drawing P16_03 and save it as P18_04.
   B. Draw a circle centered on the flange with a radius of 300.
   C. Move the circle 200 units in the Z direction.
   D. Using the **ANIPATH** command, link the camera to the circle and the target to the center of the flange.
   E. Preview the animation and adjust the animation settings as necessary. Due to the materials in the scene, the preview may play slowly, depending on the capabilities of your computer.
   F. Select a visual style that your computer can handle. Set the resolution to 320 × 240.
   G. Save the animation to a file named P18_04.avi (or the file format of your choice).
   H. Save the drawing.

5. In this problem, you will create a flyby of the building that you created in Chapter 16.
   A. Open drawing P16_01 and save it as P18_05.
   B. Create a perspective view of the scene that shows the building from slightly above it. Save the view.
   C. Start the **3DFLY** command. Practice with the movement keys to make sure you know how to fly around the building. Then, cancel the command.
   D. Restore the starting view and select the **3DFLY** command.
   E. Record the flyby and save the animation as P18_05.wmv (or the file format of your choice).
   F. Save the drawing.

You can load, or attach, a raster image in AutoCAD and trace it to create a vector image, as shown here. This is the raster image and resulting vector image from **Figure 19-9.**

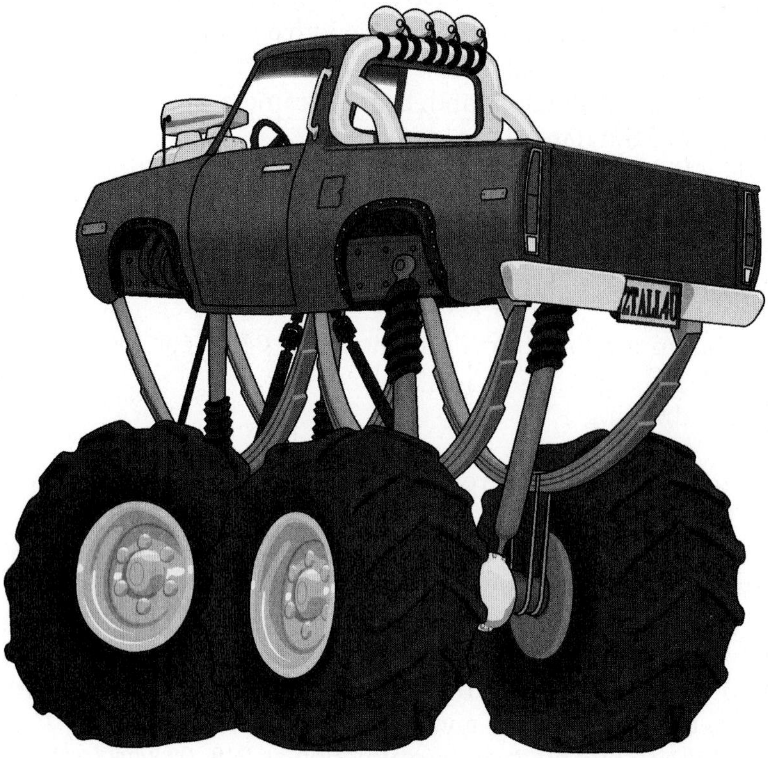

CHAPTER 19

Using Raster, Vector, and Web Graphics

Learning Objectives

After completing this chapter, you will be able to:
- ✓ Compare raster and vector files.
- ✓ Import and export raster files using AutoCAD.
- ✓ Import and export vector files using AutoCAD.
- ✓ Set image commands to manipulate inserted raster files.
- ✓ Create DWFx and DWF files.
- ✓ Create PDF files.

One of the important aspects of drawing in AutoCAD is the ability to share information. Generally, this means sharing drawing data and geometry between CAD software, either other AutoCAD workstations or workstations using different software. AutoCAD creates drawing data files in a format known as a *vector* file. However, you can also share your work, as images, with photo editing and desktop publishing software. In Chapter 14 through Chapter 18, you learned how to create realistic scenes and render them to files. A scene rendered to a file is a *raster* image. However, raster images used in AutoCAD do not have to be created in AutoCAD. They may also come from digital photographs, scanned images, or Internet sources. This chapter introduces using AutoCAD to work with raster and vector graphics files. This includes importing, exporting, and setting various parameters.

Introduction to Raster and Vector Graphics

In the world of electronic imaging, there are two basic types of files—raster and vector. AutoCAD drawings are called vector graphics. A ***vector*** is an object defined by XYZ coordinates. In other words, AutoCAD stores the mathematical definition of an object. ***Pixels*** (picture elements) are the "dots" or "bits" in the monitor that make up the display screen. When drawing vector objects in AutoCAD, your monitor uses pixels to create a representation of the object on the monitor. However, there is no relationship between the physical pixels in your monitor and a vector object. Pixels simply show the object at the current zoom percentage. Some common vector files are DWG, DXF, AI, and EPS.

Many illustrations created with drawing, painting, and presentation software are saved as raster files. A ***raster file*** creates a picture or image file using the location and color of the screen pixels. In other words, a raster file is made up of "dots." Raster files are usually called ***bitmaps.*** There are several types of raster files used for presentation graphics and desktop publishing. Some common raster file types include TIFF, JPEG, and GIF.

Working with Raster Files

EXTERNALREFERENCES

Ribbon
Blocks & References
> Reference
External References
Type
EXTERNAL REFERENCES
XREF
IMAGE
IM
Menu
Tools
> Palettes
> External References...

Raster images inserted into AutoCAD drawings are treated much like externally referenced drawings (xrefs). Therefore, they are managed in the **External References** palette. See **Figure 19-1.** Raster images are not added to the drawing database, but are attached and referenced by a path to the file's location. Any changes to the image content must be made to the original file. Settings and commands in AutoCAD can, however, control the portion of the image shown and its appearance. Images can be inserted, removed, and modified using commands found in the **Reference** panel in the **Blocks & References** tab of the toolbar and menu browser, **Figure 19-2.** These functions are discussed in detail in this section.

At the top of the **External References** palette is a drop-down list containing buttons for attaching drawings (DWG), image files, DWF files, and DGN files. The **File References** area lists all files currently attached to the drawing, whether they are drawings, images, DWF files, or DGN files. Right-clicking on an entry displays a shortcut menu that allows you to open, attach, unload, reload, and detach the files. If you hover the cursor over an entry in the palette, a preview window is displayed as help text. By default, this preview provides details related to the file and a preview of the file.

Figure 19-1.
The **External References** palette is used to manage attached images. The tooltip can be configured to display only the file name, a preview, details, or both a preview and details, as shown here.

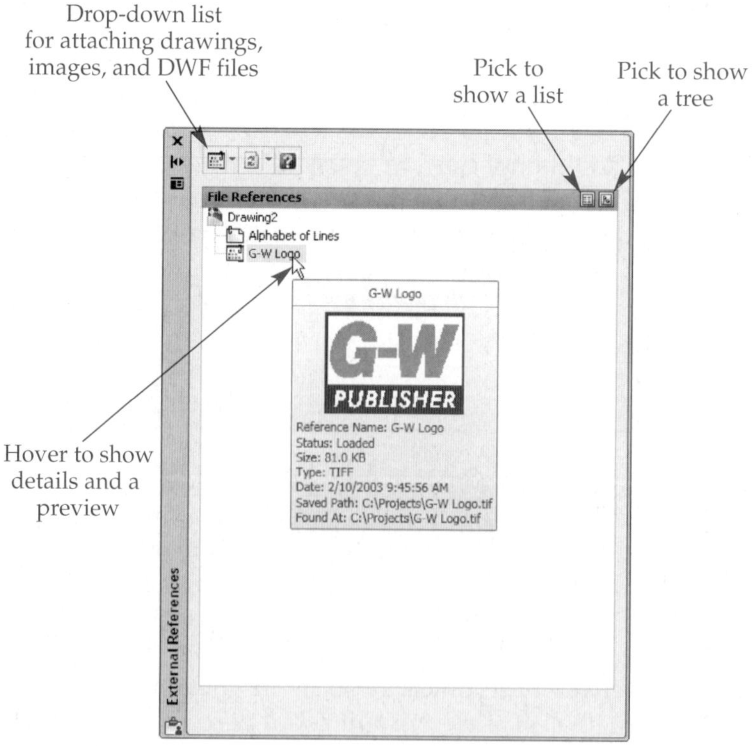

Figure 19-2.
A—Image commands located on the References panel. B—Image commands located in the menu browser.

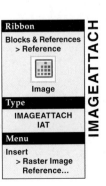

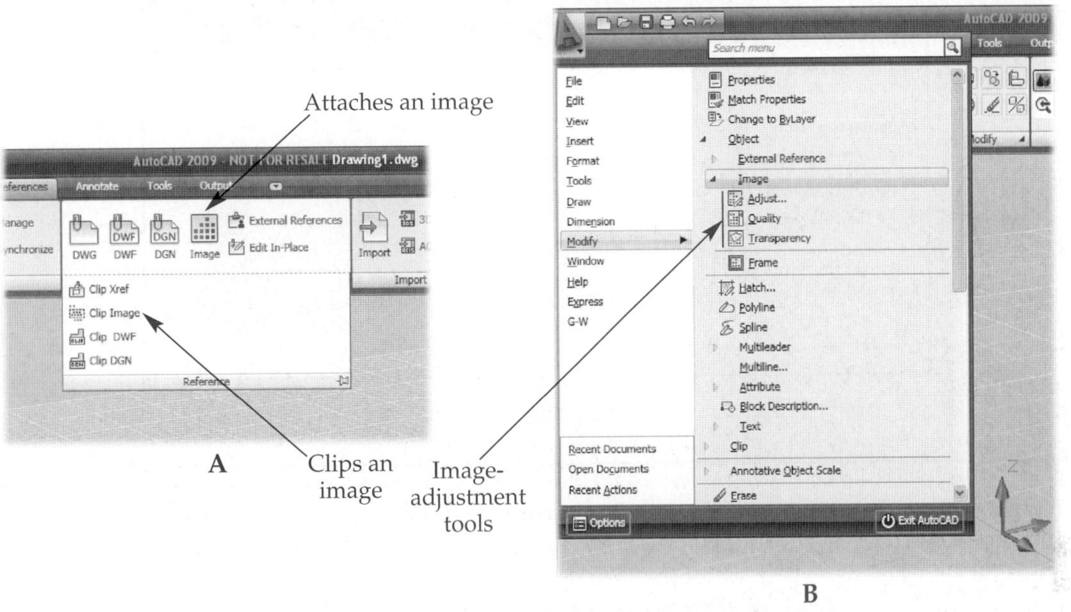

There are many different types of raster files. Some raster files used in industry today are:

- **Tagged Image File Format (TIFF).** A file format developed by Aldus Corporation and Microsoft Corporation. This is one of the most commonly used image file types.
- **Joint Photographic Experts Group (JPEG).** A highly compressed graphics image file. This type of file is very common on websites. Also known as a JPG file.
- **Graphics Interchange Format (GIF).** A file format developed to allow the exchange of graphic images over an online computer service, such as the Internet. This type of file is sometimes found on websites, often animated.
- **Portable Network Graphics (PNG).** Developed in the mid 1990s as a replacement for the GIF format. This file type is extensively used for electronic transmission, such as via e-mail or as website graphics.
- **Bitmap (BMP).** A file format developed by Microsoft Corporation. There are certain applications for this type of file. However, overall, this file type is not used much anymore.

Other raster file types can also be imported into AutoCAD. If you have a raster image that cannot be directly imported, you will need to first import the file into a paint or draw program. Then, export the image in a format that AutoCAD can read.

Inserting Raster Images

The **IMAGEATTACH** command is used to attach an image file to a drawing. When the command is selected, the **Select Image File** dialog box is displayed, **Figure 19-3**. Pick the **Files of type:** drop-down list to display all of the raster file types that can be used. If a folder contains a wide variety of raster files, you can quickly narrow your search by picking one of the file types in this list. Then, select the raster file and pick **Open**. This displays the **Image** dialog box, **Figure 19-4**.

The image name and path to the image file are displayed at the top of the **Image** dialog box. Also displayed is the path that will be saved in the drawing. You can

Ribbon
Blocks & References > Reference
Image
Type
IMAGEATTACH
IAT
Menu
Insert > Raster Image Reference...

IMAGEATTACH

Figure 19-3.
Select the image file to be attached to the drawing in the **Select Image File** dialog box. Pick the **Files of type:** drop-down list to display the raster file types that can be used.

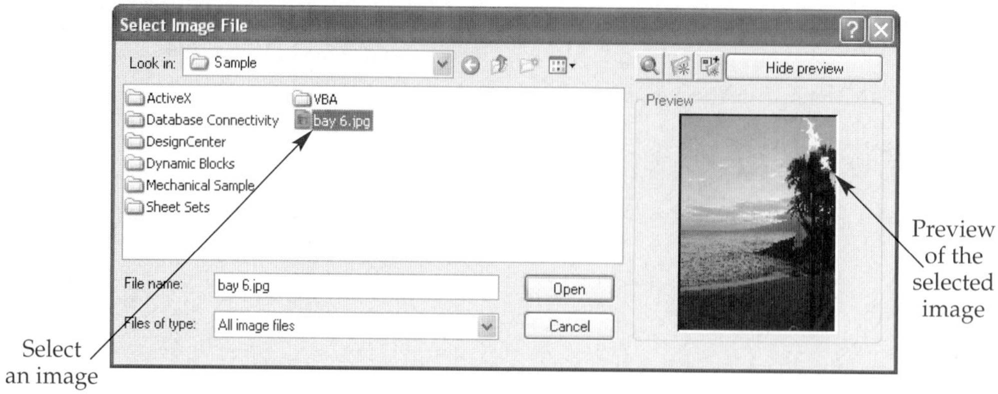

Figure 19-4.
The image name and path are displayed in the **Image** dialog box. Be sure to select the type of path to use. The dialog box expands to include the **Image Information** area when the **Details>>** button is picked.

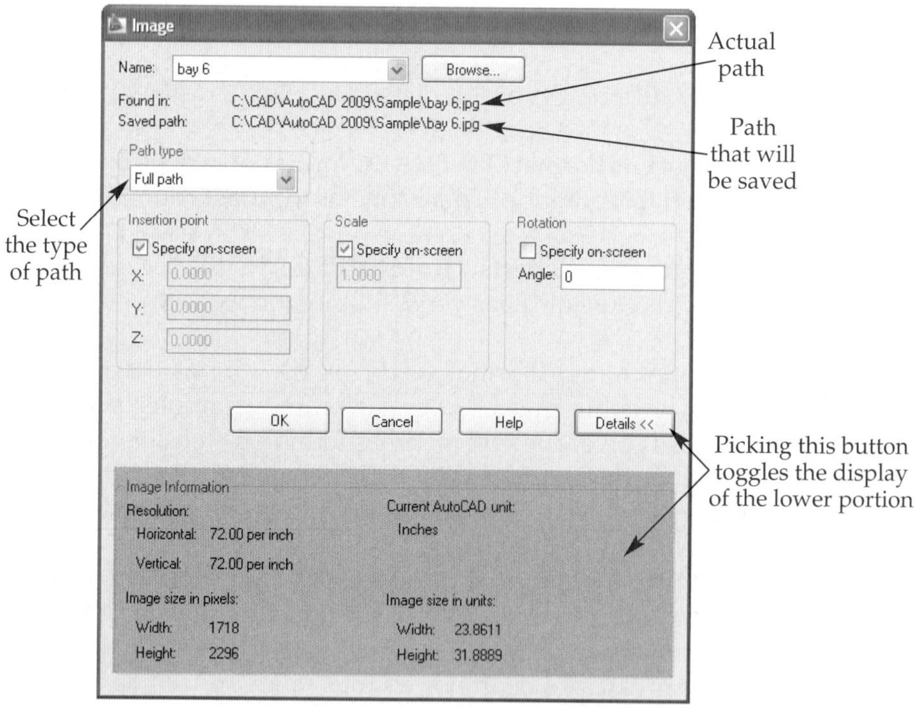

choose to save the full path, a relative path, or no path. The type of path is selected in the **Path type** drop-down list.

A ***full path*** specifies the complete location of the image file, such as c:\images\building.tif. If the image file is moved from this location, AutoCAD cannot find it.

A ***relative path*** specifies the location of the image file based on the location of the drawing file. For example, the path .\images tells AutoCAD that the image file is located in a subfolder (named images) of the folder where the drawing is located. The entry ..\images tells AutoCAD to look for the file by moving up one folder from where the drawing is stored and then in the subfolder \images. The entry ..\..\images tells AutoCAD to move up two folders and then look in the subfolder \images. The current drawing must be saved in order to specify a relative path.

The *no path* option tells AutoCAD that the image is located in the same folder as the drawing. If the image file is not found in that folder, AutoCAD looks in the path specified by the **PROJECTNAME** system variable, then in the support files search path defined in the **Files** tab of the **Options** dialog box.

You can preset image parameters (insertion point, scale, and rotation) or choose to specify them on-screen. You can view image resolution information in the **Image** dialog box by picking the **Details** button. See **Figure 19-4.** When the **OK** button is picked and the image placed, it is displayed in the drawing area. See **Figure 19-5.**

PROFESSIONAL TIP

If you are working on a project that uses xrefs and attached images, adding a "project subfolder" below the folder where the drawings are stored may be beneficial. Then, use relative paths when inserting images or xrefs. This allows all related files for a project to be found by AutoCAD, even if the folder structure is moved to a different drive or "root" folder.

Managing Attached Images

As stated earlier, the **External References** palette is used to control the raster images inserted into a drawing. The preview window displays for the image selected in the **File References** area the image name, its status (loaded or unloaded), file size, type, date the image was last saved, and the saved path. Refer to **Figure 19-1.**

Right-clicking on the image name displays a shortcut menu containing options to help you manage the image. The five options are:

- **Open.** This opens the image in the program associated with the file type of the image. For example, if Microsoft Photo Editor is associated with the TIFF file type, the TIFF image is displayed in this program.

Figure 19-5.
The raster image attached to an AutoCAD drawing.

- **Attach.** This opens the **Image** dialog box, discussed in the previous section, for attaching an additional image to the drawing.
- **Unload.** Unloads the selected image, but retains its path information. The Status column displays Unloaded if this option is selected. Display the list view to see the columns. An unloaded image is displayed as a frame until reloaded.
- **Reload.** Reloads the selected image file.
- **Detach.** Removes, or detaches, the selected image file from the drawing.

Right-clicking in **File References** area, but not on a file name, displays a different shortcut menu. See Figure 19-6. This shortcut menu contains nine options:

- **Reload All References.** Reloads any files attached to the current drawing.
- **Select All.** Selects all of the files listed in the **File References** area.
- **Attach DWG.** Allows you to attach other drawings as xrefs.
- **Attach Image.** Displays the **Select Image File** dialog box for attaching another raster image.
- **Attach DWF.** Allows you to attach a DWF file as an xref.
- **Attach DGN.** Allows you to attach a DGN file (Microstation drawing) as an xref.
- **Tooltip Style.** The tooltip (help text) that appears when you hover over one of the items is customizable. The tooltip can display the file name only, a preview only in the size you select, file details (including the name), or details and a preview.
- **Preview/Details Pane.** Turns on or off the pane at the bottom of the **External References** palette. This is not displayed by default. If the tooltip is set to display details and a preview, you probably will not need to display the preview/details pane.
- **Close.** Closes the **External References** palette.

PROFESSIONAL TIP

If drawing regeneration time is becoming long, unload attached image files that are not needed for the current drawing session.

Controlling Image File Displays

Once an image is attached to the current drawing, its display can be adjusted if needed. The **IMAGECLIP**, **IMAGEADJUST**, **IMAGEQUALITY**, **TRANSPARENCY**, and **IMAGEFRAME** commands are used to do so. These commands are discussed in this section.

Clipping an image

IMAGECLIP

Ribbon
Blocks & References > **Reference**
Clip Image
Type
IMAGECLIP **ICL**
Menu
Modify > **Clip** > **Image**

The **IMAGECLIP** command allows you to trim away a portion of the image that does not need to be seen. The clipping frame can be rectangular or polygonal. Once the command is selected, you are prompted to pick the image to clip. Then, to create a rectangular clipping frame, continue:

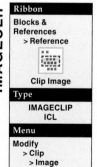

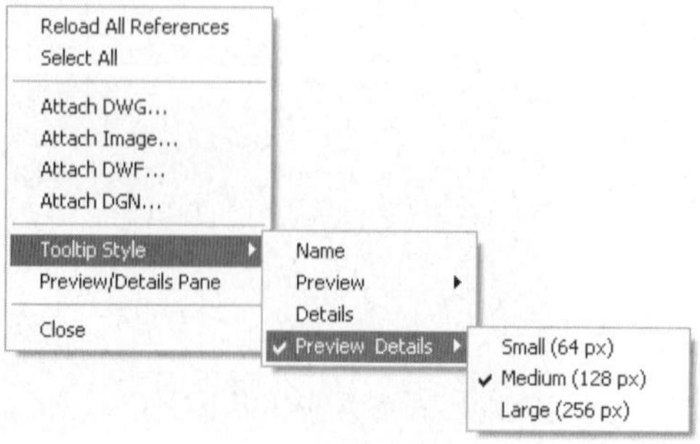

Figure 19-6.
The tooltip in the **External References** palette can be configured to display various information.

Enter image clipping option [ON/OFF/Delete/New boundary] <New>: **N**↵
Enter clipping type [Polygonal/Rectangular] <Rectangular>: **R**↵
Specify first corner point: *(pick the first corner of the clipping boundary)*
Specify opposite corner point: *(pick the second corner)*

The image outside of the rectangular frame is hidden.

The **Polygonal** option allows you to construct a clipping frame composed of three or more points. Select the command, pick the image to clip, and continue:

Enter image clipping option [ON/OFF/Delete/New boundary] <New>: **N**↵
Enter clipping type [Polygonal/Rectangular] <Rectangular>: **P**↵
Specify first point: *(pick first point to be used for the clipping boundary)*
Specify next point or [Undo]: *(pick second point)*
Specify next point or [Undo]: *(pick third point)*
Specify next point or [Close/Undo]: *(pick additional points as needed)*
Specify next point or [Close/Undo]: ↵

Figure 19-7 shows the results of using the **Rectangular** and **Polygonal** options of the **IMAGECLIP** command on a raster image. Three additional options of **IMAGECLIP** allow you to work with the display of the clipped image.

- **ON.** Turns the clipping frame on to display only the clipped area.
- **OFF.** Turns off the clipping frame to display the entire original image and frame.
- **Delete.** Deletes the clipping frame and displays the entire original image.

NOTE

You can pick an unclipped image frame to display the grips for editing. The grips are attached to the image itself. If one grip is stretched, it affects the entire image by proportionally enlarging or reducing it. On the other hand, if you select a clipped image for grip editing, the grips are attached to the clipping frame. Stretching the clipping frame does not change the size or shape of the image, but alters the frame and retains the size of the image.

Adjusting an image

The **IMAGEADJUST** command provides control over the brightness, contrast, and fade of the image. These adjustments are made in the **Image Adjust** dialog box, Figure 19-8. Once the command is selected, you are prompted to pick an image. If you want the same

Type
IMAGEADJUST
IAD
Menu
Modify
> Object
> Image
> Adjust...

IMAGEADJUST

Figure 19-7.
A—A rectangular image clip. B—A polygonal image clip. The path is shown here in color for illustration.

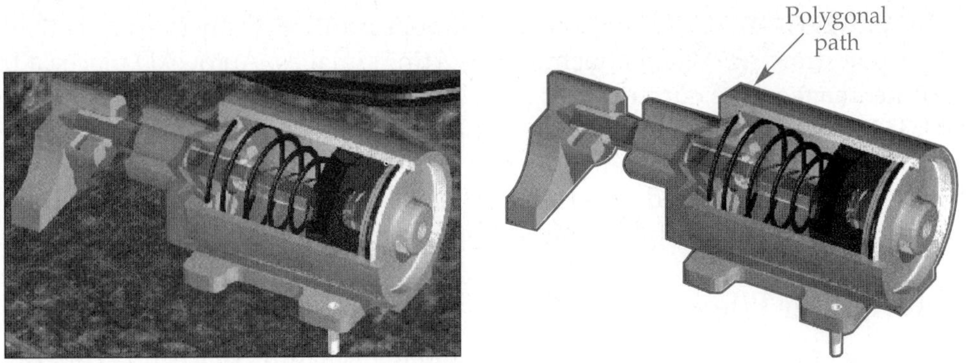

A B

Figure 19-8.
In the **Image Adjust** dialog box, brightness, contrast, and fade values can be numerically entered or set using the sliders.

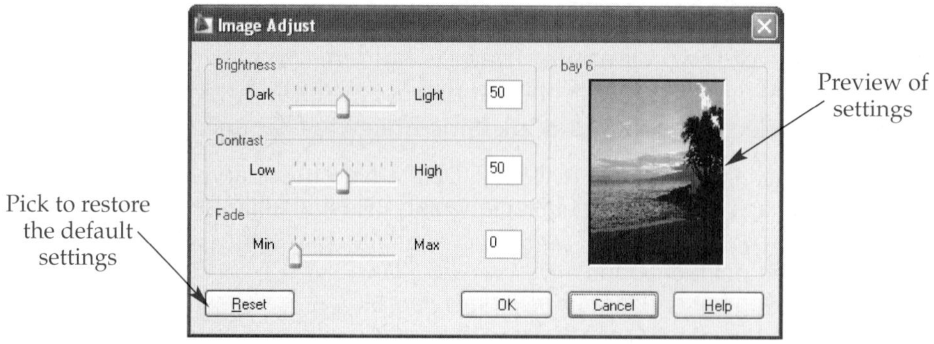

settings applied to multiple images, you can pick them all at the same time. When done picking objects, press [Enter] to display the dialog box.

Values can be changed by typing in the text boxes or by using the slider bars. The preview tile dynamically changes as the sliders are moved. Picking the **Reset** button returns all values to their defaults.

- **Brightness.** Controls pixel whiteness and indirectly affects the contrast. Values can range from 0 to 100, with 50 as the default value. Higher values increase the brightness.
- **Contrast.** Controls the contrast of the image, or how close each pixel is moved toward its primary or secondary color. Values can range from 0 to 100, with 50 as the default value. Higher values increase the contrast.
- **Fade.** Controls the fading of the image, or how close the image is to the background color. Values can range from 0 to 100, with 0 as the default value. Higher values increase the fading.

IMAGEQUALITY

Type
IMAGEQUALITY
Menu
Modify
> Object
> Image
> Quality

The **IMAGEQUALITY** command provides two options: **High** and **Draft**. The high quality setting produces the best image display, but requires more time to regenerate. If you are working with several images in a drawing, it is best to set the **Draft** option current. The image displayed is lower quality, but requires less time to display. The setting applies to all images in the drawing.

Transparency

TRANSPARENCY

Type
TRANSPARENCY
Menu
Modify
> Object
> Image
> Transparency

Some raster images have transparent background pixels. The **TRANSPARENCY** command controls the display of these pixels. If **TRANSPARENCY** is on, the drawing will show through the image background. Images are inserted with this feature turned off. The setting applies to individual images. Multiple images can be selected at the same time. Remember, only images containing transparent pixels are affected.

Image frame

IMAGEFRAME

Type
IMAGEFRAME
Menu
Modify
> Object
> Image
> Frame

The **IMAGEFRAME** command controls the appearance of frames around all images in the current drawing. When attaching (inserting) images, AutoCAD places a frame around the image in the current layer color and linetype. There are three settings for the **IMAGEFRAME** command. A setting of 0 turns off the display of the frame and the frame is not plotted. The default setting of 1 turns on the display of the frame and allows the frame to be plotted. A setting of 2 turns on the display of the frame, but the frame is not plotted. The setting applies to all images in the drawing.

Uses of Raster Files in AutoCAD

One use of raster images is as a background for sketching or tracing. For example, you may need a line drawing of an image that is only available as a continuous tone (print) photograph. The photo can be scanned, which produces a raster image. After importing the raster image with the **IMAGEATTACH** command, use the appropriate drawing commands to sketch or trace the image. After the object is sketched, the original raster image can be deleted, frozen, or unloaded, leaving the tracing. You can then add other elements to the tracing to create a full drawing. See **Figure 19-9.**

Raster files can be combined with AutoCAD drawing and modeling features in many ways to complete or complement the design. For example, company watermarks or logos can be easily added to title blocks, style sheets, and company drawing standards. Drawings that require designs, labels, and a variety of text fonts can be created using raster files in conjunction with the wide variety of TrueType fonts available with AutoCAD. Archived manual drawings can also be scanned, brought into AutoCAD, and then traced to create a CAD drawing.

You can add features to complement raster files. For example, you can import a raster file, dimension or annotate it, and even add special shapes to it. Then, export it as the same type of file. Now, you can use the revised file in the original software in which it was created. As with any creative process, let your imagination and the job requirements determine how you use this capability of AutoCAD.

Figure 19-9.
Using a raster image as a model for a drawing. A—The imported raster image. B—Use AutoCAD commands to trace the image. Then, either delete the image or freeze its layer. C—The completed drawing plotted on a title block.

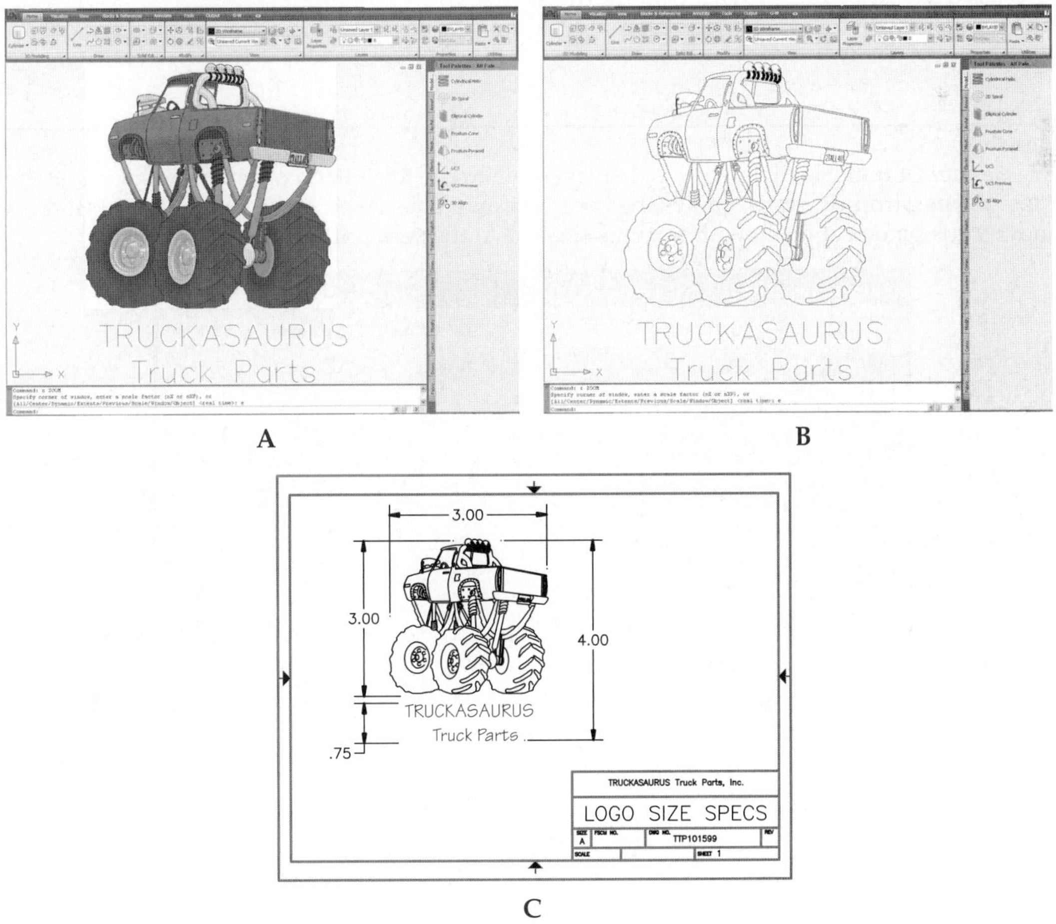

Exercise 19-1

Complete the exercise on the Student CD.

SAVEIMG

Type
SAVEIMG

Menu
Tools
>Display Image
>Save...

Exporting a Drawing to a Raster File

You can save a rendering to a raster file. This is discussed in Chapter 17. However, 2D objects are not rendered and, therefore, do not appear in the file. If you want what is displayed in the current viewport, including 2D objects, saved as a raster file, you must use the **SAVEIMG** command. This command saves the current AutoCAD viewport as an image file. What you see in the viewport is what you will get in the file, including the effect of the current visual style.

Once the command is selected, the **Render Output File** dialog box is displayed, **Figure 19-10.** This is a standard save dialog box. The **Files of type:** drop-down list displays the file types to which the image can be saved. Select the file type based on the type required for a particular process, application, job, or client. The best thing to do is ask whomever you are creating the file for which type of file will work best. After selecting the file type, give the file a name and pick the **Save** button. Another dialog box is displayed that contains settings specific to the file type. Make settings as needed and close this dialog box to save the file.

A BMP file can also be created using the **EXPORT** or **BMPOUT** command. In this manner, you can select individual objects that will be included in the image. You can also save shaded images with this method.

Figure 19-10.
The **Render Output File** dialog box is displayed when the **SAVEIMG** command is selected. The **Files of type:** drop-down list shows the file types available. After picking the **Save** button, another dialog box appears with settings specific to the selected file type.

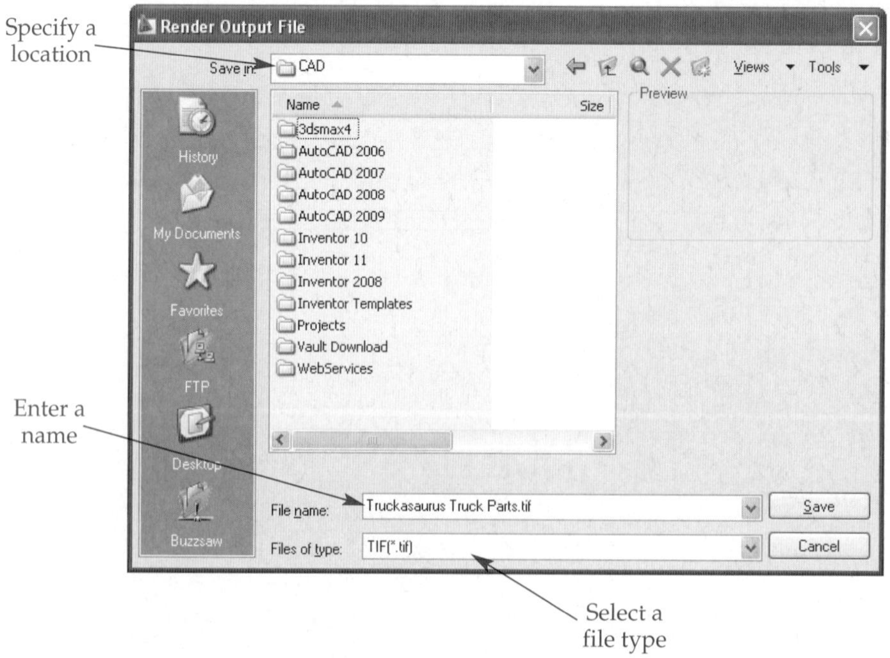

PROFESSIONAL TIP

You can use the **SAVEIMG** command to save a rendering that was rendered to the viewport. However, the result is a low-resolution image. Most images that will be in print, such as in a magazine or book, need to be high resolution. Check with the magazine or book publisher for image resolution requirements.

Exercise 19-2

Complete the exercise on the Student CD.

Working with Vector Files

A vector file contains objects defined by XYZ coordinates. AutoCAD's native file format (DWG) is a vector file. You can also work with other vector file types. These types include DXF, WMF, SAT, EPS, STL, and DXX. The two most commonly used types, DXF and WMF, are covered in the next sections.

Exporting and Importing DXF Files

DXF is a generic file type that defines AutoCAD geometry in an ASCII text file. Other programs that recognize the DXF format can then "read" this file. The DXF file format retains the mathematical definitions of AutoCAD objects in vector form. The DXF objects imported into other vector-based programs, or opened in AutoCAD, can be edited as needed.

Exporting DXF files

DXFOUT

Ribbon
Output
> Send
Export

Type
DXFOUT
SAVEAS
[Ctrl]+[Shift]+[S]

Menu
File
> Save As...

The **DXFOUT** command is used to save a DXF file. Once the command is selected, the **Save Drawing As** dialog box is displayed. See **Figure 19-11.** Select the DXF file type

Figure 19-11.
The **Save Drawing As** dialog box is used to save a DXF file.

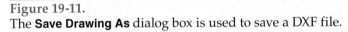

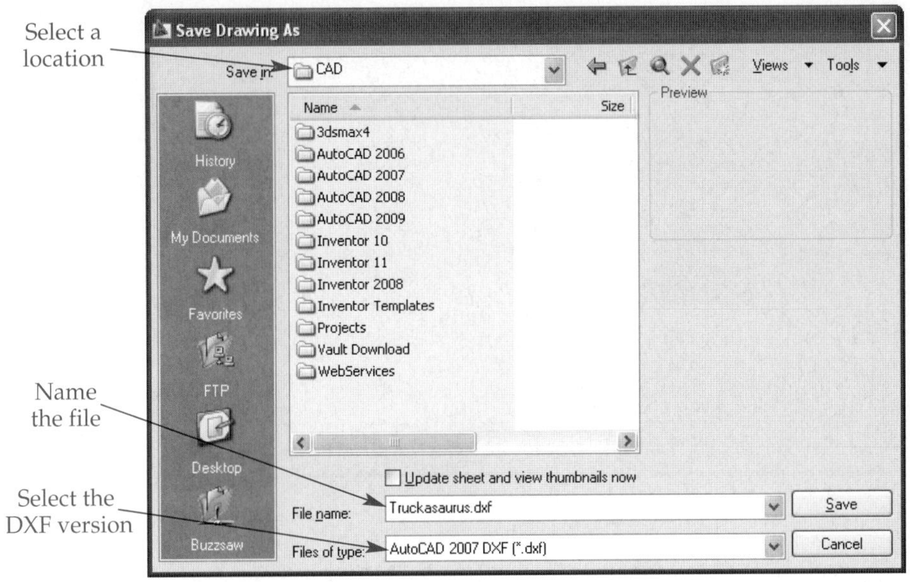

from the **Files of type:** drop-down list. Name the file and specify a location where you want to save it. Notice that you can select different versions of DXF. This is to ensure that the file you save is "backward compatible." For example, if you are sharing the file with somebody using AutoCAD 2000, save the DXF as that version to ensure AutoCAD 2000 can read the file.

Since this is a "save as" operation, the current drawing is saved as a DXF file. If you continue to work on the drawing, you are working on the DXF version, *not* the DWG version. In order to work on the original drawing, you must open the DWG file. However, if you continue to work on the drawing in DXF form and attempt to save or close the drawing, the **Save Drawing As** dialog box is displayed. You can save the drawing as a DWG or replace the previously saved DXF file. If you save the drawing as a DXF file, you are also informed that the drawing is not a DWG and given the opportunity to save it in that format.

When a DXF file is saved, all geometry in the drawing is saved, regardless of the current zoom percentage or selected objects. However, the current zoom percentage is saved in the DXF file. As explained later, this differs from the WMF format.

The DXF file format saves any surfaced or solid 3D objects as 3D geometry. When a DXF file containing 3D geometry is opened, the surfaced or solid 3D geometry remains intact. In addition, the current visual style is saved in the DXF file.

NOTE

Not all programs that can import DXF files are capable of correctly "reading" 3D objects or the visual style.

Importing DXF files

DXFIN

Type
DXFIN
OPEN
[Ctrl]+[O]

Menu
File
>Open...

Toolbar
Quick Access
Open

To open a DXF file, use the **DXFIN** command. Once the command is selected, the **Select File** dialog box is displayed, **Figure 19-12.** Select DXF (*.dxf) from the **Files of type:** drop-down list. Then, select the DXF file you want to open. Notice that there is no preview when the file is selected. AutoCAD does not support previews for the DXF file type. Finally, pick the **Open** button.

Figure 19-12.
The **Select File** dialog box is used to import a DXF file.

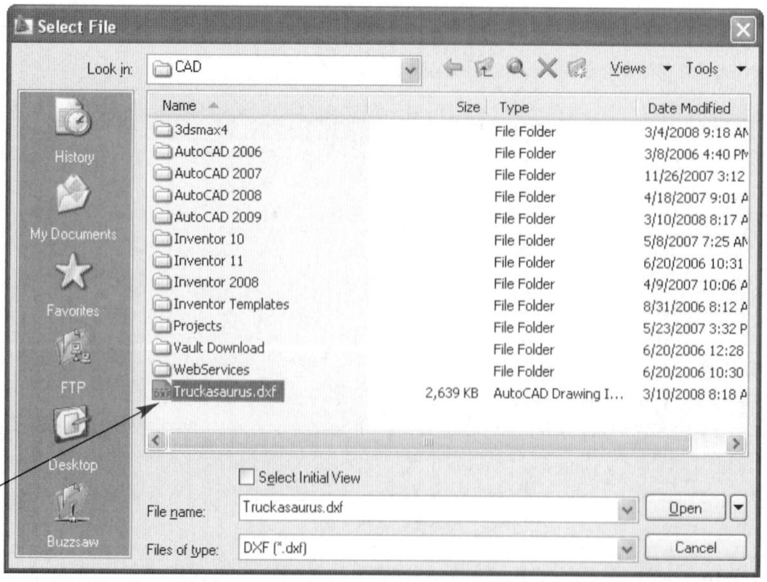

The DXF file is opened in a new document window. To place a DXF file into the *current* drawing, insert it as a block. If you do not want it inserted as a block, open the file (**DXFIN**), copy it to the clipboard ([Ctrl]+[C]), and paste ([Ctrl]+[V]) it into the current drawing.

NOTE

If you open a DXF file and try to save it, the **Save Drawing As** dialog box appears. You can save it as DXF, overwriting the existing file, or under a new name or as another file type.

Exporting and Importing Windows Metafiles

The Windows metafile (WMF) format is often used to exchange data with desktop publishing programs. It is a vector format that can save wireframe and hidden displays. Shaded and rendered images cannot be saved. Also, perspective views are saved in parallel projection.

A WMF file cannot retain the definition of all AutoCAD object types. For example, circles are translated to line segments. Also, a WMF file does *not* save three-dimensional data. The view in the current viewport is projected onto the viewing plane and saved as a two-dimensional projection.

Exporting WMF files

WMFOUT

Ribbon
Output
>Send
Export

Type
WMFOUT
EXPORT
EXP

Menu
File
>Export...

The **WMFOUT** command is used to create a WMF file. When the command is selected, the **Create WMF File** or **Export Data** dialog box is displayed. These are standard save dialog boxes. Select Metafile (*.wmf) in the **Files of type:** drop-down list. After specifying the file name and folder location and picking the **Save** button, you must select the objects to place in the file. Press [Enter] when all of the objects are selected and the WMF file is saved.

Only the portions of selected objects that are visible on-screen are written into the file. If part of a selected object is not visible on screen, that part is "clipped." Also, the current view resolution affects the appearance of a Windows metafile. For example, when **VIEWRES** is set low, circles in your AutoCAD drawing may look like polygons in the WMF file. When saved to a Windows metafile, curved objects are composed of line segments rather than defined as circles or arcs.

Importing WMF files

WMFIN

Type
WMFIN
IMPORT
IMP

Menu
Insert
>Windows
Metafile...

Use the **WMFIN** command to import a Windows metafile into a drawing. When the command is selected, the **Import WMF** or **Import File** dialog box is displayed. Select Metafile (*.wmf) in the **Files of type:** drop-down list, then select a file.

A Windows metafile is imported as a block consisting of all of the objects in the file. You can explode the block if you need to edit the objects within it. If an object is not filled, it is created as a polyline when brought into AutoCAD. This includes arcs and circles. Objects composed of several closed polylines to represent fills are created from solid fill objects, as if created using the **SOLID** command with the **FILL** system variable off.

There are two settings used to control the appearance of Windows metafiles imported into AutoCAD. Type WMFOPTS to display the **WMF In Options** dialog box, Figure 19-13. You can also pick the **Options...** button in the **Tools** drop-down menu in the "import" dialog box. The dialog box contains the following two check boxes.

- **Wire Frame (No Fills).** When checked, filled areas are imported only as outlines. Otherwise, filled areas are imported as filled objects (when **FILL** is on).
- **Wide Lines.** When this option is checked, the relative line widths of lines and borders from the WMF file are maintained. Otherwise, they are imported using a zero width.

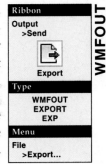

Figure 19-13.
Setting options for imported WMF files.

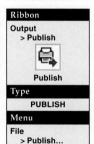

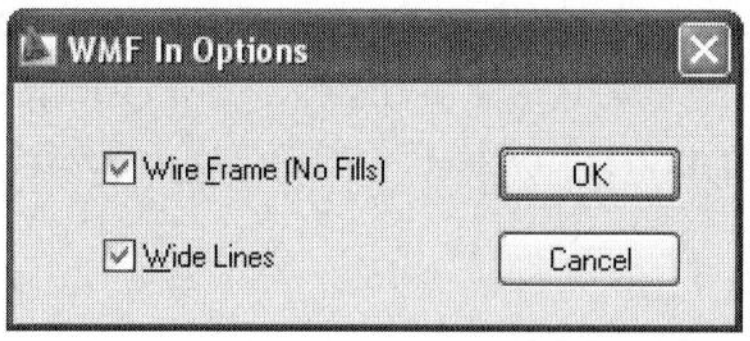

PROFESSIONAL TIP

PostScript is a copyrighted page description language developed by Adobe Systems. PostScript files are widely used in desktop publishing. AutoCAD can export PostScript files with the **PSOUT** or **EXPORT** commands. In addition, AutoCAD has several PostScript patterns that can be used as fills for closed polylines. The **PSFILL** command is used to add these patterns. However, professionals rarely use AutoCAD's PostScript functions. AutoCAD cannot import, view, or print PostScript files. In addition, any drawing that contains PostScript patterns (fills) must be sent to a printer or plotter that is PostScript compatible. These printers are not common outside of the graphics industry.

Exercise 19-3

Complete the exercise on the Student CD.

Design Web Format (DWF) Files

You can save an AutoCAD drawing as a ***Design Web Format (DWF)*** file. A DWF file is a highly compressed, vector file that can be viewed using the Autodesk Design Review 2009, Autodesk DWF Viewer, or Volo View program. In addition, when one of these programs is installed in conjunction with a supported Internet browser, you can view DWF files on the web. Autodesk Design Review 2009 is installed when AutoCAD is installed.

Beginning in AutoCAD 2009, you can also save a drawing in DWFx format. A DWFx file serves the same purpose as a "standard" DWF file, but it is based on Microsoft's XML Paper Specification (XPS) format. The DWFx format is preferred over the DWF format. The process for creating and using DWFx files is the same as for DWF files.

3DDWF
Ribbon
Output > Publish
3D DWF
Type
3DDWF

PUBLISH
Ribbon
Output > Publish
Publish
Type
PUBLISH
Menu
File > Publish...

A DWFx or DWF file is created using either the **3DDWF**, **EXPORT**, or **PUBLISH** command. If you are creating a single-sheet file, use the **3DDWF** or **EXPORT** command. If you are creating a multi-sheet file, use the **PUBLISH** command.

To use the **3DDWF** or **EXPORT** command, first enter the command. The **Export 3D DWF** dialog box is displayed. This is a standard save dialog box. Select either the DWFx or DWF format from the **Files of type:** drop-down list. Then, enter a file name, select a location, and pick the **Save** button. Once the file is saved, a message appears indicating this fact and offering you the opportunity to view the file.

To use the **PUBLISH** command, first enter the command. The **Publish** dialog box is displayed, Figure 19-14. At the bottom of this dialog box, pick the **DWF format** radio button in the **Publish to** area. Then, select the format in the drop-down list below the radio button. To change settings for the file that will be published, pick the **Publish Options...** button. This displays the **Publish Options** dialog box. See Figure 19-15.

Figure 19-14.
Using the **PUBLISH** command to create a DWFx or DWF file.

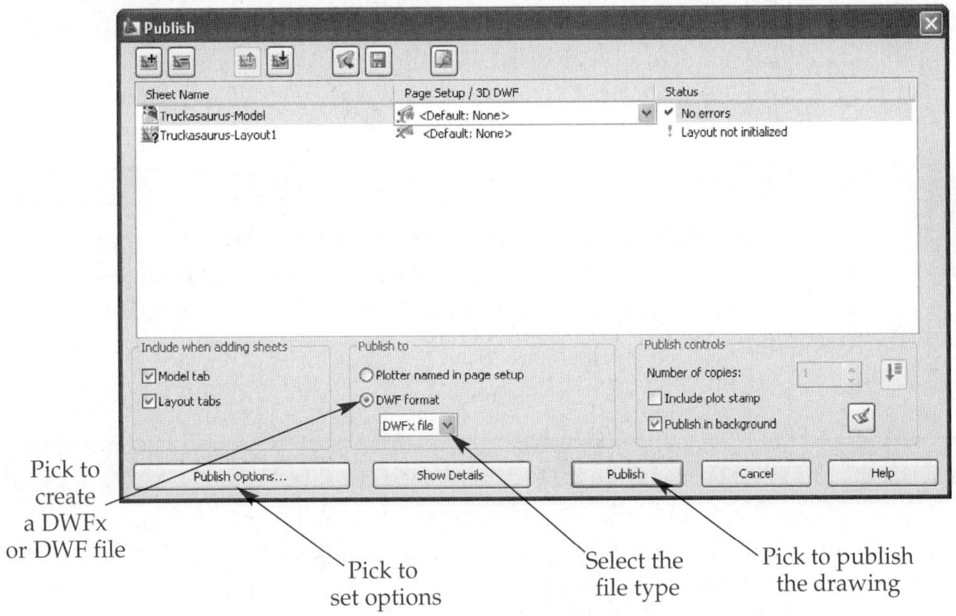

Figure 19-15.
Setting the options for a DWFx or DWF file to be created with the **PUBLISH** command.

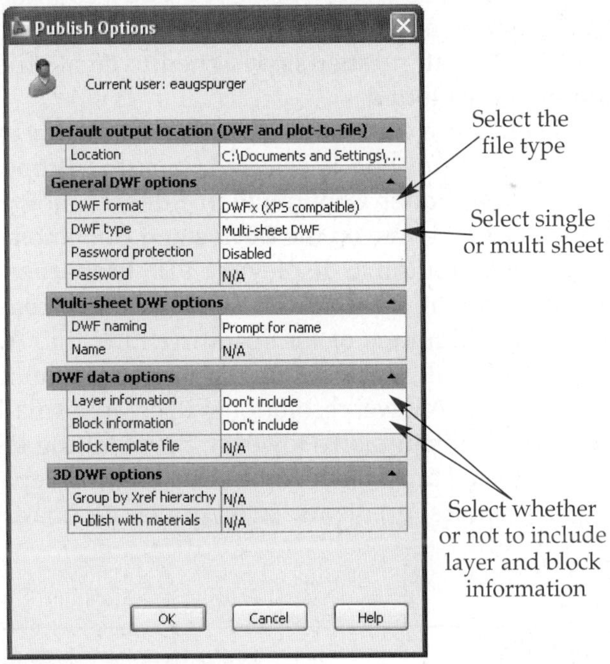

Change any settings as necessary and pick the **OK** button to return to the **Publish** dialog box.

When you are ready to create the file, pick the **Publish** button. The **Specify DWF File** dialog box is displayed. This is a standard save dialog box. Enter a name for the file, select a location, and pick the **Select** button. You cannot change the file type in this dialog box. Next, you are asked if you want to save the current list of sheets. After you make a selection in this message box, the drawing is published to a file. This may take a few seconds to complete.

NOTE

Commands that control the display of geometry on screen, such as **VIEWRES**, **FACETRES**, and **DISPSILH**, and the current visual style affect the resulting DWFx or DWF file.

PROFESSIONAL TIP

The **ETRANSMIT** command prepares a transmittal for e-mail that contains font files, plot styles, table files, and xrefs associated with the drawing. This can be a time-saving feature if you share drawings that contain xrefs.

Adobe® Portable Document Format (PDF) Files

You can save an AutoCAD drawing as a ***Portable Document Format (PDF)*** file. PDF files are vector-based files, like DWFx and DWF files. Anyone can view them using Adobe Reader. This is a free utility that can be downloaded from the Adobe website.

PLOT

Ribbon
Output > Plot
Plot
Type
PLOT
PRINT
Menu
File > Plot...
Toolbar
Quick Access
Plot

A PDF file is created using the **PLOT** command. Open the **Plot** dialog box. In the **Printer/plotter** area, select DWG To PDF.pc3 from the **Name:** drop-down list. The DWG To PDF.pc3 configuration is designed to create files that will be viewed, downloaded, and possibly plotted.

There are several settings for a PDF file that affect the final output. After the DWG To PDF configuration is selected, pick the **Properties...** button in the **Printer/plotter** area. In the **Plotter Configuration Editor** dialog box that is displayed, select Custom Properties in the tree on the **Device and Document Settings** tab. Then, pick the **Custom Properties...** button to display the **PDF Properties** dialog box, **Figure 19-16.**

The two "resolution" areas in the **PDF Properties** dialog box have settings that control the accuracy of the resulting PDF file. A medium resolution is best in most cases. A PDF file created with high resolution may be too large for practical electronic transmission. A lower resolution will create a smaller PDF file. Small files make for easy electronic transmission. However, the resulting PDF file may not display as accurately as one created at a higher resolution. You can separately set a maximum resolution for vector graphics, gradients, color/grayscale images, and black and white images. See

Figure 19-16.
Setting the properties for a PDF file in the **PDF Properties** dialog box.

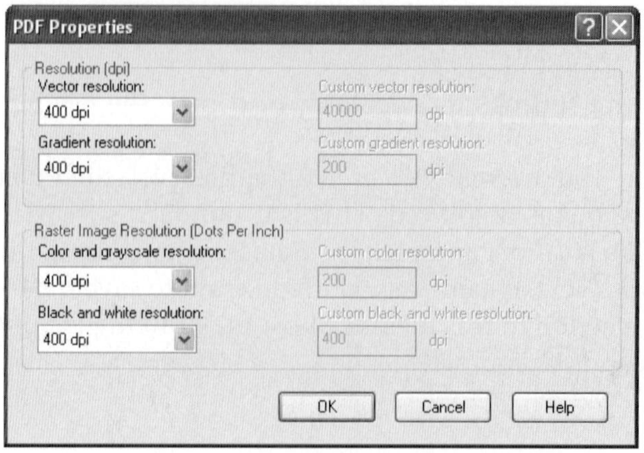

Figure 19-17 for a comparison of resolution settings in a plotted PDF file. The file size increases as the resolution increases.

Once you have made all settings as needed, pick the **OK** button in the **PDF Properties** dialog box. Then, pick **OK** in the **Plotter Configuration Editor**. If changes were made to the settings, a dialog box appears asking if you want to apply the changes on a one-time basis or save the configuration to a PC3 plotter configuration file.

Use all of the other settings in the **Plot** dialog box just as you would when plotting a hard copy. Refer to *AutoCAD and Its Applications—Basics* for detailed information on plotting. When you pick the **OK** button to "plot" the PDF, the **Browse for Plot File** dialog box is displayed. This is a standard save dialog box with only PDF available as the file type. The default filename is the drawing name and current space name separated by a hyphen. Use that name or enter a new name, navigate to the location where you want to save the PDF file, and pick the **Save** button.

PROFESSIONAL TIP

The **Plot** dialog box can also be used to create DWFx and DWF files. Instead of selecting DWG To PDF.pc3 as the output device, select either DWFx ePlot (XPS Compatible).pc3 or DWF6 ePlot.pc3.

Figure 19-17.
A comparison of low-resolution and high-resolution PDF files. A—The lines in the low-resolution file have jaggies. This is especially apparent on the windows. B—The lines in the high-resolution file are cleaner.

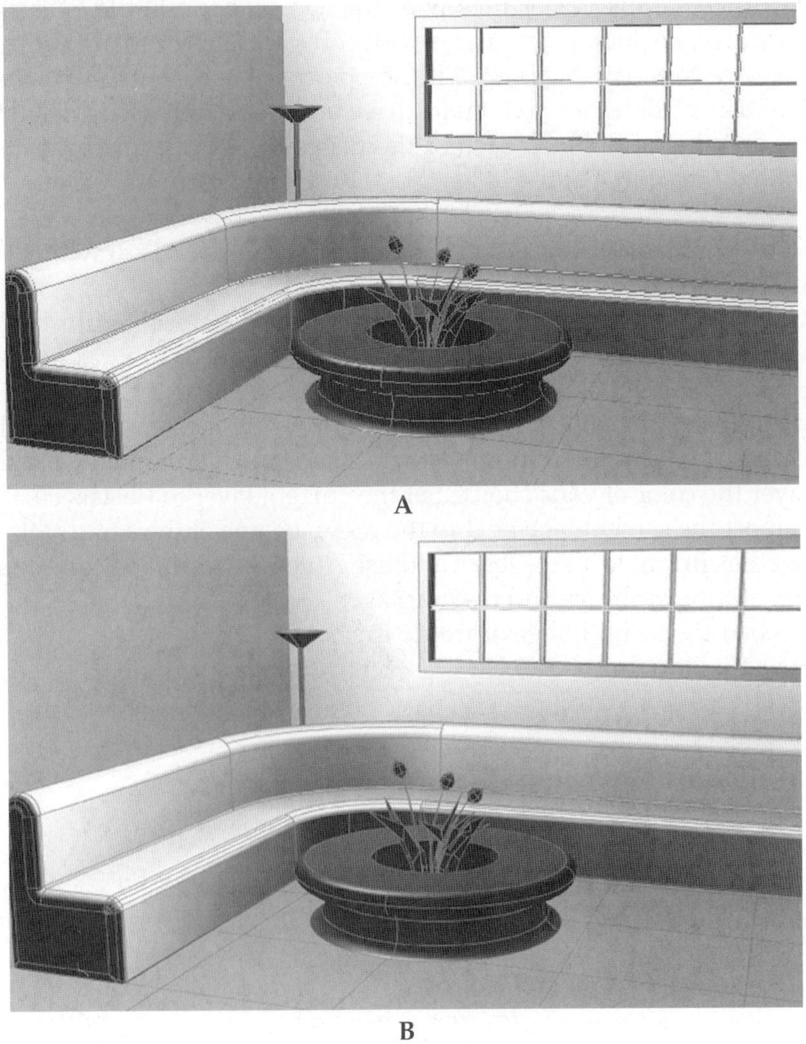

A

B

Chapter Test

Answer the following questions. Write your answers on a separate sheet of paper or complete the electronic chapter test on the Student CD.

1. Name four common formats of raster images that can be imported into AutoCAD.
2. Which command allows you to attach a raster file to the current AutoCAD drawing?
3. What is the display status in the drawing of an inserted image that has been unloaded?
4. Which two shapes can be used to clip a raster image?
5. What is the function of the **IMAGEADJUST** command?
6. Name two commands that allow you to export bitmap files.
7. Give the name and file type of the vector file that can be exchanged between object-based programs (object definitions are retained).
8. Name the commands that allow you to import and export the file type in question 7.
9. How are three-dimensional objects treated when exported to a WMF file?
10. How can a DXF file be inserted into the *current* drawing?

Drawing Problems

1. Locate some sample raster files with the .jpg, .png, or .tif file extensions. These files are often included as samples with software. They can also be downloaded as freeware from the Internet. With the permission of your instructor or supervisor, create a folder on your hard drive and copy the raster files there. Create a new drawing and attach each of the raster files. Place text below each image indicating the source of the image. Save the drawing as P19_01.

2. Choose a small raster file and attach it to a new AutoCAD drawing.
   A. Insert the image so it fills the entire screen.
   B. Undo and insert the image again using a scale factor that fills half the screen with the image.
   C. Stretch the original object using grips, then experiment with different clipping boundaries. Stretch the image after it has been clipped and observe the result.
   D. Create a layer named Raster. Create a second layer named Object. Give each layer the color of your choice. Set the current layer to Raster.
   E. Import the same image next to the previous one at the same scale factor.
   F. Set the current layer to Object and use AutoCAD drawing commands to trace the outline of the second raster image.
   G. Unload the raster image or freeze the Raster layer.
   H. Save the drawing as P19_02.

3. For this problem, you will import several raster files into AutoCAD. Then, you will trace the object in each file and save it as a block or wblock to be used on other drawings.
   A. Find several raster files that contain simple objects, shapes, or figures that you might use in other drawings.
   B. Create a template drawing containing Object and Raster layers.
   C. Import each raster file into AutoCAD on the Raster layer using the appropriate command. Set the Object layer current and trace the shape or objects using AutoCAD drawing commands.
   D. Detach the raster information, keeping only the traced lines of the object.
   E. Save the object as a block or wblock using an appropriate file-naming system.
   F. After all blocks have been created, insert each one into a single drawing and label each with its name. Include a path if necessary.
   G. Save the drawing as P19_03.
   H. Print or plot the final drawing.

4. In this problem, you will create a memo outlining your progress on a flange.
   A. Open drawing P16_03 from Chapter 16 and save it as P19_04.
   B. Set the 3D Hidden visual style current.
   C. Set the background color to white.
   D. Use the **SAVEIMG** command and save the scene as a monochrome BMP file.
   E. Render the scene using the Presentation render preset and a resolution of 320 × 480. Save the rendering as a BMP file.
   F. Open a word processor capable of importing BMP files, such as Microsoft Word or Wordpad.
   G. Write a memo related to the project. A sample appears below. The memo should discuss how you created the drawing, the BMP file, and the rendered file. Insert the BMP files as appropriate.
   F. Save the document as P19_04. Print the document.

MEMO

To:	Otto Desque
From:	Ima Drafter
Date:	Thursday, March 14
Subject:	Project Progress

Dear Otto,

I have completed the initial drawing. As you can see from the drawing shown here, the project is complying with design parameters. The drawing is ready for transfer to the engineering department for approval.

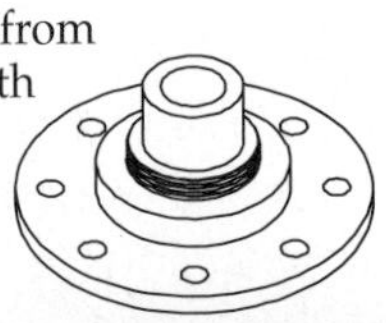

I have also included a rendered image of the project. The material spec'ed by the engineering department is represented in the rendering. This may help in evaluation of the design.

Respectfully,

Ima

5. Begin a new drawing.
   A. Insert the blocks you created in problem 3. Arrange them in any order.
   B. Add any notes you need to identify this drawing as a sheet of library shapes. Be sure each shape is identified with its file name and location (path).
   C. Create a PDF file of the drawing.
   D. Save the drawing as P19_05.
   E. Open the PDF in Adobe Reader and print it. If Adobe Reader is not installed, obtain permission from your instructor or supervisor to download and install it.

6. Add a raster image to one of your title block template drawings as a design element or a company logo. A sample is shown below. Import an existing raster image or create your own using a program such as Windows Paint. Save the template drawing.

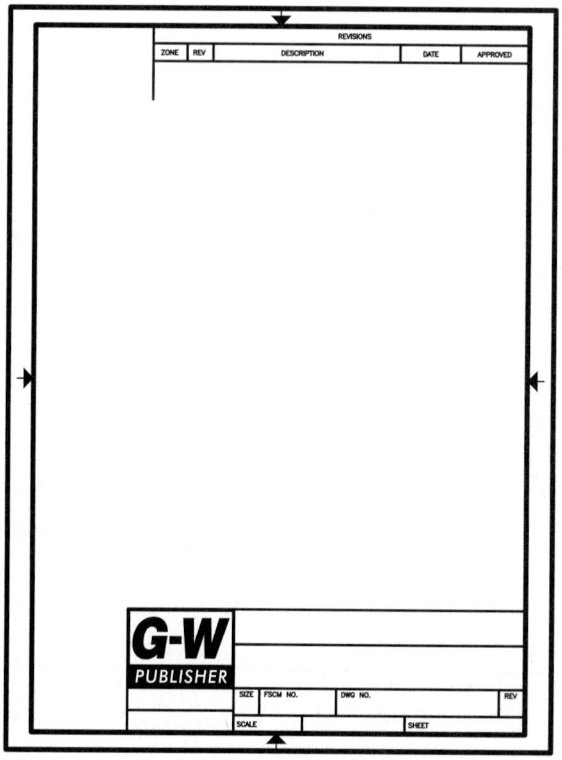

CHAPTER 20
Customizing the AutoCAD Environment

Learning Objectives

After completing this chapter, you will be able to:
- ✓ Set system variables.
- ✓ Assign colors and fonts to the text and graphics windows.
- ✓ Control general AutoCAD system variables.
- ✓ Set options that control display quality and AutoCAD performance.
- ✓ Control shortcut menus.
- ✓ Modify program icon properties.
- ✓ Set up AutoCAD for multiple configurations.

AutoCAD provides a variety of options for customizing the user interface and working environment. These options permit users to configure the software to suit personal preferences. You can define colors for the individual window elements, assign preferred fonts to the command line window, control shortcut menus, and assign properties to program icons.

The options for customizing the AutoCAD user interface and working environment are found in the **Options** dialog box, **Figure 20-1.** This dialog box is commonly accessed by right-clicking in the drawing area or command line with nothing selected and no command active and picking **Options...** from the shortcut menu. It can also be displayed by picking the **Options** button at the bottom of the menu browser.

Changes made in the **Options** dialog box do not take effect until either the **Apply** or **OK** button is picked. If you pick the **Cancel** button or the close button (**X**) before picking **Apply**, all changes are discarded. Each time you change the options settings, the system registry is updated and the changes are used in this and subsequent drawing sessions. Settings that are stored within the drawing file have the AutoCAD drawing icon next to them. These settings do not apply to other drawings. Settings without the icon indicate that the option affects all AutoCAD drawing sessions.

Setting AutoCAD System Variables

There are numerous settings that control the manner in which AutoCAD behaves in the Windows environment. These settings are made through the use of system

Figure 20-1.
The **Options** dialog box is used to customize the AutoCAD working environment. Each tab contains a variety of options and settings.

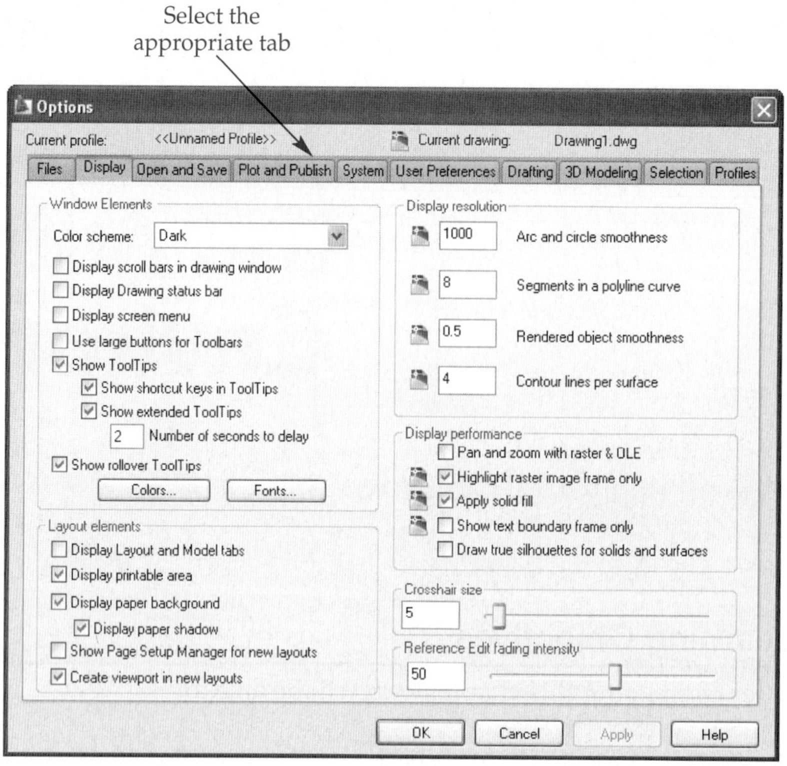

variables. ***System variables*** are used to specify such items as which folders to search for driver and menu files and the location of your temporary and support files. The default settings created during installation are usually adequate, but changing the settings may result in better performance. While several different options exist for setting many of the system variables, the simplest method is to use the **Options** dialog box.

File Locations

When AutoCAD is used in a network environment, some files pertaining to AutoCAD may reside on a network drive so all users can access them. Other files may reside in folders specifically created for a particular AutoCAD user. These files may include drawings containing blocks, external reference files, and custom menu files.

The **Files** tab of the **Options** dialog box is used to specify the path AutoCAD searches to find support files and driver files. It also contains the paths where certain types of files are saved and where AutoCAD looks for specific types of files. Support files include text fonts, menus, AutoLISP files, ObjectARX files, blocks, linetypes, and hatch patterns.

The folder names shown under the Support File Search Path heading in the **Search paths, file names, and file locations:** list are automatically created by AutoCAD during the installation. For example, **Figure 20-2** shows that the support files are stored in six different folders. Folders are searched in the order in which they are listed under Support File Search Path. As previously mentioned, some of these paths are created for a specific user. The first path listed is long and ultimately ends with the \Support folder. In the example shown, this path starts on the C: drive in a folder called \Documents and Settings. The folder listed immediately after the \Documents and Settings folder is the user-specific folder. The next folders to be searched are, in order, \Support, \Fonts, \Help, \Express, and \Support\Color. These paths are not user specific; they are located in the AutoCAD installation path.

You can add the path of any new folders you create that contain support files. As an example, suppose all of the blocks you typically use are stored in a separate

Figure 20-2.
Folder paths can be customized in the **Files** tab of the **Options** dialog box.

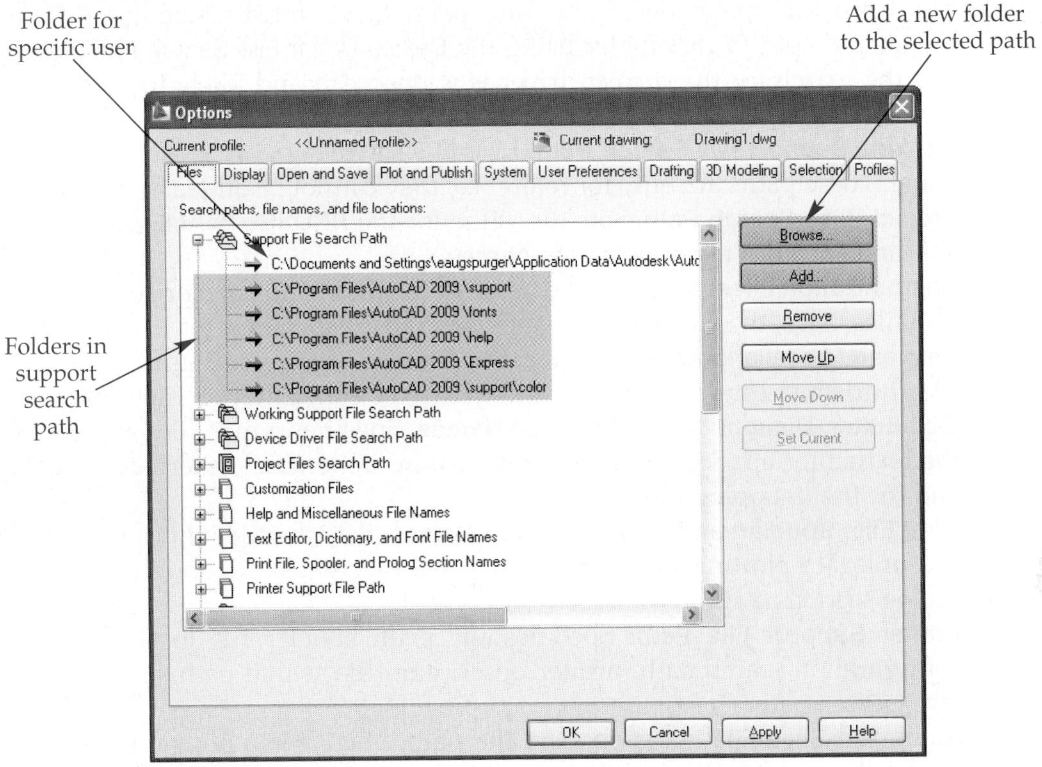

folder named \Blocks. Unless this folder name is placed in the support files search path, AutoCAD will not be able to find your blocks when you attempt to insert them, unless you specify the entire folder path. You can add this folder to the existing search path in two ways. The first method is to highlight the Support File Search Path heading and pick the **Add...** button. This places a new, empty listing under the heading. You can now type C:\BLOCKS to complete the entry. Alternately, instead of typing the path name, after picking **Add...** you can pick the **Browse...** button to display the **Browse for Folder** dialog box. You can then use this dialog box to select the desired folder. The new setting takes effect as soon as you pick **Apply** or the **OK** button and close the **Options** dialog box.

PROFESSIONAL TIP

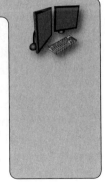

In addition to the paths listed under Support File Search Path, AutoCAD will search two other folders. The folder that contains the AutoCAD executable file, acad.exe, (typically, C:\Program Files\AutoCAD 2009) is searched, as is the folder that contains the current drawing file. These folders are searched only if the desired file name is not found in any of the listed folders. It is not advisable to store files such as block files in the AutoCAD folder. However, if you store block files in the same folder as the current drawing, you do not need to add that folder to the search path.

Other File Settings

Another setting that can be specified in the **Files** tab is the location of device driver files. ***Device drivers*** are specifications for peripherals that work with AutoCAD and other Autodesk products. By default, the drivers supplied with AutoCAD are placed in the \Drv folder. If you purchase a third-party driver to use with AutoCAD, be sure to load the driver into this folder. If the third-party driver must reside in a different folder, you should specify that folder using the Device Driver File Search Path setting. Otherwise, the search for the correct driver is widespread and likely to take longer. Some other file locations listed in the **Files** tab include:

- **Working Support File Search Path.** Lists the active support paths AutoCAD is using. These paths are only for reference; they cannot be added or amended.
- **Project Files Search Path.** Sets the value for the **PROJECTNAME** system variable and specifies the project path names.
- **Customization Files.** Specifies the name of the main and enterprise customization files. Also, the location of custom icon files is specified.
- **Help and Miscellaneous File Names.** Specifies which files are used for the help file, the default Internet location, and where the configuration file is located.
- **Text Editor, Dictionary, and Font File Names.** Specifies which files are used for the text editor application, main and custom dictionaries, alternate font files, and the font mapping file.
- **Print File, Spooler, and Prolog Section Names.** Sets the file names for the plot file for legacy plotting scripts, the print spool executable file, and the PostScript prolog section name.
- **Printer Support File Path.** Specifies the print spooler file location, printer configuration search path, printer description file search path, and plot style table search path.
- **Automatic Save File Location.** Sets the path where the autosave (.sv$) file is stored. An autosave file is only created if the **Automatic save** option is checked in the **Open and Save** tab of the **Options** dialog box.
- **Color Book Locations.** Specifies the path for color book files that can be used when specifying colors in the **Select Color** dialog box.
- **Data Sources Location.** Specifies the path for database source files (.udl).
- **Template Settings.** Specifies the default location for drawing and sheet set template files and the file name for the defaults.
- **Tool Palettes File Locations.** Specifies the path for tool palette support files.
- **Authoring Palette File Locations.** Specifies the location of authoring palette files.
- **Log File Location.** Specifies the path for the AutoCAD log file. A log file is only created if the **Maintain a log file** option is checked in the **Open and Save** tab of the **Options** dialog box.
- **Action Recorder Settings.** Specifies search and storage paths for the action recorder macro files (.actm).
- **Plot and Publish Log File Location.** Specifies the path for the log file for "plot and publish" operations. A log file is only created if the **Automatically save plot and publish log** check box in the **Plot and Publish** tab of the **Options** dialog box is checked.
- **Temporary Drawing File Location.** Sets the folder where AutoCAD stores temporary drawing files.
- **Temporary External Reference File Location.** Indicates where temporary external reference files are placed.
- **Texture Maps Search Path.** Location of texture map files for rendering.
- **Web File Search Path.** Specifies the folders to search for files associated with photometric weblight lighting.
- **i-drop Associated File Location.** Specifies the folder used by default to store downloaded i-drop content.
- **DGN Mapping Settings.** Specifies the location of the mapping files for translation to and from Microstation drawings (.dgn). This folder must have read/write file permissions enabled in order for the Microstation commands to properly function.

Customizing the Graphics Window

Numerous options are available to customize the graphics window to your personal liking. Select the **Display** tab in the **Options** dialog box to view the display control options, **Figure 20-3.**

The **Window Elements** area has a setting for the color scheme. The color scheme controls the outline color of the menu browser frame, title bar, ribbon, and status bar. Using the drop-down list, you can select between light and dark color schemes.

There are also check boxes for turning the scroll bars, status bar, and screen menu on or off; using large buttons for toolbars; showing tooltips and whether or not to show shortcut keys and extended commands in tooltips; and turning rollover tooltips on or off. The element colors and font settings can be changed using the buttons at the bottom of the **Window Elements** area.

At the bottom of the tab, the **Crosshair size** setting is a percentage of the drawing screen area. The higher the value, the further the crosshairs extend. The **Reference edit fading intensity** value determines the display intensity of the unselected objects in reference edit mode. A higher value means the unselected objects are less visible. Other options are discussed in the next sections.

Changing Colors

By customizing colors, you can add your personal touch and make AutoCAD stand out among other active Windows applications. AutoCAD provides this capability with the **Drawing Window Colors** dialog box, **Figure 20-4.** This dialog box is accessed by picking the **Colors...** button in the **Window Elements** area of the **Display** tab in the **Options** dialog box.

Figure 20-3.
Use the **Display** tab to set up many of the visual elements of the AutoCAD environment.

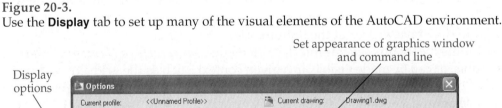

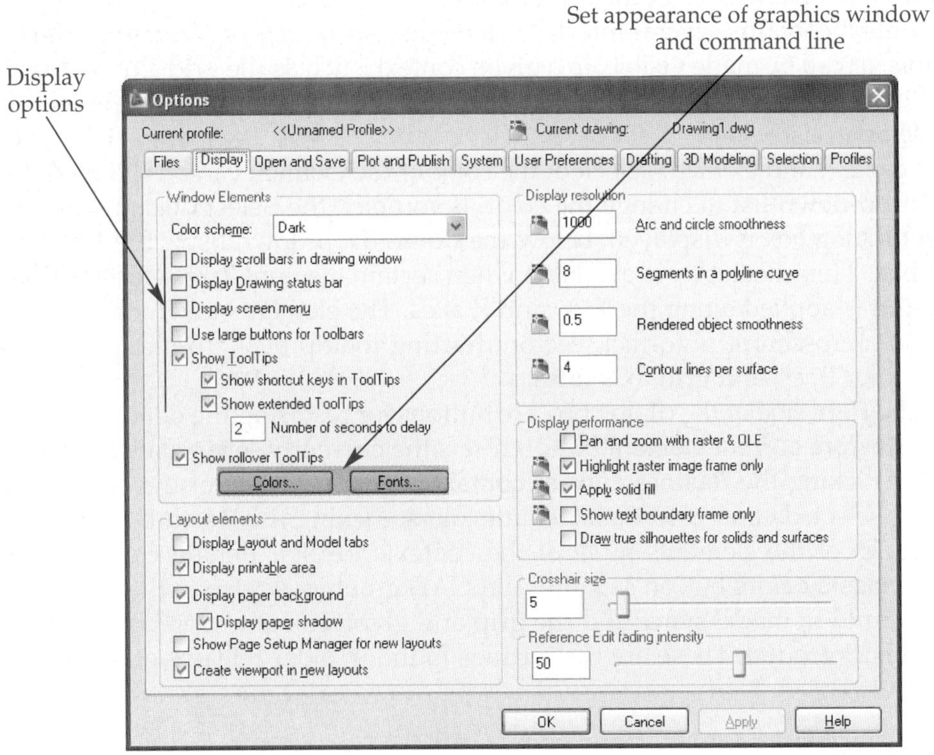

Figure 20-4.
Change AutoCAD color settings using the **Drawing Window Colors** dialog box.

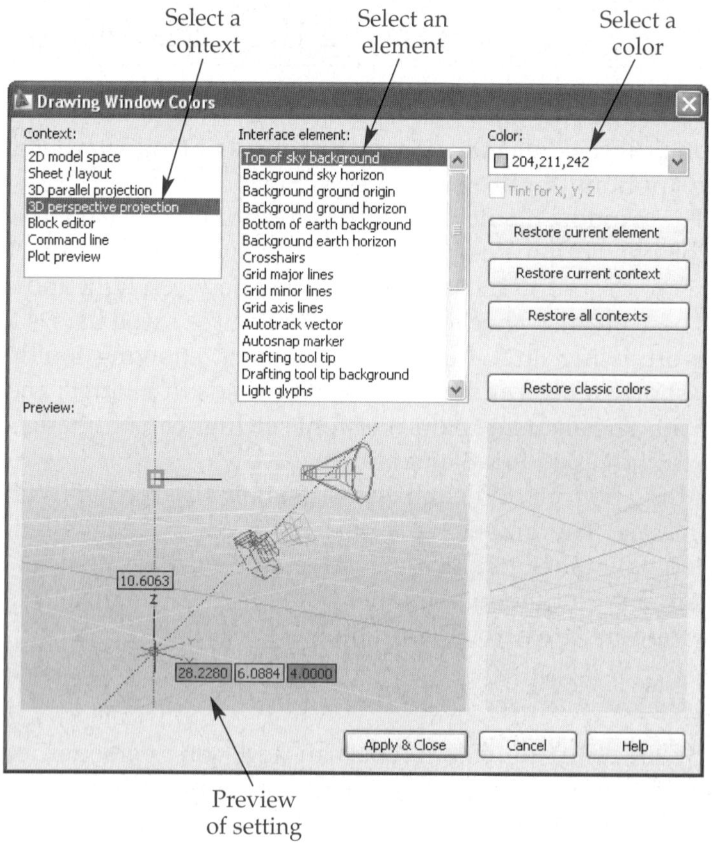

To change a color, first select a context. A ***context*** is one of the environments, or modes, in AutoCAD, such as the 3D perspective projection mode that is set current when a new drawing is started based on the acad3D.dwt template. The **Context:** list box contains the names of all contexts. The context that was current when the **Options** dialog box is opened is initially selected. A preview of the context and its settings is displayed in the **Preview:** area at the bottom of the dialog box.

Each context contains several interface elements. An ***interface element*** is an item that is visible, or can be made visible, in a given context, such as the grid axis, autosnap marker, or light glyphs. Once a context is selected, pick the element to change in the **Interface element:** list.

With a context and element selected, the color of the element can be changed. Use the **Color:** drop-down list to change the color. If you pick the Select Color... entry, the **Select Color** dialog box is displayed. Below the **Color:** drop-down list is the **Tint for X, Y, Z** check box. This check box is available when certain elements are selected. When checked, a tint is applied along the X, Y, and Z axes. The elements to which a tint can be applied are: crosshairs, autotrack vector, drafting tooltip background, grid major lines, grid minor lines, and grid axis lines.

Along the right side of the dialog box are buttons for restoring the default settings. Picking the **Restore current element** button resets the currently selected element to its default color. Picking the **Restore current context** button resets *all* of the elements of the currently selected context to their default colors. Picking the **Restore all contexts** button resets *all* of the elements in *all* of the contexts to their default colors. Lastly, the **Restore classic colors** button sets the AutoCAD graphics screen to the traditional black background in model space and the grip and glyph colors to appropriate colors for the black background. These are the settings found in older releases of AutoCAD.

Once the colors are changed as needed, pick the **Apply & Close** button. Then, pick the **OK** button in the **Options** dialog box. The graphics window regenerates and displays the color changes you made.

PROFESSIONAL TIP

When setting the background color to black, first use the **Restore classic colors** button. Then, adjust the other color settings from that point forward.

Changing Fonts

You can change the fonts used in the **Command Line** window. The font you select has no effect on the text in your drawings, nor is the font used in the AutoCAD dialog boxes, pull-down menus, or screen menus.

To change the font used in the **Command Line** window, pick the **Fonts...** button in the **Display** tab of the **Options** dialog box. The **Command Line Window Font** dialog box appears, Figure 20-5.

The default font used by AutoCAD for the graphics window is Courier New. The font style for Courier New is regular (not bold or italic) and the default size is 10 points. Select a new font from the **Font:** list. This list displays the system fonts available for use. Also, set a style and size. The **Sample Command Line Font** area displays a sample of the selected font. Once you have selected the desired font, font style, and font size for the **Command Line** window, pick the **Apply & Close** button to assign the new font.

NOTE

The Windows system "menu" font controls the font style for the text displayed in the screen menu.

PROFESSIONAL TIP

The **UNDO** command does not affect changes made to your system using the **Options** dialog box. If you have made changes you do not want to save, pick **Cancel** to dismiss the **Options** dialog box. However, picking **Cancel** does *not* dismiss changes that have been applied using the **Apply** button.

Figure 20-5.
The **Command Line** window can be changed to suit your preference.

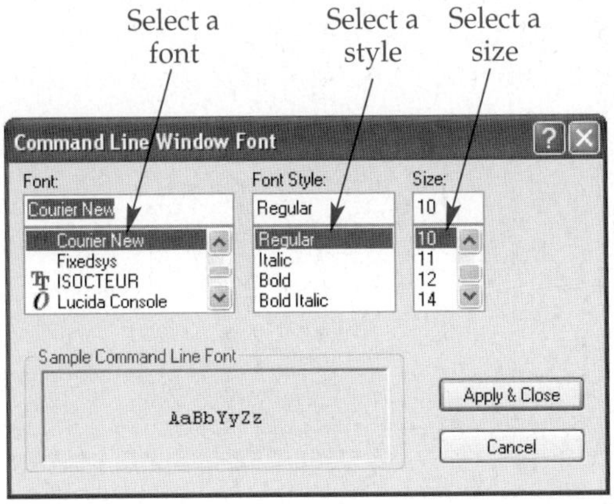

Exercise 20-1

Complete the exercise on the Student CD.

Layout Display Settings

The appearance of a layout tab is different than the appearance of the **Model** tab. The theory behind the default layout tab settings is to provide a picture of what the drawing will look like when plotted. You can see if the objects will fit on the paper or if some of the objects are outside of the margins. The following options, which are found in the **Layout elements** area of the **Display** tab in the **Options** dialog box, are illustrated in Figure 20-6.

- **Display Layout and Model tabs.** Displays the **Model** and layout tabs at the bottom of the drawing screen area. This is unchecked by default.
- **Display printable area.** The margins of the printable area are shown as dashed lines on the layout paper. Any portion of an object outside of the margins is not plotted.
- **Display paper background.** Displays the paper size specified in the page setup.
- **Display paper shadow.** Displays a shadow to the right and bottom of the paper. This option is only available if **Display paper background** is checked.
- **Show Page Setup Manager for new layouts.** Determines if the **Page Setup** dialog box is displayed when a new layout is selected or created. By default, this is unchecked.
- **Create viewport in new layouts.** Determines whether a viewport is automatically created when a new layout is selected or created. Many users uncheck this option since they will be creating their own floating viewports.

Figure 20-6.
Customizing the display of layouts. These options are set in the **Options** dialog box.

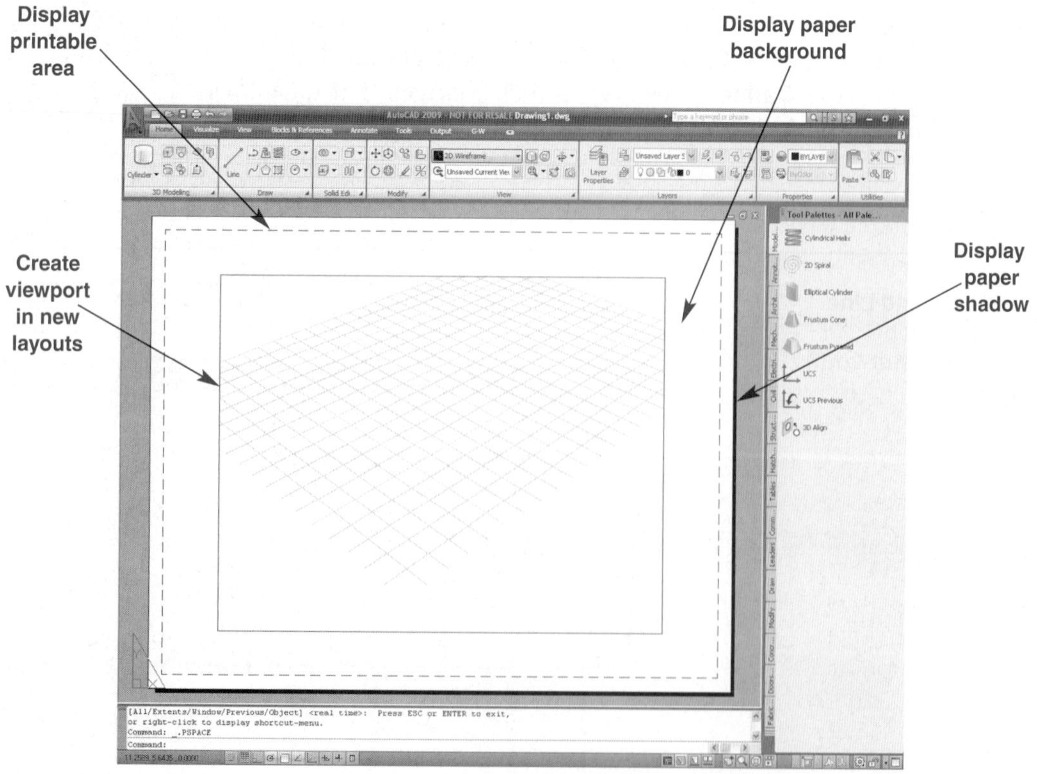

Display Resolution and Performance Settings

The settings in the **Display resolution** and **Display performance** areas of the **Display** tab in the **Options** dialog box affect the performance of AutoCAD. The settings can affect regeneration time and realtime panning and zooming. The following options are available in the **Display resolution** area. If the AutoCAD drawing icon is shown next to the setting, the value is saved in the current drawing, not in the AutoCAD system registry.

- **Arc and circle smoothness.** This setting controls the smoothness of circles, arcs, and ellipses. The default value is 1000; the range is from 1 to 20000. The system variable equivalent is **VIEWRES**.
- **Segments in a polyline curve.** This value determines how many line segments will be generated for each polyline curve. The default value is 8; the range is a nonzero value from –32768 to 32767. The system variable equivalent is **SPLINESEGS**.
- **Rendered object smoothness.** This setting controls the smoothness of curved solids when they are hidden, shaded, or rendered. This value is multiplied by the **Arc and circle smoothness** value. The default value is 0.5; the range is from 0.01 to 10. The system variable equivalent is **FACETRES**.
- **Contour lines per surface.** This value controls the number of contour lines per surface on solid objects. The default value is 4; the range is from 0 to 2047. The system variable equivalent is **ISOLINES**.

The following options are available in the **Display performance** area.

- **Pan and zoom with raster & OLE.** If this is checked, raster images are displayed when panning and zooming. If it is unchecked, only the frame is displayed during the operation. The system variable equivalent is **RTDISPLAY**.
- **Highlight raster image frame only.** If this is checked, only the frame around a raster image is highlighted when the image is selected. If this option is unchecked, the image displays a diagonal checkered pattern to indicate selection. The system variable equivalent is **IMAGEHLT**.
- **Apply solid fill.** Controls the display of solid fills in objects. Affected objects include hatches, wide polylines, solids, multilines, and traces. The system variable equivalent is **FILLMODE**.
- **Show text boundary frame only.** This setting controls the Quick Text mode. When checked, text is replaced by a rectangular frame. The system variable equivalent is **QTEXTMODE**.
- **Draw true silhouettes for solids and surfaces.** Controls whether or not the silhouette curves are displayed for solid objects. The system variable equivalent is **DISPSILH**.

NOTE

After changing display settings, use the **REGEN** or **REGENALL** command to make the settings take effect on the objects in the drawing.

PROFESSIONAL TIP

If you notice performance slowing down, you may want to adjust display settings. For example, if there is a lot of text in the drawing, you can activate Quick Text mode to improve performance. When the drawing is ready for plotting, deactivate Quick Text mode.

File Saving Options

The settings specified in the **Open and Save** tab of the **Options** dialog box deal with how drawing files are saved, safety precautions for files, how file names display in the menu browser, the behavior of xrefs, and the loading of ObjectARX applications and proxy objects. This tab is shown in **Figure 20-7.** The options in this tab are discussed in the next sections.

Default Settings for Saving Files

The settings in the **File Save** area determine the defaults for saving files. The setting in the **Save as:** drop-down list determines the default file type. You may want to change this setting if you are saving drawing files as a previous release of AutoCAD or saving drawings as DXF files.

The **Maintain visual fidelity for annotative objects** check box controls how annotative objects are displayed when the drawing is opened in AutoCAD 2007 or earlier versions. If you work primarily in model space, this can be left unchecked. If you use layouts and expect the drawing files to be opened in older versions of AutoCAD, this should be checked. When checked and the drawing is saved and then opened in an older version of AutoCAD, the scaled representations of annotative objects are divided into separate objects. These objects are stored in anonymous blocks saved on separate layers. The block names are based on the layer's original name appended with a number. When the drawing is opened once again in AutoCAD 2008 or later, the annotative objects are restored to normal. The system variable equivalent for this toggle is **SAVEFIDELITY**. Checking the check box sets this variable to 1 (on). Unchecking it sets the variable to 0 (off).

The **Incremental save percentage** value determines how much of the drawing is saved when a **SAVE** or **QSAVE** is performed. If the quantity of new data in a drawing

Figure 20-7.
The **Open and Save** tab settings control default save options, file safety features, how file names are displayed in the menu browser, xref options, and ObjectARX application options.

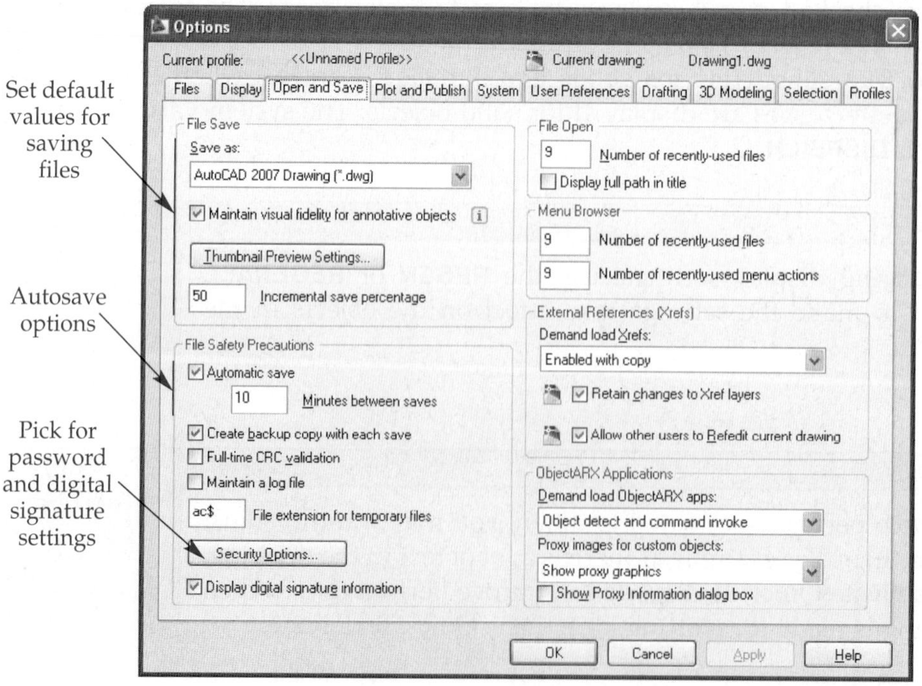

file reaches the specified percentage, a full save is performed. To force a full save to be performed, set the value to 0.

If you pick the **Thumbnail Preview Settings...** button, the **Thumbnail Preview Settings** dialog box is displayed, Figure 20-8. If the **Save a thumbnail preview image** check box is checked, a preview image of the drawing will be displayed in the **Select File** dialog box when the drawing is selected for opening. The system variable equivalent for this setting is **RASTERPREVIEW**; 1 creates a preview.

The two radio buttons below the **Save a thumbnail preview image** check box set what is used as the basis for the thumbnail. The **Use view when drawing last saved** radio button bases the thumbnail image on the last zoom location of the drawing. The **Use Home View** radio button bases the thumbnail on the view defined as the home view.

The home view can be set to the current view by picking the **Set current View as Home** button in the **Home view** area. This can also be done in the drawing area by using the view cube. See chapter 3 for a detailed explanation of the view cube. To change the home view to the default setting, pick the **Reset Home to default** button. A preview of the current home view is shown to the left of the buttons.

When the **Generate Sheet, Sheet View, and Model View Thumbnails** check box is checked in the **Thumbnail Preview Settings** dialog box, the thumbnails in the **Sheet Set Manager** are updated based on the position of the slider below this check box. The slider can be set to one of three positions. A description of the current setting appears below the slider. When the slider is in the middle position (default), thumbnails are updated when they are accessed. When the slider is in the left-hand position, thumbnails must be manually updated. When the slider is in the right-hand position, the thumbnails are updated when the drawing is saved. The system variable equivalent is **UPDATETHUMBNAIL**. The settings are:

- **0.** The **Generate Sheet, Sheet View, and Model View Thumbnails** check box is unchecked.
- **7.** The check box is checked and the slider is in the left-hand position.
- **15.** The check box is checked and the slider is in the middle position.
- **23.** The check box is checked and the slider is in the right-hand position.

Figure 20-8.
The **Thumbnail Preview Settings** dialog box.

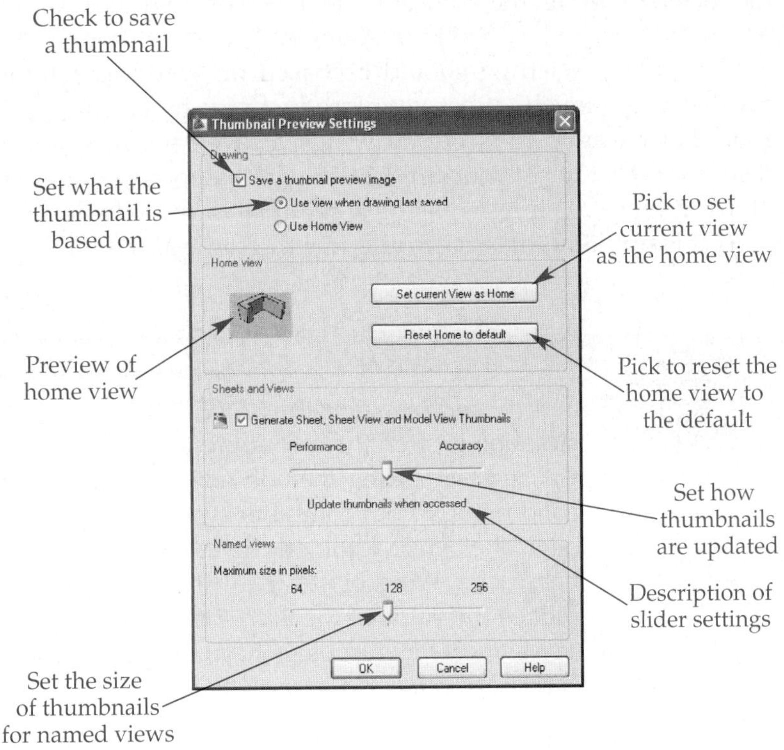

The **Maximum size in pixels:** slider controls size of thumbnails for named views. The slider can be set to 64, 128, or 256 pixels. This is the square size of the thumbnail. The system variable equivalent is **THUMBSIZE**, where a setting of 0 is 64 pixels, 1 is 128 pixels, and 2 is 256 pixels.

PROFESSIONAL TIP

To maintain forward compatibility of drawings, annotative objects should not be edited in older versions of AutoCAD. Doing so may compromise the annotative properties. For example, exploding an annotative block in an older version of AutoCAD then opening that drawing in AutoCAD 2009 results in each of the scaled representations becoming a separate annotative object.

Autosave Settings

When working in AutoCAD, data loss can occur due to a sudden power outage or an unforeseen system error. AutoCAD provides several safety precautions to help minimize data loss when these types of events occur. The settings for the precautions are found in the **File Safety Precautions** area in the **Open and Save** tab of the **Options** dialog box.

When the **Automatic save** check box is enabled, AutoCAD automatically creates a backup file at a specified time interval. The **Minutes between saves** edit box sets this interval. This is the value of the **SAVETIME** system variable. Removing the check sets **SAVETIME** to 0.

The automatic save feature does not overwrite the source drawing file with its incremental saves. Rather, AutoCAD saves temporary files. The path for autosave files is specified in the **Files** tab in the **Options** dialog box, as discussed earlier. The autosave file is stored in the specified location until the drawing is closed. When the drawing is closed, the autosave file is deleted. Autosave files have a .sv$ extension with the drawing name and some random numbers generated by AutoCAD. If AutoCAD unexpectedly quits, the autosave file is not deleted and can be renamed with a .dwg extension so it can be opened in AutoCAD.

The interval setting should be based on working conditions and file size. It is possible to adversely affect your productivity by setting your **SAVETIME** value too small. For example, in larger drawings, a save can take a significant amount of time. Ideally, it is best to set your **SAVETIME** variable to the greatest amount of time you can afford to repeat. While it may be acceptable to redo the last fifteen minutes or less of work, it is unlikely that you would feel the same about having to redo the last hour of work.

PROFESSIONAL TIP

Setting and resetting the **SAVETIME** variable according to any given situation is often the best approach. The factors that should influence the current setting include not only file size, but also the working conditions. If your computer system is experiencing frequent lockups or crashes, your automatic saves should occur often. Weather can also be a factor. Wind or electrical storms should be an immediate cue to reduce the value of the **SAVETIME** variable. In addition to automatic saves, most veteran users have developed the positive habit of "save early, save often."

Backup Files

AutoCAD can create a backup of the current drawing file whenever the current drawing is saved. The backup file uses the same name as the drawing, but has a .bak file extension. The backup is not overwritten when a different drawing is opened or saved. When the **Create backup copy with each save** check box in the **Open and Save** tab of the **Options** dialog box is checked, the backup file feature is enabled. If not checked, the file is not backed up when you save. Unless you prefer to take unnecessary risks, it is usually best to have this feature enabled.

CRC Validation

A ***cyclic redundancy check***, or CRC, verifies that the number of data bits sent is the same as the number received. **Full-time CRC validation** is a feature you can use when drawing files are being corrupted and you suspect a hardware or software problem. When using full-time CRC validation, the CRC check is done every time data are read into the drawing. This ensures that all data are correctly received.

Log Files

The log file can serve a variety of purposes. The source of drawing errors can be determined by reviewing the commands that produced the incorrect results. Additionally, log files can be reviewed by a CAD manager to determine the need for staff training or customization of the system.

When the **Maintain a log file** check box is activated in the **Open and Save** tab of the **Options** dialog box, AutoCAD creates a file named with the drawing name, a code, and the .log file extension. The name and location of the log file can be specified using the Log File Location listing in the **Files** tab of the **Options** dialog box. When activated, all prompts, messages, and responses that appear in the **Command Line** window are saved to this file. The log file status can also be set using the **LOGFILEON** and **LOGFILEOFF** commands.

PROFESSIONAL TIP

Toggle the log file open before listing any saved layers, blocks, views, or user coordinate systems. You can then print the log file contents and keep a hard copy at your workstation as a handy reference.

File Opening Settings

The **File Open** area of the **Open and Save** tab in the **Options** dialog box contains two settings. The value in the **Number of recently-used files to list** text box controls the number of drawing files listed in the **File** pull-down menu. The pull-down menus are not displayed, by default, unless the AutoCAD Classic workspace is set current. The value can be from 0 to 9. The **Display full path in title** check box controls whether the entire drawing file path (when checked) or just the file name (when unchecked) is displayed in the title bar of the AutoCAD window.

Menu Browser Settings

The **Menu Browser** area of the **Open and Save** tab in the **Options** dialog box contains two settings. The value in the **Number of recently used files** text box controls the number of drawing files displayed in the **Recent Documents** entry at the bottom of the menu browser. This value can be from 0 to 50.

The **Number of recently used menu actions** text box controls the number of actions displayed in the **Recent Actions** entry at the bottom of the **Menu Browser**. This value can be from 0 to 50. The actions in this list are only those selected from the menu browser. Actions selected from the ribbon or entered on the command line are not shown.

External Reference Settings

The external reference options in the **Open and Save** tab of the **Options** dialog box are important if you are working with xrefs. These options are found in the **External Reference (Xrefs)** area of the tab. The **Demand load Xrefs:** setting can affect system performance and the ability for another user to edit a drawing currently referenced into another drawing. You can select Enabled, Disabled, or Enabled with copy from the drop-down list. This setting is also controlled by the **XLOADCTL** system variable.

If the **Retain changes to Xref layers** option is checked, xref layer settings are saved with the drawing file. The **VISRETAIN** system variable also controls this setting.

The **Allow other users to Refedit current drawing** setting controls whether or not the drawing can be edited in-place when it is referenced by another drawing. This setting is also controlled by the **XEDIT** system variable.

ObjectARX Options

The **ObjectARX Applications** area of the **Open and Save** tab of the **Options** dialog box controls the loading of ObjectARX applications and the displaying of proxy objects. The **Demand load ObjectARX apps:** setting specifies if and when AutoCAD loads third-party applications associated with objects in the drawing. The **Proxy images for custom objects:** setting controls how objects created by a third-party application are displayed. When a drawing with proxy objects is opened, the **Proxy Information** dialog box is displayed. To disable the dialog box, uncheck the **Show Proxy Information dialog box** option. This is unchecked by default.

System Settings

Options for the pointing device, graphic settings, general system options, and dbConnect can be found in the **System** tab of the **Options** dialog box, Figure 20-9. These settings affect the interaction between AutoCAD and your operating system.

In the **3D Performance** area is the **Performance Settings** button. Selecting this button displays the **Adaptive Degradation and Performance Tuning** dialog box. The options available in this dialog box are discussed in the next section.

The **Current Pointing Device** area determines the pointing device used with AutoCAD. The default is the current system pointing device (usually your mouse). If you have a digitizer tablet, you will want to select the Wintab Compatible Digitizer option. You must configure your tablet before it can be used.

The **Layout Regen Options** setting determines what is regenerated and when it is regenerated when working with layout tabs. The following options are available in the **dbConnect Options** area.

- **Store Links index in drawing file.** When this option is checked, the database index is saved within the drawing file. This makes the link selection operation quicker, but increases the drawing file size.
- **Open tables in read-only mode.** Determines whether tables are opened in read-only mode.

The settings in the **General Options** area control general system functions. When the **Hidden Messages Settings** button is picked, the **Hidden Message Settings** dialog box is displayed, Figure 20-10. All messages hidden by the user picking the "do not show again" option in a message box are available in this dialog box. For example,

Figure 20-9.
General AutoCAD system options and hardware settings can be controlled in the **System** tab.

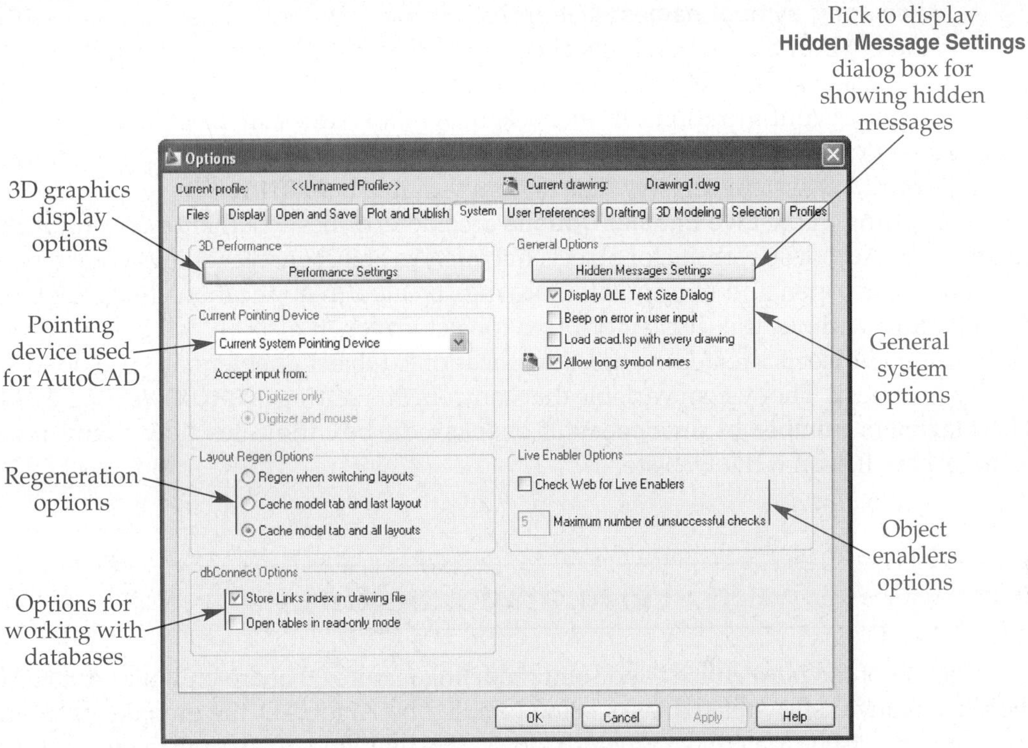

Figure 20-10.
Turning on the display of previously hidden messages.

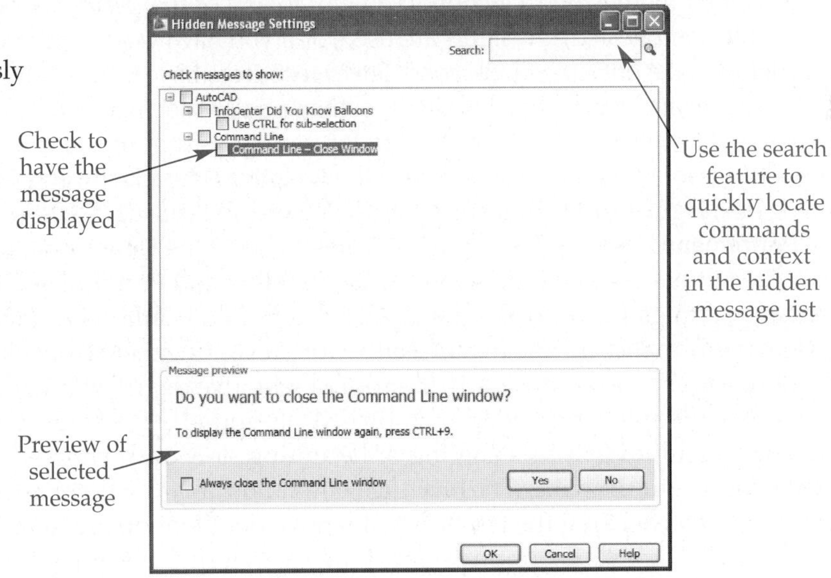

if you select a solid object, a message is displayed indicating to use the [Ctrl] key to select a subobject. If you choose to always hide this message, it appears in the **Hidden Message Settings** dialog box. Check the entry for this message in the dialog box to have it once again displayed when you select a solid. The following additional options are available in the **General Options** area of the **System** tab.

- **Display OLE Text Size Dialog.** When inserting an OLE object, the **OLE Text Size** dialog box is displayed if this option is checked.
- **Beep on error in user input.** Specifies whether AutoCAD alerts you of incorrect user input with an audible beep. By default, this is off.

- **Load acad.lsp with every drawing.** This setting turns the persistent AutoLISP feature on or off. By default, it is off.
- **Allow long symbol names.** Determines if long symbol names can be used in AutoCAD. If this option is checked, up to 255 characters can be used for layers, dimension styles, blocks, linetypes, text styles, layouts, UCS names, views, and viewport configurations. If unchecked, symbol names are limited to 31 characters. By default, this option is checked. It is also saved in the drawing, not the AutoCAD system registry. The system variable is **EXTNAMES**.

The setting in the **Live Enabler Options** area determines whether or not AutoCAD searches the Autodesk website for object enablers. An object enabler allows your version of AutoCAD to open and manipulate drawings created in applications like AutoCAD Architecture without the display of proxy object errors. It also allows the use of the custom-made objects created in those applications. Object enablers are provided for free by Autodesk. The system variable that controls this setting is **PROXYWEBSEARCH**. The **Maximum number of unsuccessful checks** edit box indicates how many times AutoCAD will search the website.

3D Performance Settings

With all of the powerful 3D and solid modeling features that are built into AutoCAD, there are many display-related tasks being handled by AutoCAD, the graphics card, and the computer itself. Materials, lights, shadows, shading, and rendering require a lot of computing power in order to project a quality representation of the model onto the monitor screen. Often there is no reduction in quality to any of the desired effects if the materials are not too complicated, few lights are used, or if you have shadows turned off. Sometimes, in order to make one effect look good, fewer resources have to be assigned to other effects. The software and hardware, working together, usually do an adequate job assigning these resources. However, it may be necessary for you to assist in this decision-making process. The settings for this process are made in the **Adaptive Degradation and Performance Tuning** dialog box, **Figure 20-11.** To display this dialog box, enter the **3DCONFIG** command or pick the **Performance Settings** button in the **Systems** tab of the **Options** dialog box.

The left-hand side of the **Adaptive Degradation and Performance Tuning** dialog box contains settings for controlling adaptive degradation. ***Adaptive degradation*** controls system performance by turning off features or preventing them from using resources. The check box at the top controls whether or not adaptive degradation is being used. When unchecked, adaptive degradation is turned off and all effects are using all resources. This may result in graphics lagging or becoming slow and "choppy" as you zoom and pan around your drawing. The orbiting commands are even more affected by this being turned off. By checking the check box, adaptive degradation is activated.

AutoCAD tracks its graphics performance in terms of frames per second (fps). Just below the **Adaptive degradation** check box is a text box for setting this value. You may enter a new value in the text box or use the arrows to increase or decrease the value. The higher the number, the sooner resources start being reassigned. If performance dips below this level, resources are taken away from the various effects that create the displayed graphics.

The effects that can be controlled while adaptive degradation is turned on are shown in the **Degradation order:** list box. Certain effects that you deem important can be unchecked so they are not degraded and operate using maximum resources. The top-to-bottom order in which the effects are listed determines the priority in which resources are removed. This order can be changed by selecting an effect and picking the **Move Up** or **Move Down** button on the right side of the list.

Figure 20-11.
The **Adaptive Degradation and Performance Tuning** dialog box is used to turn on and prioritize adaptive degradation.

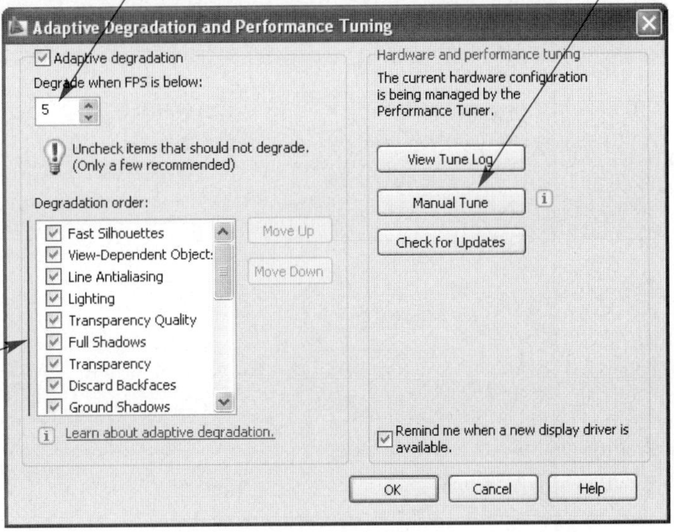

On the right side of the **Adaptive Degradation and Performance Tuning** dialog box is the **Hardware and performance tuning** area. Picking the **View Tune Log** button displays a log of any features or effects that have been turned off. Information regarding your computer, amount of RAM, and 3D graphics card are also shown. The log can be saved as a file. The **Manual Tune** button displays the **Manual Performance Tuning** dialog box. This dialog box allows control over hardware settings (hardware acceleration, graphics card driver name, and the effects the graphics card is capable of), general settings (discard back faces and quality of transparency), and dynamic tessellation settings (surface and curve tessellation settings and number of tessellations to cache). At the bottom of the **Adaptive Degradation and Performance Tuning** dialog box is the **Remind me when a new driver is available** check box. When checked, AutoCAD displays a popup message in the graphics area whenever a new graphics card driver is available.

When the settings have been adjusted as desired in the **Adaptive Degradation and Performance Tuning** dialog box, pick the **OK** button to return to the **Options** dialog box. Then, close the **Options** dialog box.

User Preferences

A variety of settings are found in the **User Preferences** tab of the **Options** dialog box. See **Figure 20-12.** AutoCAD allows users to optimize the way they work in AutoCAD by providing options for double-click editing, shortcut menu functions, **DesignCenter** units, working with fields, coordinate data entry, associative dimensions, hyperlink icon display, undo/redo control, default lineweight settings, and scale list settings. All of these are controlled in this tab.

Shortcut Menus and Double-Click Editing

AutoCAD has tools that provide easy access to commonly used editing commands and options. Two of these tools are double-click editing and shortcut menus. Double-clicking on an object calls the most appropriate editing tool for that object type, often

Figure 20-12.
The **User Preferences** tab allows you to set up AutoCAD in a manner that works best for you.

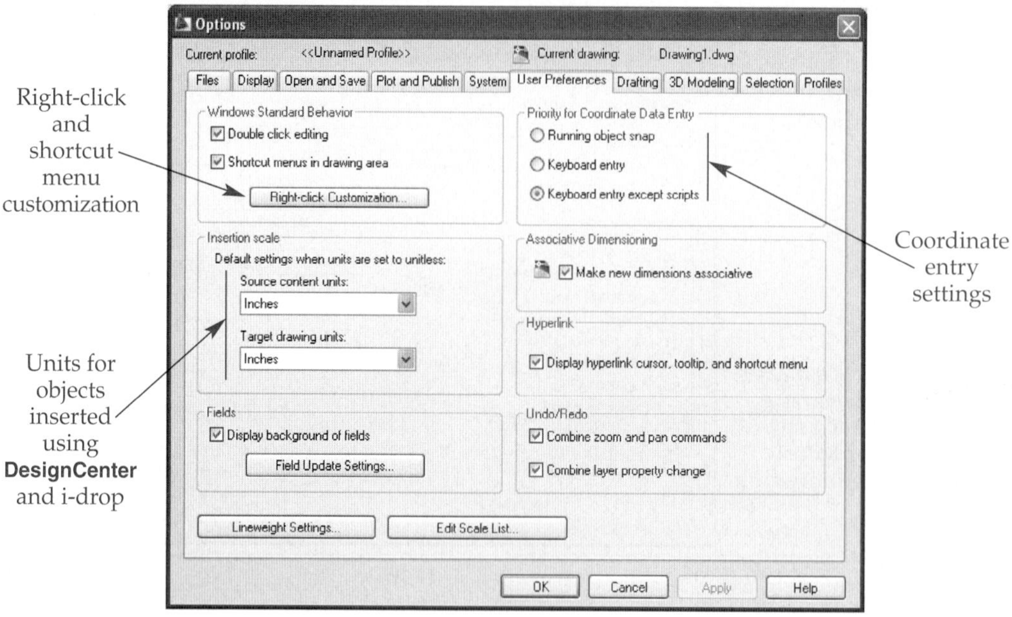

the **Properties** palette. Shortcut menus are displayed by right-clicking and are ***context sensitive***. This means the options available in the shortcut menu are determined by the active command, cursor location, or selected object.

To enable double-click editing, check the **Double click editing** check box in the **Windows Standard Behavior** area in the **User Preferences** tab of the **Options** dialog box. To enable shortcut menus, check the **Shortcut menus in drawing area** check box in the same area. Disabling the shortcut menus makes a right mouse click the equivalent of pressing the [Enter] key. In general, this is not recommended.

You can also customize the setting for the right mouse button. Pick the **Right-click Customization...** button to access the **Right-Click Customization** dialog box. See Figure 20-13. The **Turn on time-sensitive right-click:** check box controls the right-click behavior. A quick click is the same as pressing [Enter]. A longer click displays a shortcut menu. You can set the duration of the longer click in milliseconds. If the check box is checked, the **Default Mode** and **Command Mode** areas of the dialog box are disabled.

Different settings can be used for the three different shortcut menu modes. Each of the three menu modes has a separate area in the **Right-Click Customization** dialog box.

- **Default Mode.** In this mode, no objects are selected and no command is active. The **Repeat Last Command** option activates the last command issued. The **Shortcut Menu** option displays the shortcut menu.
- **Edit Mode.** In this mode, an object is selected, but no command is active. The **Repeat Last Command** option activates the last command issued. The **Shortcut Menu** option displays the shortcut menu.
- **Command Mode.** In this mode, a command is active. The **ENTER** option makes a right-click the same as pressing [Enter]. The **Shortcut Menu: always enabled** option means that the shortcut menu is always displayed in command mode. The **Shortcut Menu: enabled when command options are present** option means the shortcut menu is only displayed when command options are available on the command line. When there are no command options, a right-click is the same as [Enter]. This is the default option.

Figure 20-13.
Use this dialog box to customize the right mouse button.

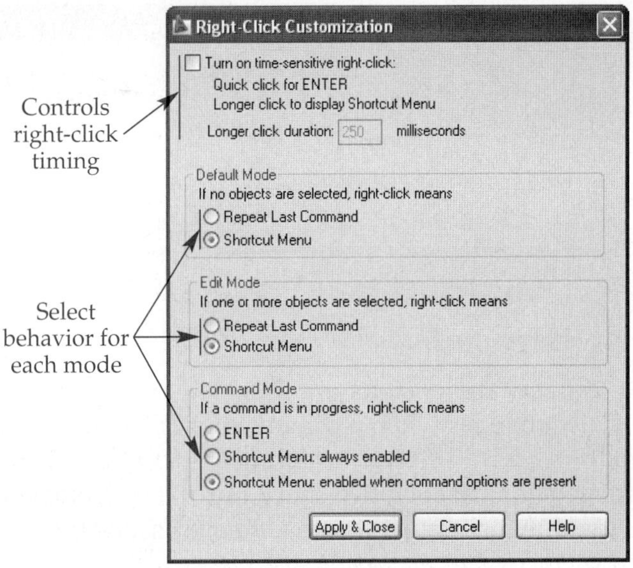

Insertion Scale

In the **Insertion scale** area of the **User Preferences** tab, unit values can be set for objects when they are inserted into a drawing. This applies to "unitless" objects dragged from **DesignCenter** or inserted using the i-drop method. The **Source content units:** setting specifies the units for objects being inserted into the current drawing. The **Target drawing units:** setting determines the units in the current drawing. These settings are used when there are no units set with the **INSUNITS** system variable.

Fields

A ***field*** is a special type of text object that displays a specific property value, setting, or characteristic. Fields can display information related to a specific object, general drawing properties, or information related to the current user or computer system. The text displayed in the field can change if the value being displayed changes. Refer to *AutoCAD and Its Applications—Basics* for more information on using fields.

In the **Fields** area of the **User Preferences** tab, you can set whether or not a field is displayed with a nonplotting background. When the **Display background of fields** check box is checked, the field background is displayed in light gray.

Picking the **Field Update Settings...** button in the **Fields** area opens the **Field Update Settings** dialog box, Figure 20-14. In this dialog box, you can set when fields are automatically updated. The five options are **Open**, **Save**, **Plot**, **eTransmit**, and **Regen**. Check as many of the options as appropriate.

Coordinate Data Priority

The **Priority for Coordinate Data Entry** area of the **User Preferences** tab controls how AutoCAD responds to input of coordinate data. The system variable equivalent for this is **OSNAPCOORD**. The three options are:

- **Running object snap.** When this option is selected, object snaps always override coordinate entry. This is equivalent to an **OSNAPCOORD** setting of 0.
- **Keyboard entry.** When this option is selected, coordinate entry always overrides object snaps. This is equivalent to an **OSNAPCOORD** setting of 1.
- **Keyboard entry except scripts.** When this option is selected, coordinate entry will override object snaps except those object snaps contained within scripts. This is the default and equivalent to an **OSNAPCOORD** setting of 2.

Figure 20-14.
Setting when fields are automatically updated.

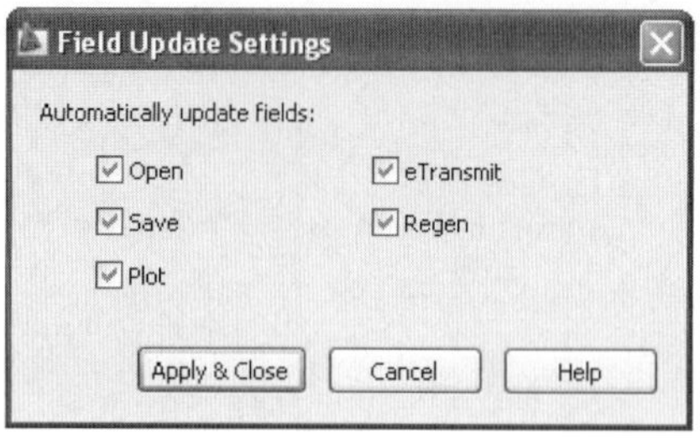

Associative Dimensions

By default, all new dimensions are associative. This means that the dimension value automatically changes when a dimension's defpoints are moved. However, you can turn this option off in the **User Preferences** tab of the **Options** dialog box. When the **Make new dimensions associative** check box in the **Associative Dimensioning** area is unchecked, any dimensions drawn do *not* have associativity. This is equivalent to a **DIMASSOC** setting of 1.

Hyperlinks

In the **Hyperlink** area of the **User Preferences** tab, you can set whether or not the hyperlink cursor and tooltip are displayed when the cursor is over a hyperlink. If **Display hyperlink cursor, tooltip, and shortcut menu** is checked, the hyperlink icon appears next to the crosshairs when the cursor is over an object containing a hyperlink. The tooltip is also displayed. Additional hyperlink options are available from the shortcut menu when an object with a hyperlink is selected.

Undo/Redo

The **Undo/Redo** area of the **User Preferences** tab allows you to control how multiple, consecutive zooms and pans are handled within the **UNDO** and **REDO** commands. By checking the **Combine zoom and pan commands** check box, back-to-back zooms and pans are considered a single operation for undo and redo purposes. In other words, performing an undo or redo undoes or redoes the entire zoom/pan sequence. Unchecking the check box allows each zoom or pan to be considered a separate operation. However, if the zoom or pan operation is launched using the menu browser, each operation is *always* considered separate.

When the **Combine layer property change** check box is checked, all changes made in the **Layer Properties Manager** palette are considered one operation. If this is unchecked, each change is considered a separate operation when using **UNDO** and **REDO**.

Lineweight Settings and Edit Scale List

At the bottom of the **User Preferences** tab are the **Lineweight Settings...** and **Edit Scale List...** buttons. The **Lineweight Settings...** button opens the **Lineweight Settings** dialog box in which you can change default lineweight settings. This is discussed in detail in *AutoCAD and Its Applications—Basics.*

A default list of scales appears in various dialog boxes related to viewports, page setups, and plot scaling. You can add custom scales to or remove scales from this list so that it is more appropriate for your application. Picking the **Edit Scale List...** button at the bottom of the **User Preferences** tab displays the **Edit Scale List** dialog box. See **Figure 20-15.** The dialog box displays the current list of scales. The buttons on the right side of the dialog box allow you to add a new scale, edit an existing scale, move a scale up or down within the list, delete a scale, or reset the list to the default set of scales.

Figure 20-15.
The **Edit Scale List** dialog box allows you to change the scale list that appears when using various viewport, page setup, and plot scaling dialog boxes.

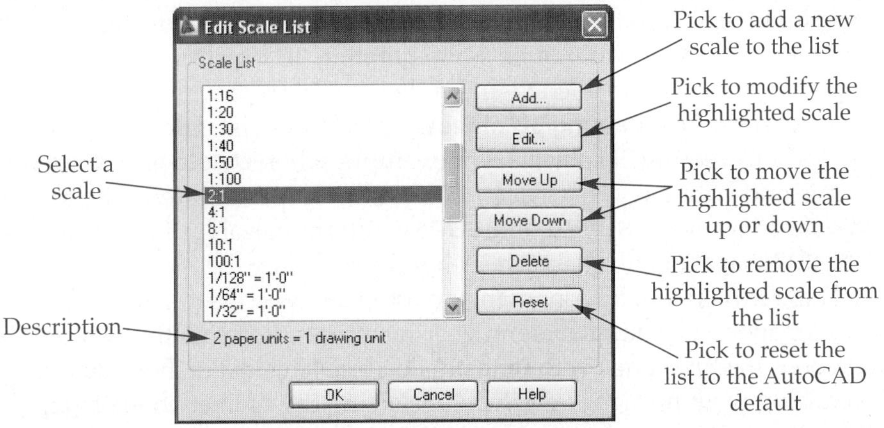

To add a scale, pick the **Add...** button. In the **Add Scale** dialog box that appears, enter a name for the scale in the **Name appearing in scale list:** text box. Then, in the **Scale Properties** area of the dialog box, enter values to indicate how many paper space units equal how many drawing units. Finally, pick the **OK** button to return to the **Edit Scale List** dialog box. The new scale appears in the list and is available wherever the scale list is displayed.

3D Display Properties

There are many ways to customize your system specifically for working in a 3D environment. The **3D Modeling** tab of the **Options** dialog box allows you to control the various settings having to do with working in 3D, **Figure 20-16.**

The **3D Crosshairs** area of the dialog box contains check boxes for displaying the Z axis on the crosshairs, labeling the axes of standard crosshairs, and labeling the axes of the dynamic UCS icon. There are three labeling possibilities from which to choose:

- X, Y, and Z.
- N (north), E (east), and z.
- Or you can specify custom labels for each axes.

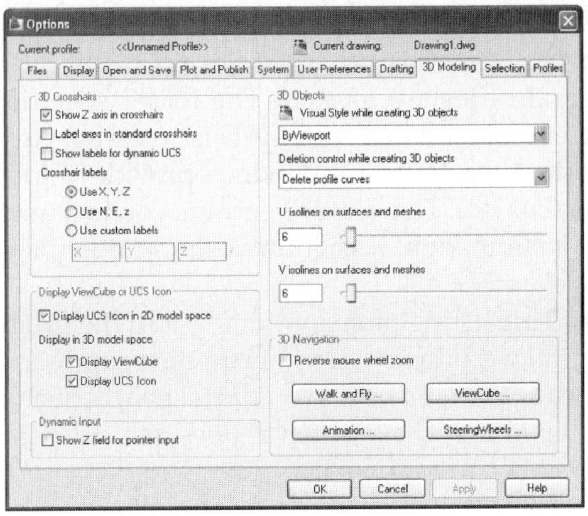

Figure 20-16.
Use the **3D Modeling** tab to customize settings when working in 3D.

The check boxes in the **Display View Cube or UCS Icon** area determine if the UCS icon is displayed in 2D model space. For a model space display in a visual style other than 2D Wireframe, you have control of both the UCS icon and the view cube. The **Dynamic Input** area has a check box for showing the Z field for dynamic input.

The setting in the **Visual Style while creating 3D objects** drop-down list in the **3D Objects** area determines which visual style is set current when objects are created. The **Deletion control while creating 3D objects** drop-down list determines how geometry is handled when creating 3D objects. For example, when **Delete profile curves** is selected, the profile and path curves are deleted after a sweep is created. The two sliders in the **3D Objects** area set the **SURFU** and **SURFV** system variables for old-style surfaces.

The **3D Navigation** area has a check box for reversing the zoom direction of the mouse wheel. There are also four buttons in this area that allow access to settings for walkthroughs/flybys, animations, the view cube, and steering wheels. Selecting the **Walk and Fly settings...** button opens the **Walk and Fly Settings** dialog box. This dialog box contains settings used when creating walkthroughs and flybys. Selecting the **Animation settings...** button opens the **Animation Settings** dialog box. This dialog box contains settings that control the actual animation of a walkthrough or flyby. The **Walk and Fly Settings** and **Animation Settings** dialog boxes are discussed in detail in Chapter 18. Selecting the **View Cube** button opens the **View Cube Settings** dialog box. Selecting the **Steering Wheels** button opens the **Steering Wheels Settings** dialog box. These dialog boxes are discussed in Chapter 3.

Changing Program Properties

When AutoCAD is first installed on your computer, the installation program automatically creates the AutoCAD group and several program items and places a program icon on the Windows desktop. If desired, you can modify the program icon properties. These properties include such things as the file attributes, the folder where AutoCAD is started, and the icon for the shortcut.

To modify the AutoCAD program icon properties, right-click on the AutoCAD 2009 icon on the desktop and then select **Properties** from the shortcut menu. See **Figure 20-17.** You can also pick the icon and then use the [Alt]+[Enter] key combination. Either action displays the **AutoCAD 2009 Properties** dialog box, **Figure 20-18.** There are three main tabs: **General**, **Shortcut**, and **Compatibility**. Additional tabs, such as **Security**, may be listed, depending on your Windows setup. The options in the **Shortcut** tab are:

- **Target.** This text box contains the name of the executable program and its path. If the folder that contains the AutoCAD executable has changed, this line can be edited so the shortcut still links to the correct file. If you are not sure of the exact path, you can pick the **Find Target...** button at the bottom of the tab to locate the executable.
- **Start in.** This text box specifies the name of the folder where the AutoCAD program files are located. The folder specified in this text box becomes the current folder when AutoCAD is running. Any new files are placed here.
- **Shortcut key.** Microsoft Windows provides a special feature called an ***application shortcut key.*** This feature permits you to launch AutoCAD with a user-defined key combination. Assigning a shortcut key for AutoCAD is described later in this chapter.
- **Run.** This listing offers options to run the program in a normal, maximized, or minimized window. Do not run the program minimized, otherwise AutoCAD appears only as a button on the taskbar when you start it. You can easily restore or maximize it, but when it does not automatically appear on screen, newer users may be confused.
- **Comment.** This is the tooltip displayed next to the cursor when it is over the icon.

Figure 20-17.
This shortcut menu appears when you right-click on an icon (shortcut) on the Windows desktop.

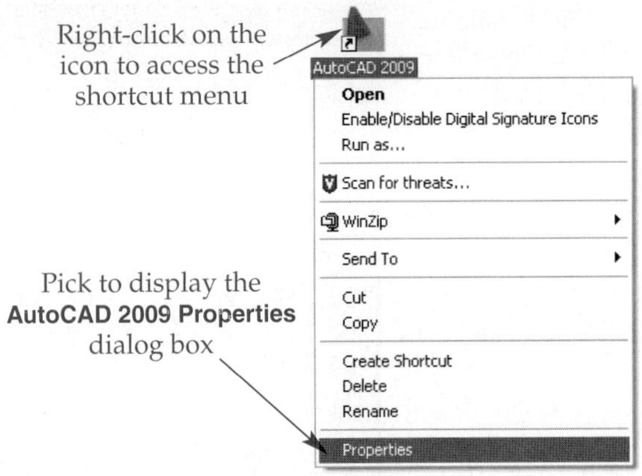

Figure 20-18.
The **AutoCAD 2009 Properties** dialog box.

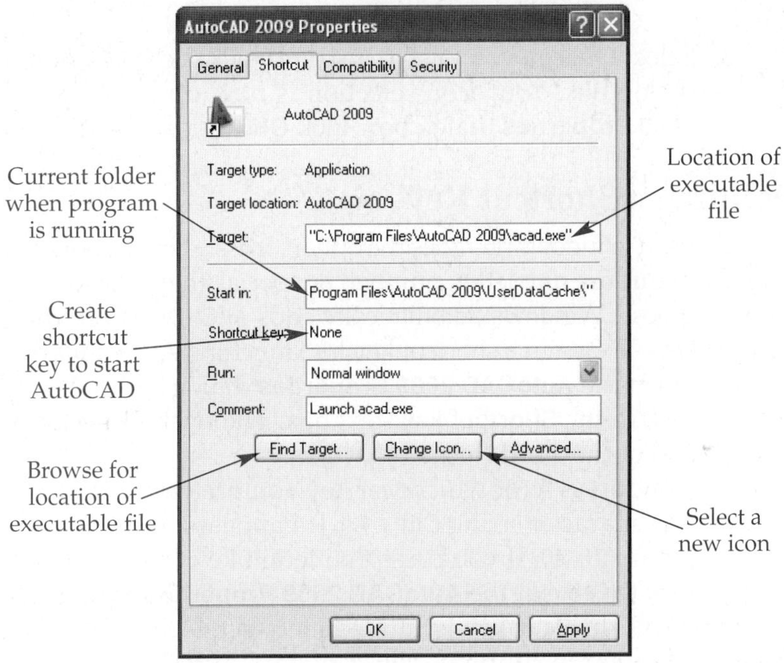

When you are finished making your changes, pick the **OK** button to exit the **AutoCAD 2009 Properties** dialog box. Any changes you make immediately take effect, so there is no need to restart Windows.

NOTE

Be sure to check with your instructor or system administrator before modifying the AutoCAD program properties.

Changing the AutoCAD Icon

The **AutoCAD 2009 Properties** dialog box provides the option to change the program icon for the shortcut. Use the following procedure to change the icon.

1. Pick the **Change Icon...** button in the **Shortcut** tab of the **AutoCAD 2009 Properties** dialog box. The **Change Icon** dialog box is then displayed.
2. To display icons for AutoCAD, use the **Browse...** button to find the file named acad.exe in the \AutoCAD 2009 folder. Pick the **Open** button to display the AutoCAD icons, as shown in **Figure 20-19**. You can also select any valid icon or library file.

Figure 20-19.
A new icon can be selected in the **Change Icon** dialog box.

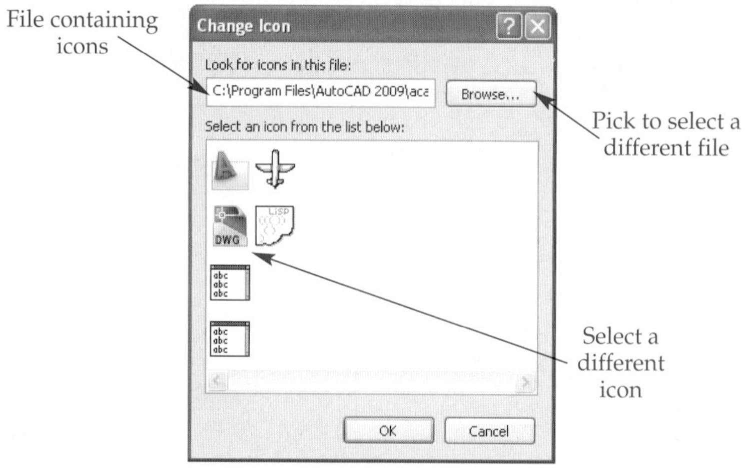

3. Select the icon you wish to use and pick the **OK** button to exit the **Change Icon** dialog box. Your icon selection is now displayed at the top of the **AutoCAD 2009 Properties** dialog box. Pick **OK** to close the dialog box.

Defining a Shortcut Key

Microsoft Windows provides the option of assigning a shortcut key that starts an application. You can use any letter, number, or special character for a shortcut key. Whichever key you choose, Windows automatically adds a [Ctrl]+[Alt] in front of it. You can also use function keys. To assign a shortcut key for launching AutoCAD, do the following.

1. Open the **AutoCAD 2009 Properties** dialog box.
2. Pick in the **Shortcut key:** text box. The flashing vertical cursor appears at the end of the word None.
3. Now, press A (or whichever key you prefer).
4. The character string Ctrl + Alt + A appears in the **Shortcut key:** text box, **Figure 20-20.** If you press a function key, the Ctrl and Alt are not added.
5. Pick **OK** to exit the **AutoCAD 2009 Properties** dialog box.

Your new shortcut key is immediately active. Now, no matter which Windows-based application is running, you can start AutoCAD with the keyboard combination [Ctrl]+[Alt]+[A] (or whatever combination you specified). Refer to the Microsoft Windows *User's Guide* or online help for more information regarding shortcut keys.

Creating Alternate AutoCAD Configurations

The information you specify for AutoCAD regarding the pointing and printing devices is recorded in a configuration file. Your pointing and printing devices are specified in the **Options** dialog box, but the information is stored in the current configuration file. The default configuration file is acad2009.cfg. You can determine the current location for this configuration file by going to the Help and Miscellaneous File Names section of the **Files** tab in the **Options** dialog box. Each time you specify a new pointing or printing device, the existing acad2009.cfg file is overwritten with the new information.

Under most circumstances, a single configuration file is all that is necessary. Some users, however, may require multiple configurations. As an example, if you use a mouse most of the time, but sometimes need a digitizer tablet, you may find it convenient to set up AutoCAD to use multiple configurations. This can save you the time required to reconfigure AutoCAD each time you need to switch your pointing devices.

To save multiple configurations, you must specify a new location for AutoCAD to store the acad2009.cfg so that it does not overwrite the previous version. This way, you actually have more than one configuration file, with each file located in a specific folder. It is recommended that these folders be placed under the AutoCAD "user"

Figure 20-20.
Setting the [Ctrl]+[Alt]+[A] key combination to automatically start AutoCAD.

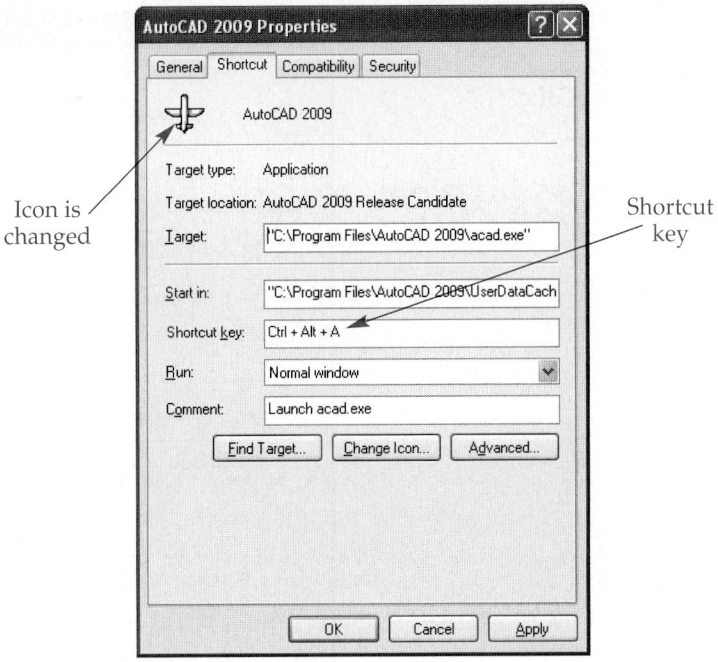

folder so they are easy to locate. For this example, create a folder named \Altcfg. Now, find the acad2009.cfg file in its current folder and copy it to the new folder.

On the Windows desktop, press the [Ctrl] key and drag the **AutoCAD 2009** icon (shortcut) to create a copy. This new shortcut is for the new configuration. Open the **AutoCAD 2009 Properties** dialog box for the new shortcut and go to the **Shortcut** tab. In the **Target:** edit box, place /c after the existing target, followed by the directory path location for the alternate configuration. For example, in Figure 20-21, the configuration folder is entered as:

"C:\Program Files\AutoCAD 2009\acad.exe" /c "C:\Documents and Settings*username*\Local Settings\Application Data\Autodesk\AutoCAD 2009\R17.1\enu\altcfg"

The *username* listing indicates the specific AutoCAD user. The new path must be placed in quotation marks due to the spaces in the path name. The /c is not in quotation marks. Command line switches (the /c) are separated by spaces. A space is interpreted as the end of the path name.

It is also recommended that you change the title of the shortcut icon on the desktop to match the configuration. For example, one shortcut icon could be called AutoCAD 2009 Original and the other could be called AutoCAD 2009 Alternate. Do this by right-clicking on the icon on the desktop and selecting **Rename**. Then, enter the new text.

When you start AutoCAD using the new shortcut, the alternate configuration file is used. This means that any configuration changes you make are stored in the new configuration file and do not affect other configurations.

NOTE

You can set up unique shortcut keys for each AutoCAD shortcut on your desktop.

PROFESSIONAL TIP

A user profile can be directly accessed from an AutoCAD shortcut on the desktop using a /p switch and the exact profile name. For example, if you created a profile called Project 0256, the **Target:** text box in the **AutoCAD 2009 Properties** dialog box may read:

"C:\Program Files\AutoCAD 2009\acad.exe" /p "Project 0256"

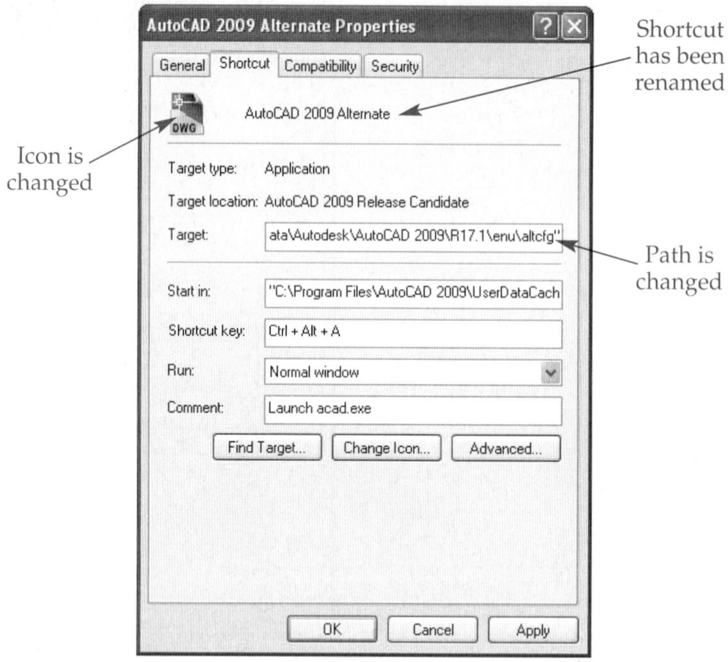

Figure 20-21.
If multiple configurations are used, the location of the alternate configuration file must be specified in the **Target:** edit box.

Chapter Test

Answer the following questions. Write your answers on a separate sheet of paper or complete the electronic chapter test on the Student CD.

1. List three methods used to open the **Options** dialog box.
2. List the tabs found in the **Options** dialog box.
3. AutoCAD resides in the C:\Program Files\AutoCAD 2009 folder on your workstation. You have created two folders under \AutoCAD 2009 named \Projects and \Symbols. You want to store your drawings in the \Projects folder and your blocks in the \Symbols folder. What should you enter in the Support File Search Path area so these folders are added to the search path?
4. How do you open the **Drawing Window Colors** dialog box to change the color of AutoCAD screen elements?
5. For which AutoCAD features can you customize the font (not within a drawing)?
6. In which tab of the **Options** dialog box can you change settings for layout tabs?
7. Briefly describe how to turn on the automatic save feature and specify the save interval.
8. How do you select the folder in which the autosave file is saved?
9. What are the advantages of toggling the log file open?
10. Name the two commands that toggle the log file on and off.
11. How would you set the right mouse button to perform an [Enter], rather than displaying shortcut menus?
12. How do you open the **Edit Scales List** dialog box from within the **Options** dialog box?
13. Which file must be copied to a separate folder before creating an alternate AutoCAD configuration?
14. How do you change the number of seconds that AutoCAD waits to display an extended tooltip?
15. How do you access the view cube setting from within the **Options** dialog box?

Drawing Problems

1. Using the methods described in this chapter, create an alternate configuration for AutoCAD dedicated to 3D modeling and rendering. Use the following instructions.
   A. Assign a different program icon for the 3D configuration.
   B. Name the program shortcut AutoCAD 3D.
   C. Define a shortcut key for the configuration.
   D. Add to the support path a folder that contains 3D shapes you have created.

2. Create an alternate configuration for AutoCAD dedicated to dimensioning. Use the following instructions to complete this problem.
   A. Assign a different program icon for the dimensioning configuration.
   B. Name the program shortcut AutoCAD Dimensioning.
   C. Define a shortcut key for the configuration.

The ribbon can be customized by adding tabs and panels. Then, you can add tools to them, either ones you have created or those that come with AutoCAD. Here, the **Customize User Interface** dialog box is shown with the custom panels. The custom tab and panels, below, allow this user to have only a single tab displayed in the ribbon, yet access the commonly used tools.

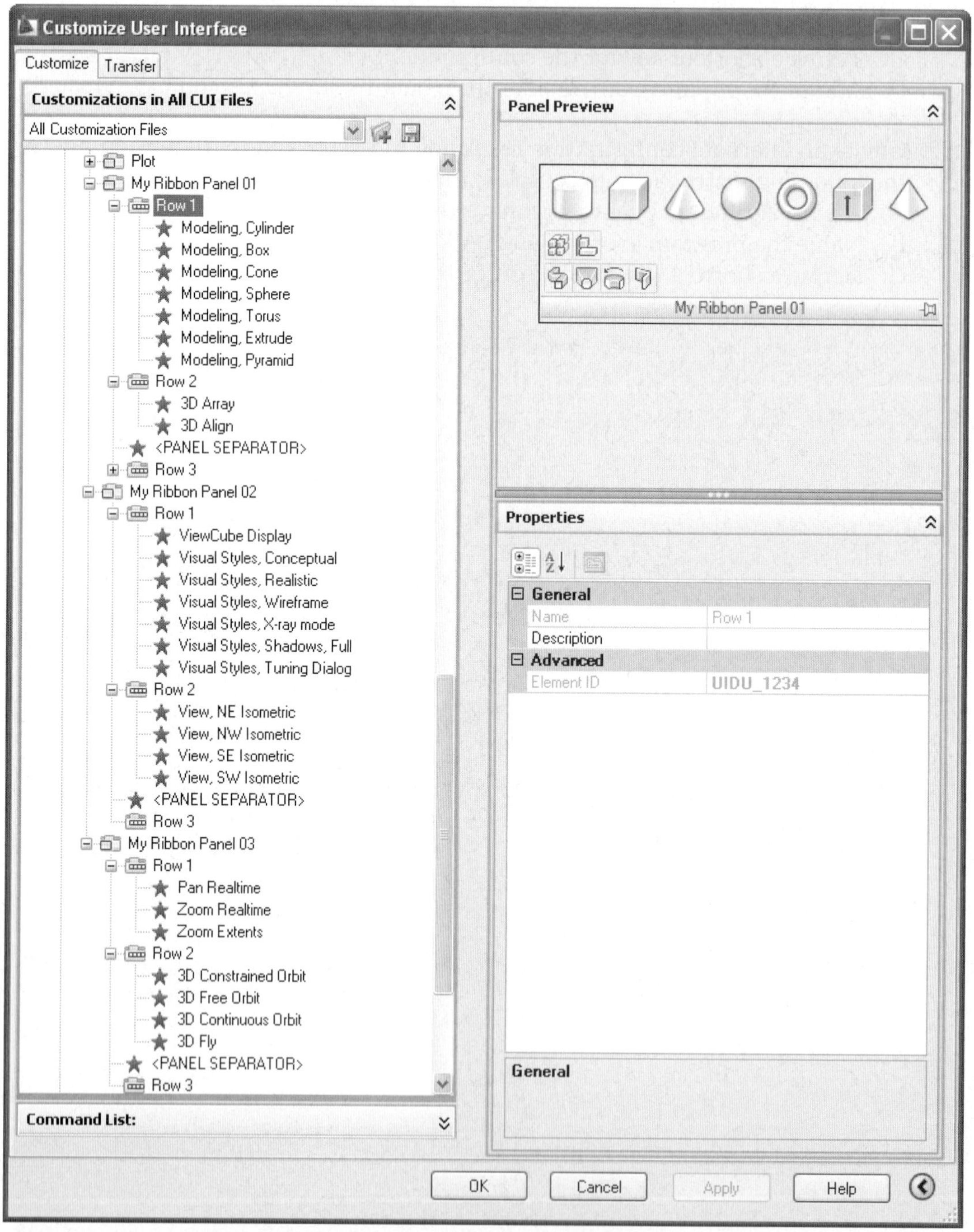

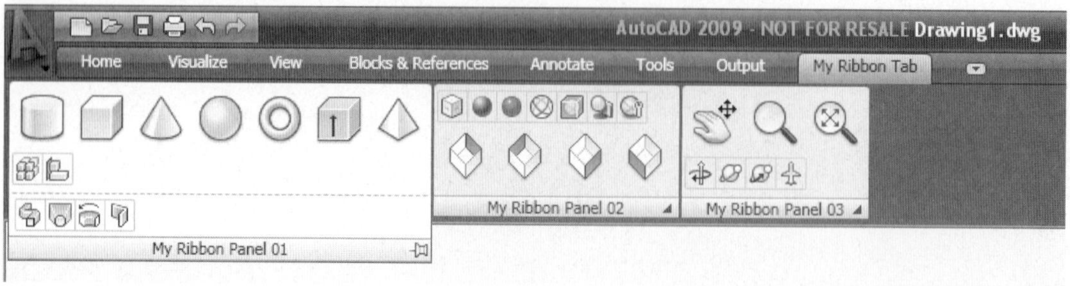

CHAPTER 21

Customizing Tools and Tool Locations

Learning Objectives

After completing this chapter, you will be able to:

- ✓ Explain the features of the **Customize User Interface** dialog box.
- ✓ Describe partial CUI files.
- ✓ Explain the **QUICKCUI** command.
- ✓ Create custom commands.
- ✓ Create new toolbars, ribbon tabs, and ribbon panels.
- ✓ Customize ribbon tabs and panels.
- ✓ Add flyouts to toolbars and ribbon panels.
- ✓ Explain how to customize menus.
- ✓ Add DIESEL expressions to menus.

One of the easiest ways to alter the AutoCAD environment is by customizing interface elements. ***Interface elements*** are graphic command-entry components of AutoCAD, such as toolbars, menus, and the ribbon. Existing toolbars and menus can be quickly modified by removing and adding commands. The panels and tabs in the ribbon can also be quickly modified. New commands can also be created and assigned to an existing toolbar, menu, or ribbon panel. The most powerful aspect of customizing toolbars, menus, and ribbon panels is the ability to quickly create entirely new functions to help you in your work. The key to good customization can be broken down into four simple rules:

- Always make a backup of the original files, such as the acad.cui file, *before* customizing.
- Do not over customize your work. Plan your customization in steps to minimize confusion and maximize productivity.
- It is best to locate customized files in folders other than the default AutoCAD folders. This makes it easier to upgrade AutoCAD in the future.
- Thoroughly test your customizations before implementing them. This will save many headaches for you and the end user.

Customize User Interface Dialog Box

The **Customize User Interface** dialog box funnels all major graphical user interface elements of AutoCAD into one central area where they can be tailored for productivity, **Figure 21-1.** All AutoCAD commands are linked for customization. The interface elements that will be discussed in this chapter are the ribbon tabs and panels, toolbars, and menus (located in the menu browser and menu bar).

CUI

Ribbon
Tools > Customization
User Interface
Type
CUI
Menu
Tools > Customize > Interface...

The **CUI** command displays the **Customize User Interface** dialog box. This can also be displayed by right-clicking on the ribbon or a toolbar and picking **Customize...** from the shortcut menu. The changes made in the **Customize User Interface** dialog box are saved in a customization file (CUI). By default, this is the acad.cui file.

The upper-left pane of the **Customize User Interface** dialog box is initially labeled **Customizations in All CUI Files**. The drop-down list located below the pane name contains the name of the main CUI file and any other currently loaded partial CUI files. Partial CUI files are discussed later. By default, the main file acad.cui and partial CUI files custom.cui, acimpression.cui, contentsearch.cui, and acetmain.cui files are installed. If you select a different entry from the drop-down list, the name of the pane changes to reflect the selection, either **All Customization Files** or **Main CUI File**.

By default, the customization file acad.cui is the main CUI file. In the box located below the drop-down list, the selected CUI file is displayed in a tree. The top level of the tree is the ACAD branch, which is the name of the selected customization file, and the AutoCAD logo icon is shown next to it. The tree under the ACAD branch lists the various customizable items. For example, to see the list of available toolbars, expand the Toolbars branch, or node, by picking the plus sign located just to its left. Any other partially loaded CUI files that have toolbars in them will be listed under the Partial CUI Files branch in the tree and can have their toolbar list similarly expanded.

The shortcut menus displayed in the **Customize User Interface** dialog box provide editing options based on the branch or item selected. Options are available for creating

Figure 21-1.
The **Customize User Interface** dialog box is used to edit existing interface elements, create new interface elements, create custom commands, and create command icons.

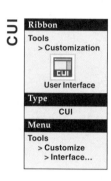

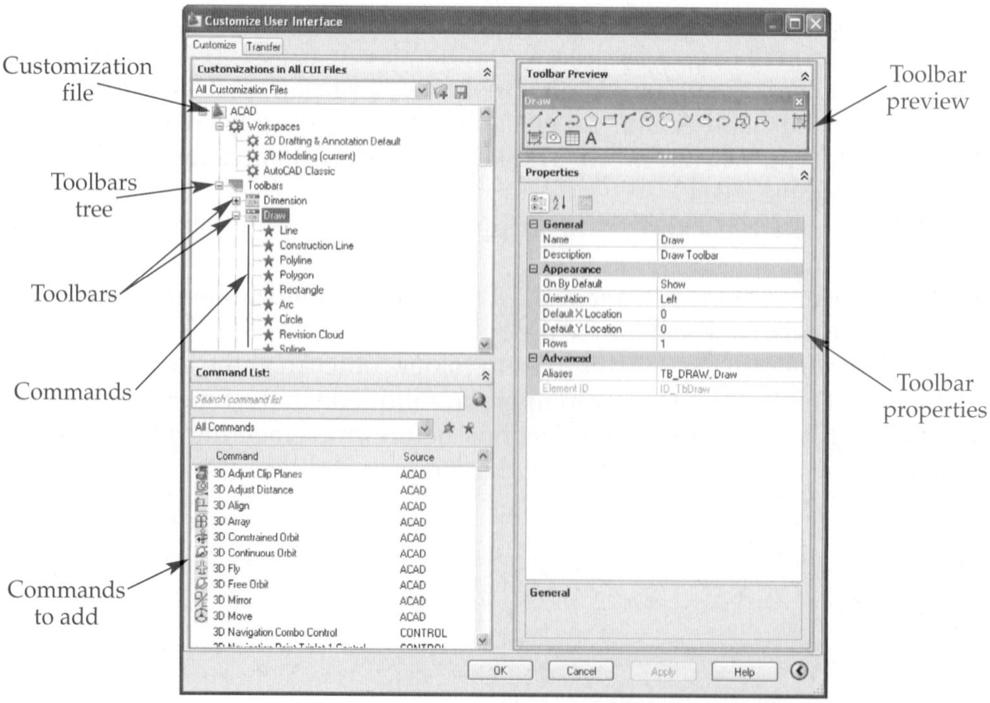

new items; renaming, deleting, copying/pasting, and duplicating items; adding menus or submenus; and inserting separators. For example, to delete a ribbon panel from the interface, select it in the Ribbon Panels branch, right-click, and pick **Delete** from the shortcut menu. When prompted, pick the **Yes** button to delete the item. Then, pick the **Apply** or **OK** button in the **Customize User Interface** dialog box to make the deletion permanent. However, a better method is to remove a ribbon panel from the workspace. This way, the ribbon panel is still available to other workspaces. Refer to Chapter 24 for complete details on workspaces.

To rename content, such as a toolbar, select the toolbar in the Toolbars branch, right-click, and pick **Rename** from the shortcut menu. The existing name of the toolbar in the tree turns into an edit box with the current name highlighted. Type a new name in the edit box and press [Enter]. The new toolbar name is displayed in the tree. You can also rename content by editing the Name property in the **Properties** pane on the right-hand side of the dialog box. Pick the **Apply** or **OK** button in the **Customize User Interface** dialog box to make the change permanent.

You can modify all existing content by deleting and adding commands. The **Command List:** pane of the **Customize User Interface** dialog box contains all commands, including those that are not installed by default. Custom commands can be assigned to all content, such as ribbons, toolbars, and menus.

The right-hand side of the **Customize User Interface** dialog box displays specific information of the highlighted content. Panes that will appear are **Information**, **Preview**, and **Properties**, depending on the selected content. It is easy to read and navigate the **Customize User Interface** dialog box by remembering the general information is stored in the upper-left pane, proceeding down to the **Command List:** pane and over to the panes on the right-hand side of the dialog box for more specific information.

NOTE

All changes made in the **Customize User Interface** dialog box are saved in the CUI file, including workspace, ribbon, toolbar, menu, and shortcut key customizations. Customizing the ribbon, toolbars, and menus is discussed later in this chapter. Customizing shortcut keys is discussed in Chapter 22. Customizing workspaces and the **Quick Access** toolbar is covered in Chapter 24.

Adding a Command to an Interface Element

All commands are available in the **Command List:** pane of the **Customize User Interface** dialog box. Included are many commands not found on the default ribbon, toolbars, or menus. Any custom commands you have created are also available in this pane.

To add a command to any interface element, first expand the tree for the element in the **Customizations in All CUI Files** pane. For example, to add a command to a toolbar, expand the Toolbars branch. Select the specific element, such as a toolbar, to which you want the command added. Then, select a command from the **Command List:** pane. The list is alphabetized. If you hover the cursor over a command, the macro or command is displayed in a tooltip. See **Figure 21-2.**

You can search the command list by picking the **Find command or text** button at the top of the **Command List:** pane. The drop-down list at the top of the pane can be used to filter the list so that only commands in a certain category appear in the list. You can also filter the list by typing in the text box at the top of the pane. Only those commands containing the characters in this text box are displayed in the list.

Figure 21-2.
The **Commands List:** pane of the **Customize User Interface** dialog box displays all predefined and custom commands. These commands can be added to interface elements.

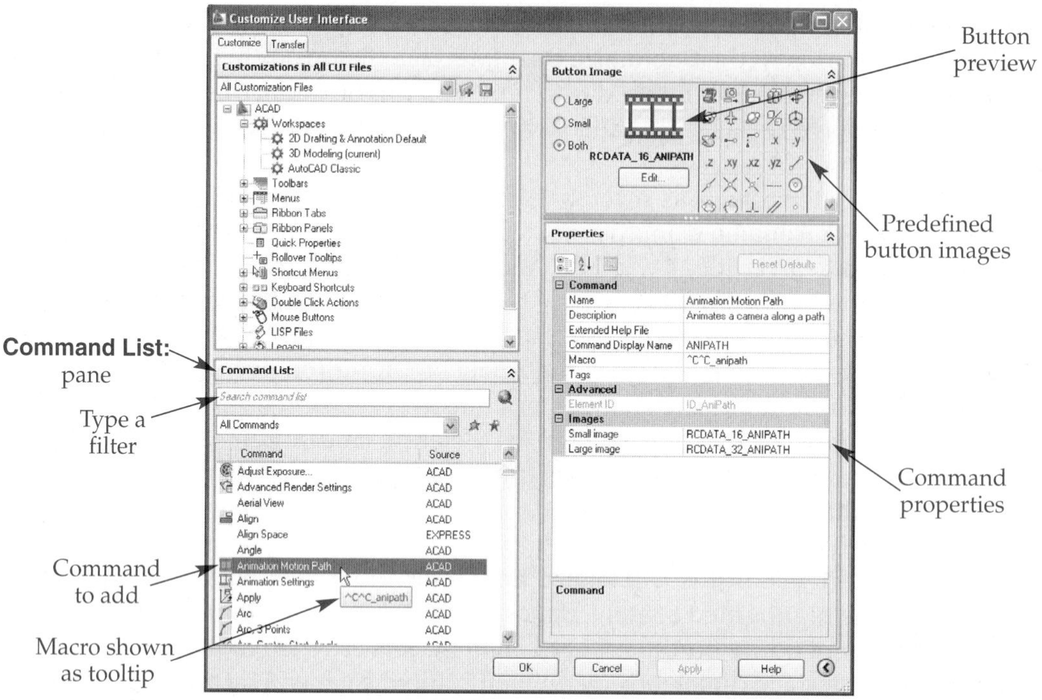

Once the command is located, pick and hold on the command in the **Command List:** pane and drag it into the **Customizations in All CUI Files** pane. A horizontal "I-bar" appears in the pane as you drag the command. This represents the location where the command will be inserted. Position the new command between the commands where you would like it to appear and release the left mouse button. The new command is added to the branch for the interface element. Pick the **Apply** or **OK** button in the **Customize User Interface** dialog box to make the addition permanent.

NOTE

Selecting the **Cancel** button in the **Customize User Interface** dialog box after selecting the **Apply** button does *not* cancel the changes made before the **Apply** button was selected.

Deleting a Command from an Interface Element

To delete a command from an interface element, expand the tree for the element in the **Customizations in All CUI Files** pane. You may need to expand more than one level to see the command you wish to delete. All of the commands currently on the interface element are displayed as branches below the element name.

Select the command you wish to delete, right-click, and pick **Remove** from the shortcut menu. You can also select the command and press the [Delete] key. Pick the **Apply** or **OK** button in the **Customize User Interface** dialog box to make the deletion permanent. The command is, however, still available in the **Command List:** pane of the **Customize User Interface** dialog box.

Moving and Copying Commands

You can move and copy commands between any interface element. First, in the upper-left pane of the **Customize User Interface** dialog box, expand the tree for both elements that you wish edit. To move a command from one element to another, pick and hold on the command and drag it to the other toolbar. The horizontal "I-bar" cursor appears as you drag. Position the cursor between the commands where you want the new command to appear and release the left mouse button. The command is moved from the first element to the second.

Use this same process to copy a command between elements, but hold the [Ctrl] key before you release the left mouse button. The command remains on the first element and a copy is placed on the second element.

You can also drag commands from the **Customize User Interface** dialog box and drop them onto toolbars and tool palettes that are currently displayed in the AutoCAD window. A command can be removed from a displayed toolbar while the **Customize User Interface** dialog box is open by dragging it from the toolbar into the drawing area and releasing. A message appears asking if you want to remove the button. Pick **OK** to remove the button. Buttons can also be rearranged on displayed toolbars while the **Customize User Interface** dialog box is open by simply dragging a button to a new position. However, it is recommended that you use the **Customize User Interface** dialog box to make edits to toolbars until you are completely comfortable with the drag-and-drop method.

PROFESSIONAL TIP

When dragging a command to a tool palette, if the desired palette is not current (on top), simply pause the cursor over the palette name until the palette is made current. Tool palette customization is discussed in detail in Chapter 23.

Adding a Separator to an Interface Element

A ***separator*** is a vertical or horizontal line that can be used in toolbars and menus to create visual groupings of related commands. On ribbon panels, a separator is a gap between tools. For example, look at the **Draw** panel in the **Home** tab of the ribbon with the 3D Modeling workspace set current. Between the **Helix** button and the **Ellipse** flyout there is a gap between the two indicating a separator. There is also a separator between the **Hatch** button and the **Circle** flyout. These separators are vertical gaps because the ribbon is docked along the top edge. If the ribbon is docked along the left or right side of the screen, the separators will be horizontal gaps. Likewise, if a toolbar is horizontal, the separator is a vertical line. If a toolbar is vertical, the separator is a horizontal line.

A ribbon panel can also have a ***panel separator.*** The commands in the tree below the panel separator appear in the expanded panel. For example, the **Draw** panel in the **Home** tab of the ribbon has a panel separator below the row of buttons containing the **Spline** and **Polygon** buttons. The panel separator is automatically added to all panels.

You can add separators to an interface element. First, open the **Customize User Interface** dialog box. Then, in the **Customizations in All CUI Files** pane, expand the branch for the element to which you want separators added.

For a toolbar or menu, right-click on the command in the tree below which you want the separator added. Select **Insert Separator** from the shortcut menu. A separator, represented by two dashes, appears in the tree below the selected command.

For a ribbon panel, right-click on the row in the panel to which you want a separator added. Then, select **Add Separator** from the shortcut menu. A separator is added to the bottom of the row's branch.

Once a separator is added, it can be dragged to a new location in the tree. When done adding and moving separators, pick the **OK** button to close the **Customize User Interface** dialog box.

NOTE

A separator can be removed from an interface element in the same manner as removing a command.

Partial CUI Files

A ***partial CUI file*** is any CUI file that is not the main CUI file. To load a partial CUI file, pick the Open... entry in the drop-down list in the **Customizations in All CUI Files** pane. Remember, the name of this pane may be different, depending on what is currently selected in the drop-down list. You can also pick the **Load partial customization file** button to the right of the drop-down list. Next, in the **Open** dialog box that is displayed, navigate to the folder where the CUI file is located, select the file, and pick the **Open** button. If the partial CUI file that has been opened contains any workspaces, the AutoCAD alert shown in **Figure 21-3** is displayed. Any workspace information contained in the CUI file is not automatically available. Workspaces are covered in Chapter 24.

Once you open the CUI file, it is automatically selected in the drop-down list. The name of the pane changes to **Customizations in Main CUI**. Now, you can manage the items contained within the partial CUI.

If you select either the main CUI or All Customization Files in the drop-down list, the Partial CUI Files branch appears in the tree. Expanding this branch, you can see the partial CUI files that are loaded. Expanding the branch for a partial CUI file, you can see the items contained within the CUI file. These items can be copied from the partial CUI file to the main CUI file as needed.

To unload a partial CUI file, select All Customization Files in the drop-down list in the "customizations" pane. Then, expand the Partial CUI Files branch, right-click on the name of the CUI file, and select **Unload CUI File** from the shortcut menu. You can also unload a partial CUI file by typing MENULOAD or MENUUNLOAD at the Command: prompt. Then, in the **Load/Unload Customizations** dialog box, select the CUI file to unload and pick the **Unload** button.

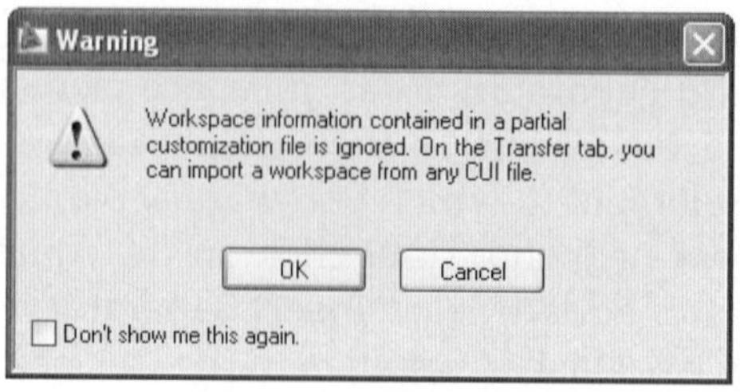

Figure 21-3.
This warning appears when loading a partial CUI file that contains workspaces. Workspaces are covered in Chapter 24.

QUICKCUI

Type
QUICKCUI

QUICKCUI

The **QUICKCUI** command opens a condensed version of the **Customize User Interface** dialog box. See Figure 21-4. The **Command List:** pane is the only visible pane. The "customizations" pane is shown minimized. The right-hand side of the dialog box is not visible, but can be displayed by picking the "expand" button at the lower-right corner. This simplified dialog can be accessed by typing QUICKCUI, right-clicking on a toolbar button and selecting **Customize...** from the shortcut menu, or right-clicking on the title bar or a blank area of the tool palette and selecting **Customize Commands...** from the shortcut menu.

The condensed dialog box allows you to more quickly perform drag-and-drop customizations. As discussed earlier, drag-and-drop operations can be done while the **Customize User Interface** dialog box is expanded. However, the expanded dialog box takes up most of the screen. The condensed version takes up less screen space, making more of the AutoCAD graphics area accessible. An advantage of the expanded **Customize User Interface** dialog box is that you can do drag-and-drop customization within the dialog box.

NOTE

Modifications made to interface elements are unaffected by the **UNDO** command. For example, if you add a panel to the ribbon, you cannot use **UNDO** to remove the panel. You have to use the **Customize User Interface** dialog box to remove the panel.

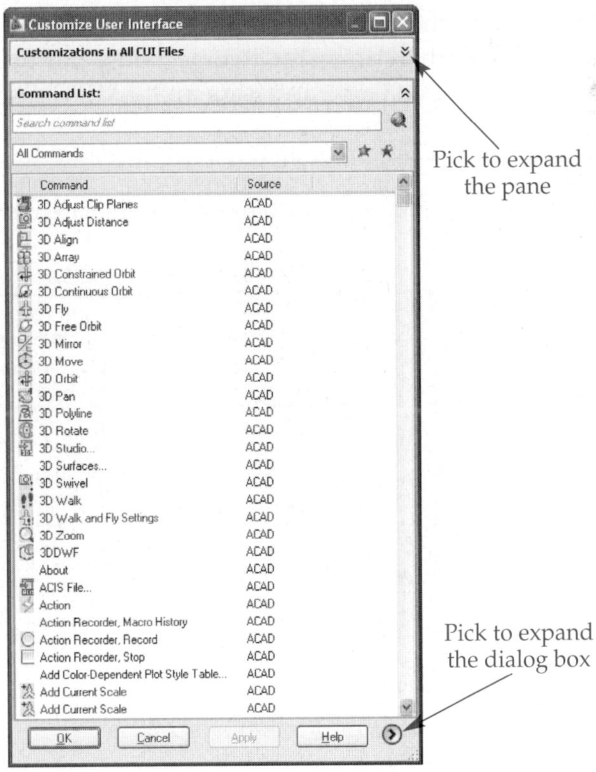

Figure 21-4.
The **QUICKCUI** command displays a condensed version of the **Customize User Interface** dialog box.

Creating New Commands

You are not limited to AutoCAD's predefined commands. ***Custom commands*** can be created and then added to ribbon panels, menus, tool palettes, and toolbars. First, however, you must create the new, custom command. To create a custom command, first pick the **Create a new command** button in the **Command List:** pane of the **Customize User Interface** dialog box. This button is to the right of the drop-down list. A new command is added to the list in the **Command List:** pane. Also, the **Button Image** and **Properties** panes are displayed for the new command. See **Figure 21-5.**

General Command Properties

By default, the new command name is **Command***n*, where *n* is a sequential number based on the number of new commands that have been added in this dialog box session. To give the command a descriptive name, highlight the command in the **Command List:** pane. Then, pick in the Name property edit box in the **Command** category of the **Properties** pane. Then, type the new name and press [Enter]. This property is displayed as the command name on the status bar and in the tooltip. The name should be logical and short, such as **Draw Box**. The entry in the Command Display Name property is what appears in the command-line section of the tooltip.

The text that appears in the Description property text box in the **Command** category of the **Properties** pane appears on the AutoCAD status line when the cursor is over the button. This text, called the ***help string***, should also be logical, but can be longer and more descriptive than the command name.

The Extended Help File property is used to specify an Extensible Application Markup Language (XAML) file to use as extended help. The ***extended help*** is displayed in the tooltip when the cursor is paused over a tool for a longer period of time. By default, if you pause the cursor for two seconds, the extended help is displayed (if the tool contains extended help). To assign an XAML file, select the property and pick the ellipsis

Figure 21-5.
The first step in adding a custom command to an interface element is to create the custom command.

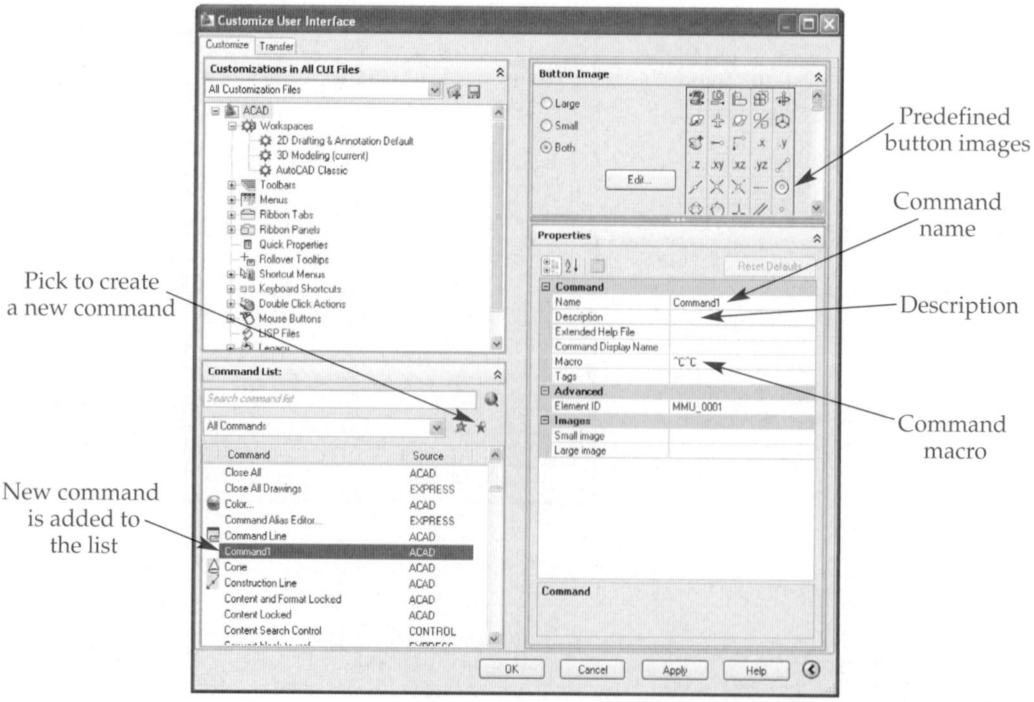

button (...) on the right-hand side of the text box. Then, in the standard open dialog box that appears, locate and open the file. For information on creating XAML files, search the Internet for resources. Many resources can be found on the Microsoft website.

Tags are used to filter commands when searching in the menu browser. The tag is what you enter in the search box in the menu browser. The tag is also displayed in the tooltip for the command. To add a tag, select the Tags property and pick the ellipsis button (...) on the right-hand side of the text box to display the **Tag Editor** dialog box, **Figure 21-6.** Then, type the tag for the command. Multiple tags can be entered by separating each with a comma. When you close the **Tag Editor** dialog box, the tag is displayed in the Tags property.

As an example, you will create a command that draws a rectangular border for an E-size sheet (44″ × 34″) using a wide polyline, sets the drawing limits, and finishes with **ZOOM Extents**. To start, create a new command and enter **E-Border** as the name. Also, enter Draws E-size border, sets limits, and zooms extents. for the Description property. In the Command Display Name property, enter Draw Border. Also, assign the tag BORDER to the command. See **Figure 21-7.** In the next sections, you will complete the command and its associated image.

Button Image

The **Button Image** pane in the **Customize User Interface** dialog box is used to define the image that appears on the command button. The image should graphically represent the function of the command. You can select one of the predefined images from the list. You can also right-click on the list of images and select **Import Image...** from the shortcut menu to import an image.

Figure 21-6.
Adding a tag to a custom command. The tag is used when searching the menu browser.

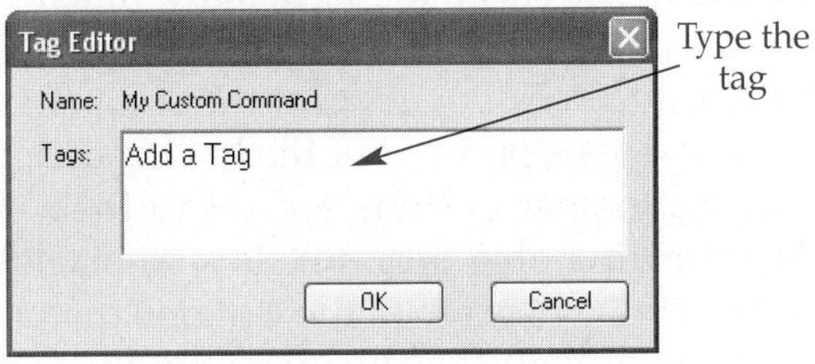

Figure 21-7.
The custom command is named and a help string and tag are assigned to it.

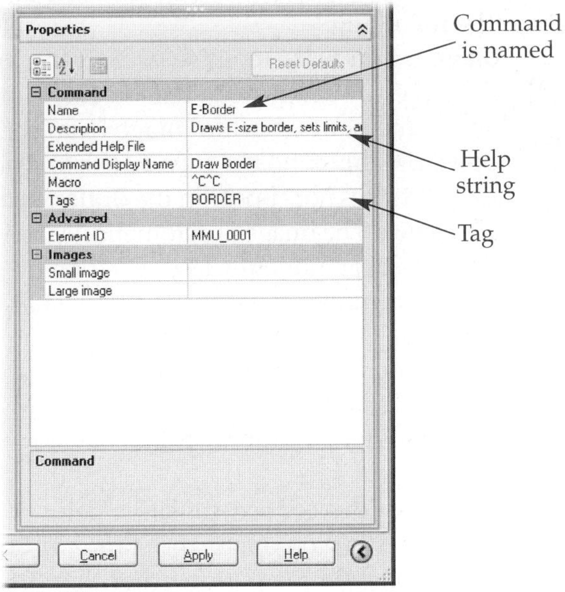

A different image can be selected for large and small buttons or you can use the same image for both button sizes. It may be a good idea for a button to have a separate image for each of the two button sizes. Pick the appropriate radio button in the pane and select an image. The name of the image appears in the **Images** category in the **Properties** pane. The small image also appears next to the command name in the **Command List:** pane.

However, confusion may arise if your custom command has the same button image as an existing AutoCAD command. It is best to create custom button images for use with your custom commands. You can either modify an existing button image or create a new image from scratch. In either case, a predefined image must be selected from the list of existing images. Then, pick the **Edit...** button in the **Button Image** pane to open the **Button Editor** dialog box. This is described in the next section.

NOTE

If you use the same image for both small and large buttons, the image is appropriately scaled as needed.

Creating a custom button image

The **Button Editor** dialog box has basic "pixel-painting" tools and several features to simplify the editing process. The four tools are shown as buttons at the top of the dialog box. The pencil paints individual pixels. The line tool allows you to draw a line between two points. The circle tool allows you to draw center/radius style ellipses and circles. The erase tool clears the color from individual pixels. The current color is selected from the color palette on the right-hand side of the dialog box and indicated by a depressed color button. Anything you draw appears in the current color.

Drawing a button image is usually much easier with the grid turned on. The grid provides outlines for each pixel in the graphic. Each square represents one pixel. Picking the **Grid** check box toggles the state of the grid. The area just above the **Grid** check box provides a preview of the button image while you draw the image.

When the toolbar buttons are set to their default, small size, the button editor provides a drawing area of 16 pixels × 16 pixels. If **Use large buttons for Toolbars** is turned on in the **Display** tab of the **Options** dialog box, then the button image drawing area is 32 pixels × 32 pixels. The images in the **Customize User Interface** dialog box are displayed at the current size setting (small or large).

There are several other tools available in the **Button Editor** dialog box. These include the following.

- **Clear.** If you want to erase everything and start over, pick the **Clear** button to clear the drawing area. This is the button you will use to clear the existing image and start a button image from scratch.
- **Open.** Use this button to open an existing bitmap (BMP) file, up to 380 × 380 pixels in size, that does not appear in the **Button Image** pane of the **Customize User Interface** dialog box. The image is automatically resized to fit the current button size.
- **Undo.** You can undo the last operation by picking this button. Only the last operation can be undone. An operation that has been undone cannot be redone.
- **Save As.** This button saves a file using a standard save dialog box. Use this when you do not want to alter the original button image.
- **Save.** Saves the current bitmap file.
- **Close.** Ends the **Button Editor** session. A message is displayed if you have unsaved changes.
- **Help.** Provides context-sensitive help.
- **More.** This button opens the standard **Select Color** dialog box. This allows you to use colors in the button other than those in the default color palette.

Once a button image is saved, it appears in the list of predefined images in the **Button Image** pane of the **Customize User Interface** dialog box. All images saved for use as button images must be stored where AutoCAD will find them. AutoCAD provides the \Icons folder within the user's support file search path. This is the default folder when using the **Save as...** button in the **Button Editor** dialog box. If you choose to use a different folder, it must be added to the support file search path, which is specified in the **Files** tab of the **Options** dialog box.

Rather than using an existing button image for the **E-Border** command, an entirely new button image will be created. With **E-Border** highlighted in the **Command List:** pane, select any one of the images in the **Button Image** pane and pick the **Edit...** button. The **Button Editor** dialog box is displayed. Now, select the **Clear** button to completely remove the existing image.

Figure 21-8A shows a 16 × 16 pixel image created for the **E-Border** button with the **Grid** option activated. Use the pencil and line tools to create this or a similar image. Save your button image with a name of E-border and store it in an appropriate location. Pick the **Close** button to return to the **Customize User Interface** dialog box. Your newly created image now appears in the list of existing images in the **Button Image** pane, as shown in Figure 21-8B. It is automatically associated with the command.

PROFESSIONAL TIP

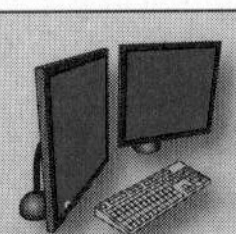

Consider the needs of the persons who will be using your custom commands when you design button images. Simple, abstract designs may be recognizable to you because you created them. However, someone else may not recognize the purpose of the command from the image. For example, the standard buttons in AutoCAD show a graphic that implies something about the command the button executes. A custom command will be most effective if its button image graphically represents the actions the command will perform.

Associating a custom image with a command

There are two ways to associate a new, custom button image with a command. You can use the **Button Image** pane or the **Properties** pane in the **Customize User Interface**

Figure 21-8.
A—A custom button image is created in the **Button Editor** dialog box. B—The new button image has been saved and appears in the list.

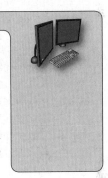

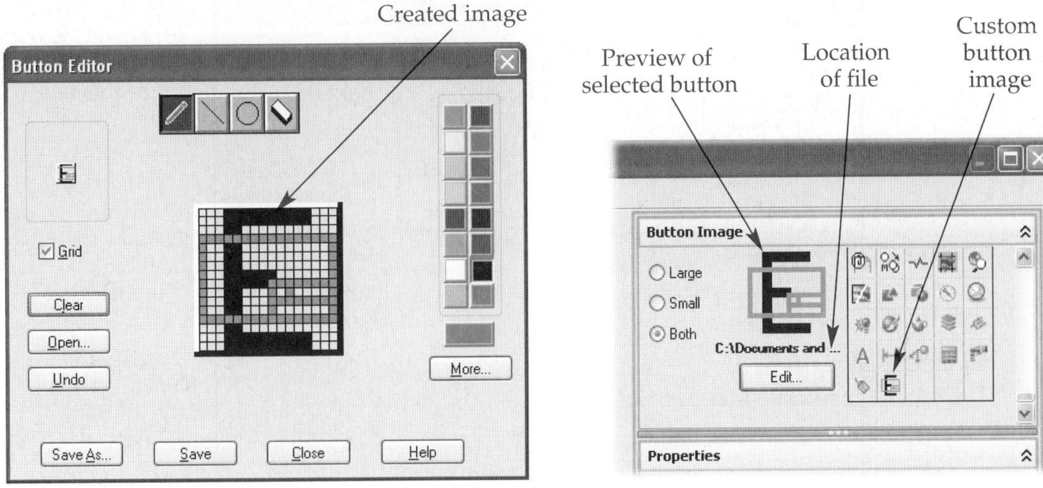

A

B

dialog box. Once a button image is associated with a command, the image is used for that command on *all* ribbon panels, menus, and toolbars where the command is inserted.

To use the **Button Image** pane to assign an image to a command, first make sure the command is selected in the **Command List:** pane. Then, select the **Large**, **Small**, or **Both** radio button in the **Button Image** pane to determine for which size of button the image will be used. Next, pick the button image in the list of predefined button images. Finally, pick the **Apply** button at the bottom of the **Customize User Interface** dialog box to assign the image to the button.

You can also use the **Properties** pane to associate a saved button image file with the command. Make sure the command is selected in the **Command List:** pane. Then, in the **Properties** pane, expand the **Images** category to display the Small image and Large image properties. If there is an image currently associated with the property, the path to the image is displayed in the text box, **Figure 21-9.** Pick in each property text box and type the path and file name of the saved image files. Alternately, you can pick the ellipsis button (**...**) to display a standard open dialog box and locate the file. This button appears when the property is selected. Finally, pick the **Apply** button at the bottom of the **Customize User Interface** dialog box to assign the image(s) to the button.

If you only designate an image file for small buttons, the button for the command will be blank when you switch to large buttons. This is because no image has been designated for that size. Be sure to specify an image for both small and large buttons.

PROFESSIONAL TIP

To open and edit a button image that is not shown in the button image list, select any button image and then pick the **Edit...** button to display the **Button Editor**. Then, use the **Open...** button to open the button image you want to edit. To assign an image that does not appear in the image list, use the **Properties** pane as described above.

Figure 21-9.
The custom button image has been assigned to the custom command.

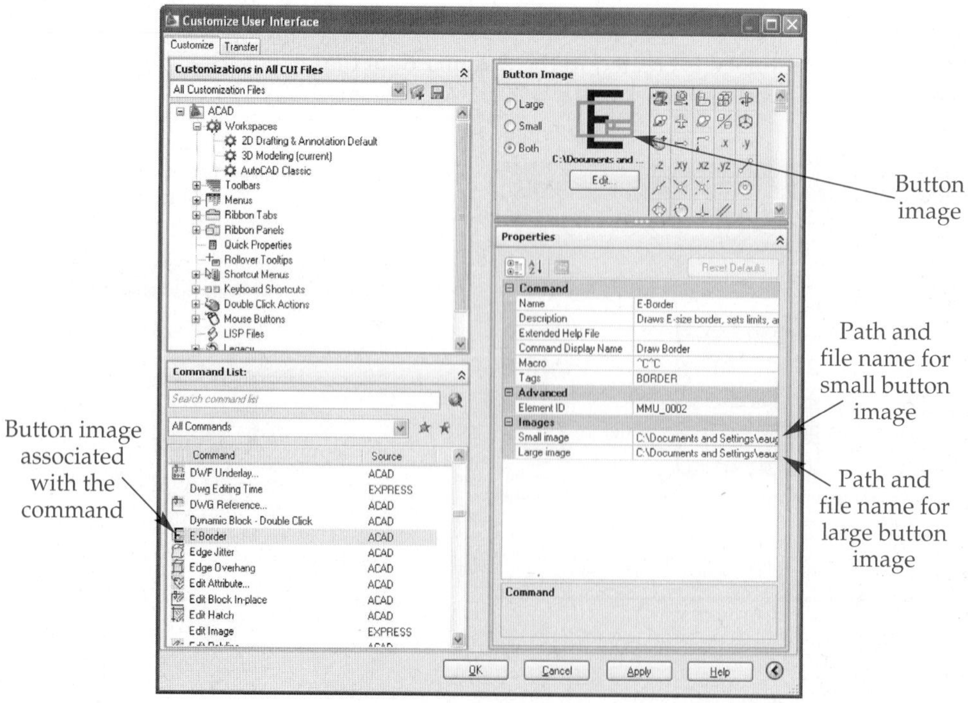

Defining a Custom Command

Now, you need to define the action that the custom command will perform. A text string called a *macro* defines the action performed by the command. This text string appears in the Macro property text box in the **Command** category in the **Properties** pane of the **Customize User Interface** dialog box. In many cases, this "command" is actually a macro that invokes more than one command. By default, the text ^C^C appears in the text box. The text ^C is a cancel command. This is the same as pressing the [Esc] key. The default text, then, represents two cancels.

Two cancels are required to be sure you begin at the Command: prompt. One cancel may not completely exit some commands. In this case, a second cancel is required to fully exit the command. Whenever a command is not required to operate transparently, it is best to begin the macro with two cancel keystrokes (^C^C) to fully exit any current command and return to the Command: prompt.

The macro must perfectly match the requirements of the activated commands. For example, if the **LINE** command is issued, the subsequent prompt expects a coordinate point to be entered. Any other data are inappropriate and will cause an error in the macro. It is best to manually "walk through" the desired macro, writing down each step and the data required by each prompt. The following command sequence creates the rectangular polyline border with a .015 line width.

Command: **PLINE**↵
Specify start point: **1,1**↵
Current line-width is 0.0000
Specify next point or [Arc/Halfwidth/Length/Undo/Width]: **W**↵
Specify starting width <0.0000>: **.015**↵
Specify ending width <0.0150>: ↵
Specify next point or [Arc/Halfwidth/Length/Undo/Width]: **42,1**↵
Specify next point or [Arc/Close/Halfwidth/Length/Undo/Width]: **42,32**↵
Specify next point or [Arc/Close/Halfwidth/Length/Undo/Width]: **1,32**↵
Specify next point or [Arc/Close/Halfwidth/Length/Undo/Width]: **C**↵
Command:

Creating the macro for your custom **E-Border** command involves duplicating these keystrokes, with a couple of differences. Some symbols are used in menu macros to represent keystrokes. For example, a cancel (^C) is not entered by pressing [Esc]. Instead, the [Shift]+[6] key combination is used to place the *caret* symbol, which is used to represent the [Ctrl] key in combination with the subsequent character (a C in this case). Another keystroke represented by a symbol is the [Enter] key. An [Enter] is placed in a macro as a semicolon (;). A space can also be used to designate [Enter]. However, the semicolon is more commonly used because it is very easy to count to make sure that the correct number of "enters" are supplied.

AutoCAD system variables and control characters can be used in menus. They can be included to increase the speed and usefulness of your menu commands. Become familiar with these variables so you can make use of them in your menus.

- **^B.** Snap mode toggle.
- **^C.** Cancel.
- **^D.** Dynamic UCS toggle.
- **^E.** Isoplane crosshair toggle.
- **^G.** Grid mode toggle.
- **^T.** Tablet toggle.
- **^H.** Issues a backspace.
- **^M.** Issues a return.
- **^O.** Ortho mode toggle.
- **^P. MENUECHO** system variable toggle.
- **^Q.** Toggles echoing of prompts, status listings, and input to the printer.

- **^V.** Switches current viewport.
- **^Z.** Suppresses the addition of the automatic [Enter] at the end of a command macro.

Keeping the above guidelines in mind, the following macro draws the polyline border.

```
^C^CPLINE;1,1;W;.015;;42,1;42,32;1,32;C;
```

Compare this with the command line entry example to identify each part of the macro.

The next steps that the command will perform are to set the limits and zoom to display the entire border. To do this at the command line requires the following entries.

Command: **LIMITS↵**
Reset Model space limits:
Specify lower left corner or [ON/OFF] <0.0000,0.0000>: **0,0↵**
Specify upper right corner <12.0000,9.0000>: **44,34↵**
Command: **ZOOM↵**
Specify corner of window, enter a scale factor (nX or nXP), or
[All/Center/Dynamic/Extents/Previous/Scale/Window/Object] <real time>: **E↵** *(this prompt will differ if the current view is perspective, but the entry is the same)*
Command:

Continue to develop the macro by adding the following text string (shown in color) immediately after the previous one.

^C^CPLINE;1,1;W;.015;;42,1;42,32;1,32;C;**LIMITS;0,0;44,34;ZOOM;E**

An "enter" is automatically issued at the end of the macro, so it is not necessary to place a semicolon at the end. The macro for the custom command is now complete.

To assign the macro to your custom **E-Border** command, first make sure the command is selected in the **Command List:** pane of the **Customize User Interface** dialog box. Then, pick in the Macro property text box in the **Properties** pane and enter the complete macro shown above. For a long macro such as this one, you can pick the ellipsis button (...) at the end of the text box to display the **Long String Editor**. See Figure 21-10. Enter the macro in this dialog box and pick the **OK** button to return to the **Customize User Interface** dialog box. Finally, pick the **Apply** button to associate the macro with the custom command.

Exercise 21-1

Complete the exercise on the Student CD.

Figure 21-10.
The **Long String Editor** dialog box can be used to write longer macros. The text string will automatically "wrap" in this dialog box, which does not affect the macro.

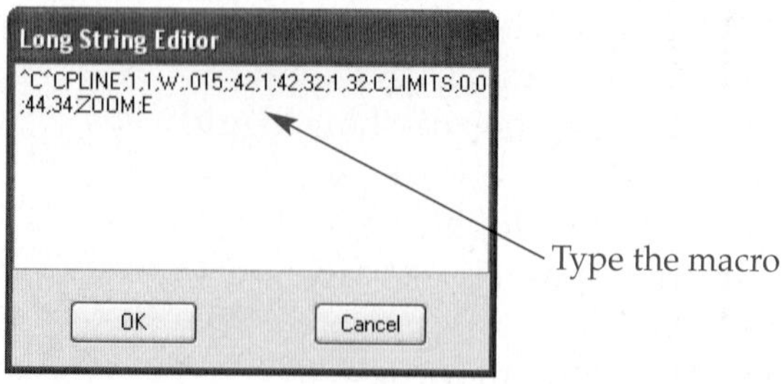

Placing a Custom Command on an Interface Element

The custom command is now fully defined. The macro has been written and associated with the command. A custom button image has also been created and associated with the command. Now, you can add the custom command to a ribbon panel, menu, or toolbar just as you would one of the predefined AutoCAD commands. This is introduced earlier and covered in detail later in this chapter in the specific sections on the ribbon, toolbars, and menus.

After adding the custom command to an interface element, it should be fully functional when you exit the **Customize User Interface** dialog box. Once you close the dialog box, test the command to make sure it works. If it does not, edit the macro in the **Customize User Interface** dialog box as needed.

Overview of the Ribbon

By default, the ribbon is docked at the top of the graphics area. The ribbon can be floating or docked to the left or right as well. The ribbon contains commands and tools on ***panels.*** The panels are grouped on ***tabs*** that can be individually displayed. Think of the tabs as the containers that hold the ribbon panels. Together, the panels and tabs make up the ribbon.

To the right of the last tab name is an arrow icon. This button is used to change the appearance of the docked ribbon. The three options are to show the full ribbon, minimize to panel tiles, or minimize to tabs. When minimized to panel tiles, hover the cursor over a title and the corresponding panel is displayed. When minimized to tabs, pick the tab name and the tab is displayed. See Figure 21-11.

A ribbon panel may contain rows of command buttons, drop-down lists, or sliders. You can choose which panels are visible by right-clicking on the ribbon to display a shortcut menu. See Figure 21-12. Select either **Tabs** or **Panels** and choose which content to display. The currently displayed items are checked in the cascading menus. The items displayed in the **Panels** cascading menu is based on which tab is current (on top). There are separate panels for each tab.

Figure 21-11.
The three display states of the ribbon when it is docked. A—Full. B—Minimized to panel titles. C—Minimized to tabs.

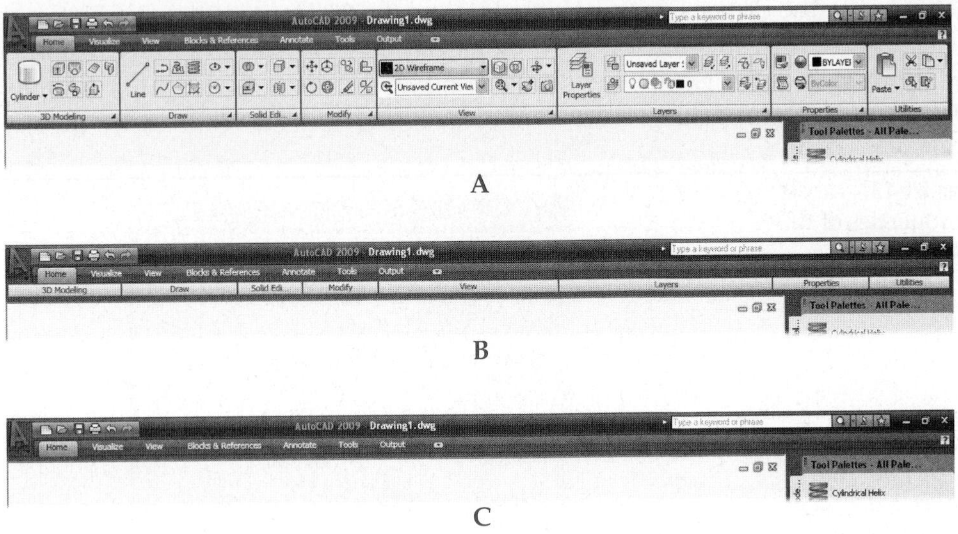

Figure 21-12.
A—The **Tabs** cascading menu is used to choose which tabs are displayed in the ribbon. B—The **Panels** cascading menu is used to choose which panels are displayed in the current tab.

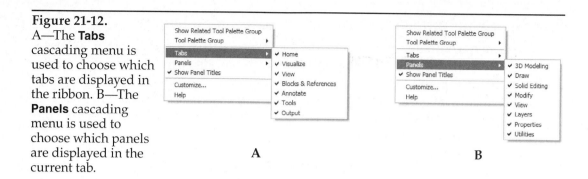

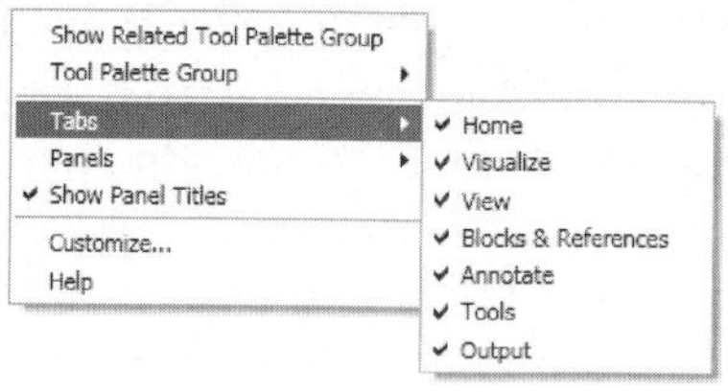

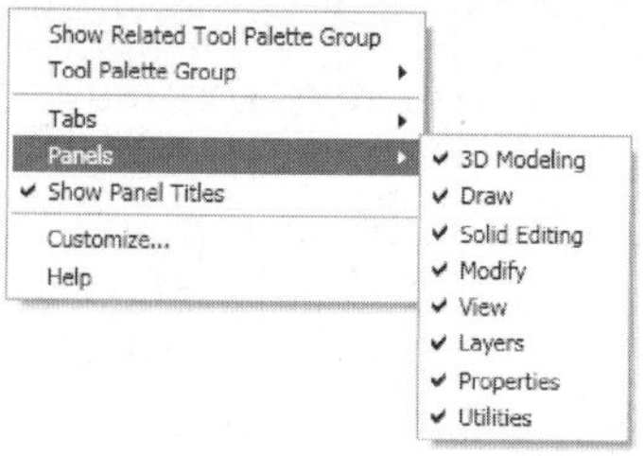

Workspaces are typically used to set which ribbon components are displayed. Chapter 24 discusses customizing workspaces.

Tabs and Panels

The ribbon has two customization areas in the **Customize User Interface** dialog box: the Ribbon Tabs branch and Ribbon Panels branch. Since the tabs contain the panels, they are displayed first in the tree. In this section, you will examine each area to gain a better understanding of the composition of the panels and how panels relate to tabs.

In the **Customizations in All CUI Files** pane, expand the Ribbon Tabs branch. There are 10 default tabs. Some tab names have the suffix 2D or 3D. These help identify the types of commands contained on the tab. They are then included in the appropriate workspace, either 2D Drafting & Annotation or 3D Modeling. For example, select the Home - 3D branch. Notice that the name of this branch does not match the name displayed on the AutoCAD screen. With the branch selected, look at the **Properties** pane, **Figure 21-13.** The name displayed on the AutoCAD screen is the value in Display Text property. The value in the Name property is the actual tab name and what appears in the **Customize User Interface** dialog box.

Expand the Home - 3D branch. It contains eight branches: 3D Modeling, Draw, Solid Editing, Modify - 3D, View, Layers - 3D, Properties - 3D, and Utilities - 3D. These branches correspond to the panels associated with the **Home** tab in the 3D Modeling workspace. Notice that there are no branches below these. The Ribbon Tabs branch contains branches for tabs and, below those, branches for panels. The Ribbon Panels branch contains branches for panels and, below those, branches for the commands on each panel.

Now, expand the Ribbon Panels branch. All of the available panels are shown as branches below the Ribbon Panels branch. Expand the 3D Modeling branch. Notice that it consists of three rows and a panel separator. See **Figure 21-14.** Any row listed after the panel separator is only visible when the ribbon panel is expanded. For the **3D Modeling** panel in the ribbon, rows 2 and 3 are located in the expanded portion of the panel.

Figure 21-13.
The properties of the Home - 3D tab.

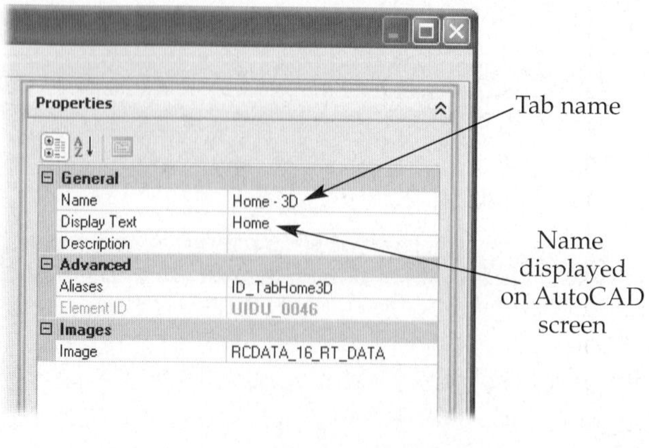

Figure 21-14.
Notice how a ribbon panel is composed in the **Customize User Interface** dialog box.

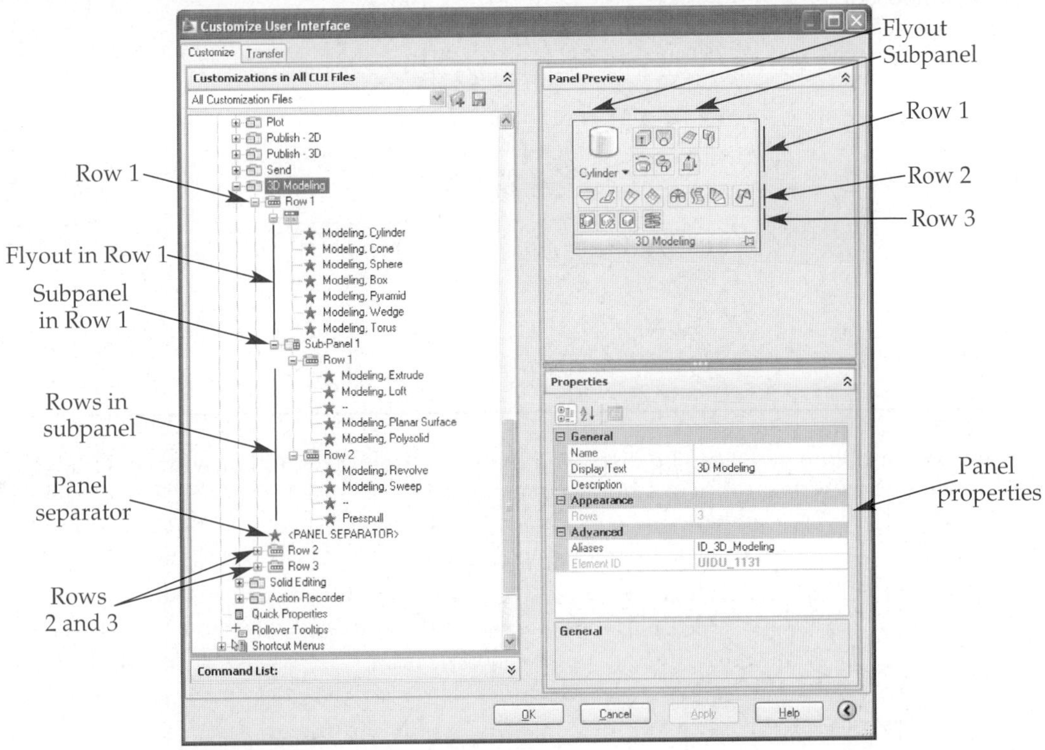

You can expand the branches for the rows in a tab. Notice row 1 contains a flyout and a subpanel. The icon for a flyout looks like a small toolbar. If you expand the branch for the flyout, you can see the commands associated with the flyout. In this case, it contains the solid primitive commands. Next, expand the branch for the subpanel. This subpanel contains two rows. Expanding the branch for each row displays the commands contained in it. Notice how the flyout and subpanel contained in row 1 of the 3D Modeling branch are fitted together in the **3D Modeling** in the ribbon. See **Figure 21-15.**

Expand the branches for rows 2 and 3 for the 3D Modeling branch. Notice these branches contain commands, but no flyouts or subpanels. Also, notice that rows 2 and 3 are below the panel separator. This means they are displayed in the expanded panel. Refer to **Figure 21-15.**

Button Properties

In the ribbon, command buttons have additional properties from the basic command properties. These are located in the **Appearance** section of the **Properties** pane.

Buttons may be displayed in one of three default sizes: standard, medium, or large. The size is set in the **Customize User Interface** dialog box. The size setting is actually the maximum display size for the button. When the subpanel is set to do so, AutoCAD adjusts the button size smaller as needed based on the space available for the ribbon.

To set the size of a command button, expand the Ribbon Panels branch in the **Customizations in All CUI Files** pane. Then, expand the branches for the panel and row that contain the command. Next, select the command in the **Customizations in All CUI Files** pane. If the panel branch is currently selected, you can also simply pick the button in the **Panel Preview** pane. Finally, set the Size property in the **Appearance** section of the **Properties** pane. See **Figure 21-16.**

You can set whether or not a label is displayed on the button. In the **Appearance** section, set the Show Label property to either Yes or No. Generally, labels are not shown on small- and medium-size buttons.

Figure 21-15.
Notice how a ribbon panel is composed.

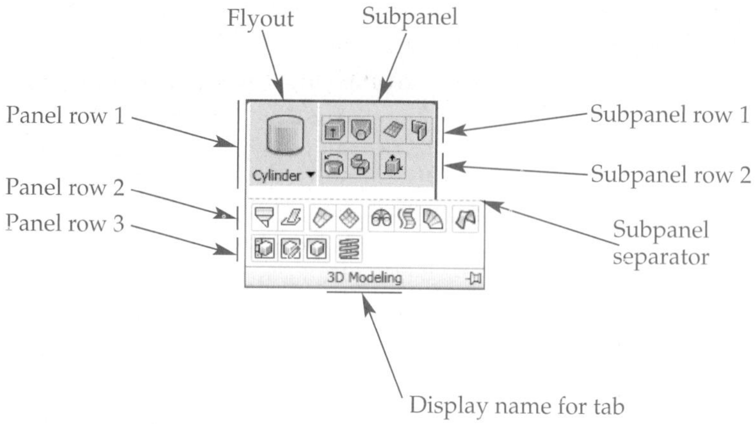

Figure 21-16.
A—Buttons in a ribbon panel can be displayed in one of three sizes, either with or without a label. B—Setting the appearance of a button in a panel.

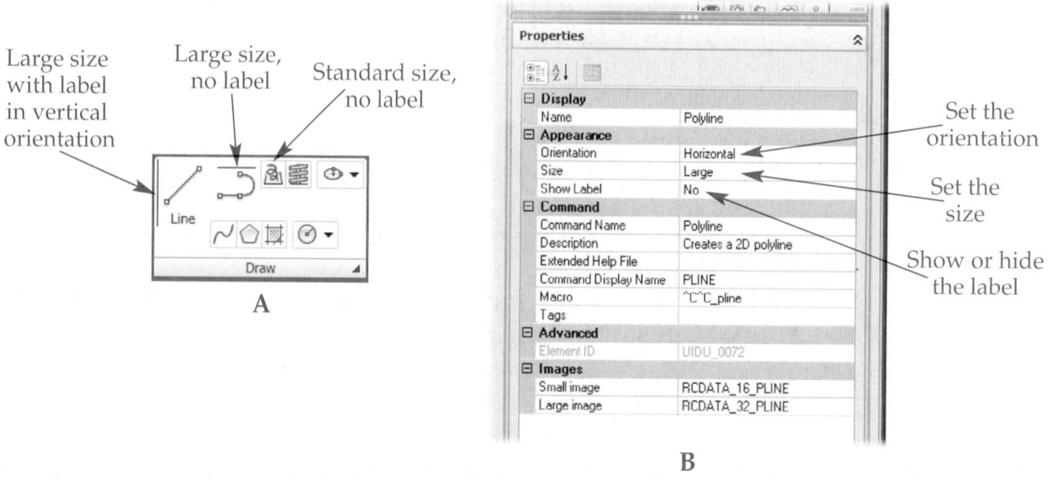

When a label is displayed, it can be either below or to the side of the button. This is referred to as the *orientation*. In a vertical orientation, the label is below the button. In a horizontal orientation, the label is to the side of the button. To set the orientation, select either Horizontal or Vertical for the Orientation property in the **Appearance** section.

PROFESSIONAL TIP

To set a subpanel to collapse large buttons, select the subpanel in the **Customizations in All CUI Files** pane, then change the Collapse large images property in the **Properties** pane to Yes. Only subpanels have this property.

Customizing a Panel

To add a command to a panel, open the **Customize User Interface** dialog box. In the **Customizations in All CUI Files** pane, expand the Ribbon Panels branch. Then, expand the branches for the panel and row to which the command will be added. In the **Commands List:** pane, locate the command to add to the panel. Drag the command from the **Commands List:** pane and drop it into position in the tree in the **Customizations in All CUI Files** pane.

To remove a command from a panel, right-click on the command in the panel's branch in the **Customizations in All CUI Files** pane and select **Remove** from the shortcut menu. You can also select the command and press the [Delete] key. There is no warning in either case; the command is simply removed.

Row 1 is the top of the panel. In addition, the top of a row branch is the left-hand side of the panel. Commands are displayed in this order on the panel. The commands in a panel can be rearranged. In the **Customizations in All CUI Files** pane, select the command to move and drag it to a new location, either within its current row or in a different row. Rows can also be rearranged by dragging them within the tree in the **Customization in All CUI Files** pane. After you drag a row to a new location, all rows are automatically renumbered. The row at the top of the panel branch is always row 1 and all other rows are sequentially numbered. The panel separator can also be dragged to a new location. Remember, rows listed after the panel separator are not displayed until the panel is expanded.

A new row can be added to a panel. In the **Customizations in All CUI Files** pane, right-click on the row *after* which you would like the new row added. To add a new first row, right-click on the panel branch name. Then, select **New Row** from the shortcut menu. The new row is added and all other rows are renumbered. Once a row is added, commands can be added to it.

NOTE

There are certain conditions in which rows in a panel cannot be rearranged. If you attempt to drag a row to a different location and you cannot, just realize you have encountered one of these situations.

Creating a New Tab or Panel

To create a new panel, open the **Customize User Interface** dialog box. Then, in the **Customizations in All CUI Files** pane, right-click on the Ribbon Panels branch and select **New Panel** from the shortcut menu. A new panel with the default name of Panel*x* is added to the bottom of the Ribbon Panels branch. The name appears in a text box in the tree. Enter a name for the new control panel, either in the tree or in the **Properties** pane. Expand the branch for the new panel and notice that Row 1 and the <Panel Separator> branches are automatically added when the panel is created. Add commands and rows to the new panel as needed. A new tab is similarly created by right-clicking on the Ribbon Tabs branch.

For example, you will now create a new ribbon panel containing the custom command you created earlier. First, create a new panel and name it My Panel. Then, in the **Command List:** pane, locate the **E-Border** command. Drag the command into the tree in the **Customizations in All CUI Files** panel. The I-bar cursor appears as you drag through the tree. When the I-bar is below the Row 1 branch, drop the command. See **Figure 21-17.**

Now, create a new tab to hold the new panel. Name the tab My Stuff. In the **Properties** pane for the new tab, change the Display Text property to Border Tools. Next, locate the My Panel branch and drag it into the My Stuff branch. As you drag, the same I-bar appears in the tree. When the I-bar is below the My Stuff branch, release the mouse button.

Close the **Customize User Interface** dialog box. After the menu compiles, the new tab is displayed in the ribbon, **Figure 21-18.** It is located on the right-hand side of the ribbon. Test the **E-Border** button on the panel to make sure the command properly functions.

Figure 21-17.
Adding a command to a custom ribbon panel.

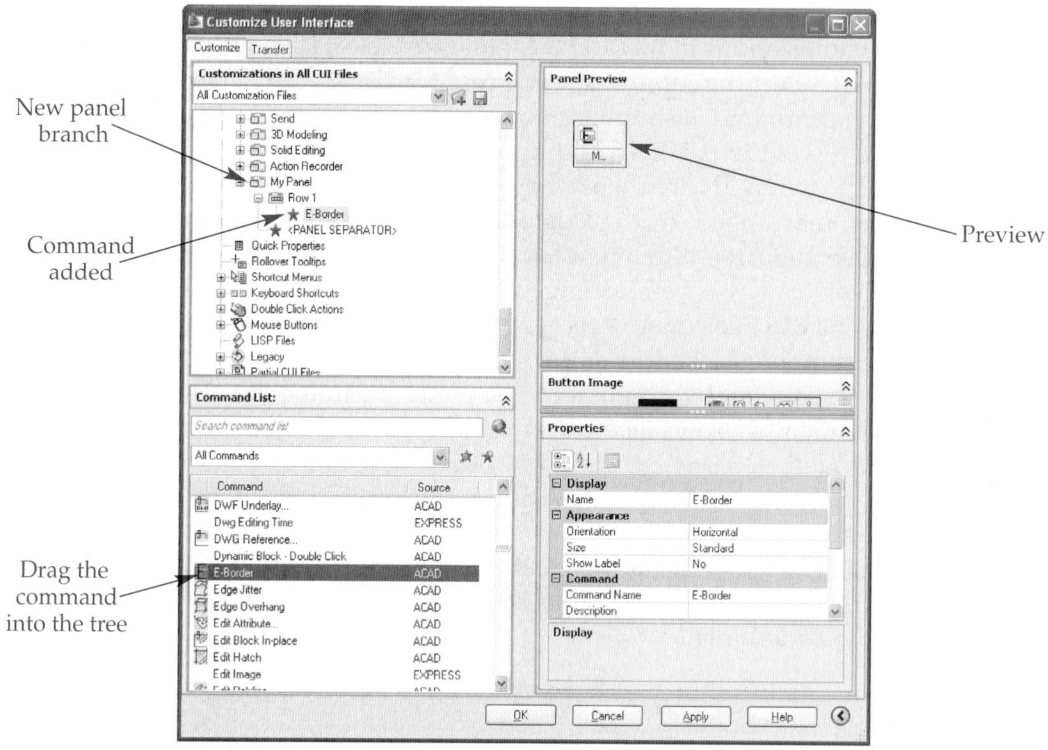

Figure 21-18.
A custom tab, panel, and command have been added to the ribbon. Notice the display name for the tab matches the **Display Text** property for the tab.

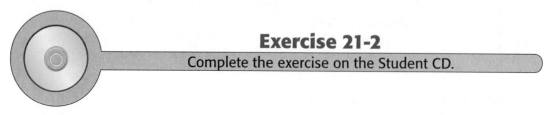

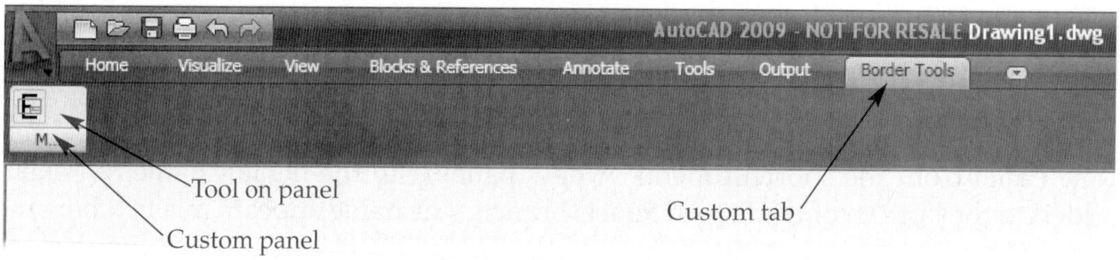

Associating a Tool Palette Group with a Ribbon Panel

A tool palette group can be associated with a panel in the ribbon. Then, the associated tool palette group is displayed in the **Tool Palettes** window when you right-click on the panel and select **Show Related Tool Palette Group** from the shortcut menu.

To associate a tool palette group with a panel, right-click on the panel in the ribbon. This is done with the **Customize User Interface** dialog box closed. Next, select **Tool Palette Group** in the shortcut menu and then the name of the group in the cascading menu. See **Figure 21-19.** You can now right-click on the panel and select **Show Related Tool Palette Group** from the shortcut menu. The tool palette group you associated with the panel is displayed in the **Tool Palettes** window.

Exercise 21-2
Complete the exercise on the Student CD.

Figure 21-19.
Associating a tool palette with a ribbon panel.

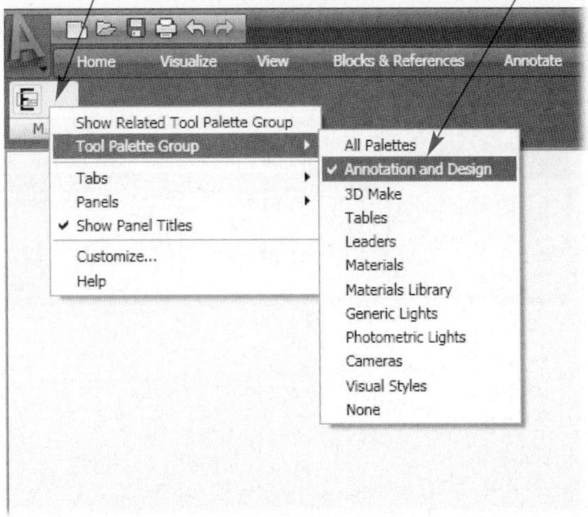

Overview of Toolbars

Although the ribbon is the primary graphic interface for accessing the main AutoCAD commands, ***toolbars*** can also provide quick access to many AutoCAD commands with one or two quick "picks." This interface provides additional flexibility, especially considering toolbars are a fraction of the size of the full ribbon. Toolbars can be quickly and easily resized, repositioned, hidden from view, or made visible. Toolbars are moved, resized, docked, and floated in the same way as in all Windows-compatible software.

In addition to positioning and sizing toolbars, you can customize the toolbar interface. In the **Customize User Interface** dialog box, all toolbars, except the **Quick Access** toolbar, are listed in the Toolbars branch in the **Customizations in All CUI Files** pane. The **Quick Access** toolbar is customized via workspaces, which are discussed in Chapter 24.

When a command is placed on a toolbar, it is represented by a button. You can add new command buttons or reposition existing command buttons for quicker access. Infrequently used commands can be removed from the toolbar or repositioned to a less prominent location. Entirely new toolbars can be created and filled with predefined or custom commands.

Toolbar Visibility

You can adjust the AutoCAD screen so that only the toolbars you need are visible. This helps conserve drawing window space. If too many toolbars are displayed, the drawing window can become small and crowded. When your drawing area is small, too much of your time is spent making display changes so you can clearly see parts of the drawing.

The length of some of the toolbars is longer than the available space. Remember this when arranging your toolbars. You should have access to all of the buttons. There is no way to "pan" a toolbar that is partially hidden from view.

By default, toolbars other than the **Quick Access** toolbar are not displayed except in the AutoCAD Classic workspace. AutoCAD provides a shortcut menu for fast and convenient control of toolbar visibility. To access the toolbars shortcut menu, right-click on any toolbar. As shown in **Figure 21-20**, a check mark is displayed next to the currently visible toolbars. Pick any toolbar name in the menu to toggle its visibility.

Another way to hide a floating toolbar is to pick its menu control button. This is the X in the corner of the toolbar. If you wish to hide a docked toolbar, you can first

Figure 21-20.
Displaying toolbars. In the **2D Drafting & Annotation** and **3D Modeling** workspaces, only the **Quick Access** toolbar is displayed by default.

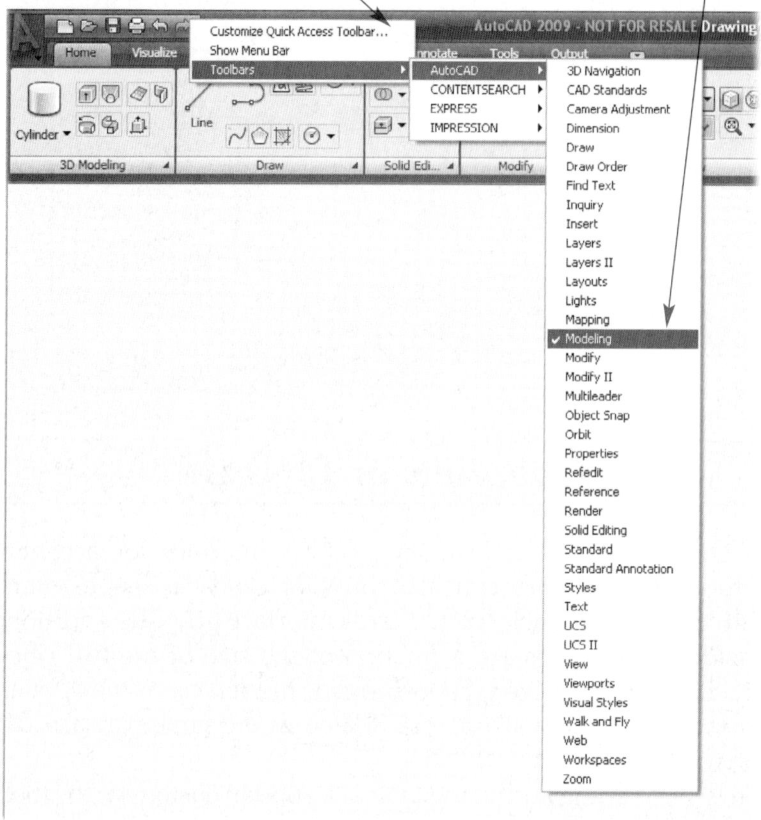

move it away from the edge to make it a floating toolbar. Then, pick the menu control button. When you hide a previously docked toolbar in this manner, it will appear in the floating position when you again make it visible.

When using floating toolbars, it is also possible to overlap the toolbars to save screen space. To bring a toolbar to the front, simply pick on it. Be sure to leave part of each toolbar showing.

Toolbar Display Options

Located in the **Window Elements** area of the **Display** tab of the **Options** dialog box are four check boxes and a text box relating to toolbars. See Figure 21-21.

When the **Use large buttons for Toolbars** check box is checked, the size of toolbar buttons is increased from 16 × 16 pixels to 32 × 32 pixels. At higher screen resolutions, such as 1280 × 1024, the small buttons may be difficult to see. At lower screen resolutions, such as 800 × 600, the large buttons take up too much of the display area.

When the **Show ToolTips** check box is checked, the name of the button to which you are pointing is displayed next to the cursor. Below this check box is the **Show shortcut keys in ToolTips** check box. When this option is checked, the shortcut key combination for the command is displayed in the tooltip. The **Show extended ToolTips** check box determines whether extended tooltips are displayed. When checked, extended tooltips are displayed when the cursor is hovered over a button for the number of seconds

Figure 21-21.
The **Display** tab of the **Options** dialog box contains settings for toolbars.

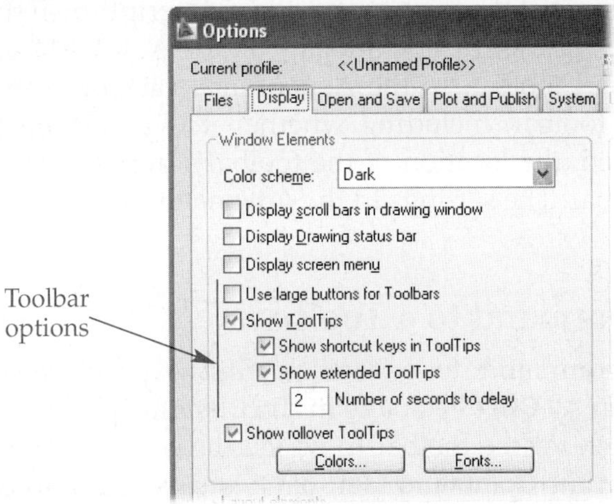

entered in the **Number of seconds to delay** text box. When tooltips are turned off, these two check boxes and the text box are grayed out.

Creating a New Toolbar

To create a new toolbar, open the **Customize User Interface** dialog box. Then, right-click on the Toolbars branch in the upper-left pane to display the shortcut menu. Pick **New Toolbar** in the shortcut menu. A new toolbar is added at the bottom of the Toolbars branch. An edit box is displayed in place of the toolbar name with a default name highlighted. Type a descriptive name for the toolbar and press [Enter].

After the new toolbar is named, it is highlighted in the Toolbars branch. The properties for the toolbar are displayed in the **Properties** pane of the **Customize User Interface** dialog box. See Figure 21-22. A preview of the toolbar also appears in the **Toolbar Preview** pane, but since the new toolbar is empty, there is not currently a preview. You

Figure 21-22.
The properties of a toolbar can be changed in the **Properties** pane of the **Customize User Interface** dialog box.

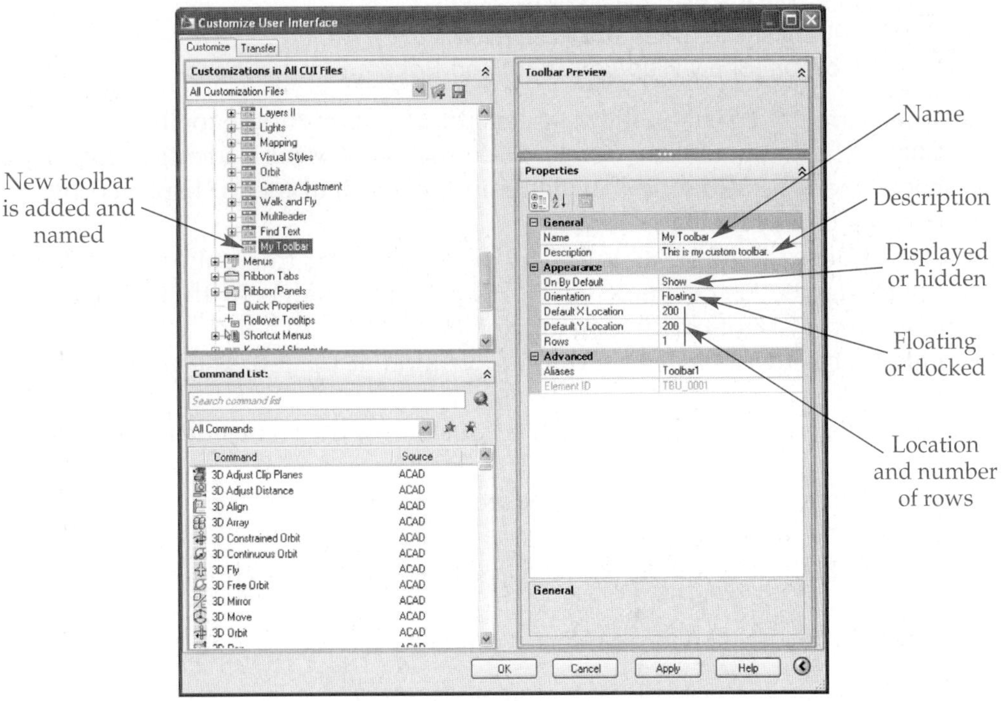

can change the name of the toolbar and add a description in the **General** category of the **Properties** pane. The description appears on the AutoCAD status bar when the cursor is over the docked toolbar. In the **Appearance** category, you can specify the default settings for the toolbar, including whether it is displayed (Show) or hidden (Hide), floating or docked, the location of the toolbar's upper-left corner, and the number of rows for the toolbar. The settings in the **Advanced** category are used for programming applications.

Adding a Command to a Toolbar

To add a command to a toolbar, first expand the Toolbars branch in the **Customizations in All CUI Files** pane in the **Customize User Interface** dialog box. Next, expand the branch for the toolbar to which the command will be added. Then, select a command from the **Command List:** pane and drag it into position in the tree in the **Customizations in All CUI Files** pane. As you drag the command in the tree, an I-bar cursor is displayed. When the I-bar is below the command where you want the new command placed, release the mouse button.

PROFESSIONAL TIP

If the toolbar branch is selected, you can also add a command by dragging and dropping the command into the **Panel Preview** pane, rather than into the tree in the **Customizations in All CUI Files** pane.

Working with Toolbars on the Command Line

Use the **-TOOLBAR** command to work with toolbars at the command line. This command is most useful when creating menu macros, script files, or AutoLISP functions to perform automated toolbar setups. When using this method, you are prompted for the toolbar name. The complete toolbar name consists of the menu group and toolbar name, separated by a period. For example, the toolbar name for the **Draw** toolbar is ACAD.DRAW. The menu group name can be omitted when only one menu is currently loaded or if the toolbar name is not duplicated in another menu group. After specifying the toolbar name (or selecting **ALL** for all toolbars), you can select an option.

Command: **-TOOLBAR**↵
Enter toolbar name or [ALL]: **ACAD.DRAW**↵
Enter an option [Show/Hide/Left/Right/Top/Bottom/Float] <Show>:

These options are used to hide, show, or specify a location for the toolbar.

- **Show.** Makes the toolbar visible. Selecting this option is identical to placing a check mark next to a toolbar name in the shortcut menu displayed by right-clicking on any toolbar.
- **Hide.** Causes the toolbar to be invisible. Selecting this option is identical to removing the check mark next to the toolbar name in the shortcut menu displayed by right-clicking on any toolbar.
- **Left.** Places the toolbar in a docked position at the left side of the AutoCAD window.
- **Right.** Places the toolbar in a docked position at the right side of the AutoCAD window.
- **Top.** Places the toolbar in a docked position at the top of the AutoCAD window.
- **Bottom.** Places the toolbar in a docked position at the bottom of the AutoCAD window.
- **Float.** Places the toolbar as a floating toolbar.

For example, to dock the **Zoom** toolbar on the left side of the AutoCAD window, use the following command sequence.

Command: **-TOOLBAR**↵
Enter toolbar name or [ALL]: **ACAD.ZOOM**↵
Enter an option [Show/Hide/Left/Right/Top/Bottom/Float] <Show>: **LEFT**↵
Enter new position (horizontal, vertical) <0,0>: ↵
Command:

The **Float** option places the toolbar in a floating position anchored at the pixels specified at the Position (screen coordinates) <0,0>: prompt. The anchor point of a floating toolbar is the upper-left corner. If you place the toolbar at 400,300, the upper-left corner of the toolbar is at this location. You are then asked to establish the shape of the new toolbar by specifying the number of rows of buttons for the toolbar.

Another capability of the **-TOOLBAR** command is to show or hide all toolbars at once. When prompted for the toolbar name, enter ALL. The only two options that appear are **Show** and **Hide**. If you use the **Hide** option, all toolbars are hidden.

Exercise 21-3

Complete the exercise on the Student CD.

Working with Flyouts

You can conserve on-screen space by using flyouts in your custom toolbars and ribbon panels. A ***flyout*** is a single command button that can display a number of other command buttons, usually for related commands. A flyout on a toolbar is really a button associated with another toolbar. A flyout on a ribbon panel is a little different. It is associated with a branch in the **Customize User Interface** dialog box. The following sections show how to add a flyout to a ribbon panel or toolbar.

To activate a command in the flyout other than the command "on top," pick the flyout (triangle) to display the pop-up menu. On a toolbar, you must hold the mouse button to display the pop-up toolbar. Move the cursor to the desired command and pick, in the case of the ribbon, or release the mouse button, in the case of a toolbar. This activates the command. Also, the selected command is displayed as the current command ("on top") in the flyout.

Adding a Flyout to a Ribbon Panel

A flyout is added to a row in a ribbon panel using the **Customize User Interface** dialog box. To add a flyout, right-click on the row branch in the **Customizations in All CUI Files** pane. Then, select **New Flyout** from the shortcut menu. The new, empty flyout is added to the bottom of the row's branch. Now you can drag commands from the **Command List:** pane into the flyout branch.

With the flyout selected in the **Customizations in All CUI Files** pane, look at the properties in the **Properties** pane. See Figure 21-23. The **Appearance** section contains several properties that control how the flyout functions. The Orientation, Size, and Show Label properties are the same as discussed earlier. The Button Style property determines whether a single pick executes the "on top" command or displays the pop-up menu. The Use Recent Command property determines which command is displayed "on top." When set to Yes, the command in the flyout that was most recently used is displayed

Figure 21-23.
Adding a flyout to a ribbon panel.

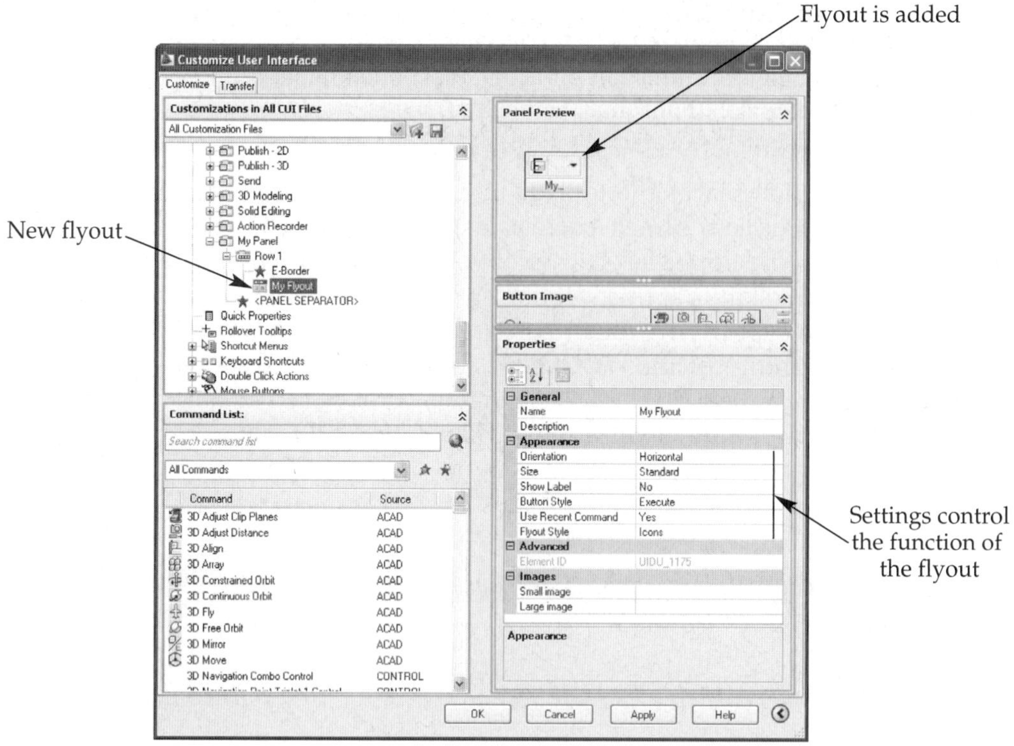

as the top button. When set to No, the default button is always displayed on top. The Flyout Style property sets how the buttons in the flyout appear. You can choose to have icons only, icons and text, icons and a description, or a gallery displayed.

Exercise 21-4
Complete the exercise on the Student CD.

Adding a Flyout to a Toolbar

In this section, you will create a custom toolbar flyout for 3D projects and add it to the **Modify** toolbar. If the **Modify** toolbar is not displayed, display it and dock it on the left side of the drawing area.

First, open the **Customize User Interface** dialog box. Then, expand the Toolbars branch in the **Customizations in All CUI Files** pane. Next, right-click on the Modify branch (or whichever toolbar you want the flyout added to), select **New Flyout** in the shortcut menu. A new toolbar is added to the bottom of the Modify branch. This is the "flyout toolbar." A toolbar with the same default name also appears in the Toolbars branch. This is the "source toolbar." Right-click on the new toolbar in the Modify branch and pick **Rename** from the shortcut menu. Change the toolbar name to **3D Tools**. This does not rename the *source* toolbar.

Next, drag and drop commands from the **Command List:** pane onto the new **3D Tools** toolbar. Use the drop-down list to filter the commands and select commands in the **Draw** and **View** categories. Refer to **Figure 21-24.** As you add command buttons to the flyout toolbar, the source toolbar is also updated. If you select the source toolbar in the Toolbars branch, you will see that the same commands are displayed in its branch.

Figure 21-24.
The **3D Tools** flyout placed in the **Modify** toolbar. Commands have been added to the **3D Tools** toolbar.

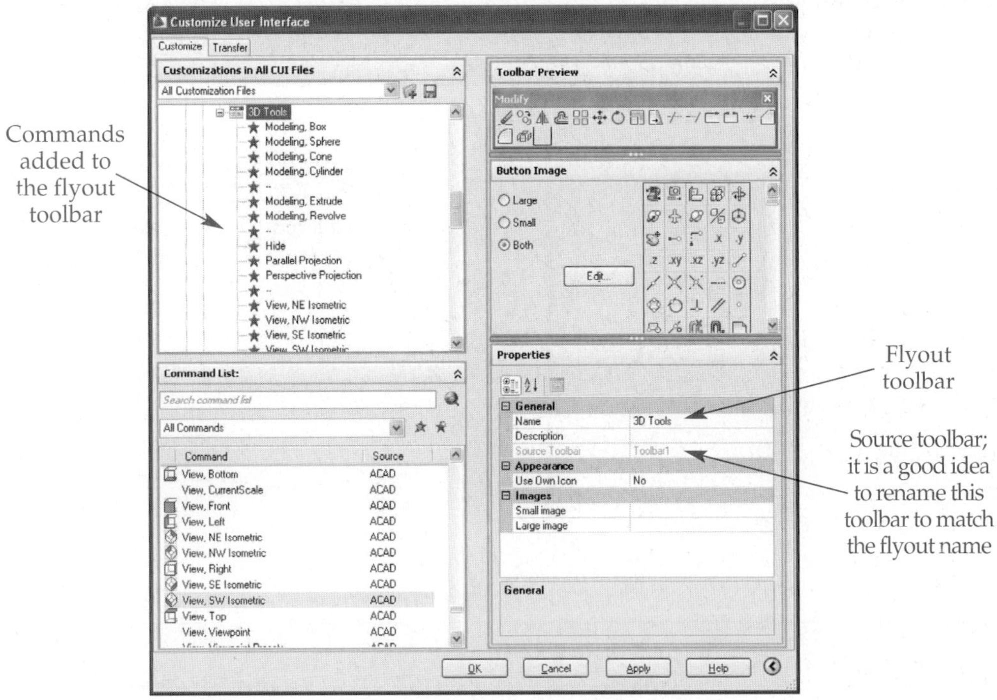

It is a good idea to rename the source toolbar to match the name of the flyout toolbar to avoid confusion.

To have the new flyout appear at the top (or left) of the **Modify** toolbar, drag it to the top position in the Modify branch. Then, select **OK** to exit the **Customize User Interface** dialog box and apply the changes. Now, when you pick the flyout button that you have added to the **Modify** toolbar, your custom **3D Tools** toolbar is displayed, as shown in Figure 21-25.

You can also turn any existing toolbar into a flyout on another existing toolbar. To do so, merely drag and drop the toolbar to be a flyout into the branch of the toolbar to contain the flyout. The original toolbar, the source, remains in the Toolbars branch. Do not use a toolbar that contains drop-down controls, such as the **Layer Control** or **Dim Style Control**, as a flyout toolbar. The resulting flyout will not properly function.

NOTE

You can delete a flyout toolbar from the toolbar branch within which it is contained. However, keep in mind that doing so does not delete the *source* toolbar, which is directly below the Toolbars branch.

Exercise 21-5

Complete the exercise on the Student CD.

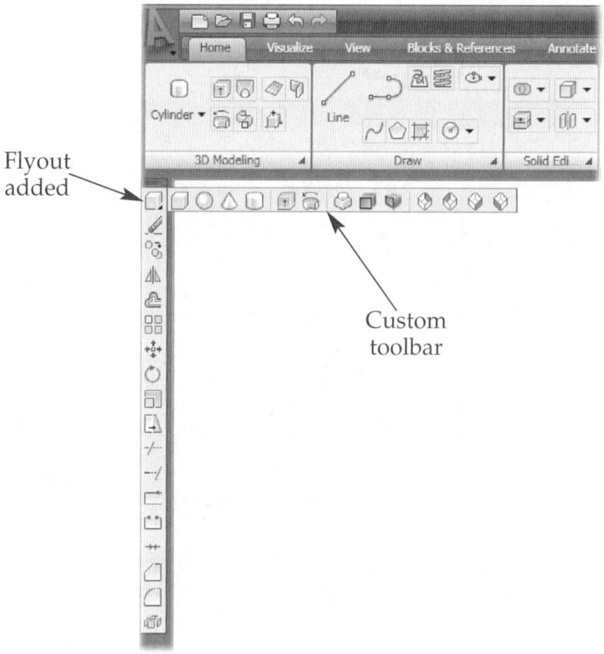

Figure 21-25.
A custom toolbar for working in 3D has been created and associated with a flyout in the **Modify** toolbar.

Overview of Menus

The names of the standard ***menus*** appear inside the menu browser and, when displayed, in the menu bar at the top of the AutoCAD graphics window. The menu bar is displayed in the AutoCAD Classic workspace. To display the menu bar in other workspaces, right-click on the **Quick Access** toolbar and select **Show Menu Bar** in the shortcut menu. Menus are selected by placing the cursor over the menu name and picking. You can also use the access (mnemonic) keys to select menus.

Once you understand how menus are designed, you can customize existing menus and create your own. Some basic information about menus includes:

- By default, AutoCAD has 12 menus displayed in the menu browser and menu bar. If the Express tools are not installed, there are 11 menus.
- If no menus are defined in the current CUI file or workspace, AutoCAD inserts default **File**, **Window**, and **Help** menus. This is similar to how AutoCAD is displayed without a drawing open.
- The name of the menu should be as concise as possible. On low-resolution displays, long menu names may cause the menu bar to be displayed on two lines, which reduces the drawing area.
- Menu item names can be any length. The menu is displayed as wide as its longest menu item name.
- Each menu can have multiple cascading menus.
- A menu can have up to 999 items, including cascading menus.
- To create an access (mnemonic) key for a menu or menu item, place an ampersand (&) before the desired access key character. Access and shortcut keys are discussed in the next section.

PROFESSIONAL TIP

In earlier releases of AutoCAD, pull-down and context shortcut menus were referred to as POP menus. In addition, a series of menu files (MNU, MNC, MNR, and MNS) were used to define the menus. Pull-down menus were defined in the POP1 through POP499 sections of the menu file. Context shortcut menus were defined in the POP500 through POP999 sections. These POP designations are still used by AutoCAD for the sake of compatibility with older menus being used in the current version of AutoCAD. In the **Customize User Interface** dialog box, the POP names appear as aliases for these menus.

Shortcut and Access Keys

Before getting started with menu customization, it is important to understand the difference between shortcut keys and access keys. ***Shortcut keys,*** also called ***accelerator keys,*** are key combinations used to initiate a command. For example, [Ctrl]+[1] displays or closes the **Properties** palette. Custom shortcut keys can be created to initiate specific AutoCAD commands or macros. Creating custom shortcut keys is covered in Chapter 22.

Access keys, also called ***mnemonic keys,*** are keys used to access a menu or menu item via the keyboard. Pressing the [Alt] key activates the access keys for the menus. The access keys are shown as underlined (underscored) letters. Most access keys (underscores) are not displayed in the menu bar until the [Alt] key is depressed. For example, notice that the letter M is underlined in the **Modify** menu name. Pressing the [M] key accesses the **Modify** menu. If the menu bar is displayed, the menu is accessed from there. If the menu bar is not displayed, the menu is accessed through the menu browser. To activate the menu browser using the access key, press [Alt]+[A]. Then use the [Tab] and arrow keys to navigate within the browser.

Any letter in the menu or menu item name can be defined as the access key, but an access key must be unique for a menu or submenu. Notice on the **Modify** pull-down menu that the M is used for **Match Properties**, so **Mirror** and **Move** use the i and v, respectively. The letter T can be used for both **Trim** and **Text** because **Text** is in the **Object** submenu, while **Trim** is in the "main" **Modify** menu. When creating custom menus, you can add custom access keys to the menu.

PROFESSIONAL TIP

Once the access (mnemonic) keys are activated, you can use the arrow keys to navigate through the menu browser or pull-down menu structure.

Creating a New Menu

A new menu is created within the **Customize User Interface** dialog box. First, a menu is added to the Menus branch. Then, commands are added to the new menu. The process is basically the same as creating a new ribbon panel or toolbar, as described earlier in this chapter. The basic procedure is:

1. Open the **Customize User Interface** dialog box.
2. In the **Customizations in All CUI Files** pane, expand the Menus branch. All of the existing menus are displayed.
3. Right-click on the Menus branch to display the shortcut menu. Pick **New Menu** from the shortcut menu. A new menu is added to the bottom of the list of existing menus. See **Figure 21-26A.** The name is highlighted in an edit box so the default name can be changed.

Figure 21-26.
A—Adding a new menu. B—Commands have been added to the new menu.

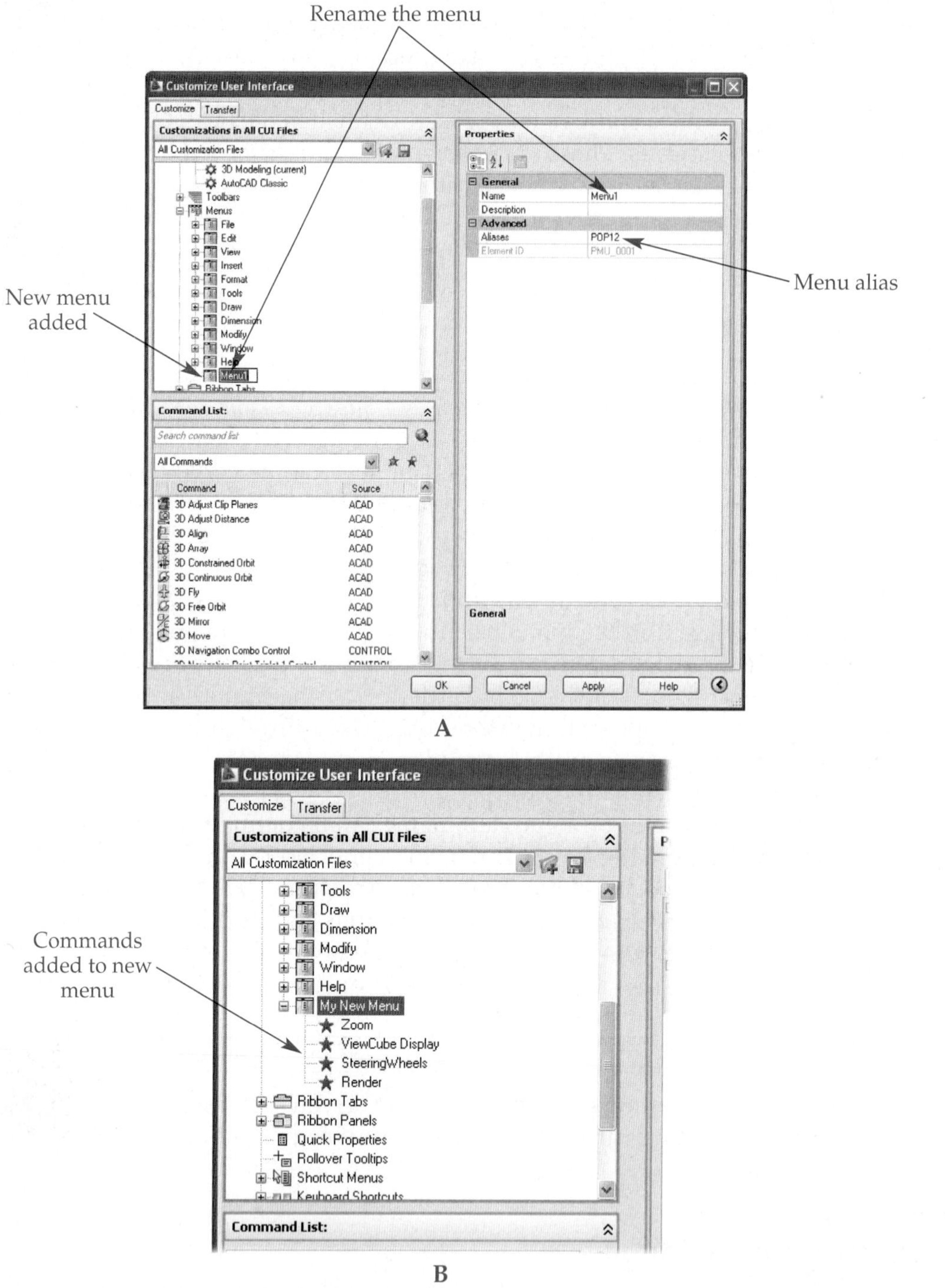

4. Give the menu an appropriate name.
5. Drag the desired commands from the **Commands List:** pane and drop them into the new menu. See Figure 21-26B.
6. To add a separator, right-click on the command below which it should be inserted and select **Insert Separator** from the shortcut menu.

By default, AutoCAD has 12 menus when the Express tools are installed. When adding a new menu, it is automatically assigned an alias of POP*n*, where *n* is the next available integer.

Exercise 21-6

Complete the exercise on the Student CD.

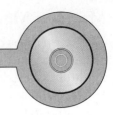

Adding a Cascading Menu

A ***cascading menu*** is a menu contained within another menu. It can be used to help group similar commands or options. For example, when **Circle** is selected in the **Draw** menu, a cascading menu appears that offers the different options for drawing a circle.

Adding a cascading menu to a menu is similar to adding a "main" menu. First, open the **Customize User Interface** dialog box. Then, in the **Customizations in All CUI Files** pane, expand the branch for the menu to which the cascading menu is to be added. Right-click on the command after which the cascading menu should appear. In the shortcut menu that is displayed, pick **New Sub-menu**. A new menu is added within the first menu. Notice that the icon in the tree indicates this item is a menu, not a command. Now, the submenu can be renamed to an appropriate name. Finally, drag commands from the **Command List:** pane and drop them into the new menu. See **Figure 21-27.**

Adding a Command to a Menu

To add a command to a menu, first expand the Menus branch in the **Customizations in All CUI Files** pane in the **Customize User Interface** dialog box. Next, expand the branch for the menu to which the command will be added. Then, select a command from the **Command List:** pane and drag it into position in the tree in the **Customizations in All CUI Files** pane. As you drag the command in the tree, an I-bar cursor is displayed. When the I-bar is below the command where you want the new command placed, release the mouse button.

Figure 21-27.
A—A cascading submenu has been added to the new menu. B—The menu displayed in the menu browser. C—The menu displayed in the menu bar.

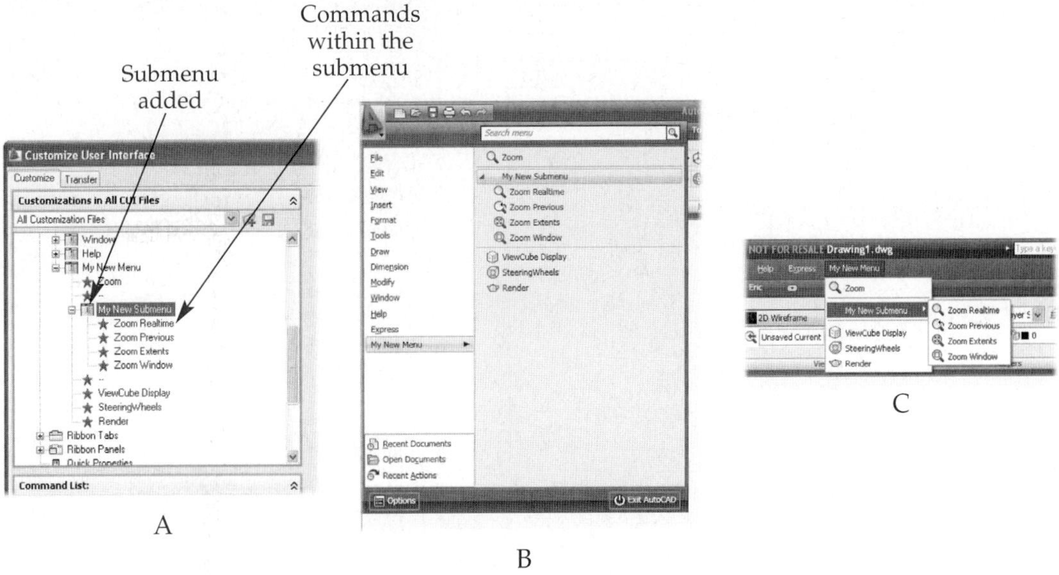

Marking Menu Items

Menu items can be marked with a check mark (✓), bullet (•) or, if an image is associated with the command, a border around the image. Marking is often related to an item that is toggled on or off, such as ortho or snap. When the item is on, it is marked. When the item is off, it is not marked.

In the menu bar, a marked item has a check mark, which is boxed, if no image is associated with it. In the menu browser, a marked item has a bullet, which is boxed, if no image is associated with it. If an image is associated with the item, the item is marked by placing a border around the image in both the menu browser and menu bar. To mark an item, place an exclamation point and period (!.) in front of its name in the **Customize User Interface** dialog box.

Menu items can also be grayed out. Any item that is grayed out in the menu cannot be selected. To gray out an item, place a tilde (~) in front of its name in the **Customize User Interface** dialog box.

Look at the sample menu shown in **Figure 21-28.** When the special characters are used in an item name, they permanently mark the item. However, as you will see in the next section, you can create *smart* menu items that can react to certain conditions. In this way, you can toggle between marked/unmarked and enabled/disabled menu items.

Figure 21-28.
Note the characters used to mark and gray out menu items.

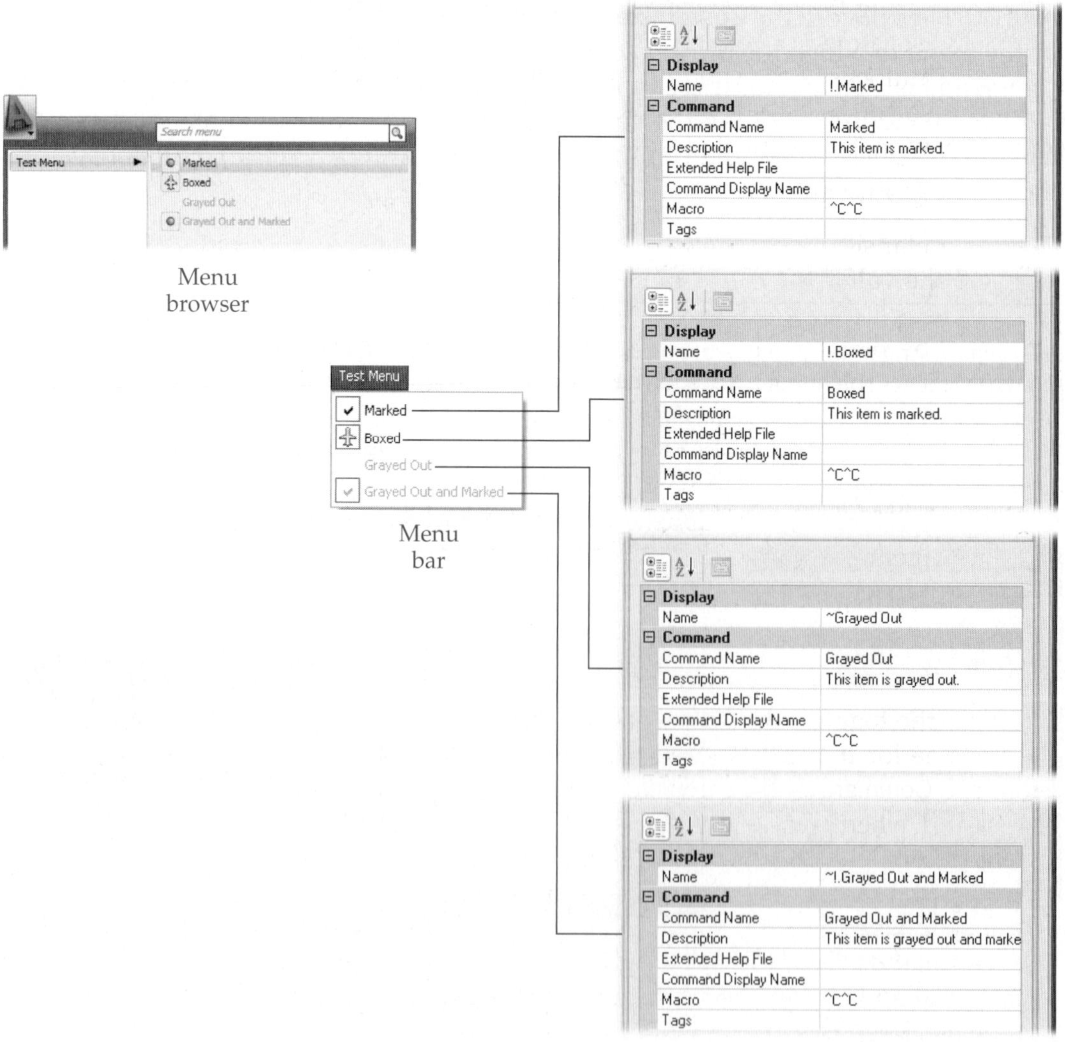

If you select the command in the Menus branch of the "customizations" pane, the **Properties** pane contains a **Display** category with a Name property, as shown in **Figure 21-28.** This is also true for commands selected in other branches, such as the Ribbon Panels or Toolbars branch. The entry for the Name property is displayed in the menu. If you entered a special, marking character for the command name, it is displayed in this property. However, notice that the Command Name property in the **Command** category does not have the marking character. If you select the command in the **Command List:** pane, the **Properties** pane does not contain the **Display** category and the Command Name property does not have the marking character. The marking characters are only placed in the Name property of the **Display** category, which is only available if the command is selected in the tree in the "customizations" pane.

Creating Smart Menu Items

You can create *smart* menu labels by using a string-expression language called ***Direct Interpretively Evaluated String Expression Language (DIESEL).*** A ***string*** is simply a group of characters that can be input from the keyboard or from the value of a system variable. DIESEL uses a string for its input and provides a string as output. In other words, you give DIESEL a value and it gives something back to you.

Adding a menu check mark or bullet is an excellent example of how DIESEL can be used for menu labels. For example, select **Lock Location** from the **Window** menu. In the cascading menu that is displayed, a mark appears next to any of the user interface items that are locked in place, such as floating toolbars, docked toolbars, floating windows (palettes), or docked windows (palettes). By default, none of these items are locked. Selecting **Docked Windows** in the cascading menu locks all docked windows in place. Also, a mark is placed next to the item in the cascading menu. Selecting that item again unlocks the docked windows and removes the mark from the menu label.

Suppose you want to create a menu item that allows the ortho mode to be toggled on and off with "on" indicated by a mark. The command label for this menu item is:

```
$(if,$(getvar,orthomode),!.)&Ortho Toggle
```

The first dollar sign ($) signals the menu to evaluate a DIESEL expression. This expression gets the value (getvar) of the **ORTHOMODE** system variable and marks the item if the value is 1 (on). If you associate an image with this custom command, the item is marked by placing a box around the image. Otherwise, a bullet or check mark is placed next to the item name in the menu. The macro for this custom command is simply ^O.

Figure 21-29 shows two DIESEL expressions in menu labels and how they would appear in the menu. The menu shows that ortho mode is off and snap mode is on.

Adding DIESEL expressions to your menu labels can make them more powerful and "intelligent." Refer to the online documentation for a complete discussion of the DIESEL language.

PROFESSIONAL TIP

In the ortho toggle example, &Ortho Toggle must be placed at the end of the line for the Name property. However, notice in **Figure 21-29** that the Command Name property is Ortho Toggle. This property is displayed when the command is selected in the Menu tree in the "customizations" pane. AutoCAD removes the special characters from the command name so that the custom command is sorted in the **Command List:** pane based on the name and appears with the other "o" commands. You may need to close the **Customize User Interface** dialog box and redisplay it for the commands to be properly ordered in the list. Keep this in mind when defining custom commands.

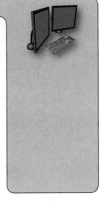

Figure 21-29.
Note the DIESEL expressions and the resulting menu items.

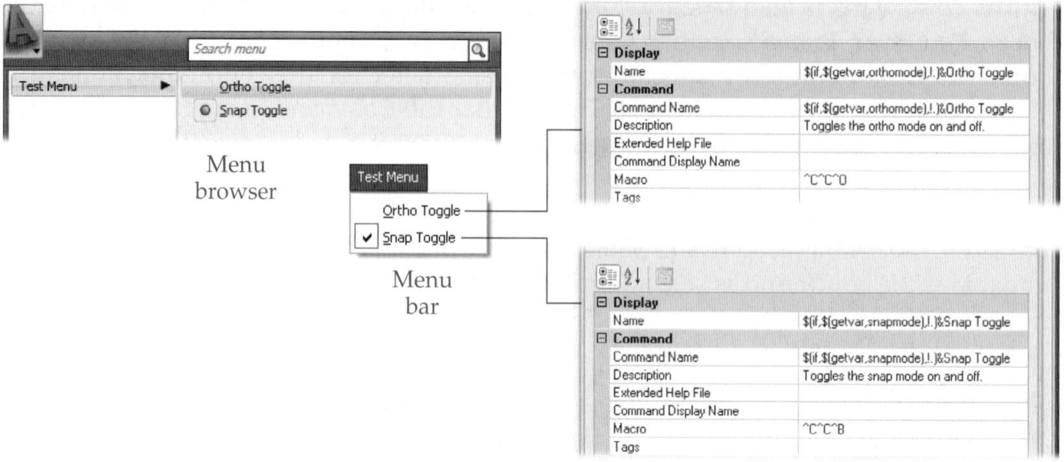

Referencing Other Menus

A menu pick can activate, or reference, another menu. A menu pick can also gray out or mark another menu item. The character codes shown in **Figure 21-30** are used for these purposes.

When referencing other menus, you can combine the characters to gray out items or mark items. Study the following menu item examples. The first example activates and displays the twelfth menu in the menu browser or menu bar. This menu may or may not correspond to the POP12 alias.

$p12=*

The next menu item marks the fourth item in the twelfth menu.

$p12.4=!.

This entry grays out the third item in the sixth menu.

$p6.3=~

The following menu item marks the second item in the eighth menu and grays it out.

$p8.2=!.~

The next menu item removes all marks and any "gray out" from the second item in the eighth menu.

$p8.2=

Numbering of menu items begins with the first line of the menu below the name and continues to the bottom of the menu. Separator lines are also counted when determining

Figure 21-30.
Character codes used for graying out or marking another menu item.

Character String	Function
$p*n*=	Makes another menu current, where *n* is the number of the menu. Alternately, any specified alias for the menu can be referenced. The alias is listed in the Aliases property text box in the **Properties** pane of the **Customize User Interface** dialog box.
$p*n*=*	Displays the currently active menu.
$p*n*.1=	References a specific item number on another menu.

line numbers. AutoCAD consecutively numbers items through all menus without considering menu levels.

The following examples show how these techniques can be combined in macros. For each of the examples, create a new command and enter the information in the **Properties** pane of the **Customize User Interface** dialog box.

Name: Insert desk
Macro: ^C^C-insert;desk;\\\\$p12=*

Name: Setup .5
Macro: ^C^Cgrid;.5;snap;.25;$p12.1=!. $p12.2=!.~

Name: Defaults
Macro: ^C^Cgrid;off;snap;off;$p12.1= $p12.2=

Figure 21-31 shows an example containing similar macros and the resulting menu.

PROFESSIONAL TIP

The method for referencing other menus described here is called *absolute referencing.* Another method, called *relative referencing,* uses the customization group and element ID. A discussion of this method is beyond the scope of this text. Refer to the online documentation for more information on relative referencing.

Figure 21-31.
Note the macros used to control the fourth item in the menu. Also note that the separators count as an item.

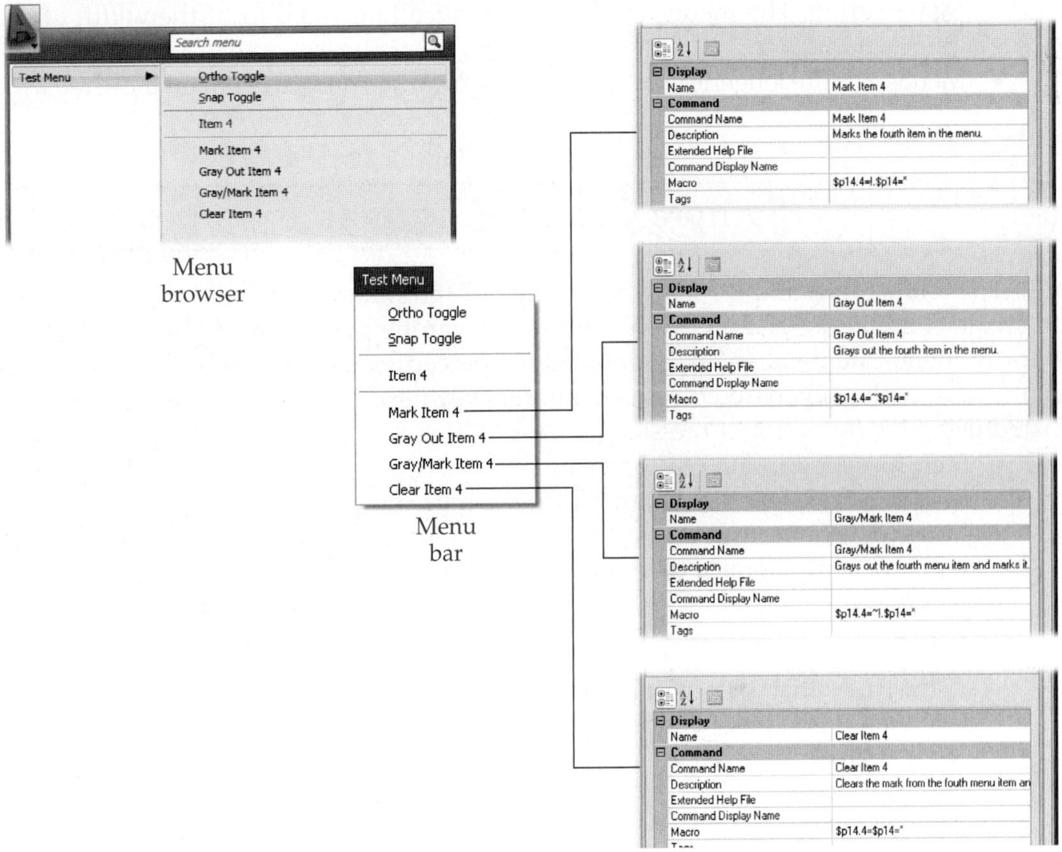

Removing a Menu

If you want to permanently remove a menu, open the **Customize User Interface** dialog box. Then, expand the tree in the **Customizations in All CUI Files** pane to display the menu to be deleted. Right-click on the menu and pick **Delete** from the shortcut menu. You can also highlight the menu in the tree and press the [Delete] key. With either method, an AutoCAD alert appears asking you to confirm the deletion. Picking **Yes** in this alert box permanently deletes the menu from the user interface.

The above procedure is not recommended because the menu is permanently removed. To "restore" the menu in the future, it must be rebuilt. A better way to remove any unwanted menus is by deleting them from the workspace. Managing workspaces is covered in detail in Chapter 24. Briefly, to remove a menu from a workspace:

1. Open the **Customize User Interface** dialog box and expand the Workspaces branch in the **Customizations in All CUI Files** pane.
2. Select the workspace from which you wish to remove a menu.
3. In the **Workspace Contents** pane, expand the Menus branch.
4. Right-click on the menu you wish to remove and pick **Remove from Workspace** in the shortcut menu.
5. Exit the **Customize User Interface** dialog box.

Now, the menu is removed from the workspace, but it is still available to other workspaces. Refer to Chapter 24 for complete details on workspaces and managing workspaces.

Some Notes about Menus

Here are a few more things to keep in mind when developing menus.

- Menus are disabled during **DTEXT** after the rotation angle is entered and during **SKETCH** after the record increment is set.
- A menu label can be as long as needed, but should be as brief as possible for easy reading. The menu width is automatically created to fit the width of the longest item.
- Menus that are longer than the screen display are truncated to fit on the screen.

Sample Custom Commands

The following examples show how AutoCAD commands and options can be used to create commands. These custom commands can be placed on ribbon panels, toolbars, or menus. Remember, an ampersand (&) preceding a character in a menu or item name defines the keyboard access (mnemonic) key used to enable it. The examples are listed using the following three-step process.

- Step 1. A description of the macro.
- Step 2. The key strokes required for the macro.
- Step 3. The name and macro for the new command as entered in the **Properties** pane of the **Customize User Interface** dialog box.

Example 1

1. This **HEXAGON** command will start the **POLYGON** command and draw a six-sided polygon inscribed in a circle.
2. **POLYGON**↵
   6↵
   (select center)
   I↵
3. Name: &Hexagon
   Macro: *^C^Cpolygon;6;\i

The asterisk in front of the ^C^C repeats the command until it is canceled. The \ in front of i indicates that the macro will wait for user input, in this case the center of the polygon, before continuing.

A return can be represented in a command or macro by using either a space or a semicolon. Notice the following two macros. Both macros perform the same function.

```
*^C^Cpolygon 6 \i
*^C^Cpolygon;6;\i
```

The first example uses spaces and the second example uses semicolons to represent pressing the [Enter] key. The technique used is a matter of personal preference, but semicolons are recommended.

Example 2

1. This **DOT** command draws a solid dot that is .1 unit in diameter. Use the **DONUT** command. The inside diameter is 0 (zero) and the outside diameter is .1.
2. **DONUT**↵
   0↵
   .1↵
3. Name: &Dot
   Macro: ^C^Cdonut;0;.1

Example 3

1. This **X-POINT** command sets the **PDMODE** system variable to 3 and draws an X at the pick point. The command should repeat.
2. **PDMODE**↵
   3↵
   POINT↵
   (pick the point)
3. Name: &X-Point
   Macro: *^C^Cpdmode;3;point

Example 4

1. This command, named **NOTATION**, could be used by a drawing checker or instructor. It allows them to circle features on a drawing and then add a leader and text. It first sets the color to red, then draws a circle, snaps a leader to the nearest point that is picked on the circle, and prompts for the text. User input for text is provided, then a cancel [Esc] returns the Command: prompt and the color is set to ByLayer.
2. **-COLOR**↵
   RED↵
   CIRCLE↵
   (pick center point)
   (pick radius)
   LEADER↵
   NEA↵
   (pick a point on the circle)
   (pick end of leader)
   (press [Enter] for automatic shoulder)
   (enter text) ↵
   (press [Enter] to cancel)
   -COLOR↵
   BYLAYER↵
3. Name: &Notation
   Macro: ^C^C-color;red;circle;\\leader;nea;\\;\;-color;bylayer

Example 5

1. This is a repeating command named **MULTISQUARE** that draws one-unit squares oriented at a 0° horizontal angle until the command is canceled.
2. **RECTANG↵**
   (pick lower-left corner)
   @1,1↵
3. Name: &Multisquare
   Macro: *^C^Crectang;\@1,1

PROFESSIONAL TIP

Some commands, such as the **COLOR** command, display a dialog box. Menu macros can provide input to the command line, but cannot control dialog boxes. To access the command-line version of a command, prefix the command name with a hyphen (-), as shown in Example 4. However, not all commands that display a dialog box have a command-line equivalent.

Exercise 21-7

Complete the exercise on the Student CD.

Chapter Test

Answer the following questions. Write your answers on a separate sheet of paper or complete the electronic chapter test on the Student CD.

1. What is an *interface element* in AutoCAD?
2. List two ways to access the **Customize User Interface** dialog box.
3. In which pane of the **Customize User Interface** dialog box can you find all predefined commands?
4. How do you add a command to an interface element?
5. How do you remove a command from an interface element?
6. How can you copy a command to a new location on a different interface element?
7. What is a *partial CUI file?*
8. Briefly describe how to create a custom command.
9. What is an *extended help file?*
10. Name the four drawing tools that are provided in the **Button Editor** dialog box.
11. What is the default, small size (in pixels) of the button editor drawing area?
12. Where is the **Use large buttons for Toolbars** check box located? What function does this check box perform?
13. How should you develop and test a new macro before entering it into a custom command definition?
14. Name two ways to specify an [Enter] in a macro. Which of the two methods is recommended?
15. Briefly describe the composition of the ribbon.
16. What determines which commands in a ribbon panel appear in the expanded panel?
17. How do you create a new ribbon tab and add a new panel to it?
18. Briefly describe how to customize a toolbar.
19. How do you create a new toolbar?
20. Explain how to display a toolbar without using a dialog box or shortcut menu.
21. Why would you use the method described in question 20?
22. What is a *flyout?*
23. How do you add a flyout to a ribbon panel?
24. How do you add a flyout to a toolbar?
25. How many items can a menu contain?
26. Provide the character(s) required to perform the following functions in a menu.
    A. Gray out a menu item.
    B. Mark a menu item.
    C. Specify the menu access key.
27. How wide is a menu?
28. What is the function of the following DIESEL expression?

    $(if,$(getvar,snapmode),!.)Snap

29. What is the function of the following menu item characters?
    A. $p3=*
    B. $p4.1=~
    C. $p6.7=!.
30. Interpret the following menu item.

    ^C^Crectang;\@1,1

Drawing Problems

Before customizing any toolbars, menus, or the ribbon, check with your instructor or supervisor for specific instructions or guidelines.

1. Create a new toolbar using the following information.
   A. Name the toolbar **Draw/Modify**.
   B. Copy at least three, but no more than six, commonly used drawing commands onto the new toolbar. Use only existing commands; do not create new ones.
   C. Copy at least three, but no more than six, commonly used editing commands onto the new toolbar. Use only existing commands; do not create new ones.
   D. Dock the new **Draw/Modify** toolbar at the upper-left side of the screen.

2. Create a new toolbar using the following information.
   A. Name the toolbar **My 3D Tools**.
   B. Copy the following solid primitive commands onto the new toolbar.
      Box **Pyramid**
      Cone **Sphere**
      Cylinder **Torus**
   C. Copy the following view commands onto the new toolbar.
      Top **Bottom** **Left**
      Right **Front** **Back**
   D. Copy the following UCS commands onto the new toolbar.
      3 Point **Object** **World**
      Face UCS **Origin** **UCS Previous**
   E. Dock the toolbar below the toolbar created in problem 1.

3. Create a new ribbon panel using the following information.
   A. The displayed name of the panel should be **Paper Space Viewports**.
   B. The panel should contain eight custom commands that use the **MVIEW** command to create paper space viewports:
      - **1 Viewport**—allow user to pick location
      - **1 Viewport (Fit)**
      - **2 Viewports (Horizontal)**—allow user to pick location
      - **2 Viewports (Vertical)**
      - **3 Viewports**—allow user to pick orientation and location
      - **3 Viewports (Right)**
      - **4 Viewports**—allow user to pick location
      - **4 Viewports (Fit)**
   C. Construct button graphics for the custom commands. Save the images in the default \Icons folder or create a new folder (be sure to add it to the AutoCAD support environment).
   D. Create a custom command that will switch from one viewport to another.
   E. Place a button on the panel that executes the **PLOT** command.

4. Create a new toolbar for inserting title block drawings. Name the toolbar **Title Blocks**.
   A. The toolbar should contain six custom commands that do the following.
      - Insert the ANSI A title block drawing (plot style of your choice)
      - Insert the ANSI B title block drawing (plot style of your choice)
      - Insert the ANSI C title block drawing (plot style of your choice)
      - Insert the ANSI D title block drawing (plot style of your choice)
      - Insert the ANSI E title block drawing (plot style of your choice)
      - Insert the Architectural title block drawing (plot style of your choice)
   B. Create button graphics for each of the custom commands. Save the images in a new folder and add the folder to the AutoCAD support environment.
   C. Dock the toolbar on the left side of the screen.

5. Add a flyout to the **Paper Space Viewports** panel created in problem 3. Add the six custom commands created in problem 4 to this flyout.

6. Create a new dimensioning menu. Place as many dimensioning commands as you need in the menu. Use cascading menus if necessary. One or more of the cascading menus should be dimensioning variables. Include menu access (mnemonic) keys.

7. Create a menu for 3D objects. Include menu access (mnemonic) keys. The menu should include the following items.
   - At least three 3D solid objects
   - **HIDE** command
   - At least three visual style commands
   - **VPORTS** command
   - **NAVSWHEEL** command

8. Create a new menu named **Special**. The menu should include the following drawing and editing commands.

   LINE **MOVE**
   ARC **COPY**
   CIRCLE **STRETCH**
   POLYLINE **TRIM**
   POLYGON **EXTEND**
   RECTANGLE **CHAMFER**
   DTEXT **FILLET**
   ERASE

   Use cascading menus, if necessary. Include a separator line between the drawing and editing commands and specify appropriate menu access (mnemonic) keys.

9. Create a menu to insert a variety of blocks or symbols. These symbols can be for any drawing discipline that suits your needs. Use cascading menus and menu access (mnemonic) keys, if necessary.

10. Create a new ribbon panel named **My 3D Tools**. Evaluate which tools you use most often for creating and rendering 3D models. Place these commands on the new panel, even if they are already contained on another panel. The purpose of this new panel is to streamline your modeling and rendering work. Use flyouts as necessary. Arrange the commands on the panel so the panel does not need to be expanded to access the most frequently used commands.

11. Create a ribbon tab with the display name **My Tools**. Set the tab name to your initials. Add the panels created in problems 3 and 10 to this tab. Review the tabs and tools to be sure they properly function.

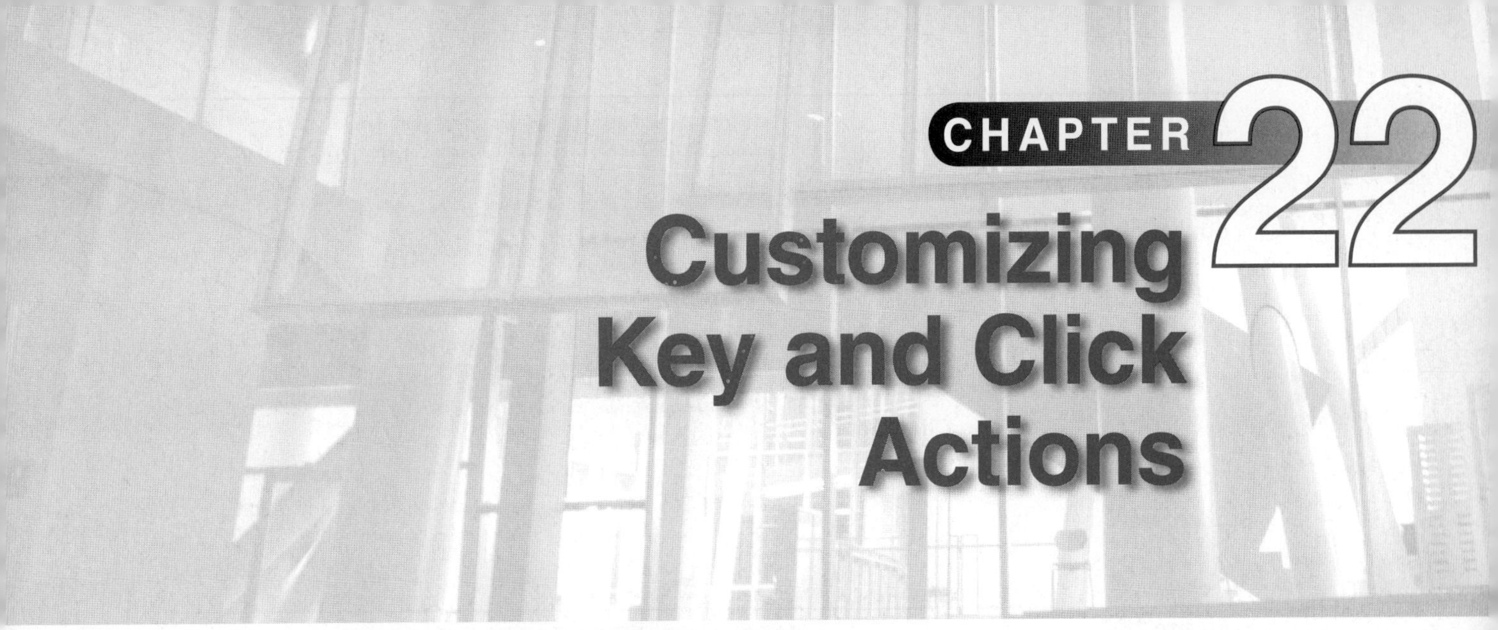

CHAPTER 22

Customizing Key and Click Actions

Learning Objectives

After completing this chapter, you will be able to:

- ✓ Assign shortcut keys to commands.
- ✓ Explain how shortcut menus function.
- ✓ Edit existing shortcut menus.
- ✓ Create custom shortcut menus.
- ✓ Customize an object's quick properties.
- ✓ Create custom rollover tooltips.
- ✓ Describe double-click actions.
- ✓ Edit double-click actions.
- ✓ Create custom double-click actions.

AutoCAD has many tools that can be used in "heads-up design." Heads-up design is a concept of working in which your eyes remain focused on the drawing area. For example, when dynamic input is on, you do not need to look at the command line to see the options for the current command. The options are displayed near the cursor in the drawing area. AutoCAD's shortcut menus and double-click actions also contribute to heads-up design. Shortcut menus are displayed by right-clicking. Double-click actions are initiated when an object is double-clicked. Like much of the graphic content in AutoCAD (the ribbon, toolbars, etc.), shortcut menus and double-click actions can be customized.

In order to use the shortcut menu and double-click action customization techniques discussed in this chapter, shortcut menus and double-click editing need to be enabled. To do this, open the **Options** dialog box and select the **User Preferences** tab. Then, check the **Double click editing** and **Shortcut menus in drawing area** check boxes, as shown in Figure 22-1.

The use of shortcut menus can be further refined by picking the **Right-click Customization...** button that appears below the check boxes. This displays the **Right-Click Customization** dialog box. See Figure 22-2. The settings in this dialog box allow you to define what a right-click does when in default mode, edit mode, or command mode. For this chapter, pick the **Shortcut menu** radio buttons in the **Default Mode** and **Edit Mode** areas. Also, pick the **Shortcut Menu: always enabled** radio button in the **Command Mode** area. Then, close the **Right-Click Customization** and **Options** dialog boxes.

Figure 22-1.
The settings for enabling shortcut menus and double-click editing are found in the **Options** dialog box.

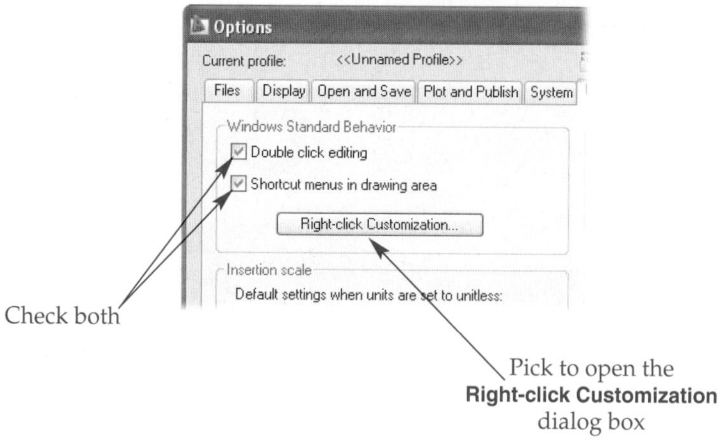

Figure 22-2.
The settings in the **Right-Click Customization** dialog box allow you to define what a right-click does when in default mode, edit mode, or command mode.

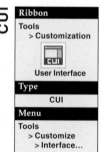

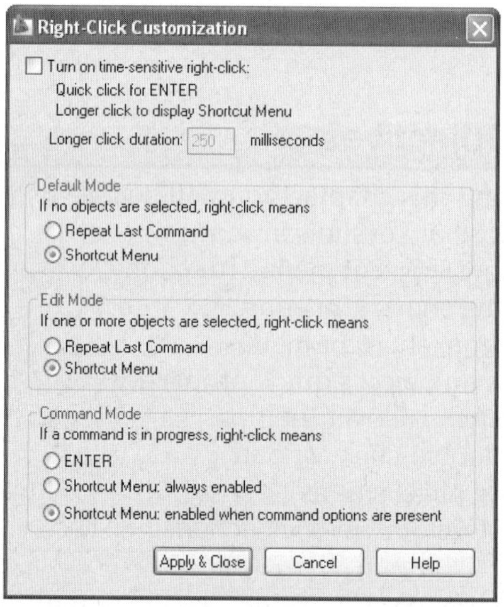

Customizing Shortcut Keys

CUI

Ribbon
Tools
> Customization
User Interface
Type
CUI
Menu
Tools
> Customize
> Interface...

You can define your own custom shortcut keys (accelerator keys) for AutoCAD commands and custom macros. The **Customize User Interface** dialog box is used to define shortcut keys. To see the commands to which shortcut keys are assigned, expand the Keyboard Shortcuts branch in the **Customizations in All CUI Files** pane. Then, expand the Shortcut Keys branch. All commands that have a shortcut key assigned to them appear in this branch. See **Figure 22-3.**

When the Shortcut Keys branch is selected, the **Shortcuts** pane is displayed in the upper-right corner of the **Customize User Interface** dialog box. A command that has a shortcut key assigned to it can be selected in this pane to display the **Information** pane in the lower-right corner of the dialog box.

Assigning a Shortcut Key

To assign a shortcut key to a command, first locate the command in the **Command List:** pane of the **Customize User Interface** dialog box. Next, drag the command into the Shortcut Keys branch in the **Customizations in All CUI Files** pane. The command is added to the list of shortcut keys (although it may not be immediately visible) and the **Properties** pane is displayed for the command. See **Figure 22-4.** In the **Access** category of the **Properties** pane, pick in the Key(s) property text box. Next, pick the

Figure 22-3.
Shortcut keys are added to commands in the **Customize User Interface** dialog box.

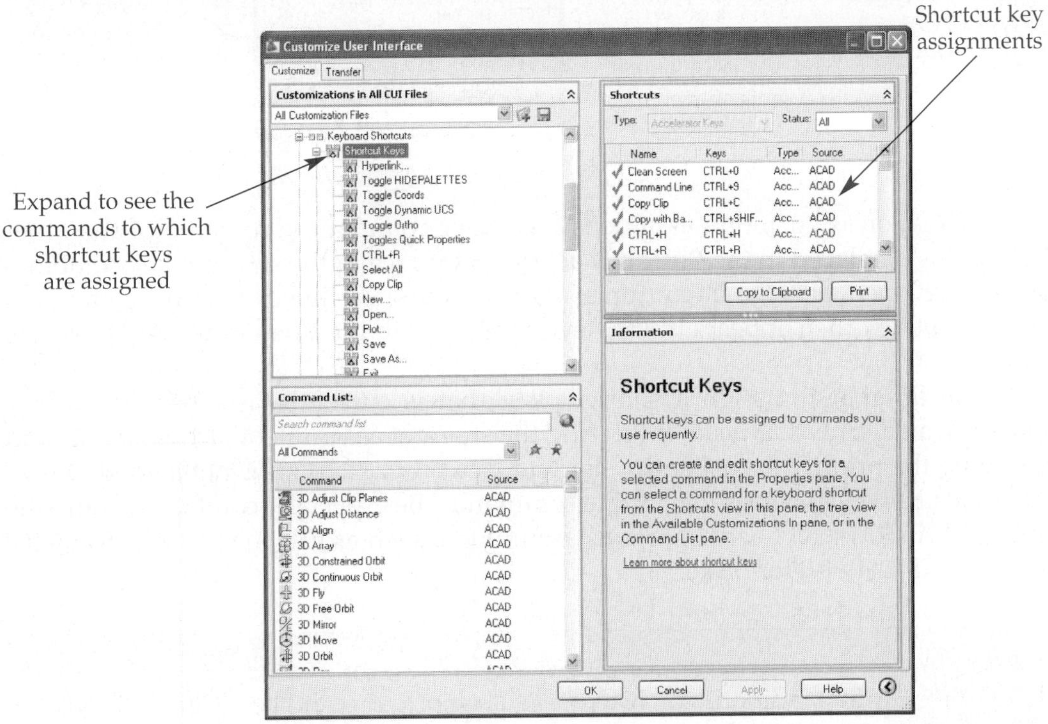

Figure 22-4.
Adding a shortcut key for the **RENDER** command. Drag the **RENDER** command up from the **Command List:** pane to the Shortcut Keys branch.

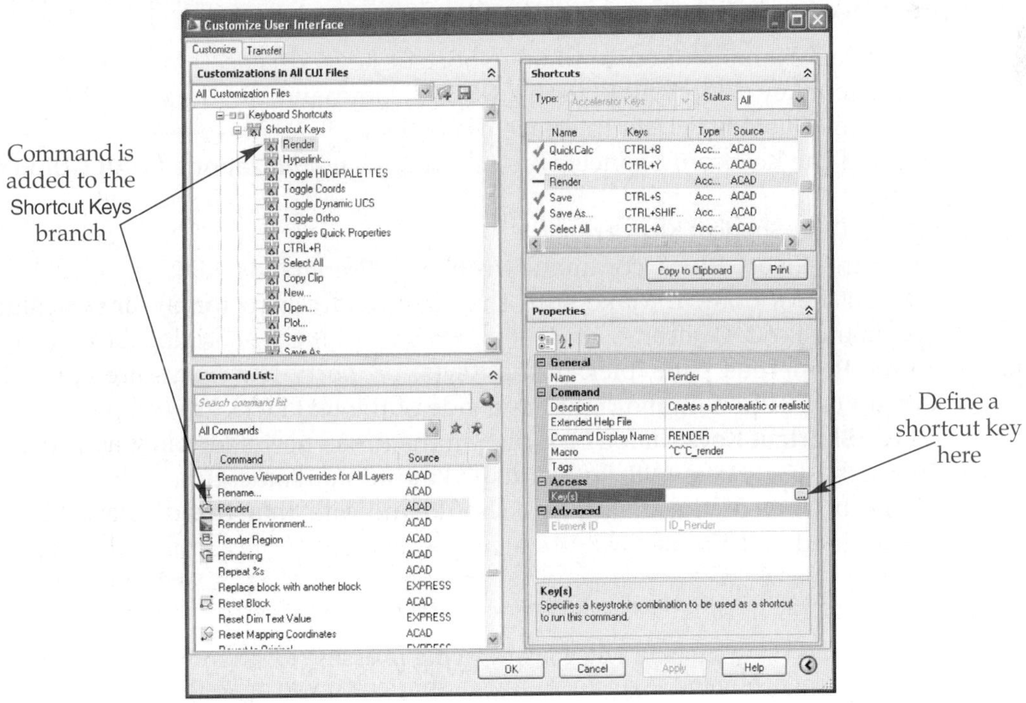

ellipsis button (**...**) on the right-hand end of the text box to display the **Shortcut Keys** dialog box. See **Figure 22-5.**

To assign a new shortcut key to the command, pick in the text box labeled **Press new shortcut key:** and press a combination of [Ctrl] + another key. If the shortcut

Figure 22-5.
The **Shortcut Keys** dialog box is where a shortcut key is specified for the command.

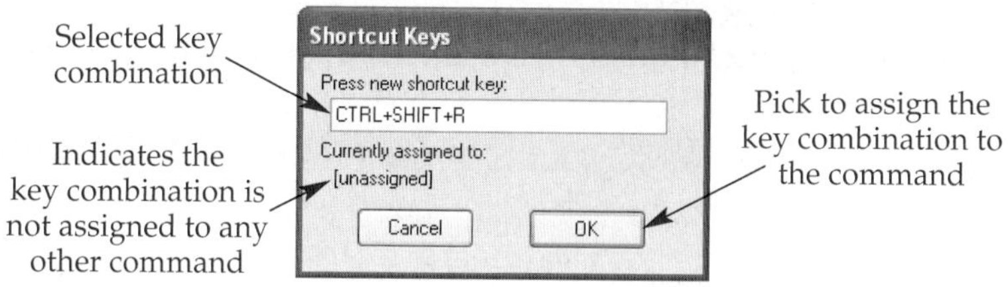

key combination is currently assigned to another command, the name of the other command is displayed in the **Currently assigned to:** area. If the shortcut key combination is unassigned, pick the **OK** button to associate the shortcut key with the command. The shortcut key then appears in the Key(s) property in the **Customize User Interface** dialog box.

If you attempt to assign a shortcut key that is currently assigned to another command, an alert box appears indicating the shortcut assignment already exists and explaining the priority for using the shortcut. See **Figure 22-6.** It is not a good idea to have a shortcut key assigned to multiple commands. Be especially careful to ensure the standard Windows keyboard shortcuts are unique, such as [Ctrl]+[X] for cut, [Ctrl]+[C] for copy, and [Ctrl]+[V] for paste.

PROFESSIONAL TIP

In addition to [Ctrl]+*key*, a shortcut can be [Ctrl]+[Shift]+*key*, [Ctrl]+[Alt]+*key*, or [Ctrl]+[Shift]+[Alt]+*key*. The [Caps Lock] key must be off in order to specify the [Shift] key in the **Press new shortcut key:** text box.

Example Shortcut Key Assignment

To provide an example of customizing shortcut keys, this section shows how to assign the shortcut key [Ctrl]+[Alt]+[I] to the **INSERT** command. Do the following:

1. Open the **Customize User Interface** dialog box.
2. Expand the Keyboard Shortcuts branch in the **Customizations in All CUI Files** pane.
3. Expand the Shortcut Keys branch.
4. Drag the **Insert Block** command from the **Commands List:** pane into the Shortcut Keys branch. Make sure the command macro for the **Insert Block** command is ^C^C_insert.
5. In the **Properties** pane, pick in the Key(s) property text box. Then, pick the ellipsis (**...**) button on the right-hand side of the text box.
6. In the **Shortcut Keys** dialog box, pick in the **Press new shortcut key:** text box.
7. Press the [Ctrl] key, [Alt] key, and [I] key at the same time. The message at the bottom of the dialog box should indicate that this shortcut key is unassigned.

Figure 22-6.
This warning appears if the shortcut key you are trying to assign to a command is already assigned to a different command. Avoid assigning a shortcut key to more than one command.

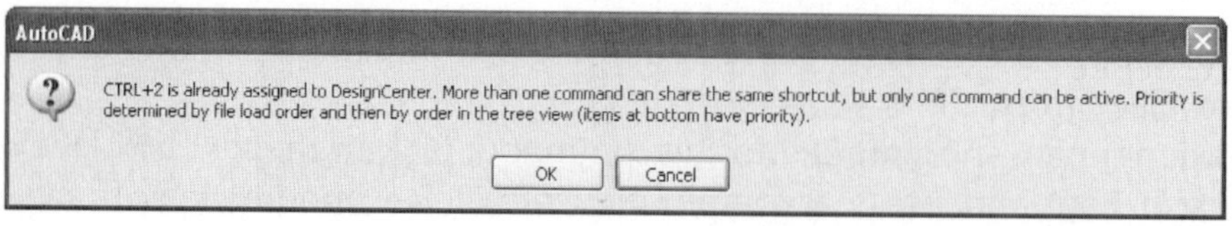

8. Pick the **OK** button to close the **Shortcut Keys** dialog box.
9. Pick the **OK** button to close the **Customize User Interface** dialog box and apply the change.
10. Test the [Ctrl]+[Alt]+[I] shortcut key. The **Insert** dialog box should appear when the shortcut key is used.

PROFESSIONAL TIP

Shortcut keys (accelerator keys) have some specific limitations. For example, a shortcut cannot pause for user input or use repeating commands. Be aware of this when assigning shortcut keys to custom commands.

Exercise 22-1

Complete the exercise on the Student CD.

Examining Existing Shortcut Menus

Shortcut menus are context-sensitive menus that appear at the cursor location when using the right-hand button on the pointing device (right-clicking). ***Context sensitive*** means that the displayed shortcut menu is dependent on what is occurring at the time of the right-click. For example, if no command is active, there is no object selection, and you right-click in the drawing area, the shortcut menu shown in **Figure 22-7A** is displayed. If no command is active and you right-click in **Command Line** window, the shortcut menu shown in **Figure 22-7B** is displayed. If the **CIRCLE** command is active and you right-click in the drawing area before any point is selected, the shortcut menu shown in **Figure 22-7C** is displayed. Other menus appear when right-clicking in other situations, too, such as when grips are being used or when an

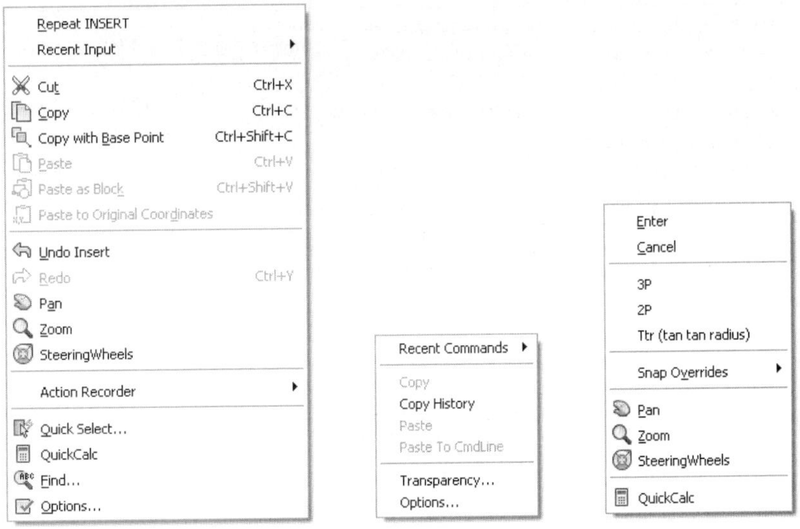

A B C

Figure 22-7. A—Displayed when no command is active and no object is selected. B—Displayed when no command is active and you right-click in the **Command Line** window. The **Transparency...** entry only appears if the window is floating. C—Displayed when the **CIRCLE** command is active and before any point is selected.

object is selected in the drawing window. In the case of a selected object, the shortcut menu is based on the type of object that is selected.

Before learning how to customize shortcut menus, examine the existing shortcut menus. Open the **Customize User Interface** dialog box and look at the **Customizations in All CUI Files** pane. The name of this pane is based on what is selected in the drop-down list. Expand the Shortcut Menus branch in the tree. All of the existing shortcut menu names are displayed as branches. See **Figure 22-8.** There are command-specific, object-specific, and generic shortcut menus. The generic shortcut menus are:

- **Command Menu.** This menu appears when right-clicking in the drawing window while a command is active. Any command options for the active command are inserted into this menu. See **Figure 22-9.**

Figure 22-8.
Existing shortcut menus are displayed as branches in the Shortcut Menus branch in the **Customize User Interface** dialog box.

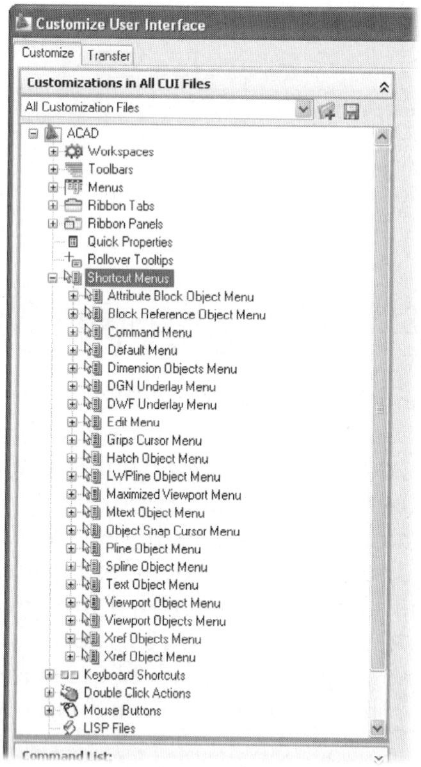

Figure 22-9.
A—The Command Menu branch in the **Customize User Interface** dialog box. B—The command shortcut menu.

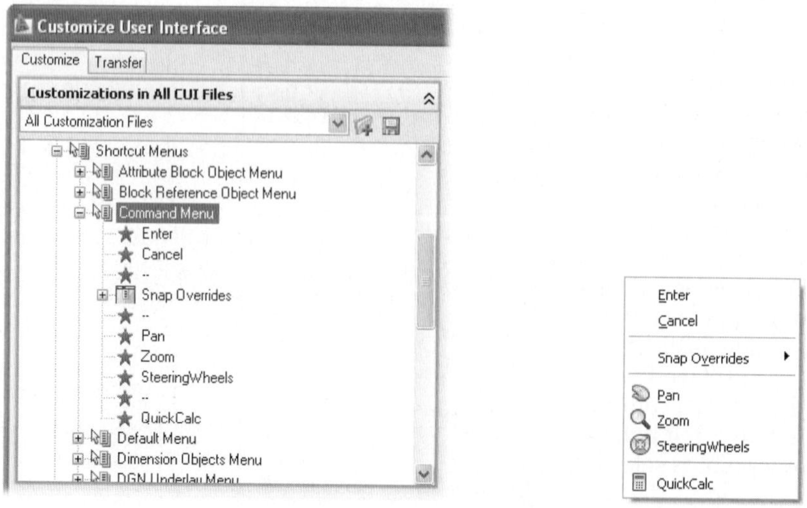

A B

- **Default Menu.** This menu appears when right-clicking in the drawing window while no command is active and no objects are selected. See **Figure 22-10.**
- **Edit Menu.** This menu appears when right-clicking in the drawing window when no command is active and an object is selected. In order for this menu to be displayed, the **PICKFIRST** system variable must be set to 1. If an object menu is available for the type of object selected, it is inserted into this menu. See **Figure 22-11.**
- **Grips Cursor Menu.** This menu appears when grips are being used. See **Figure 22-12.** An object must be selected and at least one grip must be hot.

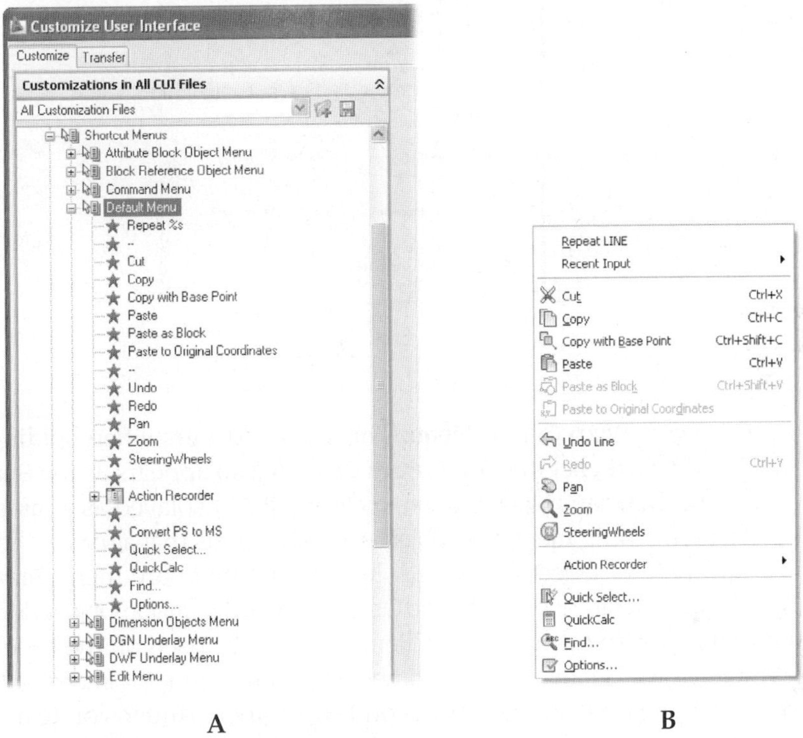

Figure 22-10.
A—The Default Menu branch in the **Customize User Interface** dialog box.
B—The default shortcut menu.

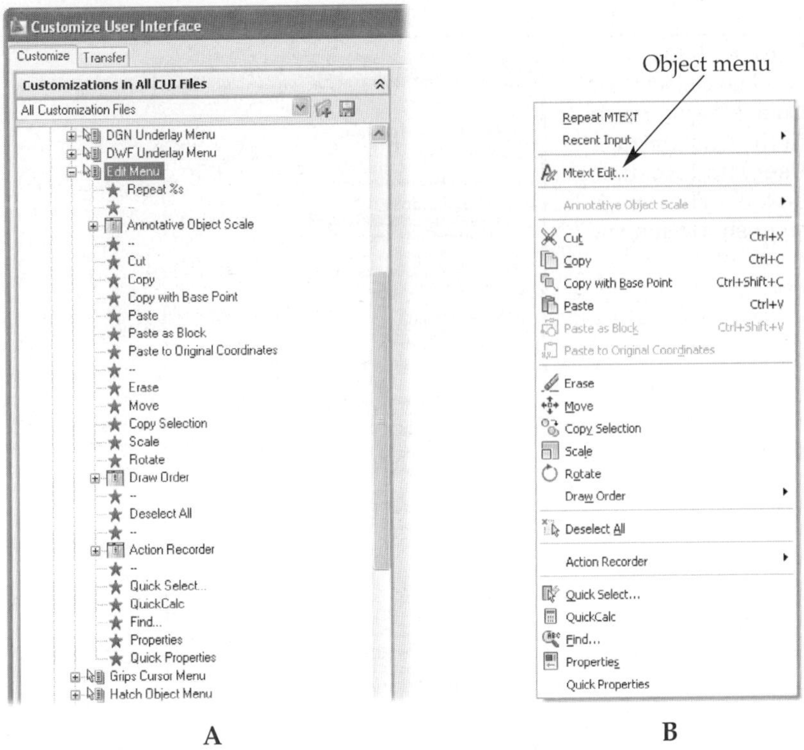

Figure 22-11.
A—The Edit Menu branch in the **Customize User Interface** dialog box.
B—The edit shortcut menu.

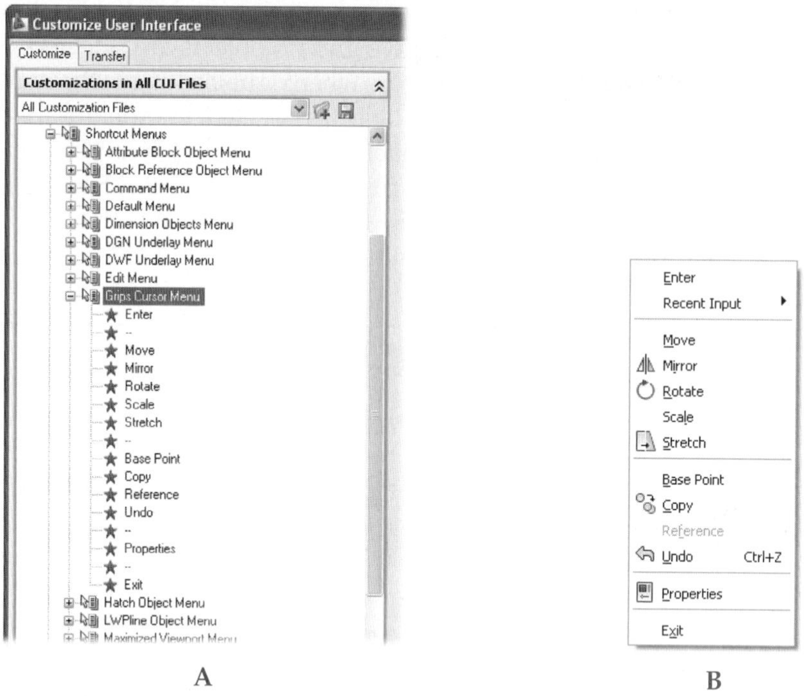

Figure 22-12.
A—The **Grips Cursor Menu** branch in the **Customize User Interface** dialog box. B—The grips shortcut menu.

- **Object Snap Cursor Menu.** This menu appears when holding the down [Shift] key and right-clicking. See **Figure 22-13.** It also appears as the **Snap Overrides** branch in the **Command Menu** branch, meaning it is displayed as a cascading menu.

The remaining menus are object-specific menus that appear when right-clicking while a certain type of object is selected. Notice that there are menu branches named **Attribute Block Objects Menu**, **Block Reference Objects Menu**, **Dimension Objects Menu**, **Hatch Object Menu**, and others. These menus contain items that can be used on the type of object selected. For example, in the **Shortcut Menus** branch, the menu branch **Dimension Objects Menu** contains commands for editing the dimension text position, dimension text precision, and dimension style.

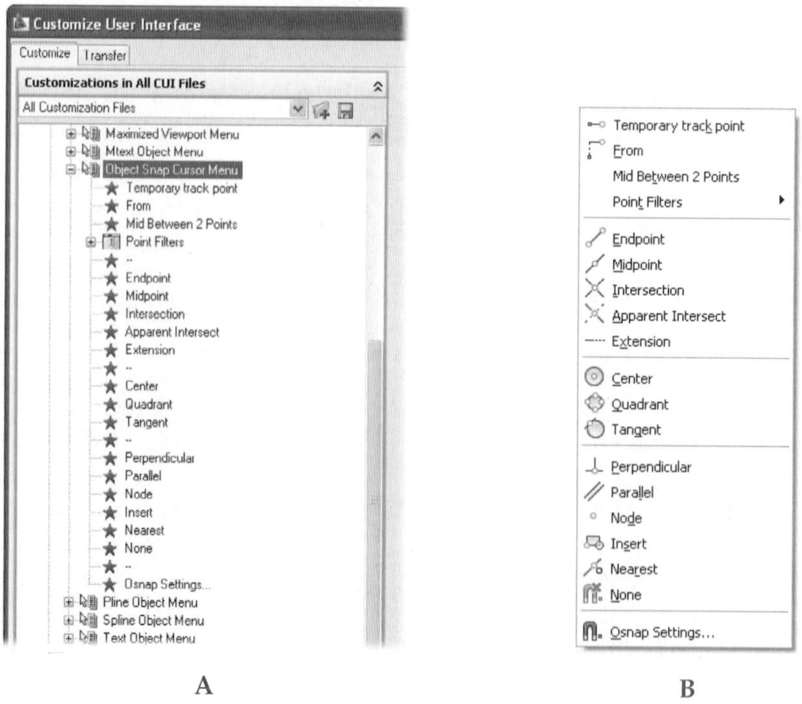

Figure 22-13.
A—The **Object Snap Cursor Menu** branch in the **Customize User Interface** dialog box. B—The object snap shortcut menu.

Exercise 22-2

Complete the exercise on the Student CD.

Customizing Shortcut Menus

The existing shortcut menus can be customized by adding or removing commands. Shortcut menus can also be customized by visually grouping commands using separators. Cascading menus can be added to shortcut menus.

To add a command to a shortcut menu, open the **Customize User Interface** dialog box and, in the **Customizations in All CUI Files** pane, expand the branch for the shortcut menu you would like to customize. Next, locate the command you wish to add in the **Command List:** pane. Then, drag the command into the desired position within the shortcut menu in the **Customizations in All CUI Files** pane and drop it when the bar appears.

To remove a command from a shortcut menu, expand the branch for the shortcut menu in the **Customizations in All CUI Files** pane. Highlight the command to be removed, right-click, and select **Remove** from the shortcut menu. You can also highlight the command and press the [Delete] key.

To add a separator to a shortcut menu, expand the branch for the shortcut menu in the **Customizations in All CUI Files** pane. Highlight the command *after* which you would like the separator to be added. Right-click and select **Insert Separator** from the shortcut menu.

To rename a shortcut menu, highlight the branch in the **Customizations in All CUI Files** pane. Then, right-click and select **Rename** from the shortcut menu. Finally, type the new name and press [Enter]. The shortcut menu can also be renamed using the Name property in the **Properties** pane.

To add a cascading menu to a shortcut menu, expand the branch for the shortcut menu in the **Customizations in All CUI Files** pane. Highlight the command *after* which you would like the cascading menu to appear. Right-click and select **New Sub-menu** from the shortcut menu. A new shortcut menu branch with the default name of Menu*x* is added to the current shortcut menu. The new menu can be renamed. Now, in the **Command List:** pane, locate the commands you wish to add to the new shortcut menu. Drag the commands into the **Customizations in All CUI Files** pane and drop them next to the name of the new shortcut menu. When the arrow appears next to the new menu name, drop the command to add it to the new shortcut menu.

Creating a new, custom shortcut menu is a two-step process. First, make a new shortcut menu and then drag commands into it. Follow these steps to make a new shortcut menu:

1. Open the **Customize User Interface** dialog box.
2. In the **Customizations in All CUI Files** pane, right-click on the Shortcut Menus branch and select **New Shortcut Menu** in the shortcut menu that is displayed.
3. Enter a name for the shortcut menu.
4. In the **Properties** pane, add a description for the shortcut menu in the **General** category.
5. In the **Advanced** category of the **Properties** pane, add an alias. This alias is in addition to the automatic, sequential POP5*xx* alias that AutoCAD creates. Select the property, pick the ellipsis button (**...**) at the right-hand end of the

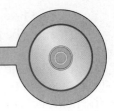

text box, and type the alias in the **Aliases** dialog box that appears. Each alias must be on its own line in this dialog box. Close the **Aliases** dialog box.
6. Drag commands from the **Command List:** pane into the new shortcut menu.
7. Pick the **Apply** or **OK** button to apply the changes.

There are two types of custom shortcut menus: object specific and command oriented. The next sections describe the two types of custom shortcut menus in detail.

Creating Object-Specific Shortcut Menus

When creating an object-specific shortcut menu, there can actually be two menus available. One menu is displayed for instances when just a single object of a given type is selected. The other menu is displayed when more than one object is selected.

The name assigned to the object menu should follow the same syntax used for naming AutoCAD's default object-specific menus: *object_type* **Object Menu** or *object_type* **Objects Menu** (with an S). In this way, when looking at the shortcut menus in the **Customizations in All CUI Files** pane in the **Customize User Interface** dialog box, you will easily recognize which object type that menu applies to and whether it is for multiple selected objects or a single selected object. The use of this syntax is optional. Menus can be named using whatever naming scheme you wish. However, it is recommended to follow the naming syntax described here.

The alias for the shortcut menu has a syntax that *must* be followed. It is this alias that AutoCAD uses in determining to which object or objects the menu applies. The syntax for the alias must take on the form of OBJECT_*type* or OBJECTS_*type* and must be exactly followed in order for AutoCAD to properly display the shortcut menu.

As an example, the following procedure creates a shortcut menu that allows access to the **LENGTHEN** and **BREAK** commands when a single line is selected.

1. Open the **Customize User Interface** dialog box.
2. Right-click on the Shortcut Menus branch in the **Customizations in All CUI Files** pane and select **New Shortcut Menu**.
3. Name the shortcut menu **Line Object Menu**.
4. In the **Properties** pane, select the Alias property in the **Advanced** category. Then, pick the ellipsis button to open the **Aliases** dialog box. On the second line, enter the alias OBJECT_LINE and then close the **Aliases** dialog box. Since the **LENGTHEN** and **BREAK** commands can only be applied to a single object, be sure to use the OBJECT_*type* syntax (without the S).
5. Drag the **LENGTHEN** and **BREAK** commands from the **Command List:** pane into the Line Object Menu branch in **Customizations in All CUI Files** pane. See **Figure 22-14A.**
6. Pick the **OK** button to close the **Customize User Interface** dialog box and apply the changes.

Now, draw a line, select it, and right-click. Notice that **Lengthen** and **Break** entries appear in the shortcut menu. See **Figure 22-14B.** Selecting either entry executes the command. If the command accepts a preselected object, it is executed on the selected line. Neither **LENGTHEN** nor **BREAK** accepts preselected objects; you must reselect the line. Having the entries in the shortcut menu provides for quicker access to the command.

Creating Command-Oriented Shortcut Menus

When a command is being executed, any command options appear in the shortcut menu. For example, when the **CIRCLE** command prompts for a radius, you can right-click and select **Diameter** from the shortcut menu. Custom shortcut menus can be created for use when certain commands are active. This allows you to add options to the shortcut menu that is displayed when a command is active. Quicker access to object snaps and object selection methods are just a couple of applications that

Figure 22-14.
A—The new object-specific shortcut menu is created. B—The **BREAK** and **LENGTHEN** commands are now available in the shortcut menu.

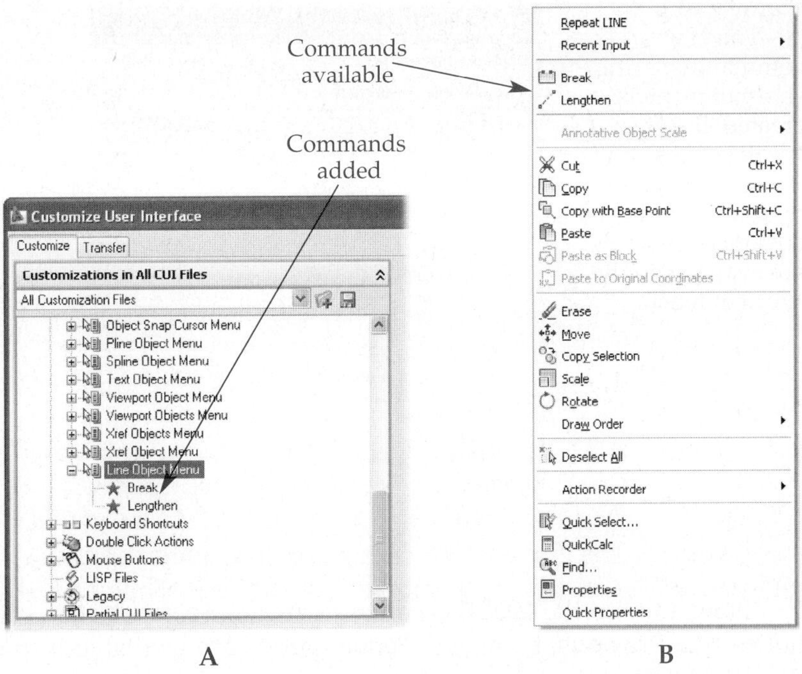

custom, command-oriented shortcut menus could allow for within commonly used commands.

A command-oriented shortcut menu is created in the same way as an object-oriented shortcut menu, as discussed in the previous section. However, the syntax for the alias is slightly different. The alias must be in the form of COMMAND_*command_name*, where *command_name* is the name of the command with which you want the shortcut menu associated.

Also, if the command step does not have any default options, such as a Select objects: prompt, right-clicking is, by default, interpreted as the [Enter] key. Therefore, in the **Right-Click Customization** dialog box, the **Shortcut Menu: always enabled** radio button must be selected in the **Command Mode** area, as described earlier.

As an example, the following procedure creates a custom shortcut menu that displays **Previous**, **Last**, and **Fence** selection options at the Select objects: prompt for the **MOVE** command.

1. Open the **Customize User Interface** dialog box.
2. Make custom commands for the three selection options. Name the commands **Previous**, **Last**, and **Fence**. For the macros, remove the ^C^C that is automatically placed in the macro and type the selection option; for example, PREVIOUS for the **Previous** command.
3. Right-click on the Shortcut Menus branch in the **Customizations in All CUI Files** pane and select **New Shortcut Menu**.
4. Name the shortcut menu **Move Command Menu**.
5. In the **Properties** pane, select the Alias property in the **Advanced** category. Then, pick the ellipsis button to open the **Aliases** dialog box. On the second line, enter the alias COMMAND_MOVE and then close the **Aliases** dialog box. The syntax of COMMAND_*command_name* must be exactly followed in order for AutoCAD to properly display the shortcut menu.
6. Drag the **Previous**, **Last**, and **Fence** custom commands from the **Command List:** pane into the Move Command Menu branch in **Customizations in All CUI Files** pane. See **Figure 22-15A**.
7. Pick the **OK** button to close the **Customize User Interface** dialog box and apply the changes.

Figure 22-15.
A—The new command-specific shortcut menu is created. B—The **Previous**, **Last**, and **Fence** "command options" (actually, custom commands) are available in the shortcut menu.

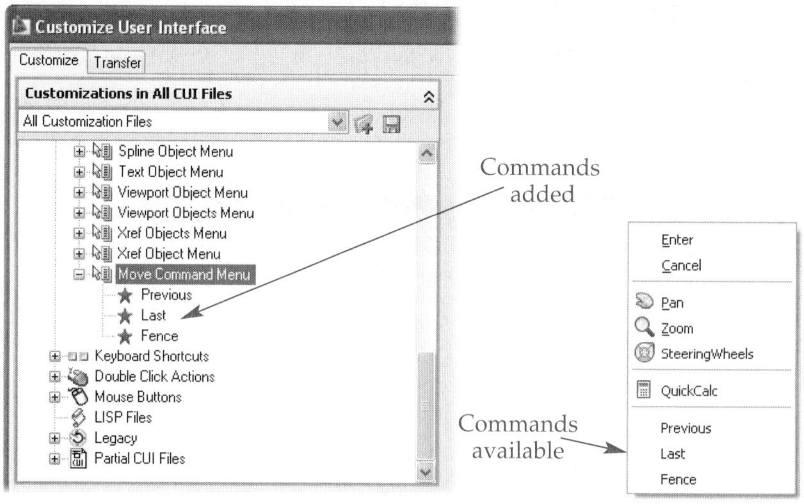

A B

Now, initiate the **MOVE** command. At the Select objects: prompt, right-click and notice that **Previous**, **Last**, and **Fence** entries are available in the shortcut menu. See Figure 22-15B. Remember, the **Shortcut Menu: always enabled** radio button must be on in the **Right-Click Customization** dialog box for this shortcut menu to appear.

Exercise 22-3

Complete the exercise on the Student CD.

Customizing Quick Properties and Rollover Tooltips

The **Quick Properties** palette appears when you select objects in the graphics area. This is a streamlined version of the **Properties** palette that displays ***quick properties,*** which provide certain information about the object. In order for the **Quick Properties** palette to be displayed, the **Quick Properties** button on the status bar must be on. The palette can also be displayed by right-clicking with an object selected and selecting **Quick Properties** in the shortcut menu so it is checked.

Rollover tooltips provide certain information about an object, also called quick properties, in a graphic tooltip. This tooltip is displayed as the cursor is hovered over the object. A rollover tooltip serves a similar purpose as the **Quick Properties** palette, but it only provides information. Properties cannot be changed in the tooltip.

The quick properties displayed in the **Quick Properties** palette and a rollover tooltip can be customized. Each object type can have different quick properties displayed. Additionally, different quick properties can be displayed in the **Quick Properties** palette and rollover tooltip for a given object type. The steps for customizing quick properties are the same for the **Quick Properties** palette and rollover tooltips, as discussed in this section.

Open the **Customize User Interface** dialog box. In the **Customizations in All CUI Files** pane, select the Quick Properties branch. Two columns are displayed on the right-hand side of the dialog box. See Figure 22-16. When you select Rollover Tooltips in the **Customizations in All CUI Files** pane, the same two columns are displayed. However,

Figure 22-16.
When the Quick Properties branch is selected in the **Customize User Interface** dialog box, the object type list is displayed on the right-hand side of the dialog box.

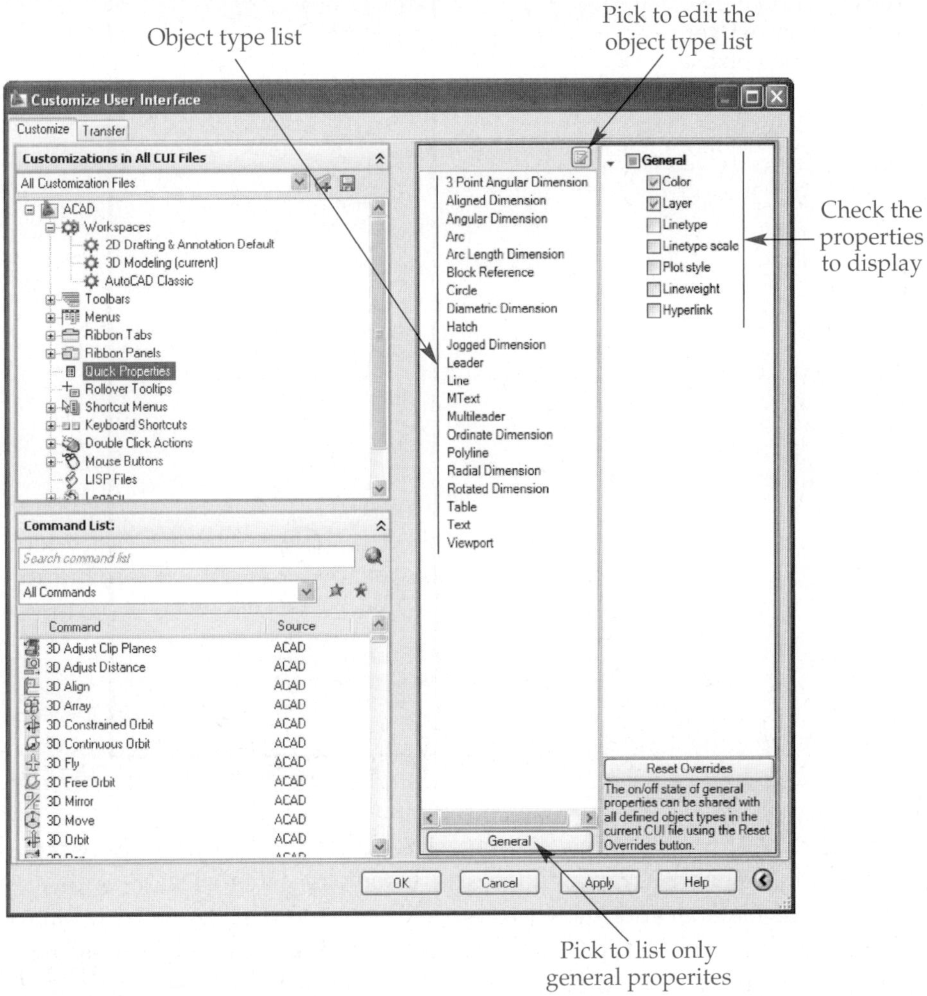

the settings may be different between the Quick Properties branch and the Rollover Tooltips branch.

The left-hand column displays the ***object type list,*** which is a list of AutoCAD object types. You may add or remove object types by picking the **Edit Object Type List** button at the top of the column. This displays the **Edit Object Type List** dialog box, **Figure 22-17.** All available AutoCAD object types are listed in this dialog box. Those that are checked appear in the object type list in the **Customize User Interface** dialog box.

The object type list controls which objects display quick properties. The right-hand column displays a list of quick properties that can be displayed. The properties that are checked appear in the **Quick Properties** palette or rollover tooltip. Remember, the palette and tooltip can display different properties.

All objects have a General category containing similar quick properties. By default, the color and layer properties are turned on for all objects in the list. To display the General category for objects that do not have defined quick properties, pick the **General** button at the bottom of the object type list.

To customize the quick properties displayed for a specific object type, select the object in the object type list. The category list in the right-hand column displays all categories and quick properties available for that object. Check the properties that you want displayed and uncheck the properties you do not want displayed.

Figure 22-17.
Determining which object types appear in the object type list in the **Customize User Interface** dialog box.

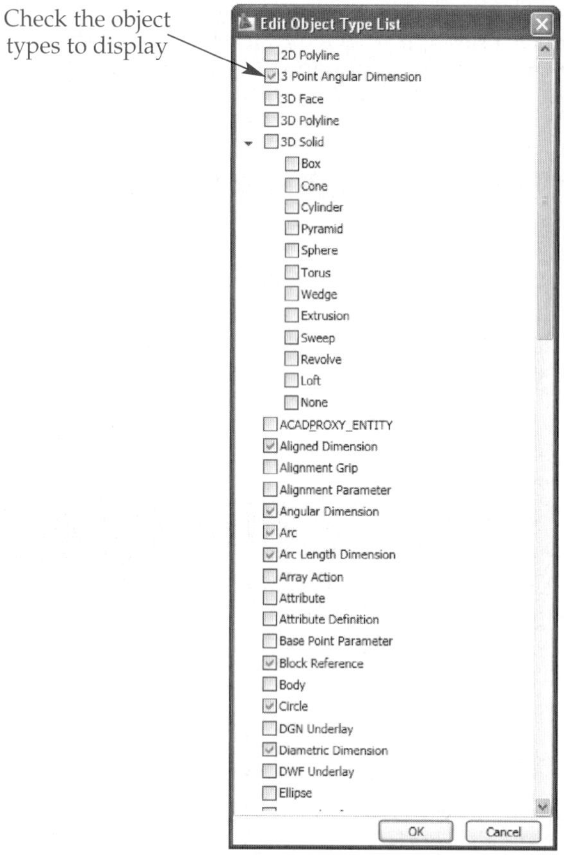

Figure 22-18A shows the line object type selected in the object type list. Notice that this object has 3D Visualization and Geometry categories, as well as the General category. The Material and Angle properties are set to display in addition to the default settings. Once you close the **Customize User Interface** dialog box to apply the changes, the new quick properties are displayed for a selected line. See **Figure 22-18B.**

PROFESSIONAL TIP

By customizing quick properties, you may improve your AutoCAD workflow by having quick access to properties throughout the design process. For example, you may wish to have the Show History property displayed in the **Quick Properties** palette for solid primitives, sweeps, lofts, and revolutions. This will allow you to quickly show or hide the history of the solid. Additionally, you may wish to have the Material property displayed in the rollover tooltip for these objects. This will provide a quick indication of which material is assigned to the object.

Customizing Double-Click Actions

By double-clicking on certain objects, an appropriate editing command is automatically executed. Which command is initiated is determined by the ***double-click action*** associated with the object type. Some AutoCAD objects have very specific

Figure 22-18.
Customizing the quick properties for a line. A—Two properties in addition to the default properties are set to display. B—The **Quick Properties** palette contains the additional properties.

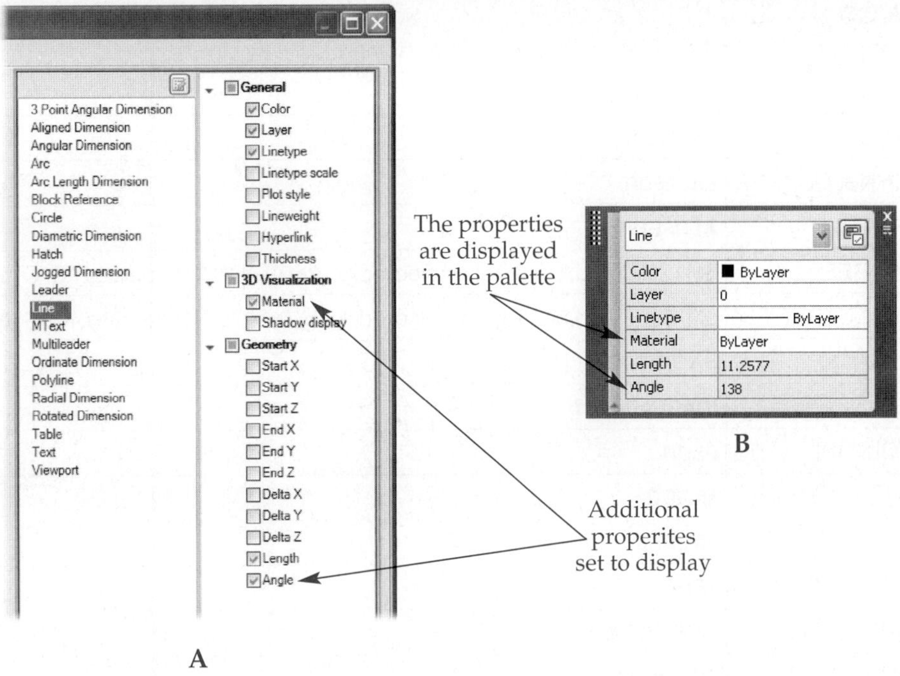

editing tools available. For example, multiline text (mtext) objects are edited with the in-place text editor and hatches are edited in the **Hatch Edit** dialog box.

A list of AutoCAD objects that have default double-click actions associated with them, other than the **PROPERTIES** command, is shown in **Figure 22-19.** If you double-click on one of the object types listed in the table, the command or macro listed in the Associated Double-Click Action column is executed. If the object type is not listed in the table, it is likely the **Properties** palette is displayed, by default, when the object is double-clicked. This is the double-click action associated with most objects.

Assigning Double-Click Actions

Double-click actions are assigned to specific object types in the **Customize User Interface** dialog box. In the **Customizations in All CUI Files** pane, expand the Double Click Actions branch. All of the AutoCAD object types are listed. See **Figure 22-20.** Expand each branch and notice that many double-click actions call the **Properties** palette, while the objects listed in the table in **Figure 22-19** have double-click actions that call the object-specific editing command.

Use the following procedure to change the double-click editing action associated with an object type. For this example, the **DDPTYPE** command will be associated with the point object type so the **Point Style** dialog box appears when a point object is double-clicked.

1. Open the **Customize User Interface** dialog box.
2. In the **Customizations in All CUI Files** pane, expand the Double Click Actions branch.
3. Expand the Point branch under the Double Click Actions branch. Notice that the **PROPERTIES** command is associated with the point object type.
4. In the **Command List:** pane, select the **Point Style...** command. This is the **DDPTYPE** command, as indicated in the **Properties** pane when the command is selected.

Figure 22-19.
AutoCAD objects to which a default double-click action other than **PROPERTIES** is assigned.

AutoCAD Object Type	Associated Double-Click Action
ATTDEF	**DDEDIT**
ATTBLOCKREF	**EATTEDIT**
ATTDYNBLOCKREF	**EATTEDIT**
ATTRIB	**ATTIPEDIT**
BLOCKREF	$M=$(if,$(and,$(>,$(getvar,blockeditlock),0)),^C^C_properties,^C^C_bedit)
DYNBLOCKREF	$M=$(if,$(and,$(>,$(getvar,blockeditlock),0)),^C^C_properties,^C^C_bedit)
HATCH	**HATCHEDIT**
IMAGE	**IMAGEADJUST**
LWPOLYLINE	**PEDIT**
MLINE	**MLEDIT**
MTEXT	**MTEDIT**
POLYLINE	**PEDIT**
SECTIONOBJECT	**LIVESECTION**
SPLINE	**SPLINEDIT**
TEXT	**DDEDIT**
XREF	**REFEDIT**

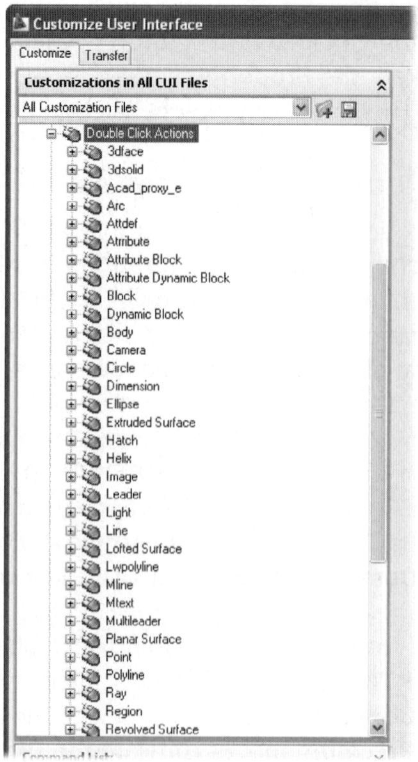

Figure 22-20.
All of the AutoCAD object types are displayed in the Double Click Actions branch in the **Customize User Interface** dialog box.

5. Drag the **Point Style...** command from the **Command List:** pane and drop it into the Point branch in the **Customizations in All CUI Files** pane. See **Figure 22-21.** The command replaces the existing command as there can only be one double-click action.
6. Pick the **OK** button to close the **Customize User Interface** dialog box and apply the change.

Now, draw a point using the **POINT** command. Double-click on the point and the **Point Style** dialog box appears. Select a new point style in the dialog box and pick the **OK** button. All existing points in the drawing should update to the new style. If not, use the **REGEN** command to update the display.

Custom Double-Click Action

You can also create a custom command and assign it to an object type as a double-click action. In this section, you will create a custom command for overriding dimension variables on the fly and applying the new settings to the dimension object that is double-clicked. Here is a breakdown of what the custom command will do:

- Cancel any commands in progress. (^C^C)
- Open the **Dimension Style Manager** dialog box, allowing the **Override** button to be used to make any changes or to create a new dimension style and set it current. The dialog box stays open until the **OK** button is picked. (dimstyle;)
- Execute a command-line version of the **DIMSTYLE** command. (-dimstyle;)
- Enter the **Apply** option. (a;)
- Select the previous selection set (the object that was double-clicked) and end the selection. (p;;)

Dimensioning variables can be overridden using the **Properties** palette. However, using the **Dimension Style Manager** dialog box may be a more-familiar means to accomplish the overrides.

Follow these steps to create a custom command and assign it as a double-click action for the dimension object type:

1. Open the **Customize User Interface** dialog box.
2. Pick the **Create a new command** button in the **Command List:** pane.
3. Name the custom command **DblClkDimEdit**.
4. In the **Properties** pane, select the Macro property. Then, enter the macro ^C^Cddim;-dimstyle;a;p;; in the text box. Use the **Long String Editor**, if needed.

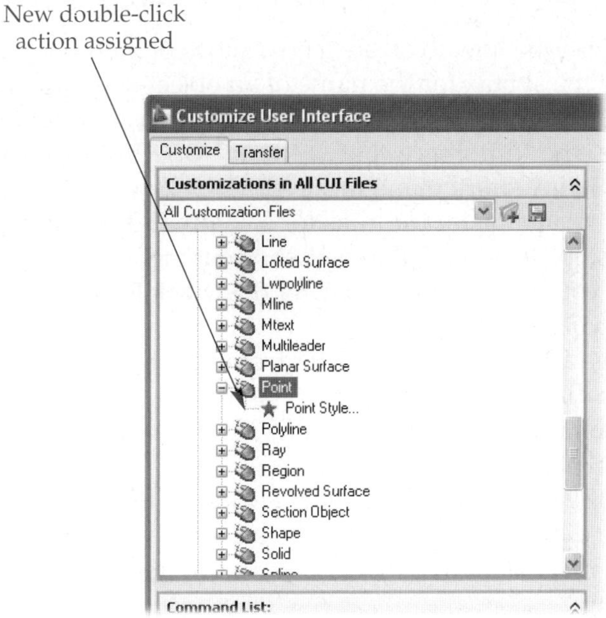

Figure 22-21.
The double-click action associated with the point object type is changed.

5. In the **Customizations in All CUI Files** pane, expand the Double Click Actions branch and locate the Dimension branch below it. Notice that the **PROPERTIES** command is associated with the dimension object type.
6. In the **Command List:** pane, select the new **DblClkDimEdit** command and drag it into the Dimension branch in the **Customizations in All CUI Files** pane.
7. Pick the **OK** button to close the **Customize User Interface** dialog box and apply the change.

Now, place a dimension using the **DIMLINEAR** command. Next, double-click on the dimension. In the **Dimension Style Manager** dialog box, select the **Override...** button. In the **Override Current Style:** dialog box that is displayed, select the **Text** tab. Using the **Text color:** drop-down list, change the text color. Pick the **OK** button to close the **Override Current Style:** dialog box. Then, pick the **Close** button to close the **Dimension Style Manager** dialog box. The dimension text should assume the new color setting. If it does not, open the **Customize User Interface** dialog box and examine the custom command macro for any errors.

NOTE

After using the custom double-click action assigned to the dimension object type, the dimension overrides remain in effect for the next dimensions placed.

Chapter Test

Answer the following questions. Write your answers on a separate sheet of paper or complete the electronic chapter test on the Student CD.

1. What is the key combination called that allows you to press the [Ctrl] key and an additional key to execute a command?
2. How can you disable all shortcut menus and all double-click actions?
3. In which dialog box can you define what a right-click does when in default mode, edit mode, and command mode?
4. Why are shortcut menus *context sensitive?*
5. When does the command shortcut menu appear?
6. What must the **PICKFIRST** setting be in order for the edit shortcut menu to appear?
7. Briefly describe how to create a new shortcut menu.
8. Describe the syntax for the name of an object-specific shortcut menu.
9. Why is CIRCLE_OBJECT *not* a valid alias for a shortcut menu?
10. Describe the difference between an OBJECT_*type* shortcut menu and an OBJECTS_*type* shortcut menu.
11. What is the syntax for the alias for a command-specific shortcut menu?
12. List the steps to add an alias to a shortcut menu.
13. How do you turn on the display of the **Quick Properties** palette?
14. What is a *quick property?*
15. How does a rollover tooltip differ from the **Quick Properties** palette?
16. In which dialog box do you select the objects that appear in the object type list in the **Customize User Interface** dialog box?
17. What is a *double-click action?*
18. What is the most common double-click action?
19. In which dialog box is a double-click action assigned?
20. List the basic steps for modifying the double-click action associated with an object.

Drawing Problems

Before customizing AutoCAD, check with your instructor or supervisor for specific instructions or guidelines.

1. Create a shortcut key for each of the drawing and editing commands listed below. Be sure not to use any existing shortcut keys.

LINE	**MOVE**
ARC	**COPY**
CIRCLE	**STRETCH**
POLYLINE	**TRIM**
POLYGON	**EXTEND**
RECTANGLE	**CHAMFER**
DTEXT	**FILLET**
ERASE	

2. In this problem, create an object-specific shortcut menu. The shortcut menu should be displayed when an arc object is selected. The shortcut menu should contain the **LENGTHEN** and **BREAK** commands.

3. In this problem, create a command-specific shortcut menu. The shortcut menu should be displayed when the **CIRCLE** command is active. Add the **Circle, Tan, Tan, Tan** command available in the **Customize User Interface** dialog box to the shortcut menu. Add two selection options, such as **Last** or **Window**, as described in this chapter.

4. By default, double-clicking on a circle displays the **Properties** palette. Take the steps necessary so that a **REGEN** is performed instead.

5. Create a custom command that changes the color of an object to blue. Then, assign this command as the double-click action for the hatch object type.

Material libraries are accessed through tool palettes. You can create your own tool palette group and new tool palettes to place within the group. This allows you to display only the palettes you wish to access for adding materials.

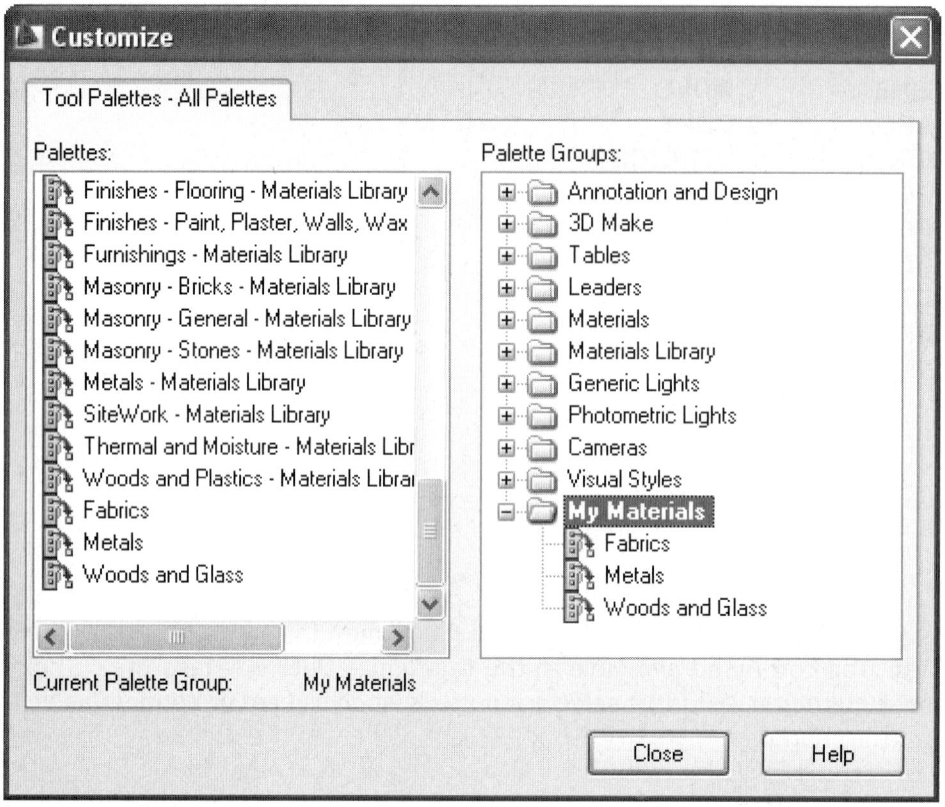

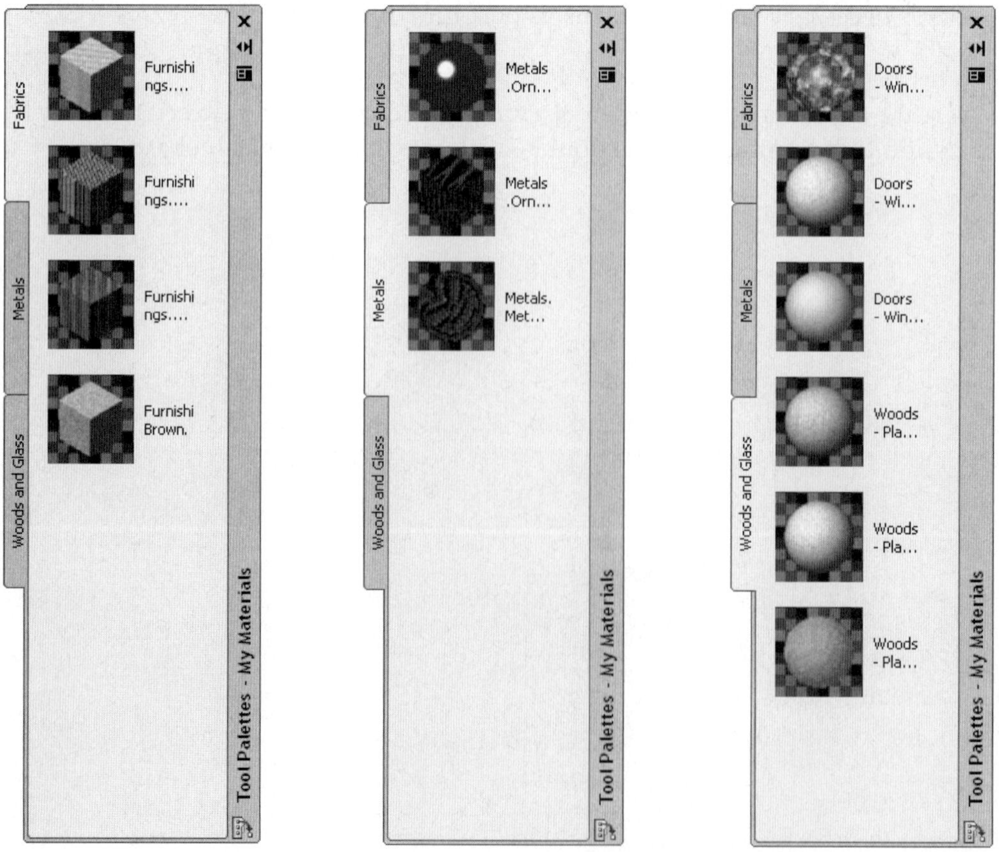

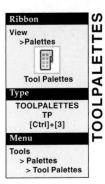

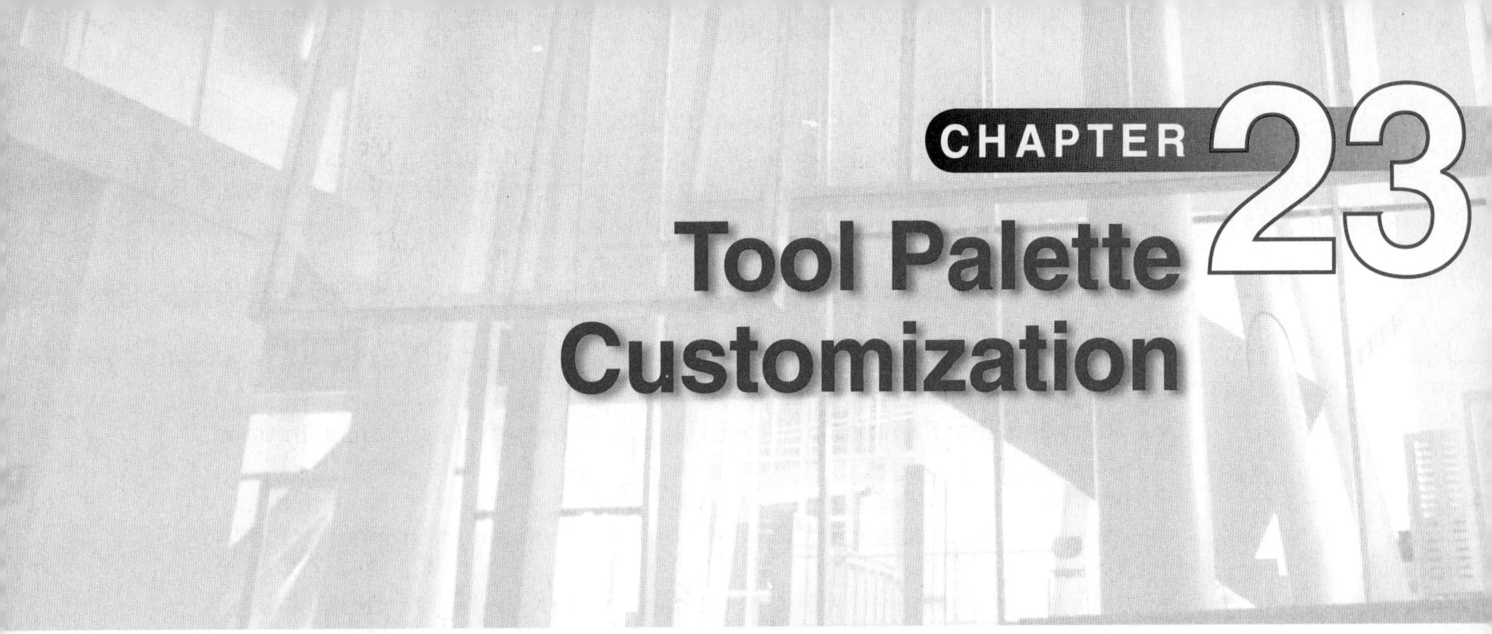

CHAPTER 23

Tool Palette Customization

Learning Objectives

After completing this chapter, you will be able to:

- ✓ Modify the appearance of the **Tool Palettes** window.
- ✓ Compare and contrast block insertion, hatch insertion, and command tools.
- ✓ Create new tool palettes from scratch and using **DesignCenter**.
- ✓ Add tools to existing tool palettes.
- ✓ Explain how tool palettes are formatted.
- ✓ Adjust the properties of tools.
- ✓ Create a flyout tool.
- ✓ Organize tool palette tabs into groups.
- ✓ Export and import tools and tool palettes.

Tool palettes are a user-interface method for the easy insertion of blocks and hatch patterns, for command entry, and for attaching materials. Blocks and hatch patterns can be simply dragged and dropped from a tool palette directly into a drawing. In addition, tool palettes serve as a materials library in AutoCAD. Tool palettes are contained within the **Tool Palettes** window.

Tool Palette Overview

TOOLPALETTES

Ribbon
View
>Palettes
Tool Palettes

Type
TOOLPALETTES
TP
[Ctrl]+[3]

Menu
Tools
> Palettes
> Tool Palettes

The **TOOLPALETTES** command is used to display the **Tool Palettes** window. Notice that the **Tool Palettes** window has a number of tabs on its edge. Each of these tabs corresponds to a tool palette. To make a tool palette active, pick its tab. If there are more tabs than can be displayed, pick on the "stack" at the bottom of the tabs to display a shortcut menu in which you can select the tool palette to display. To use a tool on any tool palette, drag it from the tool palette and drop it into the drawing.

By default, the **Tool Palettes** window contains the **Modeling**, **Annotation**, **Architectural**, **Mechanical**, **Electrical**, **Civil**, **Structural**, **Hatches and Fills**, **Tables**, **Command Tool Samples**, **Leaders**, **Draw**, **Modify**, **Cameras**, **Visual Styles**, eight material palettes (more if the materials library is installed), and five light palettes. Each of these is described below.

- **Modeling palette.** Contains tools for creating specific variations of some solid primitives. Also contains two UCS tools and a 3D align tool.

- **Annotation palette.** Contains blocks that are typically inserted in paper space.
- **Architectural, Mechanical, Electrical, Civil, and Structural palettes.** Can be used to insert blocks that are meant to be used within the discipline for which the palette is named. Certain preset properties are already attached to the symbols, such as scale and rotation.
- **Hatches and Fills palette.** Contains some commonly used hatches and sample gradient fills that can be quickly inserted into a drawing.
- **Tables palette.** Allows you to insert sample tables in US customary (Imperial) and metric formats.
- **Command Tool Samples palette.** Allows you to execute certain commands by picking the tool.
- **Leaders palette.** Allows you to place leaders with or without text, or with various types of callout balloons, in both US customary (Imperial) and metric scales.
- **Draw palette.** Contains many of the same tools found in the **Draw** panel on the **Home** tab of the ribbon and some tools for inserting blocks, attaching images, and attaching xrefs.
- **Modify palette.** Contains many of the same tools found in the **Modify** panel on the **Home** tab of the ribbon.
- **Material palettes.** The tools in these palettes allow you to quickly drag and drop various materials into the drawing. The material palettes are AutoCAD's materials library. If the materials library is not installed, eight palettes containing sample materials are available.
- **Light palettes.** Contain tools for inserting many types of lights.
- **Cameras palette.** Contains tools for inserting three different cameras into the drawing. The cameras have differing lens lengths and fields of view.
- **Visual Styles palette.** Contains tools for three variations of the default visual styles.

For detailed instruction on how tool palettes can be used to insert blocks and hatch patterns, see *AutoCAD and Its Applications—Basics.* This chapter describes how to customize existing tool palettes and create your own tool palettes.

Tool Palette Appearance

There are a number of methods for altering the appearance of the **Tool Palettes** window, either for productivity or personal preference. For example, the tabs can be renamed. Right-click on the title of the tab and select **Rename Palette** from the shortcut menu. An edit box is displayed near the current name with the name highlighted. Type a new name and press [Enter] to rename the palettes. Other methods of changing the appearance of the **Tool Palettes** window are covered in this section.

Docking

By default, the **Tool Palettes** window is floating on the right side of the screen in the AutoCAD Classic workspace, docked on the right side of the screen in the 3D Modeling workspace, and not displayed in the 2D Drafting & Annotation workspace. If docked, it can be moved to a new, floating location by picking and holding on the title bar, dragging the window to the desired location, and releasing the pick button. Moving the window to the far side of the drawing window forces the title bar to flip to the other side of the **Tool Palettes** window so the bar is toward the outer edge of the drawing window.

By default, the **Tool Palettes** window can be docked, just like a toolbar. Moving the window outside of the drawing window to the left or right docks it. The **Tool Palettes** window cannot be docked at the top or bottom. To prevent docking, right-click on the **Tool Palettes** window title bar to display the shortcut menu. Select **Allow Docking** to remove the check mark. When a check mark appears next to **Allow Docking**, the window can be docked.

The **Tool Palettes** window can be resized just like standard windows. While floating, the top and bottom edges, the vertical area just below the tabs, and the corner just below that vertical area can be used to resize the window. While docked, only the right or left edge can be used for resizing. As with standard windows, move the cursor to one of the edges of the window until a double arrow appears. Then, press and hold the pick button, drag the edge until the window reaches the desired size, and release the pick button.

Transparency

Using the **Tool Palettes** window while it is floating may cause occasional visibility problems because it covers up part of the drawing window. However, the window can be made partially transparent so that the part of the drawing under the window can be seen. Transparency will not be active when the window is in a docked position. Hardware acceleration may need to be turned off to set transparency, depending on your system configuration.

Right-click on the title bar of the **Tool Palettes** window and pick **Transparency...** from the shortcut menu. The window must be floating for this option to appear. The **Transparency** dialog box is then displayed, **Figure 23-1.** To set the level of transparency, move the slider in the **General** area to a lower value. The slider controls the level of transparency applied to the window. The further to the left that the slider is placed, the more transparent the **Tool Palettes** window, **Figure 23-2.** Placing the slider all of the way to the right actually makes the **Tool Palettes** window opaque. The slider in the **Rollover** area sets the transparency level for when the cursor is over the window. This setting must be equal to or greater than the slider setting in the **General** area. To see the transparency level when the cursor is over the window, pick the **Preview** button.

If you find a particular level of transparency that you like, but wish to make the **Tool Palettes** window opaque for a short time while you perform an operation or two,

Figure 23-1.
The **Transparency** dialog box is used to control the transparency of the **Tool Palettes** window.

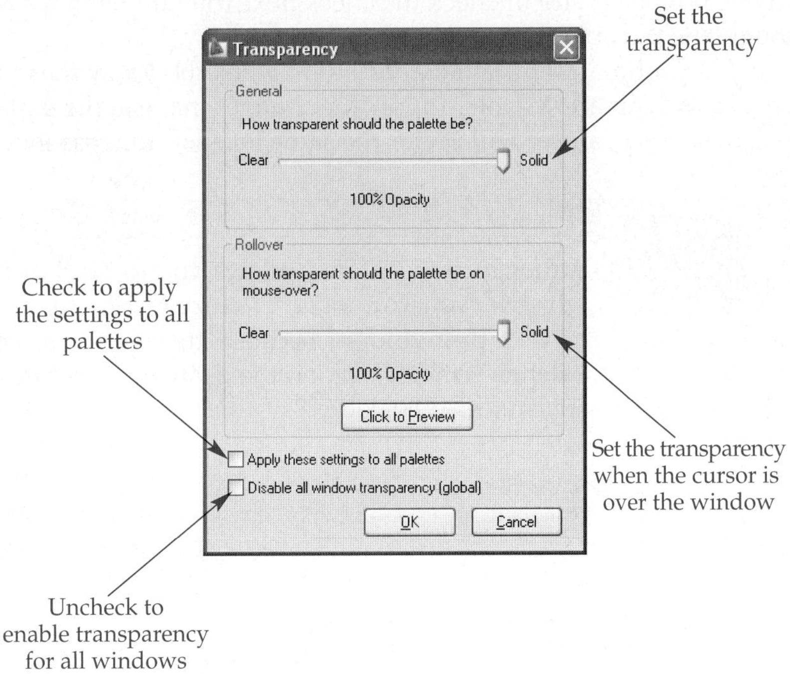

Figure 23-2.
A—The **Tool Palettes** window has a low transparency setting. B—The **Tool Palettes** window has a high transparency setting.

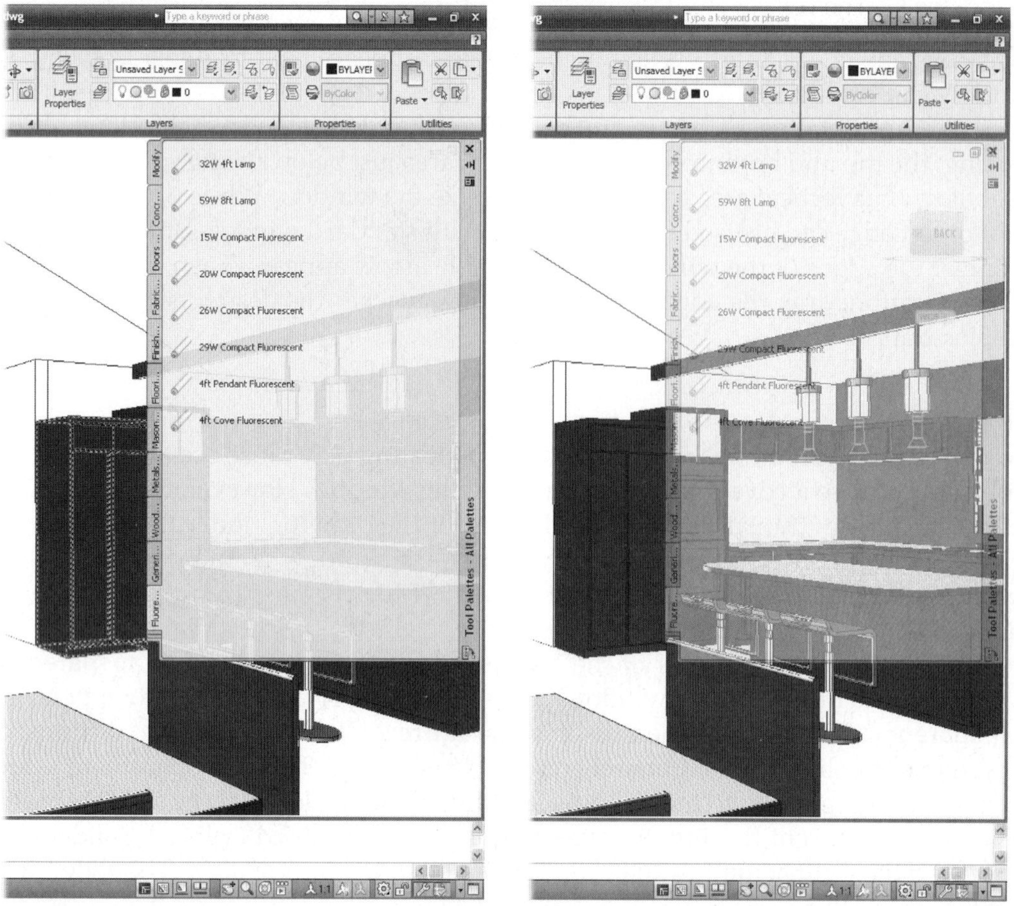

A B

you can just use the toggle to turn off transparency. Open the **Transparency** dialog box and check the **Disable all window transparency (global)** check box. Then, when you want to go back to your previous level of transparency, simply open the **Transparency** dialog box again and uncheck the check box. You will not have to adjust the slider; just toggle the transparency back on.

Also notice in the **Transparency** dialog box the **Apply these settings to all palettes** check box. This allows you to apply the changes made in the dialog box to all AutoCAD palettes. Often, a user will prefer the same level of transparency for all palettes.

PROFESSIONAL TIP

Although transparency allows you to *see* through the **Tool Palettes** window, you cannot *work* through it. You cannot access points behind the window because the cursor is actually on the **Tool Palettes** window, not on the drawing underneath it. This is true of any AutoCAD palette.

Autohide

As useful as the **Tool Palettes** window is, it does take up a large amount of valuable drawing area. The ***autohide*** feature, when enabled, compresses the **Tool Palettes** window so just the title bar appears when the cursor is not over the window, Figure 23-3. This allows the **Tool Palettes** window to take up less room when not being used.

To turn on autohide, right-click on the title bar of the **Tool Palettes** window or pick the **Properties** button at the top of the title bar to display the shortcut menu, Figure 23-4. The **Properties** button is only displayed when the window is floating. Then, select **Auto-hide** from the shortcut menu. A check mark appears next to the menu item when autohide is enabled. You can also pick the **Auto-hide** button at the top of the **Tool Palettes** window title bar.

To use the **Tool Palettes** window when autohide is enabled, move the cursor over the title bar and the window expands to its normal size. The tool palettes can then be used in the standard way. After using the **Tool Palettes** window, it is again hidden shortly after the cursor is no longer over the window.

Anchoring

The **Tool Palettes** window can also be ***anchored.*** Anchoring is a combination of docking and autohide. When a tool palette is anchored, it is docked on the right or left side of the drawing area, but it is compressed to just a title bar. See Figure 23-5. To use the **Tool Palettes** window when it is anchored, move the cursor over the anchored title bar. The **Tool Palettes** window is then displayed floating next to the anchored window. It can be used just as if autohide is enabled. Once the cursor is moved off of the **Tool Palettes** window, the window is hidden.

Figure 23-3.
When the autohide feature is enabled, the **Tool Palettes** window appears as only the title bar when the cursor is not over it.

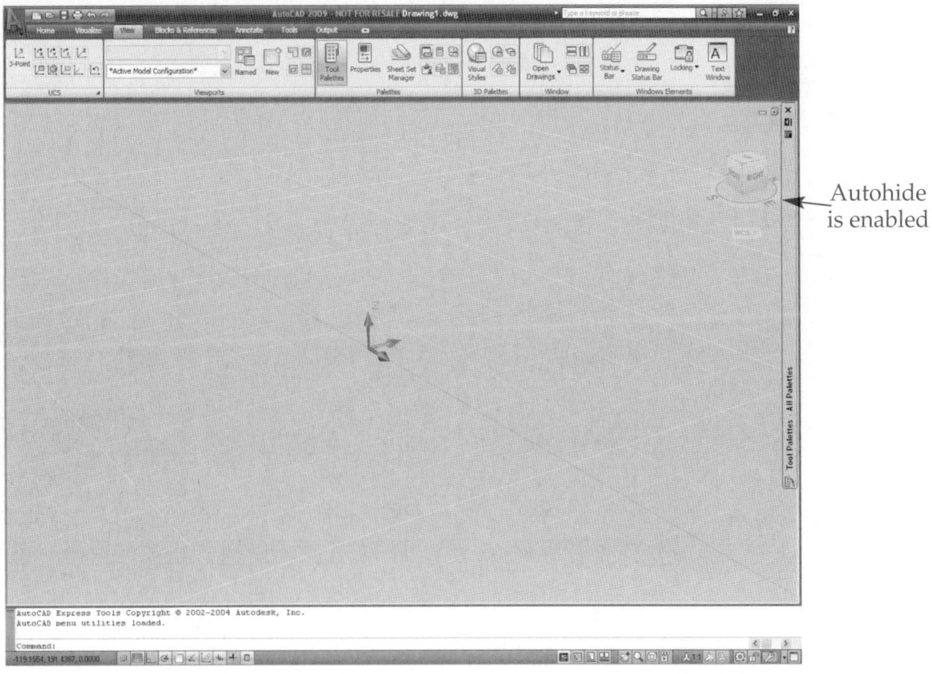

Figure 23-4.
Using the shortcut menu to enable autohide.

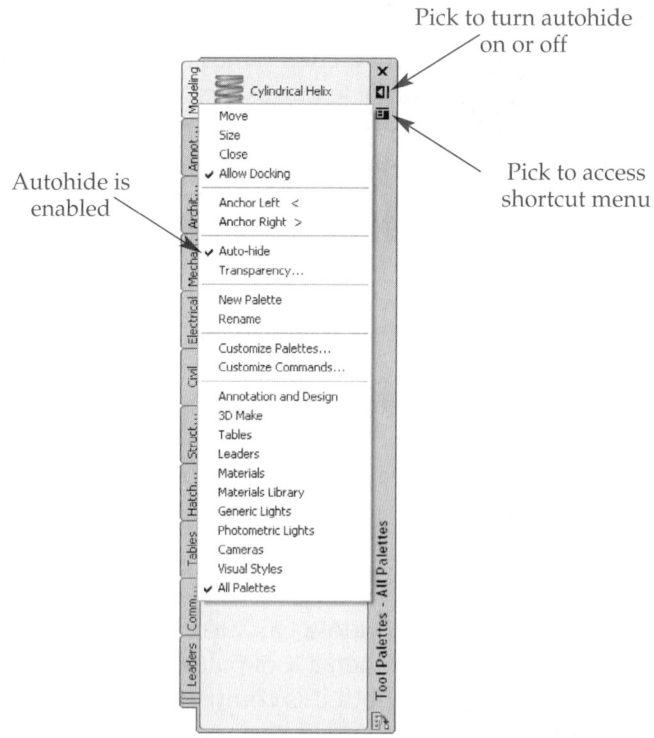

Figure 23-5.
When the **Tool Palettes** window is anchored, it is docked but compressed to just its title bar.

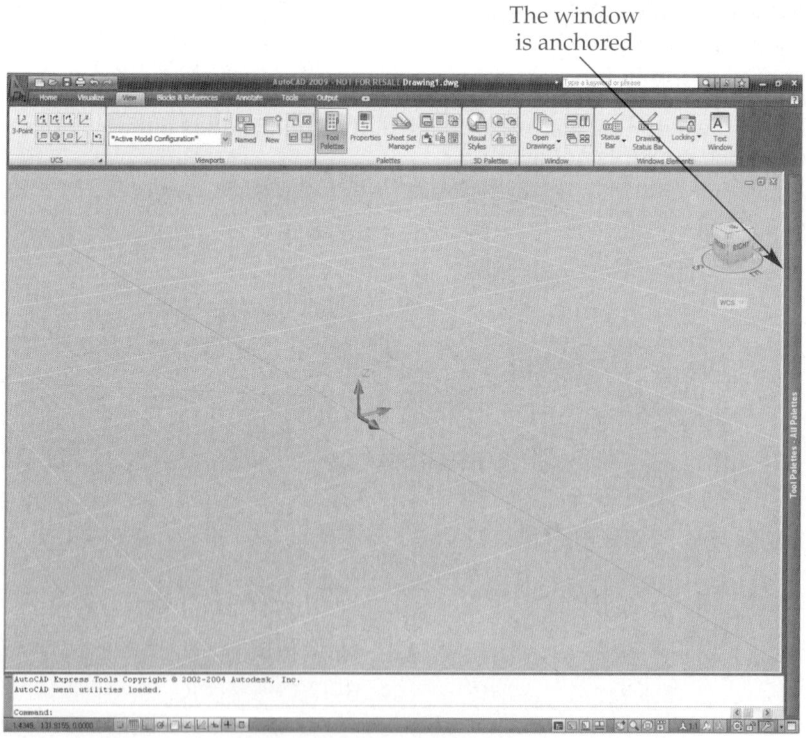

To anchor the tool palette, docking must first be enabled. Then, right-click on the title bar of the **Tool Palettes** window or pick the **Properties** button at the top of the title bar to display the shortcut menu. Next, select either **Anchor Left <** or **Anchor Right >** in the shortcut menu. To return the window to floating mode, pick and drag the title bar back into the drawing area while the window is displayed.

PROFESSIONAL TIP

The **Properties** palette, **DesignCenter**, and the ribbon also have the anchoring feature. You can create a very productive drawing window arrangement by anchoring these items along with the **Tool Palettes** window. Anchor the **Tool Palettes** window on one side of the drawing window and the **Properties** palette and **DesignCenter** on the other side. By default, the ribbon is docked at the top of the screen.

Tool Appearance

The way in which the tools are shown in the palettes can be customized. To do so, right-click in a blank area of the current tool palette (not on the title bar). Then, select **View Options...** from the shortcut menu. The **View Options** dialog box is displayed, Figure 23-6.

The **Image Size:** area of the dialog box is used to set the size of the tool icons in the palette. Drag the slider to the left or right to change the size. Dragging the slider to the left decreases the size of the icon. Dragging the slider to the right increases the size of the icon. To the left of the slider is a preview that represents the size of the icon.

The **View Style:** area controls how the tools on the tool palettes are displayed. When the **Icon only** radio button is selected, the tools are represented as an image only, Figure 23-7A. Tooltips will be displayed if you hold your cursor over a tool. Selecting the **Icon with text** radio button represents the tools with an image and the tool name below the image, Figure 23-7B. When the **List view** radio button is selected, the tools are represented with an image and the tool name to the side of the image, Figure 23-7C. This is the default view style.

The **Apply to:** drop-down list at the bottom of the dialog box determines where the settings are applied. To have the settings applied to the current tool palette, select Current Palette from the drop-down list. To have the settings applied to all tool palettes, select All Palettes from the drop-down list. When finished making settings, pick the **OK** button to close the **View** options dialog box.

Exercise 23-1

Complete the exercise on the Student CD.

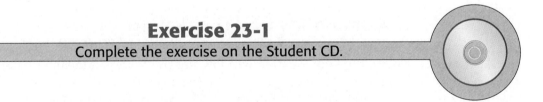

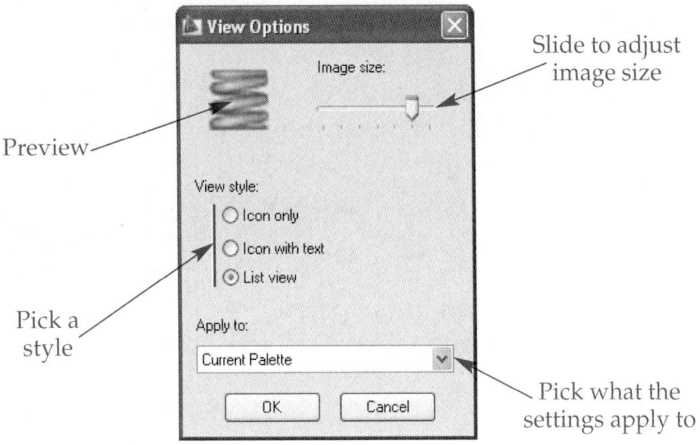

Figure 23-6.
The **View Options** dialog box is used to set how the tools appear in tool palettes.

Figure 23-7.
The various ways in which tools can appear in tool palettes. A—Icons only. B—Icons and text. C—As a list.

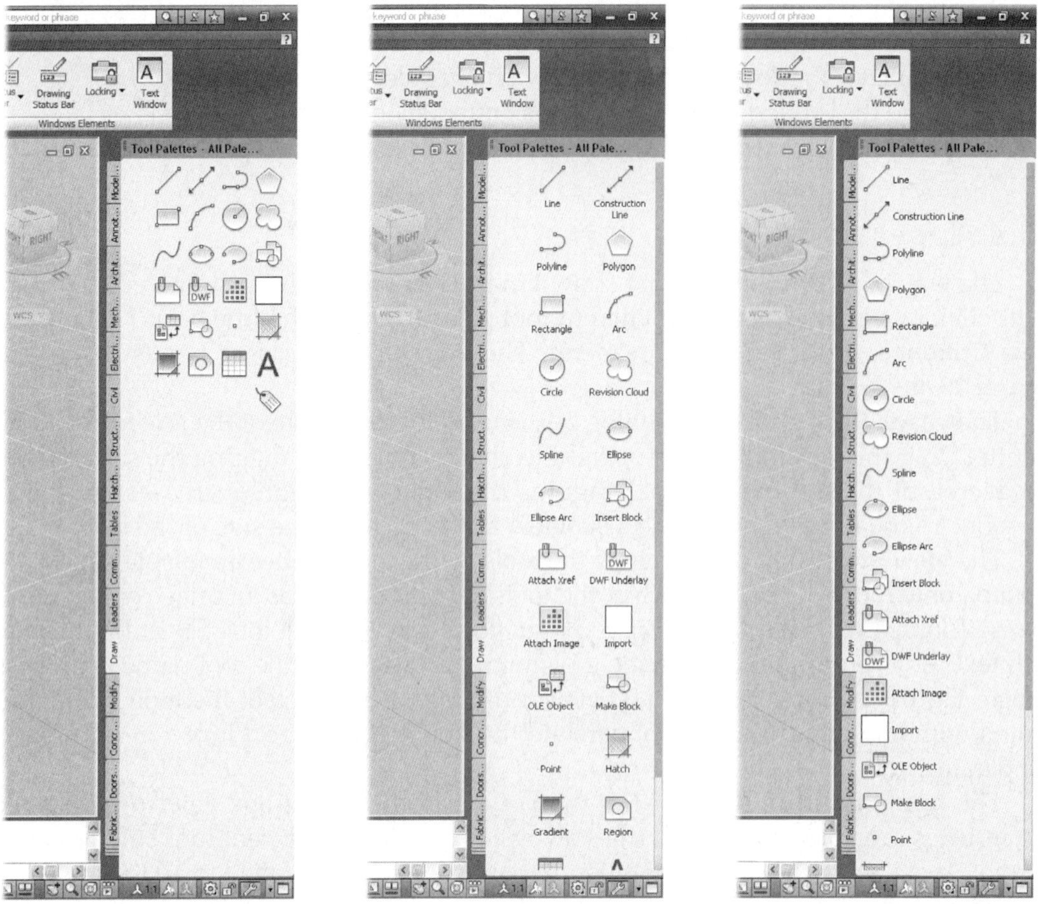

A B C

Commands in a Tool Palette

As indicated earlier, the **Tool Palettes** window not only offers a means to easily insert blocks and hatch patterns, it can be used to execute commands. Make the **Tool Palettes** window active and select the **Command Tool Samples** palette, Figure 23-8. The tools on this palette are provided to demonstrate how tool palettes can be customized by adding commands. This tool palette is provided with the intention that it will be customized by the user. Customizing tool palettes is discussed later in this chapter. The default tools provided are:

- **Line.** Executes the **LINE** command. Notice that this tool has a small triangle, or arrow, to the right of the icon. The arrow indicates that the tool acts as a ***flyout tool,*** similar to flyout buttons on the ribbon. Picking the arrow displays a graphic shortcut menu containing other command tools attached to this tool, as shown in Figure 23-8. Selecting a command tool from the shortcut menu executes the command and causes that command image to become the default image displayed in the palette.
- **Linear Dimension.** Executes the **DIMLINEAR** command. This tool is also a flyout.
- **VisualLisp Expression.** Executes the AutoLISP expression (entget (car (entsel))). The entity data list for the selected entity is displayed on the command line. AutoLISP is discussed in Chapters 26 and 27.

Figure 23-8.
A flyout tool contains other tools.

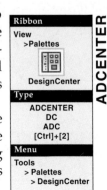

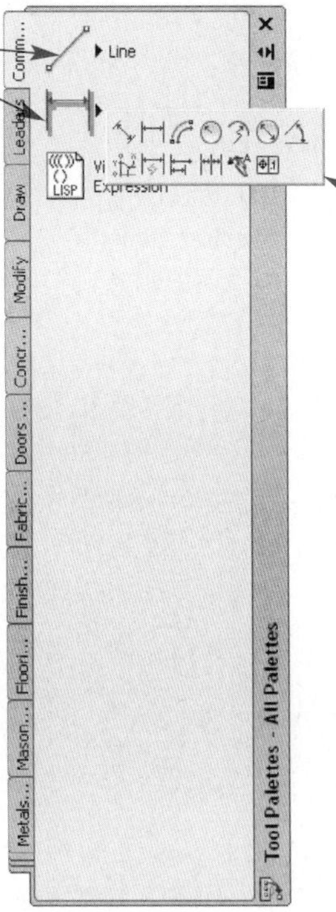

While these three tools on the **Command Tools** palette can increase productivity, this palette is included to show you examples of ways in which tools can be customized to make you more productive in your own design environment. It is meant to be customized to your own needs.

Adding Tool Palettes

As discussed later in this chapter, you can add new tools to tool palettes. You can also create new tool palettes and then add tools to them. To add a new tool palette, right-click on a blank area of an existing tool palette or on the title bar of the **Tool Palettes** window. Then, select **New Palette** from the shortcut menu. A new, blank palette is added and a text box appears next to the name. Type the desired name for the new palette and press [Enter].

Notice the help link at the top of the new tool palette, **Figure 23-9.** This link offers assistance in customizing tool palettes. It will disappear once you add a tool to the tool palette.

The new tool palette can be reordered within the tabs by right-clicking on the tab name to display the shortcut menu. Then, select **Move Up** or **Move Down** to reorder the palettes. You may need to do this several times in order to get the palette in the position you want. The other palettes can be reordered in this same manner. If you need to reorder multiple palettes, you can use the **Customize** dialog box. This dialog box is discussed in detail later in this chapter.

DesignCenter can be used to create a new palette fully populated with all of the blocks contained in a drawing. In the **Folders** tab of the **DesignCenter** palette, navigate to the drawing from which you are making the tool palette, right-click on the drawing name, and select **Create Tool Palette** from the shortcut menu. A new tool palette is added to the **Tool Palettes** window with the same name as the drawing file.

ADCENTER

Ribbon
View
>Palettes
DesignCenter

Type
ADCENTER
DC
ADC
[Ctrl]+[2]

Menu
Tools
> Palettes
> DesignCenter

Figure 23-9.
A new, blank tool palette has been created.

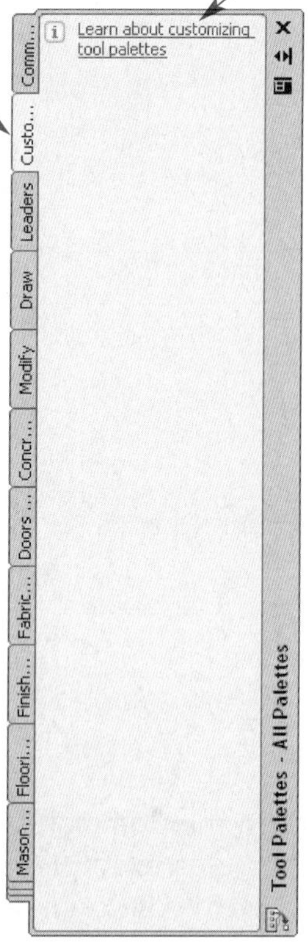

For example, open **DesignCenter** and navigate to the Fasteners-US drawing located in the \Sample\DesignCenter folder. Right-click on the file name and select **Create Tool Palette** from the shortcut menu, **Figure 23-10A.** A tool palette named **Fasteners-US** is added to the **Tool Palettes** window. All of the blocks contained in the Fasteners-US drawing are available on the tool palette, **Figure 23-10B.**

NOTE

When using any "block insertion" tool from a tool palette, the block is actually being imported from the source drawing—the drawing from which the block tool on the palette was created. An error occurs if the source file has been moved or deleted. The source file must be restored to its original location to allow the tool to work or the tool must be recreated from the source drawing in the drawing's new location.

Adding Tools to a Tool Palette

Tools can be added to a tool palette in a variety of ways. Tools can be created from toolbar buttons, geometric objects in the current drawing, and objects in other drawings (via **DesignCenter**). Tools can also be copied to and pasted from the Windows clipboard. Once tools have been added to a tool palette, they can be arranged to suit

Figure 23-10.
A—Creating a tool palette from the blocks contained within a drawing.
B—The new tool palette is added.

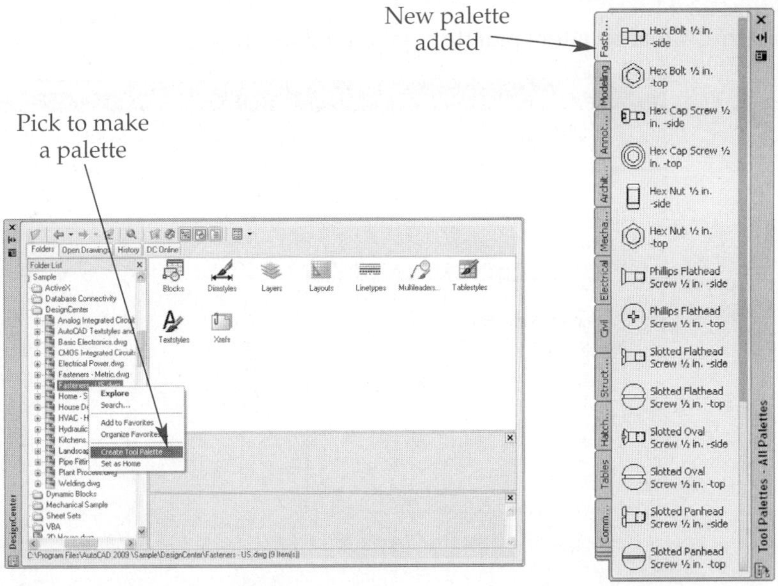

A B

your preference. Related tools can be separated into distinct areas on the tool palette and those areas can have text labels added to them.

PROFESSIONAL TIP

Tool palettes can be thought of as an extension of ribbon tabs and toolbars. You may want to add some of your favorite toolbar buttons to a tool palette.

Creating a Tool from a Toolbar

Ribbon
Tools
> Customization
Tool Palettes
Type
CUSTOMIZE
Menu
Tools
> Customize
> Tool Palettes...

CUSTOMIZE

Toolbar buttons can be directly dragged and dropped onto a tool palette. To do this, the **Customize** dialog box for tool palettes must be open. This is *not* the **Customize User Interface** dialog box that is used to customize toolbars, pull-down menus, etc., as described in previous chapters. To display the **Customize** dialog box, use the **CUSTOMIZE** command or right-click on a tool palette and select **Customize Palettes...** from the shortcut menu.

You do not actually use the **Customize** dialog box to copy a toolbar button to a tool palette, but the dialog box must be open. The **Customize** dialog box is discussed in detail later in this chapter.

Make sure the palette you want the button added to is current (on top). With the **Customize** dialog box open, move your cursor to the desired toolbar button. Flyout buttons cannot be added to a tool palette. Pick and hold on the toolbar button and drag it to the desired location in the tool palette, **Figure 23-11.** A horizontal "I-bar" appears in the tool palette to indicate where the new tool will be inserted. Drop the toolbar button when it is in the desired position. The tool is inserted in the tool palette. Close the **Customize** dialog box.

NOTE

Tools cannot be dragged from the ribbon to a tool palette, only from toolbars. Toolbars are not displayed by default except in the AutoCAD Classic workspace.

Figure 23-11.
Creating a tool on a tool palette from a toolbar button.

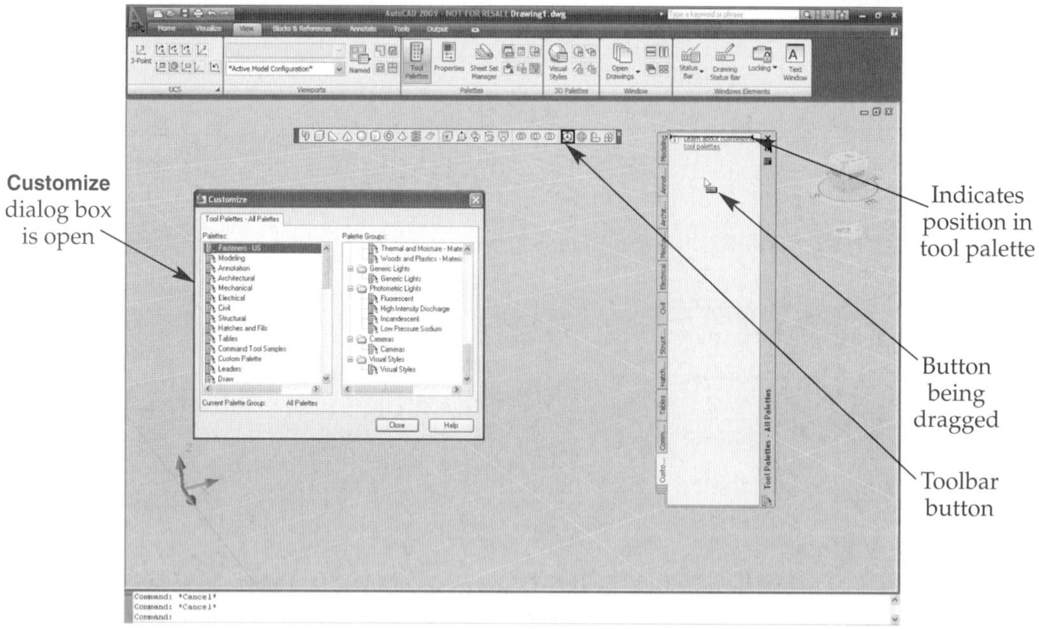

Creating a Tool from an Object in the Current Drawing

Another way to add a drawing command to a tool palette is to drag an object in the current drawing, such as a line, hatch, block, dimension, camera, or light, and drop it onto the tool palette. The appropriate command to create that object is added to the tool palette. Not all objects support this method. For example, solid primitives cannot be dragged onto a tool palette to create a tool.

First, ensure that the **PICKFIRST** system variable is set to 1. Also, make sure the tool palette to which you want the tool added to is current (on top). Next, with no command active, select the desired object. Move the cursor directly onto the selected object (not a grip). Then, press and hold down either the pick button or the right mouse button. Finally, drag the object to the desired position on the tool palette and drop it. The appropriate drawing command is inserted into the tool palette.

Using the Windows Clipboard to Create a Tool

COPYCLIP

Ribbon
Home
> Utilities
Copy Clip

Type
COPYCLIP
[Ctrl]+[C]

Menu
Edit
> Copy

The copy-and-paste feature of the Windows operating system is another way to transfer objects in the drawing to a tool palette. First, ensure that the **PICKFIRST** system variable is set to 1. Then, with no command active, right-click on the object and select **Copy** from the shortcut menu. Next, make current the tool palette to which you want the tool added. Finally, right-click on a blank area in the tool palette and select **Paste** from the shortcut menu. The appropriate command is added as the last tool on the tool palette.

The copy-and-paste technique can also be used to transfer tools from one tool palette to another. First, make current the tool palette that contains the tool to be transferred. Right-click on the tool to transfer and select **Copy** in the shortcut menu. If you want to *move* the tool from the first tool palette to the second, select **Cut** in the shortcut menu. Next, make current the tool palette to which you want the tool transferred. Right-click and select **Paste** from the shortcut menu. The tool is added to the second tool palette as the last tool on the palette.

Adding Block and Hatch Tools from DesignCenter

Earlier, you saw how to create a tool palette consisting of all of the blocks in a single drawing by using **DesignCenter**. It is also possible to add individual blocks from a drawing to a tool palette using **DesignCenter**. To do this, open **DesignCenter**. In the **Folders** tab, navigate to the drawing that contains the desired block. Expand that drawing's branch to see the named objects within the drawing. Select the Blocks branch. The blocks that are defined in the drawing appear on the right-hand side of the **DesignCenter** palette. Make sure the tool palette you want the tool added to is current. Then, select the block in **DesignCenter** and drag it to the tool palette, Figure 23-12. Move the cursor to the desired position on the tool palette and drop the block. The new block tool is inserted in the tool palette.

A tool that inserts an entire drawing into the current drawing can also be added to a tool palette using **DesignCenter**. In **DesignCenter**, navigate to the drawing in the **Folders** tab. Select the drawing on the right-hand side of the **DesignCenter** palette, drag it to the tool palette, and drop it in the desired position, Figure 23-13. The new block tool is inserted in the tool palette. When the new tool is used, the entire drawing is inserted into the current drawing as a block.

DesignCenter can also be used to add hatch patterns to a tool palette. Hatch pattern definitions are stored in two files—acad.pat and acadiso.pat. These files are located in the user's \Support folder. In the **Folders** tab of **DesignCenter**, navigate to the acad.pat file and select it. All of the hatch patterns defined within that file are shown on the right-hand side of the **DesignCenter** palette, Figure 23-14. Make sure the tool palette you want the hatch pattern added to is current. Then, select the desired hatch pattern in **DesignCenter**, drag it to the tool palette, and drop it in the desired location. The new hatch tool is inserted in the tool palette.

Adding Visual Style and Material Tools

Visual styles that are available in the drawing can be added as a tool to a tool palette. To do this, first make current the tool palette to which you want the visual style added. Then, open the **Visual Styles Manager**. Select the icon for the visual style at

Figure 23-12.
Adding an individual block contained within a drawing as a tool on a tool palette.

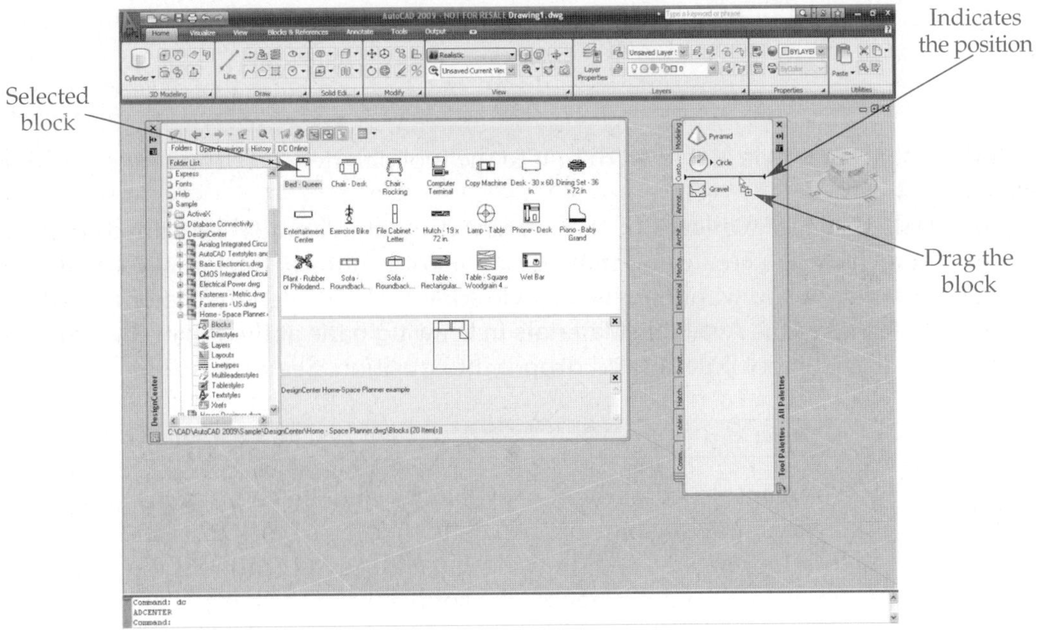

Figure 23-13.
Adding an entire drawing as a tool on a tool palette.

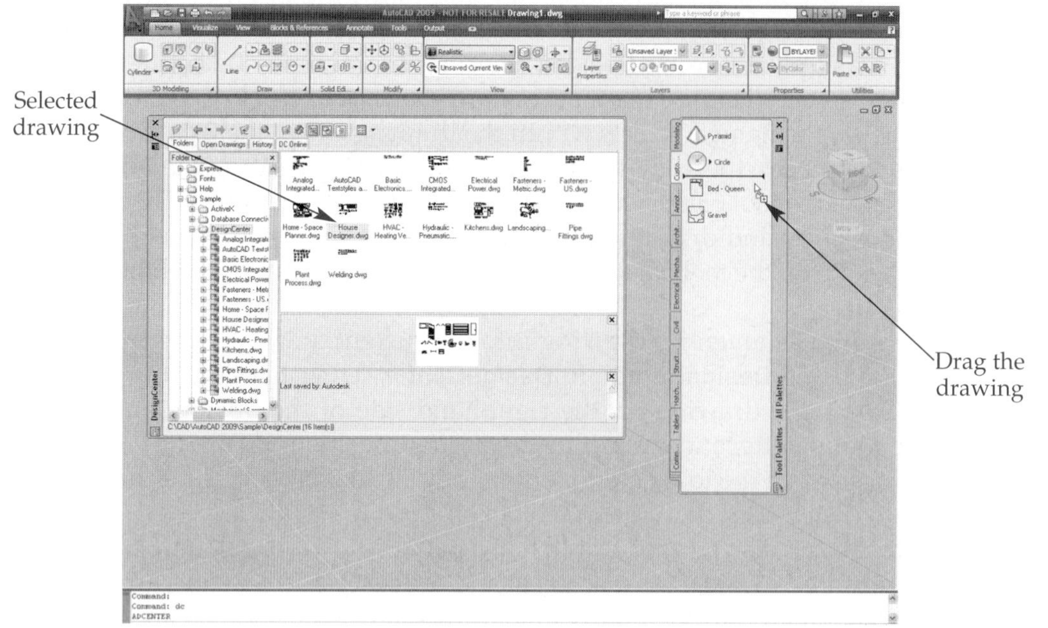

Figure 23-14.
Hatch patterns can be selected in **DesignCenter** and dragged to a tool palette to create a new tool.

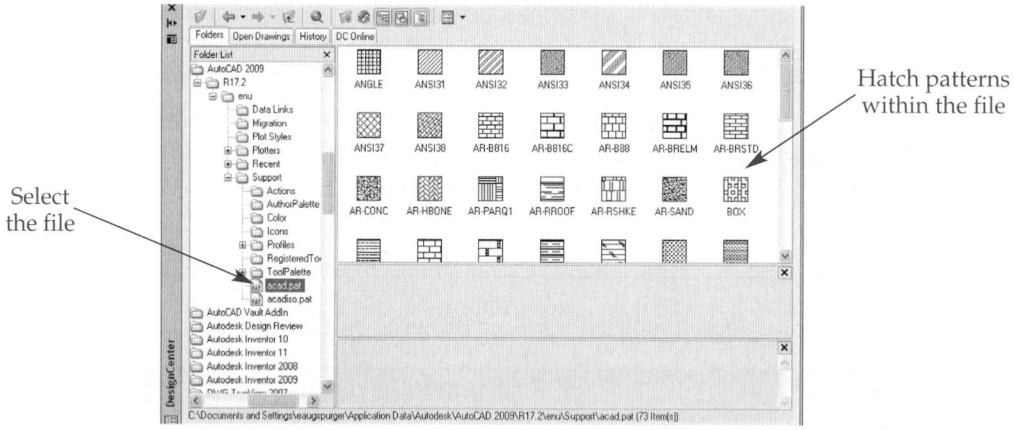

the top of the **Visual Style Manager**, drag it to the tool palette, and drop it into position. See **Figure 23-15.**

Materials that are available in the current drawing can also be added to a tool palette. This is how you create and manage a materials library. First, make current the tool palette to which you want the visual style added. Then, open the **Materials** palette. Select the material in the **Available Materials in Drawing** pane at the top of the **Materials** palette, drag it to the tool palette, and drop it into position. See **Figure 23-16.**

PROFESSIONAL TIP

You can also drag and drop blocks and hatch patterns from the current drawing onto a tool palette. To drag a block from the drawing to a tool palette, the drawing must be saved (cannot be unnamed) because the tool references the source file of the block.

Figure 23-15.
Adding a visual style as a tool on a tool palette.

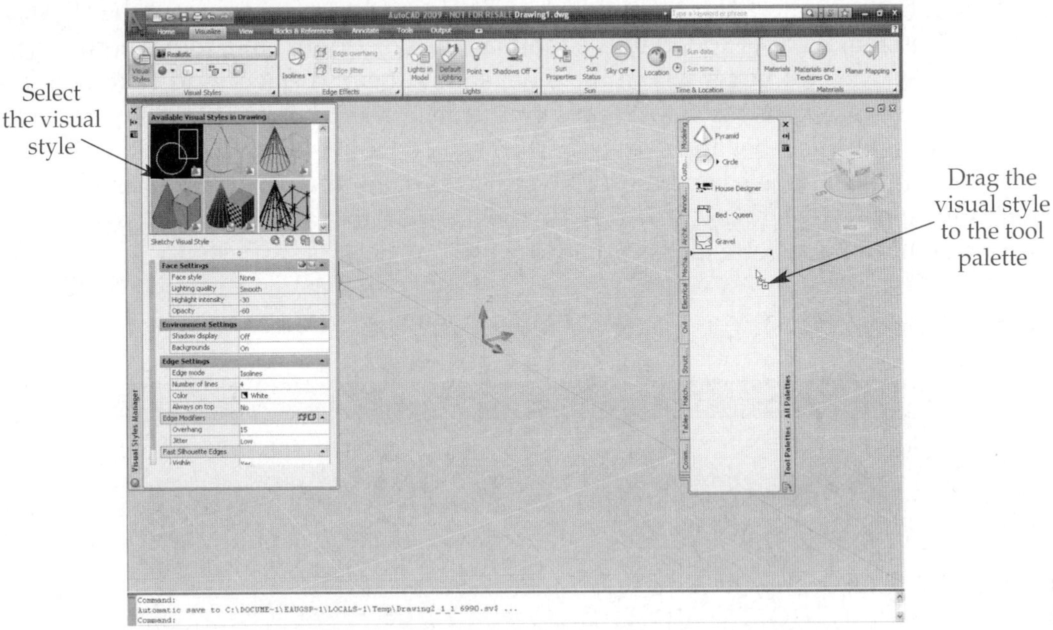

Figure 23-16.
Adding a material as a tool on a tool palette.

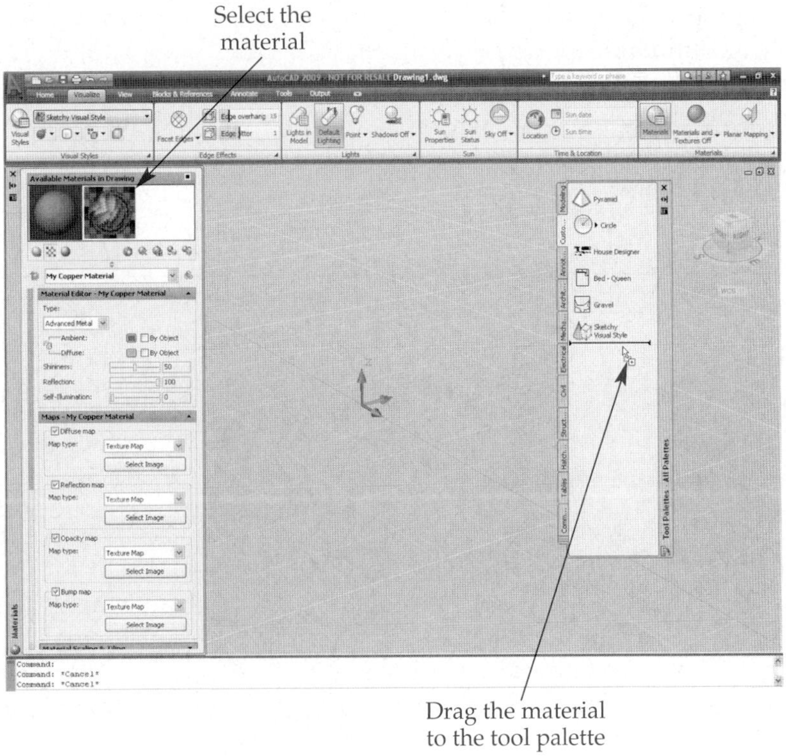

Rearranging Tools on a Tool Palette

The tools on a tool palette can be rearranged into a more productive order. To move a tool within a tool palette, simply select the tool and drag it to a new location. Remember, the horizontal I-bar indicates where the tool will be moved. In this way, you can place your drawing tools together, your block tools together, and so on.

You can further separate the tools within a tool palette by adding separator bars and text labels. Move the cursor so that it is between the two tools where you would like to add the separator. Then, right-click and select **Add Separator** from the shortcut menu. A horizontal bar is added to the tool palette. To add text to a tool palette, right-click between the two items where the label should be and select **Add Text** from the shortcut menu. A text box is displayed with the default text highlighted. Type the text that you want for the label and press [Enter]. The text label is added to the tool palette. Separators and text labels can be used together to make the visual grouping of tools even more apparent, **Figure 23-17**. You can move separators and text labels to different locations within the palette just as you can tools.

Exercise 23-2

Complete the exercise on the Student CD.

Modifying the Properties of a Tool

A tool on a tool palette can basically do one of these operations:

- Insert a block.
- Insert a hatch pattern.
- Insert a gradient fill.
- Initiate a command.
- Insert a light.
- Insert a camera.
- Apply a visual style.
- Apply a material.

Figure 23-17. Separators and text labels can be added to tool palettes to help group tools.

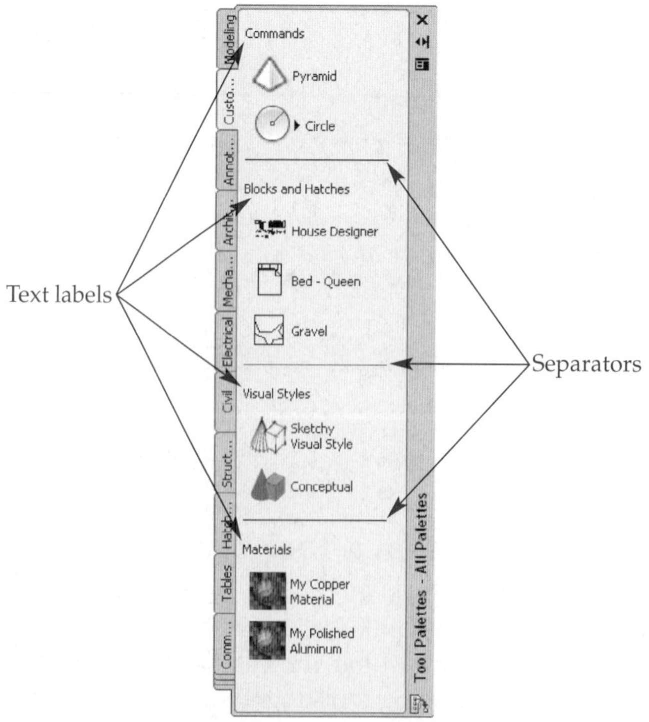

Another type of tool called a flyout is discussed later in this chapter. Each of these tools has general properties assigned to it, such as color, layer, or linetype. Each of these tools also has some tool-specific properties assigned to it, depending on the operation associated with the tool. Most of these assigned properties can be customized to your own needs.

For example, select the **Hatches and Fills** palette in the **Tool Palettes** window. Right-click on the **Curved** gradient tool and select **Properties...** in the shortcut menu. The **Tool Properties** dialog box is displayed, **Figure 23-18.** Notice that the lower half of the dialog box is divided into two sections. The **General** category contains settings for properties such as Color, Layer, and Linetype. The **Pattern** category contains settings for properties specific to this tool's operation—inserting a gradient fill. Notice that properties such as Color 1, Color 2, and Gradient angle are shown. Other types of tools will have a different category in place of the **Pattern** category. Select the **Cancel** button to close the dialog box.

Now, select the **Command Tool Samples** palette in the **Tool Palettes** window, right-click on the **VisualLisp Expression** tool in the tool palette, and select **Properties...** from the shortcut menu. The **Tool Properties** dialog box is displayed, **Figure 23-19.** This is the same dialog box displayed for the **Curved** gradient tool. However, in place of the **Pattern** category is the **Command** category. The settings in the **Command** category are

Figure 23-18.
Modifying the properties of a gradient fill tool.

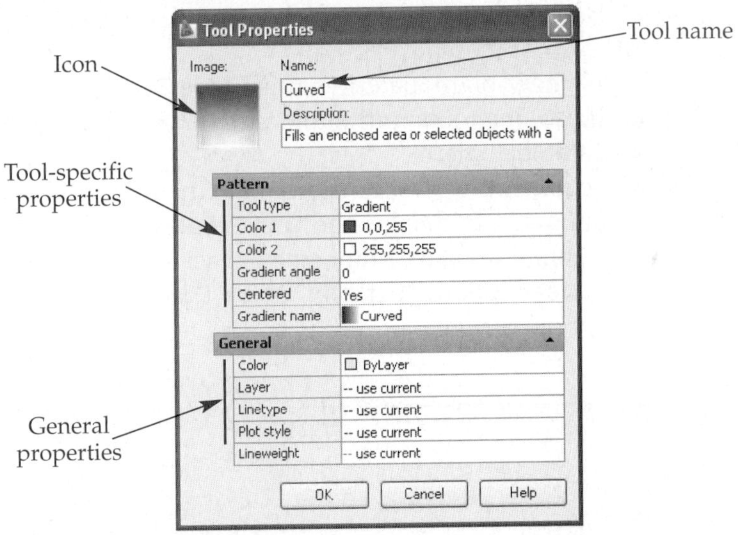

Figure 23-19.
Modifying the properties of a command tool.

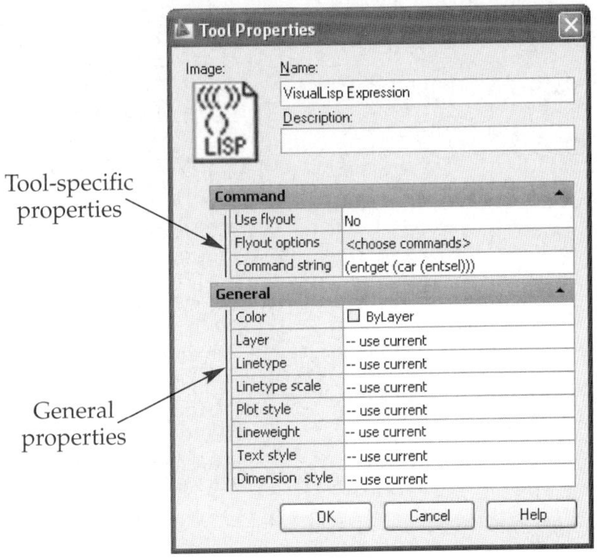

specific to the **VisualLisp Expression** tool. Notice that the **General** category contains the same properties as for the **Curved** gradient tool. There are some other general properties listed that are not applicable to a gradient (Linetype scale, Text style, and Dimension style). Select the **Cancel** button to close the dialog box.

Customizing General Properties

The three items at the top of the **Tool Properties** dialog box are available for all types of tools. The **Image:** area shows the image that is assigned to the tool. This can be modified within the dialog box for command, camera, light, and visual style tools. The **Name:** text box displays the name of the tool. You can enter a new name for the tool. The **Description:** text box displays the current description of the tool. You can change the existing description or enter a new description. The name and description appear in the tooltip that is displayed when the cursor is held over the tool, **Figure 23-20.**

The **General** category in the **Tool Properties** dialog box can be used to assign specific values to the general properties that are a part of nearly all AutoCAD objects. The properties that can be customized are Color, Layer, Linetype, Linetype scale, Plot style, Lineweight, Text style, and Dimension style. Depending on the type of tool, some of these properties may not be available.

The values assigned in the **Tool Properties** dialog box override the current property settings in the drawing when the tool is used. For instance, create three layers called Object, Hidden, and Center in the current drawing. A separate line tool can now be created for each of these layers:

1. Create a new, blank palette named **Line Tools.**
2. Add three line tools to the tool palette by copying them from the **Command Tool Samples** palette.
3. Right-click on the first of these new line tools and select **Properties** from the shortcut menu to display the **Tool Properties** dialog box.
4. In the **Name:** text box, enter Line-Object as the name.
5. In the **Description:** text box, enter Draws a line on the Object layer. as the description.

Figure 23-20.
The Name: and Description: property settings in the **Tool Properties** dialog box are used as the tooltip for the tool.

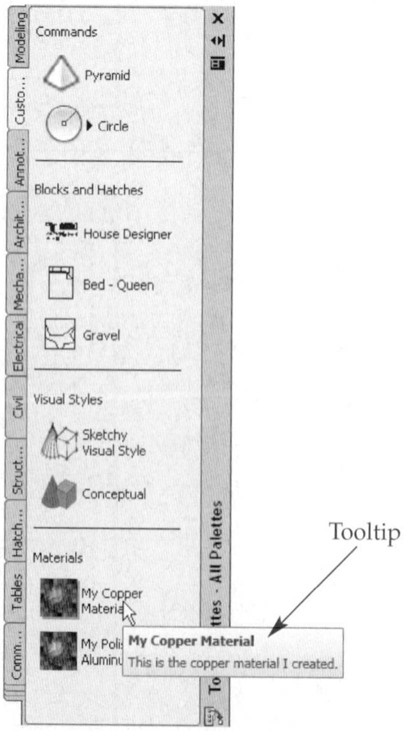

6. In the **General** category, pick the Layer property. A drop-down list appears that is set to —use current. This means that when you draw a line using the tool, the line is drawn on the current layer.
7. In the drop-down list, select Object. Now, any lines drawn with the tool are placed on the Object layer.
8. Pick the **OK** button to close the **Tool Properties** dialog box and save the changes.
9. Repeat the above steps for the other two line tools setting them to the Hidden and Center layers.

Now, use one of your new tools to draw a line. Notice that when you select the tool the current layer switches to the one assigned to the tool. When you finish using the tool, the current layer switches back to the previous layer. Try each of the other new tools. Experiment with some of the other general properties, such as Color, Linetype, and Lineweight.

Customizing Block Insertion Tools

When a block insertion tool is modified in the **Tool Properties** dialog box, properties specific to block insertion are displayed in a category labeled **Insert**, Figure 23-21. These properties are described as follows.

Name

The Name property contains the name of the block to be inserted. It is not usually modified.

Source file

The Source file property lists the name and path to the source drawing containing the block. If the drawing file has been moved to a new location, specify the correct location in the text box for this property. When you pick in the text box, an ellipses button (...) appears at the right-hand side of the box. You can pick this button to browse for the drawing file.

Scale

The Scale property value is the scale that will be applied to the block when it is inserted into the drawing. The scale is applied equally in the X, Y, and Z directions. The default value is 1.000.

Figure 23-21.
The **Tool Properties** dialog box for a block insertion tool.

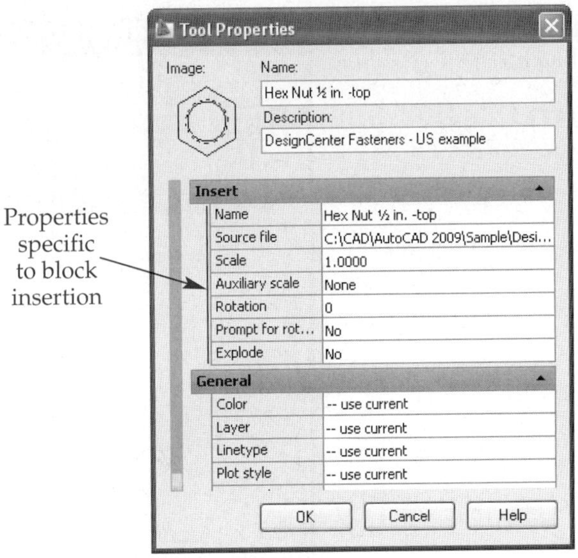

Auxiliary scale

The block is inserted at a scale calculated by multiplying the Auxiliary scale property value by the Scale property value. This drop-down list allows you to apply either the dimension scale or the plot scale to the insertion scale. The default value is None.

Rotation

The rotation angle for the block when it is inserted is set by the Rotation property. The default value is 0.

Prompt for rotation

The Prompt for rotation property determines whether or not the user is prompted for a rotation angle when the block is inserted. The default value in the drop-down list is No.

Explode

The Explode property determines whether or not the block is inserted as a block or as its component objects (exploded). The default value in the drop-down list is No, which means the block is inserted unexploded.

Customizing Hatch Pattern Tools

When a hatch pattern insertion tool is modified in the **Tool Properties** dialog box, properties specific to hatch patterns are displayed in the **Pattern** category, Figure 23-22. These properties are described as follows. Which properties are disabled or enabled is determined by the pattern type.

Tool type

The Tool type property determines if the hatch pattern is a standard hatch or a gradient fill. Choosing Gradient in the drop-down list changes the rest of the properties found in this area of the dialog box. Gradient fill properties are discussed later.

Type

The Type property determines the type of hatch pattern. To change the type, select the property and then pick the ellipses button (...) at the right-hand end of the entry. The **Hatch Pattern Type** dialog box is displayed, Figure 23-23. In the **Pattern type:** drop-down list of this dialog box, select User-defined, Predefined, or Custom.

Figure 23-22.
The **Tool Properties** dialog box for a hatch insertion tool.

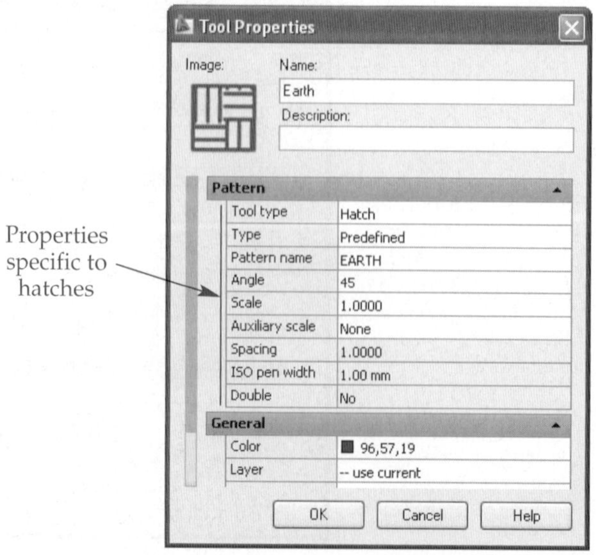

Figure 23-23.
The **Hatch Pattern Type** dialog box is used to determine the type of hatch. A predefined hatch pattern can also be selected in this dialog box.

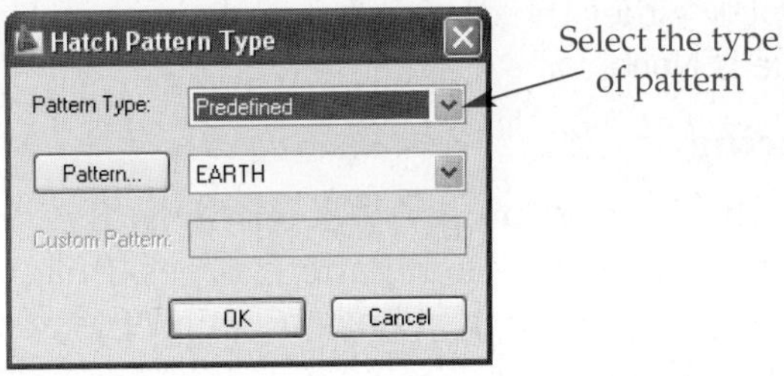

If Predefined is selected, the **Pattern...** button and drop-down list are enabled. Select a pattern from the drop-down list or pick the button to select a pattern in the **Hatch Pattern Palette** dialog box. This is the same dialog box used with the **BHATCH** command.

If User-defined is selected, the rest of the items in the dialog box are disabled. The properties for user-defined hatch patterns are set in the **Tool Properties** dialog box, as discussed next.

Selecting Custom disables the **Pattern...** button and drop-down list and enables the **Custom Pattern:** text box. In this text box, enter the name of the custom pattern to use.

Pattern name

If the pattern type is set to Predefined, you can change the pattern using the Pattern name property. Select the property and pick the ellipses button (**...**) to open the **Hatch Pattern Palette** dialog box, **Figure 23-24.** If you selected the pattern in the **Hatch Pattern Type** dialog box, you will not need to select it using this property. This property is "display only" when the type is set to User-defined or Custom.

Angle

The Angle property allows you to rotate the hatch pattern. This is the same as entering a rotation when using the **BHATCH** command. The default value is 0.

Scale

The Scale property determines the scale to be applied to the hatch pattern. Pick in the text box and enter a scale factor for the pattern. The default value is 1.000.

Auxiliary scale

The hatch is inserted at a scale calculated by multiplying the Auxiliary scale property value by the Scale property value. The Auxiliary scale drop-down list allows you

Figure 23-24.
Selecting a predefined hatch pattern.

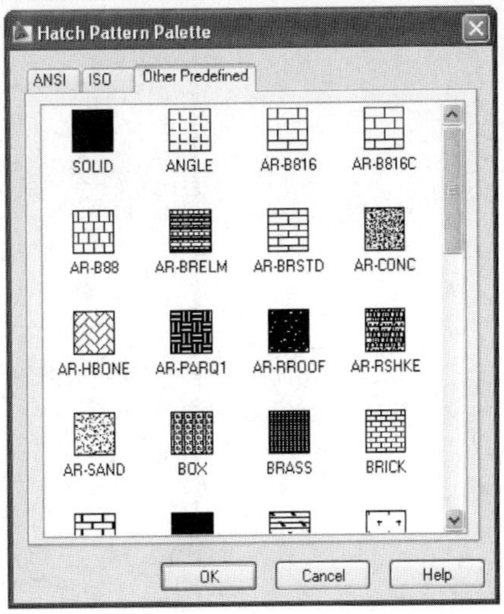

to apply either the dimension scale or the plot scale to the insertion scale. The default value is None.

Spacing

The Spacing property determines the spacing of lines in a user-defined hatch pattern. For other hatch pattern types, this property is "display only." To change the spacing, pick in the text box and enter the relative distance between lines. The default value is 1.000.

ISO pen width

The ISO pen width property allows you to set the pen width for ISO hatch patterns. It is disabled for other hatch patterns. The default value in the drop-down list is 1.00 mm.

Double

The Double property determines whether or not the user-defined hatch is a cross-hatch pattern. The default value in the drop-down list is No. To make a crosshatch pattern, select Yes.

Customizing Gradient Fill Tools

When a gradient fill hatch pattern insertion tool is modified in the **Tool Properties** dialog box, properties specific to gradient fills are displayed in the **Pattern** category, Figure 23-25. These properties are described as follows.

Tool type

The Tool type property determines if the hatch pattern is a standard hatch or a gradient fill. Choosing Hatch in the drop-down list changes the rest of the properties found in this area of the dialog box, as described earlier.

Color 1

The Color 1 property is used to specify the first color of the gradient fill. When you pick the property, a drop-down list is displayed. Pick a color from the drop-down list or choose Select Color... to pick a color in the **Color Selector** dialog box.

Color 2

The Color 2 property is used to specify the second color of the gradient fill. When you pick the property, a drop-down list is displayed. Pick a color from the drop-down list or choose Select Color... to pick a color in the **Color Selector** dialog box.

Figure 23-25.
The **Tool Properties** dialog box for a gradient fill hatch insertion tool.

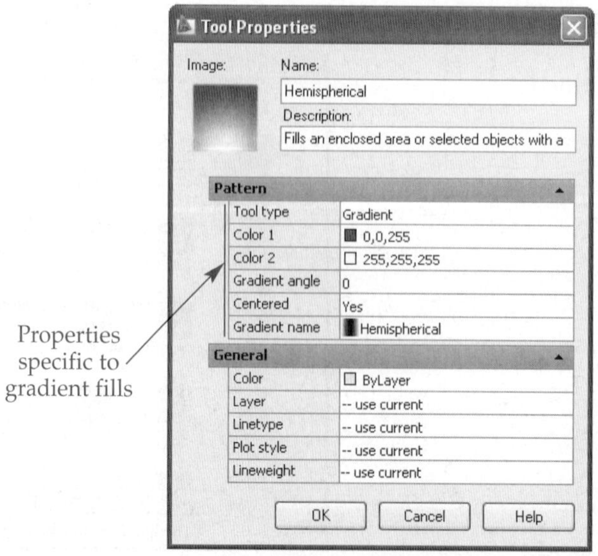

Gradient angle

The value of the Gradient angle property determines the rotation of the gradient fill. Pick in the text box and enter the number of degrees for the angle of the gradient. When the fill is created, the angle is relative to the current UCS. When you press [Enter] the **Image:** preview tile is updated to reflect the setting.

Centered

The Centered property determines whether or not the gradient fill is centered. The default value in the drop-down list is Yes. This creates a symmetrical fill. Selecting No shifts the gradient up and to the left. This is used to simulate a light source illuminating the fill from the left side.

Gradient name

The type of gradient fill is set by the Gradient name property. AutoCAD's preset gradient fills appear in the drop-down list. Select the type of gradient fill to use.

Customizing Command Tools

When a command tool is modified in the **Tool Properties** dialog box, properties specific to commands are displayed in the **Command** category, **Figure 23-26.** These properties are described as follows.

- **Use flyout.** This property determines whether or not the tool is a flyout. Flyouts are discussed later in this chapter.
- **Flyout options.** This property allows you to pick which commands are associated with the flyout, as discussed later.
- **Command string.** The command macro for the tool is entered in this text box, if the tool is not a flyout. Creating custom commands is discussed in Chapter 21. If the tool is a flyout, this text box is disabled.

For example, suppose you need a tool that will draw three concentric circles with diameters of .50, 1.00, and 1.50. Use the following procedure.

1. In the current drawing, create a circle of any diameter at any location.
2. Drag and drop the circle onto a tool palette to create a new tool.
3. Right-click on the new **Circle** tool and select **Properties...** from the shortcut menu.
4. In the **Tool Properties** dialog box, change the following properties:
   Name: Triple Circle

Figure 23-26.
The **Tool Properties** dialog box for a command tool.

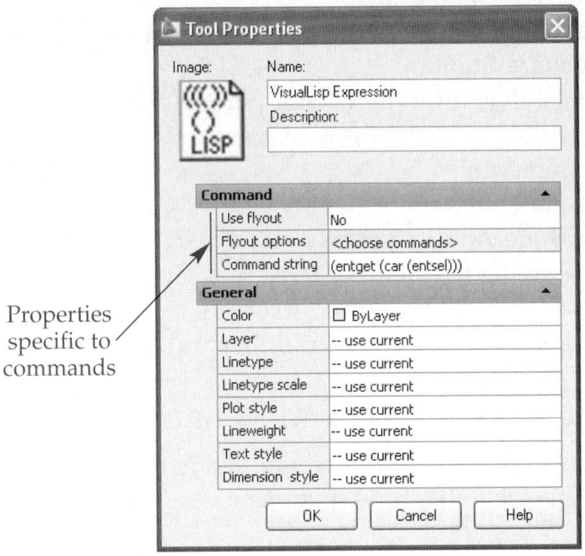

Description: Creates three concentric circles.
Use Flyout: No
Command string: ^C^Ccircle;\d;.50;circle;@;d;1.0;circle;@;d;1.5

5. Pick the **OK** button to close the **Tool Properties** dialog box.
6. Test the new tool.

Look closely at the command macro for the **Triple Circle** tool. Can you identify each component of the macro? If not, use the tool and then display the **AutoCAD Text Window** by pressing [F2]. Using the text window, determine what function each component of the macro performs.

NOTE

The **VisualLisp Expression** tool included on the **Command Tool Samples** palette is not actually a "command" tool. It is merely there to let you know that you can use a command tool to execute Visual LISP expressions. Visual LISP functions can be added in the Command string property in the **Tool Properties** dialog box. For more information on AutoLISP and Visual LISP, refer to Chapters 26 and 27 of this text and to the text *Visual LISP Programming* from Goodheart-Willcox Publisher.

Exercise 23-3

Complete the exercise on the Student CD.

Customizing Camera and Light Tools

Cameras and lights are stored in the drawing file. By placing camera and light tools on a tool palette, you can store your favorite settings for use in all drawings. Productivity is increased since you do not have to use **DesignCenter** to browse for your favorite cameras and lights within other drawings. In fact, AutoCAD provides several tool palettes with different light tools. These tools palettes are provided for lights:

- **Generic Lights**
- **Fluorescent**
- **High Intensity Discharge**
- **Incandescent**
- **Low Pressure Sodium**

AutoCAD also has a **Cameras** tool palette containing three camera tools. These tools are provided on the **Cameras** tool palette:

- **Normal Camera**
- **Wide-Angle Camera**
- **Extreme Wide-Angle Camera**

When customizing a camera or light tool, the **Tool Properties** dialog box provides all of the properties that are required to create a camera or light. See Figure 23-27. For detailed information about setting up lights and cameras, see Chapters 16 and 18.

Customizing Visual Style and Material Tools

When either a visual style or material tool is modified in the **Tool Properties** dialog box, properties specific to the type of tool appear in the dialog box. The properties avail-

Figure 23-27.
A—The **Tool Properties** dialog box for a light tool.
B—The **Tool Properties** dialog box for a camera tool.

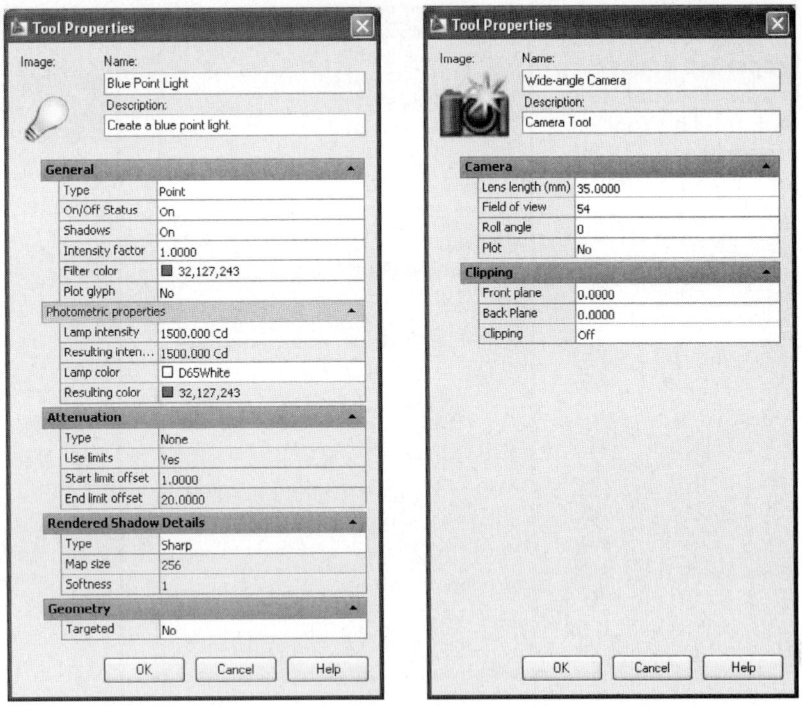

A B

able are identical to those available in the **Visual Style Manager** or **Materials** palette. See Figure 23-28. Refer to Chapter 14 for information on creating and modifying visual styles and Chapter 15 for information on creating and modifying materials.

NOTE

Modifying a material tool does not alter the material in the drawing if it has been attached to any objects.

Changing a Tool Icon

You can change the icon associated with a tool. This can be done from within the **Tool Properties** dialog box or directly on the tool palette. Right-click on the icon, either in the dialog box or on the tool palette, and select **Specify Image...** from the shortcut menu. The **Select Image File** dialog box is displayed. This is a standard "open" dialog box. Navigate to the image file, select it, and pick the **Open** button. The icon displays the new image. To change an icon back to the original image, right-click on the icon (either in the dialog box or on the tool palette) and select **Remove specified image** from the shortcut menu. The icon returns to its original image.

NOTE

Some tools, such as material tools, have an icon image based on the settings of the tool. You cannot specify an image for these tools. If the material is redefined, right-click on the tool icon in the tool palette and select **Update tool image** from the shortcut menu.

Figure 23-28.
A—The **Tool Properties** dialog box for a visual style tool. B—The **Tool Properties** dialog box for a material tool.

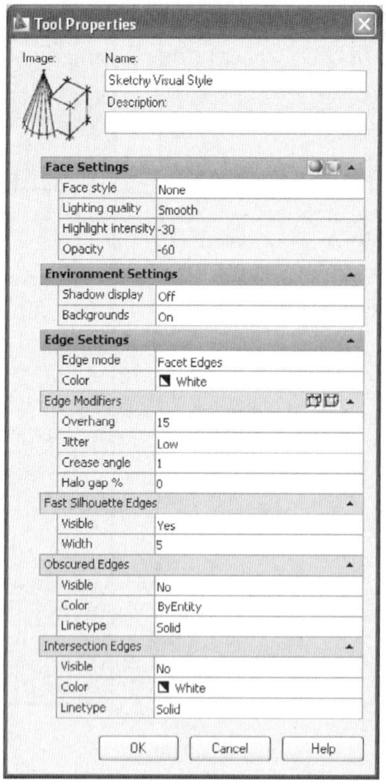

A

B

Working with Flyouts

A command tool in a tool palette can be set to function as a flyout. A flyout tool is similar to a flyout button found on the ribbon or a toolbar. The tool icon for a flyout displays a small arrow to the right of the tool. When the arrow is picked, a graphic shortcut menu is displayed that contains the command tools in the flyout.

To set a command tool as a flyout, open the **Tool Properties** dialog box for the tool. Then, in the **Command** category, set the Use flyout property to Yes. The tool is now a flyout. Notice that the **Command** string text box in the dialog box is disabled. You must now select the commands that will be displayed in the flyout.

The Flyout options property is used to specify which commands will be displayed in the flyout for a tool. This property is disabled unless the Use flyout property is set to Yes. To choose the commands to appear in the flyout, select the property and pick the ellipses button (...) at the right-hand side. The **Flyout Options** dialog box appears, Figure 23-29.

The commands that will appear in the flyout tool are indicated with a check in the **Flyout Options** dialog box. To prevent a command from being displayed in the flyout, remove the check mark next to its name. Then, close the **Flyout Options** dialog box to return to the **Tool Properties** dialog box. Finally, close the **Tool Properties** dialog box and test the tool.

The commands displayed in the **Flyout Options** dialog box depend on which command tool is being modified. Figure 23-29A shows the commands available when a dimensioning command tool is modified. When a drawing command tool is modified, the commands shown in Figure 23-29B are available. These also act as the default tools for other commands, such as modify commands or custom commands.

Figure 23-29.
A—The commands available for a dimensioning command flyout tool.
B—The commands available for a drawing command flyout tool.

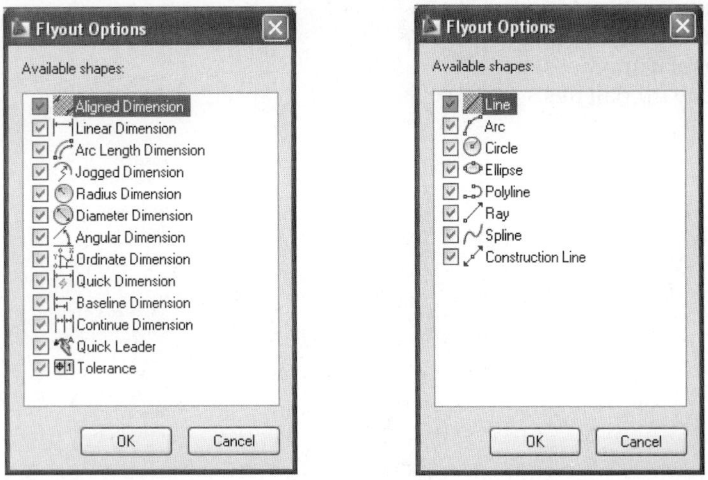

A B

PROFESSIONAL TIP

When a drawing or dimensioning command is added to a tool palette, the tool is automatically a flyout. It can then be modified to customize or remove its flyout capabilities.

Organizing Tool Palettes into Groups

Tool palettes are very useful, productive tools. You may find it beneficial to create many tool palettes to meet your design needs. However, having too many palettes visible at once can be counterproductive. The tool palette names become abbreviated in the **Tool Palettes** window or the tabs may be stacked on top of each other. This is the case if all of the default AutoCAD tool palettes are displayed. Fortunately, tool palettes can be divided into named groups and then a single group can be displayed.

By default, all of the tool palettes are shown in the **Tool Palettes** window, but the existing tool palettes are divided into named groups. Right-click on the title bar of **Tool Palettes** window and look at the shortcut menu. At the bottom of the shortcut menu, notice the **Annotation and Design**, **3D Make**, **Tables**, **Leaders**, **Materials**, **Materials Library** (if the materials library is installed), **Generic Lights**, **Photometric Lights**, **Cameras**, **Visual Styles**, and **All Palettes** entries, Figure 23-30. The check mark next to **All Palettes** indicates that all of the defined tool palettes are being displayed. Select **Annotation and Design** from the shortcut menu and notice that only the block-related tool palettes are visible. Right-click on the title bar again and select **Materials Library** from the shortcut menu. Notice that only the tool palettes related to materials are displayed. These tool palettes represent AutoCAD's materials library.

Ribbon
Tools > Customization Tool Palettes
Type
CUSTOMIZE
Menu
Tools > Customize > Tool Palettes...

CUSTOMIZE

The **Customize** dialog box is used to make new palette groups or customize existing groups. To open this dialog box, right-click on the **Tool Palettes** window title bar and select **Customize Palettes...** from the shortcut menu. You can also use the **CUSTOMIZE** command. All of the currently defined tool palettes are listed in the **Palettes:** area on the left side of the dialog box, Figure 23-31. The currently defined palette groups are listed in the **Palette Groups:** area on the right side of the dialog box. Palette groups are shown as folders. The tool palettes contained within the group are shown in the tree below the folder. The current palette group is indicated at the bottom of the dialog box and by the bold folder name in the **Palette Groups:** area.

Figure 23-30.
Select a palette group to display or choose to display all palettes.

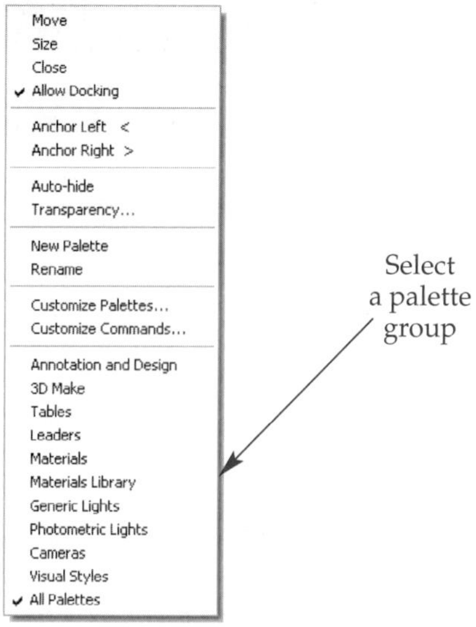

Figure 23-31.
The **Customize** dialog box is used to create and manage palette groups.

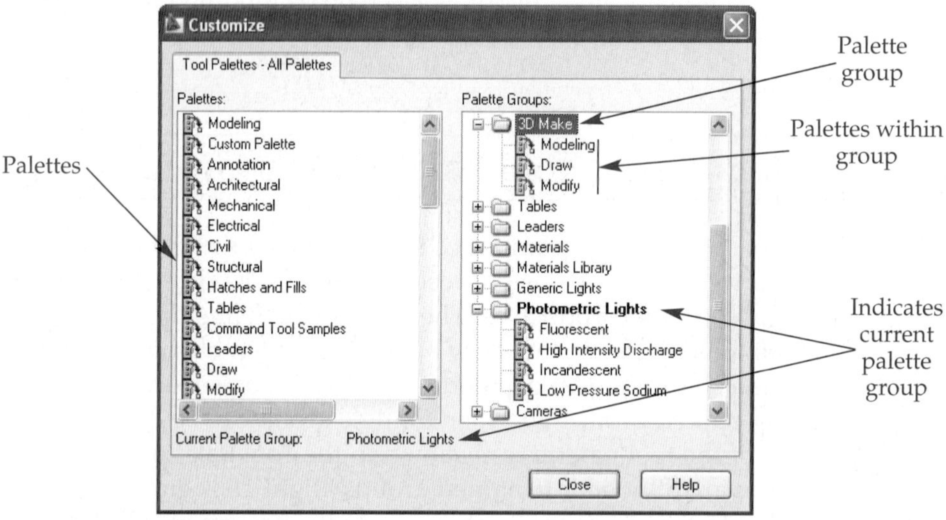

You can customize one of the existing palette groups by adding tool palettes to or removing tool palettes from the group. To remove a tool palette from a group, select the palette name under the group name in the **Palette Groups:** area. Then, press the [Delete] key or right-click and select **Remove** from the shortcut menu. To delete a palette group, select it in the **Palette Groups:** area and press the [Delete] key or right-click and select **Delete** from the shortcut menu. To add a palette to a group, simply select the palette in the **Palettes:** area and drag it into the group in the **Palette Groups:** area. A tool palette can be a member of more than one palette group.

To create a new palette group, right-click in a blank area of the **Palette Groups:** area and select **New Group** from the shortcut menu. A new folder appears in the tree with the default name highlighted in a text box. Type a name for the new palette group and press [Enter]. Then, drag tool palettes from the **Palettes:** area and drop them into the new palette group.

The order in which tool palettes appear in the **Tool Palettes** window is determined by their positions in the tree. To reorder the tool palettes, simply drag them to different positions within the palette group. To reorder the palette groups, drag the folders to different positions within the tree in the **Palette Groups:** area. The order in which the palette groups appear in the **Palette Groups:** area determines the order in which they appear in the shortcut menu displayed by right-clicking on the **Tool Palettes** window title bar. The order in which tool palettes appear in the **Palettes:** area is the order in which they are displayed when the **All Palettes** option is selected. By dragging a tool palette up or down in the tree, you can reorder the list.

PROFESSIONAL TIP

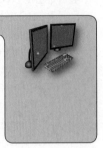

When adding a palette group, be careful where you right-click. If you right-click within a group, the new palette group is nested within that group. A cascading menu appears in the shortcut menu displayed when right-clicking on the **Tool Palettes** window title bar. If you do not want the palette group nested, simply drag the group to the top of the tree in the **Customize** dialog box.

Saving and Sharing Tool Palettes and Palette Groups

Tool palettes and palette groups can be exported from and imported into AutoCAD. Both operations are performed in the **Customize** dialog box. Some precautions about tool palette files:

- Tool palette files can only be imported into the same version of AutoCAD as the version from which the file was exported.
- Tool palette files exported from AutoCAD and imported into AutoCAD LT may have tools that will not work or behave the same. For example, color property tools using a color other than an AutoCAD Color Index (ACI) color are converted to ByLayer in AutoCAD LT. Also, gradient fill tools convert to hatch tools in AutoCAD LT. Raster image tools do not work in AutoCAD LT.

To export a tool palette, right-click on the palette to be exported in the **Palettes:** area of the **Customize** dialog box and select **Export...** from the shortcut menu. To export a palette group, right-click on the name of the group in the **Palette Groups:** area and select **Export...** from the shortcut menu. The **Export Palette** or **Export Group** dialog box is displayed. This is a standard Windows "save" dialog box. Name the file, navigate to the folder where you want to save it, and pick the **Save** button. Tool palettes are saved with a .xtp file extension. Palette groups are saved with a .xgp file extension.

To import a tool palette, right-click in the **Palettes:** area of the **Customize** dialog box and select **Import...** from the shortcut menu. To import a palette group, right-click in the **Palette Groups:** area and select **Import...** from the shortcut menu. The **Import Palette** or **Import Group** dialog box is displayed. Navigate to the folder where the file is saved, select it, and pick the **Open** button. The imported tool palette is added to the **Palettes:** area. An imported palette group is added to the **Palette Groups:** area.

Chapter Test

Answer the following questions. Write your answers on a separate sheet of paper or complete the electronic chapter test on the Student CD.

1. Name three ways to open the **Tool Palettes** window.
2. How do you dock the **Tool Palettes** window?
3. When enabled, what does the autohide feature do to the **Tool Palettes** window? How is the **Tool Palettes** window accessed when autohide is enabled?
4. Name two ways to toggle the autohide feature on the **Tool Palettes** window.
5. Describe how anchoring the **Tool Palettes** window differs from using the autohide feature or docking it.
6. How do you activate the transparency feature for the **Tool Palettes** window?
7. Name the three view styles in which tools can be displayed in the **Tool Palettes** window.
8. How do you create a new, blank tool palette?
9. How do you add a tool palette that contains all of the blocks in a particular drawing?
10. Which dialog box must be open to create a tool on a tool palette from a toolbar button? How is it opened?
11. What are the names of the two files that store hatch pattern definitions?
12. How do you rearrange tools on a tool palette?
13. Name four of the general properties that can be customized on individual tools on a tool palette.
14. What is the purpose of the auxiliary scale property for block and hatch insertion tools?
15. What are the two types of patterns that can be inserted using a tool in a tool palette?
16. If you are creating a command tool that performs a custom function, where is the command macro entered?
17. Which two types of commands can be included in a flyout tool?
18. What is the purpose of creating tool palette groups?
19. What is the extension given to an exported tool palette file?
20. How do you import a tool palette file?

Drawing Problems

Before customizing or creating any tool palettes, check with your instructor or supervisor for specific instructions or guidelines.

1. Design a complete tool palette system for your chosen discipline. Incorporate:
   - Multiple tool palettes
   - Block tools
   - Hatch tools
   - Drawing command tools (with and without flyouts)
   - Modification command tools
   - Inquiry command tools
   - Custom macro tools
   - Dimensioning command tools (with and without flyouts)

   A. On the tool palettes that use multiple types of command tools, use separators and text labels to group the types of tools.

   B. Create groups for the multiple tool palettes.

2. Export the tool palette groups created in problem 1. Copy the files to removable media or an archive drive.

A custom workspace can be created to meet your needs. Here, a workspace has been created for use when applying materials. The AutoCAD interface is stripped down to a bare minimum. Notice how this maximizes the drawing area.

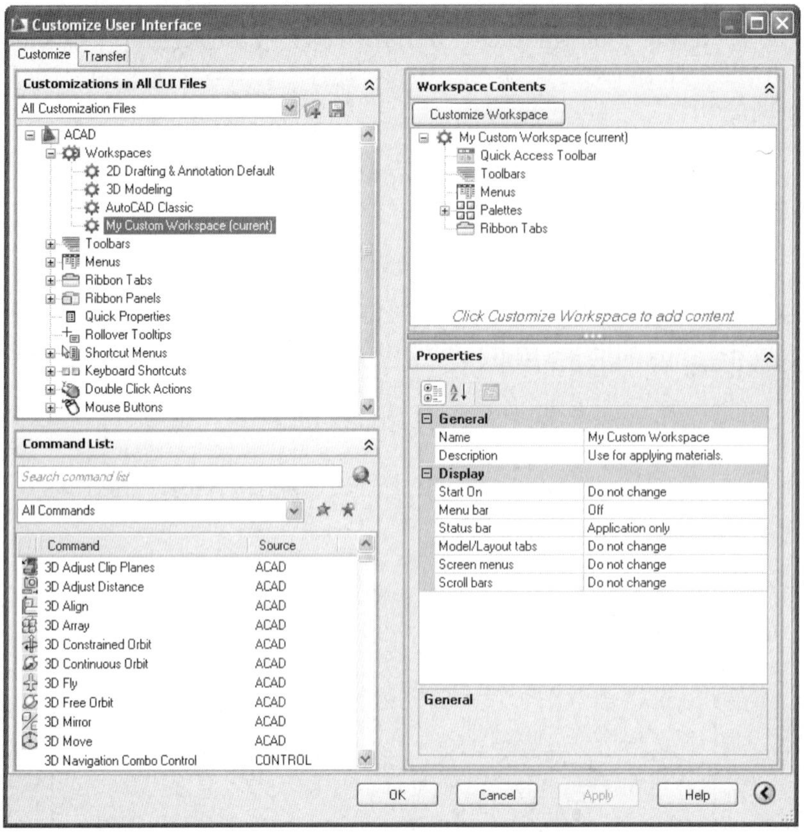

CHAPTER 24

User Profiles and Workspaces

Learning Objectives

After completing this chapter, you will be able to:

✓ Describe user profiles.
✓ Create user profiles.
✓ Restore a user profile.
✓ Describe workspaces.
✓ Explain the **Quick Access** toolbar.
✓ Create workspaces.
✓ Customize a workspace.
✓ Restore a workspace.
✓ Customize the **Quick Access** toolbar.

In a school or company, there is often more than one person who will use the same AutoCAD workstation. Each drafter has a unique style for creating a drawing. While there are often general rules to follow, many times the method used to arrive at the end result is not important. As you learned in previous chapters, there are many ways to customize AutoCAD. You can set screen colors and other features of the AutoCAD environment, create custom menus, and customize the ribbon. Many of these settings can be saved in a user profile or workspace. User profiles and workspaces allow you to quickly and easily restore a group of custom settings.

User Profiles

A ***user profile,*** which is described in detail in Chapter 20, is a group of settings for devices and AutoCAD functions. Some of the settings and values a profile can contain are:

- Temporary drawing file location.
- Template drawing file location.
- Text display format.
- Startup dialog box display.
- Minutes between automatic saves.
- File extension for temporary files.
- AutoCAD screen or pull-down menu display (on/off).
- Color and font settings for AutoCAD's text and graphics screens.

- Type of pointer and length of crosshairs.
- Default locations of printers, plotters (PC3 files), and plot styles (CTB/STB files).

Multiple profiles can be saved by a single user for different applications or several users can create individual profiles for their own use. A user profile should not be confused with settings found in a drawing. Template files are used to save settings relating to a drawing session, such as units, limits, object snap settings, drafting settings, grip settings, arc and circle smoothness, dimension styles, and text styles. A user profile, on the other hand, saves settings related to the performance and appearance of the software and hardware.

Creating a User Profile

A user profile is basically a collection of all things you have customized in AutoCAD *except* ribbon tabs and panels, menu browser and pull-down menus, tool palettes, and toolbars. These customizations are usually done to make AutoCAD easier for you to use. For example, as you gain experience in AutoCAD, you realize that you may:

- Like the crosshairs extending to the edges of the graphics window.
- Need to have the plotters and plot styles shared on a network.
- Prefer the graphics window background color to be gray.

Through the course of several drawing sessions, you have customized AutoCAD to reflect these preferences. Now, so you do not lose your preferred settings, you should create a user profile.

First, open the **Options** dialog box and pick the **Profiles** tab, Figure 24-1. Pick the **Add to List...** button on the right side of the tab. The **Add Profile** dialog box is opened, Figure 24-2. Enter a name and description. Then, pick the **Apply & Close** button to close the **Add Profile** dialog box. The current settings are saved to the user profile and the new user profile is now listed in the **Profiles** tab of the **Options** dialog box. The user profile is saved and will be available in the current and future AutoCAD drawing sessions.

Figure 24-1.
Settings can be saved in a profile.

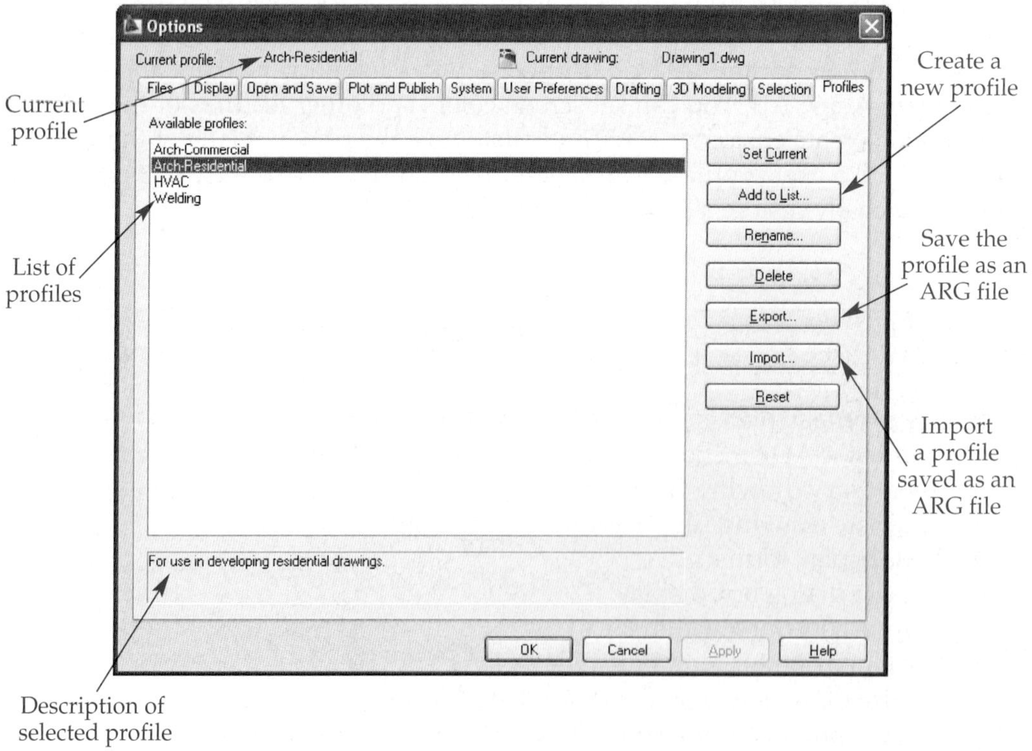

Figure 24-2.
The **Add Profile** dialog box is used to create a new profile.

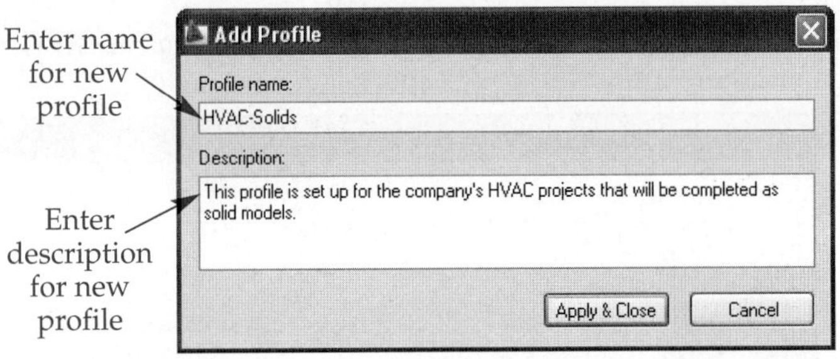

To change the name of a user profile, pick the **Rename...** button in the **Profiles** tab. In the **Change Profile** dialog box, enter a new name and description. To delete a user profile, highlight it in the **Profiles** tab and pick the **Delete** button. You cannot delete the current user profile. If you pick the **Reset** button, the highlighted user profile has all of its settings restored to AutoCAD defaults.

PROFESSIONAL TIP

Changes made to the environment (screen color, toolbar display, etc.) are automatically saved to the current profile.

Restoring a User Profile

Once a user profile is saved, it is available in the current and future AutoCAD drawing sessions. To set any saved user profile as the current user profile, first open the **Options** dialog box. The current profile is indicated at the top of the **Options** dialog box. Then, pick the **Profiles** tab. Highlight the name of the profile to restore in the **Available profiles:** list. Then, pick the **Set Current** button. You can also double-click on the name in the **Available profiles:** list to restore a profile. All of the settings in the user profile are applied while the **Options** dialog box is still open. Close the dialog box to return to the drawing editor.

Exercise 24-1

Complete the exercise on the Student CD.

Importing and Exporting User Profiles

A user profile can be exported and imported. To take your user profile to a different AutoCAD workstation, a user profile can be exported to an ARG file. A user profile is saved as an ARG file.

To export a user profile, open the **Options** dialog box and pick the **Profiles** tab. Highlight the profile to export and pick the **Export...** button. The **Export Profiles** dialog box is opened, **Figure 24-3.** Then, select a folder and name the file. When you pick the **Save** button, the user profile is saved with the .arg file extension.

To import a user profile, pick the **Import...** button in the **Profiles** tab. The **Import Profile** dialog box is displayed. This is a standard "open" dialog box. Then, navigate to the appropriate folder, select the proper ARG file, and pick the **Open** button. A second dialog box named **Import Profile** is displayed. See **Figure 24-4.** You can rename the user profile, change the description, and choose to include the file path. Pick the **Apply & Close** button to complete the process. The user profile is then available in the **Profiles** tab.

Figure 24-3.
The **Export Profile** dialog box is used to save a user profile as an ARG file, which can be transferred to another AutoCAD workstation.

Figure 24-4.
Importing a user profile.

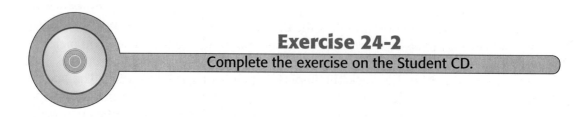

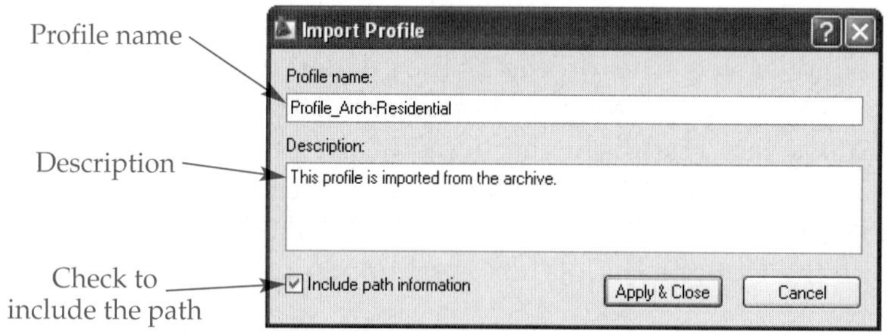

PROFESSIONAL TIP

A variety of settings can be changed in the **Options** dialog box. Settings that have the AutoCAD drawing icon located next to them can be stored in a template file (or drawing). Using the appropriate template file to begin a drawing automatically resets these settings. Settings within the **Options** dialog box that do not have the AutoCAD drawing icon next to them can typically be restored through the use of user profiles.

Exercise 24-2

Complete the exercise on the Student CD.

Workspaces

As you have seen, a user profile allows you to set and restore settings for screen colors, drafting settings, and file locations. On the other hand, a workspace allows you to set and restore settings for the **Quick Access** toolbar, ribbon, menus, and palettes (**DesignCenter**, **Properties** palette, **Tool Palettes** window, etc.), but it does not contain environmental settings. A ***workspace*** is a collection of displayed toolbars, palettes, ribbon tabs and panels, and menus and their configurations. A workspace stores not only which of these graphic tools are visible, but also their on-screen locations.

PROFESSIONAL TIP

A user profile also stores which toolbars are displayed and their location. However, the configurations of the menus (menu browser and pull-down menus) and ribbon and display status of palettes are not saved in a user profile. Therefore, if a workspace is restored, the settings for toolbar display and location override the current user profile settings.

Creating a Workspace

AutoCAD has three default workspaces—AutoCAD Classic, 2D Drafting and Annotation, and 3D Modeling. A workspace can be set current using the **Workspace Switching** button on the right-hand side of the status bar. See Figure 24-5. Picking this button displays a shortcut menu containing the names of all available workspaces. It also contains options for working with workspaces. When AutoCAD is launched, the workspace that was last active is restored. AutoCAD can be set up so that any changes made to the ribbon, toolbars, menus, and palettes are saved to this workspace. However, it is best to create your own workspaces.

The first step in setting up and storing your own workspace is to arrange the ribbon, toolbars, tool palettes, and menus to your liking. Refer to Chapter 21. Next, use the **WSSAVE** command to open the **Save Workspace** dialog box, Figure 24-6. You can easily access the **WSSAVE** command by selecting **Save Current As...** in the shortcut menu displayed by picking the **Workspace Switching** button. In the **Save Workspace** dialog box, enter a name for the workspace, such as Normal Design or Standard Arrangement, and then pick the **Save** button.

WSSAVE

Type
WSSAVE

Menu
Tools
> Workspaces
> Save Current As...

Ribbon
Status Bar

Workspace Switching

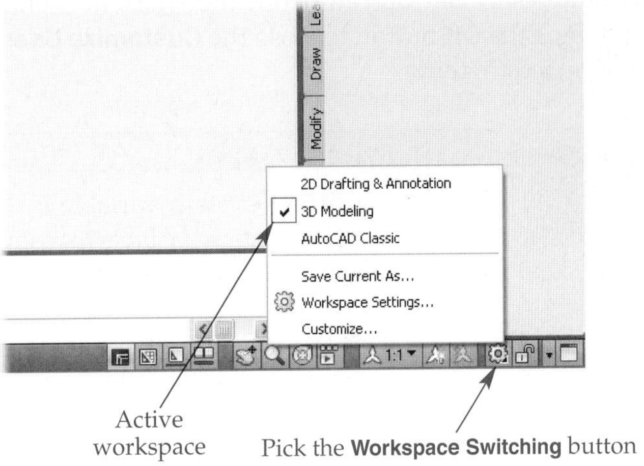

Figure 24-5.
Switching workspaces.

Figure 24-6.
Creating a new workspace.

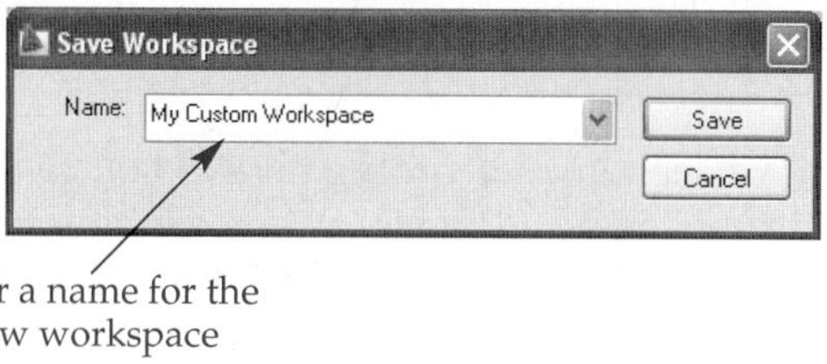

The current settings for toolbars, pull-down menus, and tool palettes are now stored in the new workspace, which is also made current. The workspace name also appears in the shortcut menu displayed by picking the **Workspace Switching** button. The current workspace is indicated in this menu by a check mark.

PROFESSIONAL TIP

Workspaces are saved in a CUI file. By default, they are saved to the main CUI file (acad.cui).

Restoring a Workspace

Once a workspace has been saved, it can easily be restored. A list of available workspaces appears in the shortcut menu displayed by picking the **Workspace Switching** button and in the **Workspaces** cascading menu in the **Tools** menu. To select a different workspace, simply pick the name of the workspace in the shortcut menu or cascading menu.

A workspace can also be restored using the command line:

Command: **WORKSPACE**↵
Enter workspace option [setCurrent/SAveas/Edit/Rename/Delete/SEttings/?] <setCurrent>: **C**↵
Enter name of workspace to make current [?] <*current*>: **MY CUSTOM WORKSPACE**↵
Command:

Notice that you can manage workspaces using this command.

You can also use the **Customize User Interface** dialog box to restore a workspace. First, open the dialog box. Then, expand the Workspaces branch in the **Customizations in All CUI Files** pane. All of the workspaces defined in the default CUI file and any open CUI files are displayed in this branch. The label (current) follows the name of the current workspace. To restore a workspace, right-click on its name in the Workspaces branch and select **Set Current** from the shortcut menu. Its name is now followed by (current). Pick the **OK** button to close the **Customize User Interface** dialog box and make the workspace current.

PROFESSIONAL TIP

The **WSCURRENT** system variable indicates the current workspace. You can use this system variable to restore a workspace. Simply set the system variable to the name of the workspace you want to restore.

Quick Access Toolbar

The **Quick Access** toolbar is located in the top-left corner of the screen to the right of the menu browser icon, **Figure 24-7.** It contains essential tools for AutoCAD. By default, it displays the **New**, **Open**, **Save**, **Plot**, **Undo**, and **Redo** tools. In addition, you can display other toolbars by right-clicking on any of the buttons to display a shortcut menu. In this menu, select the toolbars to show and hide.

Unlike the toolbars discussed in Chapter 21, the **Quick Access** toolbar is customized inside of the workspace. This is discussed in the next section.

Customizing a Workspace

An existing workspace can be customized using the **Customize User Interface** dialog box. First, select the workspace to be customized in the Workspaces branch of the **Customizations in All CUI Files** pane. Remember, the name of this pane will change based on the selection in the drop-down list. The **Workspace Contents** pane at the upper-right corner of the dialog box displays the contents of the selected workspace. There are Quick Access Toolbar, Toolbars, Menus, Palettes, and Ribbon Tabs branches. Refer to **Figure 24-8.** Expand a branch to see which components the workspace contains.

To customize the workspace, pick the **Customize Workspace** button at the top of the **Workspace Contents** pane. The tree in the pane turns blue to indicate you are in customize mode and the button changes to the **Done** button. Also, notice that the tree in the **Customizations in All CUI Files** pane has changed. Several branches have disappeared and the Menus and Ribbon Tabs branches have a green check mark next to

Figure 24-7.
The **Quick Access** toolbar is customized as part of the workspace.

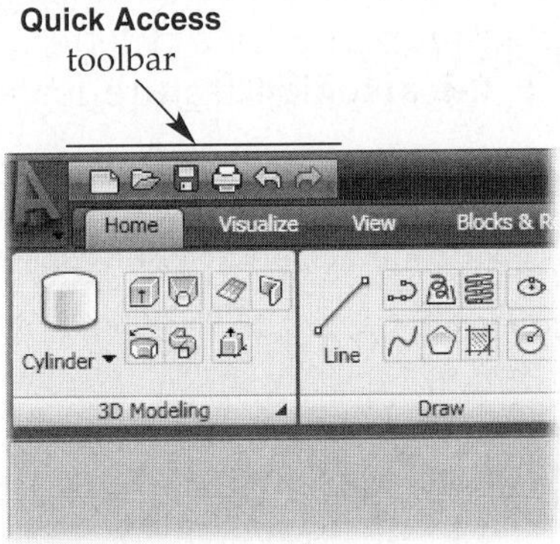

Figure 24-8.
You can customize existing workspaces.

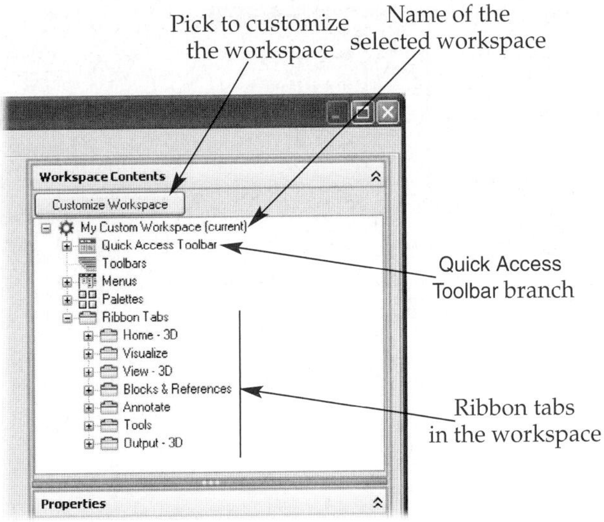

them. If you expand these branches, you will see that a green check mark also appears next to the components that currently are in the workspace. See **Figure 24-9.**

To add a component, pick the blank box in front of its name to place a check mark in the box. The component also appears in the **Workspace Contents** pane. To remove a component, pick the check mark in front of its name to clear the box. The component is also removed from the **Workspace Contents** pane.

The components in the Quick Access Toolbar branch are commands. To add a command to the Quick Access Toolbar branch, locate it in the **Command List:** pane. Then, drag and drop it into the branch in the **Workspace Contents** pane. To remove a command from the Quick Access Toolbar branch, select it in the **Workspace Contents** pane. Then, press the [Delete] key. You do not need to be in customization mode to customize the **Quick Access** toolbar.

When done customizing the workspace, pick the **Done** button in the **Workspace Contents** pane. The tree is no longer displayed in blue. Also, all branches are once again displayed in the **Customizations in All CUI Files** pane. You can now expand a branch in the **Workspace Contents** pane, select a component name, and use the **Properties** pane to adjust the component's properties. For example, suppose you have added the **Layers** toolbar to a workspace. In the **Properties** pane, you can set it to be floating, specify the location of its anchor point, and set the number of rows for the toolbar. You can also change the order in which menus appear in the menu browser and on the menu bar by dragging them to a new location in the tree in the **Workspace Contents** pane. The top of the tree is the top of the menu browser or the left-hand side of the menu bar.

You may have noticed that there is not a Palettes branch in the **Customizations in All CUI Files** pane. All palettes are automatically available in all workspaces. You can, however, specify whether a palette is displayed or hidden in a workspace. You can also change other properties of a palette, such as floating/docked status, its size, and whether or not the autohide feature is enabled. To change the properties of a

Figure 24-9.
Specifying which toolbars, menus, and ribbon tabs are included in the workspace.

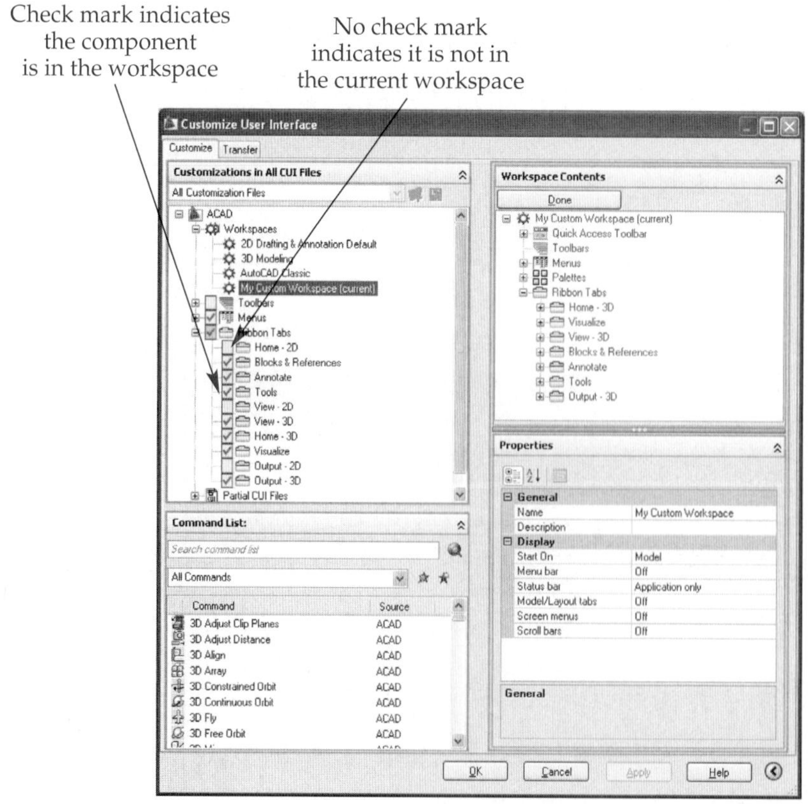

palette, first select it in the Palettes branch in the **Workspace Contents** pane. Then, in the **Properties** pane, adjust the properties as needed. When you pick **OK** to close the **Customize User Interface** dialog box, the new default properties of the palette are set for that workspace.

For example, the **Tool Palette** window in the 3D Modeling workspace is, by default, docked on the right-hand side of the screen. You can hide the **Tool Palette** window when in the drawing editor by simply picking the **Close** button (**X**). You can also drag the palette into the drawing area to float it. However, these actions do not change the default setting for the workspace. If you restore the workspace in the future, the **Tool Palette** window will again be docked on the right-hand side of the screen. You must alter the default settings for the **Tool Palette** window in the workspace. First, select Tool Palette in the Palettes branch in the **Workspace Contents** pane. Then, in the **Properties** pane, change the Show property to No. See **Figure 24-10.** Now, when you restore the workspace, the **Tool Palette** window will not be displayed by default. It can, of course, be manually displayed as needed.

You can also set up a workspace so that it displays model space or layout (paper) space when restored. By default, a workspace displays model space when it is set as current. To change this, highlight the workspace name in either the **Customizations in All CUI Files** pane or the **Workspace Contents** pane. Then, in the **Properties** pane, change the Start On property to Layout or Do not change. If Model is specified for the Start On property, model space is displayed when the workspace is restored. If Layout is specified for the Start On property, the most recently active layout tab is displayed

Figure 24-10.
Changing the default properties of a palette for a given workspace.

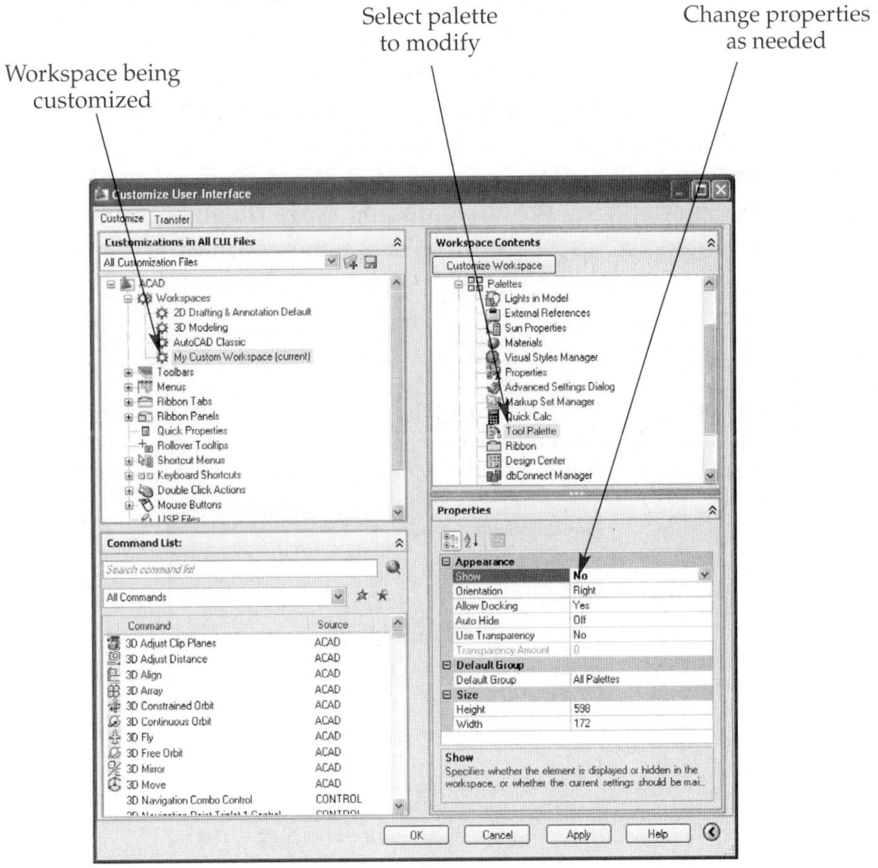

when the workspace is restored. If Do not change is specified for the Start On property, the current tab remains active when the workspace is restored.

PROFESSIONAL TIP

If the **Customize User Interface** dialog box is open, but you are not in customization mode, you can also remove a component from the workspace by right-clicking on it in the tree in the **Workspace Contents** pane and selecting **Remove from Workspace** in the shortcut menu. This is true for all component types except palettes, as all palettes are always available to all workspaces.

Workspace Settings

WSSETTINGS

Type
WSSETTINGS
Menu
Tools > Workspaces > Workspace Settings...
Ribbon
Status Bar: Workspace Switching

There are various settings related to workspaces. These are set in the **Workspace Settings** dialog box. See **Figure 24-11.** The **WSSETTINGS** command opens this dialog box. It can also be displayed by selecting **Workspace Settings...** from the shortcut menu displayed by picking the **Workspace Switching** button.

At the top of the **Workspace Settings** dialog box is the **My Workspace =** drop-down list. All saved workspaces in the CUI file appear in this list. The workspace that is selected in the list is defined as My Workspace. The workspace that is designated as My Workspace is restored when the **My Workspace** button on the **Workspaces** toolbar is picked. This can be useful if one person primarily uses a machine, but others may temporarily use the machine with their own workspace settings. You may also find this useful if you have more than one workspace, but use one more often than all of the others. This feature can only be accessed when the **Workspaces** toolbar is displayed.

The **Menu Display and Order** area of the **Workspace Settings** dialog box contains a list of all workspaces saved in the current CUI file. The order of this list determines the order of the list that appears in the **Workspace Switching** shortcut menu, the **Workspaces** cascading menu in the **Tools** pull-down menu, and in the drop-down list on the **Workspaces** toolbar. The order of the list can be modified by highlighting one of the workspaces and using the **Move Up** and **Move Down** buttons. The **Add Separator** button is used to add a horizontal line, or menu separator, to the list. A separator is

Figure 24-11.
The **Workspace Settings** dialog box is used to set which workspace is My Workspace, specify which workspaces are shown in the menu and drop-down list and their order, and set whether or not changes are automatically saved when a different workspace is restored.

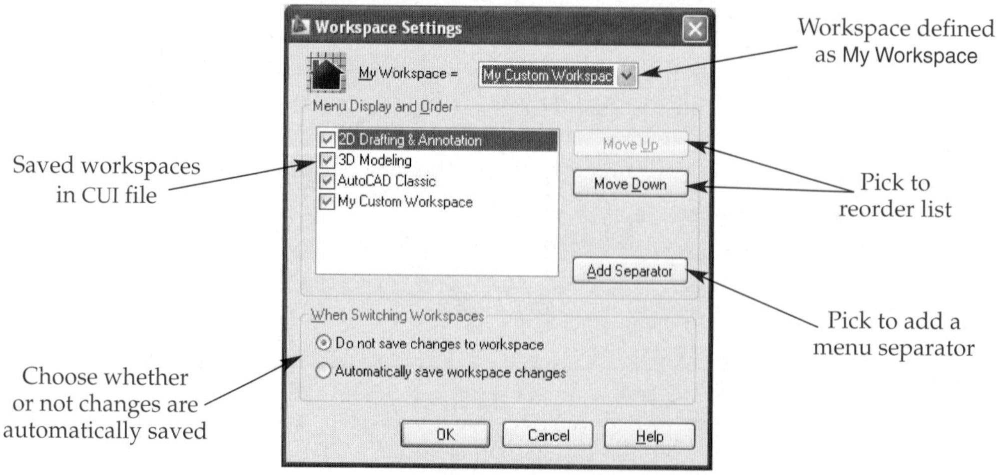

used to logically group workspace names within the list. The separator can be relocated within the list just like a workspace name.

You can prevent a workspace name or separator from being displayed in the menu or drop-down list by removing the check box next to its name. The check box next to the current workspace and the workspace designated as My Workspace can be cleared. However, these workspaces will always be displayed in the menu and drop-down list.

At the bottom of the **Workspace Settings** dialog box is the **When Switching Workspaces** area. The radio buttons in this area determine whether or not changes you have made since you last saved the workspace, such as the visibility of toolbars, are saved when you switch to a different workspace. To retain the settings as you last saved them, pick the **Do not save changes to workspace** radio button. Changes made since the workspace was last saved are discarded when a different workspace is restored. If the **Automatically save workspace changes** radio button is on, any "as you work" toolbar changes are automatically saved to the workspace when a different workspace is restored.

At any time, you can manually save the settings to the current workspace. Pick the Save Current As... selection in the **Tools**>**Workspaces** menu or the **Workspace Switching** shortcut menu. When the **Save Workspace** dialog box appears, select the current workspace from the drop-down list. Then, pick the **Save** button. An alert is displayed stating that a workspace with that name already exists and asking if you would like to replace it. Pick the **Yes** button to save the changes to the current workspace.

PROFESSIONAL TIP

Unlike a user profile, changes to the environment (toolbar display, menu configuration, etc.) are not necessarily automatically saved. To ensure the changes are only saved when you decide to save them, be sure the **Do not save workspace changes** radio button is on in the **Workspace Settings** dialog box.

Exercise 24-3

Complete the exercise on the Student CD.

Controlling the Display of Ribbon Tabs and Panels

Right-click anywhere on the ribbon to display the shortcut menu. Notice the **Tabs** and **Panels** cascading menus. See **Figure 24-12.** The default ribbon tabs in the 3D Modeling workspace are **Home, Visualize, View, Blocks & References, Annotate, Tools,** and **Output**. The **Panels** cascading menu in the shortcut menu displays the panels of the current tab. For example, the default panels of the **Home** tab in the 3D Modeling workspace are **3D Modeling, Draw, Solid Editing, Modify, View, Layers, Properties,** and **Utilities**. In the **Tabs** or **Panels** cascading menu, the currently displayed tabs and panels have a check mark next to their name. Selecting a name toggles the visibility of the tab or panel.

Figure 24-12.
A shortcut menu is displayed when you right-click on the ribbon. A—The **Tabs** cascading menu. B—The **Panels** cascading menu.

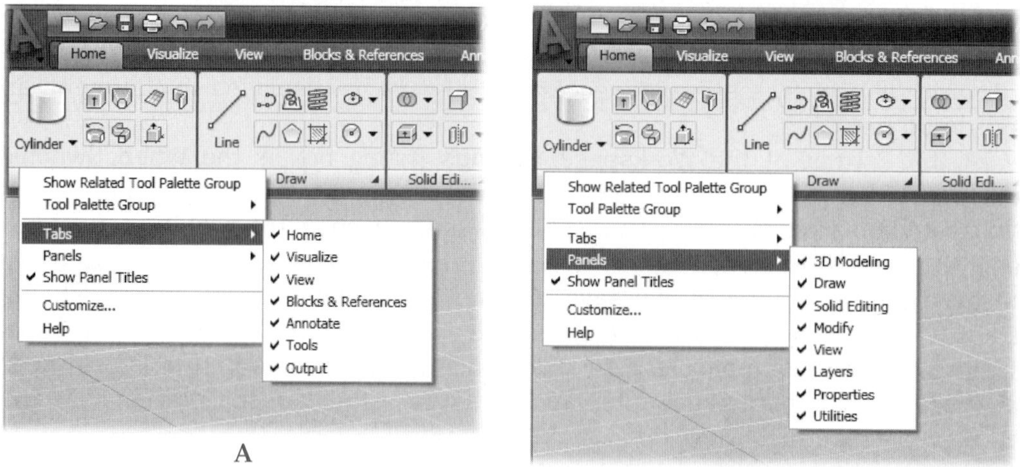

A B

While the visibility of the ribbon tabs and panels can be adjusted "on the fly" as described above, visibility can also be controlled by customizing the workspace. This is a more efficient method.

1. Open the **Customize User Interface** dialog box and expand the Workspaces branch in the **Customizations in All CUI Files** pane.
2. Select the workspace for which you wish to adjust panel visibility.
3. In the **Workspace Contents** pane, pick the **Customize Workspace** button.
4. Expand the Ribbon Tabs branch in the **Workspace Contents** pane. The tabs visible in the workspace appear in the tree. The panels visible in the workspace appear as branches below the tabs.
5. In the **Customizations in All CUI Files** pane, expand the Ribbon Tabs branch. All available tabs appear in the branch. The currently displayed tabs have a check mark next to their name. See **Figure 24-13.**
6. Check the tabs to display and uncheck the tabs to hide.
7. To control which panels are displayed for a tab, expand the tab's branch in the **Workspace Contents** pane. Then, select the panel to hide and, in the **Properties** pane, change its Show property to No. To display a panel, change the property to Yes.
8. In the **Workspace Contents** pane, pick the **Done** button.
9. Exit the **Customize User Interface** dialog box.

Tabs and panels appear in the ribbon in the order they are displayed in the tree of the **Workspace Contents** pane. Top to bottom equals left to right when the ribbon is horizontal. As you add panels to the workspace, they are added to the bottom of the Ribbon Tabs branch. Refer to Chapter 21 for information on creating custom ribbon tabs and panels. To rearrange the tabs or panels, pick and drag them within the **Workspace Contents** pane. You do not need to be in customization mode. You can also remove a tab from the workspace by right-clicking on its name in the **Workspace Contents** pane and picking **Remove from Workspace** from the shortcut menu.

PROFESSIONAL TIP

You do not need to be in customization mode to change a panel's Show property. Also, when a panel's Show property is set to No, the panel is still available in the **Panels** cascading menu in the shortcut menu displayed by right-clicking on the ribbon.

Figure 24-13.
Setting which ribbon tabs and panels are displayed for a workspace.

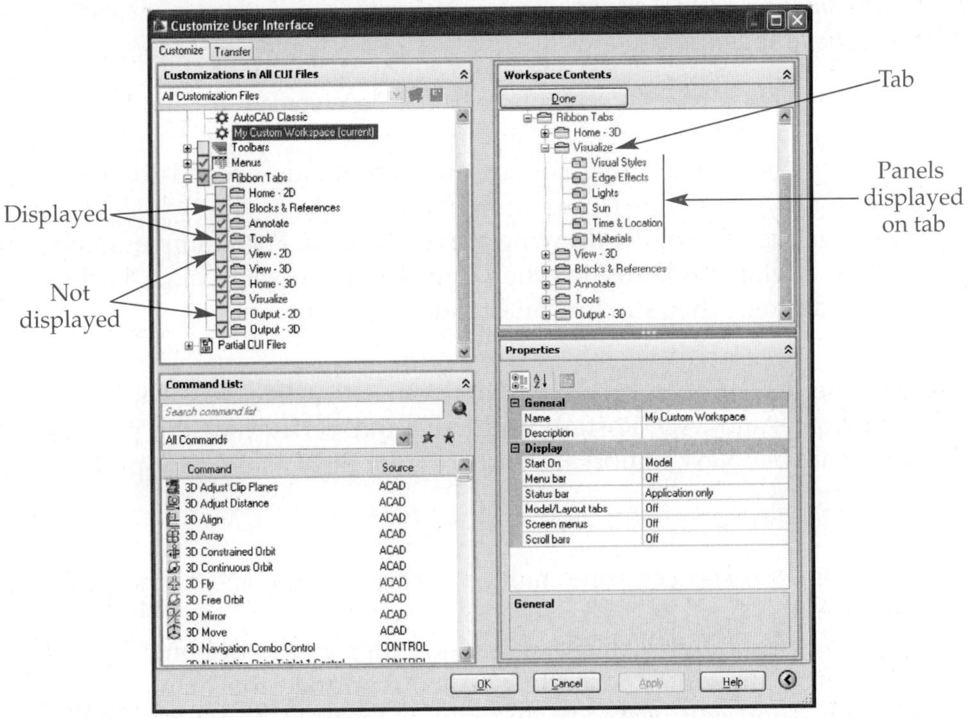

Chapter Test

Answer the following questions. Write your answers on a separate sheet of paper or complete the electronic chapter test on the Student CD.

1. What is a *user profile?*
2. How and why are profiles used?
3. What is the file extension used for a profile when it is exported?
4. In which dialog box is a user profile created?
5. How do you restore a user profile?
6. Why would you export a user profile?
7. Briefly describe how to import a user profile.
8. Define *workspace* as related to AutoCAD.
9. List three ways to open the **Save Workspace** dialog box.
10. How do you restore a workspace? List three methods.
11. When customizing a workspace, how do you determine which menus, ribbon tabs, and toolbars are displayed?
12. Briefly describe how to change the default settings for a palette for a given workspace.
13. List three ways to open the **Workspace Settings** dialog box.
14. How do you add a separator to the shortcut menu displayed by picking the **Workspace Switching** button?
15. How do you define My Workspace?
16. Briefly describe how to set up AutoCAD so that changes made to the environment are automatically saved to the current workspace.
17. Briefly describe how to add ribbon tabs to a workspace.
18. How can you add commands to the **Quick Access** toolbar?
19. Briefly describe how to control which panels are displayed for a tab in a workspace.
20. How do you set the display order of tabs and panels on the ribbon?

Drawing Problems

Before creating any user profiles or workspaces, check with your instructor or supervisor for specific instructions or guidelines.

1. Create two user profiles, one named Model Development for modeling and one named Rendering for visual styles and rendering.
   A. Display the toolbars that contain the commands needed for each type of work.
   B. Change the color of the drawing area as needed. For example, some drafters prefer a white background when drawing. However, a black background is often desired when shading and rendering the model.

2. Export the user profiles created in problem 1 to ARG files. Then, delete each profile from AutoCAD. Restart AutoCAD and verify that the profiles are no longer available. Next, import each profile from file. Restore each profile to verify the settings.

3. Create two workspaces, one named Design Development and one named Dimensioning.
   A. For the Design Development workspace, display the ribbon tabs and panels related to drawing and editing. Also, rearrange the menus to group the drawing and editing/modifying menus together. Remove any menus that are not needed.
   B. For the Dimensioning workspace, display the ribbon tabs and panels related to dimensioning the drawing. Also, remove drawing-related menus from the menu browser. You may consider removing editing/modifying menus.
   C. Create custom ribbon tabs and panels as needed. Include flyouts when advantageous.

4. Customize the two workspaces created in problem 3.
   A. Change default on/off status of any palettes to suit the purpose of the workspace. For example, you may want the **DesignCenter**, **Tool Palette**, and **Properties** palettes displayed for the Design Development workspace.
   B. Enable the autohide status of all displayed palettes.
   C. Change the Dimensioning workspace so that it starts in a layout.

5. Set up the workspaces from problem 4 so that "on the fly" changes are automatically saved when a different workspace is made current.

CHAPTER 25

Recording and Using Actions

Learning Objectives

After completing this chapter, you will be able to:

- ✓ Describe the action recorder.
- ✓ Create and store an action.
- ✓ Run an action.
- ✓ Modify an action.
- ✓ Explain the limitations of the action recorder.

In schools and workplaces, certain design elements and customizing features can be enhanced by automation. The AutoCAD ***action recorder*** is a tool that allows the user to automate a task or function by saving the steps needed to complete it. These steps are called an ***action.*** Creating a library of recorded actions allows a user to increase productivity by more efficiently working in AutoCAD.

Action Recorder Overview

The **Action Recorder** panel is located in the **Tools** tab of the ribbon. It contains five tools: **Record/Stop**, **Insert Message**, **Request User Input**, **Play**, and **Preference**. In addition, a drop-down list displays all recorded actions. See **Figure 25-1.** The expanded **Action Recorder** panel displays the action tree. The ***action tree*** displays the steps used to create the current action that is selected in the drop-down list. The steps are listed in order from top to bottom. The first step is located at the top of the tree.

The action recorder saves all steps in an action to an ACTM file. By saving the action to a file, it can repeatedly be used. The ACTM file name cannot contain spaces or special characters. Also, the name cannot be the same as an existing AutoCAD command name.

The folder where actions are stored is defined under the in the **Files** tab of the **Options** dialog box. To change the location where actions are stored, expand the Action Recorder Setting branch in the **Files** tab, **Figure 25-2.** Then, pick the Actions Recording File Locations branch, pick the **Browse...** button, and locate the new folder.

Figure 25-1.
The **Action Recorder** panel on the **Tools** tab of the ribbon with the action tree displayed.

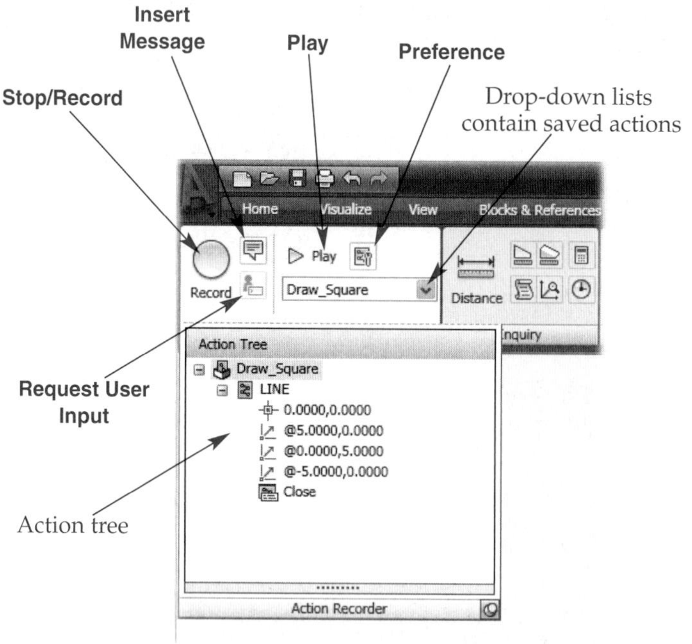

ACTRECORD

Ribbon
Tools
> Action Recorder
Record
Type
ACTRECORD
Menu
Tools
> Action Recorder
> Record

Record/Stop

The **Record** tool launches AutoCAD into record mode. Then, you can begin performing the steps needed to defined for your action. Once the **Record** tool is activated, the button changes to the **Stop** button. This is used when the steps are completed and you have finished recording your action.

ACTUSERMESSAGE

Ribbon
Tools
> Action Recorder
Insert Message
Type
ACTUSERMESSAGE

Insert Message

When in record mode or while editing a macro, the **Insert Message** tool is enabled. This tool allows you to insert a message dialog box that will be displayed for the user during action playback. A message is especially useful for directing the user's attention

Figure 25-2.
The location where actions are stored is set in the **Files** tab of the **Options** dialog box.

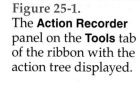

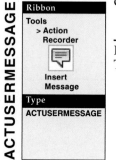

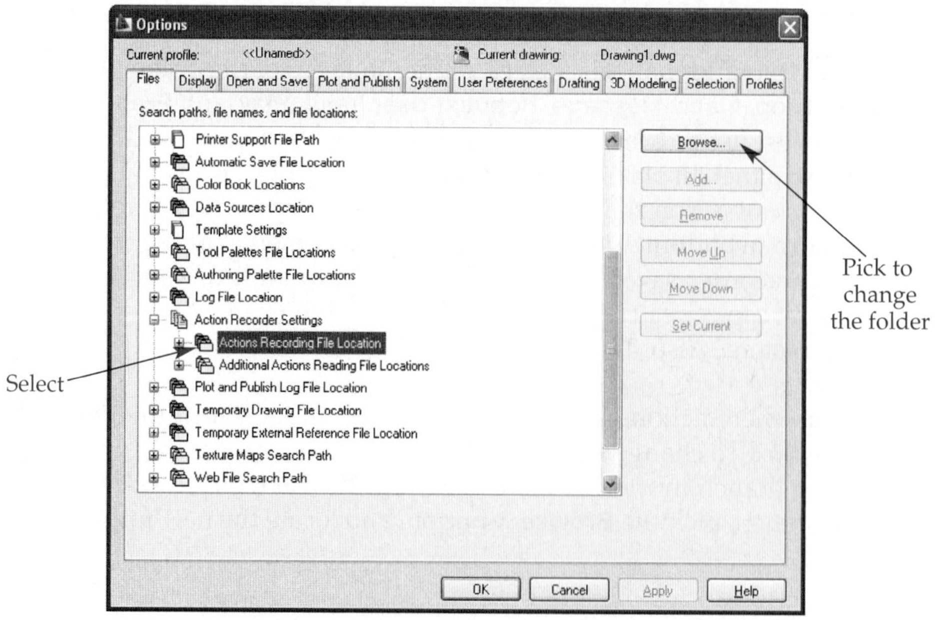

to what is required. One can also be used at the beginning of the action to introduce the user to the action and what it does.

Request User Input

When in record mode or while editing a macro, the **Request User Input** tool is enabled. Inserting a request for user input pauses the action at that point during playback. The user is prompted for input, such as selecting objects or picking locations on the screen.

ACTUSERINPUT

Ribbon
Tools
> Action Recorder
Request User Input
Type
ACTUSERINPUT

Play

The **Play** tool plays the current macro. The current macro is displayed at the top of the drop-down list in the **Action Recorder** panel. This drop-down list is discussed later.

Preferences

Picking the **Preference** tool displays the **Action Recorder Preferences** dialog box, Figure 25-3. This dialog box contains three check boxes for setting how the **Action Recorder** panel functions. When the **Expand on playback** check box is checked, **Action Recorder** panel is automatically expanded to show the action tree during action playback. This is unchecked by default. When the **Expand on recording** check box is checked, the **Action Recorder** panel automatically expands to display the action tree during action recording. This is checked by default. When the **Prompt for action macro name** check box is checked, the **Action Macro** dialog box is displayed after recording of the action is complete (the **Stop** button is picked). This dialog box prompts for the action name, which is the name of the ACTM file. See Figure 25-4.

Figure 25-3.
The **Action Recorder Preferences** dialog box is used to set certain behavior of the action recorder.

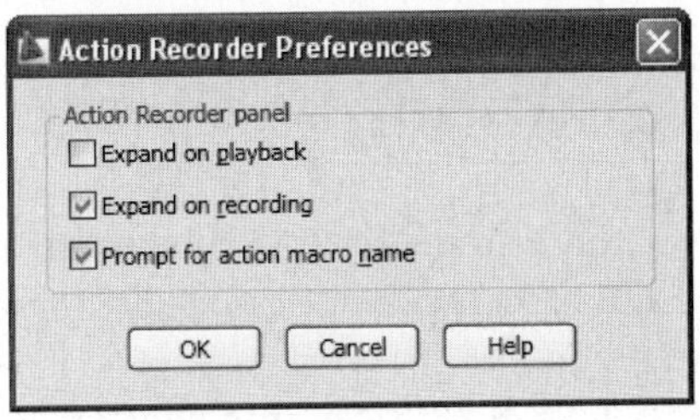

Figure 25-4.
The **Action Macro** dialog box is used to save an action.

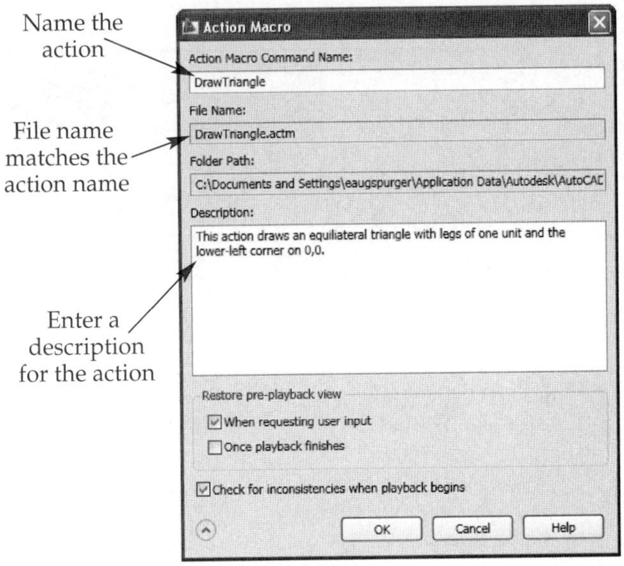

Action Tree and Available Actions

The **Available Action Macro** drop-down list displays all action files (ACTM) located in the action folder. As explained earlier, the action folder is set in the **Files** tab of the **Options** dialog box. The current action is displayed at the top of the list. To see all of the available actions, pick the drop-down list. To set a different action current, simply pick it in the drop-down list.

At the bottom of the expanded **Action Recorder** panel is the action tree. The action tree contains all of the steps in the action in a tree form. See **Figure 25-5**. The name of the action is the top of the tree. Each step is a branch in the tree. In addition, the command branches can be expanded to see the values entered into the action.

PROFESSIONAL TIP

Inserting messages is especially useful to direct the user about the steps of an action. Inserting requests for user input in an action pause the action and allows the user to select objects or on-screen points. These features make actions more dynamic and help ensure proper usage.

Exercise 25-1

Complete the exercise on the Student CD.

Creating and Storing an Action

Now that you have investigated the features of the action recorder, it is time to create an action. This example action will create a layer named A-Anno-Iden, set the layer color to orange (ACI = 30), and make the layer current. The action will also set the annotation scale to 1/4″ = 1′-0″. In this section, you will create the basic action. Later, you will modify the action to make it more interactive. Follow these steps to create the basic action named AnnoQtr.

Figure 25-5. The action tree contains all of the steps in the current action.

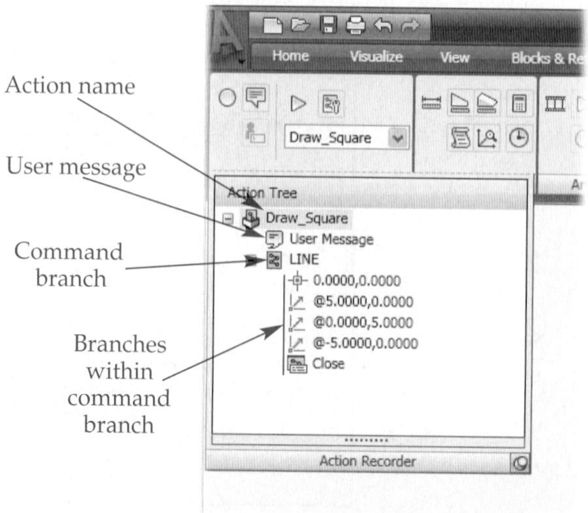

1. Start a new drawing.
2. Pick the **Record** button in the **Action Recorder** panel on the **Tools** tab of the ribbon. Notice that the panel is shaded in red and a red dot appears next to the crosshairs. These are indications that you are in record mode.
3. Pick the **Layer Properties** button on the **Layers** panel in the **Home** tab of the ribbon to display the **Layer Properties Manager** palette.
4. Pick the **New Layer** button in the palette's toolbar.
5. In the edit box, name the new layer A-Anno-Iden.
6. Pick the color swatch for the layer and, in the **Select Color** dialog box, pick color 30 on the **Index Color** tab. Then, pick the **OK** button to close the **Select Color** dialog box.
7. Right-click on the newly created layer and pick **Set Current** from the shortcut menu.
8. Close the **Layer Properties Manager** palette.
9. Using the **Annotation Scale** button on the status bar, set the 1/4″ = 1′-0″ scale current. See **Figure 25-6.** If the drawing is based on the acad3D.dwt template, you must type the **CANNOSCALE** command since the status bar button is unavailable.
10. Pick the **Stop** button on the **Action Recorder** panel in the **Tools** tab of the ribbon. This ends recording of the action.
11. The **Action Macro** dialog box appears when you pick the **Stop** button, unless you have turned off the "prompt for name" option.
12. In the **Action Macro** dialog box, type AnnoQtr in the **Action Macro Command Name:** text box.
13. In the **Description:** text box, type Creates a new layer with color 30 and sets the 1/4″ = 1′-0″ annotation scale current or a similar description.
14. Pick the **OK** button in the **Action Macro** dialog box to save the action.

The AnnoQtr action is now available to run. It is automatically selected as the current action in the **Available Action Macro** drop-down list in the **Action Recorder** panel. Also, the action tree for the action is displayed in the expanded panel. See **Figure 25-7.**

PROFESSIONAL TIP

In a design environment, saving actions in a shared folder on a network can streamline productivity. This creates an environment in which AutoCAD users can share their knowledge by creating actions drawn from their own design experiences.

Figure 25-6.
Setting the annotation scale for the action being recorded.

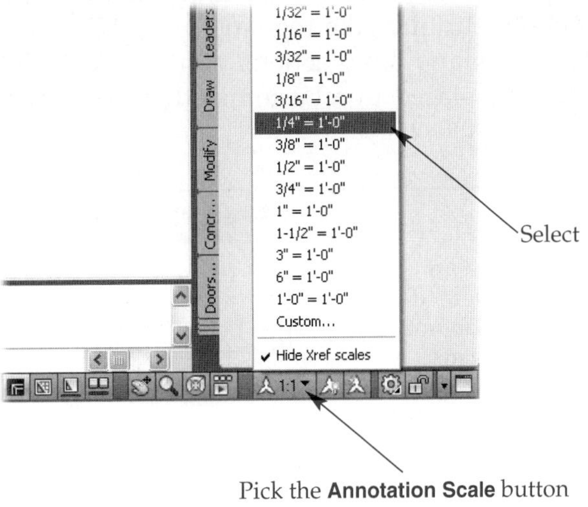

Figure 25-7.
The new action is automatically set current. Its action tree is displayed in the expanded panel.

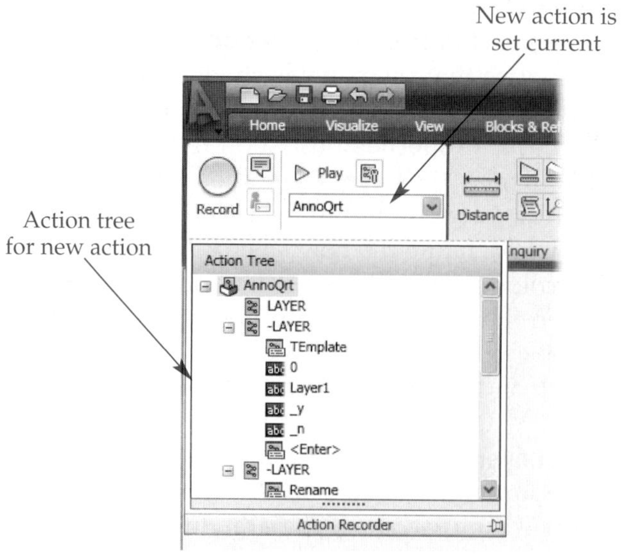

Exercise 25-2

Complete the exercise on the Student CD.

Running an Action

To run the current action, pick the **Play** button in the **Action Recorder** panel on the **Tools** tab in the ribbon. The current action is shown at the top of the **Available Action Macro** drop-down list in the **Action Recorder** panel. To run a different action, simply select it in the drop-down list and then pick the **Play** button. You can also select **Tools**>**Action Recorder**>**Play** from the menu and then select the name of the action to play. Another method of running an action is to type its name on the command line. This is why the action name cannot be the same as an existing AutoCAD command.

Before testing an action, be sure to delete all graphics from the screen unless needed for the action. To test the action recorded in the previous section, start a new drawing. Make sure the AnnoQrt action is set current in the **Available Action Macro** drop-down list. Then, pick the **Play** button and watch the action run. By default, when the action is complete, AutoCAD displays the **Action Macro—Playback Complete** dialog box, Figure 25-8. This is simply a message to the user that the action is finished. Pick the **OK** button to close the dialog box.

Actions run just like regular AutoCAD commands. Since they can be executed on the command line, actions can be made into custom AutoCAD commands. They can be placed in a customized ribbon panel, toolbar, menu, or palette. When

Figure 25-8.
This dialog box is displayed when an action is complete. If you check the **Do not show this message again** check box, this dialog box will not be displayed at the end of action playback.

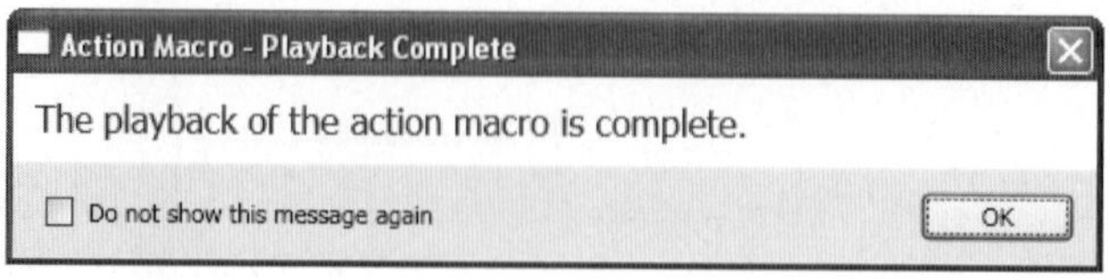

creating a custom command from an action, use the syntax ^C^C*Action_name*. Refer to Chapter 21 for information on creating custom commands.

PROFESSIONAL TIP

Actions can streamline the customization process by creating setup procedures to minimize macro writing when creating custom commands. For example, suppose you have an annotation block that you want inserted at a set scale and on a specific layer. You can create an action similar to the example above (AnnoQrt). Then, you can insert the action in the command string prior to the block insertion. This will streamline your customization process.

Modifying an Action

The action tree can be used to edit an action. Examine the action tree for the AnnoQrt example, as shown in **Figure 25-9.** At the top of the action tree is the action name. It is always the top branch of the tree. The icon to the left of the name indicates

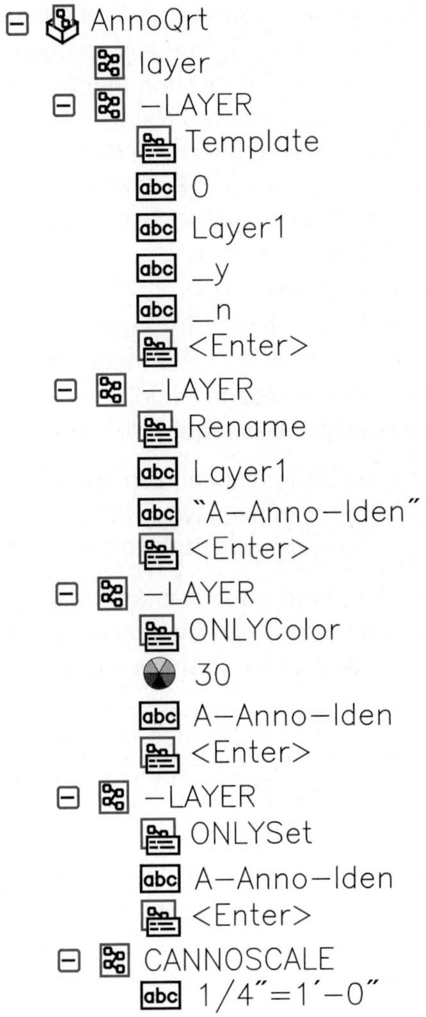

Figure 25-9.
The action tree for the recorded action prior to editing the action.

that it is an action. The branches below the action name contain the commands and steps in the action.

Notice the dash in front of the **LAYER** command. This dash indicates the command is a command-line command. Even though you used the **Layer Properties Manager** palette when recording the action, the action recorder translated your picks into the command-line version of the steps.

Branches below the command names contain the specific information used to create each item. Each branch is automatically converted to the command-line entry. The icon next to each branch indicates the type of action or input represented by the branch. These branches are also called *nodes*. For example, reviewing the **LAYER** command branches, you can see a text icon next to the name A-Anno-Iden. This icon indicates that the branch, or node, is a text entry. Additionally, the icon for the branch where the layer color is set to 30 is a color wheel. This indicates the branch is a change in color value. An icon with a head-and-shoulders image in the lower-right corner indicates the action will pause at this point to allow the user to enter information. This icon is called a user icon.

Now, you will modify the action recorded earlier. You will change some of the steps to require user input. For example, you will have the user type the annotation scale instead of automatically setting it to 1/4″ = 1′-0″ scale. So the user knows what is required, you will add a message explaining the step. Since the scale is not automatically set, the action also needs to be renamed to remove the Qtr (quarter inch scale) designation. Complete the following steps.

1. Expand the **Action Recorder** panel to see the action tree. You may want to pin the panel in the expanded state.
2. Right-click on the action name AnnoQtr and select **Rename...** from the shortcut menu. To retain the original action instead of renaming it, select **Copy...** from the shortcut menu. The **Action Macro** dialog box is displayed.
3. In **Action Macro Command Name:** text box, type AnnoUserScale and then pick the **OK** button to rename the action.
4. In the action tree, locate the CANNOSCALE branch. Right-click on the 1/4″ = 1′-0″ branch below it and select **Request User Input** from the shortcut menu. The value in the branch (1/4″ = 1′-0″) is grayed out and the icon for the branch now contains the user icon.
5. To add a message describing how to type the correct scale, right-click on the 1/4″ = 1′-0″ branch and select **Insert User Message...** from the shortcut menu. The **Insert User Message** dialog box appears, **Figure 25-10.**
6. In the **Insert User Message** dialog box, type the message:

   Enter the desired annotation scale on the command line. Please use proper syntax. For example, type 1/8″ = 1′-0″ for the 1/8″ Architectural scale. Include spaces on each side of the equals symbol.

Notice that a User Message branch is added to the action tree above the branch that was right clicked. The action is now altered. Start a new drawing and run the altered action. Notice the dialog boxes that appear to guide the user through the inputs. See **Figure 25-11.**

To remove user input, right-click on the branch and select **Request User Input** from the shortcut menu to remove the check mark. The action then uses the value set when the action was recorded.

If you would like to delete a command from the action, right-click on the command branch and select **Delete** from the shortcut menu. Once deleted, the command is permanently removed from the action. This cannot be undone.

To edit a value, right-click on the corresponding branch and select **Edit** from the shortcut menu. The value is replaced by a text box. Type the new value and press [Enter]. Careful; if you move the cursor off of the panel while the text box is displayed, whatever is displayed in the text box is entered as the value.

Figure 25-10.
Adding a user message to the action.

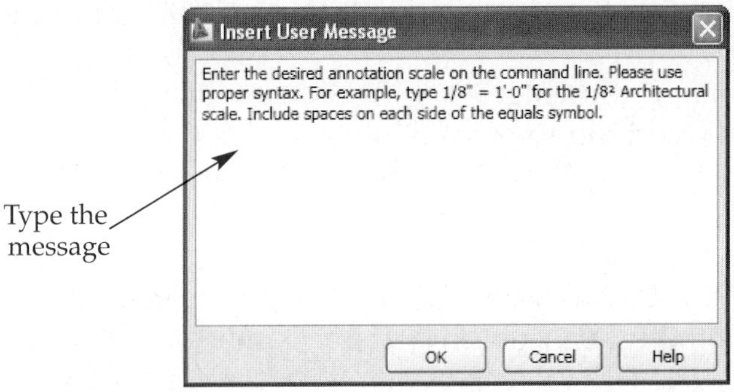

Figure 25-11.
A—The message displayed to the user during playback of the example action. B—When user input is requested, this dialog box is displayed.

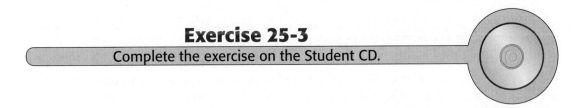

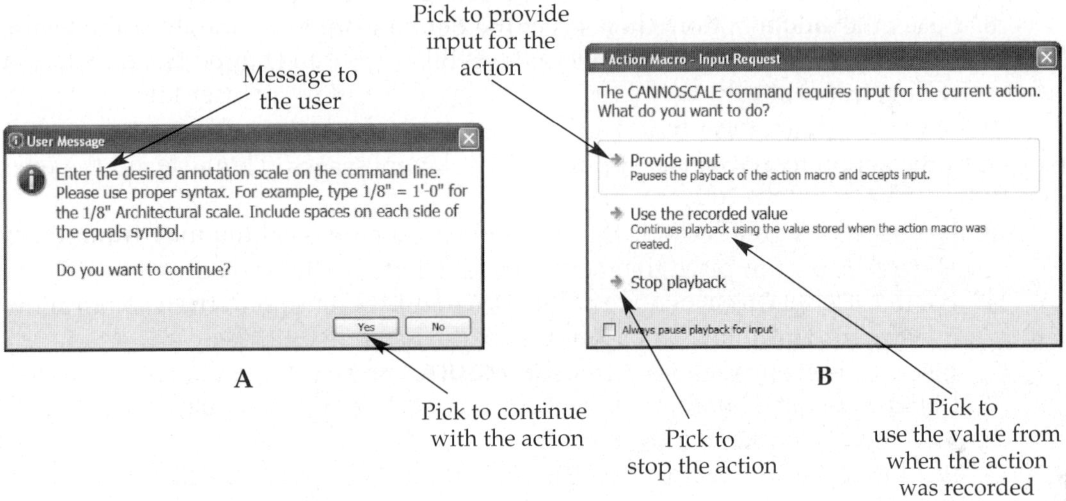

NOTE

When recording the action, use the buttons on the **Action Recorder** panel to insert messages and user-input requests.

Exercise 25-3

Complete the exercise on the Student CD.

Practical Example

This example creates a rectangle and fills it with a hatch pattern. First, you will record an action that draws a rectangle at a user-specified location and then uses the **ZOOM** command to center the rectangle. The action will draw a brick hatch pattern inside of the rectangle. Then, the hatch pattern is edited to change/reset its origin. In this example, commands will be entered on the command line. Although it is more time-consuming to create an action in this way, it allows easy access to, and editing of, the action steps.

1. Start a new drawing.
2. Begin recording a new action.
3. Type the **RECTANG** command. When prompted to specify the first corner point, pick anywhere on the screen. When prompted for the other corner point, type @120,60.
4. Type the **ZOOM** command and enter the extents option. Enter the command again and type .7x to center the rectangle on the screen.
5. Type the **-HATCH** command. Use the **Select object** option to select the rectangle.
6. Use the **Properties** option and select the hatch AR-B816. This is the architectural brick pattern. Enter a scale of 1.000 and 0° rotation angle. Finish the **-HATCH** command.
7. Type the **-HATCHEDIT** command and select the brick pattern.
8. Select the **Origin** option, then select the **Set new origin** option. Pick the lower, right-hand endpoint of the rectangle. When prompted, store this location as the default origin.
9. Stop recording of the action and name it BrickHatchEdit.

Next, edit the action to allow user input and display messages. This will aid the user in selecting points.

10. For the first point node of the rectangle, change it to allow user input. This allows the user to place the rectangle anywhere on the screen.
11. For the <Select Objects> node of the **-HATCHEDIT** command, change it to allow user input. This allows the user to pick the hatch to edit.
12. Insert a user message for the **-HATCHEDIT** command just above the <Select Objects> node. The message should read Select the brick hatch object. This gives instruction to the user.
13. For the point location under the **Set** option of the **-HATCHEDIT** command, change it to allow user input. In this way, the user selects the origin point for where the hatch pattern begins.
14. Insert a user message for the point location under the **Set** option of the **-HATCHEDIT** command. The message should read Edit the hatch and select a new origin point when prompted. This gives instruction to the user.
15. Test the action. When prompted for the new origin, select the midpoint of the lower line of the rectangle. Notice the result is different from the pattern created when recording the action.

PROFESSIONAL TIP

The action recorder works best with command-line versions of commands. Many commands can be run on the command line only by placing a hyphen (-) in front of the command name. For example, the **LAYER** command displays the **Layer Properties Managers** palette. However, the **-LAYER** command displays all options and settings on the command line without displaying a palette or dialog box. Not all commands have a command-line version.

Limitations of the Action Recorder

As a customizing tool, the action recorder is very powerful. However, as in all customization, there is syntax to follow and limitations to address. For example, the AutoCAD commands shown in **Figure 25-12** cannot be recorded in an action.

The following chapters discuss AutoLISP and other programming features of AutoCAD. Actions are able to call and run AutoLISP routines during the recording process. However, the specific AutoLISP routines, Object ARX files, VBA macros, .NET assemblies, and associated files must all be loaded into AutoCAD in order for the programming feature to function during playback of the action. See Chapters 25 through 29 for further details on programming AutoCAD.

When creating an action for use in a professional or school environment, you must always consider the source files. For example, if you create an action that reads from a template file or loads particular blocks, those external files must always be either loaded into AutoCAD or accessible to the user.

Finally, you cannot append an existing action. If you need to add steps to the action, you must re-record the existing steps along with the new steps. For this reason, it is very important to plan an action before recording it.

PROFESSIONAL TIP

You can create actions with other Autodesk applications, such as AutoCAD Architecture. If you create an action using AEC objects, for example, the action can only properly function if the action is played back in AutoCAD Architecture.

Figure 25-12.
These commands cannot be used in an action.

ACTSTOP
ACTUSERINPUT
ACTUSERMESSAGE
-ACTUSERMESSAGE
DXFIN
FILEOPEN
NEW
OPEN
PARTIALOPEN
PRESSPULL
QNEW
RECOVER
TABLEDIT
VBAIDE
VBALOAD
-VBALOAD
VBAMAN
VBANEW
VBAPREF
VBARUN
-VBARUN
VBASTMT
VBAUNLOAD
XOPEN

Chapter Test

Answer the following questions. Write your answers on a separate sheet of paper or complete the electronic chapter test on the Student CD.

1. What is an *action?*
2. What is used to record an action?
3. In which file format is an action saved?
4. By default, where are action files stored?
5. What is the *action tree?*
6. How do you set an action current?
7. Name three ways to play an action.
8. How do you pause an action for user input?
9. How can you display a custom message in an action?
10. Briefly describe how to change the value associated with a branch in an action.

Drawing Problems

1. In this problem, you will create an action that sets up a drawing for architectural work. The action will create layers and set the units. The action should:
   A. Display a message to the user indicating what the action will do.
   B. Create a layer named A-Wall and set its color to ACI 113 (or the color of your choice).
   C. Create a layer named A-Door and set its color to ACI 31 (or the color of your choice).
   D. Create a layer named A-Demo and set its color to ACI 1 (or the color of your choice).
   E. Set the units to architectural with a precision of 1/4″.
   F. Save the action as ArchSetup.actm. If the file is saved in a folder other than the default, make sure that folder is added to the AutoCAD search path.

2. In this problem, you will create an action that allows the user to select objects and then places those objects at an elevation of 12 units. The action should:
   A. Display a message to the user indicating what the action will do.
   B. Prompt the user to select objects.
   C. Change the elevation property of all objects to 12 units.
   D. Save the action as 1FtElevChange.actm. If the file is saved in a folder other than the default, make sure that folder is added to the AutoCAD search path.

3. In this problem, you will modify the action created in problem 2. Edit the action to allow the user to enter the new elevation. Be sure to display a message to the user indicating what is being asked of them. This is a good tool for flattening linework or resetting solids. Save the action as ElevChange.actm. If the file is saved in a folder other than the default, make sure that folder is added to the AutoCAD search path.

CHAPTER 26

Introduction to AutoLISP

Learning Objectives

After completing this chapter, you will be able to:

- ✓ Use basic AutoLISP functions on the command line.
- ✓ Locate, load, and run existing AutoLISP programs.
- ✓ Define new AutoCAD commands.
- ✓ Write AutoLISP programs using the **Visual LISP Editor**.

What Is AutoLISP?

AutoLISP is a derivative, or dialect, of the LISP programming language. ***LISP,*** which is an acronym for ***list processing,*** is a high-level computer programming language used in artificial intelligence (AI) systems. In this reference, the term *high-level* does not mean *complex,* rather it means *powerful.* As a matter of fact, many AutoCAD users refer to AutoLISP as the "nonprogrammer's language" because it is easy to understand.

AutoLISP is specially designed by Autodesk to work with AutoCAD. It is a flexible language that allows the programmer to create custom commands and functions that can greatly increase productivity and drawing efficiency.

Knowing the basics of AutoLISP gives you a better understanding of how AutoCAD works. By learning just a few simple functions, you can create new commands that make a significant difference in your daily productivity. Read through this chapter slowly while you are at a computer. Type all of the examples and exercises as you read them. This is the best way to get a feel for AutoLISP.

AutoLISP and AutoCAD

AutoLISP can be used in several ways. It is a built-in feature of AutoCAD and is, therefore, available on the command line. When AutoLISP commands and functions are issued inside of parentheses on the command line, the AutoLISP interpreter automatically evaluates the entry and carries out the specified tasks. AutoLISP functions can also be incorporated into the AutoCAD menu as buttons, menu items, and tablet menu picks. In addition, AutoLISP command and function definitions can be saved in a file and then loaded into AutoCAD when needed. Items that are frequently used can be placed in the acad2009.lsp file, which is automatically loaded for the first drawing (by default) when AutoCAD starts. The acad2009doc.lsp file should contain functions that are to be available in all concurrent drawings during a session.

AutoCAD also provides an integrated development environment for editing called ***Visual LISP.*** Visual LISP and the **Visual LISP Editor** offer powerful features designed specifically for writing and editing AutoLISP programs.

The benefits of using AutoLISP are endless. A person with a basic understanding of AutoLISP can create new commands and functions to automate many routine tasks. After working through this chapter, you will be able to add greater capabilities to your menu macros. You can also enter simple AutoLISP expressions on the command line. More experienced programmers can create powerful programs that quickly complete very complex design requirements. Examples of possible new functions that might be designed using AutoLISP include:

- Automatic line breaks when inserting schematic symbols.
- Automatic creation of shapes with associated text objects.
- Parametric design applications that create geometry based on numeric entry.

NOTE

For additional information on using AutoLISP, refer to *Visual LISP Programming* available from Goodheart-Willcox Publisher, which provides complete coverage of AutoLISP and Visual LISP.

AutoLISP Basics

As stated earlier, LISP stands for list processing, which indicates that AutoLISP processes lists. In the LISP language, a ***list*** can be defined as any number of data enclosed in parentheses. Each item in a list must be separated from other items by a space.

When any entry is made on the command line, it is checked to see if the first character is a parenthesis. The opening parenthesis tells AutoCAD that an AutoLISP expression is being entered. AutoCAD then sends the expression to the AutoLISP interpreter for evaluation. The initial input can be supplied as direct keyboard entry or even a menu macro. The format for an AutoLISP expression, called ***syntax,*** is:

(*FunctionName AnyRequiredData…*)

The first item in the AutoLISP expression is a ***function name.*** A function in AutoLISP is similar to a command in AutoCAD. Some functions require additional information. For example, the addition function requires numeric data:

Command: **(+ 2 4)**↵
6
Command:

Any required or optional data for a function are called the ***arguments.*** Some functions use no arguments; others may require one or more. When entering an AutoLISP expression, it is important to *close* it using a closing parenthesis prior to pressing [Enter]. When you press [Enter], the AutoLISP interpreter checks to see that the number of opening and closing parentheses match. If they do not, you are prompted:

Command: **(+ 2 4**↵
(_>

The (_> prompt indicates that you are missing one closing parenthesis. In this example, all that is necessary is to enter the single missing parenthesis and the function is complete.

```
(_> )↵
6
Command:
```

When the AutoLISP interpreter evaluates an AutoLISP expression, it *returns* a value. An expression entered on the command line instructs the system to return its value to the command line, such as 6 in the previous example. If a different prompt is active, the returned value is used as input for that prompt. For example, this next sequence uses the result of adding two numbers as the input at the Specify radius of circle or [Diameter]: prompt. Checking the **CIRCLERAD** system variable verifies that the value returned by AutoLISP was in fact applied to the circle radius.

Command: **C** *or* **CIRCLE**↵
Specify center point for circle or [3P/2P/Ttr (tan tan radius)]: *(pick a point)*
Specify radius of circle or [Diameter]: **(+ 14.25 3.0)**↵
17.25
Command: **CIRCLERAD**↵
Enter new value for CIRCLERAD <17.2500>: ↵

Basic AutoLISP Functions

The best way to get started learning AutoLISP is to enter a few functions on the command line and see what they do. The following discussion includes basic AutoLISP functions that are part of the foundation for all AutoLISP programs. Practice using the functions as you read. Then, begin using them in menus and macros. At first, these functions and expressions will be entered on the command line. Later in this chapter, and in Chapter 27, you will learn about creating and using AutoLISP program files.

AutoLISP Math Functions

AutoLISP provides many different mathematical operators for performing calculations. All real number calculations in AutoLISP are accurate to 15 decimal places. AutoLISP distinguishes between real numbers and integers, handling each data type differently. ***Real numbers*** are numbers with a decimal point, such as 1.25, 7.0, and –0.438. ***Integers*** are whole numbers without a decimal point, such as 3, 91, and –115. If a mathematical expression has only integer arguments, the result is returned as an integer. If at least one real number is used, the result is returned as a real number. The following symbols are used for the four basic math functions.

Symbol	Function
+	Addition; returns the sum of all the supplied number arguments.
–	Subtraction; subtracts the sum of the second through the last number arguments from the first number argument and returns the result.
*	Multiplication; returns the product of all the supplied number arguments.
/	Division; divides the first number argument by the product of the second through the last number arguments.

NOTE

Real numbers technically include integers and fractions, as well as decimal numbers. However, in applications involving AutoLISP and throughout this discussion, real numbers are always classified as those that have a decimal part.

The following examples illustrate AutoLISP math expressions entered on the command line. As you practice entering these expressions, use the following procedure.

1. Start with an open parenthesis.
2. Separate each item in the expression with a space.
3. End the expression with a closing parenthesis.

Using these steps, enter the following expressions on the command line. If you get lost at any time or do not return to the Command: prompt when expected, press the [Esc] key to cancel the AutoLISP entry.

Command: **(+ 6 2)**↵
8
Command: **(+ 6.0 2)**↵
8.0
Command: **(– 15 9)**↵
6
Command: **(* 4 6)**↵
24
Command: **(/ 12 3)**↵
4
Command: **(/ 12 3.2)**↵
3.75
Command: **(/ 19 10)**↵
1

An "incorrect" answer is returned in the last example. The result of dividing 19 by 10 is 1.9. When only integers are supplied as arguments, the result is returned as an integer. If the result is rounded, it rounds to 2. However, the returned result is simply the integer portion of the actual answer. The result is not rounded, it is truncated. To get the correct result in division expressions such as the one above, specify at least one of the arguments as a real number.

Command: **(/ 19.0 10)**↵
1.9

When entering real numbers between 1 and –1, you must include the leading zero. If the zero is not entered, you will get an error message:

Command: **(+ .5 16)**↵
; error: misplaced dot on input
Command:

The correct entry is:

Command: **(+ 0.5 16)**↵
16.5

Exercise 26-1

Complete the exercise on the Student CD.

Nested Expressions

The term ***nested*** refers to an expression that is used as part of another expression. For example, to add 15 to the product of 3.75 and 2.125, you can nest the multiplication expression within the AutoLISP addition expression. Notice the two closing parentheses:

```
Command: (+ 15 (* 3.75 2.125))↵
22.9688
```

Nested expressions are evaluated from the deepest nested level outward. In the previous expression, the multiplication operation is evaluated first and the result is applied to the addition operation. Here are some examples of nested expressions:

```
Command: (+ 24 (* 5 4))↵
44
Command: (* 12 (/ 60 20))↵
36
Command: (/ 39 (* 1.6 11))↵
2.21591
```

Significant Digits

AutoLISP performs all mathematical calculations to 15 decimal places, but only displays six significant digits. For example, take a close look at this expression:

```
Command: (+ 15 (* 3.75 2.125))↵
22.9688
```

The actual result is 22.96875, but AutoLISP displays only six significant digits on the command line and rounds the number for display only. This is true for large and small numbers alike. The next example shows how AutoLISP uses exponential notation to display larger numbers using only six digits:

```
Command: (* 1000 1575.25)↵
1.57525e+006
```

This final example uses a numeric printing function (real to string) set to show eight decimal places in order to indicate that the number is not actually rounded and that no precision is lost:

```
Command: (rtos (+ 15 (* 3.75 2.125)) 2 8)↵
"22.96875000"
```

Exercise 26-2

Complete the exercise on the Student CD.

Variables

All programming languages make use of ***variables*** to temporarily store information. The variable name can be used in an expression anywhere in the program. When AutoLISP encounters a variable in an expression, it uses the value of the variable to evaluate the expression. An AutoLISP variable name cannot be made up of numeric characters only, nor can it contain any of the following characters.

- Open parenthesis (()
- Close parenthesis ())
- Period (.)

- Apostrophe (')
- Quotation marks ("")
- Semicolon (;)

The **(setq)** AutoLISP function is used to set variable values. A **(setq)** expression requires a variable name and value as arguments. The following example shows an expression that creates a variable named **A** and assigns it a value of 5.

Command: **(setq A 5)**↵
5

If you try to use an illegal variable name, an error message is returned. The following example tries to create a variable named **2** with an assigned value of 7. Since **2** is not a valid variable name, an error message is returned.

Command: **(setq 2 7)**↵
; error: syntax error

Once a valid variable name has been assigned a value, the variable can be used in subsequent AutoLISP expressions or even directly accessed on the command line. To access a variable value on the command line, precede the variable name with an exclamation mark (!). For example:

Command: **C** *or* **CIRCLE**↵
Specify center point for circle or [3P/2P/Ttr (tan tan radius)]: *(pick a point)*
Specify radius of circle or [Diameter] <*current*>: **!A**↵
5
Command:

To use the value of a variable in any expression, simply include the variable in the appropriate location. The following sequence sets and uses a series of variables.

Command: **(setq A 5)**↵
5
Command: **(setq B (– A 1))**↵
4
Command: **(setq C (– A B))**↵
1
Command: **(setq D (* (+ A B) 2))**↵
18

Look closely at the example illustrated in **Figure 26-1.** Find the three separate expressions inside of parentheses. AutoLISP evaluates expression 3 first. The result is applied to expression 2, which is then evaluated. The result of expression 2 is applied to expression 1. The final evaluation determines the value of the variable **D**.

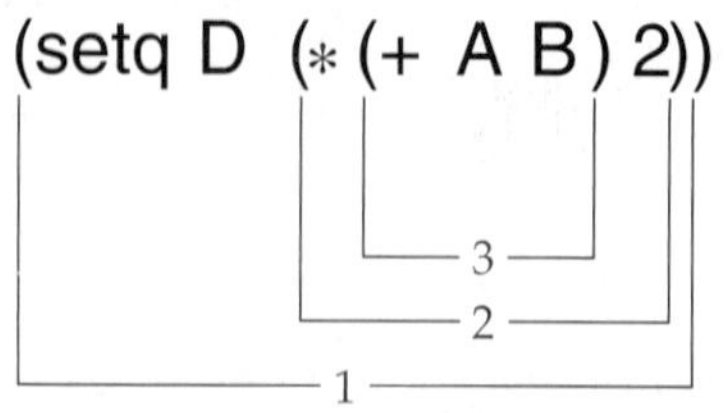

Figure 26-1.
Each AutoLISP expression must be enclosed within parentheses. In this evaluation of variable **D**, expression 3 is evaluated first, then expression 2, and finally expression 1.

PROFESSIONAL TIP

When working with AutoLISP on the command line, use AutoCAD's command line editing features to your best advantage. Remember that you can use the up and down arrow keys to display previously entered lines of code. Additionally, you can use the left and right arrow keys to position the cursor to delete or insert text within a line. You may also find it convenient to turn off dynamic input while entering AutoLISP expressions on the command line.

Exercise 26-3

Complete the exercise on the Student CD.

AutoLISP Program Files

Entering AutoLISP expressions on the command line is suitable for applications that are simple or unique. However, when more complex expressions are required or when the expressions you are using may be needed again, it is best to save them in an AutoLISP program file. This can be easily accomplished using the **Visual LISP Editor** provided with AutoCAD. AutoLISP programs can be more effectively developed using the **Visual LISP Editor**. Creating AutoLISP program files is discussed in the following sections.

A very common feature found in most AutoLISP programs is a function definition. A ***function definition*** is a collection of AutoLISP expressions that performs any number of tasks. The function is assigned a name that is used to activate the expressions. Some function definitions create new AutoCAD command names that can be entered at the command line.

Once written and saved, an AutoLISP program can be loaded and used whenever it is needed. By default, AutoCAD automatically loads the acad2009.lsp file, if it is located in the support file search path, when you first begin a drawing session. The acad2009doc.lsp file is loaded with each drawing that is opened. Any new AutoLISP commands or functions that you define in this file will be available in every drawing during a session.

An AutoLISP program file must be a "plain" text file. If you choose to edit your AutoLISP files with a word processing program such as Microsoft Word or WordPerfect, be sure to save the files as "text only." Word processing files use special codes that AutoLISP cannot understand. It is recommended that you use the **Visual LISP Editor** because it has tools specifically designed for use in writing and editing AutoLISP programs.

Introduction to the Visual LISP Editor

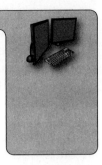

The **Visual LISP Editor** provides powerful editing features. The editor is an ***integrated development environment (IDE)*** that features AutoLISP development tools not available in standard text editing programs. The interactive nature of the **Visual LISP Editor** simplifies the task of creating AutoLISP program files. This section provides only a brief introduction to Visual LISP. For a more detailed discussion of the features and applications of Visual LISP, refer to *Visual LISP Programming* available from Goodheart-Willcox Publisher.

VLIDE

Ribbon
Tools > Applications
Visual LISP Editor
Type
VLIDE
VLISP
Menu
Tools > AutoLISP > Visual LISP Editor

The **VLIDE** command is used to open the **Visual LISP Editor**. When the **Visual LISP Editor** is first displayed, it appears as shown in Figure 26-2. The windows within the editor can be minimized or maximized. The editor itself can be temporarily closed to return to AutoCAD as necessary.

To create a new AutoLISP program using the **Visual LISP Editor**, pick the **New file** button, select **New File** from the editor's **File** pull-down menu, or press [Ctrl]+[N]. This opens a window for an untitled document on the **Visual LISP Editor** desktop. See Figure 26-3. The windows and features in the **Visual LISP Editor** are:

- **Desktop.** This is the main area of the editor window. It is similar to the main program window in AutoCAD and can be used to relocate toolbars or windowed components, such as the **Visual LISP Console** or a text editor window.
- **Text editor window.** Text editor windows are used to write and edit AutoLISP programs. Different windows can be used to create new files or view existing programs. The **Visual LISP Editor** provides interactive feedback as you enter material to help you avoid errors.
- **Visual LISP Console window.** This window provides several functions. You can use it to enter any AutoLISP expression to immediately see the results. You can also enter any AutoLISP variable to determine its value. Visual LISP commands can also be entered from this window. The text can then be copied from the window to a text editor window.
- **Trace window.** This window is minimized when you first display the **Visual LISP Editor**. It records a history of the functions within your program and can be used to trace values when developing or debugging a program.

Figure 26-2.
The primary features of the **Visual LISP Editor**.

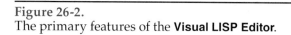

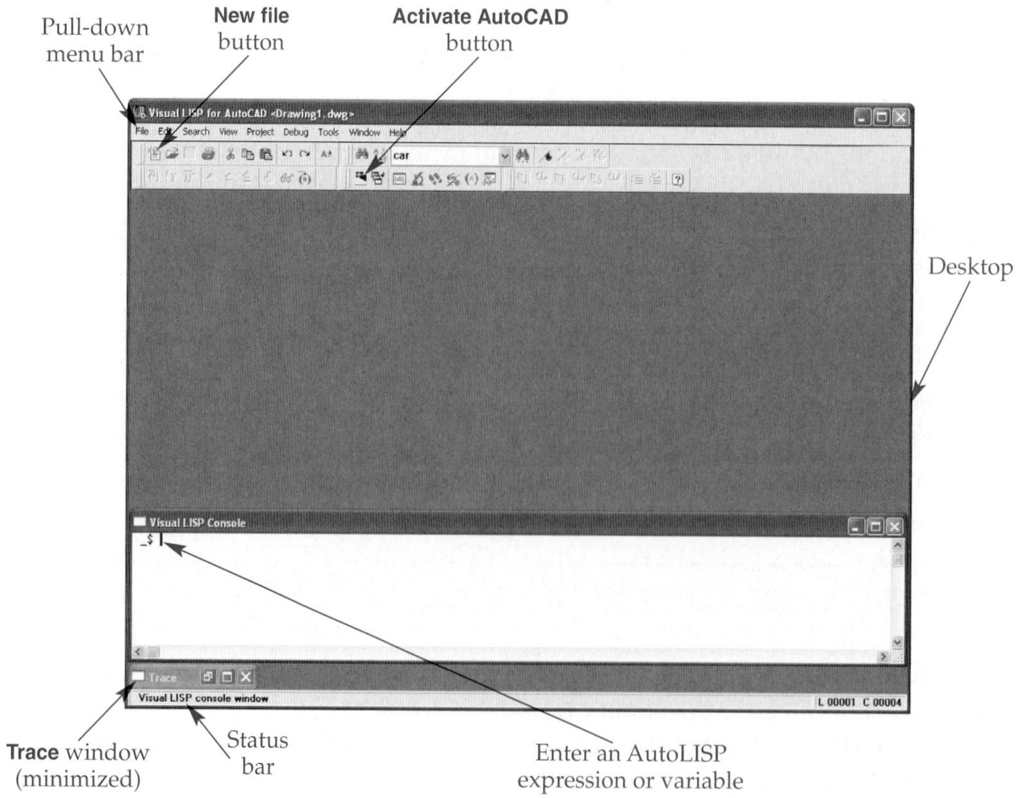

Figure 26-3.
Picking the **New file** button or selecting **New File** from the **File** pull-down menu displays a text editor window in the **Visual LISP Editor**.

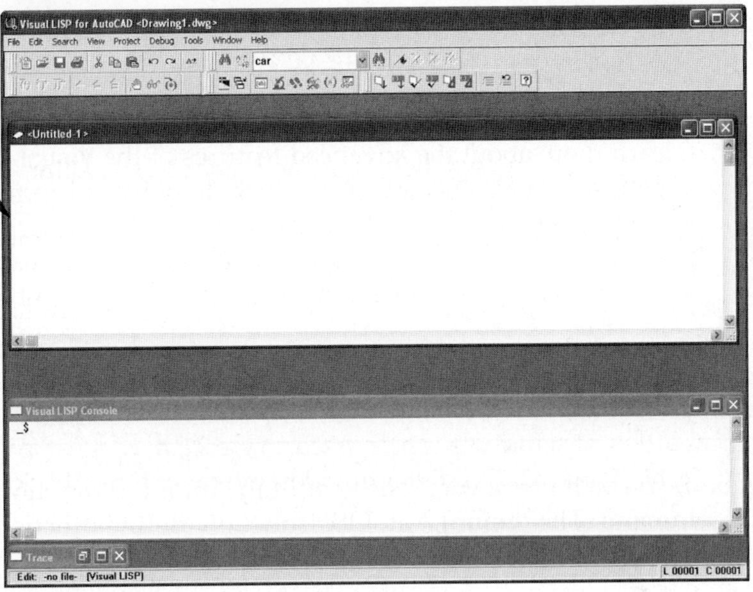

- **Status bar.** This area at the bottom of the **Visual LISP Editor** is similar to the status bar in AutoCAD's main program window. It provides feedback regarding the status of the current window or application being used.

Several visual aids are provided to help identify functions as you enter text. For example, as you construct the expressions that make up your program, a color-coding system provides immediate feedback as you type. Text for any unrecognized items, such as a user variable or a portion of a function, is shown in black. For example, if you enter the **(setq)** function, the text is shown in black until you have entered the letters set. Because AutoLISP recognizes the text entry as the valid function **(set)**, a function not covered in this book, the color of the text is changed to blue. When you have entered the full **(setq)** function name, the text remains blue because AutoLISP also recognizes this function name. The color coding can be very useful. If you enter a function name and the text does not turn blue, you know that you have made an incorrect entry. The default color coding system used in the **Visual LISP Editor** appears in the following chart.

AutoLISP Text Elements	Associated Color
Built-in functions and protected symbols	Blue
Text strings	Magenta
Integers	Green
Real numbers	Teal
Comments	Purple on a gray background
Parentheses	Red
Unrecognized items	Black

Another valuable visual aid provided by the **Visual LISP Editor** is instant parenthesis matching. When you enter a closing parenthesis in an expression, the cursor jumps to the opening parenthesis and then returns back to the current position. If the closing parenthesis does not have a match, the cursor does not jump. This helps indicate that a matching parenthesis is needed.

Once you have entered one or more expressions in the **Visual LISP Editor**, you can save the file and then test the results in the **Visual LISP Console** window. Or, you can return to AutoCAD to test your results.

PROFESSIONAL TIP

If you frequently work with AutoLISP program files, you may wish to learn more about the advanced features of the **Visual LISP Editor**. Some of these advanced features include powerful formatting and debugging tools that make your programming time much more productive. For a complete discussion of these topics, refer to *Visual LISP Programming* available from Goodheart-Willcox Publisher.

Defining New AutoCAD Commands

In this section, you will use several of the built-in AutoLISP functions to create a new AutoCAD command. The **(defun)** AutoLISP function (define function) is used for this. The syntax for this function is:

(defun *FunctionName* (*ArgumentList*)
(*Expression*)...
)

The function name can be any alphanumeric name and is subject to the same conditions as for any variable name assigned with the **(setq)** function. If you prefix the function name with **C:**, the name can be entered on the command line in AutoCAD.

You must include an argument list in every function definition, even if the list is empty. The argument list is used to declare local variables and, in more advanced applications, to indicate which arguments are required by a function. For many applications, the argument list is simply left empty.

Any number of expressions can be included in a function definition. All of the expressions contained in the definition are evaluated when the function name is called.

A very powerful, yet simple, application for a function definition is to create a shortcut command similar to one of the command aliases in the acad.pgp file. However, a shortcut command defined using AutoLISP can specify command options and even multiple commands to use. Remember that the command aliases defined in the acad.pgp file can only launch a single command; they cannot specify any command options.

This first example shows the definition for a new function named **ZX**. The function issues the **ZOOM** command and performs the **Previous** option.

```
(defun C:ZX ()
  (command "ZOOM" "PREVIOUS")
)
```

To see this function work, enter the definition at the command line as:

Command: **(defun C:ZX () (command "zoom" "previous"))**↵
C:ZX

Notice that the new function name is returned by the **(defun)** function. The **C:** prefix indicates that it can be entered at the Command: prompt.

Command: **ZX**↵
zoom
Specify corner of window, enter a scale factor (nX or nXP), or
[All/Extents/Window/Previous/Object] <real time>: previous
Command: nil
Command:

When activated, defined functions return the value of the last expression evaluated in the definition. Since the **(command)** function always returns a value of "nil," this is returned when using the **ZX** function. The "nil" value has no effect. You can suppress it if you do not want it to appear each time you use a defined function. To suppress the value, add the **(princ)** function using no arguments to the end of the definition:

```
(defun C:ZX ()
  (command "ZOOM" "PREVIOUS")
  (princ)
)
```

Entering a function definition on the command line is an inconvenient way to define custom functions. By storing such definitions in a text file, they can be loaded whenever needed.

PROFESSIONAL TIP

When defining new command names, keep in mind that most AutoCAD users are one-handed typists because the other hand is used for the pointing device. For example, when deciding on the name for a function that performs a **ZOOM Previous**, it may be easier for the user to type the [Z]+[X] key combination rather than [Z]+[P]. The [Z] and [P] keys are in opposite corners of the keyboard.

Creating Your First AutoLISP Program

As discussed earlier, a typical use for an AutoLISP program file is to hold function definitions. An AutoLISP program file can contain a single function or it can contain several. Many AutoLISP programs are created to perform a single group of specific tasks. Other AutoLISP programs hold a large number of function definitions, all of which become available when the program file is loaded. One common application for the acad2009doc.lsp file is to create a series of function definitions for shortcut commands used to speed up routine drafting tasks.

Writing the Program

To create your first AutoLISP program, open the **Visual LISP Editor** or another text editing application and start a new document (file). Begin by entering two function definitions into the program. The first is the **ZX** function from the previous example. The second defines a command named **FC** (fillet corner) that sets the fillet radius to 0 and allows the **FILLET** command to continue.

```
(defun C:ZX ()
  (command "ZOOM" "PREVIOUS")
  (princ)
)

(defun C:FC ()
  (command "FILLET" "RADIUS" 0 "FILLET" "MULTIPLE")
  (princ)
)
```

When using the **Visual LISP Editor**, the final closing parenthesis is not automatically "flush left." You will need to delete the spaces added. It is a good habit to place the final closing parenthesis flush left to help keep your program organized.

Adding the appropriate documentation to your program files is recommended. When a semicolon (;) is encountered in a program (except when it is part of a text string), any information to the right of the semicolon is ignored. This enables you to place ***comments*** and documentation in your AutoLISP programs. The example below shows the appropriate documentation for this program file, called myfirst.lsp.

```
; MyFirst.lsp
; by A. Novice

;C:ZX – To key ZOOM Previous command.
(defun C:ZX ()
  (command "ZOOM" "PREVIOUS")
  (princ)
)

;C:FC – Fillet Corner: Sets fillet radius to 0 and
;allows FILLET command to continue.
 (defun C:FC ()
  (command "FILLET" "RADIUS" 0 "FILLET")
  (princ)
)
```

After entering these functions and comments into the new LISP program, save the file as myfirst.lsp in the AutoCAD or your user's \Support folder.

Loading the Program

APPLOAD

Ribbon
Tools
> Applications
Load Application

Type
APPLOAD

Menu
Tools
> Load Application...

The **APPLOAD** command is used to load applications, such as AutoLISP program files, into AutoCAD. Once the command is selected in AutoCAD, the **Load/Unload Applications** dialog box appears, **Figure 26-4.** A list of currently loaded applications appears in the **Loaded Applications** tab. To load an application file, select it in the file-selection window near the top of the dialog box. You can highlight any number of files in the file list. Picking the **Load** button loads the currently selected application file(s).

Figure 26-4.
The **Load/Unload Applications** dialog box is used to load AutoLISP program files into AutoCAD.

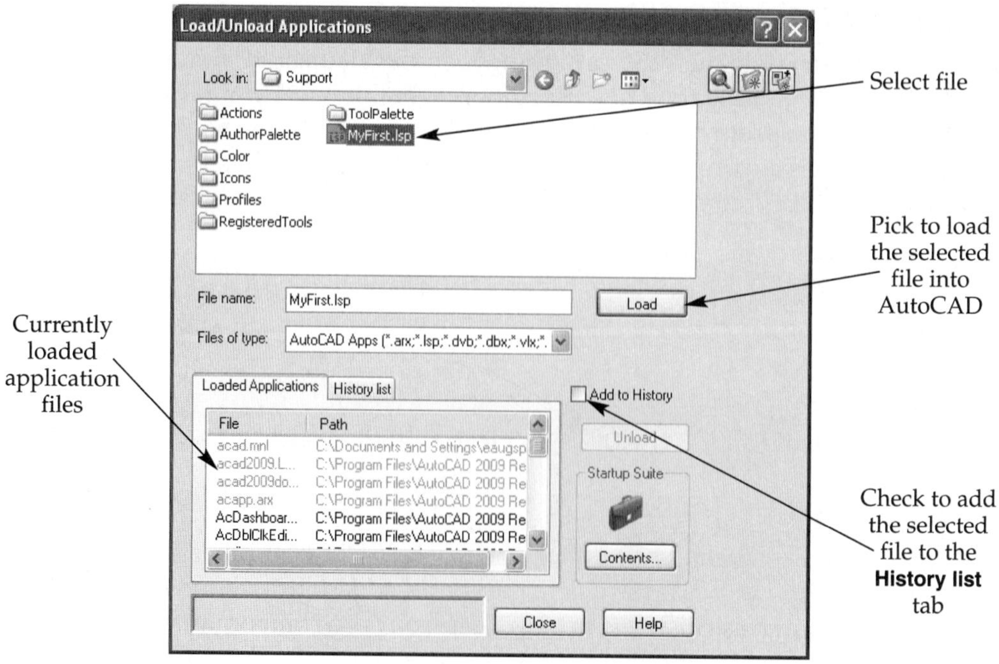

If the **Add to History** check box is activated, the loaded file(s) will be added to the list in the **History list** tab. This tab provides convenient access to saved files during subsequent **APPLOAD** sessions and keeps you from having to search for frequently used files every time they are needed. Picking the **Unload** button removes any highlighted files from the **History list** tab or **Loaded Applications** tab.

You can also load an AutoLISP file by highlighting the file in Windows Explorer and dragging and dropping it into the AutoCAD drawing area. This method is extremely convenient if Windows Explorer is open.

The **(load)** function allows you to load an AutoLISP program file on the command line. This function requires an AutoLISP file name as its argument and requires that the name be enclosed in quotation marks. To load the myfirst.lsp file using the **(load)** function, the following sequence is used.

```
Command: (load "myfirst")↵
C:FC
Command:
```

When the file has a .lsp file extension, it is not necessary to include the extension in the **(load)** expression. Therefore, you should use the standard .lsp file extension for all AutoLISP files you create. If you are loading an AutoLISP file that does not use a .lsp file extension, the actual extension must be included in the file name argument.

When an AutoLISP program file is loaded and no errors are encountered, the result of evaluating the last expression in the file is returned to the screen. In the example above, the last expression in the file is the definition for the **FC** function, so that function name is returned.

The **(load)** function locates AutoLISP files residing in the support file search path. To load a file that exists elsewhere, the path name must also be specified. In the following example, the myfirst.lsp file is stored in the C:\My Documents\AutoLISP folder.

```
Command: (load "c:/my documents/autolisp/myfirst")↵
C:FC
```

Notice that backslashes are not used in the path specification. In an AutoLISP text string, the backslash is used to specify special characters. For example, the string **\n** indicates a new line. When specifying file paths, you can use either forward slashes, as shown above, or double backslashes (\\). Therefore, in the example above, the file to load could also have been specified as c:\\my documents\\autolisp\\myfirst.

If you frequently load files that are in a folder not found in the current support file search path, it may be helpful to include the folder in the path. This is done using the **Options** dialog box. After displaying this dialog box, pick the **Files** tab and select Support File Search Path. Then, pick the **Add...** button and enter the desired folder. Refer to Chapter 20 for detailed information.

As previously indicated, when you have defined one or more functions that you want to have available in all editing sessions, the definitions can be placed in the acad2009doc.lsp file. If the acad2009doc.lsp file already exists on your system, consult your system administrator or instructor prior to editing this file. The acad2009.lsp and acad2009doc.lsp files are often used by third-party applications. Changing them or accidentally redefining existing commands or functions may render certain features unusable.

Exercise 26-4

Complete the exercise on the Student CD.

Creating Specialized Functions

Although shortcut commands are a powerful use for AutoLISP, it can also be used to create highly specialized functions. Input can specify how the program should function in any given situation. This aspect of AutoLISP allows you to customize AutoCAD to meet the specific needs of your industry or department.

AutoLISP is a versatile tool, offering many different functions for effectively working with numeric data, text data, data files, and AutoCAD drawing objects. This section introduces several basic AutoLISP functions, including some that are used for acquiring input from the user.

Providing for User Input

AutoLISP can prompt the user for various types of data. Depending on its function, a program may need numeric input, text input, or specification of a coordinate location. The **(getpoint)** function prompts for a point entry and pauses the program until the point is entered. For example:

Command: **(setq PT1 (getpoint))**↵

After you press [Enter], AutoLISP waits for a value to be input for the **(getpoint)** function and then stores the value in the **PT1** variable. A prompt can be added to the original expression to clarify what is required:

Command: **(setq PT1 (getpoint "Enter a point: "))**↵
Enter a point:

Now, pick a point on screen. The coordinates for the selected point are assigned to **PT1** and displayed on the command line. If you know the coordinates, you can enter them at the keyboard.

The following example shows how closely AutoCAD and AutoLISP work together. First, define the two variables **PT1** and **PT2** as shown below. Then, enter the **LINE** command and use AutoLISP notation to return the values of **PT1** and **PT2** as the endpoints of the line.

Command: **(setq PT1 (getpoint "From point: "))**↵
From point: **2,2**↵
(2.0 2.0 0.0)
Command: **(setq PT2 (getpoint "To point: "))**↵
To point: **6.25,2**↵
(6.25 2.0 0.0)
Command: **LINE**↵
Specify first point: **!PT1**↵
(2.0 2.0 0.0)
Specify next point or [Undo]: **!PT2**↵
(6.25 2.0 0.0)
Specify next point or [Undo]: ↵

The following is a sample function definition named **1LINE** that uses expressions similar to those given in the previous example. This function will draw a line object based on user input.

```
(defun C:1LINE ()
  (setq PNT1 (getpoint "From point: "))
  (setq PNT2 (getpoint "To point: "))
  (command "LINE" PNT1 PNT2 "")
  (princ)
)
```

The **(command)** function is used to call AutoCAD commands from within AutoLISP. Typically, an AutoCAD command that is "started" within a program is also "ended" within the program. The pair of quotation marks near the end of the fourth line is equivalent to pressing [Enter] after the second point entry, thus ending the **LINE** command.

When developing AutoLISP routines, you may need to assign the length of a line or the distance between two points to a variable. The **(getdist)** function allows you to assign a distance to a variable. A command line prompt is not added to the following example; the "second point" prompt is automatic.

> Command: **(setq LGTH (getdist))**↵
> *(pick the first point)*
> Specify second point: *(pick the second point)*
> *distance*

Use object snaps as needed or enter absolute coordinates. After the second point is specified, the distance value is shown and assigned to the variable. In this example, the distance is assigned to the variable **LGTH**. You can confirm the setting by retrieving the value of the variable.

> Command: **!LGTH**↵
> *distance*

The **(distance)** function is similar to the **(getdist)** function. However, the **(distance)** function does not require picking two points. Instead, it measures the distance between two *existing* points. This function can be used to display a distance or to assign a distance to a variable.

> Command: **(distance PT1 PT2)**↵
> *distance between* ***PT1*** *and* ***PT2***

> Command: **(setq D1 (distance PT1 PT2))**↵
> *distance between* ***PT1*** *and* ***PT2***

The first example returns the distance between the previously defined points **PT1** and **PT2**. The second example displays the distance *and* applies it to the variable **D1**.

PROFESSIONAL TIP

The sample AutoLISP expressions in this section are entered at the command line. However, AutoLISP expressions are more effective as part of a saved program file.

Exercise 26-5

Complete the exercise on the Student CD.

Assigning Text Values to AutoLISP Applications

Values assigned to AutoLISP variables do not have to be numeric. In some applications, you may need to assign a word or line of text to a variable. To do so, use the **(setq)** function and enclose the word(s) in quotation marks.

> Command: **(setq W "What next?")**↵
> "What next?"

You can also assign a word or line of text to a variable with the **(getstring)** function. This function is similar to the **(getpoint)** function in that the user must enter a value.

Command: **(setq E (getstring))**↵

Nothing is displayed on the command line because the optional prompt was not specified. AutoLISP is waiting for a "string" of characters. You can enter as many characters (numbers and letters) as needed. Once you press [Enter] or the spacebar, the string is entered and displayed. To allow spaces in the response, place the letter **T**, without quotation marks, after the **(getstring)** function:

Command: **(setq E (getstring T))**↵
HI THERE↵
"HI THERE"
Command:

The **(prompt)** function can be used to simply display a message. The resulting message has no variable value. AutoLISP indicates this by printing nil after the prompt.

Command: **(prompt "Select an object: ")**↵
Select an object: nil

You can use prompts in AutoLISP programs to provide information or to prompt the user.

CAUTION

The symbol **T** is a built-in AutoLISP constant defined as a *protected symbol.* However, it is possible to change its value using the **(setq)** function. Do *not* change its value. Be certain not to use the variable name **T** for any of your own variables or other functions referencing this symbol may not properly function. If it is accidentally changed, you can reset the value of **T** using the following expression.

Command: **(setq T 'T)**↵

Exercise 26-6

Complete the exercise on the Student CD.

Basic AutoLISP Review

Before applying the functions you have learned to an AutoLISP program, take a few minutes to review the following list. These functions are used in the next chapter, which discusses more advanced AutoLISP applications.

- **(+), (–), (*), (/).** These are the basic math functions used in AutoLISP. They must be entered as the first part of an expression. For example, (+ 6 8).
- **(setq).** The **(setq)** function allows a value to be assigned to a variable. For example, the expression (setq CITY "San Francisco") sets the value San Francisco to the variable **CITY**.
- **!.** An exclamation point entered before a variable on the command line returns the value of the variable. For example, !CITY returns the value San Francisco for the above expression.

- **(getpoint).** This function allows you to define a point location by entering coordinates at the keyboard or using the pointing device. The resulting value can be applied to a variable. For example, the expression (setq A (getpoint)) assigns a point to the variable **A**.
- **(getdist).** This function returns the distance between two points entered at the keyboard or picked on screen. The value can be applied to a variable and a prompt can be used. For example, the expression (setq D2 (getdist "Pick two points:")) allows you to determine a distance and assign it to the variable **D2**.
- **(distance).** This function returns a distance between two existing points. For example, the expression (distance P1 P2) returns the distance between the defined points **P1** and **P2**. The distance can also be assigned to a variable. For example, (setq D (distance P1 P2)).
- **(getstring).** This function returns a word or string of characters entered by the user. The resulting text can be assigned to a variable. For example, the expression (getstring) waits for a string of characters and displays the string when [Enter] or the spacebar is pressed. Spaces are allowed in the text string if **T** follows the **(getstring)** function. For example, the expression (setq TXT (getstring T "Enter text:")) assigns the text entered, which can contain spaces, to the variable **TXT**.
- **(prompt).** Messages or prompts can be issued in a program using the **(prompt)** function. For example, the expression (prompt "Select an entity:") prints the Select an entity: prompt.

PROFESSIONAL TIP

Design your AutoLISP programs to closely resemble the AutoCAD interface. For example, it is easier for the user to read "back-to-back" prompts when the prompts appear on separate lines. Use the **\n** string to specify a new line for a prompt. For example:

```
(setq PT2 (getpoint "\nTo point:"))
```

Exercise 26-7

Complete the exercise on the Student CD.

Chapter Test

Answer the following questions. Write your answers on a separate sheet of paper or complete the electronic chapter test on the Student CD.

1. What is the standard extension used for AutoLISP program files?
2. A comment is indicated in an AutoLISP file with a(n) _____.
3. When in the drawing area, what are three ways to load the contents of the AutoLISP file named chgtext.lsp that is saved in the support file search path?
4. Define the terms *integer* and *real number* as related to AutoLISP.
5. Write expressions in the proper AutoLISP format for the following arithmetic functions.
   A. $23 + 54$
   B. $12.45 + 6.28$
   C. $56 - 34$
   D. $23.004 - 7.008$
   E. 16×4.6
   F. 7.25×10.30
   G. $45 \div 23$
   H. $147 \div 29.6$
   I. $53 + (12 \times 3.8)$
   J. $567 \div (34 - 14)$
6. Explain the purpose of the **(setq)** function.
7. Write the proper AutoLISP notation to assign the value of (67 – 34.5) to the variable **NUM1**.
8. What does the **(getpoint)** function allow you to do?
9. Which AutoLISP functions allow you to find the distance between two points? Describe the difference between the two functions.
10. Explain the purpose of the **(getstring)** function.
11. Write the proper AutoLISP notation for assigning the string This is a test: to the variable **TXT**.
12. How do you allow spaces in a string of text when using the **(getstring)** function?
13. Write the proper notation for using the **PLINE** command in an AutoLISP expression.
14. Which prefix must you enter before a function name in an expression to indicate it is accessible at the Command: prompt?
15. What is a *function definition?*
16. Define an *argument.*
17. Which AutoLISP function is used to create new AutoCAD commands?
18. What is the purpose of the **Visual LISP Editor**?
19. When entering text in the **Visual LISP Editor**, which color indicates that you have entered a built-in function or a protected symbol?
20. Explain the purpose of the **\n** text string in AutoLISP.

Drawing Problems

Write AutoLISP programs for the following problems. Use the **Visual LISP Editor.** *Save the files as* P26-*(problem number) with the* .lsp *extension.*

1. Write an AutoLISP program to draw a rectangle. Use the **(getpoint)** function to set the opposite corners of the rectangle. Follow these guidelines:
   A. Set **P1** as the first corner.
   B. Set **P3** as the opposite corner.
   C. Use the **RECTANG** command to draw the rectangle using **P1** and **P3** in place of picking corners.
   D. The users should not be able to change any options in the **RECTANG** command.

2. Create an AutoLISP program to draw a square. Follow these guidelines:
   A. Set a variable for the length of one side.
   B. Set the variable **P1** as the lower-left corner of the square.
   C. Use the **RECTANG** command to draw the square.

3. Revise the program in problem 2 to draw a square with filleted corners.
   A. The fillet radius should be equal to 1/4 of the side length.
   B. After the fillet rectangle is drawn, reset the fillet radius so the next rectangle drawn with the **RECTANG** command does not automatically have fillets. Note: Use ^C to cancel a command that you do not want to complete. For example:

```
(command "LINE" PT1 ^C)
```

4. Use the program in problem 3 to create a new command that draws a square with thick lines.
   A. The line thickness should be a percentage of the fillet radius (between 5% and 10%).
   B. Reset the line thickness so that the next rectangle drawn with the **RECTANG** command does not automatically have thick lines. Note: Use ^C to cancel a command that you do not want to complete. For example:

```
(command "LINE" PT1 ^C)
```

5. Write an AutoLISP program that allows the user to draw parallel rectangles.
   A. Provide a prompt that asks the user to enter an offset distance for a second rectangle to be placed inside of the first rectangle.
   B. Use the **OFFSET** command to allow the user to draw the parallel rectangle inside the original without entering an offset distance.

AutoLISP programs do not need to be complex to be very useful. This program, which is fully documented, allows the user to select an arc and turn it into a circle. AutoCAD does not have the ability to extend an arc into a circle. At the bottom of the page, the program is shown as it appears in the **Visual LISP Editor**.

```
;;;
;;;                 ARC2CIR.lsp
;;;               by Craig P. Black
;;;           original release date: 6/7/xx
;;;
;;;  This program was written to handle AutoCAD's inability to
;;;  extend an arc into a circle. AutoCAD can trim a circle into
;;;  an arc, but not vice versa.

(defun C:ARC2CIR                            ; defines a command named ARC2CIR
    (/ CMD ARC EDATA CPT RAD LYR)           ; localizes variables used in program
    (setq CMD (getvar "CMDECHO"))           ; stores value of cmdecho sysvar
    (setvar "CMDECHO" 0)                    ; sets cmdecho sysvar to off
    (setq ARC (entsel "\nSelect arc: "))    ; allows user to select an arc
    (setq EDATA (entget (car ARC)))         ; stores the data associated with the arc
    (setq CPT (assoc 10 EDATA))             ; stores the center point of the arc
    (setq RAD (assoc 40 EDATA))             ; stores the radius of the arc
    (setq LYR (assoc 8 EDATA))              ; stores the layer of the arc
    (entdel (car ARC))                      ; deletes the existing arc
    (entmake   (list                        ; creates a new entity
                  (cons 0 "CIRCLE")         ; the entity will be a circle
                  CPT                       ; the circle will use the arc's center point
                  RAD                       ; the circle will use the arc's radius
                  LYR                       ; the circle will use the arc's layer
               )
    )
    (princ)                                 ; cleanly exits the program
)
```

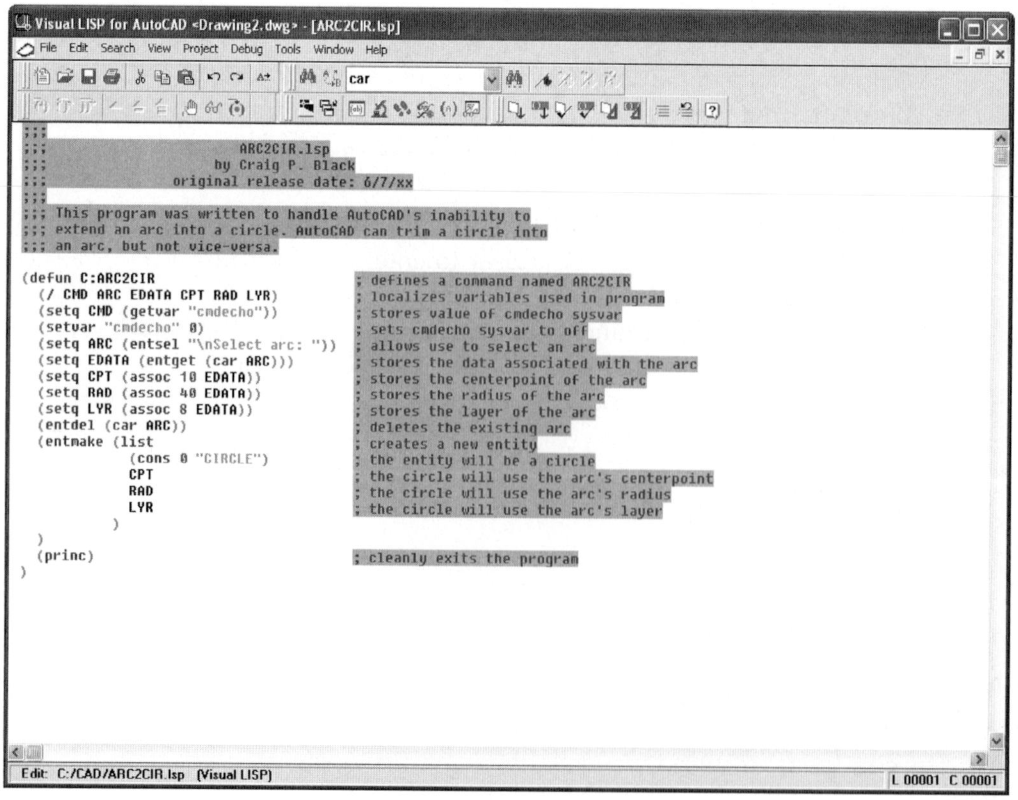

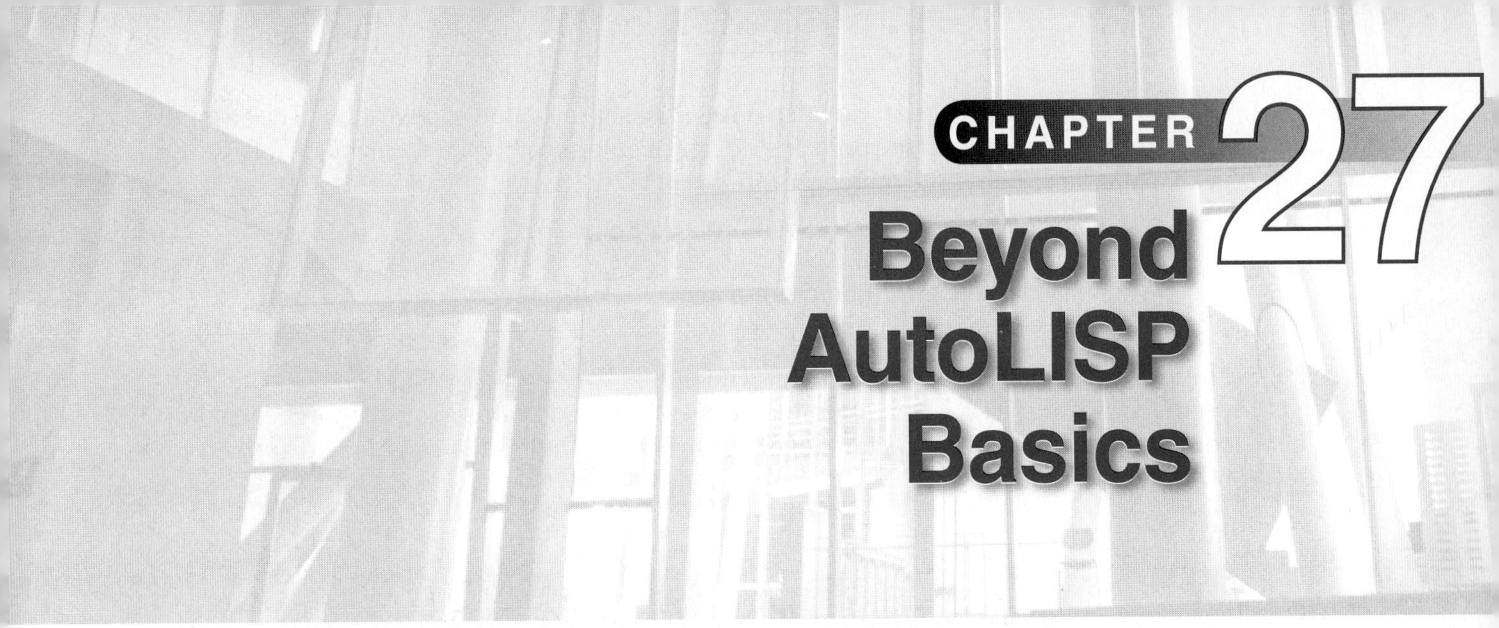

CHAPTER 27 Beyond AutoLISP Basics

Learning Objectives

After completing this chapter, you will be able to:

- ✓ Identify ways to provide for user input.
- ✓ Retrieve and use system variable values in AutoLISP programs.
- ✓ Work with lists using AutoLISP.
- ✓ Use angular input in AutoLISP programs.

As you practice using AutoLISP, you will develop ideas for programs that require additional commands and functions. Some of these programs may require that the user pick two corners of a windowed selection set. Another program may use existing points to draw a shape. You may also need to locate a point using polar coordinate notation or determine the angle of a line. All of these drawing tasks can be done with AutoLISP programs.

Providing for Additional User Input

The **(getreal)** function allows you to define a variable value by entering a real number at the keyboard. Remember, as defined by AutoLISP, real numbers are classified separately from integers. A real number is considered to be more precise than an integer because it has a decimal value.

The **(getreal)** function works with numbers as units. You cannot respond with a value of feet and inches. Once issued, the function waits for user input. A prompt can be included. The real number is returned after a response is entered. The **(getreal)** function can be used to set the value of a variable as follows.

```
Command: (setq X (getreal "Enter number: "))↵
Enter number: 34↵
34.0
```

The **(getcorner)** function allows the user to pick the opposite corner of a rectangle and define it as a point value. This is similar to placing a window around objects to define a selection set in a drawing. An existing point serves as the first corner of the rectangle. When locating the opposite corner, the screen cursor appears as a "rubber band" box similar to the window used when defining a selection set.

The **(getcorner)** function can also be used to set the value of a variable. The second corner can be picked with the pointing device or entered at the keyboard. The following is an example of using the **(getcorner)** function.

> Command: **(setq PT1 (getpoint "\nPick a point:"))**↵
> Pick a point: *(pick the point)*
> Command: **(setq PT2 (getcorner PT1 "\nPick the second corner:"))**↵
> Pick the second corner: *(pick the corner)*

Notice that the value of **PT1** is set first. The point represented by **PT1** becomes the base point for locating **PT2**. The two points (corners) located in this example can be used to construct an angled line, rectangle, or other shape. The points can also be applied to other functions.

Using the Values of System Variables

AutoCAD's system variables can be read and changed from within AutoLISP applications with the **(getvar)** and **(setvar)** functions. These functions can be useful if an application requires you to store the value of a system variable in an AutoLISP variable, change the system variable setting for your program, and then reset the system variable to its original value.

The **(getvar)** function is used to return the value of a system variable. In the following example, two system variable settings are saved as AutoLISP variable values.

> Command: **(setq V1 (getvar "TEXTSIZE"))**↵
> *current value of the **TEXTSIZE** system variable*
> Command: **(setq V2 (getvar "FILLETRAD"))**↵
> *current value of the **FILLETRAD** system variable*

The **(setvar)** function is used to change an AutoCAD system variable setting. You can assign a new value to a variable as follows.

> Command: **(setvar "TEXTSIZE" 0.25)**↵
> 0.25
> Command: **(setvar "FILLETRAD" 0.25)**↵
> 0.25

Remember, you need to add the 0 in front of .25 or an error is generated.

Suppose you need to save a current system variable setting, change the variable, and then reset the variable to its original value after the command is executed. The **(getvar)** function can be used to assign the original value to a variable, such as **V1** shown in the first example on the **TEXTSIZE** system variable above. When the program is complete, the **(setvar)** function can be used to reset **TEXTSIZE** to its original value.

> Command: **(setvar "TEXTSIZE" V1)**↵
> 0.125

This returns the value of **TEXTSIZE** to the value of the variable **V1**, which is the original system variable setting.

Exercise 27-1

Complete the exercise on the Student CD.

Working with Lists

In AutoLISP, a ***list*** is defined as a stored set of values that are enclosed in parentheses. Lists are commonly used to provide point locations and other data for use in functions. A list is created, for example, when you pick a point on screen in response to the **(getpoint)** function. The list is composed of three numbers—the X, Y, and Z coordinate values. You can tell it is a list because AutoLISP returns the numbers enclosed in parentheses. On the other hand, a number entered in response to the **(getreal)** function is returned as a real number (it is not enclosed in parentheses). A single number is not a list. The following expression returns a list.

Command: **(setq P1 (getpoint "Enter point:"))**↵
Enter point: *(pick a point)*
(2.0 2.75 0.0)

The individual values in a list are called ***atoms*** and can be used in an AutoLISP program to create new points. The **(car)** function retrieves the first atom in a list. The variable **P1** in the example above is composed of the list (2.0 2.75 0.0). Thus, using the **(car)** function with the **P1** variable returns a value of 2.0.

Command: **(car P1)**↵
2.0

The second atom in a list is retrieved with the **(cadr)** function. Find the second atom of the list stored in the variable **P1** by entering the following.

Command: **(cadr P1)**↵
2.75

You can create a new list of two coordinates by extracting values from existing points using the **(car)** and **(cadr)** functions. This is done with the **(list)** function. Values returned by this function are placed inside of parentheses. The coordinates of the first variable, **P1**, can be combined with the coordinates of a second point variable, named **P2**, to form a third point variable, named **P3**. Study the following example and Figure 27-1. The coordinates stored in the variable **P1** are (2.0 2.75).

Command: **(setq P2 (getcorner P1 "Enter second point: "))**↵
Enter second point: **6,4.5**↵
(6.0 4.5 0.0)
Command: **(setq P3 (list (car P2)(cadr P1)))**↵
(6.0 2.75)

In AutoLISP, a function is followed by an argument. An ***argument*** consists of data on or with which a function operates. An expression must be composed of only one function and any required arguments. Therefore, the functions **(car)** and **(cadr)** must be separated because they are two different expressions combined to make a list. The **(car)** value of the list stored in **P2** is to be the X value of **P3**, so it is given first. The **(cadr)** value of the list stored in **P1** is placed second because it is to be the Y value of **P3**. Notice the number of closing parentheses at the end of the expression.

Figure 27-1.
A third point identified as **P3** has been created using the **(car)** value of the list **P2** and the **(cadr)** value of the list **P1**.

Figure 27-2.
Once the third point, **P3**, is created, a triangle can be drawn.

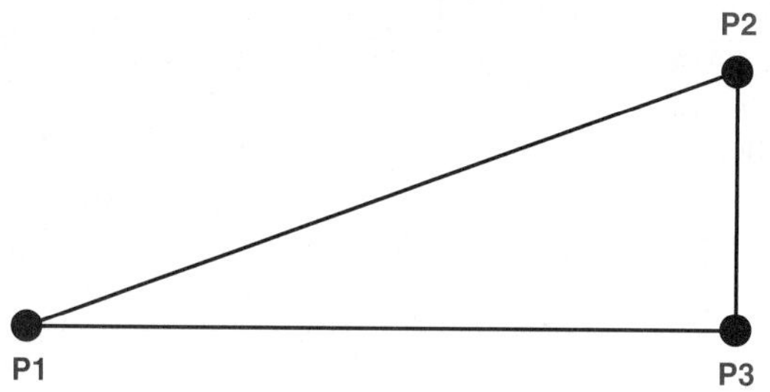

Now, with three points defined, there are many things you can do. For example, you can draw lines through the points to form a triangle, **Figure 27-2.** To do so, use the **(command)** function as follows.

Command: **(command "LINE" P1 P2 P3 "C")**↵

The **(car)** and **(cadr)** functions allow you to work with 2D coordinates. The **(caddr)** function allows you to use the third atom of a list. This can be the Z coordinate of a point. Enter the following at your keyboard.

Command: **(setq B (list 3 4 6))**↵
(3 4 6)

You have created a list of three atoms, or values, and assigned it to the variable **B**. The third value is retrieved with the **(caddr)** function.

Command: **(caddr B)**↵
6

Since 6 is a single value, not a list, it is not enclosed in parentheses. Now, use the **(car)** and **(cadr)** functions to find the other two atoms of the list.

Command: **(car B)**↵
3
Command: **(cadr B)**↵
4

The following is a short AutoLISP program that uses the **(car)** and **(cadr)** retrieval functions to place an X at the midpoint of two selected points.

```
(defun C:MDPNT ()
  (setq PT1 (getpoint "\nEnter the first point: "))
  (setq PT2 (getpoint "\nEnter the second point: "))
  (setq PT3 (list (/ (+ (car PT1) (car PT2)) 2) (/ (+ (cadr PT1) (cadr PT2)) 2)))
  (setvar "PDMODE" 3)
  (command "POINT" PT3)
)
```

The **(cdr)** function is also used to work with lists. It allows you to retrieve the second and remaining values of a list. Earlier in this discussion, the list (3 4 6) was assigned to variable **B**. In the following example, the **(cdr)** function is used to return the list (4 6).

Command: **(cdr B)**↵
(4 6)

This returns a list of two values, or coordinates, that can be further manipulated with the **(car)** and **(cadr)** functions. Study **Figure 27-3** and the following examples.

Command: **(car (cdr B))**↵
4
Command: **(cadr (cdr B))**↵
6

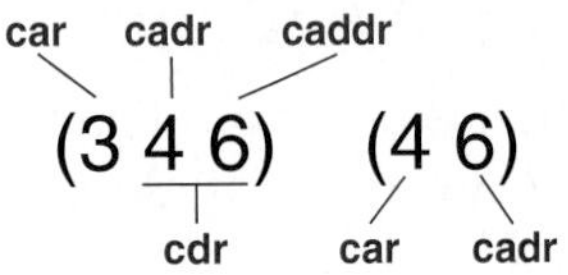

Figure 27-3.
The **(cdr)** function creates a list containing the second and remaining atoms of a list. The new list can be manipulated as necessary with the **(car)** and **(cadr)** functions.

The first example is asking for the first atom—**(car)**—of the list generated from the last two atoms—**(cdr)**—of variable **B**. In the second example, the second atom—**(cadr)**—of the list generated from the last two atoms of variable **B** is returned.

The four functions used to manipulate lists—**(car)**, **(cadr)**, **(caddr)**, and **(cdr)**—may seem confusing at first. Practice using them to see how they work. Practice with a list of numbers, coordinate values, or text strings. Remember, text strings must be enclosed in quotation marks. Try the following examples to see what happens. Enter the expressions on the command line exactly as shown and press [Enter] at the end of each line.

```
(setq NOTES (list "DO" "RE" "MI"))
(car NOTES)
(cadr NOTES)
(caddr NOTES)
(cdr NOTES)
(setq LASTNOTES (cdr NOTES))
(car (cdr NOTES))
(cadr (cdr NOTES))
(car LASTNOTES)
(cadr LASTNOTES)
```

As you continue to work in AutoLISP, you will find many uses for the functions that allow you to work with lists. Remember the following review.

- **(car).** Returns the first atom in a list.
- **(cadr).** Returns the second atom in a list.
- **(caddr).** Returns the third atom in a list.
- **(cdr).** Returns the second and remaining atoms of a list. The returned values are placed in a list. If the original list contains two atoms, only the second atom is returned and it is placed in a list.
- **(list).** Creates a list of all values entered as arguments to the function name.

Exercise 27-2

Complete the exercise on the Student CD.

Using Polar Coordinates and Angles

The ability to work with angles is vital if you plan to do much AutoLISP programming. Four functions—**(angle)**, **(polar)**, **(getangle)**, and **(getorient)**—allow you to use angles when writing program files. AutoLISP works with these functions using the radian system of angle measurement. This system of measurement is explained in the next section.

Measuring Angles in Radians

The **(angle)** function is used to calculate the angle in the XY plane of a line between two given points. The value of the angle is given in radians. ***Radian angle measurement*** is a system in which 180° equals "pi" (π). Pi is approximately equal to 3.14159.

AutoLISP functions use radians for angular measurement, but AutoCAD commands use degrees. Therefore, to use a radian angle in an AutoCAD command, it must first be converted to degrees. Conversely, a degree angle to be used by AutoLISP must be converted to radians. The following formulas are used for those conversions.

- To convert degrees to radians, use the formula:

  (* pi (/ *ad* 180.0))

  where *ad* = angle in degrees.
- To convert radians to degrees, use the formula:

  (/ (* *ar* 180.0) pi)

  where *ar* = angle in radians.

The following table gives common angles measured in degrees, the AutoLISP expressions used to convert the angular values to radian values, and the resulting values in radians to four decimal places.

Angle (degrees)	AutoLISP expression	Angle (radians)
0		0
30	(/ pi 6)	0.5236
45	(/ pi 4)	0.7854
60	(/ pi 3)	1.0472
90	(/ pi 2)	1.5708
135	(/ (* pi 3) 4)	2.3562
180	pi	3.1416
270	(/ (* pi 3) 2)	4.7124
360	(* pi 2)	6.2832

The following example illustrates how the angle between two points can be set to a variable, then converted to degrees.

```
Command: (setq P1 (getpoint "Enter first point: "))↵
Enter first point: 1.75,5.25↵
(1.75 5.25 0.0)
Command: (setq P2 (getpoint "Enter second point: "))↵
Enter second point: 6.75,7.25↵
(6.75 7.25 0.0)
Command: (setq A1 (angle P1 P2))↵
0.380506
```

The angle represented by the variable **A1** is measured in radians (0.380506). To convert this value to degrees, use the following expression.

```
Command: (/ (* A1 180.0) pi)↵
21.8014
Command: !A1↵
0.380506
```

The value 21.8014 is the angle in degrees between the coordinates in variables **P1** and **P2**. However, notice that this conversion does not set the variable **A1** to the value in degrees. Make the degree value permanent by assigning it to the variable using the following expression.

```
Command: (setq A1 (/ (* A1 180.0) pi))↵
21.8014
Command: !A1↵
21.8014
```

The variable **A1** now has a value of 21.8014.

Exercise 27-3

Complete the exercise on the Student CD.

Providing for Angular Input by the User

The **(getangle)** function allows the user to input an angular value for use in an application. This function is often used to set a variable that can be used by another function. The **(getangle)** function automatically issues a Specify second point: prompt. The following example illustrates how you can set a variable to an angular value that is input by the user.

Command: **(setq A (getangle "Pick first point: "))**↵
Pick first point: *(pick the first point)*
Specify second point: *(pick the second point)*
angle (in radians)

The angular value is given in radians. To convert it to degrees, use the formula presented in the previous section.

The **(getangle)** function uses the current **ANGBASE** (angle 0 direction) and **ANGDIR** (clockwise or counterclockwise) system variables. Therefore, if you have angles set to be measured from north (where **ANGBASE** = 90°), angles picked with the **(getangle)** function will be measured from north. If the **ANGDIR** system variable is set to measure angles clockwise, the **(getangle)** function will accept input of clockwise values, but returns counterclockwise values.

A companion function to **(getangle)** is **(getorient)**. It is used in exactly the same manner as the **(getangle)** function. However, **(getorient)** always measures angles counterclockwise from east (0°), regardless of the current **ANGBASE** and **ANGDIR** system variable settings.

Exercise 27-4

Complete the exercise on the Student CD.

Using Polar Coordinates

The **(polar)** function allows you to specify a new point based on the angle and distance from an existing point. Three arguments are required for the **(polar)** function. The first argument must contain the coordinates of the base point from which you are locating the new point. The second argument is the angular direction (in radians) to go from the base point argument. The third argument is the distance value from the base point argument to the new point. The syntax for the **(polar)** function is:

(polar *base_point angle distance*)

For example, suppose you want to specify a point as **P1** and locate another point, **P2**, at a specific distance (three units) and angle (60°) from **P1**. Enter the following expressions.

Command: **(setq P1 (getpoint "Enter point: "))**↵
Enter point: **4.0,4.5**↵
(4.0 4.5 0.0)
Command: **(setq D (getdist P1 "Enter distance: "))**↵
Enter distance: **3.0**↵
3.0
Command: **(setq A (/ pi 3))**↵
1.0472

In this example, the desired angle is 60°. However, AutoLISP uses radians for angular values. Therefore, the degree value is converted to radians. The resulting value, 1.0472, is saved as the variable **A**. Next, use the **(polar)** function to locate the second point relative to **P1** at the specified angle and distance. A line can then be drawn from **P1** to **P2** using the **(command)** function. The sequence is:

Command: **(setq P2 (polar P1 A D))**↵
(5.5 7.09808 0.0)
Command: **(command "LINE" P1 P2 "")**↵

Exercise 27-5

Complete the exercise on the Student CD.

Locating AutoCAD's AutoLISP Files

One of the best ways to become familiar with AutoLISP is to enter expressions and programs into your computer. Look for programs in the books, magazines, newsgroups, and blogs that you read. Get a feel for how the functions and arguments go together and how they work in AutoCAD. Make a habit of reading through one of the AutoCAD journals and experiment with the AutoLISP routines printed in them. Also, refer to the online documentation and developer help for other samples.

AutoLISP files are typically saved with the .lsp extension. A variety of AutoLISP programs are supplied with AutoCAD. These are saved in the AutoCAD folder structure. You can use Windows Explorer to search the AutoCAD folder structure and list the .lsp files.

The AutoLISP files found in the \Support folder are standard files that support many of AutoCAD's built-in features. When the command that starts the function is entered, the associated program file is automatically loaded. For example, the 3darray.lsp AutoLISP file is found in the \Support folder. This routine makes it possible to create an arrangement of rows, columns, and levels of an object with the **3DARRAY** command.

PROFESSIONAL TIP

For easier access to any AutoLISP program file, add its folder in the Support File Search Path listing located in the **Files** tab of the **Options** dialog box.

Sample AutoLISP Programs

The following programs are provided for you to copy and add to your acad2009doc.lsp file or to your custom menus. Practice using the routines for a few minutes a couple of times a week. This will help you begin to better understand and use AutoLISP. Train yourself to learn a new function every week. Before long, you will be writing your own useful programs.

Erasing the Entire Screen

This program sets two variables to the minimum and maximum screen limits. It then erases everything within those limits and redraws the screen. Name this program zap.lsp.

```
;;; ERASES ENTIRE LIMITS.
(defun C:ZAP ()
  (setq LMIN (getvar "LIMMIN"))
  (setq LMAX (getvar "LIMMAX"))
  (command "ERASE" "C" LMIN LMAX "")
  (command "REDRAW")
)
```

Setting the Current Layer

Similar to the built-in **Make Object's Layer Current** tool on the **Layers** panel in the **Home** tab of the ribbon, this program asks the user to pick an object on the layer to be set current. The program finds the layer of the object picked and sets it current. Name this program lp.lsp.

```
;;; AUTHOR ROD RAWLS
(defun C:LP (/ E)
  (while (not (setq E (entsel "\nSelect object on target layer...")))
        (alert "No object selected!")
  )
  (setq LN (cdr (assoc 8 (entget (car E)))))
  (command "-LAYER" "S" LN "")
  (princ)
)
```

Cleaning Overlapping Corners

This program allows you to trim the overlapping ends of intersecting lines. You are requested to pick the two lines that intersect and overlap. The points you pick are on the portion to keep. The program does the rest. Name the program cleanc.lsp. Note: The value returned at the end of the program is the original **OSMODE** setting.

```
;;; AUTHOR: GEORGE HEAD
;;; PRINTED IN CADENCE MAGAZINE
(defun C:CLEANC (/ O1 P1 P2)
  (setq O1 (getvar "OSMODE"))
  (setvar "OSMODE" 512)
  (command "FILLET" "R" 0)
  (setq P1 (getpoint "\nPick a line "))
  (setq P2 (getpoint "\nPick other line "))
  (command "FILLET" P1 P2)
  (setvar "OSMODE" O1)
)
```

Calculating the Length of Lines

This program calculates the length of all lines on a specified layer. It can be used for estimating and material takeoffs. This program only works with lines, not with polylines. Name the program linear.lsp. After loading it into AutoCAD, respond to the first prompt by entering the name of the layer that contains the lines you wish to total. The calculation is given in current drawing units. Also, the layer name is case sensitive.

```
;;; AUTHOR: JOE PUCILOWSKI
;;; COMPANY: JOSEPH & ASSOCIATES
;;; REVISED BY CRAIG BLACK
;;; NOTE: THIS PROGRAM FIGURES THE TOTAL NUMBER OF LINEAR
;;; UNITS (FEET, INCHES, ETC.) OF LINES ON A SPECIFIC LAYER.
;;;
(defun C:LINEAR ()
  (setq  TOTAL    0
         E        (entnext)
         NUMLIN   0
         LAYPIK   (getstring T "\nAdd up lines on layer: ")
  )
  (if (tblsearch "LAYER" LAYPIK)
    (progn
      (while E
        (setq  ENTTYP  (cdr  (assoc 0 (setq EG (entget E))))
               LAYNAM  (cdr  (assoc 8 EG))
        )
        (if  (and
               (equal ENTTYP "LINE")
               (equal (strcase LAYNAM)
                      (strcase LAYPIK)
               )
             )
          (progn
            (setq  LINLEN  (distance  (cdr  (assoc 10 EG))
                                      (cdr  (assoc 11 EG))
                           )
                   TOTAL   (+ TOTAL LINLEN)
                   NUMLIN  (+ 1 NUMLIN)
            )
          )
        )
        (setq E (entnext E))
      )
      (princ (strcat "\nFound "
               (itoa NUMLIN)
               " lines on layer <"
               LAYPIK
               "> with a total of "
               (rtos TOTAL)
               " linear units."
             )
      )
    )
    (princ "\nLayer does not exist.")
  )
  (princ)
)
```

Changing the Grid Rotation

The first routine, titled **S**, rotates the grid to the angle between the X axis and any picked line. The second routine, **SS**, returns the grid to zero rotation. These functions are achieved by rotating the snap. Save the file as rotgrid.lsp.

```
;;; AUTHOR: EBEN KUNZ
;;; COMPANY: KUNA ASSOCIATES ARCHITECTS
;;; REVISED BY CRAIG BLACK
;;;
(defun C:S (/ PT1 PT2)
  (setq lOSMODEl (getvar "OSMODE"))
    (setvar "OSMODE" 0)
    (setvar "ORTHOMODE" 0)
    (setq PT1 (osnap (getpoint "\nPick line to match new Grid angle: \n") "NEA"))
    (setq PT2 (osnap PT1 "END"))
    (command "SNAP" "R" PT1 PT2)
    (setvar "SNAPMODE" 0)
  (setvar "OSMODE" lOSMODEl)
  (princ)
)
(defun C:SS ()
  (prompt "\nReturn Grid to zero.")
  (command "SNAP" "R" "" 0.0)
  (setvar "SNAPMODE" 0)
)
```

Moving Objects to a Selected Layer

This routine, named la.lsp, allows you to move objects to a layer by picking an object on the destination layer. After you select an object on the destination layer, you can select multiple objects using any AutoCAD selection method.

```
;;; AUTHOR: SHELDON MCCARTHY
;;; COMPANY: EPCM SERVICES LTD.
;;;
(defun C:LA ()
  (setq 1A
          (cdr  (assoc 8
                     (entget  (car
                                (entsel "Entity on destination layer: "
                                )
                              )
                     )
                )
          )
  )
  (prompt "Objects to change...")
  (ssget)
  (command    "CHANGE"
              "P"
              ""
              "P"
              "LA"
              1A
              ""
  )
)
```

Moving Objects to the Current Layer

This simple program, titled cl.lsp, quickly changes selected objects to the current layer. You can select multiple objects using any AutoCAD selection method.

```
;;; AUTHOR: BILL FANE
;;; COMPANY: WISER, INC.
;;;
(defun C:CL (/ THINGS)
  (setq THINGS (ssget))
  (command    "CHANGE"
              THINGS
              ""
              "P"
              "LA"
              (getvar "CLAYER")
              ""
  )
)
```

Chapter Test

Answer the following questions. Write your answers on a separate sheet of paper or complete the electronic chapter test on the Student CD.

1. Name the function that allows you to return a real number and use it as a variable value.
2. Which two functions allow you to work with system variables?
3. Define the following AutoLISP functions.
   A. **(car)**
   B. **(cadr)**
   C. **(cdr)**
   D. **(caddr)**
   E. **(list)**
4. Write the proper AutoLISP notation to return the last two atoms of the list (4 7 3) as a list.
5. Write an expression to set a variable named **A** to the result of question 4.
6. Write an expression to return the second atom of the list created in question 5.
7. Compare and contrast the **(getangle)** and **(getorient)** functions.
8. Write an expression to set the angle between points **P3** and **P4** to the variable **A**.
9. Which system of angular measurement does AutoLISP use?
10. Explain the purpose of the **(polar)** function.

Drawing Problems

*Write AutoLISP programs for the following problems. Use the **Visual LISP Editor.** Save the files as P27_(problem number) with the .lsp extension.*

1. Add the following capabilities to the right triangle function developed in Exercise 27-2.
   A. Use the **(getdist)** function instead of **(getcorner)**.
   B. Allow the angle of the hypotenuse to be picked.
   C. Allow the length of a side or the hypotenuse length to be picked.

2. Create an AutoLISP program similar to that in problem 1, but write it so that it draws an equilateral triangle (with equal angles and equal sides). Use the **(polar)** function.

3. Revise the program in problem 1 in Chapter 26 to draw a rectangle using the **(getcorner)** function to find the second corner. Also, revise the program so that the **LINE** command is used instead of the **RECTANG** command.

4. Add a **Fillet 0** command to your **Modify** menu. Use menu macros and AutoLISP expressions to create the command. Follow these guidelines:
   A. Retrieve the current fillet radius setting and assign it to an AutoLISP variable.
   B. Set the fillet radius to 0.
   C. Allow the user to select two lines and automatically enter a 0 radius fillet.
   D. Reset the fillet radius to the original value.
   E. Assign an appropriate mnemonic key to the new menu command.

5. Write an AutoLISP program that allows the user to measure the distance between two points using the **DIST** command. Use AutoLISP expressions to do the following.
   A. Assign the current unit precision for read-only linear units to an AutoLISP variable.
   B. Prompt for the desired unit precision from the user and store the value as a variable.
   C. Set the unit precision with the user-defined variable value.
   D. Allow the user to measure the distance between two selected points with the **DIST** command.
   E. Reset the unit precision to the original value.

6. Write an AutoLISP program to draw a rectangle and place a circle having a user-specified diameter in the center of the rectangle.
   A. Incorporate the rectangle program from problem 3.
   B. Use the **(angle)**, **(polar)**, and **(distance)** functions to find the center point of the rectangle.
   C. Prompt the user to enter the diameter of the circle.
   D. Use the **CIRCLE** command to draw the circle at the center point of the rectangle.

7. Write a program to draw a leader with a diameter dimension having plus and minus tolerances.
   A. Issue prompts that allow the user to set the **DIMTP** and **DIMTM** system variables and save the specified values to AutoLISP variables.
   B. Set the new values to the **DIMTP** and **DIMTM** system variables.
   C. Turn the **DIMTOL** system variable on.
   D. Activate the **DIMDIAMETER** command. Use the **(entsel)** function to set the selection specification to a variable as follows.

```
(setq SC (entsel))
```

   E. Using the **(getpoint)** function, issue a prompt that allows the user to pick a location for the leader line and the default dimension text.
   F. Turn the **DIMTOL** system variable off.

8. Write an AutoLISP program to draw a leader with a bubble attached to the end.
   A. Prompt the user for the start point of the leader and set it to the variable **P1**.
   B. Prompt the user for the endpoint of the leader and set it to the variable **P2**.
   C. Prompt the user for the text height and set it to a variable.
   D. Issue a prompt that asks for the text string (specify a maximum of two characters) and set the resulting text to a variable.
   E. Calculate the circle diameter at three times the text height and set it to a variable.
   F. Set the center point of the circle to a point relative to **P2** using the **(polar)** function. Set the relative distance as the radius of the circle. Assign the center point to the variable **P3**.
   G. Use the **LEADER** command to draw a leader from **P1** to **P2**.
   H. Draw the leader line with no shoulder and no annotation text.
   I. Draw a circle with the center point at **P3**.
   J. Draw text in the center of the circle using the appropriate justification option of the **TEXT** command.

9. Develop a program that draws a line of text and places a box around it.
   A. Prompt the user for the text height and set it to the variable **TXHT**.
   B. Prompt the user for a point representing the lower-left corner of the box and set it to a variable.
   C. Prompt for the text string from the user.
   D. Set the text string length to the variable **LG1**. Use the **(strlen)** function. The following is an example of using this function.

```
(setq TEXT (getstring T "Enter Text: "))
(setq LG1 (strlen TEXT))
```

   E. Set the X length of the box to a variable using the expression:

```
(* LG1 TXHT)
```

   F. Set the Y length of the box to a variable using the expression:

```
(* 3 TXHT)
```

   G. Draw the box using the variables set in E and F.
   H. Calculate the center point of the box and set it to the variable **CEN1**.
   I. Draw the text string inside the box. Use the **MC** text justification option for point **CEN1**.

CHAPTER 28

Introduction to Dialog Control Language (DCL)

Learning Objectives

After completing this chapter, you will be able to:

✓ Describe the types of files that control dialog boxes.
✓ Define the components of a dialog box.
✓ Write a DCL file for a basic dialog box.
✓ Write an AutoLISP file to control a dialog box.
✓ Associate an action with a dialog box tile.

Programmable dialog boxes can be used to completely customize the interface of AutoLISP programs. These dialog boxes allow LISP programs to work like many of AutoCAD's built-in functions. Using dialog boxes improves efficiency and reduces data-entry errors.

Dialog boxes minimize the amount of typing required by the user. Rather than answering a series of text prompts on the command line, the user selects options from the dialog box. Dialog box fields can be filled in by the user in any order. While the dialog box is still active, the user can revise values as necessary.

AutoLISP provides basic tools for controlling dialog boxes, but the dialog box itself must be defined using the ***Dialog Control Language (DCL).*** The definition is written to an ASCII file with a .dcl file extension. When creating and editing DCL files, the **Visual LISP Editor** provides many helpful tools, including color coding.

This chapter is only an introduction to DCL. It covers basic DCL file construction and a few common tile types. For more information, refer to the online help documentation.

DCL File Formats

A DCL file is formatted as an ASCII text file with a .dcl file extension. These files can have any valid file name, but a file name with 1 to 8 characters is recommended. Writing DCL is easy. Many of the components of a DCL file are normal English words.

The components of a dialog box—such as edit boxes, images, and drop-down lists—are referred to as ***tiles.*** Tiles are defined by specifying various ***attribute*** values. Each attribute controls a specific property of the tile, such as size, location, and default values.

When writing a DCL file, you do not use parentheses as you do with AutoLISP. When defining a dialog box or tile, all of the required attributes are placed within {braces}. As with AutoLISP programs, indentation helps to separate individual elements, making the file more readable. Comments are preceded by two forward slashes (//). Semicolons are used at the end of an attribute definition line.

To view an example of DCL code, open the acad.dcl and base.dcl files in a text editor. These two files are found in the user's \Support folder, not the AutoCAD \Support folder. A portion of the acad.dcl file is shown in **Figure 28-1.**

CAUTION

The base.dcl file contains standard prototype definitions. The acad.dcl file contains definitions for dialog boxes used by AutoCAD. Do *not* edit either one of these files! Altering them can cause AutoCAD's built-in dialog boxes to crash.

AutoLISP and DCL

A DCL file simply defines a dialog box. The dialog box cannot actually do anything without a controlling application. AutoLISP is frequently used to control dialog sessions. This section shows examples using the AutoLISP dialog-handling functions.

In order to display a dialog box, the controlling AutoLISP application must first load the dialog definition. The AutoLISP **(load_dialog)** function loads the specified dialog definition file:

(load_dialog "*file name*.dc")

The file name is enclosed in quotation marks. The **(load_dialog)** function returns a positive integer that identifies the loaded DCL file. If the attempted load was unsuccessful, a negative integer is returned.

The next step is to activate a specific dialog box definition contained within the DCL file. The AutoLISP **(new_dialog)** function activates the dialog box specified, where *dlgname* is the name of the dialog box:

(new_dialog *dlgname dcl_id*)

This function is case sensitive. Suppose the dialog definition is named main. Specifying Main or MAIN will not activate this dialog box since the text string does not exactly match. The *dcl_id* argument represents the integer value returned by **(load_dialog)**. This value is often assigned to a variable, as you will see later. The **(new_dialog)** function also supports additional, optional arguments, which are not discussed here.

Figure 28-1.
A portion of the acad.dcl file.

```
acad_snap : dialog {
  label = "Drawing Aids";
  : row {
    : column {
      : boxed_column {
        label = "Modes";
        : toggle {
          label = "&Ortho";
          key = "ortho";
        }
        : toggle {
          label = "Solid &Fill";
          key = "fill";
        }
```

Dialog definition

Label attribute adds a text string

Key attribute identifies a text string that associates the dialog tile with an AutoLISP function

To actually begin accepting input from the user, the AutoLISP **(start_dialog)** function must be used:

```
(start_dialog)
```

This function has no arguments. It allows input to be received from the dialog box initialized by the previous **(new_dialog)** expression.

With these basic AutoLISP functions, it is possible to display the dialog box shown in **Figure 28-2.** You will create this dialog box in the next section. After the AutoLISP program is written and saved, it can be loaded into AutoCAD using the load function or the **APPLOAD** command. Enter the controlling AutoLISP application named EXAMPLE1.LSP as follows.

```
(setq EX1_DCL_ID (load_dialog "EXAMPLE1.DCL"))
(if (not (new_dialog "main" EX1_DCL_ID))
  (exit)
)
(start_dialog)
```

Now, take a closer look at the controlling code for this dialog box:

```
(setq EX1_DCL_ID (load_dialog "EXAMPLE1.DCL"))
(if (not (new_dialog "main" EX1_DCL_ID))
  (exit)
)
(start_dialog)
```

This expression loads the dialog definition found in EXAMPLE1.DCL and assigns the value returned by **(load_dialog)** to the variable **EX1_DCL_ID**.

```
(setq EX1_DCL_ID (load_dialog "EXAMPLE1.DCL"))
(if (not (new_dialog "main" EX1_DCL_ID))
  (exit)
)
(start_dialog)
```

If **(new_dialog)** is unable to activate the specified dialog box for any reason, the expression in the next three lines exits (terminates) the application. This is an important safety feature. In many cases, loading an incorrect or incomplete definition can cause your system to lock up and may require the system to be rebooted.

```
(setq EX1_DCL_ID (load_dialog "EXAMPLE1.DCL"))
(if (not (new_dialog "main" EX1_DCL_ID))
  (exit)
)
(start_dialog)
```

The last expression opens the dialog box indicated by the previous **(new_dialog)** expression.

Once the descriptions within a specific DCL file are no longer needed, they can be removed from memory using the AutoLISP **(unload_dialog)** function.

(unload_dialog *dcl_id*)

Do not unload a dialog definition until your application is finished using the DCL file. Otherwise, your application may fail to properly function.

Figure 28-2.
A sample custom dialog box.

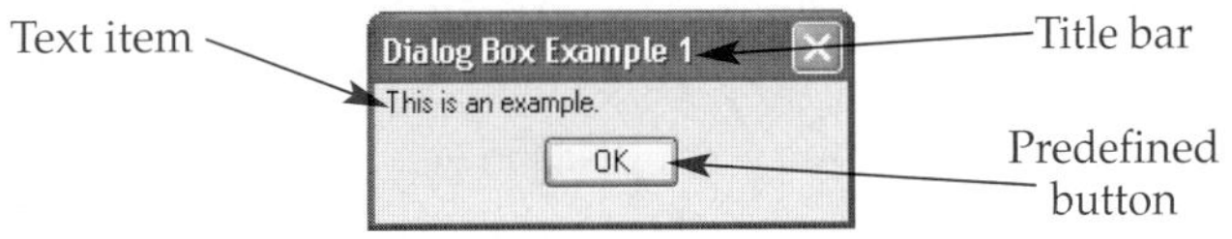

DCL Tiles

Your work in AutoCAD has provided you with a good background in how dialog boxes function. By now, you should be familiar with the use of buttons, edit boxes, radio buttons, and list boxes. This will be helpful as you design dialog interfaces for your AutoLISP programs.

DCL tiles are used individually or combined into structures called ***clusters.*** For example, a series of button tiles can be placed in a column tile to control the arrangement of the buttons in the dialog box. The primary tile is the dialog box itself.

The best way to begin understanding the format of a DCL file is to study a simple dialog box definition. The following DCL code defines the dialog box shown in **Figure 28-2.**

```
main : dialog {
  label = "Dialog Box Example 1";
  : text_part {
        value = "This is an example.";
  }
  ok_only;
}
```

Now, take a closer look at the definition of this dialog box. The ***dialog definition*** is always the first tile definition.

```
main : dialog {
  label = "Dialog Box Example 1";
  : text_part {
        value = "This is an example.";
  }
  ok_only;
}
```

Everything within the braces defines the features of the dialog box. The word "main" indicates the name of the dialog box within the code. This name is referenced by the controlling AutoLISP application. A colon (:) precedes all tile callouts. In the case of a dialog tile, the colon separates the name from the tile callout.

```
main : dialog {
  label = "Dialog Box Example 1";
  : text_part {
        value = "This is an example.";
  }
  ok_only;
}
```

The ***label*** attribute of the dialog tile controls the text that appears in the title bar of the dialog box. The line is terminated with a semicolon. All attribute lines must be terminated with a semicolon.

```
main : dialog {
  label = "Dialog Box Example 1";
  : text_part {
        value = "This is an example.";
  }
  ok_only;
}
```

The ***text_part*** tile allows placement of text items in a dialog box. The ***value*** attribute is used to specify the text that is displayed. Just as with the dialog tile, all of the attributes are defined between braces.

```
main : dialog {
  label = "Dialog Box Example 1";
  : text_part {
        value = "This is an example.";
  }
  ok_only;
}
```

There are many predefined tiles and subassemblies in the base.dcl file. A ***subassembly*** is a cluster of predefined tiles, such as **ok_cancel** and **ok_help**. The **ok_only** tile places an **OK** button at the bottom of the dialog box, as shown in **Figure 28-2.** The statement is not preceded by a colon because it is not a specific definition. This line is terminated with a semicolon, just like an attribute. Braces are not required because the statement is a reference to a predefined tile, rather than a tile definition.

Once you have defined a dialog box, the definition must then be saved in a DCL file. For this example, the dialog definition above should be saved in the file EXAMPLE1.DCL. This is treated as any other support file and should be saved in the AutoCAD support path.

For examples of other DCL functions, look at the **Viewpoint Presets** dialog box shown in **Figure 28-3.** Various tiles of this dialog box are identified with the corresponding DCL code needed to define the tile. In older releases of AutoCAD, this dialog box was defined by a stand-alone DCL file named ddvpoint.dcl. However, this DCL file no longer exists as the dialog box is now defined by a different method.

Figure 28-3.
Some of the tile definitions and attributes associated with the **Viewpoint Presets** dialog box (this dialog box is no longer defined by a DCL file).

```
ddvpoint : dialog {
  aspect_ratio = 0;
  label = "Viewpoint Presets";
  fixed_height = true;
  fixed_width  = true;
  : column {
    : row {
      : text {
        label = "Set Viewing Angles";
        key = "ddvp_header";
      }
    }
```

```
: row {
  : radio_row {
    : radio_button {
      label = "Absolute to WCS";
      key = "ddvp_abs_wcs";
      mnemonic = "W";
      value = "1";
    }
    : radio_button {
      label = "Relative to UCS";
      key = "ddvp_rel_ucs";
      mnemonic = "U";
    }
  }
}
```

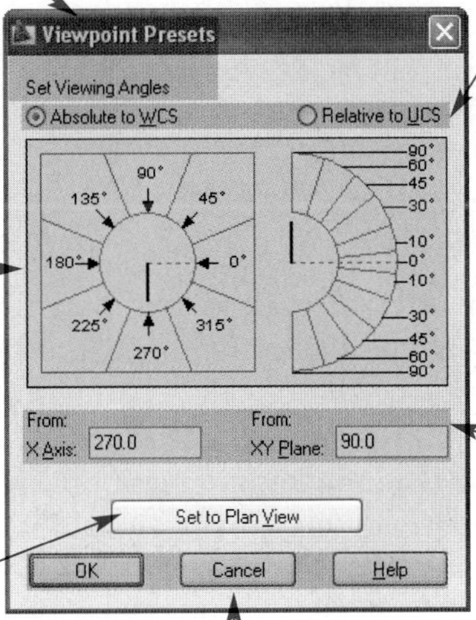


```
: row {
    fixed_width = true;
    fixed_height = true;
    : image_button {
      alignment = top;
      fixed_width = true;
      fixed_height = true;
      key = "ddvp_image";
      width  = 39;
      height = 12;
      color  = 0;
      is_tab_stop = false;
    }
  }
```

```
: row {
    : edit_box {
      label = "From:  X Axis:";
      mnemonic = "A";
      key = "ddvp_val_x";
      fixed_width = true;
      edit_width  = 6;
    }
    : edit_box {
      label = "XY Plane:";
      mnemonic = "P";
      key = "ddvp_val_xyp";
      fixed_width = true;
      edit_width  = 6;
    }
  }
```

```
: row {
    : button {
      label = "Set to Plan View";
      key = "ddvp_set_plan";
      mnemonic = "V";
    }
  }
}
```

```
spacer_1;
  ok_cancel_help_errtile;
}
```

Exercise 28-1

Complete the exercise on the Student CD.

Associating Functions with Tiles

Most tiles can be associated with actions. These actions vary from run-time error checking to performing tasks outside of the dialog box session. The **(action_tile)** AutoLISP function provides the basic means of associating tiles with actions.

(action_tile "*key*" "*action-expression*")

The *key* references the attribute assigned in the DCL file. The *action-expression* is the AutoLISP expression performed when the action is called. When the desired action requires a large amount of AutoLISP code, it is best to define a function to perform the required tasks. This function is then called within the *action-expression*. Both the *key* and *action-expression* arguments are supplied as text strings.

In order to access a specific tile from AutoLISP, the key of the tile must be referenced. The key is specified as an attribute in the DCL file. Tiles that are static (no associated action) do not require keys. Any tile that must be referenced in any way—such as setting or retrieving a value, associating an action, or enabling/disabling the tile—requires a key.

The next example changes the previous dialog box by adding a button that displays the current time when picked. The new or changed DCL code is shown in color. Save this file as EXAMPLE2.DCL.

```
main : dialog {
  label = "Dialog Box Example 2";
  : text_part {
          value  = "";
            key  = "time";
  }
  : button {
            key  = "update";
          label  = "Display Current Time";
     mnemonic  = "C";
  }
  ok_only;
}
```

Notice the addition of a key attribute to the **text_part** tile. This allows access by the AutoLISP application while the dialog box is open. Another addition is the **button** tile. A **key** attribute is provided in the **button** tile so an association can be created in the AutoLISP program with an *action-expression* argument. The **label** attribute provides the text displayed on the button. The **mnemonic** attribute underlines the specified letter within the label to allow keyboard access. The AutoLISP application used to manage this dialog session is as follows. Save the program as EXAMPLE2.LSP.

```
(setq EX2_DCL_ID (load_dialog "EXAMPLE2.DCL"))
(if   (not (new_dialog "main" EX2_DCL_ID))
      (exit)
)
(defun  UPDTILE ()
  (setq CDVAR (rtos (getvar "CDATE") 2 16)
      CDTXT (strcat "Current Time: "
         (substr CDVAR 10 2)
         ":"
         (substr CDVAR 12 2)
         ":"
         (substr CDVAR 14 2)
         )
  )
  (set_tile "time" CDTXT)
)
(UPDTILE)
(action_tile "update" "(UPDTILE)")
(start_dialog)
```

The dialog box displayed by this code is shown in **Figure 28-4.** The "time" button displays the current time when the button is picked. The mnemonic character is displayed once the [Alt] key is pressed. Note: Some AutoLISP functions not covered in this text are used in the above programming to retrieve and display the current time.

Commands that change the display or require user input (outside of the dialog interface) cannot be used while a dialog box is active. These AutoLISP functions cannot be used with DCL:

command	**getangle**	**getpoint**	**grread**	**prompt**
entdel	**getcorner**	**getreal**	**grtext**	**redraw**
entmake	**getdist**	**getstring**	**grvecs**	**ssget** (interactive)
entmod	**getint**	**graphscr**	**menucmd**	**textpage**
entsel	**getkword**	**grclear**	**nentsel**	**textscr**
entupd	**getorient**	**grdraw**	**osnap**	

Exercise 28-2

Complete the exercise on the Student CD.

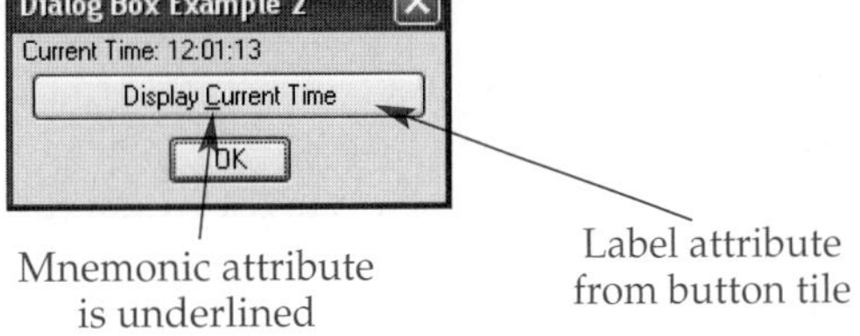

Figure 28-4.
The dialog box defined by EXAMPLE2.DCL and controlled by EXAMPLE2.LSP.

Working with DCL

There are many types of DCL tiles available. You can provide edit boxes for users to directly enter information, such as numeric or text information. You can create lists and drop-down lists to allow users to choose from preset selections. You can also add buttons to provide a simple means of initiating an action.

Images can be used to enhance dialog boxes. For example, you can place company or personal logos in your dialog boxes. An interactive image, such as the one that appears in the **Viewpoint Presets** dialog box shown in **Figure 28-3,** can also be used. Tools such as text tiles, sliders, and clusters are used to control the layout of tiles in a dialog box.

A wide variety of attributes are available for controlling the appearance and function of a dialog session. In addition, several AutoLISP functions are provided to control your dialog session. You can disable or enable tiles and change the active tile. It is even possible to change the value or state of a tile based on an entry in another tile.

You have already seen two examples of dialog boxes created using DCL and AutoLISP. The following sections provide two additional applications that use various dialog boxes. Study these examples for additional insight into the creation of dialog boxes. Be sure to have an appropriate reference handy, such as the online documentation, to look up DCL and AutoLISP terms. You can adapt or modify these programs to produce dialog sessions of your own.

Dialog Example 3

Create the following DCL and AutoLISP programs. Save the programs as EXAMPLE3.DCL and EXAMPLE3.LSP. Then, load the AutoLISP program file. To open the dialog box, type DRAW. The dialog box is shown in **Figure 28-5.**

```
;EXAMPLE3.LSP
;This file displays the dialog box defined in EXAMPLE3.DCL and begins the
; selected drawing command as specified by the user.
;
(defun C:DRAW (/ EX3_DCL_ID)
  (setq EX3_DCL_ID (load_dialog "EXAMPLE3.DCL"))
  (if (not (new_dialog "draw" EX3_DCL_ID))
    (exit)
  )
  (action_tile "line" "(setq CMD $key) (done_dialog)")
  (action_tile "circle" "(setq CMD $key) (done_dialog)")
  (action_tile "arc" "(setq CMD $key) (done_dialog)")
  (action_tile "cancel" "(setq CMD nil) (done_dialog)")
  (start_dialog)
  (unload_dialog EX3_DCL_ID)
  (command CMD)
)
```

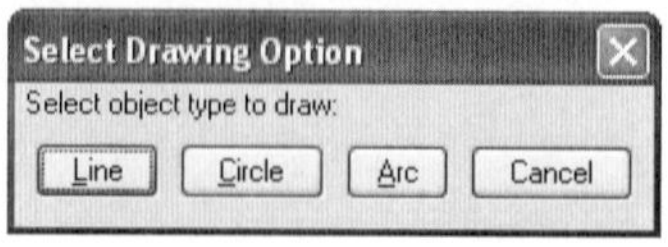

Figure 28-5.
The dialog box displayed using the EXAMPLE3 DCL and LSP files.

```
//EXAMPLE3.DCL
//Defines a dialog box that presents three drawing options to the user.
//
draw : dialog {
  label = "Select Drawing Option";
  :  text_part {
     label = "Select object type to draw: ";
  }
  : row {
     : button {
        key           = "line";
        label         = "Line";
        mnemonic      = "L";
        fixed_width   = true;
     }
     : button {
        key           = "circle";
        label         = "Circle";
        mnemonic      = "C";
        fixed_width   = true;
     }
     : button {
        key           = "arc";
        label         = "Arc";
        mnemonic      = "A";
        fixed_width   = true;
     }
     : button {
        key           = "cancel";
        label         = "Cancel";
        is_cancel     = true;
        fixed_width   = true;
     }
  }
}
```

Dialog Example 4

This example allows you to select a new current layer from a drop-down list in a dialog box. Save the files as EXAMPLE4.DCL and EXAMPLE4.LSP. Then, load the AutoLISP file. To access the dialog box, type GOFOR. The dialog box is shown in **Figure 28-6.**

```
;;EXAMPLE4.LSP
;;
(defun CHECKOUT ()
   (setq LD (tblsearch "LAYER" (nth (atoi (get_tile "lyr_pop")) LL))
      LN (cdr (assoc 2 LD))
      LS (cdr (assoc 70 LD))
   )
   (if (and
         (/= 1 LS)
         (/= 65 LS)
      )
      (progn
         (setvar "CLAYER" (nth (atoi (get_tile "lyr_pop")) LL))
         (done_dialog)
      )
      (alert "Selected layer is frozen!")
) )
(defun C:GOFOR ()
   (setq EX4_DCL_ID (load_dialog "EXAMPLE4.DCL"))
   (if (not (new_dialog "fourth" EX4_DCL_ID)) (exit))
   (start_list "lyr_pop")
   (setq LL '()
      NL (tblnext "LAYER" T)
      IDX 0
   )
   (while   NL
         (if (= (getvar "CLAYER") (cdr (assoc 2 NL)))
            (setq CL IDX)
            (setq IDX (1+ IDX))
         )
         (setq LL (append LL (list (cdr (assoc 2 NL))))
            NL (tblnext "LAYER")
   )     )
   (mapcar 'add_list LL)
   (end_list)
   (set_tile "lyr_pop" (itoa CL))
   (action_tile "lyr_pop" "(if (= $reason 4) (mode_tile \"accept\" 2))")
   (action_tile "accept" "(CHECKOUT)")
   (start_dialog)
   (unload_dialog EX4_DCL_ID)
   (princ)
)
```

Figure 28-6.
The dialog box displayed using the EXAMPLE4 DCL and LSP files.

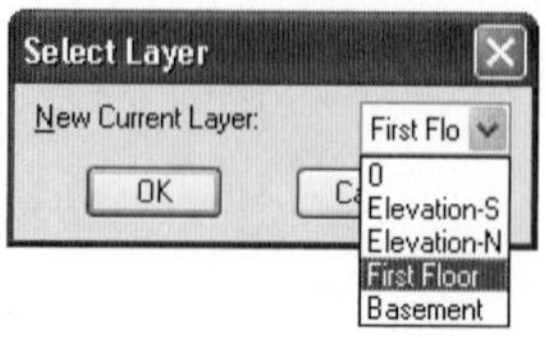

```
//EXAMPLE4.DCL
// Presents a list of layers to the user.
fourth : dialog {
  label = "Select Layer";
  : popup_list {
    label          = "New Current Layer:";
    mnemonic       = "N";
    key            = "lyr_pop";
    allow_accept   = true;
    width          = 32;
  }
  ok_cancel;
}
```

Chapter Test

Answer the following questions. Write your answers on a separate sheet of paper or complete the electronic chapter test on the Student CD.

1. What are the two types of files that must be created to construct a functioning dialog box?
2. When referring to a dialog box, what is a *tile?*
3. When defining a dialog or tile, inside of which character are all of the required attributes for a tile definition placed?
4. Which symbol indicates a comment inside of a DCL file?
5. Write the appropriate notation for the first line of a DCL file that defines a dialog box named **Test**.
6. Write the appropriate notation in a DCL file that defines the text in the title bar of a dialog box named **Select Application**.
7. Write the notation in a DCL file for defining a cluster of four buttons labeled **OK**, **Next**, **Cancel**, and **Help**.
8. Which type of file is commonly used to control a DCL file?
9. Write the notation that would appear in the file in question 8 that loads a dialog file named **PICKFILE**.
10. What is a *key* in a DCL file?
11. What is the function of a *mnemonic* attribute?
12. Write the proper DCL file notation for the first line that identifies a button.

Drawing Problems

1. Create a dialog box that contains the following items. Write the required DCL and AutoLISP files.
   A. Title bar—**Dialog Box Test**
   B. Label—**This is a test.**
   C. **OK** button

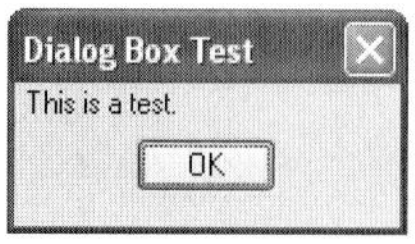

2. Create a dialog box that contains the following items. Write the required DCL and AutoLISP files.
   A. Title bar—**Date**
   B. Label—**Current Date:**
   C. Action button—**Display Current Date**
   D. **OK** button

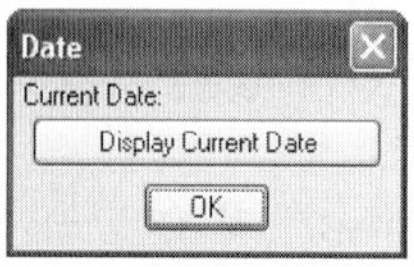

3. Create a dialog box that performs the following tasks. Then, write the required DCL and AutoLISP files.
   A. Displays the current date.
   B. Displays the current time.
   C. Contains buttons to display and update current date and time.
   D. Displays the current drawing name.
   E. Contains an **OK** button.

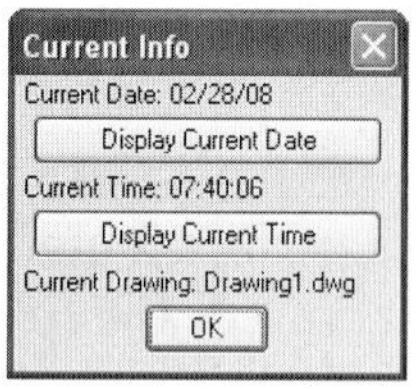

CHAPTER 29

Introduction to Visual Basic for Applications (VBA)

Learning Objectives

After completing this chapter, you will be able to:

- ✓ Explain object-oriented programming.
- ✓ Describe the AutoCAD object model.
- ✓ Change an object's properties.
- ✓ Use an object's methods.
- ✓ Use the **VBA Manager**.
- ✓ Develop a VBA project using the **Visual Basic Editor**.
- ✓ Explain the data types used in VBA.
- ✓ Store data in variables.
- ✓ Run a VBA macro.
- ✓ Create a form (dialog box) in a VBA project.

Visual Basic for Applications (VBA) is a version of Microsoft's Visual Basic (VB) programming language that is built into AutoCAD. All of the features of the full version of VB are included, in addition to functions and procedures that are specific to programming the AutoCAD application. This chapter is intended to give you an overview of the basics of VBA. You will learn how easy to use, and yet powerful, the language is. This chapter is by no means an in-depth look at VBA. For more complete discussions and study of VBA within AutoCAD, refer to *VBA for AutoCAD* published by The Goodheart-Willcox Company, Inc.

Object-Oriented Programming

VBA is an *object-oriented* programming language. Although lines, arcs, and circles are objects, AutoCAD entities are not the only objects. The many "parts" that make up the AutoCAD application itself are considered objects. The whole program and all that it is composed of are considered the *object model.* The AutoCAD object model contains all of the objects and provides access to their methods, properties, and events in a tree-like hierarchy. See **Figure 29-1.** To display this object model, select **Help**>**Additional Resources**>**Developer Help** in the menu browser. In the left-hand pane (**Contents** tab) of the help that is displayed, select **ActiveX and VBA Reference**. Finally, in the right-hand pane, select **Object Model**.

Figure 29-1.
The object model for AutoCAD.

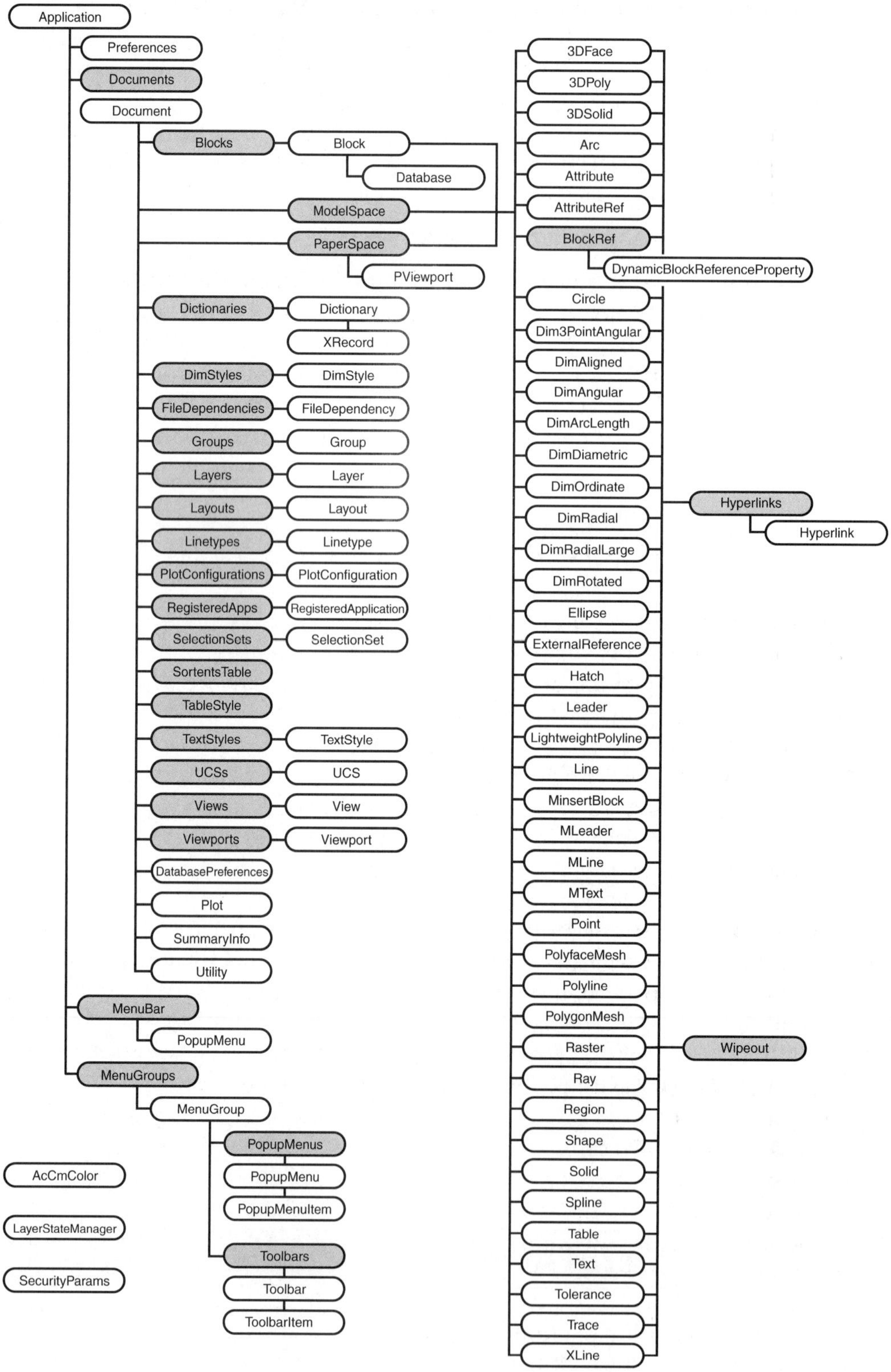

Notice that the AutoCAD **Application** object itself is the upper-most object in the hierarchy. The application is considered the *root* of the tree. Under the application are branches for **Preferences**, **Documents**, **Document**, **MenuBar**, and **MenuGroups**. Each of these is considered an object. Through the **Application** object and then through these five objects (branches of the tree), all of the methods, properties, and events can be accessed for all of the objects in the AutoCAD program.

For example, to change the size of the pick box to four, you must go through the hierarchy to get to that object's properties using the following code. Each level, or branch, of the object model is separated by a period.

```
Application.Preferences.Selection.PickBoxSize = 4
```

The above code introduces another level in the hierarchy: **Selection**. The **Selection** object is a subobject of the **Preferences** object. The **Preferences** object holds those options in AutoCAD's **Options** dialog box that are stored in the registry. The **Preferences** object is made up of subobjects that represent each of the tabs in the **Options** dialog box. Working from AutoCAD's point of view, rather than VBA's point of view, the pick box size is set on the **Selection** tab of the **Options** dialog box in the AutoCAD application.

Methods, Properties, and Events

Each object within the object model has various methods, properties, and events associated with it. The set of available methods, properties, and events is unique for each object. However, some methods, properties, and events are available to multiple objects. Some objects do not have any methods, properties, or events available to them.

Methods are functions built into the objects that allow the object's properties to be modified. Some examples of methods that are available to a few objects include:

- The **Circle** object has a **Move** method and 18 other methods.
- The **Layer** object has a **Delete** method and three other methods.
- The **ModelSpace** object has an **AddLine** method and 51 other methods.
- The **Document** object has a **Close** method and 19 other methods.

Properties are the "settings" associated with an object, similar to the properties of AutoCAD entities that are found in the **Properties** dialog box. Other, non-AutoCAD-entity objects have properties, too. Some examples of properties that are associated with a few objects include:

- The **Circle** object has a **Layer** property and 20 other properties.
- The **Layer** object has a **Freeze** property and 19 other properties.
- The **ModelSpace** object has a **Count** property and six other properties.
- The **Document** object has an **ActiveSpace** property and 48 other properties.

Events are actions that occur while a VBA program or macro is running. An event can be monitored (continuously checked) and, if it occurs, another action can be triggered. An event can be as simple as the user picking the **OK** button to close a dialog box. For example, you can create a VBA program that changes the linetype scale setting when the user switches from model space to paper (layout) space. Some examples of events that are associated with a few objects include:

- The **Circle** object has a **Modified** event.
- The **Layer** object has a **Modified** event.
- The **ModelSpace** object has a **Modified** event.
- The **Document** object has a **LayoutSwitched** event and 27 other events.

Events are beyond the scope of this text. For more information on using events in VBA macros, refer to *VBA for AutoCAD* published by The Goodheart-Willcox Company, Inc.

Exercise 29-1

Complete the exercise on the Student CD.

Understanding How a VBA Program Works

VBA programs are actually called projects. A ***project*** consists of the forms and modules necessary to obtain the desired outcome. VBA refers to dialog boxes as ***forms. Modules*** are the **Sub** procedures that actually contain the program code. ***Sub procedures*** are subroutines, or small programs, that can be called from within other procedures. A ***macro*** is a **Sub** that is declared as **Public**, meaning it will show up in AutoCAD's **Macros** dialog box. The terms *projects, modules, macros, subs,* and *forms* are used throughout this chapter.

Projects can be stored in two locations: in a file or in a drawing. A project stored in a drawing is considered ***embedded.*** That project is automatically loaded and its macros are available each time the drawing in which the project is embedded is opened. A project stored in a file has a .dvb file extension and must be loaded in order for its macros to be available in the drawing. A project stored as a DVB file is considered ***global*** as it can be loaded into any drawing from any computer that has access to the DVB file. If the project is saved as a file named acad.dvb and the file is in the AutoCAD search path, it is loaded each time a drawing is opened. Interestingly, once a project has been loaded into one drawing, its macros are available to all open drawings, as long as the drawing into which the project was loaded remains open.

Using the VBA Manager

VBAMAN

Ribbon
Tools
> Applications
VBA Manager
Type
VBAMAN
Menu
Tools
> Macro
> VBA Manager...

The **VBA Manager** dialog box allows a project to be loaded or embedded. See **Figure 29-2.** It also allows a project to be created or saved to a file. The **VBAMAN** command opens the dialog box.

The active drawing file is shown at the top of the dialog box. Any other open drawings are available within the drop-down list. Just below the drop-down list, the name of the embedded project is shown, if a project is embedded in that drawing. Only one project can be embedded in a drawing at a time.

The **Projects** area in the middle of the dialog box lists all of the projects that are currently loaded. This list shows the name and location of the project. If the project is stored as a DVB file, the file name and path are shown. If the project is embedded in a drawing, the drawing name and path are shown.

On the right side of the dialog box are several buttons. These buttons are described below.

- **Extract.** Picking this button removes the embedded project. A message box appears asking if you would like to save the project to a file before extracting it from the drawing.
- **Embed.** This button allows a project to be embedded in a drawing. A project must be selected from the **Projects** list and the drawing in which you want to embed the project must be selected in the **Drawing** drop-down list. Only one project can be embedded in a drawing at a time.

Figure 29-2.
The **VBA Manager** in AutoCAD.

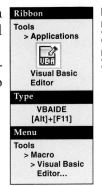

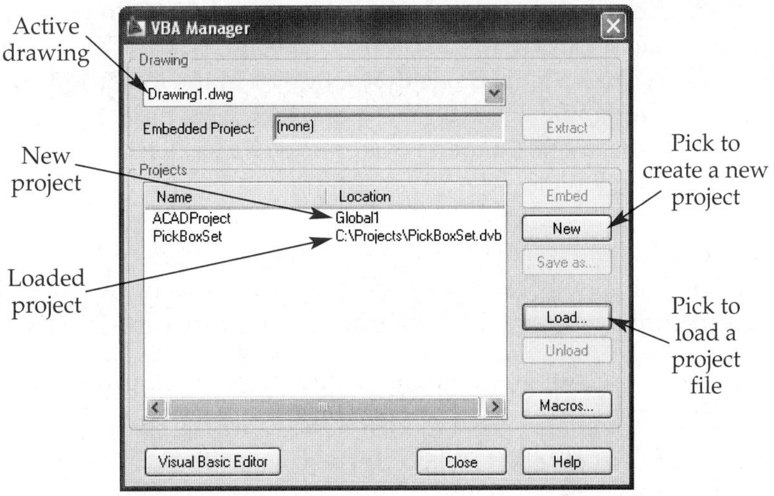

- **New.** Picking this button creates a new project and adds it to the **Projects** list. The new project has the default name ACADProject name and is generically listed as Global*n*, where *n* is a sequential integer. The project name can only be changed in the **Visual Basic Editor**, which is covered in the next section. The Global*n* location is updated when the project is saved as a file or embedded in a drawing.
- **Save as.** Use this button to save to a file the project highlighted in the **Projects** list. A standard Windows "save as" dialog box appears when the button is picked.
- **Load.** Picking this button displays a standard Windows "open" dialog box in which you can select a project file (DVB) to be loaded. The project is loaded into the drawing selected in the **Drawing** drop-down list.
- **Unload.** This button allows a project to be unloaded, making its macros unavailable. Highlight the project to unload in the **Projects** list and then pick this button.
- **Macros.** Picking this button closes the **VBA Manager** dialog box and opens the **Macros** dialog box. The available macros are listed in the **Macros** dialog box. The **Macros** dialog box has a **VBA Manager...** button that displays the **VBA Manager** dialog box.

There is also the **Visual Basic Editor** button in the lower-left corner of the **VBA Manager** dialog box. Picking this button opens the **Visual Basic Editor**, which is covered in the next section.

Using the Visual Basic Editor

The **Visual Basic Editor** is a full featured, built-in editor for VBA programming in AutoCAD. The **VBAIDE** command displays the **Visual Basic Editor**. It can also be opened by picking the **Visual Basic Editor** button from within the **VBA Manager** dialog box.

VBAIDE

Ribbon
Tools
> Applications
Visual Basic Editor

Type
VBAIDE
[Alt]+[F11]

Menu
Tools
> Macro
> Visual Basic Editor...

Now that you have been introduced to VBA terminology and have a basic understanding of how to manipulate projects, you will create a project to allow you to examine the **Visual Basic Editor**. To avoid confusion, first unload all loaded projects:

1. Open the **VBA Manager**.
2. Select a project in the **Projects** list.
3. Pick the **Unload** button.
4. Do the same for all other projects until the **Projects** list is empty.

5. Pick the **New** button. A project named ACADProject is added to the **Projects** list and its location is shown as Global*n*.
6. Pick the **Visual Basic Editor** button in the lower-left corner of the **VBA Manager** dialog box.

The **Visual Basic Editor** has several key areas. See **Figure 29-3.** At the upper, left is the **Project Explorer** window. All loaded projects are listed in this area, as well as the AutoCAD objects, forms, and modules associated with the project. The project name is shown and next to the name in parentheses is the project location. The objects, forms, and modules are shown in a tree below the project name. At the lower, left of the **Visual Basic Editor** is the **Properties** window. This window is used to set the various object properties used in the program. It will be most often used when creating forms. The right-hand side is the "desktop" where the **Code** window will be displayed while writing the program.

You will create a short macro for enlarging the size of the pick box. The macro will be stored in a project called PickBoxSet.dvb. Later, you will add another macro to the project to change the pick box to the default size. Notice the **Project Explorer** window shows the project as ACADProject and the project location as Global*n*. Also, notice the ThisDrawing branch listed under the AutoCAD Objects branch in the tree. Continue as follows.

1. Select ACADProject in the **Project Explorer** window. Notice that ACADProject is now shown in the **Properties** window next to the (Name) property.
2. Pick in the text box next to the (Name) property in the **Properties** window, change the name to PickBoxSet, and press [Enter]. Notice that the **Project Explorer** window now shows the project name as PickBoxSet. This named the project within the drawing; it did *not* save the project to a file.
3. Select **Module** from the **Insert** pull-down menu in the **Visual Basic Editor**. The **Code** window is opened on the **Visual Basic Editor** desktop. Also, notice that a Modules branch has been added in the **Project Explorer** window and Module1 is listed in this branch. Module1 is highlighted in the **Project Explorer** window and listed in the **Properties** window.
4. In the **Properties** window, change the name of Module1 to PickBoxBig. Notice that the module name is updated in the **Project Explorer** window and in the title bar of the **Code** window.

Figure 29-3.
The **Visual Basic Editor**.

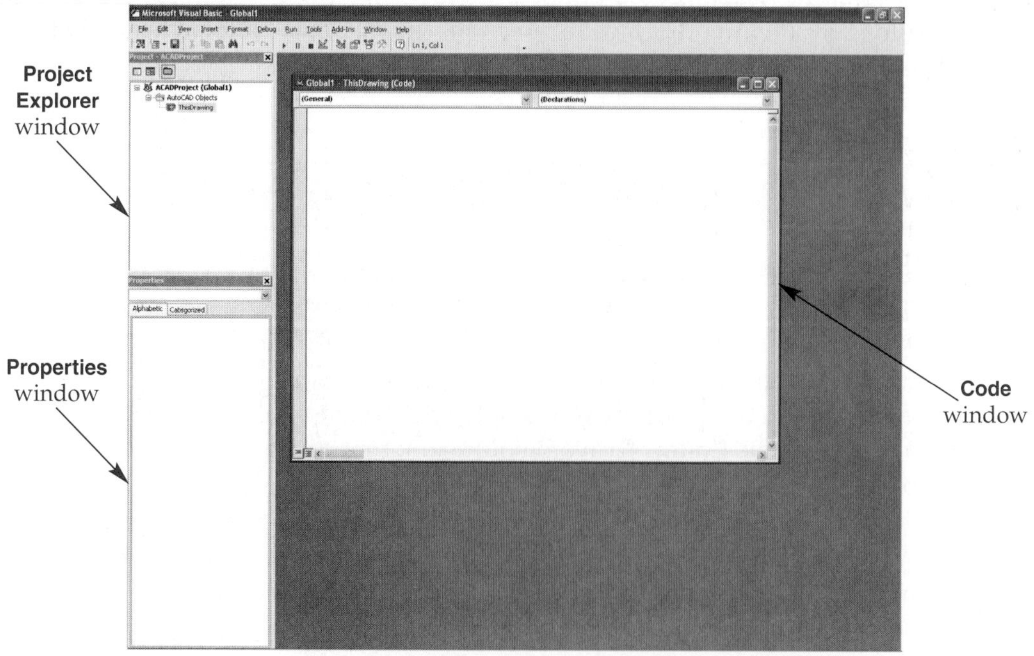

Figure 29-4.
Adding a procedure.

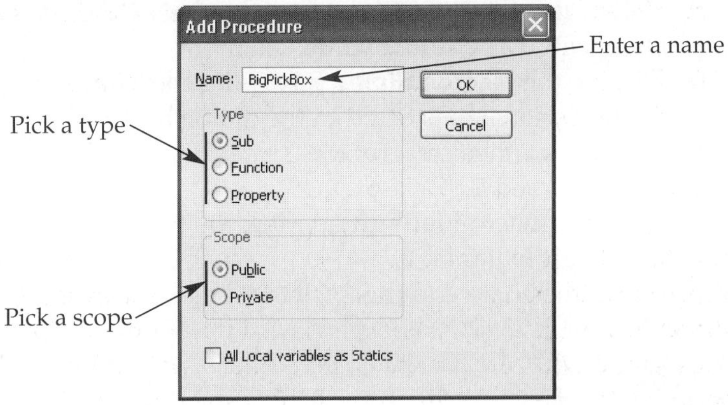

5. Pick inside of the **Code** window. Notice the blinking, vertical cursor in the window, similar to how it would appear in a text editor.
6. Select **Procedure...** from the **Insert** pull-down menu in the **Visual Basic Editor**. The **Add Procedure** dialog box appears, **Figure 29-4.** Enter BigPickBox in the **Name:** text box. Pick the **Sub** and **Public** radio buttons. Then, pick the **OK** button to close the dialog box.

Notice that some code is automatically entered in the **Code** window. The Public Sub BigPickBox () line is the syntax for the beginning of a **Public Sub**. The End Sub line is the syntax used for the ending of a **Sub**. The remainder of the code for the **Sub** is entered between these two lines of code. Continue as follows.

7. On the first line after Public Sub BigPickBox (), type:

```
Application.Preferences.Selection.PickBoxSize = 7
```

Notice that the editor has a feature called **Auto List Members**. After you type the period following the object name, a list of methods and procedures associated with that object appears. Typing the first letter of the method or property you want scrolls the list to that letter. You can continue typing or use the up and down arrow keys to highlight the word you want. When the word you want is highlighted, press the [Tab] key and the word is entered for you. If you want to select a method or property of the new object, type another period and the **Auto List Members** feature is displayed for the new object. This greatly reduces the amount of typing needed to get to nested objects. The module (macro) is now complete. Test the macro in AutoCAD:

8. Return to AutoCAD by picking the **View AutoCAD** button in the **Visual Basic Editor**. See **Figure 29-5.**

Figure 29-5.
Picking the **View AutoCAD** button returns you to AutoCAD.

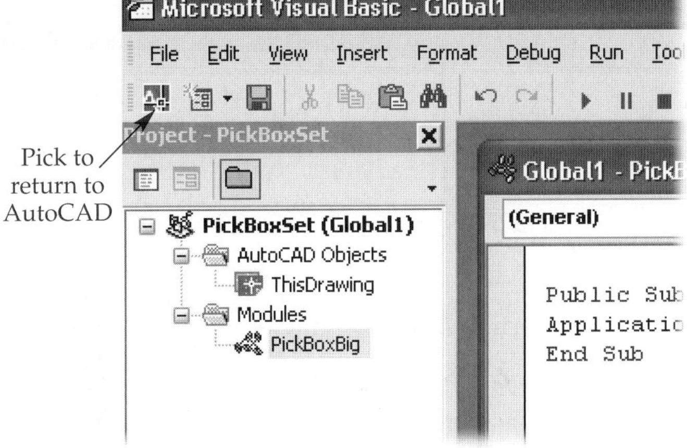

VBARUN

Ribbon
Tools > Applications

Run VBA Macro
Type
VBARUN
Menu
Tools > Macro > Macros...

9. Determine the current setting for the **PICKBOX** system variable. If it is 7, change it to a different value.
10. Display the **Macros** dialog box using the **VBARUN** command. Notice that the BigPickBox macro is listed in the dialog box. See **Figure 29-6.** The name shows that it is a global macro, it is stored in a module named PickBoxBig, and the **Sub** is named BigPickBox.
11. With the macro highlighted, pick the **Run** button. Notice that the pick box is now slightly larger.
12. Verify the change to the **PICKBOX** system variable.

PROFESSIONAL TIP

Be sure that the **PICKFIRST** system variable is set to 1 (noun/verb selection enabled) so that the pick box is displayed with the cross-hairs. Also, you can use a higher value in the macro to make the change in the pick box size easier to see.

You have just created your first VBA macro! You will now add another module to change the pick box back to the default size and then save the project as a DVB file. Follow these steps:

1. Display the **Visual Basic Editor**.
2. Pick inside of the **Code** window to make it active.
3. Select **Procedure...** from the **Insert** pull-down menu.
4. In the **Add Procedure** dialog box, enter NormPickBox as the name of the new **Sub**. Also, pick the **Sub** and **Public** radio buttons, then pick the **OK** button.
5. Enter the following code in the new **Sub**. Remember, type the code between the Public Sub and the End Sub lines.

```
Application.Preferences.Selection.PickBoxSize = 3
```

6. Display AutoCAD.
7. Display the **Macros** dialog box. Notice the new macro is now listed along with the first macro. Select the new macro and pick the **Run** button.
8. Notice that the pick box size is now set to the default size. The default **PICKBOX** value is 3.

Figure 29-6. The **Macros** dialog box is used to select a macro to run.

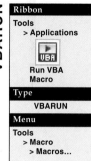

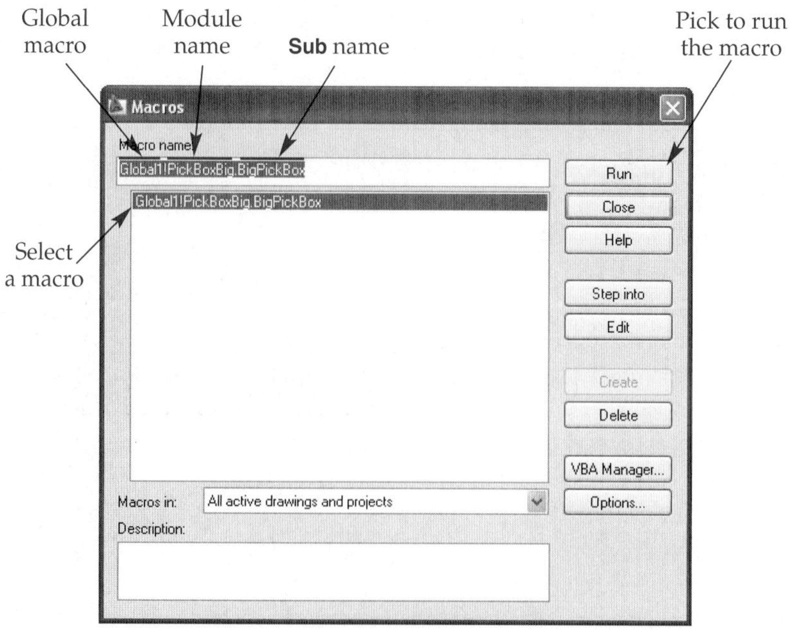

9. Display the **Visual Basic Editor**.
10. Pick the **Save** button on the toolbar in the **Visual Basic Editor**. A standard Windows "save as" dialog box appears. Save the file under the name PickBoxSet in the folder of your choice. The .dvb extension is automatically added.

As you work through the rest of the chapter, enter each example in the **Code** window in the **Visual Basic Editor**. Then, test each example using **Macros** dialog box in AutoCAD.

Exercise 29-2

Complete the exercise on the Student CD.

Dealing with Data Types

The concept of programming revolves around gathering, storing, and reusing data. The data used by programs come in various ***data types.*** In the previous project, the macro set the pick box size by providing an integer. An integer is considered a data type. As you learn to use VBA to manipulate the AutoCAD environment in other ways and to create and modify AutoCAD entities, you will need to use other data types.

Although there are many data types available and needed while programming in VBA, only a few are often used while working in AutoCAD. The more common data types used in AutoCAD are strings, integers, real numbers, and variants. Integers and real numbers are each further broken down into two types covering different ranges of numbers.

Data type	Range	Description
String		Text characters.
Integer	–32,768 to 32,767	Small integer values.
Long	–2,147,483,648 to 2,147,483,647	Large integer values.
Single	1.4E–45 to 3.4E+48	Single precision floating point numbers.
Double	4.94E–324 to 1.8E+308	Double precision floating point numbers.
Variant		Typically used to denote coordinates.

For the examples in the rest of this chapter, you will use the **String**, **Integer**, **Double**, and **Variant** data types. The practical applications for these data types are:

- **String.** Used for command names, prompts, AutoCAD system variables, and so on. When using strings within a program, the characters making up the string are enclosed in quotation marks "like this".
- **Integer.** Used for counting. Often, the program has to progress through a list in increments. Integers are used to do so.
- **Double.** Used for lengths; distances; and X, Y, or Z coordinate values (when dealing with X, Y, and Z separately).
- **Variant.** Used for point coordinates (when working with X, Y, and Z values together).

Using Variables

A ***variable*** is a named memory location that holds a value. The name given to a variable should have a prefix based on the type of data that it is holding. Refer to the following table.

Data type	Prefix	Example
String	str	strFirstName
Integer	int	intCount
Double	dbl	dblDist1
Variant	var	varCenterPoint

In VBA, before a variable name is assigned a value, it must be ***declared*** as to which type of data will be stored. The syntax to do this is:

Dim *variable_name* As *data_type*

Applying this syntax to the examples in the above table:

```
Dim strFirstName As String
Dim intCount As Integer
Dim dblDist1 As Double
Dim varCenterPoint As Variant
```

Once a variable has been declared, a value can be assigned to it. This is accomplished with the **=** assignment operator. The syntax for assigning a value to a *data variable* is:

variable_name = *value*

Examples of how this looks in the **Code** window of the **Visual Basic Editor** are:

```
strFirstName = "John"
intCount = 10
dblDist1 = 135.75
```

Allowing for User Interaction

The last examples in the previous section are referred to as *hard coding* of variables. The variables are not really "variable," rather they are being directly set by the programmer. Look at this line of code:

```
strFirstName = "John"
```

This would work great if everyone in the world was named John. VBA provides methods that allow prompting the user for values and retrieving those values. There is a specific method for each data type that a program may need. To handle the **String**, **Integer**, **Real**, and **Variant** data types, there are the **GetString**, **GetInteger**, **GetReal**, and **GetPoint** methods, respectively.

There are also data-conversion methods for changing the data type of a variable when this is necessary. Most of these methods are found in the **Utility** object, along with most of the user-interaction methods. The **Utility** object is a subobject of the **ActiveDocument** object, which, in turn, is a subobject of the **Application** object.

PROFESSIONAL TIP

To make coding a little easier, the **ThisDrawing** object can be used as an alias for the **Application.ActiveDocument** object.

To store a string supplied by the user, the **Utility** object's **GetString** method is used. The **GetString** method has one required argument, which must come first, and one optional argument, which must come second. An ***argument*** is additional information that can be passed to the method. The arguments are listed within parentheses immediately after the method. Each argument is separated by a comma. This additional information is required in some instances and optional in other instances.

In the case of the **GetString** method, the first argument is a **TRUE** or **FALSE** test and determines whether or not the string that the user enters can contain spaces. Actually, it determines whether the space bar is interpreted as a space or as the [Enter] key. If the argument is **FALSE**, spaces are not allowed. If the user presses the space bar, the text input is ended. If the argument is **TRUE**, spaces are allowed in the input string.

The second argument for the **GetString** method is an optional prompt. If included, it must be a string. The provided string is displayed on the command line when the method is called. This can be used to let the user know what is expected of them. Even though this argument is optional, it is almost always included.

The following code gets a string input by the user and stores it in a variable. Notice that spaces are not allowed in the string.

```
Dim strName as String
strName = ThisDrawing.Utility.GetString(FALSE,"First name only: ")
```

Now that the value is stored, it can be used in some way. For the test macro, it will just be sent to the command line using the **Prompt** method. The **Prompt** method requires one argument, which must be a string. The data stored in the strName variable represent a string, so pass this variable to the **Prompt** method:

```
ThisDrawing.Utility.Prompt (strName)
```

Another feature of the **Visual Basic Editor** becomes apparent as you enter functions that can have arguments passed to them. The **Auto Quick Info** feature displays information about the arguments as soon as you type the opening parenthesis. The argument that you are "working on" is in bold. Arguments that are optional are shown enclosed in brackets. Required arguments are shown without brackets.

The following shows additional example code for the **GetInteger**, **GetReal**, and **GetPoint** methods. For each method, the variable is passed to the **Prompt** variable.

```
Sub GetSamples ()

  Dim strName as String
  strName = ThisDrawing.Utility.GetString(FALSE,"First name only: ")
  ThisDrawing.Utility.Prompt (strName)

  Dim intNumber as Integer
  intNumber = ThisDrawing.Utility.GetInteger("Enter an integer: ")
  ThisDrawing.Utility.Prompt (intNumber)

  Dim dblNumber as Double
  dblNumber = ThisDrawing.Utility.GetReal("Enter a real number: ")
  ThisDrawing.Utility.Prompt (dblNumber)

  Dim varPoint as Variant
  varPoint = ThisDrawing.Utility.GetPoint(, "Pick a point: ")
  ThisDrawing.Utility.Prompt (varPoint(0) & ", " & varPoint(1))

End Sub
```

Some items of note regarding the **GetPoint** code:

- The **GetPoint** method can have two arguments, but in this case only a prompt string argument needs to be supplied. However, this must be the second argument. The first argument is left blank, but still separated from the second argument with a comma.
- The **GetPoint** method returns (produces) a set of X, Y, and Z coordinates. These three values are stored in what is called an *array* in VBA, which is similar to an AutoLISP list. The items in an array are indexed beginning with 0, rather than 1. So, the X value is in the array at an index of 0, the Y value at index 1, and the Z value at index 2. Each item can be passed as an argument by using its index in the array. In the above example, the X and Y values (at index positions 0 and 1) are passed to the **Prompt** method.
- The **Prompt** method can only have one argument, a string, passed to it. Multiple strings can be *concatenated* (added together) using the ampersand (**&**). In the above example, only the X value varPoint(0) and Y value varPoint(1) are supplied and they are separated by a comma and a space (", ").

Exercise 29-3

Complete the exercise on the Student CD.

Creating AutoCAD Entities

AutoCAD entities can be created using VBA. The following sample code creates a circle. Later in this section, sample code is provided that creates a line.

```
Sub CreateCircle()

Dim objCircle As AcadCircle
Dim varCP As Variant
Dim dblRadius As Double

varCP = ThisDrawing.Utility.GetPoint(, "Center point for circle: ")
dblRadius = ThisDrawing.Utility.GetReal("Enter circle radius: ")

Set objCircle = ThisDrawing.ModelSpace.AddCircle(varCP, dblRadius)

End Sub
```

The **Set** statement and **=** assignment operator are used to assign a reference to a particular object type. This is how you store a value in an *object variable.* The **AddCircle** method is used to create a circle, in this case as a member of the **ModelSpace** collection (created in model space). This example also introduces a new data type. **AcadCircle** is an object data type exclusive to AutoCAD. Variables for use with object data types have their names prefixed with obj. A list of all AutoCAD-specific object data types is located in the developer's help:

1. In AutoCAD, select **Help>Additional Resources>Developer Help** from the menu browser.
2. In the left-hand pane (**Contents** tab), select **ActiveX and VBA Reference.**
3. In the right-hand pane, select **Objects.**

4. The right-hand pane now displays a list of all AutoCAD-specific data types. Picking on an object name displays information specific to that data type.

The next example creates a line between two points that the user selects. This example is similar to the previous example.

```
Sub CreateLine()

Dim objLine As AcadLine
Dim varFP As Variant
Dim varNP As Variant

varFP = ThisDrawing.Utility.GetPoint(, "Select first point for line: ")
varNP = ThisDrawing.Utility.GetPoint(varFP, "Select last point for line: ")

Set objLine = ThisDrawing.ModelSpace.AddLine(varFP, varNP)

End Sub
```

The only new concept introduced in this macro is that the first selected point, which is stored in a variable as a **Variant** data type, is being passed as the first argument for the second use of the **GetPoint** method. By including this, a "drag line" is shown from the first point to the cursor location until the second point is picked or entered.

Exercise 29-4

Complete the exercise on the Student CD.

Editing AutoCAD Entities

Editing an AutoCAD entity typically involves changing one of its properties. In order to do that, the user must be allowed to select the entity. Then, the properties of the entity can be accessed. The **GetEntity** method allows the user to pick an entity, returns the object and the point used to select it, and provides for a prompt that can be used to let the user know what to do. The following code allows the user to specify a radius and then to select a circle to change.

```
Sub ChngCirRad()

Dim objCir As AcadCircle
Dim varPt As Variant
Dim dblCirRad As Double

dblCirRad = ThisDrawing.Utility.GetReal("Enter new circle radius: ")
ThisDrawing.Utility.GetEntity objCir, varPt, "Pick a circle: "

objCir.Radius = dblCirRad

End Sub
```

The **GetEntity** method assigns both the selected object and the selection point to the variable. This is similar to the argument-passing concept. A third argument is the prompting string. Notice how the **Radius** property of the variable objCir, which is an **AcadCircle** data type, is set equal to the value of the dblCirRad variable.

Exercise 29-5

Complete the exercise on the Student CD.

Creating a Dialog Box Using VBA

When programming using VBA, dialog boxes are called ***forms.*** The command buttons, option buttons, labels, text boxes, and other items that are found on forms are called ***controls.*** Adding forms to your programs and controls to your forms is rather easy. If you are familiar with AutoLISP and Dialog Control Language (DCL) programming, you will find VBA's approach to dialog box creation much simpler.

This section shows you how to add a form to a VBA project, use some of the available controls, add code to those controls, and create a macro that will call the dialog box. It is not meant to be an in-depth discussion on forms and their many possible uses. When you have completed this section, you will have a good overview of the concepts of forms and controls, as well as created a very handy program. For more detailed information on VBA forms, refer to *VBA for AutoCAD* published by The Goodheart-Willcox Company, Inc.

The example in this section creates a program that adds and subtracts the areas of circles and polylines selected by the user. The program has a dialog box (form) interface, which has buttons to be used for adding and subtracting objects. The area of the last object selected is shown in the dialog box along with the running total area. See **Figure 29-7.**

Step 1: Begin a New Project

1. In AutoCAD, open the **VBA Manager** dialog box. Pick the **New** button. Make note of the location.
2. Pick the **Visual Basic Editor** button to open the **Visual Basic Editor**.
3. In the **Project Explorer** window, highlight the ACADProject that was just created. The location appears at the end of the name.
4. In the **Properties** window, pick in the (Name) property text box.
5. Change the name of the project to AreaCalc.
6. Pick the **Save** button on the toolbar in the **Visual Basic Editor** to save the project.
7. Name the project AreaCalc.dvb and put it in a folder of your choice. Notice that the location is changed in the **Project Explorer** window.

Figure 29-7.
This is the dialog box you will create using VBA.

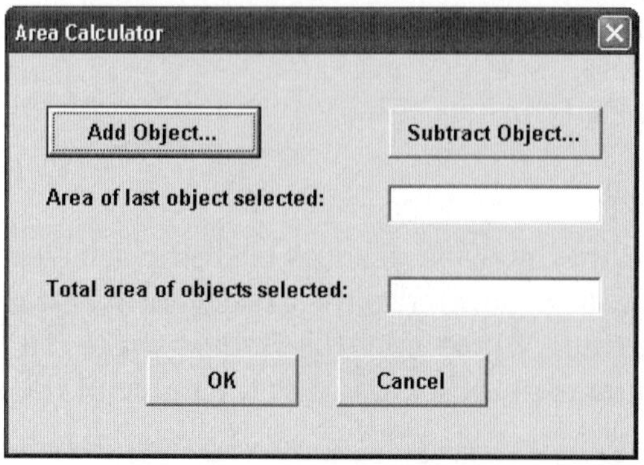

Step 2: Add a User Form

1. In the **Visual Basic Editor**, select **Insert>UserForm** from the pull-down menu. The **UserForm** window, containing a blank user form, is opened on the **Visual Basic Editor** desktop. A **Toolbox** window also appears, which contains controls that can be placed on the form.
2. The **Properties** window shows all of the various properties of the form. Change the (Name) property to frmAreaCalc. Also, change the Caption property to Area Calculator.

The Caption property is the name that appears in the title bar of the form (dialog box). The form is an object and, for the sake of clarity, is usually given a name with the standard form prefix frm. Other standard prefixes will be used later when you provide names for the controls that are placed on the form. The project should now look similar to **Figure 29-8.**

Step 3: Add Controls to the Form

1. From the **Toolbox** window, drag a **CommandButton** object onto the form and drop it anywhere. If you pause the cursor over an object in the **Toolbox** window, the name of the object is displayed as help text.

The default size of the command button may be quite large or small in comparison to the default size of the form. The form and controls can be resized. The controls can also be repositioned on the form.

2. In the **UserForm** window, pick on the form to make it the active object. Resizing grips appear along the edges and at the corners.
3. Move the cursor to the lower-right corner. When the standard Windows resizing cursor appears, drag the corner down and to the right to increase the size of the form.
4. From the **Toolbox** window, drag three more **CommandButton** objects, two **Label** objects, and two **TextBox** objects onto the form.

Figure 29-8.
A new form has been added to the project. Its name and caption have been changed.

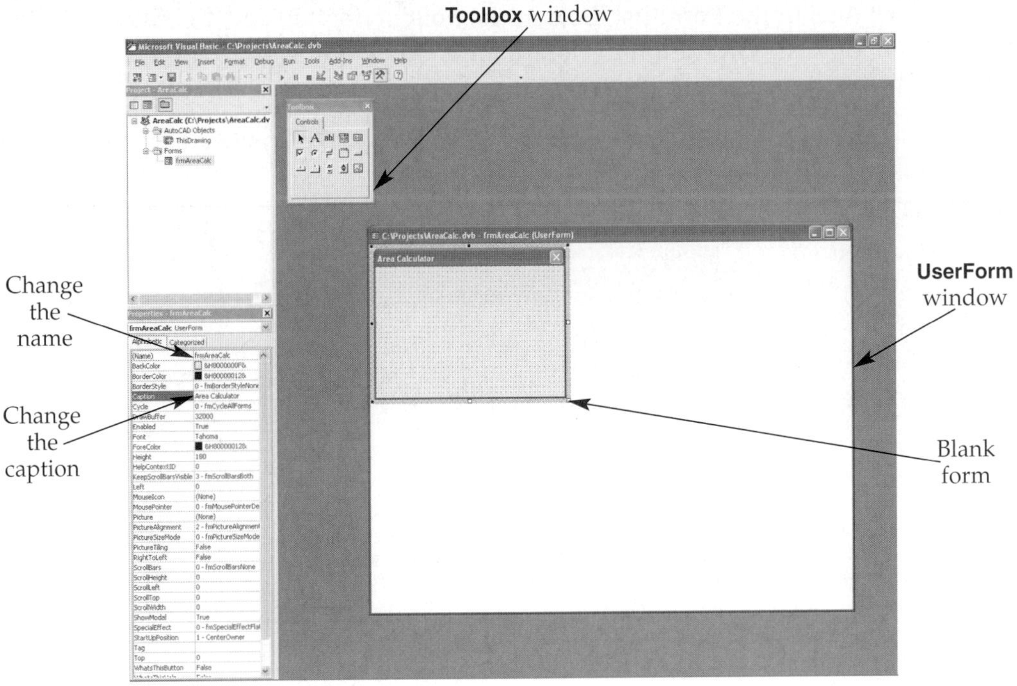

5. The controls can be moved around on the form by picking on the object and dragging it to a new location. Multiple controls can be selected by pressing the [Ctrl] key before picking the objects. Arrange the controls as shown in **Figure 29-9.**

Step 4: Set the Properties of the Controls

1. Select the upper-left command button to make it active. Notice that its properties are now shown in the **Properties** window and the resizing grips are displayed on the object.
2. Change the Caption property to Add Object... and the (Name) property to btnAddObject. The btn prefix is used for the names of button objects.
3. Select the upper-right command button. Change its Caption property to Subtract Object... and its (Name) property to btnSubtractObject.
4. Change the (Name) property of the top label to lblLastArea and its Caption property to Area of last object selected:. The lbl prefix is used for the names of label objects.
5. Change the (Name) property of the bottom label to lblTotalArea and its Caption property to Total area of objects selected:.
6. Change the (Name) property of the top text box to txtLastArea. Leave its Text property blank. The txt prefix is used for the names of text box objects.
7. Change the (Name) property of the bottom text box to txtTotalArea. Leave its Text property blank.
8. Change the (Name) property of the bottom-left command button to btnExit. Change its Caption property to OK.
9. Change the (Name) property of the bottom-right command button to btnCancel. Change its Caption property to Cancel.

Next, you will change the font used to display text on the objects. This can be done "globally" by selecting all of the objects. Press the [Ctrl] key and pick each of the eight objects on the form. The properties that are common to the selected controls are displayed in the **Properties** window. Continue as follows.

10. Pick in the Font property text box and select the **...** button at the far right. The **Font** dialog box is displayed.
11. Select Arial in the **Font:** list, Bold in the **Font style:** list, and 10 in the **Size:** list. Then, pick the **OK** button to close the **Font** dialog box.

Figure 29-9.
Controls have been added to the form and arranged.

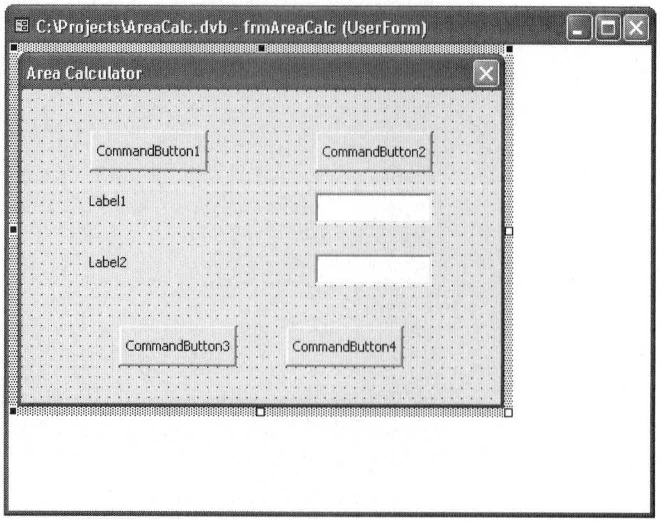

When the form (dialog box) is being used, the two text boxes will be displaying numeric values. It is common practice to display numeric data right justified. Select the two text box controls and continue as follows.

12. In the **Properties** window, select the TextAlign property. Pick the drop-down arrow and select 3–fmTextAlignRight from the list.
13. Individually select, resize, and relocate each of the controls until the form appears as shown in **Figure 29-10.**
14. Pick the **Save** button on the toolbar in the **Visual Basic Editor** to save the project.

PROFESSIONAL TIP

It is important to use logical names with standard prefixes for objects on a form. These names are used to reference the objects within code. Using logical names and standard prefixes help to keep everything organized and easily identified.

Step 5: Add Code to the Form

So far, you have created the visual interface for the program, but the form cannot yet do anything. You are now ready to add code to the form. Double-click anywhere on the form (not on a control). This opens the **Code** window for the form where code can be added for the form itself and the objects (buttons, text boxes, etc.) it contains. The window contains some default code. This code is associated with an action, or event. In this case, the default code is a **Private Sub** associated with the action of picking (clicking) on the form. This default code should be removed since no actions will be performed when the form is picked.

1. Highlight all of the existing code and press the [Delete] key.
2. Be sure (General) is selected in the top-left drop-down list in the **Code** window and (Declarations) is selected in the top-right drop-down list.
3. Enter the following lines of code:

```
' Declaration of variables for use in the program
Dim objOBJ As AcadObject        ' The object (circle or polyline) that will be selected
Dim varPNT As Variant           ' The point that was used when selecting the object
Dim dblObjectArea As Double     ' The area of the selected object
Dim dblTotalArea As Double      ' The running total of the area of all the selected objects
Dim strType As String           ' The type of object (circle or polyline) that is selected
```

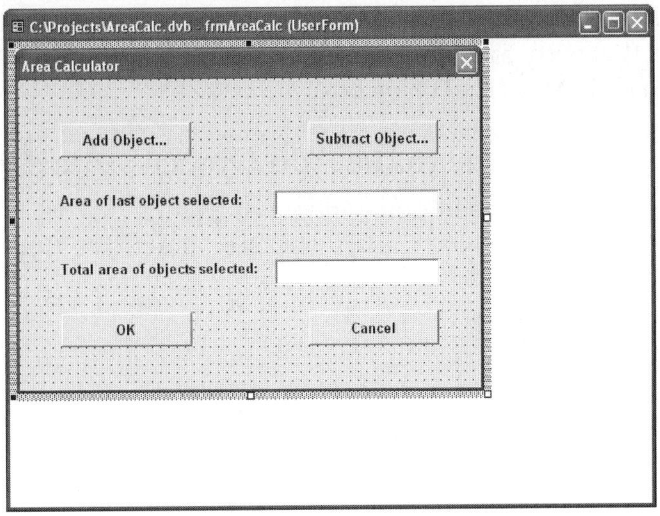

Figure 29-10.
The controls have been edited and resized.

4. Pick the **Save** button on the toolbar in the **Visual Basic Editor** to save the project.

The code you just entered declares the variables needed to do the area calculations. Also, note the comments added to the code. Adding ***comments*** is very important because it informs you or anyone else reading the code as to the purpose of the code. Anything after an apostrophe (') is ignored by VBA. Comments are usually added to a line above code or at the end of a line of code, as shown above.

Step 6: Add Code to the Exit Button

1. With the **Code** window active, select btnExit in the upper-left drop-down list.

The upper-right drop-down list changes to the Click action. A **Private Sub** is added that will be executed when the **Exit** button on the form is picked. Also, notice the horizontal line between the declarations and the beginning of the **Private Sub**. This automatically appears before each **Sub** to help visually separate the program into blocks. It is also common practice to use tabs and blank lines to visually separate logical blocks of code. Continue as follows.

2. On the blank line between the Private Sub line and the End Sub line, type:

   ```
   Unload Me
   ```

   This line of code closes the dialog box and removes from memory all of the code associated with the form.
3. Save the project.

Step 7: Add Code to the Cancel Button

1. Activate the **UserForm** window. This can be done by picking on the window (if it is visible) or selecting the window in the **Window** pull-down menu of the **Visual Basic Editor**.
2. Double-click on the btnCancel control. Make sure you do not double-click on the label displayed on the object.

This displays the **Code** window and adds a **Private Sub** that will be executed when the **Cancel** button on the form is picked. In the last section, you used the left-hand drop-down list in the **Code** window to accomplish the same thing. Use whichever method you prefer. Continue as follows.

3. Add the Unload Me line of code to the **Private Sub**. The **Code** window should appear as shown in **Figure 29-11.**
4. Save the project.

In the **Area Calculator** dialog box (form) you are creating, there will be no difference between the actions of the **OK** button and the **Cancel** button. Both are included for consistency, since most AutoCAD dialog boxes have an **OK** and a **Cancel** button. Users quickly become accustom to the consistent locations of features in the software. Try to mimic this with your programs by always including **OK** and **Cancel** buttons located near the bottom of the dialog box.

Step 8: Add Code to the Add Object... Button

1. Make the **UserForm** window active.
2. Double-click on the btnAddObject object. The **Code** window is displayed and a **Private Sub** is added that will be executed when the **Add Object...** button on the form is picked.

Figure 29-11.
Variables have been declared and code has been added for the **Cancel** and **Exit** buttons.

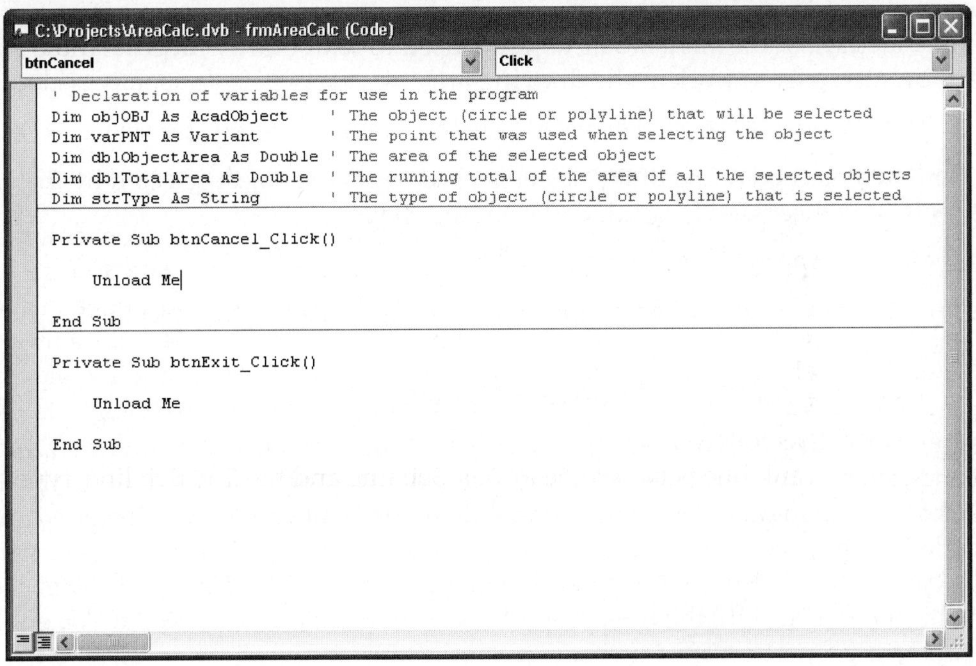
C:\Projects\AreaCalc.dvb - frmAreaCalc (Code)
btnCancel
Click
' Declaration of variables for use in the program
Dim objOBJ As AcadObject ' The object (circle or polyline) that will be selected
Dim varPNT As Variant ' The point that was used when selecting the object
Dim dblObjectArea As Double ' The area of the selected object
Dim dblTotalArea As Double ' The running total of the area of all the selected objects
Dim strType As String ' The type of object (circle or polyline) that is selected
Private Sub btnCancel_Click()
Unload Me
End Sub
Private Sub btnExit_Click()
Unload Me
End Sub

3. Between the Private Sub line and the End Sub line, type the following lines of code. Notice how blank lines and tabs are used to visually organize the code.

```
frmAreaCalc.Hide

ThisDrawing.Utility.GetEntity objOBJ, varPNT, "Pick a circle or a polyline: "
strType = objOBJ.ObjectName

If strType = "AcDbCircle" Or strType = "AcDbPolyline" Then
    dblObjectArea = objOBJ.Area
    dblTotalArea = dblObjectArea + dblTotalArea
    txtLastArea.Text = Str(dblObjectArea)
    txtTotalArea.Text = Str(dblTotalArea)
    frmAreaCalc.Show

Else

    MsgBox ("Object must be a circle or a polyline")
    frmAreaCalc.Show

Exit Sub

End If
```

4. Save the project.

Here is a description of each line of code for the **Add Object...** button:

```
frmAreaCalc.Hide
```

The **Hide** method of the frmAreaCalc object is used to temporarily hide the dialog box. This allows the user to work in the drawing area.

```
ThisDrawing.Utility.GetEntity objOBJ, varPNT, "Pick a circle or a polyline: "
```

The **GetEntity** method of the **Utility** object is used to get the object selected by the user. This method is discussed in detail earlier in the chapter.

```
strType = objOBJ.ObjectName
```

This line stores the **ObjectName** property of the selected AutoCAD object in the strType variable.

```
If strType = "AcDbCircle" Or strType = "AcDbPolyline" Then
```

This line is the first line of the **If** function. The **If** function checks a condition and, if the condition is true, it executes all of the code after the **Then** statement up to the **Else** statement. The **Else** statement is optional, so if an **Else** statement is not included, all of the code after the **Then** statement is executed until the **End If** statement is encountered. In the case of this program, the condition being tested is the object type. This check has to be performed since the **Area** property will be used and not all AutoCAD entities have an **Area** property.

At this point, the program branches. If the selected AutoCAD object is a circle or polyline, then the next line is executed. Otherwise, execution jumps to the **Else** statement.

```
dblObjectArea = objOBJ.Area
```

This line stores the value of the selected object's **Area** property in the dblObjectArea variable.

```
dblTotalArea = dblObjectArea + dblTotalArea
```

This line adds the value of the dblObjectArea variable to the value of the dblTotalArea variable and stores the result in the dblTotalArea variable. The first time this line is performed, the dblTotalArea variable does not have a value, so 0 is used.

```
txtLastArea.Text = Str(dblObjectArea)
```

This line sets the **Text** property of the txtLastArea object (labeled **Area of last object selected:**). The text to appear in the text box is the value that is stored in the dblObjectArea variable. That variable is a numeric value, but text boxes can only display string values. The **Str** function is being used to convert the data type from a number to a string. This is done by passing the dblObjectArea variable as an argument to the **Str** function.

```
txtTotalArea.Text = Str(dblTotalArea)
```

This line is doing the same as the previous line, but it applies to the txtTotalArea object (labeled **Total area of objects selected:**).

```
frmAreaCalc.Show
```

The **Show** method of the frmAreaCalc object is used to display the dialog box.

If the selected AutoCAD object is not a circle or polyline, code execution jumps from the **If** statement to the **Else** statement:

```
Else
```

This line begins the lines of code that are to be performed if the condition being checked is false. The condition being checked is whether or not the selected object is a circle or a polyline. If the selected object is not either of these object types, the **MsgBox** function is called.

```
MsgBox ("Object must be a circle or a polyline")
```

The **MsgBox** function takes a string as an argument and shows that string as a message to the user in a small dialog box with an **OK** button at the bottom. The message informs the user that a circle or a polyline was not selected. When the user picks the **OK** button, the next line of code is executed.

```
frmAreaCalc.Show
```

This line uses the **Show** method of the frmAreaCalc object to display the dialog box, allowing the user to pick the **Add Objects...** button to select another object or **Subtract Object...** button to remove an object.

```
Exit Sub
```

This line exits the **Sub** routine that was called when the user picked the **Add Object...** button the first time.

```
End If
```

This line signals the end of the code within the **If** function.

Step 9: Add Code to the Subtract Object... Button

1. Activate the **UserForm** window.
2. Double-click on the btnSubtractObject object. The **Code** window is displayed and a **Private Sub** is added that will be executed when the **Subtract Object...** button on the form is picked.
3. Between the Private Sub line and the End Sub line, type the following lines of code. Notice how blank lines and tabs are used to visually organize the code.

```
frmAreaCalc.Hide

ThisDrawing.Utility.GetEntity objOBJ, varPNT, "Pick a circle or a polyline: "
strType = objOBJ.ObjectName

If strType = "AcDbCircle" Or strType = "AcDbPolyline" Then
    dblObjectArea = objOBJ.Area
    dblTotalArea = dblTotalArea – dblObjectArea
    txtLastArea.Text = Str(dblObjectArea)
    txtTotalArea.Text = Str(dblTotalArea)
    frmAreaCalc.Show

Else

    MsgBox ("Object must be a circle or a polyline")
    frmAreaCalc.Show

Exit Sub

End If
```

   The only difference between these lines of code and those for the **Add Object...** button is this line:

```
dblTotalArea = dblTotalArea – dblObjectArea
```

   This line subtracts the area of the selected AutoCAD object from the total area.

4. Save the project.

NOTE

As you double-click to add code for the various objects on the form, the **Private Subs** are added to the **Code** window in alphabetical order. The **Private Subs** can be rearranged using cut-and-paste editing to more closely follow the flow of the program, if desired. For example, you may wish to rearrange the **Private Subs** for the controls on the frmAreaCalc form as:

```
Private Sub btnAddObject_Click()
   lines of code
End Sub

Private Sub btnSubtractObject_Click()
   lines of code
End Sub

Private Sub btnExit_Click()
   lines of code
End Sub

Private Sub btnCancel_Click()
   lines of code
End Sub
```

Step 10: Create a Macro to Call the Form

The form is complete, as is the code attached to the command button controls on the form. The last task is to create a macro to call the form so the dialog box will be displayed on the screen.

1. In the **Visual Basic Editor**, make sure the AreaCalc project is selected in the **Project Explorer** window.
2. Select **Insert**>**Module** from the pull-down menu.

The **Code** window for the module is opened on the **Visual Basic Editor** desktop. This is not the same **Code** window for the form, which is why it currently is blank. Also, notice that a Modules folder is added to the tree in the **Project Explorer** window with Module1 listed below it. Continue as follows.

3. Select Module1 in the tree in the **Project Explorer** window.
4. In the **Properties** window, change the (Name) property to RunAreaCalc.
5. In the module **Code** window, type:

```
Public Sub RunAreaCalc()

  frmAreaCalc.Show

End Sub
```

6. Save the project.

Step 11: Load the Project and Run the Macro

If you have been following along with the text, the macro is available at this point and you can skip to step 3. Otherwise, the project needs to be loaded. In this case, begin with step 1.

1. Open the **VBA Manager** dialog box.
2. In the **VBA Manager** dialog box, pick the **Load...** button. Navigate to the AreaCalc.dvb file and open it. The project name and location are shown in the dialog box. If the file is already loaded, you do not need to reload it.
3. Switch to AutoCAD.
4. Draw a couple of circles, polylines, lines, and arcs.
5. Open the **Macros** dialog box. The macro that was created in the AreaCalc project is listed.
6. Highlight the RunAreaCalc macro and pick the **Run** button.

The form (**Area Calculator** dialog box) created in the project appears. Pick the **Add Object...** button; the dialog box is hidden. Select one of the circles you drew. The dialog box is displayed and the area of the circle appears in both text boxes in the dialog box. Pick the **Add Object...** button again and select a different circle. The area of that circle appears in the top text box and the combined area of the two circles appears in the bottom text box. Experiment with using the **Subtract Object...** button, selecting a line or arc, and using the **OK** and **Cancel** buttons.

CAUTION

This routine is not error proof. It will break down if you do not select an object when prompted to do so. Error checking is an important feature of programming. For information on adding error checking to your VBA programs, refer to *VBA for AutoCAD* published by The Goodheart-Willcox Company, Inc.

Running a VBA Macro from the Keyboard

One drawback of the VBA language is that there is no way to create a command out of a VBA macro or project. Additionally, there is no way to create a keyboard shortcut for a VBA macro or a project. There is, however, a way to create a command from a VBA project through the use of AutoLISP.

Create the following AutoLISP program using the **Visual LISP Editor**. A couple of AutoLISP functions are used that are not covered in this text. You can research these functions in the online documentation if you want to explore them deeper.

```
; For use with AreaCalc VBA project
(defun c:AreaCalc ()
  (vl-vbaload "c:/vba projects/AreaCalc.dvb")
  (vl-vbarun "RunAreaCalc")
  (princ)
)
```

The first line of code after the comment defines a function called **AreaCalc** that can be used on the command line. The second line of code after the comment loads a VBA project file. The path needs to match the location of your file, so adjust this line as needed. The next line runs the macro that calls the dialog box from the loaded project. The next line creates a clean exit from the AutoLISP program. The last line just closes the **(defun)** function. Now, this LISP program can be saved, loaded into AutoCAD, and run. Refer to Chapters 26 and 27 for more information.

Chapter Test

Answer the following questions. Write your answers on a separate sheet of paper or complete the electronic chapter test on the Student CD.

1. What does *VBA* stand for?
2. Briefly describe the AutoCAD object model.
3. What is the root object of the AutoCAD object model?
4. What are the five objects that branch from the root object in the AutoCAD object model?
5. Which branch off of the root allows access to most of the objects stored in AutoCAD's **Options** dialog box?
6. Which branch off of the root allows access to the objects stored in model space and paper space?
7. What is a VBA *method?*
8. What is a *property,* in terms of VBA?
9. What are *events,* in terms of VBA?
10. What is a VBA *project?*
11. What is a *form?*
12. Describe the difference between an *embedded* project and a *global* project.
13. How do you access to the **Macros** dialog box, **VBA Manager**, and **Visual Basic Editor** using the ribbon?
14. Describe the **Auto List Members** feature of the **Visual Basic Editor**.
15. Name six common data types used in VBA programming.
16. Define *variable.*
17. What is *declaring* a variable?
18. What does the term *hard coding* mean?
19. The **ThisDrawing** object is an alias for _____.
20. In which object are most of the user-interaction methods stored?
21. Name the methods that will obtain each of the following data types: **String**, **Integer**, **Real**, **Point**.
22. Given ThisDrawing.Utility.Prompt (strName), which term describes the (strName) portion of the code?
23. Describe the **Auto Quick Info** feature of the **Visual Basic Editor**.
24. Describe the difference between storing a value in an object variable versus storing a value in a data variable.
25. Command buttons, option buttons, labels, text boxes, and other items that are found on forms are called ____.

Drawing Problems

1. Create a VBA macro that will ask the user to select an object. Then, display a message box indicating the type of object selected. Name the macro P29_01_ObjectType.

2. Create a VBA macro that will ask the user to select a line. Then, display the length of the selected object in a message box. If the selected object is not a line, display a message informing the user of this. Name the macro P29_02_LineLength.

3. Create a VBA macro that will draw three circles.
   A. Draw the first circle using a center point and radius provided by the user.
   B. Draw the second circle using the same center point and a radius 25% larger than the first circle.
   C. Draw the third circle using the same center point and a radius 25% smaller than the first circle.
   D. Provide prompts for the user for the center point and radius.
   E. Name the macro P29_03_DrawCircles.

4. Create a VBA macro that will reduce the radius of a selected arc or circle to half of its original radius. If the selected object is not an arc or circle, display a message informing the user of this. Name the macro P29_04_ChangeRadius.

Index

B

D

E

Index–Advanced

V

W

X

Index—Advanced